Short Story Criticism

Guide to Gale Literary Criticism Series

For criticism on	Consult these Gale series
Authors now living or who died after December 31, 1999	*CONTEMPORARY LITERARY CRITICISM (CLC)*
Authors who died between 1900 and 1999	*TWENTIETH-CENTURY LITERARY CRITICISM (TCLC)*
Authors who died between 1800 and 1899	*NINETEENTH-CENTURY LITERATURE CRITICISM (NCLC)*
Authors who died between 1400 and 1799	*LITERATURE CRITICISM FROM 1400 TO 1800 (LC)* *SHAKESPEAREAN CRITICISM (SC)*
Authors who died before 1400	*CLASSICAL AND MEDIEVAL LITERATURE CRITICISM (CMLC)*
Authors of books for children and young adults	*CHILDREN'S LITERATURE REVIEW (CLR)*
Dramatists	*DRAMA CRITICISM (DC)*
Poets	*POETRY CRITICISM (PC)*
Short story writers	*SHORT STORY CRITICISM (SSC)*
Literary topics and movements	*HARLEM RENAISSANCE: A GALE CRITICAL COMPANION (HR)* *THE BEAT GENERATION: A GALE CRITICAL COMPANION (BG)*
Asian American writers of the last two hundred years	*ASIAN AMERICAN LITERATURE (AAL)*
Black writers of the past two hundred years	*BLACK LITERATURE CRITICISM (BLC)* *BLACK LITERATURE CRITICISM SUPPLEMENT (BLCS)*
Hispanic writers of the late nineteenth and twentieth centuries	*HISPANIC LITERATURE CRITICISM (HLC)* *HISPANIC LITERATURE CRITICISM SUPPLEMENT (HLCS)*
Native North American writers and orators of the eighteenth, nineteenth, and twentieth centuries	*NATIVE NORTH AMERICAN LITERATURE (NNAL)*
Major authors from the Renaissance to the present	*WORLD LITERATURE CRITICISM, 1500 TO THE PRESENT (WLC)* *WORLD LITERATURE CRITICISM SUPPLEMENT (WLCS)*

ISSN 0895-9439

Volume 88

Short Story Criticism

Criticism of the
Works of Short Fiction Writers

Rachelle Mucha
Thomas J. Schoenberg
Lawrence J. Trudeau
Project Editors

THOMSON

GALE

Detroit • New York • San Francisco • San Diego • New Haven, Conn. • Waterville, Maine • London • Munich

THOMSON
GALE

Short Story Criticism, Vol. 88

Project Editors
Thomas J. Schoenberg, Lawrence J. Trudeau and Rachelle Mucha

Editorial
Jessica Bomarito, Kathy D. Darrow, Jeffrey W. Hunter, Jelena O. Krstović, Michelle Lee, Russel Whitaker

Data Capture
Frances Monroe, Gwen Tucker

Indexing Services
Factiva®, a Dow Jones and Reuters Company

Rights and Acquisitions
Margaret Abendroth, Lori Hines, Timothy Sisler

Imaging and Multimedia
Dean Dauphinais, Leitha Etheridge-Sims, Lezlie Light, Mike Logusz, Dan Newell, Christine O'Bryan, Kelly A. Quin, Denay Wilding, Robyn Young

Composition and Electronic Capture
Amy Darga

Manufacturing
Rhonda Dover

Associate Product Manager
Marc Cormier

LIBRARY OF CONGRESS CATALOG CARD NUMBER 88-641014

ISBN 0-7876-8885-1
ISSN 0895-9439

Printed in the United States of America
10 9 8 7 6 5 4 3 2 1

Contents

Preface vii

Acknowledgments xi

Literary Criticism Series Advisory Board xiii

Preface

Short Story Criticism (*SSC*) presents significant criticism of the world's greatest short-story writers and provides supplementary biographical and bibliographical materials to guide the interested reader to a greater understanding of the authors of short fiction. This series was developed in response to suggestions from librarians serving high school, college, and public library patrons, who had noted a considerable number of requests for critical material on short-story writers. Although major short-story writers are covered in such Thomson Gale series as *Contemporary Literary Criticism* (*CLC*), *Twentieth-Century Literary Criticism* (*TCLC*), *Nineteenth-Century Literature Criticism* (*NCLC*), and *Literature Criticism from 1400 to 1800* (*LC*), librarians perceived the need for a series devoted solely to writers of the short-story genre.

Scope of the Series

SSC is designed to serve as an introduction to major short-story writers of all eras and nationalities. Since these authors have inspired a great deal of relevant critical material, *SSC* is necessarily selective, and the editors have chosen the most important published criticism to aid readers and students in their research.

Approximately four to five authors are included in each volume, and each entry presents a historical survey of the critical response to that author's work. The length of an entry is intended to reflect the amount of critical attention the author has received from critics writing in English and from foreign critics in translation. Every attempt has been made to identify and include the most significant essays on each author's work. In order to provide these important critical pieces, the editors sometimes reprint essays that have appeared elsewhere in Thomson Gale's Literary Criticism Series. Such duplication, however, never exceeds twenty percent of an *SSC* volume.

Organization of the Book

An *SSC* entry consists of the following elements:

- The **Author Heading** cites the name under which the author most commonly wrote, followed by birth and death dates. Also located here are any name variations under which an author wrote, including transliterated forms for authors whose native languages use nonroman alphabets. If the author wrote consistently under a pseudonym, the pseudonym will be listed in the author heading and the author's actual name given in parentheses on the first line of the biographical and critical introduction. Uncertain birth or death dates are indicated by question marks. Single-work entries are preceded by the title of the work and its date of publication.

- The **Introduction** contains background information that introduces the reader to the author and the critical debates surrounding his or her work.

- A **Portrait of the Author** is included when available.

- The list of **Principal Works** is ordered chronologically by date of first publication and lists the most important works by the author. The first section comprises short-story collections, novellas, and novella collections. The second section gives information on other major works by the author. For foreign authors, the editors have provided original foreign-language publication information and have selected what are considered the best and most complete English-language editions of their works.

- Reprinted **Criticism** is arranged chronologically in each entry to provide a useful perspective on changes in critical evaluation over time. All short-story, novella, and collection titles by the author featured in the entry are printed in boldface type. The critic's name and the date of composition or publication of the critical work are given at the beginning of each piece of criticism. Unsigned criticism is preceded by the title of the source in which it appeared. Footnotes are reprinted at the end of each essay or excerpt. In the case of excerpted criticism, only those footnotes that pertain to the excerpted texts are included.

- Critical essays are prefaced by brief **Annotations** explicating each piece.

- A complete **Bibliographical Citation** of the original essay or book precedes each piece of criticism. Source citations in the Literary Criticism Series follow University of Chicago Press style, as outlined in *The Chicago Manual of Style,* 14th ed. (Chicago: The University of Chicago Press, 1993).

- An annotated bibliography of **Further Reading** appears at the end of each entry and suggests resources for additional study. In some cases, significant essays for which the editors could not obtain reprint rights are included here. Boxed material following the further reading list provides references to other biographical and critical sources on the author in series published by Thomson Gale.

Indexes

A **Cumulative Author Index** lists all of the authors that appear in a wide variety of reference sources published by Thomson Gale, including *SSC*. A complete list of these sources is found facing the first page of the Author Index. The index also includes birth and death dates and cross references between pseudonyms and actual names.

A **Cumulative Nationality Index** lists all authors featured in *SSC* by nationality, followed by the number of the *SSC* volume in which their entry appears.

An alphabetical **Title Index** lists all short-story, novella, and collection titles contained in the *SSC* series. Titles of short-story collections, separately published novellas, and novella collections are printed in italics, while titles of individual short stories are printed in roman type with quotation marks. Each title is followed by the author's last name and corresponding volume and page numbers where commentary on the work is located. English-language translations of original foreign-language titles are cross-referenced to the foreign titles so that all references to discussion of a work are combined in one listing.

In response to numerous suggestions from librarians, Thomson Gale also produces an annual paperbound edition of the SSC cumulative title index. This annual cumulation, which alphabetically lists all titles reviewed in the series, is available to all customers. Additional copies of this index are available upon request. Librarians and patrons will welcome this separate index; it saves shelf space, is easy to use, and is recyclable upon receipt of the next edition.

Citing *Short Story Criticism*

When citing criticism reprinted in the Literary Criticism Series, students should provide complete bibliographic information so that the cited essay can be located in the original print or electronic source. Students who quote directly from reprinted criticism may use any accepted bibliographic format, such as University of Chicago Press style or Modern Language Association (MLA) style. Both the MLA and the University of Chicago formats are acceptable and recognized as being the current standards for citations. It is important, however, to choose one format for all citations; do not mix the two formats within a list of citations.

The examples below follow recommendations for preparing a bibliography set forth in *The Chicago Manual of Style,* 14th ed. (Chicago: The University of Chicago Press, 1993); the first example pertains to material drawn from periodicals, the second to material reprinted from books:

Morrison, Jago. "Narration and Unease in Ian McEwan's Later Fiction." *Critique* 42, no. 3 (spring 2001): 253-68. Reprinted in *Short Story Criticism.* Vol. 57, edited by Janet Witalec, 212-20. Detroit: Gale, 2003.

Brossard, Nicole. "Poetic Politics." In *The Politics of Poetic Form: Poetry and Public Policy,* edited by Charles Bernstein, 73-82. New York: Roof Books, 1990. Reprinted in *Short Story Criticism.* Vol. 57, edited by Janet Witalec, 3-8. Detroit: Gale, 2003.

The examples below follow recommendations for preparing a works cited list set forth in the *MLA Handbook for Writers of Research Papers,* 5th ed. (New York: The Modern Language Association of America, 1999); the first example pertains to material drawn from periodicals, the second to material reprinted from books:

Morrison, Jago. "Narration and Unease in Ian McEwan's Later Fiction." *Critique* 42.3 (spring 2001): 253-68. Reprinted in *Short Story Criticism.* Ed. Janet Witalec. Vol. 57. Detroit: Gale, 2003. 212-20.

Brossard, Nicole. "Poetic Politics." *The Politics of Poetic Form: Poetry and Public Policy.* Ed. Charles Bernstein. New York: Roof Books, 1990. 73-82. Reprinted in *Short Story Criticism.* Ed. Janet Witalec. Vol. 57. Detroit: Gale, 2003. 3-8.

Suggestions are Welcome

Readers who wish to suggest new features, topics, or authors to appear in future volumes, or who have other suggestions or comments are cordially invited to call, write, or fax the Associate Product Manager:

Associate Product Manager, Literary Criticism Series
Thomson Gale
27500 Drake Road
Farmington Hills, MI 48331-3535
1-800-347-4253 (GALE)
Fax: 248-699-8054

Acknowledgments

The editors wish to thank the copyright holders of the excerpted criticism included in this volume and the permissions managers of many book and magazine publishing companies for assisting us in securing reproduction rights. Following is a list of the copyright holders who have granted us permission to reproduce material in this volume of *SSC*. Every effort has been made to trace copyright, but if omissions have been made, please let us know.

COPYRIGHTED MATERIAL IN *SSC*, VOLUME 88, WAS REPRODUCED FROM THE FOLLOWING PERIODICALS:

ANQ, v. 9, fall, 1996. Copyright © 1996 by Helen Dwight Reid Educational Foundation. Reproduced with permission of the Helen Dwight Reid Educational Foundation, published by Heldref Publications, 1319 18th Street, NW, Washington, DC 20036-1802.—*College Literature,* v. 16, fall, 1989. Copyright © 1989 by West Chester University. Reproduced by permission.—*Dickens Quarterly,* v. 8, June, 1991; v. 17, March, 2000. Copyright © 1991, 2000 by the Dickens Society. Both reproduced by permission.—*Dickensian,* v. 83, spring, 1987 for "'To Be Read at Dusk'" by Ruth Glancy. Reproduced by permission of the author.—*English Language Notes,* v. 20, May-June, 1983; v. 32, March, 1995. Copyright © 1983, 1995, Regents of the University of Colorado. Both reproduced by permission.—*Essays in Arts and Sciences,* v. 29, October, 2000. Copyright © 2000 by the University of New Haven. Reproduced by permission.—*Essays in French Literature,* v. 27, November, 1990. Copyright © Department of French Studies, University of Western Australia. Reproduced by permission.—*Explicator,* v. 47, winter, 1989; v. 53, fall, 1994. Copyright © 1989, 1994 by Helen Dwight Reid Educational Foundation. Both reproduced with permission of the Helen Dwight Reid Educational Foundation, published by Heldref Publications, 1319 18th Street, NW, Washington, DC 20036-1802.—*Fabula,* v. 44, 2003 for "Framing the Brothers Grimm: Paratexts and Intercultural Transmission in Postwar English-Language Editions of the *Kinder- und Hausmärchen*" by Donald Haase. Copyright © 2003 by Donald Haase. All rights reserved. Reproduced by permission of the author.—*French Cultural Studies,* v. 4, June, 1993. Copyright © Sage Publications, 1993. www.sagepub.co.uk. Reproduced by permission of Sage Publications, Ltd., Thousand Oaks, London and New Delhi.—*French Review,* v. 68, December, 1994; v. 69, December, 1995. Copyright © 1994, 1995 by the American Association of Teachers of French. Both reproduced by permission.—*German Quarterly,* v. 77, winter, 2004. Copyright © 2004 by the American Association of Teachers of German. Reproduced by permission.—*Germanic Review,* v. 68, winter, 1993 for "Feminist or Anti-feminist? Gender-Coded Role Models in the Tales Contributed by Dorothea Viehmann to the Grimm Brothers *Kinder- und Hausmärchen*" by Maureen Thum. Copyright © 1992 Helen Dwight Reid Educational Foundation. Reproduced by permission of the author.—*Nineteenth-Century Fiction,* v. 22, March, 1968 for "Art and Nature in 'The Masque of the Red Death'" by Kermit Vanderbilt. Copyright © 1968 by The Regents of the University of California. Reproduced by permission of the publisher and the author.—*Papers on Language & Literature,* v. 29, spring, 1993. Copyright © 1993 by The Board of Trustees, Southern Illinois University at Edwardsville. Reproduced by permission.—*Poe Studies/Dark Romanticism,* v. 16, June, 1983 for "'The Masque of the Red Death': Yet Another Source" by Michael Tritt. Reproduced by permission of the author./ v. 34, June-December, 2001 for "Deliberate Chaos: Poe's Use of Colors in 'The Masque of the Red Death'" by Eric H. du Plessis. Reproduced by permission of the publisher and the author.—*Romanic Review,* v. 95, January-March, 2004. Copyright © 2004 by the Trustees of Columbia University in the City of New York. Reproduced by permission.—*Southern Literary Journal,* v. 37, spring, 2005. Copyright © 2005 by the University of North Carolina Press. Used by permission.—*Sprachkunst,* v. 13, 1982. Copyright © Osterreichische Akademie der Wissenschaften. Reproduced by permission.—*Studies in English Literature, 1500-1900,* v. 32, autumn, 1992. Copyright © 1992 The Johns Hopkins University Press. Reproduced by permission.—*Studies in Short Fiction,* v. 19, winter, 1982; v. 21, spring, 1984; v. 25, summer, 1988; v. 26, winter, 1989; v. 28, fall, 1991; v. 30, spring, 1993. Copyright © 1982, 1984, 1988, 1989, 1991, 1993 by *Studies in Short Fiction.* All reproduced by permission.—*Studies in Twentieth Century Literature,* v. 19, summer, 1995. Copyright © 1995 by *Studies in Twentieth Century Literature.* Reproduced by permission.—*SubStance,* v. 13, 1984; v. 20, 1991. Copyright © 1984, 1991 by the Board of Regents of the University of Wisconsin System. Both reproduced by permission.—*Technology and Culture,* v. 42, July, 2001. Copyright © 2001 The Johns Hopkins University Press. Reproduced by permission.—*Victorian Studies,* v. 42, winter, 1999-2000; v. 43, spring, 2001. Copyright © 1999, 2001 Indiana University Press. Both reproduced by permission.

COPYRIGHTED MATERIAL IN *SSC*, VOLUME 88, WAS REPRODUCED FROM THE FOLLOWING BOOKS:

Bottigheimer, Ruth B. From *Grimms' Bad Girls & Bold Boys: The Moral & Social Vision of the Tales.* Yale University Press, 1987. Copyright © 1987 by Ruth B. Bottigheimer. Reproduced by permission of the author.—Edwards, Rachel. From

"Michel Tournier: 'Les Suaires de Véronique,'" in **Short French Fiction: Essays on the Short Story in France in the Twentieth Century.** Edited by J. E. Flower. University of Exeter Press, 1998. Copyright © University of Exeter Press 1998. Reproduced by permission.—Freedman, William. From **The Porous Sanctuary: Art and Anxiety in Poe's Short Fiction.** Peter Lang, 2002. Copyright © 2002 Peter Lang Publishing, Inc., New York. All rights reserved. Reproduced by permission.—McGlathery, James M. From **Fairy Tale Romance: The Grimms, Basile, and Perrault.** University of Illinois Press, 1991. Copyright 1988 by the Board of Trustees of the University of Illinois. Used with permission of the University of Illinois Press.—Murphy, G. Ronald, S.J. From **The Owl, the Raven, & the Dove: The Religious Meaning of the Grimms' Magic Fairy Tales.** Oxford University Press, 2000. Copyright G. Ronald Murphy. Used by permission of Oxford University Press, Inc.—Nayder, Lillian. From "Dickens and 'Gold Rush Fever': Colonial Contagion in *Household Words*," in **Dickens and the Children of Empire.** Edited by Wendy S. Jacobson. Palgrave, 2000. Selection and editorial matter copyright © Wendy S. Jacobson 2000. Text copyright © Palgrave Publishers Ltd., 2000. Reproduced with permission of Palgrave Macmillan.—Perry, Dennis R. From **Hitchcock and Poe: The Legacy of Delight and Terror.** The Scarecrow Press, Inc., 2003. Copyright © 2003 by Dennis R. Perry. All rights reserved. Reproduced by permission.—Petit, Susan. From **Michel Tournier's Metaphysical Fictions.** John Benjamins Publishing Company, 1991. Copyright © 1991 John Benjamins B.V. Reprinted with kind permission by John Benjamins Publishing Company, Amsterdam/Philadelphia. www.benjamins.com.—Platten, David. From **Michel Tournier and the Metaphor of Fiction.** St. Martin's Press, 1999. Copyright © 1999 David Platten. Reprinted by permission of St. Martin's Press, LLC.—Redfern, Walter. From **Michel Tournier: Le Coq de bruyère.** Fairleigh Dickinson University Press, 1996. Copyright © 1996 by Associated University Presses, Inc. All rights reserved. Reproduced by permission.—Roberts, Martin. From "Inversion and Androgyny: *Le Coq de bruyère*," in **Michel Tournier: Bricolage and Cultural Mythology.** ANMA Libri, 1994. Copyright © 1994 by ANMA Libri and Department of French & Italian, Stanford University. All rights reserved. Reproduced by permission of the publisher and the author.—Tatar, Maria. From **The Hard Facts of the Grimms' Fairy Tales.** Expanded second edition. Princeton University Press, 2003 paperback edition. Copyright © 1987 Princeton University Press. Reprinted by permission of Princeton University Press.—Tatar, Maria M. From "Beauties vs. Beasts in the Grimms' *Nursery and Household Tales*," in **The Brothers Grimm and Folktale.** Edited by James M. McGlathery, Larry W. Danielson, Ruth E. Lorbe, and Selma K. Richardson. University of Illinois Press, 1988. Copyright 1988 by the Board of Trustees of the University of Illinois. Used with permission of the University of Illinois Press.—Vescovi, Alessandro. From "The Bagman, the Signalman and Dickens's Short Story," in **Dickens: The Craft of Fiction and the Challenges of Reading.** Edited by Rossana Bonadei, Clotilde de Stasio, Carlo Pagetti, and Alessandro Vescovi. Edizioni Unicopli, 2000. Copyright © by Edizioni Unicopli. Reproduced by permission.—Zipes, Jack. From **The Brothers Grimm: From Enchanted Forests to the Modern World.** Palgrave Macmillan, 2002. Copyright © Jack Zipes, 2002. Reproduced with permission of Palgrave Macmillan.—Zipes, Jack. From **Fairy Tales and the Art of Subversion: The Classical Genre for Children and the Process of Civilization.** Routledge, 1991. Copyright © Jack Zipes 1983. Reproduced by permission of Routledge/Taylor & Francis Group, LLC and the author.

PHOTOGRAPHS APPEARING IN *SSC*, VOLUME 88, WERE RECEIVED FROM THE FOLLOWING SOURCES:

Dickens, Charles, photograph, c. 1840-60, photograph. © Bettmann/Corbis.—Edgar Allan Poe, photograph. The Library of Congress.—Grimm, Wilhelm, and Jacob Grimm, photograph. The Library of Congress.—Tournier, Michel, photograph. © Jerry Bauer. Reproduced by permission.

Thomson Gale Literature Product Advisory Board

The members of the Thomson Gale Literature Product Advisory Board—reference librarians from public and academic library systems—represent a cross-section of our customer base and offer a variety of informed perspectives on both the presentation and content of our literature products. Advisory board members assess and define such quality issues as the relevance, currency, and usefulness of the author coverage, critical content, and literary topics included in our series; evaluate the layout, presentation, and general quality of our printed volumes; provide feedback on the criteria used for selecting authors and topics covered in our series; provide suggestions for potential enhancements to our series; identify any gaps in our coverage of authors or literary topics, recommending authors or topics for inclusion; analyze the appropriateness of our content and presentation for various user audiences, such as high school students, undergraduates, graduate students, librarians, and educators; and offer feedback on any proposed changes/enhancements to our series. We wish to thank the following advisors for their advice throughout the year.

Charles Dickens
1812-1870

(Full name Charles John Huffam Dickens; also wrote under the pseudonym Boz) English novelist, short fiction writer, and essayist.

The following entry provides an overview of Dickens's short fiction. For additional information on his short fiction career, see *SSC,* Volume 17; for discussion of his novella *A Christmas Carol* (1843), see *SSC,* Volume 49.

INTRODUCTION

Widely regarded as the quintessential English novelist of the Victorian era, Dickens also wrote a great deal of short fiction throughout his career, most notably the beloved classic *A Christmas Carol.* Most of his stories originally appeared either in various periodicals, including his own weekly miscellanies, or as inset stories in some of his novels, and he rarely collected his short fiction for publication as separate volumes during his lifetime. In his sketches, tales, and short stories, Dickens typically blended genial humor and benevolence with pathos and macabre imagery to render highly detailed portraits of ordinary but colorful people and places. His early short fiction comprises brief, usually comic sketches of middle- to lower-class characters and manners drawn from the teeming streets of London. Many critics have described these sketches as verbal equivalents of the pictorial art of George Cruishank, whose illustration work often accompanied Dickens' writings. As with his novels, Dickens designed many of his mature tales to expose the injustices of Victorian society and to promote social reform in his own time. These stories often reflect a concern about evils caused by poverty, inhumane social institutions, and industrial progress, and they replace comedy with satire while exhibiting the dense, metaphoric prose style that characterizes all of his work.

BIOGRAPHICAL INFORMATION

Born near Portsmouth, England, Dickens was the second of eight children fathered by a well-paid navy payroll clerk whose foolish habits continually threatened his family's domestic stability and financial security. Nonetheless, at age six, Dickens entered school, where he developed a love of reading and a passion for theater

as well as a fondness for ghost stories and the Christmas season. In 1824 Dickens' parents and most of his younger siblings were imprisoned for debt; Dickens was forced to withdraw from school and work in dreadful conditions at a blacking (shoe polish) warehouse where he glued labels on bottles. For nearly a year he lodged in squalid quarters and often went hungry, enduring poverty so extreme that it made a lasting impression on him.

Upon his family's release from debtor's prison, Dickens returned to school but soon left again and continued his education on his own at the British Museum library. During his late teens he clerked at a lawyers' office for two years and then for the next four years prepared shorthand court reports with such accuracy that the *Morning Chronicle* newspaper hired him in 1834 as a reporter on Parliament politics and personalities. Meanwhile, Dickens also began contributing stories and sketches of daily life on London's streets to such magazines as the *Monthly Magazine* and *Bell's Weekly.*

In 1836 Dickens gave up legal reporting when he published the two-volume *Sketches by Boz,* a compilation of his London tales. Also that year he married Kate Hogarth, with whom he would have ten children. In 1837 Dickens became a literary celebrity with the novel *The Posthumous Papers of the Pickwick Club,* which was first published serially, a practice he would use for all of his novels. Following the popular success of *Oliver Twist* (1838) and *The Life and Adventures of Nicholas Nickleby* (1839), Dickens compiled his first self-published weekly miscellany, *Master Humphrey's Clock* (1840-41), which included the serial novels *Barnaby Rudge* and *The Old Curiosity Shop.*

In 1842 Dickens and his wife spent five months touring the United States, which he documented in the essay collection *American Notes for General Circulation* (1842) and to a lesser extent, in the novel *The Life and Adventures of Martin Chuzzlewit* (1844). About this time, he also began writing annual Christmas stories, beginning with *A Christmas Carol, The Chimes* (1844), and *The Cricket on the Hearth* (1845).

Despite his lucrative career, Dickens struggled to maintain a large, growing household, so he moved his family in 1844 to Italy and in 1846 to Switzerland, where living expenses were cheaper than in London. In 1849-50 Dickens published the semi-autobiographical novel *The Personal History of David Copperfield,* and during the next decade his literary themes perceptibly turned darker in such works as *Bleak House* (1852-53), *Hard Times* (1854), and *Little Dorrit* (1855-57). Between 1850 and 1859, Dickens co-owned and edited his second weekly miscellany, the popular *Household Words.* Although Dickens wrote much of the miscellany's contents, notably contributing the serial novel *Hard Times* and many short stories, especially those for its annual Christmas numbers, he also solicited contributions from such authors as Wilkie Collins and Edward Bulwer-Lytton. However, frequent quarrels with his partners prompted Dickens to buy them out and rename the periodical *All the Year Round.* The miscellany continued to issue annual Christmas numbers and serially published *A Tale of Two Cities* (1859) and *Great Expectations* (1861), his literary masterpiece.

Throughout his career, Dickens periodically staged public readings of his works with dramatic flair and to great popular acclaim, but from the mid-1850s onward family obligations forced him to increase their frequency. Consequently, his marriage suffered, and in 1858 he and his wife separated, leaving Dickens to care for their children with the help of his sister-in-law and eventually his mistress. During the 1860s he continued his public readings but wrote less often, publishing only the short story collection *The Uncommercial Traveller* (1861) and the novel *Our Mutual Friend* (1864-65). In

June 1865 Dickens survived a deadly railroad accident, which brought him anxiety attacks for the rest of his life. In the summer of 1870, after a long day working on his incomplete novel *The Mystery of Edwin Drood* (1870), Dickens suffered a stroke and died the next day, which coincidentally marked the fifth anniversary of his railroad accident.

MAJOR WORKS OF SHORT FICTION

Like most literature of the Romantic period, Dickens' short fiction illustrates the need for imagination, sympathy, and emotional release in an increasingly practical world; but his journalist's objectivity also places his work within the tradition of literary realism. His sketches, tales, and novellas evince a thorough acquaintance with the London streetscape and Victorian vernacular, a capacity for memorable characterization, a powerful storytelling technique, and a unique, highly creative prose style.

Subtitled "Illustrative of Every-Day Life and Every-Day People," *Sketches by Boz* gathers nearly sixty brief, often comic pieces, most of which were previously published between 1833 and 1836. These sketches, bearing such titles as "The Boarding-House," "Making a Night of It," and "Mr. Minns and His Cousin," vividly describe the street life of London as seen by a ruminative pedestrian who observes the domestic misadventures and bungling social aspirations of lower- to middle-class citizens. The narrator's simultaneous attraction to and distancing from his subjects reflects the work's journalistic objectivity but creates an uneven tone, swinging from sentimental or sympathetic to facetious or ironic. Several sketches in this collection are more properly termed short stories, including such tales as "The Black Veil," a psychological study of a wife who calculates her self-worth based on her husband's net worth, and "The Drunkard's Death," an unsentimental account of a once-prosperous alcoholic's demise.

Among the better-known stories of Dickens' oeuvre are his Christmas books, including *A Christmas Carol, The Chimes,* and *The Cricket on the Hearth,* which feature fallen protagonists who realize their mistakes after witnessing remarkable, even supernatural events. Most of these tales appeared in his miscellanies' annual Christmas numbers, which typically revolved around a single theme suggested each year by Dickens to contributing authors, with whom he sometimes collaborated. For instance, the theme of the 1856 Christmas number of *Household Words* centers on the plight of British seamen, which inspired "The Wreck of the Golden Mary," a collaborative effort between Dickens and Wilkie Collins. Based on actual events of the shipwreck of the title vessel during the California Gold Rush, this tale recounts the crew's heroic efforts to maintain sanity and civilized order by swapping stories. In the 1866 Christmas number of *All the Year Round,* the theme is railway operations and safety, which informs "The Signalman," one of Dickens' more popular short stories. In it, the narrator doubts the sanity of a railroad signalman who believes that the phantom he earlier saw on the tracks presages his own death. When the narrator finds the signalman dead the next day, he begins to question his initial skepticism of a supernatural world.

A fascination with supernatural phenomena extends beyond Dickens' Christmas numbers. In the novella *The Haunted Man and the Ghost's Bargain* (1848), the protagonist accepts a ghost's offer to erase his memories in order to escape the pain of past injuries; but he soon learns the real cost when people around him also lose their memories. "To Be Read at Dusk" focuses on the powers of hypnosis and premonitions of loved ones' deaths, both subjects of popular fads during the nineteenth century.

Dickens' last story collection, *The Uncommercial Traveller,* draws upon memories of his own life in such stories as "Dullborough Town," which describes his childhood home, and "City of London Churches," which recalls the circumstances of his first love.

CRITICAL RECEPTION

Dickens has commanded the attention of critical and general audiences alike since the beginning of his literary career. Commentators have praised his comedy and his realism, his endearing characters and their moving plights, and the journalistic integrity and morality of his narratives. They have also widely recognized the influence of Dickens' stories on the contemporary mythology surrounding the Christmas season. Many critics have examined Dickens' narrative techniques in his short fiction—particularly what Michael E. Schiefelbein has called the "detail overload" characterizing his prose style—and have investigated the role his miscellanies played in the development of his fiction.

Another area of critical endeavor has involved attempts to articulate Dickens' aesthetic theory of the short story genre, an especially difficult task, since Dickens' thoughts on the subject consist of scattered references in his correspondence. Some critics have explicated Dickens' depiction of a number of social evils within the context of contemporary medical diagnoses of such disorders as post-traumatic stress and alcoholism; others have explained the ideological significance of Dickens' treatment of class resentment and discontent as symptoms of a disease. For many, the narrative implications of the unconscious and the memory upon the structures, characterizations, and images of Dickens' short stories has occupied a major portion of their scholarship.

PRINCIPAL WORKS

Short Fiction

Sketches by Boz, Illustrative of Every-Day Life, and Every-Day People [as Boz] 1836
Master Humphrey's Clock 1840
A Christmas Carol, in Prose: Being a Ghost Story of Christmas 1843
The Chimes: A Goblin Story of Some Bells That Rang an Old Year Out and a New Year In 1844
The Cricket on the Hearth: A Fairy Tale of Home 1845
The Haunted Man and the Ghost's Bargain: A Fancy for Christmas-time 1848
To Be Read at Dusk 1852
The Seven Poor Travellers 1855
The Wreck of the Golden Mary [with Wilkie Collins] 1856
The Perils of Certain English Prisoners and Their Treasure in Women, Children, Silver, and Jewels [with Collins] 1857
The Haunted House 1859
Christmas Books 1860
Hunted Down: A Story 1860
The Uncommercial Traveller 1861
*Mugby Junction; and Dr. Marigold's Prescriptions 1867
Selected Short Fiction [edited by Deborah A. Thomas] 1976
Sketches by Boz and Other Early Papers, 1833-39 [edited by Michael Slater] (1994)

Other Major Works

The Posthumous Papers of the Pickwick Club [as Boz] (novel) 1836-37
Oliver Twist (novel) 1838
The Life and Adventures of Nicholas Nickleby (novel) 1838-39
The Old Curiosity Shop (novel) 1840-41
Barnaby Rudge: A Tale of the Riots of 'Eighty (novel) 1841
American Notes for General Circulation (essays) 1842
The Life and Adventures of Martin Chuzzlewit (novel) 1842-44
Dealings with the Firm of Dombey and Son, Wholesale, Retail, and for Exportation (novel) 1846-48

The Personal History of David Copperfield (novel) 1849-50
Bleak House (novel) 1852-53
Hard Times: For These Times (novel) 1854
Little Dorrit (novel) 1855-57
A Tale of Two Cities (novel) 1859
Great Expectations (novel) 1861
Our Mutual Friend (novel) 1864-65
The Mystery of Edwin Drood (novel) 1870

*This work contains eight individual short stories, four of which are by Dickens.

CRITICISM

Ruth Glancy (essay date spring 1987)

SOURCE: Glancy, Ruth. "'To Be Read at Dusk.'" *Dickensian* 83, no. 411 (spring 1987): 40-7.

[*In the following essay, Glancy explicates Dickens' concern with altered states of consciousness in "To Be Read at Dusk," drawing parallels between its narrative elements and paranormal influences.*]

'To Be Read at Dusk' is one of Dickens's least known short stories, having been almost entirely neglected since its first publication in 1852. This neglect is unfortunate, because although the little piece has the failings common to much of the fiction written for popular journals, it is also a recognizably Dickensian story, dealing very simply with some of the central issues of his better known works, in particular the workings of the mind under unusual conditions.

The manuscript of **'To Be Read at Dusk'** is now in the Royal Library at Windsor, having been placed there on 21 January 1903 by Queen Mary, then Her Royal Highness the Princess of Wales, 'to be preserved in the Royal Library till further command'.[1] The library does not know how Queen Mary came to obtain the manuscript. The story first appeared in Miss Power's annual, *The Keepsake,* in 1852, from which it was hastily pirated by *Harper's* in New York, appearing there in January 1852. It was not published again until 1882, when it appeared in R. H. Shepherd's edition of *The Plays and Poems of Charles Dickens.* Its best-known re-printing, however, was by F. G. Kitton, who titled his useful 1898 collection of Dickensian oddments **To Be Read at Dusk and Other Stories, Sketches and Essays.**[2] The story has seldom been republished until recently, when a new interest in Dickens's short-story work, and in the genre of the ghost story in particular, has made it much more accessible.[3]

'To Be Read at Dusk' is structured in the style of Dickens's favourite short-story collection, *The Arabian Nights.* A framework provides the essential ingredients of a ghost story: a narrator who is rational, believable, and detached from his story; an audience; and a setting which establishes the necessary atmosphere and mood. As Dickens stipulates in his title, ghost stories belong to dusk, when, as he says in **The Haunted Man,**

> . . . twilight everywhere released the shadows, prisoned up all day, that now closed in and gathered like mustering swarms of ghosts. . . . When these shadows brought into the minds of older people, other thoughts, and showed them different images. When they stole from their retreats, in the likenesses of forms and faces from the past, from the grave, from the deep, deep gulf, where the things that might have been, and never were, are always wandering.[4]

'To Be Read at Dusk' contains two short supernatural stories, narrated by two mountain couriers to their fellow couriers, and to the eavesdropping first-person narrator of the whole piece. The manuscript shows that at proof stage Dickens altered the setting to make it more appropriately eerie. In the manuscript the couriers are sitting on a bench outside the Hotel de Loucher; the location of the hotel in Switzerland is hard to decipher but appears to be a corruption of Chamonix, perhaps Chamonny. The hotel's name translates as 'to squint', its adjectival form meaning 'suspicious' or 'shady'. At proof stage Dickens cancelled this setting for the convent of the Great Saint Bernard, which he had visited in September 1846. The new setting allowed him to introduce the macabre element of the nearby shed, open to the public, which contained the slowly decaying bodies of people who had been lost in the snow.[5] At proof stage Dickens removed a direct reference to the location, changing Mount Blanc to general references about 'the mountain'. The lonely, still, chilly exterior of the convent is made eerier still by the presence of the dead bodies, described in Dickens's letter as 'holding ghastly possession of the mountain where they died', and by the description of the setting sun staining the mountain-tops red. Although the German courier likens the stain to wine, the language evokes blood: the snow is 'stained' where the wine appears to have been broached, but 'had not yet had time to sink into the snow' (p. 66).[6] Soon the snow is 'reddened', and then the wine soaks in completely and the mountains return to white, like the gradual draining of a dead man's face. Because the metaphor is juxtaposed to the reference to the 'belated travellers' who 'slowly wither away, knowing no corruption in that cold region', it casts a chilly sense of deadness, or loss of consciousness, over the story. What better setting for ghost stories, or stories of unusual states of consciousness, as are about to be narrated by the couriers?

The germ of the first story can be clearly traced to Dickens's mesmeric relationship with Madame de la Rue in

1844 and 1845. The courier relates how he was employed to accompany a young English couple on their honeymoon to Italy. With a maid they settle into an old palace near Genoa, the description of which identifies it clearly as the Villa Doria, recommended by Emile de la Rue as the ideal place for the Dickens family to stay. Angus Fletcher, who was making the arrangements, did not take it, much to Dickens's regret. The house, isolated, dark and gloomy with its thick surroundings of woods, was near the sea and, according to Dickens, 'full of the most unaccountable pictures and the most incredible furniture'.[7] To this strange holiday home the carefree husband takes his pretty new bride, despite his knowledge that she is 'haunted' by the dream of a face, which had come to her on the three nights preceding her wedding. The face 'of a dark, remarkable-looking man, in black, with black hair and a grey moustache', with 'a reserved and secret air' who is 'looking at her fixedly, out of darkness' (p. 69) haunts her still; she fears that she will find the face among the old pictures in the palazzo. When her fears prove groundless she begins to relax; the dream, not forgotten, loses its intensity. But when a stranger appears and is entertained by the husband, the bride recognizes him instantly as her dream man. She collapses and is haunted all night by fearful hallucinations. Her husband, charmed by the attentive and well-mannered Signor Dellombra, treats his wife's fears as 'fancies', and urges her sternly to '[resist] her strange weakness' (p. 73). He believes that by encouraging Dellombra's friendship and ignoring his wife's fears, he will rid her of her delusion. But on a visit to Rome for the carnival, the bride suddenly vanishes. The courier and the husband pursue her, but lose the trail at a post-house whose horses had been hired twelve hours previously by Signor Dellombra. In his carriage was 'a frightened English lady crouching in one corner' (p. 74). She is never seen again.

Many details link the story to Dickens's experiences with mesmerism in Genoa. Madame de la Rue, his 'patient', was suffering from a nervous disorder which had become centred on a 'bad spirit',[8] a male figure which appeared to her, threatening, fearful and above all powerful. At first Dickens refers to it in letters to Emile de la Rue as the phantom,[9] the name he selected for Redlaw's *doppelgänger* in **The Haunted Man**. But he came to call it also the shadow, which in Italian is 'l'ombra'.[10] In the manuscript the mysterious stranger's name is di l'Ombra, an even more obvious identification with 'the shadow' than the published form, Dellombra. Dickens mesmerized Madame de la Rue a number of times during the winter of 1844-1845 in Genoa, and the treatment became increasingly a battle of wills between Dickens and the shadow. Dickens was clearly flattered that because of his patient's trust in him, he could overcome this mysterious and powerful antagonist. When the Dickenses left on a tour of Italy, Dickens kept in constant touch with de la Rue, fearing that

in his absence the phantom would gain control of Madame de la Rue's mind. He urged him to bring her to Rome to meet Dickens, adding 'I see af[ar] off, how *essential it is that this Phantom should not regain its power* for an instant'.[11] Dickens's frequent letters to de la Rue emphasize the novelist's sense of his power over Madame de la Rue and the phantom; he evidently gloried in the knowledge that he alone could combat the evil spirit. Without him, Madame de la Rue was doomed to madness:

> That figure is so closely connected with the secret distresses of her very soul—and the impression made upon it is so entwined with her confidence and trust in me, and her knowledge of the power of the Magnetism—*that it must not make head again.* From what I know from her, I know there is more danger and delay in one appearance of that figure than in a dozen fits of the severest bodily pain. Believe nothing she says of her capacity of endurance, if the reappearance of that figure should become frequent. Consult that, mainly, and before all other signs. I shudder at the very thought of the precipice on which she has stood, when that Fancy has persecuted her. If you find her beset by it, induce her to be got to me by one means or other; for there the danger lies so deep, that she herself can hardly probe it, even now.[12]

Separated from his patient, Dickens became increasingly fearful that the phantom would regain control, perhaps by making Madame de la Rue believe that Dickens himself was threatened.[13] Dickens's power over her seemed to be waning, as on the occasion when she deliberately stayed out late at a Casino Ball to avoid a pre-planned long-distance mesmeric transference from Dickens. He again urged de la Rue to bring her to Rome: 'I *cannot* beat [the phantom] down, or keep it down, at a distance. Pursuing that Magnetic power, and being near to her and with her, I believe that I can shiver it like Glass'.[14] When they met in Rome in March, Dickens mesmerized Madame de la Rue constantly, continuing the treatment during their travels in Italy afterwards, to his wife Catherine's increasing annoyance and jealousy. When Dickens left Italy in June, he felt his influence over the Phantom to be so great as to almost ensure his success. He wrote to de la Rue from Brussels that Madame de la Rue had admitted to seeing 'a Shadow for an instant—the Shadow of the Bad Shadow—passing in a great hurry: escaping observation; hanging its head; and nearly worn away'.[15] Dickens considered this more promising than if she had seen no shadow at all.

In returning to the winter of 1844-45 in his 1852 story, Dickens was clearly playing with the potentialities of Madame de la Rue's subservience to a delusion that took the form of a threatening man. The story fulfils Dickens's frequent speculation on what would happen if the phantom were allowed to take over. The loving but practical and essentially unsympathetic husband in the story brings about the catastrophe by his flippant attitude, so markedly at variance with the intense seriousness of Dickens as mesmerist and Emile, the long-suffering and eternally patient and understanding husband. Dickens saw his relationship with Madame de la Rue's phantom as very much a battle for her psyche, a battle which he would lose if he were not a constant aggressor. The fictional husband, in contrast, regards his wife's fears as a 'strange weakness' which can be easily overcome. He actually encourages Dellombra's visits, thinking that his wife's dread of the stranger is merely 'fanciful' (p. 73). Because the husband fails to recognize Dellombra's power over his wife, he loses her.

A constant obsession for Dickens in his mesmeric experiences, in his public readings, and in his fiction was the power which a person, real or imagined, could exert over another.[16] The critics of mesmerism in the nineteenth century were concerned with the nature of mesmeric power, and in particular its strong sexual foundation: most mesmerists were men; most patients, young women. Because of the hold which Dellombra maintains over the young wife, Michael Slater sees him as a clever blending of phantom and mesmerist. In the girl's dream Dellombra is 'looking at her fixedly, out of darkness', (p. 69), just as the mesmerist relies heavily on eye contact. In the story the mesmerist thus becomes the sexual victor and justifies Catherine's increasing uneasiness and jealousy of her husband's relationship with young Madame de la Rue.[17] But this would place Dickens in opposition to Emile de la Rue, whose friendship with Dickens extended well beyond 1852, and whose lack of jealousy and constant support was admirable throughout the relationship between his wife and Dickens. Although Dellombra exerts a certain mesmeric power in the story, he is rather Madame de la Rue's equally powerful 'shadow', given more substance. Dickens must have felt that the phantom's hold over her was more than just fear, as Dellombra is very clearly attractive as well as terrifying. He is handsome but secretive; that he is both dark-haired and grey moustached suggests that he combines the sexual energy of a young man with the experience and maturity of an older one. At proof stage Dickens added an important line to the bride's reaction to him: she is primarily frightened, but to the description of her casting down her eyes before him Dickens added the line 'or would look at him with a terrified and fascinated glance' (p. 73). He then added 'evil' to the remaining phrase, 'as if his presence had some evil influence or power upon her'. The phlegmatic English husband borrows a phrase from Dickens's letters when he then assures that her 'apprehension is broken like glass'. The manuscript shows that this simile was originally 'apprehension is dispersed forever'. This again identifies Dellombra very clearly with the phantom, and suggests that her husband could have freed his wife from the mysterious foreigner's grasp, just as Dickens freed Madame de la Rue. The

implication in 'fascinated' is that the young bride half welcomes Dellombra's advances, and the story elucidates a subject kept hidden by Victorian propriety, but well-known to a writer such as Dickens. The bride is the victim, not so much of Dellombra, as of the rational, staid husband. For a married woman to be attracted to a handsome, accomplished foreigner was unthinkable; but such an attraction, while not allowed to be considered by an English gentlewoman, appeared subconsciously in her dream before her marriage, and eventually conquered the unimaginative and self-assured husband. Dickens is here asserting deeply-buried responses in the woman to an attraction which society, and her own conscience, could not allow. She is last seen 'crouching' in a corner of the carriage because she herself would be afraid to face such a deeply repressed sexual attraction for another man. But the implication is very strongly that the woman is not abducted; she goes against her conscious will, while subconsciously wishing to replace her conventional marriage with a more passionate relationship.

The transformation of a dream or hallucination into a real person was partly a convention of the supernatural story, and one which Dickens admitted borrowing from Elizabeth Gaskell. Writing to her about it, he called it 'a very remarkable instance of a class of mental phenomena . . . certainly the best known, and the best certified, and among the most singular class out of many'.[18] According to Forster, Dickens had exactly this experience himself, in May 1863. He dreamed of a lady in a red shawl, unknown to him, who called herself Miss Napier. The following night, after his public reading, a friend came in to his dressing room and introduced a lady with the same appearance and the same name.[19] Dickens does not attempt to explain the phenomenon. The second story told in **'To Be Read at Dusk'** describes another well-known psychic occurrence in which the apparition of a dying man, Mr John, appears to his brother James shortly before John's death. Dickens told Mrs Gaskell that he believed the story to be 'in the slightest incident, perfectly true'.[20] In the same letter Dickens wrote that 'ghost stories, illustrating particular states of mind and processes of the imagination, are common property . . . except in the manner of relating them, and O who can rob some people of that!'. Undoubtedly the appearance of a person near death to someone emotionally close to them is a common psychic phenomenon. One telling of such an incident, which may have influenced Dickens's story, is provided by Daniel Defoe in his *History and Reality of Apparitions,* a long essay which Dickens would have read in his Scott edition of Defoe's works. One of the many apparition stories told by Defoe concerns a murdered man who appears to his brother when the latter is lying in bed, but 'broad awake'. The narrator relates how

> my brother, or an apparition of my brother, came to the
> bed's feet, and opened the curtain, looking full in my

face, but did not speak. I was very much frighted, but however I so far recovered as to say to him, Brother, what is the matter with you?

He had a napkin-cap on his head, which was very bloody, he looked very pale and ghastly, and said, I am basely murdered by—, (naming the person,) but I shall have justice done me; and then disappeared.[21]

Dickens's little story, though less dramatic, has certain parallels with Defoe's. Although the dying brother is suffering only from gout and the apparition does not speak to James, it appears, like Defoe's, in the night when James is lying awake: '. . . it came into my room, in a white dress, and, regarding me earnestly, passed up to the end of the room, glanced at some papers on my writing-desk, turned, and, still looking earnestly at me as it passed the bed, went out at the door' (pp. 75-76). James assures his servant that the apparition is merely a sign that he himself is ill, and that it had no 'external existence' outside himself. Dickens achieves his supernatural shiver, however, by concluding the story with the news of John's illness. When James then rushes to his bedside, John's last words to his brother are 'James, you have seen me before, to-night—and you know it!'. Dickens's interpretation of the incident differs from Defoe's, however. In *The History and Reality of Apparitions* Defoe argues that the apparition of a person now or once living has no connection with that person. Apparitions are good angels or evil spirits who take on the appearance of an actual person to serve their ends. Dickens's story, on the other hand, depends for its effect on this connection; the dying brother could know about the apparition's visit only if he had some psychic link with it.

For Dickens the appeal of the supernatural story was always its special ability to reveal unusual states of consciousness or heightened thought transferences. He deliberately avoided giving psychic occurrences religious significance, and ridiculed those who did in **The Haunted House**. The purpose of **'To Be Read at Dusk'** was primarily to entertain the readers of a fashionable magazine, but at the same time the story allowed Dickens to demonstrate unusual states of mind and the way in which paranormal occurrences can reveal the breadth and complexity of the mind's operation.

Notes

1. I acknowledge the gracious permission of Her Majesty the Queen to quote from the manuscript.

2. The subtitle 'now first collected' indicates that Kitton had overlooked Shepherd's earlier volume. In his introduction Kitton refers to a 'pamphlet' publication of the story which, he says, appeared in 1852 and which in 1898 was so scarce that a copy had recently fetched twenty-five guineas. Kitton and other early bibliographers were un-

aware that this pamphlet was a forgery, first spotted in 1934, and presumed now to be dated around 1890. See John Carter and Graham Pollard, 'Charles Dickens', in *An Enquiry into the Nature of Certain Nineteenth Century Pamphlets* (London, 1934), pp. 185-187, reprinted (London, 1984).

3. It appears, for example, in *The Short Stories of Charles Dickens,* ed. Walter Allen (New York, 1971); Charles Dickens, *Selected Short Fiction,* ed. Deborah A. Thomas (London, 1976); *The Supernatural Short Stories of Charles Dickens,* ed. Michael Hayes (London, 1978); *The Complete Ghost Stories of Charles Dickens,* ed. Peter Haining (London, 1982).

4. *The Christmas Books,* ed. Michael Slater (London, 1971), II, 250.

5. For Dickens's description of the convent see *The Letters of Charles Dickens,* ed. Kathleen Tillotson (Oxford, 1977), IV, 618-620. Dickens returned to this grisly scene to great effect in *Little Dorrit.*

6. Bracketed page numbers following quotations refer to the Deborah Thomas edition of the story, see note 3. A similar description of the setting sun's colour as blood-like is found at the beginning of Book II, chapter 8 of *A Tale of Two Cities.* Here the staining of the Marquis's face and hands by the sun is both a sign of his guilt (he is 'steeped in crimson') and a foreshadowing of his own murder ('It will die out', said Monsieur the Marquis, glancing at his hands, 'directly'.).

7. *The Letters of Charles Dickens,* IV, 316. For a detailed discussion of Dickens's relationship with Madame de la Rue see Fred Kaplan, *Dickens and Mesmerism: The Hidden Springs of Fiction* (Princeton, 1975).

8. *The Letters of Charles Dickens,* IV, 248.

9. *Ibid.*

10. *Ibid.,* IV, 260.

11. *Ibid.,* IV, 250.

12. *Ibid.,* IV, 255.

13. *Ibid.,* IV, 259.

14. *Ibid.,* IV, 261.

15. *Ibid.,* IV, 323.

16. Dickens described to his wife the power he felt when he reduced Charles Macready to tears by reading *The Chimes* to him. See *The Letters of Charles Dickens,* IV, 235. In the fiction, two striking examples are Miss Havisham's control over Estella in *Great Expectations,* and in *The Lazy Tour of Two Idle Apprentices* the villain's successful willing of his young bride to die simply by ordering her to do so.

17. *Dickens and Women* (London, 1983), pp. 124-125.

18. *The Letters of Charles Dickens,* ed. Walter Dexter (London, 1938), II, 359-360.

19. John Forster, *The Life of Charles Dickens,* ed. A. J. Hoppé (London, 1966), II, 402.

20. *The Letters of Charles Dickens,* ed. Walter Dexter, II, 360.

21. *The Novels and Miscellaneous Works of Daniel Defoe,* ed. Sir Walter Scott (Oxford, 1840), XIII, 170.

Michael E. Schiefelbein (essay date June 1991)

SOURCE: Schiefelbein, Michael E. "Narrative Experience and Specificity: Reading Dickens's 'Boarding-House.'" *Dickens Quarterly* 8, no. 2 (June 1991): 57-67.

[*In the following essay, Schiefelbein investigates the role of "detail overload" in Dickens's fiction, demonstrating how the details affect reader engagement with the plot, themes, and emotional resonance of "The Boarding-House."*]

In engaging its audience in a hypothetical world, a narrative promises both emotional and cognitive experience, as Mary Louise Pratt suggests in her description of the story teller's purpose, which is

> to produce in his hearers not only belief but also an imaginative and affective involvement in the state of affairs he is representing and an evaluative stance toward it. He intends them to share his wonder, amusement, terror, or admiration of the event. Ultimately, it would seem, what he is after is an *interpretation* of the problematic event, an assignment of meaning and value supported by the consensus of himself and his hearers.
>
> (136)

Yet, despite her acknowledgment of the emotion-evoking aspect of narrative, Pratt focuses on its cognitive component throughout her study, in which she ultimately equates the "point" of narrative with the evaluation process and neglects both to account for the "wonder, amusement, terror, or admiration" that a story inspires and to explain how emotion is connected to our judgment process. Perhaps this failure occurs because Pratt abandons her discussion of the similarities between oral and written narratives—the very premise for her speech act theory of literature[1]—in order to explore the more sophisticated characteristics of novels, particularly the discrepancies between the message of the author and the message of the narrator. Her investigation of literary irony (some very old territory) leads her far away from the wonder or terror that oral narratives often provoke.

This is unfortunate because providing sensory-based, emotional experience is also an important function of narrative. Not only does such experience involve the reader in the story, but it is also intricately linked to the reader's evaluation. In other words, the "point" of reading a narrative is both to imagine and to evaluate, and the latter activity often follows form or is reinforced by the former. Ross Chambers, another theorist whose premise that narrative is an experience-producing speech act, does a better job of accounting for narrative's emotional component than does Pratt. Chambers understands narration as a seductive act performed by the storyteller, who derives his or her authority from the ability to lure readers into identifying with specific narrative situations embedded in the tale. Chambers calls these narrative mirrorings "self-referential apparatus" that provide the context for experiencing the story. Through analyzing the desires of the audience of the embedded narrative, readers cast their own narrative desires into relief and find themselves satisfied or frustrated by the turns taken by the tale.

Chambers's self-referential theory is valuable not only because it accounts for the emotional component of the narrative experience, but also because it grounds that experience in features unique to a given text. It seems to suggest that we can talk about the Wharton experience, the Borges experience, the Dostoevsky experience, and the Bronte experience. The narrative experience thus becomes a richer, more liberating concept, being defined by, rather than defining, individual stories.

As it stands, however, I do not think that Chambers's theory actually allows us to describe the experience offered by just any author. By restricting self-referential apparatus to instances of narrative mirrorings, it limits the stories we can examine to those with embedded narratives—the only kind of story that Ross treats in his study. But many texts contain no stories-within-stories or other narration-reflective devices that figure prominently in their narratives, and these texts would receive no attention if we accepted Chamber's limited definition of self-referential apparatus. It would be much more fruitful to recognize any textual feature that calls attention to itself as a determinant of narrative experience,[2] for then we could describe the experiences afforded by all narratives and distinguish authors according to the unique ways their narratives involve the reader.

I. THE SELF-REFERENTIAL IN DICKENS: SPECIFICITY

In the remainder of this essay, I intend to demonstrate this larger understanding of self-referentiality by focusing on the Dickens experience, at once cognitive and emotional. Many features present themselves as prominent in a Dickens narrative—the intrusive narrator, humor, melodramatic devices, and convoluted plots, to name just a few. Although any of these could be singled out as a contributing determinant of the Dickens experience, I would like to focus on a feature which I take to be much more basic: specificity. When we think of the Dickens narrative what usually comes to mind are those 800-page novels of twenty numbers, packed with idiosyncratic minor characters (who have varying degrees of relevance to the plot), lengthy descriptions of London's nooks, and an abundance of other superfluous information that resists integration into a larger meaning. In a word, it is easy to equate the Dickens narrative with detail "overload."

Rather than understanding the piling of facts upon facts as an obstacle to appreciating Dickens, however, I want to argue that the challenge to negotiate details is an essential part of the Dickens experience. Moreover, I would like to suggest that engagement in the Dickens narrative occurs at three levels, two of which are rational—involving memory and intellect—and one of which is emotional. I would further propose that though the experiences at these levels are at once interdependent and concurrent, we can, for the sake of convenience, consider them separately. Let me briefly describe these three experiences before demonstrating them in a particular Dickens narrative.

THREE EXPERIENCE LEVELS

An obvious level of experiencing a Dickens narrative occurs at the level of the plot, where we must keep track of a great deal of information about character qualities and background in order to isolate the various strands of action. That is, before we can define events and the nature of their connection, we must first connect information to the participants in these events. Sometimes we must sort through the background of several characters within a few pages or keep track of character information over a span of many paragraphs or chapters laden with detail. (In a Dickens novel we must also connect the various threads of convoluted plots.) This plot level challenges the memory primarily: it is a mental exercise that yields its own kind of experience, both frustrating and pleasurable.

At another level, we attempt to organize plot information into thematic elements. In the thicket of information, we search for details that stand out, usually because they encourage, rather than resist, categorization and thereby suggest a thematic pattern. The process at the second level begins as an intellectual activity, but as it becomes conditioned by images, it takes on emotional significance. Image formation constitutes the third level of experience. We construct basic images from details about characters and from the descriptions of cities and neighborhoods. We also fashion more abstract images on the basis of the plot. For example, we can isolate a sequence of images that we construct from the *Bleak House* narrative, from the opening image of fog to the closing image of the Woodcourt hearth. As our imagination is engaged, so are our emotions since images are positive or negative—uplifting, reassuring, gloomy, or frightening. As images merge, negating or modifying one another, so do our emotions, until we settle on an overall sense of the narrative.

These three experiences, as I have mentioned, occur both interdependently and concurrently: while we absorb and connect plot information, we forge thematic links and shape images. We insert images into plot, bestowing them with temporal and causal relations that we have borrowed from the story line. The Dickens narrative thus transforms itself into a narrative of images, if you will, which weaves itself into the story. As we integrate these three processes, we experience the fullest power of the narrative. We do more than achieve simply an intellectual understanding of the futility and despair engulfing the victims of the Chancery system in *Bleak House,* for example: from narrative elements we actually construct an emotional experience of it.

Because of the impracticality of tracing these three levels of experience in a bulky Dickens novel, I will demonstrate them in a tale from *Sketches by Boz.* **"The Boarding-House,"** replete with the characteristic Dickensian prolixity of detail, serves as an excellent model of the more complex narratives of the Dickens novels.

II. EXPERIENCING "THE BOARDING-HOUSE"

FIRST LEVEL: PLOT AND MEMORY

In his famous essay on Dickens, George Orwell concludes that one of Dickens's distinguishing features—which both lends an element of surprise to his novels and mars them as art—is his attention to the *unecessary details* (ch. 1, pt. IV). Two questions arise over such a judgment: how do we decide what is unnecessary, and what do we mean by a "work of art"? The answer to the latter question naturally determines the answer to the first. In suggesting that for a work to be art it must establish careful perimeters around details, Orwell espouses a Jamesian idea of art, according to which details are ordered to an aesthetic design. But if we understand art as a function of one kind or another, rather than as an aesthetic object, unecessary details especially ones that surprise the reader, require a reexamination—particularly when they characterize a set of narratives. Our task is to consider how unecessary details attached to characters in **"The Boarding-House"** lend themselves to a certain experience of the story.

As are many of the Dickens characters, the participants in this tale are caricatures. Mrs. Tibbs is summed up in the first sentence of the story as "the most tidy, fidgety, thrifty little personage that ever inhaled the smoke of London . . ." (275). She is also the stereotypically loquacious, dominating wife. Mr. Tibbs is to his wife merely "what the 0 is in 90—he was some importance *with* her—he was nothing without her" (275). Tibbs plays the stock role of the bumbling henpecked husband, straining to get a word in edgewise. The boarders are similarly characterized by neat descriptions: Mrs. Maplesone is "an enterprising widow" (280); young Hicks, "a poetical walker of the hospitals" (278); and Simpson, one of those "empty-headed" young men who "dressed according to the caricatures published in the monthly fashions" (278).

How uncomplicated it should be to process information about these stock characters. A proper name ought simply to signal typical role attributes that evoke a mental configuration of the character, but textual details often keep this from happening. For example, we read not only that Tibbs received a pension, but that it was "about £43. 15s. 10d. a year" (276). We also learn the precise year in which he was a member of the volunteer corps—1806. As for O'Blearly, though the narrator is content to describe him in stereotypical terms as the happy-go-lucky Irishman in "shepherd's-plaid inexpressibles," he makes a lame attempt to individuate the character by tossing in a single idiosyncrasy: the Irishman "used to look under all the ladies' bonnets as he walked along the streets" (298).

The second chapter, which characterizes Mrs. Bloss as "vulgar, ignorant, and selfish" (294), seems to allow the reader to effortlessly slip subsequent information about her into this clearly defined category. But what does he or she do with an entire paragraph about Mrs. Bloss's deceased husband, the cork-cutter, who, as revenge against his nephew—who, supporting "himself and two sisters on 100£ a year," had shown "the insolence one morning to ask for the loan of fifteen pounds" (294) and then run away with the Blosses's cook (Mr. Bloss's only friend)—had left his whole property with Mrs. Bloss? Not only does this surplus of information neglect to advance the reader's understanding of Mrs. Bloss's delineated character, but it surpasses a simple informative function: the reader "needs" to know only that Mrs. Bloss can afford to live at the boarding house because of her inheritance.

In addition to managing strangely precise and superfluous information about caricatures, the reader of **"The Boarding-House"** must often reconnect information to them across dense stretches of text. Between the passage in which young Simpson is introduced and that in which Matilda Maplesone remarks upon the magnificence of his attire—a space of only about two pages—Dickens has stuffed an amazing amount of colorful material to be mulled over. There is the scene in which the young gentlemen (with no textual allusions to their dis-

tinguishing traits) are introduced to the ladies. There is the description of the pantomime performed over the fish by Mrs. Tibbs and her servant. There is Julia's good figure to consider, and the discussion about hackney coachmen between Mrs. Maplesone and Mrs. Tibbs. There is a joke about Tibbs's request for clean linen and a lengthy description of Mr. Carlton's moral and financial history, as well as of his intentions towards Mrs. Maplesone. Finally, there is paragraph of data about Mrs. Maplesone herself. By the time we read the exchange between the two Maplesone girls over "the magnificent individual" in a "maroon-coloured dresscoat, with a velvet collar and cuffs of the same tint" (281), we may well have forgotten whether Simpson is the "poet" or the "empty-headed" young man and will probably need to thumb back for a clarification in order to attach the details to the correct configuration.

Tracking information about characters is so difficult because the narrative does not provide the materials for an easy synthesis of generalizations and idiosyncrasies; characters refuse to cohere as complete entities. The reader constructs two separate lists, as it were, of characterizing labels and individuating details, which, when juxtaposed, elude integration. Moreover, the frustrated reader finds no assistance in commentary, implicit or explicit, by character or narrator, that explains how highly specific information expands, complicates, or simply reinforces the reader's configurations of caricatures. (As Chambers would put it, the text provides no "code models" for interpreting these characters.) Much information presents itself as gratuitous, and keeping it attached to individual caricatures seems an exercise for its own sake.

Naturally, if the reader strains to keep the characters straight, he or she struggles all the more to distinguish the relationships between characters—essential for appreciating the humor of **"The Boarding-House."** The summaries from the two chapters demonstrate how much work the reader needs to do in making connections between characters. I quote them in full here:

> On the following morning, Mr. Septimus Hicks was united to Miss Matilda Maplesone. Mr. Simpson also entered into a "holy alliance" with Miss Julia; Tibbs acting as father, "his first appearance in that character." Mr. Carlton, not being quite so eager as the two young men, was rather struck by the double discovery; and as he had found some difficulty in getting anyone to give the lady away, it occurred to him that the best mode of obviating the inconvenience would be not to take her at all. The lady, however, "appealed," as her counsel said on the trial of the cause, *Maplesone v. Carlton,* for a breach of promise, "with a broken heart, to the outraged laws of her country." She recovered damages to the amount of £1,000, which the unfortunate knocker was compelled to pay. Mr. Septimus Hicks having walked the hospitals, took it into his head to walk off altogether. His injured wife is at present residing with

her mother in Boulogne. Mr. Simpson, having the misfortune to lose his wife six weeks after marriage (by her eloping with an officer during his temporary sojourn in the Fleet Prison, in consequence of his inability to discharge her little mantua-maker's bill), and being disinherited by his father, who died soon afterwards, was fortunate enough to obtain a permanent engagement at a fashionable haircutter's.

(290)

We must leave the scene that ensued to the reader's imagination. We could tell how Mrs. Tibbs forthwith fainted away, and how it required the united strength of Mr. Wisbottle and Mr. Alfred Tompkins to hold her in her chair; how Mr. Evenson explained, and how his explanation was evidently disbelieved; how Agnes repelled the accusations of Mrs. Tibbs by proving that she was negotiating with Mr. O'Bleary to influence her mistress's affections in his behalf; and how Mr. Gobler threw a damp counterpane on the hopes of Mr. O'Bleary by avowing that he (Gobler) had already proposed to, and been accepted by, Mrs. Bloss; how Agnes was discharged from that lady's service; how Mr. O'Bleary discharged himself from Mrs. Tibb's house. . . . The lady whom we have hitherto described as Mrs. Bloss is no more. Mrs. Gobler exists: Mrs. Bloss has left us forever. . . . Mr. and Mrs. Tibbs have separated by mutual consent. . . .

(310)

At the end of the first chapter we find two characters marrying and then divorcing one another, and two characters separating from one another when one partner retracts the proposal. In the second chapter we also find marriages and broken relationships (including maidmistress and boarder-landlady relationships). Unless we take notes, however, we struggle to remember who marries whom and who leaves whom.

Many factors hinder the reader from connecting characters. Because the characters taken individually resist gelling into whole configurations, their relationships with others do the same. One list of generalizations about a character juxtaposed to a list of peculiarities has been associated (through union or separation) with another list of generalizations juxtaposed to still another list of peculiarities. Add to this the appearance of distracting information like the mantua-maker's bill and Mrs. Tibb's fainting fit, as well as the density of information, and it is easy to see the impossible task facing the reader. Paradoxically, however, at this level the story demands that the reader forge connections: Mrs. Maplesone sues Mr. Carlton because he declines to marry her since he cannot get Hicks or Tibbs to give the bride away, for one will be occupied marrying one of Mrs. Maplesone's daughters while the other will be giving away the second daughter in her own marriage to Simpson, the only other possible candidate for giving away Mrs. Maplesone.

If the interconnections in this sequence seem bewildering, examine the situation that leads to the dissipation of boarders at the end of the second chapter: Mrs. Tibbs

and Mr. Evenson eavesdrop outside the kitchen door on Agnes and O'Bleary who seem to be discussing a scheme to murder Mrs. Bloss and steal her money so that they can run away together, when suddenly Tompkins and Wisbottle, spying on Mrs. Tibbs and Evenson, advance on their suspects and startle Agnes and O'Bleary, who separate and provide occasion for Mr. Tibbs to corner Agnes and for Mrs. Tibbs to be horrified on hearing her husband's advances and at the thought of being discovered by Wisbottle and Tompkins, who by now have made such a racket that they wake Mrs. Bloss, who wakes Mr. Gobler and proceeds with him to Mrs. Tibbs's door only to find her missing from her room and swooning near Evenson.

Of course, these interlocked elements, as well as the surprising details that resist crystallization create much of the humor for which Dickens is famous. Idiosyncratic detail, though it does not necessarily succeed in realizing a complete character, does entertain us, as does a network of amazing connections. But we experience more than humor on the level of plot. The work of wading through a deluge of unrelated and overly related information turns an apparently simple story of stock characters into a complex reading process. We take on the task of inventing memorable characters with the materials at hand and of analyzing the distinct components of relationships. The story itself, as a result of our own complex interpretive work, takes on a remarkable texture. What at first seemed a simple story of character types acquires a depth derived from our own complicated experience.

SECOND LEVEL: THEMATICS AND INTELLECT

If the abundance and fluidity of detail on the first level of experience sweeps the reader up like a river, the second level offers islands where he or she can land to catch a breath. The second self-referential feature of the Dickens narrative is an element of stability; it is the information that becomes familiar through repetition. While on the first level the reader is overwhelmed by the accumulation of idiosyncratic detail and, paradoxically, by the hyperconnectedness of detail, on the second level he or she finds clarity and reassurance. Certain details stand out from the mass of information in **"The Boarding-House"** because they recur and refer to one another, suggesting patterns of organization or thematic concepts.

Take, for example, Mrs. Tibbs's tidiness first described in the tale's initial paragraph:

Mrs. Tibbs was, beyond all dispute, the most tidy, fidgety, thrifty little personage that ever inhaled the smoke of London; and the house of Mrs. Tibbs was, decidedly, the neatest in all Great Coram Street. The area and the area-steps, and the street-door and the street-door steps, and the brass handle, and the door-plate, and the knocker, and the fan-light, were all as clean and bright, as indefatigable white-washing, and hearth-stoning, and scrubbing and rubbing, could make them. The wonder was, that the brass door-plate, with the interesting inscription "MRS. TIBBS," had never caught fire from constant friction, so perserveringly was it polished.

(275)

This information draws attention to itself for two reasons: the multiple repetitions within it encourage the reader to take it as a unit, and its placement at the beginning of the tale alerts the reader to its function as a possible abstract. I say there are repetitions, because each of details within the paragraph serves to simply restate the assertion in the beginning. By abstract, I am referring to William Labov's concept of a statement, usually located at the beginning of a narrative, which in some sense summarizes the point of the story (see ch. 2 in Pratt).

That Mrs. Tibb's concern with cleanliness is a central element of the story's meaning is reinforced by the repeated reference to it throughout the tale. When the Maplesones first arrive, Mrs. Tibbs furnishes "warm water for the ladies to wash in" and bustles about "distributing towels and soap, like a head nurse in a hospital" (277-78). Before Mrs. Bloss's initial visit to inquire about a room, the "drawing room [is] forthwith dusted for the third time that morning" and Mrs. Tibbs dashes upstairs "'to make herself tidy'" (292). In preparation for Mrs. Bloss's arrival as a boarder, the landlady "devoted all her energies" to cleaning a room for her: "The second-floor front was scrubbed, and washed, and flannelled, till the wet went through to the drawing-room ceiling" (295).

Mrs. Tibbs's preoccupation with housekeeping necessarily affects her husband. He is found either duplicating her concern by requesting clean linen before dinner or being dominated by it, as he is when he hides the gravy he has spilt on the clean tablecloth out of fear of her wrath, or when he is found unhappily "cleaning the gentlemen's boots in the back kitchen" (291). Tibbs's general state of subjugation to his wife is another much repeated piece of information in the narrative. Whenever he begins to tell his volunteer corps story, Mrs. Tibbs "very quickly and loudly" cuts him off. In the dinner scene of the first chapter, the landlady, angry that Tibbs has requested more of the limited supply of fish, commands the servant to take away her husband's knife so that he will not be able to touch the precious entree. At the end of the first chapter she confines him to the kitchen for standing up to her and forces him to clean boots. The inscription of only Mrs. Tibbs's name on the door-plate is "interesting," as the narrator notes, because so telling about her own domination over the household.

Perhaps Mrs. Tibbs's mistreatment of her husband explains his excessive concern with food and drink, about

which the reader continually receives information: in the fish scene, in which, once his knife has been taken, he settles for a crust of bread, "more hungry than ever"; in the breakfast scene in the second chapter, in which "Tibbs sat down at the bottom of the table, and began eating water-cresses like a Nebuchadnezzar" (298); and in the frequent scenes of his drunken bouts, including the final scene in which, "under the influence of gin-and-water" (309) he accosts Agnes. Tibb's advances toward Agnes have not been without warning; he tries to kiss her soon after she arrives, according to Agnes's report to Mrs. Bloss, and in the same report Agnes reveals that Tibbs has been tickling the servants. These bouts of flirtation show that Tibbs is also starving for affection.

The reader naturally connects repeated details. Perhaps he or she will interpret Mrs. Tibbs's continuous bustling and friction-producing scrubbing and compulsive cleaning as misplaced sexual energy that corresponds to the "misplaced attachment" (309) Tibbs forms for Agnes, as well as for food and drink. Such an explanation of the alienation between the Tibbses seems inevitable, but one might interpret their disharmony differently. The point is that repeated information in this narrative provides a solid ground for interpretive work in a sea of details. It draws boundaries around itself, while information on the first level seems to dissolve boundaries in the fluid connection of details. Movement on this second level offers the security of repetition and intelligible interreferentiality, while on the first level it accumulates details chaotically and winds through a confusing labyrinth of connections determined arbitrarily by the narrator.

I have mentioned only a portion of the repeated information that demands the reader's attention in **"The Boarding-House."** The pattern of marriages and divorces also needs to be reckoned with, as does the phenomena of connectedness in general. Do the boarders mirror the Tibbses in some ways, or does the narrative oppose their connectedness to the alienation between the owners of the house? Does their presence simply provide vicarious intimacy for the Tibbses? Or are they just another example of Mrs. Tibbs's reduction of people to objects that will bring money?—after all, the boarders carry on in secret largely because they know the landlady is horrified that someone will get married and leave the boarding house. However individual readers explain the repeated information, whatever oppositions or mirrorings, ironies, or symbols they detect, they will experience confidence that corresponds to their own abilities to see conceptual patterns.

THIRD LEVEL: IMAGES AND EMOTION

Details in this Dickens narrative, whether prominent because they evade synthesis or because they define patterns, trigger images, whose construction constitutes another level of experience for the Dickens reader. Whereas the two levels of experience discussed so far have been primarily rational, depending most heavily upon memory and intellect, this third level of experience is fundamentally emotional, depending upon the imagination. For Dickens, "fanciful treatment" is exactly what distinguished a tale as art, as Deborah Thomas notes in her study of Dickens's short stories.[3] According to Thomas, Dickens measured the effectiveness of his short stories by their imaginative value. Though Dickens never elaborated a systematic philosophy of composition for his short stories, he did indicate in his letter to Reverend James White that they were "supposed to be told by a family sitting around the fire" (quoted in Thomas 4)—an atmosphere most conducive to flights of fancy.

The dominant images evoked by **"The Boarding-House"** correspond to the themes that the reader abstracts from the story because they are derived from the same details. If, for example, details from the tale have suggested the opposing themes of alienation and unity, they will also evoke images of those condition. We form strong images from textual clues as we read—Mrs. Tibbs polishing the brass door-plate, Mr. Tibbs struggling to cover the gravy spill, the deal being stuck in Carlton's room, Tibbs stuck in the kitchen all alone after the marriages. But we also form images from information that is void of explicit sensory detail. After the marriages take place at the end of the first chapter, and after we learn that the house no longer has guests and that Tibbs had been banished to the kitchen, we experience the emptiness associated with the image of a house abandoned by its inhabitants and with the image of married partners who sleep at opposite corners of their abode.

Image formation also differs substantially from the way themes are abstracted. Whereas the second level of experience is one of definition and categorization, the third level reproduces in the imagination the sense of fluidity of the first level. Images derived from a Dickens narrative merge together. They modify one another, negate one another, and build on one another, producing an overall sense of movement, an overall sense of the story. We "see" the boarding house in all its original order and tidiness, the bell lamp "clear as a soap-bubble," the tables where "you could see yourself" and the stair wires that "made your eyes wink, they were so glittering" (275). When we "see" Mrs. Tibbs chastising her husband for putting his feet on the fender and for suggesting that the boarders might be attracted to each other, when we "see" meek Tibbs himself returning each day from the city where he has no job and no real purpose, "with an exceedingly dirty face, and smelling mouldy" (277), and then see him glowing in Mr. Carlton's room over the topic of marriage, we sense the great sterility of the Tibbses's marriage. Perhaps our image of the narrator—controlled, confident, undisturbed—mitigates the severity of the vision (the narrator models an attitude of distance, and thus amusement through the impersonal "we" and through condescending commentary), but we still feel the sadness.

We also feel the life and variety the boarders bring to the boarding house: the awkwardness of Hicks and Simpson who begin "to slide about with much politeness, and to look as if they wished their arms had been legs" (279) in the presence of the coy Maplesone sisters, who sing duets in the parlor, accompanying themselves on guitars. We hear the chatter and clinking at the dinner table and feel the surprise and secrecy of the meeting in Mr. Carlton's room, where marriages are planned. As life that invades the boarding house rushes to a peak, the narrator sums up all the connections that have been constructed and broken, and all the details of the summary—specific names connected to specific names and then separated again—make the unions and divorces palpable. The final image is of a solitary Tibbs, sleeping on a "turn-up bedstead" in the kitchen. This movement from sterility and estrangement to life/clutter/connection/community/chaos and back to estrangement repeats itself again in the second chapter. Again we sense the contrast between distance and intimacy, sheer endurance of a spouse and pursuit of one, tolerance and passion. We sense the limits of order and the freedom of disorder. The power of **"The Boarding-House"** ultimately resides in its ability to evoke these senses.

Thus, the reader of this simple Dickens narrative experiences a complex interweaving of memory, conceptualization, and imagination triggered by the self-referential detail. What has been said about experience on the first level can be extended to the overall reading process, though on a larger scale: a simple story—certainly not a Dickens masterpiece—of characters who lack psychological depth takes on a complexity and rigor borrowed from our own complicated experience; the whole is more than the sum of its parts. Our activity transforms the store of details confronting us in **"The Boarding-House"** into a collage of characters, events, themes, images, and finally an overall sense of the tale.

Notes

1. Pratt drawn on John Searle's elaboration of speech act theory, introduced by John Austin. Speech act theory understands utterances as performative. The particular function that an utterance performs (e.g., to inform, apologize, command, etc.) depends on the situational context in which it occurs. Pratt correctly, I think, extends the concept of "speech act" to the larger narrative utterance, arguing that not just one narrative sentence but the whole narrative occurs within a specific context and is understood to function in a certain way.

2. This is an extension of William Labov's notion of narrative's evaluative component, discussed by Pratt in the second chapter of her book. Labov in-

dicates that wherever the narrator departs from simple present or past tense recounting, he or she is drawing attention to the story's point.

3. See ch. 1 in Thomas, "Imaginative License." Thomas takes the phrase "fanciful treatment" from John Forster's defense of imaginative freedom, quoted on p. 5.

Works Cited

Austin, John L. *How to Do Things With Words*. Oxford: Clarendon Press, 1962.

Chambers, Ross. *Story and Situation: Narrative Seduction and the Power of Fiction*. Vol. 12 of *Theory and History of Literature*. Minneapolis: U of Minnesota, 1984.

Dickens, Charles. *Sketches by Boz*. New Oxford Illustrated Dickens. London: Oxford UP, 1957.

Orwell, George. "Charles Dickens." *Dickens, Dali & Others*. New York: Harcourt, Brace & World, 1946. 1-75.

Pratt, Mary Louise. *Toward a Speech Act Theory of Literacy Discourse*. Bloomington: Indiana UP, 1977.

Searle, John R. *Speech Acts: An Essay in the Philosophy of Language*. Cambridge: Cambridge UP, 1969.

Thomas, Deborah A. *Dickens and the Short Story*. Philadelphia: U of Pennsylvania Press, 1982.

Scott Moncrieff (essay date fall 1991)

SOURCE: Moncrieff, Scott. "Remembrance of Wrongs Past in *The Haunted Man*." *Studies in Short Fiction* 28, no. 4 (fall 1991): 535-41.

[*In the following essay, Moncrieff explains the content of* The Haunted Man and the Ghost's Bargain *in relation to Dickens's memory of his personal experience at a blacking warehouse.*]

At the 1989 MLA Convention, in a panel on "Dickens: Death and/of the Author," Robert Patten argued against understanding Dickens as an isolated genius writing out of strictly personal experience, and instead encouraged study of Dickens's collaborations with artists, other writers, and publishers who shaped his fiction, particularly the early work. "I suggest that we do not attribute every word or myth Dickens projects," says Patten, "to his own artfully contrived Autobiographical Fragment." On the other hand, Patten's fellow panelists Stanley Tick and Elliot Gilbert returned to the focus that has fascinated so many students of Dickens, the Blacking Warehouse episode, the Autobiographical Fragment, and the relation of Dickens's autobiography to his fiction.

And why not? Though these foci themselves are old, and have been critically abused, they continue to produce some of the most illuminating readings of Dickens's fiction and Dickens himself. Patten's implication that the Warehouse has become a sort of PX for card-carrying Dickensians is no doubt correct, yet the interpretive leverage of the Autobiographical Fragment remains indispensable, and in the present case persuades yet another critic to its use.

One may reasonably read the theme of memory as the be-all and end-all of *The Haunted Man*. After all, the plot revolves around Redlaw's loss of memory and his propensity to spread his loss to others. And the story ends with the embroidered refrain "Lord, keep my memory green" (353). Such a reading is posited by Ruth Glancy, who says "memory's restorative power became the dominant concern of the Christmas work" (57). Specifically referring to Redlaw, Glancy writes that "without memory he becomes a man without a soul, as incapable of compassion, artistic sensitivity or spiritual understanding as the abandoned waif whose neglected short life is equally barren of memories" (57). As important as memory admittedly is, however, such a reading tends to overemphasize the process without paying sufficient attention to the product: what matters most, I would argue, is not only memory itself—though at times even Dickens seems to think so—but also what is remembered.

At the story's heart we once again find one of Dickens's bachelor loners. His "habitual reserve, retiring always," and his "solitary and vault-like" dwelling (246-47) confirm that Redlaw is cut off from his fellow man. Whereas Scrooge appears to enjoy a positive zest in his pre-conversion cruelty, Redlaw, like Jackson (of *Mugby Junction*) after him, has a silent, brooding and inward focus. And much more than Scrooge, Redlaw seems to stand in for Dickens himself.

In his especially perceptive essay "The Love Pattern in Dickens' Novels," Harry Stone notes that *The Haunted Man* was composed under particular stress, planned in the summer of 1848 while Dickens's sister Fanny was dying of consumption, and written in the aftermath of her September 2 death (14). Stone argues that

> Dickens used his Christmas novelette to probe some of his most profound dissatisfactions, dissatisfactions which went back to the old Chatham days and earlier, dissatisfactions which had been stirred up and intensified by his sister's death.
>
> (14)

Stone goes so far as to claim that "if one makes allowances for fictional license, Redlaw's history is Dickens' history" (15). Admirably using Dickens's eccentric euphoria about Browning's forgotten play, *A Blot in the*

'Scutcheon (1842), in which an orphan brother and sister show particular fidelity to each other, Stone works out a demonstration of the importance of the idealized brother-sister relationship as a replacement for Dickens's unsatisfactory relations with his parents and spouse.

Stone's argument is undoubtedly impressive, and could have been even more so, had he integrated Dickens's Autobiographical Fragment into his study, which, depending on whom one believes, was written just prior to or about the time of the writing of *The Haunted Man* (Collins 87-89). Redlaw's Specter speaks for Dickens as well as Redlaw when he says

> Look upon me! . . . I am he, neglected in my youth, and miserably poor, who strove and suffered and still strove and suffered. . . . No mother's self-dying love, . . . no father's counsel, aided *me*. . . . My parents, at the best, were of that sort whose care soon ends, and whose duty is soon done; who cast their offspring loose, early, as birds do theirs; and, if they do well, claim the merit; and, if ill, the pity.
>
> (266; original italics)

Thoughts and even words tie directly into the Fragment, where Dickens writes of "the sense I had of being utterly neglected and hopeless" (Forster 1: 22), of having "no advice, no counsel, no encouragement, no consolation, no support, from anyone that I can call to mind, so help me God" (24). In no small sense, then, Dickens uses *The Haunted Man* to continue the very direct exploration of his past he had been recently carrying out in the Fragment and was to continue almost without cessation in the early numbers of *David Copperfield*.

By failing to balance the story by the developing pattern—from the Fragment, to *The Haunted Man,* to *David Copperfield*—Stone misunderstands the sister's role, giving her too much credit for fulfilling the author's needs, at the expense of not sufficiently appreciating the sense of lack, the antagonism arising from resentment toward the parents. There is no indication, in the Fragment, that Fanny affected Dickens's feelings during the Warehouse episode other than negatively—when she received a music scholarship while he was made to do hard labor. And although Redlaw's sister dies "gentle as ever; happy; and with no concern but for her brother," her idealized increase in brother-centered-ness (from what Fanny could credibly have possessed) still leaves Redlaw desiring to blot out the past. David Copperfield, in contrast to Redlaw, is sisterless. The admittedly loving sister is not enough, not nearly enough, to compensate Dickens or the Dickens personae for ruptured relations with the parents. For further demonstration of the sister's inadequacy, and in order to understand *The Haunted Man,* we must turn

to three characters Stone barely touches: Redlaw's old fiancée, her husband (and Redlaw's former best friend) Mr. Longford, and their son, Edmund.

In simple plot terms, Mr. Longford jilted Redlaw's sister in order to marry Redlaw's fiancée; Edmund is the son resulting from this marriage. The act of betrayal by the best friend and fiancée is the "great wrong done that could never be forgotten" by Redlaw (262). It is worth asking why the friend-fiancée combination perpetrates the betrayal. Stone associates Dickens's blacking-warehouse days, his mother's insensitivity to his suffering, and his frustrated adult loves with the great wrong, but in such a loose and unspecific manner that the reader is left without any direct connections or intelligence (17). A clearer understanding of the nature of the wrong is vital to understanding both Dickens and this story.

Valentina Poggi calls attention to the "umptieth" appearance of the "'betrayed-by-mistress-and-friend' cliché" in Dickens's contribution to *The Haunted House* (101). Yet Poggi fails to understand the significance in this important pattern. This "cliché" appears in **"The Poor Relation's Story,"** Dickens's contribution to the 1852 Christmas number, *A Round of Stories by the Christmas Fire*; it appears in the framework of the 1855 Christmas number, *The Holly-Tree Inn,* though it turns out at the end to be the narrator's delusion—his fiancée and friend actually remained true to him—and, to employ Poggi's counting system, it appears for the "umptieth" and last time in *Mugby Junction* (1866). Incomplete antecedents of the pattern appear in *Oliver Twist* and *Nicholas Nickleby,* where the bachelor uncles are robbed of the fiancée by death and elopement (but not by a best friend) respectively. By its very ubiquity, the bachelor protagonist "betrayed-by-mistress-and-friend" pattern calls for interpretation. But because this pattern has no direct biographical counterpart—no best friend ever eloped with Dickens's fiancée—as does, say, the death of the protagonist's sister, this puzzle continues to mystify.

Discussing "The Three Feathers" fairy-tale in *The Uses of Enchantment,* Bruno Bettelheim enters into an analysis of fairy-tale numerology, specifically as to the reason why the abused child in fairy-tales is so often the third child, with two "hardly differentiated" older siblings. Bettelheim concludes that the child, regardless of birth order, is always third on the family totem pole in relation to his parents. Bettelheim goes on to explain the apparently gratuitous pair of older siblings by arguing that

> surpassing the two stands in the unconscious for doing better than the two parents. In respect to his parents the child feels abused, insignificant, neglected; to excel them means coming into his own, much more than triumphing over a sibling would. But since it is difficult

for the child to admit to himself how great this desire to surpass his parents is, in the fairy tale it is camouflaged as outdoing the two siblings who think so little of him.

(106)

Bettelheim concludes that the two siblings do not make sense as siblings, but as parent stand-ins they make perfect sense.

Knowing, as we do know from the Autobiographical Fragment and other sources, that Dickens considered being sent to the Blacking Warehouse (and being asked to return there by his mother) as the great betrayal of his life, the great wrong done him that could never be forgotten or forgiven, and knowing that the bachelor protagonists, with whom Dickens demonstrably identifies, find their "great wrong" in the betrayal-by-mistress-and-friend, we may well hypothesize that the mistress and friend are substitutes for mother and father. Bettelheim's analysis of sibling-for-parent substitution provides a sound analogy of support. In other words, the betraying pair make little sense as Redlaw's or Dickens's peers, but, as I argue, they make perfect sense as stand-ins for Dickens's parents—that is, as an accommodating psychologically motivated recasting of his parents, in their presumed betrayal of Dickens.

In the Autobiographical Fragment, Dickens manipulates his parents' silence about wronging him—no doubt they never viewed the offense as he did—into the most accommodating scenario possible; he casts them as the victims of Biblical judgment, saying, in reference to the occasion when his parents decided not to return him to the Warehouse, "from that hour, until this, my father and my mother have been stricken dumb upon it [his suffering at the Warehouse and their culpability]" (Forster 1: 32-33). In *The Haunted Man,* the family of Redlaw's betrayers shows an obsessive guilt about the betrayal that Dickens would presumably have found very becoming in his parents. Redlaw first hears of Edmund as one muttering in his sleep about "some great wrong that could never be forgotten" (262), an initial recognition that the betrayers find the crime as memorable and reprehensible as Redlaw. This projected recognition of the magnitude of his suffering, the outside validating source, stands in for what Dickens misses intensely in the Fragment, where he pleads that "no man's imagination can overstep the reality" of his suffering (25).

In *The Haunted Man,* the guilty family lives out a combination of suffering for the betrayal and desire to make reparation. Edmund tells Redlaw that his parents' marriage "has not proved itself a well-assorted or a happy one" (298). Indeed, by the son's report, Mrs. Longford continually speaks of Redlaw "with honour and respect—with something that was almost rever-

ence" (298). Thus, the wife and son are loyal to Redlaw, not the real father. In a sense, young Longford grows up idolizing Redlaw as the ideal father of the Family Romance; his real father is just a poor stand-in. And, in what would seem ludicrous if the Longfords were Redlaw's peers, but makes perfect sense as Dickens's recasting of his role with his parents, the betraying husband does not resent his family's glorification of Redlaw; he seconds it. Redlaw's ability to forgive the father is immeasurably aided, no doubt, by the father's having suffered excruciatingly as a "natural" result of betraying Redlaw.[1] Milly points out the betrayer to Redlaw, saying "See how low he is sunk, how lost he is!" (346). The rival fully allows the justice of Redlaw's presumed "rising sense of retribution" at the sight of him, confesses "I made my first step downward, in dealing falsely by you," and begs Redlaw's forgiveness (348-49).

That the betraying father—and, by report, the mother—grovels before Redlaw, humbled and punished, allows Redlaw to become magnanimous in forgiving him. Dickens's parents apparently never groveled, never asked forgiveness, and thus Dickens felt forced to proclaim himself loudly as the injured plaintiff. He could not be both prosecutor and bearer of mercy, which explains why Redlaw's betrayers are forgiven, since they are so good as to accuse themselves, while Dickens's parents, in the Fragment, remain unforgiven.

Redlaw's reclamation is completed when, after regaining his memory, he falls on young Longford's neck, "entreating [Longford and his fiancée] to be his children" and vowing to "protect," "teach," and "reclaim" the little ragged boy (351). Thus he parallels Scrooge's reunion with nephew Fred and his wife, and his assumed parenthood over the ragged children under the Ghost's of Christmas Present robe, as well as his clear benevolence toward Tiny Tim. From this sentimental scene the restored community retires to the festivities of Christmas Dinner, under the benevolent patronage of their newly asserted "Uncle," Redlaw.

There is no need to detail the repetition of *The Haunted Man*'s plot in *Mugby Junction,* but a sweeping pass may serve to remind us that Dickens was reworking the same problems 18 years later. Gordon Spence has demonstrated artistic improvement in the latter version, but the emotional issues remain remarkably similar, though the protagonist's sense of injury seems softened (or deadened) by time. Jackson, the protagonist, is a man "within five years of fifty either way" (Dickens was 53 at the time), "grey too soon . . . a man of pondering habit, brooding carriage of the head, and suppressed internal voice; a man with many indications on him of having been much alone" (1).

Led by the betraying pair's innocent child, Jackson encounters his old fiancée. She tells Jackson her husband "is very, very ill of a lingering disorder. He will never recover" (14). The fatal disorder turns out to be at least indirectly tied to the husband's incessant guilt about having wronged Jackson: "it preys upon him, embitters every moment of his painful life, and will shorten it" (14). Indeed, the husband has reason to fear, for, as he believes, the couple's first five children "all lie in their little graves" under a curse presumably resulting from the betrayal. Such terrible vengeance by nature or God on the protagonist's behalf permits him, once again, to be the magnanimous forgiver instead of the injured plaintiff. Jackson raises the penitent fiancée off her knees (we are not told how long she has been down) and soothes her "as a kind father might have soothed an erring daughter" (15). He calmly forgives the dying father and becomes a sort of godfather to the child, all in a more subdued and controlled sense than appeared in **The Haunted Man.** Jackson, in the end, moves from being another Haunted Man, with nowhere to go, no roots, no human connections, and a running sore from an old wound, to become the last version of Dickens's ideal Uncle, the final Pickwick.

Ironically, Dickens was only able to work out successful revisions of "the old wrong" in a fictional scenario, in which the betraying parents are fully cognizant of their "crime," terribly punished, and becomingly penitent to the son. Only when the son's vengeance has full indirect license under the aegis of "natural causes" or divine punishment, can the son become the forgiver instead of the accuser. Then he can become godparent to himself, the adult rescuer of himself—himself repeated as the offspring of the betrayers—in Dickens's uniquely self-contained version of the Family Romance.

Note

1. Alexander Welsh's chapter "Forgiveness," in *The City of Dickens,* provides a broader background on the whole topic of forgiveness, as well as some excellent insights on its exposition in *The Haunted Man.*

Works Cited

Collins, Philip. "Dickens's Autobiographical Fragment and *David Copperfield*." *Cahiers Victoriens* 20 (1984): 87-96.

Dickens, Charles. *The Haunted Man. The Christmas Books.* Vol. 2. New York: Penguin, 1971. 240-353.

———. *Mugby Junction. Household Words.* Extra Christmas Number. December 1866: 1-25.

Forster, John. *The Life of Charles Dickens.* 2 vols. London: Dent, 1966.

Gilbert, Elliot L. "Dickens: Autobiography as Suicide." Dickens: Death and/of the Author [Program of the Div. on Prose Fiction]. MLA Convention. Washington, DC, 29 Dec. 1989.

Glancy, Ruth F. "Dickens and Christmas: His Framed Tale Themes." *Nineteenth-Century Fiction* 35 (1980): 53-72.

Patten, Robert L. "Dickens, Cruikshank, and the Death of the Author." Dickens: Death and/of the Author [Program of the Div. on Prose Fiction]. MLA Convention. Washington, DC, 29 Dec. 1989.

Poggi, Valentina. "Christmas Ghosts and Deprived Bachelors: An Aspect of the Fantastic in Dickens." *Quaderni di Filologia Germanica* 1 (1980): 85-105.

Spence, Gordon. "The Haunted Man and Barbox Brothers." *Dickensian* 76 (1980): 150-57.

Stone, Harry. "The Love Pattern in Dickens' Novels." *Dickens the Craftsman: Strategies of Presentation.* Ed. Robert B. Partlow, Jr. Carbondale: Southern Illinois UP, 1970. 1-20.

Tick, Stanley. "Dickens and the Two Autobiographies." Dickens: Death and/of the Author [Program of the Div. on Prose Fiction]. MLA Convention. Washington, DC, 29 Dec. 1989.

Welsh, Alexander. *The City of Dickens.* New York: Oxford UP, 1971.

Rosemary Mundhenk (essay date autumn 1992)

SOURCE: Mundhenk, Rosemary. "Creative Ambivalence in Dickens's *Master Humphrey's Clock*." *Studies in English Literature, 1500-1900* 32, no. 4 (autumn 1992): 645-61.

[*In the following essay, Mundhenk discusses the significance of* Master Humphrey's Clock *within the context of Dickens's literary career, focusing on his experiments with the creative tension between imaginative freedom and artistic discipline in several tales and sketches.*]

A tenuous balance between improvisation and design, creative exuberance and narrative control, free play and thematic unity, characterizes Charles Dickens's greatest novels. Dickens's imagination often contended with his growing desire to unite and control his narratives. Sairey Gamp, for instance, interrupts the thematic coherence of *Martin Chuzzlewit*; Mrs. Sparsit threatens *Hard Times.* The creative tension between imaginative freedom and artistic discipline is particularly evident in those early works in which Dickens consciously attempted greater coherence and unity. One such work is **Master Humphrey's Clock,** the critically neglected miscellany that contained within its elaborate narrative frame *The Old Curiosity Shop* and *Barnaby Rudge* as well as several short tales and sketches.[1]

Published weekly in 1840 and 1841, the threepenny miscellany was meant to release Dickens from the rigors of writing full-length novels.[2] The *Clock*'s flexible narrative machinery—Humphrey's reading of tales and sketches composed by himself and his aging associates and stored in an old clock case—seemed to provide a format for unrestrained novelty and experimentation with numerous narrators and short pieces. Within the first few numbers, however, the miscellany evolved into a work far more limited and limiting than Dickens's original conception. Partly in response to declining sales, but largely because of his own dissatisfaction with his creation, Dickens transformed the miscellany into a vehicle for two novels. He expanded a short sketch, appearing in number 4, into *The Old Curiosity Shop* and all but dropped the machinery of the storytelling club in number 11. When the *Shop* concluded in number 45, he briefly revived the clock club to create a narrative bridge to *Barnaby Rudge*; and, when that novel ended in number 88, he resuscitated the club only to describe its demise and the conclusion of the miscellany. These changes, especially the development of Master Humphrey's story about Nell into a novel, introduced many inconsistencies and contradictions into *Master Humphrey's Clock* as a whole and *The Old Curiosity Shop* in particular.[3] With its false starts and inconsistencies, all terribly apparent because publication of the weekly numbers closely followed their composition, the *Clock* reveals much about Dickens's imagination, about his contradictory inclinations to improvise freely and to impose narrative order and unity.

Dickens confided his early plans for *Master Humphrey's Clock,* his "rough notes of proposals," to John Forster in a July 1839 letter. The weekly's variety seemed limitless:

> I should propose to start, as *The Spectator* does, with some pleasant fiction relative to the origin of the publication; to introduce a little club or knot of characters and to carry their personal histories and proceedings through the work; to introduce fresh characters constantly; to reintroduce Mr. Pickwick and Sam Weller, the latter of whom might furnish an occasional communication with great effect; to write amusing essays on the various foibles of the day as they arise; to take advantage of all passing events; and to vary the form of the papers by throwing them into sketches, essays, tales, adventures, letters from imaginary correspondents and so forth, so as to diversify the contents as much as possible.[4]

Among its "veins of interest and amusement," Dickens planned to include the apparently long-contemplated **"Chapters on Chambers"** series on London's past, present, and future, "an almost inexhaustible field of fun, raillery, and interest," narrated by the Guildhall giants Gog and Magog; a series of satirical papers describing "the administration of justice in some country that never existed . . . something between *Gulliver's*

Travels and the *Citizen of the World*"; and, "to give fresh novelty and interest," a series of travel sketches, modeled on Irving's *Alhambra,* from America or Ireland (*Letters,* 1:564). These exuberant plans promised unrestricted novelty and flexibility of subject and tone.

The early numbers, published in April and May 1840, resemble at least in format the original plans. In the first number, for example, Humphrey introduces himself and his club in **"From His Clockside in the Chimney-Corner,"** and the first tale from the Clock Case, **"Introduction to the Giant Chronicles,"** appears. Yet, although the opening numbers contain several of the features envisioned in Dickens's plans, much is missing: the "amusing essays on the various foibles of the day," the allusions to passing events, the satire, the travel sketches. There are few signs of that "almost inexhaustible field of fun, raillery, and interest" forecast in the 1839 letter. In place of the promised variety of tone is the meditative and somber monotone of Master Humphrey. In place of the great diversity of contents is a series of tales and sketches surprisingly alike in subject and theme.

The limitation of flexibility, novelty, and breadth has much to do with Dickens's decision in the months following the July letter to center his "little club or knot of characters" around the figure of old Master Humphrey. In January 1840 Dickens explained the change of plans to Forster: "Then I mean to tell how he has kept odd manuscripts in the old, deep, dark, silent closet where the weights are; and taken them from thence to read (mixing up his enjoyments with some notion of his clock)" (*Letters,* 2:4). Deliberately drawing upon eighteenth- and early nineteenth-century models, Dickens creates in Master Humphrey his own version of the man of moral feeling: benevolent, acutely sensitive to the sufferings of others, reclusive, nostalgic, and often melancholic.[5] A "mis-shapen, deformed, old man,"[6] Humphrey has led "a lonely, solitary life" (1.1) and inhabits an ancient house, "a silent shady place" (1.12), filled with ghostly echoes and secret memories. Harboring a sorrow from the past, he has all but retired from the society of men and the light of day.

The club, created in January and February of 1840, is composed of men astonishingly like Humphrey himself: "men of secluded habits with something of a cloud upon our early fortunes, . . . whose spirit of romance is not yet quenched, who are content to ramble through the world in a pleasant dream, rather than ever waken again to its harsh realities" (1.5). The deaf gentleman harbors a secret misfortune, and, like Humphrey, is a "great thinker from living so much within himself" (3.29). The gentle Jack Redburn has been "bred to a profession for which he never qualified himself, and reared in the expectation of a fortune he has never inherited" (3.30). Finally, the irascible Owen Miles: despite the comic possibilities of his mental slowness and "amusing prejudices" (3.31), he too is a reclusive, disappointed man, who after his wife's death left his successful business to retire to the quiet life. The additions of Mr. Pickwick and the Wellers do little to dispel the monotony. Pickwick is, in Garrett Stewart's words, "killed by context."[7] Sam and Tony Weller, who with Humphrey's housekeeper and barber form their own storytelling club in parody of Humphrey's club, provide insufficient variety. Like Humphrey, the club members prefer dreams to actuality. Their characters and their stories, with the possible exception of **"A Confession,"** allowed Dickens to take, as Deborah Thomas contends, "his most direct and disastrous plunge into what he evidently viewed as the world of fancy," into "sustained remoteness from actuality" and "imaginative escapism and sentiment."[8] What Thomas regards as a self-indulgent plunge into fancy results in a surprisingly limited range of tellers and narrative situations.

This sameness undermines Dickens's experiment with multiple tellers. For example, the deaf gentleman, estranged from his beloved daughter, tells a bi-level tale mirroring his own pain and disappointment: his story of Joe Toddyhigh's unsuccessful attempt to revive an old friendship shares the qualities of loneliness and loss with the personal history of its creator; Magog's tale, overheard by Toddyhigh, is a self-reflexive narrative of a loving father's and a prospective husband's disappointment over Alice's elopement with an unworthy rake. Audrey Jaffe's observation that in *The Old Curiosity Shop* the story of the self is retold, over and over, as another's[9] may be extended to the miscellany. In the identification of club members with their tales, Dickens was experimenting with the subjective narration he later developed more skillfully in the sustained narrations of David Copperfield, Pip, and Esther Summerson. But the uniformity of theme and tone among the tales and the histories of the tellers also reveals Dickens's growing concern with unity and subverts the experimentation.

Between the letter to Forster and the publication of the first few numbers of the *Clock,* Dickens avoided almost all opportunities for variety and attempted to craft a miscellany complementary in tone and theme to the reminiscences and meditations in **"Master Humphrey from his Clockside."** A desire for greater unity probably accounts for the exclusion of satire and topical writing and for the limitation of raillery and fun. It surely explains the rearrangement of existing *Clock* material. Dickens delayed the publication of Mr. Pickwick's "witch-story," originally planned for number 3, until numbers 5 and 6, precisely because he felt that Pickwick's tale interrupted the tone set by Humphrey: "I have determined not to put that witch-story into number 3, for I am by no means satisfied of the effect of its contrast with Master Humphrey. I think of lengthening Humphrey, finishing the description of the society, and

closing with the little child-story, which is SURE to be effective, especially after the old man's quiet way" (*Letters,* 2:40). Consciously amending the *Clock* in order to avoid sharp contrasts to the "old man's quiet way," Dickens expressed an evolving desire to unify his fiction tonally and thematically. In a 9 March letter to Chapman and Hall, he revealed his wish "to connect the stories more immediately with the Clock, and to give the work a less discursive appearance" (*Letters,* 2:41). As Dickens later explained in the 1848 Preface to the First Cheap Edition of *Old Curiosity Shop,* before the publication of number 4 he "had already been made uneasy by the desultory character" of the *Clock.*[10]

As many have observed, the unifying structural principle of *The Old Curiosity Shop* is contrast: most obviously the contrast between Nell and her environment (initially the curiosities of the shop and later the grotesque crowd of characters and things that she encounters on her journey to death), but also the contrasts between age and youth, quiet seclusion and the noisy world, city and country, innocence and evil, neoclassical beauty and grotesque ugliness, warmth and cold, vitality and death. Robert L. Patten has shown that these oppositions are present in the opening episode of the novel, the **"Personal Adventures of Master Humphrey"** in *Clock* 4: "The whole story, indeed, is a static but effective composition of opposites."[11] Malcolm Andrews has demonstrated further that the contrasts Dickens explores in the **"Personal Adventures"** were introduced in the first few numbers of the miscellany.[12] The dominance of contrast as a structural principle in both the miscellany and the novel may seem at odds with my contention that, in the evolution of the first several numbers of the *Clock,* Dickens was striving for thematic and tonal unity. Indeed, Humphrey's imagination is triggered by contrasts. But in dwelling on contrasts, meditating upon them, Humphrey reduces their starkness, throwing over them a "hazy unreality."[13] Finding incongruous juxtapositions everywhere, Humphrey subsumes contrasts and conflicts in his rueful speculations upon the paradoxes of the human condition. Transforming contrast into paradox, Humphrey's meditative voice has a leveling, subdued, and subduing quality about it, a quality that led G. K. Chesterton to remark that *Master Humphrey's Clock* is "for the most part somewhat more level and even monotonous than most of [Dickens's] creations."[14]

The gradual thematic and tonal concentration of *Master Humphrey's Clock* reached its limit in *Clock* 7 and 8, when Dickens scuttled his miscellany format and made the *Clock* a vehicle for *The Old Curiosity Shop.* As that novel took shape, Dickens's imagination paradoxically seemed to move centrifugally toward variety and flexibility, a dynamic quite opposite to the increasingly centripetal movement that characterized the evolution of early numbers of the *Clock.* Ironically, the novel offered Dickens more opportunity for improvisation and imaginative free play than did the miscellany. Whereas the miscellany evolved from an open-ended work, characterized by diversity, to one marked by sameness and monologue, the novel begins in monotone and in the first few chapters moves toward multiplicity and dialogue. Despite the thematic continuities, discussed by Andrews and others, between the miscellany's opening numbers and the novel,[15] the narration of *The Old Curiosity Shop* becomes, within the first few chapters, freer and more varied in tone, voice, and incident.

The first three chapters reveal both the narrator's unsuitability to the evolving novel and a progressive shift in emphasis away from Master Humphrey's subjective experiencing of events and toward a more variable and more distanced, though hardly objective, narration. As the novel opens, point of view is unified ideologically, phraseologically, spatially/temporally, and psychologically in the person of Master Humphrey.[16] Yet, although his narration presents a consistent, unified point of view, the reader soon senses a straining, a tension between Humphrey's subjective narration and its object.

"The Personal Adventures of Master Humphrey," the vignette in *Clock* 4 that will become the first chapter of the novel, focuses as much on Humphrey as on Nell. He speaks in the first person, "speculating on the characters and occupations of those who fill the streets" at night (4.37), filtering and coloring what he sees. His descriptions of his encounters with Nell and her grandfather balance what is perceived (a child mysteriously alone and lost in the dark maze of London streets; her grandfather in the shop) and the consciousness of the perceiver (Humphrey's curiosity and sympathy). As Humphrey guides Nell home, for example, he reflects: "While we were thus engaged, I revolved in my mind a hundred different explanations of the riddle and rejected them every one. I felt really ashamed to take advantage of the ingenuousness or grateful feeling of the child for the purpose of gratifying my curiosity" (4.39). Even when Humphrey adopts the passive role of observer and the dramatic mode of reported speech, his physical presence, consciousness, and ideology remain explicit in phrases such as "I looked in astonishment" (4.44) and "I was rejoiced to hear" (4.42). The vignette ends with a balance of subject and object: Humphrey meditates on the contrast between his "quiet, warm and cheering" home and the "gloom and darkness [he] had quitted," but he is troubled by the images of the curiosity shop's "dark murky rooms" and the dreaming child (4.46-47).[17]

In the second chapter, in *Clock* 7, the balance between Humphrey's unifying consciousness and his material becomes uneasy. After the first few paragraphs, in which Humphrey recounts his decision to revisit Nell and describes his entry into the curiosity dealer's warehouse,

where Nell's grandfather and brother are arguing, Humphrey gradually retires to the background. He takes center stage only briefly: at the beginning of the chapter as he returns to the shop and during the argument when the grandfather "drew closer to me" (7.81). As he describes the argument and the entrance of Dick Swiveller, Humphrey's presence is much less central than it was in chapter 1. Phrases like "I supposed," "I think," and "I looked" decline significantly. In their place are first-person plural pronouns—"Mr Swiveller, after favoring us with several melodious assurances" (7.83)— and more distanced, third-person observations, such as "he was understood to convey to his hearers" (7.81). Despite the distancing, Humphrey's presence at the scene is intermittently evident. Dialogue and description are clearly provided by a witness, who describes the other characters externally, surmises their thoughts and motives, and evaluates them from his own ideological stance with a mingling of curiosity and sympathy. Yet the difference between Dickens's use of point of view in this chapter and in the first chapter is striking. Humphrey is uneasy in this scene: "I—who felt the difficulty of any interference, notwithstanding that the old man had appealed to me, both by words and looks— made the best feint I could of being occupied in examining some of the goods that were disposed for sale, and paying very little attention to the persons before me" (7.83). Although Humphrey's uneasiness makes literal sense, given the explosive family argument he has interrupted, it also seems to reveal Dickens's own discomfort with his narrator.

Before Dickens dismisses his narrator at the end of chapter 3 (*Clock* 8), we witness a dramatization of the tension between Humphrey's narration and the evolving novel. The narration in chapter 3 remains spatially/temporally, psychologically, and ideologically bound to Humphrey, as he describes the entrance of the menacing Daniel Quilp, the continued performance of Dick Swiveller, the angry departure of Nell's brother, the grandfather's affectionate confession to Nell that he may "'have dealt hardly by thee'" (8.89), and the comedy of Kit's writing lesson. But, despite the consistent perspective, Humphrey's presence is de-emphasized. As in chapter 2, first-person pronouns appear rarely and third-person narration predominates. Humphrey's few contributions to conversations are reported indirectly. We learn in summary that he tries to leave but is stopped by the grandfather: "I had several times essayed to go myself, but the old man had always opposed it and entreated me to remain" (8.88). Twice Quilp draws attention to him: first when Quilp demands to know who Humphrey is (8.85) and second when the departing Quilp leers at him. Indeed, the contrast between Quilp's hostility to Humphrey and the grandfather's desire that he remain may dramatize Dickens's contradictory attitudes toward his beloved yet burdensome narrator.

In the final scene of chapter 3, Dickens once more but briefly focuses directly on Master Humphrey, as he responds to the grandfather's whispered defense that "All is for her sake" (8.89):

> All that I had heard and seen, and a great part of what he had said himself, led me to suppose that he was a wealthy man. I could form no comprehension of his character, unless he were one of those miserable wretches who, having made gain the sole end and object of their lives and having succeeded in amassing great riches, are constantly tortured by the dread of poverty, and beset by fears of loss and ruin.
>
> (8.89)

Within the novel, this is Humphrey's swan song, recalling for a moment the prominence of his curiosity and meditations in the first chapter. Ironically, his judgment that the grandfather is a rich miser is wrong. One paragraph later, he retires from the *Shop* permanently and from the Clock temporarily (he reappears briefly in number 9 of the **Clock** to introduce **"Weller's Watch"** and again in number 45, when the storytelling club forms a bridge to *Barnaby Rudge*): "I shall for the convenience of the narrative detach myself from its further course, and leave those who have prominent and necessary parts in it to speak and act for themselves" (8.90).

In addition to the gradual de-emphasis of Humphrey and the distancing of his narration, Dickens's introduction of such explosive characters as Daniel Quilp and Dick Swiveller strains Humphrey's monotonal narration in chapters 2 and 3. Quilp's simultaneously comic and menacing sadism challenges Humphrey's ideology of sentiment and sympathy; Quilp's satiric aggressiveness breaks through the monotone. That he is, like Humphrey, physically deformed makes him seem a grotesquely inverted parody of Humphrey. Even Quilp's lascivious gazes at Nell seem to parody Humphrey's sympathetic voyeurism. A greater challenge to Humphrey's narration, Swiveller bursts into the narrative, interrupting and jostling Humphrey's monologue with boisterous wit and verbal play. In Swiveller, readers sense Dickens's desire for more latitude, for greater freedom from Humphrey's monotonal, subdued narration. A. E. Dyson remarks that "the author's chief delight in the early stages was with Dick Swiveller."[18] Swiveller's energetic, playful language challenges and undercuts Humphrey's contemplative, often sentimental prose. The street-smart wit, the excessive rhetoric, the fractured clichés and metaphors, and the cacophonous mixture of slang with poetic and polysyllabic flourishes disrupt Humphrey's monotonal narration, bring linguistic variety to the narrative, and revitalize the prose. By means of Swiveller's language, dialogue and "heteroglossia"—the coexistence of different languages, reflecting social and ideological differences—are incorporated into the embryonic novel.[19] In chapter 2, Swiveller even retells Humphrey's story of Nell from a different ideological perspective, in a different language:

> "Here is a jolly old grandfather . . . and here is a wild young grandson. The jolly old grandfather says to the wild young grandson, 'I have brought you up and educated you, Fred; I have put you in the way of getting on in life; you have bolted a little out of the course as young fellows often do; and you shall never have another chance, nor a ghost of half a one.' The wild young grandson makes answer to this and says, 'You're as rich as rich can be; . . . you're saving up piles of money for my little sister that lives with you in a secret, stealthy, hugger-muggering kind of way and with no manner of enjoyment—why can't you stand a trifle for your grown-up relation?' The jolly old grandfather unto this, retorts, not only that he declines to fork out with that cheerful readiness which is always so agreeable and pleasant in a gentleman of his time of life, but that he will blow up, and call names, and make reflections whenever they meet. Then the plain question is, an't it a pity that this state of things should continue, and how much better would it be for the old gentleman to hand over a reasonable amount of tin, and make it all right and comfortable."
>
> (7.83-84)

Monologue approaches dialogue. In fact, Humphrey's narration is influenced by the disruptive entrance of Mr. Swiveller. Swiveller has already occasioned the most detailed physical description of a character in the novel so far (7.82; *OCS* [*The Old Curiosity Shop*] 2)—a description complete with the loose laying-on of details and the playful inventiveness characteristic of Dickens's comic style and very uncharacteristic of Humphrey's sedate prose. And the reporting of Swiveller's verbal performances in indirect discourse embeds Swiveller's language and parodies the rhythms of his speech. Humphrey begins to sound less like Humphrey. Little wonder that, as chapter 3 ends, the superfluous, burdensome narrator exits from the novel in order to "leave those who have prominent and necessary parts in it to speak and act for themselves" (8.90).

Humphrey's retirement "for the convenience of the narrative" allows the narrator of *The Old Curiosity Shop* freedom in space and time. Unburdened by the physical limitations of Master Humphrey, the disembodied narrator can invade Quilp's Tower Hill parlor to witness the long-suffering Mrs. Quilp's persecution and follow Quilp to his counting house, Kit to his home, Swiveller to the Brasses' den and the mysteries of the Marchioness, and Nell to her adventures and death in the country. The new freedom is not merely spatial and temporal, but ideological and psychological as well. Humphrey's successor, who occasionally refers to himself as a "historian" or "chronicler," retains much of Humphrey's ideological stance—his sympathy, his concern for the alienated, his tendency to look for the good in all. Yet, when he generalizes about human nature, this narrator's voice sounds with new irony and anger at injustice. For example, Kit's simple generosity to Nell occasions a scathing rebuke of "unfeeling creditors, and mercenary attendants upon the sick" (13.151; *OCS* 11). When the narrator reports the antics of Swiveller, Quilp, Kit, or the pony, he does so without the mediation of Humphrey's quieting tone. Moreover, he also reports the thoughts and observations of Nell, her grandfather, Quilp, Kit, and Swiveller. Thus, the novel attains a dialogic quality, offering within its generally authoritative and omniscient narration a variety of ideologies, psychological perspectives, languages, and tones. Similarly, the narrator of the next novel within the **Clock,** *Barnaby Rudge,* relishes his omniscience and spatial/temporal freedom—"Chroniclers are privileged to enter where they list, to come and go through keyholes, to ride upon the wind, to overcome, in their soarings up and down, all obstacles of time and place" (50.284; *BR* [*Barnaby Rudge*] 9)—but also often narrows the perspective to the subjectivity of individual characters, like Barnaby, Hugh, and Gabriel, whose voices vary the language, ideology, and psychology of the narration.

In number 45 of the **Clock,** a narrative bridge between the *Shop* and *Barnaby Rudge* briefly revives Humphrey and friends in a penultimate **"Master Humphrey from His Clockside in the Chimney-Corner."** Speaking in the first person, Humphrey reports the club's final discussion of Nell's story, meditates on the great clock at St. Paul's Cathedral, in whose every stroke he finds a moral, a theme that connects the completed novel with the one about to begin. In terms of both the fluctuation in point of view and the tension between variety and unity, this narrative bridge is significant. An early manuscript draft, apparently the first of two, is narrated in the third person rather than the first.[20] Still toying with point of view, still saddled with the inconsistencies he created, Dickens first continued the third-person narration of most of the *Shop,* but then, perhaps recognizing that Humphrey's first-person voice was more consistent with the **Clock** frame, he revised to first-person. Furthermore, in both versions Humphrey announces that he is the brother of Nell's grandfather, the "single gentleman, the nameless actor," who, returning from a life abroad to search for Nell and her grandfather, has played a large role in the novel (45.225). The sudden identification of Humphrey with the Single Gentleman seems a blunder. Despite their common goodness and old wounds, the Single Gentleman and Humphrey are physically and temperamentally opposite. Unlike the quiet, retiring Humphrey, the Single Gentleman is gruff, choleric, irascible, and occasionally given to growling.[21] Despite some trouble in fashioning the Single Gentleman's account of his genealogy and boyhood for chapter 69,[22] Dickens made no effort to soften the contrast between the two; even in the concluding chapter of the novel, the Single Gentleman is portrayed as an energetic traveler, now journeying to the countryside to reward those who helped his brother and his grandniece, Nell.

Why at the novel's completion did Dickens introduce this unbelievable identification of the two characters? Robert L. Patten suggests that "Dickens, at the last minute, was straining his ingenuity beyond credible limits to provide some explanation of the novel's original title."[23] Furthermore, the blunder reveals, perhaps was motivated by, the artistic tensions that plagued the composition of the **Clock** from its inception. Having released the *Shop* from the confining, monotonal narration of Humphrey, Dickens faced a partially disassembled **Clock** frame as he concluded the novel. The lack of closure and coherence in the miscellany must have bothered him. So he sacrificed one kind of coherence, the narrative unity of the novel and the consistency of two characters, for another kind of coherence, that of the **Clock.** Then, obviously dissatisfied with this "solution" and aware that the Humphrey at the beginning of the novel could not have metamorphosed into the Single Gentleman, Dickens compounded the blunder with Humphrey's assertion that the opening adventures of the novel, in which Humphrey took part, were "fictitious" (45.224). Humphrey's revelation, calling into question the authority of the novel's narration (when do we stop believing Humphrey and start believing him again?), is a startling move for a novelist so concerned about his relationship of trust with his readers. Paradoxically, the double blunder destroys coherence while it reveals Dickens's concern with coherence and unity.

Dickens tried to disentangle the knot of inconsistencies in two public statements about his intentions, specifically in the Preface to the first published volume of the **Clock** and the October 1841 announcement that the weekly periodical would cease with the conclusion of *Barnaby Rudge.* Both are tortured efforts to explain the **Clock.** The Preface attempts to circumvent the problematic change of plans and the obvious incoherence of the volume it introduces—the juxtaposition of the short **Clock** material with the longer *Old Curiosity Shop.* As if to de-emphasize the **Clock,** Dickens asserts that he had entertained the possibility of publishing some of the stories separately "at some distant day."[24] In an unsuccessful effort to explain Master Humphrey's stint as narrator of the novel, Dickens states that "It was never the author's intention to make the Members of Master Humphrey's Clock, active agents in the stories they were supposed to relate" (iii). He thus glosses over the disappearance of Humphrey and company, and asks readers to leave "Master Humphrey and his friends in their seclusion" (iv). But Dickens, obviously unhappy with this Preface's inability to explain the volume's inconsistencies and lack of coherence, confessed in a 6 September 1840 letter to Forster, "I have been blundering over the Preface so long that I'm deadly stupid" (*Letters,* 2:124).

In the October 1841 announcement, "TO THE READ-ERS OF 'MASTER HUMPHREY'S CLOCK,'" pub-lished in *Clock* 80, the same straining to explain ap-pears with greater intensity. Here Dickens reveals his plans to terminate the *Clock* with *Barnaby Rudge,* to visit America, and to publish a new book in his "old and well-tried plan" of monthly parts, beginning in No-vember 1842.[25] Much of this announcement addresses one reason for closing the *Clock,* his dissatisfaction with weekly publication:

> I have often felt cramped and confined in a very irk-some and harassing degree, by the space in which I have been constrained to move. . . . I have found this form of publication most anxious, perplexing, and dif-ficult. I cannot bear these jerking confidences which are no sooner begun than ended, and no sooner ended than begun again.
>
> (80)

Dickens labored over this announcement. Two heavily revised proofs preceding the published version suggest his difficulty both with the form of the *Clock* and with his explanation. His complaints about the cramped space of weekly issue notwithstanding, the announcement re-veals contradictory inclinations—centripetally, his con-cern for thematic unity and, centrifugally, his desire for freedom to improvise.

Dickens's experiment in narration and form in *Master Humphrey's Clock* left him with a prematurely trun-cated miscellany and a flawed novel whose initial nar-rator deserts in chapter 3. But the experiment seems to have taught, or to have played a role in teaching, Dick-ens several things.

First, after the *Clock,* Dickens attempted to avoid pub-lishing his fiction in weekly installments. When he did return reluctantly to weekly publication with *Hard Times* (1854, in *Household Words*), *A Tale of Two Cities* (1859, in *All The Year Round*) and *Great Expectations* (1860-61, in *All the Year Round*), he still abhorred the com-pression that weekly publication demanded.[26] And when he did publish his novels weekly, he did so with consid-erably more planning before publication.

Second, after his experience with improvising *The Old Curiosity Shop* within the *Clock,* Dickens never again began publishing a novel with so little forethought. One mark of his mature attention to design is the inception of his regular use of number plans, which sketched out the contents of numbers he had yet to write, summa-rized what he had already written, and played with pos-sible themes, narrative strategies, and titles.[27] The earli-est extant full set of working notes is for *Dombey and Son* (1846-48), but Dickens actually began the practice earlier, perhaps with *The Old Curiosity Shop.* The earli-est notes to survive are three sheets pertaining to the end of that novel: 1) notes for chapters 61-72, leading

to Nell's death; 2) the brief account of the brotherhood of the Single Gentleman and Nell's grandfather, a sketch that Dickens expanded into the Single Gentleman's rev-elation of his history in chapter 69; and 3) a list of characters, which Dickens seems to have used in com-posing the concluding chapter. Possibly the improvisa-tional creation of *Old Curiosity Shop* and the problems resulting from lack of planning led Dickens to use work-ing notes.

Third, after the *Clock,* Dickens's novels are character-ized by more control of the design of the whole, by fuller integration of theme and plot through metaphor, analogy, and juxtaposition. With *Martin Chuzzlewit* Dickens attempted to "resist the temptation of the cur-rent Monthly Number, and to keep a steadier eye upon the general purpose and design."[28] Although the attempt was not totally successful—the controversial American chapters mar the novel—*Chuzzlewit* bears witness to Dickens's increased care with the general design. With its exploration of societal and personal selfishness, *Chuzzlewit* represents a progressive, though somewhat faltering, development of Dickens's skill in themati-cally unifying his sprawling fictions and integrating his plots while simultaneously leaving room for improvisa-tion. In the next novel, *Dombey,* the pervasive theme of pride, social and individual, integrates plot, social criti-cism, and character portrayal.

Finally, Dickens's experiments with point of view in *Master Humphrey's Clock,* particularly his struggle with the stranglehold of Humphrey's narration, led him to choose future narrators more wisely. From *Barnaby Rudge* onward, Dickens's narrators are more appropri-ate for his fictions. With increasing control in *Martin Chuzzlewit, Dombey and Son, Little Dorrit, A Tale of Two Cities,* and *Our Mutual Friend,* he used a loosely omniscient, multiple-focus narration, at times exploiting spatial and temporal freedom, at times limiting knowl-edge and perspective for narrative effect. When Dickens again chose first-person character-narrators in *David Copperfield, Bleak House,* and *Great Expectations,* he selected narrators whose youth, personality, and mobil-ity allow more breadth, more freedom in plot and char-acter development, more variety in tone. Unlike the meditative Humphrey, who filters all experience through his somber philosophical sieve, they are open to experi-ence and to the knowledge that narrating one's experi-ence can bring. David, though haunted by memories of his unfortunate youth and somewhat blind to his illu-sions, nevertheless revels in the re-creation of his life. His energetic portrayal of figures from his past, like Micawber and Heep, grants them semiautonomous voices that save his story from monologue. Pip, how-ever severe his self-judgment and however somber his recapitulation of experience, is capable of exuberance as a narrator. Even Esther, whose self-effacement and limited vision annoy many readers, enjoys a flexibility and sense of humor that Humphrey lacks; moreover, her narrative is dialogically counterbalanced by the prose of the present-tense narrator.

The experiment of **Master Humphrey's Clock** was in many respects a failure. Dickens called his miscellany "one of the lost books of the earth—which, we all know, are far more precious than any that can be read for love or money."[29] But the lessons of the struggle that Dickens encountered in its composition were not lost to him. Nor indeed is the miscellany's value in illuminating the tension between Dickens's natural talents for improvisation and free play and the maturing novelist's desire for narrative design and unity lost to us.

Notes

1. Despite the *The Old Curiosity Shop*'s popularity, the miscellany in which it appeared has attracted little attention. G. K. Chesterton, in *Appreciations and Criticisms of the Works of Charles Dickens* (London: J. M. Dent, 1911), claimed that the *Clock* shows the "unconscious trend of Dickens, the stuff of which his very dreams were made" (p. 237). Recent scholars who give the *Clock* more than passing attention are Malcolm Andrews, "Introducing Master Humphrey," *Dickensian* 67, 364 (Spring 1971): 70-86; K. A. Chittick, "The Idea of a Miscellany: *Master Humphrey's Clock*," *Dickensian* 78, 398 (Autumn 1982): 156-64; Carol De Saint Victor, "*Master Humphrey's Clock*: Dickens' 'Lost' Book," *TSLL* 10, 4 (Winter 1969): 569-84; Tony Giffone, "Putting *Master Humphrey* Back Together Again," *JNT* [*Journal of Narrative Theory*] 17, 1 (Winter 1987): 102-106; Audrey Jaffe, "'Never be Safe but in Hiding': Omniscience and Curiosity in *The Old Curiosity Shop*," *Novel* 19, 2 (Winter 1986): 118-34; Robert L. Patten, "'The Story-Weaver at His Loom': Dickens and the Beginning of *The Old Curiosity Shop*," in *Dickens the Craftsman*, ed. Robert B. Partlow, Jr. (Carbondale: Southern Illinois Univ. Press, 1970), pp. 44-64; Deborah A. Thomas, *Dickens and the Short Story* (Philadelphia: Univ. of Pennsylvania Press, 1982), pp. 26-31.

2. John Forster, *The Life of Charles Dickens,* 3 vols. (London: Chapman and Hall, 1872-74), 1:168-69. Between 1836 and 1839, Dickens produced *Pickwick Papers, Oliver Twist,* and *Nicholas Nickleby.*

3. Among these narrative problems are the change in narrators that occurs early in *Old Curiosity Shop* and the last-minute identification of Humphrey with the *Shop*'s Single Gentleman. Much material in the first *Clock* numbers suggests further development of characters and later installments: the introduction of Jack Bamber (a possibility mentioned in number 7), a tale from Owen Miles, and Joe Toddyhigh's return to the Guildhall for another giant's tale.

4. Charles Dickens, *Letters,* The Pilgrim Edition, ed. Madeline House and Graham Storey (Oxford: Clarendon Press, 1965-), 1:563-64; hereafter cited parenthetically as *Letters.*

5. Paul Schlicke, in "The True Pathos of *The Old Curiosity Shop*," *DQ* [*Dickens Quarterly*] 7, 1 (March 1990): 189-99, reminds us that the precedents Dickens cited (*The Tatler, The Spectator,* Goldsmith's *Bee,* and Irving's *Alhambra*) were "by noted masters of sentimental literature" (p. 195). K. A. Chittick notes that "However deliberately Dickens may have intended Master Humphrey's Club to recall Mr. Spectator's, he has come closer to that of Mr. Bickerstaff" (p. 163) in *Tatler* 132.

6. *Master Humphrey's Clock* (London: Chapman and Hall, 1840-41; facsimile rprt., London: Nottingham Court Press, 1983-84), 1.3. Subsequent references to this first edition by weekly number and page number are noted parenthetically in the text. Parenthetical references to *The Old Curiosity Shop* within the *Clock* also include chapter numbers unless the chapter reference is clear in my text.

7. Garrett Stewart, *Dickens and the Trials of Imagination* (Cambridge, MA: Harvard Univ. Press, 1974), p. 45.

8. Thomas, pp. 26-29.

9. Jaffe sees in the omniscient narration of *Old Curiosity Shop* a complex self-defeating fictional "displacement: the hiding, but not the removal, of the self" (p. 121).

10. Charles Dickens, *The Old Curiosity Shop,* ed. Angus Easson (Harmondsworth: Penguin, 1972), p. 41.

11. Patten, p. 54. Among critics attending to the structural function of contrast, Michael Hollington, in *Dickens and the Grotesque* (Totowa, NJ: Barnes and Noble, 1984), pp. 79-95, identifies the central pattern as the child amid grotesque curios and characters, within the shop and without in the "new curiosity shop" of industrial England. Similarly, Paul Schlicke, in the article previously cited and in *Dickens and Popular Entertainment* (London: Allen and Unwin, 1985), pp. 96-131, discusses the relationship between Nell and her context, the inanimate and animate curiosities, most particularly the world of showfolk; and Nancy K. Hill, in *A Reformer's Art* (Athens: Ohio Univ. Press, 1981), pp. 98-110, analyzes the juxtaposition of Nell's neoclassical beauty and the grotesquerie created by industrialization.

12. Andrews, pp. 76-85.

13. "Hazy unreality" is the dominant quality of the miscellany according to Thomas, p. 30.

14. Chesterton, p. 229.

15. For discussions of the continuities, see Andrews, pp. 73-85, De Saint Victor, pp. 579-81, and Schlicke, "True Pathos," p. 195. Andrews, in particular, argues that the *Clock*'s elegiac disenchantment with the world and retreat to the past are assimilated into the novel and finds "no real alteration of pace and tone" (p. 81) between the *Clock* material and the first chapter of *Shop*, and I agree. I disagree with Andrews, however, in seeing a noticeable change in tone and pace when Humphrey's presence is de-emphasized (in chapters 2 and 3) and then dropped.

16. Boris Uspensky, *A Poetics of Composition,* trans. Valentina Zavarin and Susan Wittig (Berkeley: Univ. of California Press, 1973). I use Uspensky's terms for the planes of point of view.

17. In 1841, while preparing *The Old Curiosity Shop* for issue as a separate volume, Dickens added four new paragraphs to the first chapter, which appear in subsequent editions. These paragraphs, immediately preceding the final paragraph, foreshadow later events in Nell's life and "provide additional evidence of a design that grew . . . gradually and unconsciously" (Patten, p. 56).

18. A. E. Dyson, "*The Old Curiosity Shop*: Innocence and the Grotesque," *CQ* [*Critical Quarterly*] 8, 2 (Summer 1966): 111-30, 113. Similar responses to Swiveller's entrance are found in S. J. Newman, *Dickens at Play* (New York: St. Martin's Press, 1981), pp. 83-86; Garrett Stewart, pp. 89-113; and Monica Feinberg, "Reading *Curiosity*: Does Dick's Shop Deliver," *DQ* [*Dickens Quarterly*] 7, 1 (March 1990): 200-211. Dickens told Forster of his enchantment with Swiveller: "I mean to make much of him" (*Letters,* 2:70).

19. M. M. Bakhtin, "Discourse in the Novel," *The Dialogic Imagination,* ed. Michael Holquist, trans. Caryl Emerson and Michael Holquist (Austin: Univ. of Texas Press, 1981), pp. 301-31.

20. MS of *The Old Curiosity Shop,* 47A, John Forster Collection, Victoria and Albert Museum, London. At the novel's end, Dickens drew a line across the manuscript page and then wrote the short, third-person version, which begins as follows: "When Master Humphrey had finished the reading of this manuscript, and again deposited it with his clock, he returned to the table where his friends were seated." I thank the Director of the Victoria and Albert Museum for permission to quote from the manuscript.

21. The illustrations support the contrast established by the text; see, for instance, the illustrations for chapters 34 and 37.

22. Dickens's fragmentary number plans for *The Shop* include an abbreviated sketch of the relationship between the Single Gentleman and Nell's grandfather (MS. *Old Curiosity Shop,* 47A, Forster Collection). The existence of this sketch suggests Dickens's need to work out the convoluted biography before writing the chapter.

23. Patten, p. 63.

24. Preface, *Master Humphrey's Clock* (London: Chapman and Hall, 1840), 1:iii; hereafter cited parenthetically.

25. The heavily revised announcement was published on the back of the front wrapper of no. 80 (9 October 1841); rprt., John Butt and Kathleen Tillotson, *Dickens at Work* (London: Methuen, 1957), pp. 88-89. Two sets of revised proofs are bound with the proof sheets of the *Clock,* 47E27, Forster Collection. The new novel is *Chuzzlewit*; its first number actually appeared in January 1843.

26. Dickens agreed to write *Hard Times* for weekly publication in *Household Words* only after his publishers convinced him to do so in order to increase sales of the periodical. Although he originally planned to publish *Great Expectations* in monthly parts, he changed his mind in order to bolster sales of *All The Year Round.*

27. Harry Stone has reproduced and transcribed the extant notes, including those for the *Shop,* in *Dickens' Working Notes for His Novels* (Chicago: Univ. of Chicago Press, 1987), pp. 3-13.

28. 1844 Preface, *Martin Chuzzlewit* (Oxford: Clarendon Press, 1982), p. lxix.

29. Preface to the First Cheap Edition (1848), *The Old Curiosity Shop,* pp. 41-42.

Graeme Tytler (essay date fall 1994)

SOURCE: Tytler, Graeme. "Dickens's 'The Signalman.'" *Explicator* 53, no. 1 (fall 1994): 26-9.

[In the following essay, Tytler explores the narrative implications of the mental disorder "monomania" in "The Signalman."]

Charles Dickens's short story **"The Signalman"** (1866) has elicited a good deal of critical discussion recently both as to its supernatural, sociological, psychological, psychiatric, and psycho-metaphysical interest and as to its possible meaning.[1] No scholar, however, has yet acknowledged it to be a story about a man evidently suffering from a type of partial insanity commonly designated in the nineteenth century as "lypemania" or "monomania."[2]

That such an interpretation is not altogether implausible is suggested by the fact that Dickens was well informed about mental illnesses and their treatment in his day, enjoying as he did friendships with various asylum doctors, notably John Conolly (1794-1866), who practiced the humane methods of therapy established in France by Pinel and Esquirol.[3] It is noteworthy that Esquirol includes "excessive night-watching" among the causes of lypemania, for his words remind us that the signalman "so often passed long winter nights there, alone and watching" (18). A more important cause in Esquirol's eyes would be the signalman's persistent unease and guilt about being a helpless functionary and a social failure. As for the symptoms of the hero's lypemania (or monomania), these are manifest not only in his auditory and visual hallucinations, his haggard appearance, his "fixed look" (18) and his obsession with words, but, curiously enough, in the very rationality with which he talks about the ghost and carries out his duties. It is this rationality which, as Esquirol and others recognized, tends to deceive all but medical experts as to the real condition of the partially insane, including the narrator of **"The Signalman,"** who with hindsight ironically remarks, "I have speculated since whether there may have been infection in his mind" (13).[4]

The advantage of this nosological interpretation is that it has some bearing on Dickens's apparent intent here to suggest, not least through his compassionate exposition of the hero's personal background, that ghostly apparitions are to be understood in some sense as the consequence of a failure in human communication. It is surely no accident that Dickens should have used the Victorian railway system for his story, inasmuch as it provided him with a metaphor for his central theme, namely, society as a complex signalling system whereby mental illness is a glaring instance of a breakdown within that system. Like any railway organization, Victorian society is here presented as a rigid hierarchy in which each individual knows his place and understands the social signals exchanged therein. Thus the narrator is immediately recognized as a gentleman, whom the signalman (middle class) and the railway men (lower class) address as "sir." This code of politeness is further seen in the handshaking between narrator and signalman and in the diplomatically urbane manner in which the narrator speaks to the hero, or disagrees with him, sometimes even by "forcing a smile" (13). Because society, like any signalling system, depends on the universal recognition of particular signals, it follows that communication within society presupposes imitation. This is especially true of gestures, stances, postures, attitudes, even touching, all of which serve specific signalling functions in the story. Thus the signalman, the narrator, the train driver, and the ghost all use, or understand, the gesticulation warning of danger, namely, placing of one arm across the face and the frantic waving of the other. Noteworthy, too, are the different ways

in which the signalman "signals" to the narrator with his body, a striking instance being his standing between the rails in a position bespeaking deep suspicion of the narrator approaching him. Again, just as flags, lamps, and telegraph are a signalman's main means of communication, so the main medium of communication in ordinary society is the word, whereby vocal utterances, which in the story range from the ghost's shouting or the train passengers' screaming to the signalman's whispering, depend for their effect on comprehension and response. Hence the narrator's surprise when the signalman fails to respond to his opening words to him in a manner normally expected.

The idea of language as a universal signalling system is nowhere better illustrated than by the story itself. That **"The Signalman"** is par excellence a story to be *read* may be gathered from the highly self-conscious use of punctuation—block letters, italics, and, above all, parentheses—as if the narrator were at pains to ensure that his readers understood the messages conveyed. Moreover, not unlike the algebra, fractions, decimals, foreign language, and "natural philosophy" (14), which, as Dickens is careful to mention for thematic purposes, the hero has studied on and off, the narrative itself is a kind of signalling system, comprehension of which depends on the readers themselves becoming, as it were, signalmen of no mean intelligence. Thus, aside from being characterized by a necessary conciseness—through, say, the narrator's elegant, if affected, use of reported speech—the story is strewn with symbolic devices that serve sundry structural functions. For example, is not the tendency of both narrator and signalman to repeat their own as well as one another's words and phrases somehow symbolic of the signalling system in general and the specter's haunting in particular? Consider, too, the repetitive use of "up," "down," "above," and "below" in the early paragraphs, and phrases such as "low voice," "lower shades," and "fallen colour," which, aside from symbolizing the contrast between the signalman's social comedown and the narrator's privileged status, ironically foreshadow the hero's tragic death, as confirmed especially when the railwaymen speak of the hero's having been "cut *down* by an engine" and of the engine's whistle being turned off "when [they] were running *down* upon him" (23). A similar function is fulfilled by the narrator's earliest reference to a passing train as a "violent pulsation" and an "oncoming rush," which causes him to "start back, as though it had force to draw [him] *down*" (11); and, shortly before, when he speaks of the signalman's figure being "foreshortened and shadowed *down* in the deep trench" (11). (All italics mine.)

To the extent that the narrative contains the signs and signals that portend the signalman's death, the narrator may, then, be regarded as a sort of signalman himself, but one who, punctilious by nature, has certain limitations. For though the narrator is good at verbal and written communication, and observant enough of the signalman's physically to suspect some disorder, and even read the latter's attitude toward him, his failure to take timely action seems due to his being misled not only by the signalmen's rationality but also by his own. And yet, how rational is the narrator? Despite his ostensible reliance on sense data and reason, he exhibits a markedly superstitious nature, not only through the "irrational" language he uses to describe his nervous reactions to the passing train, the signalman's manner, the accounts of the specter, and the signalbox area itself, which last makes him feel "as if [he] had left the natural world" (12), but even through his use of phrases such as "Heaven knows" (16) and "for God's sake" (17). That the narrator's language is by no means always "rational" is further suggested when, for instance, he finds himself at a loss to describe his emotional responses and, more particularly, when he resorts to anthropomorphism, personification, and pathetic fallacy ("angry sunset" [11], "The wind and the wires took up the story with a long lamenting wail" [19]). Accordingly, since Dickens is suggesting through his narrator that language in sometimes either inadequate or excessive for a purely rational interpretation of the world of so-called reality, he may at the same time be exposing the roots of Victorian man's susceptibility to the supernatural.

In the light of the foregoing, then, would it be too much to assert that, at the same time as he keeps us in marvelous suspense throughout, the author is hinting that the supernatural experience is somehow inseparable from the idea of society qua signalling system? When, for example, the narrator, in his one-sentence epilogue, pedantically remarks on the coincidence of the engine-driver's words resembling those uttered by the ghost and those he himself has used to describe the latter's gesticulations as imitated by the signalman, is Dickens not thereby simply underlining the idea of the universality of specific social signals, whether verbal or gestural, particularly in moments of extreme emotion? For, if our reading of the story is correct, then it would appear that the ghost's unmistakenly human utterances and gestures are, as any modern psychologist might agree, merely expressions of a partially insane signalman's unconscious, wherein lie stored up memories of all the codes of social behavior he has ever acquired.[5]

Notes

1. See especially Helmut Bonheim, "The Principle of Cyclicity in Charles Dickens' 'The Signalman,'" *Anglia* 106 (1988): 380-92; Jacques Carré, "'The Signalman' de Dickens," *Les Langues Modernes* 70 (1976): 359-68; Gary Day, "Figuring out 'The Signalman': Dickens and the Ghost Story," *Nineteenth-Century Suspense: From Poe to Conan Doyle,* ed. Clive Bloom et al. (New York: St. Martin's Press, 1988) 26-45; Daniel J. Greenman, "Dickens' Ultimate Achievement in the Ghost Story: 'To be taken with a grain of salt' and 'The Signalman,'" *The Dickensian* 85 (1989): 40-48; Henri Justin, "The Signalman's Signal-Man," *Les Cahiers de la Nouvelle* 7 (1986): 9-16; Ewald Mengel, "The Structure and Meaning of Dickens' 'The Signalman,'" *Studies in Short Fiction* 20 (1983): 271-80; John Daniel Stahl, "The Source and Significance of the Revenant in Dickens' 'The Signalman,'" *Dickens Studies Newsletter* 11 (1980): 98-101.

2. See Erwin Ackerknecht, *A Short History of Psychiatry,* tr. Sala Wolf, 2nd rev. edn. (New York and London: Hafner, 1968) 42-59.

3. See Susan Shatto, "Miss Havisham and Mr. Hopes the Hermit: Dickens and the Mentally Ill," *Dickens Quarterly* 2 (1985): 82; John Conolly, *The Treatment of the Insane without Mechanical Restraints,* introd. Richard A. Hunter and Ida Macalpine (London: Smith, Elder, 1856) 17-18; John Conolly, *An Inquiry concerning the Indications of Insanity,* Facsimile of London: John Taylor, 1830 (London: Dawson, 1964) 1-6; Richard A. Hunter and Ida Macalpine, "Dickens and Conolly: An Embarrassed Editor's Disclaimer," *Times Literary Supplement* (11 August 1961): 534-35.

4. Quotations from "The Signalman" are taken from *The Penguin Book of English Short Stories,* ed. Christopher Dolley (Harmondsworth: Penguin Books, 1967). For the symptoms and causes of partial insanity and the rationality of the lypemaniac/monomaniac, see Etienne Esquirol, *Mental Maladies. A Treatise on Insanity,* tr. E. K. Hunt (Philadelphia: Lea and Blanchard, 1845) 106-09, 200-12, 240.

5. For Dickens's skepticism toward supernatural experiences, see Philip Collins, "Dickens on Ghosts: An Uncollected Article," *The Dickensian* 59 (1963): 13.

James R. Simmons Jr. (essay date March 1995)

SOURCE: Simmons, James R. Jr. "Scrooge, Falstaff, and the Rhetoric of Indigence." *English Language Notes* 32, no. 3 (March 1995): 43-6.

[*In the following essay, Simmons notes rhetorical similarities between a speech uttered by Falstaff in Shakespeare's* Henry IV *and a comment spoken by Ebenezer Scrooge in* A Christmas Carol.]

During his lifetime, Charles Dickens read a vast array of literature, and none influenced him more than the plays of William Shakespeare. Dickens so revered

Shakespeare's work that his friend John Forster noted that they celebrated Shakespeare's birthday "always as a festival,"[1] and in fact Dickens's prize possession was a pocket edition of Shakespeare's plays that he carried with him constantly. Forster had given him the book as a gift, and Dickens later wrote to Forster to thank him, commenting, "What an unspeakable source of delight that book is to me!"[2]

Of all of Shakespeare's characters, Dickens's favorite was by far Falstaff from *1 Henry IV, 2 Henry IV,* and *The Merry Wives of Windsor.* Dickens often quoted or paraphrased Falstaff in his letters and in conversation, as for example when he told Forster of a speaking engagement at which "He would try, he said, like Falstaff, 'but with a modification almost as large as himself,' less to speak himself, than to be the cause of speaking in others."[3] In his letters, he often did the same, as for example when he wrote W. H. Wills in 1853 and used what he called "a phrase of Falstaff's"[4] to express a thought, or when he wrote Mark Lemon that same year, ". . . I became quite an impersonation of Falstaff's wonderful simile, and my face was 'like a wet cloak all laid up.'"[5] Dickens's admiration for the old knight went so far that he even bought a house at Gad's Hill because of its association with Falstaff. Thereafter, one of Dickens's favorite pastimes was to take his guests onto the lawn and point out the place where Falstaff had committed his robbery in *1 Henry IV.*[6]

Given his obvious veneration for Falstaff as one of Shakespeare's greatest comic creations, it would not have been surprising if Dickens had based one of his own characters on Falstaff. Yet for all of the wonderfully amusing characters in Dickens's works, no individual seems overly reminiscent of Falstaff. However, there is one instance in which it seems that Dickens did copy one of Falstaff's rhetorical patterns, but he used it in such a way that it is almost unnoticeable. It appears that he took a short passage spoken by Falstaff in *2 Henry IV,* and altered it so that it could be used as dialogue by, not a comic character, but by that paradigm of avarice, Ebenezer Scrooge.

In Act 1, Scene ii, of *2 Henry IV,* Falstaff is attempting to avoid the Lord Chief Justice when that personage sends his servant to bring Falstaff to him. Falstaff, fully aware that the servant has been sent by the Lord Chief Justice, attempts to make his escape on the grounds that he believes that the servant is a beggar. As the "beggar" attempts to speak to him, Falstaff offers this rebuke for his "begging":

> What? a young knave, and begging? is there not wars? is there not employment? doth not the king lack subjects? do not the rebels need soldiers? Though it be a shame to be on any side but one, it is worse shame to beg than to be on the worse side, were it worse than the name of the rebellion can tell how to make it.
>
> (1.2 72-78)

Falstaff in essence says that surely there is some gainful employment for a young man other than begging, and based on the opinions he expresses here in his first appearance in this play, we are immediately able to size up his character (that is, assuming that we do not know him already from *1 Henry IV*). We can see that Falstaff holds the poor in low esteem, that he sees them as expendable, and that his principles are not those that we would commonly expect of a knight in the King's army. Thus, we have quickly become familiar with his character in the course of only a few lines.

In *A Christmas Carol,* Dickens has used almost the identical rhetorical pattern to familiarize us with Scrooge's character and his beliefs. Approached by two philanthropists attempting to raise money for the poor, Scrooge berates them for begging in proxy, and offers his options for the indigent:

> Are there no prisons . . . ? And the Union workhouses? Are they still in operation . . . ? The treadmill and the poorlaw are in full vigor then . . . ?[7]

Told that these are still options as opposed to begging, Scrooge says that he is ". . . Very glad to hear it." One of the men says that many of the poor would rather die than suffer these indignities, upon which Scrooge says, "If they had rather die . . . they had better do it, and decrease the surplus population."[8] Scrooge, like Falstaff, declares in effect that anything, even death, is preferable to begging. Here too, we have a situation where we are able to sum up a character by just a few lines of dialogue, and we see the low regard that Scrooge has for the poor, that he too regards them as expendable, and that his principles are not what we would commonly consider attributable to a decent member of society.

Although upon first glance Scrooge's comments are not as overtly funny as Falstaff's, there is a certain underlying humor here in spite of the malice. Clearly, Dickens used Falstaff's rhetorical pattern for ostensibly a different effect than humor, but the discourse does actually appear to be comic in a rather twisted sort of way. As Ackroyd notes, "If Dickens knew Shakespeare well enough to be heavily influenced by him (and all the signs of his fiction demonstrate this), he also understood him well enough to want to parody him."[9] Obviously, Dickens found a way to emulate his favorite Shakespearean character in an unusual way, by making something seemingly serious out of something that was already comic. Thus we have a rather tragicomic effect, but this brief passage serves to shape every perception that we have of Scrooge throughout the rest of the book. In any event, it appears that an obscure comment by one of Shakespeare's most famous comic creations was the basis for a well known saying by one of Dickens's most infamous characters.

Notes

1. Forster made this comment, and Kathleen Tillotson points this out in reference to a letter that Dickens wrote to Foster planning their celebration of Shakespeare's birthday: See Kathleen Tillotson, ed., *The Letters of Charles Dickens,* 7 vols. to date (Oxford: Clarendon, 1977) vol. IV: 110.

2. Tillotson vol. III, 165.

3. George Gissing, ed., *Forster's Life of Dickens* (London: Chapman and Hall, 1903) 317.

4. Tillotson vol. VII, 47. Here Dickens thinks that the words "the receipt of fern seed" were spoken by Falstaff in *1 Henry IV* 2.1 87, but Tillotson points out that the words were in fact spoken by Gadshill. All references to Shakespeare refer to William Shakespeare, *The Riverside Shakespeare* ed. G. Blakemore Evans (Boston: Houghton, 1974).

5. Tillotson vol. VII, 96. Here Dickens is quoting from *2 Henry IV,* 5.1 85.

6. Peter Ackroyd, *Dickens* (New York: Harper, 1990) 781.

7. Charles Dickens, *A Christmas Carol* (New York: Bantam, 1986) 11.

8. Dickens 11.

9. Ackroyd 142.

Robert L. Patten (review date fall 1996)

SOURCE: Patten, Robert L. Review of *The Dent Uniform Edition of Dickens' Journalism, Vol. 1: Sketches by Boz and Other Early Papers, 1833-39,* by Charles Dickens, edited by Michael Slater. *ANQ* 9, no. 4 (fall 1996): 52-6.

[*In the following review of Michael Slater's edition of* Sketches by Boz and Other Early Papers, *Patten provides a brief overview of Dickens' early journalistic career.*]

Professor Michael Slater is doing all students of Victorian literature a great service in producing four volumes of Dickens's journalism at a reasonable price. This first volume reprints **Sketches by Boz** (1836) from the 1868 Charles Dickens edition, which is also the version the co-publisher J. M. Dent has issued for nearly ninety years in its Everyman's Library. The other early periodical contributions included in this volume are five papers from *Bentley's Miscellany* (1837-39) and the pamphlet *Sunday Under Three Heads* (1836). Slater confines his textual editing to correcting misprints and eliminating Victorian hyphens in words such as "to-day." He then supplies a brisk, informative introduction that sets out the compositional and publishing history of the material; heads every individual selection (including each installment in **Sketches by Boz**) with a more detailed account of its publication; reprints from *The Dickens Index* (Oxford UP, 1988) a chronology of Dickens's life and times to 1839; gives a brief annotated bibliography; and, at the end of the text, prints a twenty-six page double-column index and glossary that identifies people and places and explains obsolete, colloquial, or slang terms. All this, more than 600 pages plus 42 of George Cruikshank's illustrations and a map of London in 1837, can now be obtained in hard cover for under $40!

In his October 1850 preface to the Cheap Edition, Dickens apologized for the "imperfections" of the sketches: "I am conscious of there often being extremely crude and ill-considered, and bearing obvious marks of haste and inexperience." However much Dickens by midcentury wanted to denigrate these early efforts, at the time of their publication he was extremely proud of them. Moreover, whereas for the first few stories contributed to the *Monthly Magazine* he was paid nothing, by the time the sketches and tales had been printed in various periodicals, then collected into a First Series in two volumes (reprinted twice) and a Second Series in one volume, and then all republished in monthly parts, Dickens had received more than 500 pounds, sometimes selling the same paper twice or thrice. The success of these pieces, confirmed by the early reviews and by the fact that every reprinting seemed to increase the audience and sales, suggests that Dickens struck a responsive nerve in the minds, hearts, and pocketbooks of his urban readers. **Sketches by Boz** registers Dickens's literary apprenticeship and simultaneously records the efforts of Grub Street to forge a new style and subject matter for a post-Romantic, post-Regency, post-rural culture.

When he started to write, Dickens appropriated several literary models. One was tales—short, often comic stories about domestic mishaps in love and entertaining—many of which first appeared in the *Monthly Magazine.* There was precedent for them in the periodicals of the day and in various collections of stories illustrated by George Cruikshank, such as *Mornings at Bow Street.* Dickens began writing about the comfortable middle class: Mr. Minns, protagonist of his first tale, has a "good and increasing" salary as a Somerset House clerk plus 10,000 pounds in the funds. Gradually the tales dropped into the lower middle class, whose Boswell, as some reviewers assumed the pseudonym "Boz" indicated, Dickens became.

These stories about the scrapes the middling classes got into when they maladroitly imitated the well-to-do were also theatrical staples. Dickens kept **"The Great**

Winglebury Duel" out of the December 1835 *Monthly Magazine* because he was arranging to dramatize it. And although it was published in February 1836 in the First Series of *Sketches,* the tale still hit the stage seven months later as *The Strange Gentleman* and ran for more than fifty nights. Such productions, either in boards or on them, relied on stock characters, snappy dialogue, quick action, and some smart turn of events.

Another model Dickens refurbished had a more complex background and arguably more significant descendants. Verbal and visual "sketches" of London characters and street scenes had become popular after the war, as the metropolis became a tourist's town. Pierce Egan's brand of racy, knowing slang and familiarity with upscale and downscale pleasures had been combined with the Cruikshank brothers' equally racy and knowing etchings in the 1820-21 bestseller *Life in London.* This tradition of smart-alecky narrative was carried on in Egan's newspaper, which was bought by the weekly *Bell's Life in London* a few years before it commissioned Dickens's work. In *Bell's Life* Dickens published under a different pseudonym, "Tibbs," and there, as Slater notes, he perfected his tales: the narratives are more sharply observed and focused and rely less on conventional situations. Also in *Bell's Life* Dickens published a number of "sketches," street scenes witnessed by a speculative pedestrian whose simultaneous attraction to and distancing from the subjects he describes produces that vacillating narrative voice, sometimes sentimental and sympathetic, and sometimes facetious or ironic or coolly callous, that marks Dickens's first tentative experiments to find the right style.

In both the tales and the sketches, Dickens learned too from the graphic precedents of William Hogarth and especially George Cruikshank, whose depictions of London lower-class life, Geoffrey Tillotson observed years ago, pre-created the world Dickens claimed through his pen. The same thing is true of the independent publication reprinted here, Dickens's polemic against Sir Andrew Agnew's Sabbath Observance Bill, *Sunday Under Three Heads* (1836). Cruikshank had done something very similar three years earlier, collaborating with the Fleet Street reporter John Wight on an illustrated pamphlet entitled *Sunday in London* that denounced Agnew's bill by exposing its class-based bias. Bringing Dickens's pamphlet into conjunction with the metropolitan sketches therefore clarifies the extent to which Boz's early publications derive from and adapt the politics and representational strategies of his contemporaries.

Slater's choice of the Charles Dickens edition as copy text means that readers will see none of the earlier solecisms, fumblings, vulgarities, slang, topicalities, and literary models betraying the experimental origins of these pieces. It will, therefore, be more difficult for novice readers to understand what caused Dickens's later defensiveness. But on the other side of the ledger, reading them in their cleaned-up state allows more direct access to the writer's matured imagination and prose.

Understandably, this handy edition emphasizes Dickens's agency. Nevertheless, the succession of editors and publishers who bought these productions, designed them for their differing markets, married them to illustrations, sold them in many formats, and solicited reviews and publicity had much to do with the making of Boz and his *Sketches.* And the readers and reviewers of morning newspapers, sporting gazettes, monthly magazines, bound volumes, and serial parts also participated in shaping these pieces into representations of a newly rhetoricized subculture.

In their initial versions these sketches betray the instability of visual and verbal relations at a time when artists and writers were trying to express the unprecedented dislocations and violence of urban life. To steer us through Boz's city, Slater reproduces a (barely legible, alas) detail from Joseph Cross's 1837 *London Guide,* which sets forth information about locations and routes according to traditional cartographic formulas. But however much the metropolis was represented by such visual formulations of physical features, it was also represented by its inhabitants in verbal terms. Here are the directions to his cousin's house given to Mr. Minns in Dickens's first published story:

> You turn down by the side of the white house till you can't go another step further—mind that!—and then you turn to your right, by some stables—well; close to you, you'll see a wall with 'Beware of the Dog' written on it in large letters—(Minns shuddered)—go along by the side of that wall for about a quarter of a mile—and anybody will show you which is my place.

As Richard L. Stein has shown so brilliantly in his book, *Victoria's Year,* imagining oneself at the beginning of Victoria's realm, either on the map or in prose and picture, entailed reconceiving the projects of representation.

Tales, when Boz had done with them, became narratives about original characters and situations rendered in a densely and fundamentally metaphoric prose. Sketches were transformed from verbal equivalents of pictorial art to incisive, open-ended renderings of the evanescent and transitory that characterize the last pieces Dickens wrote for the Second Series of *Sketches.* In just over a month in the autumn of 1836, at the end of his journalistic career, Dickens composed what Slater so rightly calls "four little masterpieces of the genre": **"Meditations in Monmouth Street," "Scotland Yard," "Doctors' Commons,"** and **"Vauxhall Gardens by Day."** Three of these inspired Cruikshank to some of his best etchings in the two series. The artist gets scant attention from the editor, but it is understandable that, in a project devoted to Dickens's journalism, writing should take precedence. In the "Scenes," "Characters," and "Tales" that make up these *Sketches,* we witness Dickens, along with his publishers, readers, and illustrator, creating the voices and topics and modes of representation that will characterize early Victorian literature. To have this evidence, cleanly and clearly set forth by one of the world's leading Dickensians, is indeed cause for rejoicing.

Anthea Trodd (essay date winter 1999-2000)

SOURCE: Trodd, Anthea. "Collaborating in Open Boats: Dickens, Collins, Franklin, and Bligh." *Victorian Studies* 42, no. 2 (winter 1999-2000): 201-25.

[*In the following essay, Trodd demonstrates how* The Wreck of the Golden Mary *fulfills its dual purposes of defending the reputation of British seamen and justifying Dickens's literary collaboration with Wilkie Collins.*]

> Therefore, as a means of beguiling the time and inspiring hope, I gave them the best summary in my power of Bligh's voyage of more than three thousand miles, in an open boat, after the Mutiny of the Bounty, and of the wonderful preservation of that boat's crew. They listened throughout with great interest, and I concluded by telling them, that, in my opinion, the happiest circumstance in the whole narrative was, that Bligh, who was no delicate man either, had solemnly placed it on record therein that he was sure and certain that under no conceivable circumstances whatever, would that emaciated party who had gone through all the pains of famine, have preyed on one another. I cannot describe the visible relief which this spread through the boat, and how the tear stood in every eye. From that time I was as well convinced as Bligh himself that there was no danger, and that this phantom, at any rate, did not haunt us.
>
> Now, it was a part of Bligh's experience that when the people in his boat were most cast down, nothing did them so much good as hearing a story told by one of their number. When I mentioned that, I saw that it struck the general attention as much as it did my own, for I had not thought of it until I came to it in my summary.

—Charles Dickens and Wilkie Collins, *The Wreck of the Golden Mary* (143)

The Wreck of the Golden Mary (1856) was the seventh of Charles Dickens's Christmas numbers, the supplements of stories by several contributors, which went out each December from 1850 with an issue of his journal, *Household Words.* The narrative framing the stories for 1856 tells of how the survivors of a ship wrecked en route to the California Gold Rush of 1849 maintain order and morale by collaborating in storytelling. The

overtaxed captain eventually sinks into unconsciousness, yielding both the command of the lifeboat, and the first person narrative, to his inferior but adequate mate. This collapse occurs shortly after the passage above in which he cites the notorious William Bligh as an authority on cannibalism and on storytelling. This was the story Dickens devised for his first published collaboration with Wilkie Collins. Between them, they provided the shipwreck narrative as a frame, within which the stories of the other four contributors appeared (see Lohrli 236, 256).

It was the first time Dickens had yielded to another writer part of the narrative frame by which he directed readers' responses to the contributions to the Christmas numbers. To validate this new collaborative enterprise, he invoked the collective moral authority of the British seafaring community in a story told by two seamen. "I am the Captain of the Golden Mary: Mr. Collins is the Mate," he told Angela Burdett-Coutts (*Letters* 8: 231). At the same time, this was one of several writings in which Dickens rebutted a charge of cannibalism recently brought against an elite group from that community by asserting the incomparable gifts for leadership, fidelity, and self-sacrifice found among British Tars. The link between the two defenses, the rebuttal of cannibalism and the justification of collaboration, is consolidated in the insistence on storytelling as a powerful prevention against cannibalism, with the citation of Bligh as authority: "[T]he example of Bligh and his men, when they were adrift like us, was of unspeakable importance in keeping up our spirits" (151).[1] ***The Wreck of the Golden Mary*** is thus engaged in a complex double operation, defending the reputation of British Tars by invoking them as the strongest possible example of collective moral authority to justify an adventure in collaboration.

I

The collaboration of Dickens, at the height of his powers, with Collins, a junior and still relatively unknown writer, is one of the most remarkable instances of literary collaboration. It was a collaboration first imagined in nautical terms, drawing on popular constructions of the British Tar to present him both as a model for collaboration and as an exemplar to civil society. Within the story a group of ill-assorted, mostly derelict, people bound for the California Gold Rush, a destination implying unrestrained self-interest, are formed into a well-disciplined community by the direction and example of the Captain and Mate. This was precisely what Dickens was hoping to effect with his latest Christmas number. In 1855, he had complained that he found contributors to that year's Christmas number, ***The Holly-Tree Inn,*** unresponsive and recalcitrant: "[T]he way in which they don't fit into that elaborately described plan, so simple in itself, amazes me" (*Letters* 7: 753). Collins's imagined role as Mate in the latest Christmas number was apparently to provide a contributor more directly accountable and subordinate to the lead writer. At this stage in his career, Dickens was strongly attracted to collaboration; in January 1857, he wrote of the pleasures of rehearsing a play as like "writing a book in company" (*Letters* 8: 256). It was, however, collaboration imagined in hierarchical terms. This latest Christmas number was to be an example of well-led and disciplined writing in company.

To imagine this ideal literary collaboration, comradely yet hierarchical, Dickens turned for reassurance and authority to the figure of the Tar. It is accurate in this first collaboration to attribute the plan entirely to Dickens. He had written his section before Collins was enlisted: "I never wrote anything more easily, or I think with greater interest or stronger belief" (*Letters* 8: 222). Collins shared Dickens's enthusiasm for nautical literature, and the fact that he was a yachting enthusiast was probably an additional qualification for his role as Mate, but at this time the junior writer was "a willing instrument and extension of Dickens" (Peters 168).

The national dependence on the seaman during the preceding century had fostered a rich range of cultural representations to express that dependence, notably the nautical fictions and melodramas of the 1820s and 1830s. The use of those representations, in the first Dickens and Collins collaboration, is highly suggestive both about what Dickens hoped for from collaboration, and about the significance of the Tar in cultural imaginings of the period. A few years later, William Makepeace Thackeray, imagining the possibility of collaboration in the essay, "On a Peal of Bells" (1860), invoked an analogy with business:

> I confess I would often like to have a competent, respectable and rapid clerk for the business part of my novels; and, on his arrival at eleven o'clock, would say, "Mr Jones if you please, the archbishop must die this morning in about five pages. Turn to article 'Dropsy' (or what you will) in Encyclopedia."
>
> (295)

Thackeray was musing about the criticisms of Alexandre Dumas's industrial production, the most notorious contemporary example of collaboration. When Dickens, who habitually referred to himself as "the Inimitable," turned to collaboration, he invoked not a mundane business analogy but the more dignified and heroic image of endeavor associated with the British Tar. He also managed his anxieties about collaboration by responding to current fears that the seaman might not be as disciplined a figure as the idealized Tar. Significantly, the major nautical authority cited for the value of collaboration is the ship's captain who was the subject of the most famous breakdown of order in British nautical an-

nals, and particularly identified with catastrophically bad relations with his mate. It was an unforced citation by Dickens: as we shall see later, there was no storytelling in the open boat of the *Bounty*.

Most specifically, the collaboration began in attempts to defend the reputation of one of Britain's most famous Tars, and in anxieties about loss of order and hierarchy aroused by the attack on his reputation. In 1845, the Arctic explorer Sir John Franklin had disappeared into the Polar wastes with two ships and 128 British seamen. In 1854, Dr. John Rae of the Hudson Bay Company reported that Inuit traveling on the shores of the Polar Sea had found evidence that the expedition had degenerated into anarchy and cannibalism (see Beattie and Geiger; Marlow; Nayder; Owen; Spufford; Stone, "Contents"). The suggestion that Franklin and his men had suffered such a moral collapse was likely to be acutely painful to those who, like Dickens, had grown up relishing the myths of the golden age of British maritime supremacy. The sixty-year-old Franklin was a relic of that time, and his expedition represented a continuation into the present of the heroic age of Trafalgar. Dickens's first response to the suggestion that a Trafalgar veteran and the flower of the British navy had succumbed to cannibalism under the gaze of the Inuit was the series of four articles in *Household Words,* which appeared under the running title, **"The Lost Arctic Voyagers"** (1854). In these, Dr. Rae became his first, reluctant, collaborator on the topic, his account framed by the arguments Dickens marshals against the likelihood of cannibalism in any well-led expedition of civilized men, and especially of British seamen. (Dickens yields no ground to that alternative tradition, in which cannibalism in extremity was an accepted practice among the nineteenth-century seafaring community [see Simpson], a practice which surfaces in polite literature in Thackeray's 1845 ballad, "Little Billee.") Rae, a Scotsman long resident in Canada, and working for a company at odds with the expedition's sponsor, the Admiralty, is skeptical about the vaunted discipline of British seamen, and their ability to resist extreme conditions, but his arguments are neutralized by the weight of examples with which Dickens surrounds him. From within the obscurity to which Dickens has consigned him, he protests that he cannot be expected to hold his own against a writer "of great ability and practice" (458).

Rae obviously had his limits as a collaborator. Dickens's next collaborator in rebutting the charges against Franklin and his sailors was Collins. *The Wreck of the Golden Mary* was the later-conceived of two collaborations emerging in the Christmas season of 1856, in which Dickens and Collins defended the reputation of Franklin and his crews. Since April, Collins had been working under Dickens's direction on the play *The Frozen Deep* (1856), in which Dickens enjoyed his greatest success as an actor in the role of a seaman and explorer whose selfless behavior refutes the atrocious, though inexplicit, allegations brought against him. By the time *The Wreck of the Golden Mary* was being written, rehearsals of the play were under way. The two works shared obvious features: a self-sacrificing hero, a group undergoing great hardship and suffering, and a celebration of the best qualities of Englishness as demonstrated primarily by seamen and secondarily by families. In the play, Dickens and Collins acted the two principal sailors. In *The Wreck,* their sailor narrators frame the story, opening with **"The Wreck"** and concluding with "The Deliverance." In the middle section, "The Beguilement in the Boats," the stories of the other contributors are presented as examples of how storytelling, the ultimate mark of civilization, enables those involved to resist the inhumanity of cannibalism: "Spectres as we soon were in our bodily wasting, our imaginations did not perish like the gross flesh on our bones" (143-44).

II

Nautical life thus offered Dickens a model for collaboration, with opportunities both to emphasize his self-sacrifice in communal endeavors and to support extension of his authority over such activities. In particular, it offered a model for the kind of direction and control he felt he had so far failed to impose on the Christmas numbers. In the first four Christmas numbers (1850-53), the contributors had addressed the central theme of Christmas without an organizing narrative frame. Dickens first provided this kind of organizational structure in 1854 for *The Seven Poor Travellers,* for which he distributed a plan of his frame to prospective contributors in an attempt to create a more coherent number. *The Wreck of the Golden Mary* was an attempt to exert closer control over the entire number by extending the frame at the expense of the framed tales. The tales exist to demonstrate the importance of storytelling in extremity, but the real story is the frame, and Dickens was anxious not to compromise the excitement it was to generate, finding "the Narrative too strong (speaking as a reader of it; not as its writer) to be broken by the stories" (*Letters* 8: 222).

The Wreck of the Golden Mary for the first time dispensed with Christmas as a topic in order to record a more urgent occasion for storytelling: survival in an open boat. Peter Brooks has described the importance of the framed tale to Balzac, in the opportunity the frame offered of "enabling expansion of fiction into the lives it touches," its ability "to make us reflect on the substance of life and its principles" (*Melodramatic Imagination* 151). The frame of *The Wreck of the Golden Mary* was designed to compel reflections on the sheer necessity of storytelling to the maintenance of life and civilized behavior. In the *Arabian Nights,* Dickens's basic model for frame narrative, Scheherezade

postpones her own death with her stories, within which other narrators ward off death and placate figures of death-dealing power, genii and despots, with their own stories (see Glancey). An endless proliferation of linked narratives ensures that a conclusion—and death—is never reached. Indeed, in **"The Lost Arctic Voyagers,"** Dickens offers as his final, clinching rebuttal of Rae's report that, in the *Arabian Nights,* despite its many sea voyages and desert journeys, there is no reference to cannibalism (392). Where stories are consumed, the tellers are not; the survivors of the *Golden Mary* stage their own Barmecide banquet.

The purpose of the frame, however, was not only to celebrate storytelling but to control it, to offer directives to the reader on what readerly role to assume in interpreting the narrative (see Ong, "Writer's Audience"). The frame was doubly important to Dickens in collaborative narratives, allowing him to control the reader's response to the other writers, the most extreme example being **"The Lost Arctic Voyagers,"** where the frame neutralized Rae's disturbing account. Dickens's original plan for the 1856 Christmas number, outlined to prospective contributors on 30 September 1856, was to provide the frame himself as before, but, by the end of October, he had worked out an alternative. There would be two open boats, not one, and a Mate commanding the second. Collins, in the person of this Mate, John Steadiman, would take over the frame narrative at the point when the Captain sinks into unconsciousness, and words finally fail him. The previous model of collective storytelling controlled by Dickens's frame was to be replaced by a frame which emphasized collaboration within a chain of command. Part of the attraction of the nautical model of collaboration for Dickens was probably the way in which existing cultural representations emphasized the possibilities of heroic endeavor for all within a strongly hierarchical framework. The establishment of a Mate figure, working under Dickens's direction, introduced a clear hierarchy into the assembly of narratives. Moreover, Collins's first job upon assuming the narrative was to make Steadiman praise the leadership qualities of the unconscious Captain.

By 1 November 1856, Dickens had already written his section of **"The Wreck,"** and wrote to Collins proposing that they walk the following Tuesday, "through the fallen leaves in Cobham Park," where he would explain "how I think you can get your division of the Christmas no. very originally and naturally" (*Letters* 8: 218). That momentous walk on 4 November, the founding moment of a collaboration which was to last until 1867, was later described by Dickens to Angela Burdett-Coutts:

> Of course he could not begin until I had finished, and when he read the Wreck he was so desperately afraid of the job that I began to mistrust him. However, we went down to Gad's Hill, and walked through Cobham

Woods to talk it over: and he then went at it cheerfully, and came out as you see.

(*Letters* 8: 234)

Collins, whose desperation may have been related to fears about being submerged by Dickens which he had indicated to Dickens's co-editor Wills in September, had been accumulating the qualifications for Mate for some time (*Letters* 8: 189). He was working on *The Frozen Deep*, providing Dickens with his greatest dramatic role as the self-sacrificing sailor, Richard Wardour. He had written two pieces for *Household Words* in the past year that Dickens had particularly admired. His short story, "The Diary of Anne Rodway" (1856), published in July, had convinced Dickens of his abilities for pathos, and in the previous December, Dickens had admired the "plain storytelling merit" of a nautical piece, "The Cruise of the Tomtit" (1856) (*Letters* 8: 161-62, 7: 763).

Collins's junior status and amenability to direction made him an appropriate Mate, but his attraction for Dickens also included his association with Bohemianism, both in a familiarity with the sexual underground, and in the bachelor freedom of his main hobby, sailing. "The Cruise of the Tomtit" describes how, after piratical raids for provisions on the households of married friends, Collins and his companion set out to enjoy the exhilaration of being "jolly tars" at sea (493). The newish leisure world of yachting described, with its modulation of the "jolly tar" into the genteel amateur, was a long way from Trafalgar and from the Arctic, and from Dickens's own imagined nautical world of heroism, wreck, and loss, but it shared an emphasis on comradeship and on storytelling. Collins's lighter holiday interpretation of the sea is acknowledged in Dickens's writing of the "frisky" persona of Mate Steadiman. This initial nautical emphasis was maintained in the partnership's later collaborations, in the marines and seamen versus pirates story of **The Perils of Certain English Prisoners** (1857), and in another shipwreck story, **A Message from the Sea** (1860). Collins's contributions to the Christmas numbers, **The Haunted House** (1859) and **Tom Tiddler's Ground** (1861), were also nautical stories; when he eventually republished them as "Blow Up with the Brig" and "The Fatal Cradle" in *Miss or Mrs? and Other Stories* (1872), his Preface claimed that they were particular favorites with Dickens.

III

The collaboration at its inception thus called on the virtues of the Tar of the heroic maritime age to give authority to the venture. The attraction of the Tar as interpretative figure for the collaboration was founded in the two writers' common admiration for the nautical narratives of Frederick Marryat, James Fenimore Cooper, and Richard Henry Dana, and in the extraordinary cul-

tural focus upon the sailor in the decades following the Napoleonic Wars. Papers and magazines on both sides of the Channel carried extensive reports of shipping and nautical disasters, and there were specialist magazines entirely devoted to these subjects (see Corbin 229-30; Palmer). The nautical melodrama was an extremely popular genre in the theater. In these plays, the hero was usually a common seaman, a figure who became "the most powerful instrument of imperial ideology on the nineteenth century stage" (Bratton 33). The theater found in the Tar a potent image of the incorporation of the working-class man in the advantages and status of an imperial nation.

Through the 1820s and 1830s, the nautical novel, in which the hero was usually genteel, answered an enormous demand for narratives about the heroes who had saved the country, and who at this period enjoyed an iconic status comparable to that of the Few in British films of the 1940s and 1950s. One of the surviving men of Trafalgar was Franklin, the most famous example of the postwar propulsion of unemployed naval heroes into intensive Arctic exploration (see Lopez; Owen). In the three decades following the Napoleonic Wars, most of the Arctic was mapped, and the public's interest in nautical adventure shifted north toward the Polar seas. A leading agent of the shift was Sir John Barrow, Secretary to the Admiralty between 1804 and 1845, who, in 1831 in a non-Arctic mood, wrote *The Mutiny of the "Bounty"*, a major source for **"The Lost Arctic Voyagers,"** and for the Bligh citations in **The Wreck of the Golden Mary.**

When Dickens and Collins began their formal collaboration as Captain Ravender and Mate Steadiman, they were working within the type of the Tar as it had been established in those decades. The sailor was already known by 1740 for his distinctive appearance—the gait, complexion, and dialect which made him instantly recognizable to the shore population, and to the press gang—but it was not until the early-nineteenth century that this distinctive appearance acquired its status as a moral icon (see Rediker 10-12). The eighteenth century, Marcus Rediker suggests, retained a grasp of the harsh realities of the seaman's life, and of his disruptive potential, which later generations worked to obscure (4-5). On his voyage to Lisbon, for example, the dying Henry Fielding sees the seamen as representative of the kind of disorder he had devoted his life to clearing from the London streets; brave and capable in their shipboard duties, on land they "think themselves entirely discharged from the common bonds of humanity, and [. . .] seem to glory in the language and behaviour of savages" (44). This is a far remove from the domesticated Tar of 1830s writing.

Greg Dening has suggested that the creation of the Tar, initially imagined as a child, was a defensive response to recognition of the utter indispensability of the sea-man to the continuing extension of Britain's commercial and industrial power and maritime supremacy:

> Georgian England invented the jolly, simple, incongruous Tar. The more the country became dependent on the exploitation of seamen's brilliant skills, the more sure it became that seamen were "children"—improvident, intemperate, profligate.
>
> (56)

But if the high casualty rates in battle during the Napoleonic Wars intensified the public's recognition of the sailor's indispensability to the British cause, the mutiny at the Nore naval base demonstrated the sailor's potential for disruption as well. This awareness of both the sailor's usefulness and his capacity for disruption augmented public anxieties about Britain's dependence on seamen, and, in turn, deepened the need for reassuring myths about them. Royal Gettman, in his history of Bentley's, the publishing house most closely associated with the vogue for the nautical novel, ascribes much of that popularity to the "guilty conscience" (167) of a public aware of the high demands made on the sailor, as well as his necessary presence in extending and maintaining the Empire. Seamen themselves received the new images of the Tar enthusiastically. Charles Dibdin's sentimental ballads, immensely popular with both public and seamen, circulated between them the image of the noble and patriotic Tar. Herman Melville, commenting in 1850 on their continuing popularity, described how Dibdin created the image of the Tar as "the most carefree, contented, virtuous and patriotic of mankind" from and for "felons and paupers," and added, "no wonder Dibdin was a government pensioner at two hundred pound per annum" (402). Theatrical representations of the sailor during the Napoleonic Wars invoked dual perceptions of him as a paradigm of both fidelity and potential disruption, perceptions highly influential as models for Victorian depictions of the working class (see Russell). The Tar in nautical melodrama enabled the incorporation of the disruptive, often press-ganged, seaman within the myth of national supremacy (see Bratton; Russell). He also offered Dickens a heroic model for the containing and directing of the creative energies of his collaborators on the Christmas numbers.

Both Dickens and Collins liked to play with the self-conscious fictionality of the Tar. Dickens enjoyed parodying the nautical dialect popularized in the theater (see *Letters* 4: 182-85). Moreover, not only did he play seamen in Collins's plays *The Lighthouse* (1855) and *The Frozen Deep,* but many of the reminiscences about him stress his everyday seamanlike appearance. George Augustus Sala, Percy Fitzgerald, and Frederick Locker-Lampson all recorded impressions of him as likely to be taken in the street for a ship's captain (see Collins,

Charles Dickens). Collins, an enthusiastic amateur yachtsman, relished playing the "jolly tar" as gentleman in his articles for *Household Words,* "The Cruise of the Tomtit" and "My Black Mirror" (1856). *The Wreck of the Golden Mary,* however, treated a shipwreck in a year when 1153 ships were lost around Britain's coasts alone, and addressed a serious allegation made against the flower of the British Navy (see Palmer 40). The Tars whom Dickens and Collins adopted as narrative personae, both to rebut those allegations and to add authority to their collaboration, exemplified the qualities which were seen to make the Tar vitally instructive to the shore population, as well as to the contributors and readers of *Household Words,* whom Dickens was seeking to form into a community. These qualities were openness of feeling, comradeship, self-sacrifice, and yarning.

The Tar's imagined openness, his evident honesty and fidelity, made him an appropriate hero for melodrama, which, Brooks has suggested, was organized around "the admiration of virtue" (*Melodramatic Imagination* 25). Melodrama, Brooks argues, strives toward "total visibility" of the sign of virtue (27), and performance skills in the genre were directed by the belief that emotions were "susceptible of complete externalization" (47). The Tar, however, was presumed to have by nature this melodramatic transparency. Instantly recognizable even in a society where appearances were increasingly unrevealing and identity perceived as mystified, imbued with the moral power of decades of indispensability, the Tar alone made manifest his identity at first glance. In *A Message from the Sea* (1860), Captain Jorgan's instant identifiability as a seaman is indistinguishable from his moral authority. The stage melodramas sought to decipher the mysteries of identity with which the city streets confronted the curious: "[T]he stage tells a truth the street no longer tells" (Sennett 174). The Tar was already identifiable in the street; translated to the theater he redoubled his truthtelling. When Dickens's friends persistently compared his appearance to that of a sea-captain, they were not commenting on an amiable eccentricity, but paying the clearest possible tribute to his status as moral icon, as instantly recognizable sign of virtue in a mystified world.

The Tar was a sign of manly virtue, but his openness of feeling allied him with women and children, not with the reserve expected of men. Thus, there was a contest over the gender alliances of the Tar. In his 1849 Preface to *The Pilot* (1823), the novel usually accepted as beginning the vogue for nautical fiction, Cooper suggested that his novel might be read as a corrective to Walter Scott's 1822 novel of the seaboard, *The Pirate.* Whereas Scott had displayed ignorance or uninterest in the technicalities of ships and navigation, and in the distinctive nautical dialect which expressed these, Cooper's novel relied on such expertise. He accepted that such extensive attention to nautical technicalities lost him his female audience: "The Pilot could scarcely be a favourite with females. The story has little interest for them, nor was it much heeded by the author of the book in the progress of his labours" (7). Cooper is outlining a clear program for the nautical novel as exclusively masculine, confirmed in that masculinity by extensive displays of technical expertise in the appropriate language. Insofar as the appeal of the Tar lay in his escape from domesticity into adventure and technical expertise, the nautical novel followed Cooper's program, as did Collins in "The Cruise of the Tomtit."

Paradoxically, however, the Tar was also in this period especially associated with the domestic sphere, and mediated complex gender tensions (see Russell). A figure of masculine action, he was also associated with open displays of feeling customarily assigned to the female, and with accompanying qualities of obedience and naivete. William, the Tar in Douglas Jerrold's *Black-Eyed Susan* (1829), the most famous of all nautical melodramas, deploys a highly distinctive nautical dialect, but directs most of his attention to the home from which he is separated, and talks readily and directly about his feelings. Indeed, in his attachment to domestic values, and his emotionality and obedience to authority, he renders Susan herself virtually redundant, encompassing all the domestic qualities she might be supposed to represent. Nautical melodrama, during its heyday in the 1820s and 1830s, served as a transition from the earlier Gothic melodrama to the domestic melodrama dominant in the Victorian period (see Booth). "That charming representative of home life abroad, the indefatigable British Tar" was shown to direct all his feelings to the home he was occupied in defending (Donohue 116). The Tar, with his adventurous spirit and expertise, and his perpetual yearnings toward home, dissolved the boundaries between the external world and the domestic. As editor of a family magazine, Dickens would hardly have wished to engage in Cooper's attempt to alienate the female audience, and the Tar offered a unique opportunity for reconciling the worlds of adventure and domesticity. The Captain and Mate of the *Golden Mary,* then, are Tars with access to the world of adventure and endurance, but licensed unlike other men to express openly emotional natures, and to represent an especially intense and poignant relation to the idea of home.

The Tar's exceptional capacity for comradeship was his key to survival. For Dickens, one crucial piece of evidence in support of Franklin was the expression of loyal friendship by John Richardson, the naval surgeon who had accompanied Franklin on earlier Arctic expeditions:

> Lady Franklin sent me the whole of that Richardson memoir, and I think Richardson's manly friendship, and love of Franklin, one of the noblest things I ever knew in my life. It makes one's heart beat high with a kind of sacred joy.
>
> (*Letters* 8: 66)

Richardson's tribute illustrated seamen's capacity for comradeship, and thus guaranteed the impossibility of Franklin having succumbed to cannibalism. It also provided the line eventually used as the epitaph on the statue commemorating Franklin and his expedition: "They forged the last link with their lives" (*Letters* 8: 66). The chain forged was officially the North West Passage, but, more emotive than the reference to that geographically mobile and commercially useless route, was the suggestion of a chain of collaborative friendship, working in self-sacrificing unison. In **"The Wreck,"** Dickens speaks of how "the shining of a face upon a face" maintains morale in the open boat (145). He used the shining face as image of restorative friendship at least twice in his letters the following year. He wrote to his American sailor friend, Captain Elisha Morgan, "I wonder whether Morgan will ever bring one of those big ships back, and beam upon me with the light of his bright face" (*Letters* 8: 453). Morgan was to be the model for Captain Jorgan in *A Message from the Sea,* and figured for Dickens as the ideal type of ship's captain, the kind for whom he was doubtless gratified to be taken in the street. A letter from Collins elicited a similar response: he notes that his "face has been shining ever since" (*Letters* 8: 294). The image suggests the reassurance Dickens sought from collaboration at this stage. Collins's role in their first collaboration was to play Richardson to Dickens's Franklin, to pay tribute to the leader's extraordinary selflessness.

By the 1830s, the high level of self-sacrifice which had been demanded of seamen over the preceding century was increasingly viewed as intrinsic to their characters. The heavy price they paid for the extension of British maritime supremacy was reinterpreted as a voluntary sacrifice; this capacity for sacrifice, furthermore, was itself seen as proof of British moral superiority, which justified such supremacy. Marryat's sailors are the major fictional examples of this. Patrick Brantlinger has described how Marryat's narratives move "to submerge language, reason, selfhood, in the 'destructive element' of death. Despite their naive, hearty good cheer, or perhaps because of it, Marryat's novels are informed by a spirit of 'altruistic suicide'—of an ultimate self-sacrifice ending in silence" (54). In Emile Durkheim's later formulation of the concept of altruistic suicide, "this aptitude for renunciation, this taste for impersonality, develops as a result of prolonged discipline" (234). Durkheim found a higher level of suicide in the armed forces than among the general population, and explained it by the training of the sailor or soldier to be willing to submerge personality in a greater communal whole. In Marryat's work, the major example is provided by his most enduringly popular novel, *Masterman Ready* (1840). In the opening shipwreck, Ready, an omnicompetent old seaman, chooses not to go in the lifeboat, but to stay with a family of six who are passengers on the ship. His skills sustain them on a nearby desert island, where he directs them in creating a reasonable replica of domestic life, and he eventually gives his life to enable them to escape back home. His reasons for this series of sacrifices are frequently given: as a man who sacrificed his own hope of domestic happiness to a vagrant life, he feels it is his duty to preserve the family even at the cost of his own death. Captain Ravender, a single man with no domestic base, is in the model of Marryat's altruistically suicidal old seaman.

The last quality of the Tar which was instructive to the shore population, and on which Dickens and Collins drew, was his fabled skill in yarning. In "The Storyteller," Walter Benjamin discusses the traditional association of the sailor with the values of archaic storytelling, that storytelling which seeks to transmit a body of practical wisdom founded in experience to an identifiable audience in need of that wisdom. Marryat's novels foreground the continuing value of such archaic storytelling. In *Peter Simple* (1834), the description of naval battles is regularly interpolated with the yarns which the midshipman hero's older shipmates tell him, yarns of their past experience which are shown to be as instructive in nautical life and survival skills as the direct experiences of action with which they alternate (see Sussman). Masterman Ready, on his desert island, sustains the Segrave family not only with his building and provisioning skills, but with the yarns of past experience he tells them nightly, yarns of adventure which both recount past survival strategies and forever yearn back to the home life he sacrificed.

Marryat's stories thus recreate not simply the yarns, but the occasions for which they were urgently needed, and the dependence of identified listeners upon them for the transmission of survival skills. Dickens's fascination with such occasions for storytelling is demonstrated in his collaboration with Dr. Robert McCormick on an article in *Household Words* for Christmas 1850, "Christmas in the Frozen Regions," based on McCormick's recollections of Christmas storytelling and theatricals in Antarctica in 1841 on board the *Erebus* and *Terror,* the very ships in which Franklin's expedition later disappeared. The article looks back to the magazines and theatricals organized by William Parry's Polar expedition of 1819, and hopes that the current crews of the *Erebus* and *Terror* are similarly engaged in celebrating Christmas. They were, in fact, all dead by then, but throughout that Christmas the crews of the ten ships of the rescue expeditions variously sponsored by the Admiralty, and by private subscription in Britain and the

United States, produced and exchanged newspapers and stories, and put on theatricals for each other, as they all lay icebound in the Polar archipelago (see Owen).

What such activities in part demonstrated was a community for archaic storytelling usually lost to the modern writer, the storytelling Benjamin describes, which addresses an audience which depends vitally on the story to sustain a culturally deprived existence. In 1827, Heinrich Heine recorded how the sailors and fishermen of the seaboard community of Nordeney perpetuated this archaic storytelling tradition:

> They sit cosily round the fire in their low-roofed cottages, huddling together when the weather grows cold: they see by each other's eyes what each man is thinking, and read on the lips the words before they are uttered; all the common relations of life are stored in their memories, and a single sound, a single look, a single dumb gesture enables them to excite such laughter, tears or religious fervour as no orator could arouse in us without hours of expounding, expectorating and perorating.
>
> (79)

This is a context of utter intimacy for storytelling, where the slightest inflection or gesture is instantly interpreted as loaded with significance. It was this transparent intensity of meaning which melodrama sought to recreate, this urgent intimacy of community toward which the framed tale yearned. Alain Corbin suggests, however, that Heine is as much repelled as attracted by this archaic yarning (219-20). This is a community where there can be no secrets, where yarns are understood as much in gesture and close physical proximity as in language, where there is no space or privacy for storytellers, and no opportunity for them to control the story by the withholding or reinterpretation of information. Nautical writing of the period sometimes demonstrates a similar ambivalence. There is a telling episode in Dana's autobiographical *Two Years Before the Mast* (1840), a work much admired by both Dickens and Collins, in which Dana, after pages of praising the seamen's creativity, is unable to face another evening of rambling repetitive yarning, and organizes a reading of Scott's *Woodstock* (1826), seeking to instill some sense of hierarchy in narrative quality in the communal entertainment (210).

Dickens's attitude to archaic storytelling is similarly ambivalent. In the late 1850s, he was seeking to increase a relation of intimacy with his readership by appearing in plays, and by the series of readings from his novels which began in 1858, and which have been described as "repristination," the attempt to recreate the archaic values of oral narration (Ong, *Orality and Literacy* 115). With **The Wreck of the Golden Mary,** however, he was also writing to reject the claims of a particular archaic narrative, the reports of the Inuit that

Franklin's men had descended to cannibalism. **"The Lost Arctic Voyagers"** attempts to control and nullify Rae's insistence that the Inuit are reliable narrators, that, although they express themselves in a manner which may seem archaic and picturesque to Europeans, their testimony is to be depended upon. Dickens organizes a legalistic framework of documented evidence to combat what he describes as the "vague babble of savages" (364).

IV

The Wreck of the Golden Mary attempts to recreate the values of archaic yarning associated with nautical life, but in a disciplined and civilized manner. The hope that Franklin and his men were still somewhere in the frozen wastes warding off hunger by swapping yarns was gone, but it remained important to commemorate that possibility, to renew the pattern of narrative and performance maintained by McCormick's Antarctic Christmas, and by the rescue ships. Those celebrations had demonstrated not only the importance of storytelling in life-threatening situations, but the discipline of well-led men. Both the Christmas collaborations of 1856 sought to emulate that tradition, and the high quality of civilization it embodied, to restore the distance between savage and Tar threatened by Rae's report.

The personalities of the two narrators—who embodied the instructive qualities of the Tar as well as the leadership and discipline essential to survival—were outlined by Dickens in **"The Wreck"** before Collins was signed up for the voyage. Captain Ravender, despite his seadog competence and the utter reliance employers and crew place in him, is from the beginning a figure touched by melancholy, a man who has lost his chance of a home life, who is too ready to overwork, to sacrifice himself for others. Harry Stone has pointed to the suggestive fusion of "ravenous" and "provender" in Ravender's name (546). Ravender's anxieties, however, center on the effect fears of cannibalism may have on the passengers, "having such a terrific idea to dwell upon in secret" (143). While Dickens constructs his own persona as a classic model of altruistic suicide, he turns for his depiction of Mate Steadiman, credited with Collins's physical appearance, to an altogether less problematic figure, the jolly Tar of popular construction. With Steadiman's first appearance, Dickens allows for both adult and family versions of this figure. When Ravender seeks his Mate, Steadiman is on a "frisk" in Liverpool. The word probably manages a covert allusion to Collins's familiarity with the sexual underworld, but our expectations of sexual adventurism are dissipated, and the "frisk" is made acceptable for Marryat's juvenile audience, when Steadiman is found buying a toy for a child accompanying two pretty women met in the street.

Ravender and Steadiman are both single men; the *Golden Mary* is full of fragments of families, people who have lost their loves, like Ravender and Miss Coleshaw, or are seeking them, like Mrs. Atherfield. Indeed, although the passengers are officially engaged on a quest for gold, this is alluded to only in the figure of Mr. Rarx, in whom all the potential avarice of the expedition is concentrated, and who is eventually washed overboard. The real objective of the other characters is to acquire or reacquire family. This is emphasized not only in the frame, but in the narratives of three of the four contributors in "The Beguilement in the Boats." The main purpose of these stories, which are much more subordinated to the frame narrative than in previous Christmas numbers, is simply to demonstrate the frame's thesis of the vital importance of storytelling, but they also reiterate the theme of lost family. Harriet Parr's black sheep, "poor Dick," shipped abroad by his family, remembers his lost sweetheart and the hymn she used to sing. Adelaide Anne Proctor's sailor recalls how he returned home after many castaway years to find another man at his hearth, and was forced back to the sea. James White's fey ship's apprentice remembers how his drowned sister returned to the family's window on the anniversary of her birthday, and imagines himself accompanying her on her next journey home.

During the earlier part of the journey, however, the presence of the child, the Golden Lucy, enables a surrogate family to be created, in which Ravender plays father. Significantly, the account of her death is immediately followed by Ravender's reflections on cannibalism, as if the loss of the semblance of domesticity represented by the child brings the catastrophe closer. In an 1853 article in *Household Words*, "The Long Voyage," Dickens had described "the most beautiful and affecting incident I know associated with shipwreck" (411), the story of the survivors of the wreck of the *Grosvenor*, who, in their journey across African desert, devote themselves to caring for the child in the party, and are thus enabled to resist the temptations to cannibalism to which shipwrecked people described earlier in the article succumb. Even the most celebrated location of cannibalism, the raft of the *Medusa,* carried a child; J. B. Savigny and Alexandre Correard's *The Wreck of the Medusa* (1818), of which Dickens owned a copy, describes how twelve-year-old Léon sustained the compassion of the more sensitive survivors, including the writers, until "he died away like a lamp which ceases to burn for want of aliment" (71).

With the Golden Lucy's death, only storytelling stands between the survivors and cannibalism. As in *Masterman Ready,* it is the role of the Tar, who has sacrificed home life, to instruct members of derelict and fragmented families how to live as a family and eschew cannibalism, and the method he uses to unite his frag ments is to organize storytelling. Garrett Stewart has described how in *Master Humphrey's Clock* (1840-41) Dickens uses storytelling to create a family out of a group of old bachelors:

> The chief aesthetic appliance of Victorian domesticity, the novel as reading event, is hereby espoused—by this coterie of familyless readers—as their only form of the domesticity that reading is otherwise meant to replenish rather than replace.
>
> (177)

In the open boats, storytelling is, again, the means by which family is created from isolated fragments. Similarly, in *A Message from the Sea,* Captain Jorgan exemplifies the sailor whose personal sacrifice of family, and professional skills in yarning, enable him to reunite families:

> I make up stories of brothers brought together by the good providence of GOD. Of sons brought back to mothers—husbands brought back to wives—fathers raised from the deep.
>
> (415)

Early in Collins's part of **"The Wreck,"** Steadiman boards Ravender's boat, and finds the unconscious captain supported between Mrs. Atherfield, who has just lost her child, and Miss Coleshaw, who is journeying in search of her lost fiancé. This tableau of the self-sacrificing bachelor between the childless blonde and the husbandless brunette is conceived in terms of stage melodrama, one of those moments where the physical staging makes manifest "meanings that might otherwise be unavailable to representation because they are somehow under the bar of repression" (Brooks, "Melodrama" 18). It reminds us that Ravender has been filling the role of husband and father left vacant by the men absent at the Gold Rush. This motif is repeated in the next Christmas collaboration, *The Perils of Certain English Prisoners,* where a group of marines and sailors protect women and children in the absence of most of their menfolk. In both stories, we begin with a group of people engaged in the accumulation of precious metals, and our attention is entirely diverted to their need to acquire or reacquire family relations, a shift which is formalized in the substitution of Golden Lucy for Gold Rush, and the subtitle of *Perils, Their Treasure in Women, Children, Silver and Jewels.* Jenny Sharpe has described how the emphasis on the suffering of British women in narratives of the Sepoy Mutiny enabled a shift from imperial identity as self-interest to imperial identity as self-sacrifice, and this maneuver is clear in *Perils.* In *The Wreck of the Golden Mary,* however, it is the Tar in whom self-sacrifice is primarily concentrated. His capacity for feeling exceeds that of the women and children; his self-sacrifice enables the reintegration of families. He can thus compensate for the domestic failings of absent men, who are away accumulating precious metal, and efface a national narrative of treasure-hunting with one of exemplary nobility and self-sacrifice.

Dickens's division of the frame narrative allows special emphasis on these qualities. The final section of **"The Wreck,"** left for completion by Collins, is an extensive tribute to Ravender's self-sacrifice, with poignant references to the shoeless feet he has concealed, and to his last unreadable scrawl. By giving Collins the narrative at this point, Dickens arranges an opportunity to envision the world without himself, to imagine the loss and despairing gratitude of those he had sustained. Collins/Steadiman does for Dickens/Ravender what Sydney Carton has to do for himself at the end of *A Tale of Two Cities* (1859), to elaborate on the gratitude of all the people for whom Ravender has sacrificed himself. Collins was effectively being asked to write Dickens's obituary; his desperate fears in Cobham Woods are hardly surprising.

Collins went on to write the whole of the further side of the frame, "The Deliverance," which describes the protracted arrival of the rescue ship, with circumstantial nautical detail. Deborah Thomas has suggested that Collins changed the concept of his narrator, making Steadiman a more capable figure than Dickens had presented him, and relying more on descriptions of action than **"The Wreck"** had done (85). This would seem, however, to be built into the transfer. It is difficult to imagine how the jolly Tar, as described by Dickens—naive, unreflecting, childlike—could be internalized as a first person narrator. Moreover, the personalities of the altruistic Captain and his jolly Tar Mate, as planned by Dickens, referred to the existing maritime interests of the two men. Dickens's maritime world was one of danger, heroism, self-sacrifice, wreck, and loss. Collins's sea, in "The Cruise of the Tomtit," and later with the figure of Allan Armadale in *Armadale* (1866), marks the transition of the Tar into the genteel amateur yachtsman, for whom the sea represents not necessary danger, but therapeutic risk, not sacrifice of home, but an escape from domestic respectability. Dickens was to wreck and Collins to deliver. It was Collins's deputed job to rescue the open boats tossing in the sea where Dickens had left them. In subsequent Christmas collaborations, *The Perils of Certain English Prisoners, A House to Let* (1858), and *A Message from the Sea,* it was again Collins's task, as allotted by Dickens, to provide the action which would resolve the situation Dickens had created. It can be argued that Collins, far from bringing to the partnership existing plot-oriented skills, not especially evident in his pre-1856 work, learned them in the Christmas numbers in filling in the portions of narrative, the "business part" of the stories, in which Dickens had lost interest.

V

Dickens's plan for *The Wreck of the Golden Mary* effectively allowed two alternative narratives to emerge which revealed his ambivalence about the nature of collaboration. He invoked the moral authority of a community united in collective activity, an idealized nautical world of discipline and leadership. The main nautical authority cited, however, is Bligh, the subject of a famous mutiny. Moreover, although Bligh had successfully navigated the open boat of the *Bounty,* with its crew of non-mutineers, to landfall in Timor with only one casualty, the voyage had not been conducted in the climate of sweet reasonableness and unquestioning obedience found in the **Golden Mary**'s boats. Ravender exercises command effortlessly, and enjoys perfect understanding with his Mate. He experiences no difficulties, for instance, in distributing the very limited rations in the boats among the unrepining survivors of the **Golden Mary.** Bligh's distribution of the similarly limited rations in the open boat of the *Bounty,* on the other hand, was conducted amidst exchanges of nagging and recrimination habitual to his command.

Bligh is, however, crucial to Dickens's strategy as authority for both the improbability of cannibalism, and the importance of storytelling as a preventive. Cannibalism had been a sufficiently unspeakable topic for Bligh to omit the reference from his published account, but his reflection on its improbability in his manuscript record was quoted in Barrow's *The Mutiny of the "Bounty"* (127). Dickens's references to storytelling sessions in the open boat of the *Bounty* must have surprised readers familiar with the legend of Bligh's autocratic temper—and there was, in fact, no record of such storytelling. The false memory probably has its source in Barrow, who, shortly after the cannibalism passage, describes the journey of the *Bounty*'s open boat as a feat of unparalleled endurance, and in a long footnote awards second prize to the open boat of the *Centaur,* wrecked in 1782. The footnote describes how Captain Inglefield maintained morale by encouraging "the men, when the evenings closed in [. . .] to sing a song, or relate a story, instead of a supper" (133).

Dickens discusses the *Centaur* immediately after the *Bounty* in **"The Lost Arctic Voyagers"**; the proximity in Barrow of the footnote on the *Centaur* crew's Barmecide banquets to that on cannibalism probably initiated the transference of the storytelling sessions from *Centaur* to *Bounty.* Bligh would perhaps not have shared the views of Dickens and Captain Inglefield that storytelling cemented the social order. There were soon several narratives by *Bounty* survivors in circulation, and Dening has argued that their highly articulate character and skillful plotting suggest that the kind of yarning available on the *Bounty* probably contributed to the mutiny (73-74). Bligh and Barrow do record activities more susceptible to tight control, such as a round game used to distribute food, but the only sustained verbal sessions in the boat were the daily lessons in which Bligh sought to instruct his crew in navigation, so that in the event of his death they might still make land in Timor.

These lessons may have sustained morale, but, as it was generally agreed that the boat's journey was an extraordinary feat of navigation, they must also have served to demonstrate that Bligh was the one indispensable person in the boat. **"The Wreck"** remembers Bligh as organizing communal storytelling, not as giving lessons in skills exclusive to him, but in the distance between what Bligh did, and what Dickens remembered him as doing, may have lain his attraction to Dickens. Just as Bligh strove conscientiously to impart his supreme navigational skills in a situation where it was urgent that less skilled companions could believe in their ability to navigate, so Dickens seeks to impart his storytelling skills to Collins and the other collaborators. In doing so, he imposes a fiction of collaborative storytelling on the *Bounty* boat, and then uses it as authority for his story of a captain who presides effortlessly over his cooperative boatload. Behind that false memory, however, lies the other story of a boat driven on by one man's will power and exceptional skills, and that story also informs the collaboration.

Dickens wrecked and Collins delivered. It was the only time Dickens chose not to collaborate on the further side of the frame, and the narrative frame pointedly recognizes the possibility of catastrophe in the transfer of command. Captain Ravender is persuaded to take some much-needed rest; as he reluctantly leaves the deck of the **Golden Mary** he hears something strange in the sound of the sea not evident to Steadiman, who, though ordinarily capable, lacks his Captain's superior intuition. Disaster thus strikes the ship when the Mate is in command. Ravender's last thoughts in the open boat, before he sinks into unconsciousness and relinquishes the narrative, are a wish to excuse his Mate of any negligence: "I tried to write it down in my pocket-book, but could make no words, though I knew what the words were that I wanted to make" (146). While *The Wreck of the Golden Mary* extols the values of cooperation and collaboration as exemplified by British Tars, the references to Bligh, as well as to Dickens's absence from "The Deliverance," suggest another narrative, about the indispensability of exceptional men with rare skills. It was this narrative which appeared in the only book versions of the story available until recently. Collected editions of Dickens carried only his section, **"The Wreck"** (with Collins's additional valedictory pages): thus the boats were left tossing in the open sea with an unconscious captain, and, it might seem, no more chance of survival than the open boat of the *Bounty* would have had without Bligh. Dickens's first collaboration with Collins, with its nautical story, allowed him to experiment with the excitement of "writing a book in company." It also enabled him to imagine a world of writing from which he was, catastrophically, absent.

Notes

I would like to thank John Bowen and Deborah Wynne, my collaborators in studying the collaboration of Dickens and Collins, for their comments on this article.

1. This last citation of Bligh is within the section of "The Wreck"—the opening frame narrative of *The Wreck of the Golden Mary*—assigned to Collins by the *Household Words* Office Book (Lohrli 236). Harry Stone attributes this paragraph to Dickens on stylistic evidence (Dickens, *Uncollected Writings* 364). "The Wreck" is, in any case, very much under Dickens's control.

Works Cited

The Arabian Nights. Trans. Husain Haddawy. London: Everyman, 1992.

Barrow, John. *The Mutiny of the "Bounty."* London: Oxford UP, 1914.

Beattie, Owen, and John Geiger. *Frozen in Time: The Fate of the Franklin Expedition*. London: Grafton, 1989.

Benjamin, Walter. "The Storyteller." *Illuminations*. Trans. Harry Zohn. London: Collins, 1973. 83-109.

Bligh, William. *An Account of the Mutiny on Board HMS Bounty*. New York: Signet, 1961.

Booth, Michael. *English Plays of the Nineteenth Century*. Vol. 1. Oxford: Clarendon, 1969.

Brantlinger, Patrick. *Rule of Darkness: British Literature and Imperialism*. Ithaca: Cornell UP, 1988.

Bratton, J. S. "British Heroism and the Structure of Melodrama." *Acts of Supremacy: The British Empire and the Stage 1790-1930*. Ed. J. S. Bratton, et al. Manchester: Manchester UP, 1991. 18-61.

Brooks, Peter. "Melodrama, Body, Revolution." *Melodrama: Stage, Picture, Screen*. Ed. J. S. Bratton, et al. London: British Film Institute, 1994. 11-24.

———. *The Melodramatic Imagination: Balzac, Henry James, Melodrama, and the Mode of Excess*. New Haven: Yale UP, 1995.

Collins, Philip. *Charles Dickens: Interviews and Recollections*. 2 vols. London: Macmillan, 1981.

Collins, Wilkie. *Armadale*. New York: Dover, 1977.

———. "Blow Up with the Brig." *Miss or Mrs?*. Stroud: Sutton, 1993. 89-104.

———. "The Cruise of the Tomtit." *Household Words* 12 (1855): 490-99.

———. "The Fatal Cradle." *Miss or Mrs?*. Stroud: Sutton, 1993. 104-26.

———. *The Frozen Deep. Under the Management of Mr Charles Dickens: His Production of* The Frozen Deep. Ed. Robert Brannan. Ithaca: Cornell UP, 1966. 91-160.

———. "My Black Mirror." *Household Words* 14 (1856): 169-75.

Cooper, James Fenimore. *The Pilot: A Tale of the Sea*. Albany: State U of New York P, 1986.

Corbin, Alain. *The Lure of the Sea: The Discovery of the Seaside in the Western World*. Trans. Jocelyn Phelps. Harmondsworth: Penguin, 1995.

Dana, Richard Henry. *Two Years Before the Mast*. Ware: Wordsworth, 1996.

Dening, Greg. *Mr Bligh's Bad Language: Passion, Power and Theatre on the Bounty*. Cambridge: Cambridge UP, 1992.

Dickens, Charles. "The Long Voyage." *Household Words* 8 (1853): 409-12.

———. *Pilgrim Edition of the Letters of Charles Dickens*. Ed. Madeline House, Grahame Storey, and Kathleen Tillotson. 11 vols. to date. Oxford: Clarendon, 1965-.

———. *A Tale of Two Cities*. London: Oxford UP, 1949.

———. *Uncollected Writings of Charles Dickens: Household Words 1850-59*. Ed. Harry Stone. Bloomington: Indiana UP, 1969.

Dickens, Charles, and John Rae. "The Lost Arctic Voyagers." *Household Words* 10 (1854): 361-65; 385-93; 433-37; 457-59.

Dickens, Charles, and Robert McCormick. "Christmas in the Frozen Regions." *Household Words* 2 (1850): 306-09.

Dickens, Charles, and Wilkie Collins. *A Message from the Sea*. Glancey, *Charles Dickens* 342-417.

———. *The Perils of Certain English Prisoners*. Glancey, *Charles Dickens* 173-256.

———. *The Wreck of the Golden Mary*. Glancey, *Charles Dickens* 121-171.

Donohue, Joseph. *Theatre in the Age of Kean*. Oxford: Blackwell, 1975.

Durkheim, Emile. *Suicide*. Trans. John Spaulding and George Simpson. London: Routledge, Kegan Paul, 1968.

Fielding, Henry. *Journal of a Voyage to Lisbon*. London: Oxford UP, 1907.

Gettmann, Royal. *A Victorian Publisher: A Study of the Bentley Papers*. Cambridge: Cambridge UP, 1960.

Glancey, Ruth, ed. *Charles Dickens: The Christmas Stories*. London: Everyman, 1996.

———. "Dickens and Christmas: His Framed Tale Themes." *Nineteenth Century Fiction* 35 (1980): 53-72.

Heine, Heinrich. "Nordeney." *Travel Pictures*. Trans. Francis Storr. London: Bell, 1887. 79-115.

Jerrold, Douglas. *Black-Eyed Susan.* Booth 151-200.

Lohrli, Anne. *Household Words: A Weekly Journal 1850-59.* Toronto: U of Toronto P, 1973.

Lopez, Barry, *Arctic Dreams: Imagination and Desire in a Northern Landscape.* London: Macmillan, 1986.

Marlow, James. "The Fate of Sir John Franklin: Three Phases of Response in Victorian Periodicals." *Victorian Periodicals Review* 15.1 (1982): 2-11.

Marryat, Frederick. *Masterman Ready; or The Wreck of the Pacific.* London: Macmillan, 1901.

———. *Peter Simple.* London: Dent, 1896.

Melville, Herman. *White Jacket or The World in a Man of War.* London: Oxford UP, 1966.

Ong, Walter J. *Orality and Literacy: The Technologizing of the Word.* London: Methuen, 1982.

———. "The Writer's Audience Is Always a Fiction." *PMLA* 90.1 (1975): 9-21.

Owen, Roderic. *The Fate of Franklin.* London: Hutchinson, 1978.

Palmer, William. "Dickens and Shipwreck." *Dickens Studies Annual.* New York: AMS, 1989. 39-92.

Peters, Catherine. *The King of Inventors: A Life of Wilkie Collins.* London: Minerva, 1992.

Rediker, Marcus. *Between the Devil and the Deep Blue Sea: Merchant Seamen, Pirates and the Anglo-American Maritime World.* Cambridge: Cambridge UP, 1993.

Russell, Gillian. *Theatres of War: Performance, Politics and Society 1793-1815.* Oxford: Clarendon, 1996.

Savigny, J. B. H., and Alexandre Correard. *The Wreck of the Medusa.* London: Cape, 1931.

Sennett, Richard. *The Fall of Public Man.* London: Faber, 1977.

Sharpe, Jenny. *Allegories of Empire: The Figure of Woman in the Colonial Text.* Minneapolis: U of Minnesota P, 1993.

Simpson, Brian. *Cannibalism and the Common Law.* Harmondsworth: Penguin, 1986.

Spufford, Francis. *I May Be Some Time: Ice and the English Imagination.* London: Faber, 1996.

Stewart, Garrett. *Dear Reader: The Conscripted Audience in Nineteenth Century British Fiction.* Baltimore: Johns Hopkins UP, 1996.

Stone, Harry. *The Night Side of Dickens: Cannibalism, Passion and Necessity.* Columbus: Ohio State UP, 1994.

Stone, Ian. "The Contents of the Kettles: Dickens, Rae and Cannibalism." *Dickensian* 83 (1987): 7-16.

Sussman, Herbert. *Victorian Masculinities: Manhood and Masculine Poetics in Early Victorian Fiction.* Cambridge: Cambridge UP, 1995.

Thackeray, William Makepeace. "Little Billee." *Ballads and Tales.* London: Smith, Elder. 1876. 228-29.

———. "On a Peal of Bells." *Roundabout Papers.* London: Smith, Elder, 1876. 286-97.

Thomas, Deborah. *Dickens and the Short Story.* London: Batsford, 1982.

David J. Greenman (essay date March 2000)

SOURCE: Greenman, David J. "Alcohol, Comedy, and Ghosts in Dickens's Early Short Fiction." *Dickens Quarterly* 17, no. 1 (March 2000): 3-13.

[*In the following essay, Greenman explains contradictory portrayals of, and attitudes about, alcohol consumption in Dickens's early stories, highlighting the comic link between alcohol and the supernatural.*]

> Gin, cursed fiend, with fury fraught,
> Makes human race a prey;
> It enters by a deadly draught,
> And steals our life away.
> Virtue and Truth, driven to despair
> Its rage compels to flee;
> But cherishes, with hellish care,
> Theft, murder, perjury.
> Damned cup, that on the vitals preys,
> That liquid fire contains;
> Which madness to the heart conveys,
> And rolls it through the veins.
>
> —James Townley, 1751

> O, Willie brewed a peck o'maut,
>   And Rob and Allan cam to prie.
> Three blyther hearts that lee lang night
>   Ye wad na found in Christendie.
>
> Here are we met three merry boys,
>   Three merry boys I trow are we;
> And monie a night we've merry been,
>   And monie mae we hope to be! . . .
>
> Wha first shall rise to gang awa,
>   A cuckold, coward loun is he!
> Wha first beside his chair shall fa',
>   He is the King amang us three!
>
> —Robert Burns, 1789

These two eighteenth century poems display the contrasting and contradictory attitudes towards alcohol consumption that came down to Charles Dickens as he launched his literary career. From the first, he was aware of both the debilitating and convivial effects of heavy drinking, as **Sketches By Boz** (1836) and *The Pickwick Papers* (1836-7) reveal. But it is unsettling to find such ambivalence, such starkly different portrayals and attitudes side by side with no explanation from the author about why he seems quite content to play the stern moralist at one moment and the jolly companion at the next. I hope to provide an explanation, but first let me note some pertinent facts about the use of alcohol in England up to Dickens's day.

According to Berton Roueché:

> The first brandy aqua vitae reached England by way of troops returning from an expedition to the low countries in 1585 . . . in 1690 a kindly government passed "An Act for the Encouraging of the Distillation of Brandy and Spirits from Corn." . . . Within four years the annual production of distilled liquors, mostly from gin, reached a million gallons. By 1714 the output had been doubled. By 1733 the output had increased to 11 million gal. . . . In 1742 the production of English spirits reached 20 million gal.
>
> (174)

Chaim Rosenberg notes that "in 1788 Thomas Trotter presented his thesis on drunkenness for the degree of Doctor of Medicine at Edinburgh University. In 1804, Benjamin Rush, the American physician, published a paper on the same topic. These pioneer medical researchers described the increased dependence and withdrawal syndromes as well as the changes in behavior associated with chronic alcoholism" (802).

Rosenberg further notes that:

> until the beginning of the 19th century, the traditional belief stressed the virtues of alcoholic liquors. However, the rapid spread of habitual drunkenness gave rise to considerable public concern. . . . With the spread of the temperance movement, a literature was developed aimed at combating the spread of alcoholism. These "Temperance Tales" presented an image of the alcoholic as a social outcast and physically debilitated derelict. Alcohol was the demon that dragged a person from respectability and affluence into degradation and poverty. The alcoholic was seen as someone living in the shabbiest corners of human society, beyond the reach of medical practice, and fit only as an object of scorn or of charity.
>
> (802-03)

Two pieces in *Sketches By Boz* and one inset story in *The Pickwick Papers* show the young Dickens graphically depicting the brutal results of excessive drinking. The first is a scene from **"Gin-Shops"** in *Sketches*:

> It is growing late, and the throng of men, women, and children, who have been constantly going in and out, dwindles down to two or three occasional stragglers—cold, wretched-looking creatures, in the last stage of emaciation and disease. The knot of Irish labourers at the lower end of the place, who have been alternately shaking hands with, and threatening the life of each other, for the last hour, become furious in their disputes

> . . . a scene of riot and confusion ensues . . . the barmaids scream; the police come in; the rest is a confused mixture of arms, legs, staves, torn coats, shouting, and struggling. Some of the party are borne off to the station-house, and the remainder slink home to beat their wives for complaining, and kick the children for daring to be hungry.
>
> (186)

The moral Dickens applies is not to condemn the wretches he has just described, but to take society to task for allowing "wretchedness and dirt" to prevail. He exclaims "If Temperance Societies would suggest an antidote against hunger, filth, and foul air, or could establish dispensaries for the gratuitous distribution of bottles of Lethe-water, gin-palaces would be numbered among the things that were" (187). Dickens consistently maintained this attitude, although a dozen years later, when he reviewed Cruikshank's series of cautionary plates, *The Drunkard's Children,* in *The Examiner,* he focused on the government in calling for correction of these same societal evils.

However, in two detailed stories about men in the last stages of alcohol abuse—**"The Drunkard's Death"** in *Sketches* and **"The Stroller's Tale"** in *Pickwick*—Dickens, without a shred of pity for them, exposes them as bestial, sub-human creatures who ruin not only themselves but their families as well. **"The Drunkard's Death"** depicts the case of a once "respectable tradesman, or a clerk, or a man following some thriving pursuit with good prospects and decent means" (484) who has lost everything except his family and whose wife lies dying at the outset of the story. Undramatically, but emphatically, Dickens exclaims:

> Alas! such cases are of too frequent occurrence to be rare items in any man's experience: and but too often arise from one cause—drunkenness—that fierce rage for the slow, sure poison, that oversteps every other consideration; that casts aside wife, children, friends, happiness, and station; and hurries its victims madly on to degradation and death.
>
> (484)

The man soon mistreats his sons who run off into lives of crime, and he tyrannizes his daughter so she will work to provide him with money for drink. Years later when one son, fleeing from the law, returns home to hide out, the father is easily duped by lawmen offering free drinks into revealing the fugitive. Without changing his drunken behavior he endures his captured son's curse and his daughter's flight before he descends into beggary. Finally, in despair, he drowns himself in the river. The last we see of him is as a "body washed ashore, some miles down the river, a swollen and disfigured mass" (494).

In **"The Stroller's Tale"** (*Pickwick,* chapter three) Dickens switches from the grim naturalistic style of description he had used in the previous story to a starkly impressionistic approach that emphasizes the grotesque-ness of the drunken "low pantomime actor" (105) whom Dickens expressly associates with death itself:

> Never shall I forget the repulsive sight that met my eye when I turned round. He was dressed for the panto-mime, in all the absurdity of a clown's costume. The spectral figures in the Dance of Death, the most fright-ful shapes that the ablest painter ever portrayed on can-vas, never presented an appearance half so ghastly. His bloated body and shrunken legs—their deformity en-hanced a hundred fold by the fantastic dress—the glassy eyes, contrasting fearfully with the thick white paint with which the face was besmeared; the gro-tesquely ornamented head, trembling with paralysis, and the long, skinny hands, rubbed with white chalk—all gave him a hideous and unnatural appearance, of which no description could convey an adequate idea, and which to this day I shudder to think of.
>
> (106)

The "clown" rises from his sick bed to perform on stage one last time, returns to bed, and experiences hideous hallucinations of his wife transformed into a demon, rooms full of insects and reptiles, and distorted faces of his acquaintances. At last, he recognizes those around him. "He grasped my shoulder convulsively, and, strik-ing his breast with the other hand, made a desperate at-tempt to articulate. It was unavailing—he extended his arm towards them, and made another violent effort. There was a rattling noise in the throat—a glare of the eye—a short stifled groan—and he fell back—dead!" (110). Even more than the death of the isolated and abandoned suicide of the *Sketches* story, this man's death, though he is surrounded by those dear to him, exposes the excruciating isolation and guilt experienced by a person who has allowed himself to degenerate into unreclaimable alcoholism.

The grim stories just discussed appeared in print ahead of a series of five comic tales saturated with alcohol. This group includes **"The Bagman's Story"** (*Pickwick,* chapter fourteen), **"A Story about a Queer Client"** (*Pickwick,* chapter twenty), **"The Story of the Goblins Who Stole a Sexton"** (*Pickwick,* chapter twenty nine), **"The Story of the Bagman's Uncle"** (*Pickwick,* chap-ter forty nine), and **"The Baron of Grogzwig"** (*Nicholas Nickleby,* chapter six). Each provides differ-ent amounts and kinds of humor. All but the **"Queer Client"** (a two-pager) are well developed narratives. **"The Goblins Who Stole a Sexton"** is a moral fable and **"The Bagman's Story," "The Story of the Bag-man's Uncle,"** and **"The Baron of Grogzwig"** are sto-ries of jolly good fellows trying to enjoy life. In addi-tion to alcohol consumption, all five share two significant traits. The first is that they are all described as having taken place in the past. **"A Story about a Queer Client"** relates an incident which occurred "forty years ago now" (363); **"The Story of the Goblins Who Stole a Sexton"** occurred "a long, long while ago"

(480); **"The Bagman's Story"** dates from an incident "eighty years ago" (259); **"The Story of the Bagman's Uncle"** arose at least a generation before the telling: "Gentlemen, I wish your fathers and mothers had known my uncle" (775); events in **"The Baron of Grogzwig"** go back to events "three or four hundred years ago" (130). The other shared trait or common denominator is that they are all ghost stories. Before I draw conclu-sions and make judgments about these boozy comedies, I will very briefly delineate them.

In **"A Story about a Queer Client"** a poor lawyer rents "an old, damp, rotten set of chambers . . . and was sitting down before the fire at night, drinking the first glass of two gallons of whiskey he had ordered on credit" (363) when there appears the ghost of a man who claims ownership of the room in which he had died after suffering through an interminable lawsuit. Comically, the lawyer persuades the ghost to leave for a more agreeable locale, and to share this idea of moving with other ghosts who haunt spots where they were once miserable. He says:

> "it does appear to me somewhat inconsistent, that when you have an opportunity of visiting the fairest spots of earth—for I suppose space is nothing to you—you should always return exactly to the very places where you have been most miserable." "Egad, that's very true; I never thought of that before," said the ghost . . . "we must be dull fellows, very dull fellows in-deed; I can't imagine how we can have been so stu-pid."
>
> (364-5)

The story ends on that amusing note.

Gabriel Grubb, the grave-digger sexton of **"The Story of the Goblins Who Stole a Sexton"** is "an ill-conditioned, cross-grained, surly fellow—a morose and lonely man" (480) who especially enjoys having people to bury at Christmas time. After he raps his lantern sev-eral times on the head of "a young urchin roaring out some jolly song about a merry Christmas" (481), he digs a grave, then regales himself with a quart of gin, a grisly verse about corpses being "a rich juicy meal for the worms to eat," and the exclamation "A coffin at Christmas! A Christmas Box. Ho! ho! ho!" (482)—whereupon a grotesquely fantastical goblin appears to mock and deride old Grubb. Soon "whole troops of goblins; the very counterpart of the first one, poured into the churchyard and began playing at leap-frog with the tombstones" (486). They plunge Grubb underground into a hellish cavern, pour a large amount of "liquid fire" down his throat, and subject him to several visions of people both happy and sad at Christmas, the object of which is to teach Grubb to appreciate life. Though this treatment works, Grubb goes away in shame for ten years before returning "a ragged, contented, rheumatic old man" (490).

The next three stories may be grouped together. Tom Smart (**"The Bagman's Story"**), Uncle Jack (**"The Story of the Bagman's Uncle"**), and Baron Von Koëldwethout of Grogzwig (puns on cold booze without water and swigging grog intended by Dickens) are all jolly topers who have crucial but positive encounters with spirits after imbibing much liquor. Tom Smart, a weary travelling bill collector, stops at an inn, admires the buxom widow-hostess, drinks heavily, and converses with a humorous old chair who comes to life and helps him drive away a philandering fellow with designs on the widow. Tom marries her himself and becomes a happy innkeeper. Uncle Jack, also a traveling bill collector, carouses all night with friends whom he literally drinks under the table, then experiences an old junkyard for mail coaches suddenly come to life as a busy thoroughfare of a bygone era. Jack swashbuckles his way into saving the life of a pretty woman who is being abducted by villains. Then, just as he is furiously driving away with the grateful lady, everything instantly reverts to its mouldy junkyard status. The Baron and his retainers "drank Rhine wine every night till they fell under the table" (131). Eventually he marries, begets thirteen children, and becomes so uxorious and mother-in-law ridden that he considers suicide. While smoking and drinking in contemplation of the prospect "a wrinkled hideous figure, with deeply sunk and bloodshot eyes, and an immensely long cadaverous face" (135) appears—the "Genius of Despair and Suicide" (136). A lively dialogue ensues in which, though the apparition urges the Baron to dispatch himself quickly, the Baron instead plucks up his resolve and vows, "I'll brood over miseries no longer" (138). Then he reorders his life by putting wife and in-laws in their places and resuming his long-since halted convivial sports "and died many years afterwards, not a rich man that I am aware of, but certainly a happy one" (139).

Unfortunately, my outlines of these stories do little justice to the lively and witty style in which they are written. The comedy of these pieces ranges between drollery and hilarity. And always, alcohol consumption is central. Now it is time for some sober consideration.

Although **"A Story about a Queer Client," "The Bagman's Story,"** and **"The Story of the Goblins Who Stole a Sexton"** differ markedly from each other in tone, the protagonists are all outsider figures who feel alienated enough from life to rely on drink to ease the pains of their discontentment. The poor lawyer in the first of these stories has ordered "two gallons of whiskey . . . on credit, wondering whether it would ever be paid for, and if so in how many years' time" (363). He, however, is the least despondent of this trio, for he is drinking only his first glass when he encounters the ghost. Tom Smart, on the other hand, endures the hard-

ships of traveling on the wintry Marlborough Downs, and then, while trying to enjoy the comforts of an inn, is mortified to find a tall man cozying up to the attractive hostess.

> "Confound his impudence!" said Tom to himself, "what business has he in that snug bar? Such an ugly villain too!" said Tom. "If the widow had any taste, she might surely pick up some better fellow than that." Here Tom's eye wandered from the glass on the chimney-piece, to the glass on the table; and as he felt himself becoming gradually sentimental, he emptied the fourth tumbler of punch and ordered a fifth.
>
> (263)

Gabriel Grubb is the most alienated and by far the worst-tempered of this trio. His "old wicker bottle which fitted into his large deep waistcoat pocket" (480) is his only source of companionship. His anger at the singing boy and his delight in burying people at Christmas are his defense-mechanisms against despondency and signs of his defiance of society.

Alcohol perhaps assists the lawyer to speak cheekily to the ghost, though he hasn't even finished his first glass. Undoubtedly, alcohol consoles Tom Smart whose exposé of the tall man as already married derives from the contents of a letter found in the man's pocket—ostensibly through information received from the spirit of the old chair. Yet Tom's enemies "said he was drunk, and fancied it, and got hold of the wrong trousers by mistake before he went to bed" (273). As for Grubb, alcohol is no real consolation; the "liquid fire" the goblins make him drink is emblematic of that. And those who are skeptical of his tale "murmured something about Gabriel Grubb having drunk all the Hollands [gin], and then fallen asleep on the flat tombstone" (491).

Each of these outsider characters does manage to come to terms with his problem of belonging. The lawyer gets rid of the ghost and settles into his chambers, Gabriel Grubb returns contentedly to his town years later, and Tom Smart experiences much bliss with his new wife and inn. To some degree, Dickens has made alcohol the catalyst in their success. He never disparages their drinking in his own voice. In Tom Smart's case the alcohol is probably responsible for the most creative and interesting part of the story: Tom's long dialogue with the chair, which takes up five pages at the heart of the narrative. In fact, the chair is as much the story's protagonist as Tom is, but would he have appeared at all if Tom had not imbibed so much punch?

Uncle Jack in **"The Story of the Bagman's Uncle"** and the Baron of Grogzwig can hardly be classified as outsiders. The Baron is ensconced in his own castle from youth to old age and Uncle Jack, though he travels between London, Edinburgh, and Glasgow in his bill-collecting job, enjoys gathering with cronies in these cities. The two stories differ from the other comedies in that Dickens depicts drink not as a crutch or a consolation, but as the stimulus for much *joie de vivre*. In these tales we are poles apart from the debilitating and horrific results of drinking that we saw in **"The Drunkard's Death"** and **"The Stroller's Tale."**

In the Baron of Grogzwig's case, heavy drinking first brings on his trouble but then, eventually gets him out of it. After over-indulging among his jovial retainers, having "swallowed huge bumpers of wine . . . the more he swallowed, the more he frowned" (131). This discontentment brings on his resolve to wed, which in turn brings on about a quarter of a century of domestic misery: "by the time he was a fat hearty fellow of forty-eight or thereabouts, he had no feasting, no revelry, no hunting train, and no hunting—nothing in short that he used to have . . . snubbed and put down by his own lady, in his own castle" (133). The Baron drinks enough before his colloquy with the Genius of Despair and Suicide that Dickens confidently attributes his new resolve to take charge of his life to the salutary effects of deep drinking:

> And my advice to all men is, that if ever they become hipped and melancholy from similar causes (as very many men do), they look at both sides of the question, applying a magnifying glass to the best one; and if they still feel tempted to retire without leave, that they smoke a large pipe and drink a full bottle first, and profit by the laudable example of the Baron of Grogzwig.
>
> (139)

Uncle Jack, the bagman's uncle, is the most prodigious of all the drinkers in Dickens's ghost stories, be they jolly men or morose. "My uncle, gentlemen," said the bagman, "was one of the merriest, pleasantest, cleverest fellows that ever lived" (775). His ability to mix and drink down punch is one of his greatest virtues. Having met Tom Smart:

> They made a bet of a new hat before they had known each other half an hour, who should brew the best quart of punch and drink it the quickest. My uncle was judged to have won the making, but Tom Smart beat him in the drinking by about half a salt-spoon full. They took another quart a-piece to drink each other's health in, and were staunch friends ever afterwards.
>
> (775)

While in Edinburgh visiting friends Uncle Jack's usual routine includes "a dozen or so of bottle ale, and a noggin of whiskey" (776) at lunch. He boasts "that he could see the Dundee people out, any day, and walk home afterwards without staggering, and yet the Dundee people have as strong heads and as strong punch, gentlemen, as you are likely to meet with, between the poles" (776-77). Just prior to his heroic encounter with the spirits of the old mail coaches, Uncle Jack fortifies himself mightily at a banquet:

> I don't quite recollect how many tumblers of whiskey toddy each man drank after supper; but this I know, that about one o'clock in the morning, the baillie's grown-up son became insensible while attempting the first verse of "Willie brewed a peck o'maut;" and he having been, for half an hour before, the only other man visible above the mahogany, it occurred to my uncle that it was almost time to think about going: especially as drinking had set in at seven o'clock, in order that he might get home at a decent hour. But, thinking it might not be quite polite to go just then, my uncle voted himself into the chair, mixed another glass, rose to propose his own health, addressed himself in a neat and complimentary speech, and drank the toast with great enthusiasm. Still nobody woke; so my uncle took a little drop more—neat this time, to prevent the toddy from disagreeing with him—and, laying violent hands on his hat, sallied forth into the street.
>
> (777-8)

Uncle Jack's gargantuan intake of food and alcohol provides him the wherewithal to defeat the antiquely dressed rapscallions who would abduct the fair maiden. That the entire entourage suddenly disappears is unfortunate, but far from tragic. Unlike Tom Smart who marries the woman of his dreams, Uncle Jack "remained staunch to the great oath he had sworn to the beautiful young lady: refusing several eligible landladies on her account, and dying a bachelor at last" (792). His drinking habits are neither debilitating nor restorative, but they are clearly salutary and keep his life running on an even keel.

Earlier I noted that Dickens's comic stories of excessive drinking shared two features—they are tales of the past and they are ghost stories. What is the significance of these traits? As we saw in **"The Drunkard's Death"** and **"The Stroller's Tale,"** the young Dickens was quite aware of the dark side of drunkenness. The former story, though set in the past, has a time-frame purposely kept vague. At the end, the dead man's corpse has "long since" mouldered away, although perhaps not more than several years prior to the narrative's present. The grotesquely contorted death of the clown in the latter story has a contemporary feel to it. The narrator has long been a close friend of the "low pantomime actor" and he "traced his progress downwards step by step, until he reached that excess of destitution from which he never rose again" (105). **"Gin Shops,"** of course, describes a scene to be noticed any day that one walks the streets of London with open eyes. Clearly, when Dickens wants to emphasize the evils of alcoholism he presents contemporary life.

But when he wants to have some fun—with heavy drinking as the base and springboard of action in his stories—he deflates any real reader-concern by locating the events quite safely in the past, from a generation before to hundreds of years before the present of the narrator's voice. In these tales, despite prodigal drinking, we do not find any alcoholism per se. Except for Gabriel Grubb, the characters are very sociable and their drinking is a measure of their good natures and their conviviality.

The fact that the comic stories are also ghost stories is another sign that (to cast no negative aspersions on the author's considerable narrative skills) these are light, good humored tales. The appearance of ghosts, goblins, animated chairs and mail coaches is kept squarely in the realm of fantasy and alcohol is explicitly cited in several cases as the reasonable person's way of accounting for the supernatural incidents. At the outset of his career Dickens could obviously move freely between a serious and a comic view of excessive alcohol consumption.

This would change, however. After *Nicholas Nickleby* there are some pathetic drinkers in Dickens's fiction—for instance Betsy Trotwood's husband, Stephen Blackpool's wife, Krook, Mr. Dolls—but no more outright jolly topers (not excepting Micawber in *David Copperfield,* who is jolly while mixing punch but hardly an inveterate toper). By the 1840s Dickens began to write ghost stories that grew increasingly serious and in which spectral visitors could no longer be explained away by alcohol-induced delusions. A long time passed before Dickens again associated alcohol with a ghost story. When he did, in a short, untitled piece in *The Uncommercial Traveller,* published in 1860, the narrative is rather droll, but the ambiance is bleak.

Mr. Testator, in debt and hiding "occupied chambers of the dreariest nature in Lyons Inn" (143). Testator finds furniture in the basement and outfits his rooms with it. A man appears "sodden with liquor" and lays claim to the furniture. Testator serves him gin and the man drinks a decanter of it before leaving with the promise of a return next day to repossess the furniture. But:

> Whether he was a ghost, or a spectral illusion of conscience, or a drunken man who had no business there, or the drunken rightful owner of the furniture, with a transitory gleam of memory; whether he got home safe, or had no home to get to; whether he died of liquor on the way, or lived in liquor ever afterwards; he never was heard of more.
>
> (146)

This little story forms a kind of book-end with **"A Story About a Queer Client."** But whereas both tenants in the tales are down on their luck, Testator has a guilty conscience while the lawyer does not. The lawyer is engaged in drinking when the ghost steps out of a cabinet. Testator is not drinking at all; it is his visitor who is intoxicated instead. In the 1860 story Dickens is not taking alcohol lightly, for while the situation may be slightly humorous, the drunken visitor—ghost or man—is pathetic, not in the least charming.

It is quite evident that after the Baron of Grogzwig triumphed over the Genius of Despair and Suicide, Dickens triumphed over his youthful penchant to trivialize both alcoholism and the ghost story. The two ghost stories he wrote near the end of his career in the mid 1860s are masterpieces of psychological realism, their events occur in the immediate present. Ghosts are very disturbing entities in **"To Be Taken with a Grain of Salt"** and **"The Signal-Man,"** and there is not a drop of liquor anywhere on the horizon.

Works Cited

Burns, Robert. "Willie Brew'd A Peck O'Maut." Poems and Songs of Robert Burns. Ed. James Barke. London and Glasgow: Collins, 1955. 522.

Dickens, Charles. "Gin-Shops" (182-87) and "The Drunkard's Death" (484-94). *Sketches by Boz. The Oxford Illustrated Dickens.* Oxford, New York, Toronto, Melbourne: Oxford UP, 1957.

———. "The Stroller's Tale" (105-10); "The Bagman's Story" (259-73); "A Story about a Queer Client" (363-65): "The Story of the Goblins Who Stole a Sexton" (480-91); "The Story of the Bagman's Uncle" (775-92). *The Posthumous Papers of the Pickwick Club.* Ed. Robert L. Patten. Harmondsworth, Middlesex, England, and New York: Penguin Books, 1972.

———. "The Baron of Grogzwig." *Nicholas Nickleby.* Ed. Michael Slater. Harmondsworth, Middlesex, England, and New York: Penguin Books, 1978. 129-39.

———. ["Mr. Testator and the Ghost"]. *The Uncommercial Traveller and Reprinted Pieces. The Oxford Illustrated Dickens.* Oxford, New York, Toronto, Melbourne: Oxford UP, 1958. 43-46.

Rosenberg, Chaim. "The Paraprofessionals in Alcoholism Treatment." *Encyclopedic Handbook of Alcoholism.* E. Mansell Pattison and Edward Kaufman, Eds. New York: Gardner Press, 1982. 802-09.

Roueché, Berton. "Alcohol in Human Culture." *Alcohol and Civilization.* Salvatore Pablo Lucia, Ed. New York, San Francisco, Toronto, London: McGraw Hill Book Company, Inc., 1963. 167-182.

Townley, James. "Gin, cursed fiend, with fury fraught." In *Alcohol and Civilization.* Salvatore Pablo Lucia, Ed. New York, San Francisco, Toronto, London: McGraw Hill Book Company, Inc., 1963. 175.

Lillian Nayder (essay date 2000)

SOURCE: Nayder, Lillian. "Dickens and 'Gold Rush Fever': Colonial Contagion in *Household Words.*" In *Dickens and the Children of Empire,* edited by Wendy S. Jacobson, pp. 67-77. Basingstoke, England: Palgrave, 2000.

[In the following essay, Nayder analyzes the ideological significance of Dickens's characterization of class re-

sentiment and discontent as symptoms of a disease in The Perils of Certain English Prisoners *and* The Wreck of the Golden Mary.]

What would it mean if you were discontented with your job in Victorian Britain, and resentful of class privilege? If you were tired of watching the rich enjoy their luxuries while having none yourself? If you felt that you were being exploited by your employer, and complained of the gap separating capital from labour? One does not have to be Karl Marx or Frederick Engels to interpret these classic signs of disaffection and labour unrest—a result of the inequities and divisions that characterize the capitalist system, in their view.

Yet in a number of articles and stories published in his weekly journal *Household Words,* Charles Dickens offers a very different way of explaining the discontent and resentment of the Victorian have-nots—or, rather, a way of 'diagnosing' their ills. Describing a type of 'yellow fever' spreading from California and Australia to other portions of the globe in the 1850s—a fever unusually sudden and violent in its onset—these works attribute the discontent and resentment of British workers to a remarkable colonial phenomenon—the discovery of gold ('A Golden Newspaper', p. 207). The resentful workers they represent are not victims of an oppressive economic and political system; rather, they suffer from an infectious disease—'gold rush fever'.

A self-proclaimed social reformer, Dickens declared himself opposed to imperialism which deflected attention and resources away from pressing social problems at home. In what is perhaps his best-known critique of Empire, his parody of 'telescopic philanthropy' in *Bleak House,* missionaries and empire-builders are represented as irresponsible 'housekeepers', too near-sighted to notice the plight of their own children and their own poor. Asked for her opinion of these 'telescopic philanthropists' by Mr Jarndyce, Esther Summerson replies: '"We thought that, perhaps . . . it is right to begin with the obligations of home, sir; and that, perhaps, while those are overlooked and neglected, no other duties can possibly be substituted for them"' (6.60-1). As Dickens argued in 1848, when reviewing William Allen's narrative of the Niger expedition (1841), 'the work at home must be completed thoroughly, or there is no hope abroad. To your tents, O Israel! but see they are your own tents! Set *them* in order; leave nothing to be done *there*; and outpost will convey your lesson on to outpost, until the naked armies of [African Kings] . . . are reached, and taught' (p. 125).

Despite these objections to colonial enterprise and missionary zeal, however, Dickens used imperial ideology to his own ends. In his fictional works, as in those he published in his weekly journals, colonial relations and colonial events provide a means imaginatively to re-

solve England's political woes. In **'The Perils of Certain English Prisoners'**, a story he wrote with Wilkie Collins for the 1857 Christmas Number of *Household Words*, Dickens creates a narrator who loudly voices his feelings of class resentment. Sent to an English colony to protect its store of silver, private Gill Davis of the Royal Marines threatens to rebel against his officers, and against the members of the idle class on the island. '"I had had a hard life," he tells us, "and the life of the English on the Island seemed too easy . . . to please me"':

> 'Here you are,' I thought to myself, 'good scholars and good livers; able to . . . eat and drink what you like, and spend what you like, and do what you like; and much *you* care for a poor, ignorant Private in the Royal Marines! Yet it's hard, too, I think, that you should have all the halfpence, and I all the kicks; you all the smooth, and I all the rough; you all the oil, and I all the vinegar.'

(p. 241)

Yet in this imperial outpost, as in others that Dickens describes, feelings of class resentment are short-lived. Luckily for the privileged Englishmen in **'The Perils'**, the natives soon attack, enabling private Davis to identify the dark-skinned rebels as his *real* enemies, and to join forces with his social superiors against them. In a story written shortly after the Indian Mutiny, and partly modelled upon it, Dickens displaces feelings of class resentment with the nascent but virulent racism of private Davis. He uses the Empire—specifically, the sepoy revolt—to transform socially subversive feelings of class injury into a socially quiescent hatred of natives.[1]

In the stories he wrote and published about the gold rush, Dickens does not *resolve* characters' feelings of class resentment so much as explain them in non-political terms, as symptoms of madness and disease. He describes a 'golden' rather than social revolution ('Shadows of the Golden Image', p. 313), representing class resentment out of context, obscuring its political and economic origins, and calling it by another name: 'gold rush fever'. Responding to the 'Blue-Jacket Agitation' of sailors in the British merchant marine in his *Household Words* story, **'The Wreck of the Golden Mary'**, Dickens spreads this strain of 'yellow fever' among his characters, making their labour unrest seem both understandable and pathological.

On 6 March 1851, the London *Times* reported that a group of Merchant seamen, angered by the newly adopted Mercantile Marine Act, had appeared before the Board of Trade the previous day to state their grievances, requesting that certain portions of the Statute be suspended. Their statement outlined 'some of the causes of discontent and dissatisfaction extensively felt by master mariners and seamen of the united kingdom' ('New Mercantile Marine Act', 5). Told that the Act was designed 'to benefit and improve their condition' ('New Mercantile Marine Act', 5), they protested that, under the guise of encouraging moral and professional improvement among sailors, the Act imposed fines and penalties for misbehaviour, to be levied at the discretion of their captain, and thus reduced the men 'to the condition of slaves' ('New Mercantile Marine Act', 5). For insolence, or for not being 'clean shaved' on Sundays, for example, a captain could dock a sailor one day's pay ('Blue-Jacket Agitation', p. 40). The Act also allowed the captain to report on the character of his men in the logbook, while preventing sailors from responding to charges, granting him 'tremendous . . . unconstitutional' powers, in their view ('New Mercantile Marine Act' 5). 'When an entry was made in the log against a man . . . the man should have it read over to him . . . have the power of entering his defence, and the names of parties who could speak in his behalf' ('New Mercantile Marine Act', 5).

Within a month, the Merchant sailors found a spokesman in Charles Dickens, who took up their cause in *Household Words,* publishing nearly twenty articles, with titles such as 'We Mariners of England', 'Modern Human Sacrifices' and 'The Life of Poor Jack'. Providing detailed accounts of 'the Blue-Jacket Agitation', these articles describe the miseries suffered by the common sailor, and suggest that the men have valid reasons for resenting their officers and ship owners, and for deserting their ships. Describing dangers to which the men are exposed, many of which are deemed unnecessary, these articles call attention to the negligence of captains and their mates, and the greed of middle-class ship owners. More concerned with profit than with the safety of the ships, owners fail to repair rigging and spars, yet 'lie snug from censure' when sailors are killed and ships wrecked: 'The world is very slow to connect a respectable citizen of Liverpool with a wreck happening in the Bermudas, while he sat at tea in his own parlour, innocently happy with his wife and family' ('Modern Human Sacrifices', p. 562). All too often, these articles suggest, ships and their instruments are blamed for disasters caused by irresponsible officers and greedy owners:

> Can any blame by any possibility attach to any human creature? No. Obviously it must be laid upon the compasses. And this is a convenient thing, because there is no fine payable by compasses, and they are case-hardened against imprisonment. . . . We have great consideration for the feelings of a captain as a captain, of an owner as an owner, and generally of the gentlemen hidden behind the compasses. We regret, therefore, that this matter should be of a solemn kind that will not bear the consideration of those feelings any more. There must be defined responsibilities and no evasion; there must be not only moral and sentimental, but material and legal motives for the utmost care on the part of all who send or take men down to the sea in ships.
>
> ('Modern Human Sacrifices', p. 563)

While Dickens complains of 'evasion' on the part of ship owners, he can be equally evasive in his treatment of the sailors' plight. Although seamen are defended in 'Voices from the Deep' (p. 424), the editor of *Household Words* proves a reluctant champion of maritime labour. His publication of James Hannay's 'Blue-Jacket Agitation' for example, reinforces our sense of what Myron Magnet terms 'the *other* Dickens' (p. 1), the social disciplinarian rather than the social reformer. Thus sailors are portrayed as exploited members of the working class, and also as undisciplined and ignorant men responsible for their sorry state. The article that outlines the sailors' grievances and justifies their resentment and complaints also compares them to uncivilized tribes, and *endorses* legislation to which they object. The time has come for 'the meshes of law' to draw around 'that noble animal', 'the nautical leviathan', we are told ('Blue Jacket Agitation', p. 39). While sailors find the new rules and regulations dehumanizing and restrictive, they are nonetheless necessary, and will work to the men's advantage: 'Doubtless, a coat and trousers would be an intolerable restraint to a Tahitian at first, but by-and-by he would value these articles as he progressed in civilization' ('Blue-Jacket Agitation', p. 40).

In comparing discontented and resentful English sailors to uncivilized Tahitians who should be forced to wear coats and trousers, Dickens uses imperial allusion to undermine their political cause. In **'The Wreck of the Golden Mary'**, his story about labour unrest at sea, he infects sailors with 'gold rush fever', a colonial contagion that explains, yet discredits, their discontent.

'The Wreck of the Golden Mary' first appeared as the 1856 Christmas Number of *Household Words*. Like all the stories published as Christmas Numbers in Dickens's journals, it was a collaborative undertaking. Dickens composed the first section, narrated by the ship's Captain, and Collins the third, narrated by the First Mate. But Percy Fitzgerald, Harriet Parr, Adelaide Anne Proctor, and James White contributed as well in a series of interpolated tales narrated by the ship's crew members, and included in the middle section. For each collaborative Christmas Number prospective contributors were provided with a plot summary for the story before they began writing.

The officers, crew, and passengers on board the *Golden Mary,* a newly-built merchant vessel of 300 tons, are bound from Liverpool to San Francisco. The ship is manned by Captain William George Ravender, First Mate John Steadiman, and Second Mate William Rames, and a crew of 18, carrying 20 passengers. Among these, four are characterized in detail: Mrs Atherfield, 'a bright-eyed, blooming young wife who was going to join her husband in California'; their 3-year-old daughter Lucy is affectionately nicknamed 'The Golden Lucy' on the voyage out; Miss Coleshaw, a 30-year-old spinster 'going out to join a brother'; and

Mr Rarx, an 'old gentleman . . . who was always talking, morning, noon, and night, about the gold discovery' (p. 3). Taking out cargo to diggers and emigrants in California to be exchanged for gold (p. 2), the ship collides with an iceberg in the North Atlantic after more than two months at sea, and quickly sinks. All on board escape in two boats, and, in spite of the hardship, most survive; little Lucy Atherfield, the 'Golden Lucy', does not. After spending nearly 30 days in open boats, they are picked up by an English ship and transferred to a California coasting vessel. They arrive at their destination soon after their rescue at sea.

When one reads **'The Wreck of the Golden Mary'**, as a story in *Household Words,* what seems most striking is its *idealization* of the British Merchant Marine. Published alongside articles that describe capitalist exploitation and labour unrest at sea, **'The Wreck'** reveals Dickens's desire to deny or suppress such material. In the articles already discussed, sailors complain that laws are 'made for [ship] owners' rather than for the men 'before the mast' ('Sailors' Homes Afloat', p. 529). Compared to notorious rebels from English history, they threaten to desert, and to organize labour strikes—with good reason. But in **'The Wreck'**, Dickens gives his sailors no grounds for complaint. Unlike the ship owners described elsewhere in *Household Words,* the owner of the *Golden Mary* is generous and humane: 'a wiser merchant or a truer gentleman never stepped', the captain says, in Dickens's portion (p. 2). The captain is set apart from his irresponsible and abusive cohorts: he is brave, kind, and well prepared. Similarly idealized, Dickens's sailors are 'as smart, efficient, and contented, as it was possible to be' (p. 5). Manned by this idealized crew, the *Golden Mary* sets sail in a fair wind, bound on a voyage that promises well: 'And so, in a good ship of the best build, well owned, well arranged, well officered, well manned, well found in all respects, we parted with our pilot at a quarter past four o'clock in the afternoon of the seventh of March, one thousand eight hundred and fifty one, and stood with a fair wind out to sea' (p. 3).

Like many idealizations, **'The Wreck of the Golden Mary'** reveals the unpleasant realities it is designed to transcend. 'Part[ing] with [their] pilot' on 7 March 1851, Dickens's crew leaves England two days after the Merchant seamen first voiced their complaints to the Board of Trade, and these complaints are indirectly acknowledged in many details. Subtle signs of discontent and rebellion are present, despite the captain's insistence that his men are wholly 'contented', and Dickens repeatedly pairs disavowals of mutiny with admissions of it. Although Captain Ravender believes he hears his men humming at their work, for example, Dickens pauses to consider the possibility that they may actually be moaning (p. 8). The captain concedes that he 'had more than one rough temper with [him] among [his] own people' (p. 8), and repeatedly compares his own

experience with that of Captain Bligh and the mutiny of the *Bounty* (p. 9). Although a mutiny does not actually occur while the men are at sea, they desert their captain once they reach port. That the *Golden Mary* founders suggests there is trouble among them; for, as William J. Palmer points out, shipwreck is one of Dickens's favourite metaphors for social revolution (pp. 59-60).

As these details suggest, Dickens cannot wholly exclude from his story the social realities that inspired it. Yet he can explain the men's resentment and unrest in a reassuring way which obscures their political and economic origins. Sending his officers and crew to California during the days of the gold rush, and bringing them into contact with the 'infectious' Mr Rarx, Dickens makes their mutinous behaviour seem both natural and pathological by invoking the disease mechanism of 'gold rush fever'.

Dickens's readers were prepared to accept this diagnosis by an extensive series of articles published on the gold rush in *Household Words.* 'Off to the Diggings' (17 July 1852), for example, describes the widespread and irrational desertion of posts by workers who have no reason to complain of their lot. Not only are the poor and unemployed drawn to the gold fields; so, too, are 'clerks on eighty pounds a year':

> Go where you will, everybody appears to be going 'off to the Diggings'. . . . There are sixty young men rushing frantically away from their employers' counters in Saint Paul's Churchyard, and there are at least as many more longing to follow them. Fully five score of both sexes have bid adieu to Oxford Street and High Holborn: and it is computed that quite one hundred and ten have migrated from the warehouses about Cheapside and Cripplegate . . . a respectable quota of clerks on eighty pounds a year . . . are thirsting to handle the pick and the spade. I can't say how many youths at the Custom House and the Docks have drawn their last quarter's salary. . . . Legions of bankers' clerks, merchants' lads, embryo secretaries, and incipient cashiers; all going with the rush.
>
> (p. 405)

In 'A Digger's Diary' (29 January 1853), similarly, a contented apprentice who believes his 'prospect as a silversmith [is] too good to leave' (p. 457) is transformed by gold rush fever into a thoroughly unsettled and insubordinate figure. William Dixon, a silversmith's apprentice, recounts how he has been infected with feelings of discontent by the gold rush fever of his friend, Isaac Waits. Waits himself is 'giv[ing] up seventy-five pounds a year' and a possible partnership in his firm to leave for the gold fields, when the following dialogue takes place:

> A sudden thought flashed upon me. 'You are going to the Diggings!' said I.
>
> 'Of course I am,' said he, relaxing his hard features into a sort of commiserating smile, 'Of course I am! all the pluck of London's going there, or will be, soon.'

'All the dissatisfied pluck of London, you mean,' said I.

'Well,' said he, 'are you satisfied? I am not . . . Mr. William Dixon,' said he, in a rather formal, but impressive tone, 'you are nearly out of your time—you are over one-and-twenty—and you don't expect to come into a fortune. . . . In short, you are not born with a silver spoon in your mouth—you must polish 'em up for the use of others—an't it true? You can't expect to set up for yourself, because yours is a business that needs a goodish capital.'

(pp. 457-8)

Gold rush fever gives well-treated workers the *delusion* they are being exploited by those with capital, and denied their own fair share of wealth.

In **'The Wreck of the Golden Mary'**, unlike 'A Digger's Diary', 'Californian gold' rather than Australian provides the source of contagion. In March 1851, when Dickens's crew sets sail, gold had not yet been discovered in Australia. Yet Californian gold produces the same symptoms in Dickens's characters as the Australian variety, and is profusely displayed in London, as Captain Ravender explains: '"There was Californian gold in the museums and in the goldsmiths' shops, and the very first time I went upon 'Change, I met a friend of mine (a seafaring man like myself), with a Californian nugget hanging to his watch-chain. I handled it"' (p. 1). Exposed to gold at the outset of the story, the captain proves immune to infection: '"gold in California was no business of mine"' (p. 1). The same cannot be said of the captain's men. Listening to Mr Rarx in his 'delirium' about discoveries of gold, the sailors 'catch' his fever, which manifests itself in 'ungovernable' behaviour (p. 9); while Mr Rarx dies at sea, the sailors survive to desert their captain. 'Bitten by old Mr Rarx's mania for gold', they go off to the diggings and refuse to return to port (p. 36). In so doing, they exhibit the 'symptoms' of lawlessness first described to Captain Ravender by the thoughtful owner of the *Golden Mary*—a lawlessness 'as special as the circumstances in which it is placed', a unique type of rebellion wholly unrelated to the treatment the sailors receive, yet also wholly inevitable. 'Crews of vessels outward-bound, desert as soon as they make the land,' the ship owner warns the captain. 'Crews of vessels homeward-bound, ship at enormous wages, with the express intention of murdering the captain and seizing the gold freight; no man can trust another, and the devil seems let loose' (p. 2). Sending his mariners to the gold regions, Dickens presents us with a paradoxical idyllic instance of labour unrest—idyllic because the actions of managers and capitalists make no difference to the condition of the workers. Whether sailors are well or poorly paid, well or poorly treated, they become deserters and mutineers all the same.

In yet another sense, **'The Wreck of the Golden Mary'** proves to be a Dickensian idyll—not only in its use of

'gold rush fever', but also in its metaphoric associations of women and children with gold.[2] While social order on board the *Golden Mary* is disrupted by unruly sailors, it is also threatened by emancipated women who travel to California alone.[3] Indeed, the ship herself, to whom Captain Ravender is 'married', breaks her vows and deserts her husband and children (those she 'carrie[s] in her lap' [p. 4]) when she sinks in the North Atlantic.[4] Although Captain Ravender compares his ship to an angelic woman named Mary whom he was to wed years before (p. 2), the *Golden Mary* is not an angel but a whore. Adorned with ribbons and 'little bits of finery' by Lucy Atherfield, who dresses the ship like a 'doll' (p. 4), the *Golden Mary* recalls a familiar figure from the gold regions—the prostitute with the 'heart of gold'—except that her heart seems far from golden.[5]

Yet little Lucy Atherfield and the woman who gave birth to her reclaim the image of golden womanhood for Dickens. A 'little gentle woman', Mrs Atherfield remains devoted to her husband although far away from him. Defining the faithful wife against the unruly and autonomous *Golden Mary*, Dickens uses her to represent 'true gold': female sexuality as a resource that can be claimed, renewed and controlled by men.[6] Unlike the *Golden Mary*, who is built for work in the public domain and whose character as 'a very fast sailor' (p. 4) suggests both promiscuity and independence, Mrs Atherfield is last seen sitting sedately at her husband's side. Although little golden Lucy dies at sea, we learn that Mr Atherfield has mined 'another Golden Lucy' (p. 36) from his wife's abundant reproductive stores, albeit with some mixture of an alloy: 'Her hair was a shade or two darker than the hair of my poor little pet of past sad times; but in all other respects the living child reminded me so strongly of the dead, that I quite started at the first sight of her' (p. 36). Replacing the image of deserters in the gold fields with that of Mr Atherfield, a second 'Golden Lucy' by his side, Dickens suggests that Englishmen, whatever their class differences, share common ground. For husbands and fathers in patriarchy, he implies, there will always be enough wealth to go around.

Notes

1. For a detailed discussion of this transformation see my 'Class Consciousness and the Indian Mutiny'.

2. Barker-Benfield discusses the use of this metaphor, explaining that precious minerals serve as 'common images for . . . woman's and the continent's body' in Victorian writing, 'areas viewed . . . as exploitable in the same way, and as expressions of man's mastery over his own resources' (p. 382).

3. In numerous articles Dickens published or himself authored, America is described as a 'Utopia' for women ('Rights and Wrongs of Women', p. 158),

a nation in which 'strong-minded' women 'run amuck' ('Sucking Pigs', p. 146), and California in particular as a place where 'a woman . . . can earn as much, or more than a man' ('A "Ranch" in California', p. 471). See also, 'Chips: a Woman's Experience in California'.

4. Dickens represents the captain's relationship to his ship as a marriage when the ship owner first introduces them: 'On the next morning but one we were on board the *Golden Mary*. I might have known, from his asking me to come down and see her, what she was. I declare her to have been the completest and most exquisite Beauty that ever I set my eyes upon. We had inspected every timber in her, and had come back to the gangway to go ashore from the dock-basin, when I put out my hand to my friend. "Touch upon it", says I, "and touch heartily. I take command of this ship, and I am hers"' (p. 2).

5. Goldman discusses these 'golden women' and their reputed 'strivings for adventure and autonomy' (p. 4) in a history of prostitution in the American West.

6. In a number of *Household Words* articles, the mineral riches of the earth are compared to the reproductive resources of womankind. 'Mines are spoken of in the feminine gender', one article notes ('If This Should Meet His Eye', p. 598), while another compares a woman's devotion to 'all the gold in the creeks of Victoria' ('Gold-Hunting', p. 478). In 'Change for a Sovereign', Mother Earth appears as a subservient yet generous woman who freely serves gold to the men sitting at her table (p. 280).

Works Cited

G. J. Barker-Benfield, 'The Spermatic Economy: a Nineteenth-Century View of Sexuality', in *The American Family in Social-Historical Perspective,* second edition, edited by Michael Gordon (New York: St. Martin's Press, 1978), pp. 374-402.

John Capper, 'Off to the Diggings', *Household Words,* 5 (17 July 1852), 405-10.

Charles Dickens, 'Review: *Narrative of the Expedition . . . to the River Niger in 1841*' (*The Examiner,* 19 August 1848), in *'The Amusements of the People' and Other Papers: Reports, Essays, and Reviews (1834-51),* The Dent Uniform Edition of Dickens' Journalism, in 3 vols, edited by Michael Slater (London: Dent, 1996), 2.108-26.

———, 'Sucking Pigs', *Household Words,* 4 (8 November 1851), 145-7.

———, *Bleak House* (1853), edited by Andrew Sanders (London: Dent, 1994).

———, with Wilkie Collins et al., 'The Wreck of the Golden Mary', *Household Words,* Extra Christmas Number (1856).

———, with Wilkie Collins, 'The Perils of Certain English Prisoners', *Household Words,* Extra Christmas Number (1857), in *The Lazy Tour of Two Idle Apprentices and Other Stories* (London: Chapman and Hall, 1890), pp. 237-327.

Edmund Saul Dixon, 'If This Should Meet His Eye', *Household Words,* 4 (13 March 1852), 598-600.

Marion S. Goldman, *Gold Diggers and Silver Mines: Prostitution and Social Life on the Comstock Lode* (Ann Arbor: University of Michigan Press, 1981).

James Hannay, 'The Blue-Jacket Agitation', *Household Words,* 3 (5 April 1851), 36-41.

Richard H. Horne, 'A Digger's Diary: in Occasional Chapters', *Household Words,* 6 (29 January 1853), 457-62.

William Howitt, 'Gold-Hunting', *Household Words,* 13 (24 May 1856), 448-54; (31 May 1856), 472-9.

Eliza Lynn, 'Rights and Wrongs of Women', *Household Words,* 9 (1 April 1854), 158-61.

Myron Magnet, *Dickens and the Social Order* (Philadelphia: University of Pennsylvania Press, 1985).

Louisa Anne Meredith, 'Shadows of the Golden Image', *Household Words,* 15 (4 April 1857), 313-18.

Henry Morley, 'Chips: Change for a Sovereign', *Household Words,* 5 (5 June 1852), 279-80.

———, 'The Life of Poor Jack', *Household Words,* 7 (21 May 1853), 286-8.

———, 'Chips: Voices from the Deep', *Household Words,* 8 (31 December 1853), 424.

———, 'Modern Human Sacrifices', *Household Words,* 8 (11 February 1854), 561-4.

———, with Samuel Rinder, 'Sailors' Homes Afloat', *Household Words,* 6 (19 February 1853), 529-33.

———, with Samuel Rinder, 'We Mariners of England', *Household Words,* 6 (26 February 1853), 553-7.

Lillian Nayder, 'Class Consciousness and the Indian Mutiny in Dickens's "The Perils of Certain English Prisoners"', *Studies in English Literature,* Vol 32, No 4 (Autumn 1992), 689-705.

'The New Mercantile Marine Act: Deputation to the Board of Trade', The London *Times* (6 March 1851), 5.

William J. Palmer, 'Dickens and Shipwreck', *Dickens Studies Annual,* 18 (1989), pp. 39-92.

W. H. Wills, with G. B. Harrold and [Miss] Harrold, 'Chips: a Woman's Experience in California', *Household Words,* 2 (1 February 1851), 450-1.

———, with [Miss] Harrold, 'A "Ranch" in California', *Household Words*, 3 (9 August 1851), 471-2.

———, with J. Keene, 'A Golden Newspaper', *Household Words*, 4 (22 November 1851), 207-8.

Alessandro Vescovi (essay date 2000)

SOURCE: Vescovi, Alessandro. "The Bagman, the Signalman and Dickens's Short Story." In *Dickens: The Craft of Fiction and the Challenges of Reading*, edited by Rossana Bonadei, Clotilde de Stasio, Carlo Pagetti, and Alessandro Vescovi, pp. 111-22. Milan: Edizioni Unicopli, 2000.

[*In the following essay, Vescovi surveys the evolution of Dickens's narrative approach to short-story writing, contrasting "The Story of the Bagman's Uncle" and "The Signalman" in terms of their respective themes, structures, and social relevance.*]

When we talk of the evolution of a great writer like Dickens we immediately think of comparing his first novel with the novelistic production of his late years. What I propose in this article is a survey of the evolution of Dickens's narrative technique with regard to the short story. To this effect I shall proceed to compare two ghost stories published in *Pickwick Papers* and in the Christmas 1866 number of *All Year Round*, entitled **Mugby Junction**. The two narratives, **"The Story of the Bagman's Uncle"** (hereafter **"Bagman's Uncle"**) and **"The Signalman"**[1], share the theme of the uncanny, very popular with Victorian readers, but present major differences as to narrative techniques and awareness of the short story genre. Another difference which constitutes a novelty in the Victorian short story is the social engagement shown in **"The Signalman"**.

Dickens never in fact makes use of the traditional Gothic setting of the ghost story, but rather introduces ghosts for three different purposes, namely comic effects (**"Bagman's Uncle"**), conversion from evil to good (**"A Christmas Carol"**, **"The Goblins Who Stole a Sexton"**), and exploration of altered states of mind by which he was fascinated in the last part of his life, when the writer himself conducted experiments in mesmerism with M.me de la Rue (**"To Be Read at Dusk"**, **"The Signalman"**). Even when present in Dickens's narrative, Gothic effects, horror and terror are undermined by irony. In **"A Christmas Carol"**, for instance, Scrooge is actually startled by the sudden apparition, but the reader is not supposed to share his fear:

> At this, the spirit raised a frightful cry, and shook his chain with such a dismal and appalling noise, that Scrooge held on tight to his chair, to save himself from falling in a swoon. But how much greater was his hor-

ror, when the phantom taking off the bandage round its head, as if it were too warm to wear in-doors, its lower jaw dropped down upon its breast!

(***Christmas Books***: 21)

In **"A Christmas Tree"** the narrator comments on traditional ghost stories showing what seems to be the position of Dickens himself:

> There is no end to the old houses, with resounding galleries and dismal state-bed chambers, and haunted wings shut up for many years, through which we may ramble, with an agreeable creeping up and back, and encounter any number of ghosts but (it is worthy to remark perhaps) reducible to a very few general types and classes, for ghosts have little originality, and walk in a beaten track.

(13)

The existence of ghosts was, in Dickens's time, debated in extremely serious terms, and even intellectuals were divided on this point. Dickens took a clear stance in an anonymous[2] review appearing in *The Examiner* in 1848 entitled "The Night Side of Nature; or Ghost and Ghost Seers by Catherine Crowe". Dickens acknowledges the sincerity of those who claim to have witnessed preternatural phenomena, but denies their reliability:

> They [the ghosts] always elude us. Doubtful and scant of proof at first, doubtful and scant of proof still, all mankind's experience of them is, that their alleged appearances have been, in all ages, marvellous, exceptional and resting on imperfect grades of proof; that in vast numbers of cases they are known to be delusions superinduced by a well understood, and by no means uncommon disease.

Apart from the unreliability of the sources, Dickens supports his thesis with an interesting narratological proof: when dealing with a true story one can take out any detail and the story is still acceptable. Even if Nelson did not die as it is told, exemplifies Dickens, still the Battle of Trafalgar still took place on that very day with the very same historical consequences. But if one takes out a detail from a ghost story the whole edifice collapses.

Given these assumptions it is no wonder that Dickens often has his stories told by narrators whose reliability is severely compromised. Both **"The Signalman"** and **"The Bagman's Uncle"** are full of details to avoid the accusation of being implausible on account of their elusiveness. In both cases the narrators (not the witnesses) are comparably reliable and those who have actually witnessed the supernatural events are in earnest, though not very credible, the one being drunk and the other psychologically under stress.

"The Bagman's Uncle" tells the story of an adventure that occurred one night to the narrator's uncle. After a jolly evening spent drinking with friends, the protagonist sat by an old mail coaches cemetery and was invited by some ghosts to take a trip with them in one of the coaches. Among the passengers the bagman's uncle finds two suspicious men who have just kidnapped a young lady; the protagonist heroically defeats the kidnappers by stabbing them with a sword, thus causing the young lady to fall in love with him. He falls in love too and promises never to marry anyone else. Eventually the uncle wakes up in the morning, sitting on an old mail coach in the coaches cemetery and decides to keep faith with his promise never to marry anyone else.

The story of the Signalman is of quite another tenor: a railway employee works all the time in a "deep trench" by the mouth of a tunnel, where the sun never shines. His task consists in keeping a logbook, making signals to the passing trains and sending messages by telegraph from time to time. The narrator in this story has quite an active part; he gains the confidence of the railwayman who eventually tells him that he has twice seen a ghost, always in connection with a fatal accident on the line. In those days the ghost has resumed his apparitions and the signalman asks himself with anguish what is going to happen this time. As the narrator comes back for the third time to talk with the signalman, he finds him dead, knocked out by a locomotive. What is the more remarkable is that the engineer had shouted the same words and behaved in exactly the same way as the ghost.

Although both tales can now be found published separately, they first appeared within narrative frames, in the extremely wide and complicated one of *Pickwick Papers* and in the rather succinct one of **Mugby Junction.** In the first case there is no discontinuity (unless typographical) between the main narration and the bagman's story, which is a direct discourse, with frequent hints to the gentlemen who form his fictitious audience. **"The Signalman"** on the other hand presents a writing narrator—according to the intentions declared in the frame story—who demands a reader rather than a listener.

The bagman's narrative is rather chaotic, though it follows a classic scheme of presentation of the main character, followed by his adventures. Often during the story, the narrator offers his own remarks:

> Gentlemen, there is an old story—none the worse for being true—regarding a fine young Irish gentleman, who being asked if he could play the fiddle, replied he had no doubt he could, but he couldn't exactly say, for certain, because he had never tried. This is not inapplicable to my uncle and his fencing. . . .
>
> (*Pickwick*: 695)

The telling is thus much longer than the story, whose interpretation is guided by the narrator's style. As often happens in oral cultures the story, the diegesis, loses

importance compared with the narration, *mimesis*. Rapid narrative passages, Genette's summaries[3], are absent (which is not rare in the short story) and the diegesis is made of scenes, where the time taken by the story and the time taken by the narration remain comparable. Oral style is rendered through an imitation of colloquial syntax and pronunciation and the frequent use of pauses and digressions. Though we are dealing with a short story, we find no ellipses, which will be the standard in modern short fiction and are extensively used in **"The Signalman"**. No particular effort is required on the part of the reader (or rather listener) in making the text signify: nothing is given for granted, even the common places on which the comprehension depends are fully stated. It is interesting to note how, at the end of the long introduction, the narrator tells his audience what use they are supposed to make of the information just received:

> I am particular in describing how my uncle walked up in the middle of the street, with his thumbs in his waistcoat pockets, gentlemen, because, as he often used to say (and with great reason too) there is nothing at all extraordinary in this story, unless you understand at the beginning that he was not by any means of a marvellous or romantic turn.
>
> (*Pickwick*: 686)

As for the use of space in this story it should be noted that it is not used to create a particular atmosphere, but is rather described only as far as necessary to allow the action to take place. The Gothic elements lose all their evocative force as they are dealt with in a rather humorous way. The description of bleak streets is far from being frightening.

> On either side of him, there shot up against the dark sky, tall gaunt straggling houses, with time stained fronts, and windows that seemed to have shared the lot of eyes in mortals, and to have grown dim and sunken with age. Six, seven, eight storeys high, were the houses; storey piled upon storey, as children build with cards—throwing their dark shadows over the roughly paved road, and making the dark night darker. [. . .] Glancing at all these things with the air of a man who had seen them too often before, to think them worthy of much notice now, my uncle walked up the middle of the street, with a thumb in each waistcoat pocket, indulging from time to time in various snatches of song, chanted forth with such good will and spirit that the quiet honest folk started from their first sleep and lay trembling in bed till the sound died away in the distance.
>
> (*Pickwick*: 685-686)

The image of cardboards castles deflates the tension of bleak atmosphere, which definitely ceases to be frightening when the narrator adds that the protagonist was singing with a thumb in each waistcoat pocket. After this, insistence on the darkness becomes an ironic device, which produces a sort of mock ghost story, which is coherent with the character of the bagman, as described in *Pickwick Papers.*

The very ghostly image *par excellence,* the cemetery, is here radically transformed, becoming a cemetery of old coaches; the typical bleak haunted house at which they arrive in the dead of night is described as "the most ruinous and desolate place my uncle had ever beheld", but it provokes an unusual comment:

> A mail travelling at the rate of six miles and a half an hour, and stopping for an indefinite time at such a hole as this, is rather an irregular sort of proceeding I fancy. This shall be made known. I'll write to the papers.
>
> (*Pickwick*: 694-695)

The structure of **"The Signalman"** is much more complex. To begin with, there is none of the oral discourse which characterised the early Dickens; on the contrary the structure is perfected like a clockwork mechanism and offers us a cyclical structure repeated three times with slight differences:

Narrator's arrival to the trench.

Identification/recognising

Descent

Discussion about the work of the signalman and the uncanny

Description of the place

Farewell ascent

Narrators comment

This cyclical structure (see Bonheim 1988) is extremely interesting because it interweaves the two main themes of the story in an inextricable way, and at the same time it makes the signalman and the narrator reliable. In the third part of the story, when the narrator recognises the corpse of the signalman, there are no explicit references to the preternatural, the dialogue with the dead man's colleagues is extremely realistic, but the cyclical structure forces the reader to read the scene as an analepsis, thinking back to the two previous visits and therefore adding the missing uncanny element. Thus, in this third part the credibility of the story does not depend on the reliability of one character, but rather on the reader's ability to fill in the narrative gaps.

In order to obtain this effect, to train the reader to read the third part analeptically, the first two visits are characterized by a number of prolepses, whose ultimate meaning varies slightly at each occurrence and can only be fully grasped at a second reading. Such prolepses can be found on three narrative levels:

In direct speech (discursive prolepses)

In actions (proairethic prolepses)

In the descriptions of places and in the narrator's reactions to such descriptions (descriptive prolepses).

Instances of the three kinds can be found in the very first paragraph, which opens the tale with the greetings of the narrator-character: "Halloa. Below there". Such words, as we shall learn after a few pages, are attributed to the ghost and actually spoken by the engineer whose train kills the signalman, as is also the case of the warning: "For God's sake, clear the way!".

As for proairethic prolepses, in the first paragraph we find the act of covering one's face with one arm, an act performed twice more, once by the ghost and once by the engineer. Furthermore, death is mentioned in coincidence with this gesture (beside the memory of past incidents) as the narrator thinks of stone figures on tombs. Another prolepsis, partly descriptive and partly proairethic, consists in looking toward the tunnel instead of looking upwards when the signalman first hears the narrator's call.

The third prolepses chain, dedicated to description, is less objective, since it is filtered by the narrator's consciousness. Nevertheless, the narrator seems to be aware of his own implausibility, thus enhancing his reliability, as the narrating-I is scrupulous in recording what the narrated-I perceived. In the first paragraph we find the comment "There was something remarkable in his manner of doing so", later supported by the "monstrous thought" that the signalman is no real man:

> The monstrous thought came into my mind, as I perused the fixed eyes and the saturnine face, that this was a spirit and not a man.
>
> (490)

The cyclical structure and the repetition of certain motives with different meanings recalls what Derrida calls *différance;* that is difference and deferring of meaning and comprehension. The above mentioned prolepses take on different meanings, as the opening sentence does, but each meaning has a wider range than the immediate context would lead us to think, thanks to repetition, that creates a sort of resonance.

Thus the nearest literary antecedent to this short story is not, from a formalistic point of view, the oral tale, but rather the ballad. In fact there are two characteristics of the ballad which we find here: reiteration and reproducibility. The first refers to the repetition of textual elements, whose meaning becomes clearer as the story goes on, the second refers to the fact that the ballad is usually learnt by heart and, though there are dozens of different variants, it is repeated without variations each time. Such variants are quite negligible if compared with those of an oral tale. Another characteristic of the ballad is that it is not supposed to be "told" only once, but several times. Thus the text is not comprehended during the performance, but, synchronically, outside of it, after the end, and the accretion of meaning implied by repetition works for the ballad exactly as it does for **"The Signalman"**.

Let us consider one of the most famous English ballads, "Lord Randal," known all over Europe in different translations:

> 'O where ha you been, Lord Randal, my son?
> And where ha you been, my handsome young man?'
> 'I ha been at the greenwood; mother mak my bed
> soon,
> For I'm wearied wi hunting, and fain wad lie down'
>
> 'An wha met ye there, Lord Randal, my son?
> An wha met you there, my handsome young man?'
> 'O I met wi my true-love; mother, mak my bed soon,
> For I'm wearied wi hunting, and fain wad lie down.'

The basic scheme is the classic dialogue between mother and son, and the story told is about murder; by asking question the mother will find out that the youth had been poisoned by the fiancée and consequently questions him about his last will. The last two lines of each stanza are the same throughout the text, but change their meaning as we understand that the young man has been poisoned by his fiancée. In the version quoted here in the last stanza the man says "I am sick at the heart and fain wad lie down" instead of repeating the hunting refrain, thus correcting his first impression of tiredness. The epithet "true-love" appears twice in the text, but it has a radically different meaning: the first time it is romantic, the second sarcastic. Both "Lord Randal" and **"The Signalman"** share the scheme of the detective story, in which the truth comes out through a number of details—the ghost's words, the meal in the wood—which can be fully grasped only at the end of the text. Thus only repetition allows the reader/listener to grasp the hints to the final murder.

Such a complicated structure allows the story to *mean* on different levels and to mingle different themes. Thus the ghost tradition is here mingled with a sort of protest for the working conditions of the signalman, a protest that can be described in the Marxian terms of estrangement and alienation. According to the German philosopher the worker in the capitalist economy is alienated because he becomes a commodity and his work (meant both as process and product) no longer belongs to him.

> What, then, constitutes the alienation of labour?
>
> First, the fact that labour is *external* to the worker—i.e., it does not belong to his essential being; that in his work, therefore, he does not affirm himself, but denies himself, does not feel content but unhappy, does not develop freely his mental and physical energy, but mortifies his body and ruins his mind. The worker therefore only feels himself outside his work, and in his

work feels outside himself. He is at home when he is not working, and not at home when he is working. His labour is, therefore, not voluntary but forced, it is *forced labour*.[4]

The signalman seems to fall into this category, since he works alone in a bleak place communicating with other people only through the telegraph and receiving orders by an electric bell. What seems to distress the poor man most is that he is not master of his work: he can do nothing to prevent the incident foretold by the spectre:

> 'If I telegraph Danger on either side of me, or on both, I can give no reason for it,' he went on, wiping the palms of his hands. 'I should get into trouble, and do no good. They would think I was mad. This is the way it would work,—Message: "Danger! Take care!" Answer: "What Danger? Where?" Message: "Don't know. But for God's sake, take care!" They would displace me. What else could they do?'
>
> (497)

It has been said that the signalman might be suffering from monomania, a mental disease that Dickens could have known about from his acquaintance with a psychiatrist, Dr. John Conolly (1794-1866) (see Tytler 1994). It is also probable that the writer was influenced by the railway accident in which he himself was involved in 1865 and that was provoked by the carelessness of a signalman. Dickens died five years later on the same day of his accident: as he says in **"The Signalman"**, "remarkable coincidences do continually occur".

The ghost seen by the signalman could be his own creation, a projection of his fears, a sort of *alter ego* which appears as a ghost because the signalman himself is dehumanised. His work giving him no self realisation, the signalman seeks some kind of interest in other activities:

> He had taught himself a language down here,—if only to know it by sight, and to have formed his own crude ideas of its pronunciation, could be called learning it. He had also worked at fractions and decimals, and tried a little algebra. . . .
>
> (491)

The alienation of his work is the ultimate reason for his death. It is curious that no critic has ever tried to answer the question why the railwayman doesn't clear the way. In fact "no man in England knew his work better", according to the train driver who had killed him and he was "one of the safest men to be employed in that capacity", according to the narrator. It is impossible that the signalman did not hear the approaching train because, apart from his experience and the engineer's shouts, the train is very loud, as described at the beginning of the story:

Just then there came a vague vibration in the earth and air, quickly changing into a violent pulsation, and an oncoming rush that caused me to start back, as though it had force to draw me down.

(489)

Last, it is not possible that the signalman did not have time to clear the way, because the engineer had had all the time to see the danger and shout out several times. The signalman's death, therefore, can be no mere accident; the mysterious apparition must be somehow connected with it. We can make two hypotheses: the signalman let himself be killed by the train in order not to witness powerlessly somebody else's death. The second, more likely, possibility is that the signalman mistook the engineer for the ghost and deliberately decided to ignore him. In any case, alienating work is the ultimate cause of the man's death. There is a sort of bitter irony in the fact that the man who worked as interpreter of signals could not use his competence to see the human sign that would have saved his life. Such is the distance, Marx would say, between the man and the worker.

Given the double reading offered by this story (the uncanny and social engagement) it is interesting to note how the use of space fits them both. On the one hand the description of the cutting and the tunnel recall a Gothic setting, on the other the precision in details and the choice of the railway (the symbol of progress *par excellence*) put the story on an extremely realistic level.

At the beginning of the story there is a distinction between high and low, clearly established by the initial words "Halloa. Below there!". The world of the signalman is confined and shrunk to the bottom of the cutting, whereas the narrator is the *trait d'union* between the world of the signalman and ours. To get to the signalman's it is necessary to walk down a winding path, which represents the threshold between the two separated worlds. Dickens's insistence on the above/below relationship is a way to underline the desolation of the workplace. In the very first page of the story there are nine spatial hints at the signalman's location:

below there	raising his eyes
looking up to where I stood on the top	high above him
down into the deep trench	I looked down
high above him	I called down to him
halloa below	

It has been suggested that this polarisation between high and low is a symbol of the social fall of the signalman who had once been a student (Tytler 1994). This is not impossible, but seems rather far fetched if we consider how simply mimetic the description can be.

Some details of the trench seem to be taken from Gothic literature:

The cutting was extremely deep, and unusually precipitate. It was made through a clammy stone, that became oozier and wetter as I went down.

(489)

On either side, a dripping-wet wall of jagged stone, excluding all view but a strip of sky; the perspective one way only a crooked prolongation of this great dungeon; the shorter perspective in the other direction terminating in a gloomy red light, and the gloomier entrance to a black tunnel, in whose massive architecture there was a barbarous, depressing, and forbidding air. So little sunlight ever found its way to this spot, that it had an earthy, deadly smell; and so much cold wind rushed through it, that it struck chill to me, as if I had left the natural world.

(490)

The setting seems to be a sort of objective correlative of the signalman's mental health. How can a man who lives most of his time down there be completely healthy? On the other hand the space outside the cutting is never described. When the narrator reports his thoughts outside the trench, he fails to give the slightest detail of the surroundings. In fact reference to, say, a sunny and windy place might have deflated the narrative tension.

The narrative time is also much more modern than in **"Bagman's Uncle"**; here there is never a descriptive pause, the narrative concentrates on the cyclical scenes, with an ellipsis of what happens between two scenes, that is for instance what the signalman does when not on duty. Such ellipses, though, call for the reader's co-operation, giving the text greater unity. The story is longer than the telling, the opposite of what happens in **"The Bagman's Uncle"**. Another interesting point is the order in which the events are presented: we must first of all understand that this story is about two people, the signalman and the narrator. The story begins when an apparition has already taken place, but the reader only learns about it when the narrator does. This is exactly the same pattern as in the detective story where the narrator plays the part of the detective.

This double narrator has induced some critics to consider the signalman a *Doppelgänger* of the narrator, a secret sharer, since the two possess some common traits such as the fact of having been shut "within narrow limits" for a long time. In fact, if we think of the signalman as a kind of detective story in which one character is both the murderer and the victim, it is no wonder that the detective sympathises with the victim and thinks like the murderer.

We have seen that there is a considerable evolution between the extremes of **"The Story of the Bagman's Uncle"** and **"The Signalman."** The first is linear and relatively simple as an oral tale can be. The second is much more complex, both in themes and narrative techniques. What is relevant to our discourse is that the technical complexity makes the thematic complexity possible: the bagman as a narrator would not be able to mingle social issues and the uncanny in one single story. The narrator in **"The Signalman"** is able to do it because he relies on the reader's capacity to read different melodies at the same time. In particular at the end, when the story becomes merely descriptive and thus realistic, it is the reader who adds the ghostly element, by means of the technical device of cyclicity.

Notes

1. In modern reprints the story always bears this title, but originally it was "Branch Line no. 1: the Signalman".

2. The Attribution to Dickens is nevertheless beyond doubt since the author himself sent a copy of it to M. de la Rue accompanied by a letter in which he called the Swiss friend's attention on the article and hinted to his wife. See Philip Collins, "Dickens on Ghosts: An Uncollected Article", *The Dickensian,* 49:1, 1963, pp. 5-14.

3. I follow Genette (1972), who distinguishes three different kinds of narrative pace, that he calls (from the slowest) pause, scene, summary.

4. From *Economic And Philosophic Manuscripts of 1844,* edited with an introduction by Dirk J. Struik, translated by M. Milligan, London, Lawrence and Wishart, 1970, p. 110-111.

Bibliography

Dickens, Charles, *Christmas Books,* Everyman's Library, London 1907.

Dickens, Charles, *Christmas Stories,* Everyman's Library, London 1910.

Dickens, Charles, *Pickwick Papers,* Everyman's Library, London 1907.

Bonadei, Rossana (ed.), Dickens Charles, 1991, *Mugby Junction: un treno per Nessun-Luogo,* Studio Tesi, Pordenone.

Bonheim, Helmut, "The Principle of Cyclicity in Dickens's 'The Signalman'", in *Anglia,* 106: 3/4, 1988.

Caporaletti, Silvana, "Metamorfosi di un testo narrativo: 'The Signalman' di Charles Dickens", in *Strumenti Critici,* XII, 1, Jan. 1997.

Day, Gary, "Figuring out the 'Signalman': Dickens and the Ghost Story", Beeom Clive *et al.* (eds.), *Nineteenth Century Suspense,* MacMillan, London 1988.

Genette, Gerard, *Figures* III, Éditions de Seuil, Paris 1972.

Greenman, David J., "Dickens's ultimate achievements in the Ghost Story: 'To be Taken with a Grain of Salt' and 'The Signalman'", in *The Dickensian,* no. 417, vol. 85, 1, Spring, 1989.

Justin, Henry, "The Signalman's Signal-man", *Journal of the Short Story in English,* no. 7, Autumn 1986.

Mengel, Ewald, "Structure and Meaning in Dickens's 'The Signalman'", in *Studies in Short Fiction,* 20:4, 1983.

Seed, David, "Mystery in Everyday Things: Charles Dickens's 'The Signalman'", in *Criticism,* XXIII: 1, 1981.

Thomas, Deborah A., *Dickens and the Short Story,* University of Pennsylvania Press, Philadelphia 1982.

Tytler, Graeme, "Dickens's 'The Signalman'", *The Explicator,* 53:1, 1994.

Jill L. Matus (essay date spring 2001)

SOURCE: Matus, Jill L. "Trauma, Memory, and Railway Disaster: The Dickensian Connection." *Victorian Studies* 43, no. 3 (spring 2001): 413-36.

[*In the following essay, Matus draws on Victorian discourses on nervous shock and unconscious memory to focus on the ways "The Signalman," both anticipates and articulates twentieth-century theories about traumatic experience.*]

In 1865 Charles Dickens narrowly escaped death when the train on which he was traveling from Folkestone to London jumped a gap in the line occasioned by some repair work on a viaduct near Staplehurst, Kent. The foreman on the job miscalculated the time of the train's arrival; the flagman was only 550 yards from the works and unable to give adequate warning of the train's approach. The central and rear carriages fell off the bridge, plunging onto the river-bed below. Only one of the first class carriages escaped that plunge, coupled fast to the second class carriage in front. "It had come off the rail and was [. . .] hanging over the bridge at an angle, so that all three of them were tilted down into a corner" (Ackroyd 1013). Dickens managed to get Ellen Ternan and her mother, with whom he was traveling, out of the carriage and then behaved with remarkable self-possession, climbing down into the ravine and ministering to the many who lay injured and dying. With further aplomb, he climbed back into the dangerously unstable carriage and retrieved his manuscript, an account of which is offered in the memorable postscript to *Our Mutual Friend* (1865).

Once back in London, however, Dickens began to develop the symptomatology that today we would recognize as typical of trauma.[1] He was greatly shaken and lost his voice for nearly two weeks: "I most unaccountably brought someone else's out of that terrible scene," he said. He suffered repeatedly from what he called "the shake," and, when he later traveled by train, he was in the grip of a persistent illusion that the carriage was down on the left side. Even a year later, he noted that he had sudden vague rushes of terror, which were "perfectly unreasonable but unsurmountable." At such times, his son and daughter reported, he was unaware of the presence of others and seemed to be in a kind of trance. His son Henry recalled that he got into a state of panic at the slightest jolt; Mamie attested that her father's nerves were never really the same again: he "would fall into a paroxysm of fear, tremble all over and clutch the arms of the railway carriage." An uncanny repetition also characterizes his death, falling as it did on the anniversary of the accident five years later.[2]

It is well known that Dickens was engaged throughout his literary career in representations of the railroad and used it to various effects, often combining the "humorous and the horrific" (Atthill 134).[3] It would be unwise to claim, therefore, that the accident must have provoked his short story about railway disaster, **"The Signalman"** (1866), which appeared a year later as part of *Mugby Junction,* the special Christmas issue of *All the Year Round.* Yet there is, I want to argue, an integral connection between Dickens's experience of accident trauma and this ghost story. While the fact of Dickens's own experience of the train crash has sometimes been acknowledged in discussions of **"The Signalman,"** it is usually by way of a closing gesture to the grim and eerie irony that he died on the same day as the accident. To read **"The Signalman"** through the lens of current trauma theory, however, is to see that Dickens's story uncannily apprehends the heart of traumatic experience in its focus on the uncoupling of event and cognition, on belatedness, repetitive and intrusive return, and on a sense of powerlessness at impending disaster. The question that this reading of the story then raises is whether there was a discourse of trauma in the 1860s which could have provided Dickens with a hermeneutic through which to respond to his experience. That question draws us to consider both the pre-Freudian history of trauma and the relation between literature and the psychological and medical discourse of its day.

Trauma has in recent years commanded great interest across a range of disciplines. As trauma theory continues "perking" in literary studies, critics are beginning to think about why trauma should now be claiming such attention (Hartman 537). In a century that has seen cataclysmic and catastrophic activities of many kinds, a concern with aftermath—events and their representation and reconstruction—should come as no surprise. Although no one could claim that the twentieth century has the monopoly on horrific experience, trauma theory, it has been suggested, rose as a response to "modern"

experiences such as shell shock. The writings of Freud and the beginnings of psychoanalysis are often the starting point for trauma theorists who see the interest in and awareness of trauma as part of modernity itself. But the material conditions and technologies we associate with modernity began well before the twentieth century. What of earlier conceptions of psychic trauma? How did Victorians think about experiences of near death, of miraculous survival? How did they understand the effect on consciousness and memory of events and experiences that "went beyond the range of the normal"—events so overwhelming and unassimilable that the ordinary processes of registration and representation were suspended or superseded?

In order to historicize the trauma theory of the twentieth century, it is useful to look at the earlier coincidence of trauma theory and the conditions of modernity manifested in industrial technologies of the Victorian period. As Freud himself remarked in *Beyond the Pleasure Principle* (1920), there is "a condition [which] has *long been known and described* [and] which occurs after severe mechanical concussions, railway disasters and other accidents involving a risk to life; it has been given the name of traumatic neurosis" (12, my emphasis).[4] During the nineteenth century the technology of the railway not only revolutionized travel and conceptions of time and space but gave rise to large-scale, disastrous accidents. The damage to life and limb resulting from such accidents provoked claims against the railroad companies, and these in turn produced the need for insurance companies. Insurance companies were reluctant to pay damages for anything except demonstrable physical injury consequent on the accident. Medical practitioners called upon to verify injury found their attention focused on hitherto unexamined forms of suffering. As a result, the question of injurious effects not consequent on gross mechanical injury but apparently the result of the shock of the accident became a vexed and contentious one in mid-Victorian medicine. Exploring the effects of modernity in the form of railway travel, its disasters, and the statistical risks associated with indemnification and insurance, we encounter an emerging discourse of "psychic shock" that stands behind the development of trauma theory.[5]

Occupied as it is with trains and railway disaster, this essay follows a number of different tracks. First I map the development of a discourse about trauma or "psychic shock" in the 1860s. I am not arguing that before technological accidents there was no trauma, but rather that trauma came to be viewed as a medical condition worthy of notice and study as a result of modern technology and its effects. (This position does not preclude the possibility that the technology was indeed responsible for an increased incidence of trauma.) Freud was interested in what happened to the traumatized patient's memory—whether shocking events were processed and available to recall in the same way as other experiences. The focus on memory and flashback enabled Freud to remark on the peculiar bypassing of conscious memory that characterizes response to trauma. In contrast, the Victorian discourse of nervous shock focused mainly on the effects on the nervous system; the effect of shock on memory is not something that particularly occupies Victorian doctors probing the psychic damage of railway accidents. Why did the Victorians not turn their attention to the connection between trauma and memory dysfunction? What conceptions of memory and particularly "unconscious" memory were prevalent in the mid-Victorian period? In order to probe these questions, I then switch tracks to examine those psychological domains where the Victorians *did* study memory. Of particular relevance here are Victorian constructions of memory under extraordinary but not necessarily traumatic conditions—altered states, such as somnambulism, trance, mesmerism, hypnotism.[6] Under what circumstances is memory lost or retrieved? How is it that knowledge unavailable to the conscious mind can emerge in unusual situations? How, in sum, did Victorians formulate the relationship between conscious memory and what Christopher Bollas has aptly called "the unthought known"? These two tracks connect Victorian psychology (in hindsight) to the discourse of trauma from Freud on to the late-twentieth-century theorizings of Cathy Caruth, Shoshana Felman, Dori Laub, and others, which is increasingly focused on memory and its dysfunctions, on belatedness, repetition, flashback, and hallucination. The last section of this essay will turn to Dickens's story **"The Signalman"** to uncover a subterranean route or switch whereby these two apparently distinct tracks come together (and thus are more nearly resonant with current trauma studies). I will suggest that **"The Signalman"** is a kind of literary missing link between the Victorian discourse of nervous shock and Victorian conceptions of unconscious memory. The discursive development of trauma studies in the mid-1860s may have provided Dickens with a hermeneutic through which he could respond to his own experience, but, more significantly, his sensitivity to altered states and the literary possibilities of the ghost story—a favored genre—helped him to articulate what the nascent study of trauma at this time was not quite yet poised to formulate.

1. MID-VICTORIAN CONCEPTS OF PSYCHIC SHOCK

In or around the mid-1860s, the concept of psychic trauma began to percolate in Victorian Britain. And what brought it to consciousness was, arguably, the railway.[7] To place the railway more squarely within the history of trauma, we may say that the railway accident was to Victorian psychology what World War I and shell shock were to Freudian. The railway accident was the exemplary instance for Victorian medical discourse that propelled the prevailing pathological bias in relation to injury in the direction of a psychic interpretation of injury.

Industrialization and the rise of the insurance company were the twin economic factors in the development of medical interest in this subject. As Henri Ellenberger notes in his magisterial history of the discovery of the unconscious, "the development of industry and the multiplication of industrial accidents on the one side, and the development of insurance companies on the other," meant that "more and more 'official medicine' was on the search for new theories and new therapeutic methods for these neuroses" (245). Similarly, Wolfgang Schivelbusch's 1978 study of the railway journey, which lays the tracks for all future studies in this line, points out that in England by 1864 railroad companies had become legally liable for their passengers' safety and health (134); since only "pathologically demonstrable damage" qualified victims for compensation, those victims who suffered damages without a demonstrable cause created "a legal and medical problem whose solution in the courts depended on the medical profession" (134-35).

In the 1860s the "phenomenon of accident shock," the traumatization of a victim without discernible physical injury, became the object of systematic investigation by the medical profession.[8] Thomas Buzzard, for example, a doctor whose series of articles appeared in the *Lancet* in 1867, was very interested in cases where external injuries were negligible but effects on the nervous system were severe. In one case, he noted, the shock changed the very national constitution of an individual, who transformed from "the most thorough Englishman in all his habits to the manner of the most coxcombical Frenchman" (I: 624). Herbert Page, whose work of the 1880s and 90s is influential, is interested primarily in fright or shock, but he pays attention largely to its effects on the nervous system—hysterical fits, spasms, vomiting, pulse rate, and so on. And though he notes the effect of shock on memory, it is merely to say that it affects energy and concentration rather than the recall of events and incidents of past life (*Railway Injuries* 44). But he does record that patients suffering from traumatic hysteria sometimes have a "great dread of impending evil" (*Injuries of the Spine* 153). They usually sleep badly and are constantly troubled by distressing dreams: "Depend upon it that the man who can sleep naturally and well after a railway collision has not met with any serious shock to his nervous system" (158). He notes too the element of delay or belatedness which will become so important in the Freudian conceptualization of trauma: "Warded off in the first place by the excitement of the scene, the shock is gathering, in the very delay itself, new force from the fact that the sources of alarm are continuous, and for the time all prevalent in the patient's mind" (148). The emphasis on a "continuous" and "prevalent" source of alarm suggests the possession of the patient by the shocking event. William James explained delay by means of the following example in his 1894 review of Pierre Janet's work:

> The fixed ideas may slumber until some weakening of the nervous system favors their morbid activity. E.g., Col. is victim of a railroad accident, and passes six months in the hospital with a grave abdominal injury [. . .] [Six years later] if the old scar be touched, [he suffers] an hysterical attack [. . .] consisting in hallucinations of the railroad tragedy.
>
> (197)

Even this very brief history serves to contextualize and explain Freud's references in *Beyond the Pleasure Principle* to "a condition [which] has long been known and described" (12). Having acknowledged the lengthy history of traumatic neurosis, Freud then proceeds to offer the recent war as the defining moment for diagnosis of psychic shock. On the one hand, Freud indicates a familiarity with the phenomenon of railway trauma; on the other, he seems not to acknowledge the medical studies that had already, for some decades, focused on the absence of gross mechanical force:

> The terrible war which has just ended gave rise to a great number of illnesses of this kind, but it at least put an end to the temptation to attribute the cause of the disorder to organic lesions of the nervous system brought about by mechanical force. [. . .] In the case of the war neuroses the fact that the same symptoms sometimes came about without the intervention of any gross mechanical force seemed at once enlightening and bewildering.
>
> (12)

Freud's study of the dreams of shell-shocked soldiers of the 1914-1918 war provided him with an important insight into the nature of dreams. He noticed that the dreams of the traumatized were markedly different from those of ordinary dreamers in that they woke the patient up "in another fright" (13); they returned him to the scene of horror, reproducing it repeatedly and literally, whereas ordinary dream work consisted of creating scenarios to express fears and desires. Dreaming allowed ordinary patients to release anxieties and so keep sleeping; traumatic dreams woke the patient, and were therefore unable to appease anxiety. This insight in relation to traumatized soldiers allowed Freud to theorize what he had remarked in a less obvious way in his earlier work on traumatic neurosis. The hallmark of trauma, Freud decided, was the inability to possess memory, to make the event the subject of narrative. The memory seemed to possess the sufferer rather than the other way around. Hence Caruth's rearticulation of Freud: "to be traumatized is to be possessed by an image or event" (*Trauma* 5). It has been suggested that trauma involves

the collapse of witnessing and understanding, in that the event can only be witnessed at the cost of recognizing oneself as a witness. "Central to the very immediacy of this experience, that is, is a gap that carries the force of the event and does so precisely at the expense of simple knowledge and memory. The force of this experience would appear to arise precisely [. . .] in the collapse of understanding" (Caruth, *Trauma* 7). Trauma, then, comes to be theorized as the experience in which knowledge and cognition are disjoined. Geoffrey Hartman describes this as the missed encounter, the event "registered rather than experienced" in that "the traumatic event bypasses perception and consciousness, and falls directly into the psyche" (537). The knowledge that the traumatized subject stores is inaccessible to ordinary memory, but signals its presence in the form of intrusive return. It is as if the encounter, having been missed, demands recognition through reenactment rather than recall.

2. Memory, "Unconscious Cerebration" and the "Unthought Known"

> If any one faculty of our nature may be called *more* wonderful than the rest, I do think it is memory. There seems something more speakingly incomprehensible in the powers, the failures, the inequalities of memory, than in any other of our intelligences. The memory is sometimes so retentive, so serviceable, so obedient—at others, so bewildered and so weak—and at others again, so tyrannic, so beyond controul! We are to be sure a miracle every way—but our powers of recollecting and of forgetting do seem peculiarly past finding out.
>
> —Jane Austen, *Mansfield Park* (188)

Fanny Price's awareness of the vagaries of memory serves to indicate what, by the mid-nineteenth century, had become the focus of much scrutiny—those aspects of memory that seemed "peculiarly past finding out": our powers of "recollecting and forgetting," and the operations of unconscious memory. From the first, Freud's work, unlike that of his Victorian predecessors, emphasized the effects of shock on memory. In the review mentioned earlier, James writes also of the studies of two "distinguished Viennese neurologists" for whom hysteria "starts always with a shock, and is a 'disease of the memory'" (199). Although Victorian medical treatises on railway shock and injury move toward a focus on psychic rather than mechanical injury, very little attention is paid to the effect on memory of traumatic shock. Physiologists and psychologists writing about memory are also little interested in the effect of shock, though physical blows to the head prove perennially engaging (see Carpenter, for example, 443-44). In his 1860 treatise, *On Obscure Diseases of the Brain, and Disorders of the Mind,* Forbes Winslow does give some examples of the disruptions in memory after shock, but these are in effect a cabinet of curiosities drawn from cases reported in the previous century rather than a thoroughgoing investigation of what makes one remember or forget in response to extraordinary stimulus. One case, for example, concerns a "lady of rank" who

> experienced a severe shock consequent upon the receipt of the melancholy intelligence of the sudden death of an only and much-beloved child. She continued for several days in a stunned and apparently dying state. She, however, recovered. For many months afterwards her memory exhibited a singular defect. She appeared to have no recollection of the cause of her illness, and of the severe loss she had sustained. When she was informed of the death of her son, for the period of a minute she appeared to realize the melancholy fact; but the impression almost instantly passed away. About nine months from this time she was found dead in her bed. Disease of the heart and brain was said to have been discovered after death.
>
> (407 For further cases, see Winslow 465-66)

In *Diseases of Memory* (1881, trans. 1882), Theodule Ribot, well known for his work in France on physiological psychology, cites cases in which memory becomes more intense in abnormal states and undergoes permanent improvement after illness and shock:

> A man with a "remarkably clear head," [. . .] was crossing a railway in the country when an express train at full speed appeared closely approaching him. He had just time to throw himself down in the center of the road between the two lines of rails, and as the vast train passed over him, the sentiment of impending danger to his very existence brought vividly into his recollection every incident of his former life in such an array as that which is suggested by the promised opening of "the great book at the last great day." Even allowing for exaggeration, these instances show a super-intensity of action on the part of the memory of which we can have no idea in its normal state.
>
> (176)

Ribot rehearses here the widely credited idea that all memory is stored and recoverable. One of the most dramatic and frequently cited instances of this notion is Coleridge's widely quoted account in *Biographia Literaria* (1817) of a young woman in Germany who could neither read nor write, but as a result of a fever began to speak in Latin, Hebrew, and Greek. It was discovered that, as a child, the woman had been looked after by a pastor who had knowledge of these languages and used to recite passages from the Latin and Greek fathers, and Rabbinical texts (Coleridge 112-13). What is critical in the passage from Ribot cited above is the assumption that the "normal state" of memory is merely a less intense version of the "superintensity" occasioned by an extreme situation. The "normal state" of memory is a happy relationship of storage and retrieval, an archive under good management. If memory was thought of as a storehouse of previous thoughts, a kleptomaniac's secret hoard, an engraving or even photograph, the assumption that unusual conditions could suddenly as-

sist in bringing to light the further reaches of such stores is understandable in its appeal. Noting that others have already commented on the remarkable and permanent development of memory after shocks, attacks of smallpox, and other diseases, Ribot concludes that "the mechanism of this metamorphosis being inscrutable, there is no reason why we should dwell on it here" (178). The case histories recited by Winslow and Ribot suggest that the erasure and recovery of memory are equally mysterious processes. Why the one occurs as opposed to the other is as inscrutable as the "mechanism of metamorphosis" itself. What seems undisputed, however, is the miraculous latency of memory.

In *Principles of Mental Physiology* (1874), William Benjamin Carpenter, probably the most authoritative voice on memory in mid-Victorian medicine, sets out the prevailing view of the latency or dormancy of all memory:

> It is now very generally accepted by Psychologists as (to say the least) a predictable doctrine, that any Idea which has once passed through the Mind may be thus reproduced, at however long an interval, through the instrumentality of suggestive action; the recurrence of any other state of consciousness with which that idea was originally linked by Association, being adequate to awaken it also from its dormant or "latent" condition, and to bring it within the "sphere of consciousness."
>
> (429)

Drawing on the image of the railway, which frequently crops up as an apt structuring metaphor in explanations of the relation between conscious and unconscious thinking, Carpenter continues:

> And as our ideas are thus linked in "trains" or "series" which further inosculate with each other like the branch lines of a railway or the ramifications of an artery, so, it is considered, an idea which has been "hidden in the obscure recesses of the mind" for years—perhaps for a lifetime,—and which seems to have completely faded out of the *conscious* Memory [. . .] may be reproduced as by the touching of a spring, through a nexus of suggestion, which we can sometimes trace-out continuously, but of which it does not seem necessary that all the intermediate steps should fall within our cognizance.
>
> (429-30)

Similarly, E. S. Dallas's *The Gay Science* (1866) draws on the idea of traffic between related spheres. The railway being such a visible aspect of modernity in Victorian life, it is not surprising that railway tracks, networks, trains of thought, and lines of communication should come to the aid of those explaining the activity of invisible modes of thought, and, indeed, influence the very way in which the mind's operations could be visualized. A study of psychology and aesthetics, Dallas's text includes a discussion of imagination—the unconscious, or the hidden soul—in its evaluation of current theories of memory. "Between the outer and the inner ring, between our unconscious and our conscious existence, there is a free and a constant but unobserved traffic forever carried on. Trains of thought are continually passing to and fro, from the light into the dark, and back from the dark into the light" (I: 207). One might phrase the matter more succinctly, as Dickens has Mr. Toodle in *Dombey and Son* (1848) sagely remark, "What a Junction a man's thoughts is [. . .] to be sure!" (449).

The idea of memory as a treasure house of stored and recuperable knowledge was notably challenged in the early 1860s by Frances Power Cobbe's emphasis on the fallacies of memory. What we remember, she argued in opposition to the idea of the permanent register, the engraved tablet, are layered reconstructions of memories, where each "fresh trace varies a little from the trace beneath, sometimes magnifying and beautifying it, through the natural bias of the soul to grandeur and beauty, sometimes distorting it through passion or prejudice; in all and every case the original mark is ere long essentially changed" (151). What Cobbe describes here is akin to that which trauma theorists such as Judith Herman (following Janet) would describe as normal, narrative memory. Narrative memory is simply memory that is available to recall and retelling. It can be made the subject of narrative. It is possessed by the subject who remembers and is inevitably shaped by distortions and biases in the process of narrativization. In contrast, traumatic memory is that which lies inaccessible and unpossessed. It is not at the disposal of the subject, but rather able itself to possess the unremembering subject by obtruding on the present in the form of dreams, flashbacks, and hallucinations. It was after all the very literalness of the traumatic memory or dream that alerted Freud to the fact that the process of registering traumatic events and experiences was out of the ordinary. On that basis, we might argue that what made it possible for Freud to recognize traumatic memory was the very normalization of distortion, or what Cobbe calls fallacy. But here, too, as we shall see in Carpenter's work on memory, the Victorians come close to anticipating Freud.

Acknowledging Cobbe's views on the fallacies of memory, Carpenter also challenges the doctrine of memory's indelibility, suggesting that it has been too generally applied; it is "questionable whether *everything* that passes through our Minds thus leaves its impression on that material instrument" (454). Carpenter suggests that we sometimes visualize so strongly that we

> realise [. . .] forgotten experiences, by repeatedly picturing them to ourselves, that the ideas of them attain a force and vividness which equals or even exceeds that

which the actual memory of them would afford. In like manner, when the Imagination has been exercised in a sustained and determinate manner,—as in the composition of a work of fiction,—its ideal creations may be reproduced with the force of actual experiences; and the sense of personal identity may be projected backwards (so to speak) into the characters which the Author has "evolved out of the depths of his own consciousness,"—as Dickens states to have been continually the case with himself.

(455)

The process Carpenter outlines is the exercise of the imagination in creating something apparently fictitious that then assumes a life of its own and, in becoming that with which the author identifies, is able to show him what was hidden or covert within him. The author both creates himself and reveals himself through his characters, an intense form of the process detectable in all memory "creation." And not unexpectedly, Dickens provides an example in Carpenter's explanations, coming to mind as the author most readily associated with imaginative intensity and creative memory.

Even though the tenor of this passage is to question the extent of the "doctrine of indelibility," Carpenter does specify that certain categories of experience are indelible. One of these is especially pertinent to Freudian views about trauma: "Single experiences of peculiar force and vividness, such as are likely to have left very decided traces, although the circumstances of their formation were so unusual as to keep them out of ordinary Associational remembrance" (454). Carpenter refers by way of example to a case (cited in the 1830s by John Abercrombie) involving a fifteen-year-old boy who, while suffering from delirium, recalled aspects of surgery he had undergone at the age of four. He was able to remember scenes he could only have "witnessed" while unconscious and very young. Carpenter's "single experience of peculiar force" indelible and yet unavailable to ordinary associative memory is not unrelated to Freud's traumatic event, the experience of which is unremembered yet belatedly, intrusively, and literally asserted. The point of Carpenter's example is that the boy was not "there" in consciousness and hence one would not have expected him to be able to remember details of the operation; in the case of trauma, the subject is apparently "there" and conscious—so it was expected that physically unscathed victims of railway accidents be able to recall their experiences.

The conundrum of presence and absence of mind was nowhere more intriguing than in states of altered consciousness. The complex history of controversy surrounding concepts such as mesmerism, hypnotism or Braidism, spiritualism, and somnambulism attests to the nineteenth-century fascination with altered states of mind, and with the relation between conscious and (as Carpenter called it) "unconscious cerebration." In part, this fascination with altered states raised the question of what it meant to be human and conscious. What kinds of activity were performed without conscious and voluntary supervision? What force was controlling mental function in states of mind that were not fully conscious? John Abercrombie had in previous decades written about the states of mind distinguished by ideas and images over which we have no conscious control: dreams, somnambulism and double consciousness, insanity and spectral illusion (198-266).[9] The century saw an array of explanations of brain function and physiology, ranging from small concessions to the reflex function of the brain, on the one hand, to theories of the brain as two separate, rigidly divided hemispheres on the other, an idea (put forward in the 1840s by Arthur Wigan) that offered a striking model for mental dissociation (see Winter; Taylor, "Obscure Recesses" 150).

No discussion of Victorian altered states can proceed far without taking account of mesmerism, a powerful if controversial influence in England from the 1830s to 60s. Proponents of mesmerism claimed a great deal on its behalf: as a manifestation of the mind's power it was evidence of the mesmerizer's capacity to transmit his thoughts to the mesmerized subject, and, in the form of "mental travelling" or clairvoyance, was able to surmount obstacles of time and space.[10] Like other new technologies—steam and electricity—which were also revolutionizing experiences of time and space, mesmerism was a technology of the mind, hailed by its adherents in England as progressive and far-reaching. Alison Winter rightly observes that "this generation, surrounded by astonishing changes wrought by science, set few limits on the powers that might be revealed in electricity, light, magnetism, and gases. [. . .] The claim that an imponderable fluid could pass from one individual to another, altering the processes of thought, was astonishing, but just as worthy of serious evaluation as other great scientific assertions" (35). Victorian theories of mesmerism tell us much about the way Victorians construed the unconscious. In his astute assessment of mesmerism and hypnosis Jonathan Miller explains the stakes in terms of the nature and extent of the territory between the "unarguably automatic and the self-evidently voluntary" (18). What was the role of the unconscious, as mid-Victorians such as Carpenter understood it, in the behavioral and cognitive capacities of human beings? Hypnotic trance was important to Carpenter and others because, as the former explained, it was in those states (like hypnosis) where the directing power of the will is suspended, that action is determined by some dominant idea which has temporarily full possession of the mind (see Miller 27). Hypnotic trance confirmed the existence among human beings of an "'automatic self' of which they have no conscious knowledge and over which they have little voluntary control" (28). Differing from the "custodial" unconscious of Freudian theory, this mid-Victorian concept of

unconscious cerebration, Miller suggests, can best be described as enabling: "If consciousness is to implement the psychological tasks for which it is best fitted, it is expedient to assign a large proportion of psychic activity to automatic control: if the situation calls for a high-level managerial decision, the Unconscious will freely deliver the necessary information to awareness" (29). Miller's emphasis on delivery accords with the transportation and railroad metaphors used by Dallas to express the relations between conscious and unconscious activity. Rather than censorship and an edict against knowing, the situation was simply one of efficient delegation and storage. When Miller considers the question of accessibility, it is to contrast the "detention" in which the Freudian unconscious holds its mental contents with the free delivery that characterizes mid-nineteenth-century concepts of the unconscious.

The question of accessibility in the context of traumatic memory is somewhat different, however. When he came to consider traumatic experience, as we have seen, Freud posited a category of experience that was inaccessible in a different way than the repressions of the unconscious. Whereas ordinary dreams were the royal road to the unconscious, the dreams and hallucinations of traumatized patients were too literal and self-referential to lead anywhere but back to the traumatic event itself. They were a reliving rather than a representation of the event, a snapshot rather than a symbology. Caruth argues therefore that trauma can be seen as a symptom of history rather than a symptom of the unconscious. Miller's distinction between Freudian and Victorian ideas of the unconscious becomes less illuminating when we reach the question of trauma. In trauma, it is not relevant whether the unconscious is characterized as censorious, on the one hand, or enabling, on the other, because the nature and effect of the "unthought known" changes. The very nature of traumatic memory as something different from repression takes the question beyond that of voluntary and automatic selves, or unconsciously repressed selves. It is instead a question of the knowing and unknowing self—of how something can be experienced so that it is not available to ordinary consciousness but may be retrieved or reexperienced under the suspension of the will or in a trancelike state.

3. DICKENS: SIGNALING TRAUMA

I turn now to Dickens, who is represented in Carpenter's work, as we saw earlier, as the writer intimately engaged with the imaginative reconstruction of the self through memory, and who also was fascinated by mesmerism over a long period and in a variety of ways. Not only was Dickens a close friend for many years of Dr. John Elliotson, the great pioneer of mesmerism in England, and witness to a large number of displays of animal magnetism, he was himself a practicing mesmerist. Fittingly, he took the role of the Doctor in Elizabeth Inchbald's eighteenth-century farce, *Animal Magnetism* (1788), a play that formed a double bill with *The Frozen Deep* (1857) and was performed in private theatricals (Winter 148).[11] According to Fred Kaplan, Dickens, by the time he went on his Italian trip in 1844, was able to magnetize a range of subjects and was primed to develop an intense relationship with Augusta de la Rue, helping to relieve her "convulsions, distortions of the limbs, aching headaches, insomnia, and a plague of neurasthenic symptoms" through frequent mesmeric therapeutics (Kaplan 77). He was in fact practicing a form of psychotherapy, and working on the assumption that her altered state revealed aspects of personality and psyche that were hidden from her ordinary consciousness. Dickens relied on techniques such as "sleep-waking" and mesmeric trance (77). Through questions to his mesmerized patient, he formulated theories of what was causing her ailments and attempted to battle the dominating phantoms that surfaced when she was in a state of altered consciousness. Though Dickens never abandoned his belief in an independent fluid as the physical basis of magnetism, it was clearly the relation between conscious and unconscious selves that fascinated him about the magnetized state. Dickens seemed to understand that the mesmerized state offered the prospect of finding out what it is we know, but do not know that we know. What later trauma theory would propose was that the traumatized subject, though not somnambulist or mesmerized, was in a state akin to these "altered states." Shock or fright could produce the effect of making memory inaccessible; trance, nightmare, or flashback could return the victim to the unprocessed and terrible knowledge of the traumatic event. Although such propositions were not part of the discourse of nervous shock at the time Dickens suffered his accident, they are nevertheless the stuff of **"The Signalman."** I want to suggest, then, that because Dickens was sympathetic to the possibility of unconscious knowledge, and because he was adept at manipulating the literary possibilities within the genre of the ghost story, in this story he is able to articulate more about the relation of trauma and memory than was available to him in the current discourse on nervous shock. In so doing, he powerfully anticipates the formulations of Freud and later trauma theory.

The genre of the ghost story and trauma narrative have much in common, since to be traumatized is arguably to be haunted, to be living a ghost story: it is "to be possessed by an image or event" (Caruth, *Trauma* 5). It may then seem tautological to say that Dickens's story of uncanny possession is a story of trauma. But even though Dickens's ghost stories frequently objectify states of mind, not all ghost stories are expressive primarily of trauma—*A Christmas Carol* (1843), for example, is a notable exception. In ghost stories, as in trauma, the sanctity of ordered time is violated as the past intrudes on the present. In its depiction of both the

signalman's distress and the narrator's responses, this story dwells on powerlessness, heightened vigilance and a sense of impending doom, uncanny reenactment, and terror at the relived intrusion. These are all legitimate aspects of a tale of horror; they are also all characteristics of trauma. Just as Augusta de la Rue's "phantoms" emerged in the mesmerized state, so in the ghost story Dickens could give play to the phantoms or specters that intruded as hallucinations to demand that the possessed subject revisit areas of experience not fully assimilated. The ghost story was a way of probing unusual psychological states. As Dickens wrote to Elizabeth Gaskell in 1851, ghost stories were illustrative of "particular states of mind and processes of the imagination" (qtd. in Schlicke 249). The possibilities in the ghost story allow Dickens in **"The Signalman"** to confront the disjunction in subjectivity that trauma occasions as he dramatizes the emphatic gap between knowledge and cognition, signing and meaning, the shocking external occurrence and its internal assimilation and representation. The story is Dickens's way of pondering that fateful and fatal gap in the tracks at Staplehurst, a creative way of articulating his personal experience of railway shock that seems, from the vantage point of the present, uncannily prescient of the direction and emphasis that trauma studies would take in the next century.

Perhaps the most compelling aspect of trauma to which the story gives voice is the feeling of powerlessness in the survivor, who may not recall the traumatic event but has an overwhelming sense of impending and unavoidable doom. In the story, the narrator one evening passes a signalman's remote box, hails the signalman, and shows that he wishes to descend to the box and talk to him. The signalman tells the narrator of a "spectre" who has been haunting him. Indeed, he takes the narrator initially to be an apparition or ghost, the very same as the one that has appeared to him on the line near his signal box a number of times. On one occasion, the "spectre" appeared before a terrible collision; then again before the death of a young lady on the train. The signalman imagines that the apparition's reappearance precedes a further tragic event. That turns out to be the signalman's own death.[12] Dickens's story focuses obsessively on the signalman's anguish at receiving a warning in time, but finding it impossible to heed because he does not know about what exactly he is being warned.

With some justification the story could be read as a fantasy of revenge against signalmen, though in the Staplehurst disaster, strictly speaking, it was not the signalman who blundered. The foreman on the job miscalculated the time of the train's arrival; the flagman was too close to give adequate warning of the train's approach. In the story, the signalman is too close to the train and does not or cannot heed the warning as the engine bears down on him. Ironically, the signalman lives in a state of heightened vigilance, yet dies because he is unable to read the precise import of the warning; he is powerless to prevent his own death on the tracks. But there is also the sense that the signalman does not want to prevent his death. In this way, he may be seen as exemplifying the death drive that Freud associates with traumatic reenactment: he does not heed the whistle and literally allows death to overtake him as the train comes upon him from behind and cuts him down. On the one hand, Freud saw traumatic reenactment as the life-affirming attempt to master the stimulus retrospectively through repetition; on the other, he later came to see the daemonic content of reenactment as evidence of the death instinct.[13] If the signalman in some sense exemplifies the death instinct, the story as a whole may be seen as a traumatic reenactment: Dickens returns imaginatively to the site of the railway accident in order to master a stimulus that resists mastery.

Dickens's story also apprehends the repetitive cycle of trauma. Based structurally on the principle of repetition, **"The Signalman"** reveals the hallmark of trauma as unbidden repetition and return. In Dickens's story the trauma repeats and accumulates. Not only is the signalman compelled to witness a terrible train disaster, he is tantalized through the "spectre's" visitations by an impossible clairvoyance. The trauma compounds as the signalman is twice forewarned but is both times unable to avert death and disaster. After the first terrible accident on the line, the signalman thinks he has recovered from witnessing the carnage: "Six or seven months passed, and I had recovered from the surprise and shock" (531). At that point, the specter appears to him again and the next calamity occurs: "I heard terrible screams and cries. A beautiful young lady had died instantaneously in one of the compartments and was brought in here, and laid down on this floor between us" (532). Now the specter has appeared again, signaling to him some further calamity about to occur on the line, and prompting, the signalman laments, "this cruel haunting of him" (533). Haunted not only by the past, but by a past that seems to project itself into the future, the signalman is subjected to relentless repetition and can avail himself of neither hindsight nor foresight.

As it is understood today, trauma is the inability to know the past as past—it is therefore a "disease of time" in which the events of the past continually obtrude on the present in the form of flashbacks and hallucinations (Young 7). Traumatic memory is the return that does not recognize itself as a return. Like the train disaster that is literally a disruption of linearity, the narrative of **"The Signalman"** disrupts linear sequence. In part, this sense arises from the clairvoyant specter, whose gestures enact and predict each of three train disasters before they occur. The sense of disturbed linearity or chronology arises also from the fact that the narrator seems to be taking part in something that has already happened. That is, the narrative is itself part of

some uncanny repetition. The fact that the narrator uses the words, "For God's sake, clear the way," themselves repeated many times in the course of the story, could suggest that the narrator has just repeated his part in the replay of a past he "knows" but does not know he knows.

In support of this line of thinking, the narrator from the outset seems inexplicably drawn to approach the signalman, all the odder because initially he says he is not someone given to starting up conversations.[14] Understandably the signalman imagines that the narrator is himself a further spectral illusion, especially since the narrator hails him with the exact words that the specter has already used. After a time the signalman seems reassured that the rational, skeptical narrator is not a ghost, and confides his story to him. By persistently dismissing as "imagination" what the signalman says he has seen, by construing recurrence as coincidence, by remaining stubbornly unbelieving, the narrator refuses to witness the signalman's hallucination or spectral illusion. He refuses, in effect, to witness the trauma. But it is arguably inscribed upon him nonetheless, and he is now (as narrator) participating in the repetition by telling the story of it. When the narrator arrives at the tracks for the third time, he is struck with a "nameless horror" because he sees the "appearance of a man" in the tunnel and clearly thinks he is seeing a ghost (535). The horror that oppresses him passes when he sees that the figure is a real man. Horror gives way to fear that something is wrong. He then learns of the signalman's death. All would appear to be resolved for the rational narrator, except for the fact that the words the engine driver called out were the very ones in the narrator's thoughts. Despite the matter-of-factness of the coda, it is clear that the narrator too will be haunted by the words, "For God's sake, clear the way."

It is this widening implication and involvement that warns the reader against focusing only on the signalman and seeing him as a pathological case. Graeme Tytler, for example, has diagnosed the signalman as suffering from monomania—a clinical condition in which the patient is obsessed by one dominating idea. A man with a one-track mind, the signalman is undeniably fixated. But he could equally well be diagnosed as suffering from Abercrombie's spectral illusion or Wigan's split self. John Stahl, meanwhile, has seen in the story a critique of industrialization in Dickens's representation of the alienated labor of the signalman and the stress his job entails. But rather than pathologizing the signalman as a "case of partial insanity" (421) or substituting an alternate diagnosis stemming from stress in the workplace, I want to emphasize how the narrator and reader are drawn into the ongoing trauma, and the way the entire narrative is shaped by and expressive of the logic of trauma.

If the specter can be seen as an articulation of the signalman's traumatized consciousness, the narrator shares characteristics of the signalman that suggest he is not just a detached interlocutor, auditor, or reporter. The signalman thinks initially that the narrator is a specter; the narrator has a "monstrous thought" that the signalman is a spirit. Each finds himself in a position that makes him feel compelled to act and assume responsibility for the general safety of those on the line. When the signalman sees the apparition for a third time, he is (literally) beside himself to interpret the warning and forestall the disaster. But he cannot. Similarly, the narrator feels himself compelled to act: "But what ran most in my thoughts was the consideration how ought I to act, having become the recipient of this disclosure" (534). The narrator is less worried about the uninterpretable spectral warnings than he is about the mental stability of the signalman and his job performance under present stress. He resolves to try to calm the signalman as much as possible and to return the next morning to visit with him the "wisest medical practitioner [. . .] and to take his opinion" (535). He is also too late. The specter appears to the signalman on three occasions; the narrator descends to the signalman's box three times; the words the narrator uses are the words that the ghost has used and the train driver will use; the gesture that the signalman describes is given words by the narrator but, significantly, he does not speak these words—"For God's sake, clear the way"—before the engine driver tells the narrator that those are in fact the words he used. The narrator, the signalman, the specter, and the engine driver are all bound together in a series of overlapping occurrences and repeated occurrences and expressions, in a history that seems to have begun before the narration begins and will continue after it ends.

Trauma vexes the boundaries between outside and inside; recent theorists have remarked that trauma is a situation in which the outside goes inside without mediation (see Caruth, *Unclaimed Experience* 59). In **"The Signalman,"** Dickens expresses the internal dislocations associated with the external accident. Measuring the distance between Dickens's article "Need Railway Travellers be Smashed?" and his story **"The Signalman"** we see—genre and overt intention notwithstanding—a shift in emphasis in Dickens's growing apprehension of railway disaster. This shift in Dickens is very much in line with what railway historian Ralph Harrington has suggested about perceptions of railway disaster in the period. Whereas the railway was associated initially with the external destruction of landscape in its construction and of people in the wake of its accidents, it came later to provoke anxieties about internal disruption. Harrington also notes that the later part of the nineteenth century saw a change in the way people viewed accidents. Rather than *private* (individualized) happenings they became *public* ones, affecting or concerning the whole of society (1-2).[15] The paradox of railway shock, then, for the Victorians, was that what seemed insignificant and hidden—delayed nervous shock without physical injury—was nevertheless public in its significance. This paradox is articulated in **"The Signalman,"** where, although the emphasis is on the internal disruption and fragmentation of trauma, there is undeniably a public dimension to the experience, both the signalman's sense of being at once responsible yet powerless, and in the communication or transmission of the trauma to the narrator.

As the editor of widely read journals, and in his novels and stories, Dickens espoused many public causes, championing the individual plight and exposing the public responsibility for what may have appeared to be merely personal or private hardship. Dickens, it is fair to say, is preeminently the Victorian writer who claims the public dimension of private trauma. No stranger to traumatic experience before the railway accident, as his continual, fictive reenactments of abandonment and childhood abuse attest, Dickens was perhaps brought through the Staplehurst accident to a sharper intimation of the nature of trauma than ever before. He lost his voice in that accident to find it later, as I have argued, in articulating in this story of ghostly clairvoyance and hindsight the characteristics of trauma barely broached in the discourse of nervous shock during the 1860s.

Notes

I would like to thank James Eli Adams, Andrew Miller, and the anonymous readers at *Victorian Studies* for their helpful comments and suggestions.

1. It was only in 1980 that the third edition of the DSM (The American Psychiatric Association's *Diagnostic and Statistical Manual of Mental Disorders*) included a detailed set of diagnostic criteria for PTSD (ctd. in Mendelson 186). Biographers have not generally remarked on the fact that Dickens suffered post-traumatic stress disorder. Ackroyd, for example, says only that "the great conceiving power of Charles Dickens was [. . .] turned into a medium for recurrent and conscious nightmare" (1017).

2. My account here draws on the fuller treatment of this incident and Dickens's reactions offered by Ackroyd (1017) and Johnson (II: 1021).

3. Most memorable perhaps is the personification of the engine in *Dombey and Son* (1848) as a bloodthirsty monster, Death itself. There the railway as a predatory fiend that licks up the tracks and whatever falls in its path is not only identified with the villain Carker, himself predatory and cat-like, but is his nemesis. Extending Robin Atthill's analysis, David Seed suggests that "from the very first the railway was for Dickens associated with violence and mystery" (47).

4. Freud repeatedly gives the railway accident as an example of the disaster that produces trauma. See for example, *Studies on Hysteria* (1893-95), *SE* 2: 213.

5. Among the historians of medicine, psychoanalysis, and technology who have focused on the pre-Freudian history of trauma and the railway, see especially Hacking; Harrington; Schivelbusch; Caplan; Drinka; Young.

6. For a useful general overview of Victorian theories of unconscious memory, see Taylor, "Obscure Recesses" (153-158).

7. The advent of the railway accident as an important moment in the genealogy of trauma has been recognized by such theorists as Hacking and Leys.

8. Schivelbusch charts this movement, drawing on testimony from Dickens himself, after the Staplehurst crash, and that of other nineteenth-century passengers who escaped unscathed but suffered shock. See also Harrington's thorough discussion of Erichsen and Page.

9. For a more detailed discussion of Abercombie's four states, see Taylor, *In the Secret Theatre of Home,* 55.

10. Taylor notes that theories like Wigan's fed into the fin de siecle's fascination with split selves such as Jekyll and Hyde ("Obscure Recesses" 149).

11. The story has attracted a wide variety of interpretations. See Day; Greenman; Mengel "Structure and Meaning"; Seed; Stahl; Tytler.

12. As the editor of popular journals Dickens had often featured articles on the railway and on railway safety. His essay "Need Railway Travellers be Smashed?" which appeared in the 29 November 1851 issue of *Household Words,* is a vigorous and strident argument for reforms in railroad safety mechanisms. This article illustrates the crusading and aggrieved tone the journal took on behalf of innocent and endangered travelers; it concerns the invention of a signaling device that may protect travelers from collisions and lessen the risks associated with train travel. (See also Mengel, *The Railway Through Dickens's World,* a useful anthology of railway literature.) Fourteen years later he was the victim of human error, still today the greatest obstacle in providing safe railway travel.

13. See Judith Herman's discussion of the death instinct and traumatic reenactment (41).

14. The identity of the narrator has been variously construed by critics. Seed, for example, sees him as one of the Barbox Brothers, who narrated the earlier parts of *Mugby Junction*; Greenman argues that the narrator should be taken as an independent (47). See also Stahl and Day.

15. Harrington is referring here to the work of Roger Cooter.

Works Cited

Ackroyd, Peter. *Dickens.* London: Minerva, 1991.

Abercrombie, John. *Inquiries Concerning the Intellectual Powers and the Investigation of Truth.* New York: Collins, 1852.

Atthill, Robin. "Dickens and the Railway." *English* 13 (1961): 130-35.

Austen, Jane. *Mansfield Park.* 1814. Oxford: Oxford UP, 1970.

Bollas, Christopher. *The Shadow of the Object: Psychoanalysis of the Unthought Known.* London: Free Association Press, 1988.

Buzzard, Thomas. "On Cases of Injury from Railway Accidents." *Lancet* (1867): I: 389-91; 453-54; 509-10; 623.

Caplan, Eric. "Trains, Brains and Sprains: Railway Spine and the Origins of Psychoneuroses." *Bulletin of the History of Medicine* 69:3 (1995): 387-419.

Carpenter, William Benjamin. *Principles of Mental Physiology.* 4th ed., 1876. New York: Appleton, 1890.

Caruth, Cathy. *Trauma: Explorations in Memory.* Baltimore: Johns Hopkins UP, 1995.

———. *Unclaimed Experience: Trauma, Narrative, and History.* Baltimore: Johns Hopkins UP, 1996.

Cobbe, Frances Power. "The Fallacies of Memory." *Hours of Work and Play.* 1867. Taylor and Shuttleworth 150-154.

Coleridge, S. T. *The Collected Works of Samuel Taylor Coleridge.* Vol. 7. Ed. Kathleen Coburn. London: Routledge and Kegan Paul, 1983.

Dallas, E. S. *The Gay Science.* 2 vols. London: Chapman & Hall, 1866.

Day, Gary. "Figuring Out 'The Signalman': Dickens and the Ghost Story." Eds. Clive Bloom, et al. *Nineteenth-Century Suspense: From Poe to Conan Doyle.* London: Macmillan, 1988. 26-45.

Dickens, Charles. *Dombey and Son.* 1848. Oxford: World's Classics, 1982.

———. "The Signalman." *Christmas Stories.* Oxford: Oxford UP, 1956.

———. "Need Railway Travellers be Smashed?" *Household Words.* 29 November 1851: 217-21.

Drinka, George. *The Birth of Neurosis: Myth, Malady and the Victorians.* New York: Simon & Schuster, 1984.

Ellenberger, Henri. *The Discovery of the Unconscious: The History and Evolution of Dynamic Psychiatry.* New York: Basic Books, 1970.

Erichsen, John Eric. *On Railway and Other Injuries of the Nervous System.* London: Walton, 1866.

Freud, Sigmund. *The Standard Edition of the Complete Psychological Works of Sigmund Freud.* Ed. James Strachey. London: Hogarth Press, 1955.

———. *Beyond the Pleasure Principle. Standard Edition.* 18: 1-65.

———. *Studies on Hysteria. Standard Edition.* Vol. 2.

Greenman, David. "Dickens' Ultimate Achievements in the Ghost Story: 'To be Taken with a Grain of Salt' and 'The Signalman.'" *The Dickensian* 85 (Spring 1989): 40-48.

Hacking, Ian. *Rewriting the Soul: Multiple Personality and the Sciences of Memory.* Princeton: Princeton UP, 1995.

Harrington, Ralph. "The Railway Accident: Trains, Trauma and Technological Crisis in Nineteenth-Century Britain." 22 June 1999. http://www.york.ac.uk/inst/irs/irshome/papers/rlyacc.htm.

Hartman, Geoffrey H. "On Traumatic Knowledge and Literary Studies." *New Literary History* (1996): 537-63.

Herman, Judith. *Trauma and Recovery.* New York: Basic Books, 1992.

James, Williams. Review. *The Psychological Review* 1 (1894): 195-200.

Johnson, Edgar. *Charles Dickens: His Tragedy and His Triumph.* 2 vols. London: Gollancz, 1953.

Kaplan, Fred. *Dickens and Mesmerism: The Hidden Springs of Fiction.* Princeton: Princeton UP, 1975.

Leys, Ruth. *Trauma: A Genealogy.* Chicago: U of Chicago P, 2000.

Mendelson, Danuta. *The Interfaces of Medicine and Law.* Aldershot: Ashgate/Dartmouth, 1998.

Mengel, Ewald. "Structure and Meaning in Dickens's 'The Signalman.'" *Studies in Short Fiction* 20 (1983): 271-80.

———, ed. *The Railway Through Dickens's World.* Frankfurt: Peter Lang, 1989.

Miller, Jonathan. "Going Unconscious." *Hidden Histories of Science.* Ed. R. B. Silvers. New York: New York Review, 1995.

Page, Herbert. *Injuries of the Spine and Spinal Cord.* London: Churchill, 1883.

———. *Railway Injuries, With Special Reference to Those of the Back and Nervous System in Their Medico-Legal and Clinical Aspects.* London: Griffin, 1891.

Ribot, Theodule. *Diseases of Memory: An Essay in the Positive Psychology.* Trans. William Huntingdon Smith. New York: Appleton and Co., 1887.

Schivelbusch, Wolfgang. *The Railway Journey: The Industrialization of Time and Space in the Nineteenth Century.* Berkeley: U of California P, 1977.

Schlicke, Paul, ed. *Oxford Reader's Companion to Dickens.* Oxford: Oxford UP, 1999.

Seed, David. "Mystery in Everyday Things: Charles Dickens' 'Signalman.'" *Criticism* 23 (1981): 42-57.

Stahl, John. "The Sources and Significance of the Revenant in Dickens's 'The Signalman.'" *Dickens Studies Newsletter* 11 (1980): 98-101.

Taylor, Jenny Bourne. *In the Secret Theatre of Home: Wilkie Collins, Sensation Narrative and Nineteenth-Century Psychology.* London: Routledge, 1988.

———. "Obscure Recesses: Locating the Victorian Unconscious." *Writing and Victorianism.* Ed. J. B. Bullen. London: Longman, 1997. 137-79.

———and Sally Shuttleworth, eds. *Embodied Selves: An Anthology of Psychological Texts 1830-1890.* Oxford: Oxford UP, 1998.

Tytler, Graeme. "Charles Dickens's 'The Signalman': A Case of Partial Insanity." *History of Psychiatry* 8 (1997): 421-32.

Winslow, Forbes. *On Obscure Diseases of the Brain and Disorders of the Mind: Their Incipient Symptoms, Pathology, Diagnosis, Treatment, and Prophylaxis.* London: John Churchill, 1860.

Winter, Alison. *Mesmerized: Powers of Mind in Victorian Britain.* Chicago: U of Chicago P, 1998.

Young, Allan. *The Harmony of Illusions: The Invention of Post-Traumatic Stress Disorder.* Princeton: Princeton UP, 1995.

Norris Pope (essay date July 2001)

SOURCE: Pope, Norris. "Dickens's 'The Signalman' and Information Problems in the Railway Age." *Technology and Culture* 42, no. 3 (July 2001): 436-61.

[*In the following essay, Pope illuminates mid-Victorian attitudes about railway operation and safety within the context of "The Signalman," emphasizing the public's growing awareness of the need for fast and reliable information.*]

This examination of public attitudes toward railway signaling and railway safety takes as its starting point a short story by Charles Dickens titled **"The Signalman."** This story first appeared as a chapter of *Mugby Junction,* the 1866 extra Christmas number of Dickens's weekly journal *All the Year Round.*[1] Its title was an obvious play on Rugby Junction, an important stop on the London and Northwestern Railway and the Midland Railway, and at the time probably the most well-known junction station in England. For Dickens, Mugby Junction served as both an organizing device and a metaphor, naming a place where multiple narratives cross and interact, and where possibilities for various beginnings and various endings are drawn together. The story's initial reception was unremarkable, apart from arousing some mild indignation on the part of a railway official and two pamphlet writers, who sought to defend the refreshment room at Rugby Junction. Dickens had a longstanding gripe about railway refreshment rooms, and an incident of rudeness that he had experienced there in April 1866 provided him with comic material for a satire on such establishments in the third chapter of *Mugby Junction.*[2] Largely in response to the railway material in *Mugby Junction,* Dickens was asked to speak at the annual dinner of the Railway Benevolent Institution in 1868, where he gave an amusing speech in praise of railway servants and in support of the institution.[3]

"The Signalman" appeared as the fourth chapter of *Mugby Junction,* under the heading "No. 1 Branch Line." It was written entirely by Dickens, and is classed among his ghost stories—a "Tale of Presentiment," as Charles Kent labeled it in a December 1866 review.[4] It has never been seriously considered, however, within the context of railway signaling technology, the system for providing advance information about traffic and line conditions on which railway safety depended.[5] This omission is puzzling, because Dickens wrote the story little more than a year after the Staplehurst accident, in which he was involved as a passenger. The result of a signaling failure, this accident was the most traumatic experience of the final decade of his life. Moreover, Dickens's weekly periodicals *Household Words* and *All the Year Round* each devoted articles to railway signaling.[6] The most interesting of these had just appeared in *All the Year Round,* in October 1866. Titled "The Hole in the Wall," this essay provided a vivid description of the workings of a very important and technologically advanced signal box that controlled access to the two lines accommodating all inbound and outbound traffic serving the Brighton Line platforms at Victoria Station.[7] **"The Signalman"** thus touched upon issues of railway operation and railway safety that closely concerned Dickens's mid-Victorian readers, the first generation to experience high-speed railway travel and high-density railway traffic.

Technological development always takes place within multiple contexts, of which public sentiment is only one. But public sentiment was especially important in the case of Victorian railways, which were created by parliamentary act and depended upon the public for patronage. Indeed, public concern about railway safety played a critical role in shaping the behavioral and regulatory context within which Victorian railways operated, just as consumer demand for greater speed and more frequent service played a part in increasing the dangers to which critics reacted. My goal here will be to help illuminate the reception of Victorian railways by emphasizing growing public awareness of the railways' unprecedented need for rapid and unfailingly accurate information handling—the precondition for safe and efficient operation within increasingly complex systems.

Although by no means a technical expert on railways, Dickens provides an instructive lens through which to view this topic. As Humphry House pointed out many years ago, Dickens was a particularly acute observer of the effects of the railway revolution, both individual and social, and he touched upon railway operations frequently in his writings from the mid-1840s onward.[8] Moreover, his standing as a literary celebrity from very early in his career guaranteed him a significant public voice. "It is scarcely conceivable," Harriet Martineau wrote in the late 1840s, "that anyone should . . . exert a stronger social influence than Mr. Dickens has in his power."[9] Relentlessly active, Dickens remained a public figure throughout his life, devoting remarkable energies to his fiction, journalism, editorial work, public speaking, reading tours, and involvement in a wide range of voluntary and philanthropic causes. If his "sentimental radicalism," as Walter Bagehot termed it, struck a highly responsive chord in large sections of his Victorian audience, it was in no small measure because his concerns were also the concerns of his readers—in this case, concerns fully justified by the safety issues surrounding the operation of mid-Victorian railways.[10]

RAILWAY ACCIDENTS

In a three-month period that included the Staplehurst accident, the London *Times* published forty-eight articles and notes concerning railway accidents (not including leaders devoted to railway safety or discussions of railway safety within articles about individual railway companies or shareholders' meetings). Only eight of these dealt with the Staplehurst accident. This total was not unusually high: in the following three months, the paper published sixty-five pieces on the same topic.[11] In light of such attention, it is easy to see why a writer for Dickens's *All the Year Round* could claim in 1862 that "railway collisions, in spite of our greater experience, become annually more disastrous and more frequent," a belief that was widely shared by the riding public in this period.[12]

Railway officials were quick to rebut the view that railway travel was becoming more dangerous, often using detailed statistics to show its safety in relation to the massive growth in passenger miles.[13] H. W. Tyler, a government railway inspector often highly critical of railway practices, concluded flatly in 1862 that "railway travelling is safer than any other mode of travelling," and Samuel Smiles, in the preface to the 1868 edition of his biography of the Stephensons, noted that more people in Great Britain were killed by lightning in 1866 than were killed as railway passengers "from causes beyond their own control."[14] But public concern mirrored the increasingly common experience of railway travel and the novel sensations of high speed and growing traffic density. Whether outwardly expressed or experienced subconsciously, anxieties about the perils of high-speed railway travel and what has been called the "technological accident" were commonplace throughout the mid-Victorian era. Advances in railway technology thus brought with them a growing awareness of the increasingly lethal consequences of technological failure.[15] And with reason: heavy passenger trains routinely ran at speeds in excess of fifty and sometimes sixty miles per hour, generally without the benefit of continuous braking—a safety feature not made compulsory for passenger trains until the Regulation of Railways Act of 1889, which insisted, among other things, that all passenger trains be equipped with air brakes that could be applied simultaneously in each carriage from the locomotive.[16] Moreover, the traffic density was truly extraordinary: Clapham Junction, for example, had to handle 700 trains per day in this period; Cannon Street, a commuter station for the South Eastern Railway, was handling upwards of 525 trains per day coming in or going out; and London Bridge Station, albeit a through station rather than a terminal station, had to handle on some days as many as 1,200 trains either stopping or passing through.[17] Unsurprisingly, the speed and complexity of Victorian railways were thus sources of both pride and alarm. In a famous treatise on railways published in 1850, for example, Dionysius Lardner—a leading if sometimes ineffectual exponent of railways (Dickens once referred to him as a "prince of humbugs"[18])—recommended against riding in express trains whenever possible.[19] And Dickens himself avoided express trains for some time after the Staplehurst accident, noting that fast railway travel left him nervously exhausted.[20]

The Staplehurst accident, which occurred on 9 June 1865, involved the Folkestone Boat Express, on which Dickens was returning from France.[21] The train derailed on a viaduct near Staplehurst, in Kent, killing ten passengers and injuring many more. **"The Signalman"** was also written only five years after the widely publicized Clayton Tunnel disaster, at the time the worst railway accident in English history, which figures briefly but importantly in Dickens's story.[22] All three of these episodes—two actual and one fictional—turned on information ambiguities and information failures within complex systems. The problematization of this issue in **"The Signalman"** thus reflects an important public question, easy to overlook today when a high degree of trust in technology and complex systems is an axiom of modernity.[23]

FICTIONAL NARRATIVE AND OFFICIAL NARRATIVE

The role of information and misinformation in Dickens's story and in the two railway accidents is easy to summarize. **"The Signalman"** has a simple but effective plot. Its narrator, out for an evening stroll along a railway line, is attracted to an isolated signal box at the bottom of a steep cutting, just outside the entrance to a tunnel. He spots the signalman below, who responds peculiarly to the sudden appearance of a figure above—a reaction that evokes the narrator's curiosity. The next evening, at a time appointed by the signalman, the narrator returns to the signal box for a second visit, and the signalman reveals the source of his agitation. Some years before, a ghostly messenger had appeared to him, hovering near the danger lamp just outside the tunnel where the narrator had stood the previous evening, signaling frantically as if trying to warn of some impending catastrophe. Shortly afterward, an appalling train wreck occurred inside the tunnel, in which many passengers perished. Some months later, the ghostly messenger reappeared, again seeming to give some kind of warning signal. A little while later, a young girl died inside a railway carriage, just as the train passed the signalman (who was obliged to signal the train to a stop, because no effective communication existed in this period between passenger compartments and train crew—apparatus not made mandatory until the 1868 Regulation of Railways Act).[24] And now the ghostly messenger has returned, but trying to warn of what impending disaster? The narrator agrees to return the next evening, to see whether he can do anything to allay the signalman's acute anxiety, which he fears might endanger public safety. But when he does, he finds a solemn group assembled near the signal box, discussing a gruesome accident: earlier that day, the signalman himself had been struck by a locomotive and killed.[25]

The Clayton Tunnel disaster, the basis for the first accident described by Dickens's signalman, occurred on 25 August 1861. There are some differences in the testimony of witnesses, so the following account of the accident is based on the conclusions of H. W. Tyler, the Board of Trade inspector who conducted the official inquiry and one of the leading experts on railway safety in this period.[26] The accident occurred on a Sunday morning, when the London, Brighton, and South Coast Railway had scheduled three trains from Brighton to London in close succession. The first was a fortnightly excursion train originating in Portsmouth; the second was an excursion train originating in Brighton; and the third was an ordinary train from Brighton. According to the advertised schedule, the trains were to have left Brighton at 8:05, 8:15, and 8:30 A.M., respectively. Because the Portsmouth train was late, however, the actual departure times from Brighton appear to have been 8:28, 8:30 or 8:31, and 8:35—thus violating in at least one case and probably two the company's rule that a minimum separation of five minutes between trains was to be enforced at all stations and signal points.

Clayton Tunnel was just over five miles outside Brighton, at the end of a curved section of line that restricted visibility for trains approaching from the south. The tunnel was the only section of the line that was operated on the block system. Under this system, a signalman was stationed at each end of the tunnel, in communication with the signalman at the other end by electric telegraph—a system in operation at the tunnel since 1842. The tunnel was also protected at both ends by distant signals that operated automatically as well as manually. Whenever a train passed one of these signals, the locomotive's wheel flanges displaced a treadle, which was designed to change the signal immediately to danger. For added safety, a bell sounded in the signalman's hut whenever a train activated the signal, and the signalman had to return the signal manually to all clear for any subsequent train, once he had been explicitly informed by telegraph that the initial train had cleared the other end of the tunnel.

At the Brighton end of the tunnel, the distant signal was located 300 yards from the signalman's hut. The sequence of miscommunication that led to the accident arose from the malfunction of this signal's self-acting mechanism—a classic "revenge effect" of a technology introduced to enhance safety.[27] When the first train passed the signal on its way into the tunnel, the signal failed to change automatically to danger for the following train. The signalman at the Brighton end, whose name was Killick, might have recognized this immediately, had he been in his hut and observed that no bell sounded. He was outside his hut, however, and did not immediately notice the signal failure. Following proper procedures, he returned to his hut as the train passed, and sent the appropriate train-in-tunnel message to the signalman at the London end of the tunnel, a man named Brown. Only then did Killick notice that his distant signal had not changed to danger—by which time the second train had already passed the signal. Killick had no home signal, so he seized his red danger flag and waved it desperately at the second train, which was just passing his hut and heading into the tunnel. Once the train had disappeared into the tunnel, Killick gave a second train-in-tunnel message to Brown. After a brief period of anxious uncertainty, he again telegraphed Brown, this time asking whether the tunnel was clear. It is not certain whether Brown simply forgot that he had

received *two* train-in-tunnel messages, or whether he assumed that Killick had sent two messages by mistake. In any event, because the first train had cleared the tunnel, he sent a message to Killick to say that the tunnel was now clear. Unhappily, however, the driver of the second train had managed to catch a glimpse of Killick's danger flag as he entered the tunnel, and he had brought his train to a halt as quickly as he could, which was perforce a considerable distance inside the tunnel. He then began backing his train slowly toward the Brighton end, to ask what the problem was. By this time, the third train was approaching the tunnel's distant signal. Having been informed that the tunnel was clear, Killick lowered the signal from the danger position, and he also gave the driver of the third train an all-clear signal with his white hand flag, as the locomotive passed his hut. The third train therefore entered the tunnel under full steam, at a speed of around 25 miles an hour, where it smashed violently into the second train, which was still moving backwards, at a point approximately 200 yards inside the tunnel. The locomotive knocked the rear brake van off the rails, but then rose up as it plowed into the final passenger carriage, eventually coming to rest on top of it. Amid escaping steam, burning coals, and hideous wreckage, the passengers in this final car, as Tyler put it, "met with an awful fate." Of twenty-four people in the car, only three were pulled out alive. In all, twenty-three people were killed and 176 more were injured in the accident, described by the *Morning Chronicle* as "without parallel in the annals of railway misfortune."[28]

The Staplehurst accident, which killed ten people almost four years later, happened during repairs to the Beult viaduct, on the main line of the South Eastern Railway.[29] The viaduct, one of three just east of Staplehurst Station, carried the line roughly ten feet above the bed of a muddy stream. It was built of brick piers linked by cast-iron trough girders, eight spans in all, with wooden timbers and rails on top. The wooden timbers, referred to as baulks, needed to be replaced. According to F. H. Rich, the railway inspector who provided the official report on the accident, the work of replacing the timbers had extended over a period of eight or ten weeks. The task was organized to allow the replacement of individual timbers and the reattachment of the rails during intervals between passenger trains, thus avoiding having the traffic run in both directions on a single line of track. This procedure had worked very smoothly for almost the entire project—so smoothly, in fact, that no printed notices about the repairs had been given to engine drivers, and no passenger trains had been delayed by the work. (The only trains to be stopped were two slow ballast trains and one locomotive traveling on its own.)

Company regulations specified that an obstructed line was to be protected during work periods by fog detonators placed at 250-yard intervals from the work site up to a distance of 1,000 yards, where someone was to be stationed with a signal flag. During work on the Beult viaduct, however, the work foreman, John Benge, had not bothered with detonators, and he had in fact placed his up-line flagman, John Wiles, at a telegraph post only 544 yards away from the viaduct. Far worse, however, Benge had failed to read his time schedule carefully for 9 June. The Folkestone Boat Express was a "tidal," which meant that it operated according to the arrival time of the channel packet, rather than at the same time each day. Benge's mistake was to take the train's projected arrival time on the 10th for its projected arrival time on the 9th, when it was due just over two hours earlier. As a result, the train reached the viaduct at a time Benge believed entirely safe for working, and when two rails had been removed. The engine driver attempted to stop the moment he saw Wiles's red flag, but he could not stop his thirteen-car train in time. The locomotive, tender, and leading brake van made it across the viaduct on the beams, but the derailed tender broke off the outside portion of one of the iron girders. The first carriage, carrying second-class passengers, stayed on the viaduct, but with its rear wheels hanging over the edge. The next carriage, a first-class carriage in which Dickens was a passenger, ended up hanging precariously, with its front end still attached to the preceding car, and the other end resting on the ground below. The next seven cars fell completely off the viaduct, ending up upside down or on their sides in the muddy stream bed below.[30]

"No imagination," Dickens wrote to Thomas Mitton four days after the accident, "can conceive the ruin of the carriages, or the extraordinary weights under which the people were lying, or the complications into which they were twisted up among iron and wood, and mud and water." Although Dickens's assistance to the injured and dying earned him recognition in the press and from the South Eastern Railway, he was reluctant to speak publicly about the experience. "I don't want to be examined at the inquest and I don't want to write about it. I could do no good either way, and I could only seem to speak about myself, which, of course, I would rather not do. . . . I instantly remembered that I had the MS. of a number [of *Our Mutual Friend*] with me, and clambered back into the carriage for it. But in writing these scanty words of recollection I feel the shake and am obliged to stop."[31] As Dickens later put it, in the final sentence of his postscript to *Our Mutual Friend*, "I can never be much nearer parting company with my readers for ever, than I was then, until there shall be written against my life, the two words with which I have this day closed this book:—The End."[32]

In his letter to Mitton, however, Dickens was not entirely candid about the reasons for his reticence: his traveling companion was his mistress, Ellen Ternan,

along with Ellen's mother.[33] The railway's signaling failure thus has an ironic analog in Dickens's own efforts to conceal information.

RAILWAY INFORMATION AND RAILWAY SAFETY

Occurring at a time when he was heavily dependent on railway travel for his public reading tours and for commuting between Gad's Hill and London, the Staplehurst accident intensified Dickens's concerns for railway safety and his awareness of the importance of efficient signaling. Signaling failure, however, was by no means the only cause of railway accidents, which were often the result of mechanical or structural failure, or of human error unrelated to information systems. Moreover, the ultimate blame for railway accidents was often hard to pin down: structures could give way, for example, because they were inadequately designed, badly built, or improperly maintained, just as mechanical parts often broke because of poor manufacture, inadequate inspection, or ill-usage. But signaling failure remains a highly important analytic category, because it underlines the central importance of information systems and coordinative mechanisms within the increasingly complex world of Victorian railways. As Dickens was acutely aware, information had to be systematically accumulated, organized, and transmitted with unfailing accuracy—and often with remarkable timeliness—in order for railways to operate safely on the scale required to serve the transportation needs of mid- and late-Victorian Britain.

This point was recognized very early on. In an 1852 paper presented to the Institution of Civil Engineers, Mark Huish, the first general manager of the London and North Western Railway, noted that all the other causes of railway accidents "do not produce a tithe of the accidents which result from inattention to signals" and the operating regulations linked to them. "There is," he noted, "no part of the system to which the railway manager looks with more anxiety, than to the efficiency of the signals on the line."[34] Indeed, signaling and information failures were almost always the cause of collisions between trains, which by the mid-1850s constituted more than half of all serious railway accidents.[35]

Both the Clayton Tunnel disaster and the Staplehurst accident raised issues about information management and the limits of information systems in markedly revealing ways. "The frightful collision on the Brighton Line," the *Times* noted in a leader on the Clayton Tunnel disaster, "has but too plain and simple an explanation." Though there were mistakes on the part of both signalmen, and though a mechanical failure rendered one signal useless, "the culpable thing was that the trains succeeded one another so rapidly that the slightest possible mistake, even an excusable mistake, was fatal." The *Times*'s view of the formidable information problems and possibilities for system overload that confronted the most heavily trafficked Victorian railways merits quoting at length:

> So we come to the too rapid succession of trains, after all, as the real blameworthy cause of this whole misfortune. It is obvious that if one train succeeds another so quickly that the head of a signalman is confused . . . the rapidity in the succession of the trains is too great. You depend on the telegraph as the ultimate corrector of all mistakes, and its ultimatum continues or stops the motion of the train. But if the succession is so quick that the telegraph itself is confused by it, and sends wrong answers, there is an end to all security. . . . Things are run so closely that nothing but the most perfect accuracy and precision can prevent a crash. . . . Your signalmen are not pieces of clockwork, upon which hurry has no effect, they are men whose nerves and brains are susceptible of disorder. . . . They are good steady pieces of *human* clockwork, but human machinery is a very different thing from the machinery which you move by steam or spring.[36]

Moreover, the *Times* urged, railway companies were not alone to be blamed for excessive traffic densities: public enthusiasm for excursion trains was responsible for the ever greater numbers of such trains. "So they must be squeezed in any how between other trains. The thing goes on gradually, and the intervals get less and less, till at last a dreadful crash shows that the power of the arrangement has been tested too sharply, and has given way." Up to that point, the *Times* noted, "nobody has any idea how very near the edge of peril the whole system has been all along."[37] The *Morning Chronicle* concurred; it was a fearful reflection, a leader noted, how hundreds of lives are routinely "placed on the verge of peril, from which nothing can save them but an infallibility of instruments and men, utterly unattainable." The Clayton Tunnel accident thus arose from "unpardonable neglect" on the part of railway officers, coupled with "over confidence in signals and signal-men."[38]

The Staplehurst accident elicited four leaders in the *Times,* all of them sharply critical of railway practices, and all emphasizing the justifiable level of public alarm about railway safety—alarm exacerbated by the fact that the accident followed by only four days another serious railway accident, which had cost twelve lives. "On what is the confidence of railway travellers to rest?" the paper asked in its first leader, after noting how few of the obvious dangers were present in the case of the Staplehurst accident.[39] The last two leaders were written after the official inquest, and they focused directly on problems of information management within complex systems. The strongest appeared on 21 June, twelve days after the accident. Not only were the railway's own safety regulations blatantly disregarded, the *Times* insisted, but, contrary to the conclusion of the official accident inspector, Captain Rich, the regulations themselves were patently inadequate. There was no point in placing for detonators at 250-yard intervals between the flagman and the obstruction, or in placing a flagman at 1,000 yards from the obstruction, because a heavy train travelling at nearly 60 miles per hour required around 1,320 yards to stop. This "arrangement appears to us the most ingenious example of 'How Not to Do It' we have seen in a long time," the *Times* concluded, deliberately echoing the famous credo of the Circumlocution Office, Dickens's satirical image of incompetent and obstructive governmental bureaucracy in *Little Dorrit*.[40]

"This is indeed," the *Times* went on to argue vigorously, "the vice of modern railway management":

> The pressure of traffic is enormous, and its safety is made to depend on a complex system, first of timing, and then of signals to counteract failures in punctuality. Such a system requires constant and unfailing care. But the officials upon whom the observance of these rules depends grow so accustomed to the danger that they slip into all manner of irregularities, which go on increasing until some frightful disaster suddenly reveals the rottenness of the whole system; and then the Directors assume an air of the most virtuous innocence because their system looks well on paper.[41]

The *Times* returned to the failures of railway management the next day, attacking what it saw as a pattern of habitual neglect of duty by railway officials. Invoking the idea of "nobody's fault"—an idea that lay behind much of Dickens's polemic against administrative inefficiency, jobbery, and lack of public accountability in *Little Dorrit* ("Nobody's Fault" was Dickens's original title for the novel[42])—the *Times* focused on evident failures of individual responsibility within the framework of the "complex system" it had identified the day before: "The shareholders trust everything to the Directors, and the Directors trust everything to a Manager, and the Manager trusts everything to the Engineer, and the Engineer to the Inspectors, and the Inspectors to the workmen, and thus everybody considers his responsibility shifted to his superior or subordinate, and the rules sooner or later fall into abeyance."[43]

Dickens could not have agreed more. In a letter to the novelist Bulwer Lytton less than a month after the Staplehurst accident, Dickens referred to England's "enormous Railway No-System," which had "grown up without guidance." "Its abuses," he went on to say, "are so represented in Parliament by Directors, Contractors, Scrip Jobbers, and so forth, that no Minister dare touch it." Several months later, in a letter to a friend in France, Dickens described "a muddle of railways in all directions possible and impossible, with no general public scheme, no general public supervision, enormous waste of money, no fixable responsibility, [and] no accountability but under Lord Campbell's Act." The Staplehurst accident served as a case in point: "Before the most furious and notable train in the four and twenty hours," Dickens expostulated, "the head of a gang of workmen takes up the rails. That train changes its time every day as the tide changes, and that head workman is not provided by the railway company with any clock or watch!"[44]

In fact, the coroner's jury inquiring into the Staplehurst accident delivered a verdict of manslaughter against the South Eastern's district inspector, Joseph Gallimore, as well as against the platelayers' foreman, John Benge, and both men were subsequently convicted and imprisoned.[45] The question of how to apportion responsibility for accidents within complex systems, however, was a vexed one. In September 1861, for example, *All the Year Round* published a strong article in support of Lord Campbell's Act (1846), which railway interests were lobbying (without success) to repeal. This act had made companies liable for paying compensation when passengers were killed in accidents arising from company neglect. As damage awards rose in amount and number, railway companies grew alarmed by the implications of the act, arguing that almost all culpable accidents were attributable to the faults of individual employees, not of the company. *All the Year Round* urged, to the contrary, that "no jury could lay the whole blame [for the recent Clayton Tunnel and Kentish Town accidents] on the signalmen immediately concerned"—one of whom (at Kentish Town) was an exhausted "boy of nineteen, at fourteen shillings a week in wages, working, under no proper oversight, fifteen hours and a half, and ten hours on alternate days, to perform the duties of a too responsible position." "The responsibility for shameful laxity of management," the writer went on to insist, "is not to be got rid of by a censure of some humble servant of the company."[46] Eight months later *All the Year Round* suggested that an excellent way to enforce railway safety would be to "insist on one of the directors of each company accompanying every train."[47]

Despite system overload and managerial failure, however, immediate responsibility for railway safety fell heavily on operating personnel, and a particularly large share fell on signalmen. Indeed, Dickens's anxious signalman in **Mugby Junction**—"intelligent, vigilant, painstaking, and exact"—was keenly aware of his individual responsibility, believing that "he held a most important trust." And although the writer for *All the Year Round* who visited the signal box at Victoria Station ("The Hole in the Wall") was baffled by the complexity of the signalman's task, he repeatedly imagined the dire consequences of even a single lapse in the signalman's attention—a common response of observers contemplating the work of signalmen.[48] This drove the narrator toward "a morbid and an increasing longing to try the experiment of turning the wrong handle and bringing two full trains into collision . . . the first warning given

me of the strain on the nerves produced by the noises and signals described."[49]

The exacting and unusually responsible nature of signalmen's work was underlined not only by railway commentators but by signalmen themselves. In the anonymous pamphlet *A Voice from the Signal Box: Or, Railway Accidents and Their Causes* (1874), a signalman with eleven years experience at a busy and complicated junction explained the daily complexity of his job, on which the safety of a great many trains depended. His shift was only eight hours long. In an ordinary twenty-four-hour period, however, nearly five hundred trains passed his signal box, "requiring the moving of four thousand eight hundred levers, and six thousand signals to be given on the block telegraph. If these are divided into three parts, it will be seen that I and my mates have each sixteen hundred levers to shift, and two thousand signals to give daily on the telegraph during the time we are on duty." If these figures were correct—and other evidence suggests they were—they mean that on average a train passed the signal box once every three minutes. If the signaling tasks were distributed evenly across an eight-hour shift, each signalman would have to move a switch lever, signal lever, or interlocking lever once every 18 seconds, and move the handle of a telegraphic instrument once every 14.4 seconds. In view of such an extraordinarily rapid exchange of information, electrical, mechanical, and visual, there can be little wonder why the signalman felt that his wages were incommensurate with his responsibilities—or why he believed that railway companies should pay greater attention to the advice of signalmen, provide better training for the job, and offer signalmen more chances for promotion.[50]

THE BLOCK SYSTEM, THE TOKEN SYSTEM, AND INTERLOCKING TECHNOLOGY

Dickens's interest in railway safety and its necessary corollary, signaling, was in fact paralleled in this period by a more technical debate among railway professionals about the best procedure for controlling traffic. This debate, which was of direct relevance to the Clayton Tunnel disaster and also of indirect relevance to the Staplehurst accident, remained unresolved through the 1860s.[51]

From a very early period, it was understood that the primary danger of collision arose from the comparative feebleness of braking power in relation to the weight and momentum of trains. As trains grew longer, heavier, and faster, this problem tended to increase rather than diminish. In 1862, for example, H. W. Tyler asserted that "trains are habitually run, on the principal lines in the country, without a suitable amount of break-power," a defect, he noted, that was "constantly pointed out."[52] Even on a double line, where the danger of a head-on collision was nearly eliminated, a train that had stalled ran a serious risk of being struck from behind if the driver of the following train had no means of knowing that the line ahead was obstructed until he was close enough to see the obstruction—a point amply demonstrated in a different context by the Staplehurst accident.

The first solution proposed for this problem was to attempt to enforce a strict temporal separation of trains. By the 1860s, this ordinarily took the form of a regulation specifying that no train be allowed to pass any signal point or station within five minutes of any previous train. Signals were thus to be kept at danger for five minutes after the passage of a train, then at caution for five minutes more.[53] As the Clayton Tunnel collision clearly showed, this system proved inadequate for accommodating the traffic density required by major lines in busy periods, and it was also unsafe in sub-optimal conditions. Its reliability was based on the margin of five minutes allowed the guard of a stalled or stopped train to move far enough back along the track on foot to signal a following train to a half before it collided with the train blocking the line. Assuming that the guard ran back at ten miles per hour at the very fastest, he would manage a distance of approximately 1,467 yards in the allotted time—an adequate stopping distance for a train moving at 60 miles per hour on dry and level track, if it carried an adequate number of brake vans or had some carriages fitted with patent brakes.[54] If, however, the guard did not set out immediately or manage ten miles per hour, or if the following train had encroached on the preceding train or lacked sufficient brake power—or if the track were wet and limited visibility prevented the guard from being seen at a distance—then the margin of safety vanished entirely.

To permit greater traffic density and a more reliable margin of safety, an alternative system emerged with a different conceptual and technological basis. Known familiarly today as the block system, this approach was based on the idea of enforcing intervals of space between trains, rather than intervals of time. Under this system, which was initially developed to preserve safety within tunnels (where engine drivers often had almost no forward visibility),[55] railway lines were divided up into sections, with the length of the sections determined by the amount of traffic that the line needed to accommodate (little over a mile in heavily trafficked areas). Entry to each section was controlled by a signal, operated by a signalman in communication with the preceding and following signalmen by electric telegraph. No train would be allowed to enter a section (at speed) until the signalman controlling it had confirmed, on the basis of information conveyed to him by the next signalman, that the section was clear of any preceding train. Dickens does not seem to have commented on the block system explicitly, but he in fact assumed an operating block system in **"The Signalman,"** since the sig-

nal box in his story had telegraphic connections to the adjacent signal boxes in *both* directions along the line.[56]

The block system represented a very considerable advance in railway safety, particularly in its "absolute" rather than "permissive" version.[57] The idea received significant public attention as early as August 1854, when it was strongly recommended in a circular issued by the Railway Department of the Board of Trade. The plan was immediately endorsed by the *Times,* which published a leader on the topic, urging "the general adoption of a scheme promising such material advantages to companies and travellers together."[58] Uniform adoption of the telegraphic block system, however, was slowed down by three concerns. The first was the expense of installing telegraphic equipment and of hiring and training signalmen capable of using what was thought to be demanding technology. The second was lack of confidence in the reliability of telegraphic communication (because of the presumed delicacy of the apparatus, along with the difficulty of using it in an unambiguous and error-free fashion, especially under great pressure).[59] And the third was concern that a reliance on telegraphic information undermined the engine driver's sense of personal responsibility for the safety of his train, thereby undermining the primary source of all railway safety.[60] Ironically, the 1861 Clayton Tunnel disaster, because it occurred on a section of line operated on the telegraphic block system, was used by critics of the system to argue against excessive reliance on an advanced technology that lessened the responsibility of drivers. Frederick Slight, secretary of the London, Brighton, and South Coast Railway, criticized Tyler's recommendation to institute telegraphic block signaling on the line precisely for this reason. The Brighton line's directors, he noted, wondered whether "the increasing practice of multiplying signals, and thus lessening the responsibility of the engine driver . . . has not resulted in reducing . . . the safety of railway locomotion."[61] In the end, it took the appalling Armagh disaster of June 1889, which led to the swift passage of the 1889 Regulation of Railways Act, to make mandatory the absolute block system on all railway lines (old as well as new), along with continuous automatic braking for passenger trains and signal and switch interlocking.[62]

Although the telegraphic block system represented the most important advance in managing train information to ensure railway safety, it was by no means the only notable innovation in this period. Track detonators, invented by E. A. Cowper in 1841, came into widespread use to indicate danger in emergencies and to serve as audible signals when visibility was severely limited.[63] Signalmen were increasingly given control of two signals: a home signal at the start of a section, to accept or deny entrance into it, and a distant signal some 500 to 900 yards before the section, to provide advance knowledge of the information conveyed by the home signal.

(The distant signal is thought to have been first introduced in Scotland, in 1846.[64]) And signals were increasingly constructed in such a way that their natural or default setting was at danger rather than at line clear. This was intended to eliminate false line-clear information resulting from mechanical failure, as well as to require signalmen to give line-clear information on an active, positive basis. (An article in Dickens's *Household Words* advocated a radical version of the latter procedure in 1856: it urged that signals should always remain at danger between trains, and that engine drivers should be required to sound a whistle as they approached within sight of any signal, at which time the signalman would change the signal to line clear, if he had knowledge that the line was indeed clear.)[65]

For single-track lines, the "train-staff" or token system was devised to guarantee that only one train could traverse a stretch of line at any one time. The staff, which was originally a guard's truncheon, had to be carried on the train by the guard or by someone on the engine; it served simultaneously as a document confirming that the line was clear and as the train's authority to proceed.[66] "Train-staff" and token instruments were later developed for station use to govern the release of staffs and tokens. In general, these instruments would permit only one staff or token to be outside the mechanism at any one time: a staff or token had to be replaced before a new one could be released (thereby guaranteeing that only one train at any one time had authority to move on the line). The principle was eventually extended to cover more complicated situations, sometimes by allowing token machines to be activated by telegraphic signals from each end of the protected line segment, rather than by the return of a token to the original point, and sometimes through a system in which tickets and a tablet were combined to permit several trains to follow in a single direction, while prohibiting any train in the opposite direction until after transfer of the tablet, carried by the final train in the original direction.[67]

The most important additional development in this area, however, was signal and switch interlocking. The earliest known device anticipating interlocking was an apparatus constructed in 1843 by Charles Hutton Gregory, at Bricklayers Arms Junction, in London. One year earlier, Gregory had built at this site the first frame and platform to consolidate both signal controls and switch controls at a single operating location. His initial experiment in mechanical coordination was to connect several signal levers together with stirrups and chains, so that the signals could not inadvertently communicate conflicting or incompatible information.[68] The next and more important step was to link signals and switches together mechanically, so that they would be altered in harmony. The initial devices designed to accomplish this goal simply provided physical connections between appropriate switches and signals for simultaneous movement. This differed, however, from true interlocking, as the latter eventually came to be understood. "Switches and signals are said to be *connected* when they are simply coupled together and have a *pari passu* motion," Richard Rapier explained in 1874; "they are said to be *interlocked* when the movement of a signal to safety cannot be *commenced* until after the necessary movement of the switches has been *completed,* and also the movement of switches cannot be commenced until after all the signals concerned by them have first been set *fully* to danger."[69] By establishing a mechanically necessary precedence of actions, true interlocking devices allowed safe control of very complicated track and switching arrangements, and in both simple and complex situations the technology proved safer than devices that depended on simultaneous parallel motion, because with the latter apparatus the mechanical failure of one motion need not prevent the other (thereby more readily allowing a switch and a signal to be in conflict). The first recorded physical linkage of signals and switches was instituted at East Retford Junction in 1852.[70] John Saxby's interlocking mechanism, which paved the way for genuine interlocking and evolved into the most popular type, was invented in 1856.[71] More modern forms of full ("successive motion") interlocking were developed by Austin Chambers at Kentish Town Junction in 1859, by Saxby and Farmer at Victoria Station and elsewhere from 1860 onward, and then by Stevens and Sons at Waterloo Station and elsewhere in the 1870s.[72]

Described as "an admirable improvement . . . introduced of late" in the early 1860s,[73] interlocking mechanisms (including locking devices designed for facing switches, which rendered points immobile while a train was passing over them) became increasingly commonplace and increasingly central to railway safety in the decades that followed. From this period onward, increasingly complicated interlocking mechanisms coordinated train movements and signals at the bulk of England's most heavily trafficked junctions—a point made abundantly clear in the description in *All the Year Round* of the signal box governing access to Victoria Station, a Saxby and Farmer device, based on Saxby's 1860 patent frame, installed in October 1860[74]:

> Bells ring, whistles shriek, hands move, and huge iron bars creak and groan apparently of their own accord, and certainly by agencies which are invisible. On the right-hand wall of the box, and on a level with the eye, are fastened four cases, which communicate telegraphically with the platforms of the station, with Battersea Park, and with Stewart's-lane junction; and the movable faces of these are full of mysterious eloquence. The furthest one strikes what seems to be a gong twice, and then, without waiting for a reply, bangs the gong four times; the needle hands of the others tick away with spasmodic vigour. . . . To the left of the window, and facing the entrance door, is an apparatus which I

can only describe as terrifying. Composed of strong and massive cranks so connected as to form a consistent whole, and resembling a tangled agricultural harrow, or one of the weird instruments of torture which racked the limbs of schismatics in bad old times, it has secret springs, and bells, and joints, which creak, and act, and tingle with a sudden directness highly discomposing to a stranger. You look mildly at one of its joints, and have a question concerning its use on the tip of your tongue, when, presto! it gives a cumbrous flap, and becomes a staring red signboard, with "Crystal Palace up waiting," or "Brighton down waiting," staring you in the face.[75]

Interlocking was an especially significant breakthrough in railway safety because it linked information and mechanical action into a unified whole. Prior to interlocking, setting a switch and providing information about it were separate and mechanically independent activities—activities that could fall into catastrophic conflict, thanks to inattention and human error. Afterward, the two were coupled in a single, mechanical sequence, with the information component embodied in the yoked switching action, and vice versa. Information and action, signifier and signified, were thus "locked" together performatively, eliminating potential conflicts and guaranteeing a very high degree of safety.

SIGNALS AND THE RAILWAY LANDSCAPE

In an 1857 article for Dickens's *Household Words,* the journalist John Hollingshead described the experience of leaving London at night behind the footplate of an express locomotive. The first thing to strike Hollingshead was the array of signals. "In front of us," he wrote, "is a brilliant galaxy of red, green, and white lights, looking like a railway Vauxhall. . . . Further on, as we leave the discs and semaphores and outbuildings behind us, . . . we appear to chase a solitary coloured lamp with lightning speed. . . . I can allow my fancy full play in looking at these signs; but to steady, patient Tom Jones, the driver, they are as the leaves of a book in which he often reads a lesson of life and death to himself and his heavy responsible charge—signal lessons of danger, caution, and safety."[76] "Perhaps to a stranger on an engine," W. M. Acworth wrote some years later, "nothing is so remarkable as the signalling and the organisation of the trains," organization made possible by the evolution of information technology.[77]

Railway signals had become omnipresent features of the railway landscape. In *The Lazy Tale of Two Idle Apprentices,* which Dickens wrote with Wilkie Collins in 1857, slotted-post semaphore signals, which were in widespread use before the Abbotts Ripton accident of 1876,[78] aptly appear as "wooden razors."

> It was a Junction-Station, where the wooden razors before mentioned shaved the air very often, and where the sharp electric-telegraph bell was in a very restless

condition. All manner of cross-lines of rails came zig-zagging into it, like a Congress of iron vipers; and, a little way out of it, a pointsman in an elevated signal-box was constantly going through the motions of drawing immense quantities of beer at a public-house bar. In one direction, confused perspectives of embankments and arches were to be seen from the platform; in the other, the rails soon disentangled themselves into two tracks, and shot away under a bridge, and curved around a corner.[79]

Nearly a decade later the "wooden razors" were still visible "shaving the atmosphere" during the daytime at Mugby Junction. At night, however, only the changes of the colored signal lights were visible, "unknown languages in the air":

> A place replete with shadowy shapes, this Mugby Junction in the black hours of the four-and-twenty. Mysterious goods trains, covered with palls and gliding on like vast weird funerals, conveying themselves guiltily away from the presence of the few lighted lamps, as if their freight had come to a secret and unlawful end. Half miles of coal pursuing in a Detective manner, following when they lead, stopping when they stop, backing when they back. Red-hot embers showering out upon the ground, down this dark avenue, and down the other as if torturing fires were being raked clear; concurrently, shrieks and groans and grinds invading the ear, as if the tortured were at the height of their suffering. Iron-barred cages full of cattle jangling by midway, the drooping beasts with horns entangled, eyes frozen with terror, and mouths too: at least they have long icicles (or what seem so) hanging from their lips. Unknown languages in the air, conspiring in red, green, and white characters. An earthquake accompanied with thunder and lightning, going up express to London. Now, all quiet, all rusty, wind and rain in possession, lamps extinguished, Mugby Junction dead and indistinct, with its robe drawn over its head, like Caesar.[80]

This evocative passage, one of Dickens's best on railways, reminds us of Dickens's own broader preoccupation with problems of knowledge—with the inevitably troubled relations between the seen and unseen, known and unknown, determinate and indeterminate. Throughout his fiction, mysteries abound and failures of communication proliferate, engendering complex problems and complicated plots. A disturbed and isolated signalman, haunted by ghostly premonitions, was thus a naturally Dickensian subject. Equally natural for an experienced railway traveler, however, was an awareness of the vital role of signals for communicating the essential information on which railway safety depended.

The growth of railway signaling clearly reflected the increasing scale and complexity of the mid-Victorian railway system, with its high-speed trains, remarkable traffic densities, and ever greater reliance on technology. But public awareness of railway signals also reflected a continuing anxiety about the dangers of high-speed railway travel, dangers for which railway signals had the double effect of providing both a reminder and reassurance.

Two years after Dickens wrote **"The Signalman,"** Samuel Smiles observed that "the electric telegraph may, indeed, be regarded as the nervous system of the railway": "By its means the whole line is kept throbbing with intelligence."[81] The goal of this article has been to use **"The Signalman"** as a starting point for examining public understandings of the varieties of operational intelligence necessary for railway safety. In a manner without historical precedent, mid-Victorian railways demonstrated the need for rapid information transfer and unfailingly accurate information management, just as they demonstrated in new ways the possibilities for system overload and for breakdowns in human and machine interaction. Victorian railway signaling, part of the revolution in communications, is thus a revealing and concrete example of the development of information technology, necessary for the growth of modern, complex systems. The evolution of mid-Victorian railway signaling clearly anticipates central aspects of modernity—a world that Victorian railways did a great deal to bring about.

Notes

1. Dickens usually provided an extra, double-length issue of his weeklies at Christmas, filled exclusively with fiction. He himself contributed only half of the contents of *Mugby Junction.* The authorship of individual chapters is indicated on the number's cover.

2. Jack Simmons, *Rugby Junction* (Oxford, 1969), 12-15. Dickens's complaints were remembered more than twenty years later: W. M. Acworth, a leading authority on late-Victorian railways, insisted that railways had "made considerable progress since the days when the tea and the soup at Mugby Junction rested substantially on the same foundation" (*The Railways of England* [London, 1889], 145).

3. K. J. Fielding, ed., *The Speeches of Charles Dickens: A Complete Edition* (Hemel Hempstead, 1988), 361-66.

4. Philip Collins, *Dickens: The Critical Heritage* (New York, 1971), 420.

5. Recent articles on "The Signalman" include John Stahl, "The Source and Significance of the Revenant in Dickens's 'The Signalman,'" *Dickens Studies Newsletter* 11 (December 1980): 98-101; David Seed, "Mystery in Everyday Things: Charles Dickens's Signalman," *Criticism* 23 (winter 1981): 42-57; Ewald Mengel, "The Structure and Meaning of Dickens's 'The Signalman,'" *Studies in Short Fiction* 20 (fall 1983): 271-80; Gary Day, "Figuring Out 'The Signalman,'" in *Nineteenth-Century Suspense: From Poe to Conan Doyle,* ed. Clive Bloom et al. (New York, 1988);

Daniel J. Greenman, "Dickens's Ultimate Achievement in the Ghost Story," *Dickensian* 85 (spring 1989): 40-48; and Graeme Tytler, "Dickens's 'The Signalman,'" *Explicator* 53 (fall 1994): 26-29. None of these provides any substantial discussion of railway signaling practices or railway safety.

6. For *Household Words* articles on railway signaling, see "Need Railway Travellers Be Smashed?" 29 November 1851, 217-21; "Self-Acting Railway Signals," 12 March 1853, 43-45; and "Signals and Engine Drivers," 6 September 1856, 179-80. Dickens's interest in railway information systems was not in fact confined to signaling. His periodicals carried detailed descriptions of railway Post-Office cars, of railways' internal accounting systems (for example, what happens to tickets once they are collected), and of the Railway Clearing House.

7. "The Hole in the Wall," *All the Year Round,* 13 October 1866, 325-29, reprinted in *The Railway Through Dickens's World,* ed. Ewald Mengel (Frankfurt am Main, 1989), 122-31. The article is attributed to Joseph Charles Parkinson. (A signal box is normally called a signal tower in the United States.)

8. Humphry House, *The Dickens World,* 2nd ed. (Oxford, 1960), 145.

9. Quoted by House, 74. Much has been written about Dickens's celebrity and his attachment to his audience. For a good overview, see the section on Dickens's public life in Paul Schlicke, ed., *Oxford Reader's Companion to Dickens* (Oxford, 1999), 161-66.

10. Walter Bagehot, *The Collected Works of Walter Bagehot,* ed. Norman St. John-Stevas (Cambridge, Mass., 1965), 2:100. Bagehot's description of Dickens's politics was originally published in an 1858 review.

11. *Palmer's Index to "The Times" Newspaper, 1865* (London, 1878).

12. "Notes of Interrogation," *All the Year Round,* 10 May 1862, 211. On the belief that railway travel was becoming more dangerous, see R. W. Kostal, *Law and English Railway Capitalism, 1825-1875* (Oxford, 1994), 311. See also "My Railway Collision," *All the Year Round,* 17 December 1859, 176-80; reprinted in Mengel, 160-68. This fictional account, attributed to George Thornbury, narrates the frightening experience of a fortunately minor collision on the London and South Western's line to Basingstoke. It anticipates Dickens's "The Signalman" in one notable way: the narrator begins his trip with a powerful "presentiment" of danger, the result of having read in the *Times* at breakfast a description of an accident the previous

day on the Eastern Counties line that claimed three lives. Both accidents were the result of signaling failures.

13. See, for example, Mark Huish, *Railway Accidents: Their Causes, and Means of Prevention* (London, 1852), 29-34, and F. G. P. Neison, *Analytical View of Railway Accidents* (London, 1853), 31.

14. H. W. Tyler, "Railway Control," *Quarterly Review,* January 1862, 4; Samuel Smiles, *The Life of George Stephenson and His Son Robert Stephenson* (New York, 1868), x. According to Smiles, nineteen people were killed by lightning in Great Britain in 1866. The number of passengers killed in railway accidents in 1866, including those excluded by Smiles for having some responsibility for their fate, was thirty-six. See Kostal, 281.

15. Wolfgang Schivelbusch, *The Railway Journey: The Industrialization of Time and Space in the Nineteenth Century* (Berkeley, Calif., 1986), 129-49. See also Michael Freeman, *Railways and the Victorian Imagination* (New Haven, Conn., 1999), 85-86.

16. Jack Simmons, *The Victorian Railway* (London, 1991), 95-97.

17. Smiles, xii, xiv.

18. Charles Dickens, *The Letters of Charles Dickens,* ed. Madeline House et al. (Oxford, 1965-), 1:359.

19. Dionysius Lardner, *Railway Economy* (London, 1850), 339. In Lardner's view, the danger of express trains did not arise from their speed per se, but rather from their speed in relation to other traffic. For similar reasons—i.e., because they represented departures from the ordinary—Lardner thought that special trains and excursion trains were also dangerous (341).

20. Simmons, *Victorian Railway,* 199. See also Dickens, *Letters,* 11:65.

21. Dickens, *Letters,* 11:49. This episode is widely discussed in biographical work on Dickens.

22. The connection between the Clayton Tunnel disaster and "The Signalman" appears to have been made first by T. S. Lascelles, in "The Signalman's Story: Had Dickens Any Particular Tunnel in Mind?" *Dickensian* 56 (May 1960): 84. The physical setting of the tunnel, the location of the wreck inside the tunnel, and the signalman's reference to the "memorable accident on this Line" make the identification conclusive.

23. On trust in abstract and expert systems as a characteristic of modernity, see Anthony Giddens, *The Consequences of Modernity* (Stanford, Calif.,

1990), 26-29, 83-92. Complex systems, however, often produce their own "revenge effects"; see Edward Tenner, *Why Things Bite Back: Technology and the Revenge of Unintended Consequences* (New York, 1996).

24. Richard Blythe, *Danger Ahead: The Dramatic Story of Railway Signalling* (London, 1951), 68.

25. Charles Dickens, "The Signalman," in *Christmas Stories* (London, 1914), 414-27.

26. *Reports of the Inspecting Officers of the Railway Department . . . Upon Certain Accidents Which Have Occurred on Railways During the Months of June, July, August, September, October, and November, 1861* (London, 1862), 87-96. A classic account of this accident (and the Staplehurst accident) is also provided in L. T. C. Rolt, *Red for Danger: A History of Railway Accidents and Railway Safety* (Newton Abbot, 1976), 51-54, 127-30. My description differs, however, in a few minor details. Finally, another good account of the Clayton Tunnel disaster may be found in Geoffrey Kichenside and Alan Williams, *Two Centuries of Railway Signalling* (Sparkford, 1998), 40-41.

27. On this kind of irony as a technological "revenge effect," see Tenner, chap. 1.

28. *Morning Chronicle* (London), 27 August 1861, 4.

29. My description of the Staplehurst accident is taken from *Reports of the Inspecting Officers of the Railway Department . . . Upon Certain Accidents Which Have Occurred on Railways During the Month of June 1865* (London, 1865), 41-44.

30. Dickens stated to the Head Station Master at Charing Cross that he was in "the first class carriage which was dragged aslant, but did not go over. . . . The Engine broke from it before, and the rest of the train broke from it behind and went down into the stream below." Dickens, *Letters* (n. 18 above), 11:53-54.

31. Ibid., 56-57. The letter to Mitton provides Dickens's fullest account of the accident, but the accident is mentioned in a number of his letters written in this period. Ibid., 49-62. Dickens's involvement in the accident was noted in the first description of the accident in the *Times*; "Dreadful Railway Accident at Staplehurst," 10 June 1865, 9.

32. Charles Dickens, *Our Mutual Friend* (1864-65; Everyman Library reprint, London, 2000), 873-74, 894. It is frequently observed that Dickens died five years to the day after the Staplehurst accident.

33. Dickens, *Letters,* 11:53.

34. Huish (n. 13 above), 24-25.

35. Alfred Ogan, *Railway Collisions Prevented* (London, 1855), 7. See also Neison (n. 13 above), 35.

36. *Times,* 27 August 1861, 6.

37. Ibid., 6.

38. *Morning Chronicle* (London), 27 August 1861, 4.

39. *Times,* 12 June 1865, 8. See also 14 June 1865, 11, for the second leader. For the initial accounts of the accident, see the *Times,* 10 June 1865, 9; 12 June 1865, 5; and 13 June 1865, 14. (The other accident was at Rednal, north of London.)

40. *Times,* 21 June 1865, 11. Charles Dickens, *Little Dorrit* (1855-57), chap. 10.

41. *Times,* 21 June 1865, 11.

42. Harry Stone, ed., *Dickens's Working Notes for His Novels* (Chicago, 1987), 267, 271.

43. *Times,* 22 June 1865, 11.

44. Dickens, *Letters* (n. 18 above), 11:68, 116.

45. *Reports of the Inspecting Officers of the Railway Department . . . Upon Certain Accidents Which Have Occurred on Railways During the Month of June 1865* (n. 29 above), 44. Dickens, *Letters,* 11:57.

46. "Rather Interested in Railways," *All the Year Round,* 28 September 1861, 17-18. For a good discussion of Lord Campbell's Act and railway opposition to it, see Kostal (n. 12 above), 310-11.

47. "Notes of Interrogation," *All the Year Round,* 10 May 1862, 211.

48. Dickens, "The Signalman" (n. 25 above), 425. For a similar view, see W. M. Acworth's discussion of this issue in *The Railways of England* (n. 2 above), 306.

49. "The Hole in the Wall," in Mengel (n. 7 above), 127. Because the switching mechanism was an interlocking apparatus, signals and switches could not in fact have been set in conflict. See the later discussion of interlocking.

50. *A Voice from the Signal Box: Or, Railway Accidents and Their Causes* (London, 1874). This pamphlet carried an introduction by Edwin Phillips, editor of the *Railway Service Gazette.* Phillips appears to cite the same signalman in his article "The Internal Workings of Railways," *Fortnightly Review,* March 1874, 381. The complexity of signaling in a busy setting is confirmed a decade and a half later by Acworth's description of the duties of signalmen in the "A" Box at Waterloo Station. This box contained 209 separate levers (for points, signals, and interlocking apparatus), and each train movement required an average of twenty-two lever movements. The box was manned by four signalmen at the busiest times of day, when they were required to pull or push 900-1,000 levers per hour—which meant that each man had to move on average one lever every fifteen seconds. Acworth, 306-7.

51. See, for example, H. W. Tyler's comments about the underlying causes of the Clayton Tunnel disaster: *Reports of the Inspecting Officers of the Railway Department . . . Upon Certain Accidents Which Have Occurred on Railways During the Months of June, July, August, September, October, and November, 1861* (n. 26 above), esp. 95. See also Tyler's important article "Railway Control" (n. 14 above), 13-14.

52. Tyler, "Railway Control," 8. The same point was still being made a dozen years later: see Phillips, "The Internal Workings of Railways," 377.

53. Tyler, "Railway Control," 13.

54. According to Tyler, "when a train is travelling at high speed, it frequently cannot be stopped in less than from half a mile to a mile," i.e. 880 to 1,760 yards. Ibid., 6.

55. Ibid., 13.

56. At the time of the Clayton Tunnel disaster, the signalmen posted at either end of the tunnel only had telegraphic contact with each other.

57. For the advantages of the "absolute" block system, whereby no train could enter a section of line until the section was clear, over the "permissive" block system, whereby greater traffic densities were achieved by allowing trains to enter sections not yet clear at reduced speeds, see Richard Rapier, *On the Fixed Signals of Railways* (London, 1874), 6.

58. The Board of Trade circular and the *Times* leader are reprinted as an appendix to Ogan (n. 35 above), 31-34. (The *Times* quotation is from p. 34.)

59. Thomas Wrigley, *Railway Accidents: Their Cause and Cure* (London, 1871), 39-40.

60. Simmons, *Victorian Railway* (n. 16 above), 97-98.

61. *Reports of the Inspecting Officers of the Railway Department . . . Upon Certain Accidents Which Have Occurred on Railways During the Months of June, July, August, September, October, and November, 1861* (n. 26 above), 96. (As a concession, however, the railway agreed to institute block signaling between Brighton and Hassock's Gate; ibid., 96.)

62. Rolt (n. 26 above), 192-93; Blythe (n. 24 above), 75. The Armagh (Ireland) disaster was only in small measure a signaling failure. A heavy excursion train leaving Armagh stalled just short of the top of a very long incline. The guard in charge of the train agreed to divide the train, to allow the locomotive to restart by pulling only the first five carriages over the top and onto a nearby siding. The train, however, lacked continuous automatic braking, and the remaining ten carriages, overpowering the comparatively feeble hand brakes, rolled backward over the stones used to block the wheels and gathered speed down the incline, soon outrunning the guards desperately trying to stop the runaway. The helpless passengers were unable to leap to safety because the carriage doors had been locked from the outside. A following train, released on the time interval system from Armagh, was at best only able to slow down before colliding into the speeding carriages. The resulting collision killed eighty people and injured many more. Rolt, 187-93.

63. Rapier (n. 57 above), 19.

64. Tyler, "Railway Control" (n. 14 above), 6; and Rapier, 6, 15.

65. "Signals and Engine-Drivers," *Household Words*, 6 September 1856, 179-80. For a vigorous polemic fifteen years later in favor of "affirmative" rather than "negative" signaling, see Wrigley (n. 59 above). Wrigley also advocated an arrangement whereby engine drivers would have to whistle as they approached every signal, and the signalman would then change the signal to all clear (if the line were indeed clear) within the engine driver's sight. (Wrigley was strongly opposed to the use of telegraphic communication for railway signaling, so it is not clear how signalmen in his system would obtain reliable information; see 37-40.) For the theoretical advantages of his system, see his summary chart comparing the "affirmative" system with the "negative" system, 51-56.

66. Tyler, "Railway Control," 17-18.

67. On token systems and machines, see Acworth (n. 2 above), 392-94, and Edward S. Hadley, *Railway Working and Appliances* (London, 1909), 38-41. See also Blythe (n. 24 above), 87-88.

68. Rapier (n. 57 above), 23.

69. Ibid., 23.

70. Ibid., 23.

71. Signalling Study Group, *The Signal Box: A Pictorial History and Guide to Designs* (Shepperton, 1986), 15. (Saxby's 1856 patent still involved "simultaneous motion," rather than "successive motion.")

72. Rapier, 23-34; Signalling Study Group, 12-16.

73. Tyler, "Railway Control" (n. 14 above), 15.

74. Kichenside and Williams (n. 26 above), 38; and Signalling Study Group, 14-15.

75. "The Hole in the Wall," in Mengel (n. 7 above), 123.

76. John Hollingshead, "Riding the Whirlwind"; reproduced in Mengel, 36-43. (Quote at 37.)

77. Acworth (n. 2 above), 80.

78. The Abbots Ripton accident, which took place during a very heavy blizzard in January 1876, was a double collision that claimed fourteen lives. Although a number of errors of judgment contributed to the disaster, the underlying cause was the failure of a number of slotted-post semaphore signals, which had become clogged with snow and ice, thereby holding the blade in the down position (inside the post), which indicated all clear. The upshot was the abandonment of signals for which a mechanical breakdown automatically resulted in false line-clear information. See Rolt (n. 26 above), 115-21.

79. Charles Dickens and Wilkie Collins, *The Lazy Tour of Two Idle Apprentices* (1857; reprint, London, 1895), 62.

80. Charles Dickens, *Christmas Stories* (n. 25 above), 429-30. (For the reference to "wooden razors," see 437.) Dickens also described signal lights at a station in *Our Mutual Friend* (n. 32 above). These comments led to a debate, beginning in 1908, on whether Dickens misinterpreted the meaning of red and green. This matter seems to me to have been settled authoritatively by T. S. Lascelles, in "Railway Signal Puzzle in *Our Mutual Friend*," *Dickensian* 18 (1922): 213-16. (I am indebted to Joel Brattin for drawing my attention to this material.)

81. Smiles (n. 14 above), xiii.

FURTHER READING

Criticism

Allingham, Philip V. "Dickens's Aesthetic of the Short Story." *Dickensian* 95, no. 448 (summer 1999): 144-53. Articulates Dickens' attitudes toward short story writing gleaned from his correspondence and offers a brief survey of twentieth century critical responses to Dickens' short fiction.

Bonheim, Helmut. "The Principle of Cyclicity in Charles Dickens' 'The Signalman.'" *Anglia* 106, nos. 3-4 (1988): 380-92.

> Analyzes three recurring plot cycles of "The Signalman," illuminating various symmetries among the images, phrases, and actions of the story.

Buckwald, Craig. "Stalking the Figurative Oyster: The Excursive Ideal in *A Christmas Carol*." *Studies in Short Fiction* 27, no. 1 (winter 1990): 1-14.

> Discusses Dickens' comparison of Scrooge to an oyster, assessing its importance to the imagery, structure, and meaning of *A Christmas Carol* as a whole.

Butterworth, R. D. "*A Christmas Carol* and the Masque." *Studies in Short Fiction* 30, no. 1 (winter 1993): 63-9.

> Examines formal similarities between *A Christmas Carol* and Renaissance masques.

Carrer, Luisa. "Trieste's Early Role in the Italian Reception of Charles Dickens." *Modern Language Review* 98, no. 1 (January 2003): 1-10.

> Traces the critical reception and literary reputation of Dickens in Italy.

Huff, Lawrence. "The Lamar-Dickens Connection." *Mississippi Quarterly* 40, no. 2 (spring 1987): 113-15.

> Discusses John Basil Lamar's story "The 'Experience' of the Blacksmith of the Mountain Pass" as a source for Dickens' "Colonel Quagg's Conversion."

Justin, Henri. "The Signalman's Signal-man." *Journal of the Short Story in English* 7 (autumn 1986): 9-16.

> Analyzes the character of the signalman and his relationship to the narrator of Dickens' short story.

Additional coverage of Dickens' life and career is contained in the following sources published by Thomson Gale: *Authors and Artists for Young Adults,* **Vol. 23;** *Beacham's Guide to Literature for Young Adults,* **Vols. 1, 2, 3, 13, 14;** *British Writers,* **Vol. 5;** *British Writers: The Classics,* **Vols. 1, 2;** *Children's Literature Review,* **Vol. 95;** *Concise Dictionary of British Literary Biography: 1832-1890;* *Dictionary of Literary Biography,* **Vols. 21, 55, 70, 159, 166;** *DISCovering Authors; DISCovering Authors: British Edition; DISCovering Authors: Canadian Edition; DISCovering Authors Modules: Most-studied Authors* **and** *Novelists; DISCovering Authors 3.0; Exploring Novels; Gothic Writers: A Gale Critical Companion,* **Vol. 2;** *Junior DISCovering Authors; Literary Movements for Students,* **Vol. 1;** *Literature and Its Times,* **Vols. 1, 2;** *Literature and Its Times Supplement,* **Vol. 1;** *Literature Resource Center; Major Authors and Illustrators for Children and Young Adults,* **Eds. 1, 2;** *Nineteenth-Century Literature Criticism,* **Vols. 3, 8, 18, 26, 37, 50, 86, 105, 113, 161;** *Novels for Students,* **Vols. 4, 5, 10, 14, 20;** *Reference Guide to English Literature,* **Ed. 2;** *Reference Guide to Short Fiction,* **Ed. 2;** *St. James Guide to Crime & Mystery Writers,* **Vol. 4;** *St. James Guide to Horror, Ghost & Gothic Writers; Short Story Criticism,* **Vols. 17, 49;** *Something About the Author,* **Vol. 15;** *Supernatural Fiction Writers,* **Vol. 1;** *Twayne's English Authors; World Literature and Its Times,* **Ed. 4;** *World Literature Criticism; Writers for Children;* **and** *Writers for Young Adults.*

Jacob Grimm
1785-1863

Wilhelm Grimm
1786-1859

(Full names Jacob Ludwig Karl Grimm and Wilhelm Karl Grimm; also published under Grimm Brothers and Brüder Grimm) German folklorists, philologists, lexicographers, and translators

The following entry provides an overview of the Brothers Grimm's short fiction. For additional information on their career, see *SSC*, Volume 36.

INTRODUCTION

Renowned in Germany for their erudite study of German philology and their ambitious contributions to German lexicography, the Brothers Grimm famously compiled the internationally beloved anthology of European folklore entitled *Kinder- und Hausmärchen* (1812-15; *Children's and Household Tales* or *Nursery and Household Tales*). Commonly known today as *Grimms' Fairy Tales,* the two-volume collection initially comprised more than two hundred stories ostensibly transcribed from the oral storytelling traditions of German peasants although some tales derive from other European sources, including literary ones. The Grimm brothers aimed to record as closely as possible the diction and syntax of the original spoken narratives. They appended copious scholarly notes explaining the peculiarities of oral folk traditions to the work's second edition, which they revised and expanded five additional times during their lifetimes. The methodology they used to compile their story collection helped to establish the philological model practiced by subsequent folklorists. Although the brothers originally intended their folk tale collection for a scholarly audience, *Grimms' Fairy Tales* has proven popular among children and adults throughout the world.

BIOGRAPHICAL INFORMATION

The oldest of six children, Jacob and Wilhelm Grimm were respectively born in 1785 and 1786 at Hanau, Hesse-Kassel, a former kingdom in present-day Germany. When their father, a lawyer, died in 1796, their mother moved the financially distressed family into her

sister's household in Kassel where the brothers attended the Lyceum Fridericianum. Close friends from an early age, they entered the University of Marburg intending to study law, but they developed an interest in medieval literature after a professor inspired them with a love of antiquarian research, which they gratified by transcribing the oral folk tales and lyrics of Hesse-Kassel, a region relatively untouched by the Industrial Revolution. Their research brought each brother his first publication, Jacob's *Über den altdeutschen Meistergesang* (1811) and Wilhelm's *Altdänische Heldenlieder* (1811; *Old Danish Ballads*), and eventually led to the publication of their *Children's and Household Tales.* In 1815 the Grimm brothers received appointments as librarians in Kassel, which let them devote their free time to scholarship. During their tenure there, the brothers completed their collaboration on *Deutsche Sagen* (1816-18;

The German Legends of the Brothers Grimm), a collection of essays on folklore, and focused on individually publishing a number of philological works. These included Jacob's *Deutsche Grammatik* (1819-37)—an extensive, highly influential study of the grammar of Germanic languages, which articulates the linguistic principle widely known as Grimm's Law—and Wilhelm's folklore studies *Über deutsche Runen* (1821) and *Die deutschen Heldensage* (1829). During the early 1830s, the Grimm brothers accepted appointments as professors of linguistics and literature at the University of Göttingen in the kingdom of Hanover, where advocates of democratic reform and German nationalism flourished. Sympathetic to these causes, the brothers signed a formal protest with six other professors against the new Hanoverian king, who had imposed restrictive civil policies. Consequently, they were discharged from their university posts in 1837. In 1840 King Friedrich Wilhelm IV of Prussia appointed the brothers as full professors at the prestigious Berlin Academy of Science, where they both lectured on German law, literature, and folklore. After Jacob published *Deutsche Mythologie* (1835; *Teutonic Mythology*), a work begun years earlier at Göttingen, and *Geschichte der deutschen Sprache* (1848), the brothers began compiling *Deutsches Wörterbuch* (1854-1961), a multi-volume etymological dictionary regarded as the German equivalent of the *Oxford English Dictionary*. Beginning in 1852, they devoted the rest of their careers to the massive work, the first volume of which appeared in 1854. Wilhelm lived to assist the project through the letter "D" before he died in 1859, and Jacob survived through the letter "F" before he died in 1863. Subsequent generations of scholars continued the brothers' lexicographic undertaking, which was finally completed in 1961.

MAJOR WORKS OF SHORT FICTION

Popularly known as *Grimms' Fairy Tales, Children's and Household Tales* comprises folk stories chiefly transcribed from oral tradition and supplemented by a number of written myths and legends, which the Brothers Grimm found during their research of old Germanic and Scandinavian manuscripts and books. The collected tales represent thirteen years of research by the brothers, who sought to preserve the simple, unadorned style and language of peasant storytellers with "faithfulness and truth," according to their preface to the second edition. Although the Brothers Grimm contributed no material of their own beyond their scholarly annotations, their fidelity to the tone, style, and detail of traditional storytelling in such classics as "The Frog Prince," "Little Red Riding Hood," and "Snow White" renders the tales at once familiar and universal. Typically set in the ancient castles, primeval forests, or enchanting cottages of medieval times, the tales feature a host of characters readily familiar to any schoolchild: beautiful princesses and dashing princes, sly fools and tricksters, evil stepmothers and crafty witches, doting but naïve fathers, talking animals of all kinds, magical fairies, bumbling craftsmen, fearless boys, and clever girls. Each narrative tends to combine imaginative adventure with practical lessons on human nature, animating the contrast between good and evil through exaggerated representations of innocence and decadence, while generally avoiding explicit didacticism. Some of the stories' plots involve weak or victimized protagonists who ultimately triumph over their all-powerful adversaries by virtue or fate, but many plots center on flawed protagonists possessing at once the best and the worst traits of human nature. For instance, in "Mary's Child," the Virgin Mary takes a curious girl up to heaven where she enters a forbidden room and witnesses a vision of the Holy Trinity. The Virgin Mary then returns the girl to earth as punishment for her disobedience. In "The Goose Girl at the Spring," a beautiful princess purposely deceives a noble prince by disguising herself as a poor peasant in order to test his humility as a worthy suitor. Indeed, many critics have attributed the charm of fairy tales to this peculiar blend of the ugly with the beautiful, not only for children but also adults. For example, "The Nixie on the Millpond" highlights the difficulties and the blessings of sexual love. In this tale, the title character tricks a downtrodden miller, who unwittingly exchanges his newborn son for his return to prosperity. When the nixie claims her part of the bargain years later, the son's wife manages to rescue her husband only to be separated from him for many more years "full of longing and sorrow" before reuniting as an old couple. Although the Grimm brothers published seven editions of their collected folk tales between 1812 and 1857, English-language translations have yet to completely and accurately reflect the Grimms' publications. Instead, selections from the original volumes began to appear within a decade of their first publication, with compilers softening the tone of the folk tales and modifying such details as character names and the titles of individual stories, as well as the original title of the collection itself.

CRITICAL RECEPTION

Widely credited by literary scholars for preserving the storytelling traditions of medieval Europe, *Grimms' Fairy Tales* has appealed to children since its initial publication, but the collection has also raised objections from certain quarters at various times throughout the nineteenth and twentieth centuries. Educators, social reformers, the clergy, and parents have sought to amend the original tales to suit their own respective agendas either by outright banning and censorship or through selection and revision. This has led, in turn, to discussion of the textual significance of various editions of the collection, producing a body of criticism on topics ranging from translation to didactic possibilities. Contradicting the Grimms' explicit certainty about the linguistic authenticity of the tales, contemporary scholars have also questioned the brothers' philological methods and ideological purposes informing the collection with the observation that the Grimms' rendered all the tales in High German despite different origins in many dialects. Some critics have contended that such editorial revision admitted various influences, conscious or otherwise, which are at odds with the collection's original purpose, including the promotion of bourgeois social norms and Christian moral doctrines. Others, however, have acknowledged the fundamental role of the editor in the process of transcribing the oral storytelling tradition. While debate about the literary significance of the tales has continued, other scholars have examined individual stories for their representation of gender and the dynamics of family relationships, demonstrating the influence of various tales upon the themes and motifs of the Grimms' collection and the fairy tale genre as a whole. In fact, *Grimms' Fairy Tales* has inspired artists of every medium and delighted generations of readers regardless of their ages.

PRINCIPAL WORKS

Short Fiction

Kinder- und Hausmärchen. 2 vols. [*German Popular Stories, Translated from the Kinder und Haus Marchen.* 2 vols.; also published as *Grimms' Fairy Tales, Children's and Household Tales,* and *Nursery and Household Tales*] 1812-15
Grimms' Household Tales, with the Authors' Notes 1884
Märchen der Brüder Grimm: Urfassung nach der Original-handschrift der Abtei Olenberg im Elsass 1927
The Complete Fairy Tales of the Brothers Grimm 1987

Other Major Works

Altdänische Heldenlieder [*Old Danish Ballads*; by Wilhelm Grimm] (folklore) 1811
Über den altdeutschen Meistergesang [by Jacob Grimm] (folklore) 1811
Deutsche Sagen. 2 vols. [*The German Legends of the Brothers Grimm.* 2 vols.] (literary history) 1816-18
Deutsche Grammatik. 4 vols. [by Jacob Grimm] (grammar) 1819-37
Über deutsche Runen [by Wilhelm Grimm] (folklore) 1821

Die deutschen Heldensage [by Wilhelm Grimm] (folklore) 1829
Deutsche Mythologie. 4 vols. [*Teutonic Mythology*; by Jacob Grimm] (folklore) 1835
Geschichte der deutschen Sprache. 2 vols. [by Jacob Grimm] (folklore) 1848
Deutsches Wörterbuch [with others] (dictionary) 1854-1961

CRITICISM

Ruth B. Bottigheimer (essay date 1987)

SOURCE: Bottigheimer, Ruth B. "Witches, Maidens, and Spells." In *Grimms' Bad Girls & Bold Boys: The Moral & Social Vision of the* Tales, pp. 40-50. New Haven, Conn.: Yale University Press, 1987.

[*In the following essay, Bottigheimer describes the characteristics of and conditions for spell-laying in* Grimms' Fairy Tales, *drawing parallels between conjuring and the natural powers of women, especially virgins.*]

Ask any three people about **Grimms' Tales** [**Grimms' Fairy Tales**] and two of them will respond, "Witches, ogres, wolves. . . ." Ask again what witches do, and the questioner will hear that witches lay spells and enchant young heroes and heroines. All of this is correct, and yet these answers obscure some rather surprising facts. Of the many supposed spell-laying verses in **Grimms' Tales,** only a few represent true conjuring.[1] Not a simple act, conjuring in the German tradition accomplishes something by invoking or commanding a spirit, a natural being, or a natural power by means of a spell or a sacred name. Of the successful spells actually laid in **Grimms' Tales,** the overwhelming majority, if not all, are performed by young, beautiful, and usually nubile girls. Furthermore, the girls' effectiveness in laying spells seems related to an inborn connection to nature itself. It takes close and careful reading to come to this conclusion, because the text often imputes fearsome powers to old women and young men. For example, Rapunzel's godmother (no. 12) was an "enchantress, who had great power and was dreaded by all the world" (Zauberin, die große Macht hatte und von aller Welt gefürchtet ward).

We also hear about witches who lay spells with dire consequences:

> But the wicked step-mother was a witch, and had seen how the two children had gone away, and had crept after them secretly, as witches creep, and had bewitched all the brooks in the forest.

("**Brother and Sister**," no. 11)

Die böse Stiefmutter aber war eine Hexe und hatte wohl gesehen, wie die beiden Kinder fortgegangen waren, war ihnen nachgeschlichen, heimlich, wie die Hexen schleichen, und hatte alle Brunnen im Walde verwünscht.

But on closer examination we see that the only magical voice heard in this text does not belong to the witch: it belongs to the brook that warns Little Sister away from its witch-enchanted waters that will turn Little Brother into a tiger or a wolf. The same is true of the witchlike enchantress in the perennial German favorite, **"Jorinda and Joringel"** (no. 69). We do not hear a single one of her seven thousand bewitchings that change virgins into caged birds, not even the one that entraps Jorinda.[2] To judge from his notes to the tales as well as from the list of verbal forms to be gathered that was included in the constitution of the Wollzeilergesellschaft,[3] spell-laying generally escaped both Grimms' editorial sifting, though on at least one occasion Wilhelm added an invocation to a fairy tale.[4]

Spell-laying is a quite specific act that has to satisfy several formal requirements to fit the traditional Germanic model. First, the conjurer must be human. Second, the spell itself should consist of three parts: naming the deity or natural force invoked, describing a past act that proves the effectiveness of the power invoked, and finally requesting in the imperative form. Since none of the spells laid in *Grimms' Tales* includes a description of a past act, the requirements here are reduced: the invocation of a natural force followed by a command.

Some apparent spells do not fulfill the principal criterion that the conjurer be human, as in the toad's verses in **"The Iron Stove"** (no. 127).[5] The spell itself must incorporate a command. Pure wishing does not constitute conjuring, though wishes accompanied by unintended results appear often in *Grimms' Tales.*[6] They usually reflect character deficiency—greed or short temper—and comically undermine the character's true desires.[7] The fact that a wish leads to the desired result should not obscure the more important fact that basic conditions for laying a spell have not been met.

Although wishing itself does not meet the formal requirements for laying a spell, conjuring can apparently develop out of a wish. In **"The Knapsack, the Hat, and the Horn"** (no. 54), the youngest of three brothers astonishes himself with the effectiveness of simply wishing for food. Climbing down a tree, tormented by hunger, he thinks to himself: "If I could but eat my fill once more" (Wenn ich nur noch einmal meinen Leib ersättigen könnte). Immediately he finds a richly spread table beneath the tree. Keeping the tablecloth when he has finished, he later tests its powers, saying: "I wish you to be covered with good cheer again" (So wünsche

ich, daß du abermals mit guten Speisen besetzt wärest). His wish works, and the third time he settles into the imperative spell-laying form, though he does not address it to a natural power, saying only: "Little cloth, set [RBB] yourself" (Tüchlein, deck dich).

Traditional German spells require the imperative, not the interrogative form. The stepmother's questions to the mirror in **"Snow-White"** (no. 53) do not constitute conjuring or spell-laying on two counts: the object addressed is neither a natural force nor a deity and the mood is not imperative. Nonetheless she addresses her mirror formulaically seven separate times:

> Looking-glass, Looking-glass, on the wall,
> Who in this land is the fairest of all?

> Spieglein, Spieglein an der Wand,
> wer ist die Schönste im ganzen Land?

More remarkably, it responds seven times, varying its reply to suit the circumstances.

Three modalities characterize a genuine spell in *Grimms' Tales,* when it makes one of its rare appearances. At its most powerful, conjuring power resides within the conjurer, who generates her own incantation rather than having it prescribed for her. At a slight remove is conjuring that depends on specific incantations passed on to the conjurer by a knowledgeable individual. These incantations lose their efficacy if the conjurer deviates even slightly from the prescribed form. And finally there are spells whose efficacy derives from a magical object presented to the conjurer.

Good examples of the three types of conjuring surface in **"The Goose-Girl"** (no. 89), **"The Two King's Children"** (no. 113), **"Cinderella"** (no. 21), **"One-Eye, Two-Eyes, and Three-Eyes"** (no. 130), and **"Sweet Porridge"** (no. 103). Each of the spells in these tales conforms to the requirements that a sacred name or the spirit of a natural force or being be invoked together with a command to perform a specific act, followed in the text by the result requested or commanded. Furthermore, each of these spells proceeds from a woman and links the conjurer to basic natural processes: chthonic, physical, or biological.

The characteristics of the Grimms' spells join them to the oldest preserved German literature, the pre-Christian Merseburg Spells (Merseburger Zaubersprüche), which bear witness to an early and perhaps continuous belief—or at least continuous reference to—a peculiarly female ability to control, direct or affect natural powers. In one, warrior women, the Idise, are invoked to help release prisoners taken in battle, and in the other, two pairs of sisters, Sintgunt and Sunna, Frija and Volla, whose past help has cured Baldur's steed, are invoked to effect a present cure.

The simple act of commanding may be understood within many different contexts. In his elaboration of speech act theory, John L. Austin suggests that "a necessary part of [a command] is that . . . the person to be the object of the verb 'I order to . . .' must, by some previous procedure, tacit or verbal, have first constituted the person who is to do the ordering an authority, e.g. by saying 'I promise to do what you order me to do.'"[8] The intimate link between women and natural powers may be viewed as part of a tacit pact between ancient Germanic society and women, that natural processes be understood to be under feminine control, while acts of aggression and governing fall to the male sphere.[9] Clearly, neither wind, birds, nor pots can enter a pact with women and agree to perform responsively. Nonetheless, Austin's suggestion—even though made in an entirely different context—evokes the possibility both in the Germanic past and in Grimm's day of a relationship between women and natural forces understood as reciprocal by women and their society.[10] By uttering the right words, a girl causes birds to peck (**"Cinderella"**), winds to blow (**"The Goose-Girl"**), and trees to bend down (**"One-Eye, Two-Eyes, and Three-Eyes"**).

The most dramatic spell in *Grimms' Tales* appears in **"The Goose-Girl,"** where a princess made to take her maidservant's place nonetheless retains her abilities to converse with her horse, Falada, and to conjure the winds to blow. Its alliterative verses, internal rhyme, and archaic vocabulary betray its ancient origins:

> Blow, blow, thou gentle wind, I say,
> Blow Conrad's little hat away,
> And make him chase it here and there,
> Until I have braided all my hair,
> And bound it up again.

> Weh, weh, Windchen,
> nimm Kürdchen sein Hütchen,
> und laß 'n sich mit jagen,
> bis ich mich geflochten und geschnatzt
> und wieder aufgesatzt.

This spell, like all others in *Grimms' Tales,* lacks an integral component of the Merseburg Spells, namely, the initial description of a former and successful conjuration. Instead, it opens directly with an address to the force to be activated together with a command. In its first published appearance in volume 2 of the *Kinder- und Hausmärchen* (1815), Wilhelm emphasized that the line "Weh, weh, Windchen" was a command, not an exclamation, apparently wanting his readers to understand the precise nature and importance of this construction.[11] The goose-girl needs no magical object to enable her to conjure; nor does her loss of marital queenship affect her abilities. Her power inheres in her queenship over nature, which one may consider a legacy from her mother, the old queen, who opens this tale:

> There was once upon a time an old queen whose husband had been dead for many years, and she had a beautiful daughter.

> Es lebte einmal eine alte Königin, der war ihr Gemahl schon lange Jahre gestorben, und sie hatte eine schöne Tochter.

Cinderella similarly derives her power from her mother. Though long dead, she transmits magic capabilities to the upper world through the tree sprig her daughter planted on her grave. Watered with Cinderella's tears, it grows into a beautiful tree from whose boughs a little white bird flutters to her assistance or casts down whatever she wishes for. Twice Cinderella calls on the entire avian kingdom to pick lentils from the ashes where her stepmother, intending to set an impossible task, has scattered them. And twice the birds heed her call:[12]

> You tame pigeons, you turtle-doves, and all you birds beneath the sky, come and help me to pick

> The good into the pot,
> The bad into the crop.

> Ihr zahmen Täubchen, ihr Turteltäubchen, all ihr Vöglein unter dem Himmel, kommt und helft mir lesen,

> die guten ins Töpfchen,
> die schlechten ins Kröpfchen.

Cinderella also conjures the tree itself:

> Shiver and quiver, little tree,
> Silver and gold throw down over me.

> Bäumchen, rüttel dich und schüttel dich,
> wirf Gold und Silber über mich.

The third verse in the Grimms' **"Cinderella"** is not a spell but a message from the birds to the prince, twice informing him that he has chosen the wrong bride, and finally confirming his choice:

> Turn and peep, turn and peep,
> No blood is in the shoe,
> The shoe is not too small for her,
> The true bride rides with you.

> Rucke di guck, rucke di guck,
> kein Blut im Schuck:
> der Schuck ist nicht zu klein,
> die rechte Braut, die führt er heim.

The preponderance of trees in spells reiterates their special importance in conjunction with women, while the trees' connection with gold and silver unites them to an ancient Western tradition.[13] In the three tales **"The Goose-Girl," "Cinderella,"** and **"One-Eye, Two-Eyes, and Three-Eyes,"** the power of the conjurer over the tree appears in progressively attenuated form.[14] In the first tale, we are left to infer that the goose-girl's magic powers over the wind that blows Conrad's hat and bends the trees derive from her femaleness, while this notion is further developed in **"Cinderella"** by the image of the tree growing out of the mother's grave (for which "out of the mother's body" may be read), while in **"One-Eye, Two-Eyes, and Three-Eyes"** a real woman appears on the scene to instruct Two-Eyes in how to address her goat to obtain food.[15]

Then the wise woman says: "Wipe away your tears, Two-Eyes, and I will tell you something to stop your ever suffering from hunger again; just say to your goat:

Bleat, my little goat, bleat,
Cover the table with something to eat,

and then a clean well-spread little table will stand before you, with the most delicious food upon it of which you may eat as much as you are inclined for, and when you have had enough, and have no more need of the little table, just say,

Bleat, bleat, my little goat, I pray,
And take the table quite away."

Sprach die weise Frau: "Zweiäuglein, trockne dir dein Angesicht, ich will dir etwas sagen, daß du nicht mehr hungern sollst. Sprich nur zu deiner Ziege:

Zicklein, meck,
Tischlein, deck,

so wird ein sauber gedecktes Tischlein vor dir stehen und das schönste Essen darauf, daß du essen kannst, soviel du Lust hast. Und wenn du satt bist und das Tischlein nicht mehr brauchst, so sprich nur:

Zicklein, meck,
Tischlein, weg."

Whatever power the girl displays must first be communicated by the real holder of the power, the wise woman, and can only be potentiated in the presence of a second being, a goat. But Two-Eyes has not become a simple conduit for power from natural sources, for she seems to possess magic powers of her own formulation. Later in the tale, she introduces an original incantation to send her sister off to sleep, although the second time she tries to lay this spell it fails her, an indication within the plot of an attenuated connection between women and natural powers. This failure leads her jealous sisters to kill Two-Eyes' goat, but the wise woman appears once more and directs Two-Eyes to request the goat's innards. Buried in front of the threshold, they produce a magical tree with silver leaves and golden apples, inaccessible to anyone but Two-Eyes, before whom the tree bends to yield its precious fruit.

The image of the tree is more socialized in **"One-Eye, Two-Eyes, and Three-Eyes"** than in **"The Goose-Girl."** In the former, the tree provides the heroine with a treasure trove. Thus its story emphasizes the achievement of high social status conferred by possessions rather than the immanent personal power evident in

"The Goose-Girl." In these three stories there is a clear pattern: the heroine's immanent power bears an inverse relationship to the presence of Christian elements. Just as there are no tears in **"The Goose-Girl,"** there also is not a single Christian element. In the second tale, the reader is told that Cinderella cried and prayed three times a day at her mother's grave, while in **"One-Eye, Two-Eyes, and Three-Eyes"** the reader is not only told that Two-Eyes, the weakest of the spell-layers in these tales, says a prayer before eating, but is also given the text of the prayer: "Lord God, be our Guest forever, Amen" (Herr Gott, sei unser Gast zu aller Zeit, Amen). Since female conjuring and Christianity seem to be in some way incompatible in *Grimms' Tales,* it is consistent that when a prayer appears in a tale about a girl who can lay spells, it should be the shortest one Two-Eyes knows, even though the text credits its brevity to her extreme hunger.

The primacy of possessions evident in **"One-Eye, Two-Eyes, and Three-Eyes"** may account for a transitional form of conjuring, which requires a magical object rather than a creature from the natural world to potentiate a command. Such an object appears in **"Sweet Porridge,"** where an aged woman meets a starving girl (poor but good) and gives her a magic pot, which will produce sweet porridge when she says: "Cook, little pot, cook" (Töpfchen, koche), until she stops it with the words "Stop, little pot" (Töpfchen, steh). The tale's humor grows out of the inexhaustible store of porridge that fills the village up to the last house, because the girl's mother, who starts the pot, doesn't know how to stop it. The girl, with her knowledge of the correct words, comes home just in time to stop the pot, but we are told that "whosoever wished to return to the town had to eat his way back" (wer wieder in die Stadt wollte, der mußte sich durchessen). Such tales can be found in many cultures throughout the world and over great periods of time, but here its significance lies in the fact that the girl, though the inheritor of the aged woman's knowledge, nonetheless requires an object to perform her magic, while the real magical powers lie not in her, or in her mother, but in the correct words themselves. Without them, the conjurer is powerless. This represents a marked change from the conjurings in **"The Goose-Girl," "Cinderella,"** or **"One-Eye, Two-Eyes, and Three-Eyes,"** for whom no such exactitude is required.

A different object, a magic knotted handkerchief analogous to the magic wand in French and English tradition, potentiates the invocation in the Low German tale "The Two King's Children." Confusingly composite, it unites familiar motifs from disparate traditions in a meandering literary fairy tale (*Kunstmärchen*). Three princesses live in a world populated by men: their father's masculine height is emphasized when he is described as a great tall man on his first appearance; the sisters' bedroom doors are guarded by statues of Saint Christopher; and the youngest sister has sway over numbers of little earth-men, whom she calls forth by taking her handkerchief, tying a knot in it, and striking it three times on the ground while saying; "Earthworkers, come forth" (Arweggers, herut!), and whom she dismisses with the words, "Earthworkers, go home" (Arweggers, to Hus!).

The earthworkers perform the stock impossible tasks for the hapless prince to help him win the youngest daughter as his bride. The king's wife, who materializes quite suddenly in midtale, pursues the fleeing couple and thus occupies the same position that witch figures do in analogous tales. But in an abrupt character reversal she later becomes a helpful maternal figure and provides her daughter with three walnuts, within each of which a beautiful gown is hidden. With them, the mother explains, her daughter can help herself when she is in greatest need. In the meantime, the prince returns home and announces his engagement, but his mother's kiss erases all memory of his betrothed, and he takes another bride. However, with her gowns, the young princess regains her betrothed's love; the prince's mother is declared to be false and must go away together with the false bride; and the two lovers have a merry wedding.

A highly confused picture of the two queens emerges from this tale. The narrator appears to have dimly remembered that old queens pass on magical powers and injects that motif in a timely manner in conjunction with the princess' mother. On the other hand, the prince's mother is made to waffle between an intentionally witchlike mother-in-lawdom and an unwittingly untoward influence on her son. Despite this confusion one element remains in its familiar channel: the earthworkers called forth by the young girl conform to the requirement that effective female conjuring grow out of an ultimate association or connection with the earth.

Men and magic coexist comfortably in *Grimms' Tales*. On occasion a man in a forest encounters an old woman who turns out to be a witch or who passes on important information in her incarnation as a wise woman. In **"Donkey Salad"** (RBB) (no. 122), for instance, an ugly woman meets a jolly hunter one day and tells him that if he eats the heart of a certain bird he will find a gold piece under his pillow every morning. It becomes clear from the tale, however, that whoever has the heart has the gold, and that the old woman has passed on no magic power to the hunter. All magic remains in the heart, which mindlessly enriches whoever has eaten it.

Men occasionally appear to share in women's spell-laying powers in the tales, but a close examination of these powers suggests that such tales derive from earlier forms with female protagonists or else are modern inventions. Male conjurations with a character distinctly

their own exist in three of the tales. The incantation that produces food in **"One-Eye, Two-Eyes, and Three-Eyes"** reappears in **"The Wishing-Table, the Gold-Ass, and the Cudgel in the Sack"** (no. 36), but it represents a derivative form. It offers, first of all, a shortened form of the incantation. Second, the magic clearly resides completely in the object rather than in the person. Third, two elements joined in **"One-Eye"** [**"One-Eye, Two-Eyes, and Three-Eyes"**]—the goat and the incantation—appear logically separated in **"The Wishing-Table."** [**"The Wishing-Table, the Gold-Ass, and the Cudgel in the Sack"**] And fourth, two elements—the goat and gold—remain linked but in altered form. In **"The Wishing-Table"** the narrator rather than a mysterious figure describes how one lays a spell:

> His master presented him with a little table which was not particularly beautiful, and was made of common wood, but which had one good property; if anyone set it out, and said: "Little table, spread yourself," the good little table was at once covered with a clean little cloth, and a plate was there, and a knife and fork beside it, and dishes with boiled meats and roasted meats, as many as there was room for, and a great glass of red wine shone so that it made the heart glad.

> [Der Meister] schenkte ihm ein Tischchen, das gar kein besonderes Ansehen hatte und von gewöhnlichem Holz war; aber es hatte eine gute Eigenschaft. Wenn man es hinstellte und sprach: "Tischchen, deck dich," so war das gute Tischchen auf einmal mit einem saubern Tüchlein bedeckt und stand da ein Teller und Messer und Gabel daneben und Schüsseln mit Gesottenem und Gebratenem, soviel Platz hatten, und ein großes Glas mit rotem Wein leuchtete, daß einem das Herz lachte.

The text hints at no particular link between the eldest son and chthonic powers; it is the table that possesses unmediated powers, like the lamps and rugs in the tales of *Thousand and One Nights*.

At first glance **"Ferdinand the Faithful and Ferdinand the Unfaithful"** (no. 126) seems to offer a clear example of successful male conjuring. Yet the natural creature, the talking white horse, represents an attenuated link with nature, for as the last sentence reveals, the horse is in reality a prince. Nonetheless, in his equine state, the horse tells Ferdinand how to calm dangerous giants and large birds, which he will encounter on his travels:

> When the giants come say:
> "Peace, peace, my dear little giants,
> I have had thought of ye,
> Something I have brought for ye."

> And when the birds come, you shall again say:
> "Peace, peace, my dear little birds,
> I have had thought of ye,
> Something I have brought for ye."

> Wenn dann de Riesen kümmet, so segg:
> Still, still, meine lieben Riesechen,

ich habe euch wohl bedacht,
ich hab euch was mitgebracht.

Un wenn de Vüggel kümmet, so seggst du wier:
Still, still, meine lieben Vögelchen,
ich hab euch wohl bedacht,
ich hab euch was mitgebracht.

Ferdinand himself, however, never utters these words in the text of the tale, neither in the First Edition nor in any subsequent edition. If he had, then one could cite at least one example of a male who successfully lays a spell, which grows out of a male association with an apparently natural being, for the form of the spell fits the requirements if one allows for an implied imperative form, "Be" (Sei) before the word "peace" (still).

The final spells laid by men occur in **"Brother Lustig"** (no. 81) and suggest that men's verbal efficacy derives from different sources than women's. Here a soldier watches Saint Peter resurrect a dead princess by dismembering the corpse, boiling the bones, rearranging them properly, and saying three times: "In the name of the holy Trinity, dead woman, arise" (Im Namen der allerheiligsten Dreifaltigkeit, Tote, steh auf). However, when Brother Lustig tries to revive another dead princess in a separate episode, he fails dismally, because he cannot put the bones in the proper order. His flawed knowledge of nature thus prevents the formula from working.

First impressions deceive. It would seem that *Grimms' Tales* is sprinkled with conjuring witches, but instead it is young and beautiful women who call forth and direct powerful natural forces. Each of these young females is also unmarried, and within the terms of these tales, presumably virgin. The forms spells take and the conjurers apparently regarded as licit in the Grimms' collection point toward a latent belief in the natural powers of women, especially of virgins. Unlike the more familiar and thoroughly Christianized French medieval image of the virgin with her inherent ability to attract the magical mythical unicorn, German tradition as it appears in *Grimms' Tales* defines a sharp boundary between female spell-laying powers and Christian belief.[16]

Notes

1. Throughout this chapter, *conjuring* is used interchangeably with *spell-laying* in a verbal sense, rather than with the connotation of manual legerdemain.

2. Upon her return, the enchantress "said in a hollow voice: 'Greet you, Zachiel. If the moon shines on the cage, Zachiel, let him loose at once'" (sagte mit dumpfer Stimme: "Grüß dich, Zachiel, wenn's Möndel ins Körbel scheint, bind los, Zachiel, zu guter Stund"): a rare, perhaps unique, example of an old woman actually using words magically. She is, perhaps significantly, disenchanting Joringel with her words rather than laying a spell.

3. Founded by Jacob Grimm while he attended the Vienna Congress in 1815 as a member of the Hessian legation.

4. In both the 1810 and 1812 versions of "Hansel and Gretel," the children return home on their own, but in the 1819 edition, Wilhelm added the white duck, whom Gretel summons by calling: "Oh, dear duckling, take us on your back" ("Ach, liebes Entchen nimm uns auf deinen Rücken"). Grimm later elaborated this brief command into a quasi spell, perhaps unwittingly but correctly putting it in a young girl's mouth. That this spell is an invention becomes clear from a comparison with true conjurings, which are always part of a link with nature mediated by a wise woman.

5. She addresses a "little green waiting maid, Waiting-maid with the limping leg, little dog of the limping leg" (Jungfer grün und klein, Hutzelbein, Hutzelbeins Hündchen), telling her to "Hop hither and thither, / And bring me the great box." (hutzel hin und her, / bring mir die große Schachtel her.) The conjuring form remains, perhaps because a female, even though a toad, is speaking.

6. It is not sufficient for an impatient mother to cry out, curselike, to her naughty little daughter, "I wish you were a raven and would fly away, and then I would have some rest" ("Ich wollte, du wärest eine Rabe und flögst fort, so hätt ich Ruhe") (no. 93, "The Raven"), nor for an impatient father to cry angrily about his seven sons, "I wish the boys were all turned into ravens" ("Ich wollte, daß die Jungen alle zu Raben würden") (no. 25: "The Seven Ravens"). See also Belgrader, "Fluch, Fluchen, Flucher."

7. A good example occurs in "The Poor Man and the Rich Man" (no. 87), when the greedy, irascible rich man uses up his three wishes apoplectically and fruitlessly, first responding to his horse's capering about by wishing it would break its neck, then wishing his wife to be stuck to the saddle he is carrying, and finally having to use his third wish to unstick her again.

8. *How to Do Things with Words,* 28-29. The separate chapters constituted the William James lectures of 1955 at Harvard University.

9. In *Das Recht in den Kinder- und Hausmärchen der Brüder Grimm,* Jens Christian Jessen understands the word-immanent power of magic in different terms, as an aspect of promising (*Versprechen*) (27).

10. According to Tacitus (*Germania,* 10), natural forces were believed to confer mantic powers on women by informing them of future events.

11. In the First Edition Wilhelm routinely placed notes on the tales in an appendix, but in this case he as-

terisked the line to a footnote appearing on the same page: "D.h. Windchen wehe! nicht die Ausrufung eher!"

12. The 1810 version of this tale is assumed to have been lost when the Grimms sent their collection to Clemens Brentano, but in the 1812 version this verse appears, requesting beautiful clothes ("wirf schöne Kleider herab für mich"). The spell took its present form in the 1819 edition, possibly to bring it into conformity with the gold- and silver-bearing tree of "One-Eye, Two-Eyes, and Three-Eyes" (no. 130). In the 1856 volume of notes to the collection, Wilhelm mentions a variant, "Hohe Weide, thu dich auf, / gib mir dein schön Geschmeide raus," which evokes precious metals without mentioning them. At this remove it is impossible to know whether the alteration to the spell resulted from his own invention or from a variant form, since the volume of notes that appeared in 1822, i.e., after the 1819 revision, does not mention the verses. The verses addressed to the tree and the one spoken by the birds remain unchanged through all editions from 1812 to 1858.

13. See a more detailed discussion of this subject in Bottigheimer, "The Transformed Queen."

14. As magic power is attenuated, expressions of grief increase. The goosegirl invokes the wind matter-of-factly; Cinderella waters the grave with her tears; and Two-Eyes weeps "so bitterly that two streams ran down from her eyes."

15. In "The Goose-Girl," trees have no textual association with the goosegirl's conjuring, but the illustration tradition accompanying this tale, begun by Ludwig Emil Grimm, displays trees prominently in the pictorial rendering of her conjuring. See Bottigheimer, "Iconographic Continuity in Illustrations of 'The Goosegirl.'"

16. This is all the more fascinating, since the Church had attempted, often successfully, to Christianize incantations used in daily life in Germany. For a recent discussion of this subject, see Robert Scribner, "Cosmic Order and Daily Life."

Bibliography

PRIMARY SOURCES

Grimm, Jacob. *Circular wegen Aufsammlung der deutschen Poesie.* 1815; Ed. Ludwig Denecke. Cassel: Brüder Grimm Gesellschaft, 1968.

———. *Deutsche Mythologie.* 1835; Graz: Akademische Druck- und Verlagsanstalt, 1953.

———. *Deutsche Rechtsalterthümer.* 2 vols. 1828; Darmstadt: Wissenschaftliche Buchgesellschaft, 1965.

———. *Kleinere Schriften.* 8 vols. 1882-90; Hildesheim: Georg Olms, 1966.

Grimm, Jacob and Wilhelm. *Altdeutsche Wälder.* 3 vols. 1813-16; Darmstadt: Wissenschaftliche Buchgesellschaft, 1966.

———. *Deutsche Sagen.* 2 vols. 1816-18; Philadelphia: Institute for the Study of Human Issues, 1981.

———. *Deutsches Wörterbuch.* 33 vols. Leipzig: S. Hirzel, 1852-1960.

———. *Sechs Märchen aus dem Nachlaß.* Ed. Johannes Bolte. Berlin: Brandus, 1918.

———. *German Legends.* 2 vols. Trans. Donald Ward. Philadelphia: Institute for the Study of Human Issues, 1981.

———. *German Popular Stories.* Trans. Edgar Taylor. London: John Camden Hotten, 1969.

———. *Grimms' Fairy Tales.* Trans. Margaret Hunt and James Stern. New York: Pantheon, 1944, 1972.

———. *Kinder- und Hausmärchen.* Large Editions: 1812-15; 1819; 1837; 1840; 1843; 1850; 1857. Small Editions: 1825, 1833, 1836, 1839, 1844, 1847, 1850, 1853, 1858.

SECONDARY WORKS

Austin, John L. *How To Do Things with Words.* The 1955 William James Lectures. Cambridge: Harvard University Press, 1962.

Belgrader, Michael. "Fluch, Fluchen, Flucher." *Enzyklopädie des Märchens* 4:1315-28.

Bottigheimer Ruth B. "Iconographic Continuity in Illustrations of 'The Goosegirl' (KHM 89)." *Children's Literature* 13. Ed. Margaret R. Higonnet and Francelia Butler. New Haven: Yale University Press, 1985. 49-71.

———. "The Transformed Queen: A Search for the Origins of Negative Female Archetypes in Grimms' 'Fairy Tales.'" *Amsterdamer Beiträge* 10 (1980): 1-12.

Jessen, Jens Christian. "Das Recht in den 'Kinder- und Hausmärchen' der Brüder Grimm.'" Diss., Kiel, 1979.

Scribner, Robert W. "Cosmic Order and Daily Life: Sacred and Secular in Pre-Industrial German Society." *Religion and Society in Early Modern Europe, 1500-1800.* Ed. Kaspar von Greyerz. London: George Allen and Unwin, 1984. 17-32.

Maria Tatar (essay date 1987)

SOURCE: Tatar, Maria. "Born Yesterday: The Spear Side." In *The Hard Facts of the Grimms' Fairy Tales,* pp. 85-105. Princeton, N.J.: Princeton University Press, 1987. Reprint. 2003.

[In the following essay, originally published in 1987, Tatar describes typical character traits of male protagonists in Grimms' Fairy Tales, *assessing the extent to which the plots of the stories correspond to their epithets and predicates.]*

> "There comes an old man with his three sons—"
>
> "I could match this beginning with an old tale."
>
> —Shakespeare, *As You Like It*

Identifying fairy-tale heroes by name is no mean feat. In the Grimms' collection, only one in every ten actually has a name. But it is also no secret that the most celebrated characters in fairy tales are female. Cinderella, Snow White, Little Red Riding Hood, and Sleeping Beauty: these are the names that have left so vivid an imprint on childhood memories. With the exception of Hansel, who shares top billing with his sister, male protagonists are exceptionally unmemorable in name, if not in deed. Lacking the colorful descriptive sobriquets that accord their female counterparts a distinctive identity, these figures are presented as types and defined by their parentage (the miller's son), by their station in life (the prince), by their relationship to siblings (the youngest brother), by their level of intelligence (the simpleton), or by physical deformities (Thumbling).[1]

Most people may be at a loss when it comes to naming fairy-tale heroes, but few have trouble characterizing them. "In song and story," writes Simone de Beauvoir, "the young man is seen departing adventurously in search of woman; he slays the dragon, he battles giants." And what are this young man's attributes? One commentator on the Grimms' collection describes him as "active, competitive, handsome, industrious, cunning, acquisitive." That list sums up the conventional wisdom on the dragon slayers and giant killers of fairy-tale lore.[2]

That conventional wisdom, however, proves to be a fairy tale so far as German folklore is concerned. A reading of the first edition of the *Nursery and Household Tales* reveals that there are exactly two dragon slayers and only one giant killer in the entire collection of some 150 tales.[3] One of those stories, **"Johannes-Wassersprung and Caspar-Wassersprung,"** rehearses the classic story of the slaying of a seven-headed dragon and the liberation of a princess, but (for unknown reasons) the tale never made it to the second edition of the *Nursery and Household Tales.* The other dragon-slaying hero bears the distinctly unheroic name Stupid Hans (Dummhans), and the contest in which he dispatches three dragons, each with a different number of heads, is less than gripping. As for the giant killer, he

succeeds in decapitating three giants, but only because the proper sword is placed directly in his path. If there is any attribute that these heroes share, it is naiveté. Like so many other heroes in the Grimms' collection, they are decidedly unworldly figures. "Innocent," "silly," "useless," "foolish," "simple," and "guileless": these are the adjectives applied repeatedly to fairy-tale heroes in the Grimms' collection.

Among folklorists, it is the fashion to divide heroes into two distinct classes. There are active heroes and passive heroes, "formal heroes" and "ideal heroes," dragon slayers and male Cinderellas, tricksters and simpletons.[4] According to theory, the oppositions active/passive, seeker/victim, brave/timid, and naive/cunning serve as useful guides for classifying fairy-tale heroes. In practice, though, it is not always easy to determine whether a hero relies on his own resources or depends on helpers. Does he have a zest for danger or does he simply weather the various adventures that befall him? Just what is his level of intelligence? What at first blush appear to be straightforward choices turn out to be fraught with complexities. The happy-go-lucky simpleton who appears to succeed without trying is not always as doltish as his name or reputation would lead us to believe, and the roguish trickster does not always live up to his reputation for shrewd reasoning.

There is a further complication. Despite their seeming artlessness, the *Nursery and Household Tales* are not without occasional ironic touches that subvert surface meanings. In particular, the epithets and predicates reserved for their protagonists can highlight utterly uncharacteristic traits. The eponymous heroine of **"Clever Else"** ranks high on the list of dull-witted characters; **"Hans in Luck"** charts a steady decline in its hero's fortunes; and the brave little tailor in the story of that title displays more bravado than bravery.[5] In the world of fairy tales, a simpleton can easily slip into the role of a cunning trickster; a humble miller's son can become a king; and a cowardly fool can emerge as a stout-hearted hero. Character traits display an astonishing lack of stability, shifting almost imperceptibly into their opposites as the tale unfolds. Bearing this in mind, let us take the measure of male protagonists in the Grimms' collection to determine what character traits they share and to assess the extent to which the plots of their adventures follow a predictable course.

If the female protagonists of fairy tales are often as good as they are beautiful, their male counterparts generally appear to be as young and naive as they are stupid. Snow White's stepmother may be enraged by her stepdaughter's superior beauty, but the fathers of male heroes are eternally exasperated by the unrivaled obtuseness of their sons. To the question, Who is the stupidest of them all? most fairy-tale fathers would reply: my youngest son. Yet that son is also the chosen son, the son who ultimately outdoes his older and wiser siblings. In an almost perverse fashion, fairy tales featuring male protagonists chart the success story of adolescents who lack even the good sense to heed the instructions of the many helpers and donors who rush to their aid in an attempt to avert catastrophes and to ensure a happy ending. "You don't really deserve my help," declares one such intercessor in frustration after his sage advice has been disregarded on no less than three occasions.[6]

In fairy tales all over the world, the one least likely to succeed paradoxically becomes the one most likely to succeed. Merit rarely counts; luck seems to be everything. Aladdin, the prototype of the undeserving hero who succeeds in living happily ever after, begins his rise to wealth and power under less than auspicious circumstances. The introductory paragraphs of his tale give the lie to the view that classical fairy tales reward virtue and punish evil. "Once upon a time," begins the story "Aladdin and the Enchanted Lamp," "there lived in a certain city of China an impoverished tailor who had a son called Aladdin. From his earliest years this Aladdin was a headstrong and incorrigible good-for-nothing." When he grows older, he refuses to learn a trade and persists in his idle ways until his father, "grieving over the perverseness of his son," falls ill and dies. Yet this same Aladdin, who becomes ever more wayward after having dispatched his father to the grave, ultimately inherits a sultan's throne. As one critic correctly points out, the story of Aladdin and his enchanted lamp exalts and glorifies "one of the most undeserving characters imaginable." It is telling that Aladdin made his way so easily from the pages of German translations of *The Thousand and One Nights* to the oral narratives of one region of Germany. Once his exotic name was changed to Dummhans, he was evidently quickly assimilated into Pomeranian folklore, so much so that it was difficult to distinguish him from native sons.[7]

The heroes of the *Nursery and Household Tales* may, for the most part, be unlikely to win prizes for intelligence and good behavior, but they are even less likely to garner awards for courage. Their stories chronicle perilous adventures, but they often remain both cowardly and passive. When summoned to discharge the first in a series of three tasks, the simpleton in **"The Queen Bee"** simply sits down and has a good cry. In **"The Three Feathers,"** the hero sits down and "feels sad" instead of rising to the challenges posed by his father. Fairy-tale heroines have never stood as models of an enterprising spirit, but it is also not rare for fairy-tale heroes to suffer silently and to endure hardships in a hopelessly passive fashion.

For all their shortcomings, the simpletons in the Grimms' fairy tales possess one character trait that sets them apart from their fraternal rivals: compassion. That compassion is typically reserved for the natural allies and benefactors of fairy-tale heroes: the animals that inhabit the earth, the waters, and the sky.[8] Even before the simpleton embarks on a journey to foreign kingdoms or undertakes diverse tasks to liberate a princess, he must prove himself worthy of assistance from nature or from supernatural powers by displaying compassion. Of the various tests, tasks, and trials imposed on a hero, this first test figures as the most important, for it establishes his privileged status. Once he exhibits compassion—with its logical concomitant of humility—he can do no wrong, even when he violates interdictions, disregards warnings, and ignores instructions. This preliminary test of the hero's character comes to serve the dual function of singling out the hero from his brothers and of furnishing him with potential helpers for the tasks that lie ahead.

Two fairy tales from the Grimms' collection illustrate the extent to which compassion is rewarded. In **"The Queen Bee,"** the youngest of three sons defends an anthill, a bevy of ducks, and a beehive from the assaults of his mischievous brothers. "Leave the animals alone," he admonishes his elders on three occasions. Compassion pays off in the end, for this youngest son is also the one to escape being turned to stone—a punishment that perfectly suits the crimes of his callous siblings. With the help of his newly won allies, the simpleton of the family discharges three "impossible" tasks written for him on a stone slab. He gathers a thousand pearls that lie strewn about the forest, fetches a bedroom key from the sea's depths, and succeeds in identifying the youngest of three "completely identical" sisters. To be more precise, the ants gather the pearls, the ducks fetch the key, and the bees identify the youngest sister. Yet the simpleton is credited with disenchanting the palace in which the trio of princesses resides; he thereby wins the hand of the youngest and earns the right to give the other two sisters in marriage to his brothers.

The hero of **"The White Snake,"** like the simpleton of **"The Queen Bee,"** hardly lifts a finger to win his bride. Once he displays compassion for wildlife by coming to the rescue of three fish, a colony of ants, and three ravens, he joins the ranks of the "chosen," who receive assistance from helpers as soon as they are charged with carrying out tasks. Although male fairy-tale figures have customarily been celebrated for their heroic feats, their greatest achievement actually rests on the passing of a character test. By enshrining compassion and humility, which—unlike intelligence and brute strength—are acquired characteristics rather than innate traits, the Grimms' tales make it clear to their implied audience (which gradually came to be adolescents) that even the least talented youth can rise to the top.[9]

Once the hero has proven himself in the preliminary character test, he is braced for the tasks that lie ahead.

The grateful beneficiaries of his deeds are quick to even out the balance sheet. As soon as the hero finds himself faced with an impossible task—emptying a lake with a perforated spoon, building and furnishing a castle over-night, devouring a mountain of bread in twenty-four hours—help is at hand. For every task that requires wisdom, courage, endurance, strength, or simply an ap-petite and a thirst of gargantuan proportions, there is a helper—or a group of helpers—possessing the requisite attributes. And ultimately the achievements of the helper redound to the hero, for he is credited with having drained the lake, built the castle, and consumed the bread.

Passing the preliminary test and carrying out the basic tasks are sufficient to secure a princess and her king-dom. Nonetheless, a number of fairy tales mount a third act in keeping with the ternary principle governing their plots.[10] The final trial the hero must endure is motivated by the reappearance of the fraternal rivals who vexed the hero in his earlier, preheroic days. The brothers seize the earliest opportunity to pilfer the hero's riches, alienate him from his beloved, malign his good name, or banish him from the land. Yet they are no match for the hero, who deftly outwits them and survives their as-saults. Although the hero is rarely instrumental in carry-ing out the tasks imposed on him, in the end he ac-quires the attributes of his helpers and gains the strength, courage, and wit needed to prevail.

Just as the humble male protagonist matures and is el-evated to a higher station in life, so his antagonists are demeaned and demoted in the final, optional segment of the tale. If the hero often distinguishes himself by show-ing mercy for animals, he remains singularly unchari-table when it comes to dealing with human rivals. "Off with everyone's head but my own," proclaims the hero of **"The King of the Golden Mountain."** And he makes good on that threat. Even brothers and brides are dispatched by fairy-tale heroes without a moment's hesitation once their deceit comes to light. The hero of **"The Knapsack, the Hat, and the Horn,"** for example, does away with his wife once he uncovers her duplicity. Treachery is punished as swiftly and as predictably as compassion is rewarded. This third phase of the hero's career endows his story with a symmetry and balance for which all tales strive. Like the first two acts, the fi-nal act stages a contest between a youth and his two older, but morally inferior brothers. Both dramatic con-flicts culminate in the rewarding of good will and the punishment of treachery; the last act simply intensifies the reward (a princess and a kingdom) and the punish-ment (death). In doing so, it adds not only moral reso-nance, but also a measure of finality to the tale. The hero has not only attained the highest office in the land, but has also eliminated his every competitor. For that office, he was singled out in the tale's first episode,

made singular in the tale's second part, and celebrated as the sole and single heir to the throne in the tale's coda.

The trajectory of the hero's path leads him to the goal shared by all fairy tales, whether they chart the fortunes of male or female protagonists. In keeping with the fun-damental law requiring the reversal of all conditions prevailing in its introductory paragraphs, the fairy tale ends by enthroning the humble and enriching the im-poverished. The male heroes of fairy tales are humble in at least one, and often in both, senses of the term. More often than not they are low on the totem pole in families of common origins. But whether born to the crown or raised on a farm, they are also frequently humble in character; without this special quality they would fail to qualify for the munificence of helpers and donors. Thus, humility seems to be the badge of the fairy-tale hero. And since humbleness, in one of its shades of meaning, can inhere in members of any social class, both princes and peasants are eligible for the role of hero in fairy tales.

Humility also comes to color the psychological makeup of fairy-tale heroines. Female protagonists are by nature just as humble as their male counterparts, but they dis-play that virtue in a strikingly different fashion and at a different point in their fairy-tale careers. Fairy tales of-ten highlight psychological characteristics by translating them into elements of plot; in the case of female hero-ines, this proves especially true. Daughters of millers and daughters of kings alike are not merely designated as humble; they are actually humbled in the course of their stories. In fact, *humbled* is perhaps too mild a term to use for the many humiliations to which female protagonists must submit.

Since most fairy tales end with marriage, it seems logi-cal to assume that a single tale suffices to illustrate the contrasting fates of male and female protagonists. Yet though there is often a happy couple at the end of a fairy tale, the fate of only a single, central character is at stake as the tale unfolds. That pivotal figure stands so firmly rooted at the center of events that all other char-acters are defined solely by their relationship to him and consequently lack an autonomous sphere of action. In **"Cinderella,"** for instance, even the bridegroom, for all the dashing chivalry attributed to him by Walt Dis-ney and others, remains a colorless figure. The tale tells us nothing more about him than that he is the son of a king. Lacking a history, a story, and even a name, he is reduced to the function of prince-rescuer waiting in the wings for his cue. The brides in stories of male heroes fare little better. Relegated to subordinate roles, they too fail to engage our interest. Still, there are exceptions to every rule, and the Grimms' collection provides one noteworthy variation on the principle that only one character can occupy center stage in fairy tales. **"The Goose Girl at the Spring"** weaves together the fates of both partners in the marriage with which it concludes. To be sure, there are signs that the tale is not of one piece, that at some historical juncture it occurred to one teller of tales to splice two separate plots.[11] Nonetheless, the two plots conveniently dovetail to create a single narrative. The story of the humble count and the humbled princess who marries him offers an exemplary study in contrasts between the lot of males and that of females in fairy tales culminating in wedding ceremonies.

"The Goose Girl at the Spring" commences with an account of the heroine's future bridegroom. The young man is handsome, rich, and noble, yet he must—like the most lowly fairy-tale heroes—prove his mettle by displaying compassion and humility. Without these virtues, his otherwise impeccable credentials would prove utterly worthless. And indeed, we learn that the young count is not only able to "feel compassion," but that he is also, despite his noble station, not too proud to translate compassion into action. Once he demonstrates his humility by easing the burdens of a feeble old hag shunned by everyone else, he earns himself a passport to luck and success. Like his many artlessly benevolent folkloric kinsmen, the count becomes the recipient of a gift that accords him a privileged status among potential suitors of a princess. The emerald etui bestowed upon him by the old hag ultimately leads him to his bride—a princess masquerading as a shepherdess.

Neither the count nor his rustic bride can boast humble origins. The unsightly girl tending geese at the beginning of the tale is not at all what she seems. At the well, she peels off her rural costume along with her rough skin to reveal that she must be a princess. Despite her aristocratic origins, she too can ascend to a higher position, for her fairy-tale days are spent in the most modest of circumstances. Unlike her groom, however, she was pressed into assuming a humble position when her own father banished her from the household. Like countless folkloric heroines, she suffers a humiliating fall that reduces her from a princess to a peasant, from a privileged daughter to an impoverished menial. Fairy-tale heroes receive gifts and assistance once they actively prove their compassion and humility; heroines, by contrast, become the beneficiaries of helpers and rescuers only after they have been abased and forced to learn humility.

There are many well-known tales of victimized female heroines who rise to or return to the ranks of royalty once they have been humbled and humiliated.[12] But no tales more explicitly display the humiliation prerequisite to a happy ending than **"King Thrushbeard," "The Mongoose,"** and **"The Six Servants."** King Thrush-

beard's bride furnishes a classic example of the heroine who earns a king and a crown after straitened circumstances break her arrogance and pride. It is not enough that she curses the false pride that led to her downfall; her husband must also solemnly state: "All of this was done to crush your pride and to punish you for the haughty way in which you treated me." When King Thrushbeard generously offers to reinstate her to a royal position, she feels so deeply mortified that she declares herself unworthy to become his bride. The princess in the tale known as **"The Mongoose"** also finds herself humbled by her prospective husband. Nonetheless, she takes the defeat in stride and observes to herself with more than a touch of satisfaction: "He is cleverer than you!" The princess-heroine of **"The Six Servants"** is also cheerfully repentant and resigned to her fate by the end of the story. Reduced to tending swine with her husband (a prince who has duped her into believing that he is a peasant), she is prepared to accept her lot: "I've only got what I deserved for being so haughty and proud." After revealing the true facts of his life, her husband justifies the deception by declaring: "I suffered so much for you, it was only right that you should suffer for me."

As the tale **"The Six Servants"** makes clear, young men "suffer" by taking the credit for tasks carried out by animal helpers, human servants, or supernatural assistants. Women suffer by being forced into a lowly social position. In short, male heroes demonstrate from the start a meekness and humility that qualify them for an ascent to wealth, the exercise of power, and happiness crowned by wedded bliss; their female counterparts undergo a process of humiliation and defeat that ends with a rapid rise in social status through marriage but that also signals a loss of pride and the abdication of power.

Before moving to another category of heroes, a quick review of our first class is in order. The naive hero in tales of three sons lacks the brains and brawn conventionally associated with heroic figures; he must rely on helpers with superhuman or supernatural powers to carry out every task demanded by a king in return for the hand of the princess. Instead of slaying dragons, he offers to louse them; instead of killing giants, he befriends them and makes himself at home in their dwellings. His demonstrations of compassion set the stage for the reversal of fortunes characteristic of fairy-tale plots. Only from a position of humility can he be elevated to the loftiest office in the land. Just as this hero works his way up the social ladder by climbing down it, so too he acquires intelligence and power by displaying obtuseness and vulnerability. Although it is never explicitly stated that he becomes smart and strong in the end, most fairy tales imply that their heroes have acquired the attributes of royalty right along with the office of king.

The youngest of three sons makes his way through magical kingdoms where an ant might plead for a favor, an enchanted princess could call on his services, or a dwarf might demand a crust of bread. But a second group of heroes in the Grimms' *Nursery and Household Tales* moves in what appears to be the more realistic setting of folk tales: villages and the roads connecting them. The cast of characters in tales with these heroes includes kings and princesses, yet the tales lack the supernatural dimension of fairy tales and tend to be more earthy in humor and down-to-earth in tone. The heroes are often far enough along in life to have a profession; many are apprentices, but some are tailors, foresters, tradesmen, or mercenaries. Many are men and not boys. (One is so old that he finds himself obliged to choose the eldest of twelve princesses when a king offers him one of his daughters in marriage.) Still, these heroes do not seem equipped with much more intelligence, strength, or valor than the young simpletons of fairy tales. They may not be village idiots, but in accordance with the general tendency of German folklore to avoid endowing male protagonists with heroic traits, their strengths are rarely described in much detail.

Naiveté also appears to be the principal hallmark of village boys and men. But what appears to be a character defect is in fact turned to good account once the protagonist determines to seek his fortunes in the world. Nietzsche once observed that fear is an index of intelligence, thus confirming the old saw that fools rush in where wise men fear to tread.[13] The more naive the hero, the more foolhardy and fearless he is, and the more likely he is to rise to the challenges devised to foil the suitors of a princess. Naiveté implies fearlessness, which in turn can take on the character of courage.

In much the same way that naiveté can shade into courage, it can translate into cunning. A hero's stupidity can take such extreme forms that it utterly disarms his antagonists. A young man who starts out handicapped by naiveté may in the end triumph over his adversaries by outwitting them. The protagonist unwise to the ways of the world can therefore be in the best possible position to exhibit heroic qualities by the close of the story.

Heroic feats performed by figures with clear character defects—lack of wisdom and wit—can end by producing comic effects. Blockhead, Numbskull, and Simpleton rush into one hazardous situation after another; they get the upper hand by putting their dim-wittedness on display, taking every word of advice that they hear literally; but they also escape harm because they are so naive that they confound their opponents. It may be true that they succeed in accomplishing the tasks laid out for them, but there is more than a touch of vaudeville to their every move.

The burlesque effect produced by tales chronicling the deeds of fearless heroes is perhaps most pronounced in **"The Fairy Tale of One Who Went Forth to Learn Fear."** The hero of that tale tries in vain to learn to be afraid, or more precisely, to shudder. Through one hair-raising episode after another he preserves his equanimity and coolly turns the tables on his would-be terrorizers. In one last desperate attempt to discover what it is to feel fear, he spends three nights warding off and ultimately exorcising the demons haunting a castle. His reward is the hand of a princess, but still he feels no fear. Only in his marriage bed does he finally learn to shudder, when his resourceful wife pulls off his covers and pours a bucketful of live minnows on him. Bruno Bettelheim is surely right to read psychosexual implications into the final act of the tale, particularly since the art of shuddering rather than the actual experience of fear constitutes the overt tale value. But the hero's inability to feel fear ought not to be construed as a negative trait; Bettelheim asserts that "the hero of this story could not shudder due to repression of all sexual feelings."[14] It is precisely the absence of the capacity to fear that enables the sprightly hero to withstand the horrors of a haunted castle and consequently to win the hand of his bride. Indeed, the inability to fear comes so close to courage here that the protagonist, for all his unflinching artlessness, begins to take on heroic attributes. Unlike his humble and helpless kinsmen in classical fairy tales of three sons, he breezily accomplishes one task after another without receiving aid from foreign agents. Were it not for the comic overtones to his adventures, it would seem entirely appropriate to place him in the class of heroes who live by their courage and wits.

If naiveté and courage are virtual synonyms in the folkloric lexicon, naiveté and cunning are also not far apart in meaning.[15] The more hopelessly naive and obtuse the hero of a tale, the more likely it is that he will triumph over his adversaries and that his adventures will be crowned with success. The Brave Little Tailor, who decorates himself for having dispatched seven flies with one blow, seems to stand as the very incarnation of fatuous vanity. Yet his bravado endows him with the power to outwit giants, to complete the tasks given by his bride's belligerent father, and to subdue a blue-blooded wife who is repelled by the thought of a marriage below her social station. In this tale, the line dividing naiveté from shrewdness and bravado from bravery has been effaced. The naive hero without fear and intelligence becomes virtually indistinguishable from the trickster.

By now it should be clear that the humble and naive youngest of three sons is a not-so-distant cousin of the fearless and naive hero. In fact, the hero of the Grimms' **"Crystal Ball"** combines the attributes of humble heroes and fearless fools; he possesses the simplicity and humility that go hand in hand with his familial status as the youngest of three sons, and he is also said to have "a heart without fear." It is above all his foolishly dauntless spirit that gives him the audacity to line up as the twenty-fourth suitor to seek out a princess imprisoned in the "Castle of the Golden Sun" and to undertake her liberation. And it is precisely his slow-wittedness that provides him with the means for arriving in the kingdom inhabited by the princess. He "forgets" to return a magical hat to two giants and thereby receives just the right means for transporting himself to that kingdom. In fairy tales, brashness can accomplish as much as bravery; naiveté is as effective as craft. The manifest lack of a virtue often translates into its possession. Just as Cinderella proves to be the fairest and the noblest of them all despite her shabby attire and her station at the hearth, so the simpleton of the family ultimately prevails over older and wiser antagonists.

As noted, the rigors of a fairy-tale hero's life endow him in the end with the attributes commonly associated with royalty. Even if the humble simpleton never lifts a sword and is incapable of answering a single question, let alone a riddle, he becomes a prince in more than just name. The feats of each and every woodland helper become his own deeds and accomplishments; he becomes a figure with all the qualities of dragon slayers and giant killers. Since our other class of tales, those featuring the comic adventures of heroes without fear, generally dispenses with tests of compassion, it also does away with the helpers responsible for elevating humble protagonists to heroic stature. Fearless heroes must rely wholly on their own mental and physical resources, however modest these may be. It is those resources that are put to the test in the opening paragraphs of the tale, where brashness achieves more than bravery, and artlessness proves more effective than artifice.

Since the hero without fear displays a greater measure of self-reliance than his humble kinsmen, the plot of his adventures contains the potential for greater realism. Gone are the encounters with talking animals, supernatural counselors, and other exotic agents. Instead, the hero meets hunters, locksmiths, sextons, innkeepers, and similar folk. He may not marry a peasant's daughter, but the castle in which he finally takes up residence has the distinct odor of the barnyard. Again, we are in the village rather than in an enchanted forest. Yet it would be misleading to label these tales realistic. They do not strive to hold up a mirror to the social conditions of the age or culture in which they were told. These are tall tales, stories that take advantage of exaggeration, punning, parody, and literalism to produce comic effects.

The many realistic touches in these folk tales, in tandem with their farcical aspects, point to their basic affinity with tales of tricksters, where professional fools, tradesmen, discharged soldiers, and youths of various other callings conspire to thwart their masters, creditors, or any other members belonging to the species of the overprivileged. Through ingenious disingenuousness they succeed in coming out on top. An open-ended episodic principle organizes the plot of both tall tales featuring heroes without fear and trickster stories. One absurd skirmish follows another, with no distinctive growth, development, or maturity. By contrast, the humble hero's adventures take the form of a three-act drama, with a test in the first act, tasks in the second, and a final trial crowned by success in the third. The goal may be the same for both types of heroes, but the paths bear little resemblance to each other.[16]

Tales charting the adventures of male protagonists posit from the start one dominant character trait that establishes a well-defined identity for the hero even as it proclaims his membership in the class of heroic figures. The verbal tag attached to the character ("Dummy," "the youngest of three sons," "Blockhead") ensures that he is recognized as the central character of the narrative. But in the course of the hero's odyssey, his dominant character trait begins to shade into its opposite through a process of inversion. The humble hero weds a woman of royal blood; the brazen fool proves his mettle; the naive simpleton outwits just about anyone. In fairy tales and folk tales, the youth lacking a good pedigree, a stout heart, and a sharp wit is precisely the one who wins a princess and a kingdom.

Inversion of character traits is a common occurrence in folkloric narratives. A reversal of the conditions prevailing at the start is, after all, manifestly the goal of every tale. The folktale in general, as Max Lüthi has observed, has "a liking for all extremes, extreme contrasts in particular." Its characters, he further notes, are either beautiful or ugly, good or bad, poor or rich, industrious or lazy, and humble or noble.[17] Yet much as readers and critics insist on the folk-tale's low tolerance for ambiguity and stress the inflexibility of the attributes assigned to heroes and villains, the frequency with which inversion appears suggests that they overstate their case. Just as "Beast" can be at once savage and civilized, so the youngest of three sons can be both simpleton and sage, humble lad and prince, coward and hero. Both character attributes and social conditions can rapidly shift from one extreme to the other.

That character traits are not as standardized or programmed as would appear becomes evident if we analyze the fate of one character who does not figure prominently in the pantheon of folkloric heroes. The eponymous protagonist of **"Hans in Luck"** might, in fact, well be called an anti-hero. In the course of his travels, he outwits no one; he instead becomes the victim of numerous transparently fraudulent transactions. His fortunes, rather than rising, steadily decline. And at the end of his journey, he seems no wiser and is decidedly less prosperous than he was at the beginning. Still, Hans is said to be lucky, and he feels he is among the happiest men on earth. The steps of Hans's journey to felicity are easy enough to retrace. After serving his master loyally and diligently for seven years, Hans winds his way home with a weighty emolument: a chunk of gold the size of his head. Hans happily barters this monetary burden for a horse that will speed him on his way. In the further course of his journey, he exchanges the horse for a cow, the cow for a pig, the pig for a goose, and the goose for a grindstone and rock. Even after these two worthless rocks land at the bottom of a well, leaving him nothing to show for seven years of labor, Hans remains undaunted. He literally jumps for joy and praises God for liberating him from the burdens that slowed his journey. Unencumbered by earthly possessions and with a light heart, Hans heads for his mother's home.

Conventional wisdom has it that the happy-go-lucky hero of this tale stands as the archetypal fool. The very title of the tale, **"Hans in Luck,"** is charged with irony: only a fool would delight in parting with the hefty wages Hans receives from his master. Yet on closer inspection, it becomes clear that the story of lucky Hans may also celebrate freedom from the burden of labor. On the last leg of his journey, Hans jettisons grindstone and rock—the tools of the trade that was to secure for him a steady flow of cash; at the outset of his journey, he rids himself of the gold with which his labor was compensated. In a stunning reversal of the value system espoused in fairy tales, Hans's story not only substitutes rags for riches, but also supplants marriage to a princess in a foreign land with a return home to mother. In short, it ends where most tales begin. Instead of charting an odyssey toward wealth and marriage, it depicts the stations of a journey toward poverty and dependence. But in remaining wholly indifferent to the wages of labor and freeing himself from its drudgery, Hans displays a kind of wisdom that invalidates ironic readings of his tale's title. Bereft of material possessions yet rich in spirit, he turns his back on the world of commerce to embrace his mother.[18]

The story of lucky Hans dramatically demonstrates the impossibility of establishing a fixed set of character traits shared by male heroes. Like Hans, who is both foolish and wise, poor and rich, lucky and unfortunate, the heroes of numerous fairy tales possess attributes that imperceptibly shade into their opposites. All the same, it is clear that certain oppositions (humble/noble, naive/cunning, timid/courageous, compassionate/ruthless) are encoded on virtually every fairy tale with a male hero. It is, then, difficult to draw up an inventory of immutable character traits, largely because a single figure within a tale can—and usually does—have one character trait and its opposite. But it is equally diffi-

cult, if for different reasons, to establish precise models for the plots of tales featuring male heroes. For every score of heroes who wed princesses and inherit kingdoms, there is one who returns home as an impoverished bachelor. For ten heroes who receive assistance and magical gifts by demonstrating compassion, there is one who acquires aid and magical objects through an act of violence. For every animal bridegroom who is released from a curse through the love and devotion of a woman, there is one who is disenchanted by the callous treatment he receives at the hands of his bride. To be sure, there is a measure of predictability in these plots, but only if we bear in mind that every narrative norm established can be violated by its opposite. Thus the preliminary test of good character at the start of tales with a ternary plot structure can be replaced by a demonstration of the hero's ruthlessness. The story of a hero dependent on magical helpers in carrying out appointed tasks can exist side by side with the tale of a hero who acts autonomously and takes on the characteristics of helpers.[19]

Recognizing and appreciating the fairy tale's instability—its penchant for moving from one extreme to another—is vital for understanding its characters, plots, and thematic orientation. Fairy-tale figures have few fixed traits; they are re-formed once they reach the goals of their journeys, when they become endowed with the very qualities in which they were once found wanting. Male protagonists may adhere slavishly to the ground rules of heroic decorum, or they may break every rule in the book; either way, their stories end with accession to the throne. And finally, the conditions prevailing at the start of the tales are utterly reversed by the end. The fairy tale, in sum, knows no stable middle ground. Inversion of character traits, violation of narrative norms, and reversal of initial conditions are just a few of the ways in which it overturns notions of immutability and creates a fictional world in which the one constant value is change.

In this context, it is worth emphasizing once again some of the disparities between folkloric fantasies and social realities. The radical reversals that lift fairy-tale heroes from humble circumstances to a royal station were virtually unknown during the age in which fairy tales developed and flourished, but they undeniably correspond to childhood fantasies of past ages and of our own day. If in real life the youngest of three sons rarely had the wherewithal to succeed in life or to transcend his station in life, fairy tales held out the promise that humility and other virtues might well outweigh the benefits of an inheritance. But beyond offering consolation to underprivileged sons who lived in an era when primogeniture was custom or law, fairy tales more generally respond to the insecurities of every child. Even the eldest child is likely to perceive himself less gifted or less favored than his siblings and can thereby readily identify with simpleton heroes. Fundamental psychological truths, rather than specific social realities, appear to have given rise to the general plot structure of those tales.

A stable plot still leaves much room for variation. Skillful raconteurs can take the same story line and give it unique twists and turns. The tone may vary from one tale to the next, and the hero may be presented in different lights. As Robert Darnton has shown, comparing different national versions of a single tale type can be a revealing exercise. Reading through various tellings of "Jack the Giant Killer," one can register the changes from "English fantasy to French cunning and Italian burlesque." More important, there are subtle shifts in the character of the protagonist as he slips from one culture into another. Darnton has observed that the trickster figure is especially prevalent in French folklore and literature.[20] By contrast, as we have seen, the simpleton or (to put it in more flattering terms) the guileless youth figures prominently in the Grimms' collection. These differences between the folkloric heroes of the two cultures may, however, be more apparent than real, for the roguish Gallic trickster and his naive Teutonic counterpart have more in common than one would suspect. Even the names most frequently bestowed in the *Nursery and Household Tales* on the two types (Dummling for the simpleton and Däumling for the trickster) suggest that they are kindred spirits. Both the simpleton and the trickster ultimately make good by outwitting or outdoing their seemingly superior adversaries. Still, the shift in emphasis from cunning to naiveté as one moves across the Rhine is telling, suggesting that the French celebrate cleverness and audacity while the Germans enshrine the virtue of guilelessness.

If we take a closer look at German literary traditions—both oral and written—it becomes clear that the naive hero is by no means a folkloristic aberration. He fits squarely into a long tradition of such figures. Wolfram von Eschenbach's Parzival, who comes to incarnate the highest chivalric ideals, is described as *der tumme* (the young and inexperienced one). Dressed by his mother in the costume of a fool, he mounts a wretched nag to seek his fortune in the world. Although there are hints that he is something of a dragon slayer (he arrives at Munsalvæsche during the feast of Saint Michael, the vanquisher of Satan as dragon), the only dragons he slays are emblazoned on his opponent's helmet. But like folkloric heroes, Parzival knows no fear and consequently displays valor on the battlefield. Although he fails the initial test of compassion, in the course of his adventures he develops that quality and learns humility.

Remaining in the same poetic climate but moving to another era, we find that Richard Wagner's Siegfried also launches his heroic career as a naive youth without fear. The resemblances between his story and the **"Fairy**

Tale of One Who Went Forth to Learn Fear"** are unmistakable. To his cantankerous guardian, Mime, Siegfried confides that he wishes to learn what it is to fear, to which Mime responds that the wise learn fear quickly, the stupid have a harder time of it.[21] Siegfried clearly belongs in the latter category. Like the one who went forth to learn fear, he discovers that emotion in the experience of love. As he sets eyes on the sleeping Brünnhilde, he feels a mystifying quickening of emotions:

> How cowardly I feel.
> Is this what they call fear?
> Oh mother! mother!
> Your fearless child!
> A woman lies in sleep:
> She has taught him to be afraid!

> *(Siegfried, act 3)*

No one was more surprised by the resemblances between the Grimms' fairy-tale character and the heroic Siegfried than Richard Wagner. In a letter to his friend Theodor Uhlig, he wrote: "Haven't I ever told you this amusing story? It's the tale of the lad who ventures forth to learn what fear is and who is so dumb that he just can't do it. Imagine my amazement when I suddenly realized that that lad is no one else but—young Siegfried."[22]

It would not be difficult to identify countless other guileless fools and lads without fear in German literature. From the baroque era through the romantic period to the present, naiveté is the signature of many a literary hero. The protagonist of Grimmelshausen's *Simplicius Simplicissimus* may be a clever rogue, but his name is telling. Like Parzival, he moves from foolish innocence to an understanding of the ways of the world, though his story ends in disillusion. Goethe's *Wilhelm Meister's Apprenticeship,* perhaps the finest exemplar of the *Bildungsroman,* that most hallowed of German literary traditions, gives us a naive innocent who happens to be fortunate enough to stumble into the right circles. We do not have to look far in the romantic era for heroes pure in heart and innocent in spirit. Each and every one of them—from Novalis's Heinrich von Ofterdingen to Josef von Eichendorff's Florio—begins the first leg of his journey into the wild blue yonder as a charming young man wholly untutored in worldly matters.

Twentieth-century German literature has no shortage of similar types. In a belated introduction to *The Magic Mountain,* Thomas Mann makes a point of bowing in the direction of Hans Castorp's literary antecedents. Mystified by the way in which the weight of literary tradition—without his knowing it—determines his protagonist's character, he is also flattered by the company in which literary critics placed his hero. Both Parzival and Wilhelm Meister, he notes, belong to the class of "guileless fools," and his Hans Castorp is no different.

His "simplicity and artlessness" make him a legitimate literary cousin of those two quester figures. Yet Hans Castorp can also display all the wisdom of an innocent: when he wants something, he can be "clever," "crafty," and "shrewd." That Mann further emphasizes resemblances "here and there" between Hans Castorp's story and fairy tales comes as no surprise.[23]

It may seem to be stretching a point to suggest that fairy tales can tell us something about what historians of the *Annales* School call *mentalités*. Yet, throughout the ages, storytellers have embroidered the narratives passed on to them with the cultural values as well as with the facts of their own milieu. Every subtle change can be significant, so long as it takes place on a large scale and does not simply represent one idiosyncratic telling of a tale. What the Grimms' collection tells us about heroes does not deviate fundamentally from what other German folkloric and literary sources declare. There is far more to naiveté than meets the eye.

Notes

1. Max Lüthi asserts that the disproportionately large number of female heroines in fairy tales can be traced to the prominent role women played in shaping the plots. See "The Fairy-Tale Hero," in *Once upon a Time: On the Nature of Fairy Tales,* trans. Lee Chadeayne and Paul Gottwald (Bloomington: Indiana University Press, 1976), pp. 135-46. By contrast Ralph S. Boggs asserts that 80 percent of German tales have a hero and that only 20 percent have a heroine ("The Hero in the Folk Tales of Spain, Germany and Russia," *Journal of American Folklore* 44 [1931]: 27-42). Neither Lüthi nor Boggs identifies his statistical sample.

2. Simone de Beauvoir's characterization appears in *The Second Sex,* trans. H. M. Parshley (New York: Bantam, 1952), pp. 271-72. For the list of heroic attributes, see Jack Zipes, *Fairy Tales and the Art of Subversion: The Classical Genre for Children and the Process of Civilization* (New York: Wildman Press, 1983), p. 57.

3. The first edition is reprinted in *Die Kinder- und Hausmärchen der Brüder Grimm: Vollständige Ausgabe in der Urfassung,* ed. Friedrich Panzer (Wiesbaden: Emil Vollmer, 1953).

4. On the various types of heroes, see Katalin Horn, *Der aktive und der passive Märchenheld* (Basel: Schweizerische Gesellschaft für Volkskunde, 1983); August von Löwis of Menar, *Der Held im deutschen und russischen Märchen* (Jena: Eugen Diederichs, 1912); Ralph S. Boggs, "The Hero in the Folk Tales of Spain, Germany and Russia," pp. 27-42; Vincent Brun, "The German Fairy Tale," *Menorah Journal* 27 (1939): 147-55; and

Louis L. Snyder, "Cultural Nationalism: The Grimm Brothers' Fairy Tales," in *Roots of German Nationalism* (Bloomington: Indiana University Press, 1978), pp. 35-54.

5. Constance Spender makes this point. See "Grimms' Fairy Tales," *The Contemporary Review* 102 (1912): 673-79.

6. These are the words of the fox in the Grimms' version of "The Golden Bird."

7. *Tales from the Thousand and One Nights,* trans. N. J. Dawood (Harmondsworth, Middlesex: Penguin Books, 1973), p. 165. Robert Crossley makes the point about Aladdin's lack of merit ("Pure and Applied Fantasy, or From Faerie to Utopia," in *The Aesthetics of Fantasy Literature and Art,* ed. Roger C. Schlobin [Notre Dame, Indiana: University of Notre Dame Press, 1982], pp. 176-91). On Aladdin's fortunes in Germany, see Erich Sielaff, "Bemerkungen zur kritischen Aneignung der deutschen Volksmärchen," *Wissenschaftliche Zeitschrift der Universität Rostock* 2 (1952/53): 241-301.

8. On the ethnographic significance of animals in fairy tales, see Lutz Röhrich, "Mensch und Tier im Märchen," *Schweizerisches Archiv für Volkskunde* 49 (1953): 165-93.

9. Eugen Weber finds that the celebration of compassion in fairy tales reflects the rareness of that virtue during the age in which the tales flourished: "Kindness, selflessness is the greatest virtue (perhaps because there is so little to give, perhaps precisely because it is so rare)." See "Fairies and Hard Facts: The Reality of Folktales," *Journal of the History of Ideas* 42 (1981): 93-113.

10. On the three phases of action in classical fairy tales, see E. Meletinsky, S. Nekludov, E. Novik, and D. Segal, "Problems of the Structural Analysis of Fairytales," in *Soviet Structural Folkloristics,* ed. P. Maranda (The Hague: Mouton, 1974), pp. 73-139. The authors divide the action of fairy tales into a preliminary test, a basic test, and an additional, final test.

11. Note the use in the tale of such heavy-handed transitions as "But now I must tell you more about the king and the queen, who had left with the count." On the presence of only one single sharply defined plot in classical fairy tales, see Max Lüthi, *The European Folktale: Form and Nature,* trans. John D. Niles (Philadelphia: Institute for the Study of Human Issues, 1982), p. 34. Lüthi uses the term *Einsträngigkeit* (single-strandedness) to designate the absence of digressive plot lines in fairy tales. *Einsträngigkeit* is the term that Walter A. Berendsohn also uses to characterize the fairy tale's

one-track plot structure in *Grundformen volkstümlicher Erzählkunst in den Kinder- und Hausmärchen der Brüder Grimm: Ein stilkritischer Versuch* (Hamburg: W. Gente, 1921), p. 33. The term has its origins in Axel Olrik's essay of 1919, which has been translated as "Epic Laws of Folk Narrative," in *The Study of Folklore,* ed. Alan Dundes (Englewood Cliffs, N.J.: Prentice-Hall, 1965), pp. 129-41.

12. On abasement as "a prelude to and precondition of *affiliation*" in "Cinderella," see Madonna Kolbenschlag, *Kiss Sleeping Beauty Good-bye: Breaking the Spell of Feminine Myths and Models* (New York: Doubleday, 1979), p. 72.

13. Friedrich Nietzsche, "Morgenröte," bk. 4, in *Friedrich Nietzsche: Werke in drei Bänden,* ed. Karl Schlechta (Munich: Hanser, 1954), vol. 1, p. 1172.

14. Bruno Bettelheim, *The Uses of Enchantment: The Meaning and Importance of Fairy Tales* (New York: Random House, Vintage Books, 1977), p. 281.

15. Stith Thompson emphasizes the ambiguous nature of the trickster's intellect: "The adventures of the Trickster, even when considered by themselves, are inconsistent. Part are the result of his stupidity, and about an equal number show him overcoming his enemies through cleverness." See *The Folktale* (1946; rpt. Berkeley: University of California Press, 1977), p. 319. In *World Folktales: A Scribner Resource Collection* (New York: Charles Scribner's Sons, 1980), Atelia Clarkson and Gilbert B. Cross confirm the ambiguity when they point out that "the most incongruous feature of the American Indian trickster is his tendency to become a dupe or play the buffoon even though he was the wily, clever trickster in a story told the day before" (p. 285).

16. Variants of the tale of the courageous tailor demonstrate that a single core theme can lend itself to two types of narratives: a biographical tale that focuses on the life of a hero and on his attempt to win the hand of a princess and an episodic tale that focuses on the various pranks played by a trickster. See the seven variants of "Das tapfere Schneiderlein," in Leander Petzoldt, *Volksmärchen mit Materialien* (Stuttgart: Ernst Klett, 1982), pp. 42-72.

17. Max Lüthi, *The European Folktale,* pp. 34-35.

18. For a reading of the story along similar lines, see Roderick McGillis, "Criticism in the Woods: Fairy Tales as Poetry," *Children's Literature Association Quarterly* 7 (1982): 2-8.

19. As Vladimir Propp puts it, "when a helper is absent from a tale, this quality is transferred to the hero." See *Morphology of the Folktale,* trans. Laurence Scott (Austin: University of Texas Press, 1968), p. 83.

20. Robert Darnton, "Peasants Tell Tales: The Meaning of Mother Goose," in *The Great Cat Massacre and Other Episodes in French Cultural History* (New York: Basic Books, 1984), pp. 9-72. The quoted phrase appears on p. 44.

21. The retort is in Wagner's first version of *Siegfried* (Richard Wagner, *Skizzen und Entwürfe zur Ring-Dichtung,* ed. Otto Strobel [Munich: F. Bruckmann, 1930], p. 113).

22. The letter, dated 10 May 1851, appears in Richard Wagner, *Sämtliche Briefe,* ed. Gertrud Strobel and Werner Wolf (Leipzig: VEB Deutscher Verlag für Musik, 1979), vol. 4, pp. 42-44. Heinz Rölleke discusses Wagner's dependence on the Grimms' fairy tale in "Märchen von einem, der auszog, das Fürchten zu lernen: Zu Überlieferung und Bedeutung des *KHM* 4," *Fabula* 20 (1979): 193-204.

23. Thomas Mann, *The Magic Mountain,* trans. H. T. Lowe-Porter (New York: Knopf, 1964), pp. 719-29. Castorp is described, in German, as a "Schalk"; he is "verschmitzt" and "verschlagen." Mann's remarks on the fairy-tale quality of Castorp's story appear on p. v. Unfortunately Helen Lowe-Porter translated Mann's term *Märchen* (fairy tale) as "legend."

Maria M. Tatar (essay date 1988)

SOURCE: Tatar, Maria M. "Beauties vs. Beasts in the Grimms' *Nursery and Household Tales*." In *The Brothers Grimm and Folktale,* edited by James M. McGlathery, Larry W. Danielson, Ruth E. Lorbe, and Selma K. Richardson, pp. 133-45. Urbana: University of Illinois Press, 1988.

[*In the following essay, Tatar examines the textual history of the Bluebeard folktale in* Nursery and Household Tales, *contrasting narrative elements of "Mary's Child" and "Fowler's Fowl."*]

Fairy-tale beauties may all be very much alike, but there are two quite different types of beasts in the Grimms' **Nursery and Household Tales.** First, there are the animal-grooms who make life unpleasant for many a female protagonist: these are the frogs, bears, hedgehogs, and other creatures that press themselves on attractive young girls. But these beasts invariably turn out to be handsome young princes in disguise and generally prove to be perfect gentlemen. The real fairy-tale beasts, even if they are beasts in only the figurative rather than the literal sense of the term, turn out to be murderers masquerading as civilized men: Bluebeard, the Robber Bridegroom (in the tale of that title), and the wizard in **"Fowler's Fowl" ("Fitchers Vogel")** are the most prominent examples in the *Nursery and Household Tales*.

Bluebeard, the most infamous of this entire lot of beasts, entered the pages of the Grimms' collection, but only in its first edition. For the second, revised edition of 1819, the Grimms eliminated the tale, evidently because it was too close in both substance and verbal realization to its French source. Still, Bluebeard was not done away with entirely. He stood as model for at least one villain in the Grimms' collection, and his wife lent her traits to more than one fairy-tale heroine. For this reason, it will be useful to take a brief detour into the realm of Perrault's Mother Goose, then to trace our way back to a path that leads directly into the world of the Grimms' *Nursery and Household Tales*.

The heroine of Perrault's "Bluebeard" may be a woman of "perfect beauty," but her character is flawed by the nearly fatal sin of curiosity. When her husband tests her by entrusting her with the key to a forbidden chamber, she is so plagued by curiosity that she "rudely" leaves the guests in her house to their own devices, then nearly breaks her neck in her haste to reach the forbidden door. At the door she hesitates as she meditates on the possible consequences of being "disobedient." But the temptation is too great, and she unlocks the door to witness a grisly scene of carnage in the forbidden chamber: "the wives of Bluebeard, whose throats he had cut, one after another."[1] When Bluebeard discovers the evidence of his wife's transgression, he flies into a rage and swears that this woman too will die by his sword. The heroine's brothers arrive in the nick of time to prevent their sister from joining the victims in Bluebeard's chamber.

Perrault harbored no doubts about the meaning and message of this story. "Bluebeard" has two different "moralités" appended to it. The first warns women of the hazards of curiosity, a trait that "costs dearly" and brings with it "regrets." The second reminds us that Bluebeards no longer exist in this day and age: "The time is long gone when there were strict husbands, / And no man will demand the impossible / Even if he is plagued by jealousy and unhappiness."[2] Perrault's description of Bluebeard as a "strict" husband who demands "the impossible" squares with the facts of the text. But his declaration that Bluebeard is "plagued by jealousy and unhappiness" gives us an extratextual piece of evidence concerning the motivation for testing his wives. Bluebeard, Perrault implies, is the victim of sexual jealousy—hence his need to subject each successive wife to a test of absolute obedience. In that test, which becomes as much a test of fidelity as of obedience, Bluebeard's new wife, like all the others before her, fails miserably.

Nearly every reader and rewriter of Bluebeard has fallen in line with the interpretation implicit in Perrault's two morals to the tale. Bruno Bettelheim's view is representative. In Bluebeard he sees a cautionary tale armed with the message "Women, don't give in to your sexual curiosity; men, don't permit yourselves to be carried away by your anger at being sexually betrayed." For Bettelheim, the bloodstained key (in some versions it is an egg) that Bluebeard's wife is obliged to surrender to her husband clinches the argument that she has had "sexual relations" and symbolizes "marital infidelity."[3] For another reader, that key becomes a symbol of "defloration," revealing the heroine's sexual betrayal of her husband during his absence.[4] For a third, it marks the heroine's irreversible loss of her virginity.[5]

What Bettelheim and others do with few hesitations, reservations, and second thoughts is to turn a tale depicting the most brutal kind of serial murders into a story about idle female curiosity and duplicity. These critics follow Perrault's lead and invite us to view the heroine's quite legitimate *cognitive* curiosity (what does her husband have to hide?) as a form of sexual curiosity and sexual betrayal that can only bring in its wake serious "regrets." The genuinely murderous rages of Bluebeard and his folkloric cousins would presumably never have been provoked had it not been for the symbolic infidelity of his wives. As horrifying as those multiple murders may be, they do not succeed in deflecting attention from the heroine's single transgression. That transgression, like the opening of Pandora's box, comes to function as the chief source of evil. In Ludwig Tieck's "Ritter Blaubart," even Bluebeard's wife is appalled by her inability to resist temptation. "O curiosity," she declaims, "damned, scandalous curiosity! There's no greater sin than curiosity!" Her self-reproaches are uttered in full view of the scene of carnage for which her husband bears responsibility. Bluebeard himself confirms his wife's appraisal of her high crimes (by contrast to his misdemeanors): "Cursed curiosity! Because of it sin entered the innocent world, and even now it leads to crime. Ever since Eve was curious, every single one of her worthless daughters has been curious. . . . The woman who is curious cannot be faithful to her husband. The husband who has a curious wife is never for one moment of his life secure. . . . Curiosity has provoked the most horrifying murderous deeds."[6] This is surely a case of the pot calling the kettle black. Whether intentionally or not, Tieck revealed the extent to which literary retellings of Bluebeard blame the victim for the crimes of the villain. Is it any wonder that in the nineteenth century Anatole France attempted to rehabilitate Bluebeard by pointing out that there never really were any corpses in the forbidden chamber: Bluebeard's wife headed for that room with such breakneck speed because a handsome young man was waiting for her on the other side of the door.[7] Here, once again, the heroine's cognitive curiosity in the folktale is taken as a sign of sexual curiosity, while Bluebeard's murderous sexual curiosity (he takes one wife after another) is taken as rage at his wife's sexual curiosity.

As Bluebeard became appropriated by the literary culture of the nineteenth century, it was transformed from a folktale describing the rescue of a maiden from a murderous ogre (AT [Aarne-Thompson] 312) into a text warning of the evils of female curiosity. Oral folktales (even those of relatively recent vintage) rarely embroider on the theme of curiosity and disobedience; instead the tales' narrative energy is funneled into the mounting dramatic tension that arises as the heroine's brothers race to Bluebeard's castle while the heroine stalls for time, resorting to various tactics to keep her husband from cutting her throat or decapitating her before the arrival of her brothers. A related tale type (AT 311) focuses on the clever ruses mounted by the youngest of three sisters to outsmart and defeat an ogre who has slaughtered her sisters.[8] It was Perrault, in his literary version of an orally transmitted tale, who took the first steps in the direction of converting a dramatic encounter between innocent maiden and barbaric murderer into a moral conflict between corrupt woman and corrupted man.

That female curiosity has been enshrined as the central subject of this tale is confirmed by a brief glance at the pictorial history of Bluebeard. One illustrator after another emphasizes one of two "key" scenes in the tale: the arousal of curiosity is masterfully put on display in Gustave Doré's illustration for Perrault's "Bluebeard"; the satisfaction of curiosity is depicted in one of ten sketches prepared by Otto Brausewitz. Again and again these two scenes capture the attention of the tale's illustrators. Walter Crane's drawing of Bluebeard's wife on her way to the forbidden chamber is also revealing. As the curious heroine slips away from her guests, she passes by a tapestry that provides a moral gloss on her action: Eve is shown succumbing to temptation in the Garden of Eden. The sin of Bluebeard's wife originated with Eve, and all of Eve's daughters (as the tableau of inquisitive guests opening cupboards, chests, and drawers tells us) suffer from it. "Succumbing to temptation," as one commentator on Bluebeard feels obliged to remind us, "is the sin of the Fall, the sin of Eve."[9] When women give in to temptation, they symbolically reenact the Fall, committing a deed tainted with the evil of sexual curiosity. Like Eve, they may begin their quest in a search for cognitive knowledge, but it ultimately ends in the desire for carnal knowledge.

In light of the interpretive vicissitudes of Bluebeard, it is easy enough to see why the Grimms may have had moral reservations—in addition to their other objections—for including that story in the second edition of the *Nursery and Household Tales.* The second edition, after all, was rewritten with a view toward producing a collection of tales suitable for children's ears. And Perrault's version of the tale, as we have seen, lent itself all too easily to interpretations that veered off into areas that most parents preferred to avoid for bedtime reading. For whatever reasons the Grimms decided against including in their collection the tale of Bluebeard that had come into their hands, they were not at all opposed to including variants of that tale type, even in their second edition. Those variants, however, branch out into two radically different directions.

Let us begin with the variant that makes of the tale type a cautionary tale pure and simple—one in which the evils of curiosity are writ even larger than in Perrault's "Bluebeard" and in which the figure substituted for Bluebeard is beyond reproach. **"Mary's Child"** **("Marienkind")** gives us a remarkable recasting of the story of a forbidden chamber. The Grimms' heroine, who has been rescued from starvation and taken up to heaven by the Virgin, cannot resist the temptation to unlock a door to which Mary has given her the key. Behind the door, she sees the blinding splendor of the Holy Trinity and touches it with her finger, which becomes gilded. When Mary discovers the evidence of the girl's transgression, she makes the unrepentant child mute and sends her back down to earth. In one tale variant heard by the Grimms and recorded in their annotations, the Virgin silences the girl by slapping her on the mouth so hard that blood gushes forth. That the Virgin Mary could slip with ease into the same functional slot occupied by Bluebeard is telling and does much to explain why it became easy for rewriters and critics of the tale type to let Bluebeard off the hook. The heroine's disobedience is so unattractive a trait that violence and bloodshed pale by comparison. What is even more remarkable than Mary's adoption of Bluebeard's role is her assumption of the part, in the second half of **"Mary's Child,"** ordinarily played by an ogress. After the heroine's marriage to a king, the Virgin returns on three occasions to demand a confession, each time kidnapping the queen's latest newborn in retaliation for her failure to tell the truth. When the queen confesses at last (just before she is about to be burned at the stake), Mary releases her and restores the three children to her. "Now that you have told the truth," Mary declares, "you are forgiven." The Virgin spells out one lesson of the story; the other lesson has to do with the perils of curiosity, with the girl's inability to avoid taking a peek at the forbidden.

In this story, we have something of a reversal of the ground rules operating in classical children's fairy tales. In the final analysis, it is the heroine's antagonist who wins; the heroine, stubborn as she may be, must admit defeat in the end. **"Mary's Child"** is only one of several such cautionary tales that side with adults. **"Frau Trude,"** one of the less well known texts in the *Nursery and Household Tales,* is a story that few children could find satisfying. "Once there was a girl who was stubborn and insolent, and disobeyed her parents." In addition, she is unable to curb her curiosity and is driven to see with her own eyes Frau Trude, a "wicked" woman who does "godless things." In the end, the girl is turned into a block of wood that Frau Trude casually throws into the fire to provide heat. Here, the evil witch wins for once. But more than that, the world of adults wins out over the child, taking revenge for childish stubbornness, insolence, and disobedience. There is only one other story in the *Nursery and Household Tales* that surpasses **"Frau Trude"** in its stark portrayal of the punishment of children. **"The Stubborn Child"** ("Das eigensinnige Kind") tells of a naughty youngster who refuses to do what its mother commands. "God was displeased and made it fall sick." The child dies, is buried, but still asserts itself even beyond the grave by thrusting an arm into the air. Only when the mother makes her way to the grave and whips the arm with a switch does the child find peace.

Each of these three stories preaches a straightforward lesson about the virtues of telling the truth, suppressing curiosity, and practicing obedience. It is therefore surprising to hear the Grimms declare, in the preface to the *Nursery and Household Tales,* that their stories were never intended "to instruct, nor were they made up for that reason." These tales seem consciously designed to impart specific lessons framed by adults for children. As cautionary tales, they demonstrate how children with undesirable traits—deceitfulness, curiosity, insolence—come to a bad end.

We have seen how the breathtaking, bloodcurdling story of an ogre's murderous schemes against a young woman could be recast to create a didactic tale celebrating the triumph of adult authority over childish deviousness and deviance. But the conversion took place only with time, as oral folktales moved from *Spinnstuben* and workrooms into the nursery and household, as the audience for the stories shifted from adults to children.[10] The revisions in the Grimms' second edition were motivated in part by harsh contemporary criticism of the first edition, which was deemed adult entertainment rather than children's literature.[11] For the second edition it was logical to replace **"Bluebeard,"** with its forbidden chambers, bloody keys, and maimed corpses, with **"Mary's Child,"** a story that few adults in the Grimms' day and age would have found offensive. There, the figure who incarnates authority in its most tyrannical form is turned into a saint and therefore becomes impossible to associate with villainy. Instead, evil emanates solely from the tale's obstinately disobedient protagonist, who in the end is punished for her transgression. The quick-

est way to "teach someone a lesson," as our language puts it, is to punish them. **"Mary's Child,"** with its foregrounding of the transgression/punishment pattern, stands as one of the most striking examples of a fairy tale crafted to teach a lesson both to its protagonist and to its youthful readers.

There is another story in the Grimms' collection that belongs virtually to the same tale type as Bluebeard, yet its conclusion moves in a very different direction, and it is therefore designated as AT 311 rather than 312. **"Fowler's Fowl"** casts an evil wizard in the role of Bluebeard and features three sisters, two of whom succumb to curiosity, disobey the wizard, discover a bloodbath behind the door forbidden to them, and are executed by their cold-blooded fiancé. The third and youngest sister is "clever and sly." She has the foresight to put into a safe place the egg that her two sisters dropped in their fright at witnessing the scene of carnage. With not a single shred of evidence for her transgression, the wizard loses his power over the heroine, and she is able both to resurrect the mutilated corpses of her sisters and to engineer the downfall of the wizard. The plot of this story follows the classic lines of children's fairy tales: it begins with a display of weakness and victimization at the hands of an all-powerful adversary and ends with a tableau of revenge and retaliation.

In the Grimms' *Nursery and Household Tales,* we have few dragon slayers and giant killers. What we have instead are endless variations on male Cinderellas: Hans Dumm, the youngest of three sons, or a fearless simpleton. Helplessness and abject self-pity are the characteristic poses struck by these figures. Female heroines fare little better: Cinderella, Thousandfurs (Allerleirauh), Snow White, King Thrushbeard's wife, and a variety of princesses must wash dishes, haul firewood, scrub floors, polish boots, and carry out all manner of domestic chores before they are translated into a higher social sphere. But the tables are turned before the tale ends. The hero's accession to wealth and power drains the strength of his adversaries, who become helpless targets of revenge. Punishments overshadow nearly all else in the coda to a large number of the Grimms' tales. The description of Cinderella's wedding is almost wholly devoted to an elaborate account of how doves peck out the eyes of the stepsisters. Snow White's wedding really has only one central event: the death of the stepmother after she is forced to dance in red-hot iron shoes. The king, the queen, and her six brothers may all live happily ever after in **"The Six Swans,"** but not until the queen's wicked mother-in-law has first been burned at the stake. The hero of **"The Knapsack, the Hat, and the Horn"** triumphs in the end by blowing on his horn until everything around him collapses, crushing to death the duplicitous king and princess of the tale. "Revenge can be as sweet as love," Musäus points out in the version of "Snow White" that he published in his *Volksmärchen der Deutschen.* Revenge comes to function as the main motor of the plot in countless fairy tales.[12]

The protagonists of classic children's fairy tales have never placed a premium on good manners and virtuous behavior. The hero of **"The Golden Bird"** lies, cheats, and steals his way to success, all the while ignoring the advice of his helper. Rapunzel deceives her enchantress-guardian by arranging secret meetings with a prince. And the princess of **"The Frog King"** dashes against the wall the importunate amphibian who once came to her aid. Fairy-tale heroes are also rarely prepared to forgive and forget. Wicked stepmothers are forever being stripped and rolled down hills in barrels embedded with nails or turned out into the woods to be devoured by wild animals. That Two-eyes forgives her sisters in the story **"One-eye, Two-eyes, and Three-eyes"** is a startling exception to the rule of fairy-tale conduct. Virtually any tactic used to work one's way up the ladder of social success is considered legitimate; once on the top rungs, the protagonist has no reservations about toppling those above him. Still, from Perrault on, there has been no end to inscribing moral lessons even on tales that clearly have no moral. When Wilhelm Grimm was preparing the second edition of the *Nursery and Household Tales,* for example, he gave the father of the princess in **"The Frog King"** an additional line of dialogue: "[The frog] helped you when you were in trouble and you mustn't despise him now." But the father's pronouncements on the importance of keeping promises and remaining loyal move against the grain of the story itself. The Frog King is not released from his enchanted state until the princess displays her contempt for him through an act of physical violence. Passion rather than compassion leads to a happy ending. The protagonists of fairy tales rarely achieve their ends by observing strict ethical codes.

The textual history of **"Bluebeard"** in the Grimms' *Nursery and Household Tales* illustrates clearly the way in which a single plot can be channeled into two separate and distinct types of stories. The one trusts Perrault's tale and its literary "moralité" on the hazards of curiosity; the other relies on the oral folktales on which Perrault himself probably based his text. What started out as a story pitting a Beauty against a Beast was turned, on the one hand, into a story staging a struggle between a pathological liar and a saint. **"Mary's Child"** shows us how adult patience wins out over childish disobedience, deception, and stubbornness. Children are guilty of transgressions; adults visit punishments on the transgressors. Power is invested solely in adults, who use their superior strength and intelligence to teach children a lesson. These stories, with their single-minded focus on the transgression/ punishment pattern, their unique power relationships, and their explicit morals, belong to a breed apart—one that is best designated by the term cautionary fairy tale.

"Bluebeard," as we have seen, also took another course in the Grimms' collection, one that resulted in the demonization of the figure named in the story's title. **"Fowler's Fowl"** (along with its variant known as **"The Robber Bridegroom"**) sets up a conflict between a wholly innocent young girl and an evil mass murderer. The contrast between heroine and villain could not be more striking. Against all odds, the helpless heroine triumphs over her powerful adversary. It is easy enough to see just why this particular story would prove attractive to children. A sense of utter vulnerability in the face of a seemingly capricious all-powerful figure replicates perfectly the feelings of the young child toward adults. The movement in this fairy tale, and in others, from victimization to retaliation gives vivid but disguised shape to the dreams of revenge that inevitably drift into the minds of every child beset by a sense of weakness and inconsequence. Fairy tales such as **"Fowler's Fowl"** put on display the victory of children over adults—power is ultimately put into the hands of the powerless. For the transgression/punishment pattern of cautionary fairy tales, these tales substitute its obverse: victimization/retaliation. They do not have a lesson to preach; if a general truth or moral precept is enunciated in the course of the narrative, it rarely squares with the actual facts of the text. What **"Fowler's Fowl," "The Robber Bridegroom,"** and other such stories give us are classic children's fairy tales—stories in which innocent young Beauties (male or female) always defeat the adult Beasts.

Notes

1. "Bluebeard," in *Perrault's Complete Fairy Tales,* trans. A. E. Johnson et al. (New York: Dodd, Mead, 1961), p. 81.

2. Ibid., p. 88. I have taken the liberty of modifying the translation slightly to make it more literal.

3. Bruno Bettelheim, *The Uses of Enchantment: The Meaning and Importance of Fairy Tales* (New York: Random House, Vintage Books, 1977), pp. 301-2. Bettelheim's interpretation and those of other critics are discussed in my book *The Hard Facts of the Grimms' Fairy Tales* (Princeton, N.J.: Princeton University Press, 1987), pp. 158-61.

4. Alan Dundes, "Projection in Folklore: A Plea for Psychoanalytic Semiotics," in his *Interpreting Folklore* (Bloomington: Indiana University Press, 1980), p. 46.

5. Carl-Heinz Mallet, *Kopf ab! Gewalt im Märchen* (Hamburg: Rasch und Rohring, 1985), p. 201.

6. Ludwig Tieck, "Ritter Blaubart," in *Werke,* ed. Richard Plctt (Hamburg: Hoffmann und Campe, 1967), pp. 226, 238.

7. Anatole France, *The Seven Wives of Bluebeard and Other Marvelous Tales,* trans. D. B. Stewart (London: John Lane, 1920), pp. 3-40.

8. For summaries of or references to printed versions of "Bluebeard," see Antti Aarne, *The Types of the Folktale: A Classification and a Bibliography, Translated and Enlarged by Stith Thompson* (Helsinki: Academia Scientiarum Fennica, 1961), pp. 101-4; Paul Delarue, *Le Conte populaire français* (Paris: Erasme, 1957), I, 182-99; and Johannes Bolte and Georg Polívka, *Anmerkungen zu den Kinder- und Hausmärchen der Brüder Grimm,* vol. 1 (Leipzig: Dieterich, 1913), 398-412.

9. J. C. Cooper, *Fairy Tales: Allegories of the Inner Life* (Wellingborough, Northhamptonshire: Aquarian Press, 1983), pp. 72-73. The illustrations are discussed in my book, *The Hard Facts of the Grimms' Fairy Tales,* pp. 161-63.

10. On this point, see Jack Zipes, *Fairy Tales and the Art of Subversion: The Classical Genre and the Process of Civilization* (New York: Wildman Press, 1983), p. 31.

11. See the first chapter of my *Hard Facts of the Grimms' Fairy Tales.*

12. Johann Karl August Musäus, *Volksmärchen der Deutschen* (Munich: Winkler, 1976), p. 115. On revenge in fairy tales, see also Bettelheim, *Uses of Enchantment,* pp. 133-34.

Selected Bibliography

Editor's Note: This list represents a selection of items from the notes to the individual essays, together with additional references included to enhance its usefulness as a guide to further reading on the subject of the Grimms and folktale.

I. Translations

Grimm, Jacob, and Wilhelm Grimm. *Grimm's Fairy Tales: Complete Edition.* Translated by Margaret Hunt and [revised by] James Stern. Introduction by Padraic Colum. Afterword by Joseph Campbell. New York: Pantheon, 1944. (Paperback ed., New York: Random House, Pantheon Books, c. 1972.)

Perrault, Charles. *Perrault's Complete Fairy Tales.* Translated by A. E. Johnson et al. New York: Dodd, Mead, 1961.

II. Editions

Grimm, Jacob, and Wilhelm Grimm. *Die älteste Märchensammlung der Brüder Grimm: Synopse der handschriftlichen Urfassung von 1810 und der Erstdrucke von 1812.* Edited by Heinz Rölleke. Cologny-Genève: Fondation Martin Bodmer, 1975.

———. *Kinder- und Hausmärchen der Brüder Grimm in ihrer Urgestalt: Vollständige Ausgabe in der Urfassung [1812/1815].* Edited by Friedrich Panzer. Wiesbaden: Emil Vollmer, [1955].

———. *Kinder- und Hausmärchen: Gesammelt durch die Brüder Grimm. Vergrößerter Nachdruck der zweibändigen Erstausgabe von 1812 und 1815 nach dem Handexemplar des Brüder Grimm-Museums Kassel mit sämtlichen handschriftlichen Korrekturen und Nachträgen der Brüder Grimm sowie einem Ergänzungsheft, Transskriptionen und Kommentare.* Edited by Heinz Rölleke with Ulrike Marquardt. 3 vols. Göttingen: Vandenhoeck & Ruprecht, 1986.

———. *Brüder Grimm: Kinder- und Hausmärchen, nach der zweiten vermehrten und verbesserten Auflage von 1819, textkritisch revidiert und mit einer Biographie der Grimmschen Märchen versehen.* Edited by Heinz Rölleke. Cologne: Eugen Diederichs, 1982.

———. *Kinder- und Hausmärchen: Kleine Ausgabe.* Berlin: Reimer, 1825.

———. *Kinder- und Hausmärchen: Ausgabe letzter Hand mit den Originalanmerkungen der Brüder Grimm, mit einem Anhang sämtlicher, nicht in allen Auflagen veröffentlichter Märchen.* Edited by Heinz Rölleke. 3 vols. Reclams Universal-Bibliothek, 3191-93. Stuttgart: Reclam, 1980.

———. *Märchen aus dem Nachlaß der Brüder Grimm.* Edited by Heinz Rölleke. Wuppertaler Schriftenreihe Literatur, 6. 3d rev. ed. Bonn: Bouvier, 1983.

III. General

Aarne, Antti, and Stith Thompson. *The Types of the Folktale: A Classification and Bibliography.* (See Thompson, Stith)

Bettelheim, Bruno. *The Uses of Enchantment: The Meaning and Importance of Fairy Tales.* New York: Alfred A. Knopf, 1976; New York: Random House, Vintage Books, 1977.

Cooper, J. C. *Fairy Tales: Allegories of the Inner Life.* Wellingborough, Northhamptonshire: Aquarian Press, 1983.

Delarue, Paul. "Les contes merveilleux de Perrault et la tradition populaire." *Bulletin folklorique d'île-de-France,* 14 (1953), 511-17.

Dundes, Alan. *Interpreting Folklore.* Bloomington: Indiana University Press, 1980.

Mallet, Carl-Heinz. *Kopf ab! Gewalt im Märchen.* Hamburg: Rasch und Rohring, 1985.

Thompson, Stith. *The Types of the Folktale: A Classification and Bibliography. Antti Aarne's Verzeichmis der Märchentypen Translated and Enlarged by Stith Thompson.* Helsinki: Suomalainen Tiedeakatemia, 1961.

Zipes, Jack. *Fairy Tales and the Art of Subversion: The Classical Genre and the Process of Civilization.* New York: Wildman, 1983.

IV. THE GRIMMS AND FOLKTALE

Bolte, Johannes, and Georg Polívka. *Anmerkungen zu den Kinder- und Hausmärchen der Brüder Grimm.* 5 vols. Leipzig: Dieterich, 1913-32; rpt. Hildesheim: Georg Olms, 1963.

Jeffrey Alan Triggs (essay date winter 1989)

SOURCE: Triggs, Jeffrey Alan. "Fevers Deeply Burning. Sexuality in the Brothers Grimm's 'Nixie of the Millpond.'" *Studies in Short Fiction* 26, no. 1 (winter 1989): 86-90.

[In the following essay, Triggs analyzes the treatment of human sexuality in "The Nixie of the Millpond," focusing on the tale's representation of sexual love.]

One of the rare Grimm's stories that deserves greater attention is **"The Nixie of the Millpond."**[1] Rich in symbolic detail and psychological depth, embodying in Joseph Campbell's phrase "a world of magic . . . symptomatic of fevers deeply burning in the psyche," it well repays close critical study.[2] Like **"East of the Sun and West of the Moon"** and other tales from the so-called "animal groom" sequence, **"The Nixie of the Millpond"** is steeped in the mysteries of human sexuality, with which it deals simply but not simple-mindedly. In the tradition of romantic comedy, to which most fairy stories adhere, it offers hope in the ultimate benignancy of the human condition without understating the dangers and the difficulties we all know to be a part of that condition. **"The Nixie of the Millpond"** celebrates in festive terms a full, rounded view of sexual love towards which so many in the latter twentieth century grope with increasing anxiety and frustration.

The plot is fairly complicated for a fairy tale. It begins with a miller who has lost his fortune through one of those quirks of fate common in fairy tales as in life. One day, as he wanders near his mill, he sees a beautiful woman rising from the water. Although he rightly takes her to be a water spirit and reacts at first with fear, she cunningly wins his confidence and offers to restore his fortune in return for "the young thing which has just been born" in his house. Unwittingly, he consents to this bargain, and only later discovers that his wife has just given birth to a baby boy. The miller is remorseful and brings up his son to fear the water and the nixie. But over the years, as his fortune returns and the nixie does not appear to claim her part of the bargain, the miller begins to feel at ease about the nixie. The boy grows up to be a fine huntsman and is married to a "true-hearted maiden" from the village. Everything is fine until he accidentally ventures near the pond to wash his hands after hunting. The nixie ascends, "smilingly" wraps her arms around him, and drags him under. The huntsman's wife goes to the millpond when her husband does not return and, finding his hunting pouch by the shore, guesses what has happened. Vainly, she curses the nixie and paces around the pond. After many hours, she falls asleep and dreams that she climbs a mountain and visits an old woman who lives in a little cottage. Upon waking, she resolves to act in accordance with her dream and indeed discovers the old woman in her cottage.

On three occasions, the woman offers the wife gifts to take to the millpond. Whenever the wife leaves one of the gifts at the water's edge, she sees part of her husband's body appear above the water. Each time, however, a wave rises from the pond and drags him down again. The third time, the husband manages to escape with his wife, but the couple are threatened by a tidal wave. In desperation, the wife calls on the old woman for help, and she responds by turning the wife into a toad and her husband into a frog. They thus escape the flood, though the water separates them, and when they regain their human form, they cannot find each other. In their need, they both turn to tending sheep and drive their flocks for years, "full of sorrow and longing." One spring they meet by chance but do not recognize each other. They do feel comforted in each other's company, however, and so continue their friendship. One day the man pulls out a flute and begins to play. The woman weeps on hearing this and, when questioned, replies that the air was one she had played on a golden flute (one of the wife's gifts to the nixie) on one of the occasions when she had seen her husband rise from the water of the millpond. The two then recognize each other and live happily thereafter.

The plot is composed of three loosely connected sections: the story of the miller inadvertently offering up his child, the story of the son's capture and his wife's valiant efforts to free him, and the story of the couple's separation and eventual reunion. The miller's story, a common motif in fairy tales, is curiously incomplete. He does not undergo any development and indeed disappears from the story completely after the first part. And since the husband plays a relatively passive role throughout, the main focus of interest is on two characters, the nixie and the wife. Interestingly, their parts overlap—the nixie appearing in the first two thirds of the story, the wife in the last two thirds. The miller and the old woman balance each other in the first two sections and are completely absent from the last section, which is left to the husband and wife alone. The progress of the plot is to isolate and make autonomous the married pair. The story's symmetry derives from its balancing of characters: the miller against the old woman, the nixie against the wife, and ultimately the wife with the husband.

The miller and the old woman function at strategic moments to propel the plot. In effect, they represent the harmful and helpful influence of an older generation on the young couple. The miller's foolish greed in trading his son for gold—an act he regrets but does not disclaim (he accepts the nixie's gold in spite of the probable consequences of this action)—predestines his son's bad fortune. The old woman balances the miller's greed with her own generosity. Her golden gifts—a comb, a flute, and a spinning wheel—enable the wife to pay back the nixie for the gold she gave the miller. The old woman, whose white magic counters the black magic of the nixie, acts also as a mother figure to the young wife, duplicating in her relation to the wife the miller's relation to his son. Together they suggest the ambiguous relation of the older generation to the younger often found in comedy. The miller is a blocking character, or *senex iratus,* while the helpful old woman is a type of *eiron,* facilitating the young lovers' escape to a festive conclusion.

The nixie and the wife are the characters most interesting in themselves. They are described in such opposite terms that one is almost tempted to think of the old Victorian dichotomy of the whore and the angel of the house. In a certain sense, such a symbolic opposition suggests a splitting of character and thus essential identity. The nixie and the wife are negative images of each other. The wife has long black hair. The nixie has long hair also, and although its color is not specified, we may imagine from her obvious association with figures like the Lorelei, that her hair is blonde. The nixie is always described in what are essentially sexual terms. When the miller meets her, she is presumably naked and holds her long hair "off her shoulders with her soft hands." She is described as having a "sweet voice," which she uses to manipulate the miller. Her taking of the huntsman is described as an erotic act: "Scarcely, however, had [the huntsman] dipped [his hands] in than the nixie ascended, smilingly wound her dripping arms around him, and drew him quickly down under the waves." The wife, on the other hand, seems completely asexual. She is "a beautiful and true-hearted maiden" when she marries the hunter, and we are given no reason to suppose that she changes until her husband is taken from her. Though the two "loved each other with all their hearts," they have no children, and one may infer that their domestic paradise is innocent of its sexual component. At this point, the "love" of the huntsman and the "true-hearted maiden" is more akin to *agape* than *eros.*

Indeed, this is the heart of the story. Bruno Bettelheim has argued interestingly that all good fairy tales suggest some moral or emotional development on the parts of

their heroes and heroines.[3] The development of the huntsman and his wife is a matter of accepting sexual maturity. The huntsman must learn to become a husbandman (suggested by his career change from hunter to shepherd, from predatory male, as it were, to nurturing protector), while the wife must learn to acquire some of the nixie's arts, in other words to found and embrace the sexual side of her nature. Until they do this, they are embroiled in what is essentially a love triangle. Lacking a sexual component in his marriage, the huntsman, like many other men, has gone hunting for it and wound up in the clutches of the nixie. The fact that he is captured while washing his hands after having disemboweled a deer reinforces this notion. The location of such drives in the unconscious is suggested by his visiting the pond, the natural habitat of the nixie. The wife too has to come to terms with her unconscious sexual drives; she must visit the pond three times to dicker with the nixie and ultimately learn to survive in some form in the watery element.

The wife's development is the most interesting part of the tale. It begins with her dream of the old woman, suggesting that the route she must take is through the unconscious. From the old woman she learns how to be a woman, and the implication of the dream is that this growth is achieved only by a fuller understanding of herself. The three gifts she receives from the old woman are fairly commonplace in fairy tales (one thinks, for instance, of the similar gifts in **"East of the Sun and West of the Moon"**), but they are of interesting symbolic significance in this context. The comb, flute, and spinning wheel suggest three important aspects of a woman's love, if not woman herself: sexual attractiveness, a spiritual component, and domestic industry (the spinning wheel, I dare say, was more commonly used in its day by women of a certain class than the microwave oven in our own time). The flute is also of special significance, implying that in order to rise above empty sex, love must have a spiritual element—a "primal sympathy," to borrow a phrase from Wordsworth. Indeed, it is this primal sympathy, suggested by the remembered melody of the flute, which brings about the festive *anagnorisis* and *peripeteia* of the conclusion.

The primal sympathy was always there, as we know— "they loved each other with all their hearts"—but to achieve a mature and lasting love, the couple must first learn to deal with and domesticate the sexual sides of their natures. They must deal with and escape from the nixie. It is interesting that their escape is made possible by their being changed into amphibian creatures. Bettelheim contends persuasively that amphibians in fairy tales are almost always sexual symbols, primitive creatures associated with the primitive drives of the id as well as "our ability to move from a lower to a higher stage of living."[4] The transformation to amphibians suggests that the couple are at last able to deal with their sexuality and indeed to transcend it. The process is not easy, however, and the husband and wife must spend years as shepherds (a symbolic wandering in the desert) before they recognize each other in terms of mature love. The act of shepherding represents the effort to domesticate their drives, the symbolic husbanding of sexual energy necessary for the social ideal of a family. This is not a limiting of sexual possibility, nor the imposition of unrealistic expectations, but the hope of a healthy society, the hope of renewal and regeneration which the greatest comic art dramatizes and predicts.

Notes

1. All references to "The Nixie of the Millpond" are to *The Complete Grimm's Fairy Tales,* trans. Margaret Hunt and James Stern (New York: Random House, 1972), pp. 736-741.

2. Joseph Campbell, "The Question of Meaning," in *The Complete Grimm's Fairy Tales,* p. 863.

3. Bruno Bettelheim, *The Uses of Enchantment: The Meaning and Importance of Fairy Tales* (New York: Vintage Books, 1977).

4. Bettelheim, p. 101.

James M. McGlathery (essay date 1991)

SOURCE: McGlathery, James M. "Fathers and Daughters." In *Fairy Tale Romance: The Grimms, Basile, and Perrault,* pp. 87-112. Urbana: University of Illinois Press, 1991.

[*In the following essay, McGlathery explores the erotic implications of the father-daughter relationship in the romantic folktales of the Brothers Grimm, Giambattista Basile, and Charles Perrault, highlighting common plot scenarios.*]

As the stories discussed thus far show, emotional involvement between parents and children is a frequent object of portrayal in folktales. That this is especially true of the romantic tale should come as no surprise, for in love plots generally the requisite hindrance to the fulfillment of young desire often takes the form of parental objection or intervention. There are surprises to be found here, however. In particular, the romantic folktale offers the possibility of hinting, with seeming innocence, at erotically tinged undercurrents in the relationship between parent and child that do not lend themselves to tasteful direct portrayal.

Fairy tale romance often depicts the child's first experience of leaving home and venturing out on its own, usually in connection with choosing a mate. In the stories of the brother and sister type, resistance to the tak-

ing of this step is reflected in a desire to return to the bosom of the family or, failing that, to retain the devoted company of one's siblings. Thus, we have seen how Hansel and Gretel, while prepared to survive together in the forest if need be are overjoyed at being able to live with their father, and how the sister in **"The Seven Ravens"** succeeds in restoring her brothers to human form and bringing them home with her. Or when the situation at home precludes returning there—as in **"The Twelve Brothers," "The Six Swans," "The Little Lamb and the Little Fish,"** and **"Little Brother and Little Sister"**—the siblings set up housekeeping together elsewhere or the sister marries and the brother joins the new household.

The aspect of such stories that occupies us at present, though, is the nature of the parents' feelings toward the children in this crisis, especially those of a father toward a daughter. Although the frequent role of the evil stepmother primarily serves to provide occasion for the brothers and sisters to demonstrate their devotion to one another, the stepmother's intervention may also point to the question of the father's degree of attachment to the children. The answer is almost always that the father's love is unquestioned, but that the changed circumstances in his household render him powerless to take effective action. Thus, the father in **"Hansel and Gretel"** reluctantly agrees to abandon the children in the forest; his counterpart in **"The Six Swans"** fails in the attempt to hide the children from the stepmother; in **"Fundevogel"** the devoted father is simply away from the house when his lady cook—the stepmother-figure there—sets about to do the mischief; and in Basile's "Ninnillo and Nennella" the father's attempt to leave a trail for the children in the forest fails when a donkey eats the clover.

In the stories in which leaving home involves the prospect of marrying, the emotional situation is rendered potentially more complex by the possibility of a degree of erotic attachment between parents and children of the opposite sex. To the extent that the Beauty and the Beast type focused simply on the girl's panic—or surprising lack of it—at the thought of marrying, the issue of her possible attachment to the father was incidental, and was indeed precluded in a number of instances. The girl in **"The Hare's Bride,"** for example, does not appear to have a father and simply runs home to mother. In **"Fitcher's Bird,"** the girls' eagerness to get home likewise has nothing to do with thoughts of their father. And the sisters Snow-White and Rose-Red are the daughters of a widow—although this very lack contributes to their attachment to the bear as houseguest and avuncular playmate. In some of these stories, however, and in a number of others as well, the child's arrival at marriageable age provides the occasion for a display of intensified devotion between a parent and a child of the opposite sex, and occasionally even of jealous or incestuous passion on the part of the parent.

I. PATERNAL DEVOTION

The crisis in the relationship between a father and his daughter may involve nothing more than his parental concern that she make a proper marriage, often in connection with his desire to become a grandfather. Even these decidedly innocent depictions, however, place the father in a position of concerning himself with a matter of most intimate importance to the daughter, the prospect of surrendering her virginity. This degree of intimacy is heightened, moreover, by the almost-universal circumstance that the father is a widower, or that the mother at least plays little or no role or is not mentioned. Thus, as we have seen, the father in **"King Thrushbeard"** teaches his daughter humility by forcing her to marry a troubadour, while the father in Basile's "Pinto Smalto" finds himself accepting as his son-in-law a magical doll fashioned by the daughter's own hand. The charm of these portrayals lies largely in the wide range of possibilities provided by the ingredient of fairy tale magic.

The father in **"The Frog King"** (*KHM* [*Kinder- und Hausmärchen*] 1) does not suggest that the daughter should marry the animal, to be sure, but he does insist that she keep her promises to the creature and is indeed delighted to accept him as son-in-law once he has been restored to princely human form; nor does he object to their having consummated the union prior to the wedding. The father may even unconsciously identify with the young man as having succeeded, under magical circumstances and against great odds, in gaining entry to the daughter's bedroom. By contrast, in **"The Iron Stove"** (*KHM* 127), where the daughter's promise concerns marriage, the father conspires with her to avoid fulfilling it. His shock is understandable, considering that she made the promise to an iron stove; but there are hints that the attachment between father and daughter is quite strong, especially on her part. She does not tell the father, for example, that the promise was made actually to a young man imprisoned in the oven who claimed to be a prince. One thus may imagine that she fears that the father would then have considered the fellow a suitable match and have insisted that she keep the promise. This impression that the princess is ambivalent about surrendering the role of daughter for that of wife is reinforced by her desire, after she has finally kept her promise to rescue the prince from the oven, to return home to say a few words to her father.

Unlike the daughters in **"The Frog King"** and **"The Iron Stove,"** the girl in Basile's "Cannetella" (III, 1) avoids marriage, preserves her virginity, and apparently resumes her former role in her father's household. Here we have the case, as in "Pinto Smalto," that the father, wanting progeny, begs the daughter to marry, whereas she is devoted to remaining a virgin, and in this instance has indeed dedicated her virginity to the goddess Diana. The type of the haughty virgin, Cannetella attempts to avoid marriage by setting what she considers to be an impossible condition: the head and teeth of the prospective husband must be of gold. As fate would have it, the condition is satisfied by the king's mortal enemy, the sorcerer Fioravante, to whom the king, not recognizing him, gives the daughter as bride. Fioravante, though, does not appear interested in consummating the union, since he simply locks up Cannetella in a stall, intending to keep her there seven years while he is away. She is rescued by her father's loyal blacksmith; and, fearing that the sorcerer will attempt to abduct her, she has the father put seven iron doors on her room. This measure does not prevent Fioravante from gaining entry, but the spell he has placed on the castle is broken just in time to prevent the abduction. The sorcerer is slain, and the daughter's express desire now to remain forever with the father apparently achieves its fulfillment (though the story ends simply with the would-be abductor's death).

While it is hard to know what to make of Cannetella's adventure, the evident result is that the father is made to forget his desire for progeny and is rendered content to live out his days with the unmarried daughter, whom he clearly adores and who seems equally devoted to him. A possible reading of the story is thus that the sorcerer's role serves to fulfill a secret desire on the father's part for an excuse to retain the status quo in his relationship with the daughter, or a similar wish on the daughter's part, or both. The names of the characters, indeed, may hint at a subterranean eroticism: the father is king of "beautiful little hill" (*bello poggio*; cf. *mons veneris*) and sires the daughter with his wife Renzolla (*renna zolla* 'lump of sand'?), yet only with the magical aid of the goddess Siringa ('lilac' or 'syringe'), after whom he promises to name the daughter, in memory of the goddess's having transformed herself into a *canna* ('pipe', 'tube', etc.; from this imagery it would almost appear that he sired the daughter with the goddess herself, or at least with the goddess in mind). The name of the father's enemy perhaps suggests "flower in front" (*fiore avanti*), referring to the sorcerer's apparent contentment to abduct the girl without then possessing her sexually or, by extension, an unconscious desire on the part of the father himself to retain her virginal presence. Finally, the father's readiness, in the face of the magical threat from outside, to bar the way to the daughter's room with seven iron doors may hint that he is secretly happy to have just cause for joining her in her jealous guardianship of her virginity.

Indications of a particular attachment between father and daughter are provided in a different way in **"The**

Skilled Huntsman" (*KHM* 111). Here the daughter marries in the end, quite happily and very much with her father's blessing. Yet there is the interesting circumstance that the means of identifying the young man who has rescued her from impending abduction by greedy giants include, among other things, two tokens of love and devotion between the king and his daughter that were found by the young huntsman in the tower bedroom where she was in a deep slumber: a pair of slippers under the bed, one with her name on it, the other with that of her father, and a large neckerchief with her father's name on the right side and hers on the left. Moreover, the father seems almost to have set the stage for the daughter's rescue by an eventual bridegroom, which may indicate a degree of anticipatory, vicarious identification with whoever is destined to become the lucky suitor. In an antechamber the young man finds a saber with the king's name on it, which he uses then to slay the giants, and on a table next to the saber a sealed letter in which it is said that "whoever had the saber could slay anything he encountered." Also, there is the curious circumstance that the huntsman finds the slumbering maiden completely sewn into her nightshirt, suggesting that the father envisions her rescue as being such that she will not be violated. And the huntsman fulfills this evidently desired role, for he is content to cut off a small piece of the nightshirt: "Then he went away and allowed her to sleep on undisturbed."[1] That he also takes along all three of the items with the father's name on them—the saber, the slipper for the right foot, and the right-hand half of the neckerchief—indicates that the young man thinks of himself, if only unconsciously, as assuming the father's role as the maiden's fetishistic admirer, since slippers and neckerchiefs—not to forget nightshirts—belong to the more intimate sphere of a maiden's wardrobe.[2] Finally, the father's rage at the daughter's rejection of the—false—rescuer, an unbearably ugly captain, as bridegroom serves as a final hint, perhaps, that the "rescue" represents the fulfillment of a secret, guilty dream on the father's part.

Often, the father's devotion is a decidedly minor, though still not insignificant, element. In **"The Goosegirl at the Spring"** (*KHM* 179), the king banishes the youngest of his three daughters for having responded in a seemingly insulting, though actually quite devoted, way to his demand that the daughters express their love for him—a scene reminiscent of that in *King Lear*, of course. In **"Rumpelstiltskin"** (*KHM* 55) the girl's predicament is caused by her miller father's unfounded boast that she could spin straw into gold, a fantastic claim that likely is motivated as much by his excitement over her beauty as by his hope of gaining favor with the king; indeed, it is possible to view Rumpelstiltskin's magical role in getting the daughter out of this mess as related to her father's having gotten her into it, especially since the dwarf's demand to have her

child bears resemblance to the concern of widower—and in that sense "bachelor"—fathers in folktale that their daughters produce children. And in **"Cinderella"** (*KHM* 21), the father's seeming lack of devotion in failing to protect Cinderella from the stepmother's abuse or otherwise to concern himself with his daughter stands in odd contrast to his awareness of her appeal. Twice, with playful teasing, Cinderella escapes the prince's pursuit. First she leaps into the dovecote (cf. the dove as a symbol of Aphrodite), and then into a pear tree (cf. the association of fruit trees with women's seductive wiles, and the resemblance of the pear's shape to that of a woman). Each time, on hearing the prince's report of this, the father asks himself, "Could it have been Cinderella?"

Portrayals of devotion between father and daughter are more pronounced and frequent in Basile's *Pentamerone*. Reference has already been made to the depictions in "Pinto Smalto" and "Cannetella." In Basile's version of the Cinderella story, "The Cat Cinderella" (I, 6), a perfidious governess exploits Zezolla's place in her father's affections to achieve her aim of becoming his wife. Then, Zezolla herself makes use of the father's devotion in getting him to bring home from his travels the magical present that enables her to win her prince, and thereby to escape the oppression of the governess become stepmother.

The circumstances of the magical adventure on which the daughter sends her father are particularly suggestive regarding emotional undercurrents in their relationship. In her misery, Zezolla is confronted by a dove (as symbol of Aphrodite?) who tells her that if she desires anything she should let it be known to "the fairy dove on the island of Sardinia." When, as then happens, the father (a prince) sets out for Sardinia on state business and inquires of Zezolla what present he should bring her, she asks only that he give her greetings to the fairy dove and beg her to send something, but adds the warning that if he neglects to do this for her he will not be able to leave that island. The father does indeed forget and must be reminded of his promise through the good agency of—love's—magic, hinting at a need on his part to suppress all thoughts of the daughter and his paternal duty toward her, perhaps precisely because his devotion to her is secretly still quite intense. The result of his curious mission on the daughter's behalf is that she is provided with the magical means for nurturing and fulfilling her dream of marriage to a prince: through the date twig the father brings her (together with the magical implements for cultivating it), she obtains the magnificent raiment she uses to captivate the beloved.

In the Grimms' Cinderella story (*KHM* 21), the father's mission in bringing such a present to the daughter is likewise of crucial importance. The situation, though, is complicated by the fact that the magical twig's role results from its having been planted on her mother's grave, not from its having been the gift of an exotic fairy. Here the spirit of the dead mother, embodied in the white bird (a dove, evidently) that visits the hazel tree which has grown from the twig, serves as the agent of fulfillment of the girl's dream of marriage (cf. *in die Haseln gehen* = *fensterln* 'paying a nocturnal visit to a girl's room' and *Haselnuß* 'hazel nut' as a symbol of fertility). But the father's—unwitting—contribution to this magical adventure may suggest that he secretly harbors a devotion to the dead wife that has transferred itself to the daughter. In particular, Cinderella's condition that the hazel twig he is to bring her shall be the first one that knocks off his hat as he rides along on his trip points to something like loss of dignity, as though the mother or daughter were magically playing a trick on him or trying to make him "come to his senses." For her part, Cinderella seems initially to have no idea of why she wants such a twig (much less any guarantee that one will indeed happen to knock off the father's hat), and certainly no inkling that planting it on the mother's grave will lead to her winning a prince.[3]

The same sort of magical mission is found also in "The Little Slave Girl," the second tale of the Cinderella type in Basile's collection (II, 8).[4] In this case, however, the relationship is that between a girl, Lisa, and her uncle, the baron of Selvascura ("Dark Forest"). Moreover, the uncle's feelings toward the niece are complicated by the fact that she is the daughter of his dead young sister, Lilla, to whom he was most devoted, who conceived the child in an unusual and magical fashion during a game with her playmates in which the girls were to jump over a rose without knocking off any of the petals. The pregnancy occurred as a result of Lilla's having cheated at the game, by swallowing the petal she had knocked off without the other girls' having noticed it. The implication is that the pregnancy was a punishment for having committed a shameful, dishonest, or forbidden act—an act, though, that bears some resemblance to the usual way of becoming pregnant, in view of the rose symbolism. This magical circumstance must contribute, one would assume, to a romanticization of Lilla in the brother's eyes, for whom she, as virgin mother, must appear as something like a secular counterpart to the Queen of Heaven. Indeed, since the baby was conceived without being sired, the baron may secretly fancy himself to be the niece's father "in the spirit," so to speak, as a sublimation of forbidden incestuous desire (see the tales of the brother and sister type).

This impression of the uncle as doting on the niece out of an incestuous devotion to his sister is reinforced by subsequent magical events in the story. As a result of a fairy's curse at her christening (the motif especially familiar from the Sleeping Beauty story), Lisa, having reached the age of seven, dies when her mother forgetfully leaves the comb in her hair with which she has

been grooming her (cf. the use of this motif in the Snow White story). The girl's corpse is placed inside seven crystal boxes, fitted within one another, and then put in a remote room of the castle. Her mother, Lilla, soon dies out of grief over her loss. That Lilla, on her deathbed, makes her brother promise never to open the room containing the crystal coffins, as she gives him the key to it, implies that she senses he will feel the urge to do just that, out of passionate adoration of the niece, the magically conceived offspring and image of his beloved sister. (The uncle is thereby placed somewhat in the position of the wife or potential bride in the stories of the Bluebeard type.) That it is instead the wife he takes, after a year of grieving over the loss of his sister, who succumbs to the temptation does not lessen the suspicion that the uncle is passionately devoted to the niece. On the contrary, the wife's surrender to curiosity about the forbidden room results in her jealous belief—surely not so very wide of the mark—that the baron has been worshipping the beautiful dead maiden, who has now magically become fully grown (the crystal boxes have grown right along with her).

It is at this point that "The Little Slave Girl"—which, as we have seen, combines elements of the Sleeping Beauty, Bluebeard, and Snow White stories—becomes the Cinderella type. Having inadvertently revived the girl, in her jealous rage, by grabbing her hair and pulling her out of the coffin, the uncle's wife abuses her and turns her into a kitchen maid. On his return from a hunting trip, the uncle does not recognize Lisa, whom the wife presents to him as an African slave girl. When the baron then goes off on another journey, Lisa asks him to bring back three presents for her—a doll, a knife, and a sharpening stone—and warns that should he forget to do her bidding, he will be prevented from completing the trip.

As then becomes clear, Lisa's request reflects her thoughts—perhaps only unconscious—of her uncle as her potential angel of rescue. In the kitchen she repeatedly laments her fate to the doll as though it were a live person, demanding from it a response. When the doll does not answer, she sharpens the knife and threatens to kill it, whereupon the doll gives the—evidently desired—reply that it has heard her better than a deaf person (meaning the uncle?). Finally, the uncle overhears the niece speaking in this manner to the doll and looks through the keyhole into the kitchen. This time, though, Lisa threatens to kill herself if the doll does not answer. The uncle, who has recognized her from the story she has been telling to the doll, kicks open the door, takes the knife, restores the niece to her blossoming beauty, sends the wife back to her relatives, and marries the niece to a young man of her choice. Thus, in the end the uncle has returned to a bachelor life such as he led prior to his sister's death. And most important, his relationship to the beloved niece has been restored. To be sure, he has lost his status as her guardian and custodian, but he has surely gained an even greater place in her affections for having served as her angel of rescue.

Similarly interesting, though rather incidental, depictions of paternal devotion are found in other tales of Basile's collection. In the frame story itself, the tale of Princess Zoza's love for Prince Thaddeus of Roundfield, there is the example of a father who, being a widower, desires nothing more than to see his beautiful daughter laugh. He attempts to cure her melancholy by having a fountain of oil built to amuse her with the sight of people hopping around it to avoid soiling their clothes. The indirect result is that the princess soon turns her thoughts to marrying, a development which suggests that such serious-mindedness in a girl is a sign of latent desire and that the father is bound to lose her someday to a husband. In this sense, then, a father's passionate desire to see his daughter laugh involves something of a secret, forbidden wish to have her relate to him as to a lover. In another story, "Peruonto" (I, 3), the father reacts to his daughter's unexplained pregnancy with a rage colored by irrational thoughts of himself as having been thereby not only dishonored but cuckolded as well. He tells his council, "You all know already that the moon of my honor has gotten horns." Ultimately, the father becomes reconciled to his new role as grandfather, as does the father in "The Raven" (IV, 9), a sorcerer who at the end arrives in a cloud just in time to prevent his daughter from throwing herself from a window and to explain that all of the magical adventures that have beset her, her husband, and his brother were wrought by him as punishment for the brothers' abduction of her and for her susceptibility to the temptation of fine raiment that led to it.

II. JEALOUS PASSION

In the stories discussed above, we have already seen elements or tinges of jealous passion intruding occasionally into otherwise innocent feelings of paternal devotion. There are, however, certain tales in which the father's feelings about the daughter, or his actions in connection with her role as bride, exceed the bounds of propriety. This is perhaps most evident in those stories in which the father one way or another becomes involved in what transpires in the bridal chamber on the wedding night. To be sure, in **"Hans My Hedgehog"** (*KHM* 108) this involvement occurs at the bridegroom's request: he tells the old king that he should have four men stand guard before the door and make a large fire, in which they are to burn the skin the hedgehog will shed just before he climbs into the marriage bed. Once this has happened and Hans is lying in the bed "completely in human form, but . . . black as coal as though he had been burned," the king calls for his physician, who washes the bridegroom "with good salves and covers him with ointments" so that he is transformed into a

handsome young man, very much to the daughter's delight. In **"The Two Royal Children"** (*KHM* 113), though, a father's jealous love of his daughters, and accompanying envy of the suitor as prospective bridegroom, is indicated by his condition that if the young prince is to have one of the daughters to wife, he must remain awake in her bedroom for nine hours—from nine in the evening to six in the morning—without falling asleep. The—ironic—implication of the father's odd demand may be that he imagines that in this way the young man will be prevented from "sleeping" with the daughter and will thus have to suffer the torments of unfulfilled desire.

As it happens, the eldest daughter and the two younger ones after her trick the father by having the statues of St. Christopher standing in their rooms answer each hour for the young man, who thereby passes the test despite having fallen asleep in the girls' bedrooms (there is no indication that he engages in any intimacy with them, except the laconic reports that he "laid himself on the threshold"). That the father, each of the first two times, goes back on his word by refusing to give the daughter to the prince in marriage and by making him repeat this great accomplishment with the next youngest daughter reinforces the impression that the king harbors a forbidden love for the daughters, as does the circumstance of his hourly visits outside the bedroom doors to insure that the suitor is still awake, and that he subsequently sets three further seemingly impossible tasks once the prince has passed the original test with each of the three girls in succession. Moreover, the presence of a statue of St. Christopher, the guardian saint for children, in the bedroom of each of the girls suggests that the father may think of them as susceptible to the temptations of desire (St. Christopher, if not Daddy, will see what you are doing in your bedrooms), as does the fact that the younger the daughter, the larger her St. Christopher's statue, especially since it is the youngest daughter who proves the most "fetching"—both in the appeal she holds for the prince and in her determination to win him as husband. This impression of the statues' role is strengthened, if anything, by the girls' use of St. Christopher as accomplice in their deceit of the jealous father.

In Basile's *Pentamerone* there are several stories in which the father's attention similarly becomes focused on the daughter's bedroom or on the bridal chamber. The father in "The Beetle, the Mouse, and the Cricket" (III, 5) stipulates that, although Nardiello, the simpleton son of a rich farmer, has met the challenge of making his melancholy daughter laugh, the marriage will be valid only if the youth succeeds in consummating it within the space of three nights. The king, who does not consider Nardiello a suitable mate for a princess, then slips him a sleeping potion each night to prevent the marriage's consummation. In "The Serpent" (II, 5) the king, who has similarly been forced to betroth his daughter to an unwanted suitor (in this case understandably so, since it is a snake), peers in through the keyhole to discover what transpires on the wedding night, and then breaks down the door in order to do away with the snakeskin that the bridegroom has shed in emerging as a handsome prince. And in "Sapia Liccarda" (III, 4) a rich merchant, fearing that his daughters might invite young men into their bedrooms while he is away on a business trip, boards them up in the house—but to no avail, of course.

One of the most intriguing examples of a father's resistance to the thought of his daughter marrying is found in **"Old Rinkrank"** (*KHM* 196). A king has a glass mountain built and tells his daughter's beloved that whoever can succeed in running over the mountain without falling can have his daughter to wife. Out of a burning desire to be wed to her beloved, the princess eagerly offers to join him in attempting this feat, in order to catch him should he begin to fall. The result is that she falls, the mountain opens up, and she disappears into it, becoming the prisoner of an old man with a long gray beard (the title role) who tells her she must choose between becoming his maidservant and being killed. As the years pass, their relationship develops into something like that of an old married couple, though their cohabitation remains chaste. Eventually, she escapes from the gnomic captor and is reunited with the father and the beloved. The father, daughter, and her beloved succeed in killing Old Rinkrank and, made rich by his gold and silver, live happily on together.

Is there a secret, or ironic, connection between the roles of the father and the gnome, who is perhaps a projection of the father's guilt over a subterranean desire to steal the daughter's youth by keeping her for himself? Rinkrank cohabits—celibately—with the girl until she has grown old; then, the time for jealous love on a father's part having passed, the father, daughter, and bridegroom live happily together under the same roof.

In a number of stories depicting a father's feelings about a daughter, the focus is on the circumstances of her birth. In **"The Twelve Brothers"** (*KHM* 9) the father, passionately hoping that, contrary to superstition, thirteen will be his lucky number and his wife will finally bear him a daughter, has coffins made for his twelve sons, so that the child may be his sole heir, should it be a girl. The impression is thus created that from the outset he has been yearning to have a daughter and therefore resents the sons, whose successive births have brought him a series of a dozen disappointments.[5] As we have noted, there is a similar, though less drastic, portrayal at the beginning of **"The Seven Ravens"** (*KHM* 25), where the father, who has yearned for a daughter, is so aggrieved over the prospect that the

baby girl might die that he utters the fateful wish that his seven sons be transformed into ravens when they fail to return immediately with water for her emergency baptism. One also finds cases in which the wish for a daughter is fulfilled in an almost fantastic manner, recalling, say, Athene's springing full-grown from the head of Zeus. Thus, in a variant opening of the Snow White story, a count has no sooner expressed the wish, as he is out riding with his wife in their carriage one winter day, that he might have a daughter with skin as white as snow, etc., than such a girl indeed appears, as if by magic, at the side of the roadway.[6] And in Basile's "Viola" (II, 3) an ogre, having emitted a loud fart and then discovered a beautiful young maiden standing behind him, imagines that he has sired her in this manner and dotingly takes her in as his daughter.

There are, to be sure, exceptions to the rule that fathers in romantic folktales are depicted as being devoted to their daughters. In **"Rapunzel"** (*KHM* 12), the father does not display any remorse over having to surrender the baby daughter to the hag, to whom he has promised his pregnant wife's child in exchange for the rampion required to satisfy the wife's lust for that leafy salad vegetable. And in **"The Robber Bridegroom"** (*KHM* 40), the miller offers no objection to his daughter's going out alone to visit the fiancé's house in the forest, at the latter's insistence. The points of these stories, though, lie elsewhere.

In the tales of the Sleeping Beauty type, depiction of the father as longing for a daughter becomes related to a crisis involving her eventual arrival at marriageable age. The father's yearning in **"Little Briar-Rose"** (*KHM* 50) is answered by a frog's announcement to the queen, as she is bathing, that she will give birth to a daughter before the year is out (a travesty, perhaps of the Annunciation to Mary?). The ironic point of this "miraculous" conception is perhaps that with a passion so intense wishing alone might suffice to produce a pregnancy, or even that the king's desire is more to obtain a daughter than to sleep with his wife. The matter of the hag's curse of the baby girl, and the twelfth fairy's amelioration of it, may likewise be viewed as secretly related to the father's doting wish for a daughter since the result is that, befitting a princess, the girl remains ignorant of the onerous distaff chore of spinning. She is thereby also prevented from indulging in the traditionally concomitant pastime of building romantic castles in the air (cf. German *spinnen* in the sense of "fantasizing"). And, most important, she does not take a husband when she reaches marriageable age, but remains in the stage of blossoming maidenhood for fully a hundred years.[7]

The intensity of the father's devotion to the daughter is more evident in two versions of the Sleeping Beauty tale found in Basile's collection. In "Sun, Moon, and

Talia" (V, 5), when the girl, in fulfillment of the curse, falls down as though dead, the grieving father locks up her corpse in the sylvan palace where they have been living together and leaves, never to return, in the hope that he might thus forget the great misfortune that has befallen him. At her birth, the father—her mother is not mentioned—gave her the name Talia (i.e., Thalia, Greek *Thaleia* 'the blossoming one'), testifying no doubt to his yearning for a daughter and his anticipation of her arrival at maidenhood. Once Talia has fallen into the deathlike sleep and the father leaves, he plays no further role in the story.

The subsequent events, however, concern a similarly intense passion for the daughter on the part of another older man, a king who is unhappily married. While out hunting one day he discovers the seemingly dead girl and, filled with passionate desire, carries her to a bed in the abandoned palace, "and plucked the fruits of love," as we are told. When he later returns, he finds that she is alive and has given birth (while still in the deathlike sleep) to fraternal twins (a boy and a girl), and he promises to come back for them. The degree to which the girl represents for him an ideal beloved is attested by his subsequent mumbling of her name and those of their children (Sun and Moon) in his sleep, thereby leading to his wife's discovery of his infidelity. The king then, in turn, discovers his wife's plan to do away with the rival and her offspring (she intends to have the children fed to him). He has her thrown on the fire she has prepared for Talia, and lives happily ever after with the beloved and their children.

One suspects that the fulfillment of the king's passion may be in some sense an ironic substitute for similar fulfillment of the part of the aggrieved father, especially since the father's departure from the scene is followed immediately by the king's entry into the story. Had the father acted as this king does upon his discovery of the seemingly dead maiden, he would of course have violated the incest taboo, whereas this king is guilty simply of an act of adultery rendered excusable in view of his wife's evil or jealous nature. At the same time, though, the king's deed amounts to a form of rape and of necrophilia, so that a degree of vice attaches to it after all. His act is thus not so very different from the case in which the father, had he not left the secluded palace immediately after the daughter's apparent death, might have succumbed to the same temptation. The odd circumstance that the father does not bury Talia further suggests that his departure forever from the castle was the product not only of grief but of secret fear that the same passionate devotion that renders him incapable of consigning her remains to the grave might cause him to violate her corpse.[8] This possibility, though, is otherwise not indicated in the text, and thus remains pure conjecture.

In Basile's other tale of this type, "The Face" (III, 3), one does not actually have a *sleeping* beauty. Indeed, only the opening of this story belongs to that type, and as such constitutes rather a travesty of it. Here it is made quite clear that the mysterious danger awaiting the daughter is, first and foremost, simply her arrival at womanhood, with the attendant awakening of desire. And the father responds in a transparently jealous or possessive way, building a tower to house the daughter after it has been prophesied that she is in danger of having "the main sluice of life (*la chiavica maestra della vita*) uncorked by the thighbone of an animal (*per un osso maestro*)."[9] The effect of her incarceration with twelve ladies-in-waiting and a governess and of the king's order that only meat with no bones be brought to her is, if anything, to fan the flames of desire. She flirts shamelessly with the first eligible male she spies from her tower and promises on the spot to run off with him. The magical means of her rescue, not surprisingly, is a bone (a thighbone that a dog brings into her tower); and she immediately rides off with her prince.

The coupling of a father's wish for a daughter with the prospect that she will then leave him is quite plain in another of Basile's stories, "The Three Crowns" (IV, 6), where a king hears a voice ask him whether he prefers to have a daughter who would flee from him or a son who would destroy him. The fact that this voice actually leaves him no choice makes one suspect that he secretly wishes for a daughter. Once the girl is born, he locks her up until he has arranged to marry her off. But the moment she is released from captivity, the prophecy nonetheless comes true, as she is carried off by a stormy gust of wind. This magical event, which prevents her marriage to the bridegroom her father has selected for her, may project her resentment of the father's possessive control of her destiny. In any case, the eventual result of her magical abduction—her marriage to a king whom she, disguised as a boy, has served as a page—suggests that her experience of having been locked away by the father made her yearn all the more to bask in the devotion of an older man. The effect of the mysterious, magical prophecy made to the father is thus to ensure that he will succeed in alienating and thereby losing the daughter, just as in the Sleeping Beauty story the father's doting concern to keep the daughter innocent of anything having to do with spindles ensures that when she first encounters one she will be all the more drawn to it. In this sense, we are dealing in each instance with the proverbial self-fulfilling prophecy.

In yet another of Basile's tales, "The Flea" (I, 5), the devotion that fathers in folktale commonly exhibit toward daughters is transferred to a pet flea. Since the father's fascination with the flea, however, becomes entwined with the question of whom—and whether—the daughter shall marry, it may be suspected that the flea is in some measure a substitute for the daughter. The father's involvement with the flea begins one day when he discovers it biting him on the arm and is about to kill it, but instead suddenly develops an infatuation with the creature. He feeds it daily with blood from his arm until it has grown quite large (here one may be reminded that the daughter represents his own flesh and blood that he has nurtured and raised to maturity). He then—implausibly—has the flea skinned and the hide tanned, and offers to give the daughter in marriage to any man who can guess from what animal the hide has been taken. It is at this point, particularly, that an association of the flea with the daughter, and a hint of repressed jealous passion on the father's part, suggests itself. The father must consider it practically impossible that anyone should be capable of guessing the truth; and he therefore would have a rationalization, of sorts, for not giving the daughter away in marriage. In this sense, the daughter is the pet whom he has nurtured with his life's blood and then "skinned," or cheated, in hopes of retaining possession of her.

As the examples discussed thus far indicate, a father's passionate love for a daughter is a subject that, in view of the incest taboo, calls for delicate handling and veiled depiction. Portrayed openly, the matter is simply too offensive. There is, for example, in a tale of the brother and sister type, **"The White Bride and the Black Bride"** (*KHM* 135), the case of the widower king who wanted to remarry only if the woman were as beautiful as his dead wife, and then was fortunate enough to find her exact image, yet still more beautiful, in the young sister of his coachman. Thus, one is dealing in that case only with spiritual, as opposed to physical, incest. There is, however, one great exception to this avoidance of portraying a father's openly incestuous desire for his daughter. And the tale in question is represented in all three classic literary collections of folktales: in Basile, Perrault, and the Grimms.

In the Grimms' version of this story, **"Allerleirauh"** (*KHM* 65), a widower king conceives the mad plan of marrying his daughter.[10] This forbidden, if not entirely unnatural, wish is motivated in part by lingering grief over the death of his beautiful wife, to whom he was passionately devoted. The dying spouse's request that he promise never to take another wife unless he should find a woman as least as beautiful as she is likely an expression of her confidence in the incomparability of her beauty, for the request makes sense only as indirect testimony to a desire on her part that he not remarry (this is her explicit motivation in Perrault's version). The king's promise to the wife is likewise a confession of his eternal devotion, but it subsequently provides as well a justification for his assertion of his right to marry the daughter. In the context of the story, the circumstance of the wife's request and the king's promise offers an explanation of the secret desire that fathers feel toward their daughters. By the time a daughter has

reached adolescence, the mother's beauty has begun to fade, or she is in any case no longer the nubile, virginal maiden with whom the father once fell in love (it is of course not necessary, as happens here, that the mother actually has died). The king's failure, during the years that the daughter is growing to adulthood, to find a prospective bride as beautiful as the dead wife may be counted as evidence that his secret desire is for the daughter. That such guilty passion is involved is also indicated by the likely element of repressed awareness in the father's failure to notice, until the daughter has reached marriageable age, that she is equal in beauty to her dead mother. At this point, in any event, the issue is joined. If the father does not marry the daughter, she will leave his household and wed another, as then happens in the ensuing course of the story.

The king's councillors react with horror to his announcement that he intends to wed the girl, admonishing him that "God has forbidden that a father should marry his daughter; nothing good can come of sin, and the kingdom will be dragged along into ruin." The daughter's horror at the prospect is all the greater, of course. Yet the plan she conceives for dissuading the king from his mad folly suggests that she is secretly delighted by the intensity of his passion. The extravagant request she makes as the condition for acceptance of his proposal of marriage amounts to an unconscious invitation to him to demonstrate the degree of his devotion. In stipulating that he must first provide her with three dresses—one as golden as the sun, one as silver as the moon, and one as shining as the stars—and then with a fur coat made from a piece of hide from each and every animal in his kingdom, she is making the sort of demand, only much exaggerated, that one might expect from a spoiled daughter or a haughty bride or vain courtesan. If the girl's secret, unconscious wish is to test how far the father's passion for her will carry him, it certainly is fulfilled; and once he has complied with her demands, she has no choice but to flee. The father's sinful passion is not punished, other than by the loss of the daughter, and with her flight from his castle he disappears from the story. This indicates that the opening episode is, in the last analysis, a roguishly comic depiction of certain aspects of the emotional crisis experienced by many a father and daughter with the latter's arrival at marriageable age.[11]

In Perrault's and Basile's versions of the Allerleirauh story, the focus is so completely on the intensity of the father's passion, and the disgust and revulsion it produces in the daughter, that there is little reason to suspect that she may secretly share his dream. The father in Perrault's "Donkey-Skin" ("Peau d'Ane") displays not the least hesitation in squandering all the riches of his kingdom in the vain hope that the daughter will agree to marry him. In particular, he accedes immediately to her ultimate demand, born of desperation, that he sacrifice the source of his kingdom's wealth, a magical donkey in whose straw each morning golden coins are found (in place of the usual excremental matter). The king's willingness to have the miraculous donkey slaughtered so that the daughter might have its hide (hence Perrault's title) can fairly well be said to offer final proof, as it were, that the father's foolish passion has made an ass of him. Meanwhile, the daughter in this version is removed from suspicion that she unconsciously desires to test the heat of the father's passion, insofar as it is not she herself but the fairy godmother from whom she seeks advice in her adversity who is responsible for suggesting the series of demands to be made in an effort to dissuade him. Since the godmother, though, is possessed of supernatural powers, she may be seen to that extent as a creature of fantasy and a magical mentor. The advice she gives may therefore reflect, after all, a secret desire on the daughter's part to take the measure of her father's devotion.[12]

In Basile's version of the Allerleirauh story, "The She-Bear" (II, 6), the daughter has no opportunity to pose seemingly impossible demands that may satisfy a secret desire to know just how much the father is captivated by her. The father, enraged by her rejection of his proposal, simply orders her to come to his bedroom that evening to consummate the union. The matter of unrestrained and forbidden sexual passion is very much out in the open. As the old woman who serves here as the daughter's adviser puts it, the father, who is behaving like an ass (cf. the symbolism in Perrault's "Peau d'Ane" referred to above), would like this evening "to play the stallion." To punish the father for his outrageous demand and thereby also enable the daughter to escape the fate envisioned for her, the hag gives her a splinter which, when she puts it into her mouth, transforms her into a she-bear. The odd—though certainly most effective—character of this magical remedy likely represents a continuation of the sexual imagery in this episode, especially the hag's words about the father being an ass who would like to play the stallion. The father's unnatural command, in effect, reduces the daughter to the role of a concubine or female animal, since she is offered no choice in the matter. Were the daughter actually to join him in bed, she would feel herself, at best, to be no better than a she-bear.

As in Perrault's and the Grimms' versions of the Allerleirauh story, in Basile's "She-Bear" the new raiment, or in this case the transformed appearance of the daughter that formed a part of her efforts to defeat the father's plan to marry her subsequently plays an indispensable role in her captivation of her eventual husband. Here the princess's use of her magical appearance as an animal in winning her prince casts retrospective doubt on the complete purity or chasteness of her initial employment of this guise to thwart her father's plan. She

appears to enjoy this role of female bear; at least she makes use of it in order to enter into a relationship with a prince as his pet. The prince, "finding himself confronted with this female bear, was about to die of fright; but then, seeing that the animal, all the while crouching and wagging its tail like a little pet female dog, was circling around him, he regained his courage." The implication is that the girl's acquiring of the ability to change herself into a she-bear, which she first used to defeat her father's immoral purpose, is in part a symbolic representation of her nubility. With this new, magical role as she-bear the princess has simultaneously acquired the mating instinct and mastered the art of flirtation. It is as though the father's mad plan to make her his wife served to awaken the woman in her, in this sense.

III. SONS AND MOTHERS

Basile's "She-Bear" is of further interest for its depiction of a mother's involvement in her son's choice of a bride. The portrayal of the mother-son relationship, in this aspect, is much less common in the romantic folktale than the like situation between father and daughter. In Basile's story, the matter is highly comical. The intensity of the mother's devotion is evidenced by her consent, at her lovesick son's request, to allow the pet bear to serve as his nurse. Preziosa is thereby able to demonstrate her own devotion to the prince and her virtue as a prospective wife, thus winning the mother's blessing for their union. Most striking, though, is that Preziosa's resumption of her human form occurs in connection with her granting of the mother's request (at the son's urging) that she kiss the prince in his sick bed to keep him from fainting, out of unfulfilled desire. As the she-bear is kissing him, the splinter falls out of her mouth—"I don't know how," so the narrator roguishly avers. Thus, the mother's role here, like that of the father in a number of stories of the animal suitor type, is that of matchmaker or go-between (the type of the *ruffiana* from the *commedia dell'arte*); and the fun concerns the point that a doting mother would accept even a female animal as a daughter-in-law should this be her beloved son's passionate wish. A variation on this theme of the mother as go-between is found in another of Basile's stories, "Belluccia" (III, 6), where the mother helps the son discover whether the youth who has been sent to keep him company during an illness, and with whom he has fallen in love at first sight, is not in reality a maiden.

Portrayals of mothers bending their efforts to see that their sons are not disappointed in love appear to be lacking in the Grimms' collection. There are, however, depictions of true and tender love between a mother and a son. In **"The Little Shroud"** (*KHM* 109) a mother grieves so over her seven-year-old son's death that he appears to her in his funeral dress and begs her to desist, because her tears prevent the shroud from drying and he thus can find no peace in the grave. Prior to this scene, the child returned from the grave at night to visit the places where in life he had sat and played, and when the mother wept, he wept too. A similarly touching love between mother and son is depicted, as we have seen (Chap. 1), in **"The Juniper Tree"** (*KHM* 47). There the mother's wish for "a child as red as blood and as white as snow" is fulfilled with the birth of a son (not a daughter, as in the Snow White story). Her joy at his birth is so great, though, "that she dies" and, according to her wish, is buried beneath the juniper tree under which her cutting of her finger while peeling an apple gave rise to the wish for a child. Moreover, she appears to have identified with that tree during her pregnancy as she watched it, too, blossom and bear fruit. When the son then suffers under the resentment and abuse of his stepmother, his half-sister Marleenken's devotion compensates him for the loss of the mother whom he never knew. The association of the stepsister with the dead mother is suggested, however, only after the stepmother has murdered the boy. Marleenken ties up his bones "in her best silken scarf" and lays them on the grass under the juniper tree: "And when she had laid them there, she felt at once so much better and did not weep any longer. Then the juniper tree began to stir, and the branches spread themselves apart and then came back together again, just as when someone is so very overjoyed and does the same with his hands." A mist came forth out of the tree, and out of the mist a beautiful bird that "sang so magnificently and flew high into the air; and when it was gone the juniper tree became again as it was before; and the scarf with the bones was gone. Marleenken though became quite happy and delighted, just as though the brother were still alive." The half-brother's reincarnation as a bird and his subsequent return to human form, after his revenge on the stepmother, thus result from a collaboration between Marleenken and the dead mother, and as a token of their shared devotion to him. The half-sister therefore appears almost to be the dead mother's agent, as the boy's angel of rescue (cf. *Marleenken* as "Little Mary Ann," i.e., as a little heavenly and virginal mother).

Portrayals of a mother's reunion with her son in connection with his discovery of a bride are found in at least two of Basile's stories. In "The Padlock" (II, 9) there is, indeed, a hint that the mother's feelings for the son, on his arrival at manhood, involve a tinge of incestuous desire, since at the end we learn that the son's absence from home and his amorous involvement with his eventual bride resulted from a witch's curse to the effect that he "should wander about far from his homeland until he might be embraced by his mother and the rooster would not crow any longer." The spell is broken only after the following events have occurred: the girl

with whom he has slept finds her way unwittingly to his mother's castle; she gives birth to a beautiful son, whom her former lover comes mightily to adore; a lady-in-waiting overhears him exclaim during these secret visits, "Oh, my most beautiful little son, if my mother knew! She would wash you in a basin of gold; she would wrap you in swaddling clothes of gold. If the song of the roosters were silent, I would never leave you"; and the youth's mother, on hearing about this from the lady-in-waiting, has all the roosters in the city killed, and when the son returns the following night, she embraces him. As the narrator reports, "As soon as he found himself in his mother's arms, the spell was broken and his affliction was ended."

This enigmatic close of the tale suggests that the earlier developments in the story—which concern the youth's appearance to the girl at the well as a handsome Moorish slave boy, her seduction by him, his rejection of her when she contrives to discover his true appearance, and her subsequent wanderings while pregnant with his child—are the result of an emotional crisis regarding his attachment to his mother and his awakening sexual desire. What causes him to show himself again to the girl is the birth of the son, and evidently because the boy's arrival fills him with sweet memories of his relationship with his mother. The words of devotion he addresses to the infant son project his longing to be adored and embraced by his mother; and now that he has become a father, this proves indeed to be possible again. That the mother, though, first takes the precaution of seeing that all roosters in the town have been slaughtered suggests that she feels the danger of incestuous desire is still present. In any case, it would appear that the son had to become a father before the "curse" of an incestuous desire could be broken, laid to rest, or sublimated.

In Basile's other tale of a mother's happy reunion with her son, "The Dragon" (IV, 5), the nature of her relationship to the youth appears far less enigmatic, and seemingly quite innocent. Here the mother, Porziella, is protected from starvation and death, and ultimately released from solitary imprisonment, through the loyal efforts of a magical bird. The bird is actually a fairy whom Porziella, in turn, had saved from being dishonored by a satyr as she lay slumbering in a forest. The fairy's motivation in her efforts on Porziella's behalf is somewhat ambiguous, however. In rescuing her benefactress, the fairy also wins Porziella's son Miuccio as her husband. Moreover, it is odd that the fairy did not manage, or even attempt, to repay Porziella in kind by preventing the latter's violation by the misogynous king of Altamarina. Instead, she only restrained the king's arm when he attempted to slay Porziella with a dagger after he had raped her.

Miuccio is the fruit of the king's violation of Porziella; and the fairy's secret feeding of her during her ensuing imprisonment makes possible the boy's birth and his survival. Therefore, we may suspect that desire for an ideal mate lies behind the fairy's actions. When Miuccio reaches adolescence, he is "adopted" by the king as his page. The queen's envy of this rival for the king's affection is thereby aroused; and this paves the way for the happy ending. The envious queen is destroyed; the king marries Porziella; the fairy asks, as her reward, to have Miuccio as her husband; and the two couples presumably live happily ever after.

The whole of the fairy's involvement in the story may be read, too, as magical wish fulfillment on Porziella's part. Her rescue of the fairy from violation by the satyr may hint at virginal sexual fantasy in anticipation of her own rape by the king. The fairy's restraint of the king when he is about to slay Porziella after having violated her may reflect a fantasy on Porziella's part that her beauty alone would suffice to save her from death (the king, at least, believes that it is Porziella's beauty that held back his arm). Her rescue through the magical powers of the fairy may represent a dream of being saved by her son. And the fairy's marriage to Miuccio may fulfill Porziella's own vicarious wish.

In the stories discussed above, the mother tends to be instrumental in bringing about the son's marriage to his beloved. One also finds, however, the opposite situation in which the mother somehow stands in the way of the son's further involvement with, or marriage to, the maiden of his choice. This potentiality of the mother-son relationship is usually depicted in connection with the motif of the false bride. Thus, in **"The Drummer"** (*KHM* 193), a youth who has just rescued a maiden from imprisonment by a witch takes leave of the girl to go home so that he may tell his parents where he has been. The girl warns him not to kiss his parents on the right cheek; but then, in his joy at seeing them again, he fails to think of her admonition. Having greeted his parents with that fateful kiss, he promptly forgets the beloved entirely. The mother meanwhile has selected a bride for him; and as a devoted and obedient son, he agrees to marry the girl of his mother's choosing. This same situation is found in Basile's "The Dove" (II, 7). Here, though, it is specifically a kiss from the youth's mother that causes him to lose all conscious memory of the maiden he has just rescued from the clutches of a jealous witch (in this case, the witch is the girl's mother). Moreover, the girl's mother, because of her own possessiveness regarding the daughter, is responsible for that result, because it is she who places a curse on the youth to the effect that with the first kiss Prince Nardaniello receives—from whomever—he will forget his beloved Filadoro completely.

In another of Basile's tales, "The Golden Tree Stump" (V, 4), the youth's mother—here it is she who is the

witch—sets about openly to destroy his desired beloved and attempts to marry him to a repulsive bride who brags about her promiscuity. The youth, Tuoni-e-lampi ("Thunder-and-Lightning"), takes both his beloved and the revolting bride to the wedding chamber, slays the bride with a knife, and sleeps instead with Parmetella. His mother, on discovering this (and that her sorceress sister and her child have perished in an oven) repeatedly rams her head into a wall until she has burst her skull. Finally, in Basile's "The Face" (III, 3) another case of direct intervention by the mother ends tragically. On the wedding night, the son stabs himself after having kissed the false bride and then having recognized, in the page whom he had invited into the bridal chamber, the true bride (she died of a broken heart at witnessing his betrayal of her love). The mother, having already picked out a wife for the son, had summoned him home with a letter claiming she was on the point of death—a letter that arrived when the lovers were, as the storyteller reported, "in the midst of their pleasures."

As we have observed, depiction of fathers' attachments to their daughters is more typical of the romantic stories in Basile's collection than in the Grimms' tales of love. Moreover, such depictions as are found in *Grimm's Fairy Tales* tend to occur in stories that the later German collection has in common with the earlier Neapolitan one, such as Sleeping Beauty, Cinderella, and Thousandfurs (Allerleirauh). The reason is surely that the subject easily offended the sensitivities of a later age and more northern, puritanical climate. In late Renaissance Italy, by contrast, a father's, guardian's, or uncle's foolish love for his pretty daughter, ward, or niece became the dominant subject for comedy. Pantalone, the old fool in love, was the principal figure in the *commedia dell'arte* of Basile's time.

While magic usually plays a role in Basile's tales of the father and daughter type, it is not employed to veil the father's passion nearly to the extent it does in the Grimms' stories. The Neapolitan Renaissance author depicts the older man's devotion or jealous love openly as well as more frequently. In Basile's Sleeping Beauty tale, "Sun, Moon, and Talia," as in the Grimm and Perrault versions, the daughter pricks her finger and falls into a magical, deathlike sleep. Basile, though, has the father and daughter in a more intimate relationship, living together in a secluded sylvan palace, while Perrault and the Grimms have her living with both parents in the father's royal residence. And in Basile's other story about a father's worry over a curse or prophecy about his daughter, "The Face," the father goes so far as to lock her away in a tower. The Cinderella tale, meanwhile, represents a case in which the father's devotion emphasized in Basile's "The Cat Cinderella" has been transferred almost entirely to the dead mother in the Grimms' story, while Perrault completely did without this element in his version. Further, Basile employs the

Cinderella story a second time, in "The Little Slave Girl," to depict an older man's devotion to a maiden, in this case an uncle's passion for his adored sister's daughter.

To be sure, both the Grimms' **"Allerleirauh"** and Perrault's "Donkey-Skin" baldly depict a father's incestuous love of his daughter, as did Basile earlier in "The She-Bear." Here the exception proves the role, though, because this tale renders the father's passion less offensive as resulting from his grief over the death of his beautiful, beloved wife, with whose beauty only the daughter can compare. Moreover, Perrault and the Grimms made the fathers' feelings toward the daughter very tender. Thus, Basile's father does not bother to prove his devotion and try to win his daughter with gifts, as he does in the Grimms' and Perrault's versions, but simply and immediately orders the daughter to come to his bed.

Whereas the existence of a type of story focusing on a father's devotion to, or jealous love of, a daughter is evident, the same cannot be said for the theme of a mother's passion for a son. There are, to be sure, occasional depictions of at least innocent devotion of a mother to her son, as in the second half of Basile's "She-Bear"; and his "The Padlock" and "The Dragon" may hint enigmatically at even deeper, illicit emotional currents. Yet while fathers are expected, by popular tradition, to be sweet on daughters and mothers to dote on sons, and while, in a patriarchal society, a father might be excused or accepted as a fit subject for comedy if his passion for the daughter exceeded the bounds of propriety, depiction of a mother's incestuous feelings toward a son was wholly unacceptable, in the poetic imagination as well as in the prose of everyday life in early modern Europe (and basically remains so even today). Thus, in the *commedia dell'arte* the older woman's role was quite different from that of Pantalone, the older man chasing "sweet young things" who were usually his daughters, nieces, or wards. Instead, the older woman was typically the *ruffiana*, or matchmaking hag, who participated only vicariously in young love. This role as go-between, or facilitator, is indeed that played by the mother in Basile's "The She-Bear." The older woman's place in fairy tale romance, however, usually was involvement rather in the affairs of young maidens in love; and it is to the description and analysis of this role that we now turn.

Notes

1. In their notes the Grimms refer to another version in which the young huntsman impregnates the princess as she sleeps (in this version she is lying naked on the bed). On discovering that the daughter is pregnant, yet claims not to know by whom, the father has her thrown into prison. This version

thus appears to lack the symbolic depiction of the father's devotion to the daughter, though it may, at the same time, carry an even stronger suggestion that he is preoccupied with her as an object of desire. See Jacob Grimm and Wilhelm Grimm, *Kinder- und Hausmärchen,* ed. Rölleke, III, 192-93; and cf. Bolte and Polívka, *Anmerkungen zu den Kinder- und Hausmärchen der Brüder Grimm,* II, 503. As Maria Tatar has observed, the eroticism in this version of the tale "must have struck the Grimms as unsatisfactory"; see her *Hard Facts of the Grimms' Fairy Tales,* p. 7.

2. Bruno Jöckel judged that the young huntsman loses his courage as prospective lover because the symbolism of the names on the slippers and neckerchief "leaves no doubt that the daughter is bound to her father by strong ties of love." Jöckel also calls attention to the somewhat contrary implication that the king was seeking a suitor for his daughter: "That the father's name becomes a threat to the huntsman precisely at the point when his passion makes possession of the daughter its object is understandable. Less clear, though, might be the resulting reversal of the position of the huntsman vis-à-vis the king, since through the letter the king made him, on the latter's entry into the castle, the executor of his child's fate, as it were." Jöckel also suggests that the girl's tender age, symbolized by her virginal sleep, may play a role in the huntsman's reticence as a lover: "What does more to prevent him from going further, her sleep—that is, the girl's immaturity—or his fear of her father, is hard to say." See Jöckel, *Der Weg zum Märchen,* pp. 101-2.

3. In Bruno Bettelheim's view, "Cinderella's asking her father for the twig she planned to plant on her mother's grave is a first tentative re-establishment of a positive relationship between the two." Bettelheim, though, interprets the story as depicting, ultimately, the process of becoming independent of one's parents: "If Cinderella is to become master of her own fate, her parents' authority must be diminished. This diminution and transfer of power could be symbolized by the branch knocking the father's hat off his head, and also the fact that the same branch grows into a tree that has magical powers for Cinderella." See *Uses of Enchantment,* pp. 256-57.

In the Grimms' first edition (1812), the father had no role in procuring the twig. The mother, on her deathbed, tells the daughter to plant a tree, and indeed why she should do so: when she shakes the tree she shall have whatever she wishes, or help in necessity or adversity. In her grief over her mother's death, the girl waters the tree with her tears. Thus, in that version the focus, in this part of the story, is entirely on the devotion between the mother and daughter. See Rölleke, *Die älteste Märchensammlung,* pp. 298-317, esp. p. 299.

4. Folkloristic monographs on all known variants of the Cinderella story were done by Marian Roalfe Cox, *Cinderella: Three Hundred and Forty-Five Variants of Cinderella, Catskin, and Cap o' Rushes, Abstracted and Tabulated, with a Discussion of Mediaeval Analogues, and Notes,* with an introduction by Andrew Lang, Publications of the Folk-Lore Society, 31 (London: Folk-Lore Society, 1892; reprint, Nendeln/Liechtenstein: Kraus, 1967), and, more recently, by Anna Birgitta Rooth, *The Cinderella Cycle* (Diss., Lund, n.d. [1951]; Lund: Gleerup, n.d. [1951]).

August Nitschke uses the Cinderella story to exemplify his historical-behavioral approach to folktales as a source of information about life in prehistoric times; see his "Aschenputtel aus der Sicht der historischen Verhaltensforschung," in Brackert, ed., *Und wenn sie nicht gestorben sind . . . ,* pp. 71-88.

5. The father's passion for the daughter is of course not the chief object of depiction, which is instead the girl's relationship with her brothers, although the father's mad desire for a daughter introduces the underlying theme of incestuous attachment. As Ruth Bottigheimer observed, from a feminist viewpoint, "The basic premise of 'The Twelve Brothers' is that disposing of the brothers will allow for a greater accretion of wealth and power to the sister. Therefore it is surprising that once this statement has set the whole tale moving, no more is heard about the father's (and mother's) kingdom, which the princess is to inherit"; see Bottigheimer, *Grimms' Bad Girls and Bold Boys,* p. 38. The explanation is that the incestuous yearning that seized the father has passed to the children, in the devotion of the brothers to their sister and hers to them.

6. See Jacob and Wilhelm Grimm, *Kinder- und Hansmärchen,* ed. Rölleke, III, 87-88.

7. For a similar interpretation of the father's role in "Dornröschen" as symbolically depicting "his romantic attachment to the daughter," see Jöckel, *Der Weg zum Märchen,* esp. p. 44: "the girl is hindered by her own father in that development which leads, after all, to another man." Bettelheim, meanwhile, takes the view that "the central theme of all versions of 'The Sleeping Beauty' is that, despite all attempts on the part of parents to prevent their child's sexual awakening, it will take place nonetheless"; see *Uses of Enchantment,* p. 230.

8. Bettelheim's interpretation of Basile's "Sole, Luna e Talia" is similar, but he sees the father's romantic attachment to the daughter, and the other king's attraction to her, as arising in response to seductive behavior on her part: "Might these two kings not be substitutes for each other at different periods in the girl's life, in different roles, in different disguises? We encounter here again the 'innocence' of the oedipal child, who feels no responsibility for what she arouses or wishes to arouse in the parent"; see *Uses of Enchantment,* p. 228.

The view that Basile's tale concerns incestuous and illicit desire is indirectly supported by Ester Zago's argument that Basile, here and in his Allerleirauh tale "L'orsa" (II, 6), de-emphasized these themes, compared with his possible sources, out of discretion and a personal reserve regarding sexual matters; see "Giambattista Basile: Il suo pubblico e il suo metodo," *Selecta: Journal of the Pacific Northwest Council on Foreign Languages* (formerly: *Proceedings of the Pacific Northwest Conference on Foreign Languages*), 2 (1981), 78-80.

9. For a psychoanalytic study of puberty rites as reflected in folktale, where girls are made outcasts, secluded, put in towers or in the care of an older woman, protected from imagined dangers, or instructed in the domestic arts, see Alfred Winterstein, "Die Pubertätsriten der Mädchen und ihre Spuren im Märchen," *Imago,* 14 (1928), 199-274.

10. As we know from their notes to another tale, "Das Mädchen ohne Hände" (*KHM* 31), the Grimms were familiar with a version of that story in which the father wants to marry his daughter. When she refuses, he personally cuts off her hands—and her breasts as well—and chases her off into the world. See Jacob Grimm and Wilhelm Grimm, *Kinder- und Hausmärchen,* ed. Rölleke, III, 57-60; and cf. Bolte and Polívka, *Anmerkungen zu den Kinder- und Hausmärchen,* I, 295-96. In the version the Grimms used in their collection, the father does not conceive a passion for the daughter, but instead unwittingly promises her to the devil (trying to get the daughter to commit incest with him, as in the other version, would amount to offering her to Satan, too). As noted earlier (Chap. 1), in Basile's related tale, "La bella dalle mani mozze" (III, 2), the girl has her manservant cut off her hands in order to thwart her brother's mad plan to marry her. The Grimms' "Das Mädchen ohne Hände" is cited by Renate Meyer zur Capellen as an example of how folktales reflect men's feelings about women, and the position of women, in a male-dominated society; see "Das schöne Mädchen: Psychoanalytische Betrachtungen zur 'Form-

werdung der Seele' des Mädchens," in Brackert, ed., *Und wenn sie nicht gestorben sind . . .* , pp. 89-119.

11. Jöckel makes a somewhat similar interpretation of the beginning of "Allerleirauh": "In our opinion . . . the father represents for the daughter men in general, the representative of the male principle, toward which the girl must first have adopted a clear, and therefore affirmative, attitude before she goes about choosing for herself that man with whom she would like to share her life"; see *Der Weg zum Märchen*, p. 62.

12. An analysis of the story using deconstructionist notions of intertextuality was done by René Démoris, "Du littéraire au littéral dans 'Peau d'âne' de Perrault," *Revue des Sciences Humaines,* 166 (1977), 261-79.

Maureen Thum (essay date winter 1993)

SOURCE: Thum, Maureen. "Feminist or Anti-Feminist? Gender-Coded Role Models in the Tales Contributed by Dorothea Viehmann to the Grimm Brothers *Kinder- und Hausmärchen*." *The Germanic Review* 68, no. 1 (winter 1993): 11-21.

[*In the following essay, Thum studies the themes, motifs, behaviors, and attributes of female protagonists in Dorothea Viehmann's contributions to* Grimms' Fairy Tales, *demonstrating a heterogeneity of narrative voices with respect to questions of gender roles.*]

Long ago, a beautiful princess was bewitched and shut up in an iron stove deep in a dark forest. There she passed many years until a handsome king's son lost his way and, coming upon that very spot, he heard a voice coming from the stove, saying: "I will help you get home again if you make me a promise. I am an enchanted princess. If you return and free me, I will marry you." But love for enchanted princesses in fairy tales never runs smooth. And although her lover freed her and was dazzled by her beauty, he left her there to say good-bye to his father. When he returned, the iron stove had disappeared. The beautiful princess was gone. Heartbroken, he sought her, traveling through the dark forest without food or drink or rest. After nine days had passed, he met a tiny toad who spoke to him in these words: "You must climb a high glass mountain; you must pass over three piercing swords, and you must cross a great lake. If you fulfill all of these tasks, you will find your true love once again."

But when he finally accomplished the tasks and arrived in the distant kingdom where the princess now lived, she had been charmed by another. In desperation, the prince used magic in order to spend a night in the room of his beloved. But her false lover had given her a sleeping potion, and she did not awake. A second night he waited in vain by her bedside. But the third night,

the princess, having heard of the long vigil of a mysterious stranger, threw away the potion. As she lay in bed, her lover entered the room. It was a joyful reunion. The two lovers, united at last, fled from this kingdom and lived happily ever after.

The above sounds like a typical, even "stereotypical" fairy tale:[1] aggressive, adventuresome male frees passive, imprisoned princess. He then sets out alone and undergoes a series of adventures in his quest to find her. Her role consists simply in being beautiful and in waiting. The above tale certainly would fit the widely held stereotype of fairy tales were it not for one rather startling fact: In the retelling, I have intentionally reversed the gender roles of the original tale. In the real version, the active protagonist who undertakes a difficult quest in search of a lover is not a prince but a princess. And the passive victim-lover who must be freed from an iron stove and rescued while sleeping in bed is not a princess but a prince. Is this a modern-day ironic role reversal, a feminist version of an old fairy tale? Not at all. In its barest schematic outlines, this is **"Der Eisenofen"** (KHM [*Kinder- und Hausmärchen*] #127),[2] one of the fairy tales contributed by Dorothea Viehmann to the Grimm brothers' collection *Kinder- und Hausmärchen.*

The active heroine who sets out alone, and who depends on her intelligence, persistence and courage to make her way in life is not simply an exception, a strange occurrence in the midst of the more "conventionally" depicted heroines that we have come to expect from fairy tales. Instead, she is in many ways representative of the type of heroine and the view of women that emerge if one examines the more than thirty tales that Dorothea Viehmann contributed to the Grimm brothers' collection. It is a view quite different from that presented by such tales as **"Schneewittchen"** (KHM #53) and **"Dornröschen"** (KHM #50), where a passive heroine is portrayed as waiting for deliverance by a prince, king or other male figure of authority.

Contrary to the general consensus about gender questions in the Grimm tales, the norms and stereotypes of passive, submissive womanhood are not reinforced in the tales contributed by Dorothea Viehmann; instead, they are subverted and even contradicted. Nor do the editorial changes made by the Grimm brothers—particularly by Wilhelm Grimm—follow what has come to be seen as the tendency to impose an increasingly normative view of gender roles on the tales, beginning with the 1812 edition and culminating in the final edition of the tales in 1857. In the case of the Viehmann contributions, quite the contrary is frequently the case.[3]

In her essay on silenced women, Ruth Bottigheimer has expressed what may be seen as a general critical consensus concerning gender-related themes in the Grimms' tales. According to Bottigheimer, gender-coded themes and motifs in the collection frequently express a normative view of women:

> One must concede that fairy tales offered an apparently innocent and peculiarly suitable medium for both transmitting and enforcing the norm of the silent woman. To the extent that these tales corroborated and codified the values of the society in which they appear, they reinforced them powerfully, symbolizing and codifying the status quo and serving as paradigms for powerlessness.[4]

("Silenced" 130)

Because they have focused primarily on motif and on structural and ideological patterns, critics such as Bottigheimer and Maria Tatar have, of necessity, looked at the collection as a relatively homogeneous whole. They have tended to treat the individual tales for the most part somewhat schematically as carriers of specific motifs and repeated patterns on the one hand and as reflections of a particular mind-set imposed upon them to a great extent by Wilhelm Grimm on the other.[5] This critical approach has certainly been fruitful and enlightening, leading to a much deeper understanding of stereotypes embedded implicitly in the tales. However, the approach is not without certain limitations because it emphasizes some aspects of the collection without taking into account other, equally important factors that also bear upon the gender question. The almost exclusive focus on the congruence among particular motifs in the overall collection—an approach influenced both by the Jungian emphasis on autonomous archetypes and by Vladimir Propp's attempt to find invariant sequences common to all fairy tales—has led many critics to deemphasize the specific and very-telling configuration of motifs, themes and functions as they appear within the context of the individual tales themselves.[6] In addition, the tendency to focus almost exclusively on the—albeit fascinating and very problematic—editorial voice of Wilhelm Grimm, has led critics, with the exception of Heinz Rölleke, to mention at best only in passing the equally fascinating and problematic voices of the various original tellers who provided the Grimm brothers with the initial versions of the tales.[7]

One of the problems in dealing with the various informants is that up until recently the entire question of the transmitters has been clouded by myth, by misunderstanding and by inadequate information regarding the various sources. Heinz Rölleke's marvelous detective work has helped to establish the identity of the numerous original tellers and has thereby provided the groundwork for examining the gender question in relation to individual transmitters. As Rölleke has stressed, many voices speak in the Grimms' tales:

> Methodologically, the ***Grimms' Fairy Tales*** do not reflect the intentions of a single author, as literary masterworks otherwise do, but the highly divergent purposes of two imitative collectors and revisors and about forty different contributors, as well as thirty different published or manuscript sources spanning six centuries and almost all of the German-speaking areas.

("New Results" 101)

Seconding Rölleke's findings, Jack Zipes, Bottigheimer and others have more recently acknowledged, either explicitly or implicitly, the presence of a variety of voices that should be taken into account in any study of the Grimms' tales. However, no critic has as yet explicated these voices or gone beyond Rölleke's brief but very telling comments on the relationship of the different voices to gender considerations.[8]

In looking at the picture of women in the tales contributed by different original tellers, I wish to use as a point of departure Rölleke's very telling but only briefly sketched argument that the view of women changes according to the sex, the age, the marital status and the social class of the teller.[9] Going beyond Rölleke's more general comments, I will examine in detail the female protagonists in several representative tales contributed by Dorothea Viehmann in order to demonstrate that the Grimm brothers' final versions of the tales do not speak with a single, relatively unified voice in questions of gender.

At this point, it is necessary to define briefly what I mean by the term "voice." The term is derived from Mikhail M. Bakhtin's concept of "heteroglossia" or "multi-voicedness," that is, the concept of a multiplicity of fictive voices, overt and implicit, within a single work.[10] I have found this metaphorical term particularly apt as a means to characterize the interplay or polyphony of quite different, often conflicting overt and implicit voices that may be detected in the multi-layered tales of the Grimms' collection.[11]

In stressing the importance of multiple speakers and corresponding multiple perspectives in the Grimms' tales, I by no means wish to deemphasize the "editorial" role of Wilhelm and Jacob Grimm. They attempted quite consciously to speak in the projected voice of a kind of mythic story teller, after the model of Clemens Brentano and Phillip Otto Runge. In realizing this editorial goal, they transformed the tales stylistically, often to a very marked degree, as even a superficial comparison of the original transcriptions with later edited versions immediately reveals (Rölleke "New Results" 107).[12] For instance, the Grimm brothers added details, improvised dialogue, inserted "folk sayings" and conflated various sources to form mosaic-like individual tales (Rölleke "New Results" 108-9). Nevertheless, in questions of gender, they did not consistently shape the tales according to a single, discernible—conscious or unconscious—ideological intent.

The problems posed in dealing with the implicit voices of the various transmitters are considerable. For the most part, the informants provided the Grimm brothers only with the barest schematic outlines of the tales. Thus, their voices cannot be identified stylistically, as in the case of Wilhelm and Jacob Grimm themselves. However, the difficulties involved in detecting these concealed voices are not insurmountable; Rölleke has suggested a very fruitful method of approach, or perhaps process of "detection" might be a better word here. As his discussion of the "woman question" suggests, the voices of the various transmitters may be identified indirectly if one examines the configuration of themes and motifs as well as the behavior and attributes of female protagonists within the individual tales that they contributed.

If the tales are analyzed in relation to their known contributors, certain patterns emerge. For instance, the stories transmitted by young, educated—and unmarried—women of the upper-middle class reveal certain role-oriented expectations that seem to have played a decisive role in their predilection for the tales that they remembered and chose to pass along.

Marie Hassenpflug, who belonged to the Grimms' circle of friends in Kassel, exemplifies the correlation between personal and social circumstances and the choice of material. In the nine tales that she contributed, women play a dominant role in seven, more than two-thirds of the narratives. In four of the tales—nearly half of her contributions—a passive, obedient heroine is portrayed as undergoing a process of maturation or socialization during which she waits for deliverance by a prince, a king or other male authority figure. In **"Dornröschen"** and **"Schneewittchen"** (two of the above stories) the heroine literally sleeps her way into womanhood. The paradoxical message of such tales is that passivity is a source of power, a means to achieve emotional and economic rewards.

Of the fourteen stories transmitted by Dortchen Wild, the later wife of Wilhelm Grimm, twelve (86 %) present women in the main role, an even higher percentage than in the case of Marie Hassenpflug. Seven of these figures are represented as undergoing trials and suffering in preparation for marriage. In two tales, relatively active, independent women are portrayed as negative and in need of punishment. In one story, **"Frau Holle,"** the young woman meets the test of her maturity and is rewarded for proving her capabilities as the ideal housewife who knows how to cook, clean and carry out daily chores with thoroughness and consistency. Her counterpart, who fails to fulfill the specifically gender-oriented tasks, is punished in a horrible manner. She is covered with pitch.

The contributions of Marie Hassenpflug and Dortchen Wild seem to fulfill to a great extent some of the stereotypes of fairy tales that have remained with us until

the present. It is indicative that, as Rölleke astutely points out, none of the young bourgeois women in the circle of the Grimms' acquaintances continued to provide tales for the Grimm brothers after their marriage—that is, after the coming of the "prince" who was to usher them into womanhood.[13]

However, if one turns to other contributors to the Grimms' collection, to those who were not unmarried bourgeois girls with a relatively good formal education, quite a different picture emerges. Sergeant of the Dragoons, J. F. Krause and the "market woman," Dorothea Viehmann, are cases in point. Six tales have been attributed with varying degrees of certainty to the retired soldier, Sergeant Krause.[14] Although unmarried young women play a central role in the majority of the contributions of Marie Hassenpflug and Dortchen Wild, in Krause's tales, only men (in one case a male animal) play the leading role. With one exception, the women are all princesses, and all of them are the booty or reward of the active and aggressive lower-class male protagonist, who through magic and cunning manages to assume a role of political and economic power. The two princesses who are portrayed positively are both depicted in a totally passive role—asleep—and both are dismissed with a perfunctory sentence or two. They function primarily as the object of the protagonist's quest, assuming no autonomous role whatsoever in the story. They are anonymous figures symbolizing his rise to power. The remaining three princesses play an actively and aggressively evil role as the antagonists of their lower-class husbands. The picture of womanhood that emerges in these tales may be said at the very least to suggest strongly misogynistic tendencies; it corresponds neither to the view of women of the Grimm brothers themselves nor to the view held by other contributors, and certainly not to that expressed in the Viehmann contributions.

If one examines the contributions of Dorothea Viehmann, one finds a picture of the female protagonists that is far more complex and in some cases even markedly different from that so frequently attributed to the tales of the Grimms' collection. One of the most important single sources for the tales, she had just reached the age of 60 when the Grimm brothers first met her. The daughter of an innkeeper, of Huguenot origin, she had married a tailor in Niederzwehren, a little village near Kassel. Although she was certainly not an uneducated peasant,—she spoke both French and German and could read and write—she could by no means be termed a member of the relatively wealthy rising bourgeoisie. Her life had not been easy. Her husband was an alcoholic. After the unrest caused by the Napoleonic wars, the family—she had six children—fell upon hard times, and she was forced to support them by carrying market wares on her back into the homes of the Kassel gentry (Seitz 61; Rölleke "New Results" 103-5).

It was during her visits to the Grimms' household that she told the brothers many of the 37 tales that she supplied for their collection. By the time of the 1857 edition, 31 of the narratives had been included in the text of the *Kinder- und Hausmärchen* itself, while the remaining six of her 37 contributions were related in the notes to the 1857 edition.

If one examines her contributions in some detail, particularly in comparison to those of Marie Hassenpflug and Dortchen Wild, certain patterns emerge that suggest that her background, her personal experiences of the realities of existence in a small town, as well as her knowledge of the conditions and limitations faced by the women of her time, seem to have played more than just a minor role in her choice of tales. One must, of course, tread carefully here. Dorothea Viehmann herself did not invent the stories that she told. It is important to keep in mind that we are not dealing here with a "Kunstmärchen" or literary fairy tale—one in which the author incorporates fairy tale motifs into an original work. We are looking at Viehmann primarily as a source and asking what tentative observations can be made about her view of women, given the make-up of the tales that she contributed. It must also be stressed that we have the original transcription for only a few. In my discussion, I will focus primarily on these tales as they provide the best evidence that one can indeed speak of an implicit "voice" in reference to a transmitter such as Viehmann.

Viehmann's hidden voice may be deduced from certain recurring patterns in her contributions. A careful examination of the tales in which women appear suggests that Dorothea Viehmann had few illusions about the limitations facing any woman within the social context that she had observed in the more than a half-century of her life in a small German town. Of the 31 tales she contributed to the collection, only 10 have female protagonists, in other words, women who play a leading or decisive role. In the remaining two-thirds, the protagonists are male. Women appear only peripherally, if at all. The ratio of male to female is the *reverse* of what we find in the case of Marie Hassenpflug and Dortchen Wild. In the case of Sergeant Krause, whereas 50% of the tales have an active and evil female antagonist, none of the tales have a woman as the central figure of the tale. This numerical comparison of the ratio of heroes to heroines is certainly significant, as Rölleke has suggested ("Frau" 226-7). However, even more telling is the role played by the heroines within the specific context of individual Viehmann tales. If we look carefully at the 10 Viehmann contributions in which women play a leading role, we find that the depiction of the female protagonists not only subverts but often contradicts the stereotype of the passive, obedient, submissive heroine whom we have come to expect from fairy tales and who present to us what Bottigheimer refers to as "para-

digms of powerlessness" ("Silenced" 130). Thus, the roles of various female protagonists are far more varied than one might expect, especially given the fact that they are clearly locked into a patriarchal society in general and limited by the gender-coded normative roles required by a specific social class in particular.

The role models provided by Dorothea Viehmann's tales are quite different from those suggested by passive princesses sleeping their way to marriage and maturity. Indeed, in only 3 of the 37 tales she narrated to the Grimm brothers—that is in less than 10% of her tales—is the protagonist a princess. And none of these three resemble their passive and far better known counterparts in **"Dornröschen"** and **"Schneewittchen."** Instead, they are women who, while limited by their clearly defined roles of the time, are very positive figures. They are shown as intelligent, as prepared to take the initiative, as capable of change, and in at least two of the three instances, as prepared to take a role usually assigned in fairy tales to their male counterparts.

The remaining seven of the ten female protagonists are "ordinary" women, peasants for the most part. Of them, four marry princes or kings in order to escape very unpleasant circumstances at home, the misery of overly hard work and poverty, the brutality of their stepparents or of natural parents. Their escape and rescue is depicted as occurring by chance, or through the direct intervention of God and the angels—a fact strongly suggesting how unlikely such an escape was considered to be in real circumstances. A fifth, **"Die faule Spinnerin"** (**KHM** #128) remains a peasant, but through her considerable ingenuity, she tricks her husband into allowing her to do very little housework and, thus in effect, lives as a "princess"—or a parasite, because her husband must work all the harder as she does nothing at all. Unlike the lazy sister in **"Frau Holle,"** this woman is not punished for her failure to fulfill household tasks; overt moralizing comment in the tale concerning the "proper" role of women is quite absent in the earlier, 1812 edition. Only later does Wilhelm Grimm add the statement "Aber das musst du selbst sagen, es war eine garstige Frau" (**KHM** 1857 Vol. 1 207). It is with this sort of comment, of course, that Grimm has earned the reputation of imposing normative values upon the tales!

The two remaining female characters, both peasant women, who fail to escape from their social circumstances, are depicted as pitiable figures. Both are mentally disturbed, and both are propelled into madness—whether intentionally or not—by their husbands.

Viehmann's choice of tales appears to reflect a clear knowledge of the social position of women in her time. Very few are princesses. Most are lower class. Compared to men, women of both the upper and lower classes seldom play the leading role. In the tales where women are the protagonists, their life is not easy. They are able to survive against very great odds only through their deep inner strength, and through an ability to assert themselves despite the handicap of their gender, and despite numerous adversities. These are the survivors. The others who fail to exercise their will and intelligence, and who are thus unable to cope with the realities of their situation, are not. The passive, submissive role in the Viehmann tales appears as a danger and a trap.

In order to see how the role models presented in Dorothea Viehmann's tales break the stereotype and contradict the normative view of women so often associated with the Grimm tales, it is necessary to look at the female protagonists within the context of individual tales. Three of her tales may be seen as representative: **"Die zwölf Brüder"** (KHM #9), **"Die kluge Bauerntochter"** (KHM #94) and **"Die kluge Else" (KHM #34)**. (I wish to note here that according to the source Jack Zipes cites, he is incorrect in attributing **"Die zwölf Brüder"** to Julia and Charlotte Ramus and claiming that it was not contributed by Dorothea Viehmann.)[15]

In the tales Viehmann related, the princess as protagonist is seen, within the very real limitations of her position, as a relatively autonomous figure who is capable of exercising her will and intelligence in her relationship to her male counterpart, even when she is forced into what appears, at least physically, to be a passive role. Such is the case in **"Die zwölf Brüder."** The irony of the title, which boasts of not just one but twelve male protagonists, becomes very quickly apparent: the focus of the tale is not on the twelve princes and two kings, but rather on a young girl, their sister, who is the only one aside from her mother to assume a positive role or to take any real initiative in this male-dominated world, a world in which the "natural," accepted order has been overturned by the caprice of a maniacal king.

The father, to whom we are introduced in the opening of the story, is a gruesome, twisted man whose unquestioned power as absolute monarch permits him to realize his delusions and to fashion a distorted world that corresponds to his mental aberrations. Thus, he reverses the feudal order of succession, according to which the eldest male—in the case of two or more daughters, the eldest—inherits the throne. He proclaims to his pregnant wife that if her thirteenth child is a girl "so sollen die zwölf Buben sterben, damit sein Reichtum gross wird und das Königreich [dem Mädchen] allein zufällt" (**KHM** 1857 Vol. 1 71). As we have the original manuscript version of this tale, we can compare it to the later-edited versions of Wilhelm Grimm. The change Grimm makes in the opening is not, as Tatar has suggested, incomprehensible (31-32). While Viehmann's version emphasizes the utter caprice and irrationality of the king, Wilhelm Grimm intensifies the focus on the social implications and the king's personal motivation by substituting intentionality for accident.

The king underlines the seriousness of his brutal and absurd intention by having twelve coffins made in preparation for the little girl's birth. He had them brought to a locked room, "dann gab er der Königin den Schlüssel und gebot ihr, niemand etwas davon zu sagen" (**KHM** 1857 Vol. 1 72). As a consequence of their sister's birth, the twelve brothers must flee into the forest. In their rage at their enforced exile, they are as capricious and wrong-headed as their crazy father: they project the blame for their plight not on the king, who perpetrated this evil deed, but rather on all of womankind: "Sollten wir um eines Mädchens willen den Tod leiden!" (72). Out of revenge, they swear an oath to kill every young woman that they encounter, an act that they carry out in Viehmann's version of the tale. The focusing of their anger on an improper target prevents them from countering their father's move or from taking revenge on the real culprit, and leaves them in a state of embittered powerlessness.

As the little girl comes on the scene, through no fault of her own, the hallowed social order has been destroyed: Time is out of joint, and she must be the one to set it right. When she first hears about the existence of her banished brothers, her reaction is neither egotistical nor is it passive. Although it would be in her "interest" to accept the royal position awaiting her, and thus to forget about the brothers that she has never seen, she does not even consider this possibility. Nor does she simply lament their banishment or bewail her lot. Instead, she takes the initiative, assuming what normally would be the role of the male in such a story: she ventures out alone into the forest to find and rescue them. The changes made by Grimm in this case emphasize rather than reduce the active role of the princess, since they show that her trek into the forest is not merely an accidental journey undertaken out of boredom as in the 1810 manuscript (Rölleke: *Älteste Märchensammlung* 64). Instead, it results directly from her curiosity, her deductive abilities and her decision to find her brothers in order to comfort her mother.

Although the young girl precipitates her brothers' transformation into ravens after she has found them, her deed is no more intentional than was her birth, which was technically the immediate cause of their becoming outcasts in the first place. She is innocent of any wrongdoing. One might infer from her inculpability that she is no more than an accidental victim of chance or fate, suffering wrongly in expiation for the crimes of others. However, the role she now plays once more goes beyond the mere passive bearing of undeserved fate. A woman in the forest tells her that her brothers may only be saved by a person who vows to keep silent, neither to laugh nor to speak under any condition for seven years. For a second time, she takes upon herself a difficult task in order to restore order. The fulfillment of her vow of silence is a morally free act, one undertaken without any considerations of pleasure or self-advancement. She suffers by choice in order to restore the rule of law and morality and thus to right the wrongs committed by her father, wrongs visited upon his sons not only in the form of banishment, but in the guise of a distorted view of the world—suggested by their state of enchantment.

Like her original act of entering the forest alone, her silence is by no means passive. She can uphold it only by extreme strength of will, as it is tested again and again by slander, false accusations and finally condemnation by her own husband, who decrees that she be burned to death. Even when the flames are licking at her body, she does not speak. Her husband, the king, who looks on with tears rolling down his cheeks as he obeys his mother's wishes to kill her, is an abject figure in comparison to the young woman in her strength and courage. The twelve brothers who "rescue" her from the fire are able to do so only because her action has restored them to human form.

Bottigheimer mentions the silence of the princess in this tale as one of the instances where the female figure provides a paradigm of powerlessness; however, if one looks at her silence within the context of the entire tale, the princess, despite the limitations of the role of silence, is by no means powerless. Already in Viehmann's original version, and even more so in Wilhelm Grimm's later versions, the princess is not only a positive figure, but she is the only figure shown as capable of inducing change in a world gone mad. Her male counterparts, by contrast, are shown as powerless to provoke change: the king because of his madness, the brothers because of their inability to assess the real nature of their position and the final king of the story because he is easily manipulated by his mother into acting against his own very real inclinations.

The fact that princesses as protagonists play a relatively autonomous role in the contributions of Dorothea Viehmann suggests an awareness of the fact that social class and relative autonomy are closely linked. Peasant heroines in Viehmann's contributions are, for the most part, less independent because of economic and social limitations. However, of the seven peasant girls, the five who do improve or maintain their present position are certainly not passive. On the contrary, they demonstrate strength of will as well as initiative. In four of the five cases in which the peasant heroine successfully copes with adversity, marriage to a king represents an escape from the misery imposed by the often trying and even brutal circumstances of their lives. In none of the cases does mere passive waiting, obedience or beauty bring about positive results.

In **"Die kluge Bauerntochter,"** for example, beauty, obedience and various "housewifely" virtues play no role at all in her rise in status. Instead, the king, who is rather more enlightened than the usual feudal creature of his sort, is drawn to her intelligence, seeking in her an equal and companion, not merely an ornament for his throne. (This does not mean that he is without ambivalence in this regard, as the events of the story demonstrate. He is, after all, a feudal king.) The king first desires to see her when he finds that she has predicted his behavior very accurately without ever having seen him. She had told her father that if he presents the king with a mortar made of gold, which he has found in his field, the king will demand to have the pestle as well. She has astutely assessed the king's greed as well as his mistrust for those in his power. She knows that he will resort to violence and injustice out of sheer covetousness.

Instead of being shocked and angered at her insight, the king, an unusually tolerant monarch, becomes intrigued by this woman who understands the mechanisms of human behavior, and particularly the mechanisms governing relationships between those who have power and those who do not. He is certainly not the stereotype of the feudal ruler who listens only to his courtiers. This man is curious to see himself through the eyes of the "people"—in this case, the peasant's wise daughter. Another surprising characteristic is that he is not afraid of, but rather appreciates, an intelligent wife and queen. Thus, he presents a riddle to her, promising to marry her if she can find the answer. Here is the riddle: "Komm zu mir, nicht gekleidet, nicht nackend, nicht geritten, nicht gefahren, nicht in dem Weg, nicht ausser dem Weg, und wenn du das kannst, will ich dich heiraten" (**KHM** 1857 Vol. 2 58). The young woman's answer is highly ingenious:

> Da ging sie hin und zog sich aus splinternackend, da war sie nicht gekleidet, und nahm ein grosses Fischgarn und setzte sich hinein und wickelte es ganz um sich herum, da war sie nicht nackend; und borgte einen Esel fürs Geld und band dem Esel das Fischgarn an den Schwanz, darin er sie fortschleppen musste, und war das nicht geritten und nicht gefahren; der Esel musste sie aber in der Fahrgleise schleppen, so dass sie nur mit der grossen Zehe auf die Erde kam, und war das nicht in dem Weg und nicht ausser dem Wege.

> (58)

This picture is certainly a far cry from that of the elegant, passive, obedient beauty of dubious insight and intelligence, the stereotypical fairy tale heroine. Her intellect is her most important asset, so important, in fact, that her appearance is not mentioned at all.

When the king places her in charge of the royal possessions, she is portrayed as humanizing the government by ameliorating conditions caused by excesses of the feudalist regime. She is seen by peasants as gracious, "weil sie auch von armen Bauersleuten gekommen (war)" (**KHM** 1857 Vol. 2 59).

In the course of the story, however, she angers her husband by causing him to lose face; he has made a capricious and unfair decision in a judicial case between two peasants. Her advice to one of the peasants who approaches her secretly, asking for her counsel, causes her husband to see the absurdity of his own decree but nonetheless to feel injured in his pride. Thus, he repudiates her, sending her home again to her hovel with the stipulation that she may take with her the thing most precious to her in his palace.

The resolution again comes about through the young woman's initiative and intelligence: she drugs the king, and takes him with her to her hut. When he awakes, wondering where he is, she says to him, "Ihr habt mir befohlen, ich sollte das Liebste und Beste aus dem Schloss mitnehmen, nun hab ich nichts Besseres und Lieberes als dich, da hab ich dich mitgenommen." Tears come into the king's eyes as he hears these words, and he replies, "Liebe Frau, du sollst mein sein und ich dein" (**KHM** 1857 Vol. 2 60).

It is noteworthy that Wilhelm Grimm himself felt a little uncomfortable with the figure of the peasant's wise daughter, even though he left her relatively intact and allowed her to speak for herself. In the notes to the 1857 edition, he is careful to explain that a peasant girl could surely not be quite as intelligent as the young woman depicted here. "Sie ist über ihren Stand und ihre Eltern weise," protests Wilhelm Grimm (**KHM** *Anmerkungen* 170). Therefore, he continues, this is not actually a story about an ordinary woman. Instead it is a Brunhilde figure in peasant guise! It is hard to avoid the suspicion that the notes in this case were not only of literary interest, but, at least in part, Grimm's means of dealing with an image of womanhood that implicitly contradicted his own.[16]

Unlike the peasant's wise daughter, and the other heroines who manage to cope through initiative and intelligence, the two female protagonists who fail to cope with reality, and who are thus seen as piteous outcasts by the end of the story, demonstrate neither intelligence nor initiative, despite their good intentions. One of these is **"Die kluge Else."**

"Die kluge Else" is a tale that appears, on the surface, to be simply a farce in a long tradition of tales about "clever" characters whose behavior is absurd, ludicrous or stupid because they fail to follow the simplest requirements of common sense. However, the dark conclusion of the tale—Else's loss of identity—forces the reader to reexamine his or her assumptions about the ludicrousness of the characters presented in the tale. In

this sense, the tale is relatively sophisticated, since the teller consciously presents an ending that is contrary to expectations and that thus causes the entire story to appear in quite a different light. This reversal is in line with other Viehmann tales, which are satirical and often ironic rather than naive in the telling. In light of the ending, the story becomes a rather disturbing and telling analysis of a communal and individual aberration.

It is highly indicative that in choosing **"Die kluge Else"** as part of their collection, the Grimm brothers moved not toward but *away* from a more normative view of gender roles. **"Die kluge Else,"** a highly complex tale that subverts the expected farce, appeared for the first time in the 1819 edition, replacing a different variant of the story, which had appeared in the 1812 edition under the title **"Hansens Trine"** (***KHM in ihrer Urgestalt [Kinder- und Hausmärchen der Brüder Grimm in ihrer Urgestalt]*** #34). **"Hansens Trine,"** which Wilhelm Grimm relegated to the notes of the 1857 edition, presents the expected gender-coded stereotypes. The tale consists of the brief account of Trine who was "faul und wollte nichts thun" (***KHM in ihrer Urgestalt*** Vol. 1 104-05). As a punishment, her husband takes a knife and cuts off her long dress at the knee. When she runs away from home, no longer knowing who she is, she is described as "vergnügt" (105). The story concludes with the judgmental statement: "und Hans war die Trine los" (105). In this case, contrary to the normative tendencies frequently attributed to his editing practices, Wilhelm Grimm prefers the tale that breaks the stereotype. With one exception, an excellent analysis by Erika Metzger, previously published critical commentary on the tale has failed completely to note the difference between the two versions and dismisses **"Die kluge Else"** as a straightforward tale about a young woman who is called "clever" but is actually unbelievably stupid.[17]

In **"Die kluge Else,"** all of the members and servants of the relatively well-off peasant household are in apparent agreement about the meaning of the word "clever" in reference to Else. The father's claim to her potential suitor, Hans, that his daughter "hat Zwirn im Kopf" (i.e., is "very sharp") is seconded by her mother. And while Else's mother concurs with her husband, her words unwittingly point to her daughter's exaggerated, if not pathological, sensibility: "Ach, die sieht den Wind auf der Gasse laufen und hört die Fliegen husten" (**KHM** 1857 Vol. 1 189). Whatever their reservations, spoken or unspoken, both her parents and the two servants exclaim how intelligent she is, as they join her to wail communally in the basement over a future possibility, which Else has fantasized and which could be easily prevented by making a few common sense moves. As Else sits in the cellar drawing beer, she sees a pickaxe left by the masons in the masonry and says to herself: "Wenn ich den Hans kriege, und wir kriegen ein Kind, und das ist gross, und wir schicken das Kind in den Keller, dass es hier Bier zapfen [soll], so fällt ihm die Kreuzhacke auf den Kopf und schlägt's tot." (**KHM** 1857 Vol. 1 189) Her false assessment of reality causes her to begin to wail and scream with all her strength, as if she were facing an inevitable occurrence. For Else, conjecture has as much power as the concrete reality of the everyday physical world. She is unable to distinguish between reality and her own hallucinations. Thus, she seems to feel overwhelmed by the objects around her, investing in them a power they do not have and failing to see her own role as exercising any rational, practical control over her environment. Her parents and the servants seems to share, at least in part, her failure to come to grips with reality because it does not occur to any of them to remove the axe and thus avert any possible accidents in the future.

The behavior of both the parents and Hans is presented ambiguously. Is Else's overwrought fantasizing, which distorts her relationship to reality, the individual expression of a communal aberration? Or is the family intent on proving to the potential groom that Else is indeed normal and desirable as a wife in order to ensure her a future despite her strange behavior? Or is this simply the protective mode into which many families fall who cannot deal with the strange behavior of one of their members and who, therefore, attempt to pretend that it does not exist? The teller leaves all of these possibilities open. Judging by Else's behavior and her family's response, her distorted relationship to reality is of long-standing, and if it is not shared by her family, it has certainly not been discouraged. Hans's response is also ambivalent: "mehr Verstand is für meinen Haushalt nicht nötig; weil du so eine kluge Else bist, so will ich dich haben" (**KHM** 1857 Vol. 1 191). Does he prefer to have a stupid wife who does not threaten his feeling of authority and power? Is he willing to assent to the communal delusion because he is too limited to see the implications of her behavior, or is he just as aberrant and thus incapable of judging with common sense? Perhaps it is indicative that this suitor came from "far away." Those in the area could not be induced to marry her.

The brief, telling episode that follows occurs "als sie den Hans eine Weile hatte" (**KHM** 1857 Vol. 1 191). One would assume that he knows his wife by now, as well as her aberrations; but his role in this regard is somewhat ambiguous. When he goes out to earn some money, he sends her alone into the field, where, as we have seen in the episode above, her behavior is highly consistent and thus predictable. She fails at each turn to come to grips with reality, and although she is able to cook a broth and fulfill simple household tasks, she appears to be unable to cope with a new situation, working in the field. Thus she reverses the usual, practical order of things. She eats, then sleeps all day long.

The event has unpleasant consequences. Hans, understandably angry at his wife's apparent laziness, and very probably unaware of the consequences of his act, plays a rather cruel trick on her. He hangs a fowler's net about her as she sleeps, then runs home and shuts the door to wait. This practical joke is the immediate cause for Else's mental crisis. Waking in the dark and hearing the bells ringing all about her, Else is filled with fear: Her already tenuous relationship to reality is broken completely, as she loses her sense of self and identity. "Da erschrak sie, ward irre, ob sie auch wirklich die kluge Else wäre" (**KHM** 1857 Vol. 1 192). Unable to reorient herself, she runs home to her husband, hoping that he will help her to cope with this frightening mental state. Finding the door shut, she knocks at the window and makes her plea: "Hans, ist die Else drinnen?" His answer, "Ja . . . sie ist drinnen" indicates, on the one hand, Hans's abandonment of his wife in her suffering, and on the other, the personality split that takes place in the form of acute neurosis and madness (**KHM** 1857 Vol. 1 192). The individual seems to depart into a realm of chaos and meaninglessness, and the rational mind is no longer in control. Her identity as "Clever Else" has been called into question by the realities of married life, and she has found no other "self" that would allow her to cope with the world that she has encountered, once she has left the protection of her parents' home, where her failure to come to terms with reality was neither remarked upon nor discouraged.[18]

The last few lines picture the abandoned Else, going from door to door, searching for someone to help her in her suffering and madness. But, as is the case when one is mad or disturbed, her neighbors are too frightened to reach out to her and bring her into their homes: "sie konnte nirgend unterkommen" (**KHM** 1857 Vol. 1 192). The conclusion of the story remains open: Does Else return to her parents? Does she perhaps find a new identity and new means to cope elsewhere? Or is the break with reality and the loss of self irreversible? The reader knows only that Else's future is shadowed by foreboding and that she never appeared in the village again.

Else's mental instability, as well as that of her counterpart in the tale **"Der Frieder und das Catherlieschen"** (**KHM** #59), suggests that the woman who is unable to exercise her strength of will, her initiative and intelligence runs the danger of losing her identity altogether when faced with the realities of a peasant's life. Else is simply too vulnerable to survive the circumstances in which she lives.

The three female figures in the tales just discussed are certainly a far cry from the young women whose obedience and passivity are shown to be the only means of survival. They bear little resemblance to the stereotypical role of the female protagonist that has become entrenched in popular imagination as the epitome of the fairy tale heroine. In the stories of Dorothea Viehmann's repertoire, women face difficult, often harsh circumstances, and yet, like Dorothea Viehmann herself, they survive through their own strength and inner resources. They are not unlike this surprising woman who carried market wares on her back into town to support six children and a husband but who managed to preserve her dignity and find expression for a keen intellect and insight in her preservation of the many tales that she told to the Grimm brothers. And despite the fact that the Grimm brothers' editing, particularly that of Wilhelm Grimm, has been associated with tendencies to provide a more normative view of gender roles than one finds in the initial versions of the tales, in the case of Viehmann's contributions, their editorial policies are clearly more complex, and less clear-cut or obvious than has frequently been assumed.

The question raised by the title of this essay must now be addressed: "feminist or anti-feminist?" I wish to stress that the results of any study based on the recognition of the multiple voices both overtly and implicitly present in the numerous, multi-layered texts of this collection must be, at best, tentative. But it has not been my purpose to resolve the riddle posed by the gender question in the Grimm brothers' collection. Instead, I have attempted to follow—and to suggest for further research—a fruitful line of investigation that provides no simple answers to the question of my title but that takes into account the complexity of the often paradoxical gender portrayals in this multi-faceted collection. Instead of giving answers, the present discussion strives to point out unanswered questions and to uncover concealed voices that run counter to any general conclusions about the nature of this work, considered as a univocal "product" of the Grimm brothers' editing or of the patriarchal society whose assumptions are clearly embedded in the tales themselves.

Notes

1. Since the tales of the Grimm brothers tend to shift between the generic classifications designated in German by the two terms "Märchen" and "Kunstmärchen," finding satisfactory designation of the tales has posed a problem. I use the terms "tale" and "fairy tale" throughout to refer to the "Märchen" in the Grimms' collection, and "literary fairy tale" to designate the "Kunstmärchen."

2. I will be using the numbering of the 1857 edition, indicating the number in *Kinder- und Hausmärchen* (KHM) in parentheses in the text. See Rölleke's excellent three-volume scholarly edition of the 1857 *Kinder- und Hausmärchen*. The third volume includes notes and tables indicating the various sources, dates of inclusion in the editions,

as well as other important information for evaluating the editorial changes in the collection from the 1810 manuscript to the final version in 1857.

3. See also Rölleke's statement that the Grimm brothers let the tales speak essentially ("im wesentlichen") for themselves ("Frau" 223). Despite certain demonstrably normative tendencies in the Grimm brothers' editing, Rölleke's assessment is certainly not far off the mark, particularly in reference to the tales that I will be discussing below.

4. In a somewhat later essay, Bottigheimer modifies her stance, indicating that the gender stereotyping derives as much from the folk tradition itself as from Wilhelm Grimm's editing of the stories ("From Gold" 196-97).

5. Ruth Bottigheimer's provocative studies, for instance, have explored a number of gender-related themes. See her discussion of the silence and silencing of women at several levels in the tales ("Silenced" 119-20). See also her chapter "Prohibitions, Transgressions and Punishments" in which she suggests that men and women are rewarded or punished according to the extent to which they fulfill preconceived, gender-coded roles. Bottigheimer concludes that one can detect a "general pattern of exculpating men and incriminating women" that "permeates Grimms' Tales" (*Grimms' Bad Girls* 81-94).

For a discussion of the role played in the stories by passive and aggressive female figures, by witches, wise women and wicked stepmothers, see particularly Bottigheimer's chapter "Witches, Maidens and Spells" (*Grimms' Bad Girls* 40-50) and Tatar's chapter "From Nags to Witches" (*Hard Facts* 137-55). Tatar discusses the "wicked stepmother" as villain in the class of "ogres and fiends" (141-42) as part of the elaboration of "variations on the theme of maternal domestic tyranny" (155).

Still others have detected overall misogynistic tendencies in the Grimms' collection, tendencies which they attribute to the Grimm brothers themselves or to the folk tradition of which the tales were originally a part. See Tatar (137-55). See also the discussions of Andrea Dworkin and Robert Moore. Rölleke was the first to point out that the misogynistic tales may be seen to reflect the voice of the informant perhaps even more than that of the Grimm brothers ("Frau" 225-26). See also Bottigheimer ("From Gold" 198).

6. The general approach to the tales as a relatively homogeneous collection in which motifs, themes, figures and functions may be removed from the

wider context of the tales and discussed as autonomous "entities" is strongly influenced by Propp, as both Bottigheimer (*Grimms' Bad Girls* x-xi) and Tatar (66-71) indicate in their studies. One of the limitations of Propp's structuralist and formalist approach, despite the very real insights it offers, is the tendency to see the various elements of fairy tales as virtually interchangeable and to deemphasize, to a great extent, the context of the individual tale in which the various themes and motifs appear. Peter Steiner has pointed to the shortcomings inherent in such an approach, despite the advantages for comparative studies: "Because a fairy tale is not an empirical but an intentional object, the static elements and their relations must be taken into account if we are to grasp the unity of the fairy tale in its process of transformation" (95).

7. Although the original tellers, particularly Dorothea Viehmann and Sergeant of Dragoons Krause, have been mentioned with greater and greater frequency, especially since Heinz Rölleke's 1986 article on the role of the transmitters in relation to gender considerations, no critic has as yet continued Rölleke's line of argument. In reference to gender questions, the transmitters have been discussed only in passing. See for instance comments by Bottigheimer on Krause ("From Gold" 198) and Tatar's references to Viehmann (109-10).

8. In a recent essay, Bottigheimer emphasizes the fact that it is difficult to attribute a single voice to the Grimm brothers or even to assign particular voices, as has been the tendency in some critical discussions, since the gender stereotypes in the tales derive as much, if not more, from the folk tradition and the sixteenth-century literary tradition of the "Schwank" as from any possible prejudices of the Grimm brothers themselves. ("From Gold" 195-97). Zipes also comments: "We must constantly bear in mind that we are dealing with multiple representations and voices within the narrative structure of each tale." (*Brothers Grimm* 50).

9. See Rölleke's comments in "Die Frau in den *Märchen der Brüder Grimm*."

10. In his discussions of Dostoevsky, Bakhtin uses a somewhat different generic application of "multivoicedness"; that is, he employs this term to characterize the interplay of relatively "autonomous" fictive voices in works by a single author. However, Bakhtin also sees the "dialogic orientation" of discourse in a broader sense as the "natural orientation of any living discourse" (*Dialogic* 279). For Bakhtin's discussion of the complex interrelationship of voice and context in what he perceives as primarily dialogic (multi-voiced) as opposed to monologic (univocal) works of fiction, see *Problems of Dostoevsky's Poetics* and *The Dialogic Imagination: Four Essays*.

11. The generic application that I propose is clearly somewhat different from that of Bakhtin's well-known discussions of Dostoevsky's, as opposed to Tolstoy's, novels. Unlike Dostoevsky and Tolstoy, the Grimm brothers were certainly not the authors of the tales themselves; nevertheless, they were more than mere "editors," since they shaped the tales in their collection by editing practices that were far more radical than one would expect of the compilers and editors of tales contributed by others (Rölleke "New Results" 107-9). That is, by conflating and rewriting the tales, they took part in the writing process itself. We must therefore continually bear in mind that their relationship to the material in their collection remains far more tenuous and ambiguous than either that of an "editor" or that of an "author." Indeed, their role lies somewhere between the usual modern definitions of these two terms. In using the term "voice" and "multi-voicedness" in reference to the Grimms' collection, I am referring both to the "voices" of the Grimm brothers as demonstrated in their editing methods and to the concealed voices of various contributors to this hybrid, heavily edited work. As my discussion will suggest, the "voices" of the informants may be deduced often only indirectly through recurring patterns in the configurations of the tales that they contributed.

12. Although the Grimm brothers destroyed all of their original hand-written manuscripts, Clemens Brentano fortunately failed to return a manuscript containing early handwritten transcriptions of the tales that the Grimm brothers sent to him in 1810. The 46 original transcriptions have been preserved and are among the only records of the earliest form of the tales in later editions (Rölleke "New Results" 102). See Rölleke's comparative presentation of the texts of the tales preserved in the Brentano manuscript, alongside the texts of the revised tales as they appeared in the first edition of 1812 (*Älteste Märchensammlung der Brüder Grimm*, 1975).

13. See note 9 above. My discussion of the numerical ratios is indebted to Rölleke's astute observations and his scholarly research that has made possible the assignment of various tales with some certainty to particular tellers. For a very judicious assigning of the tales to the original tellers, see the tables in Rölleke's edition of the Grimm brothers' notes to the 1857 edition (KHM *Anmerkungen* 559-74) and see the essays in his collection *Wo das Wünschen noch geholfen hat.*

14. We have very little information about Sergeant Krause (1747-1828). See Fink (147), Schindhütte (100-02) and Schoof (88). Six tales have been attributed to him, four with some certainty and two more tentatively. See particularly Rölleke's tables in KHM *Anmerkungen* (559-74). See also Fink (147-48).

15. See Zipes (*The Brothers Grimm* 49-50). The reference Zipes cites in Rölleke indicates that the Ramus sisters gave the tale to the Grimm brothers but then specifies that the Ramus sisters had received the tale from Dorothea Viehmann (*KHM Anmerkungen* 445-46). Dorothea Viehmann is corroborated as the source for the tale in two other places. See Rölleke's table, attributing #9 ("The Twelve Brothers") to Viehmann with the comment "vor Okt. 1810; durch Ramus vermittelt" (*KHM Anmerkungen* 571). See also Wilhelm Grimm's notes to the 1857 edition (*KHM Anmerkungen* 20).

16. See Rölleke's highly informative commentary on the Grimm brothers' view of women, based on biographical details and on the one tale that they are known to have put together themselves ("Die Frau" 220-23).

17. Lutz Röhrich sums up the figure of Else with the comment that tales in the collection portray intelligent women but also those who are like the "so-genannte kluge Else, die in Wirklichkeit strohdumm ist" (84). Metzger, on the other hand, analyzes both "Der Frieder und das Catherlieschen" (KHM #59) and "Die kluge Else" as tales traditionally characterized as "farce" but that actually describe the mental illness of a peasant woman, an illness masked in the story by the supposed stupidity of the female protagonist (100-01). Metzger notes the frightening conclusion: "Das Märchen endet mit den Sätzen, die das ganze Elend der unschuldigen Kranken . . . beschreiben" (110). Whereas I agree with Metzger's suggestion that the earlier variant "Hansens Trine" already contains the frightening possibilities of "Die kluge Else," these possibilities are set aside by the words of the text itself, which judge the peasant woman, Trine, as lazy, and which suggest that the ending is "happy" for both Trine and her punitive husband. Roderick McGillis's unpublished paper, with the apt title "She Has No Voice to Speak Her Dread" is the only other discussion, to my knowledge, that presents a serious and sensitive account of Else's mental breakdown.

18. See also Metzger 108-09.

Works Cited

Bakhtin, Mikhail M. *Problems of Dostoevsky's Poetics.* Trans. and Ed. Caryl Emerson. *Theory and History of Literature.* Vol. 8. Minneapolis: U of Minnesota P, 1984.

———. *The Dialogic Imagination: Four Essays.* Trans. Caryl Emerson and Michael Holquist. Ed. Michael Holquist. Austin: U of Texas P, 1981.

Bottigheimer, Ruth. "From Gold to Guilt: The Forces Which Reshaped the *Grimms' Tales.*" *The Brothers Grimm and Folktale.* Ed. James M. McGlathery. Chicago: U of Illinois P, 1988. 192-204.

———. *Grimms' Bad Girls and Bold Boys: The Moral and Social Vision of the Tales.* New Haven: Yale U P, 1987.

———. "Silenced Women in the Grimms' Tales: The 'Fit' between Fairy Tales and Society in Their Historical Context." *Fairy Tales and Society: Illusion, Allusion and Paradigm.* Ed. Ruth Bottigheimer. Philadelphia: U of Pennsylvania U P, 1986. 115-31.

Dworkin, Andrea. *Woman Hating,* New York: Dutton, 1974.

Fink, Gonthier-Louis. "The Fairy Tales of the Grimms' Sergeant of Dragoons J. F. Krause as Reflecting the Needs and Wishes of the Common People." *The Brothers Grimm and Folktale.* Ed. James M. McGlathery. Chicago: U of Illinois P, 1988. 146-63.

Grimm, Jacob and Wilhelm. *Kinder- und Hausmärchen. Ausgabe letzter Hand mit den Originalanmerkungen der Brüder Grimm.* Vol 3. (1856) Ed. Heinz Rölleke. Stuttgart: Philipp Reclam, 1980.

———. *Kinder- und Hausmärchen der Brüder Grimm in ihrer Urgestalt.* 2 vols. Ed. Friedrich Panzer. Hamburg: Stromverlag, 1948.

McGillis, Roderick. "She Has No Voice to Speak Her Dread." Unpublished Paper. Midwest Modern Language Association Convention. Chicago, October 26, 1986.

Metzger, Erika A. "Zu Beispielen von Depersonalisation im Grimmschen Märchen." *Fairy Tales as Ways of Knowing: Essays on Märchen in Psychology Society and Literature.* Bern: Peter Lang, 1981. 99-116.

Moore, Robert. "From Rags to Witches: Stereotypes, Distortions and Anti-humanism in Fairy Tales." *Interracial Books for Children* 6 (1975): 1-3.

Propp, Vladimir. *Morphology of the Folktale.* 2nd ed. Trans. Laurence Scott. Austin: U of Texas P, 1975.

Röhrich, Lutz. "Das Bild der Frau im Märchen und im Volkslied." *Das selbstverständliche Wunder: Beiträge germanistischer Märchenforschung.* Ed. Wilhelm Solms. Marburg: Hitzeroth, 1986. 83-108.

Rölleke, Heinz. ed. *Die Älteste Märchensammlung der Brüder Grimm: Synopse der handschriftlichen Urfassung von 1810 und der Erstdrucke von 1812.* Jacob and Wilhelm Grimm. Cologny-Genève: Foundation Martin Bodmer, 1975.

————. "Die Frau in den *Märchen der Brüder Grimm.*" *Wo das Wünschen noch geholfen hat: Gesammelte Aufsätze zu den Kinder- und Hausmärchen der Brüder Grimm.* Bonn: Bouvier Verlag, 1985. 220-35.

————. ed. *Kinder- und Hausmärchen. Originalanmerkungen. Herkunftsnachweise. Nachwort.* Vol 3. *Brüder Grimm: Kinder- und Hausmärchen.* Stuttgart: Philipp Reklam Jr., 1980.

————. "New Results of Research on *Grimms' Fairy Tales.*" *The Brothers Grimm and Folktale.* Ed. James M. McGlathery. Chicago: U of Illinois P, 1988. 101-11.

————. *Wo das Wünschen noch geholfen hat: Gesammelte Aufsätze zu den Kinder- und Hausmärchen der Brüder Grimm.* Bonn: Bouvier Verlag, 1985.

Schindhütte, Albert, ed. *Krauses Grimm'sche Märchen.* Kassel: Johannes Stauda, 1985.

Schoof, Wilhelm. *Zur Entstehungsgeschichte der Grimmschen Märchen.* Hamburg: Dr. Ernst Hauswedel Co., 1959.

Seitz, Gabriele. *Die Brüder Grimm: Leben-Werk-Zeit.* München: Winkler Verlag, 1984.

Steiner, Peter. *Russian Formalism: A Metapoetics.* Ithaca: Cornell U P, 1984.

Tatar, Maria M. *The Hard Facts of the Grimms' Fairy Tales.* Princeton U P, 1987.

Zipes, Jack. *Breaking the Magic Spell: Radical Theories of Folk and Fairy Tales.* New York: Methuen, 1979.

————. "Dreams of a Better Bourgeois Life: The Psychosocial Origins of the Grimms' Tales." *The Brothers Grimm and Folktale.* Ed. James M. McGlathery. Chicago: U of Illinois P, 1988. 205-19.

————. *Fairy Tales and the Art of Subversion: The Classical Genre for Children and the Process of Civilization.* New York: Wildman, 1983.

G. Ronald Murphy (essay date 2000)

SOURCE: Murphy, G. Ronald. "Scholars and the Religious Spirit of the Tales," and "Snow White." In *The Owl, the Raven, & the Dove: The Religious Meaning of the Grimms' Magic Fairy Tales,* pp. 17-29; 113-32. Oxford: Oxford University Press, 2000.

[*In the first essay that follows, Murphy surveys contemporary scholarship on religious meaning in* Grimms' Fairy Tales *within the context of Christian theology. In the second essay, Murphy identifies Germanic oral and literary sources of "Snow White," explicating the tale's textual history and interpolated Christianity.*]

SCHOLARS AND THE RELIGIOUS SPIRIT OF THE
TALES

My interest in religious meaning in the *Grimms' Fairy Tales* began with the appearance of Bruno Bettelheim's *The Uses of Enchantment, the Meaning and Importance of Fairy Tales.*[1] Bettelheim's application of psychological models to explain the tales struck me then, and now, as a brilliant work of interpretation, even though there are places, such as his reading of the seven dwarfs, where it seems he got carried away. Bettelheim consistently maintains a Freudian-Oedipal approach throughout the book and forcefully defends the therapeutic usefulness of the stories in raising children, but he also repeatedly makes reference to his feeling that the tales have unexplored religious significance. In referring to the return journey of Hansel and Gretel after they have defeated the witch, he comments: "Their way home is blocked by a 'big water' which they can only cross with the help of a white duck. The children do not encounter any expanse of water on their way in. Having to cross one on their return symbolizes a transition, and a new beginning of a higher level of existence (as in baptism)."[2] When he comments briefly on **"The Seven Ravens,"** Bettelheim speaks more fully on what he sees as baptismal symbolism in the tale:

> In the Brother Grimm's story **"The Seven Ravens"** seven brothers disappear and become ravens as their sister enters life. Water has to be fetched from the well in a jug for the girl's baptism, and the loss of the jug is the fateful event which sets the stage for the story. The ceremony of baptism also heralds the beginning of a Christian existence. It is possible to view the seven brothers as representing that which had to disappear for Christianity to come into being. If so they represent the pre-christian, pagan world in which the seven planets stood for the sky gods of antiquity. The newborn girl is then the new religion, which can succeed only if the old creed does not interfere with its development. With Christianity, the brothers who represent paganism become relegated to darkness. But as ravens, they dwell in a mountain at the end of the world, and this suggests their continued existence in a subterranean, subconscious world.[3]

When he discusses the possible survival of Greek mythology in Basile's tale of Talia, mother of the sun and the moon, who does not know that she had intercourse nor that she has "conceived without pleasure or sin," Bettelheim first comments that Basile is probably being influenced by the story of Leto, lover of Zeus, who bore him Apollo and Artemis, and then, thinking of the Virgin Mary, Bettelheim adds: "Most fairy tales of the Western World have at some time included Christian elements, so much so that an account of those underlying Christian meanings would make another book."[4] Thinking of the white birds which are present in so many of the Grimms' classical fairy tales, he comments on the dove in **"Hansel and Gretel,"** "The behavior of the birds symbolizes that the entire adventure was arranged for the children's benefit. Since early Christian times the white dove has symbolized superior benevolent powers. . . . Another white bird is needed to guide the children back to safety."[5]

In **"The Three Languages"** a young man learns to speak the languages of the frogs, the dogs, and the birds, which Bettelheim reads as mastering the urges of sex, violence, and the superego. Having achieved this mastery of self and created internal harmony, the young man is made pope, since he now deserves the "highest office on earth." At the end of the tale the young man celebrates his first Mass, and has no trouble with the Latin, nor perhaps even with the sermon, because two white doves alight on his shoulders and whisper into his ears everything that he has to say and do. Bettelheim adds an integrating comment:

> Learning the language of the birds follows naturally from having learned that of the dogs. The birds symbolize the higher aspirations of the superego and ego ideal. . . . White doves—which in religious symbolism stand for the Holy Ghost—inspire and enable the hero to achieve the most exalted position on earth; he gains it because he has learned to listen to the doves and do as they bid him. The hero has gained personality integration.[6]

What Bettelheim does not notice is the similarity of the image of the whispering doves perched on the shoulders of the young pope to the standard iconography of Woden and his two ravens, Hugin and Munin "mind and memory," standing on his shoulders and whispering into his ears all that happens on the earthly middle world below.

Though Bettelheim can be criticized for using an amalgam of each tale for his interpretation of it, it is also interesting to note that he is biased in favor of the French version of tales for psychological interpretation, and yet his observations on the religious symbolism of water and baptism in the fairy tales are almost without exception references to the versions of the brothers Grimm.

The most distinguished scholar of the textual history of the Grimm versions is Heinz Rölleke, who has published not only the final versions of the tales with the notes on the fairy tales made by the brothers Grimm themselves, but more important, the earliest Grimm versions in the manuscripts and earliest printed editions, enabling scholars to examine the scope of the rewriting of several of the tales from the earliest versions of 1810 to the final edition of 1857. It is interesting, therefore, to contrast Rölleke's ideas on the religious element in the tales with the ideas of Bettelheim. In an essay published in 1985 he addressed the question of the role of God in the *Grimms' Fairy Tales.*[7] He gives four categories of ways in which God is present in the Grimms'

versions of the tales. First, God is present in colloquial expressions (*redensartlich*), and as is appropriate to this form of presence, no one is really concerned with Him, and He is just as unconcerned about anything at all. He gives examples such as "Oh God," "dear Lord," and so on. Second, God is present in certain middle-class, Victorian exclamations that have made their way into the fairy tales via the middle-class Christian Zeitgeist incarnate in Wilhelm's quill, not in order to move the plot forward, but simply to be an adjunct contributor to general atmosphere.[8]

He gives examples from **"Hansel and Gretel."** Hansel reassures Gretel, "God will not abandon us," and "Don't cry Gretel, go to sleep, God will help us." Rölleke assures us that it is not God in the story but the dumbness of the witch and the cleverness of the children which make the happy end possible. It is not God, he says—in contrast to Bettelheim's suggestion about the significance of the way the children come home over the water—who brings the children home to their father, but a magic duck. Christianity in the tales is just a layer of varnish.

In his third category, Rölleke maintains much the same concerning the rare personal appearances of God in the two hundred tales. He plays a totally insignificant role and never one that is critical of society. God is like the exclamations addressed to Him: a cliché, an insignificant add-on. In his fourth category, however, Rölleke acknowledges the intrusion of Christianity deep into several of the tales. This is for Rölleke a melancholy matter. In the story of **"The Goose Girl,"** he sees a story line deeply structured by the intrusion of a Christian philosophy of life: an interconnected plot of guilt, healing, and reconciliation. At the end of the tale the thirsty princess bends over the flowing water of a brook and drinks. As she drinks, the little cloth with the three magic drops of blood falls out of her bosom, and, without her noticing it, disappears forever downstream. The magic is gone as she drinks from the waters. For a moment even Rölleke is allowing himself to see in the flowing water something of Bettelheim's baptismal vision, albeit in a negative version. With the waters, he believes, the old pagan magic is gone.[9] Rölleke regrets that the tales have not remained in a pure animistic form. He sees the Christianity in them as an "add-on," usually harmless, and does not see the animistic-pagan and Christian elements in the stories in transhistorical, mutually supportive synthesis.

Rölleke also brings up a theological/aesthetic question that justifies the non-inclusion of Christianity in the Grimms' tales as he sees them. He refers to the realization of the brothers Grimm concerning the nature of fairy tales: "Fairy tales are survivals of an ancient faith that goes back to the earliest times, a faith which is expressed in the pictorial representation of things that go beyond the senses" (*Märchen sind Überreste eines in die älteste Zeit hinaufreichenden Glaubens, der sich in bildlicher Auffassung übersinnlicher Dinge ausspricht*).[10] In other words, the oldest levels of the fairy tale faith go back to animism, Christianity is intrusive if one wishes to read the tales for their oldest level. "Oldest," however, is a term that needs a great deal of clarification. The oldest written European tales go back to Basile, older yet are those in the Norse tradition, still older are the Greek myths. The "oldest level" of a Grimm tale could mean anything from the above available myths, such as the Norse *Snaefrið* as the oldest form of **"Snow White,"** or a manuscript version of 1808, or a projected "oldest level of the tale *an sich*" which would be a Platonic abstraction created by the scholar. This latter would be of dubious helpfulness and objectivity, not to mention antiquity, and it would not get at the poetic religious nature of the stories as published by the brothers Grimm, where many ages or levels are skillfully woven together.

Theologically, Rölleke maintains, Christianity in fairy tales would have the problem of the Incarnation. In Christian belief, in the life of Jesus of Nazareth the eternal God entered into the world of time and was restricted by his humanity to a specific time and place, whereas the fairy tale hero is beyond time ("Gott ist in diese Zeit gekommen, der Märchenheld aber steht außerhalb jeder Zeit").[11] Granted that this is so, were Christianity to be present theologically in the tales, following the Grimms' insight above, it would be present in perceptible images of faith, *in bildlicher Auffassung* and in the depiction of the supernatural in natural things or symbolic persons intruding into the plot. In other words, Christ incarnate could not be depicted in the tales except in the form of faith-caused outcomes of the plot, or as the symbolic rescuer, or even in the form of "things" such as water, trees, and birds, when used to indicate the presence of spiritual awareness and providence. I maintain that this is indeed the case and that Wilhelm realized the aesthetic-theological problem which Rölleke has broached. Wilhelm solved the problem in good medieval Christian style: Christ is depicted not in biblical glory but rather in plotlines and endings that reflect Christian faith, in a rescuing prince coming from "beyond" the forest, and in things, magic things (the water of the river, doves)—in which the invisible is depicted happening—things that depict the spiritual and supernatural in a sacramental view of the natural world. This we will take up again when we examine Wilhelm Grimm's spirituality.

Rölleke's view is markedly different from Bettelheim's, and rests on the acceptance of the tales' rootedness in reconstructed unknown oral "Germanic" versions of the tales that are not merely pre-Wilhelm Grimm, but also pre-medieval. Such core versions would have to be scholarly reconstructions. Non-reconstructed tales which

are that old do exist: the written tales of the classical Greeks and Romans. Most important, however, Rölleke is persuaded that, even if the word "the Lord" is a meaningless nineteenth-century addition in the fairy tales, the religion and faith, especially the ancient animistic form of faith, found in them is constitutive of their power of enchantment. Christianity, he maintains, as a later addition, often of Wilhelm, is not constitutive of the magic of the ***Grimms' Fairy Tales.*** In this he offers reassurance against the fear of historical-analytic scholars that in their attempts to find the earliest recoverable written versions of the Grimms' tales, they will lose the very magic that drove them to study the tales in the first place.[12] The earliest manuscript versions presumably, from 1808, before Wilhelm rewrote them, one must conclude from Rölleke's exhortation, are the ones that contain in pure form the familiar Grimm fairy-tale "magic." In this I disagree with him entirely.[13] For me it is the stories as rewritten by Wilhelm (and Jacob) in their final versions which are the works of art that charm us all with diachronic religious magic. In the words of Donald Ward, "Had Wilhelm Grimm not revised and restored the tales, no one other than a handful of philologists and narrative researchers would have heard of them today."[14] In general for researchers on the literary side of the fence this sentiment is agreeable, regardless of point of view. The "handful of philologists" and folklore researchers, however, are not of the same sentiment and have found rather explosive expression in the writing of John M. Ellis. Their disappointment is acute that the Grimms' tales are not literally preserved remnants of ancient lore passed on in oral form by the "folk" from generation to generation, but rather that many of them are also in part what the title of most translations imply: "the Fairy Tales of the Brothers Grimm." This knowledge of the Grimms' rewriting of the tales leads Ellis to call the Grimms liars about their collected folklore and to call their stories "fakelore." His shock that these famous paragons of the simple *Märchen*, unadorned folk tales, are actually *Kunstmärchen*, tales that are deliberate works of art, is quite apparent. Ellis writes:

> The Grimms, it will be remembered, said in their preface that Dorothea Viehmann was the ideal story teller, a German peasant who told from her memory ancient tales from the old tradition of the Hessen region—"from the heart of the German-speaking area," as Gerstner later put it. But the facts were shockingly different: Dorothea Viehmann's first language was French, not German, and she was a member of a large community of Huguenots who had settled in the area, in which the language of church and school was still French. She was not a peasant but a thoroughly middle-class woman; she was not an untutored transmitter of folk tradition but, on the contrary, a literate woman who knew her Perrault; she was not a German but of French stock. The discrepancy between the Grimms' account of her and the real facts is astonishing, but what is just as astonishing is the way in which scholars have al-

luded to some of those facts seeming not to notice the way in which they made nonsense of what the Grimms had said. Already in 1959, Schoof reported: "She was the daughter of the innkeeper Johann Isaak Pierson and came from an old Huguenot family . . . . Frau Viehmann whose source was Perrault, just like the Hassenpflugs."[15]

It is immediately clear why this gradual realization would disconcert two groups of scholars. For one thing, if the fairy tales were really works of Wilhelm Grimm's creative art, *Kunstmärchen,* then the proper literary study of them would necessarily treat each one of them as an individual aesthetic entity, would insist on the priority of the final version of 1857 as the proper object of study, and would subject them, as poetry, to literary analysis and interpretation involving their place, and Wilhelm Grimm's place, in the history of German literature. Folklorists would have to abandon any idea that the final versions of 1857, nor even the earliest versions of 1810 and 1812, would provide them with a royal road to ancient Germanic mythology via the generational continuity of the simple voice of the people. The reticence of the first group and the angry disappointment of the second (the Grimms are considered the founders of the scientific study of folklore) is what Ellis expresses. The anger of the second group may have abated somewhat as other scholars reasonably pointed out that it is foolish to expect that the Grimms would have had tape recorders and video cameras to do the literal collecting of storytelling as one might imagine it in our world. The Grimms did indeed acknowledge in their second preface, 1819, that they were responsible for the way in which the tales were expressed. Even in the example that Ellis gives,[16] it is clear that the brothers carefully copied down the plot of the story which they were told, accepting in good Aristotelian fashion that the plot contained the essence of the story, so that they could later re-create the full tale. What they copied down from the teller is little more than a sketch, somewhat useful perhaps to the folklorist, but completely unappealing as a work of art. Even Jacob wrote critically in the margin of one tale "the ending isn't right" (*"Endung stimmt nicht"*), a judgmental statement unambiguously calling for restorative or creative work (or both) to get the ending right. If then there are strong Germanic and Christian plot elements in the completed final versions of the tales, and not just some reworking in the realm of morals and language, and if these elements did not come down through history by way of Perrault via the Huguenot German families of the Viehmanns and the Hassenpflugs, then they must be the additions of Wilhelm (and Jacob) Grimm. If the final versions of the tales are the creative reworkings of traditional story material, as Goethe reworked the Faust tradition to the point of giving it a "happy end," then it is important to study Wilhelm Grimm as someone engaged in a task no more reprehensible than Goethe's.

Ruth Bottigheimer approaches the task of interpreting the corpus of 210 tales in the Grimm collection with a realistic view of their authorship. Quoting from a legal brief in which Wilhelm's sons, after Wilhelm's death, attempted to claim right of ownership of the collection she then gives her opinion of the importance of the Grimms' reworking of the tales:

> "Their collection came to be the mother of all subsequent collections. . . . In it lies the distinct individuality which authors manifest, [and] if any claim of authorship may be asserted it lies with them. Not in the sense that they composed and invented an uncomposable, uninventable material, but far more in the higher [sense] that they understood how to save this material from degeneration and how to breathe new life into it."

This letter is meant to define the tales legally not literally, but it nonetheless clearly sets forth the terms in which Jacob Grimm understood their, and particularly Wilhelm's effort. The letter states that this collection legally belongs to them because of the formative effort they had upon it, an evaluation that provides the basic premise of my study, namely, that any consideration of the content of the **Kinder- und Hausmärchen** [the **Grimms' Fairy Tales**] must include an appreciation of the extent and nature of Wilhelm Grimm's reformulation of the text.[17]

I could not possibly agree more.

When it comes to the actual religious nature of the tales and of the extent to which they have been Christianized by Wilhelm, Bottigheimer comes to a conclusion that I find wide of the mark. First, in her chapter entitled "Christian Values and Christian Narratives," she accepts Rölleke's views that God in the tales is merely a very occasional and completely irrelevant intruder, and even then only in the form of a pious exclamation. She does state that "German and Christian are two concepts that have been inextricably linked in Germany for centuries,"[18] but instead of going back to the instances in medieval or later German literature, which might have led to consideration of Wilhelm's love of Wolfram's *Parzival,* and the *Heliand*'s first edition being dedicated to Jacob, Bottigheimer gives a number of household examples, accurate enough, but from the realm of mottos and other clichés taken from parlor samplers or lintels rather than from literature. Her point, however, is clearly made: the concept of German and Christian have been linked in German culture, whether in harmony or in discord, for a millennium. While I agree with her observation that **"Hansel and Gretel"** does not become a Christian tale by the addition of a few pious exclamations, it becomes quite necessary to examine the symbolism and the plot alterations, as well as Wilhelm's own spirituality, to come to a more rounded poetic judgment on the religious spirit of the tale. If Wilhelm Grimm is the principal agent in this process, it might be appropriate to examine what he did of substance to the tales in reworking them, especially to the one he reworked the most, **"Snow White,"** rather than accepting that **"The Sparrow and His Children"** is the most Christian tale in the collection on the basis of the presence of the virtue of humility in a sparrow.

On the other hand, however, Bottigheimer speaks favorably or at least neutrally of a suggestion concerning Christian narrative material in the *Handwörterbuch des deutschen Märchens* which contradicts the view that a thoroughly non-Christian mentality underlies folk narrative:

> Dietz-Rüdiger Moser represents the antipodal position in "Christliche Erzählstoffe," which claims that the extent of Christian material in oral narrative has been underestimated in the past, citing the Catholic church's active role in disseminating Christian tales that then entered the oral tradition, especially during the Counter Reformation. The final word on this subject is not yet in.[19]

If one is open to the suggestion that both a symbolic approach and an examination of Wilhelm Grimm's spirituality are appropriate tools for ascertaining the role of religion in the tales, then it might be possible to determine which tales have been religiously modified, and to what degree and in what particular direction Christianized. Bottigheimer's view might then be open to the suggestion of rejecting Rölleke's sweeping negative judgment and of reexamining the basis for the use of the term "Christian" as applying par excellence to the sparrow tale. It might then be appropriate to modify her conclusion that "Christianized tales in the Grimms' collection separate the characters not so much into good and evil as into male and female, their fates determined and defined not according to the ethical and moral quality of their lives, but according to their sex."[20] The surprise in all of this might well be that it is precisely the most Christianized tales (without excluding the two earlier faith forms) which have become the most popular throughout the world.

In a brief but perceptive aside, moreover, Bottigheimer noted what I think is the very heart of Wilhelm's religious style of poetic composition:

> In **"The Juniper Tree"** (no. 47), an elaborately intricate and beautiful symbol links classical allusions to immortality with Germanic and Biblical ones and narrates the first stage of the murdered boy's return to life:
>
> "Then the juniper tree began to stir itself, and the branches parted asunder, and moved together again, just as if someone were rejoicing and clapping his hands [Germanic, the tree Yggdrasil]. At the same time a mist seemed to arise from the tree, and in the center of this mist it burned like a fire, and a beautiful bird flew out of the fire singing magnificently [Classical, the phoenix], and he flew high up in the air, and when he was gone, the juniper tree was just as it had been before, and the handkerchief with the bones was no longer there [biblical, Resurrection]."[21]

In other words, Wilhelm does indeed speak of immortality, but through a beautifully complex interweaving of the mytho-poetic imagery of three ancient faiths, which he both finds present and also weaves in, and in no way can his transcendent religious poetry be restricted to the pious exclamations found in a few very circumscribed and relatively unknown "Christian tales." When writing his comments on the meaning of the phoenix in **"The Golden Bird"** (**"Vom goldenen Vogel"**), a tale in which brothers toss their youngest brother into a well from which he is later rescued by a compassionate fox, Wilhelm's poetic faith sees "the falling into the well" in this Germanic fairy tale as related to the biblical story of Joseph who was thrown by his brothers into a well. He then adds "and Joseph himself is none other than the phoenix, the golden bird."[22] The religious spirit in the tales, or religious faith as the Grimms maintained, is an ancient one and speaks in diachronic pictures of the unseen. The pictures, moreover, in strikingly close parallel to the Grimms' method of defining a word in their German dictionary, are arranged in a harmonized historical order, and this harmony we will examine in five of the most well-known stories.

Max Lüthi, looking at the Grimms' tales in the context of German literature, wrote: "The fairy tale is the poetic expression of the confidence that we are secure in a world not destitute of sense, that we can adapt ourselves to it and act and live even if we cannot view or comprehend the world as a whole."[23] He furthermore considers the authors of fairy tales to be great religious poets dealing with the great question, "What is man?" "Fairy tales certainly do not originate among simple folk but with great poets; and, in a sense, they provide an answer. . . . The fairy tale . . . presents its hero as one who, though not comprehending ultimate relationships, is led safely through the dangerous world."[24] In considering Mircea Eliade's view that listening to fairy tales was a sort of initiation rite, a baptism of the imagination, he cites with approval,

> "The folk tale transposes the initiation process into the sphere of imagination. . . . Without rendering account to ourselves but rather in the full belief that we are merely relaxing and being entertained, modern man too enjoys the imaginative initiation that the fairy tale affords us." How correct this scholar's assertion is can be shown in any folk fairy tale. It is not surprising that it becomes especially clear in the best known, most popular tales.[25]

It is precisely in these tales that the hero-heroine is led by supernatural forces acting through natural ones and that Wilhelm Grimm has most advanced the notion of divine providence acting through nature.

Other critics, however, see either relatively little of the religious in the tales or a very great deal. An example of the first is Jack Zipes, who feels that the tales have a socially liberating function that he characterizes as the "progressive pursuit of home." This is a very appealing and insightful notion, one that could readily find authorial confirmation in the dogged pursuit of home which was a regular occurrence, and one of the sadder ones, in the lives of the brothers Grimm.[26] It certainly is a driving force in many of the most popular tales. Zipes, however, does not list religious spirituality in the form of a sublimated pursuit of home as one of the contributions of Wilhelm to the tales. In his introduction to his remarkable translation of the Grimms' tales he lists Wilhelm's authorial/editorial contributions as: stylistic smoothness, concern for sequential structure, liveliness and imagery, reinforcement of motives for action, infusion of psychological motifs, and the elimination of non-rustic elements from the tone.[27] When he ends his introductory essay, however, Zipes adds, "Though the Grimms imbued the tales with a heavy dose of Christian morality, the Protestant work ethic, and patriarchalism, they also wanted the tales to depict social injustices and possibilities for self-determination."[28] Is it really Christian morality and Protestant work ethic that give Wilhelm's revised versions of the tales their universal power of enchantment—or is it their multiple strands of spiritual faith?

On the other side, Norbert Glas seems to feel that the tales are entirely Christian. He gives a reading of them in which he remarks, "The fairy stories collected by the brothers Grimm are an infinite source of . . . pictures of events taking place within the human soul."[29] He is described with some annoyance by Dundes as interpreting **"Little Red Riding Hood"** in such a way that the grandmother is an old woman weak and in need of help. Red Riding Hood comes to her aid bringing bread and wine, just as in the Church Christ comes to the weak in the Bread and Wine to bring healing. The huntsman signifies wisdom. In the end the grandmother eats the cake, the bread, and the wine, thus receiving Holy Communion. The fairy tale **"Little Red Riding Hood"** describes thus in a most wonderful way the victory of the human soul over the wild and tempting forces of the wolf which want to prevent it from treading the true path into the future.[30] In my opinion Glas' reading may do justice to the Christian element in the tales, but at the fatal price of blindness to the importance of the religious charm that comes from the lively presence of the pagan figures and poetry in the narrative.

Maria Tatar, who has studied so extensively the surprising level of violence and grisly behavior in many of the tales, comes to a very interesting conclusion that final success does not go to those in the fairy tales who are brave and strong, neither the wolf nor the hunter, so to speak, but to the humble and the compassionate.[31] In this regard she emphasizes that the help that comes from the natural-supernatural world often comes after the humiliation of the heroine, such as Cinderella, has

taken place. She also mentions from the history of German literature that the initial failure of Parzival at Munsalvaesche on the feast of St. Michael is his lack of compassion.[32] Wilhelm Grimm would have heartily agreed.

Two recent scholars have commented on the influence of Herder, the theologian of Romanticism. Judith Ryan comments on form: "The German Romantic poets followed in Herder's footsteps by combining an interest in oral traditions with scholarly research into written traditions.[33] Their familiarity with a wide variety of literary works from earlier periods provided models for the mixed-form texts they developed."[34] Christa Kamenetsky's admirable *The Brothers Grimm and Their Critics, Folktales and the Quest for Meaning*,[35] gives an additional basis for accepting the role of compassionate human feelings in the Grimms' tales, the influence of the humanistic thought of the theologian Herder. In her very encompassing and useful study, she highlights Herder's belief in the symphonic harmony of the ancient and natural poetry of all nations. "He believed that each ancient nation's voice was lovely in its own way, yet in harmony with the songs of other nations, they created a symphony that was symbolic of God's creation of the world."[36] The Grimms certainly must have been inspired with regard to the presentation of diverse images in the tales in harmonized, diachronic form, and by Herder's insistence in the story on rewarding the good and punishing the bad, but they differed from Herder as well. Herder thought little of violence in the tales and made a great deal more out of biblical stories and their usefulness than did the Grimms. They were completely with him, however, throughout their lives and their scholarly work, in balancing a love for their own nation's tradition with a belief that other nations should equally treasure their own poetry's role in the human "symphony." Kamenetsky quite rightly takes to task those scholars who accuse the Grimms of ethnocentricity and nationalism, citing the Grimms' prominent work on Irish and Slavic tales in particular, and deplores the presence of a certain scepticism that has crept in among the folklore-oriented critics with regard to the Grimms' work. Her final conclusion is that literary and psychological studies offer the most enlightened perspectives on the Grimms' tales.

Marina Warner sees both the Christian and the classical in the tales: "The Grimm Brothers worked on the **Kinder- und Hausmärchen** in draft after draft after the first edition of 1812, Wilhelm in particular infusing the new editions with his Christian fervor. . . . Just as [*King Lear*'s] Cordelia is a fairytale heroine, a wronged youngest child, a forerunner of Cinderella, so Goneril and Regan are the wicked witches, ugly sisters; the unnatural women whom fairy tales indict."[37]

From all of this it seems very important to determine as clearly as possible just what the religious outlook of the brothers was and to apply it to the reading of the final version of the Grimms' tales. This is especially true, of course, for Wilhelm. There are two sources that we can turn to for this information and evidence. The first are the two autobiographies written by the brothers, and the second and truly invaluable source is the copy of the Greek New Testament that Wilhelm read early in the morning to begin his day, and in which he carefully underlined more than seventy-one passages.

. . . . .

SNOW WHITE

In their commentary on the origins of their version of **"Snow White,"** the brothers Grimm wrote: "taken from many diverse Hessian stories" (*nach vielfachen Erzahlungen aus Hessen*).[38] They remark on how well known this story is and on the many varieties in which it is told in the Germanies, including the retention everywhere of a North German version of the heroine's name, Sneewitchen, even if in garbled form, in the High German-speaking regions of the south. In one of the several German versions of the story which they describe, a king and queen are riding along in a sleigh, and as the queen tries to peel an apple she accidentally cuts her finger, causing blood to spill on the snow. In others, it is a count and a countess in the sleigh. The countess makes a wish for a baby girl as white as the snow piles, as red as three pools of blood which they pass, and as black as three ravens who fly overhead. In still another version, the queen drives Snow White into the forest, has the carriage stop, and suggests that Snow White get out to pick a bouquet of red roses; as the girl is gathering them the carriage quickly drives off, abandoning Snow White in the woods. In yet another, the queen takes Snow White to dwarfs in the forest who kill young girls, but they decide not to kill her in exchange for her doing household work. In this version, while with the dwarfs, Snow White had left her pet dog, named "Mirror" (*Spiegel*) back in the castle. When the queen returns to the castle, she asks the dog:

> Mirror under the bench,
> Look in this land, look in that land,
> Who is the fairest in England?

> (Spiegel unter der Bank,
> sieh in dieses Land, sieh in jenes Land:
> wer ist die schönste in Engelland?)

After hearing the disconcerting answer, the queen plots Snow White's death again as in the other versions. Whoever retold this tale and in retelling decided that the mirror would be better as a pet dog, while implausibly retaining "Mirror" as a canine name, demonstrates a peculiar, if animal-loving, imagination.

Another German source acknowledged by the Grimms is the much lengthier story of *Richilde* in Musäus's collection of German fairy tales, *Volksmärchen der Deut-*

schen, published initially in 1782, some thirty years prior to their own first edition. Musäus's style has much of the ironic and even satirical air of Perrault and Basile and seems far more destined to appeal to the rationally and sophisticatedly cynical adult reader than to children. His version begins with an un-Grimm-like lampoon of piety and devotion in the person of the excessively pro-clerical Count of Brabant, Gunderich der Pfaffenfreund (Gunderich the Clergy-friend) who is always at Mass or walking in processions, and who, thus restricted in his time for procreation, has no children. It is intimated that the understandably childless countess of Brabant finally achieves pregnancy only after a very private sacramental confession to one of her husband's esteemed clergyman visitors, renowned Dominican Albertus Magnus. Albertus Magnus in turn, his remarkable interest in the future child noted by court gossip, then fashions a magic mirror through his knowledge of the black arts as a gift for the child. This child is Richilde, who becomes the jealous mother of Blanca,[39] the persecuted heroine. The mother uses the enchanted mirror in the traditional manner to find out who is "the most beautiful in the land of Brabant."[40] The mirror, however, is not capable of magic speech, but answers sensibly by showing an image, as mirrors will do. As Richilde's behavior toward her more beautiful child deteriorates, in a nice touch the mirror darkens and rusts to a degree that its images become faint and useless. The mother attempts three times to poison her daughter, first with a half-poisoned apple (*Granatapfel,* pomegranate), the second time with perfumed soap, and the third time with a loving letter from herself laced with poisonous salts. She has forced the court doctor, Sambul the Jew, to concoct the poisons by bullying and by the offer of money, but each time his conscience gets the better of him and he merely injects a sleeping potion or a strong narcotic into the apple and the soap, and smears only sleep-inducing aromatic salts on the letter. He is punished by Richilde for his lack of success at causing the death of her child by having his beard pulled out and his ears cut off. In contrast to the Grimms, therefore, Musäus eschewed the mystical or magical, made the conscience of the professional doctor the instrument of mercy, and thereby enabled Blanca, "Snow White," to awaken reasonably each time from the casket on her own. By turning her apparent death into a medically induced sleep, Musäus makes the moment of crisis in the narrative fully responsive to reason and avoids any real need for supernatural agency to overcome death. The story's religious content is thus not found in the realm of the spiritual or mystical, but is in the realm of morality and conscience.

The dwarfs are present, but they are demythologized and described as "court dwarfs" presumably kept in the castle for the service and amusement of the nobility. They are, however, honest and helpful. They are not asked to make a glass casket for Blanca, but they insert a little glass window in it above the face of the "corpse" so that they can watch her, and eventually they see the rosy color returning to her face.

The need for rescue by the prince is diminished by the doctor's successful preventive efforts, but it is not done away with entirely. The prince appears when Blanca is lying in her third occasion of sleep. On arrival he applies a papally blessed relic to her heart and, lo, just at that moment the effect of the salts wears off, Blanca awakes and gets her prince, who is neither mythical nor timeless, as Rölleke might have liked it, but rather Gottfried of Ardenne. The ending follows very much in the same spirit of the Enlightenment. The countess, Richilde, is invited to the wedding of her daughter, having been deceived into believing that she herself is to be the bride. After fainting at the shock of seeing Blanca alive and in the bridal veil, she is forced to dance at the wedding feast in glowing hot shoes, but at the end of the dance is discovered to have suffered only burns and blisters to the feet. She is thrown into a tower to give her time to repent. Death is avoided even in her case, with the liberal and enlightened hope that imprisonment will work her eventual rehabilitation. The concluding lines of the story do not serve as the place for the ritual statement about "happiness ever after" for the young couple. In an effective twist, the last lines treat the conscientious Jewish doctor as the real hero, in the style of Lessing, and comment approvingly on his new position as prime minister to the king of Morocco, describing him as being blessed with children and grandchildren, and promising that it is he who will live happily ever after.[41] The Grimm version, in contrast, will reinterpret the fundamental narrative in the style of Romanticism and retain the death of Blanca (and her mother), thus returning the religious level of the story from the moral to the transcendental.

Because of its age and provenance, the most remarkable version of *Snow White* to the Grimms was the medieval Norse story of *Snaefrið* in the *Haraldsaga* of Snorri Sturluson's *Heimskringla*. Snorri lived from 1179 to 1241, and Harald Fairhair of the saga lived in the ninth and early tenth centuries, thus establishing the great antiquity of the roots of the story.[42] The name *Snaefrið* might be translated "Snow Lover,"[43] and this story bears some remarkable resemblances, as well as differences, to the Grimms' version. I have italicized some significant similarities.

> King Harald went *one winter* a-feasting in the Uplands and had a Yule feast made ready for himself in Toftar. On the eve of Yule, Svasi came to the door whilst the king was at the table and he sent a messenger to the king to come out to him. [The king is annoyed but goes out, crosses the stream with the man and goes to his hut.] There *Snaefrid*, Svasi's daughter, stood up, the most beautiful of women, and she offered the king a cup full of mead; he drank it all and also took her

hand, and straightway it was as though fire passed through his body, and at once he would lie with her that same night. But Svasi said that it should not be so except by force, unless the king betrothed Snaefrid and wed her according to the law. The king took Snaefrid and wed her, and he loved her so witlessly that he neglected his kingdom and all that was seemly for his kingly honor. [They then have four sons] Afterwards *Snaefrid died*, but *the color of her skin never faded* and *she was as rosy as before when she lived*. The king always *sat over her* and thought that she would come to life again, and thus it went on for three winters that he *sorrowed* over her death and all the people of his land sorrowed over his delusion. And to stop this delusion Torleiv the Wise came to his help, he did it with prudence in that he spoke to him first with soft words, "It is not strange, O king, that thou shouldst remember so bright and noble woman and honor her with down [blankets] and precious coverlets as she bade thee. But thy honor and hers is still less than it seems, in that she has *lain for a long while* in the same clothes, and it is fitter that she should be raised and the clothes changed under her." But as soon as she was raised from the bed, there rose from the body a rotten and loathsome smell and all kinds of evil stink; speedily a funeral bale was then made and she was burned. But before that, all the body waxed blue and out crawled worms and adders, frogs and paddocks and all manner of foul reptiles. So she sank into ashes, and the king came to his wits and cast his folly from his heart and afterwards ruled the kingdom and was strengthened and gladdened by his men, and they by him, and the kingdom by both.[44]

The similarities are as remarkable as the Grimms thought. The location of the story in winter, the closeness of "Snow White" to "Snow Lover," the corpse that maintained its rosy red color and promise of life, the long watch over the body, the hope of resurrection are all there. However, the story is more a clash of religious thought than a harmony. The story stems from the time when Norway was still pagan—"Yule" is repeated twice, but there is no hint of Christmas; the king's love of the queen is not favored by all; his attitude of continuing fidelity to his wife is "witless." When the king sits by her corpse awaiting its resurrection, he is described as being in a state of delusion. Reasonable people have to persuade him to examine the hideous state of the body, and when the body is "raised," there is a rotten and loathsome smell and an exodus of reptiles. Harald then quickly forgets his idling over resurrection and returns to his senses and rules his kingdom as a proper king should. The tale could easily be seen as an attack on those in the North who were dawdling with the new Christian religion's central tenet by exposing belief in resurrection as an intoxicated lover's self-delusion. When he is cured of his Christian-style dreaming, Harald becomes a good and sensible man once again.

In Wilhelm's eyes, however, the story would probably have been seen as striking evidence of religious consciousness from pre-Christian times, a Germanic prayer of hope and waiting for a beloved dead princess to rise, as one waits for spring to rise from beneath the white snow of winter. It is Rölleke's view, based on the Grimms' commentary discussed here, that the German word itself used for the name of the heroine of the story, *Sneewittchen,* was derived by the Grimms from *Snaefrið,*[45] thus they could be confident that they were aware of the oldest Germanic form of the story. Wilhelm's "restoration" of the tale of **"Snow White"** is thus not a return to the pre-medieval original, nor a simple retelling of what they wrote down in 1808 from their Hessian sources, nor a combination of the two. By insertion of the birds, the resurrection, the prince, and the huntsman, and by reinterpreting the dwarfs and the apple, the tale will become a story of salvation told in a harmony of Christian spirituality and Germanic myth with a Classical element as well.

The other older work noted by the Grimms as containing part of the story of **"Snow White"** is in Basile's *Pentamerone.* In the story, called **"The Kitchen Maid"** by the Grimms and "The Young Slave" by Burton, a young girl, Lilla, jumps over a rose bush on a dare. To prove she cleared it completely and thus to get the prize, she deceptively eats the petal of a rose which she had actually touched and knocked to the ground. She becomes pregnant by the rose leaf and gives birth secretly. She sends the baby, Lisa, to the fairies for their help, and when they come to see her, each gives the girl a charm. However, in a twist similar to that of **"Sleeping Beauty,"** the last fairy to come was running and tripped and fell, painfully spraining her ankle. In her "anguish of pain she cursed the child, saying that when she had reached her seventh year, her mother in combing her hair would forget the comb sticking in the hair on her head, and this would cause her to die." It happens in the seventh year, and in her agony, Lilla, the mother, "ordered seven glass chests one within the other, and had Lisa put within them." The chest was then placed in a distant chamber in the palace, but the mother kept the key, giving it only when death approached to her brother, the baron.

The mother dies. The baron, her brother, takes a wife a year later, gives his wife the key, and begs her above all never to open the room. Being asked not to open the door makes the wife feel suspicious and jealous, which leads to uncontrollable curiosity. In a fit of jealousy (Basile's favorite vice to target), the wife opens the door and finds the glass casket: "She beheld the seven crystal chests, through which she could perceive a beauteous child lying as it were in a deep sleep." Curiously, and conveniently for the beauty of the child, the glass caskets had grown in size as the child grew. In a fit of wild jealous rage, thinking the child to be her husband's and herself cuckolded, the stepmother pulls the child out of the glass chest by her hair in order to beat her black and blue, which she does; but as she pulls Lisa by the hair, the comb falls out, and Lisa comes to life again. After an incident with the traveling father bringing home gifts, including a knife, he eventually realizes through magic that this slave girl is his sister's child, who had been locked in the room! He learns of his wife's abuse of his niece and restores her to health and beauty, and sends the jealous wife home to her family.[46] The story thinly hints at incest, but this the Grimms ignored for other elements.

What Wilhelm saw here, I think, were elements of a timeless tale: a fated incident, an accidental dislodging of the item causing death-sleep, the overtones of Classical religion, Christianity's fear of the corroding sin of jealousy, and Germanic religion's hope in the casket made of crystal through which the person in the sleep of death could be seen as potentially revivable. The paradox of love is there as well. As in the case of Cinderella what a mother sees as beautiful and to be protected, even in death, an insecure (step)mother can imagine as a living memory of time past and a threat to herself.

The red of the rose petal may have impressed him as analogous in all three tales: the rosy red color of the dead Snaefrid, the red rose petal that Lisa swallowed, the roses that Snow White was sent to pick, the rose color of her cheeks. The spiritual common thread is the deep human helplessness and grief over the death of someone loved, expressed in Norse, Neapolitan, and German versions of these tales. The patient waiting of King Harald for three winters gives forlorn expression to the hope that somehow human love possesses a supernatural vitality that can transform death into a temporary sleep from which one be can awakened by love. It is this fragmentary hope of King Harald that Wilhelm restored to life as he reworked the remnants of ancient religious poetry come down to us as "almost historical" (as he referred to *Snaefridr* [his spelling]).

The very earliest version of this story which the Grimms themselves wrote down is in a manuscript from 1808 taken down by Jacob and sent to Savigny, the main source for which must have been an oral telling of the story by Marie Hassenpflug. The detail of the half-poisoned red and white apple in the manuscript of 1808, which Jacob Grimm took down from her, indicates that she may have known of Musäus's version. There is no Perrault in the background in this case, since he does not have the **"Snow White"** story. By the final version in 1857, it is the first part of the story and the last which have been most extensively reworked by Wilhelm. The middle part, the events at the house of the seven dwarfs, with the three visits by the jealous queen, has been changed the least. The version of 1808:

> Once upon a time, it was winter and it was snowing down from heaven, a queen was sitting at an ebony window & was sewing. She wanted a child very very

much. And while she was thinking about this she poked herself more or less in the finger with the needle, so that several drops of blood fell on the snow. She made a wish and said: Oh if only I had a child as white as this snow, as red-cheeked as this red blood & as black-eyed as this window frame.

Soon after she got a wonderfully beautiful little daughter, as white as snow, as red as blood & black-eyed as ebony & the daughter was called Snow White. My lady the queen was the most beautiful lady in the land, but Snow White was still a hundred thousand times more beautiful & when the queen asked her mirror:

  Mirror, Mirror, on the wall,
  Which lady in England is fairest of all?

The mirror answered: My lady the queen is the most beautiful, but Snow White is still a hundred thousand times more beautiful.

My lady the queen couldn't stand that a moment longer because she wanted to be the most beautiful in the kingdom. When now my lord the king had journeyed off to war, she had her coach hitched up and gave the order to drive into a dark forest far away & she took Snow White along. In this very same forest there were many very beautiful red roses. Now when she had arrived there with her little daughter she said to her: Oh Snow White, why don't you get out and gather me some of those beautiful roses! And as soon as she had gotten out of the coach to carry out this command, the wheels [turned and] drove off at the greatest speed, but my lady the queen had arranged all of this because she hoped that the wild animals would soon devour the child.

Now Snow White was all alone in the great forest and so she cried very much and kept on walking & kept on walking & and got very tired until she finally came to a little house.

In this first part, compared to the final version, there is no alliterative verse in the first line, it is the mother herself who becomes jealous of the very child she had wished for, the child is driven into the woods with the mother directing the coach, there is no hunter and therefore no request for a sign of the child's death, nor is there any mercy shown. The roses are the ruse for facilitating the abandonment of the child in the woods and speeding off.

In the second part of the manuscript version, Snow White finds the house empty because the seven dwarfs were at the time working in the mine. She goes inside and finds the seven dishes along with the seven spoons, forks, knives, and glasses on the table and the seven beds. She takes a little bit from each plate and a drop from each glass, tests each bed and finds the seventh fits her. When the dwarfs come home, each asks the ritual question, "Who's been eating from my dish, drinking from my mug . . . ?" When they find her in the seventh bed, they have compassion on her and let her stay. The seventh dwarf does as well as he can shar-

ing the bed of the sixth. When she awakes she tells them the story about how her mother the queen drove off and abandoned her in the forest. Out of sympathy for her, the dwarfs invite her to stay and to cook their supper for them, and they warn her to be careful and not let anyone in the house. The queen disguises herself and comes three times to tempt Snow White. The first time as an old peddler woman selling bodice laces, Snow White falls to the temptation to buy them, and the queen laces them up so tight that Snow White collapses and is left for dead. The dwarfs come home, loosen the laces in time, and save her.

The second time, the queen comes with a beautiful comb. Again Snow White falls to the temptation, but is rescued by the returning dwarfs who remove the comb, and at that Snow White comes back to life. The third time, disguised as a farm woman selling apples, she tempts Snow White to bite into the poisoned red half of an apple. The dwarfs are helpless this time. However, "they laid Snow White in a glass casket in which she completely maintained her former appearance, they wrote her name and her ancestry on it, and watched over it carefully day and night." As is clear from this description, there is very little in this part that was later altered or inserted by Wilhelm with the important exception of his insertion of the queen's jealous questioning of the mirror on the wall, repeated in ritual style, marking off her three attempts to destroy Snow White as moral temptations.

The third part of the story, the ending, as related to them by Marie Hassenpflug, quite clearly disappointed Jacob and Wilhelm. In the manuscript they put a long line next to it, which included the entirety of the conclusion, and wrote the following comment in the margin:

(The ending included is not correctly told and is too skimpy. In other versions the dwarfs revive Snow White by striking her 32 times with little magic hammers. I don't know it very well though. Some of the material is in Musäus's Richilde.)

(Das eingeschloßene End ist unrecht erzählt u. zu mangelhaft. Nach andern machen die Zwerge das Schneeweißchen wieder lebendig, indem sie mit kleinen Zauberhämmerchen 32 mal anklopfen ich weiß es aber nicht recht. ein Stück des Stoffs ist auch in Musäus Richilde.)[47]

It is indeed interesting to see that the Grimms judged the quality of the materials told them both from the point of view of narrative form (Does the end flow appropriately from the plot as given?) and whether there is a fullness in the ending that satisfies. These are, of course, aesthetic criteria for "rightness" and, like Cinderella's slipper, the ending must not be artificially forced into place; it must, naturally, fit. The criterion for what "fits" is something that can be different from author to author of the stories, but for the brothers, it seems, it must include above all adequate expression of the ancient spirituality which they find in fragmentary form in the fairy tales, and thus "fulfill" the story. The following is the ending from the 1808 manuscript which the brothers found both incorrectly told and too skimpy:

> One day the king, Snow White's father, was returning to his kingdom & had to go through the same forest where the 7 dwarfs lived. When he saw the casket and read its inscription he felt great sadness about the death of his beloved daughter. In his entourage, however, he had with him very experienced physicians who requested and obtained the corpse from the dwarfs, took it and tied a rope to the 4 corners of the room & Snow White came back to life. Thereupon everyone went home, Snow White was married to a handsome prince, & at the wedding a pair of shoes were heated in the fire to glowing which the queen had to put on and in them dance herself to death.

The ending seems vapid indeed. The rope's connection to the corpse is not clear. The revival from death through the efforts of trained physicians and their four ropes seems totally out of place, inappropriate both to the rationalist and the romantic. The princely husband has no connection to any earlier part of the plot and is brought in pro forma. There is no presence of the spiritual, nor does it serve any rescuing function. There are, so to speak, no helpful birds in the ending. The father, to be sure, rescues his own, which must have pleased Wilhelm, but the ending is quick and contrived—the result is flat and does not arouse interest. The glowing shoes seem like an afterthought except for one item, the poignant use of the reflexive verb "dance herself" to show the lonely self-punishment of the jealous.

Let us look now at the Grimms' final version of 1857, a world masterpiece.

> Once upon a time in the midst of winter as the snow-flakes were falling like feathers from heaven, a queen sat at a window which had an ebony frame and sewed. And as she was sewing, she looked up at the snow and she stabbed herself in the finger with the needle and three drops of blood fell onto the snow. And since the red looked so beautiful in the white snow she thought to herself, "I wish I had a child as white as snow, as red as blood, and as black as the wood of the window frame." Soon thereafter she had a child which was as white as snow, as red as blood, and as black-haired as ebony wood, and therefore was called Snow White. And as the child was born the queen died.

The first thing is, of course, the famous "fairy-tale style" of Wilhelm Grimm. In the German original the lines flow in the measured pace of poetic prose. The almost hypnotic rhythm, with its repeated use of "and" to begin sentences, deliberately creates a biblical and religious feeling around a most everyday occupation, sewing. The first sentence has been rewritten by Wilhelm so that it ushers in the story with alliterative verse, recalling medieval epic poetry as much as does the queen's position, sewing at a castle window. The alliteration of *f* is luckily the same in English as in the original: flakes, falling, feathers; *flocken, fielen, federn*. The single seemingly insignificant action in the scene, a pinprick, occurs by inadvertence. As the queen looks at the falling snow, and wishes for a child sent from heaven, she is distracted and stabs herself with the sewing needle and her blood falls on the snow. The accident causes life to come from a love-wounded person, and thus Wilhelm begins to rework the story into a framework. As the story begins, so will it end, by inadvertence. A servant will stumble and the apple core will fall from Snow White's mouth, and she will live again. What or who controls these accidents? They happen by chance. "Chance" (or, really, "necessity") was revered by the ancient Greeks as the ultimate divine force driven by the fates.

By changing the drops of blood from "several" to "three"—and the brothers did that at a very early date; it had already been changed in the second manuscript version in 1810—the story's beginning contains an allusion to Wolfram von Eschenbach's medieval epic *Parzival*. In one of the central scenes, Parzival is fighting for his life but cannot take his eyes off three drops of blood which have fallen into the snow. They remind him of Condwiramurs, his truly beloved wife, whose name means "love leads," or "love shows the way." Thinking of her, his strength is redoubled, and he is able to fight off his attackers if just to see her again. Bettelheim sees the needle and the blood as suggesting sexual intercourse, which is one thing that it does. But the scene also recalls a need for the fidelity of love and companionship even when distance make it physically, but not spiritually, impossible. Condwiramurs comes "leaping over five countries" to be at his side when Parzival is pressed so hard that he could be killed. Blood dripping in the snow is profoundly ambiguous. It can mean that death is coming, or it can mean life and love is on its way. In the case of Snow White's mother, it meant both.

For Snow White herself, the blood in the snow designates her identity as a person. She will be named Snow White because of those three colors. Wilhelm's revision, however, has removed the possibility of identifying the colors solely with her external beauty as in the 1808 text in which the mother clearly wanted a child who is "red," meaning the color of her cheeks, who is "white as snow," which by combination with the other colors can only refer to her skin, and who is "black" in the sense that she has eyes or hair of black. If "beauty" is "worth" in Wilhelm's revisions of the tales, then he obvious wishes her beauty to be on more levels than the physical alone, and thus he does not specify exactly what part of her body the three colors might refer to.

The imagination of the reader is not entirely without guidance however. The medieval and biblical tone of the opening lines immediately suggest that there are more levels to beauty than skin color alone, and that the visible colors should be interpreted as revealing her invisible internal beauty.

Snow White's mother wishes for a child who will be a beautiful human being, one red as blood: loving and warm; white as snow: innocent and heaven-connected; and black as ebony wood: mortal, at home with the dark earth, living within the familiar framework of the tree. Mortality is the framework of the window through which the queen looks out on her world. She looks up and sees snowflakes falling gently, but falling, to the black earth. By the end of this short paragraph their fate will be hers. "And as the child was born the queen died." The mystery of the story will be: what is the meaning of the life of such a beautiful creature, born at such a cost to life, and made of such beautiful components?

As the story continues, the king takes another wife. The Grimms, under pressure from contemporary criticism that parents should not be depicted so severely, as would be the case if the mother herself became jealous of her daughter, yielded and changed the mother of the Hassenpflug version to a stepmother. On the one hand this is not out of accord with the tradition of Basile, but on the other it does not quite carry the force of acting in an "unnatural" manner as it does when the jealous person is the child's own parent. When the mirror is asked the fatal question, the formulation has been changed in order to give it an air of timelessness and a sense that it is unrestricted to any geography. The queen does not ask who is the fairest in England or in Brabant, but simply, "in the land." The answer allows the reader's fantasy to supply a real or imaginary place:

> My lady the queen, you are the most beautiful woman
>   on the site,
> but a thousand times more beautiful than you is Snow
>   White.

Unlike Musäus's mirror, this one can indeed speak. Being a mirror, and not a paid portrait artist, it always "tells the truth." Wilhelm lets this hidden metaphor justify the magic of the talking mirror in the story, making it unnecessary to resort to the rationalist use of mirror images alone.

Wilhelm then introduces an incident that is not at all in the manuscript. When the queen calls the huntsman to take Snow White out into the woods and kill her, the story verges off in the direction of Classical mythology. When Jocasta the queen, the mother of Oedipus, wanted to get rid of her child, she too ordered one of her herdsmen to take the infant out into the wilderness and to

abandon him on a wild mountainside to be devoured by the wild animals. The herdsman, however, took pity on the helpless young child and spared him. The herdsman returns to her and says nothing to the queen about letting the baby go free. Wilhelm Grimm then interweaves another ancient myth with this one. There is no substitution of an animal for the baby in the Oedipus myth. This brief allusion to the Oedipus story is therefore deftly interwoven with the biblical story of Abraham in which an animal is substituted (by the parent) for the child who is spared. In Genesis 22, Abraham lowers his knife and does not kill his son Isaac on the altar but lets his son go free and substitutes a wild ram caught in a nearby thicket for the child. The herdsman in **"Snow White"** kills a nearby wild young boar in order to bring back its lungs and liver (*Lunge und Leber*—the alliteration helps make the act seem northern and medieval) to Snow White's mother, the queen. Wilhelm then completes the incident by giving it a Germanic twist at the end. In the myth of Sigurd (Siegfried) the Dragon Slayer, the same request is made by the treacherous Regin who shows Sigurd how to kill the dragon by digging a camouflaged pit in the earth and striking up from below. Regin hopes, however that the venomous blood will then pour into the pit and destroy the hero, and the treasure will be his. This is the passage in Padraic Colum's retelling:

> Then did Regin, hearing the [death-]scream that let him know that Fafnir was slain, come down to where the battle had been fought. When he saw that Sigurd was alive and unharmed he uttered a cry of fury. For his plan had been to have Sigurd drowned and burnt in the pit with the stream of Fafnir's envenomed blood. But he mastered his fury and showed a pleased countenance to Sigurd. . . . "Fafnir is slain," Sigurd said, "and the triumph over him was not lightly won. Now may I show myself to king Alv and to my mother, and the gold from Fafnir's hoard will make me a great spoil."
>
> "Wait," said Regin cunningly, "you have yet to do something for me. With the sword you have, cut through the Dragon and take out the heart for me. When you have taken it out roast it that I may eat of it and become wiser than I am." Sigurd did what Regin would have him do and cut out the heart of the dragon and he hung it from stakes to roast.[48]

When the equally cunning queen sees the cut-out lungs and liver provided by the hunter, she has them roasted triumphantly as if she were incorporating Snow White's magic beauty into herself, just as Regin wished to incorporate into himself the magic wisdom of the serpent. What the stepmother eats, however, is the life of a pig.

The harmony of the three mythologies under Wilhelm's hand in this passage is a work of art. In David Luke's translation:

> So she sent for a huntsman and said: "Take that child out into the forest, I'm sick of the sight of her. You are to kill her and bring me her lungs and liver as proof."

The huntsman obeyed and took Show White with him, but when he had drawn his hunting-knife, and was about to thrust it into her innocent heart she began to cry and said: "Oh, dear huntsman, let me live; I will run away into the wild forest and never come home again." And because she was so beautiful the huntsman took pity on her and said: "Run away then, you poor child." The wild beasts will soon have eaten you, he thought, and yet it was as if a stone had been rolled from his heart because he did not have to kill her. And when a young boar happened to come bounding up he slaughtered it, cut out its lungs and liver and took them to the queen as the proof she wanted. The cook was ordered to stew them in salt and the wicked woman devoured them, thinking she had eaten the liver and lungs of Snow White.[49]

With this ingenious interweaving of the three mythologies Wilhelm ends the first part of the story.

For the middle part of the story we are on familiar ground, the archetypal and mythic place of biblical religious consciousness, the place of the experience of temptation, fall, and salvation: the Garden of Eden, woven together with the garden of Easter, redone as Wilhelm Grimm's forest with the little house which is as old as the hidden room in which the queen concocts her poison, and into which Hansel and Gretel, Red Riding Hood, and now Snow White are destined to enter. The satanic role of the tempting serpent, played by the witch in **"Hansel and Gretel"** and by the wolf in **"Red Riding Hood,"** both of whom wish to devour the little hero and heroines, is played in **"Snow White"** by the wicked queen and stepmother, who also was interested in devouring the lungs and liver of Snow White. Because she covets being the most beautiful of all, Wilhelm constantly associates her with evil and wickedness, uses the colors green and yellow of her (in contrast to Snow White's red, white and black) to describe her as the stunningly beautiful embodiment of jealousy, absolutely incapable of tolerating any rival—not even one for whom she should feel love.—She is, in other words, Lucifer. Wilhelm's close approximation of the character of the (step)mother to the character of the angel Lucifer ("light-bearer"), second only to God in beauty, rests upon the cause of his fall in the biblical myth because of his infatuation with his own beauty and his refusal to accept that anyone else was "the most beautiful in the land."

In church preaching tradition it is often taught that Lucifer tempts human beings out of jealousy and that he always tempts with some form of the same temptation to self-infatuation to which he himself succumbed. "You will be like God," and "You will be as beautiful as God" are the poisonous and deadly apple. Wilhelm's retention of the hellish fire-heated shoes at the end and his placing of the apple temptation in the third and climactic position in the narrative reinforce the image of the queen as the consummately beautiful, jealously ruth-less Lucifer. She is loveless but beautiful, and Wilhelm refers to her true identity when he calls her "godless." To the little house she comes disguised as someone plain-looking and of no great consequence, and is that not a wry description of the camouflaged nature of Wilhelm's reworked tale?

What of the temptations themselves? I believe that Bettelheim's reading, that the three temptations are all attempts to deceive Snow White into accepting her mother's concept of the nature of personal beauty, is correct. If she becomes like her (step)mother, she will be dead, her very great personal beauty will wither. Lucifer baits with each of the three gifts: "You will become like me." Snow White's soul, seen through the eyes of her real mother and through the eyes of the owl, the raven, and the dove, is a thousand times more beautiful than the most beautiful person in the land. Her personality, her very soul, is red: loving and warm, white: innocent and faithful, and black: mortal. But those colors can also be seen through her stepmother's eyes. If Snow White can be tempted to exchange her spiritual sense of what about her is worthwhile, to adopt material criteria only, she will lose her personal beauty, she will die. The tighter, in other words, she tightens the bodice strings for the sake of her figure, the closer she comes to asphyxiating her self. The more intently she lets the queen properly fashion her hair with the black comb, the more its poison takes effect on her person.

The colors too warn of the mortal danger of externalizing the nature of beauty / worth. Snow White's soul is beautiful because it is "white"; to tempt her to buy the bodice lacings and to tighten them provocatively in order to let more of her skin show is to tempt her to embrace the queen's interpretation of the beauty of "white." Snow White's "redness," her warmth and loving nature, are very attractive and will appeal to a prince. Can she be tempted to interpret the attractiveness of her self as "red" as a reference to her mouth's apple color? Snow White's real beauty is also "black." If she can be made to act as if that color refers primarily to her hair rather than to her mortality, her ultimate vulnerability, she will cease to value what makes her ultimately attractive to God. If she were to accept such an un-magical mirror's notion of beauty, then, should even the prince most beautiful come down from his father's castle at the time when the snowflakes fall like feathers from heaven, she would find him plain-looking and uninteresting. Each Lucifer-like deception is a threat to her soul because each one leads her further away from spiritual awareness of what about her person makes her a thousand times more beautiful than the most beautiful person in the land.

Each temptation enables her to rationalize her way out of heeding the sound advice of the dwarfs, and in some sense it shows an innocent "lack of faith" on Snow

White's part that the magic mirror is telling the truth—something the queen knows to be the case. Each time she submits—to the bodice strings, to the comb, and to the apple—she is showing a lack of faith in the message of the magic mirror. If Snow White is already, naturally, "a thousand times" more beautiful than the stepmother, then there is no need whatsoever to put faith in the artificially created improvements of lacings and combs, nor for eating (suspiciously like her stepmother's attempt to eat beauty) the beautiful apple. Snow White, like Cinderella, is the most beautiful person in her family regardless of her appearance.

She does eat the apple, however, as did Eve in the Garden. The good dwarfs are able to rescue her from the consequences of the laces and the comb, but not from the consequences of eating the apple. "She was dead and she remained dead" (*das liebe Kind war tot und blieb tot*). Wilhelm certainly put this line into the text to distinguish himself from Musäus's heroine's narcotic-induced sleep. The good dwarfs and, presumably, the adept physicians, were Wilhelm to have allowed them into his tale, are now quite helpless.

Just who are these dwarfs who can do so much rescuing but cannot save from death? Their house, as we have seen, is the place of religious experience and of testing. Wilhelm makes this point again when in addition to the seven forks, and plates, and cups of the seven dwarfs, he mentions that when they come home at night they light their seven little lamps. The seven lamps recall the menorah in the temple and the seven lamps of the seven Christian churches. Immediately before the lamp lighting Snow White got into the seventh or Sabbath bed and "commended herself to God." The dwarfs offer her protection and kindness, asking only that she do her part in the daily work. They themselves live a life of goodness and labor in the mines. All of this Bettelheim treats unusually, seeing only the "working in the mine shafts" and their small stature as identifying characteristics:

> So dwarfs are eminently male, but males who are stunted in their development. These "little men" with their stunted bodies and their mining operation—they skillfully penetrate into dark holes—all suggest phallic connotations. They are certainly not men in any sexual sense—their way of life, their interest in material goods to the exclusion of love, suggest a pre-oedipal existence.[50]

I suggest that pre-Freudian thoughts might be possible in the context of Wilhelm Grimm's mind-set as well. Dwarfs are characters from Germanic religious thought and story, and very often they are associated with both magic and the ability to make the greatest of swords and rings and armor. They are always associated with fine and magical workmanship, but they are not gods, and they do not always have a fine disposition. The

seven of this tale are a mixture of Germanic workers and Christian disposition. The fact that they are celibate, carry the seven lamps, give the heroine good advice on the intent and persistence of the Lucifer-like queen, rescue her twice from death at the queen's hands, point to the familiar mix of Germanic and Christian. In some senses, their daily working is not unlike that of medieval Benedictine monks whose motto was, and is, *ora et labora,* pray and work! To see them only as stunted "little men" is to look at them through the eyes of Cinderella's father—or Snow White's stepmother! More importantly the reason for the appearance of the prince on the scene is not by accident but is connected with the presence of the dwarfs. In the Grimm version the third part of the story, the ending with the prince, is introduced rather solemnly: "And it came to pass that a prince was traveling through the forest and he came to the house of the dwarfs[51] in order to stay there overnight" (*Es geschah aber, daß ein Königssohn in den Wald geriet und zu dem Zwergenhaus kam, um dort zu übernachten*). In other words, the prince is acquainted with the house of the dwarfs and feels it is a place where he can stay overnight, perhaps not unlike a monastery, a place of refuge for the soul. What the king's son finds is the body of Snow White, which the dwarfs had washed "with water and wine," but which they did not wish to "sink into the black earth." It is curious how that passage evokes both Christian myth and ritual with water and wine, and also, combined with the "black" earth, the three colors of Snow White's personality. As in the Passion, which the scene has now evoked, there were three days in which all stopped work and kept watch over the body.

It is in this context that we come to the glass casket. Not the small window above the face of *Richilde*'s Blanca, not the expanding glass cases of Basile, nor even the open air bier of King Harald's Snaefrid, but the dwarfs love Snow White so much that "they had a glass casket made, so that she could be seen from all sides, they laid her in it and wrote her name on it in golden letters and said that she was the daughter of a king." They not only refuse to bury her, but one of them is constantly on vigil where she is, and they place the casket on top of a mountain, so that all the world and God above can see the one whom they love so much. There are three glass objects in this tale associated with seeing, only two of which are transparent and transitive, the other is reflexive. The first to be encountered is the window, through which Snow White's mother can look and admire the beauty of the world and nature's falling snow, the transparency of the glass giving her sight of the beauty of the outside world and suggesting the tragic wonder of the world coming to be within her. The second is the non-transparent glass of the mirror into which the queen can look, continually observing how beautiful she is, or appears to be. She prefers the mirror, glass rendered opaque, to the appreciation of anything beyond the castle window, reflecting only her admired light image back to herself. The third is something that is an appeal to heaven: a casket of glass placed on a mountain, so designed as to not impede being looked into, a transparent display of human mortality and its beauty, an appeal and an invitation to the provident eye of God and a benevolent nature to look upon the black ebony frame of mortal goodness. The glass casket is an invitation to those who love the beauty of a good soul to be moved as was King Harald centuries ago, to hope that the red and white of life will come back to her. "Blessed are those who mourn, for they will be comforted." The glass of the casket is the second beatitude turned into an appeal, a prayer like the one she said before she laid herself down to sleep when she first found the spiritual house in the forest. "she commended herself to God," as now does the transparency of the coffin.

And who comes to stand watch and to see if this very open appeal of a glass casket on a mountain is answered? The answer is, I think, one of Wilhelm Grimm's finest, and in it he reveals in slightly veiled form the heart of the magic of his fairy tales: "And the animals came too, and cried over Snow White, first an owl, then a raven, last a little dove" (*Und die Tiere kamen auch und beweinten Schneewittchen, erst eine Eule, dann ein Rabe, zuletzt ein Täubchen*).

Nature, which always recognized her as one of her own, now cries over her loss. Only those who did not love do not mourn. Cinderella knew that, even pets and animals know that. But of all the animals of the forest (Disney will have many more), why these three? For millennia the three religions have accompanied the good human being with hope for rescue for as far as they can go, up to the grave. The Classical, the Germanic, and the Christian religions can now only mourn, keep watch over the body as they have always done, and hope. Where do these spirits of hope come from? Where in the forest is their real place of origin? Their colors tell much. The owl is reddish brown, the raven is black, the dove is white. They are the colors of Snow White's soul, her person itself, and it is from the soul of the good person that religion's spirit originates, from its red loving warmth, from its white loyal innocence, and from its humbling, black and earthlike, mortality. The three birds are the soul of mankind keeping watch over the body to see if it can come to life again, to see if there is a "resurrection of the body and life everlasting," to see if death is a sleep. As they keep their long vigil over her, the owl dreams of her rescue by some provident accident, the raven dreams of her rescue by a tree, and the dove dreams that one day the king's son will come for her.

And the king's son does come, and when he looks through the glass casket and sees her he realizes why he came into the woods, he cannot live without her.

Faith, hope, and love write the ending. The prince is surely the Christ figure of Wilhelm's many readings in the New Testament on the Resurrection. Christ is the friend of the Germanic religious dwarfs, and he sees the beauty of the dead Snow White. Wilhelm seems almost to be thinking of St. Paul's famous equation of death with sleep as the prince asks if he can take her with him: "But we do not want you to be uninformed, brothers and sisters, about those who have fallen asleep, so that you may not grieve as others do who have no hope. For since we believe that Jesus died and rose again, even so, through Jesus, God will bring with him those who have fallen asleep"[52] (1 Thes 4:13-15).

As the prince is about to bring her with him and has the servants lift up the casket to carry it, one of them—by chance—stumbles over a shrub and the bit of poisoned apple flies from Snow White's throat. All three birds of the spirit must be happy, since it is the Spirit of God over time that guided them, the good human spirit, to this point. Each now contemplates its prescribed role in the raising of Snow White. As the bearers of the glass casket stumble, Athena's owl sees the event as one fated to happen "by accident." Woden's raven fixes its gaze upon the cause of the accident, a small "tree." Christ's dove contemplates the loving arrival of the prince, whose love, with the help of a tree and an accident, caused Eden's poisoned apple to be spit out. As Snow White opens her eyes, lifts the lid of the casket and sits upright, she says, "Oh God, where am I?" The answer which Wilhelm wrote is Christ's, the answer hoped for for millennia, "the king's son says, 'You are with me,'" and he tells her that he loves her more than anything in the world and immediately invites her to follow him into the eternal world of the Father. "Come with me into my father's castle, you will be my wife." The story comes to a mystical Trinitarian ending as the good soul, led by the Spirit in the owl, the raven, and the dove, is brought to a meeting with the Son, who conducts the person in love beyond death to his Father's house.

The last lines of the story do not end with this promise of eternal life in the heaven from which the snowflakes were falling at the beginning of the tale, in a sort of Christmas to Easter sequence, but rather with the punishment of the evil queen. Her first shock, taken from Musäus's version, is the sight of Snow White alive and in the bridal veil. Her second is to realize that she is not among the blest invited to the wedding feast of the king's son. The shoes are made glowing hot for her and, instead of just getting a few blisters, she is made to dance until she falls down dead. This quick introduction of a second death in the story, the queen's, suggests the Christian concept that there is nothing for the good person to fear from "the first death," rather it is the second death that is serious. The death of the unloving queen-mother is another kind of death. It is the death of the red and white aspect of the personality, an ignoring of the humility suggested by the black framework, in sum, the spiritual consequence of her preference of the mirror to the window. The queen's misuse of her mirror nourishes a corrosive envy of the beauty of others, creates a poisonous apple in the secret chamber of her soul, and maintains a closed circuit of reflection that excludes the love of neighbor and precludes any real interest in the coming of the King's Son.

Notes

1. Bruno Bettelheim, *The Uses of Enchantment, the Meaning and Importance of Fairy Tales* (New York: Random House, 1976). I am here using the Vintage Books paperback edition.

2. Bettelheim, p. 164.

3. Bettelheim, pp. 12-13, 14.

4. Bettelheim, p. 228. See also his discussion of "safe" stories, p. 8: "'Safe' stories mention neither death nor aging, the limits on our existence, nor the wish for eternal life. The fairy tale, by contrast, confronts the child squarely with the basic human predicaments."

5. Bettelheim, p. 164.

6. Bettelheim, p. 102.

7. In "Wo das Wünschen noch geholfen hat," *Gesammelte Aufsätze zu den "Kinder- und Hausmärchen" der Brüder Grimm* (Bonn: Bouvier Verlag, 1985).

8. "Wo das Wünschen," p. 212. "Also darf man auch diese intensiven und inständigen Nennungen und Anrufungen Gottes nicht als handlungsfördernd, sondern lediglich als atmosphärisches Beiwerk betrachten."

9. "Wo das Wünschen," p. 217.

10. "Wo das Wünschen," p. 215.

11. "Wo das Wünschen," p. 216.

12. See "New Results of Research on Grimms' Fairy Tales," in *The Brothers Grimm and Folktale*, ed. James M. McGlathery (Urbana: University of Illinois Press), p. 109.

13. An effective example of how spare the first Grimm versions can be is given by Ellis in his *One Fairy Story Too Many, The Brothers Grimm and Their Tales* (Chicago: University of Chicago Press, 1983), pp. 54ff.

14. In "New Misconceptions about Old Folktales" in *The Brothers Grimm and Folktale*, ed. James M. McGlathery (Urbana: University of Illinois Press), p. 95. See also in the same volume the essay of

Lutz Röhrich on the need to interpret the tales, "The Quest of Meaning in Folk Narrative Research," pp. 1-15.

15. John M. Ellis, *One Fairy Story Too Many*, p. 32.

16. Ellis, p. 54.

17. Ruth B. Bottigheimer, *Grimms' Bad Girls and Bold Boys, The Moral and Social Vision of the Tales* (New Haven: Yale University Press, 1987), p. 7.

18. Bottigheimer, p. 144.

19. Bottigheimer, p. 143.

20. Bottigheimer, p. 155.

21. Bottigheimer, p. 27.

22. "Das Stürzen in den Brunnen . . . ist mit der Sage von Joseph, der ja auch sonst selbst der Phönix, (d.h. der Goldvogel) ist. . . ." Rölleke, *Synopse*, p. 331. I am indebted to Colin Bezener, a graduate student of mine, for noting this comment made by Wilhelm.

23. Max Lüthi, *Once Upon a Time, On the Nature of Fairy Tales* (New York: Ungar, 1970), p. 145.

24. Lüthi, p. 142.

25. Lüthi, p. 60.

26. See Jack Zipes, "Dreams of a Better Bourgeois Life: The Psychosocial Origins of the Grimms' Tales," in McGlathery, *The Brothers Grimm and Folktale*, pp. 205-19.

27. *The Complete Fairy Tales of the Brothers Grimm*, trans. Jack Zipes (New York: Bantam, 1987), p. xxv.

28. *Complete Fairy Tales*, p. xxxi. Zipes too agrees that the Grimms substantially revised the tales, but for purposes of "sanitizing" them for the "bourgeois socialization" of children. "The Grimms gathered their tales primarily from petit bourgeois or educated middle-class people, who had already introduced bourgeois notions into their versions. In all cases the Grimms did more than simply change and improve the style of the tales: they expanded them and made substantial changes in characters and meaning." Jack Zipes, *Fairy Tales of the Brothers Grimm, The Classical Genre for Children and the Process of Civilization* (New York: Wildman Press, 1983), "Who's Afraid of the Brothers Grimm," pp. 45-70; citation, 47.

29. Cited by Alan Dundes in his "Interpreting Little Red Riding Hood Psychoanalytically," in McGlathery, ed., *The Brothers Grimm and Folktale*, p. 29.

30. Dundes. Cf. Glas' *Red Riding Hood* (East Gannicox: Education and Science Publications, 1947), p. 3; and *Once Upon a Fairy Tale: Seven Favorite Folk and Fairy Tales by the Brothers Grimm,* translated and interpreted by Norbert Glas (Spring Valley, N.Y.: St. George Publications, 1976).

31. Maria Tatar, "Born Yesterday," in *The Hard Facts of the Grimms' Fairy Tales* (Princeton: Princeton University Press, 1987), pp. 85-105.

32. Tatar, "Born Yesterday," pp. 103-104.

33. Herder's collection of folksongs, "natural poetry" in his description, as opposed to "work-of-art poetry," was published in 1778-1779.

34. In "Hybrid Forms in German Romanticism," *Prosimetrum, Crosscultural Perspectives on Narrative in Prose and Verse,* ed. Joseph Harris and Karl Reichl (Cambridge: D. S. Brewer, 1997), p. 165. Ryan emphasizes the "wildness" of variety encouraged here, using the example of the English garden rather than the French. This is useful when thinking of the hidden variety involved in Wilhelm's weaving of diverse religious traditions in his retelling of the fairy tales.

35. Christa Kamenetsky, *The Brothers Grimm and Their Critics, Folktales and the Quest for Meaning* (Athens: Ohio University Press, 1992).

36. Kamenetsky, pp. 56-57.

37. Marina Warner, *From the Beast to the Blonde,* pp. 211, 228.

38. Rölleke, *Jubiläumsausgabe,* III, 87. Much of the following review of sources taken from the Grimms' commentary on the tale which is on pp. 87-90 of this volume.

39. *Blanca* means white in Spanish, and therefore is partly related to "Snow White." It is almost as though "Snow White," were a combination of the "snow" of *Snae-frið* and the "white" of *Blanca.* Another Spanish curiosity in *Richilde* is the use of *dueña* for the mistress of a castle, perhaps to evoke the time of the Spanish rule of the Lowlands.

40. Wilhelm seems to have seen a connection here to Wolfram's *Parzival.* In his copy of *Parzival* which he used for his lectures in Marburg he underlined the following two lines from the end of the epic: vil liute in Brabant noch sint, / die wol wizzen von in beiden ("there are many people in Brabant who still know about both of them"). He may suspect then that the story of Lohengrin is still remembered, through folktale continuity with epic of the medieval past, as the happy couple of Brabant at the end of the fairy tale *Richilde.*

41. See Musäus, J. K. A., *Volksmärchen der Deutschen* (Darmstadt: Wissenschaftliche Buchgesellschaft, 1961), pp. 75-117.

42. The Grimms were deeply impressed by the story, even rhapsodizing over it in their commentary as being "almost historical" (*fast historisch*). Despite the age of the story, which delighted the brothers as collectors of folklore, the original ending with its religiously satirical tone received no attention from Wilhelm whatsoever when the religious poet in him re-created the story of *Snow Lover* as *Snow White.*

43. In Old Norse, *snæ* is "snow," *frið* is, as a noun, "peace," "serenity," "friendliness," as an adjective it can mean "beautiful," "friendly," or even "alive." The Grimms' entry in their German dictionary admits to the puzzling nature of *fried* when used as a component of names. As a given name it seems to me to be a parental wish, that the child will be someone who enjoys something—for example, Siegfried "enjoys victory," Winfried "enjoys friends," Godfried "enjoys God," "friend of God." "Snaefrid" could mean "Snow Friend," or perhaps "Snow Beauty." I think it is best understood as someone who will love the snow and share the snow's loveliness. The names Snow White and Snow Lover are, therefore, quite close. In medieval literature, white skin was considered to be very desirable as a sign of great, and aristocratic, beauty.

44. Snorri Sturluson, *Heimskringla* or *The Lives of the Norse Kings,* ed. and with notes by Erling Monsen (New York: Dover, 1990), 61-62.

45. *Synopse,* p. 384. Curiously, in their earliest manuscript of the story, 1808, the Grimms entitled the story *Schneeweißchen* and gave the expected *Sneewittchen* merely as a variant along with *Unglückskind* (*Child of Misfortune*). Later, I believe because of the existence of the early medieval Nordic story of *Snaefrið,* they came to prefer and settle on the North German form, *Sneewittchen,* as more geographically suggestive of northern ancestry than the South German *Schneeweißchen.* The Grimms claimed to have encountered both variants everywhere in Germany, but the word, except for "White"(*Blanca*), is inexplicably absent in Musäus' *Richilde,* and the suspicion must arise that they themselves are responsible for the word in its two main forms by translating and combining "Snaefrið" and "Blanca" into "Sneewitt," "Snow White."

46. Taken from Giambattista Basile, *Il Pentamerone,* pp. 169-73.

47. Rölleke, *Synopse,* p. 383.

48. Padraic Colum, *Nordic Gods and Heroes* (New York: Dover, 1996), pp. 227-28. This is the scene where the hero inadvertently (again!) lets a drop

of blood from the dragon's heart fall on his finger. When he puts his finger into his mouth to ease the burning pain and tastes the blood he can from that moment understand the speech of birds. This is an episode of which Wilhelm seems to have been very cognizant.

49. *Jacob and Wilhelm Grimm, Selected Tales,* trans. with introduction and notes by David Luke (London & New York: Penguin, 1982), p. 75.

50. Bettelheim, *The Uses of Enchantment,* p. 210.

51. There is a connection suggested between the helpful doves and the helpful dwarfs. It is indicated by the similarity of the compounds used in the German for both places where the heroines take refuge, Cinderella in the *Taubenhaus,* Snow White in the *Zwergenhaus.*

52. Unfortunately, in modern translations the poignant metaphor of sleep is often ignored and the Greek original "those sleeping" and "those having fallen asleep" (*koimonenon* and *koimethentas*) are bluntly rendered "the dead."

Select Bibliography

PRIMARY SOURCES

Kinder- und Hausmärchen, gesammelt durch die Brüder Grimm. Bd.1, 1812; Bd. 2, 1815. Berlin: in der Realschulbuchhandlung [Reimer]. [contains first brief source information and comment given by the brothers; at the Beineke Library, Yale]

Kinder- und Hausmärchen, 2. Auflage, Bd. 1 & 2, 1819; Bd. 3, 1822. Berlin: Reimer. [vol. 3 contains expanded annotations and Wilhelm's essay on the nature of fairy tales; at the Firestone Library, Princeton University]

Kleine Ausgabe. Berlin: Reimer, 1825. [contains illustrations by Ludwig Emil Grimm guided by Wilhelm; a later reprint at Firestone Library, Princeton]

Novum Testamentum Graece, ed. Schott. Leipzig: 1811. [at the Humboldt University Library, Berlin]

Die Heilige Schrift in berichtigter Uebersetzung mit kurzen Anmerkungen. Johann Friedrich von Meyer. Frankfurt am Main: Verlag der Hermannschen Buchhandlung, 1819. [at the Grimm Museum in Haldensleben]

SECONDARY LITERATURE

Basile, Giambattista. *Lo Cunto de Li Cunti,* a cura di Ezio Raimondi. Milan-Naples: Einaudi, 1960.

Bettelheim, Bruno. *The Uses of Enchantment, The Meaning and Importance of Fairy Tales.* New York: Random House, Vintage Books, 1977.

Bottigheimer, Ruth B. *Grimms' Bad Girls and Bold Boys, The Moral and Social Vision of the Tales.* New Haven: Yale University Press, 1987.

Colum, Padraic. *Nordic Gods and Heroes.* New York: Dover, 1996.

Dundes, Alan. "Interpreting Little Red Riding Hood Psychoanalytically." *The Brothers Grimm and Folktale,* ed. James M. McGlathery.

Ellis, John M. *One Fairy Story Too Many, The Brothers Grimm and Their Tales.* Chicago: The University of Chicago Press, 1985.

Glas, Norbert. *Red Riding Hood.* East Gannicox: Education and Science Publications, 1947.

Herder's Werke, ausgewählte Werke in einem Band. Stuttgart und Tübingen: Cotta, 1844.

Kamenetsky, Christa. *The Brothers Grimm and their Critics, Folktales and the Quest for Meaning.* Athens, Ohio: Ohio University Press, 1992.

Lüthi, Max. *Once Upon a Time, On the Nature of Fairy Tales,* trans. Lee Chadeayne and Paul Gottwald. New York: Frederick Ungar Publishing Company, 1970.

Musäus, Johann Karl August. *Volksmärchen der Deutschen.* Darmstadt: Wissenschaftliche Buchgesellschaft, 1961.

Rölleke, Heinz. *Wo das Wünschen noch geholfen hat: Gesammelte Aufsätze zu den Kinder- und Hausmärchen der Brüder Grimm.* Wuppertaler Schriftenreihe Literatur, 23. Bonn: Bouvier, 1985.

————. "New Research on Grimms' Fairy Tales." *The Brothers Grimm and Folktale,* ed. James M. McGlathery.

Ryan, Judith. "Hybrid Forms in German Romanticism." *Prosimetrum, Crosscultural Perspectives on Narrative in Prose and Verse,* ed. Joseph Harris and Karl Reichl. Cambridge: D. S. Brewer, 1997.

Sturluson, Snorri. *Heimskringla or The Lives of the Norse Kings,* ed. Erling Monsen. New York: Dover, 1990. [contains the story of Snaefrið]

Tatar, Maria M. *The Hard Facts of the Grimms' Fairy Tales.* Princeton: Princeton University Press, 1987.

Ward, Donald. "New Misconceptions about Old Folktales: The Brothers Grimm." *The Brothers Grimm and Folktale,* ed. James M. McGlathery.

Warner, Marina. *From the Beast to the Blonde, On Fairy Tales and their Tellers.* New York: Farrar, Straus and Giroux, 1995.

Wolfram von Eschenbach. *Parzival, (Studienausgabe) mittlehochdeutscher Text nach der 6. Ausgabe von Karl Lachmann.* Berlin: Walter de Gruyter, 1998.

Zipes, Jack. "Dreams of a Better Bourgeois Life: The Psychosocial Origins of the Grimms' Tales." *The Brothers Grimm and Folktale,* ed. James M. McGlathery.

Jack Zipes (essay date 2002)

SOURCE: Zipes, Jack. "From Odysseus to Tom Thumb and Other Cunning Heroes: Speculations about the Entrepreneurial Spirit." In *The Brothers Grimm: From Enchanted Forests to the Modern World,* pp. 91-106. New York: Palgrave Macmillan, 2002.

[*In the following essay, Zipes studies different types of male protagonists in Grimms' Fairy Tales, demonstrating how their behavior reinforces bourgeois ideals of male gender roles.*]

In her introduction to the 1976 Insel edition of the Grimms' *Kinder- und Hausmärchen* (*Children's and Household Tales*), the noted ethnologist Ingeborg Weber-Kellermann states:

> The triumphal procession of the *Children's and Household Tales* succeeded only because the nurseries of bourgeois homes formed the well-disposed circle of consumers. With its strong bourgeois sense of family the nineteenth century was receptive to the Grimms' fairy tales as a book that mothers and grandmothers could read aloud and that children could read to themselves. . . . The possibilities for identification involved nationalist thought and German *Volkstümlichkeit,* and all of this was considered to be perfectly captured in the Grimms' *Children's and Household Tales.* The success of their book cannot be understood without studying the social history of the nineteenth century.[1]

Some years later, Heinz Rölleke, the foremost scholar of the Grimms' tales in postwar Germany, reiterated Weber-Kellermann's point in his book *Die Märchen der Brüder Grimm* (1985), with a slightly different twist:

> The bourgeoisie has continually accepted the possibilities for identification in these texts beyond national boundaries, texts which effectually represent their own virtues and ideals and can be used effectively for pedagogical purposes. The bourgeois sense of family, an entirely new and high estimation of the child as autonomous personality, a moderate *biedermeier* world-view in keeping with the European social history of the nineteenth century, but also more or less with the Japanese of the late twentieth century—these were and continue to be the significant factors for the enthusiastic reception of the Grimms' fairy tales from generation to generation. Hence, it was not the joy about the "German essence" of the tales that brought about the international success of the *Children's and Household Tales* as a book but much more the respective affinity between the social and cultural givens in a particular country with those of Germany at the beginning of the nineteenth century.[2]

Whereas Weber-Kellerman finds that the reasons for the success of the *Children's and Household Tales* are due to the growing nationalist and bourgeois climate in nineteenth-century Germany, Rölleke points to the international bourgeois reception and endeavors to discount the "German essence" of the tales. Both are in agreement, however, that the tales offer bourgeois models or narrative paradigms that reinforce social, moral, and political codes that have become common to modern nation-states. Surprisingly, neither Weber-Kellermann nor Rölleke have endeavored to explore the so-called bourgeois appeal of the tales in depth, even though the key to their reception and celebration in the modern world today lies there.

As I have demonstrated in previous chapters and also in *Fairy Tales and the Art of Subversion,*[3] there is a clear connection between the rise of the civilizing process, standards of civility and *Bildung* (education) set largely by the bourgeoisie, and the origins of the fairy tale as institution in the eighteenth and nineteenth centuries. The connection accounts for the continued appeal not only of the Grimms' tales but of most classical fairy tales that received approbation by the middle-class reading public because of the manner in which the tales constructed solutions to moral and political conflicts. As devout Calvinists dedicated to the principles of the enlightened German *Bildungsbürgertum,* the Grimms were the perfect pair to stamp the fairy-tale genre with the imprint of the Protestant ethic. If today we continue to value the tales that they collected and revised, it is because they stylistically formulated those norms and gender roles that we have been expected to internalize psychologically and ideologically, from childhood to old age. Or, to put it another way, the "contagious" charm of the Grimms' fairy tales emanates from the compositional technique and ethics developed by the Brothers Grimm to stress fundamental bourgeois values of behavior and moral principles of Christianity that served the hegemonic aspirations of the rising middle classes in Germany and elsewhere. As various critics have noted, these values and principles are also oriented toward male hegemony and patriarchy.[4] Consequently, most critical attention has been paid to sexism and female role expectations in the Grimms' tales and classical fairy tales,[5] and there has curiously been very little research on male heroes, stereotypes, and role expectations.[6] This is unfortunate, since I believe that an understanding of the different roles played by the male protagonists in the Grimms' tales might enable us to gain a deeper understanding of the bourgeois content, popular appeal, and endurance of the Grimms' tales. Let us then see what can be done here with a little speculation.

In his essay "Die Frau in den *Märchen der Brüder Grimm,*"[7] Rölleke has argued that there is a danger in generalizing about a gender type, for there is no single female type consistently depicted in the same manner throughout the tales. Indeed, there are many different types of women at different stages in their lives, and they have various occupations and social backgrounds. At best, one could select the dominant characteristics of heroines in the most popular tales to illustrate readers' preferences in the portrayal of acceptable female behavior. The different types of women and their various modes of action in the tales have all been leveled in the cultural *reception and use* of the tales. For instance, among the Grimms' tales there are only a few "heroines" who stand out in the public's memory today—such as Cinderella, Sleeping Beauty, Snow White, Little Red Riding Hood, Rapunzel, the miller's daughter in **"Rumpelstiltskin,"** and the princess in **"The Frog King."** For the most part these heroines indicate that a woman's best place is in the house as a diligent, obedient, self-sacrificing wife. In the majority of these tales and their imitations, the male is her reward, and it is apparent that, even though he is an incidental character, he arrives on the scene to take over, to govern, and control her future. (We tend to forget the tales in which women are strong, intelligent, and brave, and outwit men. Such tales as **"Clever Gretel," "The Clever Farmer's Daughter,"** or **"The True Bride"** have not become part of the fairy-tale canon.)

But what about the tales in which the male is the protagonist? What about the tales in which the male is largely concerned with his own fate? In the 211 tales of the last edition of 1857 and in the additional 28 tales that had appeared in previous editions but were omitted for various reasons at a later date, we encounter such types as the magician, drummer, thief, goldsmith, shoemaker, woodcutter, servant, Jew, shepherd, blacksmith, fisherman, huntsman, elf, gnome, dwarf, journeyman, cook, army surgeon, king, prince, hermit, soldier, tailor, giant, hedgehog, donkey, Thumbling, youngest son, and farmer/peasant. Their behavior varies according to their situation, occupation, and class; though magic and miraculous events do occur, these types all evince characteristics that correspond realistically to representative figures of the eighteenth and nineteenth centuries. Therefore, it is important to gather historical information about social conditions during these centuries if we are to grasp both differences and similarities among the heroes. As we saw in chapter 3, historical data enables us to comprehend to a certain degree why the soldiers in the Grimms' tales display a distinct dislike for the army and their superiors; we saw why they are often bent on revenge after having been mistreated and why they want nothing more to do with soldiering. We also grasped why tailors in Grimm tales are anxious to abandon their craft: because at the time the guilds were declining and tailoring was no longer profitable. Similarly, history tells us a good deal about the third or youngest son, who is denied property and inheritance due to primogeniture and must prove his worth alone in the wide

world. What unites these types—the soldier, tailor, and youngest son—is the will for survival and a strong desire to improve their lot, no matter what risks they have to face.

Here the specific can be linked to the general: The male heroes in the Grimms' tales tend to be adventurous, cunning, opportunistic, and reasonable. They take "calculated" risks and expect these risks to pay off. And, for the most part, their *Fleiß* (industriousness) and aggressive behavior are rewarded. Contrary to what one might expect, the majority of the male heroes in the Grimms' tales are *not* princes—at least, not at the outset, nor can we say that their conduct is "princely" or aristocratic in any way. If anything, the majority of the male heroes reveal a definite bourgeois entrepreneurial spirit, and even the princes must toe the bourgeois line.

But what is meant by bourgeois entrepreneur? What is meant by the "bourgeois line" that the Grimms' protagonists must toe? Here I would like to turn to Theodor Adorno and Max Horkheimer for some help—two unlikely critics at first glance, and yet I believe that they open up a general view of male protagonists in western culture that may prove invaluable for the study of male behavior in the Grimms' tales and their favorable reception in Western societies up to the present.

In the second chapter of their book *Dialectic of Enlightenment,*[8] Adorno and Horkheimer discuss Homer's *Odyssey* in relation to their notion of bourgeois enlightenment and myth with the intention of showing how the struggle for self-preservation and autonomy has been linked to sacrifice, renunciation, and repression ever since the beginning of western thought. For Adorno and Horkheimer, Odysseus is the prototype of the bourgeois individual, and they analyze his struggles philosophically as representing both the general and particular form that the struggle against nature takes. Odysseus battles his way home while demonstrating what qualities one needs in order to retain control over inner and outer nature. According to Adorno and Horkheimer, Odysseus is mostly concerned with his own vested interests and self-preservation, not with the welfare of the collective. Yet, at the same time, these concerns entail the repression of his own instincts and immediate needs, for

> the nimble-witted survives only at the price of his own dream, which he wins only by demystifying himself as well as the powers without. He can never have everything; he always has to wait, to be patient, to do without; he may not taste the lotus or eat the cattle of the Sun-god Hyperion, and when he steers between the rocks he must count on the loss of the men whom Scylla plucks from the boat. He just pulls through; struggle is his survival; and all the fame that he and the others win in the process serves merely to confirm that the title of hero is only gained at the price of abasement and mortification of the instinct for complete, universal, and undivided happiness.[9]

In the eyes of Adorno and Horkheimer, each trial and test experienced by Odysseus represents a stage in self-mastery. During the course of his voyage, Odysseus learns how to dominate by developing and making instrumental a personal system of rational calculation. The authors argue that this mythic model became general and historical for Western bourgeois men by the nineteenth century. For instance, when Odysseus arrives home, he has completed a voyage or course in civilization that appears to be one of fulfillment, but it is actually the culmination of self-renunciation and self-alienation. By withstanding the forces of magic, chaos, nature, and sensuality, Odysseus acts in the name of civilizing rationality, which constitutes the very essence of the bourgeois individual. Adorno and Horkheimer continually underline how cunning leads Odysseus to mark the formation of the bourgeois entrepreneur:

> From the standpoint of the developed exchange society and its individuals, the adventures of Odysseus are an exact representation of the risks which mark out the road to success. Odysseus lives by the original constitutive principle of civil society: one had the choice between deceit and failure. Deception was the mark of the ratio which betrayed its particularity. Hence universal socialization, as outlined in the narratives of the world traveler Odysseus and the solo manufacturer [Robinson] Crusoe, from the start included the absolute solitude which emerged so clearly at the end of the bourgeois era. Radical socialization means radical alienation. Odysseus and Crusoe are both concerned with totality—the former measures whereas the latter produces it. Both realize totality only in complete alienation from all other men, who meet the two protagonists only in an alienated form—as enemies or as points of support, but always as tools, as things.[10]

As discussed by Adorno and Horkheimer, *The Odyssey* is about its male hero's civilizing rationality. This same kind of "bourgeois" male self-mastery, one that flowers in the Enlightenment, informs male behavior in the Grimms' tales. Here I would like to maintain that the *magic* fairy tales of the Grimms were designed by them as literary products to put an end to magic (deus ex machina, good fairies, supernatural luck, spells)—perhaps first even told by others with this end in mind—and to establish the significance of cunning and rational enlightenment. A "male" principle of literacy is at work here, for to become literate and sophisticated is to learn to exploit the distinction between word and fact and to deceive the outside world in order to conquer it. The principles of literacy in the West have been formulated largely by men in their enterprise to deceive, for men know that their principles are not based on fact or on nature but on their own vested interests for power and survival. To know the world is to conceive narratives to control cognition when it is apparent that the truth and essence of the world can never be known. Consequently, men, especially rulers and their advisers, must use their cunning to concoct words so as not to be found out—

just as Odysseus does in his encounter with Polyphemus, where he pretends to be nobody. By playing with words Odysseus shows his intellectual superiority, but he is also compelled to deny his identity to escape and make his way home. The escape toward home as a realm of nonalienation is opposed to the deceitful discourse that enables the hero to succeed. The escape toward home marks the narrative purpose of most fairy tales in the Grimms' collection, and the tension in the compositional technique of fairy tales resides in the self-consciousness of the narrator, who knows that words can be used to maintain domination over nature in the interests of men but can also be employed to liberate humankind from deceitful myths that cause the enslavement of humankind. If we focus on how different male heroes in the Grimms' tales use cunning in securing their realms, we shall see that reason is used instrumentally to banish magic and establish male governance that appears to be home.

In contrast to the structural approach to fairy tales that tends to homogenize the hero according to an aesthetic function, the sociohistorical approach must try to differentiate and grasp the action of the hero in the Grimms' tales in light of his predicament—the German term *Not* (need) is often used—and social class. Moreover we must bear in mind at all times that the Grimms selected tales according to the manner in which they exemplified customary behavior and language and revealed truths about all strata of the German people and their social laws. However, as the Grimms recorded and revised the tales, there is no doubt that they framed all conflicts and normative resolutions within the general Protestant ethic and code of the bourgeois enlightenment. The quest for self-preservation in the tales—and almost all the quests are for self-preservation and the resolution of a conflict—involves adventures that show how the hero is *graced,* and how he uses his wits and reason and exhibits industriousness and valor to succeed in acquiring a fortune. Paradoxically, magic is extolled and used by the hero to ban magic. Nothing is to be left to chance at the end. Home is the overcoming of self-alienation marked by a rational closing of the narrative, which is also the rational enclosure of the future. Becoming king or prince at the end of a Grimms' tale is a socially symbolic act of achieving self-mastery—as well as mastery over outside forces that include women and nature.

How are self-mastery and mastery represented by the male heroes in the Grimms' tales? Let us glance at several examples related to one another by their rational design: resolving conflicts in a calculated way to serve the interests of male domination. The compositional strategy of the tales is closely connected to the theme of cunning and calculation.

In **"The Boy Who Set Forth to Learn about Fear,"** a peasant boy's apparent naiveté and self-restraint enable him to survive various encounters with a ghost, hanged men on a gallows, and an assortment of ghoulish creatures in a haunted castle. It is his fearlessness along with his self-control that allow him to survive, discover a treasure, and marry a princess. Whereas the peasant boy is a "pure soul," whose curiosity and adventurous spirit are rewarded—in contrast to women, who are punished for the same tendencies—the tailor in **"The Brave Little Tailor"** achieves his goals through his deft use of words, first by announcing his skills (he can kill "seven with one blow"), which are deceptive because the words are ambivalent, and then by using the spoken word to get himself out of difficulties. Like Odysseus, he is a boaster who outwits giants, dangerous animals, and a king and his court to become a king himself. In **"The Riddle,"** it is a prince this time who desires to see the world, and after escaping from a witch he uses his wits in a battle of words to pose a riddle to a princess and win her for his bride. In **"The Magic Table, the Gold Donkey, and the Club in the Sack,"** the use of cunning again is important: The tailor's youngest son diligently learns the trade of a turner and then employs his brains to outwit the innkeeper who had stolen the magic table and donkey from his brothers. Again, it is knowing how to use words that gives the hero power over others and objects. The youngest son restores his brothers' rightful property to them, and they can now lead prosperous lives. In a variation on this theme, **"The Knapsack, the Hat, and the Horn,"** the youngest of three poor brothers uses magic gifts and cunning to punish his brothers, a king, and the king's daughter, to become king himself. Knowing the right incantation gives him power to devastate his opponents. Most youngest sons are compelled to become facile with words and exploit their meanings in deceitful ways to set their own rules for attaining success. In **"The Golden Goose,"** another youngest son, known as a simpleton, reveals that his naiveté merely concealed his cunning. With the help of a dwarf and the magic goose, he tricks all those around him so that he can eventually marry a king's daughter and inherit a kingdom. In **"The King of the Golden Mountain,"** a merchant's son manages to save himself from the devil and outfoxes three giants to regain his kingdom. He becomes a ruthless, revengeful ruler at the end by commanding a magic sword to chop off all the heads of the guests at his wife's wedding—except his own, of course. The establishment of his realm is determined by his word as law. Another protagonist, the soldier in "Bearskin," also meets the devil. However, in stark contrast to the merchant's son, he displays remarkable self-control and piety for seven years by keeping his word. His reward is a bride, who exhibits patience and faithfulness, and a fortune. His self-denial and deception lead to a "cleaning up" of his own messiness followed by blessed days.

In the tales discussed thus far, we have a peasant boy, a tailor, a prince, a turner, a poor boy, a simpleton, a merchant's son, and a soldier, all of whom outwit their adversaries largely through their capacity to use words cunningly in order to deceive others and gain their objectives. The emphasis in the tales is on *cunning,* and invariably the hero orders his world and the outside world so he will not be threatened by nature, magic, or the unknown. He, the knower, who knows that he deceives through words, makes the objective world known so that he will have it at his command. In contrast to tales in which female protagonists must exhibit *silence*[11] and patience if they are to survive and wed, the male heroes must be verbally adroit and know how to use words and their wits as weapons. In most cases the protagonist as adventurer moves up in social class and improves his state of affairs. Given a chance, he uses every opportunity to economize his energies and advance himself without really giving a thought to people around him. Maria Tatar has argued that the Grimms' heroes tend to be compassionate,[12] but this is not really a striking characteristic of most heroes. They help people and animals when they believe it will be to their advantage and *expect* to be paid back in the end. More often than not, the hero is out to prove himself at all costs and to survive—and love has very little to do with his actions. (Most marriages in the eighteenth and nineteenth centuries, we should note, were based on economic arrangements and convenience.) Love and compassion are not major themes in the Grimms' tales, even though they may at times play a key role. Rather, arranging and rearranging one's life to settle down comfortably according to one's self-interests takes precedence over "noble" feelings. Survival and self-preservation—whether one is aristocrat, bourgeois, or peasant—mean acquiring, learning, and knowing how to use verbal codes to increase one's power. The tales that most attracted the Grimms as *Bildungsbürger* were those that involve the adroit use of words to gain wealth, happiness, and above all, power; these tales all show a distinct narrative bias for the underdog, the underprivileged, and those who need to display the right "civil" sense of cunning to make their way in society.

It is thus not by chance that three of the tales that captured the Grimms' imagination involved Tom Thumb: **"Thumbling," "Thumbling's Travels,"** and **"The Young Giant."** In fact, Wilhelm dealt with the *Däumling* figure in a scholarly article and commented on it in the introduction to the second printing of the 1819 edition of the ***Children's and Household Tales***:

> The simpleton is that person who is despised, inferior, and small, and if he becomes strong, he is only sucked up by giants. In this way he is close to Tom Thumb (*Däumling*). This figure is only as large as a thumb at birth and does not grow any more than that. But the determining factor with him is cleverness: he is completely cunning and deft so that he can get himself out of any dilemma because of his small stature, and he even knows how to use his size to his advantage. He makes a monkey out of everyone and likes to tease

people in a good-natured way. In general this is the nature of dwarfs. Most likely the tales about Tom Thumb emanate from the legends about dwarfs. Sometimes he is portrayed as a clever little tailor who terrifies the giants with his incisive and quick wit, kills monsters, and wins the king's daughter. Only he can solve the riddle put before him.[13]

And the tales prove Wilhelm's point. In **"Thumbling,"** the son of poor peasants allows himself to be sold so his father can gain some money. After numerous adventures in which he is almost swallowed and killed by different animals, Thumbling uses his brains to return safely to his parents. In **"Thumbling's Travels,"** the protagonist is a tailor's son and goes out into the world where he works as a journeyman, becomes a thief, and works at an inn. Finally, he too returns home, cleverly avoiding the hazards of the outside world. In **"The Young Giant,"** Thumbling is a peasant's son who is kidnapped by a giant and then becomes a giant himself (one of the few tales in which Thumbling grows). He travels about the countryside, punishes miserly masters, and fends for himself wherever he goes.

Though each one of the Tom Thumb tales differs, they all focus on the same major concerns of *The Odyssey* as discussed by Adorno and Horkheimer: self-preservation and self-advancement through the use of reason to avoid being swallowed up by the appetite of unruly natural forces. The voyage in the Thumbling tales is an apprenticeship in which the small hero learns self-control and how to control others. This is one of the reasons why Tom Thumb is related to the thief, who must become an absolute master of self-control and capable of controlling appearances and how he is seen by other people.

Theft has something to do with being deft, and the thieves in the Grimms' tales (not to be confused with the murderous robbers) are generally admired, for thievery is an art form. It involves creating an illusion, just as the Grimms, in the composition of their tales, were seeking to create an illusion—which could transform itself into an anticipatory illumination, pointing to the way the underprivileged and disadvantaged might overcome obstacles and attain happiness.

Practically all the protagonists in the Grimms' tales must learn something about the art of thievery, especially when they are confronted by ogres, giants, tyrannical kings, or witches. A classical case is the peasant boy born with a caul in **"The Devil with the Three Golden Hairs,"** who must eventually trick the devil and a king to gain a princess and a kingdom. In the three tales that focus directly on the art of thievery, **"The Thief and His Master," "The Four Skillful Brothers,"** and **"The Master Thief,"** the young man is a peasant who learns his craft in order to survive and maintain himself against "legitimate" but unjust rulers. (Obviously, the craft of thievery was one that mainly

lower-class men learned or had to learn, since other choices were not always available to them.) In **"The Thief and His Master,"** a man named Jan is concerned about his son's future and is tricked by the sexton of a church into sending his son to learn the trade of thieving. Later, however, the son uses his skills of deception and transformation to make his father a rich man. Not only does thievery pay in this tale, but the son appears to be more considerate toward his father than the sexton. In **"The Four Skillful Brothers,"** one of the sons of a poor man becomes a master thief and joins with his three gifted brothers to rescue a princess from a dragon. There is not the slightest hint of condemnation regarding the son's profession. Only in **"The Master Thief"** is there an indication that thieving might indicate a "crooked" upbringing, when a son returns home to his peasant parents and the father tells him that nothing good will come out of his profession. In fact, the father is wrong, for the son makes a fool of the count, his servants, and his pastor, and eventually leaves his home to wander about the world.

The Grimms' apparent admiration for cunning heroes was such that they could not bring themselves to condemn or punish a hero for being a thief. In another tale, entitled **"The Robber and His Sons"**[14]—which appeared in the fifth and sixth editions of *Children's and Household Tales* in 1843 and 1850, but was omitted in the final 1857 edition because it was too closely related to the Polyphemus tale in *The Odyssey*[15]—a famous retired robber/thief recounts three adventures in order to save his sons, who had disregarded his advice against becoming robbers and tried to follow in his footsteps by stealing a horse from the queen. They are captured by the queen's men, and only by telling the queen three extraordinary tales about his days as a great robber can the father gain clemency for his sons. One of the adventures concerns his entrapment in a cave by a giant (similar to Odysseus' plight with Polyphemus) and how he managed to outwit the giant by escaping in a sheepskin. Aesthetically speaking, the text as composed by Wilhelm employs a framework similar to the one used in *A Thousand and One Nights*. Here the third-person narrative shifts to the more personal first-person narrative—in effect, a strategy for emancipation, a plea. The father adroitly uses his words to conjure pictures of his unusual adventures and thereby gains the freedom of his three sons. Cunning is again exemplified in the figure of a thief as narrator, and one who is, for the Grimms, much more than a thief; for them, he represents the spirit of bourgeois entrepreneurism and civilization.

In 1857, the very year in which **"The Robber and His Sons"** was eliminated from *Children's and Household Tales,* Wilhelm held a talk in the Berlin Academy of Sciences entitled "Die Sage von Polyphem" ("The Legend of Polyphemus"),[16] in which he drew comparisons between ten similar legends and myths based on the Polyphemus material. The main point of the talk was to prove that, despite major differences between the versions, they all stemmed from a primeval myth, an *Ur-mythos,* that dealt with the origins of the world and the struggle between good and evil forces personified by a "good" dwarf or little man and an "evil" giant, whose one eye is a mark of his divine origins that he has betrayed:

> If a greater meaning is established with such references, then we can perhaps move closer toward understanding the original figure. What else do the mythical songs of primeval times celebrate but the origins of the world and, so long as the world lasts, the movements of powerful, inimical forces that never rest? They are the battles of the elements among themselves, of heaven and the underworld, of summer and winter, of day and night, that reflect the moral opposites of benediction and corruption, love and hate, joy and sadness. The opposition between the outer, terrifying natural forces and the quiet, concealed natural forces or the opposition in the moral connection between raw power and cunning deftness is expressed in the myths about giants and dwarfs. It is here that I find the original content and meaning of the Polyphemus legend, which is articulated most clearly in the nordic tradition.[17]

Though Wilhelm's theory cannot be proved, it does reveal something important about male protagonists in the Grimms' tales and the Grimms' compositional techniques in regard to moral order. The Thumbling, the simpleton, the thief, the youngest son, and the little man are all one and the same man, who serves the same aesthetic and thematic function. He is faced with unruly forces of nature and a world that is unjust or incomprehensible, and represents the moral principle of order based on reason and cunning. His task is to enlighten himself and enlighten the world. The embarkation on a voyage is like the initial stages of the narrative composition in the Grimms' work on their tales. The hero, like the Brothers Grimm, embarks to resolve conflicts and order the world according to his basic self-interests. In the case of the Grimms, the reassembling of the tales was completed in a dialogue with moral standards and ethical principles of the German *Bildungsbürgertum,* and the tales were to be published and institutionalized as an *Erziehungsbuch* (education manual) within the bourgeois public realm governed by male regulations. Each tale they heard was a speech utterance that they sought to reshape and designate generically as fable, legend, anecdote, magic fairy tale, joke, ditty, etc. While the Grimms consciously endeavored to work within the European tradition of oral storytelling, they also tried to improve the tales and shape them into authoritative representations of their view of the world. As Mikhail Bakhtin has pointed out,

> in each epoch, in each social circle, in each small world of family, friends, acquaintances, and comrades in which a human being grows and lives, there are always

authoritative utterances that set the tone—artistic, scientific, and journalistic works on which one relies, to which one refers, which are cited, imitated, and followed. . . . This is why the unique speech experience of each individual is shaped and developed in continuous and constant interaction with others' individual utterances. This experience can be characterized to some degree as the process of *assimilation*—more or less creative—of others' words (and not the words of a language). Our speech, that is, all our utterances (including creative works), is filled with others' words, varying degrees of otherness, of varying degrees of "our-own-ness," varying degrees of awareness and detachment. These words of others carry with them their own expression, their own evaluative tone, which we assimilate, rework, and re-accentuate.[18]

By appropriating oral tales largely from female informants and reworking tales from books and texts that were sent to them, the Grimms chose words, expressions, and narrative forms of development that provided for rational cohesion and a reward system that justified male domination within the bourgeois public sphere. Even when a male does not figure prominently within the action of a tale like **"Snow White," "Cinderella," "One-Eye, Two Eyes, and Three-Eyes,"** or **"The Goose Girl,"** he brings about the proper closure by rationally, morally, or cunningly ordering her world so that it becomes *his* world. The principles of the writing of the tale and the action within the tale are the same: prudence with respect to overt sexuality, industriousness with respect to forming a new world, perseverance in seeking the right words, rationalization in championing the power of enlightenment, and equality in establishing the rights of men with the principles of enlightenment and justice.

In various kinds of dialogues with others—their informants, the legal system of their day, their national heritage, the ancient Greek and Roman tradition, the Christian faith, and between themselves—the Grimms set the tone for the development of a literary language that preferred the Odyssean principle. It is not by chance that Odysseus becomes the prototype of the bourgeois entrepreneur in the nineteenth century, and the Grimms were not the only ones to champion this spirit of rational entrepreneurism and appropriation. In the Western fairy-tale tradition there is an abundance of Tom Thumbs, Jack the Giant Killers, and swineherds—Horatio Algers, explorers, pioneers, and colonialists take center stage in bourgeois novels and stories of adventurers in the nineteenth century. What marks these adventurers is the cunning manner in which they go about their business. Women, magic, nature, and raw power are put to use to guarantee harmony in accordance with the self-interest of an individual male, whose word spoken as law appears to be the last word on justice. Ultimately, what underlies the actions of the male protagonists in the Grimms' tales is a principle of instrumental reason, and if we want to attain a fuller understanding of the bourgeois appeal of the Grimms' fairy tales, we might do well to look today at our own need for control and domination of nature, and at our manly means of fairness and order in public and private realms of action.

Notes

1. Ingeborg Weber-Kellermann, ed., *Kinder- und Hausmärchen,* vol. 1 (Frankfurt am Main: Insel, 1976), 14-15.

2. Heinz Rölleke, *Die Märchen der Brüder Grimm* (Munich: Artemis, 1985), 25.

3. Jack Zipes, *Fairy Tales and the Art of Subversion: The Classical Genre for Children and the Process of Civilization* (New York: Methuen, 1983).

4. Cf. Andrea Dworkin, *Woman Hating* (New York: Dutton, 1974); Heide Göttner-Abendroth, *Die Göttin und ihr Heros* (Munich: Frauenoffensive, 1980); and the various essays in Sigrid Früh and Rainer Wehse, eds. *Die Frau im Märchen* (Kassel: Erich Röth, 1985).

5. See Jennifer Waelti-Walters, *Fairy Tales and the Female Imagination* (Montreal: Eden Press, 1982); Jack Zipes, ed., *Don't Bet on the Prince: Contemporary Feminist Fairy Tales in North America and England* (New York: Methuen, 1986); Ruth B. Bottigheimer, *Grimms' Bad Girls and Bold Boys: The Moral and Social Vision of the Tales* (New Haven: Yale University Press, 1987); Marina Warner, *From the Beast to the Blonde: On Fairy Tales and Their Tellers* (London: Chatto & Windus, 1994).

6. For two stimulating studies on this topic, see Katalin Horn, *Der aktive und der passive Märchenheld* (Basel: Schweizerische Gesellschaft für Volkskunde, 1983) and Maria M. Tatar, "Born Yesterday: Heroes in the Grimms' Tales," in *Fairy Tales and Society: Illusion, Allusion, and Paradigm,* ed. Ruth B. Bottigheimer (Philadelphia: University of Pennsylvania Press, 1986), 95-112.

7. In Früh and Wehse, eds., *Die Frau im Märchen,* 72-88.

8. Max Horkheimer and Theodor Adorno, *Dialectic of Enlightenment*; trans. John Cumming (New York: Seabury, 1972), 43-80.

9. *Ibid.,* 57.

10. *Ibid.,* 62.

11. Cf. Ruth B. Bottigheimer, "Silenced Women in the Grimms' Tales: The 'Fit' Between Fairy Tales and Society in Their Historical Context," in *Fairy Tales and Society,* ed. Ruth B. Bottigheimer, 115-131.

12. Cf. Tatar, "Born Yesterday: Heroes in the Grimms' Fairy Tales," 98-105.

13. Gustav Hinrichs, ed., *Kleinere Schriften,* vol. 1 (Berlin: Dümmlers, 1881), 356.

14. See my translation in Jacob and Wilhelm Grimm, *The Complete Fairy Tales of the Brothers Grimm* (New York: Bantam: 1987), 708-713.

15. For a comprehensive analysis of the Polyphemus tradition and the place of the Grimms' "The Robber and His Sons" within it, see Lutz Röhrich, "Die mittelalterichen Redaktionen des Polyphem-Märchens und ihr Verhältnis zur außerhomerischen Tradition," in Röhrich, *Sage und Märchen: Erzählforschung heute* (Freiburg: Herder, 1976), 234-251.

16. Gustav Hinrichs, ed. *Kleinere Schriften,* vol. 4 (Gütersloh: Bertelsmann, 1887), 428-462.

17. *Ibid.,* 461.

18. Mikhail M. Bakhtin, "The Problem of Speech Genres," in *Speech Genres and Other Late Essays,* ed. Caryl Emerson and Michael Holquist, trans. Vern W. McGee (Austin University of Texas Press, 1986), 88-89.

Bibliography

EDITIONS OF THE BROTHERS GRIMM

Altdeutsche Wälder. 3 vols. 1813-1816. Reprint. Darmstadt: Wissenschaftliche Buchgesellschaft, 1966.

Deutsche Sagen. 2 vols. 1816-18. Reprint, Dartmstadt: Wissenschaftliche Buchgesellschaft, 1972.

German Legends. Trans. Donald Ward. 2 vols. Philadelphia: Institute for the Study of Human Issues, 1981.

Kinder- und Hausmärchen. Vollständige Ausgabe in der Urfassung. Ed. Friedrich Panzer. 1st ed. Wiesbaden: Emil Vollmer, n.d.

Kinder- und Hausmärchen. Vergrößerter Nachdruck von 1812 und 1815 nach dem Handexemplar des Brüder Grimm-Museums Kassel mit sämtlichen handschriftlichen Korrekturen und Nachträgen der Brüder Grimm. Eds. Heinz Rölleke and Ulrike Marquardt. 1st ed. 2 vols with an additional notebook. Göttingen: Vandenhoeck & Ruprecht, 1986.

Kinder- und Hausmärchen. Nach der zweiten vermebrten und verbesserten Auflage von 1819. Ed. Heinz Rölleke. 2d ed. 2 vols. Cologne: Diederichs, 1982.

Kinder- und Hausmärchen gesammelt durch die Brüder Grimm. Vollständige Ausgabe auf der Grundlage der dritten Auflage (1837). Ed. Heinz Rölleke. Frankfurt am Main: Deutscher Klassiker Verlag, 1985.

Kinder- und Hausmärchen gesammelt durch die Brüder Grimm. Intr. Ingeborg Weber-Kellermann. 7th ed. 3 vols. Frankfurt am Main: Insel, 1976.

Kinder- und Hausmärchen. Ausgabe Letzter Hand mit den Originalanmerkungen der Brüder Grimm. Ed. Heinz Rölleke. 7th ed. 3 vols. Stuttgart: Philipp Reclam, 1980.

Kinder- und Hausmärchen. Nach der Großen Ausgabe von 1857, textkritisch revidiert, kommentiert und durch Register erschlossen. Ed. Hans-Jörg Uther. 7th ed. Darmstadt: Wissenschaftliche Buchgesellschaft, 1996.

Kinder- und Hausmärchen gesammelt durch die Brüder Grimm. Kleine Ausgabe von 1858. Illustr. Ludwig Peitsch. Afterword Heinz Rölleke. 10th printing. Small Ed. Frankfurt am Main: Insel, 1985.

The Complete Fairy Tales of the Brothers Grimm. Trans. and Ed. Jack Zipes. Rev. and exp. ed. New York: Bantam, 1992.

REFERENCE WORKS

Bakhtin, Mikhail M. *Speech Genres and Other Late Essays.* Ed. Caryl Emerson and Michael Holquist. Trans. Vern W. McGee. Austin: University of Texas Press, 1986.

Bottigheimer, Ruth B., ed. *Fairy Tales and Society: Illusion, Allusion, and Paradigm.* Philadelphia: University of Pennsylvania Press, 1986.

———. *Grimms' Bad Girls and Bold Boys: The Moral and Social Vision of the Tales.* New Haven: Yale University Press, 1987.

Dworkin, Andrea. *Women Hating.* New York: Dutton, 1974.

Früh, Sigrid, and Rainer Wehse, eds. *Die Frau im Märchen.* Kassel: Erich Röth, 1985.

Göttner-Abendroth, Heide. *Die Göttin und ihr Heros.* Munich: Frauenoffensive, 1980.

Horkheimer, Max, and Theodor W. Adorno. *Dialectic of Enlightenment* Trans. John Cumming. New York: Seabury Press, 1972.

Horn, Katalin. *Der aktive und der passive Märchenheld.* Basel: Schweizerische Gesellschaft für Volkskunde, 1983.

Röhrich, Lutz. *Sagen und Märchen. Erzählforschung heute.* Freiburg: Herder, 1976.

Rölleke, Heinz. *Die Märchen der Brüder Grimm.* Munich: Artemis, 1985.

Tatar, Maria M. "Born Yesterday: Heroes in the Grimms' Fairy Tales." In *Fairy Tales and Society: Illusion, Allusion, and Paradigm.* Ed. Ruth B. Bottigheimer. Philadelphia: University of Pennsylvania Press, 1986.

Waelti-Walters. *Fairy Tales and the Female Imagination.* Montreal: Eden Press, 1982.

Warner, Marina. *From the Beast to the Blonde: On Fairy Tales and Their Tellers.* London: Chatto & Windus, 1995.

Zipes, Jack. *Fairy Tales and the Art of Subversion: The Classical Genre for Children and the Process of Civilization.* London: Heinemann, 1983.

———, ed. *Don't Bet on the Prince: Contemporary Feminist Fairy Tales in North America and England.* New York: Methuen, 1986.

Donald Haase (essay date 2003)

SOURCE: Haase, Donald. "Framing the Brothers Grimm: Paratexts and Intercultural Transmission in Postwar English-Language Editions of the *Kinder- und Hausmärchen*." *Fabula* 44, nos. 1-2 (2003): 55-69.

[In the following essay, Haase explores the paratextual dimension of Anglo-American translations of Grimms' Fairy Tales, *contrasting the cultural discourse and values characterizing these translations with the linguistic-cultural agenda surrounding the Grimms' original text.]*

Humans love not only to tell stories, but to tell stories about stories. The stories that we tell each other about Grimms' fairy tales account for much of the writing that goes on in Grimm scholarship. The conventional narrative that has been constructed to explain the worldwide reception of Grimms' **Kinder- und Hausmärchen** involves a series of transformations and paradoxes that raise interesting questions. It begins with Grimms' own alleged transformation of the oral tradition into published text, a metamorphosis that ostensibly renders the audible legible between the covers of a book. When this already transformed German original is then transmitted across cultures—to Anglo-American readers, for example—that printed text undergoes another linguistic-cultural transformation, a metamorphosis that renders into English what was uniquely and historically German[1]. The translated text is now at least two removes from the Grimms' original sources, which—according to the conventional narrative—supposedly drew their authority and value from their authenticity as oral narratives of the German folk.

Given these transformations and paradoxes, we can legitimately wonder how to account for the Grimms' continuing success abroad. That is, if oral authenticity is compromised by the printed text, and if the linguistic authority of the original is compromised through translation, what value does the English edition now have? One ready answer is that Grimms' scholarly collection for the preservation of the oral tradition has been received largely as a book of children's literature for popular consumption. In fact, the collection's ultimate success reflects simultaneously the emergence of folk-lore studies and the rise of children's literature in the nineteenth century. But that intersection of national-ethnic culture with children's literary culture only intensifies questions about the intercultural transmission of Grimms' tales. How, in Anglo-American contexts, do published translations appropriate Grimms' linguistic-cultural project and endow the stories with value and authority? How, in other words, do translators, editors, and publishers—who exercise primary, if not exclusive, control over the translated texts—come to grips with the Grimms' cultural agenda in English-language publications aimed ostensibly at the Anglo-American children's-book market?

One way of addressing these questions is to consider the linguistic process of translation, that is, the manner in which the stories are translated from the German language into English. This is the route taken principally by scholars such as Martin Sutton in his book on *The Sin-Complex: A Critical Study of English Versions of the Grimms' "Kinder- und Hausmärchen" in the Nineteenth Century* (1996) and Karen Seago in her dissertation entitled *Transculturations: Making "Sleeping Beauty". The Translation of a Grimm Märchen into an English Fairy Tale in the Nineteenth Century* (1998). Although dealing with a different cultural context, it is also worth noting Cay Dollerup's book on *Tales and Translation: The Grimm Tales from Pan-Germanic Narratives to Shared International Fairytales* (1999). Dollerup's study of Danish translations of the **Kinder- und Hausmärchen** is particularly revealing because it also illuminates the extent to which paratextual characteristics help shape the production and reception of the Grimms' tales in the recipient culture. Indeed, studying the paratextual dimension of English-language translations and editions offers another, equally important method of addressing questions about the way in which Grimms' stories are appropriated, transmitted, and received across cultures. Accordingly, it is the paratextual dimension that I explore in this paper.

Much of what we know or believe about Grimms' tales comes not only from the stories, but also through paratexts. Paratext is the term used by Gérard Genette to describe those elements of a literary text that surround it and present it as a text—titles, authorial names, dedications, forewords, introductions, and so on. "[T]he paratext", according to Genette, "is what enables a text to become a book and to be offered as such to its readers and, more generally, to the public" (1997, 1). Describing the paratext as a "threshold" and citing Philippe Lejeune's reference to "a fringe of the printed text which in reality controls one's whole reading of the text", Genette goes on to say that "this fringe, always the conveyor of a commentary that is authorial or more or less legitimated by the author, constitutes a zone between text and off-text, a zone not only of transition but

also of transaction: a privileged place of a pragmatics and a strategy, of an influence on the public, an influence that—whether well or poorly understood and achieved—is at the service of a better reception for the text and a more pertinent reading of it (more pertinent, of course, in the eyes of the author and his allies)" (1997, 2). As authors—or at least authorial agents—the Grimms carefully framed their collection with a variety of significant paratexts that sought to contextualize their fairy tales and explain to the reader a multitude of relevant and often complex issues. The title, designation of the compilers, dedication, preface, and annotations were all intended to help the recipient understand the place, nature, and function of the tales in historical, political, cultural, ethnic, mythological, scholarly, and pedagogical terms. Without these paratexts legitimizing and contextualizing them, the tales would likely have been an unremarkable assemblage of disdained stories. They became texts worthy of attention and serious reception only in light of the Grimms' larger—and enormously successful—cultural project that sought to give the stories legitimacy as primary cultural documents from oral tradition (Köhler-Zülch 1993, 42 and 51).

So one measure of how translators of Grimms' stories deal with cultural issues important to the Grimms is the extent to which their translations make use (or no use) of Grimms' paratexts. In other words, the question is how translators, editors, and publishers, in order to direct their readers' attention, frame Grimms' translated stories with their own allographic, editorial paratexts—from dust jackets and titles to prefaces and notes. What sort of cultural discourse characterizes these new paratexts, and what cultural values are foregrounded for readers? Do these paratexts attempt to duplicate and transmit the Grimms' linguistic-cultural agenda, do they appropriate the tales for the culture of the intended audience, or do they attempt to lend the tales authority by re-presenting them as culturally transcendent and universal?

It is remarkable that there is no English-language edition of Grimms' fairy tales that accurately reflects in paratextual terms Grimms' own publication. In that sense Grimms' fairy tales—the **Kinder- und Hausmärchen**—has never, not once, been translated into English. If one takes the last Large Edition published in Grimms' lifetime—the well-known seventh edition—as the standard, then only Margaret Hunt's 1884 two-volume translation comes close. Hunt's translation, which aimed in no way for the children's book market, is the only English-language edition to include all the stories of that edition as well as Grimms' pioneering scholarly annotations. Hunt, however, omits Grimms' important programmatic foreword—which amounts nearly to a manifesto of folk-narrative scholarship—and replaces it with a long introduction by Andrew Lang, which frames the German tales in broader anthropological terms and supports the theory of polygenesis and thus the universality of folktales. Moreover, as Karen Seago has demonstrated (1998, chapter 8), Hunt selectively translates and glosses the Grimms' annotations where she disagrees with their theory of folktale origins, a paratextual adjustment that is entirely invisible to the unsuspecting reader who may have faith in the fidelity of Hunt's translation of the Grimms' original scholarly commentary. By suppressing the original preface and altering the annotations, Hunt's effort to provide a translation of Grimms' work for scholars is severely compromised. One searches in vain not only here, but in any so-called complete translation for the Grimms' culturally authentic foreword or annotations—or any set of original paratexts—that attempt to direct a reader's understanding of the tales. In fact, Wilhelm Grimm's prefaces were only made fully available in English in 1987 by Maria Tatar, but even then they appeared divorced from the full corpus of tales they were intended to introduce[2].

As a consequence, there is no English-language edition of the *Kinder- und Hausmärchen* that organizes, frames, and presents—or re-presents—the stories to us in the same way as the Grimms themselves published the tales as part of their cultural project. To be sure, a number of translations present themselves as 'complete'. The publisher Pantheon has reprinted Hunt's Victorian translation, as revised by James Stern and illustrated by the German exile artist Josef Scharl, many times since 1944 as *The Complete Grimm's Fairy Tales* (Hunt 1972); but that reprint lacks not only Grimms' preface (and even Andrew Lang's substitute introduction), but also Hunt's original translation of the Grimm's annotations[3]. Decoupling the Grimms' stories from their German context might have made good sense in 1944, when the Pantheon reprint first began to appear, but the fact remains that the translation is anything but 'complete'. In 1977, Ralph Manheim published *Grimms' Tales for Young and Old: The Complete Stories,* but his translation is a similarly amputated version of Grimm. In addition to ignoring all paratexts—from the prefaces to annotations—Manheim makes no effort to represent any part of the corpus of tales and versions that belong to any edition other than that of 1857. Given the developments in German Grimm scholarship occurring in the mid-1970s, particularly the publication of the tales in the Ölenberg manuscript and their 1812 counterparts (Rölleke 1975), Manheim's 1977 translation missed an opportunity to exhibit a greater awareness of the complexity involved in representing a complete picture of Grimms' work. It is indicative of Manheim's misrepresentation of Grimms' collection that his book, which is obviously based on the tales in the Grimms' seventh edition of 1857, purports to be a translation of the "Complete Kinder- und and [sic] Hausmärchen as first published in 1819" (Manheim 1977, [iv]). Manheim's errors about the first publication of Grimms' tales and

about the edition he has translated can be attributed to his use of the misleading Winkler edition (Grimm 1989) and, more importantly, his disregard for the textual history of the *Kinder- und Hausmärchen*[4]. In contrast, and on firm scholarly ground, Jack Zipes's translation, *The Complete Fairy Tales of the Brothers Grimm,* provides not only the stories of the 1857 edition, but also thirty-two tales that had been omitted from Grimms' earlier editions, as well as eight tales selected from the annotations of 1856 (Zipes 1992). In that sense, Zipes's edition does present, as he claims, "the most comprehensive translation of the Grimms' tales to date" (1992, xxxii; emphasis added)[5]. However, once again the important paratexts have been put aside. So, despite these efforts and important advances, there is no complete translation of Grimms' fairy tales in English.

It is questionable, in fact, whether there could be such a complete translation. The problem has to do with the extraordinarily difficult nature of Grimms' text. Identifying Grimms' collection as a published text—as a book—is, perhaps surprisingly, a formidable task. While we speak without qualification and generously generalize about 'Grimms' *Fairy Tales*', as if the referent of that phrase required no elaboration, the textual and editorial history of that title makes it impossible to speak definitively of a single text. In fact, Grimms' fairy tales constitute not simply a book but many books. As Grimm scholarship over the last twenty-five years has stressed, the *Kinder- und Hausmärchen* is a dynamic publishing phenomenon that existed in seventeen different authorized editions in the Grimms' lifetime alone[6]. The collection emerged over six decades and underwent ongoing editorial revisions, deletions, substitutions, and reframings. It existed simultaneously in two fundamentally different formats: the large, multivolume annotated edition, intended primarily for scholars; and the small, illustrated edition of fifty selected tales intended for wider readership. The Large Edition, which contained ultimately over two hundred stories, appeared in differing formats throughout its seven editions, with the accumulation of important frontispieces, an epigraph, appended prefaces, and a changing selection of other paratexts illuminating the Grimms' emerging conception of their work and the tales they presented. The ten Small Editions included a consistent fifty tales, but also underwent editorial revisions and included important, authorized illustrations that added another paratextual dimension to its identity. Even the annotations to the Large Edition exist in three versions—of 1812/15, 1822, and 1856. Although we tend to think of the final Large Edition as the standard of reference, it is clear that there are multiple Grimm versions of the *Kinder- und Hausmärchen* and that these are different from each other not only in light of the individual tales that make up the central text(s)—the stories—but also in light of the diverse paratexts that direct our transaction with these stories and their original editors. In the final analysis, it might even be more accurate to think of 'Grimms' *Fairy Tales*' not even as an assortment of many books, but rather as an idea—and a postmodern idea at that[7].

Even disregarding problems of language, then, translation of the *Kinder- und Hausmärchen* can be no simple matter. The relative sensitivity of translators to the complex textual issues that I just outlined tells us something about their understanding of the stories they are mediating for us. By disregarding the textual complexity of the Grimms' work and by omitting the paratexts that were so crucial to the Grimms' own publications, translators and editors dismember the collection and represent the tales for English-speaking readers without their authentic historical context. When translators and editors speak for the Grimms, whose voices are now left out of the initial transaction between reader and authorial text, they replace the Grimms' frame with their own.

There are at least three pragmatic reasons that this occurs in English-language editions. In the first place, most translations of Grimms' stories—even the so-called complete translations—are targeted, at least in part, for the juvenile book market[8]. Publishers know that neither children nor the adults who purchase these books for them will be attracted at the point of purchase by a volume that includes the complete paratextual apparatus of the Grimms' Large Edition. The book, to be sure, must speak to the potential adult purchaser, but must not appear to be a scholarly text, which is certainly how the 'complete' text would appear. This is a purely pragmatic decision having to do with the costs of producing and marketing a book[9]. Secondly, the content of Grimms' prefaces and their annotations would make it evident that the Grimms did not primarily conceive of their collection as children's literature. This would complicate publishers' marketing strategies, which in general rely heavily on positioning fairy-tale collections as children's literature. And finally, the Grimms' prefaces raise historical, nationalistic-ethnic, and scholarly issues that are usually antithetical to the translators' mission, which is to produce a text that will resonate with contemporary readers. Pragmatically, and again for reasons of targeted reception and marketability, translations are compromised by the need to negotiate a cultural transfer by producing texts to which the receiving culture will be receptive. In transferring the text from one language and culture to another, translators find themselves much in the same position as the Grimms did when transferring oral texts into the medium of print. In the Grimms' case, they opted to speak, in print, for the folk. Similarly, rather than let the Grimms speak for themselves, translators find it more convenient to re-frame the tales in their own way.

This final point is illustrated by examining how translators deal with the Grimms' methods of collecting and editing tales. The prefaces to the *Kinder- und*

Hausmärchen contain important pronouncements by the Grimms concerning their pedagogical intentions[10], as well as their editorial methods and textual alterations. Accordingly, scholarship has focused intensively on these passages to come to grips with the question of the brothers' fidelity to the oral tradition. This, too, is an issue that resists facile generalization, but the crucial point for this discussion is that in their prefaces, the Grimms admit to editorial emendations and alterations that can give us reason to suspect, not their integrity as pioneering folklorists, but the accuracy of their stories as authentic products of the oral tradition[11]. As a result of these investigations, Grimm scholarship has gained new insights into Grimms' collection as a historical phenomenon that documents the appropriation of oral tradition and early-modern print traditions by middle-class literary consciousness of the nineteenth century. Concomitantly, this historical insight has significantly discredited the appealing romance of Grimms' tales as timeless, universal myths from the anonymous folk. Increasingly, scholarship has become more comfortable with the notion that the *Kinder- und Hausmärchen* are not folktales but a form of literary adaptation, which, in one sense, would justify the exclusion of Grimms' paratexts that frame the collection as folklore.

Still, translators and editors of English-language editions have typically framed their translations with their own prefaces perpetuating this erroneous mythic view, albeit without including Grimms' paratexts. Examples are legion, and I cite only a few to demonstrate one important way in which this framing occurs. My examples—which come from the postwar/Cold-War period—focus on a deceptive but appealing strategy that has evolved to make sense of the Grimms' own contradictory claims about the cultural authenticity of their works. Confronted with evidence of Grimms' editorial revisions, new framers of the tales have sought to rationalize the presence of the brothers' voice in the text as a superior form of the folk's own voice. Frances Clarke Sayers, writing in 1968, even cites the Grimms' admission that "the mode of telling and carrying out particular details is principally due to us"—that is, that they did in fact have a hand in the narration and composition of the tales. Yet Sayers introduces this important evidence of the Grimms' literary intrusions with a naive insistence on their fidelity to the folk voice: "The nineteenth century was the century in which folklore was acknowledged by the respectable and lettered folk. Poets, novelists, and storytellers; sociologists and theologians used and manipulated it, each to his own end. The difference with the Brothers Grimm was that they recognized the depth and breadth of the tales and were determined to transfer the integrity of their origins from the storytellers' tongues (the told story) to the preserving alchemy of print, as directly as possible, with no distortion of the cultivated and literary mind to soften the matter or invent interpolations of its own." Sayers manages this compelling slight of hand by referring to "the preserving alchemy of print", a meaningless phrase that wants us to believe that print can magically transform orality without a mediating impact. It cannot, of course; and the Grimms' editing makes it clear that they did not preserve the integrity of the oral tradition, especially when many of their texts had already originated in printed sources. As Linda Dégh has noted, the Grimms' source texts, including the orally based texts, were frequently already very much of literary origin, and it was only through their claims—presented in paratexts—that the tales assumed oral status: "Although the Grimm collection [. . .] depends on literary, sometimes translated sources, even if the source was second-hand, a reteller has read it from a book or heard it from another reader who read it from a book, its authors claim folk (primitive, rustic, illiterate) origin. With the Grimms and their supporters, the Märchen (the same body of complex tales) becomes celebrated as ancestral German heritage preserved by the peasant folk" (1990, 164).

Significantly, translators and editors who uphold the idea of oral authenticity and peasant origins typically decouple those concepts from cultural authenticity or cultural specificity—what Dégh referred to as "ancestral German heritage". Using a strategy similar to that of Sayers, the editor of a 1966 reprint of Lucy Crane's translation entitled **Household Stories** (1882) upholds the idea of Grimms' fidelity to the oral tradition while appearing to acknowledge their hand in editing: "If tape recorders had been available at the beginning of the nineteenth century the work of the Brothers Grimm would have been a lot easier. Chances are, however, that all of the generations who have enjoyed the fruits of that work would have been the losers thereby. [. . . M]uch has been made of the fact that they transcribed their tales just as they came from the lips of the people. This [. . .] is not so. A tape recorder could have done that. It took the brothers over thirteen years to collect the tales that appear in the volume you now hold and while every one of them is an authentic folk tale they have been transmuted into true literature by the humanity, love and poetic feeling of the Brothers Grimm" (G. H. 1966). Paralleling Sayers's verbal legerdemain, this editor has reclaimed the tales' discredited oral authenticity by simply declaring the very methods that deprive the stories of their claim to authenticity to be superior forms of preserving authenticity. Readers are actually encouraged to believe that Grimms' editing is more accurate than a tape recording for preserving the voice of the folk and has—like Sayers's alchemy—transformed the tales into an even higher form of humanity. This rhetorical move erases the cultural specificity of the tales and ascribes universal humanity to the authentic folk voice.

A nearly identical strategy and rationalization are used by Ralph Manheim in his 1977 translation, **Grimms' Tales for Young and Old.** In his *Translator's Preface,* Manheim writes the following: "Some students of folklore have found fault with the Grimm brothers for 'improving' on the tales they collected. The Grimms themselves claimed to have taken down the stories faithfully. Of course they improved on the spoken word; some storytellers are fluent, others hem and haw, and from the storytelling point of view there would seem to be no point in recording their hemming and hawing. But at the same time the Grimms were astonishingly faithful [. . .]. More important—and this, I believe, is the greatest mark of their genius—they make us hear the voices of the individual storytellers, and much more clearly I am sure than if they had been two tape recorders. In the German text the human voice [. . .] is a natural human voice, speaking as someone might speak [. . .]" (1977, 1). There are several rhetorical strategies at work here, but the most significant in the context I have developed is Manheim's appeal to a higher form of fidelity. That is, like the editor above, Manheim, sensing that the battle over fidelity is lost, shifts the discourse of the debate by equating the Grimms' very failure to be faithful to the oral tradition with true faithfulness to it. Drawing on the same tape recorder motif we saw earlier, Manheim irrationally declares that the Grimms have been more faithful to the oral tradition than if they had had the audio-recording technology to achieve that fidelity. This has the effect of helping us forget that the print technology on which the Grimms relied is in fact a technology. This myth of the 'natural' also turns our attention to the "voices of the individual storytellers", who speak more clearly when Grimms act as ventriloquists and speak for them. And ultimately Manheim invokes "the human voice" as "a natural human voice", thus once again naturalizing and universalizing the tales in the name of humanity.

These examples reveal a tendency among translators to re-frame Grimms' stories in ways that preserve the myth of their natural origin and their universal, transcendent nature while simultaneously ignoring their cultural specificity. Stripping the Grimms' collection of its original paratexts is a pragmatic marketing decision based on the understanding that fairy tales have a wider appeal when dehistoricized and presented not as cultural artifacts but as natural transcultural possessions. The allographic paratexts provided by translators and editors reflect this same universalizing tendency. Their introductions and prefaces frequently attempt to direct readers' attention away from historical facts that discredit the mythic origins of the tales and to portray the stories as impersonal, ahistorical expressions of a higher humanity. Marketing, however, is only one motive driving this strategic substitution of paratexts.

While English-language paratexts invoke the myth of the folk and of oral authenticity to lend the translated tales authority, they simultaneously erase the German voice by substituting a universal human voice. Given this act of ventriloquism, we can ask whether this erasure and re-appropriation may be viewed as an act of cultural colonialism. Although one would not typically think of Anglo-American-German cultural relations in a colonial or postcolonial context, it is useful to recall that the principal examples presented here are from English-language editions published during the postwar era and in the wake of British and American occupation. Just as postwar German editions attempted to recuperate the Grimms from the damage done by their conscription into the service of National-Socialist folklore and pedagogy[12], so did translations produced by occupying cultures attempt to eradicate the tales' German character by reappropriating them in the name of a higher humanity. Such is the strategy in a 1959 retelling of *Grimm's Fairy Tales* by Amabel Williams-Ellis, who uses a biographical note to defuse the Grimms' identity as German nationalists by reclaiming their tales in the name of humankind. "German patriots though they were", she writes in this postwar London publication, "[the brothers] would have been glad to know that later research suggests that this [worldwide diffusion of the tales] is in fact a humble proof of the brotherhood of man" (Williams-Ellis 1959, 333).

In his essay on *Memory and Cultural Translation,* Gabriel Motzkin notes that, "The tendency to the universalization of the collective memory has been present since antiquity, but it has been [. . .] accelerated by historical events that impinge on all peoples. All the nations that fought in the Second World War are defined by their memory of that war, however great the differences between their memories. Except for the Germans, the Germans are the other for all the peoples who fought in the war on either side, even if the Germans are a different other for each of the respective peoples" (1996, 274). I would argue that the tendency to universalize the Grimms' tales in the postwar era derives significantly from the war itself and from the Anglo-American attitude toward the German as the other—an other who must be dominated, tamed, and civilized. This form of colonialist thinking and control extended even to Grimms' fairy tales, which in eyes of the British occupying forces had contributed to the barbaric behavior of the Germans. Such were the hysterical claims of T. J. Leonard in his infamous 1947 indictment, *First Steps in Cruelty,* published in the *British Zone Review.* To dehistoricize and denationalize the Grimms' stories, the tales had to be presented not as the narratives of a specifically Germanic people, but as a collection that transcended its origins and evinced an anonymous humanity. The *Kinder- und Hausmärchen,* which were presented as the creation of—as it were—a German 'Volk ohne Buch', had simultaneously to become for its postwar Anglo-American audiences a 'Buch ohne Volk'.

There is a difference, of course, between misunderstanding and misrepresenting Grimms' tales as a strategy of cultural appropriation, domination, and homogenization, on the one hand, and intentionally reframing them as a site of intercultural contact and hybridization, on the other. In today's global context in the post-postwar era and at a time when the multicultural nature of western societies is becoming increasingly recognized, the tendency to explore and underscore the intercultural connections of Grimms' collection grows[13]. In these situations there are a similar tendency and new reason to omit original paratextual materials—not only in English-language translations, but also in post-unification-era German editions. For example, Hans-Jörg Uther's valuable edition of the *Kinder- und Hausmärchen* includes a volume of his own commentary that emphasizes the stories' international variants and reception (Uther 1996). In another internationally oriented project—*Grimms Märchen International*—Ingrid Tomkowiak and Ulrich Marzolph have reprinted ten Grimm tales in conjunction with variants from within and beyond Europe (Tomkowiak/Marzolph 1996). Most recently, if we return to English-language texts, in an anthology entitled *The Great Fairy Tale Tradition,* Jack Zipes (2001) has surrounded English translations of Grimm tales with translations of French and Italian literary variants by both men and women—a Eurocentric project to be sure, but one that simultaneously historicizes the Grimms' stories and relativizes their traditionally canonical position within a more inclusive multicultural and less gendered context. Moreover, Zipes's essay on *Cross-Cultural Connections and the Contamination of the Classical Fairy Tale,* which helps to frame the anthologized tales, reasserts the cultural specificity of individual tales while stressing that "they contain 'universal' motifs and components that the writers borrowed consciously and unconsciously from other cultures in an endeavor to imbue their symbolical stories with very specific commentaries on the mores and manners of their time" (Zipes 2001, 845). Resurrecting the term 'contamination', Zipes rejects the idea of folktale or fairy-tale purity and emphasizes the role of cross-cultural contamination—what we might want to call instead 'hybridization'—as a phenomenon that is essential for the continuing production, transmission, and reception of the fairy tale. "Though we do not realize it", Zipes argues, "we bring ourselves closer to people from many different cultures through the cross-cultural connections of the tales, even though we endow them with our own specific individual and cultural meanings as we appropriate them" (2001, 868).

As suggested by these final examples from the postunification era, the notes, titles, and essays that frame these recent editions of Grimms' tales do not seek to camou-flage the act of cultural appropriation or to erase the tales' historicity and specific cultural context. Nor do they substitute for the specifically cultural the vague idea of a homogenous humanity onto which we project our own cultural identity. Instead, these recent efforts to view Grimms' tales in international and cross-cultural contexts underscore difference and hybridity in cross-cultural transactions.

If paratexts exist, as Genette notes, in a zone of "trans-action: a privileged place of a pragmatics and a strat-egy, of an influence on the public, an influence that [. . .] is at the service of a better reception for the text and a more pertinent reading of it", then paratextual de-vices in fairy-tale translations and editions may be more important in the tales' reception than the *märchen* them-selves. And because they have a public impact on how readers understand, respond to, and evaluate written cultural artifacts, authorial and editorial paratexts have a social, cultural, and political role. Engaged in a con-tinuing debate about the identity and hierarchy of cul-tures, the paratexts that present Grimms' stories seek to direct and capture the reader's allegiance in a struggle over the tales' authority, control, and ownership[14], and—most fundamentally—in a struggle over the stories that we tell each other about them.

Notes

Paper presented at the 13th conference of the Interna-tional Society for Folk Narrative Research, July 16-20, 2001, Melbourne, Australia.

1. For a discussion of how translators attempt to ne-gotiate the transformation of Grimms' language into English, see Alderson 1993; Seago 1998; and Sutton 1996. The path into another language is not always direct, as pointed out by Tomkowiak, who notes that "Not all [. . .] translations are based on German copies[.] Japanese and South American translators for instance, frequently used English versions, some translations into Russian are based on French editions" (1987, 202). This clearly further complicates the question of trans-mission.

2. In her 1987 study of the Grimms' tales, Tatar made the prefaces to the two volumes of the first edition (1812/15) and the preface to the second edition (1819) available for the first time in full English translation (Tatar 1987, 203-233). In 1996, Gumbrecht and Schnapp also published an anno-tated English translation of the 1819 preface. They note that because of "the broad international re-ception of [the *Kinder- und Hausmärchen*] as a reader for children" the preface "has not been available in a modern English translation that gives attention to its singular historical impor-

tance" despite its standing as "one of the outstand-ing foundational documents for the academic dis-cipline of literary studies [. . .]" (Gumbrecht/ Schnapp 1996, 475). Gumbrecht and Schnapp apparently overlooked Tatar's earlier translation. Moreover, they claim to have identified a transla-tion of the preface in Edgar Taylor's translation of *German Popular Stories* (1823/26). While correct that Taylor's translation of Grimms' tales "is not available at most university libraries", they are mistaken that it includes a translation of Grimms' preface (Gumbrecht/Schnapp 1996, 488, note 1). Earlier, Peppard had provided an abbreviated translation of the 1812 preface in his biography of the Grimms (Peppard 1971, 53-55).

3. The Pantheon Hunt translation is framed by an in-troduction by Padraic Colum, which notes that "We have another past besides the past that his-tory tells us about [. . .]" (Hunt 1972, xiv), and a "Folkloristic Commentary" by Joseph Campbell, which concludes that "The folk tale is the primer of the picture-language of the soul" (Hunt 1972, 864).

4. Manheim notes that he has used the "Winkler-Verlag edition" (Manheim 1977, [iv]). This popu-lar edition (Grimm 1989) has given more than one reader the impression that it reprints the Grimms' second edition of 1819 due to the fact that the principal introductory paratext in even later edi-tions of the *Kinder- und Hausmärchen* is the pref-ace dated 1819; cf. the caution expressed in Tatar 1987, xxii.

5. However, it is not quite accurate that all these tales appear here "in English for the first time" (Zipes 1992, xxxii). Selected Grimm tales, other than those from the 1857 edition, had been trans-lated by Ruth Michaelis-Jena and Arthur Ratcliff; see Michaelis-Jena/Ratcliff 1956; and Michaelis-Jena/Ratcliff 1960.

6. The philological complexity of Grimms' texts is evidenced by the challenge scholars face in creat-ing an historical-critical edition of the tales, as demonstrated by Bluhm 1995, 59-76; see also the various editions of Grimms' tales by Rölleke (1975; 1982; 1984; 1985a; 1985b; 1986; 1987; 1989). For a concise description of the complexity of the Grimms' texts, see Rölleke 1985b, 1178-1180.

7. On Grimms' tales in postmodern contexts, see Walsh 2001. On 'Grimms' Fairy Tales' as an idea, i.e., as a variable "lexical signifier [that] carries a changing array of signifieds, different for each in-dividual imagination that conceives of it", see ibid., 18f.

8. My specific arguments here would not apply nec-essarily to all translations, of course. Zipes's im-

portant translation (1992), for example, does omit the Grimms' authorized paratexts, but provides its own scholarly apparatus that critically addresses the work's textual complexity, sociohistorical context, and editorial methods. Still, the translation does pursue its own critical agenda, as does any publication, scholarly or popular.

9. On the packaging of Grimms' tales for the children's book market, see Hearne 1988.

10. See Steinlein 1987, 117-120.

11. For diverse views of the issues related to Grimms' editorial methods, including the nature of their sources and informants, as well as questions of authenticity and fidelity, see: Bluhm 1995, 1-24; Jones 1991, Rölleke 2000; Sacchetto 1990; and Tatar 1987. For a discussion of orality and authenticity as presented within the framework of nineteenth-century collections of fairy tales and legends, see Köhler-Zülch 1999.

12. On the role of folklore and fairy tales in Nazi Germany, see Bausinger 1965; Kamenetsky 1977; and Zipes 1983, 134-169. On the postwar German reception of Grimms' tales, see Zipes 1993.

13. On the necessity of pursuing intercultural issues in Grimms' work, see Haase 1999.

14. On the question of cultural ownership of fairy tales, see Haase 1993a.

References

Alderson, Brian: The Spoken and the Read: German Popular Stories and English Popular Diction. In: Haase 1993b, 59-77.

Bausinger, Hermann: Volksideologie und Volksforschung: Zur nationalsozialistischen Volkskunde. In: Zeitschrift für Volkskunde 61 (1965) 177-204.

Bluhm, Lothar: Grimm-Philologie: Beiträge zur Märchenforschung und Wissenschaftsgeschichte. Hildesheim 1995.

Dégh, Linda: The Variant and the Folklorization Process in Märchen and Legend. In: Görög-Karady, Veronika (ed.): D'un conte . . . à l'autre: La variabilité dans la littérature orale. Paris 1990, 161-173.

Dollerup, Cay: Tales and Translation: The Grimm Tales from Pan-Germanic Narratives to Shared International Fairytales. Amsterdam 1999.

Genette, Gérard: Paratexts: Thresholds of Interpretation. Trans. Jane E. Lewin. Cambridge 1997.

Grimm, Jacob and Wilhelm: Kinder- und Hausmärchen. München 1989.

Gumbrecht, Hans Ulrich/Schnapp, Jeffrey T. (trans./eds.): Preface to Kinder- und Hausmärchen gesammelt durch die Brüder Grimm (1819). In: Bloch, R. Howard/Nichols, Stephen G. (eds.): Medievalism and the Modernist Temper. Baltimore 1996, 475-492.

H., G.: From the Editor to the Reader. In: Crane, Lucy (trans.): Household Stories from the Collection of the Brothers Grimm [1882]. Ann Arbor 1966, no pagination.

Haase, Donald: Yours, Mine, or Ours? Perrault, the Brothers Grimm, and the Ownership of Fairy Tales. In: Blatt, Gloria (ed.): Once Upon a Folktale: Capturing the Folklore Process with Children. New York 1993, 63-77 (reprint in: Merveilles et contes 7 [1993] 383-402) (= Haase 1993a).

id. (ed.): The Reception of Grimms' Fairy Tales: Responses, Reactions, Revisions. Detroit 1993 (= Haase 1993b).

id.: Re-Viewing the Grimm Corpus: Grimm Scholarship in an Era of Celebrations. In: Monatshefte 91 (1999) 121-131.

Hearne, Betsy: Booking the Brothers Grimm: Art, Adaptations, and Economics. In: McGlathery, James M. (ed.): The Brothers Grimm and Folktale. Urbana 1988, 220-233.

Hunt, Margaret (trans.): Grimm's Household Tales 1-2. London 1884 (reprint Detroit 1968).

ead. (trans.): The Complete Grimm's Fairy Tales. Revised by James Stern (1944). New York 1972.

Jones, Steven Swann: In Defense of the Grimms: The Aesthetics of Style in Oral and Printed Folktale Texts. In: Southern Folklore 48 (1991) 255-274.

Kamenetsky, Christa: Folktale and Ideology in the Third Reich. In: Journal of American Folklore 90 (1977) 168-178.

Köhler-Zülch, Ines: Heinrich Pröhle: A Successor to the Brothers Grimm. In: Haase 1993b, 41-58.

ead.: Der Diskurs über den Ton: Zur Präsentation von Märchen und Sagen in Sammlungen des 19. Jahrhunderts. In: Schmitt, Christoph (ed.): Homo narrans: Studien zur populären Erzählkultur. Festschrift für Siegfried Neumann zum 65. Geburtstag. Münster/New York 1999, 25-50.

Lang, Andrew: Introduction: Household Tales; Their Origins, Diffusion, and Relations to the Higher Myths. In: Hunt 1884, vol. 1, ix-lxxv.

Leonard, T. J.: First Steps in Cruelty. In: British Zone Review: A Fortnightly Review of the Activities of the Control Commission for Germany (B.E.) and Military Government 1, 37 (1947) 10-13.

Manheim, Ralph (trans.): Grimms' Tales for Young and Old: The Complete Stories. New York 1977.

Michaelis-Jena, Ruth/Ratcliff, Arthur (trans.): Grimms' Other Tales. Selected by Wilhelm Hansen. London 1956 (reprint Edinburgh 1984).

iid. (trans./eds.): New Tales from Grimm. Edinburgh 1960.

Motzkin, Gabriel: Memory and Cultural Translation. In: Budick, Sanford/Iser, Wolfgang (eds.): The Translatability of Cultures: Figurations of the Space Between. Stanford 1996, 265-281, 343.

Peppard, Murray B.: Paths through the Forest: A Biography of the Brothers Grimm. New York 1971.

Rölleke, Heinz (ed.): Die älteste Märchensammlung der Brüder Grimm: Synopse der handschriftlichen Urfassung von 1810 und der Erstdrucke von 1812. Cologny-Genève 1975.

id. (ed.): Kinder- und Hausmärchen 1-2: Nach der 2. vermehrten und verbesserten Auflage von 1819. Köln 1982.

id. (ed.): Kinder- und Hausmärchen 1-3: Ausgabe letzter Hand mit den Originalanmerkungen der Brüder Grimm. Stuttgart 1984.

id. (ed.): Kinder- und Hausmärchen gesammelt durch die Brüder Grimm: Kleine Ausgabe von 1858. Frankfurt am Main 1985 (= Rölleke 1985a).

id. (ed.): Kinder- und Hausmärchen gesammelt durch die Brüder Grimm: Vollständige Ausgabe auf der Grundlage der dritten Auflage (1837). Frankfurt am Main 1985 (= Rölleke 1985b).

id. (ed., in collaboration with Ulrike Marquardt): Kinder- und Hausmärchen gesammelt durch die Brüder Grimm 1-2 + Ergänzungsheft: Vergrößerter Nachdruck der zweibändigen Erstausgabe von 1812 und 1815. Göttingen 1986.

id. (ed.): Unbekannte Märchen von Wilhelm und Jacob Grimm. Köln 1987.

id. (ed.): Die wahren Märchen der Brüder Grimm. Frankfurt am Main 1989.

id.: Die Märchen der Brüder Grimm: Quellen und Studien. Trier 2000.

Sacchetto, Claudia: Deutsche Märchen zwischen J. K. A. Musäus und den Brüdern Grimm. In: Annali di Ca' Foscari 29, 1-2 (1990) 265-297.

Sayers, Frances Clarke: Introduction In: Grimm's Fairy Tales. Based on the Frances Jenkins Olcott edition of the English translation by Margaret Hunt. Chicago 1968, no pagination.

Seago, Karen: Transculturations: Making "Sleeping Beauty". The Translation of a Grimm Märchen into an English Fairy Tale in the Nineteenth Century. Diss. London 1998.

Steinlein, Rüdiger: Die domestizierte Phantasie: Studien zur Kinderliteratur, Kinderlektüre und Literaturpädagogik des 18. und frühen 19. Jahrhunderts. Heidelberg 1987.

Sutton, Martin: The Sin-Complex: A Critical Study of English Versions of the Grimms' Kinder- und Hausmärchen in the Nineteenth Century. Kassel 1996.

Tatar, Maria: The Hard Facts of the Grimms' Fairy Tales. Princeton 1987.

Tomkowiak, Ingrid: Grimms' Household Tales Abroad: Some Aspects of Cultural Mediation. In: German Studies in India 11, 4 (1987) 198-207.

ead./Marzolph, Ulrich (eds.): Grimms Märchen International 1-2: Zehn der bekanntesten Grimmschen Märchen und ihre europäischen und außereuropäischen Verwandten. Paderborn 1996.

Uther, Hans-Jörg (ed.): Kinder- und Hausmärchen 1-4: Nach der Großen Ausgabe von 1857, textkritisch revidiert, kommentiert und durch Register erschlossen. München 1996.

Walsh, Michael G.: Grimms' Kinder- und Hausmärchen in Postmodern Contexts. Diss. Detroit 2001.

Williams-Ellis, Amabel: Grimm's Fairy Tales. London 1959.

Zipes, Jack: Fairy Tales and the Art of Subversion: The Classical Genre for Children and the Process of Civilization. New York 1983.

id. (trans.): The Complete Fairy Tales of the Brothers Grimm. Expanded edition. New York 1992.

id.: The Struggle for the Grimms' Throne: The Legacy of the Grimms' Tales in the FRG and GDR since 1945. In: Haase 1993b, 167-206.

id. (ed.): The Great Fairy Tale Tradition: From Straparola and Basile to the Brothers Grimm. New York 2001.

Orrin W. Robinson (essay date winter 2004)

SOURCE: Robinson, Orrin W. "Rhymes and Reasons in the Grimms' *Kinder- und Hausmärchen*." *The German Quarterly* 77, no. 1 (winter 2004): 47-58.

[*In the following essay, Robinson examines the use and function of poetry in* Grimms' Fairy Tales *as one means of authenticating their distinctive German character, comparing linguistic aspects of tales from originally German sources with those of adaptations designed to seem German.*]

As the only linguist in a German Department filled with scholars of literature and culture, I have occasionally dabbled in literature and culture myself. My main dabble in the past few years has been a freshman seminar on the Brothers Grimm and their fairy tales. Like a literary scholar, I have addressed with the students questions concerning the cultural context in which the tales were written, their oral and/or written sources, and the values that may or may not be revealed in them. I have approached them from a number of different theoretical perspectives, including feminist and psychoanalytic ones.

As a linguist, however, I am ultimately interested in the Grimms' fairy tales for the linguistic, or, in this context, philological issues they raise. My particular interest for the purpose of this article has to do with the ways in which dialect phenomena, rather than or in addition to more standard forms, are manipulated in the fairy tales to achieve the goals of the Brothers Grimm.

It has long been recognized that the Brothers Grimm did not arrive at their world-famous fairy-tale collection by slogging through the fields, woods, and villages of German-speaking Europe, eliciting age-old folktales from peasant farmers and old spinning ladies.[1] Many of their sources are demonstrably literary, their informants were frequently acquaintances, and many of the tales are not even exclusively German. Furthermore, the *Kinder- und Hausmärchen* (*KHM*) went through seven editions while at least one Grimm was still alive, and the differences between, indeed developments in, the successive versions of the collection are wide-ranging and striking.

Nevertheless, the argument has been made, and I will reinforce it here, that the Grimms tried to give to their tales a distinctively German, and in fact, frequently, a regional German character. Indeed, to strengthen their claim for the Germanness of these tales, the Grimms obviously relied on their talents as folklorists and linguists not to actually forge, but rather to edit and add to the tales, and to emphasize aspects of them that would buttress their "authenticity."

Heinz Rölleke and his students (Rölleke 1988) have argued persuasively that one of the things the Grimms (especially Wilhelm Grimm) did which had this folkloristic effect was to add over the years hundreds of independently collected sayings and proverbs to the body of the tales. To quote Rölleke:

> Wilhelm Grimm hat gerade durch die Interpolation der dem Märchen als wesensverwandt empfundenen Parömien das meiste für die ungeheure Volkstümlichkeit seiner Textgestaltung und damit zweifellos auch einen unverächtlichen Beitrag zur Revitalisierung volkstümlichen Sprachguts geleistet.
>
> (1988: 20)

Without denying the great importance of such incorporations to the "Volkstümlichkeit" of the tales, I argue here that the Grimms used other strategies that may have played an equally important role in lending the tales a more authentic, and more oral, cast. Specifically, I examine the use of verse in their stories.

I begin with tales for which there exist clear literary sources, in order to establish those elements which in the Grimms' judgment added not only to the authenticity of a tale, but also to the likelihood of a positive reception by a general German audience. To this end, a comparative analysis of those aspects that they kept from a preexisting tale with those that they changed is called for.

When comparing the literary sources for these tales with the versions presented by the Brothers Grimm, it becomes obvious that in terms of narrative, prose is favored over verse. This may be illustrated with tale #147 **"Das junggeglühte Männlein,"** the original coming from Hans Sachs. I have presented the original, in rhymed couplets, first and further to the left, while the Grimm version from the seventh and final edition is indented:

> (Sagt "Weil Christus auff erden gieng",)
> Kehrt er eins Tags mit Petro ein,
> Woltn bey eim Schmid zu Herberg sein,
> Der nams willig zu Herberg an.
> Nun kam ein armer Bettelman
> Hinein gangen an zweyen Krucken
> Mit grawen haar und bogem rucken
> Und mit dem alter hart beschwert,
> Das Allmuß von dem Schmid begehrt.
>
> > Zur Zeit, da unser Herr noch auf Erden ging,
> > kehrte er eines Abends mit dem heiligen Petrus
> > bei einem Schmied ein
> > Und bekam willig Herberge.
> > Nun geschah's, daß ein armer Bettelmann,
> > von Alter und Gebrechen hart gedruckt
> > in dieses Haus kam
> > Und vom Schmied Almosen forderte.
>
> (cited in Rölleke 1998: 206-07)

Though I have presented the Grimm version in verse format (to capture the correspondence between the two versions) this fragment is not in rhymed verse. In the *KHM* this is entirely a prose story, without a trace of rhyme. In general, as stated above, the Grimms did not value verse in their tales for the straightforward telling of a story, however fantastic the story might be. Indeed, although many of the tales are derived more or less directly from literary sources that are entirely poetic (cf. Rölleke 1998), there is not a *single* case in which the result is even largely poetic in the Grimm versions.

This is not to say that poetic form is unimportant for the Grimms' fairy tales. As I will argue below, poetry is certainly important for the Grimms, but it serves specific functions, whether in the tales with more obvious literary sources, or in those with less obvious literary sources, or indeed oral ones. This brings us back, then, to one of the main themes of this article, namely just *how* it was that the Grimms strove to give their tales an authentic German flavor.

One way to make a fairy tale seem authentic was to render it in some form of German dialect. How could a story narrated in a German dialect not be German? This strategy can in fact be found in the *KHM,* but relatively rarely. I give below a short selection from one of the most famous such tales, #19 **"Von dem Fischer und syner Fru."** This tale, originally composed in Pomeranian dialect (i.e., Eastern Low German) by the painter Runge, is taken over in the Grimms' collection almost without change, though based upon several divergent editions of Runge's story:[2]

> "Ga doch", säd de Fru, "he kan dat recht goot un dait dat geern; ga du man hen." Dem Mann wöör syn hart so swoor, und wull nich; he säd by sik sülven: "Dat is nich recht", he güng awerst doch hen.
>
> As he an de See köhm, wöör dat Water ganß vigelett un dunkelblau un grau un dick, un goor nich meer so gröön un geel, doch wöör't noch still. Do güng he staan un säd:

> > Manntje, Manntje, Timpe Te,
> > Buttje, Buttje in der See,
> > myne Fru, de Ilsebill,
> > will nich so, as ik wol will.

> (Grimm v. 1: 121)

As a result of this strategy, the story becomes almost incomprehensible for most Germans.[3] It was, therefore, not a strategy that the Grimms followed often.

A more effective strategy, as illustrated in the quotation from tale #198 **"Jungfrau Maleen"** below, was to keep the *prose* text in more or less Standard German, but to insert dialect poetry in order to buttress authenticity:

> Der falschen Braut ward zur Vergeltung der Kopf abgeschlagen.
>
> Der Turn, welchem die Jungfrau Maleen gesessen hatte, stand noch lange Zeit, und wenn die Kinder vorübergingen, so sangen sie:

> > Kling, klang, kloria,
> > wer sitt in dissen Toria?
> > Dar sitt en Königsdochter in,
> > die kann ik nich to seen Krygn.
> > De Muer, de will nich bräken,
> > de Steen, de will nich stechen.
> > Hänschen mit de bunte Jak,
> > kumm unn folg my achterna.

> (Rölleke 1998: 536-37)

In this particular instance, the Grimms follow their source and copy all the verse, which mostly rhymes. The Grimms accidentally change one word in the poem into Standard German ("stäken" to "stechen"), which then does not rhyme. In contrast, the unsatisfactory rhyme of the last two lines is taken directly from their source.

The use of dialect still makes the poem hard to follow, even if the story, in Standard German, is comprehensible. One solution to this kind of problem is to modify the inserted poems in the direction of the Standard, while still retaining dialect characteristics. A prime example can be found in #119 **"Die Sieben Schwaben"** below, where the original poem is first, the Grimms' modification indented:

> Stoahst Zueah in allar Schwoaba Nahma,
> Sonscht weünsch i, dass ihr mächt erlahma.
> · · · · ·
>
> Bey Elament, du hauscht gueat schwätza.
> Du bischt dear leatzt beym Dracha hetza.

> > Stoß zu in aller Schwabe Name,
> > sonst wünsch i, daß ihr möcht erlahme.
> > · · · · ·
> >
> > Beim Element, du hast gut schwätze,
> > bischt stets der letzscht beim Drachehetze.

> (Rölleke 1998, 124-27)

As with the Low German cases considered earlier, the poems above employ a German that is far from Standard. Nevertheless, the poems also contain changes toward a more Standard German. The Swabian diphthongs *oa* corresponding to Standard long *o* (and here also long *a*) and *uea* for Standard long *u* are rejected, as are the vowels in *weünsch, mächt,* and *hauscht.* What the Grimms kept are elements which they clearly saw as stereotypically Swabian, without harming the comprehensibility of the couplets: Loss of final *-n* in endings, *i* for *ich,* internal *scht* for *st.* Notable about the latter, however, is that they do not keep the *scht* in *hast,* perhaps because it would hinder comprehension, and add a *sch* compared to the original in *letzscht.* Overall, it seems clear that the Grimms try to capture the dialect flavor of the dialogue without worrying much about detailed linguistic accuracy.

Importantly, words that rhyme in the original text also rhyme in the Grimms' rendition. This is true even if the spelling of the rhyming words is different, as in *schwätze* and *-hetze* above, or *Streit* and *Leut* below:

> So Ziecht dann hertzhafft an de streit,
> Hieran erkennt man tapfre Leüth.
> > So zieht dann herzhaft in den Streit,
> > hieran erkennt man tapfre Leut.

> (Rölleke 1998:126-27)

It is important to note that the latter rhyme exists in Swabia, and indeed in much of Germany, because formerly front rounded vowels have lost their rounding in these language variants, even though a conservative writing system, supported by the Standard, keeps up a distinction.

It may be useful to document how important a good rhyme was to the Grimms, with what approaches a totally Standard-language text. Note the source poem for #186 **"Die wahre Braut,"** and its ultimate form in the seventh edition:

> 'kälbchen, knie nieder
> und vergiss deiner ehre nicht, wie der
> prinz Lassmann die arme Helene vergass,
> als sie unter der grünen linde sass'

>> Kälbchen, Kälbchen, knie nieder,
>> vergiß nicht deine Hirtin wieder,
>> wie der Königssohn die Braut vergaß,
>> die unter der grünen Linde saß.

>> (Rölleke 1998:448-49)

Here, in addition to evening out the scansion, the Grimms have eliminated an obnoxious rhyme dependent on ending a poetic line at an absent syntactic boundary.

The examples given above, however, raise an obvious issue concerning the Grimms' strategy: If they preserved general comprehensibility by using more or less Standard prose for the main storyline, and relegated somewhat altered regional dialects to the interpolated poems, but also wanted the poems to be understood and to rhyme, they were often faced with a dilemma. They in fact frequently had to choose among three competing alternatives, namely among dialect-flavoring, comprehensibility, and poetic purity. And it is quite obvious that the Grimms did not always come up with an ideal, or even regularly predictable, solution. One possible solution, documented in #1 **"Der Froschkönig oder der eiserne Heinrich,"** could be termed the "footnote" solution. In the original manuscript version of this tale sent to Brentano, but never actually published by him, we find the following poem at the end of the tale:

> Heinerich der Wagen bricht!
> Nein Herr der Wagen nicht,
> Es ist ein Band von meinem Herzen
> das da lag in großen Schmerzen
> als ihr an dem Brunnen saßt
> als ihr eine *Fretsche* wart.   Frosch

>> (Rölleke 1975: 146)

The word *Frosch* floating out on the right of the manuscript was meant to tell somebody, presumably Brentano, that *Fretsche* means *Frosch*. The use of *Fretsche* in the actual poem does not improve the rhyme, but it does improve the scansion.

Having once employed the footnote strategy, the Grimms were clearly committed to it in this poem. In later versions of this tale, in fact from the first edition on, the poem reads as follows:

> Heinrich, der Wagen bricht!
> Nein Herr der Wagen nicht,

> Es ist ein Band von meinem Herzen
> das da lag in großen Schmerzen
> als ihr in dem Brunnen saßt
> als ihr eine Fretsche (Frosch) was't. (Wart)

>> (Grimm v. 1: 32)

Here *wart* has been restored to a presumably dialectal *was't,*[4] rhyme and scansion have been preserved, and the footnotes, in the form of parentheses, ensure comprehensibility.

Sometimes the Grimms were confronted in the poem with a dialect form that would lead to an actual misunderstanding, rather than incomprehension. This is what may have happened in the following poem from #188 **"Spindel, Weberschiffchen und Nadel"**:

> Spindel fein, Spindel schon
> Begrüße mir den Königssohn

>> Spindel, Spindel, geh du aus,
>> Bring den Freier in mein Haus

>> (Rölleke 1998: 464-65)

Here the nonumlauted *schon,* "already" in the Standard, rather than the intended Bavarian "beautiful" (which in the Standard is the nonrhyming *schön*), forces the Grimms to change the entire verse.

To document further the Grimms' conflicting concerns with authenticity, comprehensibility, and poetic purity, one may also look at the development of #53 **"Sneewittchen,"** with its famous woman/mirror interchanges. In the Brentano manuscript, only the queen's first question to the mirror is found rhymed, clearly flawed in terms of scansion, although Standard German in appearance:

> Spieglein, Spieglein an der Wand,
> wer ist die schönste Frau in ganz Engelland?

>> (Rölleke 1975: 244)

By the first edition this has been improved somewhat, and by the seventh edition it works in most respects (the seventh is indented):

> Spieglein, Spieglein an der Wand:
> wer ist die schönste Frau in dem ganzen Land?

>> Spieglein, Spieglein an der Wand:
>> wer ist die schönste im ganzen Land?
>> (Rölleke 1975:245, Grimm v. 1:269)

Similar improvements can be noted with respect to the mirror's first answer to this question, first found in the first edition and much improved, as far as scansion is concerned, in the seventh:

> Ihr, Frau Königin, seyd die schönste Frau im Land.

>> Frau Königin, Ihr seid die schönste im Land.
>> (Rölleke 1975:245, Grimm v. 1:269)

By the time the first edition appeared, the Grimms had also added six more rhymed questions by the queen, all identical to the first, and six more answers by the mirror. One of them is identical to the single-line answer immediately above, but the other five are as rhymed as the question. Unlike the question, they are not all identical, since they respond to the plot developments in the story. The second answer in the story, at the point when the queen discovers she has a problem, is found below; again the first edition comes first and the seventh is indented:

> Frau Königin, Ihr seyd die schönste hier,
>   aber Sneewittchen ist noch tausendmal schöner als
>   Ihr!

>   Frau Königin, Ihr seid die schönste hier,
>   aber Sneewittchen ist tausendmal schöner als
>   Ihr!

(Rölleke 1975: 247, Grimm v. 1: 270)

Simply by dropping the word *noch,* the Grimms succeeded in improving the scansion between the first and the seventh editions. But what to make of the third, fourth, and fifth answers, whose first-edition appearance follows below?

Third answer (1st edition):

> Frau Königin, Ihr seyd die schönste hier,
>   aber Sneewittchen, über den sieben Bergen
>   ist noch tausendmal schöner als Ihr!

Fourth and *fifth* answers (1st edition):

> Frau Königin, Ihr seyd die schönste hier,
>   aber Sneewittchen bei den sieben Zwergelchen
>   ist tausendmal schöner als Ihr!

(Rölleke 1975:251, 253, 255)

Obviously, there is a lot more wrong with the scansion of these poems than the word *noch* in the third answer. In these answers, the Grimms apparently attempted to incorporate new information from the story into the poems by adding two different prepositional-phrase modifiers to the word *Sneewittchen* found in the second answer. By so doing, they apparently tried to emphasize the importance of repeated formulaic rhymed utterances. Nevertheless, these lines simply do not scan very well, because the second rhyming line is so much longer than the first. A further complicating factor is the use of the Central West German (north of the Main river) double diminutive *Zwergelchen, -elchen* being found after velar stops.[5] Presumably, this provides a dialect flavor to the verse, since in the body of the text, all the way up to the seventh edition, the dwarves are referred to as *Zwerge* or *Zwerglein.*

All of this changes by the last edition, given below. The scansion is obviously much improved, the rhymes are also improved, but the Grimms have had to abandon the dialectal *Zwergelchen,* clearly losing something they originally wanted, given the addition of that form in the first edition.

Third answer (7th edition):

> Frau Königin, Ihr seid die schönste hier,
>   Aber Sneewittchen über den Bergen
>   bei den sieben Zwergen
>   ist noch tausendmal schöner als Ihr.

Fourth and *fifth* answers (7th edition):

> Frau Königin, Ihr seid die schönste hier,
>   Aber Sneewittchen über den Bergen
>   bei den sieben Zwergen
>   ist noch (fifth: doch) tausendmal schöner als Ihr.

(Grimm v. 1:272-75)

To summarize to this point: The Grimms wanted their fairy tales to appear authentic. With a few exceptions, they rejected tales in pure dialect, because the audience for this would have been small. In addition, they appear to have made the decision, given the evidence of tales like #147 **"Das junggeglühte Männlein,"** that prose should be favored over poetry as the typical form of their fairy tales. As a compromise, the body of the tale itself normally appears in more or less Standard, if antiquated, German prose, while occasional bits of verse provide the stamp of regional authenticity. The problem with such verses is twofold. Most prominently, the verses have to be at least somewhat comprehensible. This is documented clearly in #119 **"Die Sieben Schwaben,"** where adjustments toward Standard German are evident. Secondly, as verse these inserts have to meet certain poetic standards, such as proper rhyming and scanning. A number of the tales cited above illustrate this.

One of the most famous of all the Grimms' fairy tales, #15 **"Hänsel und Gretel,"**[6] illustrates how complicated the combination of all these desiderata can be. According to the Grimms' notes, this tale is drawn from "verschiedene Erzählungen aus Hessen,"[7] most likely from their acquaintances, the Wild sisters.

There are precisely three instances in this tale where verse is used. One of them, apparently added to the story by Dortchen Wild in 1813,[8] is the most transparent in terms of rhyme:

> Der Wind, der Wind,
> das himmlische Kind.

(Grimm v. 1: 144)

This verse seems a somewhat unsatisfactory reaction to a question by the wicked witch who hears nibbling on the eaves. This question, in precisely the following form, survived every revision of the tale from the very beginning as a handwritten story on Brentano's desk:

Knuper, knuper, kneischen
wer knupert an meinem Häuschen?

(Grimm v. 1:104)

Interestingly enough, most Germans whom I have reminded of this couplet have insisted on pronouncing
kneischen as if it were written *kneuschen*. Understandably so, since they want the verse to rhyme as much as
the Grimms did. The latter, however, were aware that
many of the dialect variations they were dealing with,
especially in the orally-transmitted tales, normally pronounced front rounded vowels as unrounded ones. Thus,
minimally, *Häuschen* would have been pronounced
more like *Heis[ç]en*. But in fact, it would take more
than unrounding to achieve a good rhyme here. In
kneischen the letter group *sch* stands, in the Standard,
for the sound [š]. In *Häuschen,* on the other hand, it
stands for the sound sequence [sç].

Is there no solution for this? Indeed there is, and it
makes a good case for the Hessian provenience of at
least this snippet of poetry. For there is a widespread
sound change in much of the Central German area
whereby the ich-Laut [ç] has indeed fallen together
with [š] in a sound almost identical to the latter. Thus,
these dialects pronounce *mich* ("me") like *misch*
("mix"), and *Männchen* ("little man") is pronounced
like *Menschen* ("people").[9] This latter nondistinction is
clearly of relevance to the *kneischen/Häuschen* rhyme.
Using phonetic symbols, and assuming the natural assimilation of an [s] to the following [š], these two words
would be [knaiš]/[haišn], a very good rhyme indeed.

But in fact, in most of these same dialects, and indeed
others, as I documented earlier for Swabian, the final n
of -en endings is typically dropped, leaving such words
with a bare schwa vowel. Thus the chances are good
that the rhyme here is actually [knaiš]/[haiš]. The likelihood of this increases when we consider the final two
lines of the last poetic interpolation in **"Hänsel und
Gretel,"** at the point when the children entreat a duck
to ferry them across a stream:

Entchen, Entchen,
da steht Gretel und Hänsel.
Kein Steg und keine Brücke,
nimm uns auf deinen weißen Rücken.

(Grimm v. 1: 107)

Heinz Rölleke (1985: 75-87) has made a compelling
case that these lines, and indeed many nonpoetic lines
from **"Hänsel und Gretel"** as well, were inserted into
the ***KHM*** between the fourth and fifth editions by Wilhelm Grimm, following an 1842 collection of Alsatian
folksongs and folk tales published by August Stöber. In
evidence, Rölleke notes that in the encounter with the
duck in the fourth edition, published in 1840, the
Grimms have Gretel saying "ach, liebes Entchen, nimm

uns auf deinen Rücken." It seems beyond doubt that between then and the 1843 publication of the fifth edition,
they had read Stöber's lines:[10]

Endele.
Bändele.
Kenn Stai unn kenn Brucke
Nimm eß uff dynne wysse Rucke!

(Rölleke 1985: 85-86)

In the dialect verse, *Brucke* and *Rucke* rhyme, mainly
because Alsatian is one of the *n*-dropping dialects, making the accusative singular of the word for "back" available for a rhyme with the nominative singular of
"bridge."

The Grimms are clearly counting on this southwestern
dialect phenomenon for the rhyming of their own third
and fourth lines above. Whether the umlauted <ü> is
meant to read as rounded or unrounded is irrelevant for
this rhyme. But what to make of the first two lines of
the poem from the duck-encounter, repeated below?

Entchen, Entchen,
da steht Gretel und Hänsel.

(Grimm v. 1:107)

I argue here that on some level these lines also rhyme,
and that the Grimms knew this. In order to perceive
these two lines as rhyming, one must understand *Hänsel*
as a stand-in for a disguised diminutive form
Hänsche(n). This is in line both with the claimed Hessian origin of the story (where *Hänsche* is native), and
with its original manuscript title **"Das Brüderchen und
das Schwesterchen."**[11] Additionally, for a good rhyme
one needs the Hessian change of [ç] to [š], with attendant assimilation of [s] to the following [š].

This interpretation raises at least two questions. The
first is: Why would the Grimms have picked the names
Hänsel and *Gretel* at all for an ostensibly Hessian fairy
tale, given the clearly southern dialect-provenience of
the *-el* diminutive? In answer, I reiterate a point I made
when discussing tale #119 **"Die Sieben Schwaben"**:
The Grimms were less interested in real authenticity
than in the appearance of authenticity. The names
Hänsel and *Gretel,* in the early 1800s as well as today,
bear the same kind of relationship to *Hänschen* and
Gretchen as the diminutive suffix *-lein* does to the suffix
-chen: In each case, the latter is more prosaic, more
Standard than the former, with its overtones of the archaic and dialectal.

Thus the Grimms originally picked the names *Hänsel*
and *Gretel* because they came across as more authentic
to a true folktale. Having then decided to add between
the fourth and fifth editions a little verse to make the
tale even more authentic, why didn't they change the

names back, so that the verse openly rhymed? The answer is that they could not. The whole reason that the Grimms had to publish a new edition of the **KHM** between 1840 and 1843 is that they were wildly popular, and tale #15 was one of the most popular. They could not change the names of the main characters in midcareer, as it were.

The text contains some independent evidence for my somewhat quirky interpretation of this verse, namely the order of the two names *Hänsel* and *Gretel*. These two first names actually appear eight times linked by the conjunction *und,* including in the title. Of these eight conjoinings, only the one verse above shows *Gretel* before *Hänsel.* Why, if not to achieve a kind of disguised quasi-rhyme? If closeness of rhyme were not an issue, surely *Gretel* rhymes as well as *Hänsel* with the word *Entchen*?

With regard to this particular verse, there is no explicit acknowledgment on the part of the Grimms that would support my claim. Such an acknowledgment, or indeed even an explicit statement concerning the use of dialect features and linguistic archaisms in any of their fairy-tale verses, is notably lacking from their notes. Yet I hope to have made the case here that such features played an important role in lending the fairy tales an air of Germanic authenticity. As I also hope to have shown, authenticity was frequently at odds with the equally important desiderata of comprehensibility and poetic purity. The resolution of such conflicts, as in the last verse above, was not always transparent.

Notes

1. See most polemically perhaps Ellis, but also Tatar, Zipes, Derungs, and numerous works by Rölleke.

2. Rölleke in Grimm, v. 3: 449-50.

3. Interestingly enough, this dialect makes the story more comprehensible to English speakers if read aloud.

4. I say "presumably" here because I cannot find a dialect source for the *s* in question, assuming this is a preterite form of the verb "to be" (cf. Zhirmunskii 571-74). In much of the High German area, no simple preterite exists for this verb (especially as a copula), and those dialects that have one normally show an *r* in the plural, as the pronoun *ihr* formally is. In many dialects (northern or southern) that have a preterite, as in the standard, the *r* original to the plural has conquered the singular, not the reverse (though this is not theoretically impossible). Did the Grimms just make up this form for the rhyme?

5. See Zhirmunskii 479.

6. See Grimm, v. 1: 100-08.

7. Grimm v. 3: 448.

8. Rölleke in Grimm v. 3: 448.

9. See Herrgen for a detailed discussion of this phenomenon.

10. They do give Stöber credit for a lot, though not the massive revisions between the fourth and fifth editions.

11. Curiously enough, a manuscript notation by Jacob gives the words "alias: Hänsel und Gretchen." Cf. Rölleke 1975:70.

Works Cited

Derungs, Kurt, ed. *Die ursprünglichen Märchen der Brüder Grimm. Handschriften, Urfassung und Texte zur Kulturgeschichte.* Bern: Peter Lang, 1999.

Ellis, John M. *One Fairy Story Too Many: The Brothers Grimm and Their Tales.* Chicago: U of Chicago P, 1983.

Grimm, Jacob and Wilhelm. *Kinder- und Hausmärchen: Ausgabe letzter Hand mit einem Anhang sämtlicher nicht in allen Auflagen veröffentlichter Märchen.* Ed. Heinz Rölleke. 3 vols. Stuttgart: Reclam, 1984.

Herrgen, Joachim. *Koronalisierung und Hyperkorrektion: das palatale Allophon des CH/-Phonems und seine Variation im Westmitteldeutschen.* Wiesbaden: F. Steiner, 1986.

Rölleke, Heinz. *Die älteste Märchensammlung der Brüder Grimm: Synopse der handschriftlichen Urfassung von 1810 und der Erstdrucke von 1812.* Cologny-Genève: Fondation Martin Bodmer, 1975.

———. "August Stöbers Einfluß auf die *Kinder- und Hausmärchen der Brüder Grimm*: Zur Herkunft der KHM 5 und 15." Heinz Rölleke, *"Wo das Wünschen noch geholfen hat": Gesammelte Aufsätze zu den "Kinder- und Hausmärchen" der Brüder Grimm.* Bonn: Bouvier, 1985. 75-87.

———. *Grimms Märchen und ihre Quellen: die literarischen Vorlagen der Grimmschen Märchen/synoptisch vorgestellt und kommentiert von Heinz Rölleke.* Trier: WVT Wissenschaftlicher Verlag, 1998.

———, ed. *"Redensarten des Volks, auf die ich immer horche." Das Sprichwort in den Kinder- und Hausmärchen der Brüder Grimm.* Bern: Peter Lang, 1988.

Tatar, Maria M. *The Hard Facts of the Grimms' Fairy Tales.* Princeton, N.J.: Princeton U P, 1987.

Zhirmunskii, V. M. *Deutsche Mundartkunde.* Berlin: Akademie-Verlag, 1962.

Zipes, Jack David. *The Brothers Grimm: From Enchanted Forests to the Modern World.* New York: Routledge, 1988.

Jack Zipes (essay date 2006)

SOURCE: Zipes, Jack. "Who's Afraid of the Brothers Grimm? Socialization and Politicization through Fairy Tales." In *Fairy Tales and the Art of Subversion: The Classical Genre for Children and the Process of Civilization,* revised ed., pp. 45-70. New York: Routledge, 2006.

[*In the following essay, Zipes discusses the origins of* Grimms' Fairy Tales *and its historic role in promulgating bourgeois social norms, demonstrating how contemporary revisions co-opt a countercultural socialization process.*]

> The wolf, now piously old and good,
> When again he met Red Riding Hood
> Spoke: "Incredible, my dear child,
> What kinds of stories are spread—they're wild.
>
> As though there were, so the lie is told,
> A dark murder affair of old.
> The Brothers Grimm are the ones to blame.
> Confess! It wasn't half as bad as they claim."
>
> Little Red Riding Hood saw the wolf's bite
> And stammered: "You're right, quite right."
> Whereupon the wolf, heaving many a sigh,
> Gave kind regards to Granny and waved good bye.
>
> Rudolf Otto Wiemer, *The Old Wolf* (1976)

Over 200 years ago the Brothers Grimm began collecting original folk tales in Germany and stylized them into potent literary fairy tales. Since then these tales have exercised a profound influence on children and adults alike throughout the western world. Indeed, whatever form fairy tales in general have taken since the original publication of the Grimms' narratives in 1812, the Brothers Grimm have been continually looking over our shoulders and making their presence felt. For most people this has not been so disturbing. However, during the last thirty-five years there has been a growing radical trend to overthrow the Grimms' benevolent rule in fairy-tale land by writers who believe that the Grimms' stories contribute to the creation of a false consciousness and reinforce an authoritarian socialization process. This trend has appropriately been set by writers in the very homeland of the Grimms, where literary revolutions have always been more common than real political ones.[1]

West German writers[2] and critics have come to regard the Grimms' fairy tales and those of Hans Christian Andersen, Ludwig Bechstein, and their imitators as "secret agents" of an education establishment which indoctrinates children to learn fixed roles and functions within bourgeois society, thus curtailing their free development.[3] This attack on the conservatism of the "classical" fairy tales was mounted in the 1960s, when numerous writers began using them as models to write innovative, emancipatory tales, more critical of changing conditions in advanced technological societies based on capitalist production and social relations. What became apparent to these writers and critics was that the Grimms' tales, though ingenious and perhaps socially relevant in their own times, contained sexist and racist attitudes and served a socialization process which placed great emphasis on passivity, industry, and self-sacrifice for girls and on activity, competition, and accumulation of wealth for boys. Therefore, contemporary West German writers moved in a different, more progressive direction by parodying and revising the fairy tales of the eighteenth and nineteenth centuries, especially those of the Grimms.

For the most part, the "classical" fairy tales have been reutilized or what the Germans call *umfunktioniert*: the *function* of the tales has been literally turned around so that the perspective, style, and motifs of the narratives expose contradictions in capitalist society and awaken children to other alternatives for pursuing their goals and developing autonomy. The reutilized tales *function against* conformation to the standard socialization process and are meant to *function for* a different, more just society which can be gleaned from the redirected socialization process symbolized in the new tales. The quality and radicalism of these new tales vary from author to author.[4] And it may even be that many of the writers are misguided, despite their good intentions. Nevertheless, they have raised questions about the sociopolitical function of fairy tales, and just this question-raising alone is significant. Essentially they reflect upon and seek to understand how the messages in fairy tales tend to repress and constrain children rather than set them free to make their own choices. They assume that the Grimms' fairy tales have been fully accepted in all western societies and have ostensibly been used or misused in furthering the development of human beings—to make them more functional within the capitalist system and to prescribe choice. If one shares a critique of capitalist society, what then should be changed in the Grimms' tales to suggest other possibilities? What sociogenetic structural process forms the fairy tales and informs the mode by which the human character is socialized in capitalist society?

Before looking at the literary endeavors made by West German writers to answer these questions, it is important to discuss the nature of the Grimms' fairy tales and the notion of socialization through fairy tales. Not only have creative writers been at work to reutilize the fairy tales, but there have been a host of progressive critics who have uncovered important historical data about the Grimms' tales and have explored the role that these stories have played in the socialization process.

I

Until the 1970s it was generally assumed that the Grimm Brothers collected their oral folk tales mainly from peasants and day laborers, that they merely altered and refined the tales while remaining true to their perspective and meaning. Both assumptions have been proven false.[5] The Grimms gathered their tales primarily from petit bourgeois or educated middle-class people, who had already introduced bourgeois notions into their versions. In all cases the Grimms did more than simply change and improve the style of the tales: they expanded them and made substantial changes in characters and meaning. Moreover, they excluded many other well-known tales from their collection, and their entire process of selection reflected the bias of their philosophical and political point of view. Essentially, the Grimm Brothers contributed to the literary "bourgeoisification" of oral tales which had belonged to the peasantry and lower classes and had been informed by the interests and aspirations of these groups. This is not to say that they purposely sought to betray the heritage of the common people in Germany. On the contrary, their intentions were honorable: they wanted the rich cultural tradition of the common people to be used and accepted by the rising middle classes. It is for this reason that they spent their lives conducting research on myths, customs, and the language of the German people. They wanted to foster the development of a strong national bourgeoisie by unraveling the ties to Germanic traditions and social rites and by drawing on related lore from France and central and northern Europe. Wherever possible, they sought to link the beliefs and behavior of characters in the folk tales to the cultivation of bourgeois norms.

> It was into this nineteenth century where a bourgeois sense for family had been developed that the Grimms' fairy tales made their entrance: as the book read to children by mothers and grandmothers and as reading for the children themselves. The Grimms countered the pedagogical doubts from the beginning with the argument that the fairy-tale book was written both for children and for adults, but not for the badly educated. . . . The enormous amount of editions and international circulation of the Grimms' fairy tales as literary fairy tales can also be explained by their bourgeois circle of consumers. Here is where the circle closes. Aside from the questionable nature of the "ancient Germanic" or even "pure Hessian" character of the collection, we must consider and admire the genial talents of the Brothers, who were able to fuse random and heterogeneous material transmitted over many years into the harmonious totality of the *Children and Household Tales.* They were thus able to bring about a work which was both "bourgeois" and "German" and fully corresponded to the scientific temper and emotional taste of their times. The general room for identification provided for the bourgeoisie completely encompassed the virtues of a national way of thinking and German folk spirit, and the Grimms' *Children and Household Tales*

contained all this in the most superb way. Its success as a book cannot be explained without knowledge of the social history of the nineteenth century.[6]

The sources of the tales were European, old Germanic, and bourgeois. The audience was a growing middle-class one. The Grimms saw a mission in the tales and were bourgeois missionaries. And, although they never preached or sought to convert in a crass manner, they did modify the tales much more than we have been led to believe. Their collection went through seven editions during their own lifetime and was constantly enlarged and revised. Wilhelm Grimm, the more conservative of the two brothers, did most of the revisions, and it is commonly known that he endeavored to clean up the tales and make them more respectable for bourgeois children—even though the original publication was not expressly intended for children. The Grimms collected the tales not only to "do a service to the history of poetry and mythology," but their intention was to write a book that could provide pleasure and learning.[7] They called their edition of 1819 an *Erziehungsbuch* (an educational book) and discussed the manner in which they made the stories more pure, truthful and just. In the process they carefully eliminated those passages which they thought would be harmful for children's eyes.[8] This became a consistent pattern in the revisions after 1819. Once the tales had seen the light of print, and, once they were deemed appropriate for middle-class audiences, Wilhelm consistently tried to meet audience expectations. And the reading audience of Germany was becoming more *Biedermeier* or Victorian in its morals and ethics. As moral sanitation man, Wilhelm set high standards, and his example has been followed by numerous "educators," who have watered down and cleaned up the tales from the nineteenth century up to the present.

Thanks to the 1975 re-publication of the neglected 1810 handwritten manuscript side by side with the published edition of the tales of 1812 by Heinz Rölleke, we can grasp the full import of the sanitation process in relation to socialization. We can see how each and every oral tale was conscientiously and, at times, drastically changed by the Grimms. For our purposes I want to comment on three tales to show how different types of changes relate to gradual shifts in the norms and socialization process reflecting the interests of the bourgeoisie. Let us begin with the opening of **"The Frog Prince"** and compare the 1810 manuscript with the editions of 1812 and 1857.

1810 MANUSCRIPT

The king's daughter went into the woods and sat down next to a cool well. Then she took a golden ball and began playing with it until it suddenly rolled down into the well. She watched it fall to the bottom from the edge of the well and was very sad. Suddenly a frog stuck his head out of the water and said: 'Why are you complaining so?' 'Oh, you nasty frog, you can't help me at all. My golden ball has fallen into the well.' Then the frog said: 'If you take me home with you, I'll fetch your golden ball for you.'[9]

1812 Edition

Once upon a time there was a king's daughter who went into the woods and sat down next to a cool well. She had a golden ball with her that was her most cherished toy. She threw it high into the air and caught it and enjoyed this very much. One time the ball went high into the air. She had already stretched out her hand and curled her fingers to catch the ball when it fell by her side onto the ground and rolled and rolled right into the water.

The king's daughter looked at it in horror. The well was so deep that it was impossible to see the bottom. She began to cry miserably and complain: "Oh! I would give anything if only I could have my ball again! My clothes, my jewels, my pearls and whatever I could find in the world." While she was complaining, a frog stuck his head out of the water and said: "Princess, why are you lamenting so pitifully?" "Oh," she said, "you nasty frog, you can't help me! My golden ball has fallen into the well." The frog said: "I won't demand your pearls, your jewels, and your clothes, but if you accept me as your companion, and if you let me sit next to you at your table and eat from your golden plate and sleep in your bed, and if you cherish and love me, then I'll fetch your ball for you."[10]

1857 Edition

In olden times when making wishes still helped, there lived a king whose daughters were all beautiful, but the youngest was so beautiful that the sun itself, who has seen so much, was astonished by her beauty each time it lit upon her face. Near the royal castle there was a great dark wood, and in the wood under an old linden tree there was a well. And when the day was quite hot, the king's daughter would go into the woods and sit by the edge of the cool well. And if she was bored, she would take a golden ball and throw it up and catch it again, and this was the game she liked to play most.

Now it happened one day that the golden ball, instead of falling back into the little hand of the princess when she had tossed it up high, fell to the ground by her side and rolled into the water. The king's daughter followed it with her eyes, but it disappeared. The well was deep, so deep that the bottom could not be seen. Then she began to cry, and she cried louder and louder and could not console herself at all. And as she was lamenting, someone called to her. "What is disturbing you, prin-

cess? Your tears would melt a heart of stone." And when she looked to see where the voice came from there was nothing but a frog stretching his thick ugly head out of the water. "Oh, is it you, old waddler?" she said. "I'm crying because my golden ball has fallen into the well." "Be quiet and stop crying," the frog answered. "I can help you, but what will you give me if I fetch your ball again?" "Whatever you like, dear frog," she said. "My clothes, my pearls and jewels, and even the golden crown that I'm wearing." "I don't like your clothes, your pearls and jewels and your golden crown, but if you love me and let me be your companion and playmate, let me sit at your table next to you, eat from your golden plate and drink from your cup, and sleep in your bed, if you promise me this, then I shall dive down and fetch your golden ball for you again."[11]

* * *

By comparing these three versions we can see how **"The Frog Prince"** became more and more embroidered in a short course of time—and this did not occur merely for stylistic reasons. In the original folk tale of 1810 the setting is simple and totally lacking in frills. There is no castle. The incident appears to take place on a large estate. The king's daughter could well be a peasant's daughter or any girl who goes to a well, finds a ball, loses it, and agrees to take the frog home if he finds the ball for her. He has no other desire but to sleep with her. There is no beating around the bush in the rest of the narrative. It is explicitly sexual and alludes to a universal initiation and marital ritual (derived from primitive matriarchal societies), and in one other version, the princess does not throw the frog against the wall, but kisses it as in the "Beauty and Beast" tales. Mutual sexual recognition and acceptance bring about the prince's salvation. In both the 1812 and 1857 versions the princess provides more of an identification basis for a bourgeois child, for she is unique, somewhat spoiled, and very wealthy. She thinks in terms of monetary payment and basically treats the frog as though he were a member of a lower caste—an attitude not apparent in the original version. The ornate description serves to cover or eliminate the sexual frankness of the original tale. Here the frog wants to be a companion and playmate. Sex must first be sweetened up and made to appear harmless since its true form is repulsive. The girl obeys the father, but like all good bourgeois children she rejects the sexual advances of the frog, and for this she is rewarded. In fact, all three versions suggest a type of patriarchal socialization for young girls that has been severely criticized and questioned by progressive educators today, but the final version is most consistent in its *capacity* to combine feudal folk notions of sexuality, obedience, and sexual roles with bourgeois norms and comportment. The changes in the versions reveal social transitions and class differences that attest to their dependency on the gradual ascendancy of bourgeois codes and tastes.

Even the earlier French *haute bourgeois* values had to be altered by the Grimms to fit their more upright, nineteenth-century middle-class perspective and sense of decency. Let us compare the beginning of Perrault's "Le Petit Chaperon Rouge" with the Grimms' 1812 **"Rotkäppchen"** since the French version was their actual source.

"LE PETIT CHAPERON ROUGE" (1697)

Once upon a time there was a little village girl, the prettiest that was ever seen. Her mother doted on her, and her grandmother doted even more. This good woman made a little red hood for her, and it became the girl so well that everyone called her Little Red Riding Hood.

One day her mother, having baked some biscuits, said to Little Red Riding Hood: "Go and see how your grandmother is feeling; someone told me that she was ill. Take her some biscuits and this little pot of butter." Little Red Riding Hood departed immediately for the house of her grandmother, who lived in another village.[12]

"ROTKÄPPCHEN" (1812)

Once upon a time there was a small sweet maid. Whoever laid eyes on her loved her. But it was her grandmother who loved her most. She never had enough to give the child. One time she gave her a present, a small hood made out of velvet, and since it became her so well, and since she did not want to wear anything but this, she was simply called Little Red Riding Hood. One day her mother said to her: "Come, Red Riding Hood, take this piece of cake and bottle of wine and bring it to grandmother. She is sick and weak. This will nourish her. Be nice and good and give her my regards. Be orderly on your way and don't veer from the path, otherwise you'll fall and break the glass. Then your sick grandmother will have nothing."[13]

In their article on Perrault's "Little Red Riding Hood," Carole and D. T. Hanks Jr. have commented on the "sanitization" process of the Grimms and later editors of this tale. "Perrault's tale provides a classic example of the bowdlerizing which all too often afflicts children's literature. Derived from the German version, 'Rotkäppchen' (Grimm No. 26), American versions of the tale have been sanitized to the point where the erotic element disappears and the tragic ending becomes comic. This approach emasculates a powerful story, one which unrevised is a metaphor for the maturing process."[14] The word "emasculates" is an unfortunate choice

to describe what happened to Perrault's tale (and the original folk tales) since it was the rise of authoritarian patriarchal societies that was responsible for fear of sexuality and stringent sexual codes. Secondly, Perrault's tale was not written only for children but also for an educated upper-class audience which included children.[15] The development of children's literature, as we know, was late, and it only gradually assumed a vital role in the general socialization process of the eighteenth and nineteenth centuries. Therefore, Perrault's early tale had to be made more suitable for children by the Grimms and had to reinforce a more conservative bourgeois sense of morality. This moralistic impulse is most apparent in the changes the Grimms made at the very beginning of the tale. Little Red Riding Hood is no longer a simple village maid but the epitome of innocence. It is not enough, however, to be innocent. The girl must learn to fear her own curiosity and sensuality. So the narrative purpose corresponds to the socialization for young girls at that time: if you do not walk the straight path through the sensual temptations of the dark forest, if you are not orderly and moral (*sittsam*),[16] then you will be swallowed by the wolf, ice, the devil or sexually starved males. Typically the savior and rebirth motif is represented by a male hunter, a father figure devoid of sexuality. Here again the revisions in word choice, tone, and content cannot be understood unless one grasps the substance of education and socialization in the first half of the nineteenth century.

Let us take one more example, a short section from the Grimms' 1810 and 1812 versions of **"Snow White."**

1810 MANUSCRIPT

When Snow White awoke the next morning, they asked her how she happened to get there. And she told them everything, how her mother the queen had left her alone in the woods and went away. The dwarfs took pity on her and persuaded her to remain with them and do the cooking for them when they went to the mines. However, she was to beware of the queen and not let anyone in the house.[17]

1812 EDITION

When Snow White awoke, they asked her who she was and how she happened to get in the house. Then she told them how her mother wanted to have her put to death, but that the hunter spared her life, and how she had run the entire day and finally arrived at their house. So the dwarfs took pity on her and said: "If you keep our house for us, and cook, sew, make the beds, wash and knit, and keep everything tidy and clean, you may stay with us, and you will have everything you want. In the evening, when we come home, dinner must be ready. During the day we are in the mines and dig for gold, so you will be alone. Beware of the queen and let no one in the house."[18]

These passages again reveal how the Grimms had an entirely different socialization process in mind when they altered the folk tales. Snow White is given instructions which are more commensurate with the duties of a bourgeois girl, and the tasks which she performs are implicitly part of her moral obligation. Morals are used to justify a division of labor and the separation of the sexes. Here, too, the growing notion that the woman's role was in the home and that the home was a shelter for innocence and children belonged to a conception of women, work, and child-rearing in bourgeois circles more so than to the ideas of the peasantry and aristocracy. Certainly, the growing proletarian class in the nineteenth century could not think of keeping wives and children at home, for they had to work long hours in the factories. Snow White was indeed a new kind of princess in the making and was constantly remade. In the 1810 version the father comes with doctors to save his daughter. Then he arranges a marriage for her daughter and punishes the wicked queen. In the margin of their manuscript, the Grimms remarked: "This ending is not quite right and is lacking something."[19] Their own finishing touches could only be topped by the prudish changes made by that twentieth-century sanitation man, Walt Disney.

Aside from situating the compilation of folk tales and grasping the literary transformations within a socio-historical framework, it is even more important to investigate the pervasive influence which the Grimms have had in the socialization process of respective countries. We know that the Grimms' collection (especially the 1857 final edition) has been the second most popular and widely circulated book in Germany for over a century, second only to the Bible. We also know that the tales and similar stories are the cultural bread and basket of most children from infancy until ten years of age. Studies in Germany show that there is a fairy-tale reading age between six and ten.[20] Otherwise the tales have already been read or told to the children by adults before they are six. Incidentally, this process of transmission means that certain groups of adults are constantly re-reading and re-telling the tales throughout their lives. Ever since the rise of the mass media, the Grimms' tales (generally in their most prudish and prudent version) have been broadcast by radio, filmed, recorded for records, tapes, and video, used as motifs for advertisements, and commercialized in every manner and form imaginable. Depending on the country and relative reception, these particular tales have exercised a grip on our minds and imagination from infancy into adulthood, and, though they cannot be held accountable for negative features in advanced technological societies, it is time—as many West German writers believe—to evaluate how they impart values and norms to children which may actually hinder their growth, rather

than help them to come to terms with their existential condition and mature autonomously as Bruno Bettelheim and others maintain.[21]

Here we must consider the socialization of reading fairy tales with the primary focus on those developed by the Brothers Grimm. In discussing socialization I shall be relying on a general notion of culture which is defined by the mode through which human beings objectify themselves, come together, and relate to one another in history and materialize their ideas, intentions, and solutions, in the sense of making them more concrete. By concrete I also mean to imply that there are forms people create and use to make their ideas, intentions and solutions take root in a visible, audible, and generally perceptible manner so that they become an actual part of people's daily lives. Thus, culture is viewed as an historical *process* of human objectification, and the level and quality of a national culture depends on the socialization developed by human beings to integrate young members into the society and to reinforce the norms and values which legitimize the sociopolitical systems and which guarantee some sort of continuity in society.[22]

Reading as internalization, or technically speaking as resubjectification, has always functioned in socialization processes, whether it be the conscious or unconscious "understanding" of signs, symbols, and letters. In modern times, that is, since the Enlightenment and rise of the bourgeoisie, reading has been the passport into certain brackets of society and the measure by which one functions and maintains a certain place in the hierarchy.[23] The reading of printed fairy tales in the nineteenth century was a socially exclusive process: it was conducted mainly in bourgeois circles and nurseries, and members of the lower classes who learned how to read were not only acquiring a skill, they were acquiring a value system and social status depending on their conformity to norms controlled by bourgeois interests. The social function of reading is not to be understood in a mechanistic or reductive way, i.e., that reading was solely a safeguard for bourgeois hegemony and only allowed for singular interpretations. Certainly the introduction of reading to the lower classes opened up new horizons for them and gave them more power. Also the production of books allowed for a variety of viewpoints often contrary to the ruling forces in society. In some respects reading can function explosively like a dream and serve to challenge socialization and constraints. But, unlike the dream, it is practically impossible to determine what direct effect a fairy tale will have upon an *individual* reader in terms of validating his or her own existence. Still, the tale does provide and reflect upon the cultural boundaries within which the reader measures and validates his or her own identity. We tend to forget the socio-historical frameworks of control when we talk about reading and especially the reading of fairy tales. Both socialization and reading reflect and are informed by power struggles and ideology in a given society or culture. To become literate means to learn how to operate within the laws of literacy that are class determined. The Grimms' fairy tales were products not only of the struggles of the common people to make themselves heard in oral folk tales—symbolically representing their needs and wishes—but they also became *literary* products of the German bourgeois quest for identity and power. To this extent, the norms and value system which the Grimms cultivated within the tales point to an objectified, standard way of living which was intended and came to legitimate the general bourgeois standard of living and work, not only in Germany but throughout the western world.

In all there were 51 tales in the original manuscript of 1810. Some were omitted in the 1812 book publication, and those which were included were all extensively changed and stylized by the Grimms to meet middle-class taste. This process of conscious alteration for social and aesthetic reasons was continued until 1857. The recent findings which have stressed and documented this are not merely significant for what they tell us about the Grimms' method of work or the relation of the tales to late feudal and early bourgeois society in Germany. They have greater ramifications for the development of the literary fairy tales in general, especially in view of socialization through reading and the meaning of literacy.

II

First of all, through understanding the subjective selection process and adaptation methods of the Grimms, we can begin to study other collections of folk tales, which have been published in the nineteenth and twentieth centuries, and analyze similar transcription methods in light of education and socialization. Recent attention has been paid to the role of the narrator of the tales in folklore research, but the role of the collector and transcriber is also significant, for we have seen how consciously and unconsciously the Grimms integrated their world views into the tales and those of their intended audience as well. The relationship of the collector to audience is additionally significant since printed and transcribed folk tales were not meant to be reinserted into circulation as books for the original audience. As Rudolf Schenda has demonstrated in *Volk ohne Buch,*[24] the lower classes did not and could not use books because of their lack of money and training. Their tradition was an oral one. The nineteenth-century and early twentieth-century transcription of folk tales was primarily for the educated classes, young and old. The reception of the tales influenced the purpose and style of the collectors. This remains true up through the present.

As I have noted, psychologists have explored the relationship between dream and fairy-tale production, and moreover they have endeavored to explore the special role which fairy tales have played in socialization. One of the most succinct and sober analyses of why the fairy tale in particular attracts children and functions so well in the socialization process has been made by Emanuel K. Schwartz. He argues that

> the struggle between what is perceived as the "good parent" and the "bad parent" is one of the big problems of childhood. In the fairy tale the bad mother is commonly seen as the witch (phallic mother). The great man, the father figure (Oedipus), represents the hero, or the hero-to-be, the prototype, for the young protagonist of the fairy tale. The process of social and psychological change, characteristic of the fairy tale, is childishly pursued, and magic is used to effect changes. On the other hand, experience with having to struggle for the gratification and the fulfillment of wishes results in a social adherence to and the development of an understanding of social norms and social conformities. This does not mean, however, that the reinforcement of an awareness of socialization results in submissiveness; but a certain amount of common sense, which goes into conforming with the social *mores,* is a realistic necessity for children and adults alike.[25]

To a certain extent, Schwartz minimizes the inherent dangers in such narratives as the Grimms' fairy tales which function to legitimize certain repressive standards of action and make them acceptable for children. Reading as a physical and mental process involves identification before an internalization of norms and values can commence, and identification for a child comes easily in a Grimms' fairy tale. There is hardly one that does not announce who the protagonist is, and he or she commands our identification almost immediately by being the youngest, most oppressed, the wronged, the smallest, the most naive, the weakest, the most innocent, etc. Thus, direct identification of a child with the major protagonist begins the process of socialization through reading.

Although it is extremely difficult to determine exactly what a child will absorb on an unconscious level, the patterns of most Grimms' fairy tales draw conscious attention to prescribed values and models. As children read or are read to, they follow a social path, learn role orientation, and acquire norms and values. The pattern of most Grimms' fairy tales involves a struggle for power, survival, and autonomy. Though there are marked differences among the tales, it is possible to suggest an overall pattern which will make it clear why and how they become functional in the bourgeois socialization process.

Initially the young protagonist must leave home or the family because power relations have been disturbed. Either the protagonist is wronged, or a change in social relations forces the protagonist to depart from home. A task is imposed, and a hidden command of the tale must be fulfilled. The question which most of the Grimms' tales ask is: how can one learn—what must one do to use one's powers rightly in order to be accepted in society or recreate society in keeping with the norms of the *status quo*? The wandering protagonist always leaves home to reconstitute home. Along the way the male hero learns to be active, competitive, handsome, industrious, cunning, acquisitive. His goal is money, power, and a woman (also associated with chattel). His jurisdiction is the open world. His happiness depends on the just use of power. The female hero learns to be passive, obedient, self-sacrificing, hardworking, patient, and straight-laced. Her goal is wealth, jewels, and a man to protect her property rights. Her jurisdiction is the home or castle. Her happiness depends on conformity to patriarchal rule. Sexual activity is generally postponed until after marriage. Often the tales imply a postponement of gratification until the necessary skills, power, and wealth are acquired.

For a child growing up in a capitalist society in the nineteenth and twentieth centuries, the socialization process carried by the pattern and norms in a Grimms' fairy tale functioned and still functions to make such a society more acceptable to the child. Friction and points of conflict are minimized, for the fairy tale legitimates bourgeois society by seemingly granting upward mobility and the possibility for autonomy. All the Grimms' tales contain an elaborate set of signs and codes. If there is a wrong signaled in a Grimms' fairy tale—and there is always somebody being wronged, or a relation disturbed—then it involves breaking an inviolate code which is the basis of benevolent patriarchal rule. Acceptable norms are constituted by the behavior of a protagonist whose happy end indicates the possibility for resolution of the conflicts according to the code. Even in such tales as **"How Six Made their Way through the World," "Bremen Town Musicians," "Clever Gretel,"** and **"The Blue Light,"** in which the downtrodden protagonists overthrow oppressors, the social relations and work ethos are not fundamentally altered but reconstituted in a manner which allows for more latitude in the hierarchical social system—something which was desired incidentally by a German bourgeoisie incapable of making revolutions but most capable of making compromises at the expense of the peasantry. Lower-class members become members of the ruling elite, but this occurs because the ruling classes need such values which were being cultivated by the bourgeoisie—thrift, industry, patience, obedience, etc. Basically, the narrative patterns imply that skills and qualities are to be developed and used so that one can compete for a high place in the hierarchy based on private property, wealth, and power. Both command and report[26] of the Grimms' fairy tales emphasize a *process* of socialization through reading that leads to internalizing the basic nineteenth-century bourgeois norms, values, and power relationships, which take their departure from feudal society.

For example, let us consider **"The Table, the Ass and the Stick"** to see how functional it is in terms of male socialization. It was first incorporated into the expanded edition of the Grimms' tales in 1819, deals mainly with lower middle-class characters, focuses on males, and will be the basis for a discussion about a reutilized tale by F. K. Waechter. All the incidents concern master/slave relationships. Three sons are in charge of a goat, who rebels against them by lying and causing all three to be banished by their father, a tailor. After the banishment of the sons, the tailor discovers that the goat has lied. So he shaves her, and she runs away. In the meantime, each one of the sons works diligently in a petit bourgeois trade as joiner, miller, and turner. They are rewarded with gifts by their masters, but the two eldest have their gifts stolen from them by the landlord of a tavern. They embarrass the father and bring shame on the family when they try to show off their gifts which the landlord had replaced with false ones. It is up to the third son to outsmart the landlord, bring about a family reunion, and restore the good name of the family in the community through exhibiting its wealth and power. The father retires as a wealthy man, and we also learn that the goat has been duly punished by a busy bee.

Though the father "wrongs" the boys, his authority to rule remains unquestioned throughout the narrative; nor are we to question it. The blame for disturbing the seemingly "natural" relationship between father and sons is placed on liars and deceivers, the goat and the landlord. They seek power and wealth through devious means. The elaborated code of the tale holds that the only way to acquire wealth and power is through diligence, perseverance, and honesty. The goal of the sons is submission to the father and maintenance of the family's good name. The story enjoins the reader to accept the norms and values of a patriarchal slave/master relationship and private property relations. In general, there is nothing wrong with emphasizing the qualities of "diligence, perseverance, and honesty" in a socialization process, but we are talking about socialization through a story that upholds patriarchal domination and the accumulation of wealth and power for private benefit as positive goals.

In almost all the Grimms' fairy tales, male domination and master/slave relationships are rationalized so long as the rulers are benevolent and use their power justly. If "tyrants" and parents are challenged, they relent or are replaced, but the property relationships and patriarchy are not transformed. In **"The Table, the Ass and the Stick"** there is a series of master/slave relationships: father/son, patriarchal family/goat, master/apprentice, landlord/son. The sons and other characters are socialized to please the masters. They work to produce wealth and power for the father, who retires in the end because the sons have accumulated wealth in the proper, diligent fashion according to the Protestant

Ethic. The goat and landlord are punished for different reasons: the goat because she resented the master/slave relationship; the landlord because, as false father, he violated the rules of private property. Although this remarkable fairy tale allows for many other interpretations, viewed in light of its function in the bourgeois socialization process, we can begin to understand why numerous West German writers began looking askance at the Brothers Grimm during the rise of the anti-authoritarian movement of the late 1960s.

III

Actually the reutilization and transformation of the Grimms' tales were not the inventions of West German writers, nor were they so new.[27] There was a strong radical tradition of rewriting folk and fairy tales for children that began in the late nineteenth century and blossomed during the Weimar period until the Nazis put an end to such experimentation. This tradition was revived during the 1960s, when such writers as Hermynia Zur Mühlen, Lisa Tetzner, Edwin Hoernle, and Walter Benjamin[28] were rediscovered and when the anti-authoritarian movement and the Left began to focus on children and socialization. One of the results of the general radical critique of capitalism and education in West Germany was the attempt to build a genuine, non-commercial children's public sphere which might counter the exploitative and legitimizing mechanisms of the dominant bourgeois public sphere. In order to provide cultural tools and means to reutilize the present public sphere for children, groups of people with a progressive bent tried to offset the racism, sexism, and authoritarian messages in children's books, games, theaters, tv, and schools by creating different kinds of emancipatory messages and cultural objects with and for children.

In children's literature, and specifically in the area of fairy tales, there were several publishing houses that played an active role in introducing reutilized fairy tales created to politicize the children's public sphere, where children and adults cooperated and conceived more concrete, democratic forms of play and work in keeping with the needs and wishes of a participating community.[29] Obviously the rise of a broad left-oriented audience toward the end of the 1960s encouraged many big publishers to direct their efforts to this market for profit, but not all the books were published by giant companies or solely for profit. And, at the beginning of the twenty-first century, when the so-called New Left is no longer so new nor so vocal as it was during the late 1960s, there are still numerous publishing houses, large and small, which are directing their efforts toward the publication of counter-cultural or reutilized fairy-tale books and children's literature. My discussion will limit itself and focus on the reutilized Grimms' tales published by Rowohlt, Basis, Schlot, and Beltz & Gelberg

during the 1970s and 1980s. In particular I shall endeavor to demonstrate how these fairy tales reflected possibilities for a different socialization process from standard children's books, and to a certain extent some of the ideas, plots, and practices in the tales have been realized in the children's public sphere and education.

In 1972 the large Rowohlt Verlag established a book series for children entitled '*rororo rotfuchs*' under the general editorship of Uwe Wandrey. An impressive series was developed and contained a wide range of progressive children's stories, histories, autobiographies, handbooks, and fairy tales for young people between the ages of four and eighteen. Here I want to concentrate on two of the earlier and best efforts to reutilize old fairy tales.

Friedrich Karl Waechter, illustrator and writer,[30] has written and drawn numerous politicized fairy tales and fairy-tale plays for children. One of his first books, *Tischlein deck dich und Knüppel aus dem Sack (Table Be Covered and Stick Out of the Sack,* 1972) is a radical rendition of the Grimms' **"The Table, the Ass, and the Stick."** His story takes place in a small town named Breitenrode a long time ago. (From the pictures the time can be estimated to be the early twentieth century.) Fat Jakob Bock, who owns a large lumber mill and most of the town, exploits his workers as much as he can. When a young carpenter named Philip invents a magic table that continually spreads as much food as one can eat upon command, Bock (the name means ram in German) takes over the invention and incorporates it since it was done on company time. He promises Philip his daughter Caroline if he now invents a "stick out of the sack"—the power Bock needs to guard his property. Philip is given the title of inventor and put to work as a white-collar worker separating him from his friends, the other carpenters, who had helped him build the magic table. At first Philip and his friends are not sure why Bock wants the stick, but an elf named Xram (an anagram for Marx spelled backwards) enlightens them. They decide to work together on this invention and to keep control over it. But, when it is finished, Bock obtains it and plants the magic table as stolen property in the house of Sebastien, a "trouble-maker," who always wants to organize the workers around their own needs. Bock accuses Sebastien of stealing the table and asserts that he needs the stick to punish thieves like Sebastien and to protect his property. However, Philip exposes Bock as the real thief, and the greedy man is chased from the town. Then the workers celebrate as Philip announces that the magic table will be owned by everyone in the town while Xram hides the stick. The final picture shows men, women, children, dogs, cats, and other animals at a huge picnic sharing the fruits of the magic table while Bock departs.

Like the narrative itself, Waechter's drawings are intended to invert the present socialization process in

West Germany. The story-line is primarily concerned with private property relations, and it begins traditionally with the master/slave relationship. The ostensible command of the tale—"obey the boss and you'll cash in on the profits"—is gradually turned into another command—"freedom and happiness can only be attained through collective action and sharing." The narrative flow of the tale confirms this reversed command, and the reading process becomes a learning process about socialization in capitalist society. Philip experiences how the fruits of collective labor expended by himself and his friends are expropriated by Bock. With the magical help of Xram (i.e., the insights of Marx) the workers learn to take control over their own labor and to share the fruits equally among themselves. Here the master/slave relationship is concretely banished, and the new work and social relationships are based on cooperation and collective ownership of the means of production. The virtues of Philip and the workers—diligence, perseverance, imagination, honesty—are used in a struggle to overcome male domination rooted in private property relations. Socialization is seen as a struggle for self-autonomy against exploitative market and labor conditions.

In Andreas and Angela Hopf's *Der Feuerdrache Minimax* (*The Fire Dragon Minimax*, 1973), also an illustrated political fairy tale,[31] the authors use a unique process to depict the outsider position of children and strange-looking creatures and also the need for the outsider to be incorporated within the community if the community is to develop. The Hopfs superimpose red drawings of Minimax and the little girl Hilde onto etchings of medieval settings and characters.[32] The imposition and juxtaposition of red figures on black and white prints keep the reader's focus on contrast and differences. The narrative is a simple reutilization of numerous motifs which commonly appear in the Grimms' tales and associate dragons, wolves, and other animals with forces of destruction endangering the *status quo*. *The Fire Dragon Minimax* demonstrates how the *status quo* itself must be questioned and challenged.

The story takes place during the Middle Ages in the walled town of Gimpelfingen. While sharpening his sword, the knight causes sparks to fly, and the town catches fire. There is massive destruction, and the dragon is immediately blamed for the fire, but Hilde, who had fled the flames, encounters Minimax, who had been bathing in the river when the fire had begun. So she knows that he could not have caused the fire. In fact, he helps extinguish part of the fire and then carries Hilde to his cave since he prefers to roast potatoes with his flames and sleep for long hours rather than burn down towns. The knight pretends to fight in the interests of the town and accuses Minimax of starting the fire and kidnapping Hilde. He darns his armor and goes in search of the dragon, but he is no contest for Mini-

max, who overwhelms him. The knight expects the dragon to kill him, but Minimax tells him instead to take Hilde home since her parents might be worried about her. Again the knight lies to the townspeople and tells them that he has rescued Hilde and killed the dragon. Hilde tries to convince the people that he is lying, but she is only believed by a handful of people who fortunately decide to see if Minimax is alive or dead. Upon finding him, they realize the truth and bring Minimax back to town. This causes the knight to flee in fear. Minimax is welcomed by the townspeople, and he helps them rebuild the town. Thereafter, he remains in the town, roasts potatoes for the children or takes them on rides in the sky. Hilde is his favorite, and he flies highest with her and often tells her fairy tales about dragons.

Obviously the Hopfs are concerned with racism and militarism in this tale. The dragon represents the weird-looking alien figure, who acts differently from the "normal" people. And the Hopfs show how the strange and different creature is often used by people in power as a scapegoat to distract attention from the real enemy, namely the people in power. In contrast to the dominant master/slave relationship established in the medieval community, Hilde and the dragon form a friendship based on mutual recognition. Their relationship is opposed to the dominant power relationship of male patriarchy in the town. In terms of problems in today's late capitalist society, the tale also relates to feminism and the prevention of cruelty to animals. The activism of Hilde on behalf of the dragon sets norms of behavior for young girls, when she asserts herself and uses her talents for the benefit of oppressed creatures in the community. As in Waechter's politicized fairy tale, the textual symbols of goal-oriented behavior are aimed at cooperation and collectivism, not domination and private control.

The publishing house which was the most outspoken in behalf of such general socialist goals in children's culture during the 1970s was Basis Verlag in West Berlin. Working in a collective manner, the people in this group produced a number of excellent studies on fairy tales and children's literature,[33] as well as a series of different types of books for young readers. Here I want to remark on just one of their fairy-tale experiments entitled *Zwei Korken für Schlienz* (*Two Corks for Schlienz*, 1972) by Johannes Merkel based on the Grimms' tale **"How Six Made their Way through the World."** The reutilized fairy tale deals with housing difficulties in large cities, and the text is accompanied by amusing photos with superimposed drawings. Four young people with extraordinary powers seek to organize tenants to fight against an exploitative landlord. Ultimately, they fail, but in the process they learn, along with the readers, to recognize their mistakes. The open ending suggests that the four will resume their struggle in the near future—this time without false illusions.

Most of the tales in *Janosch erzählt Grimm's Märchen* (*Janosch Tells Grimm's Fairy Tales,* 1972) are intended to smash false illusions, too, but it is not so apparent that Janosch has a socialist goal in mind, i.e., that he envisions collective living and sharing as a means to eliminate the evils in the world.[34] He is mainly concerned with the form and contents of 50 Grimms' tales which he wants to parody to the point of bursting their seams. He retells them in a caustic manner using modern slang, idiomatic expressions, and pointed references to deplorable living conditions in affluent societies. Each tale endeavors to undo the socialization of a Grimms' tale by inverting plots and characters and adding new incidents. Such inversion does not necessarily amount to a "happier" or more "emancipatory" view of the world. If Janosch is liberating, it is because he is so humanely candid, often cynical, and disrespectful of conditioned and established modes of thinking and behavior. For instance, in "The Frog Prince" it is the frog who loses his ball and is pursued by a girl. The frog is forced by his father to accept the annoying girl in the subterranean water palace. Her pestering, however, becomes too much for him, and he suffocates her. This causes her transformation into a frog princess whereupon she marries the frog prince and explains to him how she had been captured by human beings and changed herself into an ugly girl to escape malicious treatment by humans. Her ugliness prevented other humans from marrying her and allowed her to return to her true form.

Such an inversion makes a mockery of the Grimms' tale and perhaps makes the reader aware of the potential threat which humans pose to nature and the animal world. This point can be argued. But what is clear from the story is that Janosch fractures the social framework of audience expectations, whether or not the readers are familiar with the original Grimms' tales. The numerous illustrations by Janosch are just as upsetting, and the tales derive their power by not conforming to the socialization of reading the Grimms' tales as harmless stories. His anarchistic, somewhat cynical rejection of the Grimms and the norms they represent is related to his rejection of the hypocritical values of the new rich in post-war Germany created by a so-called "economic miracle." For instance, in "Puss 'n Boots," a marvelous cat exposes his young master Hans to the emptiness and meaninglessness of high society. When Hans experiences how rich people place more stock in objects than in the lives of other people, he decides to abandon his dreams of wealth and success and to lead a carefree life on a modest scale with the cat. This is not to say that the cat or Hans are model characters or point to models for creating a new society. They are symbols of refusal,

and by depicting such refusal, Janosch seeks to defend a "questioning spirit," totally lacking in the Grimms tales and very much alive in his provocative *re-visions,* where everything depends on a critical new viewpoint.

One of Janosch's major supporters of re-visions was Hans-Joachim Gelberg, who was one of the most important proponents for the reutilization of the Grimms' tales and the creation of more politicized and critical stories for children and adults. Gelberg edited special yearbooks, which included various types of experimental fairy tales and received prestigious awards in West Germany,[35] for Gelberg pointed in new directions for a children's literature that refuses to be infantile and condescending. In addition to the yearbooks, Gelberg published a significant volume of contemporary fairy tales entitled *Neues vom Rumpelstilzchen und andere Haus-Märchen von 43 Autoren,* 1976.[36] Since there are 58 different fairy tales and poems, it is difficult to present a detailed discussion of the reutilization techniques in regard to socialization in the tales. Generally speaking, the direction is the same: a wholesale rethinking and reconceptualization of traditional fairy-tale motifs to question standard reading and rearing processes. Since the title of the book features "Rumpelstiltskin," and since the motto of the book—"No, I would rather have something living than all the treasures of the world"—is taken from his tale, I shall deal with the two versions of "Rumpelstiltskin" by Rosemarie Künzler and Irmela Brender[37] since they represent the basic critical attitude of most of the authors.

Both Künzler and Brender shorten the tale drastically and take different approaches to the main characters. Künzler begins by stressing the boastful nature of the miller who gets his daughter into a terrible fix. She is bossed around by the king and then by some little man who promises to help her by using extortion. When the little man eventually barters for her first-born child, the miller's daughter is shocked into her senses. She screams and tells the little man that he is crazy, that she will never marry the horrid king, nor would she ever give her child away. The angry little man stamps so hard that he causes the door of the room to spring open, and the miller's daughter runs out into the wide world and is saved. This version is a succinct critique of male exploitation and domination of women. The miller's daughter allows herself to be pushed around until she has an awakening. Like Janosch, Künzler projects the refusal to conform to socialization as the first step toward actual emancipation.

Brender's version is different. She questions the justice in the Grimms' tale from Rumpelstiltskin's point of view, for she has always felt that the poor fellow has been treated unfairly. After all, what he wanted most was something living, in other words, some human contact. She explains that Rumpelstiltskin did not need money since he was capable of producing gold any time he wanted it. He was also willing to work hard and save the life of the miller's daughter. Therefore, the miller's daughter could have been more understanding and compassionate. Brender does not suggest that the miller's daughter should have given away the child, but as the young queen, she could have invited Rumpelstiltskin to live with the royal family. This way Rumpelstiltskin would have found the human companionship he needed, and everyone would have been content. The way things end in the Grimms' version is for Brender totally unjust. Her technique is a play with possibilities to open up rigid social relations and concern about private possession. Through critical reflection her narrative shifts the goal of the Grimms' story from gold and power to justice and more humane relations based on mutual consideration and cooperation.

Both Künzler and Brender seek a humanization of the socialization process by transforming the tales and criticizing commodity exchange and male domination, and they incorporate a feminist perspective which is at the very basis of an entire book entitled *Märchen für tapfere Mädchen (Fairy Tales for Girls with Spunk,* 1978) by Doris Lerche, illustrator, and O. F. Gmelin, writer.[38] They use two fictitious girls named Trolla and Svea and a boy named Bror from the North to narrate different types of fairy tales which purposely seek to offset our conditioned notions of sexual roles and socialization. For instance, the very beginning of "Little Red Cap" indicates a markedly different perspective from the Grimms' version: "There was once a fearless girl. . . ."[39] She is not afraid of the wolf, and, even though she is swallowed by him in her grandmother's bed, she keeps her wits about her, takes out a knife, cuts herself a hole in his stomach while he sleeps, and rescues herself and granny. In Gmelin's rendition of "Hans and Gretel," the poor parents are not the enemies of the children, rather poverty is the source of trouble. To help the parents, the children go into the woods in search for food and eventually they become lost. Then they encounter a woman who is no longer a witch, but an outcast who has learned to live by the brutal rule of the land set by others. Hans and Gretel overcome the obstacles which she places in their quest for food, but they do not punish her. They are more concerned in re-establishing strong bonds of cooperation and love with their parents. The children return home without a treasure, and the ending leaves the future fate of the family open.

IV

The open endings of many of the reutilized fairy tales from West Germany of the 1970s indicate that the future for such fairy tales may also be precarious. Given the social import and the direct political tendency of the tales to contradict and criticize the dominant socializa-

tion process in Germany, these tales were not used widely in schools, and their distribution was limited more to groups partial to the tales among the educated classes in West Germany. They were also attacked by the conservative press because of their "falsifications" and alleged harmfulness to children. Nevertheless, the production of such tales did not abate in the 1980s and 1990s, and such continuous publication may reflect something about the diminishing appeal of the Grimms' tales and the needs of young and adult readers to relate to fantastic projections which are connected more to the concrete conditions of their own reality.

Folk tales and fairy tales have always been dependent on customs, rituals, and values in the particular socialization process of a social system. They have always symbolically depicted the nature of power relationships within a given society. Thus, they are strong indicators of the level of civilization, that is, the essential quality of a culture and social order. The effectiveness of emancipatory and reutilized tales has not only depended on the tales themselves but also on the manner in which they have been received, their use and distribution in society. The fact that West German writers argued and continue to argue that it is time for the Brothers Grimm to stop looking over their shoulders may augur positive changes for part of the socialization process. At the very least, they compel us to reconsider where socialization through the reading of the Grimms' tales has led us.

Notes

1. It has always been fashionable to try to rewrite folk tales and the classical ones by the Grimms. However, the recent trend is more international in scope, not just centered in Germany, and more political in intent. For some examples see, Jay Williams, *The Practical Princess and Other Liberating Fairy Tales* (London: Chatto & Windus, 1979); Astrid Lindgren, *Märchen* (Hamburg: Oetingen, 1978), which first appeared in Swedish; *The Prince and the Swineherd, Red Riding Hood, Snow White* by the Fairy Story Collective (Liverpool, 1976), three different publications by four women from the Merseyside Women's Liberation Movement. I shall discuss this international trend in my chapter eight, "The Liberating Potential of the Fantastic in Contemporary Fairy Tales for Children."

2. My focus is on the development in West Germany only. The official attitude toward fairy tales in East Germany has gone through different phases since 1949. At first they were rejected, but there was a more favorable policy during the 1980s, so long as the tales did not question the existing state of affairs. Thus, the older fairy tales by the Grimms were accorded due recognition while re-

utilization of the tales in a manifest political manner critical of the state and socialization was not condoned. See Sabine Brandt. "Rotkäppchen und der Klassenkampf," *Der Monat* 12 (1960): 64-74. I have also written more extensively about the development in East and West Germany in "The Struggle for the Grimms' Throne: The Legacy of the Grimms' Tales in the FRG and GDR since 1945" in *The Reception of Grimms Fairy Tales: Responses, Reactions, Revisions.* Ed. Donald Haase (Detroit: Wayne State University Press, 1993). 167-206.

3. See Dieter Richter and Jochen Vogt, eds., *Die heimlichen Erzieher, Kinderbücher und politisches Lernen* (Reinbek bei Hamburg: Rowohlt, 1974) and Linda Dégh, "*Grimms' Household Tales* and Its Place in the Household: The Social Relevance of a Controversial Classic," *Western Folklore* 38 (April 1979): 83-103.

4. See Erich Kaiser, "'Ent-Grimm-te' Märchen," *Westermanns Pädagogische Beiträge* 8 (1975): 448-59, and Hildegard Pischke, "Das veränderte Märchen," *Literatur für Kinder,* ed. by Maria Lypp (Göttingen: Vandenhoeck & Ruprecht, 1977), 94-113.

5. See Heinz Rölleke's introduction and commentaries to the 1810 manuscript written by the Grimms in *Die älteste Märchensammlung der Brüder Grimm* (Cologny-Geneva: Fondation Martin Bodmer, 1975); Werner Psaar and Manfred Klein, *Wer hat Angst vor der bösen Geiss?* (Braunschweig: Westermann, 1976), 9-30; Ingeborg Weber-Kellermann's introduction to *Kinder- und Hausmärchen gesammelt durch die Brüder Grimm,* Vol. I (Frankfurt am Main: Insel, 1976), 9-18.

6. Weber-Kellermann, *Kinder- und Hausmärchen gesammelt durch die Brüder Grimm,* Vol. I, 14.

7. *Ibid.,* 23-4. This is taken from the 1819 preface by the Brothers Grimm.

8. *Ibid.,* 24.

9. Rölleke, ed., *Die älteste Marchensammlung der Brüder Grimm,* 144. Unless otherwise indicated, all the translations in this chapter are my own. In most instances I have endeavored to be as literal as possible to document the historical nature of the text.

10. *Ibid.,* 145.

11. *Kinder- und Hausmärchen gesammelt durch die Brüder Grimm,* 35-6.

12. *Contes de Perrault,* ed. by Gilbert Rouger (Paris: Garnier 1967), 113.

13. Brüder Grimm, *Kinder- und Hausmärchen: In der ersten Gestalt.* (Frankfurt am Main, 1962), 78.

14. "Perrault's 'Little Red Riding Hood': Victim of Revision," *Children's Literature* 7 (1978): 68.

15. For the best analysis of Perrault and his times, see Marc Soriano, *Les Contes de Perrault* (Paris: Gallimard, 1968).

16. The word *sittsam* is used in the 1857 edition and carries with it a sense of chastity, virtuousness, and good behavior.

17. *Die älteste Sammlung der Brüder Grimm,* 246, 248 (op. cit., note 5).

18. *Ibid.,* 249, 251.

19. *Ibid.,* 250.

20. Psaar and Klein, *Wer hat Angst vor der bösen Geiss?,* 112-36.

21. See *The Uses of Enchantment: The Meaning and Importance of Fairy Tales* (New York: Knopf, 1976). For a critique of Bettelheim's position, see James W. Heisig, "Bruno Bettelheim and the Fairy Tales," *Children's Literature* 6 (1977): 93-114, and my own criticism in the chapter, "On the Use and Abuse of Folk and Fairy Tales: Bruno Bettelheim's Moralistic Magic Wand," in *Breaking the Magic Spell: Radical Theories of Folk and Fairy Tales* (London: Heinemann, 1979), 160-82.

22. Helmut Fend, *Sozialisation durch Literatur* (Weinheim: Beltz, 1979), 30, remarks: "Socialization proves itself to be a process of resubjectification of cultural objectifications. In highly complex cultures and societies this involves the learning of complex sign systems and higher forms of knowledge as well as the general comprehension of the world for dealing with natural problems and the general self-comprehension of human beings. Through the process of resubjectification of cultural objectifications, structures of consciousness, that is, subjective worlds of meaning, are constructed. Psychology views this formally as abstraction from particular contents and speaks about the construction of cognitions, about the construction of a 'cognitive map,' or a process of internalization. In a depiction of how cultural patterns are assumed in a substantive way, the matter concerns what conceptions about one's own person, which skills and patterns or interpretations, which norms and values someone takes and accepts in a certain culture relative to a sub-sphere of a society. Generally speaking, what happens in the socialization process is what hermeneutical research defines as 'understanding'. Understanding is developed and regarded here as an interpretative appropriation of linguistically transmitted meanings which represent socio-historical forms of life. To be sure, this understanding has a differentiated level of development which is frequently bound by social class."

23. See Richard Hoggart, *The Uses of Literacy* (London: Chatto & Windus, 1957), Harvey Graff, and R. A Houston, *Literacy in Early Modern Europe: Culture and Education 1500-1800,* 2nd Ed. (London: Longman, 2002).

24. *Volk ohne Buch* (Frankfurt am Main: Klostermann, 1970).

25. Emanuel K. Schwartz, "A Psychoanalytical Study of the Fairy Tale," *American Journal of Psychotherapy,* 10 (1956): 755. See also Julius E. Heuscher, *A Psychiatric Study of Fairy Tales* (Springfield, Illinois: Thomas, 1963).

26. The terms are from Victor Laruccia's excellent study, "Little Red Riding Hood's Metacommentary: Paradoxical Injunction, Semiotics and Behavior," *Modern Language Notes* 90 (1975): 517-34. Laruccia notes (p. 520) that, "all messages have two aspects, a command and a report, the first being a message about the nature of the relationship between sender and receiver, the second the message of the content. The crucial consideration is how these two messages relate to each other. This relationship is central to all goal-directed activity in any community since all human goals necessarily involve a relation with others." Laruccia's essay includes a discussion of the way male domination and master/slave relationships function in the Grimms' tales.

27. See Dieter Richter, ed., *Das politische Kinderbuch* (Darmstadt: Luchterhand, 1973). Various writers such as Kurd Lasswitz began creating political fairy tales at the end of the nineteenth century. One of the first collections of political fairy tales published during the Weimar period is Ernst Friedrich, ed., *Proletarischer Kindergarten* (Berlin: Buchverlag der Arbeiter-Kunst-Ausstellung, 1921), which contains stories and poems as well.

28. All these writers either wrote political fairy tales or wrote about them during the 1920s and early part of the 1930s. One could add many other names to this list, such as Ernst Bloch, Bruno Schönlank, Berta Lask, Oskar Maria Graf, Kurt Held, Robert Grötzsch, and even Bertolt Brecht. The most important fact to bear in mind, aside from the unwritten history of this development, is that German writers of the 1970s began to hark back to this era.

29. See my article "Down with Heidi, Down with Struwwelpeter, Three Cheers for the Revolution: Towards a New Children's Literature in West Germany," *Children's Literature* 5 (1976): 162-79.

30. Waechter is one of the most gifted writers and illustrators for children in Germany today. He is particularly known for the following books: *Der Anti-Struwwelpeter* (1973), *Wir können noch viel zusammenmachen* (1973), *Die Kronenklauer* (1975), and *Die Bauern im Brunnen* (1978).

31. The publisher of *Der Feuerdrache Minimax* is Rowohlt in Reinbek bei Hamburg. Angela Hopf has written several interesting books related to political fairy tales: *Fabeljan* (1968), *Die grosse Elefanten-Olympiade* (1972), *Die Minimax-Comix* (1974), and *Der Regentropfen Pling Plang Pling* (1981).

32. For a thorough and most perceptive analysis of this book, see Hermann Hinkel and Hans Kammler, "Der Feuerdrache Minimax—ein Märchen?—ein Bilderbuch," *Die Grundschule* 3 (1975): 151-60.

33. Among the more interesting studies related to the fairy tale are: Dieter Richter and Johannes Merkel, *Märchen, Phantasie und soziales Lernen* (Berlin: Basis, 1974); Andrea Kuhn, *Tugend und Arbeit. Zur Sozialisation durch Kinder- und Jugendliteratur im 18. Jahrhundert* (Berlin: Basis, 1975); Andrea Kuhn und Johannes Merkel, *Sentimentalität und Geschäft. Zur Sozialisation durch Kinder- und Jugendliteratur im 19. Jahrhundert* (Berlin: Basis, 1977).

34. The publisher of *Janosch erzählt Grimms Märchen* is Beltz & Gelberg in Weinheim. Janosch, whose real name is Horst Eckert, is considered one of the most inventive and provocative illustrators and writers for young people in Germany. Among his many titles, the most important are: *Das Auto heisst Ferdinand* (1964), *Wir haben einen Hund zu Haus* (1968), *Flieg Vogel flieg* (1971), *Mein Vater ist König* (1974), *Das grosse Janosch-Buch* (1976), *Ich sag, du bist ein Bär* (1977), *Oh, wie schön ist Panama* (1978), *Die Maus hat rote Strümpfe an* (1978). Many of his books have been filmed and translated into English.

35. A good example is *Erstes Jahrbuch der Kinderliteratur. 'Geh und spiel mit dem Riesen,'* ed. Hans-Joachim Gelberg (Weinheim: Beltz, 1971), which won the German Youth Book Prize of 1972.

36. Many of the tales were printed in other books edited by Gelberg, or they appeared elsewhere, indicative of the great trend to reutilize fairy tales.

37. Translations of the tales by Brender and Künzler have been published in my book *Breaking the Magic Spell,* 180-2.

38. Gmelin, in particular, has been active in scrutinizing the value of fairy tales and has changed his position in the course of the last eight years. See Otto Gmelin, "Böses kommt aus Märchen," *Die Grundschule* 3 (1975): 125-32.

39. Lerche-and Gmelin, *Märchen für tapfere Mädchen* (Giessen: Schlot, 1978), 16.

FURTHER READING

Criticism

Kamenetsky, Christa. "Didactic Approaches to Folktales and Fairy Tales." In *The Brothers Grimm & Their Critics: Folktales and the Quest for Meaning,* pp. 215-53. Athens: Ohio University Press, 1992.

  Surveys the pedagogical purposes historically associated with children's literature, and various applications of fairy tales for educating youth.

O'Neill, Thomas. "Guardian of the Fairy Tale: The Brothers Grimm." *National Geographic* 196, no. 6 (December 1999): 103-29.

  Discusses the literary significance of the Grimm brothers to German folk traditions.

Rusch-Feja, Diann D. *The Portrayal of the Maturation Process of Girl Figures in Selected Tales of the Brothers Grimm.* Frankfurt am Main, Germany: Peter Lang, 1995, 288 p.

  Examines the representation of female development in *Grimms' Fairy Tales.*

Stephens, John, and Robyn McCallum. "Utopia, Dystopia, and Cultural Controversy in *Ever After* and *The Grimm Brothers' Snow White.*" *Marvels & Tales* 16, no. 2 (2002): 201-13.

  Explores the cultural implications of utopian/dystopian themes and motifs in the films *Ever After* and *The Grimm Brothers' Snow White,* contrasting the ideological effects of their respective narrative strategies and audience positioning.

"The Masque of the Red Death"

Edgar Allan Poe

The following entry presents criticism of Poe's short story "The Masque of the Red Death" (1842). For additional information on his short fiction career, see *SSC*, Volumes 1 and 54; for discussion of the short story "The Fall of the House of Usher" (1839), see *SSC*, Volume 22; for discussion of the short story "The Tell-Tale Heart" (1843), see *SSC*, Volume 34; for discussion of the short story "The Cask of Amontillado" (1846), see *SSC*, Volume 35.

INTRODUCTION

"The Masque of the Red Death" is revered as one of Poe's most evocative tales and cited as an exemplary work of Gothic horror literature. Noted for its unique narrative perspective, "The Masque of the Red Death" utilizes a first-person omniscient storyteller, the identity and significance of whom is the subject of scholarly debate. Though Poe's narrative is simple, his finely detailed descriptions, bold use of color, allegorical structure, and employment of biblical and literary allusions paint a complex picture of humanity's physical and psychological confrontation with mortality.

PLOT AND MAJOR CHARACTERS

In the midst of the Red Death—a terrible plague that has devastated the country, killing half its population—the wealthy Prince Prospero invites one thousand friends to join him in the seclusion of his ornate abbey. The courtiers weld the doors shut to avoid exposure to the plague, which causes horrific bleeding, seizures, and death within half an hour. For several months, they enjoy a lavish lifestyle of wine, music, and dance as the Red Death ravages the outside world. The Prince decides to throw a decadent masquerade ball, providing his guests with elaborate costumes. The suite in which the ball is held consists of seven chambers, each of which is dominated by a specific color and decorated with a stained glass window of a corresponding hue. The exception to the Prince's color scheme is the seventh and most western chamber, which features a deep crimson window to contrast its black walls and décor. This last room also contains a massive ebony clock that tolls upon the hour. As the clock strikes midnight, Pros-

pero and his guests observe a corpse-like figure, dressed in ceremonial burial attire and speckled in blood. Upon noticing the spectacle, the Prince becomes enraged at what he deems a mockery of the festivities, and orders that the intruder be seized and hanged the following morning. When none of the masqueraders obey his command, Prospero pursues the stranger through each successive room until they meet in the seventh. After the prince falls dead to the floor, his guests forcibly unmask the foreboding figure, but find nothing under the stranger's disguise. The guests begin to fall one by one, and the clock stops ticking to mark the final death.

MAJOR THEMES

Time is one of the prominent themes in "The Masque of the Red Death," and the clock in the seventh room serves as the most overt symbol of the passing of time and the inevitability of death. Even as the masquerade exhibits an air of levity and hedonism, the clock continues to tick in the background. The significance of its ominous persistence is not made fully apparent to the reader or the characters until the tolling of midnight. Likewise, Poe's exacting sequential descriptions of the rooms creates an underlying sense of progression or procession. The overall effect of such an emphasis on duration becomes a fatalistic comment on Prospero's attempt to devise an alternative reality within the abbey. This points as well to the theme of the vanity of human art and endeavor. The exquisite design of the costumes and the abbey's interior, as well as the abundance of wine, song, and food, cannot stave off the presence of the Red Death.

CRITICAL RECEPTION

Although "The Masque of the Red Death" received little critical attention during Poe's lifetime, it has since come to be acknowledged as one of the finest examples of nineteenth-century American short fiction. Scholars have devoted significant attention to the possible literary sources for the story. For example, such diverse texts as William Shakespeare's *Macbeth* and *The Tempest*, Lord Byron's *Childe Harold*, Thomas de Quincey's *Klosterheim; or, The Masque*, Giovanni Boccaccio's *Decameron*, and Thomas Campbell's *Life of Petrarch* have all been cited as inspiration for "The Masque of the Red Death."

Many critics have explored Poe's rich thematic techniques in the work, examining the incidence of religious allusions and symbols as a reversal of the Christian notion of a redemptive savior triumphing over death. Some critics have maintained that the significance of the number seven also illuminates religious motifs in the story, and scholars have related the seven chambers in the abbey to the seven deadly sins, seven cardinal virtues, and seven stages of human life. Critics have also highlighted Poe's symbolic use of the colors black and red in the tale, and have discussed the aesthetic effect of his vivid descriptions of the chambers, linking his overarching color scheme to the liturgical vestments of the Catholic Church.

Scholars have maintained that Poe addressed such archetypal conflicts as life versus death, creation versus destruction, and internal order versus external chaos through his depiction of the Red Death as victor. Critics have also examined the influence of Poe's story on a number of later works, including Henry James' novel *The Portrait of a Lady*, Alfred Kubin's novel *The Other Side*, and Alfred Hitchcock's film *The Birds*. For these reasons, along with its ability to excite the darker regions of imagination, "The Masque of the Red Death"

has advanced Poe's reputation as one of the progenitors of modern literature, and has been singled out as a prime example of American Romanticism.

PRINCIPAL WORKS

Short Fiction

The Narrative of Arthur Gordon Pym 1838
Tales of the Grotesque and Arabesque. 2 vols. 1840
Prose Romances of Edgar A. Poe 1843
Tales 1845
The Works of the Late Edgar Allan Poe. 4 vols. [edited by Rufus Wilmot Griswold] 1850-56
The Complete Works of Edgar Allan Poe. 17 vols. [edited by James A. Harrison] 1902
The Collected Works of Edgar Allan Poe. 3 vols. [edited by Thomas Ollive Mabbott] 1969-78
The Short Fiction of Edgar Allan Poe: An Annotated Edition [edited by Stuart Levine and Susan Levine] 1976
The Annotated Tales of Edgar Allan Poe [edited by Stephen Peithman] 1981

Other Major Works

Tamerlane and Other Poems: By a Bostonian (poetry) 1827
Al Aaraaf, Tamerlane, and Minor Poems (poetry) 1829
Poems (poetry) 1831
The Raven, and Other Poems (poetry) 1845
Eureka: A Prose Poem (essay) 1848
The Literati (criticism) 1850

CRITICISM

James B. Reece (essay date February 1953)

SOURCE: Reece, James B. "New Light on Poe's 'The Masque of the Red Death.'"[1] *Modern Language Notes* 68, no. 2 (February 1953): 114-15.

[*In the following essay, Reece suggests that the account of the plague and the character of Prince Prospero in "The Masque of the Red Death" were inspired by Thomas Campbell's* Life of Petrarch.]

One of the works that may have supplied Poe with raw materials for his **"The Masque of the Red Death"** appears to have been overlooked in the discussions of the backgrounds of that story. Thomas Campbell's *Life of Petrarch* was published in 1841 and Poe reviewed it in *Graham's* for September of that year (XIX, 143-144), eight months before **"The Masque"** was published in the same periodical (XX, 257-259; May, 1842). Poe's critical remarks indicate at least a general familiarity with the contents of Campbell's book. The *Life* [*Life of Petrarch*] contains occasional passages which describe the effects of the great plague which swept through Italy in the mid-fourteenth century, and Poe chose from among these passages in selecting quotations for comment.

The descriptions of the plague in the two works show several points of correspondence in regard to the symptoms and effects of the disease. Moreover, an incident related by Campbell offers a striking parallel to the essentials of Poe's plot:

> The plague now again broke out in Italy. . . . The nobles and court abandoned their capital, Galeazzo Visconti repaired to Monza, Barnabo shut himself in his strong castle at Manigno near Lodi, a place that was thought to be sheltered from pestilence by the dense woods around it. He had his retreat strictly guarded, allowing no one to approach it. A sentinel was placed in one of the towers, who had orders to ring the bell whenever he saw any one approaching on horseback. Some gentlemen entered the precincts of the castle without any one having heard the bell. Barnabo immediately sent orders to put the sentinel to death; but they found him dead beneath the bell. This event so frightened our chieftain, that he went and hid himself in the thickest depths of the forest, where he lived so sequestered as to cause a report of his death.[2]

This account of the attempt of an Italian nobleman to isolate himself from the plague-stricken world, permitting no one to enter his secluded castle, but finding his efforts futile against the power of the pestilence,[3] may have furnished Poe with all he required in the way of basic plot material for **"The Masque."**

As Poe does in **"The Masque,"** Campbell tells of merrymakers who carried on their activities while the plague raged. He, however, unlike Poe, assigns a convincing medieval reason for such behavior:

> It was the general persuasion that sadness accelerated the infection of the malady, and that pleasant amusements were the surest defence against it. People, therefore, hardened their hearts against grief for the dead by jokes and merriment. . . .
>
> In the mean time, the living, being persuaded that diversions and songs of gaiety could alone preserve them from the pestilence, kept up their revels. . . .[4]

Prince Prospero and his "hale and light-hearted" company in **"The Masque"** unsympathetically seek a safe retreat where they can defy the plague, leaving the external world to "take care of itself." Poetic justice, for which Poe had respect, is much better served in the story by the omission of any reference to the motive which Campbell attributes to the pleasure seekers, as is the overall tone of horror which Poe wanted to achieve.

Notes

1. A list of previously suggested sources for Poe's story may be found in Cortell King Holsapple, "'The Masque of the Red Death' and *I Promessi Sposi*," University of Texas *Studies in English*, XVIII, 137-139 (1938).

2. Thomas Campbell, *Life of Petrarch*, London, 1841, II, 239-240.

3. While Campbell is not explicit on this point, the idea that the sentinel died of the plague would almost certainly have occurred to Poe.

4. Campbell, *op. cit.*, I, 353-354.

Kermit Vanderbilt (essay date March 1968)

SOURCE: Vanderbilt, Kermit. "Art and Nature in 'The Masque of the Red Death.'" *Nineteenth-Century Fiction* 22, no. 4 (March 1968): 379-89.

[*In the following essay, Vanderbilt compares Prince Prospero in "The Masque of the Red Death" to William Shakespeare's character Prospero in* The Tempest, *and views Poe's story as indicative of the Romantic literary trend in mid-nineteenth-century America.*]

The intended effect and meaning of **"The Masque of the Red Death"** have challenged and eluded Poe critics over the years. Readings of the tale have advanced Poe studies by offering valuable glimpses into Poe's fictional world; but none has achieved a satisfactory account of the story in all of its significant parts.[1] An approach to Poe's meaning overlooked up to now has been a study of **"The Masque"** in the immediate context of Poe's esthetic ideas in 1842. Interpreted in the light of Poe's developing esthetic theory in this crucial year, the story, which appeared in the May issue of *Graham's Magazine,* becomes somewhat more than a tale of horror on the coming of Death. The hero Prospero, who bears an interesting resemblance to his namesake in Shakespeare's *The Tempest,* appears to be not a fear-crazed ruler but instead an exact portrait of Poe's artist-hero, and **"The Masque of the Red Death"** becomes a fable of nature and art. Placed in a larger context, the tale allowed Poe to dramatize the tensions of the "Romantic" artist in America, and helped him to discover the way which led through **"The Domain of Arnheim"** into the cosmic regions of *Eureka.*

I

The month before **"The Masque of the Red Death"** appeared, Poe explored the contention between the artist and the limits imposed by mortality. The occasion was a review of Longfellow's recent poetry.[2] In this essay, which later would be enlarged as "The Poetic Principle," Poe defined the poet or creator of Beauty as a man of "taste" rather than of "pure intellect" or "moral sense." He concerns himself not with temporal duty or earthly truth but with supernal beauty. He is thereby superior to the rest of mankind. They delight in the "manifold forms and colors and sounds" of things-as-they-are, and in the conventional record of nature fashioned by the imitative craftsman. But the true artist strives to create rather than imitate, and his vision therefore transcends mere nature. His "burning thirst" for supernal beauty, a passion approaching even to madness, is related to "the *immortal* essence of man's nature." In making this "wild effort to reach the beauty above," the artist rearranges and transforms material reality:

> Inspired with a prescient ecstasy of the beauty beyond the grave, [the imagination] struggles by multiform novelty of combination among the things and thoughts of Time, to anticipate a portion of that loveliness whose very elements, perhaps, appertain solely to Eternity.

The next month in **"The Masque of the Red Death"** Prince Prospero will exactly match this description of the artist-hero. When he isolates himself and one thousand knights and ladies of his court during the pestilence, the Prince is not following the dictates of a judicious "intellect" or a dutiful "moral sense." The Prince, as Poe notes, is a man of "taste." Though his courtiers conceive the adventure to be a well-planned escape from the Red Death itself, the Prince has motives of another order. Objective nature outside having been ravaged by the plague, Poe's hero will employ his taste and imagination to create a symbolic equivalent of nature's elements—a combination which can transform earthly reality into the artist's liberating vision of immortal beauty.

The colors of the Prince's bizarre suite, together with their ordering from east to west, establish the leading clues to Prospero's subjective world. Poe does not seem, at first, to insist that the colors are meaningful. He sketches the seven rooms with fairly rapid strokes, seemingly to illustrate that the Prince is "gaudy," "bizarre," "wanton," and "fantastic" in his artistic predilections:

> That at the eastern extremity was hung, for example, in blue—and vividly blue were its windows. The second chamber was purple in its ornaments and tapestries, and here the panes were purple. The third was green throughout, and so were the casements. The fourth was furnished and litten with orange—the fifth with white—the sixth with violet. The seventh apartment was closely shrouded in black velvet tapestries. . . . The panes here were scarlet—a deep blood color.

Prospero's suite, arranged from east to west, with the first apartment blue and the seventh black, connotes generally the daily cycle of nature and Shakespeare's

seven ages of man, as more than one critic has remarked. No one, however, has taken Poe's art seriously enough here to confirm that the pattern is deliberate and precise. Yet Poe in the same issue of *Graham's* had reviewed Hawthorne's *Twice-Told Tales* and set down his requirement that in the tale "there should be no word written, of which the tendency, direct or indirect, is not to the one preestablished design."[3]

A meaningful symmetry does develop precisely in Prospero's seven-room suite. The middle or fourth room, for example, is orange, the warmest color in Poe's spectrum, and analogous to midday. Returning to the cold, blue eastern room, one recognizes the image of dawning human life. It is succeeded by the purple room—an infusion of blue with the warmer tone of red—suggesting perhaps the quickening of life. The third room of green connotes growth, aspiration, youth; and the orange room, corresponding to the high noon of existence, becomes the harvest or fulfillment of human labor and ambition. The next room is white, at once all-color and no-color, a sudden and chill contrast which evokes decline, old age, decomposition, and approaching death. Or as Poe put it in "Tamerlane": "Let life, then, as the day-flower, fall / With the noon-day beauty—which is all." After the white apartment comes the next-to-last room of violet, a bluish blue-red colder than the corresponding purple of the second room, and prefiguring imminent death in the seventh room. In this western room, the blood-colored panes depict, of course, the dread effects of the plague, and the black tapestries represent death itself. And most prominently stands the massive ebony clock against the western wall. Its "dull, heavy monotonous clang" pervades the entire suite and further marks the ravages of time in each of the seven stages of earthly mortality.[4]

If Prospero's suite is a metaphor of nature and mortality, one naturally asks why the Prince, apparently bent on escape from death, should have patterned his suite after the very reminders of mutability, decay, and the Red Death. The previous essay on Longfellow has suggested the answer. Poe is writing a fable of the imagination striving to control and transform the corrosive elements of nature and to gain, through immortal beauty, the artist's triumph over death. Prospero has designed an imperial suite to embody, first of all, the cycle of natural life, including what Poe had termed in the Longfellow review "the things and thoughts of Time." Next, he has created the "multiform novelty of combinations" which will permit him to move through and beyond the confinements of nature, time, and finite reality. The suite, with its windings, its stained-glass windows, closed outer corridors, artificial illumination, and bizarre embellishments—its "multitude of gaudy and fantastic appearances"—represents Prospero's imaginative re-ordering of actuality. He has created a setting which can evoke the magic and unearthly visions of the liberated sensibility. These enclosed apartments, both singly and together, define the magic circle which Poe earlier had termed "the circumscribed Eden" of the poet's dreams.

Prospero's elaborate masque provides the main drama of Poe's tale. As in Shakespeare's *The Tempest,* the masque also climaxes the struggle between the hero's art and nature's opposing forces of darkness. In fact, the illuminating parallels between the two works, while they may not prove that Poe consciously used Shakespeare's play as a source, do suggest at least a way to read Poe's climactic action in the tale.[5] Shakespeare's Prospero, it will be remembered, succeeds in controlling a savage island and turning it into a land suffused with idyllic greenness and ethereal music. To achieve this triumph of his art over barbaric nature, Prospero frees Ariel from a cloven pine where he had been imprisoned by the "earthly and abhorred commands" of the witch-hag Sycorax (I, ii, 273). So liberated from the destructive element of earth, the delicate Ariel becomes the spiritual quality of nature which unites with the powers of Prospero's art to create a landscape of paradisal beauty. Ariel helps to preserve Prospero's island dominion, though he reminds his master that this magic service will presently end.

Prospero's island rule, then, is precarious, and made more so by his chief enemy Caliban, the bestial offspring of Sycorax. Caliban embodies the withering threat of destructive nature to the artist's imagination. Shakespeare brilliantly condenses this antagonism toward Prospero's higher powers by giving Caliban's curse on his master: "the red plague rid you, / For learning me your language" (I, ii, 364-365).

The climax of Prospero's reign occurs in the masque which he conjures in the fourth act. During the dance of nymphs and reapers which follows Ceres' song of harvest abundance, Prospero grows distracted and petulant. He breaks off the masque. His imagination has failed him, his worldly fears of Caliban's "foul conspiracy" have returned, and as a result of both, he gives in to a despairing vision of cosmic dissolution. In this decline of imagination, Shakespeare's artist-hero confronts utter reality and admits, in effect, that man's creative art cannot transcend the life-threatening forces of hostile nature. In particular, he concedes his failure either to elevate or to vanquish Caliban: "This thing of darkness I / Acknowledge mine" (V, i, 275-276). At the end, he owns that his liberation from darkness, death, and the limits of earth must arrive from a power greater than his own:

> Now I want
> Spirits to enforce, art to enchant
> And my ending is despair,
> Unless I be reliev'd by prayer,

> Which pierces so that it assaults
> Mercy itself and frees all faults.

> (Epilogue, 13-18)[6]

Poe's Prospero also meets the ultimate challenge to his art as he stages his bizarre masque "while the pestilence raged most furiously abroad." The Prince's "guiding taste," once again, dictates the colors and effects. Like Shakespeare's hero, also, Poe's Prospero gives character to the masqueraders themselves. And their character is such stuff as dreams are made on. They are no longer people, but have become, instead, "a multitude of dreams": "And these—the dreams—writhed in and about, taking hue from the rooms, and causing the wild music of the orchestra to seem as the echo of their steps." Prospero has combined light and color, arabesque sculpture, wild music, and the rhythms of the dance to create his dreamland, out of space, out of time. Only the measured, hourly chiming of the ebony clock threatens to dissipate the fantasy; but this brief, contrapuntal note of reality also emphasizes, by contrast, the prevailing "glare and glitter and piquancy and phantasm" of Prospero's conjured assembly of spirits:

> The dreams are stiff-frozen as they stand. But the echoes of the chime die away—they have endured but an instant—. . . And now again the music swells, and the dreams live, and writhe to and fro more merrily than ever, taking hue from the many-tinted windows through which stream the rays from the tripods.

Like Shakespeare's hero, Prospero has controlled the movements of his visitors, transcended the limitations of nature, and approached the threshold of supernal beauty. But at the midnight hour, the figure of the Red Death—the counterpart of Caliban—appears at the masque.

Prospero's failure is first signaled not by the imminent threat of death, but by his troubled reaction to its appearance. His convulsion and anger indicate the failure of imagination even before he waves his hand to end the masque. His fearful command to his courtiers, "'Uncase the varlet that we may know whom we have to hang to-morrow at sunrise from the battlements,'" is both impotent and utterly mundane, the conventional reflex of a petulant, earthly ruler. The world, in short, is finally too much with him. The mummer of Death strides majestically past him and through the seven apartments (Poe once more underscores the exact sequence of the polychromatic décor) in symbolic triumph over each stage of earthly life and over Prospero's art and aspiring imagination. As in *The Tempest,* Ariel has taken leave and Prospero alone must confront his mortality and ultimate defeat. While the courtiers shrink from the grim figure, Prospero acknowledges this thing of darkness to be his own. In a self-destructive charge, he pursues the spectre of death westward into the seventh apartment. And predictably, death gains his midnight victory in the western room where the dread clock and macabre appointments had been the artist's ultimate challenge to his powers of imagination.

Prospero's defeat becomes inevitable within the precise logic which supports Poe's esthetic fable. And it suggests one last parallel to *The Tempest*. Anticipating the return of Caliban, Shakespeare's Prospero can no longer prolong his masque. Instead, he entertains a vision of cosmic dissolution and offers the dispiriting prophecy that

> the great globe itself
> Yea, all which it inherit, shall dissolve
> And, like this insubstantial pageant faded,
> Leave not a rack behind.
>
> (IV, i, 153-156)

Poe repeats this cataclysmic vision of destructive nature and triumphant death. The outer and inner worlds of his defeated hero fade, and the final curtain lowers to the measured and fateful cadence of Poe's closing rhetoric:

> And the life of the ebony clock went out with that of the last of the gay. And the flames of the tripods expired. And Darkness and Decay and the Red Death held illimitable dominion over all.[7]

II

In **"The Masque of the Red Death,"** Poe gave fictional expression to the esthetic ideas he had been formulating in the previous months. **"The Masque"** gains further esthetic meaning when one enlarges the context of the tale to embrace Poe's writing in the months immediately afterward. In his essay on Longfellow in April, Poe had described the poetic spirit of the various arts, but made no mention of landscape gardening. The next month in **"The Masque,"** Prospero for obvious reasons does not cultivate a landscape garden. He does, however, try (and fail) to create an earthly paradise, the artist's heightened transfiguration of nature which will transcend the limits imposed by mere nature and the Red Death. Either during the composition of the tale or immediately thereafter, Poe began to develop an articulate notion of the landscape garden as the supreme expression of human art. Within weeks, he had elaborated this extension of his esthetic theory in **"The Landscape Garden"** (*Ladies' Companion*, October, 1842).[8] In this short fiction, Prospero reappears as Ellison and proclaims that in the art of landscape gardening one discovers "the fairest field for the display of invention, or imagination, in the endless combining of forms of novel Beauty." Ellison prefers the creative "artificial" landscape garden to the "natural" style which merely imitates the proportion and congruity of nature. To Ellison, such imitation recalls the negative merit of Addison's esthetic and is "better suited to the grovelling apprehension of the herd." But the artificial style calls forth the

true poetic sentiment ("the fervid dreams of the man of genius"). Working as precisely as the rational-scientific intellect, the artist's superior taste then reorders matter and form to create "special wonders or miracles" in the landscape garden. Ellison cannot prescribe the rules which the landscape-gardener as poet must follow to achieve this higher order of beauty—"it is in vain that we are told *how* to conceive a 'Tempest'"—but given sufficient wealth (and Ellison has an annual inheritance which exceeds thirteen million dollars), the landscape-artist might "so imbue his designs at once with extent and novelty of Beauty" that "the sophists of the *negative* school" could only stand amazed at the result. Here at last might human art envision "a Nature which is not God, nor an emanation of God, but which still is Nature, in the sense that it is the handiwork of the angels that hover between man and God."

Poe expanded **"The Landscape Garden,"** though how soon afterward is hard to determine. Revised and lengthened, it appeared several years later as **"The Domain of Arnheim."** Ellison's man-made pastoral paradise now has progressed from theory to actuality. On the river-journey into Arnheim one discovers at once a continuity with the symbolic landscape of **"The Masque of the Red Death."** The boat leaves early in the morning, travelling westward. During the journey, the magic landscape resembles the windings of Prospero's apartments:

> The stream took a thousand turns, so that at no moment could its gleaming surface be seen for a greater distance than a furlong. At every instant the vessel seemed imprisoned within an enchanted circle. . . .

Ellison has shaped and transformed nature so that it exhibits "a weird symmetry, a thrilling uniformity, a wizard propriety in these her works." The river maintains a Walden-like purity as it mirrors an inverted heaven. The landscape suggests "dreams of a new race of fairies" while music emanates from an "unseen origin." (Again, as in **"The Masque,"** one thinks of parallels with *The Tempest*.) Sailing toward the red sunset beside chiselled precipices draped in lush foliage and limbs of black walnut, the traveller seems to approach an enormous western gate which will bar him from the promised glimpse of paradise (shades here of Caliban and the Red Death). But the gate is illusory and the boat passes through to enter Ellison's transcendent kingdom of supernal beauty. The traveller is overwhelmed by ethereal music, exotic trees, perfumed flowers, and a bizarre assemblage of architecture which seems "the phantom handiwork, conjointly, of the Sylphs, of the Fairies, of the Genii, and of the Gnomes." Through his landscape artistry, Ellison has happily achieved the divine marriage of nature and art which Prospero earlier had attempted and then lost to the forces of darkness, death, and dissolution.

In **"The Masque of the Red Death,"** then, Poe not only gave dramatic formulation to his esthetic creed but also was tracing the shadowy outlines of a more grandiose theory of art and nature for **"The Landscape Garden"** and beyond. Prospero's symbolic chambers, together with his artful masque of the red death, became a transitional moment in Poe's estheticism in 1842. When the Longfellow essay later became "The Poetic Principle," Poe would repeat that the poetic sentiment can be satisfied in the various fine arts; but he would climax the statement this time by adding that this sense of beauty gains expression "very peculiarly, and with a wide field, in the composition of the Landscape Garden." The artist creatively re-ordering the natural landscape for his earthly paradise had become the intermediary between man and God, had moved ever closer to the role of divine Creator. And in the final stage, Poe's esthetic would extend into the cosmic reaches set forth in *Eureka.*

Equally important, **"The Masque of the Red Death"** reveals a conflict at the heart of Poe's esthetic in 1842 which throws light also on his response to America in the mid-nineteenth century. With Hawthorne, Emerson, Thoreau, Melville, and Whitman, Poe shared basic esthetic and moral concerns over the advance of scientific rationalism, technology, and urbanism, though Poe's response appears to have been the most ambivalent. On one hand, he nurtured in **"The Masque of the Red Death"** a defiant estheticism (though precisely formulated) and expanded it in the landscape tales and *Eureka*; and in these same years, he continued to write his tales of ratiocination, though his detective hero relied heavily on intuition. In this "Romantic" effort to harmonize the rational and intuitive forces contending in his esthetic and within himself, Poe met his contemporaries on common ground. Emerson, Thoreau, and Whitman, standing with feet on the earth and head bathed in the blithe air, labored to unite the lower intellect and higher intuition. Melville's heroes pursued the linked analogies between nature and mind, and Hawthorne's poet continued the quest in the woods at Blithedale. Through his artist-heroes Prospero and Ellison, Poe joined this effort to reconcile the higher claims of ideal beauty and truth with the lower demands of utility, to render nature the willing servant of man's earthly desire and his heaven-soaring intuition. With Prospero's failure to achieve this mastery, Poe was writing Romantic tragedy to corroborate the vision of Hawthorne and Melville; but in the triumph of Ellison, Poe also confirmed the American optimism of Emerson and his disciples.[9] In the conflict and the wedding of nature and art which he explored in **"The Masque of the Red Death"** and elaborated in the landscape sequels, Poe too had suggested for his audience, in 1842 and after, the highly creative, and some of the self-destructive, energies set loose by Romantic individualism in America.

Notes

1. For a selected survey of these diverse readings, ranging from clinical diagnosis to mystic impressionism, see Joseph P. Roppolo, "Meaning and 'The Masque of the Red Death,'" *Tulane Studies in English,* XIII (1963), 59-64.

2. "Ballads and Other Poems," *Graham's Magazine,* XX (April, 1842), 248-251.

3. *Graham's Magazine,* XX (May, 1842), 299. Walter Blair first remarked that Prospero's suite suggests, in a loose way, a metaphor of nature's cycle and man's mortality. See "Poe's Conception of Incident and Tone in the Tale," *Modern Philology,* XLI (May, 1944), 239. But Mr. Blair's suggestion was quickly challenged by a critic who favored a more impressionistic reading of Poe's fictional craft. The effort to assign objective and detailed meaning to Prospero's suite would limit rather than enlarge the reader's experience: "We must accept the story as we accept a piece of music: in spite of program notes which would limit the meaning of what we hear, we generally let ourselves go and create our own meaning." (Bryllion Fagin, *The Histrionic Mr. Poe* [Baltimore, 1949], p. 216.)

4. Wilson O. Clough, "The Use of Color Words by Edgar Allan Poe," *PMLA,* XLV (June, 1930), 598-613, corroborates much of the color association I have indicated. In his tabulation, Mr. Clough reveals that Poe used greens almost exclusively for vegetation and landscape settings. While yellow often connoted sickliness and decay, orange did not. Whites, blacks and reds in the tales of horror were usually associated with death. Since blue and purple had no predictable meaning among the tales, and violet was used only for the next-to-last apartment in "The Masque," one must rely here on the context. Finally, Poe applied variegated colors "most often to nature" (p. 612).

Did Poe borrow a leaf directly from *As You Like It*? One balks at the precise linking of Poe's progressive coloration and Shakespeare's seven ages of man, but the Shakespearean analogy is astonishingly close: the infant (blue), schoolboy (purple), lover (green), soldier (orange), judge (white), the piping schoolboy again (violet), and finally the dotard *"sans* everything" (black).

5. Poe, of course, knew his Shakespeare and admired Prospero and *The Tempest* in particular. He regarded *The Tempest* and its hero to be the quintessence of the poetic spirit. See *Southern Literary Messenger,* II (July, 1836), 501-503, a slight expansion of Poe's "Letter to B——," the preface to the New York edition of his *Poems* (1831). "B" was probably Elam Bliss, publisher of this second edition.

6. *The Tempest* has been interpreted as a fable of art before. Most recent is Leo Marx's highly suggestive reading of the play as an anticipation of American pastoral themes. See *The Machine in the Garden: Technology and the Pastoral Ideal in America* (New York, 1964), pp. 34-72.

7. Roppolo, "Meaning and 'The Masque of the Red Death,'" cites Poe's later *Eureka* as evidence that Poe meant to suggest in this ending not annihilation of Prospero and his world but merely the end of one cosmic cycle in an "eternal process of contraction and expansion" (p. 68). One can more safely trace the continuity of Poe's imagination here by bringing forward his "Colloquy of Monos and Una" which appeared in *Graham's* several months before. Anticipating the esthetic credo of the Longfellow review and "The Masque," Monos, speaking from beyond the grave, ascribes his death to a general decline of taste, "that faculty which holding a middle position between the pure intellect and the moral sense . . . could have led us gently back to Beauty, to Nature, and to Life." And near the end he recalls his "chamber of Death" at midnight when the impressions of "Darkness" and "Decay" were to merge into a liberation out of time and into eternity.

8. This piece was already completed in July, submitted to *The Democratic Review,* and rejected. For a discussion of the landscape vogue in America in 1842, an excitement to which Poe clearly had begun to respond, see Robert D. Jacobs, "Poe's Earthly Paradise," *American Quarterly,* XII (Fall, 1960), 405-406.

9. Suggested here is the continuing need in Poe studies to relate Poe's imagination to the currents of American life in his time. Leo Marx has recently argued that *The Tempest* is Shakespeare's "American fable," that it "anticipates the moral geography of the American imagination" by suggesting the pastoral tensions among scientism, nature, and art (*The Machine in the Garden,* p. 72). For the mid-nineteenth century, Marx stresses the conflict between nature and technology in the major writers other than Poe. As I have intimated, one discovers *Tempest* themes updated in Poe also. Briefly to amplify one pastoral configuration: In "Monos and Una" (1841), the hero bemoans that in his lifetime "huge smoking cities" had destroyed the natural landscape as "green leaves shrank before the hot breath of furnaces." This man-made pestilence, in which "the fair face of Nature was deformed as with the ravages of some loathesome disease," may well have suggested to Poe the crisis for Prospero and his art several months later. After Prospero's aborted effort to create his insular paradise comes the renewed at-

tempt by his successor Ellison. As Poe's landscape artist, Ellison achieves the pastoral harmony of the "middle landscape" (Marx, p. 71) which reconciles the contrary impulses of primitivism and modern urbanism. For the site of his landscape garden, Ellison rejects a primitive island ("I am not Timon") in favor of "a spot not far from a populous city."

Patricia H. Wheat (essay date winter 1982)

SOURCE: Wheat, Patricia H. "The Mask of Indifference in 'The Masque of the Red Death.'" *Studies in Short Fiction* 19, no. 1 (winter 1982): 51-6.

[*In the following essay, Wheat refutes a moral reading of "The Masque of the Red Death," underscoring Poe's existential tone and apathetic narrator.*]

When Prince Prospero and his thousand carefree friends shut themselves up in a fortified abbey to escape the fearful Red Death and make merry, they also shut themselves off from the sympathies of critical opinion. Thomas Mabbot believes "one cannot run away from responsibility." Stuart Levine agrees, noting that "The nobles are fiddling while Rome burns; worse, they are fiddling in great style." David Halliburton suggests that Prince Prospero sins by trying "to supplant God's creation with a creation of his own." The Prince is viewed by Edward Pitcher as "arrogantly calculating," with character traits of "egotism, . . . pride, coldness, manic superiority and tyranny." H. H. Bell calls Prospero a "feelingless ruling prince."[1] While it is difficult to entertain feelings of goodwill toward a monarch who deserts his people and stages a festive masked ball in the midst of their exposure to peril, negative attitudes toward Prince Prospero are to be found only in the writings of his modern critics and not in his story or in Poe's attitude toward him. Joseph Roppolo comes closest to Poe's meaning in **"The Masque of the Red Death"** when he discusses the isolation of man: "In the trap of life and in his death, every man is an island. If there is a mutual bond, it is the shared horror of death."[2] The Prince and his friends have no desire to share death's horror. Poe, however, expresses no disapproval of his character's actions or of his apparent attitudes. Prince Prospero's supposed pride is best seen as a protective mask, a mask of indifference with which he tries to shield himself from death.

Commentaries on **"The Masque of the Red Death"** often, rightly, describe the story's action in terms of a battle. Walter Blair views it as a battle between death and life, between time and the "gaiety which seeks to kill time by forgetting it."[3] In his comparison of Poe's story to several Hawthorne stories, Robert Regan comments that "the gaiety within is a psychological defense against a menacing antagonist. . . ."[4] The battle is inevitable for all who live. However, from the introduction of the Prince in paragraph two, his defense is not an attempt to win the battle but an attempt to avoid it. He and the courtiers begin by retiring (literally, drawing back) into the "deep seclusion" of the abbey.[5] A strong wall with iron gates surrounds the "amply provisioned" building, suggesting preparations for a siege.

Not only do the inhabitants make physical preparations as they take their stand against the coming onslaught, they must also be as mentally ready as possible. Mentally, as well as physically, the only defense is retreat. The retreat of the mind goes beyond mere forgetfulness or simple escape into "reality-denying fantasies" (Halliburton, p. 311). The Prince and his courtiers, in an unconscious defense mechanism, construct and maintain a pose of indifference to death. Gaiety, merry making, and all the joys of superficial pleasure are allowable under this pose; concern for self or others, serious thought, and strong emotion are forbidden, for they rankle the mind with the agonizing realization that when the battle comes it will certainly be lost. The only way to approximate success is to not let losing matter. The situation is something like that of the laboratory rat trained to run a maze for a food pellet. When an essential corridor is closed off, the rat will eventually stop trying to run the maze and will sit down in his hopelessness to starve. Prince Prospero differs only in that, as a human, he is able to use his inventiveness to make the best of his hopeless situation.

The weapon of indifference and its association with tightly controlled emotions are seen throughout the story. The victim of the disease is shut out "from the sympathy of his fellowmen." The bolts inside the abbey are welded shut not to keep the Red Death *out,* but to serve as a precaution against the courtiers' own "sudden impulses of despair or of frenzy." They let "The external world . . . take care of itself. In the meantime it was folly to grieve, or to think." Some critics have detected a note of authorial disapproval of the Prince in the first of these last two sentences. But the second invites a more sympathetic interpretation. Grief and thought are not only useless but are destructive, unwise, certainly not consistent with the character of the "sagacious" Prince. The external world here has the dual meaning of the worlds outside the abbey and outside the mind.

The movements of the masked ball, beginning in paragraph three, are dominated by the striking of the ebony clock in the ominous seventh apartment where "few of the company [are] bold enough to set foot." The dancers and musicians alternate between maintaining their pose of light laughter and gaiety and, when the doleful, deep-voiced clock chimes, becoming pale, uneasy, and thoughtful. The clock is the reminder of death, the enemy, and time, his companion. The musicians smile when the striking stops. They repent of their "nervousness and folly" and promise each other to let "no similar emotion" be evinced at the next sounding of the hour. It is foolish to be nervous or to give in to a despairing emotion.

One may ask, if the Prince and his friends truly have a need to feign indifference to an inevitable death, why do they bother to retreat to an abbey? Also, if the Prince wishes to forget the presence of death why has he surrounded himself and his courtiers with reminders of death and the grotesque—rooms strangely situated and lighted only by fiery torches glowing through tinted windows, bizarre masquerade costumes, and the coffin-like black room with its "blood-colored panes"? The answer to both questions lies in Prince Prospero's grand attempts to control his environment. A poor man who has just eaten can tell himself he is not concerned about food. In like manner, only within the relative security of the stone walls can the Prince and his friends act as though they are unconcerned about death. A control over their more hysterical emotions is possible only in the extremely artificial world designed and executed by the Prince. Pitcher believes Prince Prospero deliberately tries to frighten and disturb his guests with reminders of death "to test the courage of his friends and to reveal their relative inferiority" to himself (Pitcher, p. 72). A more plausible explanation, I believe, is that he is trying to duplicate the outside world on a small scale and in a nonthreatening manner. His seven rooms have been often compared to the seven stages of man's life.[6] In an imitation of life's rooms, the apartments are situated so that "the vision embraced but little more than one at a time." However, the rooms are much more fluid and accessible than are the stages of life, which cannot be retraced or explored in advance. Actual death is too horrible to be greeted with apathy, but a man-made black room, designed and furnished by the Prince himself, can be endured. Glass, even colored blood-red, can be tolerated. The clock is a constant mournful messenger of "the Time that flies," but it is also a man-made device, and within man's control. Prince Prospero, like Mithridates, seems to be taking his poison a bit at a time. Ironically, he is so obsessed with death that all his efforts are aimed at showing how little death matters to him.

There are hints throughout the story that Prince Prospero is insane. Poe says, "his conceptions glowed with barbaric lustre. There are some who would have thought him mad." The masquerade costumes "were delirious fancies such as the madman fashions. . . ." These and similar passages are often offered as additional evidence that Poe disapproves of the Prince. But these lines can also be interpreted as comments on society's view of him, as well as a reminder of the limitations of his power. To those outside the abbey, Prospero would seem mad because his actions and attitudes seem inappropriate for the situation at hand. On another level, his "conceptions," or inventive ordering of the elements of the masquerade, are "barbaric" in that they are crude and simplistic. Prince Prospero has gained temporary control over his limited environment. But his power stops with the natural laws of the world, which are able to invade any man's plans and creations. It is necessary for the Prince to retreat to the abbey and feign indifference to the outside world—he becomes a madman with "delirious fancies" if he deludes himself that he has won the battle with death rather than avoided it.

Avoidance of death can only be temporary, as transitory as the parts of a play. The courtiers become not only guests at a masquerade, but also literally masquers, players in death's court. Before the masque and the assertion of the final royal authority belonging to the Red Death, the guests are acting out a grimly comic anti-masque in a portrayal of "the unruly, of the forces and elements royalty subdues."[7]

The real test—and the final failure—of the mask of indifference comes with the entrance of the mysterious masked figure dressed exactly like the corpse of a Red Death victim. The stranger becomes visible to the masquers just after midnight. The clock, the most powerful reminder of death in the Prince's world, is at its most powerful moment of the night, since it has twelve long, suggestive strokes to sound. The guests have too much time for thought—they slip irretrievably into meditation and become aware of the presence of the stranger who has haunted the abbey from the beginning. Death is no longer avoidable, and in its actual visitation the unfeeling gaiety must give way to feelings "of terror, of horror, and of disgust."

As the company becomes aware of the deathly figure, emotion quickly takes over. The mummer is "beyond the bounds of even the prince's indefinite decorum," and the mask of indifference can no longer be retained. The challenge, the call to battle, is given in this central passage: "There are chords in the hearts of the most reckless which cannot be touched without emotion. Even with the utterly lost, to whom life and death are equally jests, there are matters of which no jest can be made." The rooms and the costumes can be carelessly lived with. The chiming of the clock can almost be dealt with. But the appearance of a representation of the specific type of fatal illness from which Prince Prospero and his friends are physically and mentally trying to escape is too much. Even the Prince has not been hardened enough by his artificial surroundings to endure without emotion the taunting apparition. He has been heretofore "reckless" (literally, without concern). Life and death have been "equally jests" to him as he has convinced himself that he favors neither in his lack of

interest. But the one matter which is not laughable has been introduced. The Prince's reaction is that of a man who prepares himself mentally for battle, as awakening emotions can no longer be restrained.

When Prince Prospero sees the intruder his initial reaction is that of the untried soldier going, at last, into a deadly serious battle after a long wait in the camp. He is "convulsed . . . with a strong shudder either of terror or distaste." Like the untried soldier first meeting the enemy, he feels an overwhelming fear which no amount of preparation could forestall. The battle is already on its way to being lost as the Prince next grows red with anger. He is now moving to fight death on its home ground, but he makes several last vain attempts to avoid conflict. His statement, "Who dares?" is at once an acknowledgement of a challenge and impending fight, and an attempt to treat the stranger as merely another courtier, a foolish courtier who has overstepped the bounds of safety for all those in the abbey. He orders the guests to "seize him and unmask him—that we may know whom we have to hang at sunrise, from the battlements!" It is obviously fruitless to try to seize, unmask, and hang a personification of death. But if only this figure can be proven merely human, if only the court can "know whom" the tasteless mocker is, then it cannot be death. Prince Prospero's reluctance for conflict is reflected in his delegation of the seizure to his friends, and in the words "whom we *have* to hang at sunrise." The hanging is unwanted but necessary. For the mask of indifference to be reassumed the impediment to indifference must be removed.

The Prince's attack upon the mummer is filled with references to intense emotions and hurried actions. He has lost his carefully nurtured self-control and foolishly attacked the unbeatable foe. He maddens "with rage and the shame of his own momentary cowardice." He "rushed hurriedly" to the stranger, approaching him "in rapid impetuosity." The stranger is, throughout, the challenger who need not fight. He approaches the Prince with "deliberate" step and later, when the Prince pursues, he simply turns and confronts him. Prince Prospero is dead before the Red Death can do its work. He is defeated in the quite literal face of death by giving in to his emotions of terror and hysteria. The fear of death has become his master. The courtiers, who summon "the wild courage of despair" and attack the stranger's mask with "so violent a rudeness," meet the fate of their leader immediately thereafter, submitting to the same lack of control over their emotions. Death's victory is complete—a victory over both the minds and bodies of the noblemen.

The Prince has been criticized for his apparent frivolity and lack of feeling. But it is evident that this frivolity, this pretended refusal to take death seriously, is all that separates the Prince from the horror of death. His personality and creations in the abbey provide an excellent illustration of Edward Davidson's description of horror as "the total freedom of the will to function, at the same time that there is nothing to will 'for' or will 'against.' Its judgments are in a vacuum because it pretends to act in a world where no discoverable controls are operative."[8] Prince Prospero can exercise his will freely within the vacuum of the abbey as long as he can deceive himself that his emotions, the world, life, and death can be controlled. When he allows his emotions to take control, the "nameless awe" of the unknown foe destroys him.

It is natural that Poe should have written a story such as **"The Masque of the Red Death"** in 1842. By this time he had lost his mother (1811); Jane Stanard, the inspiration of "To Helen" (1824); and his foster mother, Frances Allan (1829). He had experienced what David Sinclair in his biography of Poe calls a "crippling sense of powerlessness in the face of death."[9]

Most critics of **"The Masque"** interpret it as an allegory and assume that, as such, it must point to a moral truth. But the truth in the story is existential, not moral. Poe as narrator presents characters who arm themselves against death through whatever means possible. Through his art, the author is a more formidable opponent to death than is Prospero. The Prince loses control and faces defeat, but Poe remains far removed. He voices no disapproval of the characters, but neither does he show sympathy for their fate. He maintains in his tone the superiority of what he portrays as the only, although feeble, defense against death—a perfect mask of indifference.

Notes

1. Thomas Ollive Mabbot, intro. to "The Masque of the Red Death," *Collected Works of Edgar Allan Poe*, II (Cambridge: Harvard University Press, 1978), 668; Stuart Levine, *Edgar Poe: Seer and Craftsman* (DeLand, Fla.: Everett/Edwards, 1972), p. 299; David Halliburton, *Edgar Allan Poe: A Phenomenological View* (Princeton: Princeton University Press, 1973), p. 310; Edward Taylor Pitcher, "Horological and Chronological Time in 'Masque of the Red Death,'" *American Transcendental Quarterly*, 29 (1976), 72; H. H. Bell, Jr., "'The Masque of the Red Death': An Interpretation," *South Atlantic Bulletin*, 38 (Nov. 1973), 101. Kermit Vanderbilt provides a notable exception to the prevalent critical opinion of Prince Prospero. In his "Art and Nature in 'The Masque of the Red Death,'" *Nineteenth Century Fiction*, 22 (March 1968), 397, he calls the Prince "an exact portrait of Poe's artist-hero."

2. Joseph Patrick Roppolo, "Meaning and 'The Masque of the Red Death,'" *Tulane Studies in English*, 13 (1963), 65.

3. Walter Blair, "Poe's Conception of Incident and Tone in the Tale," *Modern Philology*, 41 (May 1944), 239.

4. Robert Regan, "Hawthorne's 'Plagiary'; Poe's Duplicity," *Nineteenth Century Fiction*, 25 (1970), 287.

5. I have used the text of "The Masque of the Red Death" found in *Collected Works of Edgar Allan Poe*, ed. Thomas Ollive Mabbott, II (Cambridge: Harvard University Press, 1978), 670-678.

6. See especially Bell's essay.

7. *Princeton Encyclopedia of Poetry and Poetics*, ed. Alex Preminger, enlrg. ed. (Princeton: Princeton University Press, 1974), p. 475.

8. Edward H. Davidson, *Poe: A Critical Study* (Cambridge: Harvard University Press, 1957), p. 124.

9. David Sinclair, *Edgar Allan Poe* (Totowa, New Jersey: Rowman & Littlefield, 1977), p. 9.

Peter Cersowsky (essay date 1982)

SOURCE: Cersowsky, Peter. "Allegory and the Fantastic in Literature: Poe's 'The Masque of the Red Death' and Alfred Kubin's *The Other Side*." *Sprachkunst* 13, no. 1 (1982): 141-50.

[*In the following essay, Cersowsky analyzes the allegorical function of "The Masque of the Red Death" according to the aesthetic theories of Tzvetan Todorov, Walter Benjamin, and Charles Baudelaire, and notes Poe's influence on Alfred Kubin's novel* The Other Side.]

The fantastic and allegory in literature have been described as neighbouring genres by Tzvetan Todorov[1] and by Louis Vax[2], though neither of these critics explains in what respect they are related to each other. Nevertheless the general basis of the affinity between both genres seems to me fairly obvious: Todorov himself defined the fantastic as the "hesitation experienced by a person who knows only the laws of nature, confronting an apparently supernatural event"[3], and Roger Caillois regarded an "irruption [. . .] into the real world"[4] as the major constituent of the fantastic. In his recent book on the subject Eric S. Rabkin says that the fantastic occurs "when the ground rules of a narrative are forced to make a 180° reversal"[5]. This definition is quite similar to Andrzej Zgorzelski's. To him the fantastic "appears when the internal laws of the fictional world are breached"[6]. In spite of the considerable differences between the critical approaches leading up to these definitions there is at least one aspect they have in common: I am thinking of the prevailing conception of two contrasting levels of experience that mark out different notions of reality. The applicability of this common denominator of the four quotes would only have to be questioned insofar as things appear to be different with fantastic literature in the further course of the 20th century. But this would lead us to a problem with which I shall not be concerned in the present context. What ought to be mentioned here is the fact that the broad resemblance between the fantastic and allegory lies in their dualistic structure, for the fundamental constituent of allegory is also the manifestation of two different levels of expression, namely the concrete image and the general meaning.

Todorov and Vax might accept our basic supposition, but they would undoubtedly insist on the difference between the specific dualisms of the allegorical and of the fantastic, since both theorists maintain the oppositional character of their relationship. Todorov says that the general meaning of an allegory has nothing to do with the supernatural as an essential component of the fantastic[7]. Similarly, Vax argues that in allegory "the domains of the factual and the figurative remain well differentiated"[8], which is not so with the fantastic.

These verdicts are clearly based on ahistorical genre definitions. As soon as a more narrow focus is applied to literary history, however, a non-oppositional relationship between the two genres no longer seems inconceivable. This is indicated by Walter H. Sokel's description of a "fantastic allegory"[9]. The term is meant to characterize a trend of German Expressionist prose represented by Brod, Einstein, Kafka, Kubin, Lichtenstein, Meyrink and Mynona. Yet Sokel overexpands the meaning of his category. This appears to be the case less with his implicit notion of the fantastic that seems to correspond roughly with Todorov's understanding of the supernatural[10] than with his idea of allegory. By allowing of various grades of ambiguity in allegory he neglects one of its basic, traditionally-rooted traits, namely its clear-cut meaning. In this paper I should like to draw attention towards the relationship between the fantastic and the allegorical on a more coherent textual basis without lapsing into normative genre conceptions.

As to the question whether there are allegorical elements in Poe particular attention has always been paid to **"The Masque of the Red Death"**[11]. There is, indeed, allegory in the very first sentence of the story when the plague is spoken of as the "Red Death". Personification probably has been the most significant device of allegory since the archetypal examples of the genre. Especially the incarnation of death can be said to be the allegorical figure par excellence. The introductory paragraph is written throughout in an unemotional and detached tone. The personified plague is presented as an objectively given phenomenon. Walter Benjamin described "objectivity" as the essential cognitional charac-

teristic of allegory, for the "ideas" which, as Benjamin says, are the gist of the allegorical, "are not connected with consciousness"[12]. They are severed from subjectivity. This point is valid for ancient and medieval allegory surviving in the Baroque age which Benjamin has in mind. The beginning of Poe's tale, the setting of which obviously is medieval, can be regarded as an illustration of Benjamin's conception.

It seems to me obvious that the elements of the abbey where the prince Prospero and his company lock themselves up to escape from the disease are arranged allegorically, too. The prince with the significant name is defined by his "happy and dauntless and sagacious"[13] disposition. Thus he is the true antagonist of the death figure which he fights when it finally has intruded into the abbey. The fight between two representatives of fundamental powers has been characterized as a component element of allegory by Angus Fletcher[14]. A consistent structure furthermore manifests itself in the environment of the central characters. Firstly there is the colourful gaiety of Prospero's company and the luxury allowing for all kinds of enjoyment that culminate in the "magnificence"[15] of the masked ball. Secondly there is the arrangement of space. Walter Blair pointed out that the seven rooms decorated each in a single colour stand for the seven ages of human life[16]. The last room which is draped in black and red, which is avoided by everybody and where the mortal fight against the intruder takes place later on, is obviously the room of death. The clock in this room, the chime of which momentarily causes any movement of the company to stop, is a reminder of the transitoriness of life. By saying that it is the very "heart of life"[17] that is beating in the ballrooms, the text itself clarifies what it is all about: The stylized world within the abbey is a counter allegory of life against the sphere of death.

It is, however, of crucial importance to note that the allegorical counter world is not objective like the personification in the beginning. Instead, it is Prospero's creation. "He had directed, in great part, the moveable embellishments of the seven chambers [. . .] and it was his own guiding taste which had given character to the masqueraders"[18]. As a subjective construction this sphere can no longer be described in keeping with the cognitional principle of allegory as it was formulated by Benjamin. Anyhow the manifestation of individual creativity presented here is entirely alien to the medieval or Baroque way of thinking. Nevertheless Prospero's creation does not cease to be an allegorical world.

So Poe's text illustrates two conceptions of allegory that differ fundamentally. Yet this does not imply that by the intrusion of the death figure the objective allegory still holds the field against its counter world. The intruder is integrated in the lively ball sphere by his being masked, too. Besides, the destructive development is not initiated until the figure is perceived by the company. The concept of death becoming an object of perception is incompatible with the allegorical "idea" in Benjamin's sense. As Prospero constructs a room of death in his ballrooms full of life, the power of the death-figure likewise becomes part of his subjective world.

I am well aware that an allegorical reading of **"The Masque"** contradicts Poe's own verdict against allegory in his review of tales by Hawthorne[19]. We have to allow for the fact, however, that the kind of allegory the author has in mind at best appeals to the fancy, as he says. In another review Poe claims that a work of art is fanciful "when the harmony of the combination" of its elements "is completely neglected"[20]. This definitely does not apply to **"The Masque"**, for the elements of Prospero's world are combined most harmoniously to fit into the underlying pattern of life and death. "Thorough harmony"[21] together with the "character of obviousness"[22]—of meaning, we might add—is the defining point of the work of imagination in Poe's view. Prospero's creation is the product of his own imagination, and thereby becomes a model of the imaginative faculty itself. F. H. Link is quite right in stressing this poetological quality of the text[23]. Thus the imaginative allegory of **"The Masque"** is untouched by Poe's theoretical views on the genre.

The conception of Prospero's imagination brings us right to the problem of the fantastic. The company is described as an "assembly of phantasms"[24], their "appearances" are "fantastic"[25]. Formulations like these hint at the imaginative origin of the masked ball. But the question arises whether the use of the term *fantastic* in the text is to be identified with our common denominator of fantastic literature.

Prospero's sphere certainly is different from the outside world. So there is indeed a marked dualism in the relationship between both domains. But the sphere of the masked ball is not separated by a different status of reality. Significantly, retreats from a disease into isolation can be historically verified[26]. Of course there is a new phase in the development of the story when the intruder is unmasked, revealing death incarnate. Does not Poe here after all touch upon a new level of reality that has to be regarded as supernatural on the contrasting background of the reality suggested by the text?—Here the medieval setting has to be taken into account. Roger Caillois says that the fantastic can only exist on the basis of a rationalistic world picture in which "miracles are no longer possible"[27]. Therefore a medieval setting per se neutralizes the profile of the genre, since phenomena that might count as supernatural in a modern world picture would not transgress the limits of the natural in this context. The argument is exemplified by Poe's text. The characters of **"The Masque"** do not ex-

perience the configuration of death as surreal either. If they were convinced that the intruder could not turn out to be a real death figure, their extreme terror and aggressiveness would be unmotivated. The personal existence of death is never questioned. So the terminology of the text does not correspond with the widespread critical view of the fantastic in literature.

When the text uses the word "fantastic", it merely indicates that there is a segment in the represented world which is structured through the medium of imagination. This segment is identical with subjective allegory. So if we are permitted to talk about *fantastic allegory* at all in connection with Poe's tale, it is in the sense of an imaginative allegory that is in fact established against its objective counterpart without being contrasted to some natural world as a supernatural dimension.

A widespread reception of Poe's works in German literature set in about the turn of the century[28]. One of its first representatives is young Kai, Hanno Buddenbrook's friend, to whom Roderick Usher is "the most marvellous character that has ever been invented"[29]. Hedda and Arthur Moeller Bruck's translation of Poe that appeared from 1901 to 1904[30] can count as a decisive landmark. Particularly Alfred Kubin, who himself emphasized his spiritual kinship to the American author[31], did not at all remain untouched by the wake of enthusiasm, as can be seen from numerous illustrations[32] as well as the novel *The Other Side*[33]. This text received important impulses especially from **"The Masque"**. The *other side* is a territory equally dominated by two antagonistic central characters. Patera—his name obviously has overtones of meaning, too—on the one hand is a figure of life such as Prospero. Significantly he exerts some mysterious influence on procreation in the *other side*. Whereas Poe splits up the personification of life and death in two characters, Patera himself embodies both levels of meaning. His lifeless eyes and statuesque appearance, which suggest "that Patera was not alive at all"[34], have encouraged critics to characterize him as personified death[35]. Like the "Red Death" Patera evokes mortal fear. The part of the intruder in the *other side* is played by his antagonist, Herkules Bell, though the latter is shown as a representative of vital force as soon as Patera's death-like traits predominate. But shifts like this do not blur the polarity of life and death, the allegorical structure of which is also indicated by the concluding fight between Patera and Bell. This structure is worked out by the equally consistent arrangement of the environment. In both texts the dramatis personae are of great variety. As Poe's characters' sole aim is enjoyment since it is "folly to grieve, or to think"[36], the inhabitants of the *other side* likewise live at random and indulge in excessive lust at the end. In Kubin, too, there is at times a moment of universal death-like torpor: a reminder of death amidst a panorama of life itself. Finally, the presentation of space is in accordance with this structure, too. While at first the variety of the architecture mirrors the plenitude of life, later on "the incomprehensible weaving of death"[37] dominates the urban landscape throughout. As in Poe the device of allegorical stylization is striking. By the predominant shades of gray and green and by the dim light the ambivalence between life and death is reflected. Patera's chamber, which is entirely draped with "lead-grey coloured cloths"[38], bears particular resemblance to Prospero's harmonious rooms. Altogether the *other side* is "a harmonious sight"[39] as well. There is also a big clock standing at an exposed place that draws everybody under its spell. It brings to mind the flux of time that is otherwise shut out from the dominion: by their clothing and the entire surroundings the citizens are placed in bygone times. Thereby the autonomous life of the country is to be preserved.—In both texts the intrusion of the antagonist marks the beginning of total destruction of the allegorical world and of the sole prevalence of death.—An illustration of **"The Masque"** by Kubin shows the gigantic pendulum of the clock and a pile of dying human figures[40]. Both motifs are also of emblematic relevance for *The Other Side*. Here the vacillation between life and death is characterized as "some kind of law of the pendulum"[41] and the final annihilation is presented very drastically.

Apart from these and other correspondences Kubin's allegorical world, too, is the product of its ruler. Patera has built it and regulates its "heartbeat"[42]. "Patera's rhythmic pulse beat was omnipresent. Being insatiable in his imagination, he wanted [. . .] the world and nothingness. This is why his creatures oscillated to and fro like that."[43] Like the intrusion of the "Red Death" the appearance of Bell ultimately originates in Patera's *imagination,* too. So Kubin presents an allegorical world that is equally the work of its creator's constructive imagination, or—we may add—of his dreams, for Patera, who mostly is presented as if he were sleeping, also transfers his dreaming disposition to his realm: it is called a "dream land"[44], the citizens are "dreamers"[45], each living through their own day dream[46]. Here is another detail corresponding with **"The Masque"**, since "in the seven chambers there stalked, in fact, a multitude of dreams"[47].—The traditional, objective type of allegory, however, is not taken up at all besides its imaginative counterpart in Kubin's novel.

"A Fantastic Novel" is the subtitle of *The Other Side*. Here, too, the term is motivated in the first instance by the determinant quality of an individual's imagination. In addition, however, the fantastic gains a new dimension. Patera's dominion is no longer in accordance with the *ground rules* of reality outside. Instead, it differs from that by its supernatural quality. This quality is based on the fact that the outside world of the *other side* is concrete, natural present-day reality of the early 20th century. The novel begins in modern Munich. By

the geographically detailed description of the journey into the dream land the natural background is also marked. Thus the country itself, which, needless to say, cannot be verified, is radically set off in its status of reality. Patera's allegorical identity, too, is contrasted with his natural ego as a schoolboy. The contrast between the two worlds is also reinforced by the mythical quality the allegorical world itself takes on in *The Other Side*. Patera's vitality and his resemblance to "a Greek god"[48] as well as his function as a ubiquitous originator of love and his beauty suggest his affinity to the god Eros. Accordingly, his death-like traits can be regarded as constituents of a Thanatos-figure. Besides, there are Messianic overtones crystallized in Patera's allegorical nature, e. g. when he presents himself as "the Lord [. . .] the Master"[49] who later on dies as a martyr. The complement of this element is the Satanic aspect of Bell who is given a "diabolic profile"[50] and exerts his power in the name of Lucifer[51]. A similar fusion of mythical elements is not to be found in Poe. Placed against the natural background it stresses the supernatural character of Patera's world. So here after all is the kind of dualism that constitutes our common denominator of critical views on the fantastic.

Kubin does take up Poe's conception of allegory shaped by imagination. But this structure is no longer contrasted to the objective type of allegory while conforming with the reality status of the outside world. In *The Other Side* the imagination, which remains the crucial medium in the text, achieves even more than in Poe, for the solely imaginative dimension of allegory becomes identical with the supernatural. Thus allegory constitutes one of the two basic components of the fantastic as it has been outlined at the outset of my paper. In this sense the term *fantastic allegory* is fully applicable to Kubin's text.

In contrast to **"The Masque"** *The Other Side* is a first-person narrative. The narrator admits that his presentation of the dream land includes "the description of a few scenes [. . .] which I definitely cannot have witnessed and which I cannot have learned about from anybody"[52]. So the I himself is influenced by "phenomena of the imagination"[53]. Indeed it is him who repeatedly articulates the allegorical meaning of the text. His taking part in the establishment of this structure indicates the general relevance of the imagination in Kubin's novel.

The Other Side is exemplary of its literary age, for fantastic allegories based on the supernatural were written by numerous authors of highly different rank and on a variety of subject-matters. Apart from the tradition of the city novel that brought forth Cosmus Flam's *Athanasius Comes to the City*[54] or Karl Hans Strobl's *Ghosts in the Swamp*[55], a belated offspring of which is Hermann Kasack's *The City Beyond the Stream*[56], there are seafaring tales such as Georg Heym's "The Ship"[57] and there is e. g. Thomas Mann's story "The Wardrobe"[58]. Some of these writers—though by no means all of them, of course—do owe quite a lot to Poe. "My Adventure with Jonas Barg" by Strobl[59] is about a masked ball organized by death himself for a modern club, and Georg von der Gabelentz's "The Red Dancer"[60] reveals its literary ancestor by its very title.

No matter if a fantastic allegory can be directly referred back to **"The Masque"**, its structure is anticipated by a crucial link between the American author and early 20th-century literature, namely the conception of Symbolism that already makes up the core of Baudelaire's pioneering aesthetic reflections. It is well-known that Baudelaire found a confirmation of his own ideas in Poe's works[61]. To him Poe is a writer who transforms reality into a metaphysical dimension through the medium of imagination and dream[62]. Both are central categories in Baudelaire's aesthetic theory. His famous definition of the imagination runs:

> It takes part the whole of creation and with the materials amassed and arranged according to rules whose origin can only be found in the utmost depths of the soul, it creates a new world [. . .] As it has created the world (This may well be said, I believe, even in a religious sense), it is just that it governs it[63].

Here is a most accurate description of what Patera did when he—a sheer incarnation of vital imagination himself—took to pieces buildings in Europe in order to build his dominion by arranging them in a new structure. His divine traits correspond to the religious quality ascribed to the imagination by Baudelaire. The passage also suggests the constructive element of the imaginative faculty which is present throughout in Baudelaire's writings. Both imagination and dream—the latter being conceived completely analogously with the former—bring about a derealization of reality. They constitute the art of "surnaturalism"[64]. The imaginative transformation of reality is by no means chaotic. Rather:

> All the characters, their relative disposition, the scenery or the interior as well as their clothing, everything ultimately has to contribute to the illumination of the generating idea and to continue carrying its original colour, its apparel, so to speak[65].

Even though there is not yet a transformation towards the supernatural in **"The Masque"**, it does already exemplify this passage, which clearly formulates an implicit conception of allegory. Of course Baudelaire's *generating idea* does not have anything in common with the objective *idea* described by Benjamin. Instead, allegory becomes a "spiritual genre"[66] in his eyes which is estimated as a means of representing the imaginative "surnaturalism"[67].

Thus, fantastic allegory is theoretically described by Baudelaire. This parallel indicates that the imaginative activities of the central characters illustrate the working of the imagination in general. Thereby the exemplary relevance both of **"The Masque"** and *The Other Side* is pointed out. The imagination is the determinant category of the textual structure. In **"The Masque"** it merely brings about a subjective counterpart to the traditional, objective type of allegory without transgressing the borderline of the natural. In addition, it creates a supernatural sphere in Kubin's novel which is allegorically structured, too, while the objective type of allegory is no longer present. In this way it is the imagination that makes fantastic allegory possible at all.

Notes

1. Tzvetan Todorov, *The Fantastic: A Structural Approach to a Literary Genre*, tr. Richard Howard, Ithaca, N.Y. 1975, pp. 58, 62-74. Originally published under the title *Introduction à la littérature fantastique*, Paris 1970, pp. 63, 67-79.

2. Louis Vax, *L'art et la littérature fantastiques*, Paris 1963, pp. 5, 17 f.

3. "L'hésitation éprouvée par un être qui ne connaît que les lois naturelles, face à un événement en apparence surnaturel." Todorov (zit. Anm. 1), p. 25; Original ed., p. 29.

4. "[. . .] irruption [. . .] dans le monde réel." Roger Caillois, *De la féerie à la science-fiction: Anthologie du fantastique*, ed. R. C., Paris 1966, I, p. 8.

5. Eric S. Rabkin, *The Fantastic in Literature*, Princeton 1976, p. 12.

6. Andrzej Zgorzelski, *Understanding Fantasy*, in: *Zagadniena Rodzajów Literackich*, XIV/2 (1972), p. 108.

7. Todorov (zit. Anm. 1), p. 64.

8. "[. . .] les domaines du propre et du figuré demeurent bien distincts." Vax (zit. Anm. 2), p. 17.

9. Walter H. Sokel, "Die Prosa des Expressionismus," in: *Expressionismus als Literatur: Gesammelte Studien*, ed. Wolfgang Rothe, Bern 1969, pp. 163-165.

10. For instance when a dead person's ability to speak is regarded as fantastic by Sokel, ibid., p. 163.

11. Cf. for instance Walter Blair, "Poe's Conception of Incident and Tone in the Tale," in: *Modern Philology*, XLI (May 1944), pp. 228-240, esp. pp. 239 f. Vincent Buranelli, *Edgar Allan Poe*, New York 1961, pp. 44, 63, 133. Joseph Patrick Roppolo, "Meaning and 'The Masque of the Red Death,'" in: *Tulane Studies in English*, XIII (1963), pp. 59-69. Franz H. Link, *Edgar Allan Poe: Ein Dichter zwischen Romantik und Moderne*, Frankfurt/M. 1968, p. 251.

12. "[. . .] eigne[n] nicht einem Zusammenhang im Bewußtsein." Walter Benjamin, *Ursprung des deutschen Trauerspiels*, Frankfurt/M. 1972, p. 10.

13. *The Complete Works of Edgar Allan Poe,* ed. James A. Harrison, New York 1902, IV, p. 250.

14. Angus Fletcher, *Allegory: The Theory of a Symbolic Mode,* Ithaca, N.Y. 1964, pp. 151, 157-161.

15. Poe (zit. Anm. 13), p. 251.

16. Blair (zit. Anm. 11), p. 239.

17. Poe (zit. Anm. 13), p. 255.

18. Ibid., p. 254.

19. Poe, Tale-Writing—Nathaniel Hawthorne, ibid., XIII, p. 148.

20. Poe, *American Prose Writers.* No. 2. N. P. Willis, ibid., XII, p. 39.

21. Ibid.

22. Ibid.

23. Link (zit. Anm. 11), p. 250.

24. Poe (zit. Anm. 13), IV, p. 255.

25. Ibid., p. 252.

26. Cf. for instance the compilation of Poe's sources, in: *Collected Works of E. A. P., II, Tales and Sketches, 1831-1842,* ed. T. C. Mabbott with the assistance of Eleanor D. Kewer and Maureen C. Mabbott, Cambridge, Mass. 1978, pp. 668 f.

27. "[. . .] sans miracle". Caillois (zit. Anm. 4), p. 14.

28. Cf. Harro Heinz Kühnelt, "Deutsche Erzähler im Gefolge von E. A. Poe," in: *Rivista di Letterature Moderna* 6 (1951), pp. 457-465. H. H. K., "Edgar Allan Poe und die phantastische Erzählung im österreichischen Schrifttum von 1900-1920," in: *Festschrift für Moriz Enzinger,* Innsbruck 1953, pp. 131-143.

29. "[. . .] die wundervollste Figur, die je erfunden worden ist." Thomas Mann, *Buddenbrooks; Verfall einer Familie: Gesammelte Werke in dreizehn Bänden,* Frankfurt/M. 1974, Second ed., I, p. 720.

30. Edgar Allan Poe, *Werke,* ed. Hedda and Arthur Moeller-Bruck, Minden 1901-1904.

31. Alfred Kubin, "Skizze meines Lebens," in: *A. K., Aus meinem Leben: Gesammelte Prosa,* ed. Ulrich Riemerschmidt, Munich 1974, p. 97.

32. Cf. Alfred Marks, *Der Illustrator Alfred Kubin: Gesamtkatalog seiner Illustrationen und buchkünstlerischen Arbeiten,* Munich 1977.

33. Alfred Kubin, *Die andere Seite: Ein phantastischer Roman,* Munich 1973, Second ed. (First ed., Munich 1909).

34. "[. . .] daß Patera gar nicht lebe". Ibid., p. 199.

35. Cf. for instance Anneliese Hewig, *Phantastische Wirklichkeit: Interpretationsstudie zu Alfred Kubins Roman "Die andere Seite",* Munich 1967, p. 166.

36. Poe (zit. Anm. 13), IV, p. 251.

37. "[. . .] das unfaßbare Weben des Todes [. . .]". Kubin, *Die andere Seite* (zit. Anm. 33), p. 196.

38. "[. . .] bleigrauen [. . .] Stoffen [. . .]". Ibid., p. 119.

39. "Harmonisch [. . .] anzusehen". Ibid., p. 50.

40. Edgar Allan Poe, *Das schwatzende Herz und andere Novellen: Mit 14 Bildbeigaben von Alfred Kubin,* Munich 1909, p. 23.

41. "[. . .] eine Art Pendelgesetz". Kubin, *Die andere Seite* (zit. Anm. 33), p. 132.

42. "Herzschlag". Ibid., p. 148.

43. "Allgegenwärtig war der rhythmische Pulsschlag Pateras, er wollte, unersättlich in seiner Einbildungskraft [. . .] die Welt und das Nichts. Dadurch pendelten seine Geschöpfe so hin und her." Ibid.

44. "Traumreich". Ibid., p. 8.

45. "Träumer". Ibid., p. 10.

46. Ibid.

47. Poe (zit. Anm. 13), IV, p. 254.

48. "[. . .] einem Griechischen Gott". Kubin, *Die andere Seite* (zit. Anm. 33), p. 120.

49. "[. . .] der Herr [. . .] der Meister". Ibid., p. 121. This parallel has been pointed out by Hewig (zit. Anm. 35), p. 82.

50. "diabolisches Profil [. . .]". Kubin, *Die andere Seite* (zit. Anm. 33), p. 161.

51. Ibid., pp. 164, 168.

52. "[. . .] die Schilderung einiger Szenen [. . .], denen ich unmöglich beigewohnt und die ich von keinem Menschen erfahren haben kann." Ibid., p. 7.

53. "[. . .] Phänomene der Einbildungskraft [. . .]". Ibid.

54. Cosmus Flam, *Athanasius kommt in die Großstadt oder die Tiergrube,* Breslau 1930.

55. Karl Hans Strobl, *Gespenster im Sumpf: Ein phantastischer Wiener Roman,* Leipzig 1920.

56. Hermann Kasack, *Die Stadt hinter dem Strom,* Berlin 1947.

57. Georg Heym, "Das Schiff," in: *G. H., Der Dieb: Ein Novellenbuch,* Leipzig 1913.

58. Thomas Mann, "Der Kleiderschrank," in: *Gesammelte Werke, VIII,* p. 152-161.

59. Karl Hans Strobl, "Mein Abenteuer mit Jonas Barg," in: *K. H. S., Lemuria: Seltsame Geschichten,* Munich 1917.

60. Georg von der Gabelentz, "Der rote Tänzer," in: *G. V. D. G., Verflogene Vögel,* Berlin 1909.

61. Cf. for instance Peter Michael Wetherill, *Charles Baudelaire et la poésie d'Edgar Allan Poe,* Paris 1962. Hugo Friedrich, *Die Struktur der modernen Lyrik: Erweiterte Neuausgabe,* Hamburg 1971, p. 51.

62. Charles Baudelaire, "Notes nouvelles sur Edgar Poe," in: *Œuvres complètes,* ed. Claude Pichois, Gallimard 1976, II, p. 321, 329.

63. "Elle décompose toute la création, et, avec les matériaux amassés et disposés suivant des règles dont on ne peut trouver l'origine que dans le plus profond de l'âme, elle crée un monde nouveau [. . .] Comme elle a crée le monde (On peut bien dire cela, je crois, même dans un sens réligieux), il est juste qu'elle le gouverne". Baudelaire, "Salon de 1859", ibid., p. 621.

64. "Surnaturalisme". Baudelaire, "Fusées", ibid., I, p. 658.

65. "Tous les personnages, leur disposition relative, le paysage ou l'intérieur que leurs vêtements, tout enfin doit servir à illuminer l'idée génératrice et porter encore sa couleur originelle, sa livrée, pour ainsi-dire". Baudelaire, "Salon", p. 625.

66. "[. . .] genre [. . .] spirituel [. . .]". Baudelaire, "Les paradis artificiels", ibid., I, p. 430.

67. Ibid.

Patrick Cheney (essay date March-June 1983)

SOURCE: Cheney, Patrick. "Poe's Use of *The Tempest* and the Bible in 'The Masque of the Red Death.'" *English Language Notes* 20, nos. 3-4 (March-June 1983): 31-9.

[*In the following essay, Cheney outlines Poe's reversal of biblical and Shakespearean allusions in "The Masque of the Red Death," highlighting Poe's depiction of Prince Prospero as an antihero and the Red Death as an antichrist.*]

In **"The Masque of the Red Death"** Poe's allusions to both *The Tempest* and the Bible have been widely recognized. Briefly, the allusions to *The Tempest* include

Poe's use of "Prospero" for his hero's name; his use of the romance "masque" for his story's central event; and his borrowing of Caliban's curse of the "red plague" on Miranda for his story's central idea. Poe's allusions to the Bible include his remarks about the Red Death itself: that the Red Death "out-Heroded Herod"; that he "came like a thief in the night"; and that in the end he has "dominion" over all. As yet, though, no one has examined the relation between these two sets of allusions, as they contribute to the narrative and meaning of the story.[1]

In this essay I suggest that Poe in **"The Masque of the Red Death"** uses Shakespearean and Biblical allusions to reveal a tragic and ironic reversal of a mythic pattern which *The Tempest* and the Bible have in common. Where the mythic pattern of both *The Tempest* and the Bible depicts man's victory over sin, death, and time, Poe's mythic pattern depicts the triumph of these agents of destruction over man. In Poe's "mythic parable" of man's role in the universe,[2] Prince Prospero becomes an anti-hero, an image of man misusing his will as he attempts to shape reality; and the Red Death becomes an "anti-christ," an image of the cosmic force conspiring man's failure.

While admitting to the obvious differences between *The Tempest* and the Bible, we can also see that they have much in common. In the Bible, Adam is born into the Garden of Eden; he falls from this paradise when, tempted by Satan, he misuses his will; and finally, through the miraculous powers of the "second Adam" or Christ, he returns to a new Eden. The key to recovering Eden becomes Christ, who uses the miraculous powers of love to triumph over the old law of death, figured in his resurrection. Similarly, in *The Tempest* Prospero was originally the "right Duke of Milan"; but he lost his dukedom when he retreated into the private world of his study, to become the victim of Antonio, Alonso, and Sebastian; eventually, though, exiled on an island in the Mediterranean sea with his daughter, Miranda, he uses his magical powers to triumph over the "three men of sin."[3] In his wedding masque, Prospero uses the spirit Ariel to present a vision of the world he is trying to create: a peaceful world of heaven on earth. Prospero interrupts his masque when he remembers the plot of his slave, Caliban, thus occasioning his famous speech, "Our revels now are ended," in which the "cloud-capped towers" vanish from the world "like the baseless fabric of this vision" (IV.i.151-152). Despite this apostrophe to man's futile use of his will, Prospero goes on to regain for Miranda her lost inheritance, much as Christ regains for Adam his lost inheritance in the Bible. The mythic pattern of *The Tempest,* then, corresponds to that of the Bible by presenting a view of reality in which man uses his loving will to recreate a "brave new world," invulnerable to time and death.[4]

In **"The Masque of the Red Death"** Poe's allusions to *The Tempest* and the Bible may suggest that he is responding to this mythic pattern. Like Shakespeare's Duke Prospero, Poe's Prince Prospero uses his will to confront the harsh reality of death, figured in the ghostly apparition of the Red Death itself. But Poe recasts the story so that Prince Prospero's primary action consists of retreating from the reality of the Red Death—the action of retreat being precisely what Shakespeare takes care to emend. Poe also takes away Prospero's magic powers, leaving his hero with an art that most closely resembles interior decoration—a mere "philosophy of furniture." As a consequence, Prince Prospero lacks the supernatural power that enables Shakespeare's Prospero to succeed. Taking refuge in a "castellated abbey" (II.670), Prince Prospero uses his will to create an earthly paradise that parodies the "brave new world" of *The Tempest*—a world which, rather than transcending time, embodies the very instrument of time, the sinister "clock of ebony" (II.672): Poe's Prospero, by building time into his abbey, ensures his own destruction. In the world of Prince Prospero, the governing force becomes not that of cosmic harmony and love but that of cosmic "disconcert," the musical instrument for which becomes the clock itself, that grim "sound" which hourly interrupts the dance (II.672). In hiding from death in the bosom of earthly pleasure, Poe's Prospero is like Shakespeare's Prospero if he had given up Ariel for Caliban; in a sense, Poe's story embodies Caliban's wish-fulfillment: "the red plague rid you," Caliban says to Miranda, "For learning me your language" (I.ii.364-365). The story's subtitle appropriately becomes "Our reveals now are ended"—a powerful overture to the vanity of human wishes.[5] Prince Prospero's artistically inspired masque does not marry earth to heaven, but earth to death, so that the world of the abbey becomes, not a new Eden, but a "valley of the shadow of death."

Poe's use of Biblical symbolism does not become particularly noteworthy until the last paragraph, where the language, rhythm, and allusion are unmistakably Biblical:

> And now was acknowledged the presence of the Red Death. He had come like a thief in the night. And one by one dropped the revellers in the blood-bedewed halls of their revel, and died each in the despairing posture of his fall. And the life of the ebony clock went out with that of the last of the gay. And the flames of the tripods expired. And Darkness and Decay and the Red Death held illimitable dominion over all.[6]
>
> (II.676-677)

The sentence structure, with its repetition of the word "And," is like that in the Bible. The Red Death, Poe says, comes "like a thief in the night." The phrase is a direct quotation from 1 Thessalonians 5:2 and 2 Peter 3:10, which both refer to Christ. In Poe's mythology, the Red Death replaces Christ as the reigning force in

the universe. Hence, the Red Death is said to have "dominion over all"—a reversal of Paul's statement in Romans 6:9, in which "death hath no more dominion" because of Christ's resurrection. Moreover, the halls of Poe's earthly paradise become "blood-bedewed"—suggesting a conflation of two familiar Biblical images, blood and dew: the blood of Christ's resurrection that redeems man, and the drops of dew that fall from heaven to save man from the harshness of nature (Deut. 33:28). In Poe, the blood and dew of the Red Death replace the blood of Christ and the dew of heaven.

Poe may have in mind here the Pauline conception of baptism, in which man is baptized into Christ through being baptized into Christ's death—a conception that concludes, significantly, with Paul's remark that death will have no more "dominion" because of Christ's resurrection:

> Therefore we are buried with him by baptism into death: that like as Christ was raised up from the dead by the glory of the Father, even so we also should walk in the newness of life.
>
> For if we have been planted together in the likeness of his death; we shall be also in the likeness of his resurrection. . . .
>
> For he that is dead is freed from sin.
>
> Now if we be dead with Christ, we believe that we shall also live with him:
>
> Knowing that Christ being raised from the dead dieth no more; death hath no more dominion over him.
>
> (Rom. 6:4-9)

Poe inverts the Pauline conception of baptism by presenting his characters being "bedewed" in the unholy baptismal "blood" of the Red Death: "For he that is dead is freed from sin."[7] Death becomes the grim "saviour" of this world; appropriately, the Red Death wears a "vesture dabbled in blood" (II.675)—a grim inversion of Christ in the Book of Revelation:

> And he was clothed with a vesture dipped in blood. and his name is called The Word of God.
>
> (Rev. 19:13)

The Red Death joins Herod in denying Christ as the Messiah; but the Red Death "out-Herod[s] Herod" (II.675) by spilling the blood, not merely of the innocent first born, but of everyone. The three figures presiding over the "blood-bedewed" halls—Darkness, Decay, and the Red Death—become an infernal triumvirate replacing the divine trinity as the ruling force of the world.[8]

The Biblical counterpart to the romance "masque" or "mask" is the "veil." In the Old Testament, Moses wears a veil when he speaks in the name of Yaweh (Exod.

34:29-35). In 2 Corinthians 3 Paul says that Moses' veil symbolizes the obscurity of man's knowledge of God given through the old law, which becomes for Paul the law of death. Hence, in wearing the veil, Moses is wearing the veil of death and blinding himself to the truth about man's relation to God. Paul goes on to say that the "vail is done away in Christ" (14), that is, that Christ triumphs over the law of death through his resurrection. In John 20:6-7, the beloved disciple and Simon Peter go "into the sepulchre, and seeth the linen clothes, but wrapped together in a place by itself." The details draw attention to the success of Christ's resurrection: he has taken the veil of death away. The prefigurement for this becomes Christ's raising of Lazarus from the grave: "And he that was dead came forth, *bound hand and foot with graveclothes,* and his face was bound about with a napkin. Jesus saith unto them, Loose him, and let him go" (John 11:44; emphasis added).

Poe echoes the Lazarus passage when he makes his Red Death

> *shrouded from head to foot in the habiliments of the grave.* The mask which concealed the visage was made . . . to resemble the countenance of a stiffened corpse.
>
> (II.675; emphasis added)

But Poe rejects the notion that Christ takes the veil of death away by having his masquer, the Red Death, wear a veil that cannot be taken away:

> a throng of the revellers at once threw themselves into the black apartment, and, seizing the mummer . . . gasped in unutterable horror at finding the grave cerements and corpse-like mask which they handled with so violent a rudeness, untenanted by any tangible form.[9]
>
> (II.676)

In presenting an image of man helpless against the apparition of death, Poe suggests the inefficacy of Christ's triumph over death, thus delivering man into the world of the old law: the Red Death denies Christ his power of resurrection.

As such, the Red Death qualifies for what John calls an "antichrist": he who "denieth that Jesus is the Christ . . . is antichrist" (1 John 2:22). John admonishes:

> Love not the world, neither the things that are in the world. . . .
>
> For all that is in the world, the lust of the flesh, and the lust of the eyes, and the pride of life, is not of the Father, but is of the world.
>
> And the world passeth away, and the lust thereof. . . .
>
> Little children, it is the last time: and as ye have heard . . . antichrist shall come.
>
> (1 John 2:15-18)

Prince Prospero, who is "of the world" and suffers from "the lust of the flesh, and the lust of the eyes, and the pride of life," appropriately becomes the victim of an "antichrist," that figure who in the Bible temporarily replaces Christ as the ruling force of the world. That Poe is responding to Scripture here is further indicated if, as Thomas O. Mabbott says, the story has as one of its bases the clock at Strasbourg Cathedral,

> where, shortly before the stroke of the clock, a figure representing Death emerged from the center and sounded the full hour, while at the quarter and half hours the statue of Christ came out, repelling the destroyer.
>
> (II.669)

Not surprisingly, Poe places his grim reversal of the Christian drama in an "abbey"—the Catholic bride of Christ, a holy sanctuary in which man uses religious ritual to commune with God. The abbey has seven rooms, each decked in a different color and having a "heavy tripod, bearing a brazier of fire" (II.672) opposite a window of "stained glass" (II.671). Critics have associated the seven rooms with the cycle of nature and the seven ages of man in Shakespeare. In the Bible, though, seven symbolizes fullness, completeness—man's oneness with God. The seven colors also correspond to colors of vestments worn in Catholic liturgy, as well as to the seven colors of the rainbow (Biblical symbol of hope and the new covenant between man and God).[10] And the braziers, which use coals of fire, recall the "censer full of burning coals of fire from off the altar before the Lord" that is brought "within the vail" of the Old Testament temple in Leviticus 16:12, and the "seven lamps of fire burning before the throne" of God in Revelation 4:5. Hence, in the Red Death's destruction of the abbey, Poe seems to suggest the inefficacy of man's use of religious ritual to commune with God, as a means of transcending time and of triumphing over the law of death. Poe's story can be seen to have a basis in Ecclesiastes 6:2: "this is vanity, and it is an evil disease."[11] The "Avatar" and "seal" of Prospero's world are not Christ, as in the Bible, but the "blood" of the Red Death (II.670). The shaping force of Poe's world becomes, not the Lamb of God, as in the Book of Revelation, but that type of antichrist in the fourth seal of God riding the "pale horse": "and his name . . . was Death" (6:8).

Poe's use of *The Tempest* and the Bible to shape the mythic pattern of **"The Masque of the Red Death"** is not so much the product of a wild fancy as it is of an astute reading of western literature. For, as J. L. Borges has suggested in his story "The Gospel According to Mark,"

> generations of men, throughout recorded time, have always told and retold two stories, that of a lost ship which searches the Mediterranean seas for a dearly loved island, and that of a god who is crucified on Golgotha.

According to Northrop Frye, "Borges is clearly suggesting that romance, as a whole, provides a parallel epic" to the Bible; that, in fact, romance can be seen as a "secular scripture" whose mythic pattern mirrors that of the Bible.[12] Hence, the allusions to *The Tempest* and the Bible in **"The Masque of the Red Death"** may suggest that Poe responds to the mythic pattern of the two kinds of stories which Borges and Frye suggest form the basis of western literature.

Essentially, then, Poe in **"The Masque of the Red Death"** reads Shakespeare and the Bible much as Marlowe's Dr. Faustus reads the Bible and Aristotle—out of context. He is attracted to the ideas in two speeches that are secular and sacred correlates of each other: Prospero's "Our revels now are ended" speech and the passage in the Bible about the victory of "antichrist" over man. Specifically, Poe inverts the romantic conventions of *The Tempest* and the religious tenets of the Bible. Prospero becomes, not the unifying force of love in the world, but the mere victim of a demonic opposite, the Red Death. And the Red Death replaces Christ as the shaping force of reality. In Poe's revision of the mythic pattern set forth in the secular and sacred mythologies, man is imprisoned in a world governed by the "law" of death. Hence, man's use of his will to link himself with heaven, as a means of triumphing over sin, death, and time, becomes a "masquerade" (II.671)—a futile display of self-deception that culminates only in death. Man's final marriage is not with Milan or the Church, with home or heaven—but with the mere "shadow" of these: the Red Death.[13]

Notes

1. Critics are in general agreement that Poe knew both his Shakespeare and his Bible. On *The Tempest* in "The Masque of the Red Death," see Kermit Vanderbilt, "Art and Nature in 'The Masque of the Red Death,'" *NCF* [*Nineteenth-Century Fiction*], 22 (1968), 379-389. According to Vanderbilt, p. 383, n. 5, "Poe . . . knew his Shakespeare and admired Prospero and *The Tempest* in particular. He regarded *The Tempest* and its hero to be the quintessence of the poetic spirit." No articles examine Poe's use of the Bible in "The Masque of the Red Death." However, William Mentzel Forrest, in *Biblical Allusions in Poe* (New York, 1928), p. 147, says that Poe had "considerable knowledge of the Bible." Forrest traces the circumstances in which Poe learned the Bible and concludes (p. 150): "there is no mystery about this man's familiarity with Scripture. He absorbed it from his environment; he met it in the literature he critically examined; he was taught it in childhood and youth; he studied it in mature years." Under the heading, "Quotations, Allusions, Reflections," he cites over 600 passages and 200 proper names from Scripture. Killis Campbell, in "Poe's Knowledge of the Bible," *SP* [*Studies in Philology*], 27 (1930), says that a third of Forrest's citations could have come from secondary sources or popular usage (p. 547). He finds "less

than a hundred" to have any real substance (p. 548). Nonetheless, he agrees with Forrest's conclusion about Poe's considerable knowledge of the Bible. As the present essay reveals, the subject of the Bible in Poe deserves reevaluation. For example, Forrest cites only three allusions to the Bible in "The Masque of the Red Death": 1) "Out-Heroded Herod" (Matt. 2:16); 2) "His vesture dabbled in blood" (Rev. 19:13); and 3) "He had come like a thief in the night" (1 Thess. 4:1-2). But he misses the obvious one about the Red Death having "dominion" in this world, together with others that I will introduce. Poe begins writing and out comes the Bible; even the seemingly gratuitous phrase, "harken to the sound," can be found to come from Jeremiah 6:17: whereas Poe says his masquers "harken to the sound" of the ebony clock's music (II.672), Jeremiah warns man to "Hearken to the sound" of God's trumpet. Poe's use of the Bible, however, goes beyond mere allusions, for, as Forrest remarks (p. 160), Poe's works are "saturat[ed] with Biblical style"; and, as I go on to show, he seems to have been influenced by the general narrative shape of the Bible. In the present essay, all quotations are from the *Collected Works of Edgar Allan Poe,* ed. Thomas Ollive Mabbott (Cambridge, Mass. and London, 1969-78), II.

2. Joseph Patrick Roppolo, "Meaning and 'The Masque of the Red Death,'" *TSE* [*Tulane Studies in English*], 13 (1963), 63.

3. *The Tempest,* III.iii.53, from *William Shakespeare: The Collected Works,* ed. Peter Alexander (London and Glasgow, 1951). Future citations will be included in the text.

4. Prospero is like Christ in several other ways. Like Christ (Matt. 8:24), Prospero calms a "tempest"; he embodies a doctrine of forgiveness (see V.i.27-28); he returns from the dead (at least as far as the Court Party is concerned [see V.i.104 ff.]); and he calls on man for "prayer" (Epilogue, 14).

5. Vanderbilt, "Art and Nature in 'The Masque of the Red Death,'" p. 385, says that Poe's story "repeats th[e] cataclysmic vision of destructive nature and triumphant death" envisioned in Prospero's "Our revels now are ended" speech.

6. For a similar Biblical ending, see the closing of "Morella." Other stories permeated with Biblical style include "Shadow" and "Silence."

7. For a romantic version of this baptism, see the end of "Morella," where, during a church baptism, the "second" Morella reveals herself to be the first.

8. Roppolo, "Meaning and 'The Masque of the Red Death,'" p. 68, likens Darkness, Decay, and the Red Death to the "trinity."

9. The motif of the mask or veil of death clearly fascinated Poe. It crops up in such stories as "Ligeia," "William Wilson," "The Fall of the House of Usher," "Berenice," "The Cask of Amontillado," and "The Pit and the Pendulum."

10. Both of these correlations, though striking, need not be pressed too hard; they become significant primarily within the Biblical context I introduce. The correlation between the colors of the rooms and the colors of vestments worn in Catholic liturgy runs as follows: blue (on white)—worn during celebrations of the Holy Virgin (blue is generally the color of the Virgin); purple—worn during celebrations of the Pentecostal Season; green—worn during Sundays after Pentecost; orange–gold (and white) vestments worn during joyous holidays such as Christmas and Easter (the connection between orange and gold is also made by those critics who correlate the seven rooms with the cycle of nature); white—worn during celebrations of Easter; black—worn during celebrations of the Requiem; and scarlet (red)—worn during celebrations of Pentecost, and of the Holy Spirit, and of the Martyrs. The correlation between the seven colors of the rooms and the seven colors of the rainbow is not as exact; the seven colors of the rainbow are red, orange, yellow, green, blue, indigo, and violet; they are created through white light; hence, the only color left unrepresented is black. I would also point out Esther 1:5-8:

> And when these days were expired, the king [Ahasuerus] made a feast unto all the people that were present in Shushan the Palace . . . ;
>
> Where were white, green, and blue hangings, fastened with cords of fine linen and purple to silver rings and pillars of marble: the beds were of gold and silver, upon a pavement of red, and blue, and white, and black marble.
>
> And they gave them drink in vessels of gold, . . . and royal wine in abundance, according to the state of the king.
>
> And the drinking was according to the law; none did compel: for so the king had appointed to all the officers of his house, that they should do according to every man's pleasure.

Significantly, this pleasure palace later becomes a site of destruction, when the Jews attack "all their enemies with the stroke of the sword, and slaughter, and destruction" (9.5).

11. This passage from Ecclesiastes appears shortly after the passage about the "multitude of dreams" (Eccl. 5:7)—a phrase that Poe borrows for "The Masque of the Red Death" (II.673). Suggestively, Thomas O. Mabbott glosses "multitude of dreams" with Prospero's famous phrase from *The Tempest*, "we are such stuff as dreams are made on" (II.n.

9, 678). In other words, a single phrase from Poe ("multitude of dreams") can be glossed by reference to both the Bible and *The Tempest*.

12. *The Secular Scripture: A Study of the Structure of Romance* (Cambridge, Mass. and London, 1976), p. 15.

13. It is beyond the scope of this essay to suggest that Poe's view in "The Masque of the Red Death" is not the final view he presents of man's role in the universe. As an example of how Poe transcends his view, see another story about a castellated abbey, "Ligeia," which features another magician who comes like a thief in the night, rends the veil of death away during a tempest, and has illimitable dominion over all.

Michael Tritt (essay date June 1983)

SOURCE: Tritt, Michael. "'The Masque of the Red Death': Yet Another Source." *Poe Studies* 16, no. 1 (June 1983): 13-14.

[*In the following essay, Tritt illuminates the influence of Lord Byron's* Childe Harold *on "The Masque of the Red Death," demonstrating similarities between the Duchess of Richmond's Ball and Prince Prospero's masquerade.*]

Critics propose multiple sources for Poe's **"The Masque of the Red Death."** A quick review of the key studies suggests both their number and diversity. In "Hawthorne's 'Plagiary'; Poe's Duplicity" [*Nineteenth-Century Fiction,* 25 (1970), 281-198], Robert Regan examines the influence of four of Hawthorne's "Tales of the Province House" on Poe's story, while Walter Evans looks to another Hawthorne tale in "Poe's 'The Masque of the Red Death' and Hawthorne's 'The Wedding Knell'" [*Poe Studies,* 10 (1977), 42-43]. T. O. Mabbott [*Works* (*The Collected Works of Edgar Allan Poe*), II, 667-670; this edition is cited in the text by page] mentions the influence of Boccaccio's *Decameron,* Campbell's *The Life of Petrarch,* and, probably, the description in N. P. Willis' "Pencillings by the Way" of a masked ball in Paris with a figure dressed as "The Personification of the Cholera." Harry Levin [*The Power of Blackness* (New York: Vintage, 1960), p. 150] links Pope's *The Dunciad* to the end of the Poe tale, and Burton Pollin [*Discoveries in Poe* (Notre Dame: Univ. of Notre Dame Press, 1970), pp. 75-90] traces the possible influences of both Shelley's *The Last Man* and Byron's poem, "Darkness." These studies are persuasive, yet one can never be sure one has tapped all of the sources of a given tale. As Pollin writes, "Almost every masterpiece of literature reflects a variety of sources, recent and remote, major and minor, all absorbed and held by the creative spirit in a state of dynamic but subliminal flux, until the moment of conception" (p. 75).

Within this context, I would like to suggest yet another possible influence upon Poe's tale. In Byron's *Childe Harold,* Canto III, (1817) [in *The Works of Lord Byron,* ed. Ernest Hartley Coleridge (London: John Murray, 1922), II; hereafter cited in the text by stanza] when Harold comes upon Waterloo, he describes the Duchess of Richmond's Ball in Brussels the night before the engagement at Quatre Bras. The participants, the atmosphere, and the inevitable outcome of the ball, as well as the diction used to describe it, foreshadow Poe's tale. The generally accepted influence of Byron upon Poe [for an overview, see George H. Soule, Jr., "Byronism in Poe's 'Metzengerstein' and 'William Wilson,'" *ESQ,* 24 (1978), 152-162] suggests the possibility of a relationship between this scene in *Childe Harold* and **"The Masque of the Red Death,"** which the following parallel passages dramatize. The quotations are grouped so as to move from description of the setting and atmosphere, to the repeated intrusion of and reaction to a disconcerting sound, then to the efforts of the hero, and finally to the general collapse of gaiety and concomitant death.

Childe Harold	"The Masque of the Red Death"
"A thousand hearts" (xxi)	"a thousand . . . friends" (670)
"that high hall" (xxiii)	"his castellated abbeys." (670)
"Beauty and . . . Chivalry . . . fair women and / brave men" (xxi)	"the knights and dames of his court" (670)
"with its voluptuous swell" (xxi)	"A voluptuous scene" (671)
"in Beauty's circle proudly gay" (xxviiii)	"the whole gay company" (672)
	"a gay and magnificent revel" (673)
"A thousand hearts beat happily" (xxi)	"beat feverishly with the heart of life." (674)
"full of lusty life" (xxviii)	
"a deep sound . . . like a rising knell!" (xxi)	"a dull heavy monotonous clang;" (672)
"that heavy sound" (xxii)	"chiming" (673)
"nearer—clearer—deadlier than / before!" (xxii)	"clear and loud and deep" (672)
"deep thunder peal on peal" (xxv) "Did ye not hear it?—No—'twas but the Wind, / or the car . . . / On with the dance! let joy be unconfined" (xxii)	"harken to the sound and there was a brief disconcert.. but when the echoes had fully ceased, a light laughter at once pervaded the assembly" (672-673)
"the noon of night" (xxvi) "The midnight brought the signal-sound of strife" (xxviii)	"the sounding of midnight . . . twelve strokes . . . more of thought" (674)
"Brunswick's fated chieftain . . . roused the vengeance" (xxiii)	"Prince Prospero, maddening with rage" 676)
"rush'd into the field" (xxiii)	"rushed hurriedly through the chambers" (676)
"foremost fighting fell." (xxiii)	"fell prostrate in death." (676)
"there was hurrying to and fro" (xxiv)	"threw themselves" (676)
"with terror / dumb" (xxv)	"a certain nameless awe" (676)
"And cheeks all pale" (xxiv)	"grew pale" (672)
"And gathering tears, and tremblings of / distress" (xxiv)	"gasped" (676)
	"the wild courage of despair" (676)
"Rider and horse, friend, foe, in one red burial blent!" (xxviii)	"Darkness and Decay and the Red Death . . . dominion over all." (677)

An extravagant atmosphere, disturbing reminders of time and transience, a singular hero who challenges fate and loses, the frenzied despair with which those who remain meet their fate, as well as the descriptive language, all recommend Byron's ball scene as a source for Poe. Thematic similarity is located in the ironic discrepancy between the gay revelry and the imminence of a black and irrevocable fate. With each writer, the sound which marks the end of day also signals the end of gaiety and, with Poe and to a lesser extent Byron, the end of life itself. The transformation from happiness and life to terror and death comes quickly, surreptitiously, "like a thief in the night" (Poe, **Works,** II, 676). In the larger context of *Childe Harold,* the ball scene reflects upon a well-known Byronic theme—*sic transit gloria mundi* ("And this is much, and all which will not pass away"—Byron, xxxv). Consequently, one will expect new glories in the Byronic scheme, though they must all come to an end, as does the Duchess' ball. In contrast, Poe's vision, at its most expanded, depicts a more permanent state, a universal death, which brings us back to Byron's "Darkness" and the death of the universe. The bleakness in **"The Masque of the Red Death"** is unrelieved by any sense of the cyclical, whereas in *Childe Harold,* though "the heart will break, yet brokenly it will live on" (Byron, xxxii).

Robert Lance Snyder (essay date spring 1984)

SOURCE: Snyder, Robert Lance. "A De Quinceyan Source for Poe's 'The Masque of the Red Death.'" *Studies in Short Fiction* 21, no. 2 (spring 1984): 103-10.

[*In the following essay, Snyder treats common themes of social devastation, passionate rage, and extravagant living in Thomas De Quincey's gothic novel* Klosterheim; or, The Masque *and "The Masque of the Red Death."*]

Significant correspondences both in conception and in execution exist between Poe's **"The Masque of the Red Death"** (1842) and De Quincey's Gothic novel *Klosterheim; or, The Masque* (1832). As a prose stylist Poe is often presumed to have been influenced by De Quincey, a supposition based largely on Poe's thorough familiarity with *Blackwood's Edinburgh Magazine,*[1] which published many of De Quincey's journalistic writings, and on a letter of 30 April 1835 to Thomas W. White, then owner of the *Southern Literary Messenger,* in which Poe cites De Quincey's *Confessions of an English Opium-Eater* (1821-22) as a model for his own technique in composing serial tales.[2] Despite this prevalent assumption, however, no studies have appeared which examine specific ties or borrowings among works by these two authors. The only notice given to such connections takes the form of brief observations by Thomas Ollive Mabbott and Killis Campbell: in the

Collected Works of Edgar Allan Poe Mabbott remarks in passing that "Poe seems to have had [De Quincey] in mind"[3] while writing **"Silence—A Fable"** (1832); and in *The Mind of Poe and Other Studies* Campbell hints in a footnote that "A parallel in situation between De Quincey's *Klosterheim* and Poe's **'The Masque of the Red Death'** may also be worth noting."[4] Aside from these undocumented speculations, De Quincey's imprint on Poe's work has not been explored. In the following pages I propose to demonstrate that **"The Masque"** derives a great deal of its setting, plot, climactic incident, and expression from *Klosterheim*—enough, at least, to suggest that Poe must have read De Quincey's novel before writing his own celebrated tale.

Elsewhere I have discussed De Quincey's Gothic narrative in some detail,[5] but a preliminary synopsis may provide a helpful framework for relating the work to Poe's story. Set in Germany during the Thirty Years' War, *Klosterheim* revolves around the exploits of its hero, Maximilian, as he seeks to assert his legitimate claim to succession as ruler of the city named in the title. Because he is opposed by a tyrannical Landgrave who is acting in collusion with the Swedish invaders, Maximilian disguises himself as a figure known only as "The Masque" in order to expose the usurper and generally undermine the impostor's political designs. The subterfuge works, despite the Landgrave's attempt to entrap the mysterious intruder through the stratagem of two costume balls, and in a theatrical finale the protagonist's true identity is revealed while the Gothic antihero goes down in conventional self-inflicted defeat. So outlined, the novel is clearly a formulaic moral fantasy that hearkens back to the eighteenth-century *Schauerroman* tradition. With this sketch in mind we can consider the connections to **"The Masque of the Red Death."**

The first similarity manifests itself in situation and atmosphere, elements of setting emphasized by each author. Describing at the outset the depredations of the war and the fierceness of the approaching winter in 1633, De Quincey projects the near-final exhaustion and desperation of the populace in these terms:

> Latterly, indeed, it had become apparent that entire winter campaigns, without either formal suspensions of hostilities, or even partial relaxations, had entered professedly as a point of policy into the system of warfare which now swept over Germany in full career, threatening soon to convert its vast central provinces—so recently blooming Edens of peace and expanding prosperity—into a howling wilderness; and which had already converted immense tracts into one universal aceldama, or human shambles, reviving to the recollection at every step the extent of past happiness in the endless memorials of its destruction.[6]

Besides establishing a background for what is later called "those days of tragical confusion, and of sudden catastrophe" (XII, 28), the passage also keynotes the mood of crisis and impending disaster which prevails throughout the novel. In something of the same manner Poe begins **"The Masque"** as follows: "The 'Red Death' had long devastated the country. No pestilence had ever been so fatal, or so hideous" (II, 670). Despite the obvious stylistic difference here between De Quincey's long cumulative sentence and Poe's short declarative statements, both excerpts reinforce the idea of some cataclysmic reversal in the design of human experience. The device itself, of course, is by no means unique to these writers; moreover, Poe was probably drawing as well on his firsthand knowledge of the cholera epidemic in Baltimore in 1831 and that in Paris reported by N. P. Willis in the *New York Mirror* of 2 June 1832.[7] The parallel to De Quincey's novel nevertheless remains suggestive evidence of textual filiation.

Another correlation pertains to the havens sought from the affliction in each work. Amid the encompassing destruction and "the ruins of social order" (XII, 16) resulting from the war, the "ancient and sequestered city" (XII, 45) of Klosterheim is depicted as an island of safety to which a caravan of refugees is fleeing. The town's immunity supposedly stems from its having been linked of old with the Imperial cause; and like the neighboring chateau of Falkenberg, where an early scene of Gothic intrigue occurs, it is effectively "the sole *oasis* of culture and artificial beauty" (XII, 35) in an otherwise desolate land. These details concerning the city's privileged status have their equivalence in Poe's tale. "When his dominions were half depopulated," we are told, Prince Prospero along with a thousand friends "retire[s] to the deep seclusion of one of his castellated abbeys" (II, 670), whereupon he sets about quarantining their resort from the surrounding contagion. If allowance is made for Prospero's deliberately immuring himself and his company within his stronghold, the situation closely approximates that in *Klosterheim*. In both cases a particular group seeks asylum in a place which they suppose impervious to external disruption, only to find there an emblem of all that they most wished to avoid. And in both cases, as escape turns into encounter, the sanctuaries become increasingly subject to internal upheaval, so that each finally resembles "the chaos of a dream" (XII, 56).

De Quincey's phrase aptly captures the presence of the bizarre in both works; beyond that, however, his novel's plot seems replicated in miniature by Poe's tale. As indicated earlier, *Klosterheim* centers on Maximilian's effort to reclaim what is rightfully his by deposing the autocratic Landgrave, a man of "capricious tyranny" (XII, 67) whose "sallies of passion had become wilder and more ferocious, and his self-command less habitually conspicuous" (XII, 75), as challenges to his arbitrary authority mount. Because of the Landgrave's wiliness and the city's perplexed politics, Maximilian must engage in a campaign of dissemblance and counter-scheme to overcome his foe. Now in rendering this conflict De Quincey admittedly is relying on stereotypical patterns of Gothic fiction, reading which much fascinated him during his youth.[8] But even so the main outline of his plot seems transferred directly into the fabric of **"The Masque of the Red Death."** Thinking himself secure within his fortified retreat and so able to "bid defiance" (II, 671) to the world without, Prospero soon discovers that his elaborate plans for evasion are nullified by an unknown intruder who boldly defies his will. Moreover, this figure—a "mummer" (II, 675) inspiring fear and outrage—epitomizes everything that the Prince has tried to ward off or deny, in the same way that the spectral Masque in De Quincey's novel symbolically threatens the Landgrave's presumptions of absolute power and control. Both antiheroes thus are forced to confront in supernatural guise their own deepest anxieties, and it is around this combined psychological and moral interest that the two works are structured.

The plot of *Klosterheim* reaches its formal climax with a pair of incidents, one anticipating the other, which again leave a distinctive mark on Poe's tale. In the first, attempting to check the pervasive "sense of indefinite terror" (XII, 78) caused by his mysterious enemy, the Landgrave arranges a masked ball in the hope of thereby drawing out the interloper. Twelve hundred carefully chosen guests "attired in the unrivalled pomp of that age" (XII, 94) attend the revel, but shortly after midnight it is discovered that there is one masquerader too many among the assembly. After being singled out and wrongly accused of the murder of an old seneschal, De Quincey's protagonist manages to escape amid the "universal panic" that results when he whispers the name of the actual murderer, stuns the Landgrave by privately unveiling his own countenance (an action which, as in Poe, leads to the revelers' belief that he had revealed "the fleshless skull of some forgotten tenant of the grave"), and publicly summons the Landgrave to a tribunal for his various crimes (XII, 106-07). The latter event provides the focus for the second incident, the dénouement of the novel. Maintaining his attitude of "gloomy reserve" and "haughty disdain" (XII, 139), the Landgrave plans another masked ball on an even grander scale than the first. For this occasion the wall between the castle and an adjoining convent is thrown down, the intent being to execute by guillotine all those siding with Maximilian. Predictably, however, "The Masque of Klosterheim" once more appears at the stroke of midnight and, in a series of fortuitous reversals that conclude the novel, the townspeople follow the distraught Landgrave into the Abbey of St. Agnes where they witness his final defeat, Maximilian's vindication, and the restoration of order to the city.

Several features of these episodes in De Quincey's romance are carried over into Poe's fantasia with little

modification. Most obvious, perhaps, is the detail with which the masquerade tableaux are embellished. In *Klosterheim* De Quincey dwells on the baroque magnificence of scenes "overflowing with the luxury of sound and sight" and the "turbulent delight" of a "glittering crowd" lost in "the exhilaration of the moment" (XII, 97). Similarly, in the "voluptuous" entertainment staged in Prospero's "Gothic Wonderland,"[9] as one critic calls it, Poe stresses the predominance of "much glare and glitter and piquancy and phantasm" (II, 671, 673). Although the seven varicolored rooms of the Prince's "castellated abbey" can not be traced to De Quincey's work, he like Poe directs attention to the "barriers" erected against uninvited entrance to the *fête,* the "lofty galleries or corridors which ran round the halls," the "mazes of the palace," the "variety of fanciful costume," the "confusion of colours," the "forced and intermitting gaiety" of the revelers, and, most significant of all, the knell-like tolling of the clock with its momentarily sobering effect on the orchestra and dancers (XII, 92-97, 144-46). Other possible connections can be established only through the interpretation of nuance. For example, Poe's striking comment that in all but the seventh of Prospero's chambers "beat feverishly the heart of life," along with his rendering of the celebrants' alarm over rumors concerning "the presence of the Red Death" (II, 674, 676), may owe something to the following passage by De Quincey on the report of a murder during the first ball:

> Still, so awful is the mystery of life, and so hideous and accursed in man's imagination is every secret extinction of that consecrated lamp, that no news thrills so deeply, or travels so rapidly. Hardly could it be seen in what direction, or through whose communication, yet in less than a minute a movement of sympathizing horror, and uplifted hands, announced that the dreadful news had reached them.
>
> (XII, 95)

Such a vignette, when linked to the common emphasis on the ornate décor of the masquerades and the exotic or dreamlike quality of the revelers, suggests that Poe's tale is indebted at least as much to *Klosterheim* as it is to more widely recognized sources like Boccaccio's *Decameron* and the journalistic descriptions of N. P. Willis.

The final indication of Poe's having drawn on De Quincey's novel lies in certain analogous modes of formulation and expression. As already noted, De Quincey labors hard to evoke the "feverish state of insecurity" (XII, 67) which pervades the city as a result of both the war's vicissitudes and the nightly abduction of various citizens of Klosterheim. Together, these menacing circumstances breed a conviction among the populace that "Some enemy, of unusual ferocity, was too obviously working in the dark, and by agencies as mysterious as his own purpose" (XII, 45). When "The Masque" appears within their midst, therefore, he not only confounds all rational means of apprehension but also, in so doing, becomes the objectified or demonized representation of man's fear-ridden imagination—of what Poe calls "a certain nameless awe" (II, 676) and of what Freud means in part by "the 'uncanny.'"[10] De Quincey obliquely raises these issues when he writes:

> If, then, connected with the spiritual world, was it with the good or the evil in that inscrutable region? But then the bloodshed, the torn dresses, the marks of deadly struggle . . . these seemed undeniable arguments of murder, foul and treacherous murder. Every attempt, in short, to penetrate the mystery of this being's nature proved as abortive as the attempts to intercept his person; and all efforts at applying a solution to the difficulties of the case made the mystery even more mysterious.
>
> (XII, 95)

In one of its details the excerpt anticipates the point in Poe's tale that "the redness and the horror of blood" comprised the "Avatar" and "seal" of the "'Red Death'" (II, 670), but more importantly the passage articulates the principle of indeterminacy on which the later fiction turns. Because the masked "intruders" of both works pose an unfathomable enigma to their "victims," they can not be known and thus define the limits of logical deduction or ratiocination. And when this occurs, each is anathematized—De Quincey's "Masque" is pronounced an "atrocious monster" (XII, 96), Poe's "mummer" a "blasphemous mockery" (II, 675)—as though the curses themselves will rescue the discursive mind and confer understanding.

Other features of De Quincey's novel seem directly echoed or imitated by Poe. The Landgrave, for example, like the "dauntless" (II, 670) Prince Prospero, is "not of a character to be easily duped by mystery," yet under "the sort of fear which is connected with the supernatural" his temper soon erupts in unguarded "spasms of fury" (XII, 81, 87). Such involuntary rage is heightened further in each work by contrast with the antagonists' self-possession. When "The Masque of Klosterheim" silently lures the Landgrave into a picture gallery of the castle, he proceeds at the same "solemn pace," with the same "equable and determined step" (XII, 83), that characterizes Poe's "spectral image" whose "slow and solemn movement, as if more fully to sustain its *role,*" is mentioned three times in the story (II, 675, 676). The stately bearing of these figures, moreover, has the common effect of completely discomposing their opponents: abandoning "the ceremonious decorum of his rank," the Landgrave "swelled with passion—he quickened his step, and again followed in pursuit" (XII, 84); similarly "convulsed" and "reddened with rage" at the affront to his "indefinite decorum," Prospero "rushed hurriedly through the six chambers" in "rapid impetuosity" (II, 675, 676). When the face-to-face confrontation finally

comes, Poe's borrowing is so evident that parallel citation is almost unnecessary. "There was a sharp cry," writes Poe, after which "fell prostrate in death the Prince Prospero. Then, summoning the wild courage of despair, a throng of the revellers at once . . . seiz[ed] the mummer" (II, 676). The comparable scene in De Quincey reads as follows: "With a yell, rather than a human expression of terror, the Landgrave fell, as if shot by a thunderbolt, stretched at his full length upon the ground, lifeless apparently, and bereft of consciousness or sensation. A sympathetic cry of horror arose from the spectators. All rushed towards The Masque" (XII, 106).

The conclusion to be drawn from these several instances of formal and thematic congruence seems clear. Scholars concerned with the reliable attribution of sources for Poe's fiction have noted that the best arguments have been made when we know that Poe either read or reviewed the suggested source.[11] This proviso can hardly be debated. However, in the absence of any record of Poe's having read *Klosterheim,* the evidence presented above of textual appropriation would appear to indicate irrefutable indebtedness, despite the fact that both works are examples of formula fiction. If my analysis holds, one then detects a larger irony about the case. The writer always so ready to inveigh against others for literary plagiarism not only is open to the charge himself, but also in **"The Masque of the Red Death"** is drawing much of his material from an author given to the same tactics. Like Poe, De Quincey practiced freely the art of *rifacimento,*[12] widespread during the nineteenth century, and like Poe he criticized others for doing as he himself did. The pattern constitutes an interesting study in the psychology of progenitive influence.

Notes

1. See Michael Allen, *Poe and the British Magazine Tradition* (New York: Oxford University Press, 1969), passim. Poe's familiarity with *Blackwood's,* of course, is most immediately obvious from his satirical sketch "How to Write a Blackwood Article" (1838).

2. This letter was first published in excerpted form by Napier Wilt in "Poe's Attitude Toward His Tales: A New Document," *Modern Philology,* 25 (1927), 101-05. Containing the only explicit reference to De Quincey that I have been able to find in all of Poe's writing, it is reprinted in its entirety in *The Letters of Edgar Allan Poe,* ed. John Ward Ostrom (Cambridge, Mass.: Harvard University Press, 1948), I, 57-59.

3. *Collected Works of Edgar Allan Poe,* II (Cambridge, Mass.: Belknap Press of Harvard University Press, 1978), 187. All later quotations from "The Masque of the Red Death" are taken from Mabbott's edition and will be cited parenthetically.

4. *The Mind of Poe and Other Studies* (Cambridge, Mass.: Harvard University Press, 1933), p. 175, fn. 2. Campbell also makes the same brief suggestion in an earlier essay titled "Poe's Reading," *University of Texas Studies in English,* 5 (1925), 166-96. There he anticipates as well Mabbott's conjecture that Poe's "Silence" reflects De Quincey's influence.

5. See my essay "*Klosterheim*: De Quincey's Gothic Masque," *Research Studies,* 49 (1981), 129-42.

6. *The Collected Writings of Thomas De Quincey,* ed. David Masson (London: A. & C. Black, 1896-97), XII, 5. All subsequent quotations from De Quincey's novel are taken from Masson's edition and will be documented parenthetically.

7. See, respectively, Arthur Hobson Quinn, *Edgar Allan Poe: A Critical Biography* (1941; rpt. New York: Cooper Square, 1969), p. 187; and Campbell, *The Mind of Poe and Other Studies,* p. 171, fn. 2.

8. See *A Diary of Thomas De Quincey, 1803,* ed. Horace A. Eaton (London: Noel Douglas, n.d.), pp. 156-63.

9. Joseph Patrick Roppolo, "Meaning and 'The Masque of the Red Death,'" in *Poe: A Collection of Critical Essays,* ed. Robert Regan (Englewood Cliffs, N. J.: Prentice-Hall, 1967), p. 134. This article originally appeared in *Tulane Studies in English,* 13 (1963), 59-69.

10. See his essay by that title in *The Standard Edition of the Complete Psychological Works of Sigmund Freud,* trans. and ed. James Strachey, XVII (London: Hogarth Press, 1955), 217-56.

11. Killis Campbell makes this observation in "Poe's Reading," 166-67, as does also Gerald E. Gerber in "Additional Sources for 'The Masque of the Red Death,'" *American Literature,* 37 (1965), 52. Other literary works that have been advanced as sources for Poe's tale include Shakespeare's *The Tempest,* Disraeli's *Vivian Grey,* Victor Hugo's *Hernani,* Alessandro Manzoni's *I Promessi Sposi,* Joseph von Eichendorff's *Ahnung und Gegenwart,* William Harrison Ainsworth's *Old St. Paul's,* Mary Shelley's *The Last Man,* Coleridge's "Allegoric Vision," Hawthorne's *Twice-Told Tales,* and Mally's *Voyages et aventures des trois princes de Sarendip.*

12. See Albert Goldman, *The Mine and the Mint: Sources for the Writings of Thomas De Quincey* (Carbondale: Southern Illinois University Press, 1965), esp. pp. 82-153. On p. 156 Goldman points out that *Klosterheim* itself is very likely "a *rifacimento* of some obscure German original."

Martin Roth (essay date 1984)

SOURCE: Roth, Martin. "Inside 'The Masque of the Red Death.'" *SubStance* 13, no. 2 (1984): 50-3.

[*In the following essay, Roth illustrates the "dialectic between inside and outside" in "The Masque of the Red Death."*]

This note will explore a dialectic between inside and outside in Poe's tale [**"The Masque of the Red Death"**] which seems to fit the following propositions:

1. The tale narrates the penetration of an inside space by an outside agent or force, yet, in its personification, this agent represents the deepest inside of that space;

2. The external agent is finally seen to be an outside which has no corresponding inside.

I am not tempted to identify the ghastly masquerader as anything—the plague, death, life, the Philistine world, etc.—other than an "outside." I find support for this in the fact that my ordinary notions of how one contracts a fatal illness, dies, or puts the world at defiance are not accommodated by the literal process of the tale. The identification that seems to be most excluded by the tale is the equivalence of the body and its infections.

Prince Prospero and a thousand knights and dames seek to secure themselves against the Red Death by relocating themselves in a "new" place, a place which can be effectively contained as inside space. The Red Death is described as an invader from outside: it had "long devastated the country"; it "raged most furiously abroad"; and it "had come like a thief in the night."[1] Victims of the disease are "shut out" by the "pest ban."

The place chosen is "the deep seclusion" of a castellated abbey surrounded by a "strong and lofty wall" with "gates of iron" (p. 670). The fixity and impenetrability of this boundary is seemingly assured by the strenuous work of welding the bolts. Yet the welding of the bolts is explained by a sentence that disturbs its context and creates a countermovement, a loophole in the text (the very means, perhaps, by which the Red Death enters the abbey): "They resolved to leave means neither of ingress or egress to the sudden impulses of despair or of frenzy from within" (p. 671). The text *gets it backwards,* which is often the case in Poe. The threat which was wholly outside is now balanced between outside and inside. Indeed, this sentence is dominated by the newly arisen impulse to get out which remains untexted, although it drifts into contiguity with the even more unspecified "confused revery or meditation" which besets the "more aged and sedate" during the pauses of the music (pp. 672-673).

The lines which conclusively assert the separation between outside and inside are also unbalanced. They suggest that all is now inside, that there is nothing outside, or nothing worth writing about:

> The external world could take care of itself. . . . There were buffoons, there were improvisatori, there were ballet-dancers, there were musicians, there was Beauty, there was wine. All these and security were within. Without was the "Red Death."
>
> (p. 671)

Prospero's urban planning resembles the condition of Roderick Usher's art as summarized by Joseph Riddell: "Each of Usher's works represents a rather ordinary desire for a self-sustaining, self-present inside, an inexhaustible presence."[2]

Within this "deep seclusion" there is a space, a black room, which is both a center and a periphery.[3] It is a room which lies at the center and at the end of a labyrinthine path. It is the heart of the abbey; it contains a "gigantic clock of ebony," whose chiming imposes a stop-start movement on the festive company and whose "life" goes out with the last of the company. (Poe had featured the equation of the heart and a watch in **"The Tell-Tale Heart."**) But it is also the "western" chamber; it is the last of seven rooms; and its anticipated use as a site will end the tale.

If it is a center, it is one that the occupants of the abbey fear to enter, a room which repels them, ostensibly because it is designed to reproduce symbolically the threatening aspects of the outside: it is a black room illuminated by blood-red light.

There is a confusion about the occupancy of this room which duplicates the form of earlier uncertainties. We are first told that "there were few of the company bold enough to set foot within its precincts at all" (p. 672); then that there is a stalking to and fro in all the seven chambers (p. 673); then that "there are now none of the maskers who venture" into the black room because the light has intensified; but in that sentence there is also an abstract "him whose foot falls upon the sable carpet" and who fully hears the peal of the ebony clock (p. 674).

On the level of metaphor, the inside of the abbey is totally given over to a masquerade, a play of fantastic outsides which are repeatedly identified as deeply interior entities: maskers are described as "delirious fancies" and likened to dreams. For a stretch of the text the latter becomes their proper designation: "the dreams . . . writhed . . . the dreams are stiff-frozen . . . the dreams live and writhe to and fro" (pp. 673-674).

The figure who appears at the masquerade as the Red Death represents the outside of the tale. He appears at an end; individual maskers first become aware of him just "before the last echoes of the last chime" of midnight have "utterly sunk into silence." He is outside the bounds, both spatially and psychologically. The whole company feels deeply that there is neither wit nor propriety in his costume or bearing. But the reigning standards of propriety are Prospero's, and they are nearly unlimited: "The figure in question had . . . gone beyond the bounds of even the prince's indefinite decorum" (p. 675). Poe designates a nominal boundary which cannot really be sited. And if this figure represents the Red Death, so has everyone that has ventured within the precincts of the western room. The reason why few will enter is that the firelight streaming through the blood-tinted panes produces "so wild a look upon the countenance" (p. 672); presumably, each individual sees the others with him as either the representation of the Red Death or a representation of one of its victims.

If this figure represents the successful penetration of the outside into the impenetrable abbey, he also represents the emergence of the inside. He is a characterological duplicate of both the black chamber and its ebony clock. His costume is informed by the doubling of individual and architectural structure so prominent in **"The Fall of the House of Usher."**

At the climax of the tale, the intruder retreats backwards through each of the seven rooms followed by Prospero and, at a further remove, the other inhabitants of the abbey. In the last room, his corpse-like mask is violently removed and the company gasp "in unutterable horror" at finding nothing within, nothing beneath—the clothing and mask are "untenanted by any tangible form."

The tale, then, resembles a Mobius strip or a Klein bottle. In it inside and outside are confusable and exchangeable. In **"The Domain of Arnheim,"** as the privileged visitor journeys toward Paradise, the "windings become more frequent and intricate, and seemed often as if returning in upon themselves, so that the voyager had long lost all idea of direction."[4]

The only ontological or psychological threat in the tale that I can believe in refers to blood and the fear of blood, the fear of the "essential" inside getting outside. The word blood and synonymous words and phrases are isolated, repeated, and emphasized throughout the tale. Within the fiction, however, this blood is never real; and it is ironic that Prospero dies bloodlessly. He falls prostrate in death and thus avoids all of the symptoms of the Red Death which were so clearly laid out for us in the opening paragraph.[5]

There is an analogue to this in ***The Narrative of Arthur Gordon Pym.*** It is the letter that Augustus sends to Pym in the hold of the *Grampus*. Attempting to read this text in the blackness of the hold by the momentary glimmer of some phosphorus, and tense with anxiety, Pym is only able to read the seven concluding words: "'*blood—*

your life depends upon lying close.'" This message harrows and horrifies the reader, Pym tells us, because it is fragmentary, and he adds,

> And *"blood,"* that word of all words—so rife at all times with mystery, and suffering, and terror—how trebly full of import did it now appear—how chillily and heavily (disjointed, as it thus was, from any foregoing words to qualify or render it distinct) did its vague syllables fall, amid the deep gloom of my prison, into the innermost recesses of my soul.

(Pym, p. 34)

This text is both semantically and technically (inside and out) bloody; it was written in Augustus's blood, and the word that so chills Pym refers to that still intact and vital fluid. In context, it bears a relatively casual and indifferent meaning; but displaced, isolated, and externalized, it signifies "trebly full of import."

The play of reference in **"The Masque of the Red Death,"** as a textual parable, may help to negotiate the seesaw controversy between a logocentric and a hoaxy Poe—between an ultimate and essential nothingness that is as true as our emotional investment in ontology and teleology and a nothingness that lies beneath the abstract inscriptions on the page which have become the insides of libraries and universities and which constitute the inside of our philosophy and culture.

Notes

1. *Collected Works of Edgar Allan Poe,* ed. T. O. Mabbott (Cambridge: The Belknap Press of Harvard University Press, 1978), II, 671, 676. Hereafter cited in the text.

2. Joseph Riddell, "The 'Crypt' of Edgar Poe," *Boundary 2,* VII (1979), p. 128.

3. Poe often plays with the interchangeability of center and periphery, for example, in *The Narrative of Arthur Gordon Pym,* in the rookery unit or that of the overturning of the *Grampus,* where the cherished food of the center is now discovered on the outside surface in the form of barnacles. (Edgar Allan Poe, *The Narrative of Arthur Gordon Pym,* intro. Sidney Kaplan [New York: Hill and Wang, 1960], pp. 116, 123-127). In this tale, the intruder precipitates a movement from the center to the peripheries (p. 168).

4. Edgar Allan Poe, "The Domain of Arnheim," in *Works,* III, 1279.

5. A final inside and outside constitute the domain of criticism (text and commentary), where "The Masque of the Red Death" is usually described as scaffolding or technique without "meaning"; see, for example, Joseph Wood Krutch, quoted in Joseph Roppolo, "Meaning and 'The Masque of the Red

Death,'" *Tulane Studies in English,* XIII (1963), p. 60: "merely the most perfect description of that fantastic *decor* which [Poe] had again and again imagined." And Stuart Levine, *Edgar Poe: Seer and Craftsman* (Deland, Florida: Everett/Edwards, 1972), p. 200: "One can best convey the nature of 'Red Death' by saying that it is really not about a moral issue at all, but is really 'about' the thrill of horror it hopes to produce in the reader."

Leonard Cassuto (essay date summer 1988)

SOURCE: Cassuto, Leonard. "The Coy Reaper: Unmasque-ing the Red Death." *Studies in Short Fiction* 25, no. 3 (summer 1988): 317-20.

[*In the following essay, Cassuto focuses on the unique role of the narrator in "The Masque of the Red Death," identifying him as the figure of Death.*]

Much has been written about Poe's narrators, and with good reason. Nearly always unnamed—and therefore seen as somehow unreliable—they also have disturbing tendencies that range from the unstable and the obsessed all the way to the insane.[1] In *The Narrative of Arthur Gordon Pym* and several other tales, Poe himself even enters into the fiction, commencing the atmosphere of confusion that pervades throughout. All of this indicates that Poe wants us to pay attention to his narrators. If that is his goal, he has succeeded handsomely, but not completely. **"The Masque of the Red Death"** is a notable exception.[2] The story has a narrator unique in the Poe canon. The teller of the tale is Death himself.

Substantiating such a claim must begin with locating a first-person narrator in the story. At first there does not appear to be one, but closer study reveals that an "I" is in fact relating the action. Perhaps no one has remarked upon his presence before because, unlike many of Poe's more overtly bizarre narrators, this one never steps up and introduces himself. For all of this seeming reticence, though, the raconteur of **"The Masque of the Red Death"** makes his presence known on three separate occasions.

The first of these comes after the description of the isolation of Prospero and his followers. After five or six months in the abbey that he has turned into a vault, Prospero has announced the masked ball, and all is being prepared. Here, the narrator steps forward for the first time:

> It was a voluptuous scene, that masquerade. But first let me tell of the rooms in which it was held.[3]

Who is this "me"? He must be someone who has seen the inside of Prospero's self-imposed prison, but it has been sealed "to leave means of neither ingress nor egress" (251). This fact points to the narrator's presence in the group inside the walls. One could argue that Poe is simply employing a casual reference, that "me" is simply a figure of speech, but the frequency of the narrator's direct intervention (three times in a seven-page story) precludes this assumption.

The story has a narrator, then, but this narrator may not be a character *in* the story. Perhaps Poe has adopted a familiarly omniscient first-person narrator which would allow him to achieve a compromise between first-person involvement and third-person omniscience. This is not a new device, to be sure—Hawthorne, for one, employs it in many of his stories and romances.[4] Maybe Poe does mean to have an "I" telling the story from without. The possibility certainly exists, but not to the exclusion of all others. Furthermore, such a narrator would be unique among Poe's tales of horror.[5] On the few occasions when he does employ omniscient narration,[6] it is always in the third person. All of his other first-person narrators live and breathe within their own fictional worlds; I submit that the teller of **"The Masque of the Red Death"** does so as well.

Given the presence of a narrator, it is clear that he can be nowhere else but present at the festivity. There would be no other way for him to describe a pause in the activity at midnight: "And then the music ceased, as I have told; and the evolutions of the waltzers were quieted; and there was an uneasy cessation of all things as before" (255).

The narrator's comparison proves that he has been there since the beginning of the party. His reference to what he has already told hearkens back to a previous description of how the striking of the clock would stop the orchestra. The third and final time he refers to himself further confirms his presence amidst the merriment. He compares the Red Death figure to the other masqueraders at the party: "In an assembly of phantasms such as I have painted, it may be supposed that no ordinary appearance could have excited such sensation" (255).

The Red Death is indeed extraordinary, but so must be the narrator, for he has somehow lived to tell us about it.

The narrator's survival thus presents a contradiction which allows for an alternate reading of the story, one that adds a new dimension to the grotesque scene which Poe describes.[7] According to the narrator's own account, no one survives the Red Death's "illimitable dominion." How could the narrator be present at the ball and then be able to tell about it afterwards? The only one who "lives" is Death. The narrator must be Death himself.

This discovery adds a gruesomely ironic aspect to the entire tale. Death's storytelling is marked by a smooth, deliberate, almost deadpan calm. There is a sense of in-

evitability to the scene which precludes tension because the narrator already knows what will happen. The outcome is as dependable as the passing time, symbolized by the striking clock which governs the action in the story.[8] No one escapes Death, so it is natural that Death should not perceive any suspense. Nor has Death any need for self-aggrandizement. We see the final confrontation between Death and the pursuing prince from Death's perspective, but description of the moment of truth is carefully avoided: "There was a sharp cry—and the dagger dropped gleaming upon the sable carpet, upon which, instantly afterward, fell prostrate in death the Prince Prospero" (257). Only Death could have seen all of this; Prospero has run through six rooms while the other partygoers remain shrunk against the walls in fear. Death is describing his own actions, but without telling us exactly what happens. His tone as a narrator is consistent with his character in the story: matter-of-fact, final, and anonymous.

As Death remains masked to Prospero, so Death remains masked to us. The mockingly self-deprecatory way that he hides himself in both the action and the narration furnishes a humorous tinge to the macabre that is already present in the story, giving a uniquely grotesque turn to an already grotesque creation. Harpham has elsewhere pointed out various puns in the story's structure (e.g., the guests are "dis-concerted" when the clock stops).[9] Another can now be added to the list: Death is the author of Prospero's fate in more ways than one.

Notes

1. Daniel Hoffman suggests that these nameless, unconnected narrators allow Poe to depict psychological struggle in disguise, without having to focus on family ties (Daniel Hoffman, *Poe Poe Poe Poe Poe Poe Poe* [New York: Doubleday Press, 1972], p. 226).

2. Of all the critics who have given attention to this story over the years, only one has commented upon the narrative presence in it. Geoffrey Galt Harpham sees the narrator as "an undercover agent working for the plague" whose function is to draw the reader into a "read death" (Geoffrey Galt Harpham, *On the Grotesque* [New Jersey: Princeton University Press, 1982], p. 117). Though interesting, this reading treats the narrator as a strategy, not as a character.

3. Edgar Allan Poe, "The Masque of the Red Death," in *The Complete Works of Edgar Allan Poe,* Vol. 4, ed. James A. Harrison (New York: AMS Press, 1965), p. 251. All subsequent references to this story will be made parenthetically within the text.

4. For example, *The House of the Seven Gables.* Hawthorne also uses first-person narrative frames for some of his tales.

5. And almost alone among all of the others as well. "King Pest," which has an unidentified "I" who surfaces twice, cannot properly be said to be a story of horror, grotesque as it may be. The narrator, who refers to the protagonists as "our heroes," keeps things light. "Metzengerstein" is briefly introduced by a narrator who is typically Poe-ish in his deliberate withholding of information, but who makes no appearance thereafter.

Among Poe's humorous efforts, "Bon-Bon" and "The Devil in the Belfry" have omniscient narrators who carry on from the outset, putting themselves into almost every sentence, so that they not only insert themselves into their tales, but arguably become the dominant characters in them. The result is a parody of narrative reliability.

6. Outside of the mock articles, the angelic colloquies, and other dialogues such as "Some Words with a Mummy," "A Tale of Jerusalem" is a rare example.

7. Among his few direct references to the term, "The Masque of the Red Death" contains Poe's most explicit description of his own vision of the grotesque. Wolfgang Kayser has called his portrayal of the revelers "perhaps the most complete and authoritative definition any author has given of the grotesque" (Wolfgang Kayser, *The Grotesque in Art and Literature,* trans. U. Weisstein [Indiana: Indiana Univ. Press, 1963], p. 79).

8. For a more detailed treatment of this idea, see Edward Pitcher, "Chronological and Horological Time in 'The Masque of the Red Death,'" *American Transcendental Quarterly* 29 (1976), 71-75.

9. Harpham, p. 114.

Richard D. Slick (essay date winter 1989)

SOURCE: Slick, Richard D. "Poe's 'The Masque of the Red Death.'" *Explicator* 47, no. 2 (winter 1989): 24-6.

[*In the following essay, Slick considers "The Masque of the Red Death" in light of the AIDS epidemic, concluding that "the Romantic artists have much more to teach us about AIDS and other such problems than the moralists have to teach us."*]

We are immersed these days in articles, reports, TV specials, and dramas about the AIDS problem that one fears it might eventually have the effect of becoming one more fad. In a recent issue of the *Orlando Sentinel* (23 February 87), a special piece on Latin America (A-8) highlighted fears at Rio De Janeiro in regard to AIDS and the celebrated Rio Carnival. The reporter headed the piece "A Specter at the Party." Suddenly the word "specter" with its allegorical suggestions and extensions riveted my attention. It was as though I were a contestant on the popular "Jeopardy" quiz game on television and I had been given an answer for which I had to form the correct question. And then it hit me! What could Edgar Allan Poe possibly have meant in the rather fabulous, allegorical work **"The Masque of the Red Death"**? As a specialist in American Studies, I immediately scurried for my bookshelves and my Poe volumes. Ah, yes! There it is, *Edgar Allan Poe: Poetry and Tales* by the Library of America. The Tale is only six pages, and I hurriedly re-read it. The narrator of the Tale (and we really never know how he or she managed to escape the red death in order to tell the story) does not use the term "specter" as the *Sentinel* reporter did to allegorize the red death. However, some key allegorical descriptors are worth noting in argument. The new "phantasm" that appears almost magically by *deus ex machina* after much reveling in the bizarre (sometimes grotesque) "imperial suite" of Prince Prospero arouses feelings of disapprobation and surprise—then finally, "of terror, of horror, and of disgust" (489). The narrator observes: "In truth the masquerade license of the night was nearly unlimited [images of the Rio Carnival]; but the figure in question had out-Heroded Herod, and gone beyond the bounds of even the prince's indefinite decorum." The new appearance at the revel is described particularly as "tall and gaunt, and shrouded from head to foot in the habiliments of the grave." The visage is much like that of a "stiffened corpse." His "vesture was dabbled in blood." The face "was besprinkled with the scarlet horror" (489). Prince Prospero, in a rage, makes to attack the figure with a dagger but falls dead before he can strike. The narrator, in most stately terms, proclaims in the last paragraph of the Tale: "And the life of the ebony clock went out with that of the last of the gay" (490). Poe, of course, is using the term here in its more traditional sense.

For American readers at least, Edgar Allan Poe has practically become a folk hero of the human imagination. Is it so far-fetched to hypothesize that he could have been predicting in this fabulous allegory **"The Masque of the Red Death"** something like the terrible AIDS virus that seems to appear more and more in human communities across the world? Now we hear of a more virulent form out of Africa. As the medical research groups work at a frenzied pace to discover medicines, vaccines, whatever, we hear the Poe narrator say finally: "And Darkness and Decay and the Red Death held illimitable dominion over all" (490).

One of the things we have known about Romantic artists (both literary and otherwise) for a long time is that through the power of the imagination they often appear to be able to forecast future phenomena, events, and such that escape the attention of ordinary mortals. This is particularly why we value the human imagination and foster and nurture its presence. A question that this essay raises is: Will the AIDS horror eventually "have illimitable dominion over all?" Or will the human communities of the world be able to save themselves with either short-term solutions or long-term solutions, or both?

In the short term, we are seeing the application and use of an old, existing technology—the condom—to address the problem. Whether this technology will fill the gap is questionable. As one follows the press and the media, it seems questionable that we will ever be able to advertise this technology sufficiently in the consumer market to make it work.

The long-run solutions seem to be dialectically opposed. On the one hand, AIDS might cause human sexual behavior to return to a more celibate or controlled state—some pre-1960s state where sexual behavior is more repressive and restricted. Or, on the other hand, we might see a worse-case scenario—**"The Masque of the Red Death"**—in which hedonism runs rampant until the very end, or perhaps something in between these cases.

However, we need a word for the first scenario, and we have a "goodie but oldie" in the words of the father of American psychology, William James. In his *Variety of Religious Experience: A Story in Human Nature,* James uses the term "anhedonia" (137) to describe the opposite or pathological condition in some humans to "healthy-mindedness" (137). Speaking of what he calls the "sick soul" (112), James says: "Evil is a disease; and worry over disease is itself an additional form of disease, which only adds to the original complaint" (112). The human communities across the world appear to be in such a state of mind at the present time in regard to the AIDS crisis.

"Anhedonia" can serve as the term to label the repressive and restrictive view of sexual activity as a possible scenario down the road in the AIDS crisis. James makes a most interesting analogy to explain the pathological condition of "anhedonia," which is worth repeating. He says it is like "prolonged seasickness." "One afflicted with this illness turns away with disgust from every good, terrestrial or celestial imagining" (126). In candid discussion with young people, one already senses an uneasiness with the AIDS problem and what impact it will have on them. Generally speaking, liberals for years have pointed to the good things (healthy-mindedness) that have come from the so-called sexual revolution. Now both the young and the adult are uneasy about the future. A worst case possibility comes into view with widespread "anhedonism" or melancholy over sexual behavior. However, before we embrace "healthy mindedness" as the solution, let's refer again to the great American psychologist, William James. He observes that "healthy mindedness" excludes "evil from its field of view" (87). However, he points out that "anhedonism" or "soul sickness" suffers from the same flaw.

"Soul sickness" excludes goodness from its vision. So, we seem to be looking at mutually exclusive categories of optimistic candor and cynical depression. As we view the problems of the appearance and existence of AIDS in the human communities across the world, we not only attempt to deal with it practically, medically, and contraceptively; but we also reflect on it philosophically. A question that the "healthy minded" might raise is the following: "Is there perhaps some beneficial aspect of AIDS or some good thing about it which our limited knowledge keeps from us?" James offers us only limited and enigmatic advice on the matter. He states: "It may be that there are forms of evil so extreme as to enter into no good system whatsoever, and that, in respect of such evil, dumb submission or neglect to notice is the only practical recourse" (139).

To attempt to draw some connections from this statement relative to the AIDS crises, we might conclude that although not all whales in the ocean are Moby Dicks, probably some of them are. To relate this analogy to the AIDS crisis, one might argue that although not all evils are absolute, some of them might be. Or to return to the **"Masque of the Red Death"** with which this essay began, it might be noted that there is no compromise with the "tall, gaunt, and shrouded" phantasm with the masque resembling "[t]he countenance of a stiffened corpse." As the sombre narrator tells us: ". . . the Red Death held illimitable dominion over all" (490).

Government leaders in the United States at this time are arguing over priorities and proposed budget in regard to the AIDS crisis. The large priorities seem to be: 1) care for those already afflicted with the disease; 2) medical research for vaccines and medicines; and 3) education to attempt to change behavior. Before "education" loses the battle (usually the case in this country), one hopes that education, especially that of the humanistic kind, will have its day in court and be given due consideration as priorities are set in the immediate period ahead.

Edgar Allan Poe believed that the only thing art had to do was be beautiful. **"The Masque of the Red Death"** is a provocative tale and would be effective in generating and opening discussion with young people in an instructional unit on AIDS. The central argument of this essay is that the Romantic artists have much more to teach us about AIDS and other such problems than the moralists have to teach us.

Works Cited

James, William. *The Varieties of Religious Experience: A Study in Human Nature.* New York: New American Library, 1958.

Poe, Edgar Allan. *Poetry and Tales.* New York: The Library of America, 1984.

Hubert Zapf (essay date fall 1989)

SOURCE: Zapf, Hubert. "Entropic Imagination in Poe's 'The Masque of the Red Death.'" *College Literature* 16, no. 3 (fall 1989): 211-18.

[*In the following essay, Zapf examines archetypal aspects of "The Masque of the Red Death," illuminating the conflict between creation and destruction in its narrative structure.*]

"The Masque of the Red Death" is one of the shortest and yet best-known stories by Edgar Allan Poe. Its theme, other than the cryptosymbolic worlds of sinister subjectivity in tales like **"William Wilson," "The Tell-Tale Heart"** or **"The Fall of the House of Usher,"** seems to have a more universal appeal and a more immediately recognizable human significance. Compared with the sophisticated narrative techniques and the labyrinthine psychological complexities of those other stories the meaning and structure of **"The Masque of the Red Death"** are, at least at first sight, relatively straightforward. In place of symbolism, reflexivity and textual indeterminacy we have the clarity and coherence of allegory; in place of innovation and experiment we have a traditional form of narrative which strikes us as old-fashioned. In its theme of *superbia* and of the glory and fall of a prince, it reminds us of medieval moral parables and of the tragic tales of human vanity and pride which lead to inevitable punishment and damnation, as they are exemplified, for instance, in the "Monk's Tale" of Chaucer's *Canterbury Tales*. Furthermore, the plague, which Poe uses as a metaphor in the story for the destruction of human hopes and illusions by the agency of a superhuman fate, and which is personified and becomes the "spectral image"[1] for the final emptiness and futility of earthly life, was similarly seen as a scourge of God in the historical times of the Plague. It was seen—as it is in Poe's story—as a kind of metaphysical drama, an apocalyptic *memento mori* which forcefully reminded humans of their own mortality, purging them of their delusions and their hubris which, like an evil spirit, had possessed them. In the moral logic of the plot; in the use of an allegorical figure as a central agent; in its ghost-like appearance at midnight; and in the apocalyptic imagination with which it is associated, confronting and destroying the power of the "Prince of this World"—in all of these elements the story quite heavily draws on modes of storytelling which seem to belong to a distant past rather than to the contemporary context of Poe's own literary and cultural world.

What is the reason for this historical distancing, this aesthetic anachronism in the literary method of the story? What is its function and status in the overall composition of the text?

In speaking through the language and the imagery of a remote time, Poe tries to find a formal equivalent for the theme of his text, which is at the same time universal and temporal. It attempts to approach archetypal truths of human nature and simultaneously dramatizes the fact that these "truths" are indissolubly connected with their own transitoriness, and with the continuous self-dissolution of the historical forms in which human life and culture articulate themselves. A closer look at the text reveals that the timeworn conventions of storytelling that Poe utilizes here are not employed in an "affirmative" sense but that they are strangely inverted and turned against themselves in the course of the story. The deceptively straightforward surface of the narration conceals a degree of textual complication which is in its way as interesting and as modern as anything else that Poe wrote. It is like a stylistic mask of the narrative which, like the masks of the figures in the narrated world, simultaneously hides and discloses the disappearance of its substance.

From here, the form of the story's composition can be seen as an illustration of the entropic processes of existence, which articulate themselves in the entropic processes of art. "Entropy"—which is a *mixtum compositum* between the two Greek words *energeia* (energy) and *tropé* (transformation)—is the implication of the Second Law of Thermodynamics that all energy is continually transformed in a way in which disorder increases at the expense of order in the material universe.[2] "The available energy will undergo the irresistible and irreversible process of being degraded from useful to less useful forms until . . . maximum entropy" is reached which is known as the "heat death" of the universe.[3] In the metaphorical world of Poe's fictional text, the material side of this process is seen as inseparable from its immaterial, i.e., its psychological and cultural side. Human life itself is seen in terms of a cultural artifact which contains in the specific way in which it attempts to ensure its order the dynamics that continually increases its disorder. It is shown to accelerate its self-consuming tendencies by the very act of its intended "autonomization." The "Red Death" as the determining agent of the text is not really an outside force but is inherent in the ways in which, by means of political power-structures and the structures of artistic imagination, human life tries to become independent from the forces of chaos and annihilation surrounding it.[4]

This attempt of the autonomization of life through its transformation into a cultural artifact is illustrated in the seclusion of Prince Prospero and his privileged class in the "extensive and magnificent structure" of a castellated abbey, whose architecture is a power-structure against the lower classes and against the Red Death as well as an aesthetic structure of parareligious dimensions which mirrors "the Prince's own eccentric yet august taste" (254). This is underlined by the undisturbed, self-centered life of pleasure which, through total control of external circumstances, is to be achieved by that structure. The rituals and festivities, which are accompanied by various forms of artistic entertainment, culminate in a "masked ball of the most unusual magnificence" in which the intensity of the cultural self-dramatization of human life reaches its "feverish" climax (257)—but which is recognized in the end, with the appearance of the Red Death, to have only temporarily disguised the catastrophic climax of self-dissolution which it has precipitated. In other words, the "energy" of the cultural artifacts in which human life tries to elevate and "eternalize" itself is shown to work in a way in which it undermines and counteracts the self-affirming purposes for which they were created.[5]

If the "masque" is one key image of the text, signifying the human, historical dimension of the story's world, the "Red Death" is the other key image, signifying the transhuman, universal dimension. As the title **"The Masque *of* the Red Death"** (italics added) with its linguistic ambivalence between the *genitivus subjectivus* and the *genitivus objectivus* indicates, the two sides are interrelated in a mutually defining and conditioning way. If we look at the image of the Red Death itself more closely, we realize that it is an oxymoronic variant of the traditional notion of the plague as the Black Death, linking its destructive meanings with the vitalistic connotations of the color of blood as the life-preserving element, the "liquid organ" of the body responsible for maintaining the oxygen-supply and the "heat system" of the organism.[6] The description at the beginning of the text of the peculiar symptoms of the disease which haunts the world of Poe's story makes it clear that it is no force above, beyond, or in any way separated from life but that it is life itself which has reached a crisis where it abandons its positive functions within the order of individual organisms and thereby destroys itself:

> Blood was its Avatar and its seal—the redness and horror of blood. There were sharp pains, and sudden dizziness, and then profuse bleeding at the pores, with dissolution.

(254)

Although there is an impression of violence conveyed here, it is not external violence by which blood is spilt but a violence from within which, as it were, causes the blood to spill itself—a very unusual form of illness which can only be explained by assuming a rapid waning away of the skin, indeed of the whole body. What we have here is thus not the realistic description of an illness but a figure of the entropic imagination which pervades the story on all levels.

This can also be seen in the spatial design of the text, which is characterized by an apparently clear-cut opposition between inside and outside:

> There were buffoons, there were improvisatori, there were ballet-dancers, there were musicians, there was Beauty, there was wine. All these and security were within. Without was the "Red Death."

(254)

But this opposition is undermined from the beginning by the fear of "sudden impulses of despair or frenzy from within"; by the prison-like self-immuring of this microsociety; or, on a linguistic level, by the wordplay "within/without," where the opposing worlds are marked off by the period yet immediately juxtaposed, and where the contrast of the second syllables is ironically counteracted by the parallelism of the first syllables.

Also, within the self-created insular "paradise" of the prince—which is at the same time the prison-house of his bizarre imagination—there is implicit in its very conception the presence of the counterforces of destruction and negativity which are ostensibly shut out from it. The extreme irregularity of the castle's architecture and of the way in which the individual rooms are disposed convey a sense of disorder and irrationality rather than of order and control. In a parodistic reversal of the Biblical Act of Creation, the seven differently colored rooms[7] which are arranged from East to West, and in which the masque takes place, are composed in the form of a symbolic teleology of human life which leads from the color blue to the color black, from light to darkness, from creation to destruction. More precisely, it leads to the seventh chamber which, with its black tapestries and blood-red windows, is an objective correlative in the spatial composition of the castle of the "Red Death." The unreal or only half-real atmosphere surrounding these rooms is emphasized by the unusual, highly indirect form in which each of them is lighted by a tripod from a separate corridor "that projected its rays through the tinted glass and so glaringly illumined the room" (255), suggesting a world of illusions without substance which is in a way reminiscent of the shadow-world of Plato's cave simile.

In the process of the story, of course, the seventh chamber more and more becomes the center of attention, and with it the clock of ebony which symbolizes the structure of temporality underlying and terminating all human activities. In the striking of the hours which dictates the rhythm of the festivities, time, like space, is made conscious not only as a consitutive category of narrative fiction, but as an existential manifestation of a principle which consumes itself and which, as such, is built into the events of the masque as their structuring law.

Something similar can be said about the fictional categories of action and character. The conception of life as a masque, and of the world as a stage, which underlies the scenery of the fête and the climax and turning point of the action to which it leads, is again a traditional motif which views all human behavior in the light of the *theatrum mundi*—metaphor. But again it is used here also in the more radical sense that human life is *nothing but* this masque of history, that there is no "authentic" identity behind the masks the people wear in it. Their life consists only of the fictions they have made of themselves, turning them into "a multitude of dreams" which seem somehow to have merged with the fantastic-nightmarish quality of the rooms in which they dance their "dance of death."[8]

The masque as a metaphor of human history and culture thus gains an almost postmodern, Nietzschean meaning in Poe's story, breaking down the binary oppositions of fiction and reality, of mask and identity, into a self-referential play of cultural signifiers. This is, however, not conceived of in the sense of a "free play" but as a strangely compulsive play, a theater of escalating, mutually negating forces of opposition which are finally shown to belong indissolubly together. This is particularly true of the oppositions of creation and destruction, of life and death, as they are symbolized in the two poles of the "masque" on the one hand and of the "Red Death" on the other. As for Nietzsche there is no fundamental difference between life and death, between organic and inorganic forms of existence—life representing "only another, very infrequent form of death"[9]—in Poe's story, too, the masque of the revellers is revealed in the end as merely another form in which the entropic principle of the Red Death manifests itself.

But the parallel to Nietzsche ends where the philosopher sees the transindividual process of creation and destruction as something which, in spite of its inerasable element of negativity, should be affirmed as potentially meaningful. Poe's view is far more pessimistic here in that he sees all of creation doomed from the beginning by its "predestinated" destruction, which always already overshadows all life-affirming impulses even before they can fully realize themselves. Thus the masque, in which the cultural self-affirmation of the life-impulse in the story reaches its maximum intensity, not only implicitly derives its motivating energy from the very forces of chaos and annihilation that it opposes; but from it emerges the Red Death as a kind of supermask in which the phantasmagoric world of cultural self-signification is pushed to its extreme, yet in which it is also dramatically revealed in its fundamental negativity and in the self-consuming energy of all of its activities. This super- or metamask emerges out of nowhere, or rather it seems to emanate from the scenery itself and thus to become representative of the principle of all other masks.

> And thus, too, it happened, perhaps, that before the last echoes of the last chime had utterly sunk into silence, there were many individuals in the crowd who had found leisure to become aware of the presence of a masked figure which had arrested the attention of no single individual before.
>
> (258)

But this new mask, which apparently "concealed the visage" (258) of the stranger, is shown in the end as concealing nothing at all, because the Red Death is revealed, in the final confrontation with the other masqueraders, as consisting of nothing but its mask.

The "Red Death" can thus be seen as a cultural supersign of the world of the text which, like the whole structure and the cultural artifact of the castle, is the product of the prince's imagination, but which has become an autonomous force that has turned against its human creator. And in its emptiness which is dramatically revealed at the end, it epitomizes the *horror vacui* which, like a self-fulfilling prophecy, has shaped that imagination from the beginning. It is interesting in this context to note that, for all the contrast between the "characters" of Prospero and the Red Death—between the aggressive emotionality and the fast, hectic movements of the prince, and the indifferent, mechanical movements of the Red Death which, in their inexorable regularity, resemble the swinging pendulum of the clock—there is also an affinity between the two in their dominating behavior and, indeed, in the stranger's mask itself with its "broad brow . . . besprinkled with the scarlet horror," which parallels the prince's "brow reddened with rage" (258). This is underlined by the fact that the prince dies at the very moment when the figure of the Red Death confronts him as an empty mask. The manner of the prince's death—he dies on the instant, as if he himself has been revealed in this scene of recognition as an empty mask—is significantly not identical with the character and the progress of the disease as it is described at the beginning of the text.[10] Herein, the world of the story is once more exposed as the world of a cultural artifact that consumes itself in the same way in which the fictional categories that are used by Poe to communicate this world—i.e., space, time, characters, action, and symbolism—consume themselves in the process of the text. This becomes obvious at the end when, with the death of the revellers—

> the life of the ebony-clock went out with that of the last of the gay. And the flames of the tripods expired. And Darkness and Decay and the Red Death held illimitable dominion over all.
>
> (260)

It is not necessary to share Poe's gloomy pessimism to recognize in the specific mode in which he organizes his text, in a highly self-reflexive and carefully structured way, the contours of an entropic imagination which transcends the traditional imagery of apocalypse and makes this allegorical story, for all its medieval rhetoric, in many ways appear as a strangely contemporary text.

Notes

1. Edgar Allan Poe, "The Masque of the Red Death," *The Fall of the House of Usher and Other Writings: Poems, Tales, Essays and Reviews,* ed. with an introd. by David Galloway, (Harmondsworth: Penguin, 1967) 254-260, 258.

2. This etymology is given by Rudolf Clausius (1822-1888) who, after William Thompson (1824-1907) had discovered the Second Law of Thermodynamics, coined the word *entropy,* to describe its wider implications, in his article "Über verschiedene für die Anwendung bequeme Formen der Hauptgleichungen der mechanischen Wärmetheorie," *Annalen der Physik und Chemie,* 125 (1865): 353-400, here 390. While the First Law of Thermodynamics states that all available energy within a closed system remains constant, the Second Law complements this by the observation that in all transformation processes energy is irreversibly dissipated, so that disorder continually increases at the expense of order in the universe. I am indebted in this to Peter Freese, *Surviving the End: Beyond Apocalypse and Entropy in American Literature,* (Claremont McKenna College, Center for Humanistic Studies Monograph Series 1, 1988) 18 ff.

3. Freese, *op. cit.,* 19-20.

4. The dialectic between "inside" and "outside" in the story and their final exchangeability are demonstrated by Martin Roth in his sophisticated article "Inside 'The Masque of the Red Death,'" *SubStance* 13.2 (1984): 50-53.

5. There is an affinity between Stanley Fish's concept of "self-consuming artifact" and the structure of "The Masque of the Red Death," but the point with Poe's story is that it projects this conception from the sphere of art onto the real world of human life itself and thus, in its connection with the concept of entropy in a broad sense, gains an existential meaning.

6. See *The New Encyclopedia Britannica,* Vol. 2, 1985, 290-291. Blood, which has "evolved from seawater" (290), is thus not only a metaphorical but a metonymic symbol of the "life-force."

7. The number "seven," of course, suggests the seven days of God's creation of the world, and more generally the path of human life which is inverted here into a "labyrinthine path" (M. Roth, 51) ending in the black chamber.

8. See, for this motif, Sarah Webster Goodwin, "Poe's 'Masque of the Red Death' and the Dance of Death," in *Medievalism in American Culture: Special Studies,* ed. B. Rosenthal et al. (Binghampton, N.Y., 1987) 17-28.

9. Friedrich Nietzsche, *Die fröhliche Wissenschaft* (Stuttgart: Kröner, 1976).

10. This is also noticed by M. Roth, *op. cit.,* 52.

K. Narayana Chandran (essay date spring 1993)

SOURCE: Chandran, K. Narayana. "Poe's Use of *Macbeth* in 'The Masque of the Red Death.'" *Papers on Language & Literature* 29, no. 2 (spring 1993): 236-40.

[*In the following essay, Chandran describes similarities in theme and tone between* Macbeth *and "The Masque of the Red Death."*]

The collective evidence of the range and variety of sources suggested for **"The Masque of the Red Death"** indicates that individual readers gifted with cross-citational memory often have made profitable discoveries. Such possibilities, as every student of literary sources knows, are endless.[1] And yet it seems to me strange that *Macbeth* has seldom, if ever, figured as a possible source in any discussion of Poe's story. For, in my repeated reading of **"The Masque of the Red Death,"** I can find nothing more compellingly shadowy than the presence of this Shakespeare play, especially that of Banquo's ghost and the Banquet Scene (III.iv).

There is, indeed, first-hand evidence in Poe's *Pinakidia* that he had contemplated not only the Banquet Scene but a possible theatrical manipulation of its spooky effects:

Pinakidia 7

Speaking of the usual representation of the banquet-scene in Macbeth, Von Raumer, the German historian, mentions a shadowy figure thrown by optical means into the chair of Banquo, and producing intense effect upon the audience. Enslen, a German optician, conceived this idea, and accomplished this without difficulty.

(*Collected Writings* [*The Collected Writings of Edgar Allan Poe: The Brevities*] 2: 14)

This note appeared in 1836, six years before the publication of **"The Masque of the Red Death"** in *Graham's Lady's and Gentlemen's Magazine.* During the intervening years, Poe might well have pondered Von Raumer's suggestion in order to develop appropriate rhetorical devices for his own craft that would possibly match the Enslen effect on the stage. As a matter of fact, it is conceivable that Poe's verbal account of Prince Prospero's instinctive reaction upon seeing the "spectral image" was meant to simulate something of "the intense [visual] effect" Enslen was believed to have achieved for his "audience":

When the eyes of Prince Prospero fell upon the spectral image (which with a slow and solemn movement, as if more fully to sustain its *role,* stalked to and fro among the waltzers) he was seen to be convulsed, in the first moment with a strong shudder either of terror or distaste; but, in the next, his brow reddened with rage.

(***Collected Works*** [***The Collected Works of Edgar Allan Poe: Tales and Sketches 1831-1842***] 2: 675)

The *Pinakidia* reference, however, may not be wholly essential for us to observe how Prospero's reflexes duplicate Macbeth's during the former's encounter with the Red Death. The texts themselves give us ample evidence of Poe's persistent recall and select use of details from *Macbeth* at various stages. Given the likeness and immediacy of the two situations, both Prince Prospero and Macbeth betray shock, anger, and shame in matching proportions. Macbeth, we recall, vents his anguished fury in stages:

Which of you have done this? . . .
Thou canst not say I did it. Never shake
Thy gory locks at me.
. . . . .

Avaunt, and quit my sight! Let the earth hide thee.
Thy bones are marrowless, thy blood is cold.
Thou hast no speculation in those eyes
Which thou dost glare with.
. . . . .

What man dare, I dare.
. . . . .

Hence, horrible shadow,
Unreal mock'ry, hence!

(III.iv.48-50, 93-96, 105-106)

Prospero, on his part, addresses the revelers, and just once; he never addresses the Masque:

"Who *dares*?" he demanded hoarsely of the courtiers who stood near him—"who *dares* insult us with this blasphemous *mockery*? Seize him and unmask him—that we may know whom we have to hang at sunrise, from the battlements!"

(675, emphasis added)

The verbal parallels in **"The Masque"** of Macbeth's "dare" and "mockery" are, I believe, far from fortuitous. Furthermore, both passages underscore the visual effrontery and the threat posed to the speakers by the visitants. In other words, the *burden* of their outbursts is the same: the ghost at once mocks and stultifies; its incorporeality—compare Macbeth's "take any shape but that"—makes it impossible for them to confront it physically. While Poe spells out Prospero's "Shame of his momentary cowardice," Shakespeare suggests Macbeth's embarrassment before his invited guests through a brief exchange:

LADY MACBETH

Are you a man?

MACBETH

Ay, and a bold one. . . .

(III.iv.57-58)

"Blood was its Avatar and its seal"—runs Poe's introduction of the Red Death, "the redness and the horror of blood" (670). If this alone does not constitute a sufficient mnemonic pointer towards the Banquet Scene, Poe's specific gory details, particularly the mummer's "vesture, dabbled in *blood*—and his broad brow, with all the features of the face . . . besprinkled with the scarlet horror" (675) serve to remind us specifically of Macbeth's morbidly recurrent mention of blood (as many as nine times in the Banquet Scene alone) before and after his confrontation with the ghost. I quote below three of Macbeth's memorable utterances, two of them involving particular references to blood on the face, which I believe to be more apposite to my consideration of Poe's "Scarlet horror": *Macbeth*: [to the First Murderer] "There's blood upon thy face" (l.11); [to the ghost of Banquo] "Never shake / Thy gory locks at me" (ll.49-50); [to himself] "It will have blood, they say. Blood will have blood" (l.121); "Augures and understood relations have / . . . brought forth / The secret'st man of blood" (123, 125).

It seems plausible to me, further, that Poe has drawn upon certain details from other scenes of *Macbeth* as well. Some of these correspondences or parallels are worth recording to demonstrate Poe's more insistent and direct use of *Macbeth* than he may have been conscious of.

(1) Macbeth's concluding words at the close of Act I, "Away, and mock the time with fairest show. / False face must hide what the false heart doth know" (I.vii.81-82) virtually foreshadow **"The Masque"** both verbally and thematically. Both pretense and self-delusion by turns, or one followed by the other, the "show" in Poe capitalizes on "False face": the *Masque* of Death, not Death itself; "that masquerade" (671); and the ambiguous "presence of a masked figure" (674) which mocks self-delusion only to belie it. One might only wonder why Poe did not use these lines from *Macbeth* as his epigraph to **"The Masque."**

(2) In Macbeth's apostrophe to the dagger, he calls it "an instrument I was to use" (II.i.43). Recall that Macbeth uses the dagger, but Prospero does not. Macbeth, again, sees the dagger as marshaling him the way "[he] was going" (II.i.42); Prospero, who "bore aloft a drawn dagger" (676), is marshaled in much the same manner by the Red Death.

(3) Of Prospero's material and psychic fortifications Poe comments: "All these and *security* were within. Without was the 'Red Death'" (671, emphasis added). Quite appositely, one might recall Hecate's remark on Macbeth's false and dangerous sense of security:

> He shall spurn fate, scorn death, and bear
> His hopes 'bove wisdom, grace and fear.
> And you all know security
> Is mortals' chiefest enemy.
>
> (III.v.30-33)

(4) It is possible that Poe conceived of his Red Death "with [its] deliberate and stately step" (676) as a "walking shadow," one antithetical to Macbeth's "Life's but a walking shadow" (V.v.23). This antithesis now sharpens the irony by making Prospero and the revelers "poor players" who do all the chasing and fretting. Macbeth's "walking shadow" fits the mummer more exactly than we think if we recall Burton Pollin's contention that **"The Masque of the Red Death"** evolved from Poe's earlier sketch of a "stationary" Shadow. In fact, Pollin observes how Poe's **"Shadow—A Parable"** "resembles a dress rehearsal for **'The Masque,'** which has often been likened to a theatrical performance" (104).

The details from *Macbeth* I have listed above in thematic and tonal apposition to **"The Masque of the Red Death,"** taken together, point unmistakably to *Macbeth* as a source, as plausible as any other proposed so far, for Poe's story.

Note

1. In 1983 Michael Tritt's note in *Poe Studies* on "Yet Another Source for 'The Masque'" begins with a brief review of the major discoveries; see *Poe Studies* 16 (1983): 13-14. As far as I know, the most recent article on this subject is Robert Lance Snyder's "A DeQuinceyan Source for Poe's 'The Masque of the Red Death,'" *Studies in Short Fiction* 21 (1984): 103-110. See also Snyder's note on p. 109 for a brief survey of other sources.

Works Cited

Poe, Edgar Allan. *Collected Writings of Edgar Allan Poe: The Brevities.* Ed. Burton R. Pollin. Vol. 2. New York: Gordian, 1985. 4 vols. 1981-1986.

———. *Collected Works of Edgar Allan Poe: Tales and Sketches 1831-1842.* Ed. Thomas Ollive Mabbott. Vol. 2. Cambridge, MA: Belknap-Harvard, 1978. 3 vols. 1969-1978.

Pollin, Burton R. "Poe's 'Shadow' as a Source of his 'The Masque of the Red Death,'" *Studies in Short Fiction* 6 (1968): 104-6.

Shakespeare, William. *The Tragedy of Macbeth.* In *The Complete Works.* Ed. Stanley Wells and Gary Taylor. Oxford: Clarendon, 1986.

David R. Dudley (essay date spring 1993)

SOURCE: Dudley, David R. "Dead or Alive: The Booby-Trapped Narrator of Poe's 'Masque of the Red Death.'" *Studies in Short Fiction* 30, no. 2 (spring 1993): 169-73.

[*In the following essay, Dudley discusses the paradox of the narrator in "The Masque of the Red Death," regarding the story as a parable about the inability of art to conquer death.*]

While the narrator of Edgar Allan Poe's **"The Masque of the Red Death"** never appears *in* a scene, he is always *on* the scene. He reveals himself overtly only three times, and even then only as one who tells:

> "But first let me tell of the rooms in which [the masquerade] was held."
>
> (485)

> "And the music ceased, as I have told . . ."
>
> (488)

> "In an assembly of phantasms such as I have painted . . ."
>
> (489)

Yet as understated as this narrator is, he presents a cryptic puzzle. The problem is that while he has witnessed the fatal events inside Prince Prospero's sealed abbey and survives to tell the tale, we learn at the end that everyone within the abbey dies. The narrator's survival is therefore paradoxical. I shall get to the significance of the paradox presently, but first I would like to show why efforts to dismiss the paradox are unsatisfactory.

One possible reading of the narrator in **"Red Death"** is that Poe has simply been careless—that his inclusion of three first-person pronouns is casual and meaningless. (We might call this the default reading, implicit in most of the criticism on this story that is concerned with other issues entirely.) This easiest of all solutions to our point-of-view puzzle is also the least satisfying, when one considers Poe's usual extreme sensitivity to the position of his narrators. In fact, many of Poe's tales are arguably *about* their own existence after the death of their narrators.

For instance, **"MS. Found in a Bottle"** and **"Shadow—A Parable"** both purport to be written by narrators who are on the brink of death, and who will be dead by the time we read their texts. At first they seem to offer a promising model for a reading of **"Red Death."** Could not **"Red Death"** be written—albeit in blood—by one of Prospero's dying guests? The last sentence ("And Darkness and Decay and the Red Death held illimitable dominion over all" [490]) could then be read as the equivalent of Hamlet's "I am dead. . . . O, I die, Horatio! . . . The rest is silence" (5.2.338-63). No one finds Hamlet's failure to use the future tense confusing, so why quibble over the past tense in the last sentence of **"Red Death"**?

But Poe has precluded this solution. The puzzle of the narrator is ensured by a seemingly offhand comment exactly halfway through the story. In the middle of a description of the costumes Prospero has designed for his masque ball, the narrator tells us that "[t]here were much glare and glitter and piquancy and phantasm— much of what *has since been seen in 'Hernani'*" (487, emphasis added).

Once we notice this phrase, its effect is startling. The verb tense establishes once and for all the narrator's survival beyond the end of the story. Furthermore, the reference to Victor Hugo's *Hernani* gives the narrator a surprising contemporaneity with Poe and his initial readership. *Hernani* was first performed in 1830, and Poe wrote **"Red Death"** in 1842. By contrast, the setting of **"Red Death"** seems older by at least a century or two, giving the narrator an odd, duplicitous, then-and-now quality. The narrator is simultaneously in Prospero's time, Poe's time, and the reader's time (the latter two were nearly the same thing in the 1840s but have been diverging ever since). Time, as the ominous clock in Prospero's seventh chamber reminds us, is the bringer of death; but the narrator is anachronistic, in that he is not subject to time.

Therefore, whatever this narrator is, he is not a normal human being. Leonard Cassuto makes this point in an article entitled "The Coy Reaper: Unmasque-ing the Red Death," although he does not mention the *Hernani* phrase. Cassuto argues that the narrator is "unique in the Poe canon. The teller of the tale is Death himself" (318). Yet while this reading ingeniously accounts for the narrator's endurance, its concrete personification of death dismisses one of the central themes in Poe's work: death's intolerably enigmatic nature.

The two stories mentioned earlier, **"MS."** and **"Shadow,"** suggest the way in which Poe repeatedly designed fictional experiments to see how close he could come to having a narrator speak from the vantage of the dead. Even **"Mesmeric Revelation,"** in which the narrator hypnotizes and interviews a dying man, ends ambiguously with a question: "Had the sleep-waker, indeed, during the latter portion of his discourse, been addressing me from out the region of the shadows?" (727).[1] Always in Poe there is a frustration of the effort to comprehend death; or else there is a clear tone of burlesque, as in **"Loss of Breath"** or **"How to Write a Blackwood Article."** Poe is never able seriously to domesticate death to the degree Cassuto proposes.

Even disregarding the evidence of Poe's other works, the idea that Death is the narrator of **"Red Death"** runs afoul of the image Poe gives of death near the end of the story—or rather the conspicuous lack of an image: "the grave-cerements and corpse-like mask" that the revelers tear from the intruding figure of the Red Death are "untenated by any tangible form" (490). Mortality is terrifying for Poe because death resists all cognition and ends all communication.

Moreover, if we were to accept Death as the narrator of **"Red Death,"** we would have to imagine the Grim Reaper chattily showing off his knowledge of the latest in French theater. That sounds more like Woody Allen than Edgar Allan Poe, or else like Poe in a much lighter mood than the grim tone and subject matter of **"Red Death"** indicate.

Geoffrey Galt Harpham, in his book *On the Grotesque,* offers another reading: "This tale, like many Poe works, is concerned with the implications of narrative, of the process of rendering into artifact and the living death granted by this process." Harpham calls the narrator "an undercover agent working for the plague," and says that "[p]ursuing this narrative we experience 'read' deaths." After the narrator's last first-person reference two thirds of the way through the tale, he becomes "a bodiless voice," and then goes himself one better and "expires" at the end, since "[l]ife is synonymous with articulation and death with silence" (Harpham 117).

Notwithstanding Cassuto's mild objection that Harpham's reading "treats the narrator as a strategy, not as a character" (318), a relatively abstract, strategic reading may well offer us some insight into **"The Masque of the Red Death."** But Harpham leaves an important question unanswered: What is the rhetorical effect of the narrator's projecting himself *beyond* the end of the story—beyond the point at which Harpham says he expires—by means of the reference to *Hernani*?

As I have already noted, the *Hernani* reference gives the narrator a strange then-and-now quality. This temporal duplicity indicates a more general inside-and-outside dual status. On the one hand, the narrator must be inside the story (and the abbey) as a witness to events. On the other hand, the narrator is outside the story as a reporter of events. As a witness the narrator is contained by the story, while as a reporter he contains the story.

The narrator is rather like the braziers of fire set on tripods in the "closed corridor which pursued the windings of the suite" where Prospero holds his masque ball (486). The fires create the illusion of daylight streaming through the windows from outdoors, but are actually enclosed within Prospero's bizarre architectural scheme. Likewise, the narrator illuminates and reveals the story's events, seemingly from without, but actually from within.

The importance of the narrator's ambivalent exterior/ interior status is that it allows him deviously to "over-look" the fact that he should have died at the end of the story. The reporter conveniently forgets that he must also have been a witness. This narrative booby trap is as pointed as it is mischievous because it advances the grave theme of the story.

"The Masque of the Red Death" is a *vanitas* tale, a memento mori. More specifically, it is about the failure of art to stave off death. The fact that the narrator over-looks the necessity of his own death mirrors and mocks the cherished illusions of immortality that art gives to both artist and audience. These illusions are vividly dra-matized within the tale. Prospero and his guests attempt to immure themselves safely within a world of art, but their ball becomes a danse macabre. The guests depend on art so much that it virtually animates them: when the orchestra stops playing, they freeze in terror. For most of the revelers, art is a sort of whistling in the dark, and they avoid Prospero's ominously furnished seventh chamber like the plague, dreading the hourly toll of its giant clock. But there is also the suggestion that the rare, sensitive soul may appreciate Prospero's memento mori: "and to him whose foot falls upon the sable car-pet, there comes from the near clock of ebony a muffled peal more solemnly emphatic than any which reaches *their* ears who indulge in the more remote gaieties of the other apartments" (488). Poe thus invites the reader to join him and Prospero in their aesthetic contempla-tion of mortality.

At first it may strike us as odd that in his attempt to es-cape death Prospero includes the grim seventh room, "shrouded in black velvet tapestries," glazed with win-dows of "scarlet—a deep blood color," and containing the terrifying clock (486). But while on one level the seventh chamber shows that Prospero, like Poe, has his doubts about the success of his escape, on another level the seventh chamber is part of the escape. For while a memento mori confronts us with our mortality, it also sets that mortality at a distance: the aesthetic distance. By representing death, art creates the comforting illu-sion that death is just one of art's illusions.

Doubling Poe, Prospero attempts to control death by fitting it into his own work as a motif rather than as a reality. But a memento mori's controlled and distanced image of death must fail in the end, and to Prospero's dismay the reality of death intrudes upon his masquer-ade.

To underscore the fact that his own art must fail just as Prospero's does, Poe sabotages **"Red Death"** by means of its impossible narrator. We recognize that we cannot successfully imitate the narrator's trick, for unlike him we are flesh and blood: time and death will not pause to see whether we remember their inevitability. The narra-tor is thus a fly in the soothing ointment of aesthetic distance, figuring and ridiculing both the author's and the reader's hope of escape into art.

The irony of all this is that the cynical message of **"Red Death"** is at odds with its own power as a work of art. As J. Gerald Kennedy says, "Poe's engagement with the life of writing marks, in its sardonic way, a resis-tance to the fatality of his own vision" (ix). **"The Mas-que of the Red Death"** lays bare the impotent illusions of art, but does this so artistically that our faith in art is ironically restored in the very same moment that it is lost. Thus the story simultaneously criticizes and con-firms us in our own uneasy duplicity.

Note

1. Similarly, in Poe's "The Facts in the Case of M. Valdemar," the narrator mesmerizes the dying Val-demar, who then claims (and appears) to be dead. Roland Barthes's "Textual Analysis of a Tale by Edgar Poe" explores some implications of the ut-terance "I am dead" in "Valdemar"; but as Barthes notes, the essential facts of the story "can . . . be reduced to two points: the uttering of the 'I am dead' and the abrupt liquefaction of the dead man at the moment of his hypnotic awakening" (11). Characteristically, Poe gives liquefaction the last word, subverting his own subversion of death.

Works Cited

Barthes, Roland. "Textual Analysis of a Tale By Edgar Poe." Trans. Donald G. Marshall. *Poe Studies* 10 (1977): 1-12.

Cassuto, Leonard. "The Coy Reaper: Unmasque-ing the Red Death." *Studies in Short Fiction* 25 (1988): 317-20.

Harpham, Geoffrey Galt. "Permeability and the Gro-tesque: 'The Masque of the Red Death.'" *On the Gro-tesque: Strategies of Contradiction in Art and Litera-ture.* Princeton: Princeton UP, 1982. 106-21.

Kennedy, J. Gerald. *Poe, Death, and the Life of Writ-ing.* New Haven: Yale UP, 1987.

Poe, Edgar Allan. *Edgar Allan Poe: Poetry and Tales.* Ed. Patrick F. Quinn. New York: Literary Classics of the United States, 1984.

Brett Zimmerman (essay date October 2000)

SOURCE: Zimmerman, Brett. "*Allegoria* and Clock Ar-chitecture in Poe's 'The Masque of the Red Death.'" *Essays in Arts and Sciences* 29 (October 2000): 1-16.

[*In the following essay, Zimmerman analyzes the sym-bolic correlation between a clock's face and the ar-rangement of the rooms in "The Masque of the Red Death," and evaluates the allegorical function of the story despite Poe's purported distaste for allegory.*]

Several scholars have drawn attention to the imagery of time, the foregrounded *chronographia,* in Poe's tales—clocks, watches, pendulums, hour and minute hands, ticking sounds, and the frequency of that most gothic of hours, midnight. For instance, in "The Theme of Time in 'The Tell-Tale Heart,'" Gargano, noting the "images and sounds that evoke the rhythm of time" in the story, concludes that the mad narrator has become obsessed with the passing of the hours and that "His quarrel, then, is not with a ravaged individual but with Time, which on one level is symbolized by the omnipresent 'watches' and on another by the 'tell-tale' heart" (379). Edward William Pitcher writes of "Horological and Chronological" time in **"The Masque of the Red Death"**; Dennis W. Eddings has a monograph titled *Poe's Tell-Tale Clocks,* and in "Edgar Poe or The Theme of the Clock" Jean-Paul Weber also demonstrates "the omnipresence of clocks in Poe's writings" (79), including **"The Fall of the House of Usher"** ("the House of Usher clearly represents the clock"), **"The Devil in the Belfry,"** "The Raven," **"The Scythe of Time," "A Descent into the Maelström," "MS Found in a Bottle," "The Tell-Tale Heart," "The Pit and the Pendulum," "The Black Cat," "The Cask of Amontillado," "Silence—A Fable," "Shadow—A Parable," "The Unparalleled Adventures of Hans Pfaall," "Hop-Frog," "The Gold Bug"** and **"The Business Man"** (previously entitled **"Peter Pendulum"**). Weber finishes the essay by referring to Poe as "the maniac of time" (97).

Here I am concerned specifically with Weber's observations about **"The Masque of the Red Death."** I would like to build on and extend some of Weber's insights and thus strengthen his interpretation about the time and clock imagery and the allegorical nature of that tale. It is indeed an extended instance of what rhetoricians call *allegoria,* as other scholars (such as Buranelli, May, Peithman, Watson, Wilbur, Zapf) have argued, against those (such as Ruddick and Symons) who caution against seeing **"The Masque of the Red Death"** this way. The members of the former camp, however, are not sufficiently subtle in their interpretations, insisting on one allegorical meaning (though their interpretations differ) and on one type of allegory. M. H. Abrams reminds us (4-7) that in literature we can find more than one kind of allegory: one of "ideas," literal characters representing abstractions "such as virtues, vices, states of mind, modes of life, and types of character," and one of "things," one literal thing representing itself as well as another literal thing. In **"The Masque of the Red Death"** Poe employs both types—but the work is also a *parable,* yet a third kind of allegory, illustrating a universal moral lesson. The manifold layers of suggestive meaning in this complex work almost make the "fourfold method of exegesis" desirable when interpreting it. Thus, while building on Weber's insights (which have largely been ignored), I suggest a new way of reading **"The Masque of the Red Death"** that clears

up some critical confusion and illuminates Poe's technique as an allegorist.

* * *

The many references to time passing in **"The Masque of the Red Death"**—"after the lapse of sixty minutes, (which embrace three thousand and six hundred seconds of the Time that flies), there came yet another chiming of the clock [. . .]" (253)—tell us that time figures significantly in the tale, and supporting the theme and one of the allegorical readings is the architecture of Prospero's edifice. Richard Wilbur senses that **"The Masque"** contains "an obvious example of architectural allegory" (118), but Weber was the first to argue that the abbey is shaped like "a clock or a dial plate" (85). He refers weakly to external evidence (the clock-shaped borough in **"The Devil in the Belfry"**) rather than to the internal evidence of the tale itself—and so does not go further in his interpretation to explain the significance of the seven rooms of the abbey's suite:

> The apartments were so irregularly disposed that the vision embraced but little more than one at a time. There was a sharp turn at every twenty or thirty yards, and at each turn a novel effect. To the right and left, in the middle of each wall, a tall and narrow Gothic window looked out upon a closed corridor which pursued the windings of the suite.
>
> (251)

Commentators have assumed that the words "irregularly disposed" describe a suite of rooms that twists and turns haphazardly with no real discernible pattern; Jeffrey Meyers, for instance, writes of the "zigzag construction of the rooms" (134). Certainly the suite does not "form a long and straight vista," to use Poe's own words, but the architecture has a clear and recognizable pattern. Eddings guesses that "the progression of the colored rooms is circular rather than in a straight line" (12)—but he is only partly correct. Rather, the seven rooms taken together form a *half circle,* one half of a clock's face, with each room representing one of the seven hours between six o'clock p.m. and twelve inclusive. As for the dimensions, the turn "at every twenty or thirty yards" can be taken to mean that the walls of each room—certainly the middle five—are thirty yards in length while the walls of the two endmost are twenty. Poe's minor disquisitions on mathematical reasoning in the tales of ratiocination; the complex estimates of astronomical distances in *Eureka;* the attention to precise measurement on the part of Legrand in **"The Gold-Bug"**: these show that he was an amateur mathematician, so he likely would have been very precise about the mathematics of the layout in **"The Masque of the Red Death"**—he would not have chosen the figures of thirty and twenty yards randomly. Note, also, that the suite is said to *wind.* In the diagram the rooms have easily been drawn to wind around the center of the clock-abbey while maintaining dimensions of thirty or twenty yards (three units or two). Also, the vision of someone standing well within any given room would indeed embrace "but little more than one at a time," especially if the folding doors do not slide back entirely to the walls on either side.

Some readers, going back to Walter Blair, maintain that these seven rooms stand for the "seven ages of man" (Roppolo, Ketterer, Vanderbilt).[1] Mabbott suggests "the seven days of the week, the seven deadly sins, and even seven parts of a day" (677). Pitcher (73) mentions the "seven decades of life's conventional span," probably alluding to the Bible: "The days of our years are three score and ten [. . .]" (Psalms 90: 10). Ruddick notes (271) Angus Fletcher's observation that seven is also the traditional number of planets or the "windows" (orifices) of the head, but the text has nothing that substantiates these ideas. Patrick Cheney relates seven to its significance in the Bible and to Catholic liturgy (37), and Peithman summarizes the importance of seven in Christian thought and also relates it to Shakespeare's *As You Like It* (116, n12). My interpretation does not necessarily preclude those others, but seven is the inevitable number of rooms we must have if the abbey is shaped like half a clock. I see the explanations relating to *time* as most relevant. The very structure of Prospero's gothic edifice emphasizes the theme of time's passage in terms of minutes and hours, and readers like Mabbott have already seen the seven rooms as symbolizing weekdays and decades.

Poe's concern is with the passing of the final minutes and hours of Prospero and his guests. The clock measures these temporal units, not weekdays or decades. Furthering the allegorical importance of the abbey's shape are Prospero and the phantom of the Red Death, the two central figures that move on the face of the abbey-clock. Weber suggests that they represent two hands of that clock:

> the phantom advances "with a slow and solemn movement," moves with "deliberate and stately step," with "solemn and *measured*" step, makes his way "*uninterruptedly,*" as if impelled by some kind of inner necessity: one must agree that this uninterrupted, measured, solemn, and slow gait accords strikingly with the slow, regular tempo of the hour hand.
>
> In this case Prospero must represent the *minute hand,* and a conjunction must take place between the two. [. . .] That Prospero is something of a blade, like a minute hand, the bare blade which he carries suggests at once. That he acts the part of the minute hand is apparent from the circuit he travels and from his speed: he moves successively through the same chambers which the Masque of the Red Death had traversed, but Prospero moves precipitously, not slowly. At the end of

the tale "the tall figure" stands "erect and motionless, within the shadow of the ebony clock": the hour hand (the phantom) is indeed standing erect [. . .] at about twelve o'clock. As for Prospero, he falls "prostrate in death" a few feet from the specter. [. . .]

(86)[2]

We must distinguish between literal and allegorical time, here, though. When the phantom is first seen, the ebony clock is already striking the midnight hour, literally, but at this point Poe's allegorical time becomes important as Prospero moves quickly from the blue room to the black to catch the slowly moving phantom. Yet, Prospero (the minute hand) does not begin his pursuit until the phantom (the hour hand) is almost at midnight: indeed, the figure makes it all the way "to the violet [room], ere a decided movement had been made to arrest him" (257). He and the phantom begin to "take on" their respective hour- and minute-hand significations just as the prince begins his pursuit from the blue room. On the level of *literal* time, Prospero does not take a full half hour to go from the easternmost to the westernmost room, but he does on the level of *allegorical* time. At the end of this half hour he falls dead. Thirty minutes is exactly how long it takes for someone who has caught the Red Death to die: "And the whole seizure, progress and termination of the disease, were the incidents of half an hour" (250). The Prince and his guests catch the disease at about 11:30 p.m.—literally and figuratively—and die at midnight after he enters the midnight room. The tale's apocalyptic climax comes as the literal and allegorical time spans converge. Thus we solve the confusion that has plagued Roth, Pollin, Wheat, and Zapf, the latter of whom states, "The manner of the prince's death—he dies on the instant [. . .] is significantly not identical with the character and the progress of the disease as it is described at the beginning of the text" (217). On the contrary, the red-browed Prince has been dying for half an hour; the disease finally kills him at the climactic moment when he catches up to the allegorical representative of the plague.[3]

On another stratum of meaning and action, however, Prospero can be seen to stand for humanity in general: as the head and representative of the "thousand hale and light-hearted friends from among the knights and dames of his court" (250), he is an "Everyman" figure; and the phantom represents exactly what its name implies—the Red Death—which disease contaminates all seven rooms, from blue to black. On this level, the figure functions as part of the allegory of ideas, abstractions, representing as it does the abstraction (or personification) of the plague. One cannot see a disease, only its physical manifestations. That the figure of the Red Death *is* a mere abstraction is suggested by the emptiness, the lack of a "tangible form," that the revelers find in ripping off its corpse-like mask. As Wheat points out, "It is obviously fruitless to try to seize, unmask, and hang a personification of death" (55).

The revelers do not realize that the plague has entered, but one or two lines in the tale suggest that they, and Prospero, have caught the disease: "these other apartments were densely crowded, and in them beat feverishly the heart of life" (255). We can seize upon the word *feverishly* to suggest one manifestation of disease. And when he becomes infuriated by the figure of the Red Death, Prospero's "brow reddened with rage" (256). Never mind about his "rage"—a blood-red face is one of the symptoms of the plague: earlier we are told about the "scarlet stains upon the body and especially upon the face of the victim [. . .]" (250). The Red Death has this appearance: "His vesture was dabbled in blood—and his broad brow, with all the features of the face, was besprinkled with the scarlet horror" (256).

So, the masquerade, Prospero's dance of life, has become a *danse macabre,* a medieval dance of death, and the parable ends in biblical tones accentuated by what William Mentzel Forrest (*Biblical Allusions in Poe* 86) calls the "genitive of possession" (the frequently appearing preposition *of*) and the repetition of the conjunction *And* (the rhetorical scheme *polysyndeton*):

> And now was acknowledged the presence of the Red Death. He had come like a thief in the night. And one by one dropped the revellers in the blood-bedewed halls of their revel, and died each in the despairing posture of his fall. And the life of the ebony clock went out with that of the last of the gay. And the flames of the tripods expired. And Darkness and Decay and the Red Death held illimitable dominion over all.
>
> (258)

Cheney also notes the *polysyndeton* without using the label (34); also, following in the wake of Forrest, he does a revealing exploration of how Poe employs biblical phrases, images and allusions. We might note in this context that the image of the "thief in the night" can be found several times in the Bible: "the day of the Lord so cometh as a thief in the night" (1 Thess. 5: 2; see also 2 Peter 3: 10, Job 24: 14 and Matthew 24: 43). We might guess that some weighty meaning is suggested by the biblical diction, imagery and tone: although, as Ruddick points out, the end of the tale suggests no orthodox Christian lesson or eschatology—Darkness, Decay and the Red Death constitute "a highly unorthodox trinity of deities presiding over an equally unorthodox apocalypse" (273)—nevertheless the rhythms and images do suggest a parable (about the tragic human condition) that has the weight of biblical pronouncement.

That pronouncement, the "moral" of the story, is indeed what most scholars have said it is. Prince Prospero and a thousand guests lock themselves into one of his castellated abbeys to keep safe from the contagion outside the walls. Irresponsible, they are isolated in a kind of stationary ark trying to enjoy a hedonistic forgetfulness

of death—a *carpe diem* philosophy. The variety of their masks and professions—"There were buffoons, there were improvisatori, there were ballet-dancers, there were musicians" (251)—is so great that all manner of humans is suggested, from the beautiful to the grotesque; the revelers thus represent a microcosm of the human race (what Melville liked to call an "Anacharsis Clootz deputation"). But the black clock within the black room serves the symbolic purpose of reminding ephemeral humanity that *tempus fugit*—"time flies"; the ebony clock keeps chiming the passing hours as the revelers move closer and closer to the moment of their own deaths. Frail humanity can never escape the inevitable ravages of time—*here* is the "moral," the truth of universal applicability. Supporting this theme is the allegorical architecture of the abbey itself, the gigantic type of the smaller ebony clock. Contrary to Ketterer's insistence that the "reality of time is hidden by the arrangement of the rooms" (201), the arrangement of the chambers *reinforces* the awful reality of time as it leads inexorably to disease, death, darkness and dissolution.

* * *

Poe claimed to disapprove of *allegoria.* In an often-quoted review of Hawthorne's *Twice-Told Tales,* he states, "In defence of allegory, (however, or for whatever object, employed), there is scarcely one respectable word to be said" (148). The review in which this statement appears was first published in *Graham's Magazine* in May 1842—the same edition in which **"The Masque of the Red Death"** was first published. It is almost as if, while preparing the review for publication, Poe, thinking of Hawthorne's allegories, decided to submit one for publication himself—perhaps to show the world how allegory can be done well.[4] That Poe did not disdain to write this kind of literature is shown in the subtitle for another tale, **"King Pest: A Tale Containing An Allegory."** Other scholars insist that several other tales can be read this way. Darrel Abel suggests that **"The Fall of the House of Usher"** "is a consummate psychological allegory" (185). Edward H. Davidson holds that **"The Imp of the Perverse"** is "more an allegory than a tale" (xvi) and that "'**Hop-Frog**' is almost straight allegory" (xx); he also refers to *Pym* [*The Narrative of Arthur Gordon Pym*] as a "symbolic allegory" (xxiii) and, as the interpretations of several other prominent Poe scholars (Fiedler, Levin, Kaplan, Ketterer, Beaver) demonstrate, the second half of the novel is a kind of geographical allegory. Clark Griffith maintains that **"Ligeia"** is "an allegory of terror almost perfectly co-ordinated with the subtlest of allegorized jests" (qtd. by Robert Regan, who agrees with this reading ["Hawthorne's 'Plagiary'"] 293). David Galloway reminds us of the "allegorical mannerisms" of **"The Devil in the Belfry"** (18). Walter Stepp sees the emblem in **"The Cask of Amontillado"** as having an allegorical significance (56) and is inclined to see Fortunato as representing "guileless, trusting innocence" (60). Victor Vitanza calls the heroes of several Poe tales "allegorical figures of impulse and reason: they act out a dramatic dialogue of 'body' and 'soul'" (147). **"William Wilson"** is universally recognized as *allegoria*: let us remember, for instance, the case made in Ottavio Cassale's essay "The Dematerialization of William Wilson: Poe's Use of Cumulative Allegory." Consider Liliane Weissberg's "In Search of Truth and Beauty: Allegory in 'Berenice' and 'The Domain of Arnheim.'" A most recent book-length study is Jeffrey DeShell's *The Peculiarity of Literature: An Allegorical Approach to Poe's Fiction.* Richard Wilbur summarizes more generally: "as for Edgar Allan Poe [. . .] we can make no sense about him until we consider his work—and in particular his prose fiction—as deliberate and often brilliant allegory" (98-99); "All of Poe's major stories are allegorical presentations" of his characteristic themes (102). Lastly, Regan cites as an example of Poe's duplicity his "repeated denunciations of allegory when he was a confirmed and confessed allegorist" ("Hawthorne's 'Plagiary'" 292).[5]

If we do not want to entertain the notion that Poe was deceitful, though, we still must somehow reconcile the scoffer at allegories and the author of them. Perhaps Poe was aware that in writing works such as **"The Masque of the Red Death"** he was apparently contradicting one aspect of his own theory of composition, but this may have been less of a problem for him than for us. He might have said with the Walt Whitman of "Song of Myself," "Do I contradict myself? / Very well then I contradict myself, / (I am large, I contain multitudes)"; or agreed for once with that other Romanticist, Ralph Waldo Emerson: "A foolish consistency is the hobgoblin of little minds" ("Self-Reliance"). I propose that the contradiction is not as real as it seems; and indeed, other scholars have remembered that in his review of *Twice-Told Tales* Poe says that allegory is acceptable if the literal and the suggested meanings are not connected too clearly: "Where the suggested meaning runs through the obvious one in a very profound undercurrent so as never to interfere with the upper one without our own volition, so as never to show itself unless called to the surface, there only, for the proper uses of fictitious narrative, is it [allegory] available at all" (148). Then, after making some disparaging comments about the type of shallow (and didactic) allegory he despises—*Pilgrim's Progress*—Poe offers Baron de la Motte Fouqué's *Undine: A Miniature Romance* as a work in which the allegory is subdued because the hidden meanings are seen only "by suggestive glimpses." In other words, Poe the symbolist approves of allegory only when it approaches symbolism in offering suggested meanings rather than explicit equations.

As for **"The Masque of the Red Death,"** then, the tale on the layer of the allegory of abstractions (the phan-

tom = plague; Prospero = Everyman) functions less successfully according to Poe's definition of allegory "properly handled" because these meanings are relatively accessible to the reader. On this level **"The Masque"** is more like *Pilgrim's Progress* than Poe might want to admit. On the other hand, the work on the level of the allegory of things (the phantom suggests an hour hand, Prospero a minute hand, the abbey half a clock face) functions more successfully because these meanings are less accessible. The meaning of Poe's hinted "time motif" runs "through the obvious one in a very profound under-current" indeed.

When we add the tale's parable to the mix, we see that **"The Masque"** is complex enough to warrant a "fourfold method of exegesis." Regan, in his discussion of *allegoria,* recognizes the possibility of many layers of meaning in a typical Poe tale: "approaching the tales in the spirit of the 'fourfold method' will alert us to the special way in which they operate. We shall not grasp Poe's full accomplishment in fiction until we hear each of the several voices of a tale as at once discrete and part of a harmonious totality" (Introduction 11-12). St. Thomas Aquinas and others proposed that in interpreting the Bible we distinguish between (1) the literal meaning (what happened), (2) the allegorical meaning (New Testament truth), (3) the tropological meaning (the moral truth), and (4) the anagogic meaning (spiritual/eschatological truth). In **"The Masque of the Red Death"** Poe does give us a literal series of events (Aquinas' first meaning) and something like a tropological meaning—the parable, the "moral" of the story (the third). The tale on the level of the allegory of ideas comes closest to representing Aquinas' second meaning. As for an anagogic significance, it appears either to be missing altogether or profoundly subversive: the closing words offer no hopeful Christian eschatology.

Cheney is very good on this point and elaborates considerably: "Where the mythic pattern" of the Bible "depicts man's victory over sin, death, and time, Poe's mythic pattern depicts the triumph of these agents of destruction over man" (32); "In Poe's mythology, the Red Death replaces Christ as the reigning force in the universe. Hence, the Red Death is said to have 'dominion over all'—a reversal of Paul's statement in Romans 6: 9, in which 'death hath no more dominion' because of Christ's resurrection. [. . .] In Poe, the blood and dew of the Red Death replace the blood of Christ and the dew of heaven" (34); "In presenting an image of man helpless against the apparition of death, Poe suggests the inefficacy of Christ's triumph over death [. . .]" (36). All in all, this subversive tale constitutes Poe's "grim reversal of the Christian drama"—a production perhaps more characteristic of the skeptical Melville.

It also anticipates twentieth-century atheistic existentialism as well as the existential poetry of someone closer to Poe's own day and who enjoyed reading him: Emily Dickinson. Both Poe and Dickinson present grim visions of the human condition while otherwise surrounded by the optimism of their Transcendental contemporaries and the sentimental Christianity of everyone else (but Melville). Neither Christians nor Transcendentalists would be receptive to the perverse eschatology of **"The Masque of the Red Death,"** however, so Poe camouflages his meaning in layers of allegory: like Dickinson, he would "Tell all the Truth but tell it slant—/ Success in Circuit lies" (#427). Poe was deeply familiar with the Bible, as were Dickinson and Melville (who "quarreled with God"), but at some profound level Poe, like them, seems to have intuited the possibility of a godless universe where the eschatological promises of the Christian Bible are empty, meaningless. Like the prisoner in **"The Pit and the Pendulum"** (another allegory), we grope blindly in the dark, attempting in vain to use our reason and senses to determine the nature of our environment. But, like his, our epistemology is flawed and, like him, we are tormented physically, emotionally, and psychologically, waiting for the inevitable descent of the destroying pendulum. Indeed (and this is also the perception of literary naturalism), we are left with nothing but our biological and mental selves at the mercy of indifferent and overwhelming forces over which we have no control—eternally victims of Time. *This* existential depiction of humanity's condition in **"The Masque of the Red Death"** is the most terrifying thing in all of Poe's fiction, beside which his gothic accounts of vampires, black cats, witches, metempsychosis, and reanimated mummies are mere "bugaboo tales."

Notes

1. The great clock in "The Devil in the Belfry" also has seven built into it: seven faces, one for each side of the steeple.

2. A similar thing happens in "The Devil in the Belfry": Weber suggests that the impish figure who causes temporal chaos in the Dutch borough of Vondervotteimittiss symbolizes the minute hand and that the belfry symbolizes the hour hand. I disagree with the latter assertion: rather, the belfry and its steeple simply constitute a clock within a clock (the larger clock of the borough itself—just as the large ebony clock in "Masque" is a clock within the larger clock of the abbey); it is the belfry-man, the bell-ringer, who represents the hour hand. After all, he is described as being fat (253), as the hour hand is the fatter of the two hands on a clock's face, and, when the devil figure overcomes him, he sits "upon the belfry-man, who was lying flat upon his back" (257)—just as a minute hand lies upon the hour hand when they come together to strike twelve o'clock, which is exactly what is happening (even though a thirteenth hour is about to strike, as well). Thus, the

devil figure and the belfry-man parallel Prince Prospero and the Phantom, minute and hour hands respectively.

3. Here is another interesting point: in "Hawthorne's 'Plagiary': Poe's Duplicity" Regan, looking for possible sources in Hawthorne for "The Masque of the Red Death," cites one of his *Twice-Told Tales*: "The action of 'Howe's Masquerade' opens with a reminder that 'eleven strokes, full half an hour ago, had pealed from the clock of the Old South' and it ends with the music of a dead march" at midnight (290). Regan does not make the connection, but the events of "Howe's Masquerade" begin at 11:30 p.m. and end at 12:00—the same allegorical time span that covers the climactic finale of "Red Death." If Poe was indeed inspired by Hawthorne, then, he may have taken the idea of the fatal thirty-minute time span from "Howe's Masquerade" (but see below, n4).

4. Charles N. Watson, Jr., suggests even more—that Poe in fact got some of his ideas for "The Masque of the Red Death" from reading two specific *Twice-Told Tales*: "The May-Pole of Merry Mount" and "The Haunted Mind." As well as "Howe's Masquerade," Regan considers "Lady Eleanore's Mantle" and other "legends of the Province House" additional Hawthorne tales that inspired Poe ("Hawthorne's 'Plagiary'"). The danger with all Influence Criticism, of course, is that critics risk committing the logical fallacy known as *post hoc, ergo propter hoc*—"after this, therefore because of this" (also called the fallacy of "False Cause" or "Questionable Cause"). While Poe may have borrowed from Hawthorne, scholars should not forget the possibility that both authors borrowed from a common source, if they borrowed at all.

5. In "The Hoax of the Red Death: Poe as Allegorist," Nicholas Ruddick gives us an extended and thoughtful consideration of whether the tale falls into the category of allegory or not. He concludes that we *cannot* read the tale as such; however, in trying to demonstrate this thesis, he does a better job of persuading me that the tale *is* allegorical. He quotes from Angus Fletcher's book *Allegory: The Theory of a Symbolic Mode* in noting that an allegory must have "periodic repetitions" (then shows us several in the tale) and a "kakodaemon" (then shows that Prospero "seems perfectly to fit Fletcher's description of the typical kakodaemon" [270]). Next, Ruddick notes that "The 'Masque' of the tale's title further suggests an allegorical dimension," that the "text [. . .] seems to indicate that the tale is an allegory" too (271), and finally that it "borrows the major encoding device of contagion from Christian allegory" (273). So far so

good, but then he brings us back to the essay's central premise: "should we discern even one major allegorical equation [. . .] then we must surely account in a similar manner for all the other main elements in the tale: the Prince, the courtiers, the abbey, the suite of rooms, the ebony clock, and the Red Death itself" (268). He seems to imply that if even one element does not work allegorically then the tale as a whole cannot be so read, and the one element that cannot be seen to function this way is the color imagery, Ruddick believes (while black and red have fairly clear meanings, the other colors do not). To his argument I would make two objections: first, some scholars *do* believe they have solved the riddle of the color imagery—see, for example, Pitcher (73), Vanderbilt (142 and 149n), Pope-Hennessy (141), Peithman (116-17) and Cheney (37); second, I believe Ruddick's central premise is faulty: even if we cannot come up with an explanation of the allegorical significance of the colors, that does not mean we should throw out any and all allegorical interpretations of the other elements in the tale.

Works Cited

Abel, Darrel. "A Key to the House of Usher." *University of Toronto Quarterly* 18 (January 1949): 176-85.

Abrams, M. H. *A Glossary of Literary Terms.* 5th ed. Toronto: Holt, 1988.

Blair, Walter. "Poe's Conception of Incident and Tone in the Tale." *Modern Philology* 41 (May 1944): 228-40.

Buranelli, Vincent. *Edgar Allan Poe.* New York: Twayne, 1961.

Cassale, Ottavio. "The Dematerialization of William Wilson: Poe's Use of Cumulative Allegory." *South Carolina Review* 11 (1978): 70-79.

Cheney, Patrick. "Poe's Use of *The Tempest* and the *Bible* in 'The Masque of the Red Death.'" *English Language Notes* 20.3-4 (March-June 1983): 31-39.

Davidson, Edward H. Introduction. *Selected Writings of Edgar Allan Poe.* Boston: Houghton, 1956. vii-xxviii.

DeShell, Jeffrey. *The Peculiarity of Literature: An Allegorical Approach to Poe's Fiction.* Madison: Fairleigh Dickinson UP, 1997.

Dickinson, Emily. *Final Harvest: Emily Dickinson's Poems.* Ed. Thomas H. Johnson. Toronto: Little, 1961.

Eddings, Dennis W. *Poe's Tell-Tale Clocks.* Baltimore: Enoch Pratt Free Library and the Edgar Allan Poe Society of Baltimore, 1994.

Forrest, William Mentzel. *Biblical Allusions in Poe.* New York, 1928.

Galloway, David. Introduction. *The Other Poe: Comedies and Satires.* Ed. David Galloway. New York: Penguin, 1983. 7-22.

Gargano, James W. "The Theme of Time in 'The Tell-Tale Heart.'" *Studies in Short Fiction* 5.4 (Summer 1968): 378-82.

Ketterer, David. *The Rationale of Deception in Poe.* Baton Rouge: Louisiana State UP, 1979.

Mabbott, Thomas Ollive, ed. *The Collected Works of Edgar Allan Poe.* Vol. 2. Cambridge, MA: Harvard UP, 1978.

May, Charles E. *Edgar Allan Poe: A Study of the Short Fiction.* Boston: Twayne, 1991.

Meyers, Jeffrey. *Edgar Allan Poe: His Life and Legacy.* New York: Scribner's, 1992.

Peithman, Stephen, ed. *The Annotated Tales of Edgar Allan Poe.* New York: Doubleday, 1981.

Pitcher, Edward William. "Horological and Chronological Time in 'Masque of the Red Death.'" *American Transcendental Quarterly* 29.1 (Winter 1976): 71-75.

Poe, Edgar Allan. "The Devil in the Belfry." In Vol. 3 of *The Complete Works.* Ed. James A. Harrison. 1902. New York: AMS, 1965. 247-57.

———. "The Masque of the Red Death." In Vol. 4 of *The Complete Works.* Ed. James A. Harrison. 1902. New York: AMS, 1965. 250-58.

———. Review of *Twice-Told Tales.* In Vol. 13 of *The Complete Works.* Ed. James A. Harrison. 1902. New York: AMS, 1965. 141-55.

Pollin, Burton R. "The Role of Byron and Mary Shelley in 'The Masque.'" *Discoveries in Poe.* Notre Dame, IN: U of Notre Dame P, 1970. 75-90.

Pope-Hennessy, Una. *Edgar Allan Poe: A Critical Biography.* 1934. New York: Haskell, 1971.

Regan, Robert. Introduction. *Poe: A Collection of Critical Essays.* Ed. Robert Regan. Englewood Cliffs, NJ: Prentice, 1967. 1-13.

———. "Hawthorne's 'Plagiary': Poe's Duplicity." *Nineteenth-Century Fiction* 25 (1970-71): 281-98.

Roppolo, Joseph Patrick. "Meaning and 'The Masque of the Red Death.'" *Poe: A Collection of Critical Essays.* Ed. Robert Regan. Englewood Cliffs, NJ: Prentice, 1967. 134-44.

Roth, Martin. "Inside 'The Masque of the Red Death.'" *SubStance* 13 (1984): 50-53.

Ruddick, Nicholas. "The Hoax of the Red Death: Poe as Allegorist." *Sphyinx* 4.4 (1985): 268-76.

Stepp, Walter. "The Ironic Double in Poe's 'The Cask of Amontillado.'" In *Modern Critical Interpretations: The Tales of Poe.* Ed. Harold Bloom. New York: Chelsea, 1987. 55-61.

Symons, Julian. *The Tell-Tale Heart: The Life and Works of Edgar Allan Poe.* 1978. New York: Penguin, 1981.

Vanderbilt, Kermit. "Art and Nature in 'The Masque of the Red Death.'" *Nineteenth-Century Fiction* 22 (March 1968): 379-89. Rpt. in *Edgar Allan Poe: A Study of the Short Fiction.* Charles E. May. Boston: Twayne, 1991. 140-50.

Vitanza, Victor. "'The Question of Poe's Narrators': Perverseness Considered Once Again." *American Transcendental Quarterly* 38 (Spring 1978): 137-49.

Watson, Charles N., Jr. "'The Masque of the Red Death' and Poe's Reading of Hawthorne." *Library Chronicle* 45.1-2 (1981): 143-49.

Weber, Jean-Paul. "Edgar Poe or the Theme of the Clock." *Poe: A Collection of Critical Essays.* Ed. Robert Regan. Englewood Cliffs, NJ: Prentice, 1967. 79-97.

Weissberg, Liliane. "In Search of Truth and Beauty: Allegory in 'Berenice' and 'The Domain of Arnheim.'" In *Poe and His Times: The Artist and His Milieu.* Ed. Benjamin Franklin Fisher IV. Baltimore: The Edgar Allan Poe Society, 1990. 66-75.

Wheat, Patricia H. "The Mask of Indifference in 'The Masque of the Red Death.'" *Studies in Short Fiction* 19 (1982): 51-56.

Wilbur, Richard. "The House of Poe." *Poe: A Collection of Critical Essays.* Ed. Robert Regan. Englewood Cliffs, NJ: Prentice, 1967. 98-120.

Zapf, Hubert. "Entropic Imagination in Poe's 'The Masque of the Red Death.'" *College Literature* 16.3 (Fall 1989): 211-18.

Eric H. du Plessis (essay date June-December 2001)

SOURCE: du Plessis, Eric H. "Deliberate Chaos: Poe's Use of Colors in 'The Masque of the Red Death.'" *Poe Studies/Dark Romanticism* 34, nos. 1-2 (June-December 2001): 40-2.

[*In the following essay, du Plessis claims that Poe chose clashing colors for the seven chambers in "The Masque of the Red Death" to produce a disquieting effect on the reader.*]

Blue, purple, green, orange, white, violet, black with scarlet. The specific color arrangement of the seven chambers in Prince Prospero's imperial suite has mystified Poe's readers ever since **"The Masque of the Red Death"** appeared in *Graham's Magazine* in May of 1842. Indeed, this color sequence is puzzling, for it does not follow an immediately recognizable pattern or even conform to the standard spectrum; and yet Poe

deems it important enough to devote a comparatively long segment of his introduction to its description. His narrator lays out the color pattern in intricate detail, describing the optical effects created by the interaction of additional light and the resulting variations in tones and hues: "There was no light of any kind emanating from lamp or candle within the suite of chambers. But in the corridors that followed the suite, there stood, opposite to each window, a heavy tripod, bearing a brazier of fire that projected its rays through the tinted glass and so glaringly illuminated the room. And thus were produced a multitude of gaudy and fantastic appearances" [**Works** (**The Collected Works of Edgar Allan Poe**), 2:672].

So insistent is Poe on the importance of this color distribution that he describes it twice, once at the outset of the tale and again just before Prince Prospero's fatal encounter with the masked mummer. Yet **"The Masque of the Red Death"** offers no conspicuous clue as to its possible meaning. Such a disproportion between the amount of information contained in the text and the absence of obvious interpretation has generated a number of attempts to uncover Poe's intentions. Walter Blair and H. H. Bell Jr., for example, explain the color scheme of the seven rooms as the seven ages of man, or the seven parts of Prince Prospero's life. [See Walter Blair, "Poe's Conception of Incident and Tone in the Tale," *Modern Philology* 41 (1944): 238; and H. H. Bell Jr., "'The Masque of the Red Death': An Interpretation," *South Atlantic Bulletin* 38 (November 1973): 103-4. Bell's article includes a useful architectural drawing depicting the physical layout of the seven rooms according to the text's specifications (105).] Joseph Roppolo finds the colors to be reminiscent of a life cycle: blue in the first chamber indicating birth and life, and black and red in the last apartment signifying death ["Meaning and 'The Masque of the Red Death,'" *Tulane Studies in English* 13 (1963): 66; see sec. 1 of the essay for an overview of previous scholarship on the tale.] T. O. Mabbott suggests several possibilities: from the seven parts of the day to the seven days of the week, with a possible depiction of the seven deadly sins or the opposite poles of a compass (blue and red) [**Works,** 2:677.] Hubert Zapf likens the color coding to a parodic reversal of the biblical act of creation, a symbolic teleology of human life ["Entropic Imagination in Poe's 'The Masque of the Red Death,'" *College Literature* 16 (fall 1989): 214-15]. Finally, Kermit Vanderbilt compares Poe's polychromatic sequence to a "meaningful symmetry" in the cycle of natural life, which Prospero, the artist-hero, has submitted to an "imaginative re-ordering" in his bid to prevail over earthly corruptibility ["Art and Nature in 'The Masque of the Red Death,'" *Nineteenth-Century Fiction* 22 (1968): 381, 382]. In a note to his original and incisive analysis, Vanderbilt briefly pursues the interesting possibility that Poe consciously patterns the color distribution of Prospero's rooms after Shakespeare's own sequencing of the seven ages of man in *As You Like It,* an analogy that Vanderbilt describes as "astonishingly close" [382 n. 4]. Launching his own interpretation of the color sequence, Vanderbilt asserts that no prior scholarship "has taken Poe's art seriously enough here to confirm that the pattern is deliberate and precise" [381]—an assertion that will serve as a departure point for the present analysis.

Previous interpretations, while often stimulating, are ultimately unsatisfying. They either rely on intangible elements, inferences and extrapolations not to be found in the text, or they build their argumentation on the psychological analysis of color—subjective approaches at best. Indeed, from Goethe's controversial critique of Newton's theory of color to the claims of numerous artistic movements that have come and gone during the last two centuries, color interpretation seems to have had more to do with a personal sense of aesthetics than with objective analysis. [See Johann Wolfgang von Goethe, *Theory of Colours,* translated from the 1810 *Zur Farbenlehre* by Charles Lock Eastlake (London: J. Murray, 1840); and Sir Isaac Newton, *Opticks; or, A Treatise of the Reflexions, Refractions, and Colours of Light* (London: Printed for Sam. Smith and Benj. Walford, 1704).]

When reading **"The Masque of the Red Death,"** we can readily make a few obvious observations—red, for example, is reminiscent of blood and black is traditionally associated with the funereal—but such generalizations do not adequately explain the unique color scheme so meticulously ordained by the author. Previous attempts at explanation invariably proceed from the assumption that within the complex color arrangement of the tale lies a rational and hidden coherence which can explain Poe's choices; but, I would argue, such attempts to bring order and sense to apparent anarchy have forced upon the text intentions alien to Poe's primary purpose. What emerges from an attentive reading is that the author's desire to represent aesthetic chaos and disorder leads him to choose a fittingly aberrant color distribution. Poe does retain all the colors from the Newtonian prism, but he rearranges them out of sequence, as if to make sure none of them can blend harmoniously with those adjacent. A garish succession of tones and hues is thus created. The resulting optical shock is all the more effective because the reader sees these colors in constant reflecting motion, due to the flames that throw flickering light from the corridor through the tinted window in each room.

Since the early eighteenth century, painters have customarily grouped colors into three classifications: primary (red, yellow, and blue), secondary (orange, violet, and green), and tertiary (yellow-orange, orange-red, red-violet, violet-blue, blue-green, and green-yellow),

with the addition of the two achromatic tones of black, the complete absence of color, and white, the mixture of all colors. (The invention of color photography and subsequent advances in optics would eventually identify the primary colors as red, green, and blue.) In **"The Masque of the Red Death,"** the first room is decorated in blue, a primary color, and the second in purple, a tertiary color (violet-blue) derived from blue. The next is green, a complementary or opposite color to red (a component of the preceding color since purple is obtained by blending blue with deep red) that cannot harmonize with purple. In painting, a color will appear more intense if it is directly followed by its opposite (the opposite of a primary hue is a mixture of the other two; thus the opposite to red is green, a blend of blue and yellow). Consequently the juxtaposition of green and purple creates an immediate optical shock. Painters refer to this mutual exaltation of opposites as the "law of simultaneous contrast," first formulated by the French physicist M. E. Chevreul in 1839. Chevreul's study, though primarily written as a reference book for the printing industry, had a considerable impact in the field of aesthetics; it became a frame of reference that ended a great deal of polemics among nineteenth-century European artists. [See M. E. Chevreul, *De la loi du contraste simultané des couleurs* (Paris: Pitois-Levrault, 1839), specifically pt. 1, sec. 1, chaps. 1-3, and pt. 2, sec. 1, plate 5 (showing his chromatic scales).] This study was first translated into English in 1854; it is difficult to ascertain whether Poe had seen the original French edition, which appeared three years before the publication of his tale, or whether his reading knowledge of French would have allowed him to understand this highly technical reference.

The fourth room is hung in orange, a color almost diametrically opposed to the preceding green (since yellow, one of its two components, is itself an opposite color to green). The fifth chamber is highlighted in white, an achromatic anomaly in this sequence, creating yet another optical aberration. Violet, the next color, is a secondary shade also opposed to orange. Finally black, the color of the last apartment, represents another achromatic hue that cannot blend with the preceding shade. For the last chamber Poe bows to a pragmatic necessity that lends itself to a powerful symbolic effect. In each preceding apartment the panes of the gothic window match the prevailing color of the room, but in the last the color is altered to a deep red, since black windowpanes would not allow the light from the tripods to shine through the glass and illuminate the room.

The particular color distribution chosen by Poe forces together unrelated or opposed primary, secondary, and tertiary colors, along with achromatic tones. It is as if he painstakingly arranges his palette to prevent any chromatic progression or even more remote harmonies between secondary and tertiary colors. The chaos thus created is further enhanced by a complete disregard for tonal values and their traditional use in sequencing shades of varying intensities. Poe's use of jarringly disparate nuances in **"The Masque of the Red Death"** suggests a concerted effort to breach the standards of aesthetics prevalent among the painters of his day. [When he needed documentation on scientific topics, Poe made liberal use of the sixth edition of the *Encyclopaedia Britannica* and of Abraham Rees's *Cyclopaedia* (see **Works,** 2:575, 3:847). Homogeneity between primary and secondary colors and gradation of tonal values across the spectrum were covered at length in the reference material available to Poe in 1842. See "Chromatics," in *Encyclopaedia Britannica; or, A Dictionary of Arts, Sciences, and Miscellaneous Literature,* 6th ed. (Edinburgh: Archibald Constable, 1823), 6:91-94; and "Colour," in vol. 9 of *The Cyclopaedia; or, Universal Dictionary of Arts, Sciences, and Literature,* 1st American ed. (Philadelphia: Samuel F. Bradford, 1810).]

Even the smallest detail supports an interpretation of Poe's color sequence as a carefully orchestrated masterpiece of discord: yellow, one of the three primary colors, is remarkably absent from the color scheme chosen for Prince Prospero's suite. But in fact, its absence is only apparent. Poe removes yellow from the immediate color pattern of the rooms only to restore it indirectly, but more effectively, as his one overriding primary hue. It is pervasively present in the yellow flames of the tripods that so strangely illuminate each apartment, blending with every other color in the meandering suite. The result is a stunning kaleidoscopic effect, a sort of visual nightmare that leaves an immediate and disturbing impression upon characters and readers alike: "[T]he effect of the fire-light that streamed upon the dark hangings through the blood-tinted panes, was ghastly in the extreme, and produced so wild a look upon the countenances of those who entered, that there were few of the company bold enough to set foot within its precincts at all" [**Works,** 2:672].

The tonal anomalies and resulting visual shock orchestrated by Poe make a fitting counterpoint to the other discordant elements introduced in the text: they complement Prince Prospero's unusual demeanor and his aberrant taste in clothing, entertainment, and decor; they also reinforce the decidedly odd layout of the seven rooms, which does not conform to the traditional precepts of architectural design. Thus, on an aesthetic level, the color scheme serves to reinforce the overall dissonance that permeates the tale. Poe's reference to *Hernani* (1830) further attests to his intended effect. Victor Hugo's scandalous play illustrates artistic principles formulated three years earlier in his preface to *Cromwell,* the most important manifesto of French romanticism—which had argued that, since life is a mixture of tragedy and comedy, art should in like manner combine

the grotesque and the sublime. [See Burton Pollin, *Discoveries in Poe* (Notre Dame: Univ. of Notre Dame Press, 1970), 1-5.] In **"The Masque of the Red Death,"** the disharmonious color scheme participates effectively with other jarring elements in challenging the reader's artistic assumptions. From apparent chaos, this bold juxtaposition of opposites paradoxically brings about aesthetic unity.

William Freedman (essay date 2002)

SOURCE: Freedman, William. "The Art of Incorporative Exclusion: 'The Masque of the Red Death.'" In *The Porous Sanctuary: Art and Anxiety in Poe's Short Fiction,* pp. 135-49. New York: Peter Lang, 2002.

[*In the following essay, Freedman surveys such themes as narrative self-reflexivity, the primal fear of blood, and the conflict between art and reality in "The Masque of the Red Death."*]

"The Masque of the Red Death" is Poe's paradigmatic tale of reality's threatening incursion into the uninsulable catacombs of art.[1] Almost laboriously allegorical, it weaves a network of analogues identifying Prince Prospero as an artist who, like Frost, plays at creativity for mortal stakes, his labyrinthine catacombs as a work of art in Poe's own ornately arabesque style.[2] The castellated abbey to which the prince and his thousand revelers retreat from the Red Death is "an extensive and magnificent structure" (IV, 250); as in a narrative constructed to dazzle and repeatedly surprise, "The apartments were so irregularly disposed that the vision embraced but little more than one at a time." And again, as in Poe's own diversionary, effect-oriented fictions, "There was a sharp turn at every twenty or thirty yards, and at each turn a novel effect" (IV, 251). The internal workings of this labyrinthine structure suggest the insularity and self-reflexivity of art. In the middle of one wall of each of the seven chambers a tall and narrow Gothic window looks out upon "a closed corridor which pursued the windings of the suite" (IV, 251). No light emanates from within the chambers. The only light source is the brazier of fire that glows through the stained glass windows and illuminates the room. Since in all but the seventh room the glass is already stained in the color of its room's interior decorations, each glass transmits into its own chamber the color it already contains. As in the eye or imagination, the color of transmitted light is a function of the window's tint and composition. Like Emerson's Nature, the room wears the colors of the spirit, but there is no nature here: only the hermetic catacomb, the light of whose chambers comes not from the external world but from the closed corridors that embrace them. One part of the aesthetic construct receives illumination only from another whose rays it reconstitutes according to its own interior-reflecting hue.

Within these painterly rooms there is drama, dance, and music. "It was a voluptuous scene, that masquerade" (IV, 251), and like art as Poe defined and often fabricated it, it is "an assembly of phantasms" (IV, 255) peopled by "a multitude of gaudy and fantastic appearances" (IV, 252). There are "glare and glitter and piquancy and phantasm. . . . There were arabesque figures . . . [and] delirious fancies such as the madman fashions. There was much of the beautiful ['Beauty' itself, in fact], much of the wanton, much of the *bizarre,* something of the terrible, and not a little of that which might have excited disgust" (IV, 254). Winding catacombs of art self-advertisingly reminiscent of Poe's own constructions, they are a whirling blend of all the arts. In the "scene" the narrator has "painted," there are ballet dancers, improvisatori, and musicians (IV, 251), and all these "appliances of pleasure" are directed to the production of a series of novel effects culminating in the grand effect of terror within a still wider frame of Beauty.

In this subsuming of the terrible within the beautiful and pleasing, there is an anticipation of the transforming incorporation of reality by the aesthetic construct whose escape from that reality is only a seeming failure. But we may note, before we elaborate that dynamic, the role of Prince Prospero as the conjuring artist of his aesthetic universe. As in the equation of the chambers with the narrative that describes them, there is nothing subtle or evasive here. Poe's language, like the Gothic windows, is colorfully translucent. The name Prospero of course associates him with the island conjurer of *The Tempest,* an earlier isolate who controls a world of phantasms far removed by geography and spirit from a corrupt and endangering world he has rejected. In Act IV of *The Tempest,* Prospero orders the production of a Masque, "some vanity of mine art" (IV, i, 41), for the entertainment of Ferdinand and Miranda. And the graceful dance of Nymphs and Reapers is halted not precisely by a Red Death, but by Prospero's sudden recollection of the "foul conspiracy / Of the beast Caliban and his confederates / Against my life" (IV, i, 139-141). Like the Prospero habitually identified with his creator, Poe's more exotic duke may be read as a heightened image of at least one aspect of the author. Reflecting the duke's "love of the bizarre," both the magnificent structure and the ornately winding rooms inside it are a "creation of the prince's own eccentric yet august taste" (IV, 252, 251). His tastes, we are told, were "peculiar," and though he had "a fine eye for colors and effects . . . [h]is plans were bold and fiery, and his conceptions glowed with barbaric lustre." Apparently responding to a common rumor that still persists a century and a half after his death, Poe-as-narrator acknowledges that "there are some who would have thought him mad." But he rejects the claim even as he cites it,

assuring the reader that those who know him personally know better. "It was necessary to hear and see and touch him to be *sure* that he was not" (IV, 253).[3]

Although Poe is an inveterate interloper into his own tales, his characters (as in **"William Wilson," "The Fall of the House of Usher"** and other tales) bearers of his birthdate, physiognomy, or other personal signatures, the case for authorial self-reference, however strong, remains speculative. The narrator's own self-conscious presence is demonstrable. There are but three overt narrative self-references in **"The Masque,"** all of them to the narrator in his Prospero-like role of creative artist or director. "It was a voluptuous scene, that masquerade," he tells us. "But first let me tell of the rooms in which it was held" (IV, 251). What follows is a descriptive *tour de force* that is the narrative equivalent of the duke's own directorial supervision of the "movable embellishments" of the chambers. In Poe's lavish prose the narrator speaks the rooms into vivid being. In effect the speaker's digressive swerve from the voluptuous masquerade is a narrative prefiguring of the arrangement he subsequently describes: the irregular disposal of the rooms that prevents one's seeing beyond what is before him, "the sharp turn at every twenty or thirty yards." As the arabesque decoration of the rooms is a reflection of the arabesque quality of this and other tales, the winding pattern of the apartments is an architectural image of the digressive and diverting progress of the narrative. One may even read this averting of attention from the masquerade as the narrator's own prince-like flight from the Red Death who, the narrator well knows, will make his fatal appearance at the ball.

The second self-reference likewise speaks of the narrator as teller,[4] while the third, aided by yet another art-world metaphor, calls direct attention to the speaker's role as creator—*ab ovo,* as it were—rather than as mere recounter of the tale. "In an assembly of phantasms such as I have painted," remarks the speaker, "it may well be supposed that no ordinary appearance could have excited such sensation" (IV, 255). It was the prince's "guiding taste which had given character to the masqueraders" (IV, 254); but taking credit for the painting of the assembly, the narrator arrogates to himself a share in this determining act of imagination. What the duke is to the rooms that are the equivalent of the tale that writes them, the narrator is to that tale. One expression of the convoluted structure of the abbey is the narrator's mirroring relation to the artisan whose tale he tells.

There is—or may be—a fourth reference to the narrator in the tale, but though it is indirect it is ultimately more intrusive. Now that midnight approaches, we are informed, none of the maskers may be found in the westernmost chamber with its blood-colored panes and sable decor. And yet someone is inside that room. For "to him whose foot falls upon the sable carpet, there comes from the near clock of ebony a muffled peal more solemnly emphatic than any which reaches *their* ears who indulge in the more remote gaieties of the other apartments" (IV, 253-254). Since the masked figure of the Red Death is recognized in the following paragraph, it is reasonable and customary to identify him as the inhabitant of the seventh chamber. But when seen, the masked figure is in the outer rooms and, more important, there is nothing in the account to preclude the assumption that it is the narrator himself whose ear is most attentively attuned to the deathlike knelling of the clock.

In this reading, that which was external to the tale, the ostensibly removed omniscient narrator, has, like the Red Death, invaded it. The narrator whose creative role aligns him with the prince, now anticipates the masked figure in his physical incursion into the chambers of the fiction. The ambiguity of the reference to one whose foot falls upon the sable carpet is thus part of the newly formed association between the two spectral figures assumed to inhabit a world outside the catacombs of fiction.[5] The convolutions within are reflected in the convolutions of the tale that contains them and which, I am arguing, they emblemize.

One function of such maze-like mirroring and self-reflection is a sealing enclosure akin to the avowed purpose of the structure. Like the idealized world of art as Poe construed it, the declared purpose of these rooms is to provide a pleasurable and protected refuge from the ravages of the world of mortal flesh. Girdled round by a "strong and lofty wall" with gates of iron, the abbey allows "neither ingress—or egress to the sudden impulses of despair or of frenzy from within." Like the work of art, "The abbey was amply provisioned. With such precautions the courtiers," like the writer and, for the span of their engagement, his readers, "might bid defiance to contagion. The external world could take care of itself." Improvisatori, ballet dancers, musicians, and above all "Beauty," revealingly capitalized—"All these and security were within. Without was the 'Red Death'" (IV, 251). Beauty is particularly pertinent here, for it links the duke's achievement with that of the poet as set out in "The Poetic Principle." "The Poetry of Words," writes Poe, is to be defined as *The Rhythmical Creation of Beauty*. Its sole arbiter is Taste"[6]—as in the abbey, where the "guiding taste" of the duke, elsewhere defined as "eccentric," "peculiar," and "august," alone "had given character to the masqueraders." That quest for Beauty "may develop itself in various modes—in Painting, in Sculpture, in Architecture, in the Dance—very especially in Music." But the "present theme" of the essay and the self-reflexive theme of **"The Masque of the Red Death"** is "its manifestation in words."[7] Such Beauty, writes Poe, "has no concern whatever either with Duty or with Truth."[8] It is as derelict and self-

possessed in this regard as the duke and his solipsistically indulgent revelers who, abandoning the less fortunate to the ravages of the plague, seek refuge in a denial of its reality and power.

The retreat to the castellated abbey, like the retreat into the enclosed and winding chambers of the work of art, is a retreat from the Red Death, emblem of all that is carnal, menacing, and mortal in this life, all that speaks of blood rather than of Beauty. And while the Red Death is most saliently what it seems, it is associated, as decay and blood routinely are in Poe, with woman, though perhaps in a special way.

There is much that is portentously menstrual—perhaps hymeneal—about the Red Death as the tale describes it.

> Blood was its avatar and its seal—the redness and the horror of blood. There were sharp pains, and sudden dizziness, and then profuse bleeding. . . . The scarlet stains upon the body and especially upon the face, of the victim, were the pest ban which shut him out from the aid and from the sympathy of his fellow-men. And the whole seizure, progress and termination of the disease, were the incidents of half an hour.
>
> (IV, 251)

One of the most powerful and widespread expressions of the "horror of blood" in man, as Karen Horney argues, is the horror of vaginal blood, manifest in both the menstrual and the virginal taboo. In primitive peoples, menstruation, traditionally identified as "the curse," is cause for banishment of the woman from the presence of others—the "pest ban" of the tale—and the imposition of a taboo against all contact with her. "To primitive sensibilities," writes Horney, "the woman becomes doubly sinister in the presence of the bloody manifestations of her womanhood. Contact with her during menstruation is fatal."[9] Among the more 'sophisticated,' the physical banishment from sight and contact is typically reduced to sexual prohibition, but evidence of the revulsion is as infectious and prolific as the Red Death itself. Summarizing his observations on the dread of women generally, on castration anxiety, the virginity taboo, and the horror of blood more particularly, Freud remarks: "In all this there is nothing obsolete, nothing which is not still alive among ourselves."[10] Although he finally traces the taboo on deflowering to what he regards as deeper sources, Freud begins his analysis of the taboo with an ascription to the atavistic "horror of blood." "According to this view," he argues, "the taboo of virginity is connected with the taboo of menstruation which is almost universally maintained."[11]

The horror of blood attached to defloration and menstruation is but part of a more pervasive horror of blood no less tightly linked with woman through her role as earth goddess. Embodiment of all that is associated with matter, principally with body itself, hence with physicality, decay, and death, woman is powerfully and inseparably linked with the blood that metonymizes mortality. The horror of blood, then, that defines the Red Death and the terrors it invokes in its witnesses, is the dread of woman as both sexual and mortal danger. And we may understand both the narcissism of the retreat and the instinctual revelry of the masquerade and **"Masque"** as reactions to that menace.

In the end, of course, the aesthetic sanctuary proves porous. The world of art, conceived and structured to exclude the blooded world of sex and death, is fatally invaded by it. And yet not quite, for it is a feature of Poe's art that like the ominous but unnamed threat, absences are palpable presences. What has been excluded is already within. I have already mentioned the possible intrusion of the presumably disembodied narrator into the tale's and the abbey's chambers. But more importantly and less arguably, there is the prior introduction of the Red Death into the very structuring and decoration of the aesthetic refuge. At the farthest end of the winding passages and chambers lies the seventh room. "Closely shrouded in black velvet tapestries" and sided by windows whose panes were "scarlet—a deep blood color" (IV, 252), the room is clearly a kind of tomb or death chamber, the architectural envoy, within the artistic complex, of the Red Death it presumably holds outside.[12] Long before its fateful appearance at the end of the tale, the Red Death has already invaded the abbey. And since it is the prince who is responsible for the abbey's design and whose taste its shape and decorations express, we are led to the inescapable inference that the diseased quotidian the work of art escapes is an integral, indeed the climactic aspect of its form. Absence, in other words, is an essential and defining presence. The idealized art that ostensibly shuns the mortal world sets that world at its center and points all to it. Like language, the insular world of art is defined in large measure by what it leaves behind. In the very act of deliberate exclusion, by conceiving and constructing itself as sanctuary *against* or refuge *from,* the work of art incorporates what its walls and iron gates are erected to debar.[13]

Yet neither is the exclusion the utter failure the ending of the tale at first suggests. I will return to the decimation at the end, but in the design of the rooms there is a kind of triumph in the seeming failure, for the Red Death, while clearly not banished from the duke's construction, has undergone aesthetic transformation. Redesigned as the seventh chamber, restructured as a metaphor or symbol, and gorgeously appointed and adorned, the ghastly apartment is a kind of immunizing transformation. By bringing the Red Death inside and figuring it according to "his own guiding taste," the duke-as-artist has, at least for the moment, neutralized his adversary by subsuming it. Like a child coping with its fears, the artist seeks to master the objects of his dread

not by total exclusion, but by an act of transfiguring incorporation, by converting, as Poe did, terror into a subsidiary form of Beauty.

The "gigantic clock of ebony" plays a similar double role. Situated in the same westernmost room, where the sun will finally set on all efforts to escape it, the clock is the relentlessly paralyzing reminder of "the Time that flies . . ." (IV, 252, 253). The clock's effect is even more pervasive than that of the room it stands in. For while the revelers may—and do—assiduously avoid the black and blood-tinted chamber, the echoes of the clock resound throughout the abbey, arresting every hour the festivities summoned to efface all sense of time. One may read this as a metaphorical instantiation of the trace, of the unavoidable contamination of 'escape' or 'refuge' by what is fled. But the clock is no incidental presence here. Like the room that contains it, the clock is part of the duke's pre-eminently deliberate design. Had he wished truly to exclude all traces of time, decay, and death, to create an aesthetic sanctuary impervious to the mortal world, he could have conjured otherwise.

What we see again is the artist's dilemma, his apparent recognition that a sanctuary must include—and ultimately master—what it is designed to interdict. The province of poetry is Beauty, not Truth. And although truth is admitted a place in prose denied to it in poetry, that place is subordinate to the Beauty that includes and alters it. As an allegory of the artist's struggle with and against decaying matter, **"The Masque of the Red Death"** exposes the creator's ambivalence toward a truth that terrifies and stills. Like Leontes in Plato's narrative, the artist cannot turn away from the bodies of the dead. Yet to bring them inside his dwelling, if only to drain, disinfect, and embalm them, is to risk the destruction the Red Death wreaks upon the house of art. The anodyne again is a form of subsuming transformation, for the sound of the clock is "clear and loud and deep and exceedingly musical. . . ." Ominous and peculiar, the music of the clock constrains the musicians of the orchestra "to pause, momentarily, in their performance, to hearken to the sound . . ." (IV, 253). But it is one music that inhibits another. The conflict between the insular world of art and the blooded world of time is not between the aesthetic and the real, but between two aesthetic or musical entities. Like the transmutation of the blood of the Red Death into gorgeous stained glass windows, the tolling of the "Time that flies" is rendered as a rhythmic resonance, sharing identity with the more pleasurable music it periodically interrupts. Time is outside the world of art it menaces, yet also of it, participating in its timelessness even as it chimes away its hours.

The ambiguity is caught nicely in a phrase: the notes emitted by the clock issue "when . . . the hour was to be stricken . . ." (IV, 253). The referent that first strikes us here is of the striking or tolling of the hour, the removal of one more from our dwindling allotment. And yet, if the hour is stricken it is also cancelled, stricken from existence. In this second sense it participates in the fate of the revelers stricken by the Red Death, though with an opposing consequence. For if the hour, or time, is stricken in this sense, we are privy to the death of time, a concept as applicable to art's timelessness as to human mortality. The same ambiguity is implicit in the closing observation that "the life of the ebony clock went out with that of the last of the gay" (IV, 258). Again the apparent meaning is the obliteration of temporal life and the failure of art as refuge. But since the clock also metonymizes time itself, the extinction of its life may suggest not the devastation of the sanctuary, but its triumph. Its life gone out, time has been defeated, subsumed into the timeless life of the art that contains it, that makes of its chilling sound a deeper music.

All these ambiguities culminate in the seemingly unequivocal triumph of the Red Death over the artist's retreat into the walled and castellated seclusion of his art. It is near midnight that the uninvited figure is first discovered. It is important to note that the Red Death does not first enter the abbey at that hour. Rather, he who "had arrested the attention of no single individual before" is first noticed when some of the masqueraders find leisure to become aware of him (IV, 255). As suggested, possibly, by the earlier footfalls in the otherwise uninhabited seventh room, metaphorically by the ghastly decor of that room and by the ominous tolling of the clock, the Red Death has, it seems, always been present (always already present) within the walls relied on to exclude it. As in a deconstructable text, that which is presumably absent is always within, mingling with its opposites, waiting for us to find the leisure or the attentiveness to become aware of it.

The figure is noticed and becomes the object of alarm chiefly because of its difference from the others. Although "the masquerade license of the night was nearly unlimited . . . the figure in question . . . had gone beyond the bounds of even the prince's indefinite decorum." It had violated the strictures of "wit [and]—propriety" (IV, 255). What these remarks make clear is that the banished reality or truth has been identified by its violation of aesthetic norms. The primacy of the real, in other words, has been subverted. Rather than the expectable reverse, the real is defined as that which is not art.

With this slight gesture, the seeming triumph of the Red Death over art's escapist enterprise is brought in doubt, and it is a doubt the tale encourages. That the "tall figure stood erect and motionless within the shadow of the ebony clock" (IV, 257-258) seems to place the Red Death among those subject to time's rule, to render it

no less mortal than its victims. But the tale's climactic revelation, the final sharp turn in its angular progression, is that the Red Death is bloodlessly insubstantial. When, after it has slain the duke, the revelers seize hold of it, they gasp "in unutterable horror at finding the grave-cerements and corpse-like mask which they handled with so violent a rudeness, untenanted by any tangible form" (IV, 258).

For Joseph Patrick Roppolo, the vacancy of cerements and mask is an indication that the ghostly figure is not a representation of death itself, but a product of the terrified human imagination, man's "self-aroused and self-developed fear of his own mistaken concept of death."[14] J. Gerald Kennedy, however, argues convincingly against the reduction of the specter to a mere delusion or hallucination. All the revelers, he points out, observe "the presence of a masked figure," which Poe describes in vivid concretizing detail. For Kennedy, whose reading is much closer to my own, "the cerements and mask are signs without a proper referent; they mark the semiotic impasse in which writing has begun to locate its own activity."[15] But this reading, I believe, places the spectral presence and the tale at too distant a remove from the more immediate subject of art's struggle with reality and of the tale itself as spectral presence. The Red Death, emblem of the reality of death beyond the walls, is not distinct from the revelers, but the climactic disembodiment of their escapist aspiration. The inhabitants of the abbey, like the figures in a work of art, constitute a "multitude of gaudy and fantastic appearances," "phantasms" such as the duke directs and the narrator has painted. As mere mask, untenanted by any tangible form, the Red Death, horrific envoy of the real, is at the same time the archetypal realization of the spiritual ideal of poetry and art.

In the mirror world of **"The Masque,"** all things are themselves and their inversions. The narrator, whose relation to the tale is that of the prince to the abbey, is also interchangeable with the Red Death, whose hovering between presence and absence he likewise shares. That which is excluded is at once incorporated, as death, banished to the periphery, is centered. The time that marks the limits of mortal life participates in the timelessness of eternity and art. And the Red Death, blooded emblem of the corporeal, shares with the art that would transcend it the purity of irreferable representation. The Red Death, then, which in the end holds "illimitable dominion over all," contains no single meaning. Far more than simple death, it is a bewildering fusion of mortality and permanence, carnality and pure spirit that, far more satisfyingly than the poetic principle, describes Poe's art.

These resistant mergers, fusions, and contradictions, as I read them, grow in part from Poe's skepticism about the communicativeness of language and the possibilities of knowledge, in part from his notions about the complex interrelation of the imagined and the real. But their immediate and, I would argue, most potent cause lies in the struggle the tale both literally and allegorically describes. In a number, perhaps the majority of Poe's tales, the carnal reality from which art provides insular refuge presses its way inside, exposing the futility of the exclusionary enterprise. In **"Masque of the Red Death,"** an ambivalence elsewhere only implicit in the compulsive dependability of the incursion, governs the progress of the tale. The art that would exclude the diseased decaying world wheels the rotting horse inside the gates and choreographs the fiction's dance around that rancid core. In almost all the tales that make of this conflict their overt or hidden subject, art effects a saving triumph of incorporation; but that victory seems nearer to hand in **"The Masque"** than elsewhere. Perhaps because in this tale the artist consciously encloses the enemy within his walls he is able to transform it, to make of death the archetypal phantasm even as he dies at its fleshless hand.

CONCLUSION

Poe is, unarguably, one of the American writers most likely to inspire deconstruction, and for as long as the critical habit survives his works will probably continue to prod its users into action. This is not at all inappropriate, I believe, but as I've tried to argue, the approach will remain truer to the tales, their author, and the spurs of writing if they acknowledge the extent to which the confusion of these narratives stems from the writer's embattled ambivalence toward his subjects, principally toward the feminized "truths" of sexuality, decay, and death he fitfully exposes and recoils from. The eminently deconstructive and deconstructible habits of canceling reversal and contradiction, of evasion and denial, and of a deceptively mystifying revelation pervade, identify, and frustratingly unravel Poe's narratives. Typically, however, they reflect neither Poe's nor language's epistemological commitment to indeterminacy, but the author's textually manifest anxiety toward the mortifying material reality his art, by definition and design, offers refuge from yet cannot finally exclude.

The struggle is ongoing and unending, assuming different forms, often a variety of forms, in different tales, each of which becomes a self-reflexive study of the changing shapes the battle between recognition and denial takes on and the ways an elusive victory may be at least partially or temporarily won. When it is won, victory comes not in the triumphant effacement or banishment of the corporeal, but in its transfiguring incorporation. Ultimately, the partial and difficult victory achieved in **"The Masque of the Red Death"** is not restricted to it. Like the form of the Red Death, the figures of reality in Poe's tales are typically costumed vacancies, epitomes of the fantastic whose unreality testifies to the

transformative triumph of imagination and art. The invasive return of reality, in other words, characteristically depicted as the return of the once beautiful, now carnal and terrifying woman from the dead, is often the narrative's most surreal or fanciful moment. Art turns one last time the forces of the narrative against reality by representing its own collapse under the weight of insistent reality as a flight of fantasy, arguably—as in **"Ligeia"** and **"Usher"** [**"The Fall of the House of Usher"**]—a manifestation not of reality but of the narrator's crazed imagination. The price may be sanity or stability, but the reward is the sought escape into mind and fancy. In the end the real is de-realized, the female principle de-fanged, mortality deprived of its bite. What many of the fictions delineate, then, is not, finally, their own defeat, not the failure of art to sustain itself against reality, but its contrary and quite dazzling capacity to incorporate reality within the sphere of the imagined, to offer the enactment of its apparent defeat as its greatest triumph. The psychological requirements of fiction-as-escape are not satisfactorily served by a mere denial or exclusion of reality. Such a solution, Poe implies, is too easily won to be persuasive or to perform its defensive function. Art triumphs over reality not by rising above it or by stepping aside like a skillful matador as it rushes fiercely past. Art wins its difficult victory by inviting reality in its most ominous forms inside the house of fiction and by converting and neutralizing them there.

As the incorporative transformation of reality is the triumph of art, the obfuscation of truth is the condition, or *a* condition, of beauty. To perform its function, truth in Poe's fiction cannot be merely absent. It must be sought and undiscovered; it must be promised, pursued, and denied. Not its omission, but its suppression evinces the vagueness, the uncertainty, and the silent mystery that constitute beauty in Poe's poetic art and theory. Reworking Keats, Beauty in this usage is not Truth but its suppression, while Truth, in its denied but hinted presence, is the condition of Beauty. Beauty, then, is Truth in Poe, Truth Beauty, in that the essence of Beauty is the vagueness or mystery attendant upon the suppression of Truth, while Truth, the horror of decay, carnality, and death, always contains within it the fascination of the Beautiful. The inevitable coexistence of attraction and repulsion, described in *Eureka* as the controlling principle of all existence, assures the Yeatsian interplay of mutually immanent opposites. In Poe, attraction and repulsion do not patiently alternate with one another. Like Yeats's gyres, they interpenetrate, each always present in the other. The simultaneity of attraction and repulsion, of the fascination and horror that define Poe's Gothic achievement, assures that, as in woman, the irresistibly beautiful must also contain and conceal a terrible truth. Both the containment and the concealment are essential to Beauty. When carnal woman tears through the veil of supernal beauty Poe has draped across her flesh, reality assaults the preserve of beauty, the protective sanctuary of art. Paradoxically, it is its gossamer embalmment in fantasy, its shroud of contradiction, curtailment, and uncertainty, that reconstructs the threatened walls of art. Poe's poems and tales, then, circulate within the trinitarian parameters or uterine walls of the female. The ideal subject for poetry, and the actual subject of much of the poetry and prose, is the death of the beautiful woman. Since woman's supernal beauty is the spiritualized inversion of the carnal materality she embodies, her death frees those chthonic forces pressing for release. The death of the beautiful woman, in other words, marks the forfeiture of Poe's first line of defense—the supernal sanctuary—and typically throws the text into a search for compensatory protections. The result is obscurity, the abyss or maelstrom of whirling and bottomless implication that is another of woman's sanctified if unholy identities. Since monstrosity cannot fully reveal or sustain itself without danger to the aesthetic construct or its architect, this third identity of woman—as absence, chaos, or abyss—is invoked. Like our own, Poe's universe may be created out of a chaos it is gleaned from; but it is preserved by immersion within it.

Notes

1. Most critical readings of "The Masque" align themselves with Walter Blair's more general view that the tale describes a battle between life and death, between time and the "gaiety which seeks to kill time by forgetting it" (Walter Blair, "Poe's Conception of Incident and Tone in the Tale," *Modern Philology,* 41 (1944): 239. It is, as Joseph Patrick Roppolo argued and J. Gerald Kennedy agreed, "a parable of the inevitability and the universality of death" (Joseph Roppolo, "Meaning and 'The Masque of the Red Death,'" in *Poe: A Collection of Critical Essays,* ed. Robert Regan [Englewood Cliffs, NJ: Prentice Hall, 1967], p. 142; cited by J. Gerald Kennedy, pp. 201-202). As David Halliburton articulates it, "the real interest in the story is man's relation to his own mortality" (David Halliburton, p. 310). A smaller number have, as I do, located that interest more particularly in the flight from death into the world of creativity and art. See, for example, Kermit Vanderbilt, "Art and Nature in 'The Masque of the Red Death,'" *NCF* [*Nineteenth-Century Fiction*], 22 (1968): 379-389; David Dudley, "Dead or Alive: The Booby-Trapped Narrator of Poe's 'Masque of the Red Death,'" *Studies in Short Fiction,* 30 (1993): 169-173; and, more cursorily, David Ketterer's observation that Prince Prospero "attempts to escape life and to avoid the trauma of death in a self-created world of arabesque art" (David Ketterer, p. 200).

2. Not surprisingly, a number of readers have recognized the advertised presence of *The Tempest* and its magician hero in Poe's "Masque," but most have ignored or slighted the mutual identity of both Prosperos as covert artists. See, for example, Patrick Cheney, "Poe's Use of *The Tempest* and The Bible in 'The Masque of the Red Death,'" *English Language Notes,* 20 (1983): 31-39; and G. R. Thompson, *Poe's Fiction. . . .* Cheney notes only that Poe's Prospero will "create an earthly paradise that parodies the 'brave new world' of *The Tempest . . .*" (p. 33); while for Thompson, "Prince Prospero's sinister stronghold . . . contrasts directly with the enchanted island of his namesake . . ." (p. 122). Kermit Vanderbilt, on the other hand, has richly described the relationship between the two Prosperos as transforming artists (Kermit Vanderbilt, pp. 379-389).

3. There is a portentous irony here as well, for in his advertised palpability the fantastic and fantasizing Prospero is more substantial than the incorporeal envoy of the real who invades and decimates the phantasmagoric world of art. I am arguing, here and elsewhere, for a more complex view of the interaction of life (or death) and art than one that regards the latter as the ultimately defenseless victim of the forces it seeks transcendence of and respite from.

4. "And then the music ceased, as I have told; and the evolutions of the waltzers were quieted; and there was an uneasy cessation of all things as before" (IV, 255).

5. My reading coincides here with Leonard Cassuto's interesting suggestion that "The teller of the tale is Death himself." "How," Cassuto asks, "could the narrator be present at the ball and then be able to tell about it afterwards? The only one who 'lives' is Death. The narrator must be Death himself" (Leonard Cassuto, "The Coy Reaper: Unmasque-ing The Red Death," *Studies in Short Fiction,* 25 [1988]: 318, 319).

6. Poe, "The Poetic Principle," in *Essays and Reviews,* p. 78.

7. *Ibid.,* p. 77.

8. *Ibid.,* p. 78.

9. Karen Horney, "The Dread of Woman," *International Journal of Psycho-Analysis,* 13 (1932): 476.

10. S. Freud, "The Taboo of Virginity" (1918), in *Standard Edition,* Vol. 11, p. 199.

11. *Ibid.,* pp. 196, 197.

12. The point is made and remade: In "the western or black chamber," we are told, "the effect of the fire-light that streamed upon the dark hangings through the blood-tinted panes was ghastly in the

extreme, and produced so wild a look upon the countenances of those who entered, that there were few of the company bold enough to set foot within its precincts at all" (IV, 252).

13. David Halliburton, who notes that emblems of the death presumably excluded from the abbey are built into it, believes that the Prince is blind to this; he does not perceive "that in and through the apartment . . . death is 'already here': the black apartment is his scenic presence" (David Halliburton, pp. 311-312). But as I will argue more expansively, whatever the Prince understands—and it is difficult to imagine he is blind to this—Poe recognizes, as David Dudley suggests, that "By representing death, art creates the comforting illusion that death is just one of art's illusions." For Dudley, the narrator's impossible escape to tell the story underscores the point that his art, like Prospero's must fail. "The narrator is thus a fly in the soothing ointment of aesthetic distance, figuring and ridiculing both the author's and the reader's hope of escape into art" (David R. Dudley, p. 173). But the escape of the narrator seems to me more persuasively construed as another sign of art's triumph. In art and the imagination, it implies, such escapes are possible: witness the ruse that achieves it. In effect there has been an exchange. As the Red Death is transformed at the tale's end into an artistic phantom, the narrator is given a reality outside the story and its possibilities. In one of Poe's characteristically dizzying exchanges, as life (or death) becomes an ornament of art, art takes on the cerements of reality.

14. Joseph Patrick Roppolo, pp. 142, 144.

15. J. Gerald Kennedy, p. 203.

Works Cited

Blair, Walter, "Poe's Conception of Incident and Tone in the Tale," *Modern Philology*, 41 (1944): 228-240.

Cassuto, Leonard, "The Coy Reaper: Unmasque-ing The Red Death," *Studies in Short Fiction*, 25 (1988): 317-320.

Cheney, Patrick, "Poe's Use of *The Tempest* and The Bible in 'The Masque of the Red Death,'" *English Language Notes*, 20 (1983): 31-39.

Dudley, David, "Dead or Alive: The Booby-Trapped Narrator of Poe's 'Masque of the Red Death,'" *Studies in Short Fiction*, 30 (1993): 169-173.

Freud, Sigmund, "The Taboo of Virginity" (1918), in *Standard Ed.*, Vol. 11, pp. 191-208.

Halliburton, David, *Edgar Allan Poe: A Phenomenological View* (Princeton, N.J.: Princeton University Press, 1973).

Horney, Karen, "The Dread of Woman," *International Journal of Psycho-Analysis*, 13 (1932): 348-360.

Kennedy, J. Gerald, *Poe, Death and the Life of Writing* (New Haven and London: Yale University Press, 1987).

Ketterer, David, *The Rationale of Deception in Poe* (Baton Rouge and London: Louisiana State University Press, 1979).

Roppolo, Joseph, "Meaning and 'The Masque of the Red Death,'" in *Poe: A Collection of Critical Essays*, ed. Robert Regan.

Thompson, G. R., *Poe's Fiction: Romantic Irony in the Gothic Tales* (Madison: University of Wisconsin Press, 1973).

Vanderbilt, Kermit, "Art and Nature in 'The Masque of the Red Death,'" *NCF*, 22 (1968): 379-389.

Dennis R. Perry (essay date 2003)

SOURCE: Perry, Dennis R. "Apocalypse: Crises of Fragmentation." In *Hitchcock and Poe: The Legacy of Delight and Terror*, pp. 45-66. Lanham, Md.: The Scarecrow Press, Inc., 2003.

[*In the following essay, Perry characterizes "The Masque of the Red Death" and Alfred Hitchcock's film* The Birds *as explicitly apocalyptic works that rely on biblical allusions to express social anxieties and archetypal conflicts.*]

The apocalypse in Poe and Hitchcock begins where the ratiocination stories end, at the breaking up of the rational and predictable universe. Just as the detective stories concern themselves with explaining apparently inexplicable reality, the apocalyptic stories tell of reality coming apart and the failure of human will and reason to put it back together. In *Eureka*, Poe describes how the original oneness of the universe is forced into "the abnormal condition of *Many*."[1] While unity implied homogeneity within the one, diffusion suggests "differences at all points from the uniquity and simplicity of the origin" (*Eureka*, 28). This moment of fragmentation and diffusion in the apocalyptic phase defines the frenzy of collapse in many of Poe's tales and Hitchcock's films. Sanity becomes madness, sense nonsense. The ability to analytically discern unified patterns evident in a condition of stable unity and sameness (as in the ratiocination tales) is replaced by panic in an atmosphere of rapid and violent flux. In this chapter I will explore how Hitchcock creates an audience-centered apocalypse in *The Birds* in terms of both biblical imagery and dissonances, including the irreconcilable coexistence of humor and horror as an objective correlative of sublime delight and terror. Despite the many dark scholarly assessments of the film, reading *The Birds* in the even darker context of Poe's **"Masque,"** together with Hitchcock's special use of apocalyptic imagery and humor, makes the film lighter and more optimistic than generally reckoned.

Poe's and Hitchcock's vision in **"The Masque of the Red Death"** and *The Birds* is thoroughly apocalyptic, both artists building suspense toward an impending disaster. From the shattering breakup of the unified universe and its fragmented and diffusive aftermath to the multigalactic vortex when the universe collapses back into its original unity, *Eureka*'s impending disasters are reflected microcosmically in many of Poe's tales and poems, representing, if not the collective end of the world, then the microcosmic catastrophe of an individual character. Douglas Robinson defines apocalyptic literature in theological scholarship as the future being unveiled in the present and the encroachment of a radically new order into a "historical situation that has disintegrated into chaos."[2] Thus human weakness brings on and leads to the ultimate chaos of apocalypse. So often in Poe's tales, madness is the human weakness that brings on shattering changes. Such works as **"The Fall of the House of Usher," "William Wilson," "The Black Cat," "Morella," "Ms. Found in a Bottle,"** "Ulalume," "The Raven," *The Narrative of Arthur Gordon Pym,* and "The City in the Sea" foreshadow an impending disaster that inevitably occurs. In addition to **"The Masque of the Red Death,"** more explicit collective apocalyptic works include **"King Pest," "Mellonta Tauta," "Al Aaraaf,"** *Eureka,* and others. The latter three, including **"Mesmeric Revelation,"** allude to the cyclical creation and destruction of the earth or the universe and the underlying longing in Poe's work that Wilbur describes as his insistent theme of transcending the creative, emotional, and physical limits of mortal existence.[3] Thus virtually all of Poe's more serious work is at least subtextually apocalyptic. For the narrator of **"Ligeia,"** Roderick Usher, Prince Prospero, and others, this universal spectacle is experienced in their individual lives. The essence of Poe's art is imagining the potential end of one way of being abruptly moving to another, whether insanity, sleep, or death. But this thematic dimension is only half of the apocalyptic story, since Poe invariably subverts the structural conventions of serious gothic art. Poe raises issues about what his art is by invoking an inevitable double aspect that G. R. Thompson calls "romantic irony,"[4] undercutting the gothic theme with ironic subtexts.

While *The Birds* is Hitchcock's only explicitly apocalyptic film, Hitchcock agreeing with Peter Bogdanovich that it is a "vision of Judgment Day,"[5] it isn't his only one, nor his only way of telling an apocalyptic story. In a recent article, Christopher Sharrett proposed that *The Birds* (1963), as well as *Psycho* (1960), is a forerunner to apocalyptic films of the 1960s such as *Bonnie and Clyde* (1968) and *The Wild Bunch* (1969). Like them (and Poe), these Hitchcock films subvert our ideas about what a "work of art should represent."[6] *The Birds* generated an interpretive feeding frenzy because, as Thomas Leitch has noted, it is "the only Hitchcock film to have generated radical discrepancies in interpretation."[7] The endless speculations about the film are generated primarily by (1) the inexplicability and violence of the bird attacks, (2) the seemingly loose relationship between the attacks and the human drama, and (3) the film's apparently inconclusive ending.[8] While these aspects of the film certainly point to dark purposes, the hopeful—and even humorous—signs in the film have been generally slighted or misunderstood. Attempts to take account of all sides of the complex geometry of *The Birds* are provided a helpful image in Poe's *Eureka*. In explaining how the mind can "receive and . . . perceive an individual impression" of the universe, Poe uses the following metaphor: "He who from the top of Aetna casts his eyes leisurely around, is affected chiefly by the *extent* and *diversity* of the scene. Only by a rapid whirling on his heel could he hope to comprehend the panorama in the sublimity of its *oneness*" (6). Such a panoramic view helps reveal more fully the effect of Hitchcock's sublime dissonances in *The Birds*. The darker and lighter aspects taken together in an apocalyptic context, particularly echoing Poe's similar use of biblical prophecies and visions of the end of the world in **"Masque,"** show that just as a millennial dawn follows the inevitable destruction, so Melanie Daniels and the Brenner family have cause for hope, despite the chaos in the world.[9]

Much of Hitchcock's work, like Poe's, is implicitly apocalyptic. His many spy films, for example, suggest frightening threats against Western civilization. In *The 39 Steps* (1935), *Sabotage* (1936), *Foreign Correspondent* (1940), *Saboteur* (1942), *Lifeboat* (1943), *North by Northwest* (1959), and *Topaz* (1969) the home front is threatened by foreign intrigue. Through sabotage, murder, kidnapping, and war (as in *Foreign Correspondent* and *Lifeboat*), Hitchcock creates an atmosphere of counting down to an apocalypse with suggestive signs of the times. *Foreign Correspondent* ends with war crashing down on Johnny Jones (Joel McCrea) as he reports to American listeners during the London blitz. However, Hitchcock prefers his war films to emphasize the impact of disaster as it affects individuals rather than societies. Hence, these stories are often about the protagonists becoming increasingly involved in the plots of their enemies and becoming aware of the depth of corruption in unexpected places (e.g., *North by Northwest*). In this sense, some of these films are apocalyptic in exactly the way Sharrett suggests, subverting our views of America and how it is represented on film. In films about the apocalypse of the individual, the protagonist experiences his or her world falling apart before entering a "radically new order of being." In

Shadow of a Doubt (1943), *The Man Who Knew Too Much* (1956), and *Marnie* (1964), for example, disaster is foreshadowed early on and fulfilled in the course of the film. Hitchcock's films are regularly fueled by the imaginative catastrophe, playing on audience fears (especially during World War II and the Cold War) of the very real possibility of the ground falling out from under them. But even more to the point in this chapter are Hitchcock's experimental films (*Lifeboat, Rope, Rear Window,* and *Psycho*), which challenge genre conventions and conventional space limitations. Anticipating the unique approach used in *The Birds*, these films put audiences through unparalleled cinematic ordeals outside the comfortable Hollywood formulas of the time.

While Poe's imagery resulted from a life of personal disasters, Hitchcock's apocalyptic imagination was fueled by his moment in history. Born in 1899, Hitchcock lived through World Wars I and II, the Korean and Vietnam Wars, the Cold War, and the worldwide financial depression of the 1930s. The eruption of chaos and its potential to change everything was real and immediate for him and his generation. As JoAnn James observes, "the maelstroms of the twentieth century have given contemporary urgency to a new apocalyptic literature."[10] Following the earthshaking events up to and including World War II, Hitchcock lived through an unsettling period immersed in Cold War fears of annihilation. Susan Sontag notes that

> the trauma suffered by everyone in the middle of the 20th-century [made] clear that, from now on to the end of human history, every person would spend his individual life under the threat not only of individual death, which is certain, but of something almost insupportable psychologically—collective incineration and extinction which could come at any time, virtually without warning.[11]

As a Roman Catholic, if a lapsed one, Hitchcock would have been aware of the apocalyptic visions of Mary, particularly the Fatima secret message concerning Russia that led many Catholics in the 1950s and 1960s to understand the Cold War as a religious apocalypse.[12] Beyond the nuclear threats of the period, there was the danger of an ecological holocaust that Rachel Carson warned of in *Silent Spring* (1962). In other areas of political and popular culture during the 1960s, it became obvious that America had come to the unsettling end of the "liberal consensus," punctuated by the Vietnam and civil rights protests. These protests suggested radical ideas that were echoed in anthems to a new world to come (like Bob Dylan's "The Times They Are A-Changing" [1963]). Soon Barry McGuire's "Eve of Destruction" (1965) and the Doors' "The End" (1967) took these ideas to further apocalyptic extremes. *The Birds* appeared in the middle of a period when violent change had already taken wing—Hitchcock merely lit-

eralized it. *The Birds* was released among mainstream films that also echoed apocalyptic themes: *Dr. No* (1962), *The Manchurian Candidate* (1962), *Four Horseman of the Apocalypse* (1962), *Dr. Strangelove* (1964), *Fail Safe* (1964), *Behold a Pale Horse* (1964), and *Seven Days in May* (1964).

In the decade before *The Birds* the fear of atomic holocaust was evident everywhere, particularly in B movies about giant atomic-revived monsters (*Beast from 20,000 Fathoms* [1953], *Them* [1954], *Godzilla* [1956]), apocalyptic disasters (*When Worlds Collide* [1951], *World Without End* [1956], *The Day the Sky Exploded* [1961]), postapocalyptic life (*The Day the World Ended* [1956], *Panic in the Year Zero* [1962]), alien invasion films (*The Day the Earth Stood Still* [1951], *Invaders from Mars* [1953]), and realistic nuclear dramas (*On the Beach* [1959], *The World, the Flesh, and the Devil* [1959]).[13] Peter Biskind sums up the imaginative impact of these films in the 1950s and how unique they were to their time:

> But in sci-fi, the emergencies were much more serious than they were in war films. They jeopardized the future of the race; they were not national, nor even international, but planetary. The vast scale of destruction also differentiated sci-fi from the horror films of the thirties and forties that preceded them. In *Frankenstein* (1931) and *Dracula* (1931), the scale of misfortune was small, a few villagers mugged by a monster, a little blood let by a vampire. But films like *When Worlds Collide* (1951) or *War of the Worlds* (1953) were suffused with what Susan Sontag called the "imagination of disaster," fear of the cataclysmic destruction of civilization, mayhem of an unimaginably higher order than we had ever seen before, the beginning of the end of life-as-we-know-it.[14]

Although *The Birds* is cinematically unique, it is thematically a product of its unsettled times.

While much of this cinema of worldwide disaster sets the imaginative stage for Hitchcock's supreme apocalyptic vision in *The Birds*, Poe's **"Masque of the Red Death"** anticipates Hitchcock with a dramatic framework of inexplicable sublimity and imagery for exploring the apocalypse in a manner distinct from contemporary cinematic conventions of science fiction. As Christopher Sharrett points out, few such science fiction films "address problems deeply rooted in human psychology or the constitution of civilization" ("Myth," 39). Horror films, however, are more apocalyptic in "offering a powerful critique of fundamental assumptions of much American art, including concepts such as 'human nature' heretofore treated as self-evident and sacrosanct by all genres" ("Myth," 40). From this perspective Sharrett proposes that *The Birds* raises issues about our ideas of what film art "should represent." As a literary horror precedent, down to its specific plot details, theme, and biblical allusions to end-of-the-world prophecies, Poe's **"Masque of the Red Death"** is echoed in *The Birds*. Like the Poe tale, including a devastating and deadly plague sweeping the land and throwing all into chaos, Hitchcock's characters try to hole up in a fortress and wall out the plague. Life in the **"Masque"** fortress is punctuated by the frightening chiming of the clock in the black room, while *The Birds* is punctuated by increasingly disturbing bird attacks, likewise causing eerie, confused, and terrified silences. Finally, unsuccessfully walling out the threat from without, both stories reach a climax in a final encounter that subdues the central character. In both tales, these aspects of the narrative obtain a sublime aura of apocalyptic magnitude through the imagery of biblical prophecies concerning conditions at the end of the world.

"The Masque of the Red Death"

While criticism of **"The Masque of the Red Death"** has often focused on its many possible sources, including etiquette books, the tale has not been analyzed in terms of biblical prophecies of the end of the world—including Douglas Robinson's analysis of the tale within the context of the apocalypse. Patrick Cheney's article on the use of the Bible and *The Tempest* in **"Masque"** suggests that Poe ironically reverses the mythic pattern in the Bible, depicting "the triumph of [the] agents of destruction over man."[15] In Cheney's version, the Red Death is the Antichrist, denying "Christ his power of resurrection" ("Poe's Use," 36). Further, the Red Death "replaces Christ as the shaping force of reality" ("Poe's Use," 38). Finally, Cheney downplays the significance of biblical imagery through most of the story: "Poe's use of biblical symbolism does not become particularly noteworthy until the last paragraph" ("Poe's Use," 34). While an interesting take on the tale, Cheney's study doesn't go far enough. He emphasizes narrative shape at the expense of biblical details that, in fact, challenge his idea that the story only ironically reverses biblical patterns. But even here, while the Bible is central to Cheney's reading, the apocalypse is not. I will argue that the apocalypse is a most important aspect of the biblical imagery in Poe's tale, and that it is a displaced refiguring of the Bible in dramatic and symbolic terms that reinforces traditional readings of the apocalypse, as well as inverts them. And, importantly for this chapter, pulling in two directions at once prefigures a pattern in *The Birds*.

The setting in **"Masque"** is reminiscent of a common apocalyptic pattern in the Bible. For example, Jesus tells his disciples what will precede his second coming by comparing the people to those during the time of Noah who ate, drank, and married "until the day that Noah entered into the ark" (Matt 24:38). He also tells the parable of the rich man who builds a barn for his goods and selfishly tells himself, "Soul . . . take thine ease, eat, drink, and be merry" (Luke 12:19). This par-

able is narrated with a cosmic irony that is reflected in **"Masque"** when the narrator ironically says of Prospero's plans: "All these and security were within. Without was the 'Red Death'" (671). Like the rich farmer of the parable, who is told that "this night thy soul shall be required of thee" (Luke 12:19-20), Prospero dies at the peak of his pleasure and security, as we knew he would. Also equating personal and collective apocalypse, an important biblical source for **"Masque"** is Daniel 5, where King Belshazzar meets his untimely death while making "a great feast to a thousand of his lords" and "drinking wine before the thousand" (v. 1). His doom is sealed when he has the "golden and silver vessels," which Nebuchadnezzar had taken out of the temple in Jerusalem, brought out "that the king, and his princes, his wives, and his concubines, might drink therein" (v. 2). Committing blasphemy, Belshazzar foreshadows Prince Prospero's attempts to defy mortal and divine limitations by walling out death itself. Belshazzar further seals his doom by idolizing the "gods of gold, and of silver, of brass, of iron, of wood, and of stone" (v. 4). For his part, Prospero ignores the needs of humanity and worships pleasure and his own "magnificent . . . yet august taste" (670). The end comes in stages as Belshazzar sees a message on the wall written by a disembodied hand, which causes the king's merry countenance to change: "and his thoughts troubled him, so that . . . his knees smote one against another" (v. 6). Like the sounding of the clock in **"Masque,"** the writing on the wall stops the revelry cold, and Belshazzar seeks someone to interpret the writing, ultimately finding Daniel. Unlike the mysterious and silent masked figure in **"Masque,"** Daniel is a more vocal messenger of death to the king. He first accuses the king of defiant pride and lifting himself "against the Lord of heaven" (v. 23). Daniel then interprets the writing on the wall as a message from God, declaring that Belshazzar has been found wanting and that his kingdom will be divided and given to the Medes and Persians. The chapter then ends (as in **"Masque"**) when "that night was Belshazzar the king of the Chaldeans slain" (v. 30).

The fact that Poe's **"Masque of the Red Death"** presents the apocalypse as a day of wrath and widespread death confirms, as much as it ironically reverses, biblical patterns. As one prophet puts it, "the day of the Lord is great and very terrible; and who can abide it" (Joel 2:11). Others note that the day of the Lord comes in "perilous times" (2 Tim 3:1) and is a day "his wrath is come" (Rev 6:17). Further, that day "comes upon you unawares" (Luke 21:34) and is a day of "darkness" (Matt 24:29). On this day, all will be "desolate" (Ezk 35:15) as the Lord comes to "destroy sinners" (Isa 13:9) and "sever the wicked" (Matt 13:49). Other references reinforce Poe's awareness of scripture in writing **"Masque."** The Bible defines the wicked as those "choked by the riches and pleasures of life" (Luke 8:14). Poe presents his characters as worldly courtiers, under the influence of Prospero, allegorically trying to escape death altogether. Specific biblical imagery that Poe draws on fills in the allegory. Such biblical images as a bloody sea (Rev 16:3), heat/fire (Rev 16:8), and darkness (Rev 16:10) provide image patterns for Poe. Reflecting the "wonders of blood and fire" (Joel 2: 30), the sun "blackened and the moon turned to blood" (Rev 6:12), and a "consumption decreed that shall overflow" (Isa 10:22), Poe creates settings for the **"Masque"** such as braziers of fire, blood red lighting in the black seventh room, and a plague.

Poe's numerology in **"Masque"** also echoes biblical patterns. The plagues in John's apocalypse, for example, are associated with the number seven, the number of successive rooms in Poe's tale. Just as the plagues represent an apocalyptic countdown, so the rooms Prospero and the revelers pass through to pursue the Red Death ironically become the countdown to their end. Invariably, interpreters of the tale associate the seven colored rooms with Shakespeare's "seven ages of man." However, as John represents the sealed portions of the book, each signifies not the ages of men individually but collectively, and the sixth seal reveals events preceding the end of the world, including earthquakes, darkness, and stars falling from heaven (vv. 12-13). In chapter 5, the apostle describes a book on the throne of God with seven seals, followed by a vision in which he sees Christ as a slain lamb with seven horns and seven eyes, "which are the seven Spirits of god sent forth into all the earth" (v. 6). Without trying to unpack these images with too much specificity, I would note that like the fearful striking of the clock in **"Masque,"** the opening of the seventh seal is accompanied by awed silence. Also foreshadowing the clock, chapter 8 describes seven angels with seven trumpets, each of which precipitates a new disaster, functioning as a celestial clock measuring earth's final hours.[16] Of course, the end in **"Masque"** only occurs when Prospero and death go through all seven rooms. Like the seals on the book, the angled architecture conceals one room (or time period) from another, leading inevitably to the ultimate silence and death of the seventh room. Importantly, linking the rooms in **"Masque"** to biblical precedent, the seals in Revelation are also associated with a succession of colors in a vision of white, red, and black horses (6:4-8).[17]

Finally, while Cheney links the Red Death to the Antichrist, the biblical record uses similar terms to Poe's in describing Christ himself at the second coming. The Red Death wears vesture and countenance "dabbed in blood" (**"Masque,"** 675) and comes like a "thief in the night" (1 Thess 5:2). Most tellingly, with his coming he brings death to all of the wicked (2 Thess 2:8). Similarly, Christ is described at his second coming as wearing "dyed garments" that represent the blood he shed during his own sacrificial death (Isa 63:1). He also displays the evidences of his death, including the wounds in his hands (Zech 13:6). Allegorically, then, the tale depicts Christ returning to regain dominion of the world from the real Antichrist, Prospero, whose dreamlike kingdom of selfish revelry is "found wanting." Hence, instead of being an ironic reversal of Christ, the figure of the Red Death fulfills biblical prophecy of Christ's coming in terrible wrath to destroy the wicked and end the temporary reign of Satan. Poe's tale can be read as an allegorical reframing of the biblical story. What leads to the ironic reading is that Poe stops short of the millennial dawn that Scripture indicates will follow the apocalyptic holocaust. However, since Poe's tale focuses exclusively on Prospero and his wicked courtiers, the tale doesn't exclude salvation elsewhere. Hitchcock's apocalypse includes a hopeful dawn.

THE BIRDS

The Birds, which Fellini called "an apocalyptic poem," exemplifies the moment of fragmentation described by Poe in *Eureka* in its situations and characters. *Eureka*'s "characters" and the "plot" in which they are embroiled provide glimpses into making sense of events in the film, which critics find ambiguous viewed in isolation. *Eureka*'s characters are the diffused fragments of the universe, which differ in size, kind, form, and distance from each other (*Eureka,* 29-30). These characters are both repulsed by and attracted to each other. The attraction is Newtonian gravity while the repulsion is electricity, which is "*manifested* only when bodies of appreciable difference, are brought into approximation" (*Eureka,* 34). Reflecting these patterns, Melanie's arrival in Bodega Bay manifests a repulsive response from Annie, Lydia, and others. Melanie's obvious charms elicit jealous suspicion from Annie, while her notoriety ("jumping naked into fountains") puts Lydia off. From this perspective, the bird attacks function as a violent chorus, or objective correlative reflecting the intensity of the repulsive forces unleashed. While such a relation between the bird attacks and character tensions has been recognized before, *Eureka* reminds us that the repulsive forces are only part of a larger narrative cycle:

> The repulsion, already considered as so peculiarly limited in other regards, must be understood, let me repeat, as having power to prevent absolute coalition, *only to a certain epoch.* Unless we are to conceive that the appetite for Unity among the atoms is doomed to be satisfied never; unless we are to conceive that what had a beginning is to have no end—a conception which cannot *really* be entertained, however much we may talk or dream of entertaining it—we are forced to conclude that the repulsive influence imagined will, finally, under pressure of the Unitendency . . . shall be the superior force . . . and thus permit the universal subsidence into the inevitable, because original and therefore normal, *One.*
>
> (*Eureka,* 32)

Here Poe explains the narrative (as well as physical) logic underlying "God's plot," suggesting that the diffusive power eventually must dissipate and allow the fragments to reunite. Susan Lurie's psychoanalytic perspective shortsightedly emphasizes the negative implications in which, so to speak, the diffusions taking place in the film involve "the disenfranchising and exorcism of the mother, the placement of the desired woman in the place of the helpless child, the punishing of female desire, [and] the mutilation of the love object."[18] However, the cyclical Eurekan structure suggests that the process of reunification is equally evident as barriers between Melanie and Mitch, Annie, and Lydia successively break down, a process finally completed by the end of the bird attacks. Hence the complex dynamic in the film involves simultaneous attraction and repulsion of characters that builds to the apocalyptic climax. As detailed in the biblical prophecies, the film reflects the ultimately positive apocalyptic purposes.

The visual and situational details in *The Birds*, as in **"Masque,"** echo the Bible to reinforce its apocalyptic themes. As in **"Masque,"** *The Birds* reflects Joel's prophecy of "wonders in the heavens, and in the earth, blood, and fire, and pillars of smoke" (Joel 2:30). These images are particularly evident during the mass attack on the town, as we become front-row witnesses of the horror unleashed by the apocalyptic chaos of the birds: several fires, smoke, uncontrolled horses, cars, and fire hoses, and a bloodied man unsuccessfully trying to defend himself from attacking birds. Other scenes from the film continue these images, including the smoke on the horizon Mitch and Melanie see as they board up the house, the fire seen from the bird's-eye view, and the blood graphically lining the dead Annie's face, running from Dan Fawcett's empty eye sockets, oozing from Mitch's embattled hands, and staining Melanie's once patrician face. The work of the Red Death, then, becomes that of the birds breaking through windows, pecking at wooden doors, attacking with vicious determination (Rev 6:17). They seem the very embodiment of the "vengeance" Isaiah notes as the divine motive for destroying the world (Isa 34:8), particularly considering Hitchcock's hints that the bird attacks were some sort of revenge on mankind by nature.

One of the most overtly apocalyptic sequences in the film comes during the attacks on the school and town. In both attacks the visual emphasis on the birds massing, scattering, and attacking suggests the work of the seven angels characterizing the "day of the Lord's vengeance." In the Bible, angels are God's ministers of divine and terrible justice, swooping down with plagues of fire, smoke, blood, destroying trees, grass, waters, and people as directed (Rev 16). The fact that Melanie is unaware of the birds massing in the schoolyard affirms the Bible's theme of how the destruction at the end of the world will be an unpleasant surprise, coming as a thief in the night. As the birds gather on the jungle gym and later high above Bodega Bay, like the biblical

angels they seem to be operating with purpose "out of the temple which is in heaven" with a "sharp sickle" to reap the earth (Rev 14:15-17). The ensuing attack on the running children, and later on the town, is the very image of prophesied destruction:

> And I saw an angel standing in the sun; and he cried with a loud voice, saying to all the fowls that fly in the midst of heaven, Come and gather yourselves together unto the supper of the great God.
>
> That ye may eat the flesh of kings, and the flesh of captains, and the flesh of mighty men.
>
> (Rev 19:17-18)

As the birds again begin to reap, they instill so much irrational fear in Melanie that she runs outside the safety of the café to seek shelter in an exposed phone booth. Like a diver in a shark cage, Melanie should have a perfect view of the total breakdown of order surrounding her. But her vision blurs as the hose splashes on the glass, obscuring the chaos surrounding her. Melanie's panic is shown in shots of her twisting frantically in the phone booth as if in a trap. Finally, Mitch takes Melanie back inside the café where the once complacent Bodega folk are in shock, again in fulfillment of Isaiah who prophesied that "the haughtiness of men shall be made low" (Isa 2:17). This is particularly true of Mrs. Bundy, whose scientific arrogance has been reduced to ashes. Following these scenes, Melanie and the Brenners hole up in their farmhouse and seem alone in the world, the film becoming the simple survival drama Daphne du Maurier originally wrote. Hiding in their boarded-up house, terrified and helpless, these survivors hide from the bird plague as best they can, echoing Prospero and his courtiers: "they shall go into the holes of the rocks, and into the caves of the earth, for fear of the Lord . . . when he ariseth to shake terribly the earth" (Isa 2:19).[19] Fittingly, at its fall, Babylon is described as "a cage of every unclean and hateful bird" (Rev 18:2). The bird attacks, which come as unexpectedly as "thieves in the night" also follow apocalyptic numerical protocol as there are seven attacks that we actually see in the film.

Melanie Daniels's prophetic surname and ambiguous characterization especially invokes association with biblical imagery. "Choked with her riches and pleasures" (Luke 8:14), living the idle and useless life of a rich playgirl, Melanie is identifiable allegorically as the whore of Babylon (Rev 17).[20] Lydia, referring to her as a "girl like that" whose name can't be kept out of the news, informs Mitch of Melanie's jumping into a fountain in Rome: "the newspapers said she was naked." Like the "great whore," Melanie "sitteth upon many waters" (Rev 17:1) as she rides in a motorboat and hails from that "city by the bay." In admitting to Mitch that she ran around with a "pretty wild crowd" and that "it was easy to get lost" in Rome, she confesses her sexual freedom, among the most damning sins of the great whore (Rev 17:2). While Melanie is not arrayed in scarlet and purple and an abundance of precious stones (Rev 17:4), she does dress luxuriously, flaunting a fur coat and driving an expensive sports car. And as for dwelling on "seven mountains" (Rev 17:9), hilly San Francisco becomes a suitable California stand-in for Babylon, making her a worldly outsider in the small coastal hamlet. Like the daughters of Zion in the last days, Melanie too seems "haughty, and walk[s] with stretched forth neck and wanton eyes, walking and mincing as [she] go[es]" (Isa 3:16). While many citizens of Bodega Bay eye her with wonder, if not suspicion, the hysterical woman in the café virtually equates Melanie with wickedness:

> Why are they doing this? They say when you got here the whole thing started. Who are you? What are you? Where did you come from? I think you are the cause of all this. I think you're evil! EVIL![21]

Melanie certainly functions as a harbinger of evil. Linked to the bird attacks, she is often the first to notice impending attacks (she is the first person attacked in the film, she sees the first sparrow in the fireplace, she is one of the first to see the birds attacking the schoolchildren, she is the one who notices the seagull outside the café, and she is the one to notice the noise in the attic that leads her upstairs).[22] The other shocked people huddled in the back hall of the café during the bird attack and look fearfully and suspiciously at Melanie. Finally, in becoming the last victim of the birds, like her biblical counterpart, Melanie is brought down in "torment" (Rev 18:9-10). She who was the epitome of wealth and elegance, and haughtiness, becomes a helpless and bloody catatonic, as it were, smitten "with a scab," as Isaiah warns (3:17). If Melanie isn't really as bad as the targets of biblical prophecies, she is an ambiguous figure for the audience, one with whom it is difficult to identify. Perhaps we, like Lydia, are not reconciled to her until her purifying "final ordeal" dismantles all artifice, making her helpless and in need of care and love. Like the Red Death, Melanie, a mysterious stranger, is associated with the plague and is accused of being responsible for it.

Unlike Poe's **"Masque,"** which ends as "Darkness and Decay and the Red Death [hold] illimitable dominion over all," Hitchcock's apocalypse offers light and hope, a millennial aftermath to follow the apocalyptic terrors: "for a small moment have I forsaken thee," yet "with great mercies will I gather thee" (Isa 54:7). Hitchcock, like God, literally provides "a highway" by which Melanie and the Brenners escape (Isa 11:16). The Brenners' situation, to all appearances, fulfills other prophecies that finally the "inhabitants of the earth will be burned and there will be few men left" (Isa 24:6)—at least we only see a few in the end as the "the earth is at rest and is quiet" (Isa 14:7). While **"Masque"** ends in the silence of death, *The Birds* ends in the silence of relief and possible rebirth. These hopeful millennial suggestions, which are most strongly alluded to at the end of the film, are supported throughout with humor.

Many readings of Hitchcock's *The Birds* present the gulf between the light (human relationships) and dark elements (bird attacks) of the film as supporting evidence for the view that meaninglessness itself is the point, despairing of further interpretive precision.[23] I argue, however, that comic and horrific apocalyptic elements in *The Birds* form a complete fabric of tonal and thematic dissonance that is resolved in the film's generally positive conclusion. These dissonances include the quotidian and the fantastic, love and hate between Mitch and Melanie ("I loathe you"), peaceful lovebirds and attack birds, and the ambiguous double aspects of Lydia's motives and Melanie's role. Perhaps most jarring of all is the tonal dissonance between humor and horror, which echoes the other ambiguities. On the eve of the shoot, after evaluating the script, Victor Pritchett expressed to Hitchcock some reservations about tone, arguing that "a light comedy and a terror tale . . . do not weld together."[24] Despite Pritchett's objections, Hitchcock maintained this dissonance as a central, if problematical, aspect of the film's design.

Despite interruptions of horrific and shocking violence, *The Birds* has a pervasive comic tone. Not only are there the famous set pieces like the leaning lovebirds in Melanie's car and the comic prophet in the café ("It's the end of the world!"), but the film is populated with minor comic actors like Ruth McDevitt (bird shop owner), Richard Deacon (man in the elevator), Doodles Weaver (boat rental man), and John McGovern (the gently perplexed general store proprietor). These character actors appeared most often in light television and Disney movies and provided a light and reassuring feel to much of the film despite its horrific sequences. However, they also make viewing the film an unsettling experience. This blend of comic and horrific elements gives the film an artificial quality, a constant reminder that as Hitchcock once reassured Ingrid Bergman, "It's only a movie." Not only is the comedy undercut by the violence, but the violence is undercut by the comedy, exemplified in the absurd trio of still reaction shots of Melanie interspersed with shots of fire following a gas trail toward the inevitable explosion. As an audience we don't know how to interpret such a construction of images, except that it defies our expectations of both comedy and horror. Hitchcock's trailer for the film, whatever its weaknesses may be, captures this strange blend of comedy and horror, as his television introductions had (in relation to the somber events in the teleplays themselves), and indicate how basic his British black humor is to the effect he is after. Accompanied by a light comic score, Hitchcock describes the history of bird abuse at length until he is interrupted by the ominous sounds of birds and a terrified Tippi Hedren scrambling into the room warning that the birds (*The Birds*) are coming.[25]

Melanie is an important focus for the dissonances in the film between humor and horror, creating further audience uncertainty through the unlikely blend of her characterization. As the shallow playgirl with an identity crisis, her lightly notorious reputation and antics little support the apocalyptic weight her character is called to carry in the film. She is presented at first in San Francisco as a comic heroine straight out of a 1930s romantic comedy, leading to what soon becomes a comedy of manners when she arrives as a most unlikely and overdressed visitor to unglamorous Bodega Bay.[26] This in uneasy contrast to her role as the mysterious stranger figure and "evil" harbinger of the bird attacks connected to the most horrific aspects of the film. But if Melanie seems an unlikely plague, so Bodega Bay itself is a comic reduction of Babylon with its less-than-evil complacency.[27]

Hitchcock's black humor is also expressed through visually amusing aspects of the bird attacks themselves. These anomalies complicate our experience as an audience, creating guilty glee in our enjoyment at the secret jokes Hitchcock almost whispers at us during scenes that are horrifying and funny simultaneously. There is the little girl under the fence mechanically kicking her legs with a gull on her neck at Cathy's party, the obviously fake terror of the child actors being chased by birds from the school, the bird-oppressed man approaching Melanie in the phone booth, and the mime terror of Melanie, Lydia, and Cathy during the climactic attack on the Brenner home. Paglia notes humor at the end of Melanie's final ordeal as Mitch pulls her out of the room: "Comically disappearing last from view are her high heels: it's the last dance for the wily witch of the West."[28] This element of the fun Hitchcock is obviously having as he annihilates Bodega Bay punctuates the film's fictionality, itself a reassuring gesture. This is Hitchcock's comic relief, a variation on Roger's and Eve's repartee while precariously hanging from Mount Rushmore in *North by Northwest*. Just as Hitchcock told us "don't worry, the birds are coming" with his preattack bird scenes, so his black humor reminds us not to worry, all will turn out right in the end.

In terms of the apocalyptic dismantling of film conventions, this audience dilemma between humor and horror is a powerful element in the viewing experience. The audience situation finds an objective correlative in Melanie's phone booth ordeal. While she is trapped in the phone booth, her vision is obscured, first by a flailing fire hose and then by birds smashing into the glass.[29] The high-angle shots of her twisting and turning in the booth, vainly seeking a way out, suggests the cinematic

cage in which Hitchcock has placed his audience, preventing our access into the film, either through its character, action, or tone. This image of twisting and turning, echoed by the flailing fire hose and foreshadowed by the winding road that Melanie takes to Bodega Bay, is further echoed when Melanie twists out of her seat and into the lamp during the major bird attack on the Brenner home. During that sequence, of course, the birds can be heard but not seen. Her vision is finally ended during her "final ordeal" in the upstairs room, leaving her eyes, ironically, wide open but blind. Like the audience, she is in a state of shock, no longer able to see, or guess, what comes next. These scenes remind us of Burke's sublime in terms of "obscurity," the terror of darkness, confusion, isolation, and a sense of helplessness, and "difficulty," being caught in an extremely complex and overwhelming predicament. Such states of mind describe the condition the characters and audience increasingly feel as the film relentlessly unfolds.

The film's apocalyptic dissonances are resolved in the hopeful imagery at the end of the film: the clouds are parted by a dawning sun, the family escapes the birds, and the camera focuses in on the lovebirds that Cathy insists on bringing along. These are all signs of peace—like the dove after Noah's flood. As Hitchcock himself notes, "love is going to survive the whole ordeal" and "that little couple of lovebirds lends an optimistic note to the theme."[30] The dove, which also becomes a sign of the Holy Ghost at Christ's baptism, is the ultimate lovebird and symbol of rebirth. Donald Spoto's claim that the film "simply stops" inconclusively is akin to choosing the least plausible of Hawthorne's multiple endings.[31] The ending is vintage Hitchcock, though more implicitly rendered. That it coincides with Hitchcock's thinking is shown by the two rejected endings that would have suggested no narrative ending. The first, the original ending in the screenplay, has the car being attacked by birds as the Brenner group leaves town. The second has the group arrive in San Francisco to discover the Golden Gate Bridge covered with birds. Hitchcock rejected that temptingly spectacular shot for relative narrative coherence. It simply was not a Hitchcock ending to leave the world and his characters in perpetual chaos (though he often flirted with the idea). His *Eureka*-like pattern, reiterated by Lesley Brill, is one of "loss, search, recovery," providing "the deep structure for . . . all Hitchcock's films."[32] Despite the seeming incompleteness of the ending's resolution, as Jean Douchet puts it, "for [Hitchcock] creation depends on an exact science of the spectator's reaction . . . [because] he attributes a mission to 'suspense.' And this mission is cathartic."[33] The sublime is achieved in powerfully depicting survival in the midst of the relentless horror that still seems present as the soundtrack increases the bird sounds. Despite their still apparent terror, they move forward united and healed. Whether the birds will continue to attack or not is beside the point.

The characters have survived intact, emotionally and psychologically. As Hitchcock once remarked about *The Birds,* "I believe that when people rise to the occasion, when catastrophe comes, they are all right."[34] While the characters find millennial peace at the film's end (at least internally), the audience can bask in the comfort of a relatively happy ending, restoring the faith in the Hollywood narrative Hitchcock temporarily upended.

Notes

1. Edgar Allan Poe, *Eureka: A Prose Poem* (New York: Prometheus, 1997), 28.

2. See Douglas Robinson, *American Apocalypses: The Image of the End of the World in American Literature* (Baltimore: Johns Hopkins University Press, 1985), xii.

3. Richard Wilbur, "The House of Poe," in *The Recognition of Edgar Allan Poe: Selected Criticism Since 1829,* ed. Eric W. Carlson (Ann Arbor: University of Michigan Press, 1970), 254-77.

4. G. R. Thompson, *Poe's Fiction: Romantic Irony in the Gothic Tales* (Madison: University of Wisconsin Press, 1973), xi.

5. Peter Bogdanovich, *The Cinema of Alfred Hitchcock* (New York: Museum of Modern Art, 1963), 44.

6. Christopher Sharrett, "The Myth of Apocalypse and the Horror Film: The Primacy of *Psycho* and *The Birds,*" Hitchcock Annual, 1995-1996, 42.

7. Thomas Leitch, *Find the Director and Other Hitchcock Games* (Athens: University of Georgia Press, 1991), 226.

8. Feminist assessments of the film suggest that its message is clearly negative, going back to the hostility among the female characters and apparent punishment of Melanie by the film for her moral shortcomings. Critics from more traditional perspectives discuss the film in terms of difficulties of analysis and find it mostly ambiguous. Some find the ending hopeful of healing, while others hover between one position and another. Thus the majority find the film negative, or at best, ambiguous.

9. Camille Paglia notes that "God plays no role in this film" (33) and that through the drunk in the Tides Café the "providential view of the birds as agents of wrathful supernatural power is satirized" (71). Yet the evidence of biblical echoes must be accounted for, particularly given Hitchcock's upbringing (*The Birds* [London: BFI, 1998]). I agree that Hitchcock is making no overtly religious statement through these images; however, such images subliminally raise emotional alarms, adding substantially to the sense of global disaster.

10. JoAnn James, introduction to *Apocalyptic Visions Past and Present,* eds. JoAnn James and William J. Cloonan (Tallahassee: Florida State University Press, 1988), 2.

11. Susan Sontag, "The Imagination of Disaster," in *Against Interpretation and Other Essays* (New York: Noonday, 1966), 224.

12. See Sandra L. Zimdars-Swartz and Paul F. Zimdars-Swartz, "Apocalypticism in Modern Western Europe," in *Encyclopedia of Apocalypticism,* ed. Stephen J. Stein (New York: Continuum, 1998), 13:265-92.

13. See Stephen D. O'Leary, "Popular Culture and Apocalypticism," in *The Encyclopedia of Apocalypticism,* ed. Stephen J. Stein (New York: Continuum, 1998), 3:392-426.

14. Peter Biskind, *Seeing Is Believing: How Hollywood Taught Us to Stop Worrying and Love the Fifties* (New York: Pantheon, 1983), 102. Both Paglia and David Sterritt (*The Films of Alfred Hitchcock* [Cambridge: Cambridge University Press, 1993]) have noted where *The Birds* echoes science fiction films of the 1950s. Paglia compares Hedren's movements during the house attack to "the generic gal-turned-to-jelly of 50s screamer flicks, where women were always being delectably stalked by . . . space aliens" (80). Sterritt compares the shot of Annie and Melanie looking out at the night sky to "a shot that might have come from a science-fiction epic of the 1950s" (127).

15. Patrick Cheney, "Poe's Use of *The Tempest* and the Bible in 'The Masque of the Red Death,'" *English Language Notes* 20, no. 3-4 (1983): 32.

16. Brett Zimmerman sees "Masque" as an architectural allegory of a clock with the seven rooms forming a half circle—like half of a clock face. "Allegory and Clock Architecture in Poe's 'The Masque of the Red Death,'" *Essays in Arts and Sciences,* October 2000, 1-16.

17. There is another suggestion of Poe's use of Revelation, as well as Ezekiel, for his apocalyptic tales in "Shadow." Not only are there seven characters hold up against the plague, but at the end of the tale the voice of the shadow speaks "not the tones of any one being, but of a multitude of beings" (206). This emphasis on the power and dimensionality of the voice echoes John's description of Christ's powerful voice "as the sound of many waters" (Rev 1:15). In Ezekiel the prophet refers to the voice of the "Almighty . . . as the noise of an host" (1:24).

18. Susan Lurie, "The Construction of the 'Castrated Woman' in Psychoanalysis and Cinema," *Discourse* 4 (1981): 61.

19. While Robin Wood (*Hitchcock's Films Revisited* [New York: Columbia University Press, 1989], 161) denies that it is reasonable to correlate the mild weaknesses of the characters with bird attacks, I argue that the attacks suggest at least the potential for guilt to an audience reared in a biblical tradition that associates punishment with sin (as riches suggest God's favor).

20. Theodore Price, *Hitchcock and Homosexuality: His 50-Year Obsession with Jack the Ripper and the Superbitch Prostitute—A Psychoanalytic View* (Metuchen, N.J.: Scarecrow, 1992), 191, 199, calls Melanie a "virgin-whore" in his taxonomy of Hitchcock female types and notes that Hitchcock's calling her a "fly-by-night" is equivalent to prostitute in British slang.

21. In "Lost in the Wood," *Film Comment* 8, no. 4 (1972): 51, George Kaplan (a.k.a. Robin Wood) suggests that the hysterical woman's outburst at the camera represents a message to the audience as much as to Melanie. While Wood doesn't note this, Hitchcock may have gotten the idea from Don Siegal's 1956 *Invasion of the Body Snatchers* where Kevin McCarthy screams "You're next! You're next!" hysterically at the camera. The comparison works thematically as well, since *Invasion* is another apocalyptic film about identity and nightmarish fears, which also unsettlingly involves audiences.

22. Paglia notices that whatever "communicable disease" is keeping the chickens from eating, Melanie "is what's really going around Bodega Bay!" (43).

23. Leitch, for example, suggests the attacks are a "gag" in their unrelatedness to the film's human drama (*Find the Director,* 229).

24. Quoted in Robert E. Kapsis, "Hollywood Filmmaking and Reputation Building: Hitchcock's *The Birds,*" *Journal of Popular Film and Television* 15, no. 1 (1987): 8.

25. However, our identification problems with Melanie go deeper still. While Hitchcock took great pains to encourage identification between his new star and his audience, the results are mixed. In terms of one Hollywood genre convention, Hitchcock modifies the traditional monster movie of the 1950s by undercutting traditional authority figures—cops and docs (to use Peter Biskind's terms). He revises science fiction as he had suspense films earlier (using appealing villains, daylight settings, guilt transference, etc.). In science fiction of the 1950s, conservative films make military men (cops) the heroes, while liberally oriented films make scientists (docs) the heroes. In *The Birds,* neither type prevails. The "scientist" in this film is an eccentric old woman who is blind to the idea of bird attacks ("Ridiculous!") while the local sheriff is a head-scratching hick who is equally clueless ("That's a sparrow, all right"). Though no official military types are evident, the hawkish businessman who suggests that they "get themselves guns and wipe [the birds] off the face of the earth," he is corrected by Mrs. Bundy: "that would hardly be possible [since] the five continents of the world probably contain over a hundred billion birds." Thus a military approach is also rendered futile. Further modifying clichés, the ambiguous "heroine" is not ultimately protected from the "monster," the "hero" leaving her to face the birds alone in the end. But this subtextual deconstruction of science fiction is only a side joke next to the dismantling of the overall structure of characters and narrative logic. Despite Hedren's obvious talent and potential, she doesn't garner immediate audience sympathy and identification reserved for major stars like Grace Kelly or Audrey Hepburn, either of whom would have made *The Birds* a very different film. Audiences would have easily warmed up to them, despite the playgirl persona, as audiences did with the shallow Cary Grant character in *North by Northwest.* With Hedren audiences are being asked to identify with a woman who is subtextually identified with the whore of Babylon, placing us in the same dilemma as the citizens of Bodega Bay—we are wary and suspicious. Her negative aspects stain her comic persona, causing the audience to see her double—wanting to identify with her (since she is practically in every shot and it is through her we see the action unfold) but unable to do so wholeheartedly.

26. Raymond Durgnat, *The Strange Case of Alfred Hitchcock, or the Plain Man's Hitchcock* (London: Faber & Faber, 1974), 334-35, compares these scenes to Ernst Lubisch comedy.

27. See Kapsis, "Hollywood Filmaking," 9-10, on Hitchcock's concerns about audience reception of Hedren and steps taken to get audiences to "warm up" to her.

28. Paglia, 84.

29. See Bill Nichols, "*The Birds*: At the Window," *Film Reader* 4 (1979), in which he describes how the audience perspective is aligned with Melanie's point of view.

30. Truffaut, *Hitchcock,* 218.

31. Donald Spoto, *The Art of Alfred Hitchcock: Fifty Years of His Motion Pictures* (New York: Anchor, 1992), 332.

32. *The Hitchcock Romance: Love and Irony in Hitchcock's Films* (Princeton: Princeton University Press, 1988), 4. While *The Birds* is not the clearest instance of the romance pattern Brill identifies in Hitchcock's films, yet, as in *North by Northwest,* Mitch and Melanie "are alienated, uncertain of their identities, and in need of mates. Each for the other fills voids and ends idleness" (21).

33. Jean Douchet, "Hitch and his Public," trans. Verena Conley, in *A Hitchcock Reader,* eds. Marshall Deutelbaum and Leland Poague (Ames: Iowa State University Press, 1986), 7.

34. Quoted in Bogdanovich, *Cinema of Alfred Hitchcock,* 44.

Annotated Bibliography of Poe and Hitchcock Connections

This annotated bibliography cites scholarship that in some way links the work of Edgar Allan Poe and Alfred Hitchcock, with articles ranging from passing mentions to detailed examinations of particular thematic or theoretical connections. These comments and criticisms were written between 1957 and 2000, with many having been published during the 1990s. Hitchcock scholars have become increasingly aware of Poe's importance in Hitchcock's creative imagination.

Parts of this bibliography are reprinted by the kind permission of *Hitchcock Annual* (2000-2001) and *Poe Studies Newsletter* (Fall 1999).

Paglia, Camille. *The Birds.* London: BFI Film Classics, 1998. Comparing the film to du Maurier's original story, she notes that hers, "unlike Hitchcock's, ends in intimations of catastrophe as sweeping as the carnage wrought by Poe's Red Death" (p. 10).

Price, Theodore. *Hitchcock and Homosexuality: His 50-Year Obsession with Jack the Ripper and the Superbitch Prostitute: A Psychoanalytic View.* Metuchen, N.J.: Scarecrow, 1992. In developing a psychoanalytic reading of Hitchcock, Price refers to how Freud's family romance themes in the films are hidden in the open as in Poe's "Purloined Letter." He also refers to Bonaparte's study of Poe in discussing the psychoanalytic view of crime and its relation to Hitchcock.

Spoto, Donald. *The Art of Alfred Hitchcock: Fifty Years of His Motion Pictures.* 2d ed. New York: Anchor, 1992. In his revised edition Spoto adds a passing reference to "William Wilson" in explaining the theme of the double in *Strangers on a Train.*

Sterritt, David. *The Films of Alfred Hitchcock.* Cambridge: Cambridge University Press, 1993. Sterritt notes that Marian Crane hides her stolen money in the Bates' motel in plain sight "a la Poe's 'The Purloined Letter.'"

Truffaut, Francois. *Hitchcock.* New York: Touchstone, 1967. In the introduction to his lengthy series of interviews with Hitchcock, Truffaut states that "Hitchcock belongs—and why classify him at all?—among such artists of anxiety as Kafka, Dostoyevsky, and Poe" (p. 15).

Jeffrey J. Folks (essay date spring 2005)

SOURCE: Folks, Jeffrey J. "Edgar Allan Poe and Elias Canetti: Illuminating the Sources of Terror." *Southern Literary Journal* 37, no. 2 (spring 2005): 1-16.

[*In the following excerpt, Folks concentrates on Elias Canetti's study of crowd psychology in* Crowds and Power *as it pertains to the paranoia, terror, and courage of the revelers in "The Masque of the Red Death."*]

In *The Torch in My Ear,* the second volume of his four-volume autobiography, Elias Canetti recounts an episode from his university days in which he passed an uneasy morning in chemistry laboratory with a fellow student, Eva Reichmann: "I talked about a book I had started reading the day before: Poe's tales. She didn't know them, and I told her about one, **'The Telltale Heart,'** which had really terrified me. . . . I tried to free myself of this terror by repeating the story to her" (191). In seeking to dispel the terror generated by reading Poe's tale, Canetti turns to another human being and attempts to relieve his uneasiness by communicating his frightening experience to her as they seek to analyze his fears. In its approach of uncovering and dispelling the sources of terror in human relations, the episode points toward the long and distinguished career that Canetti would enjoy, not as a chemist but as novelist, playwright, literary critic, autobiographer, and, most importantly, as author of *Crowds and Power,* the most authoritative and original of modern treatises on crowd psychology.[1]

It is hardly coincidental that Canetti should have been struck so forcefully by the writing of Edgar Allan Poe, for there is a remarkable sense in Poe's tales of a writer who anticipated many of Canetti's insights. The fact that literature is, among other things, the record of instinctual crowd behavior was apparent to Canetti at a very early point in his life, and the affinity that Canetti perceived between his and Poe's interests is connected with a life-long effort to explain and to ameliorate the destructive potential of mass behavior. In Canetti's mind, the Holocaust was the culmination of a long history of unfaced and unresolved fear. This history, characterized by increasingly tyrannical forms of control, involved precisely those psychological terrors that Poe focused on: the sense that the world was increasingly dominated by accidental forces beyond comprehension and, in response, the rise of increasingly authoritarian conceptions of history and social order. As a result, the central focus for both writers was nothing less than the fear of annihilation.

Elias Canetti's classic work, *Crowds and Power,* is a detailed analysis of the patterns of crowd behavior and of the ways in which individuals relate psychologically to crowds. Canetti begins his analysis with a classification of different crowd types under such headings as crowd flight, prohibition, and doubling. A second major section of the work analyzes the existence of the pack, a smaller and more primitive unit that anticipated the development of the crowd in civilization. Canetti then turns to the effects of the crowd in human history, with particular emphasis on the violence of the Holocaust. He studies the primitive human instincts that anticipate modern power, and he traces the rise of what he terms the "survivor," the paranoiac leader obsessed with absolute command of others. Canetti follows this analysis of the survivor with a more detailed examination of the workings of power, carefully analyzing the ways in which commands are issued and received. He also studies transformation of crowd types and psychological identification with these types. Canetti, finally, concludes with a dissection of power and an analysis of the tendency toward paranoia in rulers.

In Canetti's sympathetic reading of Poe, he intuitively focuses on the terrifying elements of fear and isolation that Poe projects. Poe's writing evinces a profound psychological intuition concerning the instinct for power underlying social relationships, particularly those relationships involving postures of dominance or victimization.

. . . . .

Like the narrator at the end of **"Usher"** [**"The Fall of the House of Usher"**], the protagonist of **"The Masque of the Red Death"** flees the site of cataclysm—in this case, an epidemic.[2] Transporting a thousand members of his court with him to a series of chambers resembling a burial vault, Prospero intends to guarantee his own survival, not that of his subjects. The court is necessary only as an echo to Prospero's rule: he summons a "thousand" (a number, Canetti points out, indicative of a stage toward the ultimate goal of the ruler—to survive "millions" and ultimately "all") to join him in "deep seclusion" within one of his castellated abbeys (485). Here the group finds apparent security, but a question remains as to why the group must engage in revelry at a time when masses of their countrymen are dying. Why should Prospero entertain his friends at a magnificent masked ball, if not to celebrate his own survival over the dead who lie without the abbey?

The scene of the revels suggests the paranoiac's familiar compulsion to control space. Prospero carefully selects the color and decoration of each of seven rooms, ranging from the eastern blue room, through purple, green, orange, white, violet, and finally the western black room that is fitted with window panes of scarlet

and the light of a fire projecting its rays—another instance of the image of a hostile microscopic crowd that haunts the survivor's mind. Though each room is lighted by a tripod bearing a brazier of fire, the horrifying rays in the west room must pass through blood-tinted panes of glass. Also in the west room, a gigantic "clock of ebony" suggests another crowd—that of hours, minutes, and even seconds—hostile to one who values his own survival above all (487). When the clock strikes the hour, all activity ceases: the orchestra is silenced and the dancers are paralyzed by the clock's reminder of a greater power than that of Prospero, a fact that the narrator makes explicit by converting the hour into three thousand and six hundred seconds.[3]

Like the Roman emperors whom Canetti recounts, Prospero directs every detail of his fete: his guiding taste controls the celebration, combining elements of the "beautiful," the "wanton," the "bizarre," the "terrible," and much that "might have excited disgust" (487-488). This explicit comment invites consideration. Poe's list of Prospero's concerns suggests the aspiration of the paranoiac toward "enlargement" and control, as does the "multitude of dreams" that stalk to and fro among the seven chambers (488). Are these actual impersonators of dreams, masked and sent through the room at Prospero's command to mystify and thus control the guests, or are they insubstantial forms that the narrator only senses? In either case, they are powerful enough to control the orchestra, which plays as an "echo" of their moods, much as the crowd echoes Prospero.

Prospero's instinctive reaction to the masked figure is that of the paranoiac confronted by a rival whose masking appears to mock the secrecy that all rulers take on. The masked figure further offends the crowd, striking it with a sort of blow as he "impersonates" the Red Death. Poe writes, "There are chords in the heart of the most reckless which cannot be touched without emotion. Even with the utterly lost, to whom life and death are both jest, there are matters of which no jest can be made" (489). The figure, dressed in black shrouds, wears the mask of a "stiffened corpse," and his form is dabbled with blood to suggest the Red Death (489). The figure passes unimpeded within a yard of Prospero, as if to violate the ruler's space, then makes his way "with the same solemn and measured step" through each of the chambers until he stands on the threshold of the last (490). At this point Prospero, either recovering from his cowardice or embracing his doom, rushes, dagger drawn, at the masked figure. As he approaches his rival, Prospero drops his dagger and falls dead to the carpet.

Why is it that at this moment the crowd recovers its courage? Perhaps it is not so much that it wishes to rescue its endangered leader as that it senses the sudden relaxation of Prospero's authority. With "the wild courage of despair" the group rushes into the last apartment and seizes the insubstantial figure, its black attire and mask falling to the ground (490). The crowd not only realizes that it is in the presence of the Red Death: perhaps more important, the victim that it seeks in exchange for its own murdered king slips beyond the crowd's vengeance. The body of the enemy, the most important object to the vengeance pack, has evaded its grasp. The crowd's terror lies not simply in its awareness that its members are in the presence of a contagious disease; it also results from their failure to secure the body of the enemy which might assure their own increase. The fundamental instinct of grasping, seizing, and incorporating (their intention of "slaying death" and "cannibalizing" it) has been frustrated (490). Poe uses a familiar simile to characterize the figure of the Red Death: he has come "like a thief in the night" (490). Indeed, in Canetti's terms, the figure is a "thief" depriving the crowd of the victim's body that is its right.

In a broader sense, **"The Masque of the Red Death"** speaks of what is most threatening to the crowd, the threat to the group's own survival that it attaches to any threat to the figure of its king. The equation of increase with survival explains the central role of "Prospero" (his very name suggesting increase) in throwing a revel at the very time when death surrounds his group of followers. The consumption of food and drink, and the vitality of dance, are mimetic acts designed to preserve the entire court and enlarge its numbers. Equally striking is the fact that, in contrast to the thousand courtiers, the Red Death appears as a single and isolated individual. If the crowd of courtiers possesses strength by virtue of their numbers, the Red Death enjoys greater power by virtue of his "density" and by the absolute secrecy that solitude enables. The masked figure paralyzes the court when he first appears; he proves daunting even to Prospero because of his singleness and density. After all, to the primordial human imagination, the most fearful crowds are the invisible crowds of spirits, and it is these that the pestilence mimics.

The significance of the ebony clock, which forms its own dense crowd of "seconds" resembling the Red Death's crowd of bacilli, is reiterated in the final paragraph, which stresses the gradual ("clock-like") but steady and complete annihilation of the revelers. With the death of the last of these, the clock stops and the flames of the tripods expire. The tripods are ritual hearths on which burnt offerings could be made, but they are also the only source of vital light in the rooms and (as fire) elemental crowd symbols that Prospero employs to invite increase. The extinction of the tripods, coming at the end of the tale, marks the complete victory of the Red Death over Prospero's crowd. As Poe writes in the final passage: "Darkness and decay and the Red Death have illimitable dominion over all" (490).

Poe's stories reveal an author focused on the destructive effects of social isolation and victimization, and on the consequent responses of paranoia and schizophrenia. In his fiction Poe was well aware of the destructive potential of instinctual responses underlying human social relationships. In all human contacts, as Canetti demonstrates, there exists a pervasive fear of exclusion and victimization in response to which humans seek security through the seizing of power, yet this response too often perpetuates the cycle of domination and victimization. An obsession with power leads to the rise of what Canetti calls "the survivor," the tyrannical personality that attempts to secure its survival at the expense of others. For Poe, as for Canetti, only a clear understanding of the instinctive nature of power offers any real hope of transforming human relationships into a healthy form of interaction and of breaking the cycle of fear and repression that governs so much of human existence.

Notes

1. Further evidence exists of the impact of Poe's imagination on Canetti. During the first days of his acquaintance with the woman who would later become his wife, Canetti was introduced to "The Raven." When Vera (Venetia Roubner-Calderou) read the poem aloud, "the bird flew into my nerves; I began to twitch in the rhythm of the poem" (*Torch* 158).

2. Canetti groups epidemics with other phenomena which produce a "heap of corpses": battle, for example, and mass suicide. One result of contagion is the altered psychology of those people who do recover. Those miraculous survivors feel that they have become invulnerable, and they often demonstrate this by aiding the sick and dying. Canetti points to the example in Thucydides' description of the plague in Athens, where those who recovered felt that they might never die of any disease.

3. As Geoffrey Harpham stresses in a valuable reading of "The Masque of the Red Death," the structure of Poe's art itself reveals a profound anxiety concerning survival. As Harpham writes: "Poe's imagination and art flourished at the margin, for only there could he interpose a fiction between himself and a fate impossible to confront directly" (118). Prospero's flight from the plague involves a self-effacement, reducing life to the abstract form of arabesque decoration and the mechanical enumeration of time. Prospero, like many of Poe's characters, seeks "the serenity of pure appearance and impersonality" (120), but he is unsuccessful because he carries with him to his retreat the hidden bacterial source of his destruction. Yet Poe was all too conscious of the futility of Prospero's flight, and much of his art is, as Harpham sug-

gests, self-parodic, "exposing his art, the only means he had of attaining unity, for the ragbag parody of real creation that it was" (120).

Works Cited

Canetti, Elias. *Crowds and Power.* Trans. Carol Stewart. New York: Farrar Straus and Giroux, 1984.

———. *The Torch in My Ear.* Trans. Joachim Neugroschel. New York: Farrar Straus and Giroux, 1992.

Harpham, Geoffrey Galt. *On the Grotesque: Strategies of Contradiction in Art and Literature.* Princeton: Princeton UP, 1982.

Poe, Edgar Allan. *Poetry and Tales.* New York: Library of America, 1984.

FURTHER READING

Criticism

Brown, Christopher. "Poe's 'Masque' and *The Portrait of a Lady.*" *Poe Studies* 14, no. 1 (June 1981): 6-8.

Notes the similar use of restrictive interiors, color schemes, and celebratory masks in Henry James' *The Portrait of a Lady* and "The Masque of the Red Death."

Cary, Richard. "'The Masque of the Red Death' Again." *Nineteenth-Century Fiction* 17, no. 1 (June 1962): 76-8.

Cites an article from an 1839 edition of the New York *Expositor* as a source for "The Masque of the Red Death."

Goodwin, Sarah Webster. "Poe's 'Masque of the Red Death' and the Dance of Death." In *Medievalism in American Culture: Special Studies,* edited by Bernard Rosenthal and Paul E. Szarmach, pp. 17-28. Binghamton, N.Y.: Center for Medieval & Early Renaissance Studies, 1987.

Explores the narrative structure of "The Masque of the Red Death" and medieval sources for the story.

Haugen, Hayley Mitchell, ed. *Readings on the Short Stories of Edgar Allan Poe.* San Diego: Greenhaven Press, 2001, 220 p.

Includes three critical essays on "The Masque of the Red Death."

Additional coverage of Poe's life and career is contained in the following sources published by Thomson Gale: *American Writers*; *American Writers: The Classics,* **Vol. 1;** *American Writers Retrospective Supplement,* **Vol. 2;** *Authors and Artists for Young Adults,* **Vol. 14;** *Beacham's Encyclopedia of Popular Fiction: Biography & Resources,* **Vol. 3;** *Beacham's Guide to Literature for Young Adults,* **Vols. 5, 11;** *Concise Dictionary of American Literary Biography, 1640-1865; Dictionary of Literary Biography,* **Vols. 3, 59, 73, 74, 248, 254;** *DISCovering Authors; DISCovering Authors: British Edition; DISCovering Authors: Canadian Edition; DISCovering Authors Modules: Most-studied Authors* **and** *Poets; DISCovering Authors 3.0; Exploring Poetry; Exploring Short Stories; Gothic Writers: A Gale Critical Companion,* **Vol. 3;** *Literary Movements for Students,* **Vol. 1;** *Literature and Its Times,* **Vol. 2;** *Literature and Its Times Supplement,* **Vol. 1;** *Literature Resource Center; Mystery and Suspense Writers; Nineteenth-Century Literature Criticism,* **Vols. 1, 16, 55, 78, 94, 97, 117;** *Poetry Criticism,* **Vols. 1, 54;** *Poetry for Students,* **Vols. 1, 3, 9;** *Poets: American and British; Reference Guide to American Literature,* **Ed. 4;** *Reference Guide to Short Fiction,* **Ed. 2;** *St. James Guide to Crime & Mystery Writers,* **Vol. 4;** *St. James Guide to Horror, Ghost & Gothic Writers; St. James Guide to Science Fiction Writers,* **Ed. 4;** *Science Fiction Writers,* **Eds. 1, 2;** *Short Stories for Students,* **Vols. 2, 4, 7, 8, 16;** *Short Story Criticism,* **Vols. 1, 22, 34, 35, 54;** *Something About the Author,* **Vol. 23;** *Supernatural Fiction Writers; Twayne's United States Authors; World Literature Criticism; World Poets;* **and** *Writers for Young Adults.*

Michel Tournier
1924-

(Full name Michel Édouard Tournier) French short fiction writer, novelist, essayist, nonfiction writer, and autobiographer.

INTRODUCTION

Tournier's stylistically complex mixture of social critique, symbolism, myth, and realism has been highly influential in post-World War II French literature. Although Tournier is frequently compared to such American authors as John Barth and Thomas Pynchon, his work is often considered more accessible than that of many postmodern writers. His controversial explorations of identity and innocence through representations of sexual deviance and aberrant behavior have earned Tournier some detractors, yet the inventive and imaginative spirit of his stories continues to appeal to new generations of readers.

BIOGRAPHICAL INFORMATION

Tournier was born into a middle-class Parisian household. Tournier was a sickly child, and at the age of four he endured a painful tonsillectomy without anaesthesia. He has viewed the experience as a kind of primitive initiation rite; such rituals became an important theme for his writing in later life. Tournier excelled at theology and German studies, and felt his allegiances torn by the events of World War II. He was equally repulsed by German savagery and French collaboration with the Nazis. After the liberation of France, Tournier studied philosophy in Germany. During this time he occasionally returned to Paris to attend the anthropology lectures of Claude Lévi-Strauss, whose influence is apparent in Tournier's first novel, *Vendredi ou les limbes du Pacifique* (1967; *Friday; or, The Other Island*), in which the author revisits the story of Robinson Crusoe. Tournier eventually abandoned his doctoral studies and found work as an editor at a Parisian publishing house, preparing translations of works by Erich Maria Remarque and other German authors. Tournier also worked as a radio announcer for Europe Numéro Un and hosted the television series *La Chambre noire,* which concerned one of his lifelong passions, photography. His novel *Friday,* which he published at the age of 43, won the Grand Prix du Roman de l'Académie Française, and his second novel, *Le Roi des aulnes* (1970; *The Erl-*

King); also published as *The Ogre*), received the Prix Goncourt. In 1972 Tournier became a member of the prestigious Académie Goncourt, and he was awarded the Légion d'Honneur in 1979. Appearing frequently on French television talk shows, Tournier is a popular public personality and lectures widely in France and Africa.

MAJOR WORKS OF SHORT FICTION

In his essay collection entitled *Le Vol du vampire* (1982), Tournier describes three types of short fiction: the *nouvelle* tells a realistic story; the *fable* imparts a message or moral; and the *conte* combines elements of realism with an ambiguous or symbolic narrative. His first collection of short stories, *Le Coq de bruyère* (1978; *The Fetishist*), consisting of both *contes* and *nouvelles,* explores themes of obsession, sexual ambiguity, and adolescent angst. "Tristan Vox" from this collection borrows from Tournier's experience in the broadcasting industry. In it, an average, middle-aged man hosts a radio program in the persona of Tristan Vox—a debonair ladies' man who receives letters of admiration from his female fans. The broadcaster's wife, aware that Tristan is only a fabrication, nevertheless becomes infatuated with the character, causing the disintegration of their marriage. Rooted in reality, the story also functions as a morality tale denouncing the sin of coveting. "Les Suaires de Véronique" details the physical and psychological destruction of a male model (Hector) by his female photographer (Véronique). In this story, Tournier alludes to Greek mythology and Catholic imagery to explore good and evil, gender roles, and the artistic process. Tournier satirizes the sin of gluttony in "L'Aire du Muguet," which describes an impulsive, overweight truck driver's obsession with a girl named Marinette whom he sees in the countryside beyond a fence. Seeking immediate gratification, the protagonist hastily crosses a toll road to find her and is hit repeatedly by oncoming traffic. "La Jeune Fille et la mort" is about an apathetic, slothful young woman who becomes so bored with life that she plans to kill herself. When fate brings her face-to-face with a functioning guillotine, the ambiguous stroke of luck causes her to die of laughter. Some of the collection's more fantastic stories include "La Famille Adam," a retelling of the biblical creation myth including the story of Cain and Abel, and a modern updating of Charles Perrault's "Tom Thumb" entitled "La Fugue du petit Poucet" ("Tom Thumb's Escape"). "Amandine ou les deux jardins" ("Amandine, or The Two Gardens"), which was also published separately as a novella for children, uses a fairy-tale structure to tell of a young girl's entry into the "garden" of womanhood. Tournier exhibits his penchant for the grotesque in such stories as "Tupik," in which a young boy castrates himself due to his over-identification with women, and "Le Nain rouge" ("The Red Dwarf"), the tale of a circus dwarf whose rage leads to the murder of his mistress and the sexual assault of her husband.

The volume *Sept contes* (1984) contains five of the stories from Tournier's first collection along with two previously published novellas that were written for both a juvenile and adult audience: *Barbedor* (1980) and *Pierrot ou les secrets de la nuit* (1979). *Barbedor* is the tale of a king's search for the bird that stole his beard to make a nest, and *Pierrot ou les secrets de la nuit* concerns a baker who must work at night, yet loves a woman who is afraid of the dark. The seemingly simplistic narratives of each novella disguise such complex metaphysical notions as salvation and the duality of nature. Another collection, *Le Médianoche amoureux* (1989; *The Midnight Love Feast*), is divided between realistic stories and fables. "Pyrotechnie ou la commémoration" deals with the murder of a former officer of the French Resistance by the son of a woman whom the officer chastised. *Angus,* a morally ambiguous, novella-length reworking of Victor Hugo's poem "L'Aigle du casque," adds a folkloric element to the collection.

Some of Tournier's novellas are condensed retellings of his novels. *Vendredi ou la vie sauvage* (1971; *Friday and Robinson: Life on Esperanza Island*), based on his first novel, contemplates returning to the "primitive" existence of Robinson Crusoe as a possible solution to the problems of modern Western civilization. *Les Rois mages* (1983), a simplified version of *Gaspard, Melchior et Balthazar* (1980; *The Four Wise Men*), features three interconnected tales about racial and religious tolerance. One of the author's most notorious novellas, *Gilles et Jeanne* (1983; *Gilles and Jeanne*), mixes history and fiction in its depiction of the relationship between Joan of Arc and Gilles de Rais, a military commander under Joan who was later discovered to be a prolific pedophile and child-murderer.

CRITICAL RECEPTION

Tournier's stories are considered among the finest in modern European literature. Scholars have praised his exploration of gender and sexuality and his imaginative revisions of such disparate texts as the Bible, the poetry of Victor Hugo, and the fairy tales of Charles Perrault. Tournier's interest in photography has prompted many critics to read his stories as meditations on the metaphysical function of the artistic image. His capacity for etymological wordplay and punning is extolled by reviewers, particularly with regard to his reinvigoration of traditional narrative structures. Though many of his stories have been published for children, Tournier's work does not shy away from graphic examples of sexual violence. Many critics find this aspect of his writing to be morally troublesome, yet his ambiguous stance on the darker aspects of human nature has been cited as one of Tournier's unique strengths.

PRINCIPAL WORKS

Short Fiction

Vendredi ou la vie sauvage [*Friday and Robinson: Life on Esperanza Island*] 1971
Amandine ou les deux jardins 1977
Le Coq de bruyère [*The Fetishist and Other Stories*] 1978
La Fugue du petit Poucet 1979
Pierrot ou les secrets de la nuit 1979
Barbedor 1980

Gilles et Jeanne: Récit [*Gilles and Jeanne*] 1983
Les Rois mages 1983
Sept contes 1984
Angus 1988
†*Le Médianoche amoureux: Contes et nouvelles* [*The Midnight Love Feast*] 1989

Other Major Works

Vendredi ou les limbes du Pacifique [*Friday; or, The Other Island*] (novel) 1967
Le Roi des aulnes [*The Erl-King*; also published as *The Ogre*] (novel) 1970
Les Météores [*Gemini*] (novel) 1975
Le Vent paraclet [*The Wind Spirit: An Autobiography*] (autobiography) 1977
Des Clefs et des serrures: Images et proses (nonfiction) 1979
Gaspard, Melchior et Balthazar [*The Four Wise Men*] (novel) 1980
Le Vol du vampire: Notes de lecture (essays) 1982
La Goutte d'or: Roman [*The Golden Droplet*] (novel) 1985
Petites proses (nonfiction) 1986
Le Miroir des idées: Traité [*The Mirror of Ideas*] (nonfiction) 1994
Célébrations: Essais (essays) 1999

*This work contains "La Fugue du petit Poucet" and "Amandine ou les deux jardins," both of which were also published separately.

†This work contains *Angus,* which was first issued in 1988.

CRITICISM

Rachel Edwards (essay date November 1990)

SOURCE: Edwards, Rachel. "Initiation and Menstruation: Michel Tournier's *Amandine ou les deux jardins.*" *Essays in French Literature,* no. 27 (November 1990): 75-90.

[*In the following essay, Edwards suggests that the garden imagery in* Amandine ou les deux jardins *evokes Eden and original sin, and highlights notions of female sexual awakening in the story.*]

In addition to fiction which is obviously for adults, Michel Tournier has also written several short stories or *contes* which have been published for children. However, he insists that he does not write specifically for children: "Je n'écris pas de livres pour enfants, mais il m'arrive de tellement m'appliquer et d'avoir tant de talent que ce que j'écris puisse être lu aussi par les en-

fants. Quand ma plume est moins heureuse, ce qu'elle trace est tout juste bon pour les adultes".[1] This remark is corroborated by the fact that most of his so-called children's stories were originally published as adult literature.[2] It is also clear from what Tournier says, and from the fact that these stories are read by adults and children alike, that the nature of the *conte* is such that it retains its appeal throughout life: a fact which is appreciated by Michel Mansuy when he refers to the stories in **Le Coq de bruyère** as "contes d'enfants pour adultes".[3]

This overall attraction can largely be accounted for by two factors. Firstly, as Tournier informs us, the *conte,* like the myth, can be read on several different levels: as a simple story or as a symbol for deeper, more philosophical meanings. It can therefore hold the attention of different age groups with different interests.[4] Secondly, and perhaps even more importantly, these stories, again like myth, refer us to some fundamental aspect of our existence. This can largely be seen to revolve around the phenomenon of initiation. The *conte* has often been described as reliving, in narrative form, those initiation rituals which belong to our ancient past and which still survive in primitive societies today. In *Rite, roman, initiation,* Simone Vierne contends that "l'initiation touche la question essentielle de la condition humaine, il n'est donc pas surprenant que, du fond de l'inconscient, lorsque les pratiques et les croyances sont abandonnées, elle ressurgisse et s'exprime de façon plus ou moins voilée dans les œuvres littéraires".[5] If this is so we might now suggest that there are two initiations involved. One for the hero or heroine and by assimilation or viscerally another for the reader. The latter therefore participates in the adventure and benefits by what Perrault refers to as the *conte*'s defining feature: its "instructions cachées", to which Tournier refers in *Le Vol du Vampire.*[6]

Vierne, following in the footsteps of Eliade, argues that the initiation rites on which many stories are based comprise a three stage development which centres on death and rebirth:

> Dans toutes les cérémonies de l'initiation [. . .] on peut distinguer trois grandes séquences, d'inégale longueur, la plus fournie étant généralement la seconde, ce qui s'explique étant donné son importance dans l'ensemble du rituel. En effet, la première phase est une préparation à la seconde, la mort initiatique proprement dite. La troisième exprime la nouvelle naissance et son développement varie extrêmement suivant les cultures.
>
> (p. 13)

The symbolic death can take four main forms: literal fainting, a *regressus ad uterum,* a descent into hell or an ascent into heaven. Sometimes more than one form is included in the rite.

This pattern of death and spiritual rebirth is present throughout much of Tournier's fiction. Vierne has read *Vendredi ou les limbes du Pacifique* in these terms. A similar structure is also apparent in **Barbedor,** where the king is rejuvenated and becomes his own heir after a bird steals his beard to make a nest. His quest to find the bird, symbol of heaven, and his ascent up the tree into this heaven, are representative of a trial and a symbolic death which help the process of renewal. Like the Phoenix who is born out of his own ashes, the king is set to be resurrected in this way each time his old self is buried.

Although Tournier's *contes* draw on initiation structures, they also go beyond ritual archetypes in order to challenge the reader who is often forced to reconsider and reassess the stereotypes with which he or she is surrounded in society, and which are seen as the result of natural forces rather than as the consequence of imposed modes of thinking. This is very much apparent in the short story **"L'Aire du Muguet"** which tells of Pierre, the driver of a heavy goods vehicle. Pierre feels the solemnity worthy of an initiation ceremony every time he crosses the toll gate leading onto the motorway. "Aux yeux de Pierre, l'entrée officielle sur l'autoroute revêtait une valeur de cérémonie . . ."[7] He tells his friend Gaston, "T'as changé de monde. T'es dans du nouveau" (p. 269). But the world which Pierre enters, unlike the symbolic heaven of king Barbedor, is a kind of hell, for the motorway is described as "un enfer de bruit et de béton" and as "un long tunnel asphyxiant" (p. 271). Pierre never makes it out of this tunnel into the heavenly countryside he sees behind a fence in "l'aire du Muguet" to meet his shepherdess Marinette who lives nearby. His efforts to make contact with her without having the obstacle of the fence between them result in his being crushed on the carriageway. Pierre's initiation does not lead to resurrection but ends in death (which, according to Plato, is the ultimate initiation). In this way, Tournier ironically reworks, in modern garb, the tale of the gallant knight going to visit his lady. This kind of tale, which has undergone crude modifications since medieval times, has now become clichéd in the type of fiction read by Gaston and it is partly this which Tournier wants to expose. Furthermore, there is a sense in which Pierre belongs to the motorway and therefore to the violence and death which the road symbolizes, rather than to the serene and peaceful countryside which the motorway partly destroyed when it was being built and which it continues to pollute.

Another example of where Tournier draws on the structure of initiation rituals, but challenges us with the content of the tale, this time in a different way, is in **Amandine ou les deux jardins.** Tournier subtitles this story *conte initiatique,* and it is obvious from the straightforward symbolism that Amandine's initiation concerns the onset of menstruation. According to Vierne, initia-tion rites for women are always concerned with puberty and coincide with the first flow of blood. Very little is known about them and it appears that Tournier has used the same structure in this story as the one used in male initiation ceremonies, namely that of preparation, symbolic death and spiritual rebirth. He commented on the role of initiation in **Amandine ou les deux jardins** in an interview, "Le Sang des fillettes", which appeared in *Le Monde* shortly after the story was first published for children.[8] However, my interpretation goes beyond Tournier's commentary and might therefore be seen as an example of how the text, once it leaves the author, preys upon the imagination of the reader in order to create new meanings. Tournier's views on this can be found in *Le Vol du vampire.*[9]

Amandine ou les deux jardins can be seen as an attempt by Tournier to make the potentially traumatic experience of menstruation more accessible and more palatable. This is suggested by the epigraph at the beginning of **Le Coq de bruyère.**

> Au fond de chaque chose, un poisson nage.
> Poisson de peur que tu n'en sortes nu,
> Je te jetterai mon manteau d'images.[10]

The "poisson", in this instance, is menstruation; the story of **Amandine ou les deux jardins** is the "manteau d'images" in which Tournier clothes it, without hiding it completely, so as to make it easier to cope with.

In order to achieve his end, Tournier has chosen one of the most widespread symbols of both art and literature in which to set his story: the garden.[11] The garden is not only a familiar locus but it also has important affinities with initiation.

Although the setting is familiar, the *conte* is nevertheless unusual in that it avoids a typical fairy-tale beginning and is written in the first person by Amandine in the form of a diary. Her activities are recorded on Wednesdays and Sundays. This is presumably because in many schools in France there are no lessons on Wednesday afternoons, nor, of course, on Sundays and this gives Amandine time for other activities.[12] These activities are educational in a way that is not academic. In making Amandine discover what she does in the garden on days when there is no school, Tournier is implying that important learning does not necessarily have to take place in the classroom. In *Le Vent Paraclet,* he bemoans the fact that today education concentrates on teaching the child by means of "information" rather than "initiation". This is a process which, he argues, began in the eighteenth century, when the child, no longer thought of as "une petite bête, sale, vicieuse et stupide", began to be considered as a blank page which merely needed to be filled with useful facts. This change left little place for education by initiation which, in contrast to education by information, concentrates on moral and sentimental formation rather than on learning by facts.[13] According to Tournier, it is essentially a sentimental lesson on love that Amandine learns in the garden rather than a factual one regarding the physical nature of sex.[14] Although this is highly debatable, as we shall see, Amandine's education might be described as initiatory rather than informative, in Tournier's sense of the term, in that, as Vierne says, an initiation "se vit, elle ne s'étudie ni se comprend avec la seule intelligence" (p. 63).

The first person narrative here is important because it shows that Amandine regards her discoveries in a private, intimate way and yet these activities can be shared by others who read her story. This creates a kind of complicity between narrator and reader, one which—and this is important for the child reader—is not shared by the parents, or at least Amandine's who are too protective and therefore too restricting. As Amandine says when she decides to go into the other garden: "Je ne sais pas trop pourquoi, mais je crois que si papa et maman se doutaient de mes projets, ils feraient tout pour m'empêcher de les réaliser".[15] The role of the parents here is clear: to stop the child from growing up; the role of this child, and maybe of all children, is to discover the new at all costs and this often means defying the parents.

In this way, Amandine's initiation might, indeed, be seen as an "initiation-révolte" as Tournier suggests in "Le Sang des fillettes", for initiation rites at puberty are carried out with the aim of integrating the adolescent into society and not with the aim of challenging it. Amandine shares this type of initiation with Pierre in **La Fugue du petit Poucet,** who also defies his parents by running away into the forest where he is initiated into a world of different values by Logre. An ogre in society's eyes, he is really a peace-keeping, pot-smoking, vegetarian hippy who loves trees. Both Pierre and Amandine share what Tournier considers to be one of the major characteristics of mythological characters in that, by entering the other garden, or forest in the case of young Poucet, they, too, have found a means of saying no to society, in this case the one upheld by the parents.[16]

In **Amandine ou les deux jardins** the little girl's passage from one garden to the other mirrors her physical development. This is why Amandine is interchangeable with the two gardens in the title. Both Tournier's choice of the name Amandine, and the garden as the place of initiation, is in keeping with the very idea of initiation rituals. "Amandine" is derived from "amande", at once both seed and fruit of the "amandier". The image of the seed turning into a mature plant is central to the idea of initiation. In the modern world, the place where this process is most easily observed is in the garden, and in the story, it is Amandine's transformation from seed to fruit, from childhood to maturity, that we witness.

The first garden in the tale, "le jardin de papa", is, in many ways, similar to "la maison de maman". Amandine tells us:

> On dirait que maman dans sa maison et papa dans son jardin font un vrai concours de propreté. Dans la maison on doit marcher sur des patins de feutre pour ne pas salir les parquets. Dans le jardin papa a disposé des cendriers pour les promeneurs-fumeurs. Je trouve qu'ils ont raison. C'est plus rassurant comme ça. Mais c'est quelquefois aussi un peu ennuyeux.
>
> (p. 36)

The fact that Tournier so obviously adds his own voice to Amandine's judgmental narrative, has the overall effect of making what she says ironic. Whilst the set-up may constitute what is stereotypically considered to be the ideal environment for a healthy childhood—the order, the balanced life of two parents each doing their duties in house and garden—the situation is so stable and unchanging that it is essentially sterile and, we feel, more than just "un peu ennuyeux". The garden, like the house, provides a domesticated, rather than a natural place for Amandine to play in. "Le jardin de papa" is always well cared for and nature here is kept firmly under control. At this stage, Amandine moves freely between the male-dominated garden and the female-dominated house. This seems to suggest that gender divisions are not really important before puberty and consequently there is no need for segregation. It also implies that Amandine is quite happy living in a world which is defined in terms of others, rather than in terms of herself. After initiation there is a sense in which this changes.

In order to be initiated, Amandine has to pass from this secure and ordered world of everyday life to that of the unknown. Preparation for this actually takes place in the father's garden. Amandine has taken to getting up nearly an hour before her parents. The garden at dawn is completely different from during the day. She experiences a kind of primaeval state of affairs and feels that she is "seule au monde". Whilst papa sleeps nature is at work. She tells us that "le jardin de papa est si soigné et peigné qu'on croirait qu'il ne peut rien s'y passer. Pourtant on en voit des choses quand papa dort!" (p. 39). What she sees is described as the "remue-ménage" of the nocturnal animals crossing the paths of the diurnal ones.[17] This event represents a return to an original kind of chaos in which nature rules and domesticity is pushed aside. In this way, the garden acts as a place of learning for Amandine. This is her first taste of independence from her parents and her first experience of the disordered natural world which lurks beneath the imposed surface of the civilized one. Being in the garden at this time of day is a necessary step in her development and helps to prepare her for what is to come. She is beginning to break free from the restrictions of childhood and is now ready to venture into a new world which is symbolized by the other garden.

Motivation for entering the new garden is provided by the kitten, Kamicha, whom Amandine wants to befriend. Kamicha has become semi-wild and, in this way, is the opposite of its domesticated mother Claude, although, like its mother, it has a sexually ambivalent name. Amandine finds that the high wall completely surrounds the garden. There is no gate or hole to get through. The only way in is to climb over the top which is no easy task. Firstly, she climbs the pear tree in "le jardin de papa" which is near the wall. Here Tournier reminds us of the archetypal garden of Eden but changes the tree from apple to pear. All mention of falling is strictly literal, and although Amandine is very much in danger of doing so, she finally manages to leap from tree to wall without calling for help.

This experience complies with the heroic tests which novices are set and must succeed in. Amandine's climb is a heroic deed. Furthermore, the physical hardship which she undergoes in getting on to the wall acts as a kind of preparation for the physical labour she will have to endure in later life. Eve's punishment, we remember, in Genesis is that she, and therefore all women, will have pain in child-bearing and childbirth.

Although getting up on to the wall is difficult, getting down from it is relatively easy. Amandine writes:

> J'ai découvert ensuite quelque chose de tout à fait surprenant: posé contre le mur, comme pour moi depuis toujours, une sorte d'escalier en bois très raide avec une rampe, un peu comme les grosses échelles qui servent à monter dans les greniers. Le bois était verdi et vermoulu, la rampe gluante de limaces. Mais c'était quand même bien commode pour descendre, et je ne sais comment j'aurais fait sans cela.
>
> (p. 44)

This at once points to the fact that despite her trials there is an inevitability about her situation. It is significant that the ladder is described as being similar to those which "servent à monter dans les greniers". Bachelard points out that "l'escalier du grenier . . . on le *monte* toujours. Il a le signe de l'ascension . . .".[18] The attic, or grain loft, for Bachelard, is indicative of heavenly calm and serenity because of its position. Here, however, Amandine is descending the ladder, and the implication is that she was in the peaceful and serene loft and is now going down into something which is more akin to "la cave" than "le grenier", for the ladder she uses is not dry but moist and covered in slugs. This can be interpreted as the symbolic "descente aux enfers" common to initiation rituals. "Le jardin de Kam-

ich", as Amandine comes to call it, is, in fact, the exact opposite of "le jardin de papa". Amandine's first sight of it is from the top of the wall and she tells us:

> D'abord je n'ai vu qu'un fouillis de verdure, un vrai taillis, une mêlée d'épines et d'arbres couchés, de ronces et de hautes fougères, et aussi un tas de plantes que je ne connais pas. Tout le contraire exactement du jardin de papa, si propre et si bien peigné. J'ai pensé que jamais je n'oserais descendre dans cette forêt vierge qui devait grouiller de crapauds et de serpents.
>
> (p. 43)

The garden fulfils several conditions. Firstly, it is a place which is cut off from Amandine's everyday experience. As such, it represents the ideal location for the initiation ceremony to take place. The wild setting is reminiscent of where primitive tribes like to carry out their rituals as they consider the unleashed forces of nature to have sacred powers.

Secondly, Amandine's description of the garden is a standard image of hell into which she must now descend. Her fear of "crapauds et serpents" is reminiscent of the fear which female genitals, described in terms of a garden, have evoked in another literary figure, Sartre's Antoine Roquentin. In *La Nausée* Roquentin relates the dream he has after having sex with the *patronne* of "Le Rendez-vous des Cheminots":

> J'ai laissé aller mon bras le long du flanc de la patronne et j'ai vu soudain un petit jardin avec des arbres bas et larges d'où pendaient d'immenses feuilles couvertes de poils. Des fourmis couraient partout, des milles-pattes et des teignes [. . .] Derrière des cactus et des figuiers de Barbarie, la Velléda du Jardin public désignait son sexe du doigt. "Ce jardin sent le vomi", criai-je.[19]

Although Amandine's reaction to the garden which confronts her is not as violent as Roquentin's, she also encounters a strange odour. What she feels about this odour falls midway between enjoyment and aversion. It cannot be described as mandrakes giving off their perfume as they do in the "Cantique des cantiques", but nor is it the smell of vomit. It is a mixture of flour, which has heavenly connotations because the bread which it makes is likened to the body of Christ, and pepper, which is hot and spicy and can therefore be associated with hell. So, to the physical implications of sexuality evoked in previous literature, Tournier adds the moral dimension of good and bad which is often associated with sex.[20]

In a way, the garden can be seen as mirroring the changes taking place in Amandine's own body with the glands beginning to give off new smells as they do at puberty. Seeing it as a symbol of her own sexual organs also helps to explain why the garden is so completely cut off. Amandine's garden is "privé" and described as a "forêt vierge", whereas the *patronne*'s at the "Cheminots" is "public" and, one assumes, entered frequently, by many. On the one hand, Amandine's passage through the garden might be interpreted as an exploration of herself. On the other, her descent into the garden is similar to a *regressus ad uterum,* from which she will emerge a woman.

In this garden she meets Kamicha whom she follows down labyrinthine and overgrown paths. They stop when they reach a dilapidated pavilion surrounded by broken marble benches. Under the dome of the pavilion is a statue:

> Sous le dôme du pavillon, il y a une statue assise sur un socle. C'est un jeune garçon tout nu avec des ailes dans le dos. Il incline sa tête frisée avec un sourire triste qui creuse des fossettes dans ses joues, et il lève un doigt vers ses lèvres. Il a laissé tomber un petit arc, un carquois et des flèches qui pendent le long du socle.
>
> Kamicha est assis sous le dôme. Il lève la tête vers moi. Il est aussi silencieux que le garçon de pierre. Il a comme lui un sourire mystérieux. On dirait qu'ils partagent le même secret, un secret un peu triste et très doux, et qu'ils voudraient me l'apprendre.
>
> (p. 45)

The pavilion acts as a kind of initiation temple in which the ceremony will take place. The statue and Kamicha play the role of priest and helper. What Amandine learns there is a secret which is in keeping with the procedures of all initiation ceremonies. Those to do with women are kept especially secret and intruders are in danger of losing their lives.

The statue that she meets here is of a "jeune garçon tout nu" and, in this way, he evokes Adam in the garden of Eden. But this Adam is also Cupid which further stresses the sexual nature of what Amandine learns. It seems that Cupid has done his work and that his arrows may be responsible for the blood she finds on her leg.

However, the whole situation here seems to stress that the sexual element is really only a part of the lesson to be learned at puberty. Cupid's arrows might fire love which will lead to procreation, but they also wound, and the implication is that now Amandine has been wounded, it is only a matter of time before she dies. The whole garden is full of remnants of the past. With its pavilion, Cupid and alleys it seems to be a garden which would have flourished during the seventeenth and eighteenth centuries. This world and the people who inhabited it have long since gone. The very wildness of the vegetation suggests a kind of decadence. As Amandine says: "Tout est mélancolique ici, ce pavillon en ruine, ces bancs cassés, ce gazon fou, plein de fleurs sauvages" (p. 45).

This adds a new meaning to the sadness which Amandine and the others feel. It is more than simply the sorrow of losing the safety and security of childhood.

Amandine may experience "une grande joie", mixed with the sorrow, at becoming a woman—her body will now wake up to new sensations and she will be able to have children, but in a way, it is exactly this which pushes her, as it did the people who inhabited the garden before her, to the grave. In *Vendredi ou les limbes du Pacifique,* Robinson, having fertilized the island Speranza, meditates on procreation and concludes: "Procréer, c'est susciter la génération suivante qui innocemment, mais inexorablement, repousse la précédente vers le néant".[21] Likewise, the very passion which feeds love is one which really desires the obliteration of the lovers. For the act of lovemaking is, according to Robinson, an experience in which one forgets and renounces the self completely.

But it is not just sexuality which links the experience to death here. Menstrual blood itself has strong associations with death. Like urine and faeces it is a waste matter and can be associated with rotting flesh. It is also an amorphous slimy liquid, a substance to which, as Georges Bataille suggests, we are all inherently adverse.[22] This partly accounts for the taboo which surrounds it even in the most primitive and natural societies and most certainly in our own. It reminds us, even if this is on a subconscious level, of our own mortality and eventual decay as well as of our natural, and therefore animal, beginnings which we would really like to forget. It is partly for this reason that Amandine has to go to another garden to learn about menstruation. This is not possible in "le jardin de papa" because, obvious reasons apart, in its pristine condition, it excludes any notion of decay.[23]

Amandine's passage from one garden to the other, as well as being the journey from childhood to adulthood, is also that of immortality to mortality. For Tournier, it is the pre-pubescent stage of the individual which constitutes "la perfection humaine". This is clearly seen in the *Vendredi* [*Vendredi ou les limbes du Pacifique*] texts where Robinson gets younger the longer he spends on the island. His initiation might be seen as the inverse of Amandine's and can be referred to as "une progression à rebours". He develops spiritually as he goes back in time to a primaeval world where he lives a continuous "moment d'innocence". The island, Speranza, comes to represent Eden before the fall: the real fall being that into time and the knowledge it brings is essentially that of death.

In *Vendredi,* Robinson is beyond time and death. This is not the case of Amandine in "le jardin de Kamicha", for whilst it has resumed the naturalness of beginnings it is also the garden of endings. In it life and death are inextricably linked. Amandine's progression is forwards, her fall, marked by the onset of menstruation, is also a fall into time. She goes from the never-changing, stable world of her childhood to the garden in which time is clearly evident.[24] The overriding message of the story is one which is echoed in René Barjavel's *La Nuit des temps* and which Simone Vierne quotes in a different context: "Il serait peut-être temps de se demander si la perfection n'est pas dans l'enfance, si l'adulte n'est pas un enfant qui a commencé à pourrir".[25] What Amandine goes through in the garden and what she learns is as much about death as it is about life. All initiation-ceremonies are, in fact, to prepare the individual for the ultimate initiation, which is death. But, at the same time, at the very heart of death there is new life. And this new life springs from the blood of the womb, so the entire process comes full circle and continues round again.

Eventually Amandine panics and runs back over the wall to what she calls for the *first* time "le jardin de mon enfance". She then goes to her own room. This is essentially ambiguous. In one way, it is in keeping with Tournier's view of **Amandine** [**Amandine ou les deux jardins**] as an example of an "initiation-révolte", in that she does not refer again either to "le jardin de papa" or to "la maison de maman". The fact that she seeks her own personal space also seems to indicate that she has broken free from the stereotypical and artificial world which constituted her childhood: a world which she learnt was false during her early hours alone in one garden, and in the time she spent with Kamicha and the statue in the other. This might also be seen as part of her secret.

However, there is also a sense in which the story is in keeping with events following initiation-ceremonies; that is, the adolescent is integrated into society, for Amandine returns to the female sector of her everyday world as her room is in "la maison de maman". It is no longer fitting for her as an adult (and although she is only ten, she is one in the biological sense at least) to frequent her father's garden. Moreover, the fact that she does not articulate her secret (although she acknowledges the blood) might indicate that she, too, is keeping quiet about what has happened to her and therefore is not breaking the silence which still persists in surrounding menstruation today.

Although Tournier's remarks in "Le Sang des fillettes" refute this interpretation of **Amandine,** he does say that women, unlike men, have no alternative society to which they can belong. He goes on to say that for the female adolescent "l'initiation ne peut être qu'une fugue permanente" (p. 340) but one wonders whether this last interpretation is not more fitting of Pierre's initiation in **La Fugue du petit Poucet.** Pierre is last seen locking himself in his room, putting on the boots which Logre gave him and dreaming of being "un grand arbre".[26] This is the ultimate form of revolt given that his father is "le commandant des bûcherons de Paris".

In **Amandine** the final image is of the pregnant cat sunning itself. Amandine's education is completed and the full significance of what she has learned comes to light. She realizes for the first time that Kamicha is in fact "une chatte"—Kamichatte—and is going to have kittens. The implication is that Amandine will soon be following in her footsteps and will therefore remain what Tournier terms "une prisonnière du gynécée".[27] But again this ending is double-edged in that one might argue that it concludes with the hope of life to come rather than with a sense of death which was so pervasive in the garden. The ambiguity of this seems to be in keeping with Tournier's ambivalent feelings towards women and procreation in general, which emerge in much of his fiction as well as in "Le Sang des fillettes" where he equates women with the society he so obviously dislikes. One wonders therefore how far the ambivalence in the tale is really a reflection of Tournier's own position as a male writer who is reputedly also gay (although to my knowledge he has never actually confirmed this) rather than an objective account of this exclusively female experience.

In retrospect it is obvious why Tournier should have chosen a cat rather than any other pet to play the role it does in the story. That cats are associated with female genitals has been understood since Freud and is fully recognized by the popular imagination as the title of the James Bond film *Octopussy* indicates. This also explains why the cat is in its element in the other garden. The subconscious link in the text with female sexuality is strengthened by the fact that once in her room, Amandine falls asleep and wakes up to find that her clothes are not dirty and that nothing is amiss apart from a smear of blood on her leg. This has the effect of pushing the entire garden experience into the realm of dreams, thereby denying its reality but heightening its symbolic import.

The garden is also a useful symbol in that it can be read in a variety of ways. In fact, Tournier's treatment of it as the place of initiation in **Amandine** seems to offer a solution as to why it has played such an important role in literature in general throughout the ages. In the story, the garden emerges firstly as a place of observation where what happens in the natural environment can be witnessed. It is fitting that what Amandine learns from the cats is of a reproductive kind (even if Tournier sees fit to deny this). In primitive societies this observation takes place in the wild and it is easy to see how the cycle of the seasons and the growing of crops initially set up the link between the garden, procreation, sexuality, and, by extension, human passion. The woman's body, as bearer of children, also became symbolized by the garden, itself bearer of fruit. But this is a two-way process, as the earth is also known as mother and, in *Vendredi ou les limbes du Pacifique* becomes lover as well. The cycle of the seasons also links the garden to initiation in that it, too, displays a constant process of death and rejuvenation.

Furthermore, as can be seen from "le jardin de papa", the garden can also represent a natural space over which the human being has control. Nature, which to a large extent is beyond our control, can be subdued in the garden. And, as it is associated with sexuality, procreation and consequently death, the more one can bend the garden to one's will the more control one feels one has over these things. In this way, the garden can come to represent the mind as well as the body and is therefore often used as a metaphor for the self. It provides an ideal place for self-discovery and learning in both junior and adult fiction alike.

Its ultimate appeal, however, and this is admittedly more apparent in the *Vendredi* texts than it is in **Amandine,** perhaps lies in the desire we all have to return to an earthly paradise devoid of worry and responsibility, alongside our wish to recapture the immediacy and spontaneity of our beginnings. Like the *conte* the garden also retains its appeal throughout life and Tournier's obvious affection for his own garden is often the subject of his talks with school children.[28]

Amandine ou les deux jardins, then, not only emerges as a typical example of the *conte initiatique* but also helps us to understand why the garden has played such a prominent role as a symbol in fiction. And this might be said to constitute one of this tale's levels of meaning. On another level, Tournier has succeeded in presenting one of the most important events in the life of a female in semi-symbolic terms, and he has done so in such a way as to make this experience seem a heroic quest rather than a matter of shame. In a way, he has broken the silence and has uttered the secret (something which Amandine cannot do completely) thereby exposing our fear surrounding this taboo and consequently making it less formidable. One might say that Tournier has used the *conte* in this case, as he does in many of his other stories, to expose what we might term a contemporary myth in the sense of a stereotypical concept.

Notes

1. Michel Tournier, "Michel Tournier: écrire pour les enfants" in *Que ma joie demeure* (Paris: Gallimard Collection Enfantimages, 1982). Tournier makes a similar statement in the preface to *Vendredi ou la vie sauvage* (Paris: Folio, 1984): "Je n'écris pas pour les enfants. Jécris de mon mieux. Et quand j'approche mon idéal, j'écris assez bien pour que les enfants 'aussi' puissent me lire" (p. xvi).

2. *La Fugue du petit Poucet* first appeared in the magazine *Elle* in December 1972 under the title *Le Détournement du petit Poucet*, it was then pub-

lished in *Le Coq de bruyère* in 1978 and it finally appeared for children in Editions G.P. in 1979. *Amandine ou les deux jardins* was also originally published in *Elle* in June 1975 before it came out for children in Editions G.P. in 1977, followed by *Le Coq de bruyère* in 1978. Tournier's other *contes* were initially published in *Le Coq de bruyère*. There are two exceptions to this: *Barbedor*, which appeared in *Gaspard, Melchior et Balthazar* and in Gallimard's collection *Enfantimages* in 1980; and *Pierrot ou les secrets de la nuit* which was originally published in Editions G.P. in 1979 for children but whose comprehensive appeal was substantiated ten years later by its inclusion in *Le Médianoche amoureux* (Paris: 1989).

3. Michel Mansuy, "Trois chercheurs de paradis: Bosco, Tournier, Cayrol", *Travaux de linguistique et de littérature*, XVI, 2 (1978), p. 211.

4. This view is expressed in *Le Vent Paraclet* (Paris: Folio, 1977) where Tournier assesses Plato's *Mythe de la Caverne*. He relates the basic content of the tale and adds: "Raconté de cette façon le mythe n'est qu'une histoire pour enfant, la description d'un guignol qui serait aussi théâtre d'ombres chinoises. Mais à un niveau supérieur, c'est toute une théorie de la connaissance, à un étage plus élevé encore cela devient morale, puis métaphysique, puis ontologie, etc., sans cesser d'être la même histoire" (p. 188). Tournier makes a similar comment with regard to *Pierrot ou les secrets de la nuit* in an article entitled "Michel Tournier: comment écrire pour les enfants", *Le Monde* (21 dec, 1979). The key to the tale, he says, lies in the letter that Pierrot writes to Colombine: "Ce sont deux visions du monde qui s'affrontent: la substance contre la surface, la matière contre la forme, l'essence contre l'accident. De grands échos retentissent dans ces puérils porte-paroles. C'est Goethe et Newton séparés sur la théorie des couleurs, c'est Parménide contre Héraclite. C'est aussi mon maître Gaston Bachelard. Cela l'enfant, bien entendu, ne le sait pas. Mais il le sent, et il le comprend à sa manière".

5. Simone Vierne, *Rite, roman, initiation* (Grenoble, 1973), p. 5. Further references are to this edition and, where possible, will be included in the text.

6. Michel Tournier, *Le Vol du vampire* (Paris, 1981), p. 35. Further references are to this edition.

7. Michel Tournier, *L'Aire du Muguet* in *Le Coq de bruyère* (Paris: Folio, 1978), p. 268.

8. Michel Tournier, "Le Sang des fillettes", *Le Monde* (9 dec, 1977), and in the notes of *Le Coq de bruyère* (Paris: Folio, 1978), pp. 337-340. Further references are to the interview included in *Le Coq de bruyère*.

9. *Le Vol du vampire,* pp. 10-11.

10. Lanza del Vasto, epigraph to Michel Tournier, *Le Coq de bruyère* (Paris: Folio, 1978).

11. Gardens also play a significant role in other works by Tournier, notably in *Les Météores* (Paris: Folio, 1975); in *Vendredi ou les limbes du Pacifique* (Paris: Folio, 1972) and *Vendredi ou la vie sauvage* (Paris: Folio junior, 1984) which centre on the displaced garden—the island. All other references are to these editions.

12. In *Vendredi ou la vie sauvage,* Robinson calls the ship's boy "Dimanche" because "c'est le jour des fêtes, des rires, et des jeux" (p. 151).

13. For a more detailed account of initiation versus information see Michel Tournier, "l'Enfant coiffé" in *Le Vent Paraclet* (Paris: Folio, 1977). Further references to *Le Vent Paraclet* will be to this edition.

14. "Le Sang des fillettes", p. 338. "A la fin, la petite fille est beaucoup plus troublée et mûrie sentimentalement qu'informée sur la sexualité."

15. Michel Tournier, *Amandine ou les deux jardins* in *Le Coq de bruyère,* pp. 42-43. References are to this edition because it is paginated whereas the children's edition is not. From now on they will be included in the text.

16. In *Le Vol du vampire,* Tournier alludes to the rebellious nature of major mythological characters: "La passion adultère de Tristan et Iseut, le pacte avec le diable de Faust, le désir ardent et destructeur de Don Juan, la farouche solitude de Robinson, le rêve extravagant de Don Quichotte, autant de façons au contraire de dire *non* à la société, de briser l'ordre social" (p. 31).

17. Tournier also takes up the theme of primordial chaos in *Les Météores* (Paris: Folio, 1975) where the night rats and the day gulls fight on the rubbish tips just outside Marseille.

18. Gaston Bachelard, *La Poétique de l'espace,* 5e éd. (Paris, 1967), p. 41.

19. Jean-Paul Sartre, *La Nausée* (Paris: Folio, 1983), pp. 88-89.

20. An extended use of flour in connection with spirituality and sexuality is found in *Pierrot ou les secrets de la nuit* in which Pierrot makes a bread version of Colombine. Both he, Colombine and Arlequin then set about eating it. In *Amandine* the garden highlights the ambiguity of the experience as it is situated "à la charnière du ciel et de la terre" (*Les Météores,* p. 523), and therefore contains both carnal and spiritual qualities.

21. *Vendredi ou les limbes du Pacifique,* p. 131.

22. Georges Bataille, *L'Histoire de l'érotisme* in *Œuvres complètes,* vol. 8 (Paris, 1976), pp. 53-54.

23. For Tournier, "l'autre côté du mur" at his home at the presbytery is in fact the "cimetière" or the "jardin d'église" of which he tells us in *Le Vent Paraclet* (pp. 300-301) and *Le Vagabond immobile* (Paris, 1984), p. 17.

24. In *Le Vent Paraclet,* Tournier explains the characteristics of what he terms the "homme-jardin", as opposed to the "homme-île". The "homme-île", cradled by the freshness of a maritime climate, remains always young (this partly accounts for Robinson's eventual immortality on what seems to be, for Tournier, an inverse garden—the island). In contrast, the "homme-jardin" (or the "femme-jardin", in the case of Amandine) is destined to age. He comments on the garden: "Création continentale, il ne sort pas de la ronde des saisons. Au jardin en fleurs succède le jardin fruitier, puis il se couvre des rousseurs de l'automne, et l'un de ses plus purs avatars est le jardin-sous-la-neige. L'homme-jardin vieillit bien. Il prend de la bouteille et son visage s'enrichit de chacune de ses rides. Le cimetière qu'il voit de sa fenêtre, s'il habite un presbytère, est un autre jardin" (pp. 300-301). It becomes clear here that Tournier is talking about himself and that he, too, will share the ultimate fate which awaits both himself and Amandine in that "other" garden.

25. René Barjavel, *La Nuit des temps* (Paris, 1968), p. 274. Also quoted by Simone Vierne in *Rite, roman, initiation.*

26. *La Fugue du petit Poucet* in *Le Coq de bruyère,* p. 65.

27. "Le Sang des fillettes", p. 340.

28. In *Michel Tournier: le roman mythologique* (Paris, 1988) Arlette Bouloumié records Tournier talking to school children about his garden: "J'ai un jardin qui compte énormément pour moi. Et dès que je m'en vais, je pense à mon jardin avec tristesse parce que j'ai l'impression que je ne peux pas me passer de lui et qu'il ne peut pas se passer de moi" (p. 200).

Charles J. Stivale (essay date 1991)

SOURCE: Stivale, Charles J. "Nomad Love and the War-Machine: Michel Tournier's *Gilles et Jeanne.*" *SubStance* 20, no. 2 (1991): 44-59.

[*In the following essay, Stivale traces the social and political transformation of Gilles de Rais in* Gilles et Jeanne, *and praises Tournier's use of ambiguity.*]

In the section of Michel Tournier's intellectual autobiography, *The Wind Spirit,* entitled "The Mythic Dimension," Tournier reminisces about his association with Gilles Deleuze at the Lycée Carnot in the early 1940s: "All the tired philosophy of the curriculum passed through him and emerged unrecognizable, but rejuvenated, with a fresh, undigested, bitter taste of newness that we weaker, lazier minds found disconcerting and repulsive" (128). This perspective of the Deleuzian "fresh, undigested, bitter taste of newness" has been vastly enlarged, not only in Deleuze's philosophical works and in the ambitious project he has undertaken in collaboration with Félix Guattari entitled *Capitalism and Schizophrenia* (*Anti-Oedipus* and *A Thousand Plateaus*).

This "bitter taste of newness" also emerges in Tournier's work in the tension between *écriture* and *sens,* in what Colin Davis calls "his simultaneous identification with both nomad and sedentary, when the former values the journey and the latter only the destination" (205). It is the connection between "nomadology" (proposed by Deleuze and Guattari to conceptualize philosophical, political, ethical and textual multiplicity) and Tournier's re-mythologizing in the short *récit,* **Gilles et Jeanne,** that I propose to explore. In Tournier's tale, Jeanne d'Arc's quest and martyrdom are depicted for the transmutation they incite in the life and soul of her notorious comrade-in-arms, the sire Gilles de Rais.[1] Through the brief but intense period of military campaigns which Jeanne and Gilles share, the *chevalier* is transformed from merely one "of those country squires from Brittany and the Vendée who had thrown in their lot with the Dauphin Charles" (5; 9), into an isolated, tormented warlord waging his own private, roving battle with forces known only to him and to his henchmen. Tournier's reinscription of the myth of Gilles de Rais likens this transformation to an alchemical process of "becoming," ignited by the initial contact with Jeanne d'Arc and perpetuated through subsequent phases.

It is from the perspective of this "becoming" and its relation to "nomadology" that I will map out the textual coordinates, plotted through the Deleuzoguattarian connection,[2] which help us to understand the productive force of "becoming." I wish to consider how the deployment in Tournier's text of a textual "assemblage" which "in its multiplicity, necessarily acts on semiotic flows, material flows, and social flows simultaneously" (*ATP* [*A Thousand Plateaus*] 22-23; *MP* [*Mille plateaux: capitalisme et schizophrénie II*] 33-34), creates a tale of rupture and of displacement, even of exile, within the grip of feudal society. The particular semiotic and social perspective that the Deleuzoguattarian discourse provides will allow me to illustrate the trajectory of Tournier's *récit* through the five phases of its textual and thematic progression. This progression will see Gilles as a "war-machine" under the dominion and territoriality of the State, traversing various states of "becoming" via progressive nomadization and deterritorialization until he reaches a limit, where the "war-machine" exceeds the dictates of the State and must be sanctioned and reterritorialized—brought back fully under its control. By studying this representation of a cruel and ambiguous nomadism which has so shocked some readers,[3] I wish to suggest that it is precisely through this ambiguity, this lack of closure and finality, both textual and moral, that Tournier problematizes cultural traditions and political structures. At the same time, my use of nomadological terminology will explore the possibilities of fragmentation echoed thematically within the text.

THE WAR-MACHINE

Let us consider, first, the concept of the "war-machine" as it relates to nomadology and is developed in *Mille plateaux.* Conceived as a means of developing a thought that is not classical or arborescent—"whose relationship with the outside is [*not*] mediated by some form of interiority" such as the soul or consciousness (Patton, 61)—nomadology expresses counterthoughts, "violent in their acts and discontinuous in their appearances." The strategy of this "outside thought" is to place thought "in an immediate relation . . . with the forces of the outside, in short to make thought a war machine" (*ATP* 376-377; *MP* 467). Against the universalizing aspirations of the classical image of thought, and the striating of mental space that it effects, this nomadic thought allies itself not with "a universal thinking subject but, on the contrary, with a singular race;" it grounds itself not "in an all-encompassing totality but is, on the contrary, deployed in a horizonless milieu that is a smooth space, steppe, desert or sea" (*ATP* 379; *MP* 469). It is from this perspective that war-machines must be understood as distinct from the military institution. Deploying both a thought and a desire fundamentally at odds with the State apparatus, the war-machine is an assemblage of creative force that "in no way has war as its object," but constitutes a transformational energy that Deleuze and Guattari call "the passage of mutant flows" (*ATP* 229-230; *MP* 280).

The conflict of Gilles de Rais commences here, at the intersection of exteriority and interiority, of the dominion of the State apparatus *vis-à-vis* the war-machine. In the initial phase of the tale, he has thrown in his lot as vassal to Charles VII, and is thereby appropriated by the military objectives of the feudal State. However, Gilles de Rais's submission to the influence of Jeanne d'Arc, especially to the "purity that radiates from her face" (10; 15), will unleash the simultaneously creative and conflictual assemblage of desire, the "mutant flows" of "nomad love," which propel him toward a "becoming" entirely outside the constraints of the State. The initial contrast of Jeanne d'Arc with those around her is presented starkly: "And, indeed, she did seem to glide along on invisible wings above the animal as it furiously pounded the earth with its four iron shoes" (10; 16). This *bête* refers not only to Jeanne's new steed, but metaphorically, to the war-machine which envelops her, appropriated by the State apparatus, whose order she and it will struggle to re-establish. But the particular war-machine that Jeanne harnesses not only "bears witness to another kind of justice, one of incomprehensible cruelty at times, but at others of unequaled pity as well . . . the war machine is of another species, another nature, another origin than the State apparatus" (*ATP* 352; *MP* 435-436).

It is to this "other species" and to the possibilities it suggests that Gilles de Rais is attracted, lifting him from the "fate of a country squire from a particularly backward province" (11-12; 18) into a process of "becoming" which Tournier describes as "the intoxicating and dangerous fusion of sanctity and war" (13; 19). Under her tutelage, Gilles "followed Jeanne as the body obeys the soul, as she herself obeyed her 'voices'" (14; 21). "Jeanne," Gilles concludes, "I believe each of us has his voices. Good voices and bad voices. . . . The voices I heard in my childhood and youth were always those of evil and sin" (20; 25-26). He goes further, saying, "You have not come only to save the Dauphin Charles and his kingdom. You must also save the young lord Gilles de Rais! Make him hear your voice. Jeanne, I never want to leave your side. Jeanne, you are a saint, make a saint of me!" (18; 26).

During the subsequent campaigns, Gilles is able to express his particular kind of love for Jeanne, not merely through the perils which they share in the field, but more importantly, in this assemblage of movement, speed and affect which constitutes a war-machine, a "nomad love" which he proclaims to her as she lies wounded in the knee before the gates of Paris:

> "But I love you above all for the purity that is inside you and that nothing can tarnish." Looking down, he saw her wound.
>
> "Will you accept the only kiss that I ask of you?" He bent down and laid his lips for a long time on Jeanne's wound. He then stood up and licked his lips.
>
> "I have communicated with your blood. I am bound to you forever. Henceforth I shall follow you wherever you go. Whether to heaven or to hell!"
>
> (23-24; 33)

This vow will determine the destiny of Gilles de Rais once Jeanne d'Arc is captured by the English, tried and found guilty of heresy and witchcraft, and burned at the stake despite the futile efforts of Gilles to liberate her. Even before her execution, following her capture, his life had taken on new dimensions: "Neither war nor politics held his interest . . . all that mattered to him

now was that personal, mystical adventure that had begun on the day that he had met Jeanne" (27; 36). After witnessing her execution, with her cries, "Jésus! Jésus! Jésus!" ringing in his ears, "something had changed inside him: he had the face of a lying, pernicious, dissolute, blaspheming invoker of devils" (35; 45). The process of "becoming" a unique, malevolent and perverse war-machine, had thus begun. Tournier describes how, ". . . A beaten, broken man, he went on and buried himself in his fortresses in the Vendée. For three years, he became a caterpillar. When the malign metamorphosis was complete, he emerged, an infernal angel, unfurling his wings" (35; 45).

"Becomings"

This process of "becoming" had already commenced during Gilles's intense interaction with Jeanne, and his inspiration derived from Jeanne's mode of "becoming-woman," the molecular progression embodied by this particular girl-child. As Deleuze and Guattari observe, "The girl is certainly not defined by virginity; she is defined by a relation of movement and rest, speed and slowness, by a combination of atoms, an emission of particles: haecceity" (*ATP* 276; *MP* 339).[4] These are the very attributes of the nomadic war-machine, pursuing its fluid path. This "becoming-molecular" defines the "nomad love" between Gilles and Jeanne: an affective exchange—"atoms, particles"—valuable not for terrestrial carnality, but for the transmutation of the *chevalier* into child, woman, mystic—becomings that propel the war-machine further *dehors,* outside the striated borders of the State apparatus. So, in the tale's second segment, as Gilles comes into his huge fortune with the death of his grandfather, he finds himself quite literally "territorialized" by his inherited lands. But admitting that "these things mean nothing to me" (37; 47), Gilles rejects the sedentary implications of this territorialization and affirms his purpose in the journey inspired by his true master/mistress, the "Janus-Jeanne" (38; "Jeanne bifrons" 48). He recites:

> Jeanne the holy, Jeanne the chaste, Jeanne the victorious under the standard of St. Michael! Jeanne the monster in woman's shape, condemned to the stake for sorcery, heresy, schismaticism, change of sex, blasphemy and apostasy.
>
> (38; 48)

With his immense fortune, Gilles can turn apparent "good works" toward his own ends. By founding a community dedicated to the Holy Innocents, Gilles can devote his energies to recruiting young boys for its choir, and for his own purposes. He commissions a fresco of the massacre of the Holy Innocents for the chapel walls. The artist "had costumed the figures like the men, soldiers, women, and children of his own period, and placed them in a village that was supposed to be Bethlehem, but in which everybody could recognize the houses of Machecoul," with "their lord Rais behind the features of the cruel King of the Jews" (40-41; 51-52). Gilles thus creates a dual, aural/visual assemblage of deterritorialization and molecular dispersion of sanctity and suffering: "The anguished chants of the angel-faced choirboys moved Gilles all the more intensely when he saw those children against the background of such horror and slaughter. Overcome with emotion, he would stand there leaning against a pillar, murmuring between sobs, 'Pity, pity, pity!'" (41; 152). But this particular kind of pity, one of "immense pleasure" at "such a beautiful sight" of the suffering of the children's "tender, panting," "bloodstained" bodies (42; 53-54) recalls the ambiguous ecstasy of Gilles's "nomad love" for Jeanne, the purity and corporeality of holiness and blood.

The recruitment for the *collégiale* is but a prelude to the new pleasures of hunting "that other game, which was so special and so delicious" (44; 56). In this nomadic recruitment across Gilles's vast territory, the figure of the "horseman galloping through plains and forests" (44; 57) fuels the "dark, cruel scenes" with their traits of speed and affect in the nomadic pursuit:

> A woman rushes out after a young boy, seizes him and takes him into her house. The horseman is swathed in a large cloak, which floats around the horse. With loud beating of hooves he crosses the castle drawbridge. He is now standing, motionless, legs apart, at the entrance of the armoury. The lord's voice is heard.
>
> "Well?"
>
> The horseman opens his cloak. A young boy is clinging to him. He falls down, then tries to rise clumsily.
>
> "Well done!" says the voice.
>
> (45; 57)

This nomadic pursuit is the very stuff of legend, of myth, of fairy tales: of the witch called La Meffraye (she who arouses fear); of the woodcutter's son Poucet (Tom Thumb) who "saves" his brothers from the woods by leading them to the château of Tiffauges . . . never to emerge (46-48; 58-61). And the "torrent of black smoke, gushing out of the castle's biggest chimney" ("*torrent de fumée noire, vomi par la plus grosse chéminée du château*"), this "stink of burning flesh" (49; "*puanteur de charogne calcinée*" 62), disturb even Gilles's confused confessor, the Reverend Eustache Blanchet. He agrees to undertake a mission on behalf of his obsessed *seigneur,* "after a particularly delirious night." Having learned that in Florence "scientists, artists and philosophers, it seemed, had combined their forces and intelligence to create a new golden age that would soon spread to the whole of mankind," Blanchet is dispatched to "investigate these novelties on the spot. Perhaps he would bring back to the Vendée some teaching, some object, even perhaps some man capable of

tearing the seigneur de Rais from his dark chimeras" (50; 63). Thus, the priest is propelled into the coordinates of new "spaces" and of mutant, "ambulant science."

"Sᴍᴏᴏᴛʜ Sᴘᴀᴄᴇꜱ" ᴀɴᴅ "Sᴛʀɪᴀᴛᴇᴅ Sᴘᴀᴄᴇꜱ"

Before discussing the "spaces" and "science" that Blanchet encounters on his voyage to Florence, let us consider more fully how Tournier has situated Gilles in a "mixed state," the particularly ambiguous "space" constituted and inhabited in the early phases of the tale.[5] As a participant in the cause of Charles VII and as Jeanne's comrade-in-arms, Gilles pursues the goals of the sedentary State apparatus, which Deleuze and Guattari describe as being "to parcel out a closed space to people, assigning each person a share and regulating the communication between shares" (*ATP* 380; *MP* 472). They describe one of the fundamental tasks of the State as being "to striate the space over which it reigns, or to utilize smooth spaces as a means of communication in the service of striated space." This is what Gilles and Jeanne fought for, to assure the control of the State over nomadism and migrations, "to establish a zone of rights over an entire 'exterior,' over all the flows traversing the ecumenon" (*ATP* 385; *MP* 479). It is this "capture of flows"—"a need for fixed paths in well-defined directions, which restrict speed, regulate circulation, relativize movement, and measure in detail the relative movements of subjects and objects" (*ATP* 386; *MP* 479)—that Tournier's Gilles implicitly opposes in his multiple "becomings," and this despite (or because of) his own inscription in the striated space of the feudal hierarchy. His activities of "assemblage," i.e. the "recruitment," both for the *collégiale* and for his own ends, culminating in the ambiguous "savour of heresy or odor of sanctity" emanating from the château's chimney (50; 63), correspond to the war-machine's constitution of a "smooth space" that the nomad occupies and holds.

The smoke and odor which terrify Blanchet are but the exterior traces of this war-machine's "becoming"—"a spiritual voyage effected without relative movement, but in intensity, in one place" (*ATP* 381; *MP* 473). From this open, smooth space of speed and distribution, of multiple sensorial assemblages (aural, visual, olfactory), Blanchet travels to the opposite pole, to the striated space *par excellence* of the *polis*—the city, in which "one closes off a surface and 'allocates' it according to determined intervals, assigned breaks" (*ATP* 481; *MP* 600-601).

During his stay in Florence and his cultural initiation by the defrocked cleric, Francesco Prelati, Blanchet is dazed by the contrast between the poverty of his master's domain in the Vendée and the marvelous Florentine city space, striking for its own ascending, vertical "becoming." Furthermore, the splendor of the striated space encompasses another milieu of interiority, the spectacle of death "behind each tree, each street corner" (58; 73), and this frightening yet fascinating assemblage of graveyards, charnel houses and gibbets inspires Prelati's mesmerizing exposition of his unorthodox religious and scientific views. "Against mankind's moral wounds, the panacea is wealth," Prelati tells Blanchet. "If the good angel appeared on earth to cure all the wounds of body and soul, do you know what he would do? He would be an alchemical angel and manufacture gold!" (57; 72). Referring to Florence's charnel houses and torture chambers, Prelati proclaims, "We must plunge, Father Blanchet, we must have the courage to plunge into the darkness in order to bring back light," and further, that even the Devil "might have a purpose" (59-60; 75).

Given these predilections, this curious prelate is uniquely prepared to receive the tale that Blanchet recounts of the particular "becoming" of his master: "He surrounds himself with extravagant luxury. He eats like a wolf. He drinks like a donkey . . . he dirties himself like a pig" (63-64; 79-82). Prelati thus learns that Gilles's transformation following Jeanne's death was toward a "becoming-animal"; that upon his return from Jeanne's execution in Rouen, Gilles's face was "bestial": "There was something wild about his features, almost the face of a werewolf" (64; 81). Moreover, Prelati learns that Gilles's despair is not marked by weeping, but rather that "he laughs, he roars like a wild beast. He rushes forward, driven by his passions, like a furious bull" (65; 82). And Blanchet pleads, "Some use must be found for his strength, it must be given some direction, raised upward! Could you do that, François Prélat?" (64-65; 82). But it is when Prelati learns of Gilles's futile attempts "to force Jeanne's wandering soul" to return—first, embodied by a youthful actor in the *Mystery of the Siege of Orléans* commissioned by Gilles, then through his belief in the false Jeanne who subsequently appeared—that Prelati can admit, "I think I have understood the heart and soul of the Sirc of Rais" (68-69; 87). Blanchet concludes, "I am looking for someone who can give him back a sense of direction . . . How can I put it? Give him back the vertical, transcendent dimension that he lost when he lost Jeanne." We are told that Prelati "listened with passionate attention, realizing the role that he might play in that man's destiny" (64; 80). Despite Blanchet's protests against Prelati's science "nourished on blood and filth," the priest sadly admits that Prelati's description—"hands too strong, a head too weak"—portrays exactly the child-like quality of Gilles begging forgiveness for his crimes (73; 91), over which Prelati exults, "If there are crimes, we shall treat them with light! We shall see well enough what becomes of those swarming Gothic serpents when heated by the sunlight of Florence" (74; 92).

NOMADIC SCIENCE

The tale's fourth segment thus commences with the return of Blanchet and Prelati to the smooth, horizontal space constituted by Gilles's war-machine in the Vendée countryside, a space now set for the development of a horizontal, "nomadic science" opposed to the royal science's practice of "reproduction, iteration and reiteration" (*ATP* 372; *MP* 460). The alternate model, as Deleuze and Guattari describe it, "consists in being distributed by turbulence across a smooth space, in producing a movement that holds space and simultaneously affects all of its points, instead of being held by space in a local movement from one specified point to another" (*ATP* 363; *MP* 449-450). This model suggests an alternate "scientific procedure," an "itineration" based not on reproducing, but on "following":

> One is obliged to follow when one is in search of the "singularities" of matter, or rather of a material, and not out to discover form; when one escapes the force of gravity to enter a field of celerity; when one ceases to contemplate the course of a laminar flow in a determinate direction, to be carried away by a vortical flow; when one engages in a continuous variation of variables, instead of extracting constants from them, etc.
>
> (*ATP* 372; *MP* 461)[6]

All of these traits—the quest for "singularities" of matter; the field of celerity; the vortical flow; continuous variation of variables—characterize the alchemical "ambulant or itinerant science" that Prelati exercises. He will function as "a type of ambulant scientist whom State scientists are forever fighting or integrating and allying with" (*ATP* 373; *MP* 462). Deleuze and Guattari describe this "'savant' of nomad science" as "caught between a rock and a hard place, between the war machine that nourishes and inspires them"—that is, Prelati's and Gilles de Rais's nomadic pursuit of his particular mode of "becoming"—"and the State that imposes upon them an order of reasons" (*ATP* 362; *MP* 448), *i.e.*, an apparatus dominated by feudal and religious absolutism.

At the château of Tiffauges, Prelati encounters the male court with which Gilles surrounds himself, and dazzled at the spectacle of this "animal brutality and innocence," he wonders, "How can I convert all that brute force to my subtle ends?" (79-80; 99-100), that is, how to transform the raw material of this war-machine according to the variable precepts of a nomadic science. Prelati accompanies Gilles and his henchmen in their nomadic hunting in order to discover "the key to that desolate land that he had been seeking since his arrival" (82; 102-103). Prelati had been astonished by the striated confines of the "huge Gaulish forests," and especially by "that huge ballroom chimney in which whole tree trunks burnt" (82; 103). However, standing on the dunes overlooking the smooth space of the storm-swept sea, from which Gilles seems to derive particular strength and inspiration, Prelati realizes that "the ocean represented the tool, the weapon that he now had in his hands. . . . He now knew the direction of his mission: to touch with an ardent hand the purulent wound of that country and force it to rise, to stand up" (82-83; 103). Here the narrator renders his own judgement of the ambiguous "becoming" which would unfold:

> But Prelati was quite incapable of imagining the terrible course that this salvation would take. Gilles, stunned by Jeanne's execution, dragged himself along the ground like an animal. Prelati would raise him up, but only to encourage him in the diabolical vocation to which Gilles believed himself to have been called ever since Jeanne had been found guilty of the sixteen charges.
>
> (83; 104)

To succeed in his task, "the Florentine used everything he could lay his hands on," particularly his understanding of Gilles's taste for young boys, "to convince his master that only a curtain of flames separated him from heaven and that the alchemical science alone could enable him to cross it" (86; 107). In the heights of the alchemical laboratory in the attic of the château, Prelati and Gilles explore what Deleuze and Guattari call the "ambulant science," "the connection between content and expression in themselves, each of these two terms encompassing form and matter," a matter "essentially laden with singularities (which constitute a form of content)," and an expression "inseparable from pertinent traits (which constitute a matter of expression)" (*ATP* 369; *MP* 457). Tournier writes, for "the pilgrim of the sky—as the searching alchemist is called"—the scientific experiments with "the fundamental ambiguity of fire, which is both life and death, purity and passion, sanctity and damnation" are "an art as much as a technique," resulting in "the phenomenon of inversion, as an excess of cold causes a burning, or as the paroxysm of love merges with hate" (87; 108). Such a process, declares Prelati, explains Jeanne's destiny, her agony at the stake having been "the zero level at which a benign transmutation was to begin," preceding her eventual rehabilitation, beatification and canonization—"but the trial by fire was the ineluctable pivot of this change of direction" (88; 109). It is thus to the hunger of Barron, one of Satan's lieutenants, that Gilles must henceforth sacrifice the children so that their flesh might "open up . . . the incandescent gates of hell" (88; 110): "Instead of degrading yourself with them, you will save yourself and them with you. You will descend, like Jeanne, to the bottom of the burning pit, and you will rise again, like her, in a radiant light!" (90; 111-112).

The "Apparatus of Capture"

These "sublime labours of transmutation" (90; 112) are short-lived, however, since "sinister rumors travelled across the country" (90; 112), and the weight of the feudal and religious State apparatus came crashing down on the experiments of Gilles and Prelati. Gilles's transgressions are brought to the attention of his peers by an infraction against the feudal code, his public sacrilege in the church of Saint-Etienne-de-Mermorte. Then, besieged in his castle of Machecoul, abandoned by all his henchmen, Gilles surrenders to the troops representing both arms of the State structure—those of Jean V, Duke of Brittany, and those of Jean de Malestroit, Bishop of Nantes. Thus the "apparatus of capture" comes to bear on Gilles not only because of the public rumors of murder, sodomy and devil-worship, but because of "what was really at stake—that immense fortune, those fortresses, those lands, all that countless loot! It was high-flying banditry, with a regal quarry on which all the great wild beasts of the region were converging!" (99-100; 122-123). In response to the forty-nine articles of indictment, Gilles attacks the judges in a similar vein: "All of you here present care not a fig for crimes and heresies. . . . What is at stake is the immense loot that your quivering nostrils can scent" (103; 127). That is, the "outside thought" and "becomings" of Gilles's nomadic pursuit provide the pretext for a quite literal reterritorialization of the feudal domain from which Gilles drew his strength, but in support of which he was impelled toward the "ambulant," alchemical quest for gold.

Thus, the final segment, nearly one-third of the tale, presents a complex and ambiguous dénouement to this destiny: on one level, excerpts from the trial and the testimony of witnesses, henchmen, Prelati and, finally, the master Gilles de Rais, provide gruesome details of the latter's crimes, while revealing both the limits which the State must impose on such an eccentric war-machine and the means of this appropriation or "capture" by the State. On another level, the accomplishment of the State's royal "unity of composition," of "interior essence" (*ATP* 427; *MP* 532), is effected thanks to Gilles's willingness now to pursue his nomadic quest of "inversion" via the paths of interiority. For, "the State cannot effect a capture unless what is captured . . . escapes under new forms, as towns or war machines" (*ATP* 435; *MP* 542). On one hand, the detailed testimony in these four short, but intense chapters provides an example of the open and explicit ceremony which preceded the veiling of confessional questions after the Middle Ages (Foucault, 18). On the other hand, through this same confessional process, Gilles undergoes a penultimate sequence of "becomings": first, the "great lord, haughty, violent and relaxed" (101; 125)—the mask of his earliest incarnation before encountering Jeanne d'Arc; then, confronted with the threat of excommunication (105-106; 129-131), he appears as "a desperate wretch, both bestial and puerile, clinging to all those whom he believed could bring him help and safety" (101; 125)—the mask of himself after Jeanne's execution. Finally, having confessed to his crimes and submitted to the accusers, Gilles "stood, stiff and motionless as a statue, through the endless procession of witnesses" (108; 134), but also definitively "inhabited by the memory of Jeanne" thanks to which he "went to the stake as a Christian, radiantly at peace with himself and his God" (101; 125).

Thus, to evince the "power of metamorphosis" of war-machines, which "allows them to be captured by States, but also to resist that capture and rise up again in other forms, with other 'objects' besides war" (*ATP* 437; *MP* 545), Gilles must avoid excommunication so that his quest for ascension through conflagration can attain its ultimate goal. Confronted by this threat, Gilles reverts to an apparently child-like innocence, exclaiming, "You have no right! The Church is my mother! I appeal to my mother! . . . I have no wish to be left out in the cold far from my mother's bosom. Help! Help!" (105-106; 131). So, his subsequent submission consists of an apparently sincere, but nonetheless strategic confession of his crimes so that the decree of excommunication might be lifted:

> For my part I recognize the absolute truth of the appalling evidence brought against me. . . . I beseech you to impose without weakness or delay the heaviest possible penalty, convinced as I am that it will still be too light for my infamy. But, at the same time, I beg you to pray ardently for me and, if your charity is capable of it, to love me as a mother loves the most wretched of her children.

> (107; 132-133)

As Prelati explains the principles of nomadic "science" before the tribunal, his apparently blasphemous interpretations of scriptures, and of Gilles's destiny, still command attention—for "these theologians, great lovers of subtle disputes, could not but cock their ears." To submit Gilles to a "benign inversion, like the one that transmutes ignoble lead into gold," says Prelati, would result in his "becoming a saint of light." For the "malign inversion," *i.e.* Gilles's "crimes under the invocation of the devil," would lead directly to the "right path" of the benign (119-120; 147-148):

> Who knows whether, one day, the witch of Rouen will not be rehabilitated, washed of all accusation, honored and celebrated? Who can say whether, one day, she will not be canonized at the court of Rome, the little shepherdess of Domrémy? St. Jeanne! What light will then not fall upon Gilles de Rais, who always followed her like a shadow? And who can say whether, in this same movement, we shall not also venerate her faithful companion: St. Gilles de Rais?

> (121; 149)

This faith in the ultimate "becoming" of his "nomad love" is carried serenely by Gilles to the pyre, as he exhorts his henchmen, "I shall precede you, therefore, to the gate of heaven. Follow me in my salvation, as you have followed me in my crimes" (123; 152), and he fi-

nally invokes his guiding light, amidst the flames, with "a celestial cry that echoed like a distant bell: 'Jeanne! Jeanne! Jeanne!'" (124; 152).

Thus, the fact that "the crimes of Gilles de Rais are neither explained nor justified by Prélat's most bold hypotheses concerning the convertibility of Evil into Good" hardly qualifies *Gilles et Jeanne* as a failure (Davis 134). For the ambiguity, paradox, indeed the undecidability for which Davis criticizes this text are, in fact, a significant mark of the tale's post-modernity. What Davis calls the "core of *Gilles et Jeanne,*" "the unsolved but urgent enigma of ethical limits and the limits of ethics" (134), is the perpetually recurring dilemma of our own century as well, one that has spawned more than its share of blood-thirsty "ogres." But, the ethical ambiguity in Tournier's *récit* extends beyond malevolent individual *illuminés* to apply as well to the State apparatus, to its justice *in extremis*. Indeed, Gilles's condemnation of his judges—"you have negotiated the buying of this or that parcel of my goods on fabulously profitable terms. No, you are not judges: you are debtors. I am not a defendant: I am a creditor" (103; 127)—recalls the (post)modern conundrum of the demand for individual "ethical limits" within institutional apparatuses that reveal themselves so frequently to be indifferent to observing any such limits. As Mireille Rosello concludes, "Tournier's *récit* thus causes to appear (and perhaps to denounce) *all* forms of violence and to show that sometimes, Christian justice and the judiciary system, as they are used in a period of 'delirium,' are basically not different from the most brutal primitive sacrifice" (94; my translation). Whether the result of individual violence or State-sanctioned operations of "capture," the ethical uncertainty which Tournier maintains, and the limits of such ethics which he questions in *Gilles et Jeanne* are part of our own compromise with the "vampiric text" and context, both scriptural and existential.

Throughout this analysis, I have tried to indicate the focal elements for a reading along nomadological lines, through the key oppositions between the State apparatus (i.e. its military and religious appropriation of the war-machine by "royal science" and law) and the eccentric forces of metamorphoses, of "becomings" of the war-machine and its traits of speed, "smooth space" and "ambulant science" inspired by the initial nomad love. Such an appropriation becomes necessary whenever the war-machine is developed not through a "line of destruction" (with war as its object), but through "the drawing of a creative line of flight, the composition of a smooth space and of the movement of people in that space" (*ATP* 422; *MP* 526). While Gilles de Rais's quest required inhuman cruelty and destructive brutality, this desire, in the words of Deleuze and Guattari, "has nothing to do with a natural or spontaneous determination; there is no desire but assembling, assembled, desire"

(*ATP* 399; *MP* 497). Gilles's goals as well as Prelati's were always "beyond" the appropriation or "capture" characteristic of the State apparatus and its science. For this "beyond"—in Gilles's case, toward ascension and *dépassement* into sanctity via the limited, barbaric tools at his disposal—is extolled by the same State apparatus which arrests (and yet, ironically, helps realize) his path toward "becoming." As Deleuze and Guattari argue, "there is a relation between the affect and the weapon, as witnessed not only in mythology, but also in the *chanson de geste,* and the chivalric novel or novel of courtly love" (*ATP* 400; *MP* 498), even of the nomadic kind. This "becoming" is a movement towards the smooth space of a nomad horizon of "flight" (in sainthood or damnation), a spiritual and existential decoding which is inevitably over-coded and captured within the boundaries of the State hierarchies.

Finally, Tournier's re-mythologizing of the story of Gilles and Jeanne lends itself to an analysis that is not so much a re-reading as a re-writing, an "assembling" of nomadological connections, moving between points, seeking the metamorphoses of the Deleuzian "bitter novelty."

Notes

An early version of this paper was presented at the 1988 NEMLA convention as part of a panel on "Exile and Nomadism." I wish to thank Françoise Lionnet and Ronnie Scharfman for their advice and encouragement in developing this essay.

1. Davis outlines how Tournier alters the historical texts and documents on the life and trial of Gilles de Rais (notably, Bataille's *Le Procès de Gilles de Rais*) to his own, literary ends, "to *complete* the story told in the historical texts" (130), or as Tournier himself puts it, to write "dans les blancs laissés par les textes sacrés et historiques" ("in the blanks left by the sacred and historical texts") (*Gilles et Jeanne,* 5; 9).

2. Bogue has coined this somewhat ungainly term to reflect accurately the collaboration of Deleuze with Guattari. My study has also gained from Stephen Muecke's "The Discourse of Nomadology: Phylums in Flux," *Art & Text* 14 (1984): 24-40.

3. For example, Joseph Garreau, "Réflexions sur Michel Tournier," *The French Review* 58.5 (1985): 682-691.

4. "Haecceity" is a term which Deleuze and Guattari utilize (borrowing *haecceitas,* "thisness," from Duns Scotus) to designate the heterogeneity, the positionality, speed, duration and affects of individuated entities without subjectivization (*ATP* 260-265; *MP* 318-324).

5. Davis notes that Tournier "regards the possibility of describing mixed states ('faux sédentaire,' 'nomades sédentarisés,' 'voyageur sédentaire,' 'vaga-

bond immobile') as a triumph of the intellect over binary oppositions. He attempts to overcome the limitations of the dichotomy by rejecting absolute barriers between opposites, and so the nomad in his texts is never entirely independent of the sedentary order" (196).

6. Developing Michel Serres's insights, Deleuze and Guattari summarize the characteristics of the eccentric, nomad science: "1) First of all, it uses a hydraulic model, rather than being a theory of solids treating fluids as a special case; . . . 2) The model in question is one of becomings and heterogeneity, as opposed to the stable, the eternal, the identical, the constant. . . . 3) One no longer goes from the straight line to its parallels, in a lamellar or laminar flow, but from a curvilinear declination to the formation of spirals and vortices on an inclined plane: the greatest slope for the smallest angle. . . . 4) Finally, the model is problematic, rather than theorematic: figures are considered only from the viewpoint of the *affections* that befall them: sections, ablations, adjunctions, projections. One does not go by specific differences from a genus to its species, or by deduction from a stable essence to the properties deriving from it, but rather from a problem to the accidents that condition and resolve it" (*ATP* 361-362; *MP* 447-448). See Serres, *La naissance de la physique dans le texte de Lucrèce. Fleuves et turbulences* (Paris: Minuit, 1977).

Works Cited

Bogue, Ronald. *Deleuze and Guattari.* New York & London: Routledge, 1989.

Davis, Colin. *Michel Tournier. Philosophy and Fiction.* Oxford: Clarendon Press, 1988.

Deleuze, Gilles, and Félix Guattari. *A Thousand Plateaus.* Trans. Brian Massumi. Minneapolis: University of Minnesota Press, 1987. (Trans. of *Mille Plateaux: capitalisme et schizophrénie II.* Paris: Minuit, 1977.)

Foucault, Michel. *The History of Sexuality,* trans. Robert Hurley. New York: Pantheon, 1978. (Trans. of *La volonté de savoir.* Paris: Gallimard, 1976.)

Patton, Paul. "Conceptual Politics and the War-Machine in *Mille Plateaux,*" *SubStance* 44/45 (1984) 61-80.

Tournier, Michel. *The Wind Spirit: An Autobiography.* Trans. Arthur Goldhammer. Boston: Beacon Press, 1988. (Trans. of *Le vent Paraclet.* Paris: Gallimard, 1977.)

Tournier, Michel. *Gilles and Jeanne.* Trans. Alan Sheridan. London: Methuen, 1987. (Trans. of *Gilles et Jeanne.* Paris: Gallimard, "Folio," 1983. References to this translation appear in the text followed by page references to the French original.)

Rosello, Mireille. "Jésus, Gilles et Jeanne: 'Qui veut noyer son chien est bien content qu'il ait la rage,'" *Stanford French Review,* 13.1 (1989), 81-95.

Abbreviations Used

The following abbreviations are used for Deleuze and Guattari's texts:

ATP: A Thousand Plateaus.

MP: Mille plateaux: capitalisme et schizophrénie II.

Susan Petit (essay date 1991)

SOURCE: Petit, Susan. "The Short Fiction." In *Michel Tournier's Metaphysical Fictions,* pp. 97-122. Amsterdam: John Benjamins Publishing Company, 1991.

[*In the following essay, Petit details the plots and themes of Tournier's short fiction, underscoring the author's dedication to young readers.*]

Tournier's short fiction is worth studying both in itself and as a key to understanding the difference between his three novels published by 1975—*Vendredi ou les limbes du Pacifique, Le Roi des aulnes,* and *Les Météores*—and his two subsequent ones, *Gaspard, Melchior et Balthazar* (1980) and *La Goutte d' or* (1985). The first three use complex language and aim at a highly literate audience; the last two employ a much simpler style and are readily accessible to the average reader. The first three include sections which have shocked readers; the last two are more good-humored and comparatively nonprovocative. The first three have plots which, though simple in outline, bristle with interesting but often tangential incidents; the plots of the last two are much more straightforwardly developed.

These changes seem to have resulted, at least in part, from Tournier's concentration in the late 1970s on short fiction aimed mainly at a juvenile audience, for whom clarity and brevity are essential. If that were the only reason to consider his short fiction, it would be enough. But the fiction is worthwhile in itself; Tournier puts the same care and energy into his writing for children that he does into his novels. This dedication to a young audience is, paradoxically, the reason that he does not like to have his work divided into "adult" and "juvenile" fiction, for those categories seem to imply that children's literature is lesser than adult literature. But Tournier claims that the opposite is true. He says that when his writing is at its very best, it is so clear that it can be understood by adults and children alike; when it is not so well written, only adults can read it ("Writing" ["Writing for Children is No Child's Play"] 33-34; Bouloumié, "Tournier" 21). He also regrets the modern idea

that fiction read by children should not treat sexuality, money, or power, saying that in the "great tales" those are the main themes (Joxe 53), and he does include those subjects in his short fiction, though more indirectly than in the novels. As a result, his children's fiction is unconventional by today's standards. It is, however, in the tradition of the authors whose children's fiction he admires, including Charles Perrault, Rudyard Kipling, and Selma Lagerlöff (Bouloumié, "Tournier" 21), who also treat elemental themes.

Children now compose Tournier's major French audience, partly because his fiction is taught in many schools in France and other French-speaking countries, and he cultivates this audience by visiting school classes and corresponding with classes by tape cassette (Tournier, "Writer" ["Writer Devoured by Children"] 180). He often has said that, if he had become a teacher as he originally planned, he would have wanted to teach philosophy not when the curriculum calls for it, in the last year of the *lycée,* but to eleven-year-olds, a desire reflected in the fact that his books read by children of that age are "disguised philosophical treatises" (Joxe 51). Interestingly, just as his "juvenile" fiction is read in elementary schools, his "adult" fiction seems to be used regularly in *lycée* classes. The novelist Patrick Grainville, for example, has written of teaching *Vendredi* [*Vendredi ou les limbes Pacifique*], *Le Roi des aulnes,* and *Les Météores* in the last year of the *lycée.*

In keeping with his goal of using fiction to teach philosophy, Tournier tries through his juvenile fiction to reach the most malleable of audiences. His belief that children are deeply influenced by the fiction they read derives from his study of anthropology, which has made him keenly aware of the initiatory function of the myths and legends which children learn in many societies; he is certain that "myth is childish at its base, metaphysical at its summit" (Brochier, "Dix-huit" 11). He wants, however, through his fiction to initiate children into society not as it is but as he thinks it should be. As Joseph McMahon says, Tournier's children's fiction does show more overt "commitment" to the values of society than do his adult works ("Michel Tournier's Texts" 166), but Tournier wants not merely to help children integrate themselves into society but also to make them question some aspects of it. This is not an abstract idea; Tournier writes for children because he likes them, and he wants his fiction to be useful to them in their struggles to understand themselves and the world.

REWRITING *VENDREDI*

Tournier's first piece of fiction accessible to children, ***Vendredi ou la vie sauvage*** (***Friday, or Primitive Life***), was a revision of his first published novel, *Vendredi ou les limbes du Pacifique.* He says that he rewrote the book because the original version was too intellectual and not rooted firmly in physical life. Despite the success of *Vendredi ou les limbes du Pacifique* and *Le Roi des aulnes,* Tournier had a difficult time finding a publisher for this new book ("Writing" 33), but it was ultimately brought out in 1971 by his regular publishing house, Gallimard, which has since published it in a variety of formats. In the United States, Knopf put it out as *Friday and Robinson: Life on Esperanza Island.*

The book was not successful in the United States despite favorable reviews (Heins, Showers), but *Vendredi ou la vie sauvage* has enjoyed enormous popularity in France. Not only is it read in class by many schoolchildren, but since 1983 it has been available in a package including two cassette tapes on which Tournier reads the text—apparently the first in Gallimard's series of book-cassette packages for children. The story's popularity with young people can also be gauged by the fact that in 1973 it was made by Antoine Vitez into a stage play (Dumur) and in 1982 it was produced in a six-hour version for French television, starring Michael York, which was the basis for a special edition of the book illustrated by photographs from the show. *Vendredi ou la vie sauvage* was also the first braille book published by the French Institut National des Jeunes Aveugles, and on Christmas Eve 1982 Tournier distributed the first copies to 130 students at the Institut (Tournier, "Préface" ["Préface à l'édition en braille"] 11).

Although the rewritten *Vendredi* [*Vendredi ou la vie sauvage*] is less than half the length of the original novel, almost none of the events of the original have been removed, the notable exception being Robinson's and Vendredi's sexual relations with the island. What have been omitted are all but one of Robinson's logbook entries, Robinson's philosophical speculation, and many of the religious references. Use of a somewhat intrusive omniscient narrator reduces ambiguity but enhances clarity, and leaving out most of the philosophical reflections in the original makes the story more action-centered. A few incidents which do not appear in the long version, such as Vendredi's teaching Araucanian sign language to Robinson, should appeal to children, especially as Tournier made them up while telling the original story to children (Tournier, "Les Enfants" ["Les Enfants dans la bibliothèque"] 56). And here and there Tournier has softened the original. For example, in both versions, Robinson first sees Vendredi when the latter is running away from Indians trying to kill him, and in both versions Vendredi escapes because Robinson kills one of his pursuers. But whereas in the long version Robinson is actually trying to shoot Vendredi, in the "Junior" version he is aiming at one of the pursuers.

The clarity of the rewritten book has been admired by Michael J. Worton ("Ecrire" and "Michel Tournier") and Jean-Michel Maulpoix ("Des Limbes" 37), but I

miss the ambiguity of the original. The narrator sometimes sounds like a teacher, as when he explains that when Robinson decided not to eat any of the wheat from his first harvest he "followed a new tendency, *avarice,* which was going to do him a great deal of harm" (34), and he sounds like a parent when he explains that although Vendredi chewed maggots before feeding them to a sick vulture, meat or hard-boiled egg will do very well instead (76). Oddly, the revision is less amusing than the original, whose humor depends largely on the incongruity between Robinson's actions and his surroundings and on a deadpan style of narration.

The story's themes remain unchanged. The revision, like the original, implies that Western civilization needs to be saved by "primitive" responses to the world, just as Robinson needs to be saved by Vendredi from pointless activity. The theme of return to the womb is developed clearly, with the grotto described as "so soft, so warm, so white that [Robinson] couldn't help thinking of his mother" (55). The book's action also still retraces the story of the Bible, with Robinson associated with the Old Testament, Vendredi with the New, and the *Whitebird* with the Holy Spirit. The ram Andoar's role as both scapegoat and Christ is stressed when Vendredi says that Andoar "died saving me" (125). And as in the original book, after Vendredi leaves on the *Whitebird,* Robinson finds a millennial happiness on the island with the ship's cabin boy, who is at once an avatar of the Holy Spirit and a playmate to whom he can teach the games which Vendredi has taught him. However, although Tournier claims that the longer book is just a "rough draft" for the shorter version (Joxe 53), the latter has not generally been admired by critics (Worton, "Michel Tournier" 24). It is, in fact, much weaker than the longer book—a not entirely successful attempt at producing the clarity and simplicity he was striving for.

Tournier's Short Stories: An Overview

I find Tournier's short stories more appealing than *Vendredi ou la vie sauvage* because they are less explicit. His first collection, published in 1978, *Le Coq de bruyère* (translated into English as *The Fetishist,* 1983), includes thirteen stories and a one-act play. Several of those stories have been published individually in illustrated editions for children, including **"Amandine ou les deux jardins," "La Fugue du petit Poucet," "Que ma joie demeure,"** and **"L'Aire du Muguet."** (Another of the stories, **"Le Nain rouge,"** was published separately as an illustrated piece of mild erotica.) The stories which appeal most to children, **"Amandine ou les deux jardins," "La Fugue du petit Poucet," "La Fin de Robinson Crusoé," "La Mère Noël,"** and **"Que ma joie demeure,"** were reprinted in 1984 in *Sept contes* (*Seven Tales*) in Gallimard's "junior" series along with two other stories by Tournier, *Pierrot ou les se-*

crets de la nuit and **Barbedor,** both of which have also appeared individually as illustrated children's books. Like **Vendredi ou la vie sauvage, Sept contes** is available in book-cassette combination, with Tournier reading the stories, and **"La Fugue du petit Poucet"** is read by Raymond Gérome on a cassette which includes another children's story by Daniel Boulanger. In all of these short fictions, it is even more obvious than in the novels that Tournier is not inspired by real events; these are true *contes,* tales which begin from ideas, rather than *nouvelles,* or stories inspired by true events. The stories are rigorously constructed, with characterization subordinated everywhere to plot, and plot subordinated to theme, earning Salim Jay's praise of Tournier as a prince of tale-tellers ("Plumes" 145).

Because of their thematic connection, I will discuss together the thirteen stories and one play in **Le Coq de bruyère.** The most obvious structural device is length: each story is, roughly speaking, longer than the previous one, an increase in length which signals a gradual increase in complexity and sophistication. There is also chronological progression, for the first stories are set in the distant past and the later ones are clearly fixed in contemporary times. But there is a more important thematic unifying device, suggested by the number of the pieces, fourteen, and the stories' focus on moral choices. It seems clear that the first seven stories—the stories which children can most appreciate—each illustrate one of the seven cardinal virtues, and the next six stories and the play each illustrate one of the seven deadly sins. Taken as a whole, the book makes a comment on morality in our time.

Le Coq de bruyere: The Virtues

The seven cardinal virtues are generally considered to be composed of the three "theological virtues" of faith, hope, and charity, listed by Paul in the First Epistle to the Corinthians (13.13), and the four "moral virtues" of prudence, justice, temperance, and fortitude. The classification of the moral virtues results from the synthesis of ancient Greek ideas and Christian doctrine by the Scholastics, particularly Thomas Aquinas.

Faith, the "substance of things hoped for, the evidence of things not seen" (Heb. 11.1), is illustrated in the first story, **"La Famille Adam,"** which narrates the Creation up to Cain's murder of Abel and—an event added by Tournier—Cain's eventual reconciliation with God. Many of the events are whimsical, including the account of an Adam with both male and female genitals, whom Jehovah splits into male and female halves so he will produce children. This concept owes less to the biblical account of Eve's creation from Adam's rib than to a playful theory which Plato puts into the mouth of Aristophanes in *The Symposium.* (Although Plato presumably subscribed to the theory which Socrates devel-

ops later in *The Symposium,* in which physical love is less important than mental love, Aristophanes' robustly physical view of sex has had great appeal to many people, obviously including Tournier.) According to the idea ascribed to Aristophanes, man originally existed in three forms—all male, all female, and androgynous—but Zeus cut man apart to reduce his strength. Ever since, people have been trying through sexual relations—whether homophile, lesbian, or heterosexual—to rediscover their original wholeness (Plato, *Symposium* 30-32). In Tournier's story Jehovah is jealous of Cain's ability to cultivate fields and build houses and so to create his own "Eden II" (16). But even when God drives Cain away in punishment for the murder of Abel, Cain illustrates faith by believing Jehovah will return. And He finally does, tired of wandering around in the smelly Ark of the Covenant with the nomads.

Hope, which relies "on the readiness of [God's] almighty power to come to our assistance" (Ramirez Dulanto 140), is shown in its negative side, despair, in **"La Fin de Robinson Crusoé,"** a tale of lost paradise. Crusoe returns to England but is unable to forget his island. He finally goes searching for it, in vain, realizing only at the story's end that he has seen it without recognizing it, for it has changed just as he has (24). Hope must look toward the future; Crusoe despairs because he wants, impossibly, to recover the past.

Although charity is traditionally listed third in the theological virtues, it is considered the most important, for, as Paul says, "though I have all faith, so that I could remove mountains, and have not charity, I am nothing" (1 Cor. 13.2). Charity means loving both God and neighbor; and reconciling the love of God with the love of man is the main theme of **"La Mère Noël"** (**"Mother Christmas"**). The Breton town of Pouldreuzic is divided between the devout Christians, who attend mass on Christmas Eve, and those in the anticlerical group, who support the schoolteacher's dressing up as Father Christmas, or Santa Claus, and giving toys to the children on Christmas Eve. A new teacher seems to belong to both camps, for although she is divorced, she attends mass, and when Christmas comes, she continues the tradition of dressing as Santa Claus but lends her baby to represent Jesus in the church's "living crèche" (30). The climax shows that one can combine love of God with love of man: when the baby cannot be quieted at the mass, its mother, still dressed as Father Christmas, strides into church and, pushing aside her long white beard, nurses her child.

This vision of a man-woman nursing a baby is central to Tournier's thinking, what he calls a "fundamental fantasy" about man's nourishing function (Coulaud), and he says that she is the character in all his work to whom he feels closest (Braudeau 87). He even posed as "Mother Christmas" for a drawing on a band going around the cover of *Le Coq de bruyère* (Braudeau 88). Adam's androgynous original condition (according to **"La Famille Adam"**) seems to be recovered, for if Father Christmas turns out to be *Mother* Christmas, then sexual division is not absolute. The tale also implies that one can serve both God and man, for the teacher gives presents to the children and also supports the church's crèche, just as in nursing her own baby she is also, symbolically, serving the Christ Child, whom her baby represents. The appeal of this story is suggested by the fact that it has been offered as a model text for class use (Kirpalani).

The next four stories, illustrating the four moral virtues, are less innocent and less childlike, although they too can be read and understood by children. **"Amandine ou les deux jardins"** illustrates prudence, the "perfected ability to make right decisions" (Pieper 6), the virtue by means of which knowledge is brought "to bear on an individual course of action" (Gilby 927). Amandine is a ten-year-old girl, and the two gardens of the title are the too-well-tended one of her parents and another, secret one behind the wall of her parents' garden. As Tournier has explained in an interview reprinted in *Le Coq de bruyère,* the story is about initiation into the secret, sexual adult world symbolized by the hidden garden (337). This story also touches on androgyny by contrasting the rigid sexual separation in Amandine's parents' house with the sexual ambiguity of nature. This ambiguity is presented humorously at first, when Amandine cannot tell whether her cat is male or female because it is named Claude, but it emerges more seriously at the end when Amandine's expression is compared to that on a statue of the male god Eros (46). Amandine's passage to adulthood is symbolized, rather too obviously, by the onset of her first menstrual period at the end of the story, and less obviously by her realizing that Claude's kitten is pregnant. At the end, the reader sees that Amandine is prepared to be prudent, in the theological sense—she can bring knowledge to bear on her actions.

The second moral virtue, justice, "the strong and firm will to give to each his due," is also "the mediator in the personal order of love" (Häring 69). Justice should, therefore, be subordinated to love. **"La Fugue du petit Poucet"** (**"Little Poucet's Flight"**) contrasts repressive justice with forgiving love. The story is a whimsical variation on Perrault's "Le Petit Poucet," generally translated as "Tom Thumb," which is about a woodcutter's boy who tricks an ogre into killing his own seven daughters and steals the ogre's seven-league boots. Perrault's details are all updated by Tournier—the woodcutter in **"La Fugue du petit Poucet"** is responsible for removing trees in Paris to make room for more cars, the ogre is replaced by a hippie named Logre, and the seven-league boots turn into Logre's knee-high buckskin boots (57).

Little Poucet runs away from home on December 23 and finds himself in the forest south of Paris, close to Tournier's village of Choisel, where he discovers Logre and his seven little daughters. Logre incarnates an androgynous ideal, a man as "handsome as a woman" (57) with his long hair, heavy jewelry, and fringed clothes, and his pacifist philosophy and vegetarian diet give little Poucet an insight into love he does not see at home. On that night of the winter solstice, Logre tells a story of the fall of man showing Yahweh, the Old Testament's God of justice, as narrow and vindictive; but Logre teaches that man can live in harmony with himself and nature if, like a tree, he remains firmly linked with earth. False justice appears to triumph when police the next morning arrest Logre for "corrupting minors" (64), but Logre, looking like Christ in his long tunic, his hair "parted in the middle, fall[ing] freely on his shoulders" (63), shows love by giving Poucet his beautiful boots to wear "in memory of me" (63), a phrase echoing Christ's words at the Last Supper. At the story's end, on Christmas Eve little Poucet is wearing the "dream boots," which change him in imagination to a huge chestnut tree. The justice of the father has been replaced by Logre's love, just as the birth of Christ signals the end of the justice of the Old Testament and the coming of forgiveness through Christ.

Temperance, the third moral virtue, is illustrated in the cruel story **"Tupik,"** whose title is a phonetic rendering of a little boy's complaint when his father tries to kiss him: "Tu piques!"—"you scratch!" The boy is nicknamed Tupik because he is excessively sensitive to harshness, which he associates with adult males, such as those who use the "comfort station" in the square where he is taken on nice days to play. Because the men's side of the facility is dirty and smelly, Tupik prefers the women's side with its clean towels and sweet-smelling toilet paper. A series of misunderstandings about sexual identity, exacerbated by his nursemaid's threat to cut off his "little faucet" if he doesn't stop wetting his bed (79), results in Tupik's concluding that men can become women if they cut off their genitals. In the story's hair-raising conclusion, he does just that. True temperance is not hatred of the body; it is "selfless self-preservation" shown in "chastity, continence, humility, gentleness, mildness" (Pieper 150-55). But Tupik's world makes him hate his sexual identity. The story implies that Christianity is more than a little responsible for this attitude, for it is partly because of a painting of the Last Judgment (71) that Tupik associates the men's side of the toilet facility with Hell and the women's side with Heaven.

The last of the four moral virtues, fortitude, lets one "adhere to a reasonable course of action when faced with . . . grave peril" and includes a "willingness to endure suffering" (Kane). This virtue is exhibited by the protagonist of the funny and sad **"Que ma joie de-**

meure," named for the Bach cantata known in English as *Jesus, Joy of Man's Desiring* (which also gave its name to a well-known novel by Jean Giono). Raphaël Bidoche, whose name could be roughly rendered as "Raphael Crumb," is a talented pianist forced to earn his living by betraying his talent: he becomes a wildly successful musical parodist. He does not so much enjoy success as suffer it, for it pains him to betray his art. Nevertheless, his fortitude lets him live with his destiny. He is finally rewarded on Christmas Eve, when his piano, instead of exploding as planned while he is performing in a circus, works perfectly so that he can play *Que ma joie demeure,* and let the crowd "commune" (98) with each other and, presumably, with God. A miracle takes place at the end: the Archangel Raphael, Bidoche's namesake, emerges from under the piano lid. Bidoche, though beset by a corrupt world, remains innocent through fortitude.

LE COQ DE BRUYERE: THE VICES

The last seven fictions in **Le Coq de bruyère,** only one of which is likely to interest a child, reveal the seven deadly sins as Tournier sees them. The first three sins in the traditional listing are considered to be "cold"— anger, envy, and pride. Lucien Gagneron, protagonist of **"Le Nain rouge" ("The Red Dwarf"),** is angry because he is so short. His anger leads him eventually to murder his mistress, then to humiliate and sodomize her husband, whom he has framed for the murder. He vents his anger also in his circus act, in which he externalizes his hatred for normal life and ordinary-sized people. The story would be unrelievedly cruel, but Lucien is at least partly redeemed by his closeness to children. At the end, he treats a whole tentful of children on Christmas Eve to a private performance, where the children's applause "washed him of his bitterness, made him innocent" (121). The story implies that even someone eaten up by anger can be saved, and its title reminds us that a red dwarf is a kind of star, maybe even a Christmas star.

"Tristan Vox" illustrates the pointlessness of envy, "culpable sadness or displeasure at the spiritual or temporal good of another" (Herbst) resulting from "the belief that one cannot acquire" that which one wants (Lyman 185). Tristan Vox is the romantic performing name of a radio announcer, whose real name is the prosaic Félix Robinet ("Felix Faucet"). Robinet is balding and middle-aged, but his audience imagines him as young, handsome, and romantic. The surprise is that the listeners most caught by this false belief are Robinet's wife and secretary, who desire what they cannot have, for they are jealous of a Tristan Vox they know to be imaginary. The story begins light-heartedly, but it ends with the secretary's suicide and the wife's continuing obsession with Tristan Vox, who is now played by another announcer.

Pride, which springs from self-love and which may result in using other people "solely toward the achievement of [one's] own private ends" (Parmisano 766), is shown by the title character in **"Les Suaires de Véronique" ("Veronica's Winding-Sheets").** For the sake of photographic experiments, Véronique destroys her model, Hector. She controls his life, ruins his skin, and seems, finally, to have destroyed Hector himself by making "dermographic" reproductions (171) of him on light-sensitive linen in which she has wrapped his naked, solution-dipped body (169). The tiger's tooth she takes from Hector symbolizes her pride, or *morgue,* which has resulted in a photographic exhibit that suggests a "morgue" (171). Véronique is clearly a negative counterpart to Saint Veronica, on whose handkerchief was supposedly imprinted the countenance of Christ. The story's complexity is shown in the fact that an entire number of the journal *Incidences* was composed of six essays analyzing it (Bourbonnais et al.).

Neither cold nor warm is the fourth sin, *acedia* or sloth, "a disgust with the spiritual because of the physical effort involved" (Voll 83). Sloth is illustrated by Mélanie Blanchard, the heroine of the bizarre **"La Jeune Fille et la mort,"** named for Schubert's quartet *Death and the Maiden.* She suffers from a perpetual "crisis of boredom" (179) and can stay interested in life only through sensations and ideas suggesting death. She finally decides to kill herself to end the "nausea of existence" (198), but before she can do so, she dies of a crisis of laughter brought on by a "divine surprise" (199), the delivery of a functional scale-model guillotine. Mélanie is actually joyful when she dies on September 29, the feast of the Archangels Michael, Raphael, and Gabriel. Like Raphaël Bidoche, she may have had an angel watching over her, for her sudden death saves her from suicide.

Three pieces about the "warm" sins end the collection. The title story, **"Le Coq de bruyère,"** illustrates avarice. The Baron Guillaume de Saint-Fursy, called "le coq de bruyère" ("the woodgrouse") because of his womanizing and his bandy legs, is not avaricious for money; his avarice is the sort which takes the form of display and of "mak[ing] objects of all we touch" (Fairlie 149). The baron's life has consisted largely of displaying his prowess in swordsmanship, riding, hunting, and womanizing, and he is ultimately more interested in displaying his conquest of young Mariette than in the girl herself. His wife is avaricious, too, for she wants to display her piety, despite being warned by her priest against self-righteousness. Mariette is simply avaricious for the baron's money. The story is full of twists and turns as the baron and his wife struggle for the upper hand, the aging husband grasping at a last affair and the wife trying to keep both her husband and her belief that she is a good Christian, but the baroness seems finally to win when the baron has a stroke and becomes partially paralyzed. His body is fixed in a position which seems to mock his earlier gestures when he falsely claimed that he had found "perfect happiness" with Mariette (257), although he may have found happiness in being stripped of everything.

Gluttony is the subject of the next story, **"L'Aire du Muguet"** (**"The Lily of the Valley Rest Area"**), the one story in the second part of the book to be printed separately as a "Junior" book. Gluttony is distinguished by a desire to consume and by haste (Fairlie 168), and haste is the key to the main character, Pierre, a young truck driver. Like a typical glutton, he does not take the time to enjoy his food (273), and he also worships speed (269). Pretty Marinette's charm for him lies mainly in the fact that she is on the far side of the fence separating the rest area from the countryside. Later, his "desire for immediate satisfaction" (282) makes him act irrationally in trying to find her village. Finally Pierre is struck repeatedly as he tries to walk across the toll road, and presumably he is dying as an ambulance carries him away. (In an inside joke, her town is Lusigny-sur-Ouche, where the Tourniers went during World War II because food was easier to find there than in Paris.)

The last sin, lust, excessive love of sexual pleasure leading to "blindness of mind, rashness, thoughtlessness, inconstancy, self-love, and excessive attachment to the material world" (Regan 1081), is illustrated in the one-act, one-character play *Le Fétichiste,* which was produced in Paris in 1974 (*Coq* [*Le Coq de bruyère*] 340) and 1982 (Rev. of *Le Fétichiste*), Berlin in 1974 (*Coq* 340), England in 1983 (Hayman, "Underwear"), and the United States in 1984 (Dieckman), where Ubu Repertory Theater has published it as the third in its playscripts series. The play's punning subtitle, *Un Acte pour un homme seul,* suggests the masturbatory nature of the fetishism of Martin, whose main interest is women's underclothes. In an interview, Tournier has called fetishism "an absolutely unique kind of perversion" because a fetishist is "hyper-social," having overvalued clothing, which is a creation of civilization, unlike other sexual rebels, who he believes are antisocial (Sanzio et al. 15). The fetishist is, therefore, precisely the opposite of the rebels and "heretics" that Tournier most admires. As to lust itself, if it looks at the body rather than the whole person, it is an aggravated form of lust which looks only at the clothing on that body; or, in Tournier's words, "What is essential [the body] is rejected and only the detail counts—what for so-called normal people is the detail . . ." (Sanzio et al. 17).

Martin, who has temporarily escaped from his keepers at an asylum, explains his lust for women's "frillies" and for men's wallets, especially those carried near the heart; he used to steal men's wallets partly to pay for women's underclothes, but also because of a bisexuality of which he is not fully aware. Martin tells the audience his life story, which is full of burlesque episodes, including his extortion of a garter belt from a woman in the Paris *Métro* at the height of the Christmas rush, but his story is sad, too. As he is taken away by his attendants, he waves a pair of women's panties, saying, "I'm coming back. With my flag. The pirates' black flag. Long live death!" (333). Lust has destroyed Martin's life.

In each of these pieces, Tournier has constructed a plot illustrating the effects of having or not having a virtue, or of succumbing to or resisting a vice. Some of the vices and virtues are presented in an entirely secular context and others are seen from a religious angle, but each story presents a moral issue and shows one way in which a person may deal with it, successfully or not. Plot is crucial. Characterization is generally sketchy, although in some stories, notably **"Le Coq de bruyère,"** it is subtle and penetrating. But no matter how much realistic detail there may be, the stories derive from ideas. Their charm comes largely from whimsical humor, simplicity of language, and plotting which continually surprises with its logical but unexpected developments.

The stories all show remarkable technical virtuosity, wit, and warmth. The narration, especially, shows great skill. The omniscient narrator of **"La Famille Adam"** is authoritative but amused, but the omniscient narrator of **"Le Coq de bruyère"** is self-effacing, nearly transparent. The first-person narrator of **"Les Suaires de Véronique"** could be Tournier himself, but ten-year-old Amandine tells her story in diary form, in an entirely different voice, and the chatty Martin narrates quirkily the story of his life in *Le Fétichiste.* The tone of **"La Mère Noël"** suggests a legend; **"La Fugue du petit Poucet"** is whimsical; **"Le Coq de bruyère"** resembles a tale by Maupassant. In all of the stories, Tournier's wit is much in evidence, although it takes different forms, from wordplay to allusion to unexpected logic-twisting on the parts of characters, and the tone is much more playful than that of the previous novels. The wit is always accompanied by human warmth, even in the most painful of stories, such as **"Tupik"** and **"Le Nain rouge"**: the events may be cruel, but one always feels Tournier's compassion.

Pierrot ou les secrets de la nuit and
Barbedor

Two fine later works examine the nature of salvation while remaining adventure stories easily understood by children. In 1979, the year after *Le Coq de bruyère,* Tournier published *Pierrot ou les secrets de la nuit,* which he has often claimed is his best work. This short tale inspired by the familiar song "Au clair de la lune" is now published both in *Sept contes* and by itself in the Gallimard Enfantimages series, although it first came out in a specially designed format intended,

Tournier feels, to quarantine it from Gallimard's other children's books because its originality rendered it suspect ("Writing" 34). Tournier calls the book an "adventure-story, with a powerful metaphysical foundation" ("Writing" 34), whose main characters are inspired by the Italian *commedia dell' arte* figures of Harlequin, Pierrot, and Columbine.

Pierrot, a baker in Pouldreuzic (the setting of **"La Mère Noël"**), loves the laundress Colombine, but she is frightened by the night, which is when he must work. The house painter Arlequin charms her with his cheerful nature and bright colors, and she goes away with him; but when their love fades in winter, Colombine returns to Pouldreuzic with new insight into Pierrot and the night, whose beauty she has at last seen. At the end, Arlequin also arrives, singing "Au clair de la lune," its words given new meaning by the story's plot, and is warmly welcomed by the other two.

The story's "metaphysical foundation" centers in part on the contrast between sunlight, which bleaches the sheets Colombine washes but fades Arlequin's bright colors, and moonlight, which Pierrot loves and associates with sexuality. The tale also works against sex stereotyping, for Pierrot, as a baker, is feminized by his occupation, while Colombine's resourcefulness, strength, and independence may seem to be masculine qualities. The story, as Margaret R. Higonnet points out, "invokes traditional oppositions and themes" just as Tournier's long fiction does (154). But more important than these oppositions is the religious theme. Just as **Vendredi** rewrote the Old and New Testaments, this story presents the three persons of the Trinity through the three fictional characters. Pierrot, who provides the village with its daily bread, is like God the Father; the vivid, cheerful Arlequin is like Christ, literally bringing color to towns as he paints them, much as Christ, according to Koussek in *Les Météores*, brought "color, heat, and pain" (161) to religion. Colombine, so called because she reminds people of a dove, or *colombe* (**Sept** [**Sept contes**] 9), represents the Holy Spirit, traditionally symbolized by the dove.

The story's conclusion suggests the Last Supper, as Jean-Bernard Vray has pointed out ("L'Habit" 156-58). When Colombine returns to Pouldreuzic, Pierrot sculpts her form in *brioche* dough and bakes it, and after Arlequin joins them, Colombine tears out pieces of the *brioche* and offers them to Pierrot and Arlequin: "taste, eat the good Colombine! Eat me!" (**Sept** 32). This version of the Last Supper unites the Trinity, rather than God and man, but its most important characteristic is that not Christ but the Holy Spirit is the source of Communion and thus, by implication, of salvation. As in **Vendredi** and *Les Météores,* Tournier here insists that salvation comes through the Holy Spirit. Christ and Christianity, like Arlequin, are reduced to interesting but unnecessary steps.

The simpler story **Barbedor,** an Arabian Nights tale embedded in Tournier's novel *Gaspard, Melchior et Balthazar* (1980), also concerns salvation. Like **Pierrot** [**Pierrot ou les secrets de la nuit**], it is published separately in the Enfantimages series as well as in the collection **Sept contes.** Barbedor ("Goldbeard") is the nickname of Nabounassar III, a king with a beautiful golden beard but no heirs to the throne. Mysteriously, as soon as white hairs appear in his beard, they vanish during his afternoon nap. He finally has only one beard hair left, but he is lucky enough to see it plucked out and carried off by a white bird. King Barbedor chases the bird and discovers its nest, made entirely of his white hairs, with a single golden egg inside. Then Barbedor realizes that he is no longer a portly king; he has turned back into a little boy. When he returns to his city, carrying the egg, he sees his own funeral—or that of the person he was—and from the egg comes a bird which proclaims the now beardless Barbedor to be King Nabounassar IV.

Tournier is working with the theme of rebirth through the Holy Spirit, which is represented by the white bird that proclaims Barbedor the new king in an echo of the Holy Spirit's appearing in the form of a dove at Christ's baptism when God proclaimed Jesus to be His "beloved Son, in whom I am well pleased" (Matt. 3.17). The elderly Barbedor is symbolically reborn through this bird, as a believer is symbolically reborn through baptism. It is not hard, either, to see that Barbedor, with his full beard, is like God the Father, and the reborn Barbedor, the little boy, is like Christ: the story can be read as an allegory of Christ's birth. Because the story's last lines say that the new king had no successors and began to grow a beautiful golden beard, one must conclude that history will repeat itself: another age, presumably a rule of the Holy Spirit, will succeed Christianity.

GILLES ET JEANNE

Tournier's concern with salvation is also behind **Gilles et Jeanne** (1983), a novella-length *récit,* or narrative, which began as a scenario for a television film which was not made. Unfortunately, this story never succeeds in mastering its complex material, the personal and metaphysical relationship between Joan of Arc (Jeanne) and Gilles de Rais, a marshal of France who fought alongside Joan and who, like her, was burned at the stake for sorcery, although unlike Joan he unquestionably worshiped the Devil. The brevity of the narrative, its frequent chapter divisions, and its simple style suggest that Tournier hoped for an audience of young people—not children, perhaps, but teenagers. However, his inclusion of some of the horrifying details of Gilles's crimes (which even most historical studies did not relate until recently) makes one wonder if young people were really his intended audience. It is only fair to say, though, that he brings out those details after Gilles's crimes are over and presents them only through testimony at the trial.

The *récit* deals with many of the same themes as *Le Roi des aulnes* (Petit, "*Gilles*," and Nettelbeck, "The Return"), including the inversion of good and evil, sexual inversion, destiny, and the voluptuous power of destruction. Like Tiffauges, Gilles de Rais is obsessional, pursues a pleasure based on the subjugation of boys, and seeks metaphysical enlightenment. Tiffauges, however, is not intentionally cruel to the young boys at the *Napola*, whereas Gilles deliberately tortures, sodomizes, and murders hundreds of children, mostly boys; and Tiffauges changes for the better when he comes under the influence of Ephraïm, whereas Gilles does not repent until he is on trial for his life.

Tournier researched the lives of both Joan of Arc and Gilles de Rais, but the book is written, as the publisher's insert says, "in the blanks left by the historical records." Tournier has called this technique a game in which he "respects the letter" of the history he is telling but recounts a totally different story from the familiar one (Bouloumié, "Tournier" 22). He imagines that Gilles became a criminal precisely because of Joan of Arc's influence: Gilles swears to follow her wherever she goes, and, having seen her burned for witchcraft and apparently sent to Hell, he tries to follow her there by raping and torturing boys. Tournier conceives of Gilles as having been attracted to boys from the start (*Gilles* [*Gilles et Jeanne*] 12) and imagines that Joan's boyish appearance made her into an ideal companion for Gilles, but Gilles's homophilia is not violent until after Joan's death. And even then, the book insists on a close connection between Gilles's sadism and his religious feelings, for Gilles's emotions are most stirred by Herod's Massacre of the Innocents, and he founds and magnificently endows a school in honor of the Holy Innocents, even posing for a painting there of Herod (47).

Gilles's first act after Joan's death is to plunge into debauchery, but later he regains his sense of the sacred under the influence of the Italian Francesco Prelati, or François Prélat. Prélat is imbued with the spirit of the Renaissance, including alchemy, which in the fifteenth century often involved invocations of devils and was condemned by the Church as heretical and blasphemous. Led by Prélat, Gilles not only continues to kidnap, sodomize, torture, and kill children, but also uses their bodies in devil worship. When Gilles is ultimately arrested and tried, Prélat claims that he helped Gilles spiritually by restoring to him the sense of the sacred, "cauterizing the festering wounds" of Gilles with the fires of Hell (135), and says that he expected "benign inversion" to transform Gilles's evil into sanctity as lead is converted to gold (136). Although Prélat is an unscrupulous and cunning adventurer, the story implies that the "benign inversion" worked, for Gilles repents of his crimes and, in addition, Tournier changes some details of Gilles's execution to make it resemble more closely Joan of Arc's. He implies that, if Gilles is judged not by his acts but by his motives and his repentance, he may be a saint. Although such a conclusion is entirely possible from a Christian point of view, from which only God can know one's motives and the condition of one's soul, most readers of *Gilles et Jeanne* have been unable to accept Gilles's possible sainthood both because of the atrocity of his crimes and because of the absence of information about what he is thinking at the end of his life.

Tournier had used many of the ideas in *Gilles et Jeanne* in his previous novels, but their treatment is less satisfactory here than there. Perhaps it is the comparatively sketchy plot development which keeps one from becoming truly involved in the story and interested in the characters, who are outlines rather than developed human beings. The narrative angle of vision also helps keep one at a distance. The third-person narrator takes us freely into the mind of Gilles's confessor, Blanchet, a minor character, but he seldom lets us know what Prélat is thinking. Gilles's thoughts are revealed in the book's early sections, but even before Joan's death he becomes an enigma. And on occasion the narrator merely tells the reader what the people in the countryside see, not what is happening in Gilles's castles. These shifts reveal the book's origin as scenario and its incomplete conversion to *récit*. It is not surprising that *Gilles et Jeanne* was received coolly by many French critics (Boisdeffre, rev. of *Gilles*; Galey, "L'Ange noir"; Hue). One exception is Mireille Rosello, who considers *Gilles et Jeanne* a major novel (16).

THE WISE MEN

In the same year that *Gilles et Jeanne* appeared, 1983, Tournier published *Les Rois mages* (*The Wise Men*), a simpler and briefer version of his 1980 novel *Gaspard, Melchior et Balthazar*. This was his first revision of a novel into shorter form since *Vendredi ou la vie sauvage* and is a somewhat more successful one. In the next chapter I will discuss *Gaspard, Melchior et Balthazar*; here I will concentrate on those elements peculiar to *Les Rois mages* or necessary to understanding its form and focus. The book is composed of three self-contained but complementary tales, the stories of the three Wise Men, as imagined by Tournier: Gaspard, King of Méroé in Africa, who suffers from rejected love and needs to be reconciled to his blackness; Balthazar, King of Nipour in the Middle East, who mourns the loss of his art collection and seeks a new form of art; and Taor, Prince of Mangalore in India, who wants the recipe for pistachio Turkish delight. The adventure of each of the Wise Men is told with wit and whimsy, but Taor's odyssey, which occupies half of the book, is the one on which Tournier appears to have lavished the most care.

As in so much of his short fiction, Tournier uses an omniscient narrator. The several explanatory footnotes scattered throughout unfortunately make it sound at times a little like a textbook, but Tournier avoids preaching or overexplaining much more successfully than in **Vendredi ou la vie sauvage.** He relies more on the reader's judgment here than he did in **Vendredi,** and he usually succeeds in creating the tone of a fable. Tournier makes the most of parallels among the tales—for example, the African king has camels, the Middle Eastern king has horses, and the Indian prince has elephants—and emphasizes exotic elements while introducing occasional anachronisms to bring the story home. Gaspard's concern with skin color and race clearly has meaning for any contemporary reader, and Turkish delight is featured by the many African and Middle Eastern candy shops in Paris.

The theme of **Les Rois mages** is the quest for acceptance and fulfillment. In the first tale, Gaspard falls in love with a white slave, "discovers" his own blackness, and suffers when he finds out that she is deceiving him with the white man she has claimed is her brother. Gaspard's real problem is his rejection of his own blackness, for he thinks that his black skin makes him unlovable. Two amazing—and amusing—discoveries make him able to accept himself again: first, he realizes that the earth from which Jehovah supposedly formed Adam is the same color as his own skin, and, second, he sees that Jesus is black, although Mary and Joseph are white. This miracle—for it does seem to be a miracle—makes Gaspard see black as the color of redeemed flesh. Gaspard recounts the manger scene many years later to his great-grandchildren (39-41), so we also learn that Gaspard becomes an old man at peace with himself.

Balthazar's problem is similar. He has been devastated by the destruction of an art museum to which he had dedicated his life; because his religion, like Judaism, forbids graven images, the priests have incited the public to destroy the supposedly impious art. All of Balthazar's emotional life has been constructed around art: as a young man, he fell in love with a woman in a portrait and married the model, and when she stopped resembling her portrait, he stopped loving her and dedicated himself to collecting art. If the Incarnation redeems the flesh for Gaspard, it redeems art for Balthazar. The art destroyed in the riot was Greek, Egyptian, and Middle Eastern sculpture representing gods and heroes, supermen and superwomen (57), but at the manger Balthazar discovers the possibility of an art showing the inner beauty of ordinary people (76-77). God no longer forbids representation of the human body, because in taking human form God showed that the outward image of an ordinary, sinful person could be joined to an inner resemblance to God (73-76).

The third Wise Man, Taor, arrives in Bethlehem too late to see Jesus. Accompanied by a host of servants and five elephants, he sails up the Red Sea and marches into Judea, losing parts of his train along the way, in his quest for the recipe for Turkish delight. In Bethlehem, he gives a banquet for the hungry children, an act of love and generosity which is a better way of worshiping Jesus than giving him gifts, for serving children is a way of serving God. As Jesus says, "Inasmuch as ye have done *it* unto one of the least of these my brethren, ye have done *it* unto me" (Matt. 25.40). Taor serves others also when, near Sodom, he is moved by pity for the family of a camel driver about to be imprisoned and offers to pay the man's debt. When his treasurer informs him that there is almost no money left, Taor (who has no idea whether the 33 talents owed is a large or a small sum) offers to work off the man's debt himself (136) and is promptly sentenced to 33 years in the salt mines. The horrible conditions in the mines, which may be reminiscent of a descent into a symbolic hell in many fairy tales, are described only briefly, presumably so that they will not be too disturbing. The inhabitants of Sodom, both men and women, are sodomites in the sexual sense, but the explanation given the naive Taor is designed for children: "Everybody does you-know-what [*fait doudou*] from the front. As for the Sodomites, they do you-know-what from behind" (148). This hell becomes Taor's path to Heaven in another benign inversion, for in the mines Taor hears about Christ's teachings, so when he is finally released, he seeks Jesus. He arrives in Jerusalem after the Last Supper is finished, but he eats and drinks some of the leftovers and is carried to Heaven by two angels (158).

Gaspard discovers how to accept his flesh; Balthazar sees that redeemed human flesh can be represented in art; Taor learns how to make his redeemed flesh live forever through the Resurrection. Each Magus has made a greater discovery than the last. Gaspard finds a human happiness; Balthazar discovers immortality through art; Taor achieves literal immortality through the resurrection of the flesh promised by Christianity. I will leave fuller consideration of the implications of the story to my discussion of *Gaspard, Melchior et Balthazar,* but it should be clear that **Les Rois mages** reflects an increasing emphasis on Christian themes and represents a step toward greater limpidity of language and simplicity of organization. As Michael J. Worton says, its stylistic and organizational tactics make it resemble a parable ("Michel Tournier" 253).

SHORT FICTION IN THE NOVELS

Besides writing individual stories, Tournier increasingly encapsulates tales in his longer fiction. He began in *Gaspard, Melchior et Balthazar,* where one chapter became **Barbedor.** La Goutte d'or, published in 1985, includes two chapters which are complete in themselves, **"Barberousse ou le portrait du roi,"** published separately in *La Nouvelle Revue Française* in 1984, and **"La Reine blonde."** Another chapter, **"Un Chameau à**

Paris" ("A Camel in Paris"), although not an entirely freestanding story, was also published in *La Nouvelle Revue Française* in 1985, and yet another chapter appeared that same year in a collection under the title "**Il était donc en France**" (*Le Deuxième Sud: Marseille ou le présent incertain*). These chapters are reasonably successful at standing alone, for each has a thematic focus and dramatic shape, but I will discuss them in the section on *La Goutte d'or* so I can consider them in context.

"Le Peintre et son modèle," originally intended as a chapter of *La Goutte d'or,* was dropped by Tournier from that book, but he published it separately in the review *Masques* in 1986 (Jay, *Idriss* 101-02) and reprinted it in *Petites proses.* In Chapter 7, I will discuss it in relation to the themes of images in *La Goutte d'or,* but here I will consider it in regard to Tournier's theory of art. A painter, Charles-Frédéric de l'Epéechevalier (*Petites proses* 158), contrasts photography to painting and drawing, explaining that art has abandoned realistic representation to photography and has staked out for itself a new, less representational domain. Then, echoing the theory of art in *Les Rois mages* and *Gaspard, Melchoir et Balthazar,* l'Epéechevalier contrasts the art of the Greeks, Egyptians, and Romans, which represents gods and heroes, with Christian art, which represents ordinary people, saying that the latter type of art paradoxically attains a universal impact thanks to its emphasis on the particular because "it is the nature of creation to make the impossible not only real but necessary" (*Petites proses* 161).

Then, after briefly mentioning modern, nonrealistic art, including cubism, fauvism, impressionism, and expressionism, l'Epéechevalier explains that he wants to create a new kind of representational art which will be amusing but not arbitrary (*Petites proses* 163). Two of his drawings provide insight into Tournier's own work, the first being a floor plan of Notre Dame which shows the affinity between the cathedral and the cloth of a gambling table, revealing, as he explains, the relationship between man's belief in chance and God's plan. The other drawing represents Jean-Paul Sartre as a ghostly face taking form between a beech tree and its shadow, punning on the nearly identical sounds of the French word for "being," *l'être,* a key word in the title of Sartre's *Being and Nothingness,* and the word for "birch," *le hêtre* (*Petites proses* 165).

One can see how l'Epéechevalier's ideas about art relate to Tournier's fiction. The success of films in telling realistic stories is undoubtedly one reason that some writers have turned from realistic fiction to the experimental novel, the nonnarrative novel, the "new novel." Such books may be analogous to the works of impressionism, expressionism, cubism, and abstract art, which were in part reactions to photography's intrusion on the previous domain of art, realistic representation. But Tournier wants to reconquer lost ground by producing art which mirrors the real world but which also carries plural significations, through playfulness and ambiguity.

LE MÉDIANOCHE AMOUREUX

Tournier's second collection of short fiction, **Le Médianoche amoureux: Contes et nouvelles,** published in 1989, reflects his continued interest in the contrast between *nouvelles* and *contes*: the first ten stories are realistic, but the second ten resemble myths and legends. The arrangement is thus opposite to that in **Le Coq de bruyère,** which went from tales to realistic fiction. The overall theme of the collection is the function of art (whether literature, painting, or cooking) in people's lives.

The first story, "**Les Amants taciturnes,**" provides a framework: Nadège, an intellectual from an upper-middle-class background, and her husband, Yves, who worked his way up from cabin boy to captain in her father's cod-fishing fleet, decide to divorce because they have nothing left to say to each other. They invite their friends to a *médianoche,* a "midnight supper," to tell them the news, but the stories the guests tell during the night provide them with so much basis for future conversation that they have no need to divorce: art, in the form of the stories told, has saved their marriage. At the end, Nadège names Yves, who has provided and prepared all the food, the "high priest" of her kitchen (42). The movement of this tale from realism to ritual foreshadows the pattern of the entire book.

The first stories the guests tell are realistic ones of disappointment, vengeance, and loss. "**Les Mousserons de la Toussaint**" shows the unpredictability of individual destinies and people's inability to recover the past; "**Théobald ou le crime parfait**" is about a husband's unsuccessful attempt to frame his unfaithful wife for his own murder; "**Pyrotechnie ou la commémoration**" concerns a long-plotted revenge against a Resistance hero who humiliated a woman for consorting with the Germans; "**Blandine ou la visite du père,**" which had appeared in English in 1984 as "**Blandine, or The Father's Visit,**" shows a working-class father trying to improve his housing situation by cynically using a well-off bachelor's affection for his prepubescent daughter. Unlike almost all of Tournier's previous fiction, each story has a twist of some kind at the end; most are glossy commercial productions. Though well written, they are rather shallow; the characters are types rather than individuals. This lack of depth is deliberate, for it prepares for the seemingly simpler but deeper tales which conclude the book. These fictions are not truly art; they are like realistic photographs or painting which represents the world either as it is or as we would like to think of it. They feed—and feed on—our preconceptions.

The second five fictions, though essentially realistic, are more thought-provoking. In **"Aventures africaines,"** a well-to-do Frenchman with a predilection for young boys finds himself in an ironic situation in North Africa: his hosts' gardener wants him to take his handsome blond grandson under his protection, but the man has already lost his heart to a dark-skinned boy interested only in robbing him. **"Lucie ou la femme sans ombre"** shows the psychological power a young woman has when she accepts her shadow side and her loss of that power when psychoanalysis removes the shadow. The next three tales seem more like personal, autobiographical essays than fictions. In **"Ecrire debout,"** the narrator, an author, tells prison inmates that a writer must "write standing up," not on his knees (161); taking him literally, they send him a hand-made lectern so he can do just that. **"L'Auto fantôme"** is about deceptive appearances: returning from a centrally located rest area on a toll road to a parking lot on the wrong side, the narrator thinks his car has vanished, but he has only to cross the road to find it. Finally, **"La Pitié dangereuse"** shows how a doctor is led by pity to give up his normal life to help a dying patient. These five stories, although mostly about the negative side of life, are less discouraging than the previous ones because stereotypes have given way to real people, and there are no tidy endings to close off interpretation.

The second ten stories, *contes* provoking thought and analysis, begin with **"Le Mendiant des étoiles,"** which serves as hinge between the two parts of the book. The narrator and his friend Karl, European tourists horrified by the starving children they see everywhere in Calcutta, feed them while seeking to avoid being besieged by beggars. On Christmas Eve, however, they accept the risks to which charity can expose them and take a huge basket of food beneath Howrath Bridge, where they have previously found crowds of impoverished people. Amazingly, no one is there, and they have a private *réveillon,* or Christmas Eve supper, seeing at the end only a solitary beggar outlined against the stars, as if begging from God. The story has clear affinities with **"La Mère Noël,"** for both are Christmas stories about feeding the hungry, and, like **"La Mère Noël,"** **"Le Mendiant des étoiles"** is a key story for interpreting the collection in which it appears, for the realism of its early scenes gives way to the hallucinatory "hell" the travelers first find underneath the bridge and the unreal Christmas Eve scene with which it concludes.

Two more Christmas stories follow. In **"Un Bébé sur la paille,"** when the Mitterrand-like President of the Republic offers to help all French mothers-to-be to have their babies wherever they wish, the first person to accept is an unmarried woman named Mary, who wants her baby, due on Christmas, to be born in a stable. This potential new Christ will apparently usher in a new dispensation, for Mary is expecting a girl, "so much

calmer, more reassuring" than a boy (192). The second story, **"Le Roi mage Faust,"** might be material discarded from *Gaspard, Melchior et Balthazar,* for it concerns a Magus whose life has been devoted to truth but who discovers, through seeing the Christ Child, the value of innocence. The fact that Faust's gift to the Baby Jesus is a blank scroll (which Jesus could later write on) implies that language can reveal a path to salvation.

Angus is more complex. Published separately in an illustrated edition in 1988, it is a "revision" of Victor Hugo's famous "L'Aigle du casque," a narrative poem in which Angus, a young Scottish boy, has promised his grandfather to fight the giant Tiphaine. Hugo's Tiphaine kills Angus, but the murder of the innocent is so repugnant that the metal eagle on Tiphaine's helmet comes to life and kills Tiphaine. Unable to accept the sentimentality of Hugo's poem, as he told me when I saw him in 1987, Tournier reimagined this work of Hugo, whom he calls "the greatest French poet" in a note following the story (226).

In Tournier's version, the boy Jacques d'Angus is conceived when Tiphaine rapes Colombelle, the daughter of Lord Angus; Tournier thus provides a reason (missing in Hugo's poem) for Lord Angus to make his grandson vow to kill the giant. The adolescent Jacques wounds Tiphaine mortally in a tournament, but the victory is hollow; his real triumph comes after he learns that he is Tiphaine's son and realizes that he defeated Tiphaine only because the giant was trying not to hurt him. The boy is not angelic, as in Hugo's poem; he is a mixture of good and evil, particularly of pride and humility, but at the end of the story, in accepting his identity as Jacques Tiphaine, he "has become a man" (224). Significantly, it is through written words—a letter Tiphaine writes on his deathbed to Jacques—that Jacques learns his true situation.

The last six stories fall into three pairs. The first is composed of *Pierrot ou les secrets de la nuit,* discussed above, and **"La Légende du pain,"** in which bread again is a means of reconciliation. A rivalry between Pouldreuzic and Plouhinec takes the form of the two towns refusing to eat or drink the same things, so when the son of the Pouldreuzic baker marries the daughter of the Plouhinec baker, they cannot serve at the wedding either the soft *brioche* of Pouldreuzic or the hardtack of Plouhinec. The fiancés therefore invent French bread, which combines crust and a soft center. The new wife, who would like to invent a "vertebrate" bread (225) to complement the "crustacean" bread invented by her husband, finally succeeds by inventing *petit pain au chocolat.* Here creation, in the form of inventing new kinds of breads, is seen as a recombining of familiar elements, which is of course what Tournier does in his own fiction.

The stories of the second pair rely on whimsy. **"La Légende de la musique et de la danse,"** which had appeared in English in 1986 as **"The Music of the Spheres: A Biblical Tale,"** is another story of Eden, in which after they eat the apple Adam and Eve no longer hear the music of the spheres; as a result, they must invent music, which nevertheless does not approach the divine music in beauty. **"La Légende des parfums"** tells a more positive version of the same story from an olfactory perspective: after their original sin, Adam and Eve are aware only of smells, not scents, but the great French perfume-makers in the twentieth century are gradually re-creating "our paradisiacal past" (258). The artistic creations of music and perfume bring us closer to our prelapsarian past and to God the Creator.

The last two stories are also about Creation. In **"La Légende de la peinture,"** two artists are commissioned to decorate opposing walls of a caliph's hall, while a curtain down the middle keeps each from seeing what the other is doing. The first work revealed is a beautiful garden, but the victory goes to the second artist, who has covered his wall with a mirror: when the courtiers look at it, they see the painted garden with themselves moving in it. The story, illustrating Tournier's belief in the need for co-creation between artist and audience, implies that the greatest art is one which draws the reader into it. At the same time, it valorizes what seems to be—but actually is not—an imitation, for the second artist did not imitate what the first one did but mirrored it. Fiction is often said to hold a mirror up to life; Tournier's fiction more often holds a mirror up to other fiction, as the artist literally does in this story.

Actual imitation is the subject of the last tale, **"Les Deux Banquets ou la commémoration,"** in which two cooks compete to become a caliph's head chef. The first produces a magnificent meal; the second imitates it exactly. The caliph, in choosing the second to be his chef at home (the other will go with him when he travels), explains that the winning chef's second meal is a ritual, a commemoration of the first, for "the sacred exists only through repetition" (268), and so the copy is greater than the original. The story—and the book—end with the same words Nadège spoke to Yves at the end of the first story: "You will be the high priest of my kitchens and the conservator of the culinary and masticatory rites which give a meal its spiritual dimension" (268).

Arranging the stories so that the first ten are realistic, the second ten structured, strengthens the book by giving it a subtext: those in the first group divide Nadège and Yves because they present the venality of ordinary existence unleavened by the power of interpretation; the later stories unite them by showing the possibilities of life and by promoting discussion of the events. Unfortunately, the relation of the first story to the other nineteen is clear only from the publisher's note on the back cover (which says very much the same things Tournier told me in the interview in Chapter 8 below). And although Tournier claimed the *Decameron* as a model, the resemblance is slight, particularly as the narrators are only minimally distinguished (many of them seem to be slightly disguised versions of Tournier), and there is no discussion by the guests of the stories. Nevertheless, the internal resemblances among the stories increase their strength by encouraging a reader to look for patterns of meaning; for example, besides the stories which are obviously paired, one must contrast the two stories subtitled "The Commemoration," one about a long-plotted revenge, the other about the ritual possibilities of food, as well as the first and the last story, which are both about ritual meals.

The slight nature of many of the stories—the weakest, which are in the middle of the book, seem simply to be slightly camouflaged autobiographical narrations—is disappointing, but the concluding tales, with their provocative implications about the nature of art, are equal to any of Tournier's short fiction.

It is difficult to overestimate the effect on Tournier's novels of his work in the *conte* and short fiction generally. Writing for both adults and children in clear prose, in a very limited space, has honed Tournier's language, which tends naturally to a luxuriance which can interfere with clarity. Although this energy was effective in *Vendredi ou les limbes du Pacifique* and *Le Roi des aulnes,* it led to the overwriting of *Les Météores.* In contrast, Tournier's next novel, *Gaspard, Melchior et Balthazar,* shows great restraint, intensity, and clarity, without loss of power. And while humor has always been a major element in Tournier's fiction, the humor in the previous novels was often hidden, or underplayed, or bitter. Beginning with *Gaspard, Melchior et Balthazar,* Tournier was able to incorporate a gentle, relaxed humor into his novels and to create a lighter tone than in the earlier works.

Works Consulted

The works are in alphabetical order under each heading.

WORKS BY MICHEL TOURNIER

"Barberousse ou le portrait du roi." *Nouvelle Revue Française.* July-Aug. 1984: 1-16.

Le Coq de bruyère. Paris: Gallimard-Folio, 1982.

"Les Enfants dans la bibliothèque." *Nouvel Observateur* 6-12 Dec. 1971: 56-57.

"Extraits: 'Pages extimes.'" *Monde [des Livres]* 6 Aug. 1982: 11, 13.

Friday. Trans. Norman Denny. New York: Pantheon, 1985.

Friday, or The Other Island. Trans. Norman Denny. London: King Penguin, 1984.

Gaspard, Melchior et Balthazar. Paris: Gallimard, 1980.

Gilles et Jeanne. Paris: NRF and Gallimard, 1983.

The Golden Droplet. Trans. Barbara Wright. New York: Doubleday, 1987.

La Goutte d'or. Paris: Gallimard, 1985.

Le Médianoche amoureux: Contes et nouvelles. Paris: NRF and Gallimard, 1989.

Les Météores. Paris: Gallimard-Folio, 1981.

Petites proses. Paris: Gallimard-Folio, 1986.

"Préface à l'édition en braille [de *Vendredi ou la vie sauvage*]." *Michel Tournier.* Spec. issue of *Sud* 16 (1986): 11-13.

Le Roi des aulnes. Paris: Gallimard-Folio, 1980.

Les Rois mages. Paris: Gallimard-Folio Junior, 1985.

Sept contes. Illus. Pierre Hézard. Paris: Gallimard-Folio Junior, 1984.

Le Tabor et le Sinaï: Essais sur l'art contemporain. Paris: Belfond, 1988.

Vendredi ou la vie sauvage. Paris: Gallimard-Folio Junior, 1984.

Vendredi ou les limbes du Pacifique. Paris: Gallimard-Folio, 1972.

Le Vent paraclet. Paris: Gallimard-Folio, 1980.

Le Vol du vampire: Notes de lecture. Paris: Mercure de France, 1982.

"Writer Devoured by Children." Trans. Margaret Higonnet. *Children's Literature* 13 (1985): 180-87.

"Writing for Children is No Child's Play." *UNESCO Courier* June 1982: 33-34.

OTHER WORKS CONSULTED

Boisdeffre, Pierre de. Rev. of *Gilles et Jeanne. Revue des Deux Mondes* July-Sept. 1983: 424-25.

Bouloumié, Arlette. "Tournier face aux lycéens." Interview. *Magazine Littéraire* Jan. 1986: 20-25.

Bourbonnais, Nicole, et al., eds. Spec. issue of *Incidences* 2-3.2-3 (1979): 1-102.

Braudeau, Michel. "L'Ogre Tournier." Interview. *Express* 29 May-4 June 1978: 80-89.

Brochier, Jean-Jacques. "Dix-huit questions à Michel Tournier." Interview. *Magazine Littéraire* June 1978: 10-13.

Coulaud, Pierre. "Michel Tournier parle de son nouveau livre: *Le Coq de bruyère.*" Interview. *Dépêche du Midi* 23 Apr. 1978.

Dieckman, Suzanne. Rev. of a stage production of *The Fetishist.* Perry Street Theatre, [New York?]. 1984. *Theatre Journal* 37 (1985): 123-24.

Dumur, Guy. "Des petites filles modèles." Rev. of the stage production of *Vendredi ou la vie sauvage.* Adapt. and dir. Antoine Vitez. Théâtre National de l'Enfance, Paris. 1973. *Nouvel Observateur* 21-27 May 1973: 76-77.

Fairlie, Henry. *The Seven Deadly Sins Today.* Washington: New Republic, 1978.

Galey, Matthieu. "L'Ange noir né des flammes." Rev. of *Gilles et Jeanne. Express* 10 June 1983: 33-34.

Gilby, Thomas. "Prudence." McDonald 11: 925-28.

Häring, Bernard. "Justice." McDonald 8: 68-72.

Hayman, Ronald. "Underwear and Tear." Rev. of a stage production of *The Fetishist.* 1983. *Times Literary Supplement* 25 Nov. 1983: 1322.

Heins, Paul. "Stories for the Older Readers." Rev. of *Friday and Robinson. Horn Book Magazine* 49 (1973): 59.

Herbst, Winfrid John. "Envy." McDonald 5: 451.

Higonnet, Margaret R. "Marguerite Yourcenar and Michel Tournier: The Arts of the Heart." *Triumphs of the Spirit in Children's Literature.* Ed. Francelia Butler and Richard Rotert. Hamden, CT: Library Professional Publications, 1986. 151-58.

Hue, Jean-Louis. "Gilles et Michel." Rev. of *Gilles et Jeanne. Magazine Littéraire* July-Aug. 1983: 48-49.

Jay, Salim. "Les Plumes du *Coq de bruyère.*" *Michel Tournier.* Spec. issue of *Sud* (1980): 144-48.

Joxe, Sandra. "Michel Tournier: 'Je suis un monstre qui a réussi.'" Interview. *Autre Journal.* Nov. 1985: 50-54.

Kane, Thomas Cornelius. "Fortitude." McDonald 5: 1034.

Kirpalani, Marie-Claudette. "Usages possibles d'un texte littéraire." *Français dans le Monde* Jan. 1984: 86-91.

Lyman, Stanford M. *The Seven Deadly Sins: Society and Evil.* New York: St. Martin's, 1978.

Maulpoix, Jean-Michel. "Des limbes à la vie sauvage." *Michel Tournier.* Spec. issue of *Sud* (1980): 33-42.

McMahon, Joseph H. "Michel Tournier's Texts for Children." *Children's Literature* 13 (1985): 154-68.

Nettelbeck, Colin. "The Return of the Ogre: Michel Tournier's *Gilles et Jeanne. Scripsi* 2.4 (1984): 43-50.

Parmisano, Stanley Fabian. "Pride." McDonald 11: 765-66.

Petit, Susan. "*Gilles et Jeanne*: Tournier's *Le Roi des aulnes* Revisited." *Romanic Review* 76.3 (May 1985): 307-15.

Pieper, Joseph. *The Four Cardinal Virtues: Prudence, Justice, Fortitude, Temperance.* Trans. Richard Winston and Clara Winston et al. Notre Dame, IN: U of Notre Dame P, 1966.

Plato. *Symposium.* Trans. Benjamin Jowett. Indianapolis: Library of Liberal Arts, 1956.

Ramirez Dulanto, Jacobus M. "Hope." McDonald 7: 133-41.

Regan, Augustine Richard. "Lust." McDonald 8: 1081-85.

Sanzio, Alain, et al. "Rencontre avec Michel Tournier." Interview. *Masques: Revue des Homosexualités* Autumn 1984: 8-26.

Showers, Paul. Rev. of *Friday and Robinson. New York Times Book Review* 14 Jan. 1973: 8.

Voll, Walter Urban. "Acedia." McDonald 1: 83-84.

Vray, Jean-Bernard. "L'Habit d'Arlequin." *Michel Tournier.* Spec. issue of *Sud* (1980): 149-66.

Worton, Michael J. "Ecrire et ré-écrire: Le Projet de Tournier." *Michel Tournier.* Spec. issue of *Sud* 16 (1986): 52-69.

———. "Michel Tournier and the Masterful Art of Rewriting." *PN Review* 11.3 (1984): 24-25.

Walter Redfern (essay date June 1993)

SOURCE: Redfern, Walter. "Radio Daze and Imperishable Myth: Tournier's 'Tristan Vox.'" *French Cultural Studies* 4, no. 11 (June 1993): 185-90.

[*In the following essay, Redfern views "Tristan Vox" as a commentary on popular culture.*]

> Radio is dreamlike, precognitive, ultimate. It has less to do with politics or society than with sex, nature, and religion . . . A movie is just a picture, but people think radio is real.[1]

In the collection ***Le Coq de bruyère,*** the story **'Tristan Vox'** upturns the pattern of a more brutal partner, **'Le Nain rouge'**.[2] Its infelicitous hero comes to dread the power over thousands of others that comes his way. More usually captivated with signs and images than with sounds, Tournier has nevertheless on several occasions testified to his own state of thraldom when listening to broadcast voices. These both set the imagination

flying and yet promote a strange sense of familiarity, what we could call the *déjà entendu.* From the active side of the microphone, Tournier recalls in well-rehearsed wonderment his broadcasting experience, where pathos and crypto-divinity rubbed shoulders:

> Mystère prodigieusement excitant, . . . expérience capitale qui me faisait sentir la présence obscure mais vivante de cette hydre à un million de têtes, le 'grand public'. Expérience rendue plus bouleversante par le contact que j'eus un moment avec le courrier des auditeurs, cet énorme concert discordant, déchirant, grotesque, effrayant de voix de toutes provenances qui s'adressent à vous pour tout et pour rien, pour se plaindre en général de la maladie, du mari, . . . de la malchance, . . . de l'ennui, de la solitude, à vous . . . qui peut tout, qui est . . . Dieu. Oui, quiconque lit le courrier des auditeurs sonde toutes les plaies de ce monstre femelle et plaintif, la foule, et a une idée assez précise de ce que Dieu et ses saints entendent journellement dans les prières qui montent à eux.

(*VP* [*Le Vent paraclet*]: 167-8)

'Tristan Vox' is a serio-comic tale of mass-credulity. It displays an intense awareness of the awesome power of fabricated illusions, a power multiplied by the frantic acquiescence of the receivers.

For two reasons, no doubt, Tournier accepts cheerfully from the outset the seeming risk of datedness involved in dwelling on the era of Radio Days (or Nights). Firstly, television is but a more recent variant on such illusionism; and radio, besides, still exerts a powerful appeal over large numbers of devotees. In his presentation of the days of radio monopoly, Tournier moots that abstracted voices encourage in listeners unbridled flights of fancy. Listeners could make what they willed of those voices, or of the person projecting them. He draws an analogy with those religions where the voice of an invisible god is heard from on high. This will be the theme: the creation of a deity, the worshipping of a disembodied voice. In case such talk sounds far-fetched, we have only to recall the fully documented cultural phenomenon, whereby a great many viewers or auditors convince themselves that imaginary characters in radio or television serials, soap-operas, etc. are flesh-and-body people, for whom wreaths are sent in when they are 'killed off' by scriptwriters.

The pathetic protagonist, or agonist, of this tale is the eponymous Tristan Vox, a pseudonym suggesting blatantly both a melancholy delivery and the mythical hero of medieval literature. This voice has a dual effect on his mainly female audience: soothing/stimulating. The voice of the ideal lover, perhaps: faithful and reliable, but exciting. It sounds as if it bears some secret sorrow or wound. It has a catch in it, 'une fêlure, une cassure' ('**TV**' ['**Tristan Vox**']: 126). At this stage, then, the hero has a crack in his voice. Later he will watch a crevasse gape open in his very personality and being.

The anonymity, the facelessness, of radio enables this voice to be all things to all women. And yet, the image that collects around it betrays an amazing consensus. It is as if thousands were dreaming the same dream. The mass media can still exploit the hardy vestiges of the courtly love tradition (*amor de lonh*, quite literally): 'Tristan Vox, superbe assemblage de roman courtois et de modernisme vulgaire' (:129). That collective image is of a mature, sad-looking man with romantically long chestnut hair. It bears little relation to the actual owner of the voice, Félix Robinet. Félix (misnamed the fortunate one) contrasts with Tristan, and *robinet* is the most common-or-household of objects. Félix is nearly sixty, bald, short and pot-bellied. His voice is the by-blow of recurrent laryngitis and a wobbly double chin. After an earlier life as a comic thespian touring the provinces, he has settled into a comfortable life on the radio and his cosy bourgeois home.

His first job had been that of the Speaking Clock on the telephone, but his distinctive voice immediately captured the public interest. What or who lay hidden behind it? The pseudo-mystery was of course stoked up by the tabloid press, obsessed by the overlap between media personalities and private lives. By nature mistrustful of change, lacking in ambition and rather pessimistic in outlook, Félix is initially very dubious when his employer tells him his voice is worth a fortune. He endorses the plan, however, which is to keep his private life secret, and to let his broadcast self work its wonders. It is, Félix reflects, a funny old fate. On stage in the past, his voice had moved nobody. He accepts, then, trying to imagine that no real harm will ensue. The omniscient teller here anticipates the latter part of the story, justifiably, for it is the story of a destiny; a process, once set in motion, will prove unstoppable. The imaginary will not be kept at a safe distance, but will gradually vampirize reality, and indeed replace it. Myth will become Félix's daily bread.

It is like a fairy tale, but of the kind where things go awry, for example 'The Sorcerer's Apprentice', where the tyro cannot control the magic powers that he unleashes. Félix does not in fact have to slave in order to weave his magic: it just happens. What does he talk about in his solo chat-shows? This and that. In fact, he talks about things he has no experience or possession of: gardens, pets. As such, he emulates those authors who write of imagined events rather than from first-hand experience. If this is lying, then actors (which Félix was) are also liars: they embody non-existent characters. The difference between Tristan Vox and a stage-actor is that Tristan claims, implicitly, in his broadcasts that he is who he sounds like; he makes himself up as he goes along, instead of interpreting a script devised by someone else. Obviously, all these are

potentially dangerous games, as any swivelling between reality and illusion can become. Tristan does not as yet realize that he is playing with dynamite.

Even his secretary, the 'scrawny, horse-faced' Mlle Flavie (:131), finds it hard to disentangle Félix Robinet from Tristan Vox. It is always a great relief for Félix to escape from the studio late at night and hurry home for a late meal with his wife Amélie, a superb cook; there he feels safe. His wife, née Lamiche, embodies like a loaf of bread warmth, nourishment, security. The would-be earth-bound Tristan, well stocked by his wife's peasant Auvergnat cuisine, fears, unlike many another Tournier protagonist, being immaterialized. The first set of fan-letters he receives are gastronomical in flavour, and disclose intimate knowledge of his origins and his domestic life. They are signed Yseut. Tristan wonders whether the microphone he speaks into transmutes his voice by some diabolic means. It is, after all, shaped like a serpent's head. His studio strikes him as a tomb from which, as in several mythologies including the Christian, a new creature arises in a process of death and rebirth. (The same pattern occurs in another story of perverse initiation, in **Le Coq de bruyère**, '**Les Suaires de Véronique**'.) Tristan's broadcasts are a bridge between two insular solitudes, his own and that of his vast unseen audience—a situation akin to that of the writer Tournier, addressing unknown readers from his study.

The letters from Yseut grow more and more erotic, obscene even, and come accompanied by explicit drawings. The approach is thus two-pronged: after *l'estomac, le bas-ventre*. Then fate introduces a new twist, a more excruciating turn of the screw. In the equivalent of *Radio Times*, an editor mistakenly prints Tristan Vox's name under the photo of a tennis-star, Frédéric Durâteau.[3] A face now exists to go with the legendary name. Félix's 'Tristan Vox' has been usurped by a rival, however unintentionally. Félix, the genuine fake, working under a pseudonym, begins to feel like a real impostor; and the mind starts to boggle. Durâteau complains that his life is being wrecked and that it is somehow Félix's fault. The reader may well feel at this point that poor Félix is the only remotely sane person in a gallery of fruit-cases. We might also wonder whether ordinariness is meant to appear as just a variant form of monstrosity. Being the odd man out, even if you are approximately in the right, puts you out on a limb, beyond the pale.

Events accelerate and escalate. Mlle Flavie jumps or falls out of a third-floor window, and lies in intensive care. When Félix rushes to visit her, she murmurs through her grotesque bandages that she has a confession to make. She is Yseut. Or rather that she took over from the original Yseut (as Durâteau supplanted Félix). She had wanted desperately to see the legendary Tristan come real. All around Félix, people are recycling the

Tristan and Isolde myth. In **'Tristan Vox'**, fate dominates individuals and their relationship with others; they have small say in their own destinies. On display is not conjugal fidelity, of slender interest to Tournier, but faithfulness to a fateful, prescripted passion, updated.

On his return home, Amélie confesses to Félix that she is Yseut. Hearing her husband's voice over the radio waves had created a being different from the man she lived with. She had written letters in the guise of Yseut in order to win back the man whose life was being stolen from him and her by all his unseen admirers. The only solution he can imagine is to cut off the supply of the narcotic, 'fermer le robinet', as he says in a wry pun on his own name. He requests leave; his wife and he go back to their roots in central France. Amélie, however, has lost all interest in cooking, that is: in Félix as a bodily person. One night he catches her listening with a friend to the radio: Tristan Vox, now impersonated totally by Frédéric Durâteau. The story breaks off when Félix spots the name Tristan Vox on an envelope about to be posted, on the sly, by Amélie. She has not been cured of her delusion. For his part, will Félix himself ever escape from his phantom?

This story shares with **'Le Coq de bruyère'** the theme of ageing sexuality—Mlle Flavie, Amélie, and the hordes of largely female listeners. Félix's audience has in effect vampirized, de-realized him.[4] What state he ends up in is left to our putative compassion to imagine. He has suffered an existential split between his voice and the whole rest of his self. In addition, an interloping double, Durâteau, has taken over Félix's persona. Tournier's exploitation of the ancient Doppelgänger topos is largely joco-serious in its modernization of an old myth. As Ruthven says of such myth-conversion: 'Operating within a network of shared allusions among educated readers, you can by-pass the explicit in order to explore the tacit and ironic'.[5]

In answer to a question as to whether he is possessed by myths, Tournier punned in agreement, 'si cela peut aussi vouloir dire bouffé aux mites'. He went on to say that writing drains the author, renders him threadbare.[6] The creative hack becomes hackneyed. This process is reflected in the dematerialization of Félix. Many have always suspected that a goodly number of myths originate in some form of wordplay. Since, for Tournier, myths need to be periodically reinvented or invested with new meaning, twisting them for re-use is as central to creativity as is punning. Like fables, symbols or puns, myths are always *tantamount,* suggestive (Tournier would say 'apéritif') rather than definitive. In his view, myths provide an already constituted meaning, or set of variant meanings—*le donné*—which later-comers can make something of by hijacking, adapting, inverting, etc.—*le construit*.[7] Tournier is taken with both kinds of rustling, the plagiaristic and the auditory,

as in 'ce "bruissement" mythologique, ce bain d'images dans lequel vivent [les contemporains de l'artiste]' (*VP*: 192).

All in all, for Tournier myth is ambivalent (or multivalent):

> La notion même de mythe est frappée d'équivoque: un mythe, c'est à la fois une belle et profonde histoire incarnant l'une des aventures essentielles de l'homme, et un misérable mensonge débité par un débile mental, un 'mythomane' justement.
>
> (*VV* [*Le Vol du vampire*]: 14)

The 'débile mental' in **'Tristan Vox'** is no doubt the national audience creating its pathetic falsehoods about Félix Robinet. And yet, from another angle, and like **'Les Suaires de Véronique'**, this story could be read as a women's revenge-match.

> Les femmes d'aujourd'hui se révoltent assez contre l'image de la femmeobjet, répandue par nos mass media, précieuse, passive, déshabillée, maquillée, photographiée, vendue en effigie ou en chair et en os. Le mythe de Tristan fait de l'homme un objet aussi, sans cesse ballotté, endommagé et raccommodé par des mains de femme.
>
> (*VV*: 30)

Tournier's gesture towards asserting women's rights here secretes some traditional male stereotypes of women; and his sympathies clearly go to the endangered cynosure.

Just as Véronique in **'Les Suaires de Véronique'** could stand for any manipulatrix, so Félix is an (unwilling) dictator of the air-waves, swaying masses.[8] This story is also a typically ambivalent attack on modern commercial media, for their ability to concoct a synthetic product (the ersatz, Durâteau, serves just as well as the 'original', Félix), and to wash their hands of any disastrous consequences. The new order created by art, even low-grade art like radio chat-shows, cannot always be kept under control. Unlike Lucien Gagneron in **'Le Nain rouge'**, the artist here is at the mercy of his audience. Unlike Raphaël Bidoche in **'Que ma joie demeure'**, he experiences the wrong kind of acclaim. Like Tupik, on the other hand, Félix suffers a mutilation; he is cut down to his voice alone. Tournier has often claimed, with variable plausibility, that at some point his books escape his grasp. Like Tristan Vox, Tournier must sometimes feel that his real self has become a public cliché, a corny figment in the collective semiconscious of his public.

Tournier's 'Gothic' version of author-reader relationships shuttles confusingly between images of books as vampires feeding off the life-blood of readers, but also sucking the writer himself dry. More phallocentrically, books are cocks mounting a production-line of hens: us readers. By one of those change-arounds of signs that so fascinate Tournier, the reader (seen also at times as a vampire) can become a mere sucker, or dupe. **'Tristan Vox'** houses not only the polymorphous eroticism that surfaces continuously in Tournier's fiction, but also the dependence, the aggression, the scorn and the need that variously constitute his attitude to his readership.

Notes

1. G. Keillor, *Radio Romance* (London: Faber, 1991), 75.

2. Edition used: *Le Coq de bruyère* (Paris: Gallimard (Folio), 1978).

   'TV': 'Tristan Vox'.

   VP: *Le Vent Paraclet* (Paris: Gallimard (Folio), 1977).

   VV: *Le Vol du vampire* (Paris: Gallimard (Idées), 1983).

3. Almost certainly one of those insignificant names, with which Tournier at times teases readers he has already drilled to seek out 'speaking names'.

4. It has not, though, as in Clint Eastwood's film, *Play Misty for Me,* actually sought to kill the object of their fixation, their radio romance.

5. K. K. Ruthven, *Myth* (London: Methuen, 1976), 44.

6. J-L. Ézine, 'Michel Tournier', *Les Nouvelles littéraires,* 2-8 June 1975, 3.

7. See C. Lévi-Strauss, *La Pensée sauvage* (Paris: Plon, 1962), 27, on the link of myth and intellectual *bricolage*. He stresses oblique approach, dodging manœuvres, parasitism and yet resultant creativity in such mental operations.

8. Tournier wrote a preface to the French translation of Goebbels' diaries (Paris: Flammarion, 1977).

Susan Petit (essay date December 1994)

SOURCE: Petit, Susan. "Michel Tournier and Victor Hugo: A Case of Literary Parricide." *French Review* 68, no. 2 (December 1994): 251-60.

[In the following essay, Petit focuses on the revision of Victor Hugo's "L'Aigle du casque" in Angus *and proposes that Tournier's characterization of Tiphaine is modeled after Hugo.]*

When asked who was the greatest French poet, André Gide reluctantly answered, "Victor Hugo, alas." If asked today who is the most exciting novelist now writing in French, I would answer with alacrity, "Michel Tournier, paradoxically."

—Roger Shattuck (218 [*The Innocent Eye: On Modern Literature and the Arts*])

If innovating in literature is in some sense killing a father, radically rewriting a famous work by a famous author is still more parricidal.[1] But even parricides must come to terms with their ancestry. A recent case of literary parricide is shown in the *filiation* from Victor Hugo's "L'Aigle du casque" (1877) to Michel Tournier's *Angus* (1988), a tale which Tournier wrote, or at least published, partly for children, and which he has said fills in various blanks in Hugo's poem and thus, implicitly, corrects its "errors." Tournier's re-imagining of the story gives it a radically different theme, so that the story is not merely about its overt content, Jacques d'Angus's hidden parentage and unintentional parricide, but also about its own creation: the way in which Jacques struggles with his paternity symbolizes Tournier's own struggle with the influence of Victor Hugo, whom he has acknowledged as one of his literary masters (Bouloumié 21).[2]

Before discussing Tournier's revisions to Hugo's work, I would like to consider Hugo as literary and human father. In admitting Hugo as a literary father, Tournier is claiming a particularly difficult ancestry, for Hugo is archetypally patriarchal, bestriding nineteenth-century French literature with his massive output of poems, plays, novels, essays, and political writings, not to mention his voluminous correspondence. In fact, his production was so immense that when he virtually stopped writing after a stroke in 1878, he continued to publish a book a year until his death in 1885, drawing on unpublished material (Houston 12). His personal life was equally vigorous; he simply overwhelmed everyone around him with a self-absorption and force indicated by his motto, *Ego Hugo* (Maurois 370). At sixty he seemed only forty (Gregh 292), and his sentimental life included his wife; five children—all of whom he outlived except the gently insane Adèle—; Juliette Drouet, his "official" mistress for fifty years; and innumerable other women, notably Léonie d'Aunet Biard, who was jailed on her husband's insistence when caught *in flagrante* with Hugo. (Hugo himself escaped arrest because he had just been named a peer of France and was thus "inviolable" [Maurois 327-28].) His political activities made him a kind of father to his country: a *vicomte* after 1837 by virtue of a Spanish title (Maurois 274), he was elected to the National Assembly during the Second Republic, and under the Third Republic was first a member of the Assembly and later a senator. In between, during the Second Empire, he was of course one of the most famous of political exiles. As if all that were not enough, he was a talented sketch artist, a *chevalier* of the Légion d'Honneur, a member of the Académie Française, and the first person to be buried in the Panthéon.

Hugo seems to have coped easily with both his real father and his literary ancestors. He loved his father (Gregh 47 and 50, Houston 69) and became close to him in his father's last years, but he largely disagreed with his politics. Hugo had similarly ambivalent feelings about his literary fathers. Though he said once that he did not want to rewrite the works of others (Gregh 50), he took material from many sources, often without regard to accuracy, and transformed it through his extraordinary gift for language. "L'Aigle du casque," which appeared in 1877 in the second series of *La Légende des siècles,* derives from the twelfth-century *Geste de Raoul de Cambrai,* which is based in turn on actual events of the middle of the tenth century (Rouche 18-29; Lagarde and Michard, *Moyen Age* 40). Hugo's immediate source, however, was a version written by his contemporary Jubinal and published in 1846 in the *Journal du dimanche* as "Quelques Romans chez nos aïeux" (Dumas 838, n. 187, and 832, n. 144), while Hugo, under the influence of Ossian and Sir Walter Scott, set the action in Scotland (Lagarde and Michard, *XIX* 190; Dumas 837, nn. 183 and 186).

The link between "L'Aigle du casque" and these sources is tenuous, quite unlike that between Hugo's poem and Tournier's **Angus**. The *Geste de Raoul de Cambrai* seems to be a fairly realistic account of feuds between powerful Medieval knights. Raoul is given in fief Vermandois, which has belonged to relatives of Bernier, Raoul's former squire. To keep it, Raoul fights against the dispossessed heirs and their relatives, including Bernier, whose mother burns to death in the course of the battles. In the section Hugo drew from, Raoul chases Ernaut de Douai, who pleads for mercy, promising to give his lands to Raoul and become a monk. By swearing to kill him even if God and His saints should defend him, Raoul "vient de prononcer des paroles qui le perdront, car il a renié Dieu" (*Histoire de Raoul* CLII, 103). Ernaut cannot defeat Raoul, but Bernier, "qui a le droit pour lui" and whom God is protecting (*Histoire de Raoul* CLIV, 104), breaks open Raoul's head, and then Ernaut kills Raoul. This section of the *geste* emphasizes Bernier's moral conflict, an element Tournier used in his **Angus**.

Hugo, however, was interested not in internal struggles but in the melodrama of unequal combat between a fleeing young knight pleading for mercy and an older warrior carried away by his fury, and in God's involvement in the events; and around these themes, he created his own plot. Unlike the *geste*, "L'Aigle du casque" ostentatiously keeps secret the motive for the unequal battle: "Le fond, nul ne le sait. L'obscur passé défend / Contre le souvenir des hommes l'origine" (320) of such ancient battles, though "Les motifs du combat étaient sérieux" (325). One knows only that the aged and dying "comte Strathaël, / Roi d'Angus" (321), has made his orphaned six-year-old grandson Jacques swear to fight the giant Tiphaine once the boy becomes a knight. Ten years later, Jacques, who is now Lord Angus, challenges the giant. When they meet on a stormy winter's

day, the boy is unable to hurt the giant and flees; Tiphaine pursues him into a forest, ignores the pleas for mercy toward the boy made by a hermit, an entire convent, and a woman with a baby at her breast, and kills Angus in a "ravin inconnu" (330) despite the boy's own pleas. Then, in the poem's famous climax, the bronze eagle on Tiphaine's helmet comes to life and, to revenge the boy, kills the giant, then "s'envol[e] terrible" (331).

In entirely transforming his materials, Hugo has not so much killed a literary father as erased nearly every trace of any relationship. In contrast, Michel Tournier, in reworking Hugo's materials, calls attention to his story's literary ancestry and to his debt to Hugo. In fact, Tournier has explained in a note to the story that in 1985, spurred by the centenary of Hugo's death, he "docilement" reread "L'Aigle du casque" (*Médianoche* [*Le Médianoche amoureux*] 225) and began to wonder why the grandfather made the boy swear to kill the giant and what had happened to the boy's parents (225-26). Deciding that these questions were related, Tournier wrote **Angus,** finishing in the summer of 1987.[3] The story was published in 1988 in a children's edition and in 1989 in the collections **Le Médianoche amoureux** and **Les Contes du médianoche.** (In the latter book, also marketed for children, **Angus** is followed by all of **"L'Aigle du casque,"** further underscoring the debt and inviting close comparison of the two.) Tournier calls his revision of Hugo's poem "un humble hommage au plus grand des poètes français" (*Médianoche* 226), but it is a challenge as well.

Tournier has based many of his novels and stories on the works of others, but he has never before challenged a predecessor so directly. His *Vendredi ou les limbes du Pacifique* (1967) reconceived Defoe's *Robinson Crusoe,* and in other works he has drawn on Flavius Josephus, Dante, Jules Verne, Alain-Fournier, Robert Musil, Colette, and a host of other writers. Tournier considers natural such a *remaniement*; if he can treat a theme better than a previous writer, then he claims that the theme is rightfully his ("Vent" [*Le Vent paraclet*] 54-55). He also rewrites his own fiction, partly by revising works (as by turning *Vendredi ou les limbes du Pacifique* into **Vendredi ou la vie sauvage**) and partly by carrying themes over from work to work (his Tiphaine resembles both the similarly-named Tiffauges in *Le Roi des aulnes* and Gilles de Rais in **Gilles et Jeanne**). The rewriting of Hugo, however, is neither ordinary adaptation, unacknowledged quotation, nor playful allusion to a literary equal; it is a direct challenge, based on the premise that Hugo's poem gives rise to questions that children would naturally want answered and that Tournier's story does answer (Tomé 321).

Tournier has found those answers in part through historical research. He probably read the *gestes* which were Jubinal's sources, for in **Angus** there is some imitation of their events.[4] Certainly he knows something about the twelfth century, for he begins **Angus** with a conversation about courtly love, a subject which would be out of place in the battle-oriented *Geste de Raoul de Cambrai* and "L'Aigle du casque" but which is historically appropriate: at much the same time as the *Geste de Raoul de Cambrai* was being written, Marie de France, Bertrand de Born, and others were helping to create the *fin'amour.* Tournier thus "corrects" Hugo by going back to earlier material, as in *Vendredi* [*Vendredi ou les limbes du Pacifique*] he "corrected" Defoe by incorporating elements from Alexander Selkirk's story, which had been one of Defoe's sources ("Vent" 213-18).

Historical accuracy helps to justify the fact that **Angus** begins with old Angus's daughter, Colombelle, being lectured on courtly love by her fiancé, Ottmar, who has learned by heart "les Leys d'amors" of the court of love at Toulouse, where he participated in the *Jeux floraux* (200). This opening is especially important because it brings Hugo's biography into **Angus,** for at age 17 Hugo won first prize, the *lis d'or,* from the *Jeux floraux* in Toulouse (Maurois 67-68). This similarity is not coincidence; it is a sign pointing to how Tournier has encoded Hugo's life into Angus. Like Ottmar, the young Hugo thought that the best love was spiritual; he wrote to his future wife, "l'amour immatériel est éternel . . . Ce sont nos âmes qui s'aiment et non nos corps," although he did add that "il ne faut rien pousser à l'extrême" (Maurois 91). Ottmar too has accepted wholesale a Platonic view of love, ignoring the adultery which, as Tournier knows, was an integral part of the doctrine of courtly love.[5]

Angus attacks the naively idealistic young Hugo in the person of Ottmar. Ottmar's insistence that one must "laver les relations amoureuses de toute souillure matérielle" (200) reflects what Tournier considers the worst of Plato: "Plato says that when a man loves a boy . . . he mustn't love his body, he must love his soul, which is nonsense, isn't it? It doesn't mean anything" (Petit 182). In response to Colombelle's question "Est-ce à dire que les corps n'ont aucune part à votre fin'amour?" (201), Ottmar agrees that the soul makes the body lovable, but his spirituality is nevertheless excessive for a twelfth-century knight, as becomes clear when the giant Tiphaine and his dwarf, Lucain, encounter the couple in a deserted woods and Lucain kills Ottmar treacherously so that Tiphaine can rape Colombelle. Ottmar is too gentle and unworldly to protect Colombelle or himself; his foolish ideas of courtesy lead directly to his death. Ottmar—whose name in *verlan* would be *marotte*—reflects Hugo's youthful obsession with purity, and his replacement by the sensual Tiphaine reflects Hugo's own change from idealist to lecher; in André Maurois's

words, the "*adolescent chaste*" became a "*vieillard faunesque*" (7, italics in original), a "faune aux cent nymphes" (280) and an "amant farouche" (281).

Tiphaine's brutal sexuality has consequences: Colombelle dies giving birth to Jacques, Tiphaine's son, although the boy is presumably told, like everyone else, that Ottmar had married Colombelle and is his father (207). Tournier has thus provided Angus with the motive missing in Hugo's poem; Angus makes his grandson Jacques swear to kill Tiphaine in order to avenge Colombelle. Tournier has also given the boy three fathers he could emulate, each of them representing Hugo in some way: the official father, the gentle and chaste Ottmar; the biological one, the brutal but energetic Tiphaine; and old Angus, who believes in divine intervention, sure that God will make Tiphaine lose, even if it means God must "renverser l'ordre naturel en faisant triompher l'enfant sur le géant" (209). This attitude clearly is the one Hugo takes in "L'Aigle du casque," in which, although Jacques is killed, a miracle kills the giant. All three men are deficient as human beings as well as fathers; Hugo's idealism, sensuality, and mysticism are caricatured in Ottmar, Tiphaine, and Angus respectively.

Angus approaches "L'Aigle du casque" most closely when it recounts the joust between the sixteen-year-old Jacques and the experienced warrior Tiphaine, but the meaning of the contest is radically different. "L'Aigle du casque" recounts a battle between good and evil, and the boy is presented in strikingly feminine and angelic terms as he enters the lists:

> Un cheval d'un blanc rose
> Porte un garçon doré, vermeil, sonnant du cor . . .
> Il a la jambe nue à la mode d'Ecosse;
> Plus habillé de soie et de lin que d'acier . . .
>   Autour du comte adolescent,
> Page et roi, dont Hébé serait la sœur jumelle,
> Un vacarme charmant de panaches se mêle.
>
> (324-25)

This description represents what Tournier has called Hugo's "mythology about childhood" (Petit 177), his creation of "*l'angélisme de l'enfance*" which helped to inaugurate the Victorian myth of childhood innocence ("Vol" [*Le Vol du vampire*] 178, italics in original). Superficially, Tournier's Jacques is similar: "l'enfant blond, bleu et rose, vêtu de soie et de tartan, avait l'éclat irréel d'une apparition" (216). But in **Angus,** Jacques's decision not to wear armor is foolhardy, not noble; he wants to outdo Tiphaine, who has announced he will fight without a helmet, and Jacques is "porté par la force irrésistible de son destin" (216). Tournier's Jacques is a real boy, overconfident because he believes that right is on his side, caught up in heroic illusion.

Tournier's Tiphaine at this point becomes much more complex than Hugo's, and even his brutality takes on a kind of charm, just as Hugo's own overbearing nature did. In Hugo's poem Tiphaine is "le lord sauvage des forêts" whose origins are unknown (322), and he is pleased to be challenged to fight because he craves action; Tournier disapprovingly calls Hugo's Tiphaine "un paroxysme de virilité adulte" ("Vol" 179). Tournier's Tiphaine is more sympathetic. When Lucain tells him that someone wants to kill him in single combat, he does cry, "Enfin! . . . Quelqu'un qui me veut du bien! Je crevais d'inaction" (213), but when he learns that his challenger is his own son, he has mixed feelings: "Bon sang ne saurait mentir. Moi aussi j'aurais bien volontiers tué mon père. Seulement . . . je n'ai pas la moindre envie de mourir" (214).[6] The humor and the realism in these lines make Tiphaine come to life as a rounded, complex character.

This more interesting Tiphaine, as I have pointed out, represents the older Hugo. He even resembles him physically, for Tiphaine's "crinière de lion" and "barbe de prophète" (215) suggest Hugo's beard, which resisted all razors (Gregh 292), and his hair, which remained thick into old age. In Rodin's 1909 bust, Hugo has the fierce look of a bearded prophet (Goldscheider 19). Both Hugo and Tiphaine belong to the category of "barbus" who represent to Tournier the violently heterosexual, dominating male.[7] Although Hugo's Tiphaine is just forty (326), Tournier's Tiphaine by the story's end seems closer in age to the 75-year-old Hugo who published "L'Aigle du casque," for Tiphaine in *Angus* has hair which is a "buisson gris de cheveux" (217), and he fears that he will "mourir de décrépitude et de pourriture" (221) if he is not killed in battle. Both have outlived nearly everyone close to them but have not lost their zest for life, though Tiphaine's exploits are martial rather than literary: his favorite activities include "Egorger un cerf . . . forcer une fille . . . pendre un manant . . . saccager la demeure d'un voisin . . . brûler un clerc" (213). Like Hugo, he is an ambivalent father. Tiphaine has never acknowledged Jacques, but he secretly has had him watched, and he does not want to hurt him. Somewhat similarly, Hugo kept his children on a very tight leash but always looked after and supported them.

Tournier replaces Hugo's melodrama with an irony that encourages the reader to judge both father and son. Rather than taking place on a forbidding winter's day, the contest is held in mild weather (215), and the mood is lighter. Hugo's Tiphaine is insanely eager to kill the boy; Tournier's Tiphaine wants only to humble him but finds it hard not to hurt him because Jacques is not wearing armor. (So Jacques's overconfidence, ironically, actually serves him.) In the combat, rather than fleeing like Hugo's hero, Jacques splinters his lance on Tiphaine's breastplate, and a shard embeds itself in Tiphaine's eye, wounding him mortally; there is no need for the bronze eagle to pierce the giant's eyes and

crush his skull. One could say that Hugo's eagle, rather than having flown away before the story begins as Tournier says (*Médianoche* 226), is Tiphaine himself, who is fighting bareheaded so that his son can see his "regard d'aigle" (215). However, Jacques's real test comes not in the joust but when Lucain reads to him Tiphaine's dying letter, telling Jacques that Tiphaine is the boy's father, legitimizing him, and naming him his heir. Jacques has to accept that the despised, brutal Tiphaine is his father and that he himself is a parricide.

This twist returns to the plot the internal conflict in Hugo's sources, for when Jacques learns that he was able to kill Tiphaine only because Tiphaine refused to hurt him, he loses the "brume dorée" of youth for a "lucidité amère et désolée": "il avait tué sans gloire son propre père" (224). On the other hand, in accepting his new lands and responsibilities, as well as his true self, he becomes a man. Tiphaine has killed Jacques d'Angus after all, by turning him into Jacques de Tiphaine, an adult who accepts and acknowledges himself as a mixture of good and evil. Similarly, Tournier's Tiphaine—unlike Hugo's—is not the complete villain he seemed, for he has spared Jacques's life out of paternal feelings. As he says in his dying letter, "*si j'accepte qu'un fils tue son père—c'est dans l'ordre . . . le petit bout de morale que j'ai ne permet pas à un père de tuer son fils*" (222, italics in original). In his dying words, Tiphaine becomes sympathetic through his humor, his energy, and his impatience with the "*bondieuseries*" (221, italics in original) of the monk trying to absolve him. Even here there is a resemblance to Hugo, who refused the last rites (Maurois 563-64) because he had his own idea of God; in the words of Cardinal Guibert, Hugo "voulait bien aller à Dieu, mais . . . ne voulait pas que Dieu allât chez lui" (Maurois 564).

This portrait of Tiphaine implies Tournier's judgment of Hugo. He admires him in part for loving life, for Hugo's works have the "moralité extrinsèque" Tournier would like to see in all literature, "l'appétit de vivre" (Koster 305), but he rejects Hugo's sentimentality, his romanticism, his egoism, and his ferocious heterosexuality. Hugo's white-hot, passionate writing and public life seem at the opposite pole from Tournier's cool, ironic, allusive style and more private way of living, and it cannot have been easy for Tournier to accept Hugo's literary paternity. Clearly, this ambivalence—which leads Tournier to criticize Hugo as a thinker but also to admire him as a lover of life and a poet (*Médianoche* 226)—helps account for Tournier's admiration of "L'Aigle du casque" as well as his desire to rewrite it.

But where, in *Angus,* is Hugo the writer? He is represented by the dwarf Lucain, to whom the illiterate Tiphaine dictates his dying confession and who is the giant's "âme damnée, complice de tous ses crimes et témoin de tous ses triomphes" (213). Lucain's name even implies that he represents Hugo's political-literary side.[8] The Roman poet Lucan (Lucain in French), although once a friend of Nero, was forced to kill himself because he had supported the Piso conspiracy against the emperor. Like Lucan, Hugo changed his political orientation, being in turn a partisan of Napoleon, a constitutional monarchist under Louis-Philippe (and friend of his son, the Duc d'Orléans), and a republican; and he was of course an outspoken critic of the Second Empire. Like Hugo, Lucan was recognized as a poet from his early adulthood; like Hugo, he wrote about recent politics (his *Pharsalia* is an account of the civil war between Pompey and Cesar). Lucan's poem is an epic; Hugo's *La Légende des siècles,* in which "L'Aigle du casque" appears, is a series of small epics. The dwarf Lucain, then, is the last surviving avatar of Hugo, having killed Ottmar and outlived Angus and Tiphaine. If Hugo the author, living on in his works, is represented finally by a misshapen dwarf, *Angus* now looks like an attack on Hugo as writer.

This picture is corrected, though, when we look in *Angus* for Tournier, who must be represented by Jacques. They may even share birthdays, for Jacques is born "peu avant Noël" (207), and Tournier's birthday is December 19. Unlike the heroic and angelic boy of Hugo's poem, Tournier's Jacques is more often criticized than praised, for he is immature and foolhardy, no match for Tiphaine. The lonely Jacques feels himself to be an outsider despite his privileges, much as Tournier, whose own privileged childhood involved what he experienced as rejection ("Vent" 22-26), thinks of himself as a literary outsider, a "naturalisé, romancier au teint quelque peu basané par le soleil métaphysique" ("Vent" 195) who is committed both to maintaining and to undermining the tradition of realism. In rewriting "L'Aigle du casque," he has challenged the giant: a contemporary writer against a classic, a member of the Académie Goncourt against an "immortal" of the Quai Conti, a writer producing a novel about every five years against one of the most productive of all authors, who wrote in all major genres and even illustrated his works himself. It is significant that in *Angus,* Tournier represents Hugo by four characters, himself by only one. The struggle is so unequal that Tournier can seem to overcome Hugo only because there is no real combat, just as Jacques can win his factitious victory only because Tiphaine lets him.

In fact, when Tournier rewrites Hugo—or Defoe, or Alain-Fournier, or Dante, or any other writer—he cannot defeat him, for any rewriting means that the newer writer is standing on the older writer's shoulders. Like Jacques, Tournier must acknowledge his descent from a father he would prefer to reject and many of whose values and beliefs he cannot share, but one whose force and influence he cannot deny. Or, to use another image, if a revision is a sort of reflection, there must be some-

thing to reflect. Tournier's tale **"La Légende de la peinture"** tells of a competition in which a Greek artist erects mirrors on a wall so that they will reflect the painting of his Chinese rival (*Médianoche* 262-63); the mirrors are judged superior to the painting because they reflect both the painting and its viewers. In contrast, in **"Les Deux Miroirs,"** two mirrors, meeting and looking closely at each other, cannot understand what women find in them which is so interesting (**Contes** [*Les Contes du Médianoche*] 67). A mirror is nothing if it has nothing to reflect. Similarly, *Angus* pleases primarily by reflecting **"L'Aigle du casque,"** and it is much more dependent on its predecessor than **"L'Aigle du casque"** is on the *Geste de Raoul de Cambrai*; without Hugo's poem, *Angus* would be a mirror with nothing to reflect. The parricidal rewriting is, after all, the "humble hommage au plus grand des poètes français" (*Médianoche* 226) which Tournier called it, for in challenging Hugo, Tournier is actually calling attention to and acknowledging their relationship. Like Jacques accepting Tiphaine as his biological father, Tournier acknowledges Hugo as a literary father and accepts an ancestry which he both deplores and respects.

Notes

1. There are also literary mothers, but the ancestors concerned in this case are all male.

2. Christiane Baroche has said that *Angus* "fournit aux méchants esprits un meurtre du père hors de contestation et qu'on applaudirait presque, surtout quand on a conservé un cœur plus jeune que soi!" (79). She seems to be referring only to Angus's killing of Tiphaine, though, not Tournier's "attack" on Hugo.

3. When I saw Tournier on July 11, 1987, he told me that he had just finished writing by hand his final version of *Angus* and showed me the manuscript.

4. In the *Geste de Raoul de Cambrai,* Raoul's sword slides to the left several times on an adversary's armor, seriously wounding him in a place at which Raoul did not aim (*Histoire de Raoul* CXLII 99, CXLVI 100); in *Angus,* Jacques's lance twice slides off of Tiphaine's (217), and Tiphaine hurts Jacques while not meaning to (218). All page references to Angus are to *Le Médianoche amoureux.*

5. See his "Tristan et Iseut" in *Le Vol du vampire,* pages 25-34, and, in the same book, "Denis de Rougemont," pages 388-92.

6. Hugo's Tiphaine never refers to his father, but he does carry an axe "comme Oreste" (325), the archetypal parricide.

7. Occasionally beards are presented in a positive light in Tournier's work, notably in *Barbedor* and "Barberousse," but generally they suggest patriarchy, violence, and aggressive masculinity. See Merllié, "Histoires de barbes."

8. Lucain is not only a dwarf, but a hunchback, so perhaps he should be associated with Hugo's fellow-exile in Guernsey, Hennet de Kesler, whom Maurois almost invariably identifies as "bossu" when naming him (411, 435, 467, 489). However, this is a slim basis for identification. He may also constitute an allusion to Quasimodo in *Notre-Dame de Paris,* but they seem entirely different as characters.

Works Cited

Baroche, Christiane. "Tentation du légendaire ou l'éternel retour à l'enfance." *Images et signes de Michel Tournier.* Paris: Gallimard, 1991. 77-86.

Bouloumié, Arlette. "Tournier face aux lycéens." Interview. *Magazine Littéraire* (Jan. 1986): 20-25.

Dumas, André. Notes. In Victor Hugo. *La Légende des siècles.* Paris: Garnier, 1974. 807-82.

Goldscheider, Cécile. *Rodin: 1886-1917.* New York: Tudor, 1964.

Gregh, Fernand. *Victor Hugo: sa vie, son œuvre.* Paris: Flammarion, 1954.

Histoire de Raoul de Cambrai et de Bernier, le bon chevalier: chanson de geste du XIIᵉ siècle. Trans. R. Berger and F. Suard. Troesnes: Corps 9, 1986.

Houston, John Porter. *Victor Hugo.* New York: Twayne, 1974.

Hugo, Victor. "L'Aigle du casque." *La Légende des siècles.* Paris: Garnier, 1974. 320-31.

———. *La Légende des siècles.* Intro. Jean Gaudon. Notes André Dumas. Paris: Garnier, 1974.

Images et signes de Michel Tournier. Actes du Colloque du Centre Culturel International de Cerisy-la-Salle. Paris: Gallimard, 1991.

Koster, Serge. "Le Roi des Vernes." *Images et signes de Michel Tournier.* Paris: Gallimard, 1991. 297-309.

Lagarde, André, and Laurent Michard. *XIX Siècle: les grands auteurs français du programme V.* Paris: Bordas, 1961.

———. *Moyen Age: les grands auteurs français du programme I.* Paris: Bordas, 1964.

Maurois, André. *Olympio ou la vie de Victor Hugo.* Paris: Hachette, 1954.

Merllié, Françoise. "Histoires de barbes." *Magazine Littéraire* (Jan. 1986): 29-35.

Petit, Susan. *Michel Tournier's Metaphysical Fictions.* Purdue University Monographs in Romance Languages 37. Amsterdam: Benjamins, 1991.

Rouche, Michel. "Raoul de Cambrai . . . ou l'histoire dans l'épopée." *Histoire de Raoul de Cambrai.* Troesnes: Corps 9, 1986. 13-29.

Shattuck, Roger. "Locating Michel Tournier." *The Innocent Eye: On Modern Literature and the Arts.* New York: Farrar, 1984. 205-18.

Tomé, Mario. "Littérature pour enfants ou pour initiés?" *Images et signes de Michel Tournier.* Paris: Gallimard, 1991. 310-21.

Tournier, Michel. *Angus.* Illus. Pierre Joubert. N.p.: Piste, 1988.

———. *Les Contes du médianoche.* Illus. Bruno Mallart. Paris: Gallimard folio junior, 1989.

———. *Le Médianoche amoureux.* Paris: Gallimard, 1989.

———. *Le Vent paraclet.* Paris: Gallimard folio, 1980.

———. *Le Vol du vampire: notes de lecture.* Paris: Mercure de France, 1982.

Martin Roberts (essay date 1994)

SOURCE: Roberts, Martin. "Inversion and Androgyny: *Le Coq de bruyère.*" In *Michel Tournier: Bricolage and Cultural Mythology,* pp. 84-103. Saratoga, Calif.: ANMA Libri, 1994.

[*In the following essay, Roberts investigates the fusion of opposites and the reconstruction of familiar models in "La Famille Adam," "La Fugue du petit Poucet," and "Les Suaires de Véronique," and notes Tournier's fascination with the creation of artistic images such as photographs.*]

In *Le Vent Paraclet,* Tournier re-narrates the opening of Hans Christian Andersen's well-known fairytale, "The Snow Queen":

> Le Diable a fait un miroir. Déformant, bien entendu. Pire que cela: inversant. Tout ce qui s'y reflète de beau devient hideux. Tout ce qui y paraît de mauvais semble irrésistiblement séduisant. Le Diable s'amuse longtemps avec ce terrible joujou, puis il lui vient la plus diabolique des idées: mettre cet infâme miroir sous le nez de . . . Dieu lui-même! Il monte au ciel avec l'objet sous le bras, mais à mesure qu'il approche de l'Etre Suprême, le miroir ondule, se crispe, se tord, et finalement il se brise, il éclate en des milliards de milliards de fragments. Cet accident est un immense malheur pour l'humanité, car toute la terre se trouve pailletée d'éclats, de miettes, de poussières de ce verre défigurant les choses et les êtres. On en ramasse des morceaux assez grands pour faire des vitres de fenêtre—mais alors malheur aux habitants de la maison!—et en plus grand nombre des éclats pouvant être montés en lunettes—et alors malheur à ceux qui portent ces sortes de lunettes!
>
> (50)

He then goes on to recount how one of the shards from the shattered mirror falls into Kay's eye while he and his sister Gerda are looking at a picture-book together, with the consequences described above. Tournier explains that he has been unable to resist retelling Andersen's tale, because "il n'y a pas d'œuvre dont je regrette autant de n'être pas l'auteur" (52). It is easy to see why: the tale is a kind of Tournierian myth of the origin of *inversion maligne* (and its opposing counterpart, *inversion bénigne*), which is one of the most obsessive themes in all of Tournier's fiction. Tiffauges's account of the phenomenon in *Le Roi des Aulnes* implicitly alludes to Andersen's story:

> L'inversion bénigne. Elle consiste à rétablir le sens des valeurs que l'inversion maligne a précédemment retourné. *Satan,* maître du monde, aidé par ses cohortes de gouvernants, magistrats, prélats, généraux et policiers *présente un miroir à la face de Dieu.* Et par son opération, la droite devient gauche, la gauche devient droite, le bien est appelé mal et le mal est appelé bien.
>
> (123)

Tiffauges's theory of *inversion maligne/bénigne,* however, is only one aspect of Tournier's preoccupation with the phenomenon of inversion. Here is Tiffauges again, this time reflecting on the inversion of black and white in a photographic negative:

> Le visage aux cheveux blancs et aux dents noires, au front noir et aux sourcils blancs, l'œil dont le blanc est noir, et la pupille un petit trou clair, le paysage dont les arbres se détachent comme des plumets de cygne sur un ciel d'encre, le corps nu dont les régions les plus tendres, les plus laiteuses, en réalité sont ici les plus ombrées, les plus plombées, ce perpétuel démenti à nos habitudes visuelles semblent introduire dans un monde *inversé,* mais un monde d'images et donc sans vraie malignité, toujours redressable à volonté, c'est-à-dire exactement *réversible.*
>
> (175, Tournier's italics)

As Tiffauges continues, moreover,

> il n'y a pas que la métamorphose du noir en blanc et sa réciproque. Il y a aussi la possibilité en retournant le négatif dans le porte-vue de mettre la gauche à droite et la droite à gauche. Double inversion donc après le développement, à laquelle prélude naïvement, dans les vieux appareils, au moment de la prise de vue, le renversement—la tête en bas—du sujet.
>
> (176)

Inversion is more than just a theme in Tournier's fiction, however; as we have already seen in previous chapters, it is also a central mechanism in the thematic and narrative structure of the novels themselves: one has only to recall the numerous inversions of the *île administrée* by the *vie sauvage* after the explosion in *Vendredi* [*Vendredi ou les limbes du Pacifique*], the inverse relationships between Kaltenborn and Auschwitz in *Le*

Roi des Aulnes, or between the world of the *gadoue* and that of bourgeois heterosexual society in *Les Météores,* to confirm this point.

More interestingly for our purposes, inversion in Tournier's fiction also operates at a meta-textual level: as we saw in the case of *Vendredi,* Tournier's *bricolage* of *Robinson Crusoe* often takes the form of an inversion of its model, perhaps the most striking example being Robinson's and Vendredi's role-reversal game, in which Robinson prostrates himself before Vendredi and sets his foot on his head (210-13). The inversion in the reference to Atlas in *Le Roi des Aulnes* (135-36) will also be recalled. Inversion is a common procedure in *bricolage,* where the diversity and ill-matched nature of the materials at the disposal of the *bricoleur* may necessitate using them upside-down, back to front, or inside out, in order to incorporate them into a new project. It could be argued that the intertextual inversions I have mentioned are a common feature of *bricolage,* as well as of the symbolic manipulations of mythical thought itself. Yet given the unusual prominence of inversion in Tournier's fiction, it does seem that the predilection for inversion is one of the most distinctive aspects of Tournier's *bricolage.*

In this chapter, I will be focusing on three stories from *Le Coq de Bruyère*—**"La Famille Adam," "La Fugue du petit Poucet,"** and **"Les Suaires de Véronique"**— each a *bricolage* of a pre-existing or ready-made source, and each of which also exemplifies the intertextual inversion I have described. I will also be considering how these inversions entail corresponding ideological inversions in conventional assumptions about gender roles, for example, or the relationship between tradition and modernity.

In the domain of gender, inversion is closely associated with another important theme in Tournier's fiction: androgyny. What is an androgyne?[1] The question may be answered in two ways. If we leave aside the mythological dimension of androgyny, it may be said to consist of a reciprocal exchange by the male and female sexes of their respective gender roles, attributes, and characteristics, giving a chiasmus of male:female and female:male. A biologically male individual with female characteristics, and the reverse, are androgynous figures. Androgyny may thus be defined more simply as the coexistence of male and female within the same body. As soon as we turn to mythology and other products of the human imagination, however, we encounter the Androgyne, commonly regarded as a timeless, archetypal figure. This figure is conceived in terms of unity rather than duality, sameness rather than difference, fusion rather than juxtaposition, in which male and female cancel one another out and sexual difference as such is abolished. The archetypal Androgyne, moreover, is discerned not only in the resolution of the sexual dichotomy in particular, but of opposition in general. As Arlette Bouloumié writes,

> La conjonction des deux sexes dans un même être signifie en effet, symboliquement, la coïncidence des opposés à tous les niveaux, la réunion harmonieuse des contraires, ce qui est la définition la moins imparfaite de l'état divin. Le mythe de l'androgyne exprime le dépassement des conflits, la quête victorieuse de l'unité, et l'espoir en une humanité régénérée.
>
> ("Mythologies" 28)

Conceived thus, the Androgyne symbolizes nothing less than the abolition of difference itself.

Androgynous figures abound in Tournier's fiction, from Fabienne and Alexis, the *fille-garçon* and *garçon-fille* in *Les Météores* (258-59), to Jeanne d'Arc in **Gilles et Jeanne,** and we shall be encountering similar figures in each of the stories I shall be discussing. As for the archetypal Androgyne, I will be returning to this in the conclusion to this chapter, as well as suggesting some possible reasons for Tournier's fascination with androgyny.

"LA FAMILLE ADAM"

The fountainhead of Christian mythology, the biblical myth of Adam and Eve has proved to be one of the most fertile sources for Tournier's mythical imagination, and almost all of his fictional works include some new variation on the story, whether in the form of explanatory glosses or—as in the case of **"La Famille Adam"**—an actual rewriting.[2] These variations—which focus on various aspects of the human condition before the Fall, as well as the nature of the Fall itself and its consequences—differ markedly from conventional interpretations of the biblical text, most strikingly in their claim that the first "man" was androgynous: "A quoi ressemblait le premier homme? Il ressemblait à Jéhovah qui l'avait créé à son image. Or Jéhovah n'est ni homme ni femme. Il est les deux à la fois. Le premier homme était donc aussi une femme" (11). It should be noted that Tournier's primordial androgyne is bisexual, not asexual: the male and female sexes, although incorporated in one body, are nevertheless already distinguishable. Opposites are juxtaposed, but do not cancel out; duality is contained within unity, but remains duality nonetheless. Moreover, the divided nature of Tournier's androgyne is not confined to gender: "Il y a deux êtres en moi," Adam complains, "l'un voudrait se reposer sous les fleurs," the other "a besoin de marcher, marcher, marcher" (12). The creation of Eve, and the division of the androgyne, thus involves the separation not only of male and female but also of sedentary and nomadic impulses: while the nomadic Adam becomes free to "marcher, marcher, marcher," the sedentary Eve spends most of her time sleeping "sous l'ombre des palmiers." Tournier's androgyne, then, is already inhab-

ited by difference *before* the separation which supposedly creates such difference; the splitting of the androgyne is not a transition from unity to duality, but a sundering of opposites previously joined together, an externalization of difference. If Tournier's androgyne is not an actual fusion of opposites, however, it does nevertheless reduce the difference between them to a minimum, so to speak, and this attenuation of dichotomy makes it no less of a mythical figure.

Tournier's depiction of Adam as originally androgynous also serves a rhetorical purpose. Showing that a certain condition or state of existence was the original one is a persuasive way of arguing that it is also the most normal, natural, or authentic one. More specifically, showing that man/woman was originally androgynous is a way of arguing that androgyny is a "natural" vocation. Myth thus provides a way of arguing for the superiority of androgyny over the more familiar polarization of the sexes.

At first, it may seem that **"La Famille Adam"** is merely a confabulation of the variations on the Adam and Eve story in *Le Roi des Aulnes* and *Les Météores,* but this is not entirely true. The most immediate difference is one of tone: if the Adam and Eve references in the earlier novels have a serious purpose, in **"La Famille Adam"** the author's tongue seems to be set firmly in his cheek. Referring to Adam's bisexuality, for example, he comments: "C'était même assez commode: quand il marchait, il mettait sa queue de garçon dans son petit trou de fille, comme on met un couteau dans un fourreau" (11). On the creation of Eve, after describing how Yahweh installed Adam's female organs "dans un autre homme," he adds: "Et il appela cet autre homme: femme" (13).[3] Much of the story's humour and irony derive from the fact that Tournier pastiches his biblical model while at the same time undermining this pastiche by foregrounding its artificiality. At the outset, the story looks like a re-narration of the Genesis text itself, opening with the solemn "Au commencement . . ." and narrated in the simple, direct, style characteristic of myths. But Tournier also employs incongruously anachronistic images and analogies—the notion that Yahweh "voulait des petits-enfants," for example, or the description of the desert as "une terre de coureur de fond." This conceptualization of the story in contemporary terms insistently reminds the reader of the artificial, second-hand nature of the story, that it is a modern re-telling of an existing story rather than that story itself. This is made most blatantly apparent when, after recounting the creation of Adam and Eve, Tournier skips over the Fall and disconcertingly "fast forwards" to the Cain and Abel story, with the airy explanation: "Adam et Eve, *on le sait,* furent chassés du Paradis par Jéhovah . . ."—the story suddenly turning into a meta-textual commentary on its model. This device and the others I have mentioned, lends **"La Famille Adam"** a strongly ludic dimension: the author is playing with his subject, exploiting our familiarity with it to produce unexpected, and often amusing, results. The playfulness of Tournier's *bricolage* here may seem fairly innocuous—even frivolous—but closer examination shows it to be less ideologically "innocent" than it may appear.

In the mythologies of everyday popular culture, Adam and Eve are conventionally treated as stereotypical models for the male and female sexes in general. If Eve in Tournier's tale is similarly read as a representative of Woman, we see that it perpetuates the traditional wisdom that Woman is derived from Man, but in an even more radical sense than usual: Tournier's Eve is no more than the sum of Adam's reproductive organs— "les seins, le petit trou, la matrice"—transferred into another body ("un autre homme"); she is a mere reproductive machine. While affirming that motherhood is the natural female vocation, the tale is equally insistent that this vocation cannot be fulfilled on the move: Woman is also "naturally" sedentary. The emphasis on Eve's creation inside Paradise reinforces the "naturalness" of her vocation: the fertility of Eden is the natural setting for her sexual fertility. Tournier, then, uses Genesis to authenticate the view (also elaborated in *Les Météores* 416) that the female vocation is an exclusively sedentary and procreative one. Tournier is a defender of non-procreative forms of sexuality (as *Vendredi* and *Les Météores* amply attest), but this privilege extends exclusively to men, and is exemplified by male, not female, homosexuality. In Tournier's fiction, man can—and Alexandre enthusiastically does—explore exciting new possibilities of erotic experience; woman, however, must be content with motherhood. It is no coincidence that the woman who is arguably represented as most fulfilled and admirable in all of Tournier's fiction—Maria-Barbara in *Les Météores*—is the mother of so many children that she has lost count of them (10).

Tournier's *bricolage* of the Adam and Eve story in **"La Famille Adam"** thus proposes a view of women and their role in society which has been seriously challenged in recent decades, and with which many women today would take issue. The misogyny inscribed in **"La Famille Adam"** is not confined to this version of the Adam and Eve story alone, however. "Le Sosie de Dieu" (in *Le Vagabond immobile*) describes an intriguing case of mistaken identity: jealous of Adam's identical likeness to Yahweh, Lucifer tries to kill him, only to discover that his intended victim is Yahweh himself. Even after his expulsion from Paradise, however, Lucifer continues to plot Adam's downfall, "jusqu'au jour où il eut trouvé. Ce jour-là, il souffla à l'oreille de Dieu qu'il n'était pas bon qu'Adam fût seul. Alors Dieu créa Eve. *L'affaire était dans le sac*" (65). It could be argued, perhaps, that this ending is ironic and should not be taken at face value—that it is in reality poking fun at the popular (male) wisdom that woman caused man's downfall by offering him the forbidden fruit. However tongue-in-cheek it may be, nevertheless, the story makes a point. It ends with a *clin d'œil*, and it is hard to believe that this is directed toward female readers.

Tournier's *bricolage* of Genesis emerges more favorably in the second half of **"La Famille Adam."** The biblical story of Abel and Cain depicts Abel positively, Cain negatively: Yahweh accepts Abel's offerings but rejects Cain's; in the dispute which leads to Abel's death, Cain is the aggressor, Abel the victim. While superficially conforming to the biblical narrative, Tournier's tale inverts it by reversing the values attached to the two brothers in its model; in **"La Famille Adam,"** Cain undergoes an *inversion bénigne,* Abel an *inversion maligne.* Whereas Cain is "blond, dodu, calme," Abel is "maigre, noir et cynique" (15, 16). Cain resembles his mother and displays conventionally female attributes of docility, patience, and gentleness; Abel, however, is "tout le portrait de son coureur de père," and displays conventionally male attributes of assertiveness, impetuousness, and aggression. Cain is a sedentary farmer who belongs to the *règne végétal,* Abel a nomadic shepherd who belongs to the *règne animal*: his family are meat-eaters and "il était fier que ses enfants n'eussent jamais mangé de légumes" (16). As a child, Abel spitefully flattens his brother's flower-beds and sand castles; as an adult, it is he who is the cause of their dispute when his flocks stray onto Cain's land and destroy his crops. When the two meet, "Cain s'y montra doux et conciliant, Abel lui ricanant méchamment au nez" (17). In maximizing Abel's provocation, Tournier minimizes Cain's responsibility, effectively exonerating him of his crime: if Cain does kill his brother, the story implies, it is not his fault; Abel gets what he deserves. The rehabilitation of Cain is completed in the story's ending, when Yahweh abandons his nomadic life with Abel's sons and comes to settle in the town Cain has founded.

Tournier's taking of Cain's side is characteristically perverse, but it is more than mere provocation. Traditionally, as I have mentioned, Abel has been seen as the good, and Cain as the evil partner in their couple; correspondingly, the male stereotype which Abel embodies in Tournier's story has also been seen as the normal or natural one, the androgynous stereotype embodied by the effeminate Cain as abnormal or deviant. Tournier's inversion of the conventional hierarchy between Abel and Cain, then, entails an ideological inversion of the conventional hierarchy between the sexual paradigms they embody: in devaluing Abel, Tournier devalues the stereotypical masculinity he incarnates; in valorizing Cain, he also valorizes the co-existence of male and female attributes. Inversion becomes a means of promoting androgyny. It will be noted also that although Abel takes after his father and Cain his mother, Abel only resembles Adam in his post-androgynous (male) form;

Cain, who combines both male and female, is closer to Adam in his/her original, androgynous form. This association reinforces the ideological inversion I have described, by implying (again contrary to the prevailing view in Western culture) that Cain's ambiguous sexuality is more "natural" than Abel's. As we will now see, androgyny is also depicted positively in **"La Fugue du petit Poucet,"** where it is again closely associated with the inversion of the story's model.

"La Fugue du petit Poucet"

If **"La Fugue du petit Poucet"** is, like **"La Famille Adam,"** a rewriting of an existing narrative, both the narrative in question and Tournier's transposition of it are very different. Whereas the referent of **"La Famille Adam"** lies at the very source of Western Christianity, that of **"La Fugue du petit Poucet"** belongs to a more narrowly French cultural mythology, a particularized archive of narratives, figures, and images not necessarily held in common with neighbouring cultures.[4] Perrault's "Le Petit Poucet," indeed, is not so much "une histoire que tout le monde connaît déjà" as "une histoire que tous les *Français* connaissent déjà." Rather than taking the form of an ostensibly "straight" re-narration of its model, Tournier's tale transposes it into the contemporary world.[5] It thus invites us to read it against Perrault's tale (indeed, French readers can scarcely avoid doing so), and many of its apparently incidental motifs and details take on new meanings when the texts are compared.

"La Fugue du petit Poucet" broadly reproduces the narrative structure and thematic motifs of its model. Reference to Perrault is firmly established through the title, and the naming of Pierre's family. "Petit Pierre" is small and resourceful like his seventeenth-century prototype, and his father is a *bûcheron*. In Tournier as in Perrault, Poucet gets lost in a wood and ends up spending the night *chez* Logre (the analogy here turning on a blatant pun between the hippy's name and the word *ogre*).[6] In both tales, the ogre has seven daughters. Like his prototype also, Tournier's ogre owns a pair of magical boots, which by the end of the story have been acquired by Poucet. Tournier, however, also modifies these motifs in various ways. Pierre's father, for example, is not just a *bûcheron* but "le chef des bûcherons de Paris" (50). The ogre's boots in Tournier both resemble and differ from the seven-league boots of Perrault's ogre: they are "des bottes de rêve" (65), which also enable their wearer to travel great distances, but in imagination only.

The most important difference between Tournier's tale and its model, however, is its depiction of the ogre. Perrault's ogre is a cannibalistic giant who detects the presence of Poucet and his brothers by the smell of their flesh alone, and is only dissuaded with difficulty from devouring them on the spot.[7] Tournier's ogre, by contrast, is a peace-loving, dope-smoking, guitar-strumming hippy, characterized by "douceur" (57, 58), and most outrageously of all—in an ogre, at least—a vegetarian. The identification of Tournier's ogre with the *règne végétal* recalls Cain in **"La Famille Adam,"** and like Cain also, he is an androgynous figure: "Vous êtes beau comme une femme!" gasps Pierre, fascinated by his "longs cheveux blonds," his "yeux bleus et tendres," and when he sings, his "voix fluette, ce soprano léger" (57-58). The ogre's androgyny also contrasts strikingly with the aggressive masculinity of Perrault's ogre, and the two are equally opposed in terms of gender roles: Perrault's ogre is absent when Poucet and his brothers arrive at his house, and his wife is roasting a sheep for his supper; when he returns, he treats her like the caricatural tyrannical husband, churlishly demanding his meal, insulting her, and ordering her to feed the brothers (Perrault 192-93). Tournier's ogre, however, assumes the conventionally female—and indeed maternal—role; it is he who stays at home to take care of the children while his wife is away earning their living ("Drôle de famille, pense Pierre. C'est la mère qui travaille pendant que le père garde la maison!" (57).[8] Tournier's ogre, in short, is in many ways the antithesis of Perrault's ogre (or as Tournier might put it, his *inversion bénigne*). The same is true of his daughters: in Perrault, the ogre's daughters are miniature versions of himself, and indulge in amateur vampirism ("Elles n'étaient pas encore fort méchantes; mais elles promettaient beaucoup, car elles mordaient déjà les petits enfants pour en sucer le sang," Perrault 193). In Tournier, they are benevolent to the point—it is coyly implied—of subjecting the bewildered Pierre to a sexual initiation (62).

If Tournier's ogre proves to be a gentle giant, Pierre's father shows much of the hostility and aggression of Perrault's ogre. Gender roles in the Poucet household conform to the traditional model, as they do in Perrault's ogre's house, and Poucet *père* treats his wife in the same tyrannical fashion that the ogre treats his: Madame Poucet is afraid, for example, of contradicting "son terrible mari" over the issue of moving house (49). In Tournier's tale, then, the "ogrishness" of Perrault's ogre is not just inverted, but displaced onto Pierre's father; in **"La Fugue du petit Poucet,"** it is the father who is the ogre.[9]

The inversion and displacement I have described are closely linked with numerous narrative inversions which make Tournier's text a mirror-image of its model. Whereas in Perrault, Poucet's parents deliberately abandon him and his brothers, in Tournier, Poucet voluntarily runs away from his parents. Correspondingly, whereas in Perrault Poucet returns to his parents' home by choice at the end of the story, in Tournier Pierre has to be forced to do so by the police and his father. The contemporary tale's inversion of the ogre motif produces some amusing narrative inversions. Tournier's tale, for example, parallels its model in having the ogre offer Pierre supper; in Perrault, the ogre also has his wife serve supper to Poucet and his brothers, but for a different reason: having grudgingly agreed to postpone his meal until the following morning, he orders them to be fed, "afin qu'ils ne maigrissent pas" overnight (Perrault 193). In Perrault, the seven *ogresses* and the seven brothers sleep in separate beds in the same room, whereas in Tournier, Poucet sleeps *with* the ogre's daughters. In Perrault, Poucet steals the ogre's boots while he is asleep; in Tournier, he receives them from the ogre as a gift. At one point in both tales, there is a threatening knock at the door of the ogre's house. In Perrault, it is the ogre himself, and the seven terrified boys dive under the bed (192); in Tournier, it is Pierre's father with the police, and it is the ogre's daughters who "se dispersent comme une volée de moineaux" (62)—a symmetry which further underlines the structural parallel in Tournier between Perrault's ogre and Pierre's father.

The triangular relationships of similarity and difference between Perrault's ogre, Tournier's ogre, and Pierre's father sets up an opposition within Tournier's tale itself between Pierre's father and the ogre. As in the case of Abel and Cain, these opposing figures embody the conventional masculine stereotype on the one hand, the alternative, androgynous one on the other, and—again as in the earlier story—the positive and negative values attributed to them correspondingly valorizes and devalues what each represents: the story's sympathetic depiction of the benevolent ogre, like that of Cain, is another positive affirmation of androgyny. It is also far more than this, however, as can be seen when we turn to the other oppositions between the two figures.

Like the father in Perrault's story, Pierre's father is a *bûcheron*. Few professions, it might seem, could be more evocative of a rustic, rural, and placid lifestyle than that of a woodcutter, yet Tournier stands this bucolic image on its head: his modern-day woodcutter is an urban lumberjack, and a lumberjack's job, as Poucet makes clear, is to chop down trees. The rural ogre, by contrast, recognizably belongs to a social group noted for its ecological concerns, in particular with the protection of trees; his post-prandial rêverie reveals him, indeed, to be the proponent of a quasi-mystical cult of trees, and if this were not enough, he himself is a sort of human tree ("un vrai géant des bois" [57]).[10] The ogre's tree-cult sets him on the side of nature; Poucet's destruction of trees sets him in opposition to it, and on the side of technology. The high-rise apartment in which Poucet installs his unhappy family is defined by the totality with which it excludes the natural world: even contact with the air is prevented (the windows do not open). By contrast, the ogre's existence is characterized by its respect for nature and openness to it.

The opposition between the natural and the technological here is also a temporal opposition between the traditional and the modern, and this underlies a further contrast between the two figures. Poucet's technological utopia is a sterile world where everything is done by machines, at the centre of which stands the "télévision à couleurs." The ogre's world, on the other hand, is characterized by "traditional" creativity: everything in his house, it seems, is handmade (with natural materials, of course), from the elaborately decorated wickerwork armchair to Logre's own clothing; Pierre is also shown a weaving loom. It is a place where music is played, where "on chante, on danse," and most important of all, "on se raconte des histoires" (56). The ogre is a consummate storyteller, and his story acts as a catalyst to Pierre's own imagination: listening to him, Pierre actually starts to imagine he is a tree, and that like a tree he has achieved what is arguably the supreme good in Tournier's fiction: a direct, unmediated communion with Nature (62).

Through its story of Pierre, who rejects his father's brave new world for the traditional one inhabited by the ogre, **"La Fugue du petit Poucet"** articulates a longing for an escape from modern, urban existence, and for a return to an earlier existence of simplicity and innocence, where people lived in harmony with nature rather than at odds with it. Pierre for a time enacts such a return, before being thrust brutally back into the present. Yet **"La Fugue du petit Poucet"** still manages to produce a happy ending of sorts: while his parents watch television, Pierre, locked away in his room with his "bottes de rêve," secretly floats away on his imagination. Immobile on his bed, a prisoner in body but free in spirit, Pierre recalls Paul lying on his *chaise longue* at the end of *Les Météores,* and on a smaller scale the story's ending resembles that of the novel. Like *Les Météores,* **"La Fugue du petit Poucet"** ultimately affirms an apparently impossible victory against all odds—a victory which, however, can be no more than imaginary.

"LES SUAIRES DE VÉRONIQUE"

"Les Suaires de Véronique" brings together some of Tournier's most characteristic themes concerning sexual identity, good and evil, the status of the human image and the nature of art.[11] Although ostensibly a realist *nouvelle,* the story abounds in echoes of and veiled allusions to myths and rituals. Predictably, much has been made of the names of its two central protagonists, Hector and Véronique—the first evocative of Greek and the second of Christian (or more specifically, Catholic) mythology—and the conflict between them has been seen as a symbolic confrontation between the pagan world and the Christian one (Kaye 21-27). This by no means exhausts their symbolic resonance, however; according to one critic, Hector and Véronique's mythological avatars also include Hercules and Deianeira, Pasiphaë and the white bull of Crete;[12] the same (Spanish) critic also sees the story as a "spectacle taurin" in which the various stages of a bullfight are ritualistically played out.[13] Such readings are ingenious and often fascinating, but curiously, none of the articles written on the story directly discuss two of the story's most obvious referents—the legend of Veronica and the cult of the *Saint-Suaire* or Shroud of Turin. It is therefore on these two subjects that I want to focus here.

Like **"La Famille Adam"** and **"La Fugue du petit Poucet,"** **"Les Suaires de Véronique"** is a *bricolage* of a subject which will be immediately familiar to most of Tournier's readers: Veronica's wiping of Christ's face on the road to Calvary. As Ian Wilson explains,

> so widespread did this story become in Christian mythology that today it is rare to find a Catholic church that does not have somewhere a scene depicting Jesus, toiling on his way to Calvary, impressing the likeness of his face on Veronica's veil. The incident was made the sixth of the fourteen Stations of the Cross, and the guides in the Old City of Jerusalem today point out to the wanderer the site on the Via Dolorosa where it purportedly took place. There is an accompanying small, dark church where one can see an eighteenth-century icon of the veil, and many Catholics are under the impression that the story is recorded in the Gospels.[14]

The referent of Tournier's story is thus not textual but iconic: Veronica is familiar today, and has traditionally been so in Christian mythology, in the form of an image. The source of this image, moreover, as well as its object, is itself an image; the sixth Station of the Cross is an image of an image, or more exactly an image which depicts the making of an image. Veronica's veil, believed to bear the true likeness of Christ's face, was venerated as a sacred relic in the Middle Ages, and Veronica herself owes her name and in all probability her very existence to this *vera icona*. As André Chastel writes,

> Comme on l'a établi depuis longtemps, sainte Véronique n'existe qu'en fonction d'une image sacrée et la légende a trouvé sa diffusion en Occident au XIIIe et XIVe siècles quand . . . le voile portant l'empreinte miraculeuse du Sauveur fut mis en valeur à Saint-Pierre de Rome et exposé à la vénération des pélerins.[15]

The veil was also a work of art, of course, a self-portrait executed by the Son of God himself, and in its turn became a source of inspiration for medieval and Renaissance artists. Artistic representations of the veil, however, gradually displaced attention from their ostensible subject (the *vera icona*) onto the figure of Veronica her-

self—the Stations of the Cross image being a case in point. "Rien n'est plus frappant," as Catherine Millet observes,

> lorsqu'on . . . considère l'évolution iconographique [de la Véronique], que la présence de plus en plus triomphale de cette femme, vrai sujet de la peinture, au détriment de l'empreinte sacrée qui n'est plus bien tôt qu'un accessoire. La Véronique est presque une usurpatrice. Par son nom déjà, elle s'est appropriée les termes qui désignaient l'image de la Sainte Face, *Vera Icona*. Ainsi cette allégorie de l'art impose-t-elle le corps d'une femme quand disparaît le corps de Dieu fait homme.[16]

In the two stories I discussed earlier, Tournier's narrative progresses in parallel to its model and provides a kind of counterpoint to it. In **"Les Suaires de Véronique,"** however, the Veronica legend is a motif, and the narrative not so much parallels it as converges with it. Initially, the nature of the relationship between story and motif (postulated in the former's title) is enigmatic: it begins to become apparent as the story is read and is only fully revealed in its ending. The emergence of the motif can be compared to a photograph during the development process: at first, only small details are visible, but gradually larger shapes begin to become discernible and become increasingly well defined until the picture is complete.

The photographic metaphor is apt, given the nature of the tale's subject matter: Véronique is a photographer, lending her more in common with her legendary model than may at first be apparent. The photograph, indeed, is in many ways the modern equivalent of a *vera icona*—a true likeness of its subject. Showing her photographs of Hector to the narrator, Véronique asserts: "Voilà . . . le *vrai*, le seul Hector" (158). Like the *vera icona*, moreover, photographs are treated as sacred objects in the story, and photography in general as a pseudo-religion.[17] The main *point de rencontre* between Tournier's story and its referent, however, is the exhibition of *suaires* of the story's title. Just as the image on Veronica's veil was produced by a direct contact between the object and the medium of representation, so Véronique devises a photographic technique in which the image is produced by imprinting the body directly onto photosensitive paper, and later by wrapping—shrouding—it in specially treated photosensitive cloth.[18] Like the sixth Station of the Cross, **"Les Suaires de Véronique"** depicts the making of an image (or images); it represents representation, albeit textually rather than iconically. Tournier's tale also reproduces the shift in emphasis which I mentioned a moment ago from Veronica's veil to Veronica herself: his tale is dominated by Véronique, and her apotheosis is conditional on the effacement—and ultimately, the disappearance—of her subject.

The correspondences between Tournier's story and its model are offset by some equally important differences.

According to the legend, Veronica's veil was miraculously imprinted with Christ's image in reward for her compassion in wiping the blood and sweat from his face. In Tournier, on the contrary, the production of the image is the actual cause of Hector's death. Like Christ at Calvary, Hector endures a *via dolorosa* of physical suffering, humiliation, and eventual martyrdom, in which Véronique plays the role not of compassionate bystander but torturer and executioner. Véronique is the *inversion maligne* of her legendary counterpart, more witch than saint.[19]

As we saw at the beginning of this chapter, Tournier closely associates photography with inversion, and his transposition of the Veronica legend into a photographic context also involves an inversion of it; if the correspondence between story and legend develops like a photographic image, this image proves to be a *negative* image. The inverse relationship between story and model is embodied in Véronique's shrouds. In Western art, paintings of Veronica's veil always depict a positive image—like a developed photograph—rather than the negative one which an imprint would ordinarily be expected to produce. Véronique's shrouds, however, *are* negative images: the text speaks of "d'étranges *silhouettes* écrasées, . . . assez semblables . . . à ce qui restait sur certains murs d'Hiroshima des Japonais foudroyés et désintégrés par la bombe atomique" (169). The positive/negative inversion here in a sense metaphorically reproduces the relationship of *inversion maligne* between Tournier's tale and its model.

One obvious difference between Tournier's story and its model is that Véronique's *suaires* bear the imprint not just of a face but a whole body, and in this respect, it would seem, they more closely resemble another of Catholicism's most celebrated relics: the *Saint-Suaire* or Shroud of Turin, for centuries venerated as the burial shroud of Christ and believed to bear the miraculous imprint of his body, until it was recently exposed as a medieval fake. Photography, interestingly enough, has also played an important role in the Turin Shroud's history: like Véronique's *suaires,* the image imprinted on it is a negative image, making it, as Ian Wilson observes, "in a sense a photographic negative" (17).[20] Yet the Turin Shroud is itself closely associated with Veronica's veil, to the extent that both etymologically and historically, it is difficult to distinguish between the two. Although in modern French usage the word *suaire* (like the more common *linceul*) denotes a burial shroud, it derives from the Latin *sudarium,* "handkerchief, towel." In the Middle Ages, Veronica's veil was known as the *Sudario;* moreover, its mysterious disappearance, coupled with the emergence of the cult of the Turin Shroud around the same period, has led to speculation that the two relics were one and the same.[21]

My purpose here is not to resolve such questions—which are, in any case, ultimately irresolvable—but to give some idea of the complex network of correspondences linking Veronica's veil, the Turin shroud, and the works of art in Tournier's story. One of the most interesting aspects of these correspondences is that by turning Veronica's veil into a *suaire,* the story explicitly associates the making of images, and the creation of art, with death—specifically, the death of their object. This emphasis on the morbid nature of the image is symptomatic of a more general ambivalence on Tournier's part, already apparent in his earlier fiction. In *Le Roi des Aulnes,* photography is represented as an "œuvre au noir" both figuratively and literally, a sort of occult science:

> Il y de la messe noire . . . dans les manipulations auxquelles on soumet impunément cette émanation si personnelle d'autrui, son image, comme il y a du tabernacle dans l'agrandisseur, de l'enfer dans la lumière sanglante où l'on baigne, de l'alchimie dans les bacs de révélateur, d'arrêt et de fixage où l'on jette successivement les épreuves impressionnées.

(175-76)

Photography is also a form of cannibalism: when Tiffauges comes home to develop a new batch of photographs of children, Eugénie tartly observes that "[il] revient du marché avec sa provision de chair fraîche. Il va maintenant s'enfermer dans le noir pour manger tout ça" (180). As Daniel Bougnoux notes, Tiffauges's photography is also a sublimated form of sexual possession.[22] Yet Tiffauges also observes that "la photographie promeut le réel au niveau du rêve, elle métamorphose un objet réel en son propre mythe" (169). On the one hand the image—and the photographic image in particular—preys upon its object; on the other, it confers on it the timeless, mythical dimension of art.

This ambiguity of the image—both malevolent and benevolent—is taken up in **"Les Suaires de Véronique."** Studying Véronique's photographs of Hector, for example, the narrator speaks of "le charme assez *maléfique* de ces images" (160). Moreover, Hector tells Véronique that every time she has photographed him "quelque chose de moi m'a été *arraché* pour entrer dans votre petite «boîte de nuit»" (165); elsewhere, he refers to "ces *prelèvements* effectués chaque jour sur ma substance" which have left him variously "vidé, épuisé," "diaphane, translucide, transparent, invisible" (166). Photography is a form of rape: Hector's references to his exhaustion, to the draining of his vitality, to Véronique's "petite «boîte de nuit,»" highlight its unequivocally erotic dimension, casting Véronique in the role of *femme castratrice.*[23] Photography is also a form of vampirism: like the vampire draining its victim of its blood, Véronique drains Hector of his substance, until all that remains of him, it is implied, are the residual images on the *suaires.* But Véronique's manipulation of Hector is not entirely malevolent: her images are also consummate works of art which confer a mythical timelessness on their object. The story's ambivalence toward Véronique's photography is embodied in the equivocal position taken up by the story's narrator in relation to the events he describes.[24] Although clearly disturbed by Véronique's manipulation of Hector, he is no less fascinated by its aesthetic dimension, and does nothing to prevent it. Both repelled and attracted, he becomes a reluctant accomplice to Hector's death: hence his "angoisse" when his responsibility is made apparent in the story's final episode, and which ultimately reduces him to a guilty silence.

Tournier's ambivalence towards the image comes increasingly to the fore in his more recent fiction, as we shall see in the next two chapters. **"Les Suaires de Véronique"** differs from this fiction, however, in that it articulates the ambivalence without as yet offering an imaginary solution to it.

As in **"La Famille Adam"** and **"La Fugue du petit Poucet,"** androgyny is a prominent theme in **"Les Suaires de Véronique."** The story depicts, indeed, not only a feminine man but a masculine woman, and the reversal of gender roles in the story is striking. Véronique belongs to the androgynous type—much admired by Tournier—of the *femme forte,* displaying a conventionally masculine assertiveness and aggression.[25] Hector, although physically the very paradigm of masculinity, shows feminine attributes and connotations: frolicking in the pools of the Camargue, he recalls "Vénus émergeant des eaux," and in his relationship with Véronique it is she who assumes the dominant role, he the submissive one.[26] Androgyny figures equally prominently in other stories in *Le Coq de bruyère*: **"La Mère Noël"** features a female Father Christmas who breastfeeds the baby playing the newborn Messiah in the *crèche* at midnight mass (a disconcerting juxtaposition not just of male and female roles but also of Christian and pagan tradition, sacred and profane). In **"Amandine ou les deux jardins,"** the gender of the family's various cats is ambiguous; a "male" kitten turns out to be pregnant at the end of the story. The child in **"Tupik"** is also confronted by sexual ambiguity: a male statue in the local park is confusingly clad in a "jupe" and bears "un nom de fille: Thésée" (73); a "boy" named Dominique turns out to be a girl (82). Tupik himself rejects his male gender and catastrophically attempts to join the "monde des femmes" by self-castration.

Given the prominence of androgynous figures both in *Le Coq de bruyère* and elsewhere in Tournier's fiction, it is easy to see why critics such as Hoda Rizk and Arlette Bouloumié have seen the "mythe de l'androgyne" as one of the most important underlying his fiction. Such critics, however, would view androgynous characters such as those we have encountered in this chapter

merely as the most superficial manifestations of the Androgyne. As I mentioned earlier, the archetypal Androgyne is discerned in the synthesis of opposites in general, and from this perspective, potentially any figure—or even object—which enacts such a synthesis becomes "androgynous:" Paul at the end of *Les Météores,* Christ in *Gaspard, Melchior et Balthazar,* Colombine in *Pierrot* [*Pierrot ou les secrets de la nuit*].

I would not dispute that the trajectory of Tournier's fiction is toward a resolution of contradiction, and that this is one of its most important mythical characteristics; I would dispute, however, that this constitutes the manifestation of an archetypal figure such as the Androgyne. Such a view, it seems to me, is not only reductive, it also obscures one of the most important links between Tournier's fiction and myths. Tournier's fiction is held to be mythical on the basis of its manifestation of a timeless archetype, rather than because of the illusory, imaginary nature of its resolution of contradiction. My own purpose, on the contrary, is to define Tournier's fiction as mythical without reference to archetypal images and symbols.

Tournier's fascination with androgyny may be explained in terms of, and indeed is symptomatic of, the mythical mode of thought which we have already observed elsewhere in his fiction. Androgyny appeals to Tournier because it seems to represent the achievement of what his imagination urgently (if vainly) strives for: the resolution of antithesis into synthesis, and the abolition of difference. **"La Famille Adam"** exemplifies how in Tournier, this ideal fusion of opposites is inseparable from the theme of perfect origins (the advent of dichotomy being correspondingly equated with the Fall): in Tournier's mythological world, indeed, the first human being is an androgyne. The *filles-garçons* and *garçons-filles* who people his fiction symbolically recreate the androgyny of Adam, thereby reversing—or at least attenuating—the sexual dichotomy which is ordinarily the human condition. Thus while Tournier's fiction enacts a resolution of contradiction at a narrative level, his androgynous protagonists do the same at the thematic level.

If Tournier's world is androgynous, it is also a world turned upside-down. As we have often seen in this chapter, this inversion is also one of the most distinctive characteristics of his *bricolage* of cultural mythology. I began this chapter with Andersen's story of the Snow Queen, and in the light of the preceding pages, it is tempting to suggest that, like Kay in Andersen's tale, Tournier "a reçu dans l'œil l'une des poussières du grand miroir diabolique pulvérisé" (VP [*Le Vent paraclet*] 50)—or that he is the holder of the mirror in the first place. Each of the three stories I have discussed is in its way a *miroir déformant* held up to the narrative or image on which it is based, reversing the polarities

of good and evil, positive and negative, normal and abnormal. Cain is rehabilitated; Perrault's ogre becomes a
vegetarian; Saint Veronica becomes a witch. In each
tale, Tournier seems to take an almost perverse delight
in going against the grain both of his source and of
conventional assumptions (concerning sexual identity,
for example). The tendency is no less evident in his fictional characters. Alexandre's words in *Les Météores,*
for example, could equally be those of his creator:

> Contraint au départ à *prendre les gens et les choses
> carrément à rebrousse-poil,* tournant toujours dans le
> sens contraire de la rotation de la terre, je me suis con-
> struit un univers, fou peut-être, mais cohérent et surtout
> qui me ressemble, tout de même que certains mol-
> lusques sécrètent autour de leurs corps une coquille
> biscornue mais sur mesure.

(40-41)[27]

Like Alexandre, Tournier is drawn irresistibly to *prendre les choses et les gens à rebrousse-poil.* His fiction is
characterized by its capacity for persistently rubbing us
up the wrong way. Such a procedure is not without its
dangers; stroking an animal the wrong way also raises
its hackles. Whether we find the experience pleasurable
or irritating, however, it is certainly difficult to ignore.

Notes

1. The literature on androgyny is vast, but the fol-
lowing studies are especially useful: A. J. L. Busst,
"The Image of the Androgyne in the Nineteenth
Century," *Romantic Mythologies,* ed. I. Fletcher
(London: Routledge and Kegan Paul, 1967) 1-95;
C. Heilbrun, *Towards a Recognition of Androgyny*
(New York: Knopf, 1973); J. Libis, *Le Mythe de
l'Androgyne* (Paris: Berg International, 1980); E.
Zolla, *The Androgyne: Fusion of the Sexes*
(London: Thames and Hudson, 1981). Although
the figure of the androgyne is commonly associated with asexuality and that of the hermaphrodite
with bisexuality, the distinction between the two
is non-standardized and often depends on the
whim of individual authors; for the sake of clarity,
I will use the terms "androgyne," "androgyny,"
and "androgynous" to denote both asexuality and
bisexuality, androgynes and hermaphrodites, in
what follows.

2. See *Le Roi des Aulnes* 33-35; *Les Météores* 61-62,
65-66, 484-85; *Le Coq de bruyère* ("La Fugue du
petit Poucet") 59-60; *Gaspard, Melchior et Balthazar* 46-49, 194-96; *Le Vagabond immobile* ("Le
Sosie de Dieu") 65; *Le Médianoche amoureux*
("La Légende de la musique et de la danse," "La
Légende des parfums") 283-93.

3. Such passages are unlikely to be found funny by
feminist readers, of course; I shall be returning to
the implications of the representation of women in
the *conte* shortly.

4. C. Perrault, "Le Petit Poucet," *Contes,* ed. G.
Rouger, Classiques Garnier (Paris: Garnier, 1967)
182-98. "Le Petit Poucet" is less familiar in the
English-speaking world than some of Perrault's
other tales, notably "Le Petit Chaperon rouge"
(Little Red Riding Hood), "La Belle au bois dor-
mant" (Sleeping Beauty), "Le Chat Botté" (Puss-
in-Boots), and "Cendrillon" (Cinderella). The closest English equivalent to Poucet is Tom Thumb,
although the tales in which he figures are different
from Perrault's story. The cultural discrepancy
here exemplifies why Tournier is often so difficult
to translate: the prosaic rendering of "La Fugue
du petit Poucet" as "Tom Thumb Runs Away" in
the English translation of *Le Coq de bruyère* is
obviously unsatisfactory, yet it is by no means
clear what it could be replaced with.

5. Angela Carter does the same with another Perrault
tale, "La Barbe bleue," in her story "The Bloody
Chamber" (*The Bloody Chamber and Other Stories* [London: Gollancz, 1979] 7-41).

6. Logre's daughters invite Pierre to their house, for
example, with the phrase: "Viens, on va te
présenter *à Logre* [à l'ogre]" (56). Logre's name
(like Thomas Koussek's in *Les Météores*) is a
translator's nightmare, since the Logre/*l'ogre* pun
only works in French. This problem also extends
to critical discourse: unless discussing the tale in
French, it is impossible to convey the homology
between Tournier's figure and Perrault's. To foreground the linguistic homonymy between the two
figures, I shall refer to Logre as "the ogre" in what
follows.

7. "Il flairait à droite et à gauche, disant qu'il sentait
la chair fraîche" (Perrault 192). The celebrated
phrase is also the epigraph to the Rominten section of *Le Roi des Aulnes* (304). Perrault's ogre
here exemplifies Tournier's point (*VP* 117) that
the (archetypal) Ogre has a highly developed sense
of smell (especially where raw meat is concerned),
and both Tiffauges and, as we will see later, Gilles
de Rais exhibit this characteristic.

8. The inversion of gender roles here also entails a
corresponding inversion of the nomadic/sedentary
paradigm. In Perrault, the ogre's wife stays where
she is (sedentary) whereas the ogre moves around
(nomadic): indeed, when the brothers escape he
pursues them at terrifying speed with his seven-
league boots, which endow him with a kind of *su-
pernomadisme.* In Tournier, the pattern is reversed:
Logre stays at home (sedentary) while his wife
travels "en province" (nomadic).

9. This does not mean, however, that Tournier merely
inverts the roles of the father and the ogre in his
version of Perrault's tale. Perrault does not overtly

set the boys' father in opposition to the ogre, as Tournier does; in fact, the father is himself malevolent, since it is he who insists on abandoning his sons in the forest in the first place. Tournier's rewriting here is a good example of his tendency to polarize his materials, creating an opposition which has no antecedent in Perrault.

10. Trees play an important part in Tournier's writing, from the comparison of a tree to the human lung in *Vendredi* (203), through the sacred baobabs in *Gaspard, Melchior et Balthazar* (203-05), to the meditations in *Le Vagabond immobile* (100-03). See A. Bouloumié, "Le Thème de l'arbre dans l'œuvre de Michel Tournier," *L'Ecole des lettres,* 1 June 1986: 3-12.

11. The story is unusual in having been the subject of a book-length collection of articles: "Analyse plurielle: 'Les Suaires de Véronique' de Tournier," spec. issue of *Incidences* 2-3.2-3 (Université d'Ottawa, 1979).

12. See E. Roberto, "Du symbole taurin au complexe de Nessos," in *Incidences* 41-50. Nessus, the Centaur, tries to rape Hercules's wife, Deianeira, but is mortally wounded by one of Hercules's arrows. Before dying, Nessus tells her that if she uses a mixture of his blood and sperm to anoint Heracles's shirt, it will make him faithful to her when he wears it. Nessus's blood contains poison, however, and when Hercules wears the shirt, it burns his flesh; when he tries to tear it off, it sticks to his skin and he tears away his own flesh. In agony, he throws himself onto a pyre and is burned alive. See R. Graves, *The Greek Myths,* 2 vols. (Harmondsworth, Eng., Penguin, 1960) 2: 193, 201-02.

13. The latter reading is supported by the references to Hector's "front de taurillon" (154) or his "jactance de bel animal" (156), by the depiction of him frolicking in the lakes of the Camargue, even by his name—Hec *taure.* As Roberto also mentions, in bullfighting the *veronica* is the name given to one of the stylized passes made by the *matador,* in which he "wipes" his cape over the bull's face in a manner reminiscent of Veronica's wiping of the face of Jesus. Elsewhere in the same astonishing article, he extends the reading of the story as the symbolic sacrifice of a bull, and goes on to establish parallels with Egyptian, Sumerian and Cretan mythology.

14. I. Wilson, *The Turin Shroud* (London: Gollancz, 1978) 87. Chapter 13, "The Shroud and the Tradition of Christ's Face Impressed on the Cloth" (86-92), discusses the origins of Veronica's veil and

its cult. See also E. Kuryluk, *Veronica and her Cloth: History, Symbolism, and Structure of a "True" Image* (Cambridge, Mass.: Blackwell, 1991).

15. A. Chastel, "La Véronique," *Revue de l'art* 40-41 (1978) 71-82.

16. C. Millet, *Yves Klein* (Paris: Art Press-Flammarion, 1983) 57.

17. For further discussion of the analogy between photography and religion in the story, see Kaye.

18. Véronique's shrouds have a number of antecedents in experimentation in the visual arts. Robert Rauschenberg's "blueprint" series (1949-51) were produced on photosensitive paper by a method very similar to Véronique's (Millet 64). The shrouds also have much in common with Yves Klein's "Anthropométries" (1958-61), produced by imprinting bodies daubed in blue paint onto sheets of paper, which Millet describes as "modernes versions de la Véronique" (59). The analogy between Klein's works and Tournier's story is by no means gratuitous: some of the "Anthropométries" are executed on cloth and are titled "Suaires." Five years before "Les Suaires de Véronique" was published (*La Nouvelle Revue Française* 300 [1978] 23-39), Tournier reviewed an exhibition of Klein's work ("Yves Klein: le philosophe au bleu lessive," *Le Point,* 26 March 1973: 76-77); in a personal interview (24 February 1987), however, he denied that Klein's work had inspired his story.

19. For a fascinating discussion of Véronique as witch-turned-inquisitor, see Kaye.

20. Hence the furore when the Shroud was photographed for the first time at the turn of the century, the photographic negative producing—paradoxically—a *positive* image of the body imprinted on the cloth. The photographer thought he was "the first man for nearly 1,900 years to gaze on the actual appearance of the body of Christ as he had been laid in the tomb" (14).

21. Ian Wilson advances the ingenious theory that the shroud was folded soon after the time of Christ so that only the head was visible, and was thus mistaken for a veil until it was unfolded again at some point in the Middle Ages. Even if the Turin Shroud *is* a medieval fake, this does not exclude the possibility of such a link between the two relics.

22. D. Bougnoux, "Des Métaphores à la phorie," *Critique* 301 (1972) 527-43.

23. This role becomes most transparent in Véronique's re-appropriation, at the end of the story, of the phallic tiger's tooth which Hector wears around his neck.

24. For further discussion, see N. Bourbonnais, "'Les Suaires de Véronique'. Présences du narrateur," *Incidences* 51-74.

25. For Tournier's views on the *femme forte,* see "Le Crépuscule des masques," *Petites proses* (Paris: Gallimard Folio 1768, 1986) 81-85.

26. On the reversal of gender roles in "Les Suaires de Véronique," see M.-L. Girou-Swiderski, "Hector et Véronique ou la dialectique des sexes," *Incidences* 29-39.

27. Describing the torrent of refugees streaming past him from Paris, Alexandre later writes in similar vein: "Je ne vais pas résister longtemps à la tentation de remonter ce flot de fuyards. J'aime trop prendre les choses et les gens à rebrousse-poil pour ne pas tenter de vaincre ce courant" (336).

Bibliography

WORKS BY TOURNIER

Fiction

Vendredi ou les limbes du Pacifique. Paris: Gallimard, 1967. Rev. ed. Paris: Gallimard-Folio 959, 1972.

Le Roi des Aulnes. Paris: Gallimard, 1970. Paris: Gallimard-Folio 656, 1975.

Vendredi ou la vie sauvage. Paris: Flammarion, 1971. Illus. Pat York. Paris: Gallimard/Flammarion, 1981. Illus. Georges Lemoine. Gallimard-Folio Junior 30, 1977.

Les Météores. Paris: Gallimard-Folio 905, 1975.

Le Nain rouge. Illus. Anne-Marie Soulcié. Montpellier and Paris: Fata Morgana, 1975.

Amandine ou les deux jardins. Paris: G.P. Rouge et Or, 1977.

Le Coq de bruyère. Paris: Gallimard, 1978. Paris: Gallimard-Folio 1229, 1982.

La Fugue du petit Poucet. Paris: G.P. Rouge et Or, 1979.

Pierrot ou les secrets de la nuit. Illus. Danièle Bour. Paris: Enfantimages/Gallimard, 1979.

Barbedor. Illus. Georges Lemoine. Paris: Enfantimages/Gallimard, 1980.

Gaspard, Melchior et Balthazar. Paris: Gallimard-Folio 1415, 1980.

L'Aire du muguet. 1978. Illus. Georges Lemoine. Paris: Gallimard-Folio Junior 240, 1982.

Que ma joie demeure. Illus. Jean Claverie. Paris: Enfantimages/Gallimard, 1982.

Gilles et Jeanne. Paris: NRF and Gallimard, 1983.

Les Rois Mages. Paris: Gallimard. 1983. Illus. Michel Charrier. Paris: Gallimard-Folio Junior, 1985.

Sept contes. Illus. Pierre Hézard. Paris: Gallimard-Folio Junior 264, 1984.

La Goutte d'or. Paris: Gallimard, 1985. Paris: Gallimard-Folio, 1987.

"La Mère Noël." *Contes et nouvelles de Noël.* Ed. Marie-Claudette Kirpalani. Paris: Hachette, 1987. 49-51.

Angus. Illus. Pierre Joubert. [N.p.]: Signe de piste, 1988.

Le Médianoche amoureux: Contes et nouvelles. Paris: NRF and Gallimard, 1989. Paris: Gallimard-Folio 2290, 1989.

Non-Fiction

Le Vent Paraclet. Paris: Gallimard-Folio 1138, 1977.

Le Vol du vampire: Notes de lecture. Paris: Mercure de France, 1982.

Le Vagabond immobile. Drawings by Jean-Max Toubeau. Paris: NRF and Gallimard, 1984.

Petites proses. Paris: Gallimard-Folio 1768, 1986.

Articles

NOTE: Over the past two decades Tournier has published a large number of articles in prefaces, in periodicals and the press, the most important of which have been collected in *Le Vol du vampire* and *Petites proses.* The following list includes selected articles not already published in these works, and articles whose original publication is referred to in the text.

"Yves Klein: le philosophe au lessive bleu." *Le Point,* March 26, 1973: 76-77.

SECONDARY SOURCES

Articles

Bougnoux, D. "Des Métaphores à la phorie." *Critique* 301 (1972) 527-43.

Bouloumié, A. "Mythologies." *Magazine Littéraire,* January 1986: 26-29.

———. "Le Thème de l'arbre dans l'œuvre de Michel Tournier." *Ecole des Lettres,* June 1, 1986, pp. 3-12.

Bourbonnais, N. "'Les Suaires de Véronique.' Présences du narrateur." Spec. issue of *Incidences* 2-3.2-3 (1979) 51-74.

Girou-Swiderski, M.-L. "Hector et Véronique ou la dialectique des sexes." Spec. issue of *Incidences* 2-3.2-3 (1979) 29-39.

Kaye, F. "Ce petit Hector, on aimerait en faire quelque chose." Spec. issue of *Incidences* 2-3.2-3 (1979) 21-27.

Roberto, E. "Du Symbole taurin au complexe de Nessos." Spec. issue of *Incidences* 2-3.2-3 (1979) 41-50.

O*THER* W*ORKS* C*ONSULTED*

Carter, A. *The Bloody Chamber and Other Stories.* London: Gollancz, 1979.

Chastel, A. "La Véronique." *Revue de l'art* 40-41 (1978) 71-82.

Fletcher, I., ed. *Romantic Mythologies.* London: Routledge and Kegan Paul, 1967.

Graves, R. *The Greek Myths.* Rev. ed. 2 vols. Harmondsworth, Eng.: Penguin, 1960.

Heilbrun, C. *Towards a Recognition of Androgyny.* New York: Knopf, 1973.

Kuryluk, E. *Veronica and her Cloth: History, Symbolism, and Structure of a "True" Image.* Cambridge, Mass.: Blackwell, 1991.

Libis, J. *Le Mythe de l'androgyne.* Paris: Berg International, 1980.

Millet, C. *Yves Klein.* Paris: Art Press-Flammarion, 1983.

Perrault, C. *Contes.* Ed. G. Rouger. Classiques Garnier. Paris: Garnier, 1967.

Wilson, I. *The Turin Shroud.* London: Gollancz, 1978.

Zolla, E. *The Androgyne: Fusion of the Sexes.* London: Thames and Hudson, 1981.

Karen D. Levy (essay date summer 1995)

SOURCE: Levy, Karen D. "The Perilous Journey from Melancholy to Love: A Kristevan Reading of *Le Médianoche amoureux*." *Studies in Twentieth-Century Literature* 19, no. 2 (summer 1995): 185-205.

[*In the following essay, Levy analyzes the destructive elements of sexual desire in* La Médianoche amoureux *in light of Julia Kristeva's psychological theories.*]

Since the publication of Michel Tournier's first novel *Vendredi ou les limbes du Pacifique* in 1967, in which his protagonist Robinson makes fruitful the very earth of his desert island and eventually accedes to the cosmic transcendence embodied in his mentor and companion Vendredi, this contemporary French writer has boldly explored alternative forms of sexual expression that challenge traditional biological definitions of identity as well as norms of accepted behavior. The basis of his investigations is the anguish-ridden separation from the maternal, as experienced under diverse manifestations usually by male characters, and the irremediable solitude that then stretches over that empty space. In

each of his works, Tournier examines the problems that arise from what his protagonists perceive as abandonment or betrayal, and he explores the various ways in which these individuals seek to disavow, to mourn, or to sublimate the forlornness of their condition. His enchantment with the diffuse, polymorphous sexuality of the child (*Le Roi des aulnes*), his fascination with the exclusive intimacy between identical twins and their rapport with their mother (*Les Météores*), and his wistful admiration for the idyllic totality of an androgynal relationship (*Vendredi* [*Vendredi ou les limbes du Pacifique*], *Le Roi des aulnes,* **Le Coq de bruyère,** etc.), have become an inexhaustible subject of innovative inquiry as well as highly charged critical controversy.

In this three-part study, we shall explore Tournier's latest and perhaps most unexpected treatment of the phenomenon of separation and loss as depicted in his anthology of short stories **Le Médianoche amoureux** from the point of view of two of Julia Kristeva's most recent theoretical analyses. The intensely polemical character of her work and her rejection of stereotyped classifications to describe her critical positions reflect Tournier's own provocativeness at the thematic level. They both question the tangled process of sexualisation and, in particular, explore either marginal or openly perverse expressions of desire, one as literary critic and psychoanalyst and the other as fiction writer. Kristeva's texts probe precisely the kind of psychological wounds from which Tournier's protagonists suffer and, as we shall see, suggest possibilities for healing which significantly enhance our understanding of his fictional enterprise. Her discussion of melancholy in *Soleil noir: Dépression et mélancolie* and her demystifying analysis of the intricacies of amatory discourse in *Histoires d'amour* will enable us to discern the kind of movement that draws the disparate stories of **Le Médianoche amoureux** together and will reveal how this latest of Tournier's works greatly extends the scope of his preoccupations without closing any of the other doors he has so daringly opened.

Before turning our attention to how the melancholy and love Kristeva analyzes are inscribed in **Le Médianoche amoureux,** we must briefly examine the attitudes toward sexuality that have prevailed up to this point in Tournier's repertoire, for only then will we be able to appreciate fully the innovativeness of his latest publication. Tournier's glorification of either marginal or openly perverse sexuality has been accompanied, as one might expect, by his aggressive criticism of traditional sexual orientation and of the institution of marriage, which he sees as imprisoning both participants in stereotyped positions. In the personal meditations of *Le Vol du vampire* and *Petites Proses,* as well as in various interviews, Tournier has repeatedly emphasized the link between procreation and death and the stifling restrictiveness of marital and, indeed, all heterosexual relationships: "Le mariage s'inscrit dans le temps. Il implique fécondité, les enfants, la fatigue, le vieillissement, d'éventuelles trahisons, et possible divorce" 'Marriage is inscribed in time. It implies fecundity, children, fatigue, aging, eventual betrayals, and possible divorce' (*VV* [*Le Vol du Vampire*] 37, see also 151-52).[1] And his fictional works present a distressingly unpleasant series of either openly hostile or, at least, negative heterosexual situations in which, for the most part, ineffectual males are overwhelmed by phallic females with varying degrees of castrating power.

The texts published before *Le Médianoche amoureux* reveal the all-pervasiveness of this situation. The sexually active adult females who appear even fleetingly in Tournier's writings, beginning with Abel Tiffauges' Jewish mistress Rachel in *Le Roi des aulnes,* are portrayed as independent individualists who simultaneously attract and frighten their partners. On the one hand, Tiffauges is drawn to Rachel because of her overtly maternal appearance; she is what he calls "une femme paysage: un bassin méditérranéen . . . un corps ample, accueillant, maternel" 'a woman landscape: a mediterranean basin . . . an ample body, welcoming, maternal' (32). He is likewise fascinated by "son sens de la drôlerie, son adresse à déceler le côté profondément absurde des gens et des situations" 'her sense of humor, her skill in discerning the profoundly absurd side of people and situations' (19), and by her "gaieté tonique" 'invigorating gaiety' (19), which contrasts with his morbid pessimism. But, at the same time, Tiffauges finds her candid directness menacing, so much so that her statement concerning his premature ejaculation, although expressed "sans méchanceté aucune" 'without any spitefulness' (19), reduces him to the state of near impotence. It indicates what Tiffauges describes as "la grande mésentente du couple humain" 'the great misunderstanding of the human couple' (21), and this problem, presented as insoluble, triggers Rachel's departure, which, in turn, initiates Tiffauges' eventually fatal descent into the past.

A similar situation occurs in the opening sections of *Les Météores.* Edouard Surin, father of the identical twins Jean-Paul, has long since ceased to feel anything more than tenderness for his wife Maria-Barbara. He is attracted to his mistress Florence, also Jewish, largely because of her "lucidité drôle et amère, un trait qu'il avait attendu davantage d'un homme que d'une femme" 'her droll and acerbic lucidity, a trait which he would have expected much more of a man than a woman' (26). But, at the same time, her ability to judge and make fun of others, as well as herself, without rancor or condescension intimidates Edouard and makes him painfully aware of his own generalized weariness and overall inferiority (28-29). A more serious problem arises later in the text with the visit of Jean's fiancée Sophie, whom his twin brother Paul perceives as an alien force seeking to destroy the already threatened unity of the brothers' exclusive relationship. When he encounters Sophie for the first time on the cliff top path at the edge of the family property on the Brittany coast, Paul feels as if he has been raped: "ayant une connaissance intime de Jean, elle savait aussi tout de moi qui ne savais rien d'elle. . . . J'étais comme percé, inventorié" 'having an intimate knowledge of Jean, she knew as much about me, who knew nothing of her. . . . I was as if pierced, inventoried' (392). Hence, the invading Sophie must be made to leave, an act that Paul accomplishes with sadistic cunning as he confuses Sophie about which twin she actually slept with (411). Yet, ironically, it is precisely Sophie's panic-stricken departure that completes the destruction of the psychological cell whose purity Paul so jealously sought to preserve.

A much more dramatically violent situation occurs with the female protagonist in the short story **"Les Suaires de Véronique."** She literally reduces the substance of her lover Hector's body to nothing but stretched skin, albeit transforming him into spectacular photographic masterpieces in the process. Gazing incredulously around the chapel in Arles where Véronique is exhibiting her latest endeavors, the narrator attempts to describe the all-encompassing scene of destruction for art's sake: "Partout . . . le regard s'écrasait sur le spectre noir et doré d'un corps aplati, élargi, roulé, déroulé, reproduit en frise funèbre et obsédante dans toutes les positions . . ." 'Everywhere . . . one's gaze was overwhelmed by the black and golden specter of a body flattened, enlarged, rolled up, unfurled, reproduced as an obsessing funeral frieze in all positions . . .' (171). The psychological threat of a Rachel, a Florence, or a Sophie assumes its most grisly form in this short story, which constitutes the apocalyptic stage in the war of the sexes that is constantly waged in Tournier's works.[2]

At first glance, it may seem that the nurturing and politically committed Maria-Barbara in *Les Météores* offers a more positive image. But although she does take an active role in the Resistance during the German occupation, eventually being deported to Buchenwald, she too dominates the appealing though indecisive Edouard and is firmly locked into the role of brood mare. Maria-Barbara produces so many offspring that, as the text notes, "les grossesses . . . se fondent en une seule . . . Peu importait l'époux, le semeur, le donneur de cette pauvre chiquenaude qui déclenche le processus de procréation" 'her pregnancies . . . blended into one . . . the husband, the sower, the donor of this pathetic flick which unleashed the process of creation mattered little' (12). As archetype of the "mère innombrable," 'mother of countless children' (10) she neither remembers how many children she has nor, with the exception of the twins Jean-Paul, distinguishes any of them by name. Her children's sole function is to offer her hommage as part of an ever-present entourage, thereby sanctifying her importance as source of life and nourishment. It is true that Maria-Barbara appears as an unruffled, stabilizing force and that, as Paul stresses, she reigns peacefully up to the moment when the Gestapo agents arrest her (351, 355). But her nurturing is concentrated almost exclusively in the milk that flows so readily from her breasts, with Maria-Barbara dreaming of "un enfant qui viendrait à elle debout . . . et qui dégraferait de ses mains son corsage, sortirait la gourde de chair et boirait, comme un homme à la bouteille" 'a child who would come walking to her . . . and who would unbutton her blouse with his hands, would take out the flesh gourd, and would drink, like a man from a bottle' (10). Her attitude, therefore, ends up, in its own way, being as restrictive and confining as that of the other adult females depicted in Tournier's works, and her power over her husband as destructive.

Given the radical devalorization of heterosexual relationships in Tournier's writings, it is perhaps not surprising that a marital communication crisis forms the basis for the story-telling odyssey in **Le Médianoche amoureux.** But it is astonishing that the protagonists Yves and Nadège Oudalle decide to remain together after listening to their guests' tales. Their night-long narrative adventure both further exposes and, at the same time, begins to heal the wound of silent hostility eating away at the host and hostess. It rebuilds the psychic space of narcissism that can be playfully entered, explored, and exploited. As we shall see, this work presents Tournier's perhaps most banal and, at the same time, his most far-reaching exploration of the phenomenon of loss that haunts all of his writings. It stresses for the first time the importance of dialogue, albeit hesitant, between two differently sexed adults whose faces are turned toward one another across the mediating space of the dinner table in a gesture that indicates both attention to and recognition of the other's autonomy. The implications of this situation extend, for example, far beyond the self-deluding "écrits sinistres" 'left-handed writings' of Tiffauges' private journal in *Le Roi des aulnes,* beyond Paul's triumphant but solitary narration encompassing the cosmos at the end of *Les Météores,* and also beyond Riad's calligraphic deciphering of the image of the "Reine blonde" in *La Goutte d'or.*

Tournier's most recent work charts the perilous journey Yves and Nadège undertake from the stagnant waters of a melancholy that cannot be named or symbolized to the point of the couple's rebirth in signs. The stories the two protagonists absorb during the dinner party, ostensibly given to announce their separation, begin to renew their sorely diminished imaginary capacities and to produce a language that would act simultaneously both for and against the sadness that has sapped their psychic resources. Their relationship exemplifies the movement from morbid withdrawal to dynamic, though always

tentative participation, that Julia Kristeva analyzes in *Soleil noir: Dépression et mélancolie* and *Histoires d'amour.* She describes melancholy as a state in which one suffers "une mort vivante, chair coupée, saignante, cadavérisée, rythme ralenti ou suspendu, temps effacé ou boursoufflé, résorbé dans la peine . . ." 'a living death, flesh cut, bleeding, cadaverized, rhythm slowed down or suspended, time erased or inflated, resorbed in pain . . .' (14). Triggered by a loss that cannot be acknowledged, one sinks into a morose lethargy, unable to direct energy elsewhere or transfer desire to another object. As Kristeva maintains, both melancholy and its less severe form depression "s'étayent cependant d'une *intolérance à la perte de l'objet* et de la *faillite du signifiant à* assurer une issue compensatoire" 'are supported, however, by an *inability to tolerate the loss of the object* and of the *failure of the signifier* to insure a compensating outlet' (20). The aggressivity a person might feel toward the lost object is absorbed and recycled as sadness, keeping the wound open and never allowing any healing words to form over the surface. The melancholic's despairing pain becomes, as Kristeva notes, the sole focus of his attention (22). It suggests, as does the black sun in Nerval's sonnet "El Desdichado," which figures in the title of her work, "une insistance sans présence, une lumière sans représentation . . ." 'an insistence without presence, a light without representation . . .' (22).

At its most fundamental level, melancholy indicates what John Lechte describes in his sensitive analysis of Kristeva's work as, "an unsuccessful separation from the mother, an unsuccessful emergence of primary narcissism and the concommitant Imaginary Father" (34). Without separation from the maternal, as painful as it is, and initial identification with a combination of both parents that constitutes the phenomenon of the Imaginary Father or, as Kristeva also calls it, the Father of individual pre-history, no individualized identity can develop. She goes on to stress in this same context that Narcissus dies, not because he adores himself, but rather because he remains blocked in the borderline position of not being able to transfer some of what he feels for his own image to another individual. Although he desires an Other, he is, at the same time, incapable of opening up to that possibility.[3]

In her analysis of primary narcissism, which she sees as the first stage in separation or individualisation, Kristeva puts special emphasis on the gap, the void that comes into being once the elemental fusion between mother and child is broken, and she stresses the specifically linguistic manifestations of this phenomenon as the bar that forever separates the signifier from the signified (*Histoires* [*Histoire d'amour*] 29-30). It is this lack of coincidence that the melancholic cannot deal with. Unable to voice the signs to express his pain, he retreats into mournful silence. As Kristeva notes: "la parole du déprimé: répétitive et monotone. Dans l'impossibilité d'enchaîner, la phrase s'interrompt, s'épuise, s'arrête" 'the word of the depressed person: repetitive and monotonous. In the impossibility of making connections, the sentence is interrupted, drained, arrested' (*Soleil* [*Soleil noir*] 45). And as she further emphasizes at the end of this section of her study, "le dépressif . . . rivé à sa douleur, n'enchaîne plus et, en conséquence, n'agit ni ne parle" 'the depressed person . . . riveted to his pain, no longer makes connections, and, in consequence, neither acts nor speaks' (46). The pain Kristeva describes in this analysis corresponds greatly to that which haunts Yves Oudalle, and eventually also encompasses Nadège, in **"Les Amants taciturnes,"** the initial springboard narrative of *Le Médianoche amoureux.* Yves's defiant departure as cabin boy aboard a trawler bound for the waters around Newfoundland at the psychologically transitional age of thirteen indicates his jealous determination to outshine his elder brother, who merely fishes with his father for local varieties along the Normandy coast. It likewise signals a jubilant return to the archaic mother, under the double form of ship and sea. Despite the physical suffering and humiliation he is forced to endure at the hands of his superiors, Yves rises to the exalted rank of ship's captain and returns to shore only for the brief reorganizing periods necessary at the end of many months' long voyages.

As far as his relationship with Nadège is concerned, Yves actually sees her for the first time when he is sixteen and she and her brother, aged ten and eighteen respectively, spend two days observing life aboard the trawler at the request of their ship owner father. It is, however, nearly twenty years later, when he is recruiting sailors for his first voyage as captain, that they meet formally. For Nadège, Yves concretizes the image of the heroic deep sea fisherman whose legendary exploits she grew up with in the works of writers, such as Pierre Loti and Joseph Conrad. As she describes her initial reaction to Yves: "Massif, lent, le regard bleu sous les sourcils blonds, Oudalle paraissait aussi peu causant qu'un ours blanc du pôle nord. Je l'ai tout de suite aimé" 'Massive, slow, blue gaze beneath blond eyebrows, Oudalle seemed as talkative as a polar bear. I loved him at first sight' (16).

It is important to note that it is Yves's reserved, taciturn quality that so attracts Nadège and that, to a certain extent, characterizes their relationship from its inception. As a student preparing a degree in classical letters, she had, for a short time, been married to a philosophy student named Alexis, who had dazzled her with his rhetorical commentaries. But the events of "May 68" soon revealed the folly of Nadège's decision and the emptiness of Alexis's professionalism. His ardent speeches in favor of the revolution proved to be only reductive, self-deceptive tirades that fed greedily on the desire for control and the illusion of power they expressed: "tout

se résolvait pour lui en discours, un flot verbal incoercible qui balayait tout, obstacles, contradictions, et simple bon sens" 'everything became resolved for him in discourse, an uncontrollable verbal flow which swept away everything, obstacles, contradictions, and simple good sense' (16). Words, for Alexis, were discursive monologues whose purpose was to dominate, not tales to engage the imagination or dialogues to be shared. As Nadège notes, "il confondait prendre le pouvoir et prendre la parole . . ." 'he confused assuming power and speaking' (16).

Yves appears as a most welcome counterpoint to Alexis's power hungry verbiage and the most promising person to fulfill Nadège's dream of "une sagesse laconique, de mots pesés, rares, mais lourds de sens" 'a laconic wisdom, carefully weighed, sparse words, but heavy with meaning' (30). During his shore visits, Nadège listens eagerly, as fiancée and then as wife, to the sea tales and anecdotes Yves has stored up from so many years experience, to what he himself refers to as his "capital mythologique" 'mythological capital' (20). But these resources are soon depleted, and, more importantly, there is nothing to take their place. As Yves himself notes: "Elle m'écoutait avec passion quand j'évoquais mes campagnes. Puis le capital s'est épuisé. Sa passion s'est muée en respect. Ensuite ce n'était plus que de la patience qu'elle m'offrait. Et la patience a ses limites . . ." 'She listened to me with passion when I evoked my campaigns. Then the capital was depleted. Her passion changed to respect. Then it was nothing more than patience that she offered me. And patience has its limits . . .' (20). Despite the fact that they understand the same frame of references and appreciate the same vocabulary, Yves's words lose their evocative quality and eventually cease altogether, for neither he nor Nadège can envision any other kind of stories to share.

The event that precipitates his lapse into silence and immobilizes Nadège in respect, then patience, and finally bitter frustration, is the closing of the shipping company, which exiles Yves from the sea that had sustained him so long and makes him confront everyday married life on a full-time basis: "me voilà terrien intégral et mari à temps complet. Quel boulversement!" 'Here I am, living totally on land and full-time husband. What an upset!' (21). The text does not specify Nadège's reaction to the situation, but Yves himself emphasizes how she tries to save both him and their marriage by moving from the shipping port of Fécamp down the Normandy coast to Grouin-du-Sud near Avranches and encouraging him to explore the lower Normandy coast line. Unfortunately this second move serves only to reinforce Yves's sense of exile. At the same time, it reveals the double-sided limitations of his relationship with the ocean. Despite his years at sea, he had never learned to swim, and would have drowned if thrown overboard. Nor does he in any way enjoy the water. He scorns the weekend bathers who crowd the shores near Avranches and considers their seaside amusements to be an affront to the seriousness of what had been his way of life. As Yves puts it, speaking of the men with whom he had for so long sailed, "Nous, nous ne savons pas jouer avec l'océan" 'We don't know how to play with the ocean' (22).

Eventually, Yves does learn to explore the shore at low tide, but despite his initial good faith efforts to encourage Nadège to join him, he prefers to spend his days alone. The gratification he experiences is, as Nadège stresses, that of "plaisirs solitaires . . . joies égoïstes qu'on détruit en voulant les partager" 'solitary pleasures . . . egotistical joys which one destroys in wishing to share them' (23-24). The stories and anecdotes of the past disintegrate into the discourse of a pedagogical lesson. In the negatively charged language of "conseils" 'advice' and "objurgations" 'sharp reprimands,' that recall Alexis' philosophical rhetoric, Yves vainly tries to instruct the at this point alienated Nadège how to search out the creatures buried in the exposed sea bed, and eventually even these words cease.

The verbal reserve Nadège had admired disintegrates into grumbling minimalism, evident in the change from "taciturne" 'taciturn' to "taiseux" 'grudgingly silent' (29), and in the caricatured confrontational scenes that occur, which only further immobilize both individuals in the stereotyped marital positions Tournier has depicted in so many of his other works. Separated from the life at sea that had for so long fulfilled him, Yves, like the melancholics Kristeva describes, sinks deeper into his loss. Unable to swim and play in the water, he cannot move beyond this pain and respond to other stimuli. In keeping with Kristeva's analysis, Yves explains this dilemma in specifically linguistic terms. He believes that the words one uses should correspond to physical realities, which is why he finds the weather report so reassuring. The signifier and the signified should coincide to form a unity that cannot be contested. "Les mots qu'on prononce doivent s'accorder au ciel et à la mer" 'The words one uses must be in accord with the sky and the sea' (29), and he cannot accept the fact that this sense of plenitude, as illusory as it may have been, no longer exists: "Les paroles de Fécamp ne répondent pas à l'air d'Avranches" 'The words of Fécamp do not respond to the air of Avranches' (29-30). The move from the familiar port to the south, which aggravates his feeling of exile, is in turn reflected in the gap that separates the two elements of the sign, with which the melancholic Yves cannot cope: "Il y a ici comme un appel doux et insidieux, une demande que je ne sais pas satisfaire" 'There is here, like a gentle and insidious call, a request that I don't know how to satisfy' (30).

When he does speak, Yves can only monotonously repeat the words of the past, and Nadège cannot accept mere repetition as ever-enriching ritual: "aurais-je le cœur d'écouter la même histoire racontée indéfiniment dans les mêmes termes? Aurais-je l'imagination enfantine qu'il faut pour cela?" 'would I have the heart to listen to the same story told indefinitely in the same terms? Would I have the childlike imagination needed for that?' (34). Both protagonists lack the imaginary capacity necessary to be able to play. They are also unable to acknowledge the interdependence between the eternal and the temporary, the two poles of ritual, as evidenced by their encounter with the sculptor Patricio Lagos. Alienated and afraid, they can only react negatively to Lagos' sand sculptures and the dance he executes as the incoming tide engulfs them. When Yves and Nadège first see the embracing earth-colored forms on the beach, they both immediately think that the bodies are corpses, and the expansive movements of Lagos' dance complement a scene which to them is "une fantasmagorie mélancolique et irréelle" 'a melancholy and unreal phantasmagoria' (25). Tournier's protagonists can neither appreciate the subtle meteorological variations Lagos discovered when he emigrated to Normandy from his native Chile, nor can they respond to the possibilities the changing tides offer for celebrating what Lagos terms "la pathétique fragilité de la vie" 'the pathetic fragility of life' (28). Yves is unable to accept the invitation offered by the weather conditions of Avranches where the "rumeur océane" 'the oceanic rumor' (29) is different from that in the familiar city of Fécamp. While, for her part, Nadège cannot recognize the music of the waves as they caress the shore and comprehend how they depict the trauma of separation Yves is experiencing. She does not understand that, as the text indicates, the incoming tide is "volubile" 'voluble' in two different ways. Like the morning-glory vine, which engulfs even the sturdiest of plants with its wild profusion, the tide winds itself around all of the forms lying on the shore, including those of the sculptured couple. At the same time, the incoming waves struggle to verbalize the sense of loss created by the destruction and become a speaking subject. As Lagos explains, "Le flot enlace mes amants de limon. Et il les détruit. C'est le baiser de la mort. Mais volubile, le flot l'est encore par le babil enfantin qu'il chuchote. . . . Il voudrait parler. Il cherche ses mots" 'The wave embraces my lovers made of sand. And it destroys them. It is the kiss of death. But the wave is also voluble in the infantile babble which it murmurs. . . . It would like to speak. It is searching for its words' (28-29).

Immobilized as they both are, there is no point, Yves insists, in remaining together. But he also proposes separating in style with a dinner party for their friends, who, as Nadège adds, will also be both audience and participants in a discussion about love. The celebration that the couple organizes to announce their separation is especially significant because it is to be a communal feast and because of the dialogue to be exchanged. Even more important is the unexpected transformation that occurs in the nature of the words spoken and in the outcome of the evening. As Kristeva takes care to point out in the demystifying analysis of *Histoires d'amour,* the process which is the basis for any amatory relationship begins in a way that is characteristic of "la phase orale de l'organisation de la libido où ce que j'incorpore est ce que je deviens. . . . Je m'identifie non pas avec un objet, mais à ce qui se propose comme *modèle*" 'the oral phase of the libido's organization where what I incorporate is what I become. . . . I identify, not with an object, but with what offers itself to me as a *model*' (30-31). And she further notes the relationship between oral assimilation, a shared meal, and speech, singling out the specific importance of assimilating the words of an other, "substrat essentiel à ce qui constitue l'être de l'homme, à savoir le *langage*" 'the essential substratum of what constitutes man's being, namely, *language*' (31). What is particularly striking about Kristeva's discussion is the shift or displacement that occurs from object to words. As she puts it, "Pour que je sois capable d'une telle opération, il aura fallu un frein à ma libido: ma soif de dévorer a dû être différée et déplacée. . . . De pouvoir recevoir les mots de l'autre, de les assimiler, répéter, reproduire, je deviens comme lui: Un. Un sujet de l'énonciation. Par identification-osmose psychique. Par amour" 'For me to be capable of such an operation, my libido had to be restrained: my thirst to devour had to be deferred and displaced. . . . In being able to receive the other's words, to assimilate, to repeat, to reproduce them, I become like him: One. A subject of enunciation. Through psychic osmosis/identification. Through love' (31-32).

A similar shift occurs during the night-long feast prepared to solemnize Yves and Nadège's separation. As the guests partake of the delicacies that Yves has so lovingly harvested from the ocean, the displacement process Kristeva describes in her analysis is set in motion. The panoply of spectacular sea food courses is soon accompanied by words, which the guests formulate as they sit on the deck that extends to the edge of the shore, or, in linguistic terms, as they sit perched on the bar that separates the signifier from the signified. The sentences they speak become much more nourishing than the dishes consumed. As they are shared, their words become patterns for future innovations. Nadège imagined that the discourse that would dramatically highlight the breakup of her marriage to Yves would be that of a discussion: "Nous leur parlerons, ils nous parleront, ce sera la grande palabre sur le couple et l'amour" 'We'll speak to them, they'll talk to us, it will be the great debate on the couple and on love' (38). Although we are not dealing with a specifically psychoanalytic situation, the interaction Nadège envisages nevertheless suggests the kind of dynamic verbal exchange that can occur between analyst and analysand. As Kristeva notes when describing her vision of the

analytic process in *Histoires d'amour,* "Il valorisera le semblant, l'imaginaire. Pour un tel espace psychique ouvert, indécidable, la crise sera non pas une souffrance, mais un signe, à l'intérieur d'une trame dont la vérité est dans la possibilité d'absorber des semblants" 'It will actualize the seeming, the imagination. For such an open, undecidable psychic space, the crisis will not be a suffering, but a sign within a framework whose truth lies in its ability to absorb seemings' (354). Through the assimilation of shared words, the melancholic crisis of silence that is destroying the relationship between Yves and Nadège can begin to be transformed into a "*work in progress,*" (354, the expression is in English in the French text) which has the potential to restore meaning, albeit ever tentative, to a language suffering from the disappearance of representation.

It should also be noted, however, that the nature of discourse itself is transformed from that of discussion to fiction, a change in register that greatly accentuates the role of the imagination and its displacing capacity. Yves and Nadège listen, not to a discussion but to stories, to a "succession de fictions" 'succession of fictions' (40). As they do so, they learn, in a sense, how to become artists themselves and begin to rebuild the broken or collapsed space of their relationship with new "constructions imaginaires" 'imaginary constructions' (40). As John Lechte points out in his analysis of Kristeva's attitude toward art, she views it "less as an object, and more as a practice that 'creates' the subject. In short: art is constitutive of both the subject and the object" (24). And he goes on to stress that, "Potentially, at least, aesthetic *activity* is within the reach of every one, even if producing an object readily and broadly admired is not" (25). The inventions the guests narrate and that Yves and Nadège eagerly assimilate serve the same double-sided function of all artistic creation, which, as Kristeva emphasizes, "*fait voir ou entendre la fureur mais, par ce* mime *précisément, nous purge d'elle en la déplacant dans un* style . . ." '*which makes us see or hear fury, but precisely on account of such* miming, *cleanses us of it by displacing it into a* style . . .' (301).

The narrations to which Yves and Nadège listen are divided in the familiar Tournierian way between "nouvelles" 'short stories,' described as "âprement réalistes, pessimistes, dissolvantes [qui] contribuaient à les séparer, à ruiner leur couple" 'bitterly realistic, pessimistic, dissolving [which] worked to separate, to ruin their couple relationship' (40), and "contes" 'tales,' singled out as "savoureux, chaleureux, affables [qui] travaillaient au contraire à les rapprocher" 'savory, warm, gracious, [which] worked, on the contrary, to bring them back together' (40-41).[4] But despite the text's statements about the value of the two different kinds of inventions, it should be stressed that the "nouvelles" are just as important, perhaps even more important, to Yves and Nadège than the "contes" precisely because they speak the pain of loss and betrayal that Tournier's protagonists cannot themselves express. Listening to these narratives makes it possible for them to begin to emerge from the sadness paralyzing them, to respond to the tongue-in-cheek playfulness of the "contes," and finally to participate in the banquet described in the concluding tale. It is perhaps simplistic and naïve to call literature the panacea that Nadège claims it to be (42). Nevertheless the imaginary constructions assimilated during the night-long narrative adventure can be used as models, "matériaux" for their own story-telling odyssey. What Yves describes as the stagnant, melancholic "vase de notre vie quotidienne" 'mud of our daily life' (42) gives way to the fast moving, ever-changing rhythm of "un torrent de montagne" 'a mountain torrent' (42) in a gesture that acknowledges separation from the sea as well as from the anecdotes and stories associated with his maritime past. The monotonous repetition of the same will become the complex, multi-dimensional renewal that Tournier has so consistently admired.

The narration that most dramatically illustrates the melancholic crisis weighing upon Yves and Nadège is the "nouvelle" entitled **"Lucie ou la femme sans ombre,"** after **"Les Amants taciturnes,"** the longest text in the anthology and the one that occupies the very center of the collection. As most of the other pieces referred to as "nouvelles," this one too is a first person account which describes a traumatic experience in the narrator's youth. It relates an idyllic attachment at age ten to his exotic school mistress Lucie, ultimate embodiment of the maternal (132-33), and the destruction of both this relationship and the fragile construction of Lucie's own being by the forces of paternal vengeance and social repression. The narrator, Ambroise, is the only child of a wealthy but totally unloving father, whose stinginess and puritanical coldness drive the boy's mother away and make him seek refuge with Lucie. Ambroise arrives at her home on the evening of his mother's flight, and he soon falls blissfully asleep in the warm disorder of Lucie's bed, next to a mysterious doll named Olga. The comforting sensualness of his visit is soon transformed into pain and viciousness, however, as Ambroise's father presses for a divorce settlement that will prevent the child's mother from having any contact with the boy and packs him off to boarding school. He also makes formal charges against Lucie for sexually corrupting a minor, which provokes disastrous changes on both the professional and personal levels.

It is only many years later, when a radically transformed Lucie has become headmistress of a girls' lycée, that the narrator meets her again and then learns in a letter from her estranged husband Nicolas what had transpired as a result of paternal vengefulness. Following Ambroise's father's brutal legal action, Lucie was dismissed from the academy where she was teaching and fell into deep depression, sitting mutely and clutching

her doll Olga desperately. With psychiatric intervention, she did at first seem to improve, but the hope Nicolas began to feel soon changed to despair as he witnessed her transformation into the "femme de verre, transparente . . . froide et incolore" 'woman made of glass, transparent, cold, colorless' (152), whom the adult Ambroise had encountered. Although Lucie did learn to speak again, it was only in a fragmented and minimalistic way (155). Ironically, the therapy sessions triggered not a renewal or rebirth, but Lucie's own death and the destruction of those around her who drew their life from her as well. It was also only through repeated prodding that Nicolas was able to piece together the totally private story of Lucie's past- the "histoire secrète" 'secret story' (155), of which he had known nothing. He learned that she had had a sister, also named Lucie, who had died at age nine of spinal meningitis and whom his wife had replaced. He also began to understand the reason for her obsessive attachment to Olga, who had belonged to the dead sister and whom Lucie cherished since the day she had discovered her by chance in an abandoned attic trunk and learned, at the same time, of the existence of the first Lucie. As Nicolas explains in his letter to Ambroise, "l'ayant descendue dans sa chambre[Lucie] n'a plus cessé de la choyer" 'having taken her down into her room, [Lucie] did not cease pampering her' (156). When, after her therapy sessions, Lucie discards Olga by silently burying her at the sister's grave, she also, in a sense commits suicide. She accepts entombment in the clipped phrases and rigidity of a school disciplinarian, dressed in the grey and white dress of "une nonne de luxe" 'an expensively clad nun' (150). The doll which she treasured from the time she discovered the existence of her dead sister, plays the same role as the self-image Narcissus saw when he gazed into the pool. The fragile construction of Lucie's identity collapses because she can transfer to no Other the complex emotions she felt for Olga, at once her sister and herself, and thereby try to reconstruct that broken psychic space.

The colorful aura that had surrounded Lucie and inspired Nicolas' own artistic imagination disappears completely, reduced to the monotony of her proper clothes and to the black and white drawings Nicolas begins to execute in the draftsman job he takes after the breakup of their relationship. At the end of his letter to Ambroise, Nicolas counsels him derisively, "Il faut savoir tourner la page" 'One must know how to turn the page' (158). Ambroise blatantly rejects the words Nicolas writes out of despair, from his own position of definitive exile. Unable to recover from having lost the original source of his inspiration, Nicolas can respond to no other stimuli in order to replenish the psychic resources needed to be an artist. Like Lucie's estranged husband, Ambroise too has lost forever the presence of the one who had so generously comforted him, but unlike Nicolas, he has assimilated the force, the "ombre" 'aura' that was Lucie's. It is, as he says, "enfermée pour toujours dans mon coeur" 'locked forever in my heart' (158), not entombed like Olga. And its precisely symbolic presence or seeming now serves as model for his own inventions and for the new relationship he is able to form with the woman he describes as "la compagne de ma vie" 'my life companion' (149, also 158).

In a similar way, Yves and Nadège are likewise able to move beyond the melancholy that destroyed Lucie and Nicolas and use the materials of Ambroise's narrative to construct "une maison de mots où habiter ensemble" 'a house of words in which to reside together' (42). Although exiled from the sea, Yves can now begin to symbolize his loss, which, in turn, will help heal his wounds. Emerging from the borderline position of Narcissus, he is able to respond to different stimuli, and Nadège is able to recognize her husband's dilemma in the tide that "balbutiait à la recherche d'un langage" 'babbled in search of a language' (41). Listening to Ambroise narrate the "nouvelle" of his trauma transforms the "triste nouvelle" 'sad news' (42) of the separation Yves and Nadège had planned to announce into a shared declaration which emphasizes the importance of constructing an imaginary space in that to play together, an activity which, until now, they could not envision.

At the end of the night-long narrative adventure, Yves and Nadège embrace the *"work in progress"* of aesthetic activity Kristeva analyzes and reaffirm their commitment to the ephemeral though essential rituals of everyday life. They are able to accept the invitation extended in the two celebratory tales that close the collection, which illustrate importance of exchange and celebrate continually renewed artistic activity. The final stories likewise concretize other versions of the subtle (inter)play between the ephemeral and the eternal that so fascinated the sculptor Lagos and that constitutes yet another expression of the interdependence between the nomad and the sedentary that runs through all of Tournier's works. It should be noted that neither **"La Légende de la peinture"** nor **"Les deux Banquets"** valorize mere repetition. As the writer-narrator of the first tale emphasizes when speaking to the friend who wishes to use one of his works as part of a multi-lingual instant translation computer program, "je lui contai une parabole du sage derviche Algazel . . . un peu arrangé à ma manière, comme il est loisible de faire dans la tradition orale" 'I told him a parable from the wise man Algazil . . . reorganized a little according to my own way, as it is allowable to do in the oral tradition' (260-61). In contrast to Yves, who, in the past, could only tell his stories "dans les mêmes termes" 'in the same terms' (34), the narrator of **"La Légende de la peinture"** has assimilated the words of another and altered their configurations to correspond to the dictates of his own imagination. His behavior exemplifies what Yves

and Nadège learned in the course of *Le Médianoche amoureux,* for they too discovered how to adapt models to their own situation. The same dynamic relationship is likewise expressed in the text of the tale itself as the Greek painter unveils the mirror that reflects the idyllic garden painted by his Chinese rival and wins the artistic competition. What so impresses the calif and his court is the presence of the people who have gathered in the royal assembly hall for the unveiling of the two creations. As splendid as it is, "le jardin du chinois était désert et vide d'habitants, alors que dans le jardin du Grec, on voyait une foule magnifique avec des robes brodées, des panaches de plumes, des bijoux d'or et des armes ciselées. Tous ces gens bougeaient, gesticulaient et se reconnaissaient" 'The garden of the Chinese painter was deserted and empty of inhabitants, whereas, in the Greek painter's garden, one saw a magnificent crowd with embroidered gowns, a variegated assortment of feathers, golden jewels and embossed arms. All these people were moving about, gesturing, greeting one another' (262-63). It is the ever-modulating brilliance of the crowd and the constantly changing position of the guests against the background of the garden that decide the victory.

The tale also points up in another way the difference between timeless, though forever fixed statues sculpted in marble, and the ephemeral, living sand statues Lagos created, which are subject to change and destruction; his "sculptures de sable vivent . . . et la preuve c'est qu'elles meurent" 'sand sculptures live . . . and the proof is that they die' (27). Yves and Nadège are now able to respond affirmatively to the fragile dynamism which they had previously perceived as melancholy and menacing. As the text clearly indicates, they can now appreciate the stories "qui s'effaçaient dès le dernier mot prononcé pour faire place à d'autres évocations tout aussi éphémères. Ils songeaient aux statues de sable de Lagos. Ils suivaient le lent travail que cette succession de fictions accomplissaient en eux" 'which were erased as soon as the last word was pronounced to make room for other evocations just as ephemeral. They followed the slow work that this succession of fictions was accomplishing in them' (40). As they listen attentively, the reciprocal pole of speaking, the precarious healing process begins.

The final tale of the two banquets reveals a similar, though more subtle, (inter)play. Although the second chef wins the contest by what the text indicates is "l'exacte répétition du premier (banquet)" 'the exact repetition of the first (banquet)' (267), his feast is not necessarily precisely the same as first one. The very fact that he is using either live or perishable ingredients, which are subtly though constantly changing in composition, clearly leaves room for the unpredictable variations that can occur even when following a recipe *exactly.* Furthermore, although it is true that the tale emphasizes the heightened prestige of the second banquet, described as sacred and raised to "une dimension supérieure" 'a superior dimension' (267), it also acknowledges the importance of innovation and of being able to accept new ideas and respond to new stimuli. In contrast to Nadège, who listened for years to the same stories, told in the same words, the calif and his guests will not eat the same dishes Sunday after Sunday because he hires both of the chefs who had participated in the culinary competition. He tells the first one, "tu m'accompagneras dans mes chasses et dans mes guerres. Tu ouvriras ma table aux produits nouveaux, aux plats exotiques, aux inventions les plus surprenantes de la gastronomie" 'You will accompany me on my hunting and military expeditions. You will introduce my table to new products, to exotic dishes, to the most surprising inventions of gastronomy' (268). And he charges the second one to transform exotic feasts into sacred ritual by assimilating the models provided by the one who will travel with the calif: "Tu seras le grand prêtre de mes cuisines et le conservateur des rites culinaires et manducatoires qui confèrent au repas sa dimension spirituelle" 'You will be the high priest of my kitchens and the one who preserves the culinary and dining rituals, which add a spiritual dimension to the meal' (268). *Both* are necessary to initiate the sharing of dishes and the imaginative verbal exchange that can take place around a festive table, which Nadège herself acknowledges as she addresses these same words to Yves. She assimilates the last sentence of the final tale as the basis for the amatory discourse she and Yves will share.

As exemplified by the tale of the two banquets and further highlighted in one of the meditations in *Le Vol du vampire,* Tournier notes that the table "médiatise le contact du ciel et de la terre. . . . La table est membrane, goulot, diaphragme. Elle sépare l'inconscient du conscient, l'animalité de l'humanité, la nature de la culture, et aménage en même temps un passage entre ces niveaux" 'mediates contact between the sky and the earth. . . . The table is membrane, mouth, diaphragm. It separates the unconscious from the conscious, animality from humanity, nature from culture, and, at the same time, constructs a passage between them' (383). This is exactly what occurs around the continually replenished buffet table during Yves and Nadège's nightlong feast. They listen to, or, more precisely, open themselves to receive the recipes their guests offer and begin to adapt them to fulfill their own desires. They will now attempt to rebuild the broken psychic space of their relationship. As Kristeva notes in the final pages of *Histoires d'amour,* "Parler, écrire? N'est-ce pas encore bâtir du 'propre,' fût-il polyvalent?" 'Speaking, writing? Is that not again building "one's own," even if it be polyvalent?' (354). Although fragile, this kind of construction has the potential both to shelter them from outside hostility and to mediate or diffuse their own aggressivity as well. The words that Yves and Nadège will try to exchange will be formulated as they gaze at one another across the intimate space of the dinner table, not looking in opposite directions like the self-contained androgynous models described at Plato's banquet, which so fascinated Tournier in the past and which he appropriated under other forms in a number of his own works.[5] As Kristeva indicates, the stories Yves and Nadège will attempt to share will perhaps be "désabusé[s] mais nom déprimé[s]" 'disenchanted but not depressed' (122). Like the fragile forms of Patricio Lagos' sand sculptures, the amatory discourse Kristeva describes can renew Tournier's couple "provisoirement et éternellement" 'provisionally and eternally' (355). And it is through the reciprocal process of speaking and listening, opening oneself to the words and needs of another, that the possibilities of love she analyzes can be realized.

The task facing Tournier's protagonists is by no means an easy one, nor is their success in any way assured. The stories that Yves and Nadège have assimilated and that will now serve as models for their own creations are of greatly uneven aesthetic quality, ranging from poignant to cruel, from enchanting to ironic, from suspenseful to, at times, boring. Furthermore those recounted in the first person seem to be narrated exclusively by males and reveal distinctly autobiographical overtones, which leaves open the question of females as speaking subjects. Nevertheless, the anthology clearly emphasizes the reciprocity of active listening/speaking and looks much more to the future rather than to the nostalgic past that has figured so importantly in Tournier's repertoire. It likewise depicts a willingness to accept rather than incorporate otherness, sexually or psychologically, and it reveals a much greater openness to the risk of tenuous, ever-evolving human relationships. In so doing, the stories of *Le Médianoche amoureux* suggest options heretofore neglected in discussion of Tournier's writings and will hopefully serve as imaginary models for ever more enriching expressions of ritualistic sharing in the future.

Notes

1. Although this particular statement appears in Tournier's discussion of his reaction to the Tristan and Iseut myth, he nevertheless sees their situation as a specifically marital relationship because of their faithfulness to one another, and stresses that the fidelity that highlights their relationship is a characteristically female attitude (36-37). For another work treating this subject, see Tournier's comments on Lewis Carroll's passion for photographing little girls in the *Petites Proses* text entitled "L'Image érotique" (151-54). See also Tournier's comments in the short article entitled "En finir avec la femme et l'avortement," in *Le Nouvel Observateur* (39).

2. For an analysis of the way in which this text inverts sexual roles, of the hostility toward the female it reveals, and of the specific role of the narrator in the elaboration of the drama depicted, see Marie-Laure Girou-Swiderski's article entitled "Hector et Véronique ou la dialectique des sexes," in *Incidences* (29-39).

3. For a more detailed discussion of primary narcissism and the phenomenon of the Imaginary Father, see Kristeva's *Histoires* (22-40). See also John Lechte's analysis entitled "Art, Love, and Melancholy in the Work of Julia Kristeva" in the Collection *Abjection, Melancholia and Love* (24-41). See also Cynthia Chase's essay entitled "Primary Narcissism and the Giving of Figure: Kristeva with Hertz and de Man," in the same anthology (125-36).

4. See Tournier's discussion of Perrault in "*Barbe-Bleu ou le secret du conte*," in *Le Vol du vampire* (38-43). See also his interview with Jean-Jacques Brochier in *Le Magazine littéraire* (11-13). See also an unpublished interview with Serge Koster, undertaken soon after the publication of *Le Médianoche amoureux*.

5. For an analysis of the particular significance of androgynous images in Tournier's works, see, for example Arlette Bouloumié's work entitled *Michel Tournier: le roman mythologique* and Françoise Merllié's study entitled *Michel Tournier*, both of which present very positive images of the phenomenon. For a less enthusiastic analysis that points out the underside of the androgynous totality, see Jean Libis's essay "L'androgyne et le Nocturne," in the collection entitled *L'Androgyne* (11-26). See also Kristeva's brief discussion in *Histoires* (70-72). See also Tournier's own statements questioning the whole phenomenon of the androgyne in his discussion with André Dumas entitled "L'Obsession de Dieu," in *Foi et Vie* (17-46). Finally, see two other "contes" in *Le Médianoche amoureux*: first, "La Légende de la musique et de la danse" (249-52) and "La Légende des parfums" (253-58).

Works Cited

Bouloumié, Arlette. *Michel Tournier: le roman mythologique*. Paris: José Corti, 1988.

Brochier, Jean-Jacques. "Dix-huit questions à Michel Tournier." *Le Magazine littéraire* June 1978: 11-13.

Faivre, Antoine et Fréderick Tristan, eds. *Cahiers de l'Hermétisme: L'Androgyne*. Paris: Albin Michel, 1986.

Fletcher, John and Andrew Benjamin, eds. *Abjection, Melancholia, and Love: The Work of Julia Kristeva*. London: Routledge, 1990.

Girou-Swiderski, Marie-Laure. "Hector et Véronique ou la dialectique des sexes." *Incidences* 1-2.2-3 (1979): 29-39.

Koster, Serge. "Interview de Michel Tournier." Unpublished Interview, 1989.

Kristeva, Julia. *Histoires d'amour*. Paris: Denoël, 1983.

———. *Soleil Noir: Dépression et mélancolie*. Paris: Gallimard, 1987.

Merllié, Françoise. *Michel Tournier*. Paris: Belfond, 1988.

Tournier, Michel. *Le Coq de bruyère*. Paris: Gallimard, 1978.

———. "En finir avec la femme et l'avortement." *Le Nouvel Observateur* 12-18 Sept. 1986: 39.

———. *Le Médianoche amoureux*. Paris: Gallimard, 1989.

———. *Les Météores*. Paris: Gallimard, 1975.

———. avec André Dumas. "L'Obsession de Dieu." *Foi et Vie* 86.14 (1987): 17-46.

———. *Petites Proses*. Paris: Gallimard, 1986.

———. *Le Roi des aulnes*. Paris: Gallimard, 1970.

———. *Le Vol du vampire*. Paris: Mercure de France, 1981.

David Platten (essay date December 1995)

SOURCE: Platten, David. "Narrative Secrets: Tournier's Exemplary Tale—'Pyrotechnie ou la commémoration.'" *French Review* 69, no. 2 (December 1995): 229-45.

[*In the following essay, Platten assesses the interaction of fiction and history in "Pyrotechnie ou la commémoration," and discusses the spatial and temporal aspects of the story's narrative structure.*]

Although death hardly beckons to a sprightly septuagenarian who has recently been seen combing the Paris métro in search of material for his next novel, it is, alas, only six years hence. Michel Tournier announced some time ago that the year 2000 will be remembered in France for the magnificent cortège that will follow his coffin to its final resting-place in the Panthéon (*Petites Proses* 244). He will be 76, a good age to go he thinks, before the physical faculties have degenerated to an undignified extent, and before the probable onset of senility. This minor piece of myth-making typifies a writer who has successfully eluded the categories others have invented for him. If the above title presumes that I am about to invent more categories, it is because the title of the Tournier short story which will inform this essay invites its reader so to do. With his choice of title Tournier asks us to consider the sociological function of commemoration. However the rubric crowns an unostentatious story about a Parisian writer struggling for inspiration in a dusty provincial town, rather than a philosophical meditation. Tournier's reader will learn of the individual's need and of a nation's requirement to commemorate, and yet by dint of its unremarkable self-consciousness, so easily misread as a sop to a post-modernist writing practice, **"Pyrotechnie ou la commémoration"** stakes its own claim to commemorate something—the art of narration patented by Michel Tournier. I shall argue that **"Pyrotechnie"** [**"Pyrotechnie ou la commémoration"**] is, uniquely, Tournier's exemplary tale. In order to do this, I am obliged to start from a wider base. Therefore my analysis of **"Pyrotechnie"** is pre-empted by two short introductory sections, the first dealing with the reception of Tournier's work and the second with the justification, notwithstanding its claim to commemorate, of my choice of Tournier text.

I. TOURNIER AESTHETICS

Avais-je réellement toutes les intentions qu'on relevait dans mes textes? Y avait-il d'une de mes histoires à l'autre autant de fils, autant de passerelles? Oui et non. Car ces intentions, ces fils, ces passerelles existent bien réellement, mais par la seule vertu du commentaire et non par la volonté délibérée de l'auteur.

(Postface 396)

With these words, published as part of a brief afterword to the proceedings of the special Tournier conference held at Cerisy-la-Salle in 1990, the author himself pays a generous tribute to his academic audience, whilst at the same time maintaining a judicious distance from their perspective on his work. Tournier's theoretical position with regard to his readership is no longer a hot issue; his *abrégé* of the Cerisy conference dovetails with the argument delivered in *Le Vol du vampire* (9-24) which celebrates the constructive role of his reader(s). Tournier alludes here to a different phenomenon. Over the past ten or twenty years he has provoked a spectacularly heterogeneous reader-response; psychologists, sociologists, historians, psychoanalysts, feminists, traditional literary critics as well as supporters of intertextuality and metaphor have all found plenty to say about him. The reason for this is quite obvious. The early texts especially are monumental in their complexity, multi-layered and pluri-referential. Thus reading Tournier becomes rather like charting a course through hostile waters. Even when the ocean at last seems clear, the narrative starts to cohere and meaning appears within grasp, a stray mine will blow the vessel out of the water. This is why it is prudent, if one is to go on and talk about an exemplary Tournier, to embark on some extensive minesweeping.

When the sad day dawns, obituarists will no doubt laud the man who, with *Vendredi ou les limbes du Pacifique, Les Météores,* and above all *Le Roi des aulnes,* snatched the novel away from the jaws of the *nouveaux romanciers,* thereby upholding in this modern age the noble tradition of Balzac, Zola, and Flaubert.[1] There is some truth in this assertion. Tournier frequently eulogizes these illustrious forbears, whereas on hearing of the award of the 1985 Nobel Prize for Literature to *nouveau romancier* Claude Simon he was said to have grumbled something along the lines of "Ils ont donné le prix à un illisible."[2] He is candidly scornful of the achievements of "une certaine école moderne" (*Le Vent Paraclet* 175), preferring instead to cultivate the image of an author living amongst his peers, in tune with literary tradition, and yet with that necessary detachment from society which Balzac in particular saw as essential to the author's vocation. The fact remains, however, that Tournier's writing practice bears little relation to the material which might have been produced by Balzac, had the author of *La Comédie humaine* lived during the latter part of the twentieth century. A sideways glance at Tournier's huge non-fictional output emphasizes the absurdity of such comparisons. Including books and articles on literature, philosophy, history, and especially photography, it testifies to a man whose notion of culture is indeterminate and whose instinct is pluralistic.

A more sensible view is held by the numerous commentators who locate in the concept of myth and the world of mythology a key to the understanding of Tournier's work. Certainly the old myths glow in the Tournier fundament, and when western modernity is at its most chaotic, in *Vendredi* [*Vendredi ou les limbes du Pacifique*], *Les Météores,* and *La Goutte d'or,* as if to sharpen the contrast they are at their brightest. Of course there are many purveyors of twentieth century wisdom who have already trodden this path back to antiquity. Progenitors of Freud have come to prominence in numerous, diverse spheres of intellectual endeavour.[3] Likewise Tournier's predilection for rewriting myth should be interpreted in a wider context, in terms of the general rather than the particular, in terms of a theory of myth and mythologies and Tournier's perception of myth in the modern age. He once remarked, stealing a line from Freud, that myth is the "enfance" of literature (*La Quinzaine Littéraire* 25). This is no bland appeal to the classical roots of western literature. The word *enfance* should be read literally; it signals the importance to Tournier of the world of folklore, of children, and children's narrative.

Tournier's practice of rewriting his two most commercially successful novels, *Vendredi* and *Gaspard, Melchior et Balthazar,* for a younger audience has been well documented.[4] However his repeated proclamations to the effect that he sees pre-pubescent children in their innocence as no less sophisticated readers of his narrative art than adults have, with the exception of a brief *table ronde* discussion at Cerisy, fallen on deaf ears. Tournier refutes absolutely the notion that **Vendredi ou la vie sauvage** was written expressly for a young audience, despite the fact that it was first published in the Folio Junior series. Robinson Crusoe, the Ogre archetype, Joan of Arc, the Three Wise Men, Tom Thumb, Harlequin, and Pierrot are all in the first instance children's characters. Moreover Tournier has scaled down his writing project over the last twenty years. The novels have gotten shorter, and, as he has sought to fine-tune his favorite literary genre, the hybrid form of the *conte* (somewhere between the *fable* and the *nouvelle*), the short stories have proliferated. Child characters and the experience of others as children are common features of the two volumes of short stories, **Le Coq de bruyère** and **Le Médianoche amoureux.** Most interestingly, Tournier has taken to touring the *écoles primaires* of the Ile-de-France in order to give "live" renditions of his latest creations. It is as if by performing the stories, through their active narration, he is testing the product. What is he looking for? If success implies some sort of recognition, then what is the nature of this recognition and what are the qualities recognized by this audience that adults fail to see, or perhaps cannot see? And finally, how does this recognition change the way in which we read Tournier? What new secrets are confided to us?

II. JUSTIFICATIONS

"Pyrotechnie ou la commémoration" is one of seventeen *fables, contes,* and *nouvelles,* swapped among the guests invited to a lovers' feast. This lavish dinner is an important event. It provides for a rich fund of anecdotes and thus stands as a symbol for both the production and unity of the text; Tournier calls his collection **Le Médianoche amoureux.** Moreover the social occasion serves to regenerate the relationship of the hosts, two lovers who had lapsed into a solipsistic existence. Each narrative enjoys independent status. However it is significant that they are enveloped in a common context, reminding the lonely reader that written texts are dynamic; originating in a world populated by real men and women they are apt to engender repercussions in a world outside the text. **"Pyrotechnie"** is, as we shall see, a text which delivers a subtle message about commemoration, but it is also a text which, for a host of other reasons, would serve as a fitting commemoration of Tournier's literary achievements.

In the first sentence of *S/Z,* his celebrated exegesis of Balzac's short story "Sarrasine," Roland Barthes alludes to the meditative practice of certain Buddhist ascetes who are said to be able to see whole landscapes in a bean. There are several unconnected reasons why **"Pyrotechnie"** can lay claim to being a Tournier bean.

It is a modest short story, once airily dismissed by its author, in an unpublished interview with myself, as "un de mes polars," and yet this untroubled surface is shaded with barely perceptible references to influences acknowledged elsewhere, tributes to figures and archetypes past and present, which are all the more exquisite for their being disguised. This from an artist whose prose, in the longer, more ambitious texts, frequently gets bogged down in preposterous authorial interventions and explications.

Secondly, and this is a corollary of its textual economy, **"Pyrotechnie"** affords a genuine pleasure to Tournier readers who may, on occasions, have disagreed violently with some of his more controversial statements.[5] The analysis of pleasure in or through reading is particularly relevant to the study of Tournier, given that this self-proclaimed intellectual commands a large audience which transcends the academic community. Hence the pleasure of reading Tournier informs the simple inspiration of this article, which is to convey the spirit, if not the essence, of his writing. The simplicity stems from a belief that, in spite of the many theoretical paradigms which have been foisted upon readers, particularly in the last thirty years, all literary critics and students of philosophy strive—unconsciously perhaps but nonetheless every time they confront the word-processor—to recover some small part of their chosen author's intent. This view is less reductive than it might have appeared a few years ago. The furor in the United States surrounding the posthumous discovery of Paul de Man's "war writings" has raised once again the fifties issue of authorial intent, or rather of intention, as a legitimate object of theoretical inquiry. These days Tournier willingly consents to the creative role of the reader, but this is a theoretical concession. He prefers to reify the process of narration, to bring story-tellers and (interestingly) readers within the confines of the text. Different narrative voices predominate in the early fiction; however in **Gilles et Jeanne,** the character of Blanchet, the confessor, is cast less conventionally in the role of lost interpreter, dazzled both by the splendor of Renaissance Tuscany and by the vertiginous rhetoric of the de facto lawyer, Prélati. In *Gaspard, Melchior et Balthazar* the three magi chart the course of the comet, and are each inspired by their own creative reading, until the ass in the manger reveals himself to be the true poet. In *La Goutte d'or* the stories of **"Barberousse"** [**"Barberousse ou le portrait du roi"**] and **"La Reine blonde"** are intercalated into the body of the main text, so as to read like parables.

Tournier's desire to incorporate the figures of narrator and narratee (implied reader) into his texts indicates a concern to resurrect another tradition through his fiction, namely the classical style of story-telling, exemplified in the West by Homer and in the East by the *1001 Nights.* As we have seen, *Le Médianoche amoureux* tells of its own narrative genesis. The story-telling dinner guests in **"Les Amants taciturnes"** personify the idea of narrative, or rather narration as a form of social exchange. Here of course the emphasis is on listening. The art of reading is eclipsed, and meaning becomes almost entirely contingent on the ability of the audience to follow a coherent narrative sequence; what we think of as poetics is redundant. Walter Ong has shown how this phenomenon is both a return to the "primary orality" of the homeric age and a sign of the "secondary orality" of the modern, speed-oriented, technological era in which we now find ourselves. In truth there has been a boom in the literature industry of late. Many people now experience the classics of English and European literature via taped recordings, as they sit in motorway tail-backs or read the paper in bed. However, this apparent erosion of the written sign is a product of competing media and should not be exaggerated. The aural context of *Le Médianoche amoureux* points to something more specific. The effacement of the writing trace effectively narrows the gap between the adult and the child's respective worlds. It makes the adult's experience of the text more like the child's. To the extent that **"Pyrotechnie,"** like the other constituent parts of *Le Médianoche* [*Le Médianoche amoureux*], is designed in this way may mean that a specific textual policy has been implemented, according to which the value of narrative, of prosaic rather than poetic qualities, is paramount. My argument is that if we want to learn anything of Tournier's *engagement,* of the way in which his art relates to historical and ethical issues, then we must accept in some measure this tyranny. As Michael Worton has demonstrated, Tournier does inhibit the freedom of his readers. However, at the root of this tension there is a familiar opposition, that of the paradigm versus the syntagm, word versus sentence, poet versus novelist. *Le Médianoche* prescribes an aural context for its reception; however it is generally received in written form and therefore its readers will expect to find in it at least some of the polysemy of the written text.

The final and perhaps most important reason for my choice of **"Pyrotechnie"** as Tournier's exemplary text is that it demonstrates the allure of his particular narrating skills, and of narrative expression in general. Narrative is not a concept so obviously as central to Tournier's project as it is to that of a writer like Italo Calvino; in Tournier's case the relationship between author and narrative is deep-rooted, is more problematic even, for it reveals a concern for genre. This anxiety can be traced back to the start of his career. The tarot card preface to *Vendredi* and the "Pigeons du Rhin" *mise en abyme* of *Le Roi des aulnes* are prefigurations, proleptic accounts of what is to occur later on in the respective texts, in each case idealized contractions of the narrative proper. Tournier, so anxious to ensure that his reader is not misled, covets the essential brevity of the poet, of whose

expressive skills he declares himself bereft. But Tournier *is* a consummate narrator, and, as his career has evolved and his confidence grown, more and more of the short narratives have been left free-standing. An inveterate preacher, he enjoys reworking old fables to new effect, but the intuitive, mythical side to his personality leads him to value more highly the *instruction cachée* of the *conte,* and preferably "les contes que nos aïeux ont inventés pour leurs enfants" (*Le Vol du vampire* 35), beloved of Charles Perrault, a genuine Tournier avatar.[6]

"Pyrotechnie" is ostensibly a *nouvelle,* characterized according to Tournier's own typology of the short story by *vraisemblance.* The Ruggieri firework factory at Monteux exists, and the *épuration* is at the core of what Foucault has called "la mémoire populaire" (6) of the current generation in France, just as it forms the subtext to Tournier's short story. The narrative is seemingly authenticated because the narrator is himself embroiled in the process of learning. But this story tells of a mystery which is never quite solved. The narrator may well return to Paris with the material for his next novel stashed in his suitcase, but the harmony is more apparent than real, because the boundaries between truth and fiction remain blurred. Herein lies the secret of this narrative, and maybe of all narratives. **"Pyrotechnie"** does not create suspense; the plot is prefigured. Nor does it function according to the principle of cause and effect. Rather the reader is driven, as always, by curiosity. The pursuit of knowledge divested of its adult clothes becomes the desire to know what happens next. The grown-up world has shrunk, and the agent of this shrinking process is a pure narrative logic which informs the world of the child. The door is left open, however, to the adult who entertains the possibility of magic.

III. The Text

One of Tournier's guiding motifs is the principle of inversion. He is always on the look-out for the other side of the coin, in acknowledged symbols, or in eventful coincidences. In *Le Roi des aulnes* we learn that the Nazi swastika was a deformation, a bastardization of the Maltese Cross, traditional symbol of peace and tranquillity. In *Petites Proses* he idly ruminates on the significance of the day in the Christian calendar chosen to celebrate the Transfiguration, when Christ, in the company of his disciples at the summit of Mount Tabor, showed himself in a blaze of light to be the Son of God (216). August 6 is, for Tournier, a date admirably well chosen as it marks the height of summer, when holiday-makers throw off the cares of their working lives with their clothes and relax on the beach. Later (in conversation with me) he recounted how, a few years after writing this piece, he was lying on a beach when the awful *contresens* of the fête of the Transfiguration suddenly struck home. He remembered that it was early in the morning of August 6, 1945, that the Enola Gay took off from a United States naval base and began its flight to Hiroshima. At that moment on the beach the image of the atomic bomb became, in Tournier's mind at least, the diabolical inversion of Christ's Transfiguration. In **"Pyrotechnie"** we find abundant *contresens,* not least in the form of a self-conscious narrative which gradually becomes less rather than more conscious of itself.

Jorge Luis Borges, arguably the most famous, latter-day exponent of the short story, has refined a genre which now, more often than not, tells its own coming-into-being. In **"Pyrotechnie"** the self-conscious character of the short story is privileged, but in terms which are softly caricatured. The narrator is a Parisian writer, who has been exiled on the command of an impatient publisher to the small town of Monteux, near Carpentras, in order to get on with his next book away from the bright lights of the big city. He already has a provisional title for it ("Elle se mange froide"), a situation (the closed provincial community), and the genesis of a plot (a classic tale of revenge in which suspense will be created by the characters' expectancy of the retributive act). At the end of **"Pyrotechnie"** he duly starts writing, "cette histoire de vengeance étirée sur toute une vie dans le cadre d'une petite ville de province où tout se sait" (106). This self-reflexivity clearly circumscribes the text but its function is *not* to annihilate (gradually) the possibility of thematic interpretations, as it would be in a Borgesian narrative. Tournier is interested in the material fact of writing, in the reality of the writer's life. It is no accident therefore that in **"Pyrotechnie"** his narrator is bothered about relations with his publisher. Will he be able sufficiently to dress up the "mince canevas" of his story so as not to jeopardize his advance? The narrative flows *à rebours,* from the self-conscious act of writing back into the world of the writer. In so doing it serves three functions. First, it acts as a foil to other inconspicuously presented Tournier ideas; second, it facilitates the delivery of a sub-textual message; and third, it succeeds where all successful narratives succeed, in inspiring the imagination of its audience.

Familiar Tournier themes are prevalent in the early sections of the text. The proposed subject matter for the narrator's book is, of course, a wink in the direction of Maupassant. Care should be taken, however, not to misinterpret the comic touch of the prospective title. Tournier's narrator emphasizes a need to recreate the "eyes everywhere" community that typifies the gritty realism of Maupassant's short stories by reiterating the fact that the vendetta should be public knowledge: "de notoriété publique. Tout le monde le savait. Tout le monde attendait" (83-84). At this early stage his romanesque musings are already assuming an urgency that transcends the supposed fictional medium. This expository setting of the scene is significant. Tournier knows that the ef-

fects of any given crime are maximized when the crime occurs within a sedentary society; the people of Monteux are described as "des sédentaires absolus" (83). Now the distinction between sedentary and nomadic peoples is a key dialectic in Tournier's thinking. The biblical story of Cain and Abel is the prototype for a dozen other narratives, including the portrayal of the outcast, Abel Tiffauges, in *Le Roi des aulnes,* the gradual dissolution of the "cellule gémellaire" in *Les Météores,* and Idriss's quest in *La Goutte d'or.* Reifying this fundamental myth in **"Pyrotechnie,"** Tournier takes a leaf out of Balzac's *modus operandi.* Consider the way in which the explosion at the factory is described.

Tournier handles the description of this one big event with a typical flourish. The narrator is busy thinking socio-cultural thoughts at the local boulodrome as the final player of the group prepares to launch his one remaining projectile, intended to disperse the cluster around the cochonnet in all directions. At the precise moment of impact there is a thunderous noise, and the scattering of the boules is reproduced in macrocosm by the sight of "un feu chaotique," illuminating the sky. Seconds later people are running towards the factory. Accustomed to the sequential configurations of pyrotechnics, the townsfolk react instinctively to the psychedelic orderlessness above their heads. This account, which I have paraphrased, is clearly written after the event. As an outsider ignorant of the possible consequences of the explosion, the narrator cannot react in the same way as the townsfolk. While everyone else dashes about, he can only watch, and would only have made sense of what he had seen at a later time. Balzac, who saw his art as the ability to achieve the coincidence of "l'observation" and "l'expression," is a singular inspiration. Tournier's narrator is there, with the people at the boulodrome, yet able to stand back at the vital moment.

If there is some doubt as to whether Tournier is angling for a Balzacian acuity of observation in his depiction of the reactions of the Monteux townspeople, then we ought perhaps to revert to that traditional stamping ground of realist writing, namely characterization, or in this case the characterization of the factory manager:

> M. Capolini m'accueillit avec l'empressement d'un professionnel flatté qu'un ignorant de marque vienne de Paris s'instruire auprès de lui. Au demeurant il parlait si bien et si brillamment des feux d'artifice qu'il paraissait par moments devenir lui-même un feu d'artifice. J'ai rencontré plus d'une fois cette sorte de contamination totale d'un homme par sa profession, charcutière sculptée dans du saindoux, paysan pétri de terre et de fumier, banquier semblable à un coffre-fort, cavalier au rire hennissant. Les mains de Capolini devenaient à tout moment fusées, bouquets, fontaines de feu ou soleils tournoyants. Ses yeux paraissaient sans cesse éblouis par quelque déploiement féerique.
>
> (86)

This kind of picture-portrait is reminiscent of the way in which Balzac tended to stigmatize his characters. The personification of spinsterhood through the character of Sophie Gamard in *Le Curé de Tours* shows how such blanket representations may be construed as prejudicial. Meticulously observed details of her physical appearance are conjugated so as to support Balzac's one overriding contention, that "en restant fille, une créature du sexe féminin n'est plus qu'un non-sens: égoïste et froide, elle fait horreur" (69). In describing the effect of this condition on Sophie Gamard he pulls no punches, hinting that the dark rings under her eyes betray long hours of masturbatory activity, "accusait les longs combats de sa vie solitaire" (71). Balzac's discourse establishes a causal link between spinsterhood and sexual frustration; Sophie's petty attitudes and spiteful behavior are explained by the lack of a good man in her life! Although the description of M. Capolini shows Tournier indulging his Balzacian tendencies, here it is more a case of playful stereotyping; one is reminded of the oft-heard remark about dog-owners coming with time to look more and more like their four-legged friends. However it has a very different, underlying purpose. The effect is impressionistic. Each dash of paint—the lardy butcher, the earthy peasant, the impassable banker, the laughing cavalier, not forgetting the effusive M. Capolini—imparts the sort of crisp definition which is necessary to bring characters to life in children's fiction. Moreover Tournier puts his reader in contact with the symbolic functioning of the human mind, highlighting in this instance the figure of metonymy. The rich symbolism of the firework, through its metonymic definition of M. Capolini, comes to displace the character. M. Capolini's verbal dexterity is such that the symbol quickly eclipses the human actor.

Initially the firework signifies the intrusion of the fantastic, the irruption of the *conte* within the *nouvelle*. On the night of his arrival in Monteux the narrator witnesses from the window of his lodgings a marvellous firework display. Spectacular but odd, for he cannot understand why anyone should want to commemorate July 25, St. Anne's Day. He soon discovers that it was merely a routine product-testing operation. However, his curiosity is aroused by this "manufacture pittoresque," and even more so by the fact that a firework-display, usually symbolic of important historical or political events, should form part of the daily routine, that it should not interrupt for a second the rhythm of the towns-people's lives. This lovely equation of the "plus beau feu d'artifice" with ordinary life teases out a modest philosophical reflection on the nature of the phenomenon. Tournier shows through the reaction of his narrator how human perception and understanding of reality is conditional on factors of culture and environment, and therefore on the mythologies of specific cultures.[7] The effect in **"Pyrotechnie"** is to undermine the stable, symbolic value of the firework, its commemorative function. The narrator's experience of the staged firework display that commemorates nothing will turn out to be a prophesy. The next display witnessed turns out to be a tragic accident which *is* commemorative.

"Pyrotechnie" is the story of the narrator's investigation of the accident at the factory in which two men are killed. He is able to confirm that the incident was a case of simultaneous murder and suicide. The victim, Gilles, had a heroic reputation that dated back to the Resistance; the perpetrator of the deed, a young boy at the time of the war, held Gilles responsible for the public humiliation of his mother during the *épuration*. The explosion at the factory is eventually explained as the culmination of a vendetta which had been pursued commemoratively, the final in a series of unfortunate accidents which had befallen Gilles, usually on August 11 of any given calendar year. The key figure in the narrator's research is a retired journalist, "un maniaque de documentation," for whom modern day life is meaningless due to the absence of important historical events. His recollections of Gilles's former role as leader of the local Resistance group and account of the days following the liberation of the town in 1945 change entirely the perspective within which we read the narrative. As we come to understand how the apparently inexplicable occurred, why the explosion at the factory was an act of simultaneous murder and suicide, we also learn of unpleasant details concerning the liberation of the town in 1945—a story of scapegoats, of cruelty towards innocent people, of the rule of the mob. Suddenly there is a message in the text, introduced as it were through the back door, which says that the official view of the Resistance and the Liberation, the acceptable side to French history, is both glamourized and superficial.

This, then, is the twist in the tale of the firework factory, for the story is really about the art of the novelist. It presents him as if by accident "sur le terrain" and we read of the sparking of his imagination and subsequently of his painstaking research. Yet as the narrative unfolds, the novelist becomes historian, and the historian, in the shape of the retired journalist, becomes novelist. For the latter, history is a mere succession of names; the rest is fiction, as when he talks about the Great War, "J'ai tant entendu parler de Verdun et du chemin des Dames, que je finis par croire que j'y étais" (99). This curious *va-et-vient* gives a fascinating insight to the change in preoccupations of European novelists in the aftermath of the Holocaust, and more particularly in France, in the aftermath of the Occupation. French literature since 1945 is speckled with important works relating to the Occupation. The *témoignages* of Vailland, de Beauvoir, and Vercors preceded the semi-contemporaneous, allegorical account in Camus's *La Peste* (1947), which was itself a forerunner to the fully fictional representations contained in Modiano's *La Place de l'étoile* (1968), Tournier's *Le Roi des aulnes*, and especially in the *œuvre* of Jorge Semprun. In French cinema there has been a real sea-change. The end of the Gaullist interregnum saw a proliferation of important films, notably Louis Malle's *Lacombe, Lucien* (1973) and Marcel Ophuls's *Le Chagrin et la pitié* (first screened in 1971), which subject French society during the Occupation to uncomfortable scrutiny. These investigations into the national mythology of the French were "fathered" by Alain Resnais's path-breaking 1959 film *Hiroshima mon amour*, in which the need to make better sense of historical experience is asserted. Above all, these texts, especially *Hiroshima*, ask awkward questions. Is it possible to make sense of history if it is unlived, and do those who have lived it use memory to recover or distort sense? Tournier reveals in *Le Roi des aulnes*, and here in **"Pyrotechnie,"** that he is aware of the difficulties encountered by modern novelists who will inevitably find themselves at some stage "facing history."[8] He may be criticized for not helping, for not proposing solutions, but as a novel as complex as *Le Roi des aulnes* shows, he should not be rebuked for not endeavoring to understand. Like Vercors, Tournier realizes that understanding is possible only on a limited human scale, in the self-imposed dumbness of the girl refusing to connive with, to console even, the German officer in *Le Silence de la mer*, and in the image of the wretched, semi-illiterate Ange Crevet, the avenging angel in **"Pyrotechnie,"** standing each year in silent commemoration at the graveside of "la crevette," his humiliated mother.

If we agree with Tournier that the good novelist is as much historian as writer of fictions, and that the creativity of the latter is predicated upon the research of the former, then we should also accept the truth contained in his depiction of the retired journalist, who has imagined himself so successfully as "ancien combattant" that he has come to believe that this is what he now is, that the construction of the historian's narrative is a considerable feat of the imagination. Many historiographers including Paul Veyne, Hayden White, and Paul Ricoeur concede that any attempted return to a past state is a huge reconstructive task based on the flimsiest of empirical evidence, and that the primary agent for these reconstructions is the imagination of the author. Ricoeur has written extensively on the areas of congruence in modern analyses of historical and literary narrative. In one collaborative collection of essays he stakes out the field for investigation, declaring that, "l'enjeu commun à la théorie de l'histoire et à la théorie du récit fictif est la connexion entre figure et séquence, configuration et succession" (28). Ricoeur conceives the figure or symbol as, in one sense, the beginning or the *déclencheur*, as that which gives rise to narrative. Figures inspire tropes which can act in turn like keys; they may open the doors to a greater understanding. In **"Pyrotechnie"** there is one master figure; the secret of narrative lies in the firework.

The animated conversation of M. Capolini suggests that he is not only the manager of a firework factory, but also an enthusiastic aficionado of contemporary literary theory: "toute la pyrotechnie," he explains, "se ramène à une lutte contre le hic et nunc" (87). At the moment of detonation, of maximum presence therefore, the firework deploys both a spatial and a temporal configuration, a double property that it shares with narrative. The firework manufacturer, like the writer of narrative, must be master in each domain in order to achieve the desired effect: "cette explosion," pontificates M. Capolini in the style of the modern *rhétoriqueur*, "nous nous en rendons maîtres pour la déplacer dans l'espace et la différer dans le temps" (86).

Irresistibly, it would appear, we are drawn back to this essential function of the firework, "à différer dans le temps et à déployer dans l'espace." But historiography and literary theory only provide half-answers. When, in **"Pyrotechnie,"** the factory manager is explaining the technical side to his business, he lets the narrator into a real secret. For the detonation of the firework to occur, there needs to be a conical space hollowed out of its center, "un vide ménagé en son centre et ayant la forme d'un tronc de cône" (89). Without it there would be no firework, but nobody knows why. M. Capolini describes this phenomenon of the pyrotechnic function resistant to human conceptualization in suitably lyrical fashion. "Sachez-le bien," he exudes, "comme les femmes et comme les violons, la fusée possède une âme" (88). This figure, already three or four times significant (cf. Chagall's *The Cellist*, "le violon d'Ingres"), is philosophically exciting, because it seems to defy empirical verification. Interviewing Tournier in April 1990, the "firework question" was on the tip of my tongue, intrigued as I was to find out whether this was one of those mysteries of science that comes along occasionally to befuddle the methodology of empiricist lore. Was it true? Tournier smiled as he shook his head. His job was done. The important thing was that I had begun to half-believe the fiction. It could have been true. I, like the child who craves the instant gratification of a desire, needed to know the truth. The greater my need, the better the story, the shorter the time taken to know.

My reactions to **"Pyrotechnie"** neatly demonstrate the theory developed by Frege in his famous essay, "On Sense and Reference," in which he maintains that the action of the human mind is governed by an imperceptible and irresistible movement that takes us from the sense of the object to its reference. The sense of **"Pyrotechnie"** is in the resolution of the crime, which is wrapped up in the organic evolution of the narrative and manifested through a series of temporal coincidences. What is important here is the clarity, or perceptibility, of this structure, and not whether the events described are believable or not. Paradoxically, it is the inherent aspect to the firework which takes us outside of the text. The manager's words, seeking as they do to impose human qualities on a machine, simulate the convergence of the most fundamental antithesis—that of living and inert matter—and lead us once again to the crossroads of culture and nature, that we technologically motivated creatures insist on reliving. (Witness our fascination with robots, daleks, and the like.) This is the moment of metaphor, when the *as if* of the fictional narrative is dropped in favor of the *is* of the radical copula, when fiction impinges on and starts to redefine our conception of reality. It is only when we have finished reading that the writer's imagination makes its impact; it is only then that we begin to wonder about those fireworks. As the American poet Wallace Stevens once cryptically remarked, "the imagination is always at the end of an era."

This schema is diametrically opposed to the model proposed by Gérard Genette in his discourse on language and space. Genette considers that modern man is oriented primarily by spatial rather than temporal relations: "L'homme préfère l'espace au temps." Literary discourse in particular, he writes, "ne se dit plus qu'en termes de distance, d'horizon, d'univers, de paysage, de lieu, de site, de chemin et de demeure: figures naïves, mais caractéristiques, figures par excellence, où le langage s'espace afin que l'espace, en lui, devenu langage, se parle et s'écrive" (*Figures 1* 108). More than literature even, the cinema would seem to exemplify Genette's description of a "spatialized" culture. In Wim Wenders' 1984 film, *Paris, Texas,* Harry Dean Stanton stares out into the vast expanse of the Arizona desert and starts walking, apparently into infinity. But this journey into space (the sheer scale of the panorama on the big screen is breathtaking) has a destination; it ends in the big city. In one of the finest scenes of contemporary cinema, the Stanton character confronts his estranged wife, played by Natassia Kinski, through a one-way perspex glass pane, as she begins to perform her ritual sex act for the paying customer. He stops her, they talk, and gradually she recognizes who he is. At the end of his journey through space, the human identity of the characters involved is reaffirmed and the past relived, albeit through a perspex glass pane. A temporal framework is back in place.

Tournier's **"Pyrotechnie"** leads the reader gently, inexorably away from literary questions about narrative to a world of elementary philosophy and story-telling. In his excellent book, *The Sense of an Ending,* Frank Kermode poses the question as to what basic human set founds the various paradigms of our existence. He ventures, wrongly as it happens, that, "at some very low level we all share certain fictions about time" (43). Reverting swiftly back to familiar territory (western culture), Kermode argues that our verbalization of time as the tick-tock of the clock is the essential paradigm upon which we base our perception of reality. As he

puts it, "*tick* is our word for a beginning, *tock* our word for an end. We say they differ. What enables them to be different is a special kind of middle" (45). What Kermode is saying here is that we can perceive duration only when it is organized. The fact that we call the second of the two related sounds arbitrarily conferred on what would otherwise be pure chronicity *tock* is evidence that we use fictions to enable the end to confer organization and form on temporal structure. The clock's *tick-tock* then becomes the model of what we call a plot, an organization that humanizes time by giving it form; and the interval between *tick* and *tock* represents purely successive, disorganized time of the sort we need to humanize. The function of the story-teller is to fill this emptiness, to endow it with significant season. Within this organization, what was conceived as simply successive becomes charged with past and future: what was *chronos* becomes *kairos.* This is the time of the novelist, a transformation of mere successiveness which E. M. Forster once likened to the experience of love, the erotic consciousness that makes "divine sense out of a commonplace person." Kermode gives numerous examples in different contexts of the enormously complex fictions that we invent in order to give significance to our lives. They may be institutionalized, like those pertaining in the world of equity and law, or personal; we all live out our lives under the aegis of a series of false endings and beginnings. This is why stories are so satisfying; because reading them allows us to behave as young children do when they think of all the past as yesterday. As Michael Ignatieff once put it, short stories "assuage, within a miniature world of their own, our own anguish and uncertainty about what will happen next in our lives" (17).

The soul at the center of Tournier's rocket is an indication of the humanization of time that occurs within the paradigm of his fiction, and it therefore signifies our need to go beyond the text and project its structure of beginnings and endings on the formlessness of our own existence. It did not take me long to reassert the "truth" of Tournier's fiction. Stephen Hawking reminds us that when we throw a stone into a pond, the ripples spread out as a circle, that gets bigger as time goes on. Hawking proposes that we think of a three-dimensional model consisting of the two-dimensional surface of the pond (space measured on the horizontal axis), and the one dimension of time (measured on the vertical axis). The expanding circle of ripples will, he says, mark out a cone whose tip is at the place and time at which the stone hit the water. This is the simple model for what Hawking terms the "future (and past) light cone of an event" (25), which he uses to demonstrate how we ought to conceive of space and time in terms of the distance travelled by light-waves propagated from a certain indefinable point—not unlike the mysterious soul of the firework, whose secret resides in the hollow cone at its centre. The metaphor lives; and like the child for whom the story at bedtime is a prerequisite for sleep, its resurrection puts the critic's mind temporarily at rest.

The mind, however, should not remain inactive for long. The enduring image of **"Pyrotechnie"** is of two silent men sitting either side of a table at the heart of the factory, composing Rockets and Catherine Wheels from brightly colored powders contained in a series of vials. It suggests the medieval magic of alchemy, rather than the modern day certainties of science. If the firework with its weird chemistry harbors the secret of narrative, then perhaps the symbol of the firework, like the Figure in Henry James's carpet, takes us beyond narrative and into a timeless, mythical zone. Perhaps this journey into the realms of our own imagination is what Tournier really means when he talks of myth as "une histoire que tout le monde connaît déjà" (*Le Vent Paraclet* 184). This journey is essentially regressive, a journey back into our own memories, into childhood. In *Le Vent Paraclet* (48) Tournier identifies Hans Christian Andersen's "The Snow Queen" as the story he would most like to have written. It is, of course, a classic fairy-tale. A fragment of the Devil's Mirror pierces little Kay's heart, his moral view of the world is inverted, and he is kidnapped by the Snow Queen. Plucky Gerda sets off in pursuit and, after a series of interesting encounters, succeeds in rescuing Kay from the Ice Kingdom north of Lapland. On their return to Gerda's grandmother's house everything seems much the same: "the clock still said 'Tick tock!' and the hands still marked the hours" (142).[9] The difference is in themselves, for they are now grown-up people. The end of childhood coincides with the end of the story. The splinter of glass has long since been displaced from Kay's heart, but their adventures are somehow eternized in memory, representing another life which we all believe we once lived.

Notes

1. Philippe Sollers, novelist, founder of *Tel Quel* and now editor-in-chief of the Parisian review *L'Infini*, criticized Tournier on account of his "bankrupt traditionalism" in an interview published in *Le Nouvel Observateur* (January 19, 1981). For a discussion of Sollers's remarks, see Strickland. The issue is not lost on David Gascoigne who writes: "Tournier's fiction (. . .) has appealed less to the literary avant-garde, who have tended to dismiss his technique as nineteenth century, than to those delighted to rediscover a fiction which, like the major 'existentialist' novels of Gide, Sartre, Malraux, and Camus, was prepared to engage directly with ideology and philosophical ideas" (65).

2. Roger Shattuck suggests in an article in which he attempts to introduce Tournier's work to an English-speaking audience that this Prix Goncourt winner's career was mysteriously delayed during the late sixties and seventies, the hey-day of Parisian post-structuralism.

3. Lacan (Psychoanalysis), Heidegger, Sartre, Camus and many others (Philosophy), Barthes (Semiology), Northrop Frye (Literary Criticism), Lévi-Strauss (Anthropology), McLuhan (Media Studies), Darlington (Biology), Max Black (Philosophy of Language), and Naomi Wolf (Media Feminism) all immediately come to mind.

4. Genette (1978) and Worton (1986) share similar concerns, with Genette (419-25) arguing forcefully that Tournier, having altered his rendition of a crucial incident in the transition from *Vendredi ou les limbes du Pacifique* to *Vendredi ou la vie sauvage,* was prepared to compromise his aesthetic ideals in order to make more money.

5. Tournier has not only crossed swords with the literary avant-garde. Améry catches the mood of several reviews of *Le Roi des aulnes* that accuse Tournier of having "aestheticized" Nazism. The author has always defended his novel on the grounds that, by showing how Nazism seduced people, especially the young, he makes a contribution towards the understanding of the phenomenon, and that it is only by understanding it that the means to arrest any future re-emergence can be ascertained. Tournier scholars such as Woodhull and Platten have since tended to accept this defence on face value, and concentrated instead on the internal and external dynamics of Nazism as depicted in *Le Roi des aulnes*. Many commentators have also sensed a latent misogyny in Tournier's deployment (with one or two notable exceptions) of female characters in secondary, often submissive roles, and more particularly in his fastidious annulment of the notion of a female sexuality, notoriously (and amusingly) expressed by Alexandre in *Les Météores* (237):

"homosexualité masculine:

$1 + 1 = 2$ (amour)

hétérosexualité:

$1 + 0 = 10$ (fécondité)

homosexualité féminine:

$0 + 0 = 0$ (néant)".

Tournier's attitude to women is surmized well by Davis (83-93). These two controversial themes finally came together in an interview given to *Newsweek* (Nov. 1989), when Tournier, in what I perceived as an outrageous publicity stunt, denounced abortionists as "the sons and grandsons of the monsters of Auschwitz."

6. The article on Perrault, "Barbe-Bleue ou le secret du conte," is one of Tournier's most important

metafictions, for in it he elaborates an informative typology of the short story.

7. One of the most important though least noticed of Tournier's formative experiences was the year, 1950, he spent studying under Claude Lévi-Strauss at the Musée de l'Homme. Tournier acknowledges this debt in his short article "Lévi-Strauss, mon maître" (*Le Vol du vampire* 384-87).

8. This expression is adapted from the title of Anthony Cheal Pugh's article on Claude Simon, "Facing the matter of history: *Les Géorgiques.*"

9. For a wonderfully odd commentary which is exclusively on "The Snow Queen," see Lederer.

Works Cited

Améry, Jean. "Asthetizmus der Barbarei: Uber Tourniers Roman *Der Erlkönig.*" *Merkur* 27 (1973): 73-79.

Andersen, Hans Christian. "The Snow Queen." *Hans Andersen's Fairy Tales.* Ed. and Trans. Naomi Lewis. Harmondsworth: Penguin, 1981.

Balzac, Honoré de. *Le Curé de Tours.* Paris: Folio, 1976.

Barthes, Roland. *S/Z.* Paris: Seuil, 1970.

Davis, Colin. *Michel Tournier: Philosophy and Fiction.* Oxford: Oxford UP, 1988.

Foucault, Michel. "Anti-Rétro: entretien avec Michel Foucault." *Cahiers du Cinéma* 251-52 (July-Aug. 1974): 5-15.

Frege, Gottlob. "On Sense and Reference." *Translations from the Philosophical Writings of Gottlob Frege.* Eds. and Trans. P. Geach and M. Black. Oxford: Blackwell, 1952.

Gascoigne, David. "Michel Tournier." *Beyond the Nouveau Roman.* Ed. Michael Tilby. Oxford: Berg, 1990.

Genette, Gérard. *Figures I.* Paris: Seuil, 1966.

———. *Palimpsestes: la littérature au second degré.* Paris: Seuil, 1978.

Hawking, Stephen. *A Brief History of Time.* London: Bantam Press, 1988.

Ignatieff, Michael. "Europe's fairytale casts its spell." *The Observer* (29 July 1990): 17.

Kermode, Frank. *The Sense of an Ending: Studies in the Theory of Fiction.* Oxford: Oxford UP, 1967.

Lederer, Wolfgang. *The Kiss of the Snow Queen: Hans Christian Andersen and Man's Redemption by Woman.* Berkeley: U California P, 1986.

Ong, Walter. *Orality and Literacy: The Technologizing of the Word.* London: Methuen, 1982.

Platten, David. "The *Geist* in the Machine: Nazism in Tournier's *Le Roi de aulnes.*" *Romantic Review* 84 (1993): 181-94.

Pugh, Anthony Cheal. "Facing the Matter of History: *Les Géorgiques.*" *Claude Simon: New Directions.* Ed. Alistair Duncan. Edinburgh: Scottish Academic Press, 1985.

Ricoeur, Paul. "Le Récit de fiction." *La Narrativité.* Paris: Centre Nationale de la Recherche Scientifique, 1980.

Shattuck, Roger. "Michel Tournier: Why not the best?." *New York Review of Books* (April 1983): 8-15.

Strickland, Geoffrey. "The latest Tournier: *Gaspard, Melchior et Balthazar.*" *The Cambridge Quarterly* 10 (1982): 238-41.

Tournier, Michel. "A Writer's Rages." Interview in *Newsweek* 45 (Nov. 6, 1989): 60.

———. *Gaspard, Melchior et Balthazar.* Paris: Folio, 1980.

———. *Gilles et Jeanne.* Paris: Folio, 1983.

———. Interview in *La Quinzaine Littéraire* (1 March 1977): 25.

———. *La Goutte d'or.* Paris: Folio, 1985.

———. *Le Coq de bruyère.* Paris: Folio, 1978.

———. *Le Médianoche amoureux.* Paris: Gallimard, 1989.

———. *Le Roi des aulnes.* Paris: Folio, 1970.

———. *Le Vent Paraclet.* Paris: Gallimard, 1977.

———. *Le Vol du vampire.* Paris: Mercure de France, 1981.

———. *Les Météores.* Paris: Folio, 1975.

———. *Les Rois mages.* Paris: Folio, 1983.

———. *Petites Proses.* Paris: Folio, 1986.

———. Postface to *Images et signes de Michel Tournier.* Eds. Arlette Bouloumié et Maurice de Gandillac. Actes du Colloque du Centre Culturel International de Cerisy-la-Salle. Paris: Gallimard, 1991.

———. *Vendredi ou la vie sauvage.* Paris: Folio Junior, 1971.

———. *Vendredi ou les limbes du Pacifique.* Paris: Folio, 1967.

Woodhull, Winifred. "Fascist bonding and euphoria in Michel Tournier's *The Ogre.*" *New German Critique* 42 (1987): 79-112.

Worton, Michael. "Ecrire et ré-écrire: le projet de Tournier." *Sud* 61 (1986): 52-69.

———. "Intertextuality: to inter textuality or to resurrect it?" *Cross References: Modern French Theory and the Practice of Criticism.* Eds. David Kelley and Isabelle Llasera. Leeds: Society for French Studies, 1986: 14-23.

Walter Redfern (essay date 1996)

SOURCE: Redfern, Walter. "The Founding Myth: 'La Famille Adam'" and "Something about Nothing: 'La Jeune Fille et la mort.'" In *Michel Tournier: Le Coq de bruyère,* pp. 17-21; 73-88. Madison, N.J.: Fairleigh Dickinson University Press, 1996.

[In the following essays, Redfern regards the separation of the genders as the central crisis in "La Famille Adam" and documents Tournier's use of the Romantic concept of ennui and the philosophical basis for comedy in "La Jeune Fille et la mort."]

> You think Oedipus had a problem—Adam was Eve's mother.
>
> —Graffito on construction wall, Philadelphia, 1969

Logically enough, this first story in the collection rewrites Genesis, the founding story of the Judeo-Christian tradition. A rewriting of Holy Writ, it is humorous and pointed. Throughout, God is credited with human—all-too-human—attributes: vanity, irascibility, favoritism. Inevitably, the story begins "Au commencement." Tournier has substituted himself for the supreme dictator, God. Tournier's version of God is a narcissist. He plagiarizes himself by creating man in his own image. So at the outset lies the original paradox: creation and imitation were co-instantaneous. This is of course equally true of authors, those little gods. Even when seeking to be original, they are heavily in hock to predecessors.[1]

Tournier reworks to his taste the creation myth. The true Fall was the split-up into three of a previously and marvellously self-contained entity. The Platonic myth of severance is rampant in Tournier's work. His God is unisex, which is not news to today's feminists, to ancient glosses on the Bible which made much of the fact that the very word *Jehovah* comes from roots both masculine and feminine, and to the long Gnostic tradition of an androgynous Adam, God, and soul.[2] Though *sex* derives as probably as not from *secare,* to cut, such traditions refuse to see sex as a phenomenon of separation and opt for dual entities. The androgyne is a figure of approximation in two senses: a near-miss and a bringing-together. As Tournier views the polarization of the sexes as the root cause of myriad problems for humanity, a bisexual God fits his bill.

Tournier is a nonchalant borrower. He improves on Plato, whose Androgyne was a true, and hideous, monster: globular, one trunk, one head, two faces, two sexes, four arms, and four legs.[3] Tournier's version is more beautiful: a standard human shape with the physical attributes of both genders. Plato's hybrid carries in embryonic form, programmed, the future split. This outcome is not nearly so predetermined in Tournier's, so that the eventual breakup is much more traumatic. Twinhood, the dominant theme of *Les Météores,* provides in Tournier's general compensatory scheme of things a counterbalance to such cleavages, for twins are at their origin two-in-one, lying head-to-tail in the womb. Tournier would seem to prefer that humankind perpetuate itself by parthenogenesis or self-fecundation (the Holy Ghost cannot be everywhere): "Un serpent se mordant la queue est la figure de cette érotique close sur elle-même, sans perte ni bavure" (*VLP* [*Vendredi ou les timbes du Pacifique*], p. 12). We are, for Tournier, self-begetters.

In **"La Famille Adam,"** then, God conveniently sports both penis and vagina, as does his mirror image, Adam. This original copy could thus store the former organ in the latter when walking or running, like a knife in a scabbard (an ancient erotic emblem in many cultures). Splendidly self-contained, Adam could have impregnated himself. He has the best of both worlds. Bolshy by nature, however, Adam lets his virile side predominate, that wants to keep on the move and be forever ready for combat. In order to settle Adam down, God creates Eden with a view to increasing his progeny. Initially Adam refuses to acquiesce, while recognizing his bipartite nature: sedentary and nomadic. God therefore waits for Adam to fall asleep (as in the Bible), and then (as not) he subtracts the female parts from bisexual Adam and inserts them into another "man" made from the soil of Paradise: Woman is created. Stripped of his female half, Adam is now fully male. When God introduces Eve to him as his "other half," Adam responds solipsistically: "Comme je suis beau," which God then corrects to the right grammatical gender in the new dispensation: "Comme elle est belle" (**"FA"** [**"La Famille Adam"**], pp. 13-14). The woman *is* the better half.

The major difference between Tournier's tale and the Genesis myth is that Tournier's offers no explanation as to why Adam and Eve come to be expelled from Eden. The Fall is traditionally blamed on Eve's insatiable curiosity and vulnerability to the serpent's flattering wiles. Tournier very clearly wants to valorize Woman and devalue Man. In the orthodox telling, the Fall starts off human evolution. While grateful for the emphasis of the eminent geneticist, François Jacob, on the role of chance, games and *bricolage* in evolution, Tournier persists in preferring the Genesis version of mankind as God's self-portrait as richer in meaning than evolutionary theory (nature experimenting with itself).[4] In other words, Tournier dislikes anarchic freedom; he prefers to kick against the pricks, and react to an imposed given (though of course *bricoleurs,* too, or "tinkerers" as Jacob terms them, can also work only with what is to hand).

A further reason why Tournier leaves the consecrated Fall out of his variant story is that he wants to proceed instead in terms of character-types, contrasting modes of being, rather than significant, one-off events. In order to offset external causalism, or psychoanalysis, Tournier often turns to the rather old-fashioned pseudo-science of *caractérologie,* which can be adapted to suit his fondness for idiosyncrasy, perversity, and monstrosity. One particular set of standard pairs in *caractérologie* comprises *primaire/secondaire.*[5] Tournier asks us to forget the scholastic resonances, which are likely "de s'y attacher comme une mauvaise odeur" (*VV* [*Le Vol du vampire*], p. 232). In his use of the concepts, the *primaire* individual is uninhibitedly locked into a present perpetually reborn; the *secondaire* more introvertly into a past full of echoes. It is never clear whether Tournier emulates the binary polarities of Gide or Lévi-Strauss—two admitted mentors—or whether he *plays* between both. "Il ne faut pas céder à la tentation de valoriser l'une des catégories caractérologiques aux dépens de la catégorie opposée" (*VV,* p. 337).

After being expelled from Paradise, without explanation, Adam and Eve suffer long years of wandering in the desert. Or rather Adam is happy there and Eve miserable. Individual and habitat are virtually synonymous for Tournier, who frequently writes of his house, an ex-vicarage, as if it were some kind of living partner to himself. On their wanderings, Adam and Eve produce Cain and Abel, the latter stereotypically male and the former feminized. Cain drinks in Eve's entrancing tales about the lost Paradise. He is made for stay-at-home activities: gardening, farming, building. Meanwhile Abel, the spitting image of his father, wants only locomotion and contest. Brotherly rivalry very early turns them into "frères ennemis." Abel delights in wrecking Cain's juvenile constructions.

When Cain later starts building Eden 2 (no doubt a joky reference to all the satellite burghs of Paris), God grows angry with him, as he had earlier been with Adam, but for different reasons. Whereas Adam had disobediently not wanted to settle down and multiply, Cain is building or rebuilding what Adam and Eve had lost. Cain is in fact rivalling God by imposing order on chaos. In other versions of this myth, Cain is not normally the hero. In Hugo's poem "La Conscience," for example, after murdering his brother Cain tries ever more elaborate means of escape from God's judging eye, but even in a vault "l'oeil était toujours dans la tombe et regardait Caïn."[6] Tournier patently favors the underdog. Just as a stock theme of Westerns is the feud between cattlemen and farmers, so a vendetta festers between Abel and Cain. Betraying favoritism and thus showing himself not to be all-loving, God prefers the meat-offerings of Abel to the fruit and flowers of Cain. Eventually, after violent provocation, the pacifist, vegetarian Cain loses his temper and murders his carnivorous brother.

Now it is Cain's turn to be driven out, from his own Eden 2, and to spend many years wandering in the wilderness. Stubbornly, however, Cain returns to a spot close by the original paradise, and there builds the first city in history: Enoch, a marvellous, civilized place with, at its center, a majestic temple. He has overcome his damnation and come back to his preferred static existence, fortified by his experience of the opposite. This pattern reveals how the basic opposition of Cain and Abel can take different forms (as indeed it will in **"L'Aire du Muguet"**). As well as sharply defined antithesis, this myth can represent the coexistence, or the alternation, of the two tendencies within one person. Nomads cannot erect anything lasting: only tents, not temples. And sedentary people need the variant experience of travel, or as Thoreau said, "the tonic of wildness."[7]

God turns up. He has been brought down to earth, and is worn out by all his peregrinations with his favored sons of Abel. He has been jolted about on his long travels with the Ark of the Covenant across the deserts. He is in fact looking for a home in which to rest his weary bones. The grandson Cain welcomes the decrepit forbear. Instead of the prodigal son, "c'est le retour du père avare."[8] Grumpy God is solemnly installed in his waiting temple, which he will never again quit. Tournier's God is a clumsy, self-centered bungler: partial, not omniscient, nor even all-powerful. Just as Tournier enjoys making marginal people central, so here he revels in hijacking signs and turning the center of the Judeo-Christian tradition into a partly comic figure. The story has come full circle. At the start, original androgyny (God, Adam); at the finale a self-asserting hermaphrodite, a feminized male, Cain.

For Davis, this story "gives a concise version of the cycle of plenitude, loss and reconciliation which plays an important role in much of his writing."[9] Tournier here practices creative plagiarism, or adhocism, in tune with God's original copying. Thus Tournier induces both the sense of *déjà vu,* or *déjà lu,* and also he destabilizes such archetypes by extensions and twists.

Is there a moral to this fable, written in a mock-simple narrative style but loaded with ideas, as always with Tournier? Man, softened and feminized, teaches God a lesson and puts him in his place. The best place for God would appear to be in church, where he can do no, or less, mischief. And the best kind of human being is a harmonious admixture of the female and the male, the settler who has travelled.

. . . . .

> I sometimes feel that I have nothing to say and I want to communicate this.
>
> —Damien Hirst, sculptor

Lichtenberg sported ponderously with nothing: "A leg of mutton is better than nothing, nothing is better than Heaven, therefore a leg of mutton is better than Heaven."[10] More to my present point, Swift: "I am trying an Experiment very frequent among Modern Authors; which is, to write upon Nothing."[11] This could be a prescient comment on the possibly postmodernist games of Michel Tournier. In what he called his after-sales manual, *Le Vent Paraclet,* during a disquisition on "cosmic laughter," Tournier states: "Lorsque les lattes disjointes de la passerelle où chemine l'humanité s'entrouvrent sur le vide sans fond, la plupart des hommes ne voient rien, mais certains autres voient le rien." (*VP* [*Le Vent paraclet*], p. 199)

The name of the young protagonist of **"La Jeune Fille et la mort,"** Mélanie Blanchard, is, as so often in Tournier's work, loaded. *Melas* in Greek means black (as in melancholia); and Blanchard is self-explanatory. Her name, like that of Raphaël Bidoche in **"Que ma joie demeure,"** is an oxymoron, a yoking of opposites. Tournier's favorite form of photography is black-and-white, which he claims is capable of subtler effects than color photography. Initially virgin, Mélanie will be ultimately and with a smile on her face raped by death.

The tale begins at school, a mainly unhappy series of places in Tournier's autobiographical account, offset only by his willful playing of the class clown. Mélanie too is something of a sore thumb, an odd girl out, though not in any provocative way. Tournier, in fact, can define her only negatively: "ni difficile, ni secrète, ni mélancolique" (**"JFM"** [**"La Jeune Fille et la mort"**], p. 181). Obviously bright, she has strange habits such as sucking lemons during lessons. She has macabre interests. In history, she is drawn to famous people who were tortured and executed: Joan of Arc, Gilles de Rais, Mary Stuart, Charles I, Damiens.

The set topic of her latest essay is the stock "What I did in my holidays." She chooses a family picnic, which had to be cancelled owing to the sudden death of the grandmother. From this (fictional) opening onwards, the whole exercise is ruled by negation: the non-audition of birdsong, the non-return under a storm, the non-drying of clothes. A non-event, an exercise in imagination, which indeed often negates and offers an alternative version of reality, as Philip Larkin illustrates:

> And here we have that splendid family
> I never ran to when I got depressed,

> The boys all biceps and the girls all chest . . .
> The bracken where I never trembling sat,
> Determined to go through with it; where she
> Lay back, and "all became a burning mist" . . .

"Nothing, like something, happens anywhere."[12]

As Auden noted, "Poetry makes nothing happen."[13] Like Larkin, Mélanie is saying: "No, nothing happened." Like him, she is writing against cliché—though her essay begins "assez banalement" (p. 176)—against the same old story. Her negative invention is comic; death is from the outset wedded to laughter. Gravely, and all the more funnily for that, Mélanie joshes the whole ritual of school essays, family outings and grandmas turning their toes up. In the remainder of the story, her obsession with death will be rarely gloomy, most often excited and jubilant. In cancelling itself out, her essay asserts itself. Mélanie has quite literally, like the archetypal great artist, made something out of nothing, by an act of bravura against imposition.

The teacher is perplexed by this performance, as by the lemons. What do the disparate clues add up to? The answer, unavailable to the teacher but to which the reader is privy, is that Mélanie is bored. Not just run-of-the-mill boredom, but an essentially philosophical acedia. A kind of nausea, a sickening gray tide, covers everything, threatening her with stiflement. Like Sartre's Roquentin, she is unsure whether this nausea is in herself, or in things about her. She does not give in to it, but resists valiantly. As in her essay, normality is defamiliarized, stripped of its reassuring gloss. Tournier's version of Sartre is a perversion (in his own, nonpejorative sense). In *La Nausée,* the lone-wolf hero undergoes a series of shocks that induce nausea. Instead of the orderliness and meaningfulness he would prefer to find in the physical universe and in human affairs, he experiences in a terminal way, for he has had earlier inklings, the gratuitousness of existence. He rejects suicide as a tenable response, for that would be merely an additional absurd gesture. His retaliation against what causes his nausea, which becomes synonymous with truth, takes the dubious form of harking back to a jazz tune, and projecting a book. He is himself aware of the bad faith involved in such an enterprise of imposing artistic order on the disorder of existence.

For her part, Mélanie has no such hunger for being. Her nausea swamps her at moments when we should say that "l'être *est* le néant." As in all his borrowings, Tournier twists and capitalizes. Similarly, when Mélanie looks through variously colored windowpanes at the garden, Tournier no doubt had in mind the devil's mirror in Hans Christian Andersen's *The Snow Queen.*[14] When it shatters, some fragments become windowpanes, and deforming lenses which invert the appearance and value of all things. The ones Mélanie peers through do not deform, either rosily or blackly. The transformations run the gamut from the horrible to the lovely. The one color lacking is gray—the color of ashy boredom. What she deduces from these optical experiments is that anything can be viewed differently. Such relativity hardly shakes the earth, but she is still young, and is clearly a creature who will push everything to its limits.

When we consider nausea, we think of intake: too much or the wrong kind. Tournier never hints that Mélanie gets sick of people or of herself. It is out there that the problem lies, in things. Hence the stress from the start on sensation and observation. In Mélanie's case, it is foods most readily associated with childhood which provoke her physical nausea: cream, butter, jam. These are all soft, greasy, sticky, and signify a mass or trap to sink into (cf. "le visqueux" in Sartre). The tastes that delight and energize her include green apples, vinegar and pepper: all acid and sharp. As for drinks, milk is bad, lemonade good. She has had to give up her favorite mustard sandwiches, as they caused a riot at school breaks.

Tournier perseveres with his catalogue. He is trying to conjugate her nausea, as a means to making her strange obsessions more comprehensible to the reader, who is possibly jibbing at the idea of a young girl fixated on nausea, nothingness, and death. And so, in terms of weather, Mélanie dislikes hot, lazy afternoons, and prefers cold, dry, bright weather. Summer sun encourages passivity; sunbathing enacts a rape of her supine body. Her tastes go to the bracing. To this end, she gladly embraces both laughter and sobs, which equally shake the frame, and set up distance and control—the very antithesis of docility.

Sobbing and laughter figure strongly in her earlier exposure to death, that of her mother. Her previous experience, of dead animals, had produced disgust at rotting carrion, whereas bleached skeletons, bodies reduced to their essential structure, seem to embody "la bonne mort." Tournier makes little of Mélanie's father's lack of interest in his daughter, who got over her very real grief at her mother's death when she was twelve by picturing her body in the grave as picked clean. Mélanie had killed off a grandmother in her story. Is this a displacement to conceal a wound? Or a more positive option? Tournier has declared: "Les oeuvres sont les fruits du désert et ne s'épanouissent que dans l'aridité" (*VP*, p. 295). He tells an approving story of a corpse transported across the Sahara, becoming progressively lighter and mummified: "C'est beau, un pays où un cadavre ne pourrit pas."[15] There could be, in his mind, a connection between the clear lines of philosophical systems and the picked bones of a skeleton: the reduction to an essence, or at least a framework. Despite his contrary taste for sumptuousness, Tournier returns often to desiccation or sublimation, as in the anecdote of the blasé socialite,

Antoine Bibesco, visiting the plush house of a friend: "Oui d'accord, mais pourquoi pas plutôt rien?" (*VP*, p. 204). This is Mélanie's priceless question.

It might seem that the mother's death plays a traumatic role comparable to that of the adored sister, Drusilla, in Camus's *Caligula*.[16] Mélanie's envisioning of her mother's stark corpse enables her to "sob with laughter," and to feel "délivrée du poids de l'existence" (p. 181). For such a temperament, mortality renders all human endeavor futile. As death always wins in the end, dying properly seems a more logical goal than living properly. If she cannot be her own cause or origin, she wants to be in charge of her end: "Mine own executioner," as in Donne's *Devotions*. Living is living towards death. Tournier, in many ways a childlike optimist, must have known the temptation to think along these branch lines, to entertain the possibility of welcoming, even hastening, death: "Les hommes du oui imaginent difficilement le monde gris et haineux du non" (*VV* [*Le Vol du vampire*], p. 228). Did the yea-saying author have to wrench his mind in order to rehearse Mélanie's option, which is, however, not gray nor full of hatred (like Caligula), but as orectic towards nothingness as bulimics towards fullness? **"La Jeune Fille et la mort"** is Tournier's purest fiction.

It has its own impulsion. Even Sartre's *La Nausée* is only an adjunct, not a kick start. Similarly, in the area of intertextuality, Tournier diverges from the burden of Schubert's song, "Death and the Maiden" (based on a poem by Matthias Claudius, about sleeping softly in the arms of death), where the girl initially resists the approaches of Death, protesting that she is too young to die. Death sweet-talks her, explaining that she has nothing to fear. For her part, Mélanie needs no persuading to open herself up to dying. On similar lines to the song, the painting "Death and the Young Woman" by Nicholas Manuel "Deutsch" shows a dirty old man feeling up his prey. It is not entirely clear that she is thwarting him, for she appears to pull his head near hers and to guide his hand to the target area. Tournier presumably wishes to break away from the long tradition of the *danse macabre,* though Mélanie certainly knows the joys of *delectatio morosa.* As for intratextuality, another Schubert song (based on Goethe's poem "Der Erl-König") reveals death as a ravisher-before-time (see *Le Roi des aulnes*). One tradition, that of the *Ars moriendi,* does seem to be revived in Mélanie's hope for "une bonne mort."

Though most of the time Tournier makes Mélanie a likeable creature, on occasion and allowing for the inner logic of her desires, he introduces bleaker perspectives. For instance, at the time of the 1962 Cuban missile crisis when a third world war seemed imminent, Mélanie, quite logically, nurses genocidal dreams. There is always a temptation to generalize from an idiosyncratic case, as Tournier does with Abel Tiffauges or Gilles de Rais. Here, if death rules, why not envisage the massacre of millions? Mélanie soon learns, however, that history, like philosophy later, will not provide any recipe solution for her dilemmas.

Neither will sex, to which she is initiated brutally in the fuel cellar by a delivery boy, Etienne. The rape reads close to attempted murder. Mélanie is both repelled and attracted as her virgin body is assaulted in the dirty room (the white/black motif in another gauzy disguise). In fact, she follows up the rape by visiting Etienne in the wood mill where he works. The savage initiation seems not to have been psychically scarring, probably because of the near-death element in it. The sawdust lying about is an unnoticed foretaste of the story's ending, for it was traditionally used to soak up the blood of the guillotined. It comes, moreover, from tree trunks; and, after decapitation, all that is left of bodies is the trunk. It is at this juncture that Mélanie commissions an elaborate but unspecified machine from a master craftsman. It will be a long job, and the reader probably forgets about this order until the last pages. It is a kind of plant that will flower later.

Mélanie's sexual relationship and sweet nothings with Etienne, satisfying in themselves, continue, but are in no way proof against the death obsession. Tournier writes elsewhere: "La vie a partie liée avec la mort, et la psychanalyse a tort de prétendre opposer Eros et Thanatos comme deux pulsions diamétralement opposées" (*CS* [*Des Clefs et des serrures*], p. 173). For Tournier, Freud helps to provide terms for discussion, but no conclusive answers. When Etienne offloads her, Mélanie sinks back again into her *ennui,* from he has been a distraction only. *Ennui* has a long history in the Romantic tradition, although it is difficult to fit Mélanie into this line, as into any other. For Tournier, *ennui* attacks the young especially: "Il y a une lumière glauque d'aquarium tombant sur toutes choses d'un ciel uniformément voilé, et finalement une clameur silencieuse qui brame le désespoir d'exister" (*CS,* p. 39). He offers as reasons the lack of rootedness, the availability of the young. Mélanie's brief dreams of holocausts derive from Tournier's: "En 1938, 39, 40, j'avais treize, quatorze, quinze ans. Je me souviens de la ferveur avec laquelle je priais pour qu'une guerre éclatât et jetât cul par-dessus tête la société de cloportes où j'agonisais" (*CS,* p. 40). In comparison, adults are more preoccupied, but far less intense (ibid.). Mélanie has only loose connections with the youthful Tournier, for she bears her fellows no ill will.

Where Mélanie differs from her author or most people is that she decides the solution lies in her own hands. She attaches a rope to a ceiling beam and, like God on the seventh day of creation, she admires her handiwork. Suicide, of course, can be seen as the ultimate gauntlet

thrown down before God, or our body (I will die when I decide, not you). The simple act of setting up an exit suddenly gives her life a density it had largely lacked before. She has in effect stepped from the conveyor belt to the self-chosen path. To capture Mélanie's newfound direction, Tournier again resorts to oxymoron. She experiences *un bonheur patibulaire* (p. 187), gallows gaiety, *Galgenfreude* rather than mere passing *Galgenhumor.*

After a sexual liaison, ordinary practicing friendship diverts Mélanie for a spell from her new focus, when her friend Jacqueline asks her to live with her for a few weeks. Apart from her obsession, Mélanie is truly unremarkable, a perfectly decent being, who willingly helps Jacqueline to teach underachieving children. If her fixation is monstrous, she herself is a sympathetic monster. This period is again a truce. Jacqueline's fiancé is in the CRS, a potential death-dealer, as is made plain by his bulky service pistol. Through no fault of her own, Mélanie gets involved in the engaged couple's tiff, and indeed withdraws tactfully from the fraught scene. She is fully prepared for others to be orthodoxly happy. The glimpse of that revolver stays with her, a bulgingly phallic symbol, although it is rather its destructive potentiality that seduces her into stealing it.

Her first stab at suicide is a fiasco. The gun goes off harmlessly while she is trying to find out how it works. She is unsure whether to be relieved or sorry to survive: a wobble in volition that helps to keep her believable. She is typical only of herself. She is simply or complexly a human being with an urge to become an ex-human being. In the woods where she missed her target, she meets a man collecting mushrooms. This encounter opens up more possibilities (death is an eye-opener): self-poisoning. If the reader has not already begun to feel this, her single-minded efforts to do herself in start to become serio-comic here, joco-serious.[17] She has a curiosity about death. She is always ready to learn—about sex, mushrooms, fearsome machines—even if she disbelieves in the lessons of history. For his part, that mushroom expert can flirt safely with death. Mélanie is no tease; she is in earnest (cf. Elizabeth Barrett Browning: "We shape a figure of our fantasy, / Call nothing something, and run after it").[18]

The sexual motif recurs when Mélanie gets hold of some phallic-shaped lethal fungi. This third possible way out enables Tournier to go through, in wilfully excruciating detail, the various symbolic values of rope, gun and poisonous mushroom, all of which she lays out with the reverence of a sacristan. The pistol, of course, is blatantly erotic, and reminds Mélanie of the undeniable pleasures she had with Etienne. Sex and death, as in the "little death" of Elizabethan orgasm, have been traditional bedmates.[19] Beyond such local thrills, all three instruments of suicide seem to open different doors onto the unknown, as if death itself were the afterlife. The plethora of available methods suggests that Mélanie's nausea surfaces not from a lack of meaning, but from a surfeit.[20]

In his ebullient catalogue, Tournier proposes that mushrooms betoken a giant stomach and all the basic existential activities associated with it: digestion, sex and evacuation. Mélanie imagines dying from mushroom poisoning as an initiation ceremony. It would be like being born in reverse, a return to a primeval (not an identifiably maternal) womb. The pistol, for its share, evokes Hell: flames, noise, acrid stench. The third key to the door of the unknown, the rope, and the chair to take off from, represent Nature, trees and plants. If she chose this route, she could feel part of the landscape. In this section, as well as intentionally parodying experts like the mycologist-philosopher Coquebin, Tournier pastiches himself in this symbolic disquisition. Would Mélanie, without his ventriloquism, be up to articulating such finesses? Whether or not, she clearly wants what, in Starobinski's account, Montaigne desired: "La mort idéale, pour Montaigne, est une mort agie, une 'mort dirigée' (comme nous parlons d'accouchement dirigé) où la conscience s'applique étroitement à l'événement instantané qui se produit dans la profondeur du corps."[21]

To Mélanie's options Tournier opposes the very different views of the pedant, M. Coquebin (i.e., greenhorn). The décor of his room, with its plaster saints, indicates religiosity, and indeed a leading Catholic saint, Theresa, object of a particularly sentimental cult, lived once in the next street. When Mélanie looks quietly consternated at such talk—she entirely lacks mystical velleities—he swiftly changes to another hobbyhorse, philosophy. Immediately he runs up against her refusal to argue, to justify herself, or to proselytise. She is uninterested in the high-flown shoptalk of philosophy. Tournier is not alone, however, in thinking that "l'enfant est spontanément philosophe, métaphysicien même."[22] The frontispiece of *Le Vent Paraclet* shows Franz von Lenbach's shepherd-boy daydreaming on his back. Tournier glosses: "Il scrute le vide lumineux. Il se laisse basculer dans ce gouffre d'azur . . . C'est sa façon à lui de faire de la métaphysique." When Mélanie tells Coquebin without affectation the story of her life so far, he at once intellectualizes it and slots it into scholastic traditions.[23]

When Mélanie relates her experiment with the colored windowpanes, he knee-jerkily, by professional or amateur deformation, cites Kant's aesthetic theories. The more she tells, the more convinced he grows that she has, quite independently, reached the same conclusions as the two main philosophical currents over the ages. One stems from Parmenides—a philosophy emphasizing the static, unchanging nature of being. Mélanie's

fixation on death and mummified corpses could lodge here. The second wells from Heraclitus, the philosopher of flux; and the rest of Mélanie's discrete life incidents might tag along here. The opposition is also that of Cain and Abel, the sedentary and the nomad. But Mélanie hankers neither to roam nor to settle down. Such polarities leave her untouched. As he expatiates, Coquebin eventually realizes that his interlocutor is far more preoccupied by a single red hair jutting out of a mole on his cheek than by his pedantic lecture. She is taken with concrete particulars, not structures and systems. As such, she is the antithesis of Tournier himself at her age, who worshipped only "le système avec son insurpassable cohérence, . . . cause de tout, effet de rien" (*VP*, p. 157); and who looks back with fond amusement at "ces coups de poing tambourinant mes pectoraux de petit Tarzan métaphysicien" (*VP*, p. 180). Mélanie is no more cut out to be a willful nonconformist than a conformist. She is a nonesuch, neither etched black and white, nor dully gray.

Feminists might detect in this portrait of the girl an ancient stereotype: women, no matter how perceptive, seen as relying on intuition rather than reasoning powers. Yet we have seen how logical she is, and male rationalism as embodied or disembodied in Coquebin is lampooned. When she stops visiting him, she again becomes a prey to *ennui*. She is getting nowhere fast. The crunch is clearly coming. She cannot postpone forever a decision, accumulating instruments of death that she puts to no use. She is getting bored with her *ennui*. And so she opts for a deadline. This coincides with the feast day of St. Theresa, who died young herself, after likewise losing her mother at an early age. At fourteen, she was fascinated (like Mélanie with Damiens) by the murderer Pranzini. Her lively autobiography, *The Story of a Soul*, aimed to show that spiritual perfection could be achieved through childlike humility. Mélanie is not ostentatiously humble, but what arrogance she has is not targeted at others. It is the genuine arrogance of somebody who knows very definitely what she wants. She wants out. She will stop at nothing to have her way.

The decision reached, Mélanie is elated. She sees death as a process of transfiguration—another instance of Tournier's recycling of Christian tenets to unorthodox ends. Though she has fixed the deadline, we do not know which method she has chosen. Admittedly, she returns to her woodland cottage, where the rope waits, but she could equally well use the gun or the poisonous fungi fittingly there. Principally, she is seeking seclusion, having no desire to appall others. Two days before the appointed day, a van delivers the machine commissioned long before. Tournier uses the colloquial, revolutionary term, *la veuve* (an example of gallows humour).

Wittgenstein famously said: "What we cannot talk about we must pass over in silence,"[24] but the philosopher who declared that a wholly serious treatise consisting entirely of jokes was conceivable might well have allowed for mute, inner quaking.[25] There is a possible connection between "le rire blanc" and the narrative blank which Tournier tries to circumscribe thus:

> Absolu. Un concept qui pour exprimer le comble de la positivité emprunte une tournure négative. Ab-solu, qui n'a pas de lien, sans rapport, non relatif. Or tout ce que nous sommes, tout ce que nous connaissons est tellement relié-à, c'est-à-dire relatif, que le contraire devient pour nous inexprimable. A la limite, comme certains écrivains religieux qui se refusent à écrire le mot Dieu, laisser un blanc à la place d'absolu.[26]

The narrative blank, or blackout, in **"La Jeune Fille et la mort,"** like the elision of the Fall in **"La Famille Adam,"** or the children-only performance in **"Que ma joie demeure,"** digs a hole, introduces nothingness. The narrative switches from the arrival of *la veuve* to a doctor who has just examined Mélanie's corpse. He is tempted to a paradox, which is also an everyday idiom: she has died laughing. Ever the roguish pedant, Tournier then further bifurcates into a physiological account of the phenomenon of laughter. Anyone who has ever read the deathless prose of laboratory tests on a sense of humor will cheer Tournier's mockery. Just as Coquebin's potted history of metaphysical speculation got us nowhere towards understanding Mélanie's idiosyncratic version, so the doctor's borrowed dissection of laughter leaves untouched her special brand: cosmic hilarity. When he was a student, it was the concrete, not the abstract, aspects of philosophy that appealed to Tournier; and humor always returns or anchors us in the concrete. From the poetic materialist Bachelard especially he claims to have learned that the nearer you get to the ultimate questions (e.g., The Meaning of Life), the likelier you are to be convulsed with laughter (see *VP*, pp. 152-53). Levity and gravity coexist, cooperate.

For his contribution to the debate, Coquebin quotes the well-publicized comic theory of Bergson: comedy results when something mechanical is encrusted on the living; when, for example, people start behaving like automata. Bergson's *Le Rire* is essentially concerned with cliché, existential stereotypes. Bergson's dogmatic notions seem at home in the vicinity of the guillotine. They smack of the policeman: killjoy and punitive, a method of social correction and of imposing uniformity. Given Tournier's and Mélanie's individualism, such a comic ideology is itself risible. Arthur Koestler performed a perfect demolition of Bergson's overinfluential hypothesis:

> If automatic repetitiveness in human behaviour were a necessary and sufficient condition of the comic, there would be no more amusing spectacle than an epileptic fit. If "we laugh each time a person gives us the impression of being a thing," there would be nothing more funny than a corpse.[27]

If, as suggested earlier, Mélanie's single-mindedness is in part comic, it still involves mind, will, and imagination: she is no Bergsonian robot. Elsewhere, Tournier judges Bergson's theory adequate, but only for "le rire de société" (*VP*, p. 197). "White" or "cosmic" laughter (i.e., not sick or black, but coolly aristocratic) cuts far wider and deeper:

> Le cosmique et le comique. Ces deux mots qui paraissent faits pour être rapprochés . . . Il y a un comique cosmique: celui qui accompagne l'émergence de l'absolu au milieu du tissu de relativités où nous vivons. C'est le rire de Dieu. Car nous nous dissimulons le néant qui nous entoure, mais il perce parfois la toile peinte de notre vie.

> (*VP*, p. 198)

Death makes strange.

As so often, Tournier calls in henchmen. Nietzsche, whose whole work "est parcourue par un friselis de drôlerie qui sape les racines mêmes de l'être" (*VP*, p. 200). Tournier himself is not innocent of the "persiflage métaphysique" he finds in Thomas Mann, although he concedes that the account in *The Magic Mountain* of a patient tickled by unearthly laughter while undergoing the unspeakable agony of a pneumothorax is exactly what he means by "le rire blanc" (*VP*, pp. 202-3). In that same novel, Hans Castorp's mother "meurt tout simplement en riant, meurt de rire à la lettre, tuée par l'inénarrable drôlerie de la condition humaine."[28]

In contrast with the doctor or Coquebin, Mélanie's friend Jacqueline, an ordinary mortal, aspires to no sophisticated interpretation, and offers a novelettish version of the death. Consumed with passion for the riotsquaddy, Mélanie has sacrificed herself for her friend's happiness. Only the old craftsman, Sureau, does not waste words trying to read the event. He may be a stand-in for Tournier, who fondly describes himself as an artisan, who works long-windedly, and who has produced in his story a beautiful machine of destruction for his young heroine. Nobody in the story, starting with the teacher on the first page, has even begun to understand Mélanie. She nonplusses experts and laypersons alike. Her death's-head grin recalls that of the Cheshire cat. She dies, *aenigma intactum*.

Tournier winks to Alphonse Allais, one of the cream of French humorists, coiner of the epithet, when he has Mélanie send out "un faire-part anthume" (p. 201), which summons all who knew her, but is timed so that they will get to her forest hut too late to dissuade her. Foreign aid would be over her dead body. Her suicide note is no cry for help. The three weapons in her arsenal stand unused. She has died, in purely medical terms, of a massive heart attack (cf. "Les attaques cérébrales, si commodes pour ménager le coup de théâtre qui débarrasse l'auteur d'un personnage devenu inutile, reculent devant l'infarctus de myocarde plus moderne, plus business, plus noble aussi parce que touchant le coeur" (*VV*,

p. 326). Her dead face retains a smile. Twisting congealed syntagms as so often, Tournier switches "la joie de vivre" to "la joie de ne pas vivre."[29]

To add to the lexical stock-pot, I would offer "nihility": the opposite of plenitude; "neminity": the opposite of egoistic pride, the urge to be no one; and "nusquamity": the opposite of ubiquity, the urge to be nowhere. Such neologisms imply that negatives are real (to nill countervails to will), and have to bear thinking about.[30] They clear the way for the indescribable. Mélanie's essay, about a nonevent, represents Tournier's attempt in this story as a whole to evoke the positive desire to be nothing, the ambition to be dead. Saying "no" has its own reasons, its own consistency. Whereas death is traditionally associated with terminal coldness, repeated images of warmth accompany Mélanie's explorations (pp. 186, 193). Christian orthodoxy, of course, highlights Satan, the rebel angel who set up shop in rivalry with God (cf. Tournier's self-estimate), as the spirit who nay-says. A cipher is a letter, and a code, as well as zero. "Giotto's O" was legendarily taken to represent artistic perfection. Queneau opined mildly: "Rien. Rien offre des avantages," and his hero Jacques "s'efforce de se tarir, de se désencombrer, de s'évider. Il dégorge son trop-plein de moi . . . Il se dépeuple."[31] Piling on thick seems inextricably tied with evacuation, excess with lessness. Mélanie is another exponent of nontology.[32]

When someone in the cottage asks what is the large object wrapped in black linen, old Sureau unveils the guillotine, not as if it were a mature widow, *la veuve,* but rather as if it were a young bride he is gently undressing. It is a work of art. It embodies everything that Mélanie always valued: it is clean, cold, a perfect machine for the task in hand. It is also, divertingly, heavily decorated and somewhat ridiculous with its hodgepodge of styles: ancient Greek, late eighteenth-century. Coquebin identifies this composite, neoclassical, anti-rococo style as Louis XVl—the reigning monarch guillotined in 1793 (cf. the earlier list of famous figures executed). The ancestor of the French guillotine was the Maiden (also known as the Widow), used in Scotland in the sixteenth and seventeenth centuries for criminals. Maiden here means first, as in maiden voyage. Mélanie wants to *handsel* death, to inaugurate it with pleasure. She wants to do herself in in style. In another text, Tournier recounts the anecdote of a village carpenter who built a beautiful guillotine, placed his head in the *lunette,* and pressed the switch:

> Il faudrait réserver une place parmi les causes du suicide à la force de persuasion qui émane d'un instrument de mort du seul fait de sa perfection technique ou artistique. Pas plus qu'on ne peut se retenir de goûter à certains gâteaux ou de faire l'amour avec certains corps, on ne saurait refuser à certains poignards, à certains pistolets, l'acte qu'ils appellent de toute leur admirable forme.
>
> (*CS,* p. 173)

This instrumental persuasion presumably acts like the chasm breeding vertigo and the urge to jump in acrophobics. Dr. Louis Guillotin's machine, when first proposed, was greeted with much hilarity. Ambrose Bierce defined the guillotine as "a machine which makes a Frenchman shrug his shoulders with good reason."[33]

Whether or not Mélanie intended to use the guillotine, this object, blackly comic, has helped her to die laughing. For who needs a fabulous mechanism when an inside job, the heart attack, suffices? An infarctus round the time you choose is the ultimate form of do-it-yourself. Viewing the guillotine in all its sinister glory, a machine that symbolizes how most people probably think of death: a violent intrusion, which cuts us off in our prime, gives Mélanie the supreme occasion for active derision. "Une mort parfaite doit ressembler à la vie qu'elle couronne comme son ultime achèvement" (*CS,* p. 172). *Donnant donnant,* giff gaff, fair's fair. She dies laughing, and no mistake. From what we know of her, her final act would have been to laugh out quiet.

From another angle, typified by Robert Burns's "The best-laid schemes o' mice an' men / Gang aft agley," no one can successfully prepare for death; it will always catch us on the hop, and thus make us laugh the other side of our faces. The heart attack just happened, out of the blue: an ambush. Even then, Mélanie has still been able to die laughing, at herself and her own over-preparedness for death, because a cosmic sense of humor enables you to distance yourself and to find everything, even your own precious self, risible. No emperor has any clothes. This is clearly the rarest, the most rarefied, kind of humor. It seems inevitable for those tempted to think along such lines to conceive of mocking laughter, *dérision.* Whatever power it is that made an absurd world seems to be enjoying a good laugh at our expense. If, however, you are lucidly alive to the situation, as Mélanie intuitively is, you can join in the divine or diabolical joke. Wittingly or dimly, Tournier derides his own propensity for elaborate systems, and recognizes that master planners can always be outsmarted. In Coquebin, Tournier skits his own recurrent pretension of using philosophic categories to try to corral life's mysteries.

Tournier offers no criticism of Mélanie (unlike Véronique, Lucien, Pierre). Her excess, her longing for negation, come across as entirely positive, just as her essay on death was highly animated. "Certaines personnes m'ont dit que Mélanie c'était Amandine devenue grande, ce n'est pas une mauvaise interprétation."[34] We leave Amandine on the trembling threshold of teenage fecundity. Maybe what Mélanie is escaping is, amongst other things, her female *fatum.* She lacks maternal vocation, and Tournier does not encourage us to think that she wants to rejoin her mother. Mélanie, like other Tournier activists, experiences *amor fati,* defined as "la lente métamorphose du destin en destinée . . . d'un mécanisme obscur et coercitif en l'élan unanime et chaleureux d'un être vers son accomplissement" (*VP*, p. 242). Mélanie, however, is unusual in the panoply of heroes and heroines, in not seeking to generalize her obsession, nor even to let it affect others. Those things that human beings normally rely on to fill out their lives—love, friendship, ambition—have not been enough to anchor her. For Tournier, the mass of mankind are "suradaptés," living like fish in water, and not questioning their environment nor their mental climate. Society is a vast cliché factory, "une pensée stéréotypée," from which few withdraw their labor (*VV*, p. 51).

Perhaps she goes on to enjoy exalted company. For Nietzsche, the old gods laughed themselves to death, and Zarathustra added: "Truly it will be the death of me, to choke with laughter."[35] Like Novalis after the death of his adored Sophie or Kleist in his suicide pact with his beloved, the good die young: "Les vies les meilleures ne connaissent pas de phase adulte" (*VP*, p. 290). Death is unmistakably the last chance for initiation, as contrasted with mere sufferance. Tournier favors initiation stories over *Bildungsromane*. The latter afford *atterrissage*, whereas "l'initiation est un excellent décollage."[36] *Décollage*: unsticking (from the viscous here-and-now) and, more anciently, decapitation. Mélanie wants to initiate herself; her desire to die does without intervention by others. Above all, initiation is not confrontation nor assimilation, but transcendence.[37] Neither does Mélanie's effort chime in with the classic Existentialist angst about human mortality. Death does not spoil all but gives added spice, point, and vitality. Mélanie's living-towards-death echoes the Heideggerian idea (*Sein zum Tode*) which Sartre contradicts so fiercely in "Le Mur." Mélanie refuses Sisyphus' stoic, stick-at-it option. Even if Camus enjoins us to imagine his hero, in his living death, happy, we are not invited to picture him splitting his sides.

To counter the quotations opening this study, I bring in Aldous Huxley: "Can you really say something about nothing?"[38] Tournier has done his damnedest to do so, by thinking against himself more than usual, against his own majority instincts. That he impersonates Mélanie so persuasively is a sign that he is a truly polymorphous-perverse writer, and that she represents a temptation, a Valéry-type "mauvaise pensée" for her creator, a reverse-thrust of his mental mechanism. The fact remains that Tournier still speaks for her *ennui*; he dictates it, to her and to readers. Apart from inability, this results from his view of what is "un conte": "Une nouvelle hantée. Hantée par une signification fantomatique qui nous touche, nous enrichit, mais ne nous éclaire pas" (*VV*, p. 40). As Davis suggests, "Tournier's texts engage the reader in the quest for understanding, but never arrive at a fully intelligible conclusion."[39] Like

Mélanie's essay, Tournier has made something out of nothing, Mélanie's desire to be nothing.

Notes

1. For multiple variants on the Adam/Eve topos, see J.-B. Vray, "La Question de l'origine," in *Images et signes de Michel Tournier*, edited by A. Bouloumié and M. de Gandillac (Paris, 1991), 58-62.

2. In 1992, British Methodists voted to make God, or at least the pronouns used to refer to the deity, of optional gender.

3. It is a comic writer, Aristophanes, on whom Plato fathers the myth in his *Symposium*. Aristophanes hiccups and sneezes before performing.

4. See Tournier's review of Jacob's *Le Jeu des possibles*, *Le Monde*, 8-9 November 1981, 7; and Jacob, "Evolution and Tinkering," *Science*, 196 (1977), 1164.

5. For a conspectus, see R. Le Senne, *Traité de caractérologie* (Paris, 1963).

6. V. Hugo, "La Conscience," *La Légende des siècles*.

7. H. D. Thoreau, *Walden* (New York, 1960) 211.

8. C. Baroche, "L'Eternel Retour à l'enfance," in *Images et signes de Michel Tournier*, 80.

9. C. Davis, *Michel Tournier: Philosophy and Fiction* (Oxford, 1988), 192.

10. G. Lichtenberg, *Aphorisms*, trans. R. J. Hollingdale (Harmondsworth, 1990), 45.

11. J. Swift, *A Tale of a Tub and other Satires*, edited by K. Williams (London, 1982), 45.

12. P. Larkin, "I remember, I remember," *Collected Poems* (London, 1988), 81-82.

13. W. H. Auden, "In Memory of W. B. Yeats," *W. H. Auden* (Harmondsworth, 1958), 67.

14. Tournier discusses this story, which he envies greatly, in *VP*, 50.

15. See his interview with G. Dumur, "Portrait d'un ogre," *Le Nouvel Observateur*, 30 November 1970, 46. See also *VLP*, 28, for Robinson's waiting for his shipmates' putrescent corpses to become clean cadavers before decently burying them.

16. Cf. *CS*, 186: "Etre jeune, c'est n'avoir perdu personne encore."

17. Cf. all the animated cartoons featuring ever more elaborate and frustrated attempts to kill someone.

18. Elizabeth Barrett Browning, "Aurora Leigh," *Aurora Leigh and other poems*, edited by C. Kaplan (London, 1978), 245.

19. The more "normal" aging Baron in "Le Coq de bruyère" wonders whether his last-fling sexual bliss will finish him off.

20. I had the short-lived idea that Mélanie's stockpiling of weapons of destruction referred to the world's arms race. This is an example of over-interpretation, which Tournier, who often exceeds elegant sufficiency, seems to encourage in his readers. Little else would warrant this reading, apart from the earlier allusion to the Cuban missile crisis. . . . A further example is significant/insignificant names. Is there any need to link Etienne's surname, Jonchet, with "jonchets," the game of spillikins, just because he delivers logs? The narrative frequently mentions "tranches" (lemon, bread), "le tranchant" of machines, "couleurs tranchantes" and "lames" (the "lamelles" of fungi). There is a dubious etymological link between the hybrid beast lamia and a gaping mouth, as in laughter. I have no wish to make an issue of any of this.

21. J. Starobinski, "Montaigne en mouvement (2)," *Nouvelle Revue Française.* 1 February 1960, 266. See *CS,* 171-75 re "la belle mort" and Tournier's wish to keep doctors and medicine at bargepole length.

22. P. Péju, *La Jeune Fille dans la forêt des contes* (Paris, 1981), 118.

23. The footnote to "JFM," 196, pointing out that Coquebin's quotation about children as "ces demi-fous que nous tolérons parmi nous" comes from Pauline Réage's *Histoire d'O,* a pornographic classic, hints that his spirit of enquiry is not altogether pure.

24. L. Wittgenstein, *Tractatus Logico-Philosophicus,* translated by D. F. Pears and B. F. McGuinness (London, 1969), 3.

25. Wittgenstein, quoted in N. Malcolm, *Ludwig Wittgenstein* (Oxford, 1958), 29.

26. Tournier, "Les Mots sous les mots," *Le Débat,* 33 (1985), 97-98.

27. A. Koestler, *The Act of Creation* (London, 1964), 47.

28. Tournier, "Erudition et dérision," *Le Monde,* 6 June 1975, 18.

29. Reversing the telescope, Tournier writes of a neighbor's crying baby: "Cette petite plainte grêle me touche et me rassure. C'est la protestation du néant auquel on vient d'infliger l'existence" (*VI,* 7).

30. Cf. Beckett (after Democritus): "Nothing is more real than nothing," *Malone Dies* (London, 1968), 16, and the addendum to *Watt:* "Nothingness in words enclose" (London, 1963), 247.

31. R. Queneau, *Loin de Rueil* (Paris, 1976), 142, 145.

32. S. Fertig's coinage, in *Une Ecriture encyclopoétique: Formation et transformation chez Raymond Queneau* (University Microfilms, 1983), 27, re the musings of Saturnin in *Le Chiendent* on "le non-nête."

33. A. Bierce, *The Enlarged Devil's Dictionary* (Harmondsworth, 1967), 152

34. F. Brégis, "Michel Tournier n'est pas un romancier," *Brèves,* 10 (1983), 71.

35. F. Nietzsche, *Thus Spake Zarathustra,* trans. by R. J. Hollingdale (Harmondsworth, 1971), 201.

36. Tournier "Les Voyages initiatiques," *La Nouvelle Critique,* 105 (1977), 106.

37. Ibid. Novalis' *Heinrich von Ofterdingen* is Tournier's choice of the purest model of initiation novel.

38. A. Huxley, *Brave New World* (London, 1965), 64.

39. C. Davis, *Michel Tournier,* 8.

Bibliography

I have restricted the bibliography to those items most directly relevant to *Le Coq de bruyère* (Paris: Gallimard [Folio], 1981).

Bouloumié, A. and M. de Gandillac, eds., *Images et signes de Michel Tournier* (Paris: Gallimard, 1991).

Davis, C. *Michel Tournier: Philosophy and Fiction* (Oxford: Clarendon, 1988).

Rachel Edwards (essay date 1998)

SOURCE: Edwards, Rachel. "Michel Tournier: 'Les Suaires de Véronique.'" In *Short French Fiction: Essays on the Short Story in France in the Twentieth Century,* edited by J. E. Flower, pp. 89-101. Exeter, United Kingdom: University of Exeter Press, 1998.

[*In the following essay, Edwards discusses the symbolic significance of "good" and "evil" photography in "Les Suaires de Véronique," citing allusions to ancient Christian and pagan texts.*]

Michel Tournier has produced two collections of short stories for an adult audience—*Le Coq de bruyère* (1978) and *Le Médianoche amoureux* (1989). However, many of the stories in these works have also been published for children, which allows Tournier to reach as wide an audience as possible and suggests the widespread appeal of his narratives. Indeed, he is as well known for his children's literature as he is for his adult fiction. In terms of their form, the two collections are quite different. The first consists of 13 unrelated narratives and one play,[1] whilst in the second the stories are framed by the meal of the title and the plight of a married couple, Nadège and Yves, who are about to separate but who become reconciled at the end having listened to the stories told by the guests. Both collections consist of a mixture of *contes* and *nouvelles,* although many of the stories would be more accurately described as a mixture of both.

In *Le Vol du vampire* Tournier draws the distinction between three different types of short story: the *nouvelle,* the *fable* and the *conte.*[2] He sees the *nouvelle* as being characterized by 'sa fidélité au réel' (p. 36); the *fable* is recognizable by its obvious message, whereas the *conte* is situated 'à mi-chemin de l'opacité brutale de la nouvelle et de la transparence cristalline de la fable' (p. 37). The *conte* is 'translucide mais non transparent, comme une épaisseur glauque dans laquelle le lecteur voit se dessiner des figures qu'il ne parvient jamais à saisir tout à fait' (p. 37). What is more, the 'conte est une nouvelle hantée. Hantée par une signification fantomatique qui nous touche, nous enrichit, mais ne nous éclaire pas' (p. 37). If we take this as a guide, then many of Tournier's stories fall somewhere between the *nouvelle* and the *conte.* Often set in contemporary time with clearly recognizable places and characters, they nevertheless go beyond what is truly credible in a *nouvelle.* Michel Mansuy has perhaps found the best definition for stories like this when he refers to those in *Le Coq de bruyère* as 'contes d'enfants pour adultes'.[3] Like all *contes* they clothe in symbolic terms essential issues which concern us all and with which we are wittingly or unwittingly preoccupied throughout our lives. They also explore, on a smaller scale, those issues with which Tournier is concerned in his novels as a whole.

One of the reasons for choosing to write about **'Les Suaires de Véronique'**[4] is that the short story highlights many of Tournier's preoccupations, not least his obsession with photography which is often ambivalent in nature: on the one hand, he is fascinated by photography and the image in general, on the other, there is a genuine fear of taking pictures and of the resulting image, the latter often being seen as a malevolent force to be reckoned with. Indeed, Tournier's fiction often concentrates on the triumph of the sign (in terms of the written word) over the image, the most developed example of this being found in his exploration of photography in the novel *La Goutte d'or,* which, Tournier admitted when he was a guest on Pivot's *Apostrophes* in 1992, could have been called 'La Photographie'. Furthermore, **'Les Suaires de Véronique'**, like much of Tournier's fiction, highlights his preoccupation with rewriting. From the title we immediately recognize St Veronica who wiped Christ's face with a kerchief or veil upon which His image became miraculously im-

printed. In *Le Crépuscule des masques* Tournier points to the meaning of the name Véronique: 'Le nom de cette femme pieuse de Jérusalem veut dire: *image vraie.* Véronique a essuyé avec son voile le visage ruisselant de sang, de larmes et de sueur du Sauveur. Et le miracle s'est produit: le visage de Jésus imprima son image sur le voile de Véronique'.[5]

Véronique is therefore heralded by Tournier as the inventor of photography (this being all the more striking given the fact that she is a woman). However, in substituting 'voile' for 'suaire' in the title of his story, Tournier also refers us to the Shroud of Turin which is said to be the cloth in which Christ's body was wrapped when he was taken from the cross and which bears the image of His crucified body. (At the time of publication of **'Les Suaires de Véronique'** the mystery of the shroud was still intact given that it was not until 1988 that the cloth was proven to have been made somewhere between 1260 and 1390.) Calvin, in his *Traité des reliques,* of which Tournier is more than likely aware, considers, in the same passage, both Veronica's cloth and the various shrouds in which Christ's body was supposedly wrapped. Of the latter there were said to be at least six, accounting perhaps for the plural in Tournier's title. What is also worthy of note is that in the ancient scriptures the word 'suaire' meant 'un mouchoir, ou couvrechef', and not 'un grand linceul qui serve à envelopper le corps',[6] which justifies Véronique's cloth being referred to as a 'suaire' in Calvin's text. The old meaning of 'suaire' and its modern sense both come together in Tournier's title. Right from the outset, therefore, we know that Tournier intends to use the story of Veronica for his own purposes (just as the title of *Vendredi ou les limbes du Pacifique* prepares us for a different type of Robinson Crusoe story). It is also clear from the beginning that photography and death are closely allied.

Tournier is not only using ancient texts as intertexts for this story but he also adapts elements from his own fiction—most notably from *Le Roi des aulnes* (1970) in which the main character, Abel Tiffauges, is an ogre who hunts down children and shoots them with his camera. In fictional terms Dunblane[7] had already taken place in this novel when Tiffauges takes pictures of schoolchildren through the railings of the playground fence and shoots them down as easily as if they were animals in a cage at the zoo. Véronique is also established as an ogre-figure who systematically destroys her prey with an 'amour dévorant' which clearly mirrors Tiffauges's love of the children whom he photographs. Tournier is also playing with traditional gender roles here; the domain of the predatory ogre is no longer solely that of the male.

The process of borrowing, or even of copying, as it appears in Tournier's work (he has announced in an article: 'Je copie et j'en suis fier'),[8] can be likened to what Lévi-Strauss refers to as *bricolage* when he examines the way in which myths are constructed in primitive societies.[9] In intertextual terms, and for our purposes, odds and ends are pasted together from previous texts in order to construct a new version of a narrative. Roberts has coined the term 'autobricolage' when referring to Tournier's use of his own works in such a way.[10] Other examples of 'autobricolage' will become apparent when we look at **'Les Suaires de Véronique'** in more detail.

Although clearly written for adults, **'Les Suaires de Véronique'** it has much in common with children's *contes*. It aims to awaken primary fears within us and does so by using symbolic language. The epigraph at the beginning of **Le Coq de bruyère,** by Lanza del Vasto, makes this quite clear: 'Au fond de chaque chose, un poisson nage / Poisson de peur que tu n'en sortes nu / Je te jetterai mon manteau d'images' (p. 7). The 'manteau d'images' in **'Les Suaires de Véronique'** clothes basic unconscious fears which make up part of our collective and individual psyche. It draws on primeval fears of being eaten alive or swallowed up in both literal and figurative terms. In the story, these fears find their concretization in the tiger's tooth which is initially seen around Hector's neck and last perceived around Véronique's. On the one hand, Hector is devoured by this ogress-cum-tigress, referring us back to primitive fears relevant at the beginning of our collective history; on the other, he has been swallowed up by this woman who steals the tooth, making her, as Redfern would have it, a kind of symbolic 'vagina dentata' which equally awakens unconscious fears within us.[11]

Photography itself seems to kindle similarly irrational fears. Many peoples, especially in parts of China and Africa, believe that being photographed is tantamount to having one's soul stolen. Balzac dreaded having his photograph taken believing that he lost a layer of himself each time. Debray has termed this fear 'le complexe de l'oignon'.[12] In *Le Roi des aulnes* Tiffauges asserts that 'quiconque craint d'être "pris" en photographie fait preuve du plus élémentaire bon sens',[13] and Tournier points to the fact that there are very few self-portraits in photography, unlike painting, probably because people do not want to do to themselves that which they take great pleasure in doing to others. Tournier, however, has braved his own camera as his self-portrait in *Des Clefs et des serrures* indicates. It provides a striking contrast to Debray's favourite picture of himself in *L'Oeil naïf,* which is simply a blank page with a rectangle drawn on it to imitate the frame. Fear of being photographed therefore presents itself as a modern manifestation of the primary fears of being eaten up, swallowed or devoured.

There is also an initiatory aspect to the *conte*: initiation rites all follow a similar pattern—that of a preparatory period, followed by either a symbolic death or a return to the womb, and finally a rebirth. In 'Les Suaires de Véronique', Hector is firstly seduced by Véronique, then returns to a symbolic womb in the house in the Camargue and is finally reborn as the main exhibit in Véronique's exhibition. Most of Tournier's narratives do indeed deal with some aspect of initiation.[14] For example, Crusoé is initiated into a new way of life by Vendredi in *Vendredi ou les limbes du Pacifique*. Likewise, Tiffauges undertakes an initiatory voyage in *Le Roi des aulnes* as does Paul in *Les Météores*.

It is bearing all the above factors in mind that we can now consider **'Les Suaires de Véronique'** in some detail. When we initially start reading the story we seem to be situated in the realms of the *nouvelle* rather than the *conte*. The setting is a realistic one—we are in Arles at the Rencontres Internationales de Photographie, which Tournier himself founded. The place is littered with well-known photographers, amongst them 'Ansel Adams et Ernst Haas, Jacques Lartigues et Fulvio Foitier, Robert Doisneau et Arthur Tress, Eva Rubinstein et Gisèle Freund' (p. 153) to name some of them, and we could indeed be reading the *nouvelles*. When we turn the page we realize that the narrative is being written in the first person which seems to lend added authenticity to what is being recounted.[15] However, it is also now that we are paradoxically entering the world of the *conte* where we meet Hector and Véronique, who are simply referred to by their first names unlike the famous photographers who are given both a first name and a surname. They do not need surnames—we know who they are, for they come straight out of our literary and cultural tradition: Veronica wiped the face of Christ and Hector is one of the heroes of the *Iliad,* son of Priam and husband of Andromache, who is eventually killed by Achilles and whose body is then dragged around the walls of Troy. It is this which casts the spell of the *conte* over the narrative. Furthermore, if we suppose that the narrator is actually Tournier—there is no reason why it should not be, given his passion for and involvement with photography—then this would explain why we are plunged into a world which is bordering on the fantastic.

In encountering Hector and Véronique we come across the first of many dichotomies which are inherent in the text: that between Ancient Greece, on the one hand, and the Christian tradition, on the other. Further dualities which arise as a direct consequence of Hector and Véronique are Nature versus Culture, Antiquity versus the Renaissance, 'le pris-sur-le-vif' versus 'le pris-sur-la-mort', and eventually life and death. The setting up of various dichotomies is very important in Tournier's fiction and this is one of the reasons why it is considered to be mythological in nature. Lévi-Strauss, whose courses Tournier followed at the Sorbonne, sees myth as an attempt to resolve certain cultural contradictions. It is precisely the resolution of such opposites that comes about at the end of this story, as we shall see.

The first meeting with Hector and Véronique occurs in the Camargue where the narrator has gone with a group of people to take 'des photos de nu' (p. 154). What is immediately apparent from the outset of the session is that the narrator only notices the model, Hector, as he moves across the landscape assuming different postures. His nudity is described as 'superbe et généreuse' and he is endowed with 'chair splendide' (p. 154). He resembles a Greek god and we remember also that the ancient Greeks worshiped male as opposed to female beauty. On the other hand, he is like an animal—he has a 'front de taurillon' and we are told that he 'jouait pleinement de son animalité naturelle'. He is therefore reminiscent of 'le premier homme', from what Lévi-Strauss terms 'le temps mythique', a time when human beings, animals and gods were indistinguishable. He is at home in the essentially female elements of a mixture of land and sea, and gender distinctions are blurred in that he is like a type of Venus rising out of the waters.

Véronique provides a sharp contrast. She is 'une petite femme mince et vive' (pp. 154-5), which reads pejoratively beside Hector's 'chair splendide'. However, she is endowed with something which is clearly missing from the narrator's description of Hector: 'l'intelligence'. In what is a surprising reversal of stereotypical gender roles, Véronique can be seen in terms of mind to Hector's body. Hector is the body-object, traditionally a female role, whilst Véronique is one of the people exploiting this object, traditionally therefore in the male role. She is also armed with a surrogate penis—her camera and lenses—which she uses to exploit Hector. The camera as penis and as an instrument of violation is also explored in *Le Roi des aulnes* in which Tiffauges travels around with his camera between his thighs.

Véronique is in a bad mood and as such she seems to be a negative version, or as Robert's asserts, an 'inversion maligne', of her namesake. Hector is also the exact opposite of Christ. Whereas Christ is weak and suffering, carrying the burden of the cross when he meets Veronica, Hector is the picture of health and has no burdens. The only thing he carries or wears (*porter*) is a tiger's tooth on a leather thong around his neck, which simply adds to his nudity. And in this, too, he is diametrically opposed to Véronique who travels encumbered with all sorts of photographic paraphernalia. A further duality is therefore set up between Hector/Nature and Véronique/Culture.

Véronique is concerned with the fabricated rather than the given, which is made clear by her condemnation of the initial photographic session, its setting and Hector.

The only joy she managed to get from the session was in using a wide-angled lens which enabled her to distort his body: 'Pour peu qu'Hector tende la main vers l'objectif, il aura une main géante avec derrière un petit corps et une tête de moineau. Amusant' (p. 155). He is therefore reduced in stature: from being 'lourdement musclé'; with 'un front de taurillon' he becomes 'un petit corps' with 'une tête de moineau'. He is already a diminutive figure for Véronique, and her admission rings out ominously: 'On aimerait en faire quelque chose. Seulement, ça demanderait du travail. Du travail et des sacrifices . . .' (p. 155). But on whose part one wonders? Redfern pertinently points out that *travail* also means ordeal and comes from the Latin *tripalium* meaning an instrument of torture (p. 63). This is exactly what the physical-training equipment used to get Hector into shape becomes.

It is here for the first time that the opposites of good photography and evil photography come into being. This is, indeed, unusual in Tournier's fiction where photography is usually solely aligned with malignant forces. In this narrative, good photography does not harm its victim, it is, as Hector calls it, 'pas sérieuse'; in contrast, evil photography, or that which is 'sérieuse', is harmful. This is further explored in the rest of the narrative.

The first stage of the story ends with the narrator, and hence the reader, overhearing Hector tell Véronique about the tiger's tooth which is hanging around his neck: it is a charm which is supposed to keep him from being devoured by tigers. Significantly, this is the one and only time that we actually hear Hector speak. At this point, therefore, he still has a voice of his own. But in telling Véronique about his tiger's tooth, Hector, as Françoise Kaye points out, is like Sampson revealing the secret of his strength to Delilah.[16] Véronique's seduction of Hector has therefore been successful and the first part of his initiation has begun.

The second stage of the narrative begins the following summer, again at the Rencontres Internationales de Photographie. Whilst Véronique is 'inchangée', Hector is 'méconnaissable'. We are told: 'De sa patauderie un peu enfantine, de sa jactance de bel animal, de son épanouissement optimiste et solaire, il ne restait rien' (p. 156). Ironically, he has become more like Véronique: he has grown much thinner and has acquired her feverish energy. Later we realize why. The narrator is invited to the house which Véronique is renting in the Camargue, a house which blends in so well with its surroundings that it remains camouflaged to the point of being undetectable until one is almost upon it. This, added to the fact that behind closed doors anything but the natural life-style suggested by the exterior is taking place, lends sinister overtones to the narrative. One is reminded of the concentration camps which were kept out of sight or, when visible, masqueraded as work-camps rather than death-camps.

In this farmhouse Véronique is hatching Hector in 'une coquille d'œuf' (p. 164). The description of the room in which he is sleeping is like that of a womb. Its milky whiteness recalls the womb/tomb cave into which Crusoé slips in *Vendredi ou les limbes du Pacifique* and from which he eventually emerges like a newborn infant. The second phase of Hector's initiation is clearly underway here in this symbolic womb. However, Véronique is not just a simple matrix. She challenges the idea of the non-biological creative process being essentially a male domain, for she is the creator/artist. But her only means of creation is through destruction: Hector, rather than assuming the foetal position, is 'écrasé à plat ventre' in this womb-cum-tomb (p. 164). Paradoxically, it is also the case that in order to become, in photographic terms, more than he was, Hector has to become less than he is. This is a typical instance of Tournierian logic which is particularly evident in *Le Roi des aulnes* where it often seems that less becomes more and more becomes less.

Despite the somewhat sinister ambience of the farmhouse, the narrator has to admit that Hector has indeed become a 'beau spectacle' (p. 164). But the 'beau spectacle' has come about by the fact that Culture has worked on Nature. If Hector was 'le premier homme', Véronique is playing God, indeed more than God: not only is she creating man in her image (he has become like her) but she is transforming him beyond her image. The copy is becoming not a mere reflection of the original, but a superior creation. This is something which is also reflected in Véronique's musing on what it means to be 'beau' rather that 'photogénique'. Hector began as the former and is now the latter: from a natural being ('beau') he has been transformed into a cultural artefact ('photogénique'). Whereas his photographs were once inferior copies of himself, they are now superior. The idea of the copy being the original's superior is also a theme which is common in Tournier's work, the most striking discussion of this taking place in *Les Météores.*[17]

The natural as opposed to the created is further explored through the idea of the two schools of photography: that which practises 'le pris-sur-le-vif' as opposed to 'la nature morte' (p. 160). Tournier plays with the meanings here and inverts the terms. The narrator comments: 'J'ai presque envie de jouer sur ces mots et de dire: d'un côté la nature vive, de l'autre le pris-sur-le-mort' (p. 161). 'La nature vive' is allied to the type of photography in the initial photo session. It is synonymous with the study of the human anatomy as undertaken by the likes of Praxiteles in antiquity. Antiquity here stands in contrast to the Renaissance, which saw the birth of anatomy and which is described as 'l'ère du morbide' (p. 162), when Vesalius, in his quest for

knowledge, began dissecting bodies both dead and alive. The dissection and vivisection undertaken during this era is synonymous in the *conte* with Véronique cutting up Hector with her photography. Photography literally means writing with light, and there is a sense in which Véronique's use of light acts upon Hector's body like a laser. Whereas before we are told that 'la lumière glissait sans accrocher ni jouer' on Hector's body (p. 158), now we see that his body, 'découpé par les ombres et les plages de lumière d'une source lumineuse unique et violente, paraît figé, fouillé jusqu'à l'os, disséqué comme par un simulacre d'autopsie ou de démonstration anatomique' (p. 160). This gives new meaning to Valéry's words: 'La vérité est nue, mais sous le nu il y a l'écorché' (p. 160). Metaphor becomes concrete. She is literally beginning to flay him alive.

Writing on the body here strongly evokes Kafka's 'In the Penal Settlement' in which prisoners have the lessons to be learnt from their crimes written on their bodies by the harrow, a torture machine made up of tiny needles. The salutary statement is inscribed into their skin at an ever-increasing depth until death occurs after twelve hours by which time the prisoner has fully understood his crime. Enlightenment, however, occurs around the sixth hour which is the turning-point for the prisoner. He now has no more strength and waits to die. For Hector, enlightenment seems to come just prior to his writing the letter to Véronique. He has the strength to escape, but he is caught again, and as surely as the prisoners in Kafka's tale, he too succumbs to his fate. More recently, in his film *The Pillow Book*, Peter Greenaway has explored the erotic side to writing on the body. In Tournier's story, torture and eroticism come together in Véronique's treatment of Hector.

The textualization of the body is also relevant in the discussion that Véronique and the narrator have about the 'nu' and the importance of the 'visage'. Véronique asserts that the face is the key to the body: 'Le visage est le chiffre du corps. Je veux dire: le corps même traduit dans un autre système de signes. Et en même temps, la clé du corps' (p. 159). She complains that many photographs are spoilt by a face that is out of harmony with the body. Lucien Clergue has solved this problem 'en coupant la tête de ses nus' which is referred to as 'un procédé radical' (p. 158). According to Véronique, this only works for women and not for men. Men must keep their heads because 'l'homme sans tête devient indéchiffrable' (p. 159). Men emerge as essentially mind, whereas women are essentially body: 'La statue de la femme s'épanouit d'autant plus dans sa plénitude charnelle qu'elle a perdu la tête' (p. 159). The man/mind, woman/body dichotomy is a typical theme in Tournier's writing and one is reminded of the island Spermanza in *Vendredi ou les limbes du Pacifique* which is described as looking like 'un corps féminin sans tête'.[18] The idea that woman is in essence a body reveals a certain misogyny on the part of Tournier which is recurrent throughout his work. It is ironic, however, that in this story it is Hector who loses not only his head but also his entire body, and in this way Tournier is characteristically able to avoid being pinned down as a total misogynist. Paradoxically, therefore, for every example of misogyny in his work there seem to be others which prove just the opposite.

In this particular story, Tournier also redeems himself somewhat by the fact that he is the inventor of the 'portrait nu'. The anecdote surrounding this invention is recounted in *Des Clefs et des serrures* and is worth briefly repeating here. He tells us of a nineteen-year-old female student who was preparing a maîtrise on the ogre and who visited his home in order to interview him. She was impressed by all his photographs and agreed to let Tournier take her picture. He then set up his equipment whilst she prepared herself in the next room. When she reappeared she was 'nue comme Eve au Paradis'.[19] Tournier continues: 'En disant "photo", j'avais pensé "portrait". Elle avait compris "nu". Mais il y avait une autre surprise: ce corps n'était pas—tant s'en faut—celui qu'annonçait son visage: un corps plein de douceurs et de rondeurs, avenant, presque douillet, aussi féminin que possible.' (pp. 112-13). Her face on the contrary was 'aigu, presque coupant, sommaire, trop grave' (p. 111). Tournier, however, adhered to his original project and simply photographed her face. The result was that the body became reflected in the face. He comments: 'Il s'agit d'une sorte de rayonnement venu d'en bas, d'une émanation corporelle agissant comme une sorte de filtre, comme si la chair dénudée faisait monter vers le visage une buée de chaleur et de couleur' (p. 114). In a sense, Tournier's procedure is no less radical than Lucien Clergue's in that he cuts off the body from the head, rather than the inverse. In preserving the head rather than the body he cannot be accused of treating the student as a simple body-object.

Hector, on the other hand, up until this point in the narrative has been merely seen in terms of a body-object. When he is encountered as a thinking subject it is, interestingly enough, not through his images but in a letter which he writes to Véronique when he leaves her. The letter gives us an insight into Hector's mind and his feelings for the first time. Three days after his visit to the farmhouse, the narrator finds Véronique in an insalubrious bar drowning her sorrows because Hector has left her. His disappearance recalls Christ vanishing from the tomb and, indeed, Hector is not seen in the same form by the narrator or the reader again. In his letter we are shown that Hector can indeed think and is not merely a body. This is largely thanks to Véronique, for as Hector says: 'La photographie sérieuse instaure un échange perpétuel entre le modèle et le photographe. Il y a un système de vases communicants. Je vous dois beaucoup, Véronique chérie. Vous avez fait de moi un

autre homme' (p. 165). We remember that the aim of all types of initiation is to enable one to 'devenir autre'. From a rustic person at one with nature, Hector has become a thinking being whose spiritual side is mirrored in the fact that he can now write with elegance and grace. In return, Hector has given Véronique his body, or rather she has taken it from him. As he says: 'Vous m'avez aussi beaucoup pris. Vingt-deux mille deux cent trent-neuf fois quelque chose de moi m'a été arraché pour entrer dans le piège à images, votre "petite boîte de nuit" (*camera obscura*), comme vous dites' (pp. 165-6). He goes on: 'Vous m'avez plumé comme une poule, épilé comme un lapin angora' (p. 166). She deals with him as easily as if she were plucking a chicken or skinning a rabbit. Gone is the image of the bull. The two animals referred to here are domestic and therefore easy prey for Véronique, the tigress. She has sucked him dry like a vampire and he has become an insect in her collection. But for the moment Hector is safe and we realize why from his postscript: 'J'ai repris ma dent' (p. 166).

The next time the narrator hears of the couple, he is in Paris where he chances upon a friend, Chériau, who tells him that Véronique 'a retrouvé et repris' Hector and that she has begun experimenting with a series of 'photographies directes'. This entails preparing the photographic paper, putting Hector into a bath full of chemicals and then making him lie on the paper in different positions. Following this, all that remains to be done is to rinse the paper in an acid solution and 'envoyer le modèle à la douche' (p. 169). This final statement recalls the Jews being sent to the showers by the Nazis. What is more: 'Il résulte de tout cela d'étranges silhouettes écrasées, une projection plane du corps d'Hector, assez semblables, dit Véronique textuellement, à ce qui restait sur certains murs d'Hiroshima des Japonais foudroyés et désintégrés par la bombe atomique' (p. 169). Véronique has become the personification of evil in that her experiments combine the two ultimate atrocities of the Second World War: the genocide of the Jews and the destruction of Hiroshima. One is also reminded of Hector's fate in the *Iliad* where he is dragged around the walls of Troy. Dermography has now clearly replaced photography. Hector's body is no longer being textualized, it has become the text.

The narrator's final encounter with Véronique occurs later that year at the Rencontres Internationales de Photographie, at her exhibition entitled **'Les Suaires de Véronique'**. He explains: 'Partout, en haut, en bas, à droite, à gauche, le regard s'écrasait sur le spectre noir et doré d'un corps aplati, élargi, roulé, déroulé, reproduit en frise funèbre et obsédante dans toutes les positions. On songeait à une série de peaux humaines arrachées, puis étalées là comme autant de trophées barbares' (p. 171). One is instantly reminded again of Nazi experiments and the trophies which were made out of the human body. This scene also recalls *Le Roi des aulnes* and the Nazi doctor Blättchen's experiments on the children of the Napola, as well as Göring's emasculation of the stags and his subsequent displaying of their antlers. What also clearly comes to mind are Tiffauges's experiments with the negatives of photographs of children which he projects through an enlarger in his dark room.

As far as Hector is concerned, Véronique has indeed ended up by having 'sa peau'. Metaphor has indeed become concrete as is so often the case in Tournier's fiction. Hector's initiation is now over. He has become like Christ: all that is left of him is the image of his body on the shrouds.

Véronique is able to get away with what she has done because she has become an exhibitor at the Rencontres Internationales. She is up there now with the rest of the great photographers. She has found a way to avoid being punished and we recall what she says to the narrator when he tells her that during the Renaissance she would have been burnt at the stake: 'Il y avait alors un moyen bien simple de baigner dans la sorcellerie sans courir aucun risque . . . En faisant partie du tribunal de la Sainte Inquisition!' (p. 163). She, too, like the great names in the beginning, now forms part of the 'Gotha de la photographie' and is therefore safe.

The ending of the story succeeds in resolving certain contradictions which arise throughout the narrative. Ancient Greece and the Christian tradition come together in the Hector/Christ figure represented on Véronique's shrouds. Nature and Culture also merge in the 'suaires' in that they are fabricated using the human body. Body and soul become one in that Hector is both present and absent; he is there and yet elsewhere. Finally, life and death, creation and destruction are cancelled out: in creating/killing off Hector, Véronique has succeeded in destroying/preserving him for all time.

Notes

1. *Le Coq de bruyère* simply takes its title from the longest story in the collection. Whilst the narratives are not directly connected to each other some critics do consider them to be organized according to certain themes. See, for example, David Gascoigne's *Michel Tournier* (Oxford: Berg, 1996) pp. 20-1. Susan Petit, in her *Michel Tournier's Metaphysical Fictions* (Amsterdam: John Benjamins, 1991) pp. 101-9, has gone one step further and sees the first seven narratives as being emblematic of the seven cardinal virtues and the last seven as representing the seven deadly sins.

2. See the chapter entitled '*Barbe-Bleue* ou le secret du conte', in Michel Tournier, *Le Vol du vampire* (Paris: Mercure de France, 1981). Further references to this work will be included in the text where possible.

3. Michel Mansuy, 'Trois chercheurs de paradis: Bosco, Tournier, Cayrol', *Travaux de linguistique et de littérature*, XVI, 2 (1978), p. 211.

4. 'Les Suaires de Véronique' in *Le Coq de bruyère* (Paris: Folio, 1978). Further references are to this edition and will be parenthetically included in the text.

5. Michel Tournier, *Le Crépuscule des masques* (Paris: Editions Hoëbeke, 1992), p. 171.

6. Jean Calvin, *Traité des reliques*, in *Three French Treaties*, ed Francis M. Higman (London: The Athlone Press, 1970), p. 68.

7. In March 1996 Thomas Hamilton opened fire on a group of four- and five-year-olds in a primary school in Dunblane, Scotland. Sixteen children and their teacher were killed. Tiffauges's actions here seem like a macabre premonition of this event.

8. Michel Tournier, 'Je copie, et j'en suis fier!', *Femme* (mai, 1990).

9. For Lévi-Strauss's analysis of myth in terms of *bricolage* see his *La Pensée Sauvage* (Paris: Plon, 1962).

10. Martin Roberts in *Michel Tournier: Bricolage and Cultural Mythology*, Stanford French and Italian Studies, 79 (Saratoga, CA: Anma Libri, 1994), p. 99. Further references to Roberts are to this work and will be included in the text.

11. Walter Redfern, *Michel Tournier: Le Coq de bruyère* (Madison, NJ: Fairleigh Dickinson University Press; London and Toronto: Associated University Presses, 1996), p. 70. Further references to Redfern are to this work and will be included in the text where possible.

12. Régis Debray, *L'Œil naïf* (Paris: Editions du Seuil, 1994), p. 141.

13. Michel Tournier, *Le Roi des aulnes* (Paris: Folio, 1970), p. 167. Further references to this novel will be parenthetically included in the text.

14. Two of the best examples of initiation are found in *Le Coq de bruyère* in the stories of 'Tupik' and 'Amandine ou les deux jardins'. For a detailed examination of initiation in the latter see Rachel Edwards, 'Initiation and Menstruation: Michel Tournier's "Amandine ou les deux jardins"', in *Essays in French Literature*, no 27 (November, 1990), pp. 75-90.

15. For an analysis of the role of the narrator, see Nicole Bourbonnais, '"Les Suaires de Véronique": présences du narrateur', in *Incidences: analyse plurielle: 'Les Suaires de Véronique' de Michel Tournier*, 2-3 (1979), pp. 51-74.

16. Françoise Kaye, 'Ce petit Hector, on aimerait en faire quelque chose', in *Incidences: analyse pluri-elle: 'Les Suaires de Véronique' de Michel Tournier,* 2-3 (1979), p. 26.

17. See especially Alexandre's 'Esthétique du dandy des gadoues' in Michel Tournier *Les Métréores* (Paris: Folio, 1975), pp. 101-3.

18. Michel Tournier, *Vendredi ou les limbes du Paci-fique* (Paris: Folio, 1972), p. 46.

19. Michel Tournier, *Des Clefs et des serrures: im-ages et proses* (Paris: Chêne, Hachette, 1979), p. 112. Further references to this work will be paren-thetically included in the text.

David Platten (essay date 1999)

SOURCE: Platten, David. "The Empire of the Child." In *Michel Tournier and the Metaphor of Fiction,* pp. 185-202. New York: St. Martin's Press, 1999.

[*In the following excerpt, Platten examines the recon-ciliation of opposites in* Pierrot ou les secrets de la nuit.]

Jorge Luis Borges, arguably the most famous, latter-day exponent of the short story, has refined a genre which now, more often than not, tells of its own coming-into-being. In **'Pyrotechnie'** [**"Pyrotechnie ou la commém-oration"**] the self-conscious character of the short story is privileged, but in terms which are softly caricatured. The narrator is a Parisian writer, who has been exiled on the command of an impatient publisher to the small town of Monteux, near Carpentras, in order to get on with his next book away from the bright lights of the big city. He already has a provisional title for it ('Elle se mange froide'), a situation (the closed provincial community), and the genesis of a plot (a classic tale of revenge in which suspense will be created by the char-acters' expectancy of the retributive act). At the end of **'Pyrotechnie'** he duly starts writing, 'cette histoire de vengeance étirée sur toute une vie dans le cadre d'une petite ville de province où tout se sait' (*MA* [*Le Médi-anoche amoureux*], 96). This self-reflexivity clearly circumscribes the text but its function is *not* to annihi-late (gradually) the possibility of thematic interpreta-tions, as it would be in a Borgesian narrative. Tournier is interested in the material fact of writing, in the reality of the writer's life. It is no accident therefore that in **'Pyrotechnie'** his narrator is bothered about relations with his publisher. Will he be able sufficiently to dress up the 'mince canevas' of his story so as not to jeopar-dise his advance? Thus, the narrative flows *à rebours,* from the act of writing back into the world of the writer. What starts out as a self-conscious narrative becomes

less rather than more conscious of itself. Moreover, the fiction is seemingly authenticated as the narrator is him-self embroiled in the process of learning.

Familiar Tournier themes are prevalent in the early sec-tions of the text. The proposed subject-matter for the narrator's book is, of course, a wink in the direction of Maupassant. Care should be taken, however, not to mis-interpret the comic touch of the prospective title. Tourni-er's narrator emphasises a need to recreate the 'eyes everywhere' community that typifies the gritty realism of Maupassant's short stories by reiterating the fact that the vendetta should be public knowledge: 'de notoriété publique. Tout le monde le savait. Tout le monde attendait' (*MA,* 97). At this early stage his romanesque musings are already assuming an urgency that tran-scends the supposed fictional medium. This expository setting of the scene is significant. Tournier knows that the effects of any given crime are maximised when the crime occurs within a sedentary society; the people of Monteux are described as 'des sédentaires absolus' (*MA,* 96). Now the distinction between sedentary and no-madic peoples is a key dialectic in Tournier's thinking. The biblical story of Cain and Abel is the prototype for a dozen other narratives, including the portrayal of the outcast, Abel Tiffauges, in *Le Roi des aulnes,* the gradual dissolution of the 'cellule gémellaire' in *Les Météores,* and Idriss's quest in *La Goutte d'or.* Reifying this fundamental myth in **'Pyrotechnie'**, Tournier takes a leaf out of Balzac's *modus operandi.* Consider the way in which the explosion at the factory is described.

Tournier handles the description of this one big event with a typical flourish. The narrator is busy thinking socio-cultural thoughts at the local *boulodrome,* as the final player of the group prepares to launch his one re-maining projectile, intended to disperse the cluster around the *cochonnet* in all directions. At the precise moment of impact there is a thunderous noise, and the scattering of the boules is reproduced in macrocosm by the sight of 'un feu d'artifice, mais chaotique' (*MA,* 106), illuminating the sky. Seconds later people are run-ning towards the factory. Accustomed to the sequential configurations of pyrotechnics, the townsfolk react in-stinctively to the psychedelic orderlessness above their heads. This account, however, is written some time af-ter the event. As an outsider ignorant of the possible consequences of the explosion, the narrator cannot react in the same way as the townsfolk. While everyone else dashes about, he can only watch, and would only have made sense of what he had seen at a later time. Balzac, who saw his art as the ability to achieve the coinci-dence of 'l'observation' and 'l'expression', is a singular inspiration. Tournier's narrator is there, with the people at the *boulodrome,* yet able to stand back at the vital moment.

If there is some doubt as to whether Tournier is angling for a Balzacian acuity of observation in his depiction of the reactions of the Monteux townspeople, then we ought perhaps to revert to that traditional stamping-ground of realist writing, namely characterisation, in this case the characterisation of the factory-manager:

> M. Capolini m'accueillit avec l'empressement d'un professionnel flatté qu'un ignorant de marque vienne de Paris s'instruire auprès de lui. Au demeurant il parlait si bien et si brillamment des feux d'artifice qu'il paraissait par moments devenir lui-même un feu d'artifice. J'ai rencontré plus d'une fois cette sorte de contamination totale d'un homme par sa profession, charcutière sculptée dans du saindoux, paysan pétri de terre et de fumier, banquier semblable à un coffre-fort, cavalier au rire henissant. Les mains de Capolini devenaient à tout moment fusées, bouquets, fontaines de feu ou soleils tournoyants. Ses yeux paraissaient sans cesse éblouis par quelque déploiement féerique.

> (*MA,* 99-100)

This kind of picture-portrait is reminiscent of the way in which Balzac tended to stigmatise his characters. The personification of spinsterhood through the character of Sophie Gamard in *Le Curé de Tours* shows how such blanket representations may be construed as prejudicial. Meticulously observed details of her physical appearance are conjugated so as to support Balzac's one overriding contention, that 'en restant fille, une créature du sexe féminin n'est plus qu'un non-sens: égoïste et froide, elle fait horreur'.[1] And, in describing the effect of this condition on Sophie Gamard, he pulls no punches, hinting that the dark rings under her eyes betray long hours of masturbatory activity, 'accusait les longs combats de sa vie solitaire'.[2] Balzac's discourse establishes a causal link between spinsterhood and sexual frustration; Sophie's petty attitudes and spiteful behaviour are explained by the lack of a good man in her life! Although the description of M. Capolini shows Tournier indulging his Balzacian tendencies, here it is more a case of playful stereotyping; one is reminded of the oft-heard remark about dog-owners coming with time to look more and more like their four-legged friends. However it has a very different, underlying purpose. The effect is impressionistic. Each dash of paint—the lardy butcher, the earthy peasant, the impassable banker, the laughing cavalier, not forgetting the effusive M. Capolini—imparts the sort of crisp definition which is necessary to bring characters to life in children's fiction. Moreover, Tournier puts his reader in contact with the symbolic functioning of the human mind, highlighting in this instance the figure of metonymy. The rich symbolism of the firework, through its metonymic definition of M. Capolini, comes to displace the character. M. Capolini's verbal dexterity is such that the symbol quickly eclipses the human actor.

Initially the firework signifies the intrusion of the fantastic, the irruption of the *conte* within the *nouvelle*. On the night of his arrival in Monteux the narrator witnesses from the window of his lodgings a marvellous firework display. Spectacular but odd, for he cannot understand why anyone should want to commemorate 25 July, St Anne's Day. He soon discovers that it was merely a routine product-testing operation. However, his curiosity is aroused by this 'manufacture pittoresque', and even more so by the fact that a firework display, usually symbolic of important historical or political events, should form part of the daily routine, that it should not interrupt for a second the rhythm of the townspeople's lives. This lovely equation of the 'plus beau feu d'artifice' with ordinary life teases out a modest philosophical reflection on the nature of the phenomenon. Tournier shows through the reaction of his narrator how human perception and understanding of reality is conditional on factors of culture and environment, and therefore on the mythologies of specific cultures. The effect in **'Pyrotechnie'** is to undermine the stable, symbolic value of the firework, its commemorative function. The narrator's experience of the staged firework display that commemorates nothing will turn out to be a prophesy. The next display witnessed turns out to be a tragic accident which *is* commemorative.

'Pyrotechnie' is the story of the narrator's investigation of the accident at the factory in which two men are killed. He is able to confirm that the incident was a case of simultaneous murder and suicide. The victim, Gilles, had an heroic reputation that dated back to the Resistance; the perpetrator of the deed, a young boy at the time of the war, held Gilles responsible for the public humiliation of his mother during the *épuration*. The explosion at the factory is eventually explained as the culmination of a vendetta which had been pursued commemoratively, the last in a series of unfortunate accidents that had befallen Gilles, usually on 11 August of any given calendar year. The key figure in the narrator's research is a retired journalist, 'un maniaque de la documentation' (*MA,* 114), for whom modern-day life is meaningless due to the absence of important historical events. His recollections of Gilles' former role as leader of the local Resistance group and account of the days following the liberation of the town in 1945 change entirely the perspective within which we read the narrative. As we come to understand how the apparently inexplicable occurred, why the explosion at the factory was an act of simultaneous murder and suicide, we also learn of unpleasant details concerning the liberation of the town in 1945—a story of scapegoats, of cruelty towards innocent people, of the rule of the mob. Suddenly there is a message in the text, introduced as it were through the back door, which says that the official view of the Resistance and the Liberation, the acceptable side to French history, is both glamorised and superficial.

This, then, is the twist in the tale of the firework factory, for the story is really about the art of the novelist. It presents him as if by accident 'sur le terrain' and we read of the sparking of his imagination and subsequently of his painstaking research. And yet as the narrative unfolds, the novelist becomes historian, and the historian, in the shape of the retired journalist, becomes novelist. For the latter history is a mere succession of names; the rest is fiction, as when he talks about the Great War: 'J'ai tant entendu parler de Verdun et du chemin des Dames, que je finis par croire que j'y étais' (*MA,* 115). This curious *va-et-vient* gives a fascinating insight into the change in preoccupations of European novelists in the aftermath of the Holocaust, and more particularly in France, in the aftermath of the Occupation. French literature since 1945 is speckled with important works relating to the Occupation. The *témoignages* of Vailland, de Beauvoir and Vercors preceded the semi-contemporaneous, allegorical account in Camus' *La Peste* (1947), which was itself a forerunner to the fully fictional representations contained in novels such as Modiano's *La Place de l'étoile* (1968), Tournier's own *Le Roi des aulnes,* and especially in the *oeuvre* of Jorge Semprun. In French cinema there has been a real sea-change. The end of the Gaullist interregnum saw a proliferation of important films, notably Louis Malle's *Lacombe, Lucien* (1973) and Marcel Ophuls' *Le Chagrin et la pitié* (first screened in 1971), which subject French society during the Occupation to uncomfortable scrutiny. These investigations into the national mythology of the French were 'fathered' by Alan Resnais' path-breaking 1959 film *Hiroshima mon amour,* in which the need to make better sense of historical experience is asserted. Above all, these texts, especially *Hiroshima,* ask awkward questions. Is it possible to make sense of history if it is unlived, and do those who have lived it use memory to recover or distort sense? Tournier reveals in *Le Roi des aulnes,* and here in **'Pyrotechnie',** that he is aware of the difficulties encountered by the modern novelist who will inevitably find him/herself at some stage 'facing history'.[3] He may be criticised for not helping, for not proposing solutions, but as a novel as complex as *Le Roi des aulnes* shows, he should not be rebuked for not endeavouring to understand. Like Vercors, Tournier realises that understanding is possible only on a limited human scale, in the self-imposed dumbness of the girl refusing to connive with, to console even, the German officer in *Le Silence de la mer,* and in the image of the wretched, semi-illiterate Ange Crevet, the avenging angel in **'Pyrotechnie',** standing each year in silent commemoration at the graveside of 'la crevette', his humiliated mother.

If we agree with Tournier that the good novelist is as much historian as writer of fictions, and that the creativity of the latter is predicated upon the research of the former, then we should also accept the truth contained in his depiction of the retired journalist, who has imagined himself so successfully as 'ancien combattant' that he has come to believe that this is what he now is, that the construction of the historian's narrative is a considerable feat of the imagination. Many historiographers, including Paul Veyne, Hayden White and Paul Ricoeur, concede that any attempted return to a past state is a huge reconstructive task based on the flimsiest of empirical evidence, and that the primary agent for these reconstructions is the imagination of the author. Ricoeur has written extensively on the areas of congruence in modern analyses of historical and literary narrative. In one collaborative collection of essays he stakes out the field for investigation, declaring that, 'l'enjeu commun à la théorie de l'histoire et à la théorie du récit fictif est la connexion entre figure et séquence, configuration et succession'.[4] Ricoeur conceives the figure or symbol as, in one sense, the beginning or the *déclencheur,* as that which gives rise to narrative. Figures inspire tropes which can act in turn like keys; they may open the doors to a greater understanding. In **'Pyrotechnie'** there is one master figure; the secret of narrative lies in the firework.

The animated conversation of M. Capolini suggests that he is not only the manager of a firework factory, but also an enthusiastic *aficionado* of contemporary literary theory: 'toute la pyrotechnie', he explains, 'se ramène à une lutte contre le hic et nunc' (*MA,* 100). At the moment of detonation, of maximum presence therefore, the firework deploys both a spatial and a temporal configuration, a double property that it shares with narrative. The firework manufacturer, like the writer of narrative, must be master in each domain in order to achieve the desired effect: 'cette explosion', pontificates M. Capolini in the style of the modern *rhétoriqueur,* 'nous nous en rendons maîtres pour la déplacer dans l'espace et la différer dans le temps' (ibid). Irresistibly, it would appear, we are drawn back to this essential function of the firework, 'à différer dans le temps et à déployer dans l'espace'. But historiography and literary theory only provide half-answers. When, in **'Pyrotechnie',** the factory manager is explaining the technical side to his business, he lets the narrator into a real secret. For the detonation of the firework to occur, there needs to be a conical space hollowed out of its centre, 'un vide ménagé en son centre et ayant la forme d'un tronc de cône' (*MA,* 103). Without it there would be no firework, but nobody knows why. M. Capolini describes this phenomenon of the pyrotechnic function resistant to human conceptualisation in suitably lyrical fashion. 'Sachez-le bien', he exudes, 'comme les femmes et comme les violons, la fusée possède une âme' (ibid). This figure, already three or four times significant (cf. Chagall's *The Cellist,* 'le violon d'Ingrès'), is philosophically exciting, because it seems to defy empirical verification. Interviewing Tournier in April 1990, the 'firework question' was on the tip of my tongue, intrigued as I was to find out whether this was one of those mysteries of science that comes along occasionally to befuddle the methodology of empiricist lore. Was it true? Tournier smiled as he shook his head. His job was done. The important thing was that I had begun to half-believe the fiction. It could have been true. And I, like the child who craves the instant gratification of a desire, needed to know the truth.

My reactions to **'Pyrotechnie'** neatly demonstrate the theory developed by Frege in his famous essay, 'On Sense and Reference', in which he maintains that the action of the human mind is governed by an imperceptible and irresistible movement that takes us from the sense of the object to its reference.[5] The sense of **'Pyrotechnie'** lies in the resolution of the crime, which is wrapped up in the organic evolution of the narrative and manifested through a series of temporal coincidences. What is important here is the clarity, or perceptibility, of this structure, and not whether the events described are believable or not. Paradoxically, it is the inherent aspect to the firework which takes us outside the text. The manager's words, seeking as they do to impose human qualities on a machine, simulate the convergence of the most fundamental antithesis—that of living and inert matter—and lead us once again to the crossroads of Culture and Nature, that we technologically motivated creatures insist on reliving. (Witness our fascination with robots, daleks and the like.) This is the moment of metaphor, when the *as if* of the fictional narrative is dropped in favour of the *is* of the radical copula, when fiction impinges on and starts to redefine our conception of reality. It is only when we have finished reading that the writer's imagination makes its impact; it is only then that we begin to wonder about those fireworks.

This schema is diametrically opposed to the model proposed by Gérard Genette in his discourse on language and space. Genette considers that modern man is oriented primarily by spatial rather than temporal relations: 'L'homme préfère l'espace au temps'. Literary discourse in particular, he writes, 'ne se dit plus qu'en termes de distance, d'horizon, d'univers, de paysage, de lieu, de site, de chemin et de demeure: figures naïves, mais caractéristiques, figures par excellence, où le langage s'espace afin que l'espace, en lui, devenu langage, se parle et s'écrive.'[6] More than literature even, the cinema would seem to exemplify Genette's description of a 'spatialised' culture. In Wim Wenders' 1984 film, *Paris, Texas,* Harry Dean Stanton stares out into the vast expanse of the Arizona desert and starts walking, apparently into infinity. But this journey into space (the sheer scale of the panorama on the big screen is breathtaking) has a destination; it ends in the big city. In one of the finest scenes of contemporary cinema, the Stanton character confronts his estranged wife, played by Natassia Kinski, through a one-way perspex glass pane, as she begins to perform her ritual sex act for the

paying customer. He stops her, they talk, and gradually she recognises who he is. At the end of his journey through space, the human identity of the characters involved is reaffirmed and the past relived, albeit through a perspex glass pane. A temporal framework is back in place.

Tournier's **'Pyrotechnie'** leads the reader gently, inexorably away from literary questions about narrative to a world of elementary philosophy and story-telling. In his excellent book, *The Sense of an Ending,* Frank Kermode poses the question as to what basic human set founds the various paradigms of our existence. Kermode argues that our verbalisation of time as the tick-tock of the clock is the essential paradigm upon which we base our perception of reality. As he puts it, '*tick* is our word for a beginning, *tock* our word for an end. We say they differ. What enables them to be different is a special kind of middle.'[7] What Kermode is saying here is that we can perceive duration only when it is organised. The fact that we call the second of the two related sounds arbitrarily conferred on what would otherwise be pure chronicity *tock* is evidence that we use fictions to enable the end to confer organisation and form on temporal structure. The clock's *tick-tock* then becomes the model of what we call a plot, an organisation that humanises time by giving it form; and the interval between *tick* and *tock* represents purely successive, disorganised time of the sort we need to humanise. The function of the storyteller is to fill this emptiness, to endow it with 'significant season'. Within this organisation, what was conceived as simply successive becomes charged with past and future: what was *chronos* becomes *kairos*. This is the time of the novelist, a transformation of mere successiveness which E. M. Forster once likened to the experience of love, the erotic consciousness that makes 'divine sense out of a commonplace person'.

Kermode gives numerous examples in different contexts of the enormously complex fictions that we invent in order to give significance to our lives. They may be institutionalised, like those pertaining in the world of equity and law, or personal; we all live out our lives under the aegis of a series of false endings and beginnings. This is why stories are so satisfying; because reading them allows us to behave as young children do when they think of all the past as yesterday. In the words of journalist Michael Ignatieff, 'short stories assuage, within a miniature world of their own, our own anguish and uncertainty about what will happen next in our lives'.[8]

The soul at the centre of Tournier's rocket is an indication of the humanisation of time that occurs within the paradigm of his fiction, and it therefore signifies our need to go beyond the text and project its structure of beginnings and endings on the formlessness of our own existence. It did not take me long to reassert the 'truth' of Tournier's fiction. The theoretical physicist Stephen Hawking reminds us that when we throw a stone into a pond, the ripples spread out as a circle that gets bigger as time goes on. Hawking proposes that we think of a three-dimensional model consisting of the two-dimensional surface of the pond (space measured on the horizontal axis), and the one dimension of time (measured on the vertical axis). The expanding circle of ripples will, he says, mark out a cone whose tip is at the place and time at which the stone hit the water. This is the simple model for what Hawking terms the 'future (and past) light cone of an event',[9] which he uses to demonstrate how we ought to conceive of space and time in terms of the distance travelled by light-waves propagated from a certain indefinable point; not unlike the mysterious soul of the firework, whose secret resides in the hollow cone at its centre. The metaphor lives; and like the child for whom the story at bedtime is a prerequisite for sleep, its resurrection puts the critic's mind temporarily at rest.

The mind, however, should not remain inactive for long. The enduring image of **'Pyrotechnie'** is of two silent men sitting either side of a table at the heart of the factory, composing Rockets and Catherine Wheels from brightly coloured powders contained in a series of vials. It suggests the medieval magic of alchemy, rather than the modern-day certainties of science. If the firework with its weird chemistry harbours the secret of narrative, then perhaps the symbol of the firework, like the Figure in Henry James' carpet, takes us beyond narrative and into a timeless, mythical zone. Perhaps this journey into the realms of our own imagination is what Tournier really means when he talks of myth as 'une histoire que tout le monde connaît déjà' (VP [*Le Vent Paraclet*], 184). This journey is essentially regressive, a journey back into our own memories, into childhood.

As I stated in my introductory section, Tournier identifies Hans Christian Andersen's *The Snow Queen* as the story he would most like to have written. It is, of course, a classic fairy-tale. A fragment of the Devil's Mirror pierces little Kay's heart, his moral view of the world is inverted, and he is kidnapped by the Snow Queen. Plucky Gerda sets off in pursuit and, after a series of interesting encounters, succeeds in rescuing Kay from the Ice Kingdom north of Lapland. On their return to Gerda's grandmother's house everything seems much the same, 'the clock still said "Tick tock!" and the hands still marked the hours'.[10] The difference is in themselves, for they are now grown-up people. The end of childhood coincides with the end of the story. The splinter of glass has long since been displaced from Kay's heart, but their adventures are somehow eternised in memory, representing another life which we all believe

we once lived. In fact, this other world is tangible; it is the world of children's fairy tales, a world in which those adults who become parents have the opportunity to relive.

Daniel Pennac contrasts the pain of the solitary adolescent who cannot get past page 49 of *Madame Bovary* with the infectious pleasure of the toddler for whom any number of reading sessions is never enough:

> Son plaisir nous inspirait. Son bonheur nous donnait du souffle. Pour lui, nous avons multiplié les personnages, enchaîné les épisodes, raffiné les chausse-trapes . . . Comme le vieux Tolkien à ses petits-enfants, nous lui avons inventé un monde. À la frontière du jour et de la nuit, nous sommes devenus son romancier.[11]

Pennac sees no reason why this excitement over reading should not be extended through the school years, why books should not compete on an equal footing with television and video for the attention of the teenager, just as they do for the pre-school child. The key to achieving this regeneration of the subversive, thrilling quality to literature which used to entrance adolescent readers in bygone, more censorious eras, is in the slowing-down of the transition from a communal, oral reading situation to the solitary engagement with the text. Thus, though the child may have reached the point at which he or she can read unaided, the parent should continue to read aloud to his offspring until such a time as the child can not only spot the sections that have been skipped, but is able to fill them in without having recourse to the text. For Pennac, all literature should be infused with the fantastic, otherworldliness which Tolkien invented for his grandchildren. The dynamism of the spoken word must emanate from the written text; the oral must be encapsulated within the scriptural.

Tournier's **'Pierrot ou Les secrets de la nuit'** is situated plumb at the crossroads of the oral and the written. With **'Pierrot'** [*Pierrot ou les secrets de la nuit*], Tournier assumes his status as the Napoleon of contemporary French literature and gives the signal for his dragoons of young readers to invade the staid company of their 'elders and betters'. Predictably, when it was first published as an independent volume in 1979 **'Pierrot'** was largely ignored, in spite of Tournier's imprecations that it was the best thing he had ever written.[12] My discussion of it should be read in counterpoint to the reading of Ricardou's *Les lieux-dits* given in Chapter 1, for **'Pierrot'** foregrounds the holistic experience often associated with the oral narrative in contrast to *Les lieux-dits,* which focuses on the differential problematic of the written sign. **'Pierrot'** carries Tournier's bet on the ontological necessity of a language which speaks the world, which connects instantly with the experience of the Other. On the one hand it is a supreme piece of literary craftsmanship, on the other it reinvents the world through a child's mind's eye. Roberts treats it as one of the most multi-layered of Tournier's self-referential narratives. He concludes that the Pierrot/Arlequin opposition presents a clear bifurcation leading either to the classical, Platonic view of art or to the postmodern preoccupation with the simulacrum.[13]

We are immediately alerted to the possibility that Tournier is attempting to reconcile a huge disparity, between the superficial style of the *faux-naïf* and the underlying complexity of the metaphysical argument. If the effortlessness of the *rapprochement* in **'Pierrot'** is surprising, it is because the distance covered is much shorter than that evoked by the 'union des contraires impossibles' which Roberts and others see as the guiding principle of Tournier's fictional project. The ontological argument here is not one of postmodernist versus platonist. (I think this is a mistaken reading). Rather **'Pierrot'** tells of the origin of metaphysics, of the value of knowledge and wisdom as tools to penetrate the veneer of instant cognition. It is a fundamentally educational story, which follows a building-block pattern. The sequencing is minutely orchestrated. Anaphora and cataphora are used extensively. The narrative regularly refers back to remind the reader of important characteristics, to reinforce truths even, and it refers ahead so that the story gains a structural coherence. The text is literally knitted together as we read it. The context is ahistorical, and the characters are stock archetypes, taken from the *commedia dell'arte*. This second factor is unimportant in so far as our understanding of the story is concerned; we are given an explanation of the origin of Colombine's name in the first paragraph. But the *commedia dell'arte* does of course place a premium on the value of performance, on physicality, on entertainment—slapstick and farce—of a sort that would appeal to children. It is also essentially rural. More importantly, Tournier's narrative is generated from a number of fundamental associations that have their origins in popular mythology and folklore and are familiar conceits in a variety of children's stories. Some of these can of course be traced back to classical mythology.

The spinal column of what will emerge as a 'whole body' perception of literature is the eternal opposition of night and day. This is the first of many dualities highlighted in the text, and it immediately gives rise to another, that of work and rest. Pierrot, the baker's boy, embodies the night. He is fully a part of the night, he works when others rest. He is, therefore, a figure of the Other, often misunderstood, even feared. Naturally, it follows that he and the night are associated with scary things, such as wolves and bats. Colombine is associated with the day, or the everyday. The association is less strong than with Pierrot, but it is nonetheless represented by the concrete symbols of birds and flowers. The importance of work is reaffirmed. It takes Pierrot to two other 'obscurités encore plus inquiétantes': the cellar and the oven. The convergence of darkness and dan-

ger is reinforced by two rhetorical questions, the first of which introduces the rat: 'Qui sait s'il n'y avait pas des rats dans sa cave?' (*MA,* 259). Taboo creature and carrier of disease, the rat is the dread figure of Orwell, Camus, even David Attenborough. It is often found in cellars and is also, of course, associated with the dark. The second question—'Et ne dit-on pas: "noir comme un four"?' (*MA,* 259)—establishes a proverbial link with the oven and darkness, thereby suggesting the importance of language in developing our conceptual awareness of the environment. Rhetorical questions are a frequent occurrence in this text. Usually positioned at the end of paragraphs, they drive the narrative forward at crucial points and predispose the reader to the idea that this is a story written to be performed. Its self-affirmation is a clue to its educative function.

Throughout the narrative the reader is confronted with the physical and the concrete, with the tangible manifestations of nature. Although Pierrot comes to represent a form of spirituality, his temperament is first manifested through his physique. He is pale, with big eyes, and wears the baggy, white overalls of the baker. His look is that of the ubiquitous owl, nocturnal creature *par excellence,* and symbol, of course, of wisdom. The emphasis on clothes reminds us of the owl in **'Lucie ou La femme sans ombre'**, brushing past the children as it emerges from the disused tunnel. Also, it is suggested that Pierrot and Colombine may meet in the twilight zone, the hour of Minerva's owl. We are subtly reminded that wisdom could be defined as either the impulse or the capacity to react analytically to the vicissitudes of the world.

Pierrot is fundamentally lunar and owl-like. These two physical aspects externalise character traits. Pierrot is shy, quiet, loyal, discreet. He prefers solitude to the company of others, and writing—a solitary activity—to talking, which he finds painful and difficult. This is essentially cataphoric, because the character portrait of Pierrot refers ahead not to future encounters with Colombine but to the antithetical figure of Arlequin whom we have yet to encounter. At the same time the narrator instills in the sedentary Pierrot the capacity to change, to develop. His path leads him to Colombine. Theirs is not a promising start in life. The other villagers have always thought of them 'as an item', but the exigencies of their respective occupations enforces a schism which is hardened in Colombine's mind by the negative associations of popular myth and prejudice that prey on her at night as she hides beneath the blankets. Thus she is blinded to the most important aspect of Pierrot's character, namely that he represents knowledge.

What Pierrot knows is predicated on the two determining signs of his character, the natural phenomena with which he, unlike others, is in most contact: the night and the moon. Thus, two consecutive paragraphs each

begin, 'Pierrot connaît la nuit . . .', and 'Pierrot connaît la lune . . .' (*MA*, 260). Pierrot knows that the absence of sunlight accentuates the stimulus to the full
range of the human senses, including the optical. The
river twinkles, the undergrowth rustles, and the smells
of sea, mountains and forest are carried on the breeze.
Sensory inspiration is in inverse proportion to the 'ex-
halaisons du jour, imprégnées par le travail des
hommes' (*MA*, 260). From his moon-gazing Pierrot has
learned the value of perspective, of the need to appreciate surface and depth, of the three dimensions integral
to obtaining information by touch, but equally important in terms of optics.[14] But Pierrot is neither happy nor
content in his world, because he loves Colombine, who
inhabits a different and inimical world. What Pierrot
does not know therefore he has to imagine, and his
imagination is dominated by the figure of Colombine.
On his dawn wanderings he imagines her 'soupirant et
rêvant' in the 'moite blancheur' of her double bed (*MA*,
261). The roundness of a cheek or a breast or a buttock
is transmuted through the eternal, abiding figure of the
moon.

Through Pierrot the narrative has initiated its readers/
audience into the twin values of wisdom and knowledge, but the world of love is still beyond reach. The
problematics of desire lead Pierrot to an imaginary
world. He is at an impasse, an impasse which is broken
by the arrival of Arlequin. Arlequin signifies narrative,
the fracture of the status quo. Naturally he arrives out
of the blue, on a 'beau matin d'été . . . enluminé de
fleurs et d'oiseaux' (*MA*, 261). Flowers are heliotropic,
they turn towards the sun, which is Arlequin's sign, and
the joint flower-bird motif is anaphoric, referring back
to the initial characterisation of Colombine. Arlequin
disturbs Pierrot in the middle of the day. Having been
rudely awakened the latter appears more owl-like than
ever, 'tout-blanc, ébouriffé, yeux les clignotant à la lumière impitoyable de l'été' (*MA*, 262). Their essential
difference is channelled through bird analogies; their
fundamental, as yet undisclosed commonality, will be
emphasised in the fusion of their linguistic skills. The
mutual laughter of Arlequin and Colombine signals an
immediate and apparently naturalistic rapport. Pierrot is
left out, 'seul et triste dans sa défroque lunaire en face
de ces deux enfants du soleil que rapprochait leur commune gaïté' (*MA*, 263). He is jealous, jealousy being a
primal emotion *par excellence,* the first manifestation of
a child's emotional being, the point at which the infant
child starts to free itself from the shackles of babyhood
and the point at which he is most sensitive to the existence of his physical environment, and therefore the
point at which his cognitive skills are most intensively
employed. Arlequin woos Colombine by colouring her
in. Like a child armed with crayons before a blank
sheet of paper, he decorates the white façade of her
house. Perched on the scaffolding, he contrasts ornitho-
logically with the owlish Pierrot, 'avec son collant mul-

ticolore et sa crête de cheveux rouges, il ressemble à un
oiseau exotique' (*MA*, 264). In the space of a day the
building is transformed from *blanchisserie* to *teinturie*,
complete with a full-length portrait of Colombine
dressed in the Arlequin costume. The next morning Colombine herself has duly metamorphosed and become
'une Arlequine'. The mortified Pierrot transfers his
thoughts on to paper and pins a letter to Colombine on
his rival's scaffold.

The reflective, sedentary Pierrot is categorised according to Tournier's own *caractérologie* as 'un personnage
secondaire'.[15] On the contrary the flighty, nomadic Arlequin exudes 'primarité', and therefore will never stay in
one place for long. Indeed he lives out a Tournierian
ideal, that of the perpetual traveller who takes his own
home with him, 'le vagabond immobile'. The scaffold
collapses into what is described as his 'drôle de
véhicule', which it is, literally and metaphorically
speaking: Arlequin's mode of transport, a sort of mobile home *avant la lettre,* converts into the scaffold he
needs in order to indulge in his grandiose painting
projects. It is an image of totality, a symbol of existential and aesthetic plenitude. He lives on it, 'comme
l'oiseau sur la branche. Il n'est pas question pour lui de
s'attarder' (*MA*, 267). Neither should Colombine dither
any longer. This is because their love is destined to be
seasonal. It can only last 'le temps d'un beau temps':
the Colombine and Arlequin couple fall victim to
Tournier's most enduring of binary oppositions, contained in the pun on the word 'temps'. The autumn
rains cause their bright colours to run and fade, and the
leaves turn brown and fall. As they wake one morning,
they are confronted with the immobilising effect of
Winter in the guise of the first covering of snow, 'le
grand triomphe du blanc, le triomphe de Pierrot' (*MA*,
269). The narrator describes this first snowfall of the
Winter as 'un coup de théâtre'; with his baggy white
robes and slow, trance-like movements Pierrot is associated with Classical theatre, especially Tragedy, self-
evidently contrasting with the gaudy costume of the
dancing Arlequin, who represents the tradition of Provincial Farce. That night the crowning moment of this
'revanche du mitron' arrives in the shape of an enormous silver moon floating over the icy landscape.

The ever-more nostalgic, winsome Colombine discovers
Pierrot's note and thereby the secrets of the night, or
rather its sensuous colours; the deep blue skies and the
golden ovens, 'des couleurs vraies qui se respirent et
qui se mangent' (*MA*, 270). Colombine returns inspired
by the 'essaim de mots en f' that she associates with
Pierrot, manifesting an affinity with the symbol of the
written letter which he is seen to represent, again in
contrast to Arlequin, 'le beau parleur'. Significantly, the
stirring of Colombine's imagination is a matter of language, and in the first instance one of sounds. Riveted
by the prospect and actuality of her flight, the word

'fuite' re-enters her consciousness in the onomatopoeic description of her feet as she pads across the blanket of snow: 'Elle fuit dans la neige qui fait un doux frou-frou froissé sous ses pieds et frôle ses oreilles: fuite-frou-fuite-frou-fuite-frou . . .' (*MA,* 271). The sequence evokes a child's delight in the combination of like-sounding words. However, the emphasis shifts from phonetics to semantics, where the duality that seems carved into her existence once again plays itself out, firstly in the number of 'mots féroces', beginning with (f), which she now associates with Arlequin, and then in the congregation of 'mots fraternels' which confirms her decision to return to Pierrot.

Pierrot's note has engineered a crucial transition. Colombine can now see things differently. She is privy to another world that neither abolishes nor replaces her Arlequin-shaded existence but is somehow endowed with a subtler, deeper significance. She has learned like Idriss that 'true sight is a question of insight',[16] that the world is revealed through metaphor: 'Parce qu'elle s'est rapprochée de Pierrot, Colombine a maintenant des yeux pour voir' (*MA,* 271). Transfixed by the vision of Colombine bathed in the golden glow emanating from his oven, Pierrot decides to consecrate the magical moment. Whereas Arlequin reproduced her image in the form of a flat, two-dimensional, mimetic portrait, he will sculpt her out of dough. The story ends with an orgiastic, life-giving ritual—the doleful Arlequin having been welcomed into the cellar to form a *ménage-à-trois*—as the ogrish threesome munch on a hot, freshly-baked Colombine loaf.

The return of Arlequin is predicated on the universally-recognised nursery rhyme, 'Au clair de la lune', the encrypted text on which, it is claimed, the narrator bases his story, a story which will in its turn help elucidate the meaning of the original nursery rhyme. Arlequin returns because he needs shelter and warmth and, more importantly, because he has recognised the power of the scribe. However, the identification of 'Au clair de la lune' as a typical Tournier *hypotexte,* though already a clever device in that it fixes the narrative within both a child context and a collective and therefore truly popular adult consciousness, does not explain the pronounced eroticism of the final scene. The answer lies in the fact that the nursery rhyme lyric reprinted in almost every collection of nursery rhymes, and helpfully cited by Tournier's narrator, is only the first of four verses. Tournier has inverted the narrative of the nursery rhyme, in which Arlequin is the successful suitor and Pierrot merely his informant. However, the concluding (usually absent) verse introduces a note of coquettishness that seems rather incongruous in the context of a nursery rhyme but complements the erotic suggestivenes of Tournier's *dénouement* rather nicely:

> Au clair de la lune
> On n'y voit que peu;

> On chercha la plume
> On chercha le feu.
> Cherchant de la sorte
> Ne sais c'qu'on trouva;
> Mais je sais qu'la porte
> Sur eux se ferma.

Such a typically Tournierian disclosure should not obscure the magical qualities of **'Pierrot'** in which the simplicity of the language is distilled in an immaculate structure of complementary terms. Even the apparently unheralded eroticism of the final scene may be read in ironic counterpoint to the narrator's earlier rejection of voyeurism when he refuses to describe what the heart-broken Pierrot sees having scaled the scaffolding and peeped into Colombine's bedroom. **'Pierrot'** is a masterpiece of form which is ultimately motivated by a concern for education. From the beginning key terms and images (night-time, work, birds, flowers, etc.) are repeated, once or several times. The reader or listener is encouraged to perceive that each term has its complement. In the first instance this exists as a different word or concept of equal importance which generates its own sub-set of words, or what Lakoff and Johnson term 'entailments'. However, each concept is also liable to split into complementary halves and ultimately to form a constellation of related words. In **'Pierrot'** the narrator chooses to exploit the semantic possibilities inherent in the sub-category 'birds' because, whilst it allows him to differentiate imagistically between Arlequin and Pierrot, he can also establish important links between the key concepts of nature, wisdom and art. 'Flowers' should contain a similar abundance of conceptual potential and possibilities of metaphorical characterisation, but this particular sub-category is left unexplored. The metaphorical pattern overlays a dialectical narrative structure. The night-day equilibrium of Pierrot and Colombine is shattered by the arrival of Arlequin; the Arlequin and Colombine idyll is then progressively undermined by the seasonal anti-thesis driven by Pierrot, before synthesis is finally achieved with Arlequin's initiation into the baker's 'fournil'.

Tournier's spectacular achievement with **'Pierrot'**, given its covert patterns of reference to his own fictional work and its intricate formalistic design, is that it works as an educational, or rather educative text. In grammatical terms it is an exercise in denomination. All the key words are nouns. This helps children to name things, but it also suggests that language has or should regain an ontological force that philosophers believe existed in the pre-Socratic age when the distinction between word and object either was elided, or had yet to be recognised. It is a story which celebrates the evocative power of language through the reconciliation of the oral and written traditions. It presents an heuristic model of learning in which the process of discovering the world is equated with the organic evolution of a particular language. Learning is about making associations and connections which have already been enshrined in language. Hence, our use of language fuses with the way in which we interact with the world. The conceptual basis to this experience is, of course, what Lakoff and Johnson define as metaphorical.

Notes

1. H. de Balzac, *Le Curé de Tours,* Paris, Folio, 1976, p. 69.

2. Ibid., p. 71.

3. This expression is adapted from the title of an article on Claude Simon. See A. Cheal Pugh, 'Facing the matter of history: Les Géorgiques', in *Claude Simon: New Directions,* ed. A. Duncan, Edinburgh, Scottish Academic Press, 1985.

4. P. Ricoeur, *La Narrativité,* Paris, Centre Nationale de la Recherche Scientifique, 1980, p. 28.

5. See G. Frege, 'On Sense and Reference', *Translations from the Philosophical Writings of Frege,* ed. and trans. P. Geach and M. Black, Oxford, Blackwell, 1952, pp. 57-78.

6. G. Genette, *Figures I,* Paris, Seuil, 1966, p. 108.

7. F. Kermode, *The Sense of an Ending: Studies in the Theory of Fiction,* Oxford, Oxford University Press, 1966, p. 45.

8. M. Ignatieff, 'Europe's fairytale casts its spell', *The Observer,* 29 July 1990, p. 17.

9. S. Hawking, *A Brief History of Time,* London, Bantam Press, 1988, p. 25.

10. N. Lewis (ed. and trans.), *Hans Andersen's Fairy Tales,* Harmondsworth, Penguin, 1981, p. 142. For a splendid commentary on 'The Snow Queen', see W. Lederer, *The Kiss of the Snow Queen: Hans Christian Andersen and Man's Redemption by Woman,* Berkeley, University of California Press, 1986.

11. *Comme un roman,* Paris, Folio, 1992, p. 17.

12. He refers to his story as, 'ces trente pages . . . pour lesquelles je donnerais tout le reste de mon oeuvre', M. Tournier, 'Faut-il écrire pour les enfants?', *Courrier de l'UNESCO,* June 1982, pp. 33-34.

13. *Michel Tournier: Bricolage and Cultural Mythology,* p. 160.

14. It is precisely the lack of a third dimension, obliterated in a blanket of snowy foundation, which Barthes perceived as endowing the face of Greta Garbo with a mythical quality. See R. Barthes, 'Le visage de Garbo', *Mythologies,* Paris, Seuil, 1957, pp. 70-71.

15. Tournier draws frequently on this personality binarism, citing with obvious relish historical pairings of the 'primary' and the 'secondary'. Thus Voltaire, a man of the moment whose thinking reached out to the concerns of the day, contrasts with Rousseau, whose morose, nostalgic introspection led him to the dawn of mankind. Their relationship, their very existences—they died within weeks of each other—depended on a love-hate, admiration-scorn reciprocity. Tournier notes that a similar state of affairs existed between the great diplomat Talleyrand, whose outlook was anchored to his experience of the Ancien Régime, and the military genius of Bonaparte who had no such well-defined hinterland. For the most developed yet tapered account of the *primaire/secondaire* distinction see M. Tournier, *Le Miroir des idées,* Paris, Mercure de France, 1994, pp. 179-83.

16. L. Salkin-Sbiroli, *Michel Tournier,* ed. Worton, p. 117.

Bibliography

A: TOURNIER

1: FICTION (GALLIMARD FOLIO)

Le Roi des aulnes, 1970.

Les Météores, 1975.

La Goutte d'or, 1985.

Le Médianoche amoureux, 1990.

2: NON-FICTION

Le Miroir des idées, Paris, Mercure de France, 1994.

3: ARTICLES/INTERVIEWS

'Faut-il écrire pour les enfants?' *Courrier de l'UNESCO* (June 1982), pp. 33-34.

B: BOOKS AND ARTICLES ON TOURNIER

M. Roberts, *Michel Tournier: Bricolage and Cultural Mythology,* Saratoga, Stanford University/ANMA Libri, 1994.

L. Salkin-Sbiroli, *Michel Tournier: La Séduction du jeu,* Paris/Geneva, Editions Slatkine, 1987.

C: GENERAL

R. Barthes, *Mythologies,* Paris, Seuil, 1957.

A. Duncan (ed.), *Claude Simon: New Directions,* Edinburgh, Scottish Academic Press, 1985.

P. Geach and M. Black (ed.) and trans, *Translations from the Philosophical Writings of Gottlob Frege,* Oxford, Blackwell, 1952.

G. Genette, *Figures I,* Paris, Seuil, 1966.

S. Hawking, *A Brief History of Time,* London, Bantam Press, 1988.

M. Ignatieff, 'Europe's Fairytale Casts its Spell', *The Observer* (29 July 1990), p. 17.

F. Kermode, *The Sense of an Ending: Studies in the Theory of Fiction,* Oxford, Oxford University Press, 1967.

G. Lakoff and M. Johnson, *Metaphors We Live By,* Chicago, University of Chicago Press, 1980.

W. Lederer, *The Kiss of the Snow Queen: Hans Christian Andersen and Man's Redemption by Woman,* Berkeley, University of California Press, 1986.

N. Lewis (ed. and trans.), *Hans Andersen's Fairy Tales,* Harmondsworth, Penguin, 1981.

D. Pennac, *Comme un roman,* Paris, Folio, 1992.

J. Ricardou, *Les lieux-dits: Petit guide d'un voyage dans le livre,* Paris, Gallimard, 1969.

P. Ricoeur, *La Narrativité,* Paris, Centre National de la Recherche Scientifique, 1980.

Mikko Keskinen (essay date January-March 2004)

SOURCE: Keskinen, Mikko. "Voice Doubles: Auditory Identities in Michel Tournier's 'Tristan Vox.'" *Romanic Review* 95, nos. 1-2 (January-March 2004): 135-49.

[*In the following essay, Keskinen illustrates the etymological significance of names and the problem of romantic passion in "Tristan Vox."*]

Voice is intuitively regarded as the irreducible kernel of subjectivity, as the token of presence, and as the sign of intentionality. Voice issues from the speaker's body, proclaims its presence, and expresses the speaking subject's singular identity. The characteristics of voice, of human speech, are not, nevertheless, as unproblematic as one intuitively conceives of them. Nor are the philosophical overtones of the metaphor of voice incontestable, however pronounced they seem. One does not have to align with Jacques Derrida's well-known and at the same time controversial critique of the so-called phonocentric tradition of Western metaphysics to regard voice as a polymorphous entity in spite of its singular manifestation. In literature and criticism, voice is no less polyphonic a phenomenon or concept (cf. Bennett and Royle; Aczel).

In this article, I will trace the intertwined problems of voice and identity in Michel Tournier's short story **"Tristan Vox"** (1978).[1] On the level of its characters,

"Tristan Vox" dramatizes voice and identity as paradoxically mutable. On its textual level, the short story can be read as analogously vacillating between different articulations and identities. In probing this double problematic of **"Tristan Vox,"** I will account for such interrelated issues as characteristic voice, name and naming, intertextuality, and the very sound of language.

Radio Personalities

"Tristan Vox" is a story about a radio announcer, whose real name is Félix Robinet but who appears under the pseudonym Tristan Vox in his own midnight program. The show becomes considerably popular, and the listeners imagine Tristan, on the basis of his voice, as a romantic, handsome, and young-looking single, whereas, in reality, Félix is a balding and plump married man approaching sixty. Among his fan mail, Félix qua Tristan begins to receive letters, which refer to his private life and secret thoughts, from a woman who calls herself Yseut. Gradually Yseut's letters turn into seductive accounts, complete with graphic drawings of sexual acts.

A radio magazine accidentally publishes, in connection with Vox's name, the photograph of a tennis player, who happens to correspond to the audience's image of Tristan's physical appearance. When the athlete, Frédéric Durâteau, comes to Félix's studio in order to claim compensation for the loss of his privacy, Félix's secretary, Mlle Flavie, throws herself out of the window. Shortly before her death Mlle Flavie confesses that she had written the letters signed Yseut. Returning home, Félix learns from his wife that she, too, had been writing under the pseudonym Yseut. While the shocked Félix is on a sick leave, Frédéric Durâteau begins the host the Tristan Vox show. Surprisingly, his voice sounds exactly like the original announcer's, and Félix finds out that his wife continues writing love letters addressed to (the new) Tristan Vox.

The word *radio* stems from the Latin *radius,* "beam, ray" (*Oxford Latin Dictionary* s.v. radius). Radio in the meaning of "wireless telegraphy or telephony" or "an apparatus for receiving or transmitting radio broadcasts" is a shortened form of *radiotelegraphic* (or *-telephonic*) *transmission* or *instrument* (*Webster's* s.v. radio). Radio, hence, involves telecommunication, transmission of messages with the physical absence of one member of the process. In **"Tristan Vox,"** the most obvious form of radio communication is telephonic transmission, the voice in the absence of an interlocutor. Speaking into the microphone in his Paris studio, Félix Robinet addresses his absent audience all over France, for whom he materializes as a vocal image of Tristan Vox, rhetorically captivating the auditors within the radius of his voice and causing a variety of emotional effects. However, telegraphic transmission, i.e. telecommunication in writing, also figures in the short story, albeit more implicitly. Literary tradition, preceding fictional works and characters, inform many key aspects of **"Tristan Vox,"** including its very protagonist and title.

I will first deal with the radiotelephonic characteristics of **"Tristan Vox,"** and then proceed to its intertextual features as manifested in characters' names. These two forms of telecommunication relate to the problem of identity in the radio(ed) personalities of **"Tristan Vox."**

VOICE DOUBLES I: DISEMBODIMENT AND RE-EMBODIMENT

Tristan Vox only exists as a voice. A radiotelephonic pseudonym, Tristan Vox is in essence immaterial, a voice without a perceivable body. In Tristan's case, the disembodiment inherent in all telephonic communication manifests in an extreme form. Only a few people know the real identity of the man who articulates his words as Tristan Vox; for the millions of other listeners, the pseudonym and his voice are identical with each other. For the auditors, Tristan Vox is not, however, a voice without *some* personality or body. The quality of Tristan's voice, its *raucité tristanienne,* evokes a number of specific characteristics of the articulator: "il y avait en elle une gravité caressante et veloutée que relevait une fêlure, une cassure, quelque chose de blessé, et qui blessait aussi avec une implacable douceur ceux—et surtout celles—qui l'entendaient" (126). With a surprising conformity, the auditors picture, in letters and drawings, the detailed physical looks of Tristan: "L'image qu'on se faisait généralement de lui, d'après sa voix, était celle d'un homme dans sa seconde jeunesse, grand, mince, souple, avec une masse de cheveux châtains indomptés qui atténuaient par leur flou romantique ce que son masque noblement tourmenté, aux pommettes un peu hautes, aurait pu avoir d'excessivement sombre, malgré la douceur de ses grands yeux mélancoliques" (127). Félix Robinet's appearance is almost a diametrical opposite of these characteristics: "Il approchait la soixantaine. Il était petit, chauve et bedonnant" (127).

The irony in the discontinuity between Félix's voice and body is increased by the fact that the magically captivating tone of his voice is due to such unromantic physical defects as chronic laryngitis and a curiously vibrating double chin. Discontinuous as Félix's voice and body are, the effect of this discrepancy is not merely ironic but it also relates to the phenomenon of disembodied voices in general. The narrator opens the short story by recounting the meanings and effects of voice, besides in radiotelephonic transmission, in religion and mysticism. In many religions, the narrator points out, "les décrets de Dieu se manifestent par une voix tombant du haut d'un ciel vide" (125). Ethereal both in the physical and metaphysical senses of the word, the voices of radio "spiqueurs" get divine attributes in listeners' letters: "incorporelles et douées d'ubiquité, à la fois toutes puissantes et inaccessibles" (125). Even if the announcers themselves did not want to occupy the heightened position to which the audience had elevated them on the basis of mere voices "sans visage ni regard" (125), they would be compelled to face and acknowledge their other selves when looking at the mirror: "se regardant parfois dans une glace, ils prononçaient en tremblant le mot terrible de quatre lettres qu'on leur faisait incarner malgré eux" (126). The disembodied voice is, thus, re-embodied in a transcendented form in a body untransfigured.

Interestingly enough, the narrator abstains from articulating the divine name of that new constellation but refers to ineffable "Dieu" with a euphemism. In contrast, even the most reluctant of the announcers speak the divine name aloud, albeit tremblingly, to themselves, or rather to the reflection of themselves seen in the mirror. This incident can be read as a parody of the Lacanian mirror stage; unlike a toddler, the announcer recognizes himself as a complete stranger, a divine *totaliteraliter.* The voice pronouncing the name of that self-as-other seemingly connects the two entities but it, too, is removed from the immediately given. Voice as heard by others issues *from* the speaker's body, whereas the speaker hears his/her voice *through* the body, through the resonating cavities and vibrating membrane of the skull. This means that the speaker does not know what his/her voice sounds like, until hearing a recording of it; in a similar fashion, only a reflecting surface or recording device reveals the physical appearance of the subject to him/herself. Both voice and body are, then, too intimate for the subject to know as others know them. Therefore, both bodily and vocal identities are different for the subject and for others from the outset, opening up the discontinuity of these seeming stable phenomena in actual life, but especially so in radiotelephonic communication.

The disembodiment (and the possibility of re-embodiment) of voice inherent in radiotelephony seems to entail a rupture in the synchronization of the speaker and the sounds s/he produces. Félix Robinet's career as an actor can be seen to have prepared him for radiotelephonic incarnations; an actor's work is to "incarner aux yeux du public un personnage qu'on n'est pas" (130). On the radio and in the case of Tristan Vox, however, the situation is doubly different: the audience has no ocular proof of the synchronization between the speaking subject's body and the words he utters, and Félix does not *play* Tristan but professes to *be* him: "Il l'incarnait en affirmant sans équivoque qu'il l'était réellement, et il le créait en même temps, à chaque instant, au lieu de l'emprunter tout fait à un répertoire" (130). Félix's radio career has followed a gradual development from being a plain voice to its re-embodiment in a fictional character. He started as an anonymous "spiqueur" reading weather forecasts, news in brief, and the following day's program information. Then he lent his voice to the "speaking clock" (l'Horloge parlante), which inspired a veritable public quest to reveal the man behind the voice (127). Félix's own show finally takes the voice/body problematic to the extreme.

As the speaking clock, Félix's voice had been perfectly synchronous with the face of the timepiece. As Tristan Vox, Félix's voice belongs to an non-existent face, to an auditory image it creates in listeners, radically differing from Félix's own. The situation is a reversal of the Hollywood film musical *Singin' in the Rain* (1952). In the film, silent-screen star Lina Lamont is told: "You're a beautiful woman; audiences think you have a voice to match" (qtd. in Silverman 45). Her shrill, ungrammatical, and heavily accented voice is incompatible with Lamont's outer appearance, and the studio tries to hide this discrepancy by dubbing her lines with another, more "suitable" woman's voice. In **"Tristan Vox,"** his romantic voice contradicts Félix's mundane body, and this heterogeneity is attempted to conceal by hiding his true identity—until it is taken over by Durâteau's, to whom, in the auditors' minds, the voice seems to belong.

Postdubbing, which *Singin' in the Rain* features, adds voice to a character's image after filming (Silverman 47). The analogue of filmic dubbing to **"Tristan Vox"** is as heuristic as it is problematic. Durâteau's body is, imaginarily, compatible with the impression which Tristan's voice creates, thus formally realizing the perfect synchronization strived for in postdubbing. Durâteau in a way also acts as a stand-in or body double (*doublure*) in relation to Tristan's voice, albeit not to Félix's body, which practice, again formally, resembles the conventions of predubbing. Temporal suffixes do not, however, quite suffice to capture the voice/body problem in the Tournier short story. It could be said that Félix himself dubs all the present and future incarnations of Tristan Vox, because that fictional character primarily exists as a voice. Nevertheless, when Durâteau starts to act as a "voice double" under the pseudonym Tristan Vox in Félix's radio show, the voice and body form a perfect match in one single person. If this phenomenon is called dubbing, then Durâteau marries "his" voice to his own body in real-time performance, and one wonders whether or not the situation differs radically from actual people and their conventional speechacts. In any case, the doubling of voice in **"Tristan Vox"** functions as an auditory version of the Doppelgänger motif recurrent in Tournier's early œuvre (cf. Scheiner 168-96).

Durâteau's incarnation of a voice which is at first heard without "its ostensible source . . . visible at the moment of emission" resembles another codified deviation from synchronization, the voice-off (Silverman 48). When Durâteau's photograph and finally the man himself appear in the narrative world, the unity of the disembodied voice and its *ostensible* source seem to be recovered. By using the word "ostensible" instead of "actual" or "real" Silverman presumably emphasizes that the voice-off is a matter of viewers' impression rather than an empirical state of affairs: what appears as recovered synchronism may well have been executed with the help of postdubbing.

The radiotelephonic medium as such can be conceived of as a version of the voice-over, i.e. the voice heard (in film) without a sight of its originator. The voice-over is another deviation from the rule of synchronization, and this kind of disembodied voice is almost invariably male in classic Hollywood films (Silverman 48). Félix qua Tristan Vox attempts to remain invisible not only in the diegetic world of his show or medium but also in the extradiegetic realm of everyday life. The only image of Tristan Vox is indeed the one created by auditors' imagination, which is also the case in the pure cinematic voice-over. Durâteau's appearance in a published photograph and eventually in the flesh breaks the diegetic anonymity and recovers ostensible synchronism, thus turning the voice-over, via the voice-off, into a temporally anomalous version of dubbing.

The problematic nature of voice in **"Tristan Vox"** can emerge conceptually more manageable when conceived in cinematic terms, as I have done above. The Tournier story's analogue to the audiovisual conventions of the film should not, however, be stretched too far. **"Tristan Vox"** is literature, and the literary permeates it from the outset. In the next two sections, I will deal with naming in **"Tristan Vox"** and try to find out how it harks back to prior literature, as well as to hark at the auditory quality of the names themselves.

INTERFIGURAL ECHOES

Michel Tournier tends to name his characters in an allusive way. The name of a Tournier character typically relates either to his/her dominating personal traits or to some intertextual ancestors. It may suffice to trace the significations of Abel Tiffauges's name in *Le Roi des Aulnes* to see Tournier's onomastics at work. The family name Tiffauges is, at one level, a portmanteau of the German expression *tiefe Augen*, "deep eyes," and it gives away the character's relation to seeing and vision. Apart from natural language, the signifier Tiffauges can be conceived as an almost homophonic allusion to Tiphaine, the child-slaughtering criminal in Victor Hugo's "l'Aigle du Casque" (Bouloumié 45, 258). Abel, for its part, obviously alludes to the biblical twin brother of Cain, who eventually kills him thus making him the first martyr, but it, too, relates to other meanings than those of its mythical bearer. In Hebrew, Abel signifies a meadow, a breath, futility, and grief (Mercatante s.v. Abel). The first of those significations relates to the biblical Abel's occupation as a shepherd, whereas the other three more accurately describe Tiffauges's mode of being.

The names of Tournier's characters are not, hence, as transparent as a hasty reader might conceive of them. One single name may enclose layers of semic traits, intertextual allusions to literature, and references to mythological characters, the priority of which is not always apparent. Even the characters themselves are uncertain about the real meaning of each others' or even their own names, and often suggest alternate readings of them. For instance, in *Le Roi des Aulnes,* Abel's surname is conceived either as Tiefauge or as Triefauge, both of which refer to seeing, but with the opposite meanings of prophetically deep vision and myopia respectively (Tournier, *Le Roi des Aulnes* 276-77, 406-07).

Naming a character after an already existing literary figure is as common a feature in fiction as it is neglected in literary theory. Wolfgang G. Müller's account of the interrelations between characters of different texts provides a useful taxonomy of the phenomenon as well as coins a term, *interfigurality,* for it (101-21).[2] Naming is an economic means of establishing an interfigural relationship between fictional characters. Characters with the same name also metonymically link the whole texts in which they appear. The relationship between characters (or texts) is not, however, that of identity, for the new context inevitably causes changes in meaning. Often that contextual change is deliberately emphasized in the interfigural use of characters.

The most prominent interfigural name in Tournier's short story is, of course, that of its protagonist and eponymous title, Tristan Vox. Tristan Vox is a pseudonym, literally a given (and taken) name in its entirety. In order to protect his identity and to synchronize his voice with the (auditory) image it evokes in listeners, the radiophonic Félix Robinet is renamed as "Tristan Vox, superbe assemblage de roman courtois et de modernisme vulgaire" (129). This *bricolage* of semic and interfigural traits breaks the bond between the new name and its bearer so radically that the narrator describes it as a veritable coming into existence of a new person: "ainsi qu'était né Tristan Vox" (129). The pseudonym consciously contradicts Félix Robinet's traits as suggested by his actual name. Félix enjoys the simple pleasures of good food, modest *petit bourgeois* life, and marriage, thus realizing the meaning "happy" of his Latin given name. In contrast, Tristan interfigurally refers to the legendary hero of courtly love, epitomizing, even in popular thinking, unconditional passion. The suffering and melancholic side of passionate love can be seen as embedded in his very name; the first five let-

ters of Tristan homophonically disclose a semic trait of his sadness.[3] Félix's family name Robinet, "faucet," seems to hint at the banality of the modern life he leads. However, the surname also relates to Félix's most prominent feature: his exceptional spoken skills, characterized by a smooth flow of words. When, toward the end of the story, he thinks of giving notice of leaving, Félix puns on the aquatic and vocal meanings of his family name: "Il faut fermer le robinet" (149).

Besides a semic marker of Félix's verbal skills and the tone of his voice, *robinet* opens up an *intra*textual connection to another story in **Le Coq de bruyère.** **"Tupik"** is a story about a little boy who, taking his cue of his nursmaid's threat to cut off his "petit robinet" (Tournier, **Le Coq de bruyère** 79) in case he ever wets his bed again, castrates himself. In **"Tupik,"** the flow of liquid is urethral-genital, whereas in **"Tristan Vox"** it is hydrophilic-oral.[4] The opposite ends of the metabolic (and metaphoric) tract are partly dissolved in the discourse of the latter story's narrator. The new microphones in Félix's studio are, with definite phallic overtones, described as being snake-like: "Le nouveaux micros avaient l'air d'une tête de vipère dardée sur le visage, sur la bouche de celui qui parlait. Robinet s'avisa que c'était ce serpent électronique hostile et méchant qui opérait sa métamorphose en Tristan Vox." (133) The urethral-erotic association of speaking into the microphone is reinforced by the mention of Félix's being worth of gold to the radio station (128) and his voice as being golden (129). Hence, Félix's radiophonic discourse is not necessarily only clear and smooth as water but also toned and pressed as a golden shower.

The pseudonymic family name Vox seems a transparent sign of Tristan the radio personality's most prominent semic feature, his voice. In Latin, however, the semantic field of *vox* is considerably wide, including, in addition to the most common "human voice" and "tone and quality of voice," such significations as "the auditory effect of a word," "spoken utterance," "language," and "gnomic saying" (*Oxford Latin Dictionary* s.v. vox). Tristan Vox's radiophonic discourse is indeed characterized by the unique grain of his voice ("*raucité tristanienne*"; 126; emphasis in original), the spell it casts on the auditors, and the quotidian subjects heightened to veritable wisdom of "immense expérience" (130). His voice is thus not only *voix d'or* but, as auditory magic, it also resembles *voix d'Orphée,* leading the listeners from the dull underworld of the everyday, but also leading them astray as regards his own identity.

To sum up the relations between the protagonist's name and his pseudonym, the following observations can be made. There is a formal resemblance between the first name in the actual name and family name in the pseudonym (the Latin language), as well as between the actual family name and the pseudonymic first name (the

French language). The first names are contradictory ("happy" vs. "sad"), while the family names are (metaphorically) analogous on account of liquid symbolism. The pseudonym is not, thus, completely separate from the protagonist's real name or his mundane identity.

Félix's wife and secretary form a bodily and nominal opposition, the terms of which, not unlike in the case of his name and pseudonym, secretly share some characteristics. The spouse Amélie, née Lamiche, is voluptuous and a masterly cook; the significations of a soft rounded figure and food are embedded in her family name (*la miche*, "loaf of round bread"; *les miches*, "arse") (*Trésor de la langue française* s.v. miche). In contrast, Félix's secretary, Mlle Flavie, is thin and horselike ("chevaline"; 131). The name Flavie is phonetically close to the literary adjective *flave*, "golden blond, light in colour" (*Trésor* s.v. flave). The semic content of Mlle Flavie's name seems curiously contradictory to her general appearance; she is not a radiant beauty, or at least the narrator discloses no such evidence but rather emphasizes that Félix does not actually see or know her: "Félix Robinet ne la voyait pour ainsi dire que de dos, et la connaissait mal" (131). If there is radiance in Mlle Flavie it is of immaterial nature. Upon her self-defenestration but still unaware of the incident, Robinet sarcastically comments on the wailing sound of an ambulance with the cliché "Un ange passe" (143). Durâteau takes his cue from the phrase and lists the characteristics of an angel, meaning Tristan Vox: "Un ange se dresse, radieux, incorruptible, génial, généreux, terrible de pureté et de puissance" (143). Ironically, a moment later Mlle Flavie is being lifted ("charger") in an ambulance, and when he rushes to see her, Félix finds Mlle Flavie with her head wrapped in a turban-like white bandage (143-44, 145). After her revelation Félix sees Mlle Flavie as a new person capable of writing the Yseut letters; she is indeed pale ("blafarde"; 146) and dressed in white like an angel.

Both Mme Robinet and Mlle Flavie turn out to have used the pseudonym Yseut in their letters addressed to Tristan Vox. But do the two Iseults refer to the same interfigural character? In some versions of *Tristan et Yseut,* there are in fact two Iseults. The first one, with whom Tristan falls in love, is called Iseult the Fair ("Iseut la Bloie"); when he mistakenly assumes that she no longer loves him, Tristan marries Iseult of the White Hand ("Iseut aux Blanches Mains") for her beauty—and for her name: "pur belté e pur nun d'Isolt" (Thomas 153n). The conventional epithets attached to the two Iseults may function as telltales of Mlle Flavie's and Mme Robinet's interfigural roles in the Tournier story. It is clear that both women want to be or rather to play the role of the original Iseult, the fair object of Tristan's desire. Both women consciously assume the identity of another character. In her letters, to match Tristan's

name, Mme Robinet uses the pseudonym Yseut, which Mlle Flavie soon usurps. Mlle Flavie's assumed identity is thus doubly false; she not only uses an interfigural name but also an *intra*figural one referring to the first bearer of the pseudonym. Structurally, then, Mme Robinet seems fit in the position of Iseut la Bloie. Story-wise she is indeed prior to her impostress; as for discourse, however, Mlle Flavie qua Yseut is primary in the sense that her writing is quoted in the short story, whereas the style and content of Mme Robinet's letters remain secrets. As for their maiden names, both women are equally connected with the seme of whiteness, albeit with different connotations. The "flave" in Mlle Flavie's name relates to the semantic field of blond hair, whereas the light colour in Lamiche suggests doughy flesh. Again, the priority of the two Yseuts is nominally reversed: Mlle Flavie's blondness suggests that of Iseut la Bloie, and Lamiche's white skin that of Iseut aux Blanches Mains.

Frédéric Durâteau, the tennis player who is generally mistaken for Tristan Vox, comes to Félix to ask for economic remuneration for the loss of privacy. Trying to rake in money over the deal, Durâteau seems to fulfil the omen *du râteau* embedded in his name. Appropriately enough for his compensatory claims, Durâteau's name is also a homophone of the somewhat ungrammatical *dur à taux*. This economy in the sound of his name is analogous with Durâteau's experience of actually possessing Tristan's voice and opinions: "tout ce que vous avez dit ce soir, eh bien j'avais l'impression que c'était ma bouche que ça sortait" (143). In Durâteau's name, homophony is thus both economy of expression and an expression of economy.[5]

Durâteau finally adopts the pseudonym Tristan Vox, but his real family name has a certain nominal affinity with Félix's surname, Robinet. Water connects both "faucet" and Durât-*eau* (or even *rat d'eau*), and this aquatic resemblance in the names ties in with the metaphor of voice qua flow of water in that the two mens' voices indeed appear as identical when heard on the radio (150). There are, then, two Tristans in the story, just like there are two Iseults. Analogously, the legend of *Tristan et Yseut* features nominal doubles of its protagonists. In Thomas, Tristan l'Amoureux is accompanied by a benevolent namesake, Tristan le Nain (215n-19n). Again, the relation between the original and copy in the Tournier short story becomes complicated when interfigurality is taken into account. Félix Robinet qua Tristan Vox is both story-and discourse-wise the original bearer of the pseudonym, but his dwarfish outer appearance is that of the namesake in the legend. Analogously, Frédéric Durâteau is structurally in the position of Tristan the midget, but his handsome looks formally seem to cast him as the hero.

In **"Tristan Vox,"** all the characters are bearers of names which either give away their personal traits or interfigurally connect them with prior literature. It is, however, questionable whether the semic names disclose the characters' most prominent features or whether the names themselves summon those very characteristics. In the short story's constellation of names and the treatment of identity as a mutable entity, the latter reading is equally tenable. The pseudonym Tristan Vox is an exemplary case of this kind of nominalism in the short story. That pseudonym is taken in order to assume a new identity, and the effect it brings about is so radical that it surpasses rational realism: both Félix's wife and secretary fall in love with Tristan Vox although they are fully aware of his fictitious nature. That the name is more important than its bearer is further underlined with Mme Robinet's continuing infatuation with Tristan in spite of the fact that he is later played by another man, Frédéric Durâteau. The two Iseults, or rather, one Iseult mimicked by two women is analogous with the identity-generating force of a name found in Tristan's extreme case. The other names do not dramatize this force as radically as Tristan and Iseult but the semically motivated connection between the name and the named points to that direction. For instance, Durâteau's interest in money may rather be a function of his name than vice versa.

VOICE DOUBLES II: WHAT'S IN A NAME?

As Arlette Bouloumié quite correctly notes, the proper name has a dynamic content in Tournier (54). However, when emphasizing the metaphysical function of the proper name at the cost of poetic use or the sonority of signifier, Bouloumié muzzles the very phenomenon which makes onomastic dynamics so economical in Tournier. The one and the same graphic surface of a signifier allows for a number of possible articulations. The voice thus doubles or redoubles the "content" of a name. It is this polyphony that brings forward the polysemy of names in Tournier.

Just like the very Shakespearean question "What's in a name?" is rephraseable, upon articulation, as "What sin a name?" the lexical borders of all phonetic writing can be demarcated anew. Garrett Stewart calls this articulatory stream breaking through the graphic the "phonotext," and the kind of reading which only has access to it "phonemic reading" (28; for a critique and development of Stewart's theory, cf. Shoptaw).

The names in the Tournier short story tie in with the auditory in two ways. Either the name literally or metaphorically refers to sonic phenomena (Vox and Robinet respectively) or it can be conceived of as an auditory cryptograph, which discloses its meaning upon a reorganization of articulation (Lamiche < la miche; Durâteau < du râteau; dur à taux; durât-eau). The breakable acoustic continuum on which these puns are based is an aptly sonorous image of the dynamics of voice, name,

and identity in the short story. The sound of a name doubles its referents just like the disembodied voice of Tristan Vox is a carrier of multiple identities, articulable by more than one bodily speaking subject.

Both the main characters' names and casting in the roles of Tristan and Iseult are doubled in **"Tristan Vox."** To extend the tennis metaphor suggested by Durâteau's profession and not only rakish but also racketlike name, the short story's characters are performing a curious version of mixed doubles, with two men playing against two women—and against each other. The courtly love of the Tristan and Iseult legend can be seen as transposed into a game of love or even a love game on Tournier's metaphoric tennis court.

PHILTER AND FILTER: PHONETIC LOVE-POTION

The reason that medieval Tristan and Iseult fall madly in love is because they accidentally drink philter, love-potion, or wine of herbs meant for King Mark and his bride to be consumed as an aphrodisiac after their wedding. But, as Denis de Rougemont notes, the mistakenly drunk philter may be but a pretext for the moral acceptability of a passion which the lovers, even without the potion, strive for. Besides a perfect alibi, the philter functions as a symbol of the intoxication of love and as a seal of destiny, demonstrating the blind force external to the subjects in question (de Rougemont 22, 39, 113).

How does the idea of a love-potion relate to **"Tristan Vox"**? Phonetically. Tristan Vox's radiophonic voice gives a filtered version of Félix Robinet, and it functions as invisibly as a philter. Vox qua voice filters into the auditors' ears, creating a seductive auditory image of the absent speaking subject. The force of the philter is blind; it affects anyone who is exposed to its power. In the Tournier short story, the narrator repeatedly emphasizes that Vox's radiophonic voice lures both sexes alike and that Félix Robinet must be protected against the overzealous approaches of both male and female admirers (126, 130, 131, 148).[6] This is the reason why Robinet's connections with the outside world have to be "filtrées avec le plus grand soin" (129). This filtering is executed by Robinet's secretary Mlle Flavie, who for her part is affected by his vocal philter.

Interestingly reversing the conventions of courtly love, Mlle Flavie assumes the role of a knight who protects the chastity of the beloved: "C'était sur elle que venait se briser le flot du courrier matinal, l'artillerie lourde de cadeaux et paquets, et l'assaut intempestif des visiteurs et visiteuses" (131). Military rhetoric was by no means alien to courtly love; fight for the favor of the lady in lyric poetry or against competitors in the logic of tournaments combined erotic and violent instincts (de Rougemont 210-13). In **"Tristan Vox,"** however, there is a general reversal of roles. Passionate auditors pursue Tristan Vox (played either by Félix Robinet or Frédéric Durâteau), who wishes to remain unattainable. Both men exude vocal philter but are not affected by it themselves. Intertextually, both Robinet and Durateau are in the position of King Mark's mother, who brewed the love-potion but did not drink it herself, or Orpheus, who charmed with sound and voice without being charmed himself.

The main characters' identities arc thus complicated by the presence of voice. The vocal philter especially reverses or blends sexual identities and the stereotypic behavioral patterns they imply. So powerful is Tristan Vox's philtering voice that it surpasses the logic of marriage and adultery inherent in courtly love.

AUDITORY ADULTERY AND IDENTITY

According to Denis de Rougemont, Western literature, starting from the Tristan legend, shows a persistent tendency to prefer adultery to marriage, and deathly passion to life. In courtly love, however, the loyalty between the adulterous lovers opposes not only marriage but also any "satisfaction" of love, for love fulfilled ceases to be love. In the case of Tristan and Iseult, this can be seen in her return to her husband and his, literally, nominal marriage to her namesake, instead of indulging in mutual love (de Rougemont 11-13, 27-8). De Rougemont states that happy love has no history (11), but it is equally true that unhappy love generates literature.

In **"Tristan Vox,"** the obstacles in the way to the consummation of love are of ontological proportion. Tristan Vox is a fictional entity even within the fiction itself, and he only exists as immaterial and invisible voice. Yseut is likewise fictitious, but her mode of existence is that of an interfigural epistolary addresser. In the Tournier short story, Tristan and Yseut are doomed to remain separate for they are figures of speech and writing respectively. This also enables the multiplication of protagonists' identities; one voice can be articulated by two men, and two women can execute a single mode of writing.

The characters' multiplied identities bring about curious twists in their relationships vis-à-vis the Tristan and Iseult legend. Félix's wife, in the disguise of Yseut, is about to commit adultery with her own husband qua Tristan Vox. Félix is thus in danger of being cuckolded by himself. The constellation does not change radically when Frédéric Durâteau usurps Félix's position in radio, for Mme Robinet continues to be infatuated with the voice which is practically identical with that of Tristan Vox. Passionate love and any possibility of adultery hence appear on the disembodied level of radiophonic voice and epistolary writing, since M. and Mme.

Robinet are, as bodies in the material world, already married to one another, and Durâteau's looks are important only as a pictorial epitome of Tristan Vox's voice. Mlle Flavie is seemingly outside the marriage/adultery double bind, but, by adopting Mme Robinet's pseudonym and style, she is inevitably caught in the same constellation of sonic inconsummability. For the fictitious Tristan and Yseult, *amor de lonh* is the sole possible form of love.

In the context of courtly love, the existence of a husband is both an obstruction of passion and a prerequisite of adultery, for which reasons he is despised. On the other hand, her being married and thus unattainable makes Iseult passionately desirable to Tristan. In de Rougemont's reading, a Mme Tristan would equal a negation of passion (35-6). The basic relationship between passion and marriage found in courtly love holds partly true in **"Tristan Vox,"** albeit condensed in a doubled couple. Mme Robinet qua Yseut loves Tristan Vox (or the idea of being in love with him), because he is "not" her husband, but Félix Robinet qua Tristan Vox does not desire Yseut, because he is a man to be loved, not a loving man. Interestingly enough, Tristan Vox formally resembles Don Juan, the inverted reflection of Tristan (cf. de Rougemont 178). Like Don Juan, Tristan Vox is loved by many while not being in love himself (except possibly with himself); unlike Don Juan, however, he is unintentionally seductive, as if inadvertently spilling his irresistible phonetic philter.

Mlle Flavie dies upon revealing her double identity, and consequently Tristan Vox as articulated by Félix fades out into inexistence. When the aural being of Tristan Vox comes to an end, Mme Robinet grieves, seems suddenly older, and refuses to give her gourmand husband culinary oral pleasure (150). Tristan Vox's reincarnation as Frédéric Durâteau also revives Mme Robinet, but not her relationship with her husband. Rather, she resumes her admiration for Tristan Vox, and, as if miming the co-authoredness of the pseudonym Yseut, reverently listens to his radiophonic voice with another woman: "Les deux femmes, penchées sur le récepteur de la T.S.F., n'entendirent pas la porte s'ouvrir et se refermer" (150). The surviving couples thus repeat the initial situation. Félix as Tristan and Mlle Flavie as the other half of the doubled Yseut cease to exist, and their positions are taken over by Frédéric Durâteau and Mme Robinet's female neighbor respectively. The only person to remain in her original position is, thus, Mme Robinet. Her auditory affair with Tristan Vox continues with the difference that Félix is now only a potentially cuckolded husband, not in the same breath also his own wife's lover, as used to be the case.

Félix's final "solitude vertigineuse" (150) is emphasized by his radio silence; he presumes that he will never again speak into the microphone. His dead silence as

Tristan Vox, his refusal to speak radiophonically into ether, paradoxically throws him into the dizzying abyss of infinite ether reminiscent of *Mort d'Isolde* (cf. Barthes 16n). Ridding himself of Tristan Vox, Félix not only jettisons a vocal double but important features of his "real" identity as well. Félix escapes to his native Auvergne, substituting lively Paris for a small slumbering provincial town, active working life for extended games of billiards at a local café, and marital happiness for premature decrepitude. Withdrawn from Tristan Vox, Félix is drawn closer to death.

Etymologically, *adulterate* harks back to the Latin equivalent of "altered," "changed into another" (*adulterāt*), and *adultery* implies more directly the polluting, defiling nature of that change (*adulterāre*) (*Webster's* s.v. adulterate). There is thus a change of identity involved in adultery. In **"Tristan Vox,"** the auditory and adulterous change of identities does not only relate to characters but also to the textual status of the short story. The analogy between personal and textual identity is, of course, as alluring as it is problematic. There is, however, a strong link between the development of theories of the self and those of the text; as Owen Miller notes, "The rejection of the text as an autonomous entity, as a self-regulating organic whole, seems logically consistent with the demise in belief in the Romantic notion of a discrete, independent, enduring self" (Miller xiii). The two main meanings of identity, i.e. individuality and the state of remaining the same, are relevant to people and texts alike. The interfigurality of its main characters points to the fundamental intertextuality of **"Tristan Vox"** as a whole, problematizing the individuality of both the selves and the text in which they appear. In an analogous fashion, the phonemic instability of characters' names dramatizes the textual mutability of the short story; the graphically inscribed "text itself" does not remain the same, but is liable to change in the act of (phonemic) reading. If adultery transgresses marital contracts between individuals, intertextuality and textual "voice" break the supposedly self-same individuality of a given text.

In an interview Tournier states: "Il ne faut pas trop mépriser la répétition. L'uniforme a sa beauté. . . . Le clonage engendre une sorte de vertige" (Bouloumié 258). In **"Tristan Vox,"** uniformity is less beautiful than vertiginous. Although Tournier in general provocatively prefers the copy and subverts the idea of originality (cf. Davis 163-64), **"Tristan Vox"** demonstrates the suffering involved in the loss of singular origin. For Félix and Mlle Flavie that loss is painful because it both constitutes and undoes their identities. However, without intertextual and auditory doubling, **"Tristan Vox"** would be—if not nothing—then at least substantially less than what it is now.

Notes

1. Michel Tournier, "Tristan Vox," in *Le Coq de bruyère* (Paris: Gallimard, 1982: 123-50). Subsequent references are to this edition of the short story and will be given parenthetically in the text.

2. For proper names as allusion-markers, cf. also Hebel 136-43. For proper names and puns in *Le Coq de bruyère*, cf. Redfern.

3. It is not my intention to provide a systematic intertextual reading of "Tristan Vox" vis-à-vis *Tristan et Yseut.* Such a comparison would be an interesting project, although I doubt if the Tournier short story rewrites any single version of the legend. Rather, it is my contention that "Tristan Vox" selectively taps the whole Tristan and Iseult tradition, ranging from the complete medieval romances by Béroul and Thomas, the folios of Bern and Oxford and the *chévrefeuille* of Marie de France to the modern versions by Richard Wagner and Joseph Bédier. The Tournier short story picks up some of the motives found in the different renderings, but the ultimate referent of the Tristan myth in it is, as Denis de Rougemont puts it, "tout ce qu'il y a d'universellement émouvant dans nos littératures" (11).

4. Walter Redfern suggests that also mutilation connects the two characters, since Félix is "cut down to his voice alone" (61).

5. I hence disagree with Redfern, who claims that Durâteau's name is "almost certainly one of those in-significant names, with which Tournier at times teases readers he has already drilled to seek out 'speaking names'" (124n).

6. David Platten misreads the gender of the listeners by calling them Vox's "entirely female, lonely hearts audience" (154).

Works Cited

Aczel, Richard. "Hearing Voices in Narrative Texts." *New Literary History* 29:3 (1998): 467-500.

Barthes, Roland. *Fragments d'un discours amoureux.* Paris: Seuil, 1977.

Bennett, Andrew, and Nicholas Royle. "Voice." *An Introduction to Literature, Criticism and Theory.* London: Prentice Hall / Harvester Wheatsheaf, 1995. 57-64.

Bouloumié, Arlette. *Michel Tournier: Le Roman mythologique, suivi de questions à Michel Tournier.* Paris: Librairie José Corti, 1988.

Davis, Colin. *Michel Tournier: Philosophy and Fiction.* Oxford: Clarendon P, 1988.

Hebel, Udo J. "Toward a Descriptive Poetics of *Allusion.*" *Intertextuality.* Ed. Heinrich F. Plett. Berlin and New York: Walter de Gruyter, 1991. 135-64.

Mercatante, Anthony S. *The Facts on File Encyclopedia of World Mythology and Legend.* New York and Oxford: Facts on File, 1988.

Miller, Owen. "Preface." *Identity of the Literary Text.* Ed. Marlo J. Valdés and Owen Miller. Toronto: Toronto UP, 1985. vii-xxi.

Müller, Wolfgang G. "Interfigurality: A Study on the Interdependence of Literary Figures." *Intertextuality.* Ed. Heinrich F. Plett. Berlin and New York: Walter de Gruyter, 1991. 101-21.

Oxford Latin Dictionary. 1968 ed. Oxford: Clarendon Press, 1968.

Platten, David. *Michel Tournier and the Metaphor of Fiction.* New York: St. Martin Press, 1999.

Redfern, Walter. *Michel Tournier: Le Coq de bruyère.* Madison and Teaneck: Fairleigh Dickinson UP, 1996.

de Rougemont, Denis. *L'Amour et l'Occident.* Paris: Plon, 1962.

Scheiner, Barbara. *Romantische Themen und Mythen in Frühwerk Michel Tourniers.* Frankfurt am Main: Peter Lang, 1990.

Shoptaw, John. "Lyric Cryptography." *Poetics Today.* 21:1 (2000): 221-62.

Silverman, Kaja. *The Acoustic Mirror: The Female Voice in Psychoanalysis and Cinema.* Bloomington: Indiana UP, 1988.

Stewart, Garrett. *Reading Voices: Literature and the Phonotext.* Berkeley: U of California P, 1990.

Thomas. "Le *Tristan* de Thomas." *Les Tristan en vers.* Ed. Jean Charles Payen. Paris: Garnier, 1974. 145-244.

Tournier, Michel. *Le Coq de bruyère.* Paris: Gallimard, 1982.

———. *Le Roi des Aulnes.* Paris: Gallimard, 1970.

Trésor de la langue française: dictionnaire de la langue du XIXe et du XXe siècle (1789-1960). Paris: Éditions du CNRS / Gallimard, 1980. Vol. 8. 16 vols. 1971-94.

Webster's Encyclopedic Unabridged Dictionary of the English Language. 1989 ed. New York: Portland House, 1989.

FURTHER READING

Criticism

Davis, Colin. "Meaning and Intention." In *Michel Tournier: Philosophy and Fiction,* pp. 116-39. Oxford: Clarendon Press, 1988.
   Interprets *Gilles et Jeanne* as an ambiguous parable on the act of writing.

Easterlin, Nancy L. "Initiation and Counter-Initiation: Progress toward Adulthood in the Stories of Michel Tournier." *Studies in Short Fiction* 28, no. 2 (spring 1991): 151-68.
   Examines the appeal of Tournier's fiction to both adult and child readers.

Gascoigne, David. *Michel Tournier.* Oxford: Berg, 1996, 234 p.
   Book-length study of Tournier's writing.

Levy, Karen D. "Tournier's Ultimate Perversion: The Historical Manipulation of *Gilles et Jeanne.*" *Papers on Language & Literature* 28, no. 1 (winter 1992): 72-88.
   Analyzes the historical accuracy of *Gilles et Jeanne.*

Petit, Susan. "*Gilles et Jeanne*: Tournier's *Le Roi des aulnes* Revisited." *Romanic Review* 76, no. 3 (1985): 307-15.
   Concentrates on the similarities between *Gilles et Jeanne* and *Le Roi des aulnes.*

———. "Psychological, Sensual, and Religious Initiation in Tournier's *Pierrot ou les secrets de la nuit.*" *Children's Literature* 18 (1990): 87-100.
   Appraises the ethical, subversive, and ritualistic aspects of *Pierrot ou les secrets de la nuit.*

Worton, Michael, ed. *Michel Tournier.* London: Longman, 1995, 220 p.
   Collection of essays on Tournier's work.

How to Use This Index

CMW = *St. James Guide to Crime & Mystery Writers*
CN = *Contemporary Novelists*
CP = *Contemporary Poets*
CPW = *Contemporary Popular Writers*
CSW = *Contemporary Southern Writers*
CWD = *Contemporary Women Dramatists*
CWP = *Contemporary Women Poets*
CWRI = *St. James Guide to Children's Writers*
CWW = *Contemporary World Writers*
DA = *DISCovering Authors*
DA3 = *DISCovering Authors 3.0*
DAB = *DISCovering Authors: British Edition*
DAC = *DISCovering Authors: Canadian Edition*
DAM = *DISCovering Authors: Modules*
   DRAM: Dramatists Module; *MST: Most-studied Authors Module;*
   MULT: Multicultural Authors Module; *NOV: Novelists Module;*
   POET: Poets Module; *POP: Popular Fiction and Genre Authors Module*
DFS = *Drama for Students*
DLB = *Dictionary of Literary Biography*
DLBD = *Dictionary of Literary Biography Documentary Series*
DLBY = *Dictionary of Literary Biography Yearbook*
DNFS = *Literature of Developing Nations for Students*
EFS = *Epics for Students*
EXPN = *Exploring Novels*
EXPP = *Exploring Poetry*
EXPS = *Exploring Short Stories*
EW = *European Writers*
FANT = *St. James Guide to Fantasy Writers*
FW = *Feminist Writers*
GFL = *Guide to French Literature,* Beginnings to 1789, 1798 to the Present
GLL = *Gay and Lesbian Literature*
HGG = *St. James Guide to Horror, Ghost & Gothic Writers*
HW = *Hispanic Writers*
IDFW = *International Dictionary of Films and Filmmakers: Writers and Production Artists*
IDTP = *International Dictionary of Theatre: Playwrights*
LAIT = *Literature and Its Times*
LAW = *Latin American Writers*
JRDA = *Junior DISCovering Authors*
MAICYA = *Major Authors and Illustrators for Children and Young Adults*
MAICYAS = *Major Authors and Illustrators for Children and Young Adults Supplement*
MAWW = *Modern American Women Writers*
MJW = *Modern Japanese Writers*
MTCW = *Major 20th-Century Writers*
NCFS = *Nonfiction Classics for Students*
NFS = *Novels for Students*
PAB = *Poets: American and British*
PFS = *Poetry for Students*
RGAL = *Reference Guide to American Literature*
RGEL = *Reference Guide to English Literature*
RGSF = *Reference Guide to Short Fiction*
RGWL = *Reference Guide to World Literature*
RHW = *Twentieth-Century Romance and Historical Writers*
SAAS = *Something about the Author Autobiography Series*
SATA = *Something about the Author*
SFW = *St. James Guide to Science Fiction Writers*
SSFS = *Short Stories for Students*
TCWW = *Twentieth-Century Western Writers*
WLIT = *World Literature and Its Times*
WP = *World Poets*
YABC = *Yesterday's Authors of Books for Children*
YAW = *St. James Guide to Young Adult Writers*

Literary Criticism Series
Cumulative Author Index

Anderson, C. Farley
See Mencken, H(enry) L(ouis); Nathan, George Jean

Anderson, Jessica (Margaret) Queale
1916- .... **CLC 37**
See also CA 9-12R; CANR 4, 62; CN 4, 5, 6, 7

Anderson, Jon (Victor) 1940- .... **CLC 9**
See also CA 25-28R; CANR 20; CP 1, 3, 4; DAM POET

Anderson, Lindsay (Gordon)
1923-1994 .... **CLC 20**
See also CA 125; 128; 146; CANR 77

Anderson, Maxwell 1888-1959 .... **TCLC 2, 144**
See also CA 105; 152; DAM DRAM; DFS 16, 20; DLB 7, 228; MAL 5; MTCW 2; MTFW 2005; RGAL 4

Anderson, Poul (William)
1926-2001 .... **CLC 15**
See also AAYA 5, 34; BPFB 1; BYA 6, 8, 9; CA 1-4R, 181; 199; CAAE 181; CAAS 2; CANR 2, 15, 34, 64, 110; CLR 58; DLB 8; FANT; INT CANR-15; MTCW 1, 2; MTFW 2005; SATA 90; SATA-Brief 39; SATA-Essay 106; SCFW 1, 2; SFW 4; SUFW 1, 2

Anderson, Robert (Woodruff)
1917- .... **CLC 23**
See also AITN 1; CA 21-24R; CANR 32; CD 6; DAM DRAM; DLB 7; LAIT 5

Anderson, Roberta Joan
See Mitchell, Joni

Anderson, Sherwood 1876-1941 .. **SSC 1, 46; TCLC 1, 10, 24, 123; WLC**
See also AAYA 30; AMW; AMWC 2; BPFB 1; CA 104; 121; CANR 61; CDALB 1917-1929; DA; DA3; DAB; DAC; DAM MST, NOV; DLB 4, 9, 86; DLBD 1; EWL 3; EXPS; GLL 2; MAL 5; MTCW 1, 2; MTFW 2005; NFS 4; RGAL 4; RGSF 2; SSFS 4, 10, 11; TUS

Andier, Pierre
See Desnos, Robert

Andouard
See Giraudoux, Jean(-Hippolyte)

Andrade, Carlos Drummond de ..... **CLC 18**
See Drummond de Andrade, Carlos
See also EWL 3; RGWL 2, 3

Andrade, Mario de .... **TCLC 43**
See de Andrade, Mario
See also DLB 307; EWL 3; LAW; RGWL 2, 3; WLIT 1

Andreae, Johann V(alentin)
1586-1654 .... **LC 32**
See also DLB 164

Andreas Capellanus fl. c. 1185- .... **CMLC 45**
See also DLB 208

Andreas-Salome, Lou 1861-1937 ... **TCLC 56**
See also CA 178; DLB 66

Andreev, Leonid
See Andreyev, Leonid (Nikolaevich)
See also DLB 295; EWL 3

Andress, Lesley
See Sanders, Lawrence

Andrewes, Lancelot 1555-1626 .... **LC 5**
See also DLB 151, 172

Andrews, Cicily Fairfield
See West, Rebecca

Andrews, Elton V.
See Pohl, Frederik

Andreyev, Leonid (Nikolaevich)
1871-1919 .... **TCLC 3**
See Andreev, Leonid
See also CA 104; 185

Andric, Ivo 1892-1975 .... **CLC 8; SSC 36; TCLC 135**
See also CA 81-84; 57-60; CANR 43, 60; CDWLB 4; DLB 147; EW 11; EWL 3; MTCW 1; RGSF 2; RGWL 2, 3

Androvar
See Prado (Calvo), Pedro

Angela of Foligno 1248(?)-1309 .... **CMLC 76**

Angelique, Pierre
See Bataille, Georges

Angell, Roger 1920- .... **CLC 26**
See also CA 57-60; CANR 13, 44, 70, 144; DLB 171, 185

Angelou, Maya 1928- ... **BLC 1; CLC 12, 35, 64, 77, 155; PC 32; WLCS**
See also AAYA 7, 20; AMWS 4; BPFB 1; BW 2, 3; BYA 2; CA 65-68; CANR 19, 42, 65, 111, 133; CDALBS; CLR 53; CP 4, 5, 6, 7; CPW; CSW; CWP; DA; DA3; DAB; DAC; DAM MST, MULT, POET, POP; DLB 38; EWL 3; EXPN; EXPP; FL 1:5; LAIT 4; MAICYA 2; MAICYAS 1; MAL 5; MAWW; MTCW 1, 2; MTFW 2005; NCFS 2; NFS 2; PFS 2, 3; RGAL 4; SATA 49, 136; TCLE 1:1; WYA; YAW

Angouleme, Marguerite d'
See de Navarre, Marguerite

Anna Comnena 1083-1153 .... **CMLC 25**

Annensky, Innokentii Fedorovich
See Annensky, Innokenty (Fyodorovich)
See also DLB 295

Annensky, Innokenty (Fyodorovich)
1856-1909 .... **TCLC 14**
See also CA 110; 155; EWL 3

Annunzio, Gabriele d'
See D'Annunzio, Gabriele

Anodos
See Coleridge, Mary E(lizabeth)

Anon, Charles Robert
See Pessoa, Fernando (Antonio Nogueira)

Anouilh, Jean (Marie Lucien Pierre)
1910-1987 . **CLC 1, 3, 8, 13, 40, 50; DC 8, 21**
See also AAYA 67; CA 17-20R; 123; CANR 32; DAM DRAM; DFS 9, 10, 19; DLB 321; EW 13; EWL 3; GFL 1789 to the Present; MTCW 1, 2; MTFW 2005; RGWL 2, 3; TWA

Anselm of Canterbury
1033(?)-1109 .... **CMLC 67**
See also DLB 115

Anthony, Florence
See Ai

Anthony, John
See Ciardi, John (Anthony)

Anthony, Peter
See Shaffer, Anthony (Joshua); Shaffer, Peter (Levin)

Anthony, Piers 1934- .... **CLC 35**
See also AAYA 11, 48; BYA 7; CA 200; CAAE 200; CANR 28, 56, 73, 102, 133; CPW; DAM POP; DLB 8; FANT; MAICYA 2; MAICYAS 1; MTCW 1, 2; MTFW 2005; SAAS 22; SATA 84, 129; SATA-Essay 129; SFW 4; SUFW 1, 2; YAW

Anthony, Susan B(rownell)
1820-1906 .... **TCLC 84**
See also CA 211; FW

Antiphon c. 480B.C.-c. 411B.C. .... **CMLC 55**

Antoine, Marc
See Proust, (Valentin-Louis-George-Eugene) Marcel

Antoninus, Brother
See Everson, William (Oliver)
See also CP 1

Antonioni, Michelangelo 1912- .... **CLC 20, 144**
See also CA 73-76; CANR 45, 77

Antschel, Paul 1920-1970
See Celan, Paul
See also CA 85-88; CANR 33, 61; MTCW 1; PFS 21

Anwar, Chairil 1922-1949 .... **TCLC 22**
See Chairil Anwar
See also CA 121; 219; RGWL 3

Anzaldua, Gloria (Evanjelina)
1942-2004 .... **CLC 200; HLCS 1**
See also CA 175; 227; CSW; CWP; DLB 122; FW; LLW; RGAL 4; SATA-Obit 154

Apess, William 1798-1839(?) .... **NCLC 73; NNAL**
See also DAM MULT; DLB 175, 243

Apollinaire, Guillaume 1880-1918 .... **PC 7; TCLC 3, 8, 51**
See Kostrowitzki, Wilhelm Apollinaris de
See also CA 152; DAM POET; DLB 258, 321; EW 9; EWL 3; GFL 1789 to the Present; MTCW 2; RGWL 2, 3; TWA; WP

Apollonius of Rhodes
See Apollonius Rhodius
See also AW 1; RGWL 2, 3

Apollonius Rhodius c. 300B.C.-c. 220B.C. .... **CMLC 28**
See Apollonius of Rhodes
See also DLB 176

Appelfeld, Aharon 1932- ... **CLC 23, 47; SSC 42**
See also CA 112; 133; CANR 86; CWW 2; DLB 299; EWL 3; RGSF 2; WLIT 6

Apple, Max (Isaac) 1941- .... **CLC 9, 33; SSC 50**
See also CA 81-84; CANR 19, 54; DLB 130

Appleman, Philip (Dean) 1926- .... **CLC 51**
See also CA 13-16R; CAAS 18; CANR 6, 29, 56

Appleton, Lawrence
See Lovecraft, H(oward) P(hillips)

Apteryx
See Eliot, T(homas) S(tearns)

Apuleius, (Lucius Madaurensis)
125(?)-175(?) .... **CMLC 1**
See also AW 2; CDWLB 1; DLB 211; RGWL 2, 3; SUFW

Aquin, Hubert 1929-1977 .... **CLC 15**
See also CA 105; DLB 53; EWL 3

Aquinas, Thomas 1224(?)-1274 ...... **CMLC 33**
See also DLB 115; EW 1; TWA

Aragon, Louis 1897-1982 .... **CLC 3, 22; TCLC 123**
See also CA 69-72; 108; CANR 28, 71; DAM NOV, POET; DLB 72, 258; EW 11; EWL 3; GFL 1789 to the Present; GLL 2; LMFS 2; MTCW 1, 2; RGWL 2, 3

Arany, Janos 1817-1882 .... **NCLC 34**

Aranyos, Kakay 1847-1910
See Mikszath, Kalman

Aratus of Soli c. 315B.C.-c. 240B.C. .... **CMLC 64**
See also DLB 176

Arbuthnot, John 1667-1735 .... **LC 1**
See also DLB 101

Archer, Herbert Winslow
See Mencken, H(enry) L(ouis)

Archer, Jeffrey (Howard) 1940- .... **CLC 28**
See also AAYA 16; BEST 89:3; BPFB 1; CA 77-80; CANR 22, 52, 95, 136; CPW; DA3; DAM POP; INT CANR-22; MTFW 2005

Archer, Jules 1915- .... **CLC 12**
See also CA 9-12R; CANR 6, 69; SAAS 5; SATA 4, 85

Archer, Lee
See Ellison, Harlan (Jay)

Archilochus c. 7th cent. B.C.- .... **CMLC 44**
See also DLB 176

Arden, John 1930- .... **CLC 6, 13, 15**
See also BRWS 2; CA 13-16R; CAAS 4; CANR 31, 65, 67, 124; CBD; CD 5, 6; DAM DRAM; DFS 9; DLB 13, 245; EWL 3; MTCW 1

Arenas, Reinaldo 1943-1990 .. **CLC 41; HLC 1**
See also CA 124; 128; 133; CANR 73, 106; DAM MULT; DLB 145; EWL 3; GLL 2; HW 1; LAW; LAWS 1; MTCW 2; MTFW 2005; RGSF 2; RGWL 3; WLIT 1

Arendt, Hannah 1906-1975 .... **CLC 66, 98**
See also CA 17-20R; 61-64; CANR 26, 60; DLB 242; MTCW 1, 2

Aretino, Pietro 1492-1556 .... **LC 12**
See also RGWL 2, 3

Arghezi, Tudor .... **CLC 80**
See Theodorescu, Ion N.
See also CA 167; CDWLB 4; DLB 220; EWL 3

Arguedas, Jose Maria 1911-1969 .... **CLC 10, 18; HLCS 1; TCLC 147**
See also CA 89-92; CANR 73; DLB 113; EWL 3; HW 1; LAW; RGWL 2, 3; WLIT 1

Argueta, Manlio 1936- .... **CLC 31**
See also CA 131; CANR 73; CWW 2; DLB 145; EWL 3; HW 1; RGWL 3

Arias, Ron(ald Francis) 1941- .... **HLC 1**
See also CA 131; CANR 81, 136; DAM MULT; DLB 82; HW 1, 2; MTCW 2; MTFW 2005

Ariosto, Lodovico
See Ariosto, Ludovico
See also WLIT 7

Ariosto, Ludovico 1474-1533 ... **LC 6, 87; PC 42**
See Ariosto, Lodovico
See also EW 2; RGWL 2, 3

Aristides
See Epstein, Joseph

Aristophanes 450B.C.-385B.C. .... **CMLC 4, 51; DC 2; WLCS**
See also AW 1; CDWLB 1; DA; DA3; DAB; DAC; DAM DRAM, MST; DFS 10; DLB 176; LMFS 1; RGWL 2, 3; TWA

Aristotle 384B.C.-322B.C. .... **CMLC 31; WLCS**
See also AW 1; CDWLB 1; DA; DA3; DAB; DAC; DAM MST; DLB 176; RGWL 2, 3; TWA

Arlt, Roberto (Godofredo Christophersen) 1900-1942 .... **HLC 1; TCLC 29**
See also CA 123; 131; CANR 67; DAM MULT; DLB 305; EWL 3; HW 1, 2; IDTP; LAW

Armah, Ayi Kwei 1939- . **BLC 1; CLC 5, 33, 136**
See also AFW; BRWS 10; BW 1; CA 61-64; CANR 21, 64; CDWLB 3; CN 1, 2, 3, 4, 5, 6, 7; DAM MULT, POET; DLB 117; EWL 3; MTCW 1; WLIT 2

Armatrading, Joan 1950- .... **CLC 17**
See also CA 114; 186

Armitage, Frank
See Carpenter, John (Howard)

Armstrong, Jeannette (C.) 1948- .... **NNAL**
See also CA 149; CCA 1; CN 6, 7; DAC; SATA 102

Arnette, Robert
See Silverberg, Robert

Arnim, Achim von (Ludwig Joachim von Arnim) 1781-1831 .. **NCLC 5, 159; SSC 29**
See also DLB 90

Arnim, Bettina von 1785-1859 ...... **NCLC 38, 123**
See also DLB 90; RGWL 2, 3

Arnold, Matthew 1822-1888 ..... **NCLC 6, 29, 89, 126; PC 5; WLC**
See also BRW 5; CDBLB 1832-1890; DA; DAB; DAC; DAM MST, POET; DLB 32, 57; EXPP; PAB; PFS 2; TEA; WP

Arnold, Thomas 1795-1842 .... **NCLC 18**
See also DLB 55

Arnow, Harriette (Louisa) Simpson 1908-1986 .... **CLC 2, 7, 18**
See also BPFB 1; CA 9-12R; 118; CANR 14; CN 2, 3, 4; DLB 6; FW; MTCW 1, 2; RHW; SATA 42; SATA-Obit 47

Arouet, Francois-Marie
See Voltaire

Arp, Hans
See Arp, Jean

Arp, Jean 1887-1966 .... **CLC 5; TCLC 115**
See also CA 81-84; 25-28R; CANR 42, 77; EW 10

Arrabal
See Arrabal, Fernando

Arrabal (Teran), Fernando
See Arrabal, Fernando
See also CWW 2

Arrabal, Fernando 1932- ... **CLC 2, 9, 18, 58**
See Arrabal (Teran), Fernando
See also CA 9-12R; CANR 15; DLB 321; EWL 3; LMFS 2

Arreola, Juan Jose 1918-2001 .... **CLC 147; HLC 1; SSC 38**
See also CA 113; 131; 200; CANR 81; CWW 2; DAM MULT; DLB 113; DNFS 2; EWL 3; HW 1, 2; LAW; RGSF 2

Arrian c. 89(?)-c. 155(?) .... **CMLC 43**
See also DLB 176

Arrick, Fran .... **CLC 30**
See Gaberman, Judie Angell
See also BYA 6

Arrley, Richmond
See Delany, Samuel R(ay), Jr.

Artaud, Antonin (Marie Joseph) 1896-1948 .... **DC 14; TCLC 3, 36**
See also CA 104; 149; DA3; DAM DRAM; DFS 22; DLB 258, 321; EW 11; EWL 3; GFL 1789 to the Present; MTCW 2; MTFW 2005; RGWL 2, 3

Arthur, Ruth M(abel) 1905-1979 ..... **CLC 12**
See also CA 9-12R; 85-88; CANR 4; CWRI 5; SATA 7, 26

Artsybashev, Mikhail (Petrovich) 1878-1927 .... **TCLC 31**
See also CA 170; DLB 295

Arundel, Honor (Morfydd) 1919-1973 .... **CLC 17**
See also CA 21-22; 41-44R; CAP 2; CLR 35; CWRI 5; SATA 4; SATA-Obit 24

Arzner, Dorothy 1900-1979 .... **CLC 98**

Asch, Sholem 1880-1957 .... **TCLC 3**
See also CA 105; EWL 3; GLL 2

Ascham, Roger 1516(?)-1568 .... **LC 101**
See also DLB 236

Ash, Shalom
See Asch, Sholem

Ashbery, John (Lawrence) 1927- .. **CLC 2, 3, 4, 6, 9, 13, 15, 25, 41, 77, 125; PC 26**
See Berry, Jonas
See also AMWS 3; CA 5-8R; CANR 9, 37, 66, 102, 132; CP 1, 2, 3, 4, 5, 6, 7; DA3; DAM POET; DLB 5, 165; DLBY 1981; EWL 3; INT CANR-9; MAL 5; MTCW 1, 2; MTFW 2005; PAB; PFS 11; RGAL 4; TCLE 1:1; WP

Ashdown, Clifford
See Freeman, R(ichard) Austin

Ashe, Gordon
See Creasey, John

Ashton-Warner, Sylvia (Constance) 1908-1984 .... **CLC 19**
See also CA 69-72; 112; CANR 29; CN 1, 2, 3; MTCW 1, 2

Asimov, Isaac 1920-1992 ..... **CLC 1, 3, 9, 19, 26, 76, 92**
See also AAYA 13; BEST 90:2; BPFB 1; BYA 4, 6, 7, 9; CA 1-4R; 137; CANR 2, 19, 36, 60, 125; CLR 12, 79; CMW 4; CN 1, 2, 3, 4, 5; CPW; DA3; DAM POP; DLB 8; DLBY 1992; INT CANR-19; JRDA; LAIT 5; LMFS 2; MAICYA 1, 2; MAL 5; MTCW 1, 2; MTFW 2005; RGAL 4; SATA 1, 26, 74; SCFW 1, 2; SFW 4; SSFS 17; TUS; YAW

Askew, Anne 1521(?)-1546 .... **LC 81**
See also DLB 136

Assis, Joaquim Maria Machado de
See Machado de Assis, Joaquim Maria

Astell, Mary 1666-1731 .... **LC 68**
See also DLB 252; FW

Astley, Thea (Beatrice May) 1925-2004 .... **CLC 41**
See also CA 65-68; 229; CANR 11, 43, 78; CN 1, 2, 3, 4, 5, 6, 7; DLB 289; EWL 3

Astley, William 1855-1911
See Warung, Price

Aston, James
See White, T(erence) H(anbury)

Asturias, Miguel Angel 1899-1974 .... **CLC 3, 8, 13; HLC 1**
See also CA 25-28; 49-52; CANR 32; CAP 2; CDWLB 3; DA3; DAM MULT, NOV; DLB 113, 290; EWL 3; HW 1; LAW; LMFS 2; MTCW 1, 2; RGWL 2, 3; WLIT 1

Atares, Carlos Saura
See Saura (Atares), Carlos

Athanasius c. 295-c. 373 .... **CMLC 48**

Atheling, William
See Pound, Ezra (Weston Loomis)

Atheling, William, Jr.
See Blish, James (Benjamin)

Atherton, Gertrude (Franklin Horn) 1857-1948 .... **TCLC 2**
See also CA 104; 155; DLB 9, 78, 186; HGG; RGAL 4; SUFW 1; TCWW 1, 2

Atherton, Lucius
See Masters, Edgar Lee

Atkins, Jack
See Harris, Mark

Atkinson, Kate 1951- .... **CLC 99**
See also CA 166; CANR 101; DLB 267

Attaway, William (Alexander) 1911-1986 .... **BLC 1; CLC 92**
See also BW 2, 3; CA 143; CANR 82; DAM MULT; DLB 76; MAL 5

Atticus
See Fleming, Ian (Lancaster); Wilson, (Thomas) Woodrow

Atwood, Margaret (Eleanor) 1939- ... **CLC 2, 3, 4, 8, 13, 15, 25, 44, 84, 135; PC 8; SSC 2, 46; WLC**
See also AAYA 12, 47; AMWS 13; BEST 89:2; BPFB 1; CA 49-52; CANR 3, 24, 33, 59, 95, 133; CN 2, 3, 4, 5, 6, 7; CP 1, 2, 3, 4, 5, 6, 7; CPW; CWP; DA; DA3; DAB; DAC; DAM MST, NOV, POET; DLB 53, 251; EWL 3; EXPN; FL 1:5; FW; GL 2; INT CANR-24; LAIT 5; MTCW 1, 2; MTFW 2005; NFS 4, 12, 13, 14, 19; PFS 7; RGSF 2; SATA 50; SSFS 3, 13; TCLE 1:1; TWA; WWE 1; YAW

Aubigny, Pierre d'
See Mencken, H(enry) L(ouis)

Aubin, Penelope 1685-1731(?) .... **LC 9**
See also DLB 39

Barth, John (Simmons) 1930- ... CLC 1, 2, 3, 5, 7, 9, 10, 14, 27, 51, 89, 214; SSC 10
See also AITN 1, 2; AMW; BPFB 1; CA 1-4R; CABS 1; CANR 5, 23, 49, 64, 113; CN 1, 2, 3, 4, 5, 6, 7; DAM NOV; DLB 2, 227; EWL 3; FANT; MAL 5; MTCW 1; RGAL 4; RGSF 2; RHW; SSFS 6; TUS

Barthelme, Donald 1931-1989 ... CLC 1, 2, 3, 5, 6, 8, 13, 23, 46, 59, 115; SSC 2, 55
See also AMWS 4; BPFB 1; CA 21-24R; 129; CANR 20, 58; CN 1, 2, 3, 4; DA3; DAM NOV; DLB 2, 234; DLBY 1980, 1989; EWL 3; FANT; LMFS 2; MAL 5; MTCW 1, 2; MTFW 2005; RGAL 4; RGSF 2; SATA 7; SATA Obit 62; SSFS 17

Barthelme, Frederick 1943- ...... CLC 36, 117
See also AMWS 11; CA 114; 122; CANR 77; CN 4, 5, 6, 7; CSW; DLB 244; DLBY 1985; EWL 3; INT CA-122

Barthes, Roland (Gerard) 1915-1980 .... CLC 24, 83; TCLC 135
See also CA 130; 97-100; CANR 66; DLB 296; EW 13; EWL 3; GFL 1789 to the Present; MTCW 1, 2; TWA

Bartram, William 1739-1823 .... NCLC 145
See also ANW; DLB 37

Barzun, Jacques (Martin) 1907- ..... CLC 51, 145
See also CA 61-64; CANR 22, 95

Bashevis, Isaac
See Singer, Isaac Bashevis

Bashkirtseff, Marie 1859-1884 .... NCLC 27

Basho, Matsuo
See Matsuo Basho
See also RGWL 2, 3; WP

Basil of Caesaria c. 330-379 .... CMLC 35

Basket, Raney
See Edgerton, Clyde (Carlyle)

Bass, Kingsley B., Jr.
See Bullins, Ed

Bass, Rick 1958- .... CLC 79, 143; SSC 60
See also ANW; CA 126; CANR 53, 93, 145; CSW; DLB 212, 275

Bassani, Giorgio 1916-2000 .... CLC 9
See also CA 65-68; 190; CANR 33; CWW 2; DLB 128, 177, 299; EWL 3; MTCW 1; RGWL 2, 3

Bastian, Ann .... CLC 70

Bastos, Augusto (Antonio) Roa
See Roa Bastos, Augusto (Jose Antonio)

Bataille, Georges 1897-1962 .... CLC 29; TCLC 155
See also CA 101; 89-92; EWL 3

Bates, H(erbert) E(rnest) 1905-1974 .... CLC 46; SSC 10
See also CA 93-96; 45-48; CANR 34; CN 1; DA3; DAB; DAM POP; DLB 162, 191; EWL 3; EXPS; MTCW 1, 2; RGSF 2; SSFS 7

Bauchart
See Camus, Albert

Baudelaire, Charles 1821-1867 . NCLC 6, 29, 55, 155; PC 1; SSC 18; WLC
See also DA; DA3; DAB; DAC; DAM MST, POET; DLB 217; EW 7; GFL 1789 to the Present; LMFS 2; PFS 21; RGWL 2, 3; TWA

Baudouin, Marcel
See Peguy, Charles (Pierre)

Baudouin, Pierre
See Peguy, Charles (Pierre)

Baudrillard, Jean 1929- .... CLC 60
See also DLB 296

Baum, L(yman) Frank 1856-1919 .. TCLC 7, 132
See also AAYA 46; BYA 16; CA 108; 133; CLR 15; CWRI 5; DLB 22; FANT; JRDA; MAICYA 1, 2; MTCW 1; NFS 13; RGAL 4; SATA 18, 100; WCH

Baum, Louis F.
See Baum, L(yman) Frank

Baumbach, Jonathan 1933- .... CLC 6, 23
See also CA 13-16R; CAAS 5; CANR 12, 66, 140; CN 3, 4, 5, 6, 7; DLBY 1980; INT CANR-12; MTCW 1

Bausch, Richard (Carl) 1945- .... CLC 51
See also AMWS 7; CA 101; CAAS 14; CANR 43, 61, 87; CN 7; CSW; DLB 130; MAL 5

Baxter, Charles (Morley) 1947- . CLC 45, 78
See also CA 57-60; CANR 40, 64, 104, 133; CPW; DAM POP; DLB 130; MAL 5; MTCW 2; MTFW 2005; TCLE 1:1

Baxter, George Owen
See Faust, Frederick (Schiller)

Baxter, James K(eir) 1926-1972 .... CLC 14
See also CA 77-80; CP 1; EWL 3

Baxter, John
See Hunt, E(verette) Howard, (Jr.)

Bayer, Sylvia
See Glassco, John

Baynton, Barbara 1857-1929 .... TCLC 57
See also DLB 230; RGSF 2

Beagle, Peter S(oyer) 1939- .... CLC 7, 104
See also AAYA 47; BPFB 1; BYA 9, 10, 16; CA 9-12R; CANR 4, 51, 73, 110; DA3; DLBY 1980; FANT; INT CANR-4; MTCW 2; MTFW 2005; SATA 60, 130; SUFW 1, 2; YAW

Bean, Normal
See Burroughs, Edgar Rice

Beard, Charles A(ustin) 1874-1948 .... TCLC 15
See also CA 115; 189; DLB 17; SATA 18

Beardsley, Aubrey 1872-1898 .... NCLC 6

Beattie, Ann 1947- ..... CLC 8, 13, 18, 40, 63, 146; SSC 11
See also AMWS 5; BEST 90:2; BPFB 1; CA 81-84; CANR 53, 73, 128; CN 4, 5, 6, 7; CPW; DA3; DAM NOV, POP; DLB 218, 278; DLBY 1982; EWL 3; MAL 5; MTCW 1, 2; MTFW 2005; RGAL 4; RGSF 2; SSFS 9; TUS

Beattie, James 1735-1803 .... NCLC 25
See also DLB 109

Beauchamp, Kathleen Mansfield 1888-1923
See Mansfield, Katherine
See also CA 104; 134; DA; DA3; DAC; DAM MST; MTCW 2; TEA

Beaumarchais, Pierre-Augustin Caron de 1732-1799 .... DC 4; LC 61
See also DAM DRAM; DFS 14, 16; DLB 313; EW 4; GFL Beginnings to 1789; RGWL 2, 3

Beaumont, Francis 1584(?)-1616 .. DC 6; LC 33
See also BRW 2; CDBLB Before 1660; DLB 58; TEA

Beauvoir, Simone (Lucie Ernestine Marie Bertrand) de 1908-1986 .... CLC 1, 2, 4, 8, 14, 31, 44, 50, 71, 124; SSC 35; WLC
See also BPFB 1; CA 9-12R; 118; CANR 28, 61; DA; DA3; DAB; DAC; DAM MST, NOV; DLB 72; DLBY 1986; EW 12; EWL 3; FL 1:5; FW; GFL 1789 to the Present; LMFS 2; MTCW 1, 2; MTFW 2005; RGSF 2; RGWL 2, 3; TWA

Becker, Carl (Lotus) 1873-1945 ..... TCLC 63
See also CA 157; DLB 17

Becker, Jurek 1937-1997 .... CLC 7, 19
See also CA 85-88; 157; CANR 60, 117; CWW 2; DLB 75, 299; EWL 3

Becker, Walter 1950- .... CLC 26

Beckett, Samuel (Barclay) 1906-1989 .. CLC 1, 2, 3, 4, 6, 9, 10, 11, 14, 18, 29, 57, 59, 83; DC 22; SSC 16, 74; TCLC 145; WLC
See also BRWC 2; BRWR 1; BRWS 1; CA 5-8R; 130; CANR 33, 61; CBD; CDBLB

1945-1960; CN 1, 2, 3, 4; CP 1, 2, 3, 4; DA; DA3; DAB; DAC; DAM DRAM, MST, NOV; DFS 2, 7, 18; DLB 13, 15, 233, 319, 321; DLBY 1990; EWL 3; GFL 1789 to the Present; LATS 1:2; LMFS 2; MTCW 1, 2; MTFW 2005; RGSF 2; RGWL 2, 3; SSFS 15; TEA; WLIT 4

Beckford, William 1760-1844 .... NCLC 16
See also BRW 3; DLB 39, 213; GL 2; HGG; LMFS 1; SUFW

Beckham, Barry (Earl) 1944- .... BLC 1
See also BW 1; CA 29-32R; CANR 26, 62; CN 1, 2, 3, 4, 5, 6; DAM MULT; DLB 33

Beckman, Gunnel 1910- .... CLC 26
See also CA 33-36R; CANR 15, 114; CLR 25; MAICYA 1, 2; SAAS 9; SATA 6

Becque, Henri 1837-1899 ... DC 21; NCLC 3
See also DLB 192; GFL 1789 to the Present

Becquer, Gustavo Adolfo 1836-1870 .... HLCS 1; NCLC 106
See also DAM MULT

Beddoes, Thomas Lovell 1803-1849 .. DC 15; NCLC 3, 154
See also BRWS 11; DLB 96

Bede c. 673-735 .... CMLC 20
See also DLB 146; TEA

Bedford, Denton R. 1907-(?) .... NNAL

Bedford, Donald F.
See Fearing, Kenneth (Flexner)

Beecher, Catharine Esther 1800-1878 .... NCLC 30
See also DLB 1, 243

Beecher, John 1904-1980 .... CLC 6
See also AITN 1; CA 5-8R; 105; CANR 8; CP 1, 2, 3

Beer, Johann 1655-1700 .... LC 5
See also DLB 168

Beer, Patricia 1924- .... CLC 58
See also CA 61-64; 183; CANR 13, 46; CP 1, 2, 3, 4; CWP; DLB 40; FW

Beerbohm, Max
See Beerbohm, (Henry) Max(imilian)

Beerbohm, (Henry) Max(imilian) 1872-1956 .... TCLC 1, 24
See also BRWS 2; CA 104; 154; CANR 79; DLB 34, 100; FANT; MTCW 2

Beer-Hofmann, Richard 1866-1945 .... TCLC 60
See also CA 160; DLB 81

Beg, Shemus
See Stephens, James

Begiebing, Robert J(ohn) 1946- .... CLC 70
See also CA 122; CANR 40, 88

Begley, Louis 1933- .... CLC 197
See also CA 140; CANR 98; DLB 299; TCLE 1:1

Behan, Brendan (Francis) 1923-1964 .... CLC 1, 8, 11, 15, 79
See also BRWS 2; CA 73-76; CANR 33, 121; CBD; CDBLB 1945-1960; DAM DRAM; DFS 7; DLB 13, 233; EWL 3; MTCW 1, 2

Behn, Aphra 1640(?)-1689 .. DC 4; LC 1, 30, 42; PC 13; WLC
See also BRWS 3; DA; DA3; DAB; DAC; DAM DRAM, MST, NOV, POET; DFS 16; DLB 39, 80, 131; FW; TEA; WLIT 3

Behrman, S(amuel) N(athaniel) 1893-1973 .... CLC 40
See also CA 13-16; 45-48; CAD; CAP 1; DLB 7, 44; IDFW 3; MAL 5; RGAL 4

Bekederemo, J. P. Clark
See Clark Bekederemo, J(ohnson) P(epper)
See also CD 6

Belasco, David 1853-1931 .... TCLC 3
See also CA 104; 168; DLB 7; MAL 5; RGAL 4

Bitov, Andrei (Georgievich) 1937- ... **CLC 57**
See also CA 142; DLB 302
Biyidi, Alexandre 1932-
See Beti, Mongo
See also BW 1, 3; CA 114; 124; CANR 81;
DA3; MTCW 1, 2
Bjarme, Brynjolf
See Ibsen, Henrik (Johan)
Bjoernson, Bjoernstjerne (Martinius)
1832-1910 .... **TCLC 7, 37**
See also CA 104
Black, Robert
See Holdstock, Robert P.
Blackburn, Paul 1926-1971 .... **CLC 9, 43**
See also BG 1:2; CA 81-84; 33-36R; CANR
34; CP 1; DLB 16; DLBY 1981
Black Elk 1863-1950 .... **NNAL; TCLC 33**
See also CA 144; DAM MULT; MTCW 2;
MTFW 2005; WP
Black Hawk 1767-1838 .... **NNAL**
Black Hobart
See Sanders, (James) Ed(ward)
Blacklin, Malcolm
See Chambers, Aidan
Blackmore, R(ichard) D(oddridge)
1825-1900 .... **TCLC 27**
See also CA 120; DLB 18; RGEL 2
Blackmur, R(ichard) P(almer)
1904-1965 .... **CLC 2, 24**
See also AMWS 2; CA 11-12; 25-28R;
CANR 71; CAP 1; DLB 63; EWL 3;
MAL 5
Black Tarantula
See Acker, Kathy
Blackwood, Algernon (Henry)
1869-1951 .... **TCLC 5**
See also CA 105; 150; DLB 153, 156, 178;
HGG; SUFW 1
Blackwood, Caroline (Maureen)
1931-1996 .... **CLC 6, 9, 100**
See also BRWS 9; CA 85-88; 151; CANR
32, 61, 65; CN 3, 4, 5, 6; DLB 14, 207;
HGG; MTCW 1
Blade, Alexander
See Hamilton, Edmond; Silverberg, Robert
Blaga, Lucian 1895-1961 .... **CLC 75**
See also CA 157; DLB 220; EWL 3
Blair, Eric (Arthur) 1903-1950 .... **TCLC 123**
See Orwell, George
See also CA 104; 132; DA; DA3; DAB;
DAC; DAM MST, NOV; MTCW 1, 2;
MTFW 2005; SATA 29
Blair, Hugh 1718-1800 .... **NCLC 75**
Blais, Marie-Claire 1939- .... **CLC 2, 4, 6, 13, 22**
See also CA 21-24R; CAAS 4; CANR 38,
75, 93; CWW 2; DAC; DAM MST; DLB
53; EWL 3; FW; MTCW 1, 2; MTFW
2005; TWA
Blaise, Clark 1940- .... **CLC 29**
See also AITN 2; CA 53-56, 231; CAAE
231; CAAS 3; CANR 5, 66, 106; CN 4,
5, 6, 7; DLB 53; RGSF 2
Blake, Fairley
See De Voto, Bernard (Augustine)
Blake, Nicholas
See Day Lewis, C(ecil)
See also DLB 77; MSW
Blake, Sterling
See Benford, Gregory (Albert)
Blake, William 1757-1827 . **NCLC 13, 37, 57, 127; PC 12, 63; WLC**
See also AAYA 47; BRW 3; BRWR 1; CD-
BLB 1789-1832; CLR 52; DA; DA3;
DAB; DAC; DAM MST, POET; DLB 93,
163; EXPP; LATS 1:1; LMFS 1; MAI-
CYA 1, 2; PAB; PFS 2, 12; SATA 30;
TEA; WCH; WLIT 3; WP

Blanchot, Maurice 1907-2003 .... **CLC 135**
See also CA 117; 144; 213; CANR 138;
DLB 72, 296; EWL 3
Blasco Ibanez, Vicente 1867-1928 . **TCLC 12**
See Ibanez, Vicente Blasco
See also BPFB 1; CA 110; 131; CANR 81;
DA3; DAM NOV; EW 8; EWL 3; HW 1,
2; MTCW 1
Blatty, William Peter 1928- .... **CLC 2**
See also CA 5-8R; CANR 9, 124; DAM
POP; HGG
Bleeck, Oliver
See Thomas, Ross (Elmore)
Blessing, Lee (Knowlton) 1949- .... **CLC 54**
See also CA 236; CAD; CD 5, 6
Blight, Rose
See Greer, Germaine
Blish, James (Benjamin) 1921-1975 . **CLC 14**
See also BPFB 1; CA 1-4R; 57-60; CANR
3; CN 2; DLB 8; MTCW 1; SATA 66;
SCFW 1, 2; SFW 4
Bliss, Frederick
See Card, Orson Scott
Bliss, Reginald
See Wells, H(erbert) G(eorge)
Blixen, Karen (Christentze Dinesen)
1885-1962
See Dinesen, Isak
See also CA 25-28; CANR 22, 50; CAP 2;
DA3; DLB 214; LMFS 1; MTCW 1, 2;
SATA 44; SSFS 20
Bloch, Robert (Albert) 1917-1994 .... **CLC 33**
See also AAYA 29; CA 5-8R, 179; 146;
CAAE 179; CAAS 20; CANR 5, 78;
DA3; DLB 44; HGG; INT CANR-5;
MTCW 2; SATA 12; SATA-Obit 82; SFW
4; SUFW 1, 2
Blok, Alexander (Alexandrovich)
1880-1921 .... **PC 21; TCLC 5**
See also CA 104; 183; DLB 295; EW 9;
EWL 3; LMFS 2; RGWL 2, 3
Blom, Jan
See Breytenbach, Breyten
Bloom, Harold 1930- .... **CLC 24, 103**
See also CA 13-16R; CANR 39, 75, 92,
133; DLB 67; EWL 3; MTCW 2; MTFW
2005; RGAL 4
Bloomfield, Aurelius
See Bourne, Randolph S(illiman)
Bloomfield, Robert 1766-1823 ..... **NCLC 145**
See also DLB 93
Blount, Roy (Alton), Jr. 1941- .... **CLC 38**
See also CA 53-56; CANR 10, 28, 61, 125;
CSW; INT CANR-28; MTCW 1, 2;
MTFW 2005
Blowsnake, Sam 1875-(?) .... **NNAL**
Bloy, Leon 1846-1917 .... **TCLC 22**
See also CA 121; 183; DLB 123; GFL 1789
to the Present
Blue Cloud, Peter (Aroniawenrate)
1933- .... **NNAL**
See also CA 117; CANR 40; DAM MULT
Bluggage, Oranthy
See Alcott, Louisa May
Blume, Judy (Sussman) 1938- .... **CLC 12, 30**
See also AAYA 3, 26; BYA 1, 8, 12; CA 29-
32R; CANR 13, 37, 66, 124; CLR 2, 15,
69; CPW; DA3; DAM NOV, POP; DLB
52; JRDA; MAICYA 1, 2; MAICYAS 1;
MTCW 1, 2; MTFW 2005; SATA 2, 31,
79, 142; WYA; YAW
Blunden, Edmund (Charles)
1896-1974 .... **CLC 2, 56; PC 66**
See also BRW 6; BRWS 11; CA 17-18; 45-
48; CANR 54; CAP 2; CP 1, 2; DLB 20,
100, 155; MTCW 1; PAB

Bly, Robert (Elwood) 1926- .... **CLC 1, 2, 5, 10, 15, 38, 128; PC 39**
See also AMWS 4; CA 5-8R; CANR 41,
73, 125; CP 1, 2, 3, 4, 5, 6, 7; DA3; DAM
POET; DLB 5; EWL 3; MAL 5; MTCW
1, 2; MTFW 2005; PFS 6, 17; RGAL 4
Boas, Franz 1858-1942 .... **TCLC 56**
See also CA 115; 181
Bobette
See Simenon, Georges (Jacques Christian)
Boccaccio, Giovanni 1313-1375 ... **CMLC 13, 57; SSC 10, 87**
See also EW 2; RGSF 2; RGWL 2, 3; TWA;
WLIT 7
Bochco, Steven 1943- .... **CLC 35**
See also AAYA 11; CA 124; 138
Bode, Sigmund
See O'Doherty, Brian
Bodel, Jean 1167(?)-1210 .... **CMLC 28**
Bodenheim, Maxwell 1892-1954 .... **TCLC 44**
See also CA 110; 187; DLB 9, 45; MAL 5;
RGAL 4
Bodenheimer, Maxwell
See Bodenheim, Maxwell
Bodker, Cecil 1927-
See Bodker, Cecil
Bodker, Cecil 1927- .... **CLC 21**
See also CA 73-76; CANR 13, 44, 111;
CLR 23; MAICYA 1, 2; SATA 14, 133
Boell, Heinrich (Theodor)
1917-1985 ..... **CLC 2, 3, 6, 9, 11, 15, 27, 32, 72; SSC 23; WLC**
See Boll, Heinrich (Theodor)
See also CA 21-24R; 116; CANR 24; DA;
DA3; DAB; DAC; DAM MST, NOV;
DLB 69; DLBY 1985; MTCW 1, 2;
MTFW 2005; SSFS 20; TWA
Boerne, Alfred
See Doeblin, Alfred
Boethius c. 480-c. 524 .... **CMLC 15**
See also DLB 115; RGWL 2, 3
Boff, Leonardo (Genezio Darci)
1938- .... **CLC 70; HLC 1**
See also CA 150; DAM MULT; HW 2
Bogan, Louise 1897-1970 .... **CLC 4, 39, 46, 93; PC 12**
See also AMWS 3; CA 73-76; 25-28R;
CANR 33, 82; CP 1; DAM POET; DLB
45, 169; EWL 3; MAL 5; MAWW;
MTCW 1, 2; PFS 21; RGAL 4
Bogarde, Dirk
See Van Den Bogarde, Derek Jules Gaspard
Ulric Niven
See also DLB 14
Bogosian, Eric 1953- .... **CLC 45, 141**
See also CA 138; CAD; CANR 102; CD 5,
6
Bograd, Larry 1953- .... **CLC 35**
See also CA 93-96; CANR 57; SAAS 21;
SATA 33, 89; WYA
Boiardo, Matteo Maria 1441-1494 .... **LC 6**
Boileau-Despreaux, Nicolas 1636-1711 . **LC 3**
See also DLB 268; EW 3; GFL Beginnings
to 1789; RGWL 2, 3
Boissard, Maurice
See Leautaud, Paul
Bojer, Johan 1872-1959 .... **TCLC 64**
See also CA 189; EWL 3
Bok, Edward W(illiam)
1863-1930 .... **TCLC 101**
See also CA 217; DLB 91; DLBD 16
Boker, George Henry 1823-1890 . **NCLC 125**
See also RGAL 4
Boland, Eavan (Aisling) 1944- .. **CLC 40, 67, 113; PC 58**
See also BRWS 5; CA 143, 207; CAAE
207; CANR 61; CP 1, 7; CWP; DAM
POET; DLB 40; FW; MTCW 2; MTFW
2005; PFS 12, 22

Braddon, Mary Elizabeth
1837-1915 .... **TCLC 111**
See also BRWS 8; CA 108; 179; CMW 4;
DLB 18, 70, 156; HGG

Bradfield, Scott (Michael) 1955- .... **SSC 65**
See also CA 147; CANR 90; HGG; SUFW
2

Bradford, Gamaliel 1863-1932 .... **TCLC 36**
See also CA 160; DLB 17

Bradford, William 1590-1657 .... **LC 64**
See also DLB 24, 30; RGAL 4

Bradley, David (Henry), Jr. 1950- .... **BLC 1;
CLC 23, 118**
See also BW 1, 3; CA 104; CANR 26, 81;
CN 4, 5, 6, 7; DAM MULT; DLB 33

Bradley, John Ed(mund, Jr.) 1958- . **CLC 55**
See also CA 139; CANR 99; CN 6, 7; CSW

Bradley, Marion Zimmer
1930-1999 .... **CLC 30**
See Chapman, Lee; Dexter, John; Gardner,
Miriam; Ives, Morgan; Rivers, Elfrida
See also AAYA 40; BPFB 1; CA 57-60; 185;
CAAS 10; CANR 7, 31, 51, 75, 107;
CPW; DA3; DAM POP; DLB 8; FANT;
FW; MTCW 1, 2; MTFW 2005; SATA 90,
139; SATA-Obit 116; SFW 4; SUFW 2;
YAW

Bradshaw, John 1933- .... **CLC 70**
See also CA 138; CANR 61

Bradstreet, Anne 1612(?)-1672 ...... **LC 4, 30;
PC 10**
See also AMWS 1; CDALB 1640-1865;
DA; DA3; DAC; DAM MST, POET; DLB
24; EXPP; FW; PFS 6; RGAL 4; TUS;
WP

Brady, Joan 1939- .... **CLC 86**
See also CA 141

Bragg, Melvyn 1939- .... **CLC 10**
See also BEST 89:3; CA 57-60; CANR 10,
48, 89; CN 1, 2, 3, 4, 5, 6, 7; DLB 14,
271; RHW

Brahe, Tycho 1546-1601 .... **LC 45**
See also DLB 300

Braine, John (Gerard) 1922-1986 . **CLC 1, 3,
41**
See also CA 1-4R; 120; CANR 1, 33; CD-
BLB 1945-1960; CN 1, 2, 3, 4; DLB 15;
DLBY 1986; EWL 3; MTCW 1

Braithwaite, William Stanley (Beaumont)
1878-1962 .... **BLC 1; HR 1:2; PC 52**
See also BW 1; CA 125; DAM MULT; DLB
50, 54; MAL 5

Bramah, Ernest 1868-1942 .... **TCLC 72**
See also CA 156; CMW 4; DLB 70; FANT

Brammer, Billy Lee
See Brammer, William

Brammer, William 1929-1978 .... **CLC 31**
See also CA 235; 77-80

Brancati, Vitaliano 1907-1954 .... **TCLC 12**
See also CA 109; DLB 264; EWL 3

Brancato, Robin F(idler) 1936- .... **CLC 35**
See also AAYA 9, 68; BYA 6; CA 69-72;
CANR 11, 45; CLR 32; JRDA; MAICYA
2; MAICYAS 1; SAAS 9; SATA 97;
WYA; YAW

Brand, Dionne 1953- .... **CLC 192**
See also BW 2; CA 143; CANR 143; CWP

Brand, Max
See Faust, Frederick (Schiller)
See also BPFB 1; TCWW 1, 2

Brand, Millen 1906-1980 .... **CLC 7**
See also CA 21-24R; 97-100; CANR 72

Branden, Barbara .... **CLC 44**
See also CA 148

Brandes, Georg (Morris Cohen)
1842-1927 .... **TCLC 10**
See also CA 105; 189; DLB 300

Brandys, Kazimierz 1916-2000 .... **CLC 62**
See also CA 239; EWL 3

Branley, Franklyn M(ansfield)
1915-2002 .... **CLC 21**
See also CA 33-36R; 207; CANR 14, 39;
CLR 13; MAICYA 1, 2; SAAS 16; SATA
4, 68, 136

Brant, Beth (E.) 1941- .... **NNAL**
See also CA 144; FW

Brant, Sebastian 1457-1521 .... **LC 112**
See also DLB 179; RGWL 2, 3

Brathwaite, Edward Kamau
1930- .... **BLCS; CLC 11; PC 56**
See also BW 2, 3; CA 25-28R; CANR 11,
26, 47, 107; CDWLB 3; CP 1, 2, 3, 4, 5,
6, 7; DAM POET; DLB 125; EWL 3

Brathwaite, Kamau
See Brathwaite, Edward Kamau

Brautigan, Richard (Gary)
1935-1984 .... **CLC 1, 3, 5, 9, 12, 34, 42;
TCLC 133**
See also BPFB 1; CA 53-56; 113; CANR
34; CN 1, 2, 3; CP 1, 2, 3, 4; DA3; DAM
NOV; DLB 2, 5, 206; DLBY 1980, 1984;
FANT; MAL 5; MTCW 1; RGAL 4;
SATA 56

Brave Bird, Mary .... **NNAL**
See Crow Dog, Mary (Ellen)

Braverman, Kate 1950- .... **CLC 67**
See also CA 89-92; CANR 141

Brecht, (Eugen) Bertolt (Friedrich)
1898-1956 ..... **DC 3; TCLC 1, 6, 13, 35,
169; WLC**
See also CA 104; 133; CANR 62; CDWLB
2; DA; DA3; DAB; DAC; DAM DRAM,
MST; DFS 4, 5, 9; DLB 56, 124; EW 11;
EWL 3; IDTP; MTCW 1, 2; MTFW 2005;
RGWL 2, 3; TWA

Brecht, Eugen Berthold Friedrich
See Brecht, (Eugen) Bertolt (Friedrich)

Bremer, Fredrika 1801-1865 .... **NCLC 11**
See also DLB 254

Brennan, Christopher John
1870-1932 .... **TCLC 17**
See also CA 117; 188; DLB 230; EWL 3

Brennan, Maeve 1917-1993 ... **CLC 5; TCLC
124**
See also CA 81-84; CANR 72, 100

Brenner, Jozef 1887-1919
See Csath, Geza
See also CA 240

Brent, Linda
See Jacobs, Harriet A(nn)

Brentano, Clemens (Maria)
1778-1842 .... **NCLC 1**
See also DLB 90; RGWL 2, 3

Brent of Bin Bin
See Franklin, (Stella Maria Sarah) Miles
(Lampe)

Brenton, Howard 1942- .... **CLC 31**
See also CA 69-72; CANR 33, 67; CBD;
CD 5, 6; DLB 13; MTCW 1

Breslin, James 1930-
See Breslin, Jimmy
See also CA 73-76; CANR 31, 75, 139;
DAM NOV; MTCW 1, 2; MTFW 2005

Breslin, Jimmy .... **CLC 4, 43**
See Breslin, James
See also AITN 1; DLB 185; MTCW 2

Bresson, Robert 1901(?)-1999 .... **CLC 16**
See also CA 110; 187; CANR 49

Breton, Andre 1896-1966 .. **CLC 2, 9, 15, 54;
PC 15**
See also CA 19-20; 25-28R; CANR 40, 60;
CAP 2; DLB 65, 258; EW 11; EWL 3;
GFL 1789 to the Present; LMFS 2;
MTCW 1, 2; MTFW 2005; RGWL 2, 3;
TWA; WP

Breytenbach, Breyten 1939(?)- .. **CLC 23, 37,
126**
See also CA 113; 129; CANR 61, 122;
CWW 2; DAM POET; DLB 225; EWL 3

Bridgers, Sue Ellen 1942- .... **CLC 26**
See also AAYA 8, 49; BYA 7, 8; CA 65-68;
CANR 11, 36; CLR 18; DLB 52; JRDA;
MAICYA 1, 2; SAAS 1; SATA 22, 90;
SATA-Essay 109; WYA; YAW

Bridges, Robert (Seymour)
1844-1930 .... **PC 28; TCLC 1**
See also BRW 6; CA 104; 152; CDBLB
1890-1914; DAM POET; DLB 19, 98

Bridie, James .... **TCLC 3**
See Mavor, Osborne Henry
See also DLB 10; EWL 3

Brin, David 1950- .... **CLC 34**
See also AAYA 21; CA 102; CANR 24, 70,
125, 127; INT CANR-24; SATA 65;
SCFW 2; SFW 4

Brink, Andre (Philippus) 1935- . **CLC 18, 36,
106**
See also AFW; BRWS 6; CA 104; CANR
39, 62, 109, 133; CN 4, 5, 6, 7; DLB 225;
EWL 3; INT CA-103; LATS 1:2; MTCW
1, 2; MTFW 2005; WLIT 2

Brinsmead, H. F(ay)
See Brinsmead, H(esba) F(ay)

Brinsmead, H. F.
See Brinsmead, H(esba) F(ay)

Brinsmead, H(esba) F(ay) 1922- ...... **CLC 21**
See also CA 21-24R; CANR 10; CLR 47;
CWRI 5; MAICYA 1, 2; SAAS 5; SATA
18, 78

Brittain, Vera (Mary) 1893(?)-1970 . **CLC 23**
See also BRWS 10; CA 13-16; 25-28R;
CANR 58; CAP 1; DLB 191; FW; MTCW
1, 2

Broch, Hermann 1886-1951 .... **TCLC 20**
See also CA 117; 211; CDWLB 2; DLB 85,
124; EW 10; EWL 3; RGWL 2, 3

Brock, Rose
See Hansen, Joseph
See also GLL 1

Brod, Max 1884-1968 .... **TCLC 115**
See also CA 5-8R; 25-28R; CANR 7; DLB
81; EWL 3

Brodkey, Harold (Roy) 1930-1996 .. **CLC 56;
TCLC 123**
See also CA 111; 151; CANR 71; CN 4, 5,
6; DLB 130

Brodsky, Iosif Alexandrovich 1940-1996
See Brodsky, Joseph
See also AITN 1; CA 41-44R; 151; CANR
37, 106; DA3; DAM POET; MTCW 1, 2;
MTFW 2005; RGWL 2, 3

Brodsky, Joseph . **CLC 4, 6, 13, 36, 100; PC
9**
See Brodsky, Iosif Alexandrovich
See also AMWS 8; CWW 2; DLB 285;
EWL 3; MTCW 1

Brodsky, Michael (Mark) 1948- .... **CLC 19**
See also CA 102; CANR 18, 41, 58; DLB
244

Brodzki, Bella ed. .... **CLC 65**

Brome, Richard 1590(?)-1652 .... **LC 61**
See also BRWS 10; DLB 58

Bromell, Henry 1947- .... **CLC 5**
See also CA 53-56; CANR 9, 115, 116

Bromfield, Louis (Brucker)
1896-1956 .... **TCLC 11**
See also CA 107; 155; DLB 4, 9, 86; RGAL
4; RHW

Broner, E(sther) M(asserman)
1930- .... **CLC 19**
See also CA 17-20R; CANR 8, 25, 72; CN
4, 5, 6; DLB 28

Bronk, William (M.) 1918-1999 .... **CLC 10**
See also CA 89-92; 177; CANR 23; CP 3, 4, 5, 6, 7; DLB 165

Bronstein, Lev Davidovich
See Trotsky, Leon

Bronte, Anne 1820-1849 ..... **NCLC 4, 71, 102**
See also BRW 5; BRWR 1; DA3; DLB 21, 199; TEA

Bronte, (Patrick) Branwell
1817-1848 .... **NCLC 109**

Bronte, Charlotte 1816-1855 ...... **NCLC 3, 8, 33, 58, 105, 155; WLC**
See also AAYA 17; BRW 5; BRWC 2; BRWR 1; BYA 2; CDBLB 1832-1890; DA; DA3; DAB; DAC; DAM MST, NOV; DLB 21, 159, 199; EXPN; FL 1:2; GL 2; LAIT 2; NFS 4; TEA; WLIT 4

Bronte, Emily (Jane) 1818-1848 ... **NCLC 16, 35; PC 8; WLC**
See also AAYA 17; BPFB 1; BRW 5; BRWC 1; BRWR 1; BYA 3; CDBLB 1832-1890; DA; DA3; DAB; DAC; DAM MST, NOV, POET; DLB 21, 32, 199; EXPN; FL 1:2; GL 2; LAIT 1; TEA; WLIT 3

Brontes
See Bronte, Anne; Bronte, Charlotte; Bronte, Emily (Jane)

Brooke, Frances 1724-1789 .... **LC 6, 48**
See also DLB 39, 99

Brooke, Henry 1703(?)-1783 .... **LC 1**
See also DLB 39

Brooke, Rupert (Chawner)
1887-1915 ..... **PC 24; TCLC 2, 7; WLC**
See also BRWS 3; CA 104; 132; CANR 61; CDBLB 1914-1945; DA; DAB; DAC; DAM MST, POET; DLB 19, 216; EXPP; GLL 2; MTCW 1, 2; MTFW 2005; PFS 7; TEA

Brooke-Haven, P.
See Wodehouse, P(elham) G(renville)

Brooke-Rose, Christine 1926(?)- ..... **CLC 40, 184**
See also BRWS 4; CA 13-16R; CANR 58, 118; CN 1, 2, 3, 4, 5, 6, 7; DLB 14, 231; EWL 3; SFW 4

Brookner, Anita 1928- .. **CLC 32, 34, 51, 136**
See also BRWS 4; CA 114; 120; CANR 37, 56, 87, 130; CN 4, 5, 6, 7; CPW; DA3; DAB; DAM POP; DLB 194; DLBY 1987; EWL 3; MTCW 1, 2; MTFW 2005; TEA

Brooks, Cleanth 1906-1994 . **CLC 24, 86, 110**
See also AMWS 14; CA 17-20R; 145; CANR 33, 35; CSW; DLB 63; DLBY 1994; EWL 3; INT CANR-35; MAL 5; MTCW 1, 2; MTFW 2005

Brooks, George
See Baum, L(yman) Frank

Brooks, Gwendolyn (Elizabeth)
1917-2000 ... **BLC 1; CLC 1, 2, 4, 5, 15, 49, 125; PC 7; WLC**
See also AAYA 20; AFAW 1, 2; AITN 1; AMWS 3; BW 2, 3; CA 1-4R; 190; CANR 1, 27, 52, 75, 132; CDALB 1941-1968; CLR 27; CP 1, 2, 3, 4, 5, 6, 7; CWP; DA; DA3; DAC; DAM MST, MULT, POET; DLB 5, 76, 165; EWL 3; EXPP; FL 1:5; MAL 5; MAWW; MTCW 1, 2; MTFW 2005; PFS 1, 2, 4, 6; RGAL 4; SATA 6; SATA-Obit 123; TUS; WP

Brooks, Mel .... **CLC 12, 217**
See Kaminsky, Melvin
See also AAYA 13, 48; DLB 26

Brooks, Peter (Preston) 1938- .... **CLC 34**
See also CA 45-48; CANR 1, 107

Brooks, Van Wyck 1886-1963 .... **CLC 29**
See also AMW; CA 1-4R; CANR 6; DLB 45, 63, 103; MAL 5; TUS

Brophy, Brigid (Antonia)
1929-1995 .... **CLC 6, 11, 29, 105**
See also CA 5-8R; 149; CAAS 4; CANR 25, 53; CBD; CN 1, 2, 3, 4, 5, 6; CWD; DA3; DLB 14, 271; EWL 3; MTCW 1, 2

Brosman, Catharine Savage 1934- ..... **CLC 9**
See also CA 61-64; CANR 21, 46

Brossard, Nicole 1943- .... **CLC 115, 169**
See also CA 122; CAAS 16; CANR 140; CCA 1; CWP; CWW 2; DLB 53; EWL 3; FW; GLL 2; RGWL 3

Brother Antoninus
See Everson, William (Oliver)

The Brothers Quay
See Quay, Stephen; Quay, Timothy

Broughton, T(homas) Alan 1936- ..... **CLC 19**
See also CA 45-48; CANR 2, 23, 48, 111

Broumas, Olga 1949- .... **CLC 10, 73**
See also CA 85-88; CANR 20, 69, 110; CP 7; CWP; GLL 2

Broun, Heywood 1888-1939 .... **TCLC 104**
See also DLB 29, 171

Brown, Alan 1950- .... **CLC 99**
See also CA 156

Brown, Charles Brockden
1771-1810 .... **NCLC 22, 74, 122**
See also AMWS 1; CDALB 1640-1865; DLB 37, 59, 73; FW; GL 2; HGG; LMFS 1; RGAL 4; TUS

Brown, Christy 1932-1981 .... **CLC 63**
See also BYA 13; CA 105; 104; CANR 72; DLB 14

Brown, Claude 1937-2002 ... **BLC 1; CLC 30**
See also AAYA 7; BW 1, 3; CA 73-76; 205; CANR 81; DAM MULT

Brown, Dan 1964- .... **CLC 209**
See also AAYA 55; CA 217; MTFW 2005

Brown, Dee (Alexander)
1908-2002 .... **CLC 18, 47**
See also AAYA 30; CA 13-16R; 212; CAAS 6; CANR 11, 45, 60; CPW; CSW; DA3; DAM POP; DLBY 1980; LAIT 2; MTCW 1, 2; MTFW 2005; NCFS 5; SATA 5, 110; SATA-Obit 141; TCWW 1, 2

Brown, George
See Wertmueller, Lina

Brown, George Douglas
1869-1902 .... **TCLC 28**
See Douglas, George
See also CA 162

Brown, George Mackay 1921-1996 ... **CLC 5, 48, 100**
See also BRWS 6; CA 21-24R; 151; CAAS 6; CANR 12, 37, 67; CN 1, 2, 3, 4, 5, 6; CP 1, 2, 3, 4; DLB 14, 27, 139, 271; MTCW 1; RGSF 2; SATA 35

Brown, (William) Larry 1951-2004 . **CLC 73**
See also CA 130; 134; 233; CANR 117, 145; CSW; DLB 234; INT CA-134

Brown, Moses
See Barrett, William (Christopher)

Brown, Rita Mae 1944- .... **CLC 18, 43, 79**
See also BPFB 1; CA 45-48; CANR 2, 11, 35, 62, 95, 138; CN 5, 6, 7; CPW; CSW; DA3; DAM NOV, POP; FW; INT CANR-11; MAL 5; MTCW 1, 2; MTFW 2005; NFS 9; RGAL 4; TUS

Brown, Roderick (Langmere) Haig-
See Haig-Brown, Roderick (Langmere)

Brown, Rosellen 1939- .... **CLC 32, 170**
See also CA 77-80; CAAS 10; CANR 14, 44, 98; CN 6, 7

Brown, Sterling Allen 1901-1989 ...... **BLC 1; CLC 1, 23, 59; HR 1:2; PC 55**
See also AFAW 1, 2; BW 1, 3; CA 85-88; 127; CANR 26; CP 3, 4; DA3; DAM MULT, POET; DLB 48, 51, 63; MAL 5; MTCW 1, 2; MTFW 2005; RGAL 4; WP

Brown, Will
See Ainsworth, William Harrison

Brown, William Hill 1765-1793 .... **LC 93**
See also DLB 37

Brown, William Wells 1815-1884 ...... **BLC 1; DC 1; NCLC 2, 89**
See also DAM MULT; DLB 3, 50, 183, 248; RGAL 4

Browne, (Clyde) Jackson 1948(?)- ... **CLC 21**
See also CA 120

Browne, Sir Thomas 1605-1682 .... **LC 111**
See also BRW 2; DLB 151

Browning, Robert 1812-1889 . **NCLC 19, 79; PC 2, 61; WLCS**
See also BRW 4; BRWC 2; BRWR 2; CD-BLB 1832-1890; CLR 97; DA; DA3; DAB; DAC; DAM MST, POET; DLB 32, 163; EXPP; LATS 1:1; PAB; PFS 1, 15; RGEL 2; TEA; WLIT 4; WP; YABC 1

Browning, Tod 1882-1962 .... **CLC 16**
~~See also CA 141; 117~~

Brownmiller, Susan 1935- .... **CLC 159**
See also CA 103; CANR 35, 75, 137; DAM NOV; FW; MTCW 1, 2; MTFW 2005

Brownson, Orestes Augustus
1803-1876 .... **NCLC 50**
See also DLB 1, 59, 73, 243

Bruccoli, Matthew J(oseph) 1931- ... **CLC 34**
See also CA 9-12R; CANR 7, 87; DLB 103

Bruce, Lenny .... **CLC 21**
See Schneider, Leonard Alfred

Bruchac, Joseph III 1942- .... **NNAL**
See also AAYA 19; CA 33-36R; CANR 13, 47, 75, 94, 137; CLR 46; CWRI 5; DAM MULT; JRDA; MAICYA 2; MAICYAS 1; MTCW 2; MTFW 2005; SATA 42, 89, 131

Bruin, John
See Brutus, Dennis

Brulard, Henri
See Stendhal

Brulls, Christian
See Simenon, Georges (Jacques Christian)

Brunetto Latini c. 1220-1294 .... **CMLC 73**

Brunner, John (Kilian Houston)
1934-1995 .... **CLC 8, 10**
See also CA 1-4R; 149; CAAS 8; CANR 2, 37; CPW; DAM POP; DLB 261; MTCW 1, 2; SCFW 1, 2; SFW 4

Bruno, Giordano 1548-1600 .... **LC 27**
See also RGWL 2, 3

Brutus, Dennis 1924- ... **BLC 1; CLC 43; PC 24**
See also AFW; BW 2, 3; CA 49-52; CAAS 14; CANR 2, 27, 42, 81; CDWLB 3; CP 1, 2, 3, 4, 5, 6, 7; DAM MULT, POET; DLB 117, 225; EWL 3

Bryan, C(ourtlandt) D(ixon) B(arnes)
1936- .... **CLC 29**
See also CA 73-76; CANR 13, 68; DLB 185; INT CANR-13

Bryan, Michael
See Moore, Brian
See also CCA 1

Bryan, William Jennings
1860-1925 .... **TCLC 99**
See also DLB 303

Bryant, William Cullen 1794-1878 . **NCLC 6, 46; PC 20**
See also AMWS 1; CDALB 1640-1865; DA; DAB; DAC; DAM MST, POET; DLB 3, 43, 59, 189, 250; EXPP; PAB; RGAL 4; TUS

Bryusov, Valery Yakovlevich
1873-1924 .... **TCLC 10**
See also CA 107; 155; EWL 3; SFW 4

Buchan, John 1875-1940 .... **TCLC 41**
See also CA 108; 145; CMW 4; DAB;
DAM POP; DLB 34, 70, 156; HGG;
MSW; MTCW 2; RGEL 2; RHW; YABC
2

Buchanan, George 1506-1582 .... **LC 4**
See also DLB 132

Buchanan, Robert 1841-1901 .... **TCLC 107**
See also CA 179; DLB 18, 35

Buchheim, Lothar-Guenther 1918- .... **CLC 6**
See also CA 85-88

Buchner, (Karl) Georg
1813-1837 .... **NCLC 26, 146**
See also CDWLB 2; DLB 133; EW 6;
RGSF 2; RGWL 2, 3; TWA

Buchwald, Art(hur) 1925- .... **CLC 33**
See also AITN 1; CA 5-8R; CANR 21, 67,
107; MTCW 1, 2; SATA 10

Buck, Pearl S(ydenstricker)
1892-1973 .... **CLC 7, 11, 18, 127**
See also AAYA 42; AITN 1; AMWS 2;
BPFB 1; CA 1-4R; 41-44R; CANR 1, 34;
CDALBS; CN 1; DA; DA3; DAB; DAC;
DAM MST, NOV; DLB 9, 102; EWL 3;
LAIT 3; MAL 5; MTCW 1, 2; MTFW
2005; RGAL 4; RHW; SATA 1, 25; TUS

Buckler, Ernest 1908-1984 .... **CLC 13**
See also CA 11-12; 114; CAP 1; CCA 1;
CN 1, 2, 3; DAC; DAM MST; DLB 68;
SATA 47

Buckley, Christopher (Taylor)
1952- .... **CLC 165**
See also CA 139; CANR 119

Buckley, Vincent (Thomas)
1925-1988 .... **CLC 57**
See also CA 101; CP 1, 2, 3, 4; DLB 289

Buckley, William F(rank), Jr. 1925- . **CLC 7,
18, 37**
See also AITN 1; BPFB 1; CA 1-4R; CANR
1, 24, 53, 93, 133; CMW 4; CPW; DA3;
DAM POP; DLB 137; DLBY 1980; INT
CANR-24; MTCW 1, 2; MTFW 2005;
TUS

Buechner, (Carl) Frederick 1926- . **CLC 2, 4,
6, 9**
See also AMWS 12; BPFB 1; CA 13-16R;
CANR 11, 39, 64, 114, 138; CN 1, 2, 3,
4, 5, 6, 7; DAM NOV; DLBY 1980; INT
CANR-11; MAL 5; MTCW 1, 2; MTFW
2005; TCLE 1:1

Buell, John (Edward) 1927- .... **CLC 10**
See also CA 1-4R; CANR 71; DLB 53

Buero Vallejo, Antonio 1916-2000 ... **CLC 15,
46, 139; DC 18**
See also CA 106; 189; CANR 24, 49, 75;
CWW 2; DFS 11; EWL 3; HW 1; MTCW
1, 2

Bufalino, Gesualdo 1920-1996 .... **CLC 74**
See also CA 209; CWW 2; DLB 196

Bugayev, Boris Nikolayevich
1880-1934 .... **PC 11; TCLC 7**
See Bely, Andrey; Belyi, Andrei
See also CA 104; 165; MTCW 2; MTFW
2005

Bukowski, Charles 1920-1994 ... **CLC 2, 5, 9,
41, 82, 108; PC 18; SSC 45**
See also CA 17-20R; 144; CANR 40, 62,
105; CN 4, 5; CP 1, 2, 3, 4; CPW; DA3;
DAM NOV, POET; DLB 5, 130, 169;
EWL 3; MAL 5; MTCW 1, 2; MTFW
2005

Bulgakov, Mikhail (Afanas'evich)
1891-1940 ..... **SSC 18; TCLC 2, 16, 159**
See also BPFB 1; CA 105; 152; DAM
DRAM, NOV; DLB 272; EWL 3; MTCW
2; MTFW 2005; NFS 8; RGSF 2; RGWL
2, 3; SFW 4; TWA

Bulgya, Alexander Alexandrovich
1901-1956 .... **TCLC 53**
See Fadeev, Aleksandr Aleksandrovich;
Fadeev, Alexandr Alexandrovich; Fadeyev,
Alexander
See also CA 117; 181

Bullins, Ed 1935- ... **BLC 1; CLC 1, 5, 7; DC
6**
See also BW 2, 3; CA 49-52; CAAS 16;
CAD; CANR 24, 46, 73, 134; CD 5, 6;
DAM DRAM, MULT; DLB 7, 38, 249;
EWL 3; MAL 5; MTCW 1, 2; MTFW
2005; RGAL 4

Bulosan, Carlos 1911-1956 .... **AAL**
See also CA 216; DLB 312; RGAL 4

**Bulwer-Lytton, Edward (George Earle
Lytton)** 1803-1873 .... **NCLC 1, 45**
See also DLB 21; RGEL 2; SFW 4; SUFW
1; TEA

Bunin, Ivan Alexeyevich 1870-1953 ... **SSC 5;
TCLC 6**
See also CA 104; DLB 317; EWL 3; RGSF
2; RGWL 2, 3; TWA

Bunting, Basil 1900-1985 ...... **CLC 10, 39, 47**
See also BRWS 7; CA 53-56; 115; CANR
7; CP 1, 2, 3, 4; DAM POET; DLB 20;
EWL 3; RGEL 2

Bunuel, Luis 1900-1983 ... **CLC 16, 80; HLC
1**
See also CA 101; 110; CANR 32, 77; DAM
MULT; HW 1

Bunyan, John 1628-1688 ..... **LC 4, 69; WLC**
See also BRW 2; BYA 5; CDBLB 1660-
1789; DA; DAB; DAC; DAM MST; DLB
39; RGEL 2; TEA; WCH; WLIT 3

Buravsky, Alexandr .... **CLC 59**

Burckhardt, Jacob (Christoph)
1818-1897 .... **NCLC 49**
See also EW 6

Burford, Eleanor
See Hibbert, Eleanor Alice Burford

Burgess, Anthony . **CLC 1, 2, 4, 5, 8, 10, 13,
15, 22, 40, 62, 81, 94**
See Wilson, John (Anthony) Burgess
See also AAYA 25; AITN 1; BRWS 1; CD-
BLB 1960 to Present; CN 1, 2, 3, 4, 5;
DAB; DLB 14, 194, 261; DLBY 1998;
EWL 3; RGEL 2; RHW; SFW 4; YAW

Burke, Edmund 1729(?)-1797 .... **LC 7, 36;
WLC**
See also BRW 3; DA; DA3; DAB; DAC;
DAM MST; DLB 104, 252; RGEL 2;
TEA

Burke, Kenneth (Duva) 1897-1993 ... **CLC 2,
24**
See also AMW; CA 5-8R; 143; CANR 39,
74, 136; CN 1, 2; CP 1, 2, 3, 4; DLB 45,
63; EWL 3; MAL 5; MTCW 1, 2; MTFW
2005; RGAL 4

Burke, Leda
See Garnett, David

Burke, Ralph
See Silverberg, Robert

Burke, Thomas 1886-1945 .... **TCLC 63**
See also CA 113; 155; CMW 4; DLB 197

Burney, Fanny 1752-1840 .... **NCLC 12, 54,
107**
See also BRWS 3; DLB 39; FL 1:2; NFS
16; RGEL 2; TEA

Burney, Frances
See Burney, Fanny

Burns, Robert 1759-1796 ... **LC 3, 29, 40; PC
6; WLC**
See also AAYA 51; BRW 3; CDBLB 1789-
1832; DA; DA3; DAB; DAC; DAM MST;
POET; DLB 109; EXPP; PAB; RGEL 2;
TEA; WP

Burns, Tex
See L'Amour, Louis (Dearborn)

Burnshaw, Stanley 1906- .... **CLC 3, 13, 44**
See also CA 9-12R; CP 1, 2, 3, 4, 5, 6, 7;
DLB 48; DLBY 1997

Burr, Anne 1937- .... **CLC 6**
See also CA 25-28R

Burroughs, Edgar Rice 1875-1950 . **TCLC 2,
32**
See also AAYA 11; BPFB 1; BYA 4, 9; CA
104; 132; CANR 131; DA3; DAM NOV;
DLB 8; FANT; MTCW 1, 2; MTFW
2005; RGAL 4; SATA 41; SCFW 1, 2;
SFW 4; TCWW 1, 2; TUS; YAW

Burroughs, William S(eward)
1914-1997 .. **CLC 1, 2, 5, 15, 22, 42, 75,
109; TCLC 121; WLC**
See Lee, William; Lee, Willy
See also AAYA 60; AITN 2; AMWS 3; BG
1:2; BPFB 1; CA 9-12R; 160; CANR 20,
52, 104; CN 1, 2, 3, 4, 5, 6; CPW; DA;
DA3; DAB; DAC; DAM MST, NOV,
POP; DLB 2, 8, 16, 152, 237; DLBY
1981, 1997; EWL 3; HGG; LMFS 2;
MAL 5; MTCW 1, 2; MTFW 2005;
RGAL 4; SFW 4

Burton, Sir Richard F(rancis)
1821-1890 .... **NCLC 42**
See also DLB 55, 166, 184; SSFS 21

Burton, Robert 1577-1640 .... **LC 74**
See also DLB 151; RGEL 2

Buruma, Ian 1951- .... **CLC 163**
See also CA 128; CANR 65, 141

Busch, Frederick 1941- ... **CLC 7, 10, 18, 47,
166**
See also CA 33-36R; CAAS 1; CANR 45,
73, 92; CN 1, 2, 3, 4, 5, 6, 7; DLB 6, 218

Bush, Barney (Furman) 1946- .... **NNAL**
See also CA 145

Bush, Ronald 1946- .... **CLC 34**
See also CA 136

Bustos, F(rancisco)
See Borges, Jorge Luis

Bustos Domecq, H(onorio)
See Bioy Casares, Adolfo; Borges, Jorge
Luis

Butler, Octavia E(stelle) 1947- .. **BLCS; CLC
38, 121**
See also AAYA 18, 48; AFAW 2; AMWS
13; BPFB 1; BW 2, 3; CA 73-76; CANR
12, 24, 38, 73, 145; CLR 65; CN 7; CPW;
DA3; DAM MULT, POP; DLB 33; LATS
1:2; MTCW 1, 2; MTFW 2005; NFS 8,
21; SATA 84; SCFW 2; SFW 4; SSFS 6;
TCLE 1:1; YAW

Butler, Robert Olen, (Jr.) 1945- ...... **CLC 81,
162**
See also AMWS 12; BPFB 1; CA 112;
CANR 66, 138; CN 7; CSW; DAM POP;
DLB 173; INT CA-112; MAL 5; MTCW
2; MTFW 2005; SSFS 11

Butler, Samuel 1612-1680 .... **LC 16, 43**
See also DLB 101, 126; RGEL 2

Butler, Samuel 1835-1902 .... **TCLC 1, 33;
WLC**
See also BRWS 2; CA 143; CDBLB 1890-
1914; DA; DA3; DAB; DAC; DAM MST,
NOV; DLB 18, 57, 174; RGEL 2; SFW 4;
TEA

Butler, Walter C.
See Faust, Frederick (Schiller)

Butor, Michel (Marie Francois)
1926- .... **CLC 1, 3, 8, 11, 15, 161**
See also CA 9-12R; CANR 33, 66; CWW
2; DLB 83; EW 13; EWL 3; GFL 1789 to
the Present; MTCW 1, 2; MTFW 2005

Butts, Mary 1890(?)-1937 .... **TCLC 77**
See also CA 148; DLB 240

Buxton, Ralph
See Silverstein, Alvin; Silverstein, Virginia
B(arbara Opshelor)

Cankar, Ivan 1876-1918 .... **TCLC 105**
See also CDWLB 4; DLB 147; EWL 3

Cannon, Curt
See Hunter, Evan

Cao, Lan 1961- .... **CLC 109**
See also CA 165

Cape, Judith
See Page, P(atricia) K(athleen)
See also CCA 1

Capek, Karel 1890-1938 .... **DC 1; SSC 36; TCLC 6, 37; WLC**
See also CA 104; 140; CDWLB 4; DA;
DA3; DAB; DAC; DAM DRAM, MST,
NOV; DFS 7, 11; DLB 215; EW 10; EWL
3; MTCW 2; MTFW 2005; RGSF 2;
RGWL 2, 3; SCFW 1, 2; SFW 4

Capote, Truman 1924-1984 . **CLC 1, 3, 8, 13, 19, 34, 38, 58; SSC 2, 47; TCLC 164; WLC**
See also AAYA 61; AMWS 3; BPFB 1; CA
5-8R; 113; CANR 18, 62; CDALB 1941-
1968; CN 1, 2, 3; CPW; DA; DA3; DAB;
DAC; DAM MST, NOV, POP; DLB 2,
185, 227; DLBY 1980, 1984; EWL 3;
EXPS; GLL 1; LAIT 3; MAL 5; MTCW
1, 2; MTFW 2005; NCFS 2; RGAL 4;
RGSF 2; SATA 91; SSFS 2; TUS

Capra, Frank 1897-1991 .... **CLC 16**
See also AAYA 52; CA 61-64; 135

Caputo, Philip 1941- .... **CLC 32**
See also AAYA 60; CA 73-76; CANR 40,
135; YAW

Caragiale, Ion Luca 1852-1912 ...... **TCLC 76**
See also CA 157

Card, Orson Scott 1951- .... **CLC 44, 47, 50**
See also AAYA 11, 42; BPFB 1; BYA 5, 8;
CA 102; CANR 27, 47, 73, 102, 106, 133;
CPW; DA3; DAM POP; FANT; INT
CANR-27; MTCW 1, 2; MTFW 2005;
NFS 5; SATA 83, 127; SCFW 2; SFW 4;
SUFW 2; YAW

Cardenal, Ernesto 1925- .... **CLC 31, 161; HLC 1; PC 22**
See also CA 49-52; CANR 2, 32, 66, 138;
CWW 2; DAM MULT, POET; DLB 290;
EWL 3; HW 1, 2; LAWS 1; MTCW 1, 2;
MTFW 2005; RGWL 2, 3

Cardinal, Marie 1929-2001 .... **CLC 189**
See also CA 177; CWW 2; DLB 83; FW

Cardozo, Benjamin N(athan)
1870-1938 .... **TCLC 65**
See also CA 117; 164

Carducci, Giosue (Alessandro Giuseppe)
1835-1907 .... **PC 46; TCLC 32**
See also CA 163; EW 7; RGWL 2, 3

Carew, Thomas 1595(?)-1640 . **LC 13; PC 29**
See also BRW 2; DLB 126; PAB; RGEL 2

Carey, Ernestine Gilbreth 1908- ...... **CLC 17**
See also CA 5-8R; CANR 71; SATA 2

Carey, Peter 1943- .... **CLC 40, 55, 96, 183**
See also CA 123; 127; CANR 53, 76, 117;
CN 4, 5, 6, 7; DLB 289; EWL 3; INT CA-
127; MTCW 1, 2; MTFW 2005; RGSF 2;
SATA 94

Carleton, William 1794-1869 .... **NCLC 3**
See also DLB 159; RGEL 2; RGSF 2

Carlisle, Henry (Coffin) 1926- .... **CLC 33**
See also CA 13-16R; CANR 15, 85

Carlsen, Chris
See Holdstock, Robert P.

Carlson, Ron(ald F.) 1947- .... **CLC 54**
See also CA 105, 189; CAAE 189; CANR
27; DLB 244

Carlyle, Thomas 1795-1881 ..... **NCLC 22, 70**
See also BRW 4; CDBLB 1789-1832; DA;
DAB; DAC; DAM MST; DLB 55, 144,
254; RGEL 2; TEA

Carman, (William) Bliss 1861-1929 ... **PC 34; TCLC 7**
See also CA 104; 152; DAC; DLB 92;
RGEL 2

Carnegie, Dale 1888-1955 .... **TCLC 53**
See also CA 218

Carossa, Hans 1878-1956 .... **TCLC 48**
See also CA 170; DLB 66; EWL 3

Carpenter, Don(ald Richard)
1931-1995 .... **CLC 41**
See also CA 45-48; 149; CANR 1, 71

Carpenter, Edward 1844-1929 .... **TCLC 88**
See also CA 163; GLL 1

Carpenter, John (Howard) 1948- ... **CLC 161**
See also AAYA 2; CA 134; SATA 58

Carpenter, Johnny
See Carpenter, John (Howard)

Carpentier (y Valmont), Alejo
1904-1980 . **CLC 8, 11, 38, 110; HLC 1; SSC 35**
See also CA 65-68; 97-100; CANR 11, 70;
CDWLB 3; DAM MULT; DLB 113; EWL
3; HW 1, 2; LAW; LMFS 2; RGSF 2;
RGWL 2, 3; WLIT 1

Carr, Caleb 1955- .... **CLC 86**
See also CA 147; CANR 73, 134; DA3

Carr, Emily 1871-1945 .... **TCLC 32**
See also CA 159; DLB 68; FW; GLL 2

Carr, John Dickson 1906-1977 .... **CLC 3**
See Fairbairn, Roger
See also CA 49-52; 69-72; CANR 3, 33,
60; CMW 4; DLB 306; MSW; MTCW 1,
2

Carr, Philippa
See Hibbert, Eleanor Alice Burford

Carr, Virginia Spencer 1929- .... **CLC 34**
See also CA 61-64; DLB 111

Carrere, Emmanuel 1957- .... **CLC 89**
See also CA 200

Carrier, Roch 1937- .... **CLC 13, 78**
See also CA 130; CANR 61; CCA 1; DAC;
DAM MST; DLB 53; SATA 105

Carroll, James Dennis
See Carroll, Jim

Carroll, James P. 1943(?)- .... **CLC 38**
See also CA 81-84; CANR 73, 139; MTCW
2; MTFW 2005

Carroll, Jim 1951- .... **CLC 35, 143**
See also AAYA 17; CA 45-48; CANR 42,
115; NCFS 5

Carroll, Lewis ..... **NCLC 2, 53, 139; PC 18; WLC**
See Dodgson, Charles L(utwidge)
See also AAYA 39; BRW 5; BYA 5, 13; CD-
BLB 1832-1890; CLR 2, 18; DLB 18,
163, 178; DLBY 1998; EXPN; EXPP;
FANT; JRDA; LAIT 1; NFS 7; PFS 11;
RGEL 2; SUFW 1; TEA; WCH

Carroll, Paul Vincent 1900-1968 ...... **CLC 10**
See also CA 9-12R; 25-28R; DLB 10; EWL
3; RGEL 2

Carruth, Hayden 1921- ..... **CLC 4, 7, 10, 18, 84; PC 10**
See also CA 9-12R; CANR 4, 38, 59, 110;
CP 1, 2, 3, 4, 5, 6, 7; DLB 5, 165; INT
CANR-4; MTCW 1, 2; MTFW 2005;
SATA 47

Carson, Anne 1950- .... **CLC 185; PC 64**
See also AMWS 12; CA 203; DLB 193;
PFS 18; TCLE 1:1

Carson, Ciaran 1948- .... **CLC 201**
See also CA 112; 153; CANR 113; CP 7

Carson, Rachel
See Carson, Rachel Louise
See also AAYA 49; DLB 275

Carson, Rachel Louise 1907-1964 .... **CLC 71**
See Carson, Rachel
See also AMWS 9; ANW; CA 77-80; CANR
35; DA3; DAM POP; FW; LAIT 4; MAL
5; MTCW 1, 2; MTFW 2005; NCFS 1;
SATA 23

Carter, Angela (Olive) 1940-1992 ...... **CLC 5, 41, 76; SSC 13, 85; TCLC 139**
See also BRWS 3; CA 53-56; 136; CANR
12, 36, 61, 106; CN 3, 4, 5; DA3; DLB
14, 207, 261, 319; EXPS; FANT; FW; GL
2; MTCW 1, 2; MTFW 2005; RGSF 2;
SATA 66; SATA-Obit 70; SFW 4; SSFS
4, 12; SUFW 2; WLIT 4

Carter, Nick
See Smith, Martin Cruz

Carver, Raymond 1938-1988 ..... **CLC 22, 36, 53, 55, 126; PC 54; SSC 8, 51**
See also AAYA 44; AMWS 3; BPFB 1; CA
33-36R; 126; CANR 17, 34, 61, 103; CN
4; CPW; DA3; DAM NOV; DLB 130;
DLBY 1984, 1988; EWL 3; MAL 5;
MTCW 1, 2; MTFW 2005; PFS 17;
RGAL 4; RGSF 2; SSFS 3, 6, 12, 13;
TCLE 1:1; TCWW 2; TUS

Cary, Elizabeth, Lady Falkland
1585-1639 .... **LC 30**

Cary, (Arthur) Joyce (Lunel)
1888-1957 .... **TCLC 1, 29**
See also BRW 7; CA 104; 164; CDBLB
1914-1945; DLB 15, 100; EWL 3; MTCW
2; RGEL 2; TEA

Casal, Julian del 1863-1893 .... **NCLC 131**
See also DLB 283; LAW

Casanova, Giacomo
See Casanova de Seingalt, Giovanni Jacopo
See also WLIT 7

Casanova de Seingalt, Giovanni Jacopo
1725-1798 .... **LC 13**
See Casanova, Giacomo

Casares, Adolfo Bioy
See Bioy Casares, Adolfo
See also RGSF 2

Casas, Bartolome de las 1474-1566
See Las Casas, Bartolome de
See also WLIT 1

Casely-Hayford, J(oseph) E(phraim)
1866-1903 .... **BLC 1; TCLC 24**
See also BW 2; CA 123; 152; DAM MULT

Casey, John (Dudley) 1939- .... **CLC 59**
See also BEST 90:2; CA 69-72; CANR 23,
100

Casey, Michael 1947- .... **CLC 2**
See also CA 65-68; CANR 109; CP 2, 3;
DLB 5

Casey, Patrick
See Thurman, Wallace (Henry)

Casey, Warren (Peter) 1935-1988 .... **CLC 12**
See also CA 101; 127; INT CA-101

Casona, Alejandro .... **CLC 49**
See Alvarez, Alejandro Rodriguez
See also EWL 3

Cassavetes, John 1929-1989 .... **CLC 20**
See also CA 85-88; 127; CANR 82

Cassian, Nina 1924- .... **PC 17**
See also CWP; CWW 2

Cassill, R(onald) V(erlin)
1919-2002 .... **CLC 4, 23**
See also CA 9-12R; 208; CAAS 1; CANR
7, 45; CN 1, 2, 3, 4, 5, 6, 7; DLB 6, 218;
DLBY 2002

Cassiodorus, Flavius Magnus c. 490(?)-c.
583(?) .... **CMLC 43**

Cassirer, Ernst 1874-1945 .... **TCLC 61**
See also CA 157

Cassity, (Allen) Turner 1929- .... **CLC 6, 42**
See also CA 17-20R, 223; CAAE 223;
CAAS 8; CANR 11; CSW; DLB 105

Castaneda, Carlos (Cesar Aranha)
1931(?)-1998 .... **CLC 12, 119**
See also CA 25-28R; CANR 32, 66, 105;
DNFS 1; HW 1; MTCW 1

Castedo, Elena 1937- .... **CLC 65**
See also CA 132

Castedo-Ellerman, Elena
See Castedo, Elena

Castellanos, Rosario 1925-1974 .... **CLC 66;**
HLC 1; SSC 39, 68
See also CA 131; 53-56; CANR 58; CD-
WLB 3; DAM MULT; DLB 113, 290;
EWL 3; FW; HW 1; LAW; MTCW 2;
MTFW 2005; RGSF 2; RGWL 2, 3

Castelvetro, Lodovico 1505-1571 .... **LC 12**

Castiglione, Baldassare 1478-1529 ...... **LC 12**
See Castiglione, Baldesar
See also LMFS 1; RGWL 2, 3

Castiglione, Baldesar
See Castiglione, Baldassare
See also EW 2; WLIT 7

Castillo, Ana (Hernandez Del)
1953- .... **CLC 151**
See also AAYA 42; CA 131; CANR 51, 86,
128; CWP; DLB 122, 227; DNFS 2; FW;
HW 1; LLW; PFS 21

Castle, Robert
See Hamilton, Edmond

Castro (Ruz), Fidel 1926(?)- .... **HLC 1**
See also CA 110; 129; CANR 81; DAM
MULT; HW 2

Castro, Guillen de 1569-1631 .... **LC 19**

Castro, Rosalia de 1837-1885 ... **NCLC 3, 78;**
PC 41
See also DAM MULT

Cather, Willa (Sibert) 1873-1947 . **SSC 2, 50;**
TCLC 1, 11, 31, 99, 132, 152; WLC
See also AAYA 24; AMW; AMWC 1;
AMWR 1; BPFB 1; CA 104; 128; CDALB
1865-1917; CLR 98; DA; DA3; DAB;
DAC; DAM MST, NOV; DLB 9, 54, 78,
256; DLBD 1; EWL 3; EXPN; EXPS; FL
1:5; LAIT 3; LATS 1:1; MAL 5; MAWW;
MTCW 1, 2; MTFW 2005; NFS 2, 19;
RGAL 4; RGSF 2; RHW; SATA 30; SSFS
2, 7, 16; TCWW 1, 2; TUS

Catherine II
See Catherine the Great
See also DLB 150

Catherine the Great 1729-1796 .... **LC 69**
See Catherine II

Cato, Marcus Porcius
234B.C.-149B.C. .... **CMLC 21**
See Cato the Elder

Cato, Marcus Porcius, the Elder
See Cato, Marcus Porcius

Cato the Elder
See Cato, Marcus Porcius
See also DLB 211

Catton, (Charles) Bruce 1899-1978 . **CLC 35**
See also AITN 1; CA 5-8R; 81-84; CANR
7, 74; DLB 17; MTCW 2; MTFW 2005;
SATA 2; SATA-Obit 24

Catullus c. 84B.C.-54B.C. .... **CMLC 18**
See also AW 2; CDWLB 1; DLB 211;
RGWL 2, 3

Cauldwell, Frank
See King, Francis (Henry)

Caunitz, William J. 1933-1996 .... **CLC 34**
See also BEST 89:3; CA 125; 130; 152;
CANR 73; INT CA-130

Causley, Charles (Stanley)
1917-2003 .... **CLC 7**
See also CA 9-12R; 223; CANR 5, 35, 94;
CLR 30; CP 1, 2, 3, 4; CWRI 5; DLB 27;
MTCW 1; SATA 3, 66; SATA-Obit 149

Caute, (John) David 1936- .... **CLC 29**
See also CA 1-4R; CAAS 4; CANR 1, 33,
64, 120; CBD; CD 5, 6; CN 1, 2, 3, 4, 5,
6, 7; DAM NOV; DLB 14, 231

Cavafy, C(onstantine) P(eter) .... **PC 36;**
TCLC 2, 7
See Kavafis, Konstantinos Petrou
See also CA 148; DA3; DAM POET; EW
8; EWL 3; MTCW 2; PFS 19; RGWL 2,
3; WP

Cavalcanti, Guido c. 1250-c.
1300 .... **CMLC 54**
See also RGWL 2, 3; WLIT 7

Cavallo, Evelyn
See Spark, Muriel (Sarah)

Cavanna, Betty .... **CLC 12**
See Harrison, Elizabeth (Allen) Cavanna
See also JRDA; MAICYA 1; SAAS 4;
SATA 1, 30

Cavendish, Margaret Lucas
1623-1673 .... **LC 30**
See also DLB 131, 252, 281; RGEL 2

Caxton, William 1421(?)-1491(?) .... **LC 17**
See also DLB 170

Cayer, D. M.
See Duffy, Maureen (Patricia)

Cayrol, Jean 1911-2005 .... **CLC 11**
See also CA 89-92; 236; DLB 83; EWL 3

Cela (y Trulock), Camilo Jose
See Cela, Camilo Jose
See also CWW 2

Cela, Camilo Jose 1916-2002 .... **CLC 4, 13,**
59, 122; HLC 1; SSC 71
See Cela (y Trulock), Camilo Jose
See also BEST 90:2; CA 21-24R; 206;
CAAS 10; CANR 21, 32, 76, 139; DAM
MULT; DLB 322; DLBY 1989; EW 13;
EWL 3; HW 1; MTCW 1, 2; MTFW
2005; RGSF 2; RGWL 2, 3

Celan, Paul .... **CLC 10, 19, 53, 82; PC 10**
See Antschel, Paul
See also CDWLB 2; DLB 69; EWL 3;
RGWL 2, 3

Celine, Louis-Ferdinand .. **CLC 1, 3, 4, 7, 9,**
15, 47, 124
See Destouches, Louis-Ferdinand
See also DLB 72; EW 11; EWL 3; GFL
1789 to the Present; RGWL 2, 3

Cellini, Benvenuto 1500-1571 .... **LC 7**
See also WLIT 7

Cendrars, Blaise .... **CLC 18, 106**
See Sauser-Hall, Frederic
See also DLB 258; EWL 3; GFL 1789 to
the Present; RGWL 2, 3; WP

Centlivre, Susanna 1669(?)-1723 .... **DC 25;**
LC 65
See also DLB 84; RGEL 2

Cernuda (y Bidon), Luis
1902-1963 .... **CLC 54; PC 62**
See also CA 131; 89-92; DAM POET; DLB
134; EWL 3; GLL 1; HW 1; RGWL 2, 3

Cervantes, Lorna Dee 1954- ..... **HLCS 1; PC**
35
See also CA 131; CANR 80; CWP; DLB
82; EXPP; HW 1; LLW

Cervantes (Saavedra), Miguel de
1547-1616 .... **HLCS; LC 6, 23, 93; SSC**
12; WLC
See also AAYA 56; BYA 1, 14; DA; DAB;
DAC; DAM MST, NOV; EW 2; LAIT 1;
LATS 1:1; LMFS 1; NFS 8; RGSF 2;
RGWL 2, 3; TWA

Cesaire, Aime (Fernand) 1913- .... **BLC 1;**
CLC 19, 32, 112; DC 22; PC 25
See also BW 2, 3; CA 65-68; CANR 24,
43, 81; CWW 2; DA3; DAM MULT,
POET; DLB 321; EWL 3; GFL 1789 to
the Present; MTCW 1, 2; MTFW 2005;
WP

Chabon, Michael 1963- ... **CLC 55, 149; SSC**
59
See also AAYA 45; AMWS 11; CA 139;
CANR 57, 96, 127, 138; DLB 278; MAL
5; MTFW 2005; SATA 145

Chabrol, Claude 1930- .... **CLC 16**
See also CA 110

Chairil Anwar
See Anwar, Chairil
See also EWL 3

Challans, Mary 1905-1983
See Renault, Mary
See also CA 81-84; 111; CANR 74; DA3;
MTCW 2; MTFW 2005; SATA 23; SATA-
Obit 36; TEA

Challis, George
See Faust, Frederick (Schiller)

Chambers, Aidan 1934- .... **CLC 35**
See also AAYA 27; CA 25-28R; CANR 12,
31, 58, 116; JRDA; MAICYA 1, 2; SAAS
12; SATA 1, 69, 108; WYA; YAW

Chambers, James 1948-
See Cliff, Jimmy
See also CA 124

Chambers, Jessie
See Lawrence, D(avid) H(erbert Richards)
See also GLL 1

Chambers, Robert W(illiam)
1865-1933 .... **TCLC 41**
See also CA 165; DLB 202; HGG; SATA
107; SUFW 1

Chambers, (David) Whittaker
1901-1961 .... **TCLC 129**
See also CA 89-92; DLB 303

Chamisso, Adelbert von
1781-1838 .... **NCLC 82**
See also DLB 90; RGWL 2, 3; SUFW 1

Chance, James T.
See Carpenter, John (Howard)

Chance, John T.
See Carpenter, John (Howard)

Chandler, Raymond (Thornton)
1888-1959 .... **SSC 23; TCLC 1, 7**
See also AAYA 25; AMWC 2; AMWS 4;
BPFB 1; CA 104; 129; CANR 60, 107;
CDALB 1929-1941; CMW 4; DA3; DLB
226, 253; DLBD 6; EWL 3; MAL 5;
MSW; MTCW 1, 2; MTFW 2005; NFS
17; RGAL 4; TUS

Chang, Diana 1934- .... **AAL**
See also CA 228; CWP; DLB 312; EXPP

Chang, Eileen 1921-1995 .... **AAL; SSC 28**
See Chang Ai-Ling; Zhang Ailing
See also CA 166

Chang, Jung 1952- .... **CLC 71**
See also CA 142

Chang Ai-Ling
See Chang, Eileen
See also EWL 3

Channing, William Ellery
1780-1842 .... **NCLC 17**
See also DLB 1, 59, 235; RGAL 4

Chao, Patricia 1955- .... **CLC 119**
See also CA 163

Chaplin, Charles Spencer
1889-1977 .... **CLC 16**
See Chaplin, Charlie
See also CA 81-84; 73-76

Chaplin, Charlie
See Chaplin, Charles Spencer
See also AAYA 61; DLB 44

Chapman, George 1559(?)-1634 . **DC 19; LC**
22, 116
See also BRW 1; DAM DRAM; DLB 62,
121; LMFS 1; RGEL 2

Chapman, Graham 1941-1989 .... **CLC 21**
See Monty Python
See also CA 116; 129; CANR 35, 95

Clutha, Janet Paterson Frame 1924-2004
See Frame, Janet
See also CA 1-4R; 224; CANR 2, 36, 76, 135; MTCW 1, 2; SATA 119

Clyne, Terence
See Blatty, William Peter

Cobalt, Martin
See Mayne, William (James Carter)

Cobb, Irvin S(hrewsbury)
1876-1944 .... **TCLC 77**
See also CA 175; DLB 11, 25, 86

Cobbett, William 1763-1835 .... **NCLC 49**
See also DLB 43, 107, 158; RGEL 2

Coburn, D(onald) L(ee) 1938- .... **CLC 10**
See also CA 89-92

Cocteau, Jean (Maurice Eugene Clement)
1889-1963 .... **CLC 1, 8, 15, 16, 43; DC 17; TCLC 119; WLC**
See also CA 25-28; CANR 40; CAP 2; DA; DA3; DAB; DAC; DAM DRAM, MST, NOV; DLB 65, 258, 321; EW 10; EWL 3; GFL 1789 to the Present; MTCW 1, 2; RGWL 2, 3; TWA

Codrescu, Andrei 1946- .... **CLC 46, 121**
See also CA 33-36R; CAAS 19; CANR 13, 34, 53, 76, 125; CN 7; DA3; DAM POET; MAL 5; MTCW 2; MTFW 2005

Coe, Max
See Bourne, Randolph S(illiman)

Coe, Tucker
See Westlake, Donald E(dwin)

Coen, Ethan 1958- .... **CLC 108**
See also AAYA 54; CA 126; CANR 85

Coen, Joel 1955- .... **CLC 108**
See also AAYA 54; CA 126; CANR 119

The Coen Brothers
See Coen, Ethan; Coen, Joel

Coetzee, J(ohn) M(axwell) 1940- ..... **CLC 23, 33, 66, 117, 161, 162**
See also AAYA 37; AFW; BRWS 6; CA 77-80; CANR 41, 54, 74, 114, 133; CN 4, 5, 6, 7; DA3; DAM NOV; DLB 225; EWL 3; LMFS 2; MTCW 1, 2; MTFW 2005; NFS 21; WLIT 2; WWE 1

Coffey, Brian
See Koontz, Dean R.

Coffin, Robert P(eter) Tristram
1892-1955 .... **TCLC 95**
See also CA 123; 169; DLB 45

Cohan, George M(ichael)
1878-1942 .... **TCLC 60**
See also CA 157; DLB 249; RGAL 4

Cohen, Arthur A(llen) 1928-1986 ...... **CLC 7, 31**
See also CA 1-4R; 120; CANR 1, 17, 42; DLB 28

Cohen, Leonard (Norman) 1934- ...... **CLC 3, 38**
See also CA 21-24R; CANR 14, 69; CN 1, 2, 3, 4, 5, 6; CP 1, 2, 3, 4, 5, 6, 7; DAC; DAM MST; DLB 53; EWL 3; MTCW 1

Cohen, Matt(hew) 1942-1999 .... **CLC 19**
See also CA 61-64; 187; CAAS 18; CANR 40; CN 1, 2, 3, 4, 5, 6; DAC; DLB 53

Cohen-Solal, Annie 1948- .... **CLC 50**
See also CA 239

Colegate, Isabel 1931- .... **CLC 36**
See also CA 17-20R; CANR 8, 22, 74; CN 4, 5, 6, 7; DLB 14, 231; INT CANR-22; MTCW 1

Coleman, Emmett
See Reed, Ishmael (Scott)

Coleridge, Hartley 1796-1849 .... **NCLC 90**
See also DLB 96

Coleridge, M. E.
See Coleridge, Mary E(lizabeth)

Coleridge, Mary E(lizabeth)
1861-1907 .... **TCLC 73**
See also CA 116; 166; DLB 19, 98

Coleridge, Samuel Taylor
1772-1834 ...... **NCLC 9, 54, 99, 111; PC 11, 39, 67; WLC**
See also AAYA 66; BRW 4; BRWR 2; BYA 4; CDBLB 1789-1832; DA; DA3; DAB; DAC; DAM MST, POET; DLB 93, 107; EXPP; LATS 1:1; LMFS 1; PAB; PFS 4, 5; RGEL 2; TEA; WLIT 3; WP

Coleridge, Sara 1802-1852 .... **NCLC 31**
See also DLB 199

Coles, Don 1928- .... **CLC 46**
See also CA 115; CANR 38; CP 7

Coles, Robert (Martin) 1929- .... **CLC 108**
See also CA 45-48; CANR 3, 32, 66, 70, 135; INT CANR-32; SATA 23

Colette, (Sidonie-Gabrielle)
1873-1954 .... **SSC 10; TCLC 1, 5, 16**
See Willy, Colette
See also CA 104; 131; DA3; DAM NOV; DLB 65; EW 9; EWL 3; GFL 1789 to the Present; MTCW 1, 2; MTFW 2005; RGWL 2, 3; TWA

Collett, (Jacobine) Camilla (Wergeland)
1813-1895 .... **NCLC 22**

Collier, Christopher 1930- .... **CLC 30**
See also AAYA 13; BYA 2; CA 33-36R; CANR 13, 33, 102; JRDA; MAICYA 1, 2; SATA 16, 70; WYA; YAW 1

Collier, James Lincoln 1928- .... **CLC 30**
See also AAYA 13; BYA 2; CA 9-12R; CANR 4, 33, 60, 102; CLR 3; DAM POP; JRDA; MAICYA 1, 2; SAAS 21; SATA 8, 70; WYA; YAW 1

Collier, Jeremy 1650-1726 .... **LC 6**

Collier, John 1901-1980 . **SSC 19; TCLC 127**
See also CA 65-68; 97-100; CANR 10; CN 1, 2; DLB 77, 255; FANT; SUFW 1

Collier, Mary 1690-1762 .... **LC 86**
See also DLB 95

Collingwood, R(obin) G(eorge)
1889(?)-1943 .... **TCLC 67**
See also CA 117; 155; DLB 262

Collins, Billy 1941- .... **PC 68**
See also AAYA 64; CA 151; CANR 92; MTFW 2005; PFS 18

Collins, Hunt
See Hunter, Evan

Collins, Linda 1931- .... **CLC 44**
See also CA 125

Collins, Tom
See Furphy, Joseph
See also RGEL 2

Collins, (William) Wilkie
1824-1889 .... **NCLC 1, 18, 93**
See also BRWS 6; CDBLB 1832-1890; CMW 4; DLB 18, 70, 159; GL 2; MSW; RGEL 2; RGSF 2; SUFW 1; WLIT 4

Collins, William 1721-1759 .... **LC 4, 40**
See also BRW 3; DAM POET; DLB 109; RGEL 2

Collodi, Carlo .... **NCLC 54**
See Lorenzini, Carlo
See also CLR 5; WCH; WLIT 7

Colman, George
See Glassco, John

Colman, George, the Elder
1732-1794 .... **LC 98**
See also RGEL 2

Colonna, Vittoria 1492-1547 .... **LC 71**
See also RGWL 2, 3

Colt, Winchester Remington
See Hubbard, L(afayette) Ron(ald)

Colter, Cyrus J. 1910-2002 .... **CLC 58**
See also BW 1; CA 65-68; 205; CANR 10, 66; CN 2, 3, 4, 5, 6; DLB 33

Colton, James
See Hansen, Joseph
See also GLL 1

Colum, Padraic 1881-1972 .... **CLC 28**
See also BYA 4; CA 73-76; 33-36R; CANR 35; CLR 36; CP 1; CWRI 5; DLB 19; MAICYA 1, 2; MTCW 1; RGEL 2; SATA 15; WCH

Colvin, James
See Moorcock, Michael (John)

Colwin, Laurie (E.) 1944-1992 .... **CLC 5, 13, 23, 84**
See also CA 89-92; 139; CANR 20, 46; DLB 218; DLBY 1980; MTCW 1

Comfort, Alex(ander) 1920-2000 .... **CLC 7**
See also CA 1-4R; 190; CANR 1, 45; CN 1, 2, 3, 4; CP 1, 2, 3, 4, 5, 6, 7; DAM POP; MTCW 2

Comfort, Montgomery
See Campbell, (John) Ramsey

Compton-Burnett, I(vy)
1892(?)-1969 .... **CLC 1, 3, 10, 15, 34**
See also BRW 7; CA 1-4R; 25-28R; CANR 4; DAM NOV; DLB 36; EWL 3; MTCW 1, 2; RGEL 2

Comstock, Anthony 1844-1915 ...... **TCLC 13**
See also CA 110; 169

Comte, Auguste 1798-1857 .... **NCLC 54**

Conan Doyle, Arthur
See Doyle, Sir Arthur Conan
See also BPFB 1; BYA 4, 5, 11

Conde (Abellan), Carmen
1901-1996 .... **HLCS 1**
See also CA 177; CWW 2; DLB 108; EWL 3; HW 2

Conde, Maryse 1937- ..... **BLCS; CLC 52, 92**
See also BW 2, 3; CA 110, 190; CAAE 190; CANR 30, 53, 76; CWW 2; DAM MULT; EWL 3; MTCW 2; MTFW 2005

Condillac, Etienne Bonnot de
1714-1780 .... **LC 26**
See also DLB 313

Condon, Richard (Thomas)
1915-1996 .... **CLC 4, 6, 8, 10, 45, 100**
See also BEST 90:3; BPFB 1; CA 1-4R; 151; CAAS 1; CANR 2, 23; CMW 4; CN 1, 2, 3, 4, 5, 6; DAM NOV; INT CANR-23; MAL 5; MTCW 1, 2

Condorcet .... **LC 104**
See Condorcet, marquis de Marie-Jean-Antoine-Nicolas Caritat
See also GFL Beginnings to 1789

Condorcet, marquis de
Marie-Jean-Antoine-Nicolas Caritat
1743-1794
See Condorcet
See also DLB 313

Confucius 551B.C.-479B.C. .... **CMLC 19, 65; WLCS**
See also DA; DA3; DAB; DAC; DAM MST

Congreve, William 1670-1729 ... **DC 2; LC 5, 21; WLC**
See also BRW 2; CDBLB 1660-1789; DA; DAB; DAC; DAM DRAM, MST, POET; DFS 15; DLB 39, 84; RGEL 2; WLIT 3

Conley, Robert J(ackson) 1940- .... **NNAL**
See also CA 41-44R; CANR 15, 34, 45, 96; DAM MULT; TCWW 2

Connell, Evan S(helby), Jr. 1924- . **CLC 4, 6, 45**
See also AAYA 7; AMWS 14; CA 1-4R; CAAS 2; CANR 2, 39, 76, 97, 140; CN 1, 2, 3, 4, 5, 6; DAM NOV; DLB 2; DLBY 1981; MAL 5; MTCW 1, 2; MTFW 2005

Connelly, Marc(us Cook) 1890-1980 . **CLC 7**
See also CA 85-88; 102; CAD; CANR 30; DFS 12; DLB 7; DLBY 1980; MAL 5; RGAL 4; SATA-Obit 25

Connor, Ralph .... **TCLC 31**
See Gordon, Charles William
See also DLB 92; TCWW 1, 2

Cunningham, J(ames) V(incent)
1911-1985 .... **CLC 3, 31**
See also CA 1-4R; 115; CANR 1, 72; CP 1, 2, 3, 4; DLB 5

Cunningham, Julia (Woolfolk)
1916- .... **CLC 12**
See also CA 9-12R; CANR 4, 19, 36; CWRI 5; JRDA; MAICYA 1, 2; SAAS 2; SATA 1, 26, 132

Cunningham, Michael 1952- .... **CLC 34**
See also AMWS 15; CA 136; CANR 96; CN 7; DLB 292; GLL 2; MTFW 2005

Cunninghame Graham, R. B.
See Cunninghame Graham, Robert (Gallnigad) Bontine

Cunninghame Graham, Robert (Gallnigad) Bontine 1852-1936 .... **TCLC 19**
See Graham, R(obert) B(ontine) Cunninghame
See also CA 119; 184

Curnow, (Thomas) Allen (Monro)
1911-2001 .... **PC 48**
See also CA 69-72; 202; CANR 48, 99; CP 1, 2, 3, 4, 5, 6, 7; EWL 3; RGEL 2

Currie, Ellen 19(?)- .... **CLC 44**

Curtin, Philip
See Lowndes, Marie Adelaide (Belloc)

Curtin, Phillip
See Lowndes, Marie Adelaide (Belloc)

Curtis, Price
See Ellison, Harlan (Jay)

Cusanus, Nicolaus 1401-1464 .... **LC 80**
See Nicholas of Cusa

Cutrate, Joe
See Spiegelman, Art

Cynewulf c. 770- .... **CMLC 23**
See also DLB 146; RGEL 2

Cyrano de Bergerac, Savinien de
1619-1655 .... **LC 65**
See also DLB 268; GFL Beginnings to 1789; RGWL 2, 3

Cyril of Alexandria c. 375-c. 430 . **CMLC 59**

Czaczkes, Shmuel Yosef Halevi
See Agnon, S(hmuel) Y(osef Halevi)

Dabrowska, Maria (Szumska)
1889-1965 .... **CLC 15**
See also CA 106; CDWLB 4; DLB 215; EWL 3

Dabydeen, David 1955- .... **CLC 34**
See also BW 1; CA 125; CANR 56, 92; CN 6, 7; CP 7

Dacey, Philip 1939- .... **CLC 51**
See also CA 37-40R, 231; CAAE 231; CAAS 17; CANR 14, 32, 64; CP 4, 5, 6, 7; DLB 105

Dacre, Charlotte c. 1772-1825(?) . **NCLC 151**

Dafydd ap Gwilym c. 1320-c. 1380 ..... **PC 56**

Dagerman, Stig (Halvard)
1923-1954 .... **TCLC 17**
See also CA 117; 155; DLB 259; EWL 3

D'Aguiar, Fred 1960- .... **CLC 145**
See also CA 148; CANR 83, 101; CN 7; CP 7; DLB 157; EWL 3

Dahl, Roald 1916-1990 ...... **CLC 1, 6, 18, 79; TCLC 173**
See also AAYA 15; BPFB 1; BRWS 4; BYA 5; CA 1-4R; 133; CANR 6, 32, 37, 62; CLR 1, 7, 41; CN 1, 2, 3, 4; CPW; DA3; DAB; DAC; DAM MST, NOV, POP; DLB 139, 255; HGG; JRDA; MAICYA 1, 2; MTCW 1, 2; MTFW 2005; RGSF 2; SATA 1, 26, 73; SATA-Obit 65; SSFS 4; TEA; YAW

Dahlberg, Edward 1900-1977 .. **CLC 1, 7, 14**
See also CA 9-12R; 69-72; CANR 31, 62; CN 1, 2; DLB 48; MAL 5; MTCW 1; RGAL 4

Daitch, Susan 1954- .... **CLC 103**
See also CA 161

Dale, Colin .... **TCLC 18**
See Lawrence, T(homas) E(dward)

Dale, George E.
See Asimov, Isaac

Dalton, Roque 1935-1975(?) ..... **HLCS 1; PC 36**
See also CA 176; DLB 283; HW 2

Daly, Elizabeth 1878-1967 .... **CLC 52**
See also CA 23-24; 25-28R; CANR 60; CAP 2; CMW 4

Daly, Mary 1928- .... **CLC 173**
See also CA 25-28R; CANR 30, 62; FW; GLL 1; MTCW 1

Daly, Maureen 1921- .... **CLC 17**
See also AAYA 5, 58; BYA 6; CANR 37, 83, 108; CLR 96; JRDA; MAICYA 1, 2; SAAS 1; SATA 2, 129; WYA; YAW

Damas, Leon-Gontran 1912-1978 .... **CLC 84**
See also BW 1; CA 125; 73-76; EWL 3

Dana, Richard Henry Sr.
1787-1879 .... **NCLC 53**

Daniel, Samuel 1562(?)-1619 .... **LC 24**
See also DLB 62; RGEL 2

Daniels, Brett
See Adler, Renata

Dannay, Frederic 1905-1982 .... **CLC 11**
See Queen, Ellery
See also CA 1-4R; 107; CANR 1, 39; CMW 4; DAM POP; DLB 137; MTCW 1

D'Annunzio, Gabriele 1863-1938 ... **TCLC 6, 40**
See also CA 104; 155; EW 8; EWL 3; RGWL 2, 3; TWA; WLIT 7

Danois, N. le
See Gourmont, Remy(-Marie-Charles) de

Dante 1265-1321 .... **CMLC 3, 18, 39, 70; PC 21; WLCS**
See Alighieri, Dante
See also DA; DA3; DAB; DAC; DAM MST, POET; EFS 1; EW 1; LAIT 1; RGWL 2, 3; TWA; WP

d'Antibes, Germain
See Simenon, Georges (Jacques Christian)

Danticat, Edwidge 1969- .... **CLC 94, 139**
See also AAYA 29; CA 152; 192; CAAE 192; CANR 73, 129; CN 7; DNFS 1; EXPS; LATS 1:2; MTCW 2; MTFW 2005; SSFS 1; YAW

Danvers, Dennis 1947- .... **CLC 70**

Danziger, Paula 1944-2004 .... **CLC 21**
See also AAYA 4, 36; BYA 6, 7, 14; CA 112; 115; 229; CANR 37, 132; CLR 20; JRDA; MAICYA 1, 2; MTFW 2005; SATA 36, 63, 102, 149; SATA-Brief 30; SATA-Obit 155; WYA; YAW

Da Ponte, Lorenzo 1749-1838 .... **NCLC 50**

d'Aragona, Tullia 1510(?)-1556 .... **LC 121**

Dario, Ruben 1867-1916 .... **HLC 1; PC 15; TCLC 4**
See also CA 131; CANR 81; DAM MULT; DLB 290; EWL 3; HW 1, 2; LAW; MTCW 1, 2; MTFW 2005; RGWL 2, 3

Darley, George 1795-1846 .... **NCLC 2**
See also DLB 96; RGEL 2

Darrow, Clarence (Seward)
1857-1938 .... **TCLC 81**
See also CA 164; DLB 303

Darwin, Charles 1809-1882 .... **NCLC 57**
See also BRWS 7; DLB 57, 166; LATS 1:1; RGEL 2; TEA; WLIT 4

Darwin, Erasmus 1731-1802 .... **NCLC 106**
See also DLB 93; RGEL 2

Daryush, Elizabeth 1887-1977 ...... **CLC 6, 19**
See also CA 49-52; CANR 3, 81; DLB 20

Das, Kamala 1934- .... **CLC 191; PC 43**
See also CA 101; CANR 27, 59; CP 1, 2, 3, 4, 5, 6, 7; CWP; FW

Dasgupta, Surendranath
1887-1952 .... **TCLC 81**
See also CA 157

Dashwood, Edmee Elizabeth Monica de la Pasture 1890-1943
See Delafield, E. M.
See also CA 119; 154

da Silva, Antonio Jose
1705-1739 .... **NCLC 114**

Daudet, (Louis Marie) Alphonse
1840-1897 .... **NCLC 1**
See also DLB 123; GFL 1789 to the Present; RGSF 2

d'Aulnoy, Marie-Catherine c.
1650-1705 .... **LC 100**

Daumal, Rene 1908-1944 .... **TCLC 14**
See also CA 114; EWL 3

Davenant, William 1606-1668 .... **LC 13**
See also DLB 58, 126; RGEL 2

Davenport, Guy (Mattison, Jr.)
1927-2005 .... **CLC 6, 14, 38; SSC 16**
See also CA 33-36R, 235; CANR 23, 73; CN 3, 4, 5, 6; CSW; DLB 130

David, Robert
See Nezval, Vitezslav

Davidson, Avram (James) 1923-1993
See Queen, Ellery
See also CA 101; 171; CANR 26; DLB 8; FANT; SFW 4; SUFW 1, 2

Davidson, Donald (Grady)
1893-1968 .... **CLC 2, 13, 19**
See also CA 5-8R; 25-28R; CANR 4, 84; DLB 45

Davidson, Hugh
See Hamilton, Edmond

Davidson, John 1857-1909 .... **TCLC 24**
See also CA 118; 217; DLB 19; RGEL 2

Davidson, Sara 1943- .... **CLC 9**
See also CA 81-84; CANR 44, 68; DLB 185

Davie, Donald (Alfred) 1922-1995 .... **CLC 5, 8, 10, 31; PC 29**
See also BRWS 6; CA 1-4R; 149; CAAS 3; CANR 1, 44; CP 1, 2, 3, 4; DLB 27; MTCW 1; RGEL 2

Davie, Elspeth 1918-1995 .... **SSC 52**
See also CA 120; 126; 150; CANR 141; DLB 139

Davies, Ray(mond Douglas) 1944- ... **CLC 21**
See also CA 116; 146; CANR 92

Davies, Rhys 1901-1978 .... **CLC 23**
See also CA 9-12R; 81-84; CANR 4; CN 1, 2; DLB 139, 191

Davies, (William) Robertson
1913-1995 .... **CLC 2, 7, 13, 25, 42, 75, 91; WLC**
See Marchbanks, Samuel
See also BEST 89:2; BPFB 1; CA 33-36R; 150; CANR 17, 42, 103; CN 1, 2, 3, 4, 5, 6; CPW; DA; DA3; DAB; DAC; DAM MST, NOV, POP; DLB 68; EWL 3; HGG; INT CANR-17; MTCW 1, 2; MTFW 2005; RGEL 2; TWA

Davies, Sir John 1569-1626 .... **LC 85**
See also DLB 172

Davies, Walter C.
See Kornbluth, C(yril) M.

Davies, William Henry 1871-1940 ... **TCLC 5**
See also BRWS 11; CA 104; 179; DLB 19, 174; EWL 3; RGEL 2

Da Vinci, Leonardo 1452-1519 ..... **LC 12, 57, 60**
See also AAYA 40

Davis, Angela (Yvonne) 1944- .... **CLC 77**
See also BW 2, 3; CA 57-60; CANR 10, 81; CSW; DA3; DAM MULT; FW

Davis, B. Lynch
See Bioy Casares, Adolfo; Borges, Jorge Luis

Davis, Frank Marshall 1905-1987 ...... **BLC 1**
See also BW 2, 3; CA 125; 123; CANR 42, 80; DAM MULT; DLB 51

Davis, Gordon
See Hunt, E(verette) Howard, (Jr.)

Davis, H(arold) L(enoir) 1896-1960 . **CLC 49**
See also ANW; CA 178; 89-92; DLB 9, 206; SATA 114; TCWW 1, 2

Davis, Natalie Zemon 1928- .... **CLC 204**
See also CA 53-56; CANR 58, 100

Davis, Rebecca (Blaine) Harding
1831-1910 .... **SSC 38; TCLC 6**
See also CA 104; 179; DLB 74, 239; FW; NFS 14; RGAL 4; TUS

Davis, Richard Harding
1864-1916 .... **TCLC 24**
See also CA 114; 179; DLB 12, 23, 78, 79, 189; DLBD 13; RGAL 4

Davison, Frank Dalby 1893-1970 ..... **CLC 15**
See also CA 217; 116; DLB 260

Davison, Lawrence H.
See Lawrence, D(avid) H(erbert Richards)

Davison, Peter (Hubert) 1928-2004 . **CLC 28**
See also CA 9-12R; 234; CAAS 4; CANR 3, 43, 84; CP 1, 2, 3, 4, 5, 6, 7; DLB 5

Davys, Mary 1674-1732 .... **LC 1, 46**
See also DLB 39

Dawson, (Guy) Fielding (Lewis)
1930-2002 .... **CLC 6**
See also CA 85-88; 202; CANR 108; DLB 130; DLBY 2002

Dawson, Peter
See Faust, Frederick (Schiller)
See also TCWW 1, 2

Day, Clarence (Shepard, Jr.)
1874-1935 .... **TCLC 25**
See also CA 108; 199; DLB 11

Day, John 1574(?)-1640(?) .... **LC 70**
See also DLB 62, 170; RGEL 2

Day, Thomas 1748-1789 .... **LC 1**
See also DLB 39; YABC 1

Day Lewis, C(ecil) 1904-1972 . **CLC 1, 6, 10;**
PC 11
See Blake, Nicholas; Lewis, C. Day
See also BRWS 3; CA 13-16; 33-36R; CANR 34; CAP 1; CP 1; CWRI 5; DAM POET; DLB 15, 20; EWL 3; MTCW 1, 2; RGEL 2

Dazai Osamu .... **SSC 41; TCLC 11**
See Tsushima, Shuji
See also CA 164; DLB 182; EWL 3; MJW; RGSF 2; RGWL 2, 3; TWA

de Andrade, Carlos Drummond
See Drummond de Andrade, Carlos

de Andrade, Mario 1892(?)-1945
See Andrade, Mario de
See also CA 178; HW 2

Deane, Norman
See Creasey, John

Deane, Seamus (Francis) 1940- ...... **CLC 122**
See also CA 118; CANR 42

de Beauvoir, Simone (Lucie Ernestine Marie Bertrand)
See Beauvoir, Simone (Lucie Ernestine Marie Bertrand) de

de Beer, P.
See Bosman, Herman Charles

De Botton, Alain 1969- .... **CLC 203**
See also CA 159; CANR 96

de Brissac, Malcolm
See Dickinson, Peter (Malcolm de Brissac)

de Campos, Alvaro
See Pessoa, Fernando (Antonio Nogueira)

de Chardin, Pierre Teilhard
See Teilhard de Chardin, (Marie Joseph) Pierre

de Crenne, Helisenne c. 1510-c. 1560 .... **LC 113**

Dee, John 1527-1608 .... **LC 20**
See also DLB 136, 213

Deer, Sandra 1940- .... **CLC 45**
See also CA 186

De Ferrari, Gabriella 1941- .... **CLC 65**
See also CA 146

de Filippo, Eduardo 1900-1984 ... **TCLC 127**
See also CA 132; 114; EWL 3; MTCW 1; RGWL 2, 3

Defoe, Daniel 1660(?)-1731 .... **LC 1, 42, 108;**
WLC
See also AAYA 27; BRW 3; BRWR 1; BYA 4; CDBLB 1660-1789; CLR 61; DA; DA3; DAB; DAC; DAM MST, NOV; DLB 39, 95, 101; JRDA; LAIT 1; LMFS 1; MAICYA 1, 2; NFS 9, 13; RGEL 2; SATA 22; TEA; WCH; WLIT 3

de Gourmont, Remy(-Marie-Charles)
See Gourmont, Remy(-Marie-Charles) de

de Gournay, Marie le Jars
1566-1645 .... **LC 98**
See also FW

de Hartog, Jan 1914-2002 .... **CLC 19**
See also CA 1-4R; 210; CANR 1; DFS 12

de Hostos, E. M.
See Hostos (y Bonilla), Eugenio Maria de

de Hostos, Eugenio M.
See Hostos (y Bonilla), Eugenio Maria de

Deighton, Len .... **CLC 4, 7, 22, 46**
See Deighton, Leonard Cyril
See also AAYA 6; BEST 89:2; BPFB 1; CD-BLB 1960 to Present; CMW 4; CN 1, 2, 3, 4, 5, 6, 7; CPW; DLB 87

Deighton, Leonard Cyril 1929-
See Deighton, Len
See also AAYA 57; CA 9-12R; CANR 19, 33, 68; DA3; DAM NOV, POP; MTCW 1, 2; MTFW 2005

Dekker, Thomas 1572(?)-1632 ..... **DC 12; LC 22**
See also CDBLB Before 1660; DAM DRAM; DLB 62, 172; LMFS 1; RGEL 2

de Laclos, Pierre Ambroise Franois
See Laclos, Pierre-Ambroise Francois

Delacroix, (Ferdinand-Victor-)Eugene
1798-1863 .... **NCLC 133**
See also EW 5

Delafield, E. M. .... **TCLC 61**
See Dashwood, Edmee Elizabeth Monica de la Pasture
See also DLB 34; RHW

de la Mare, Walter (John)
1873-1956 . **SSC 14; TCLC 4, 53; WLC**
See also CA 163; CDBLB 1914-1945; CLR 23; CWRI 5; DA3; DAB; DAC; DAM MST, POET; DLB 19, 153, 162, 255, 284; EWL 3; EXPP; HGG; MAICYA 1, 2; MTCW 2; MTFW 2005; RGEL 2; RGSF 2; SATA 16; SUFW 1; TEA; WCH

de Lamartine, Alphonse (Marie Louis Prat)
See Lamartine, Alphonse (Marie Louis Prat) de

Delaney, Franey
See O'Hara, John (Henry)

Delaney, Shelagh 1939- .... **CLC 29**
See also CA 17-20R; CANR 30, 67; CBD; CD 5, 6; CDBLB 1960 to Present; CWD; DAM DRAM; DFS 7; DLB 13; MTCW 1

Delany, Martin Robison
1812-1885 .... **NCLC 93**
See also DLB 50; RGAL 4

Delany, Mary (Granville Pendarves)
1700-1788 .... **LC 12**

Delany, Samuel R(ay), Jr. 1942- .... **BLC 1;**
CLC 8, 14, 38, 141
See also AAYA 24; AFAW 2; BPFB 1; BW 2, 3; CA 81-84; CANR 27, 43, 116; CN

2, 3, 4, 5, 6, 7; DAM MULT; DLB 8, 33; FANT; MAL 5; MTCW 1, 2; RGAL 4; SATA 92; SCFW 1, 2; SFW 4; SUFW 2

De la Ramee, Marie Louise (Ouida)
1839-1908
See Ouida
See also CA 204; SATA 20

de la Roche, Mazo 1879-1961 .... **CLC 14**
See also CA 85-88; CANR 30; DLB 68; RGEL 2; RHW; SATA 64

De La Salle, Innocent
See Hartmann, Sadakichi

de Laureamont, Comte
See Lautreamont

Delbanco, Nicholas (Franklin)
1942- .... **CLC 6, 13, 167**
See also CA 17-20R; 189; CAAE 189; CAAS 2; CANR 29, 55, 116; CN 7; DLB 6, 234

del Castillo, Michel 1933- .... **CLC 38**
See also CA 109; CANR 77

Deledda, Grazia (Cosima)
1875(?)-1936 .... **TCLC 23**
See also CA 123; 205; DLB 264; EWL 3; RGWL 2, 3; WLIT 7

Deleuze, Gilles 1925-1995 .... **TCLC 116**
See also DLB 296

Delgado, Abelardo (Lalo) B(arrientos)
1930-2004 .... **HLC 1**
See also CA 131; 230; CAAS 15; CANR 90; DAM MST, MULT; DLB 82; HW 1, 2

Delibes, Miguel .... **CLC 8, 18**
See Delibes Setien, Miguel
See also DLB 322; EWL 3

Delibes Setien, Miguel 1920-
See Delibes, Miguel
See also CA 45-48; CANR 1, 32; CWW 2; HW 1; MTCW 1

DeLillo, Don 1936- ..... **CLC 8, 10, 13, 27, 39,**
54, 76, 143, 210, 213
See also AMWC 2; AMWS 6; BEST 89:1; BPFB 1; CA 81-84; CANR 21, 76, 92, 133; CN 3, 4, 5, 6, 7; CPW; DA3; DAM NOV, POP; DLB 6, 173; EWL 3; MAL 5; MTCW 1, 2; MTFW 2005; RGAL 4; TUS

de Lisser, H. G.
See De Lisser, H(erbert) G(eorge)
See also DLB 117

De Lisser, H(erbert) G(eorge)
1878-1944 .... **TCLC 12**
See de Lisser, H. G.
See also BW 2; CA 109; 152

Deloire, Pierre
See Peguy, Charles (Pierre)

Deloney, Thomas 1543(?)-1600 .... **LC 41**
See also DLB 167; RGEL 2

Deloria, Ella (Cara) 1889-1971(?) ..... **NNAL**
See also CA 152; DAM MULT; DLB 175

Deloria, Vine (Victor), Jr.
1933-2005 .... **CLC 21, 122; NNAL**
See also CA 53-56; CANR 5, 20, 48, 98; DAM MULT; DLB 175; MTCW 1; SATA 21

del Valle-Inclan, Ramon (Maria)
See Valle-Inclan, Ramon (Maria) del
See also DLB 322

Del Vecchio, John M(ichael) 1947- .. **CLC 29**
See also CA 110; DLBD 9

de Man, Paul (Adolph Michel)
1919-1983 .... **CLC 55**
See also CA 128; 111; CANR 61; DLB 67; MTCW 1, 2

DeMarinis, Rick 1934- .... **CLC 54**
See also CA 57-60, 184; CAAE 184; CAAS 24; CANR 9, 25, 50; DLB 218; TCWW 2

de Maupassant, (Henri Rene Albert) Guy
See Maupassant, (Henri Rene Albert) Guy de

Enchi, Fumiko (Ueda) 1905-1986 ..... **CLC 31**
    See Enchi Fumiko
    See also CA 129; 121; FW; MJW
Enchi Fumiko
    See Enchi, Fumiko (Ueda)
    See also DLB 182; EWL 3
Ende, Michael (Andreas Helmuth)
    1929-1995 .... **CLC 31**
    See also BYA 5; CA 118; 124; 149; CANR
    36, 110; CLR 14; DLB 75; MAICYA 1,
    2; MAICYAS 1; SATA 61, 130; SATA-
    Brief 42; SATA-Obit 86
Endo, Shusaku 1923-1996 ..... **CLC 7, 14, 19,**
    54, 99; SSC 48; TCLC 152
    See Endo Shusaku
    See also CA 29-32R; 153; CANR 21, 54,
    131; DA3; DAM NOV; MTCW 1, 2;
    MTFW 2005; RGSF 2; RGWL 2, 3
Endo Shusaku
    See Endo, Shusaku
    See also CWW 2; DLB 182; EWL 3
Engel, Marian 1933-1985 .... **CLC 36; TCLC**
    137
    See also CA 25-28R; CANR 12; CN 2, 3;
    DLB 53; FW; INT CANR-12
Engelhardt, Frederick
    See Hubbard, L(afayette) Ron(ald)
Engels, Friedrich 1820-1895 .. **NCLC 85, 114**
    See also DLB 129; LATS 1:1
Enright, D(ennis) J(oseph)
    1920-2002 .... **CLC 4, 8, 31**
    See also CA 1-4R; 211; CANR 1, 42, 83;
    CN 1, 2; CP 1, 2, 3, 4, 5, 6, 7; DLB 27;
    EWL 3; SATA 25; SATA-Obit 140
Ensler, Eve 1953- .... **CLC 212**
    See also CA 172; CANR 126
Enzensberger, Hans Magnus
    1929- .... **CLC 43; PC 28**
    See also CA 116; 119; CANR 103; CWW
    2; EWL 3
Ephron, Nora 1941- .... **CLC 17, 31**
    See also AAYA 35; AITN 2; CA 65-68;
    CANR 12, 39, 83; DFS 22
Epicurus 341B.C.-270B.C. .... **CMLC 21**
    See also DLB 176
Epsilon
    See Betjeman, John
Epstein, Daniel Mark 1948- .... **CLC 7**
    See also CA 49-52; CANR 2, 53, 90
Epstein, Jacob 1956- .... **CLC 19**
    See also CA 114
Epstein, Jean 1897-1953 .... **TCLC 92**
Epstein, Joseph 1937- .... **CLC 39, 204**
    See also AMWS 14; CA 112; 119; CANR
    50, 65, 117
Epstein, Leslie 1938- .... **CLC 27**
    See also AMWS 12; CA 73-76, 215; CAAE
    215; CAAS 12; CANR 23, 69; DLB 299
Equiano, Olaudah 1745(?)-1797 . **BLC 2; LC**
    16
    See also AFAW 1, 2; CDWLB 3; DAM
    MULT; DLB 37, 50; WLIT 2
Erasmus, Desiderius 1469(?)-1536 ..... **LC 16,**
    93
    See also DLB 136; EW 2; LMFS 1; RGWL
    2, 3; TWA
Erdman, Paul E(mil) 1932- .... **CLC 25**
    See also AITN 1; CA 61-64; CANR 13, 43,
    84
Erdrich, (Karen) Louise 1954- .. **CLC 39, 54,**
    120, 176; NNAL; PC 52
    See also AAYA 10, 47; AMWS 4; BEST
    89:1; BPFB 1; CA 114; CANR 41, 62,
    118, 138; CDALBS; CN 5, 6, 7; CP 7;
    CPW; CWP; DA3; DAM MULT, NOV,
    POP; DLB 152, 175, 206; EWL 3; EXPP;

FL 1:5; LAIT 5; LATS 1:2; MAL 5;
    MTCW 1, 2; MTFW 2005; NFS 5; PFS
    14; RGAL 4; SATA 94, 141; SSFS 14;
    TCWW 2
Erenburg, Ilya (Grigoryevich)
    See Ehrenburg, Ilya (Grigoryevich)
Erickson, Stephen Michael 1950-
    See Erickson, Steve
    See also CA 129; SFW 4
Erickson, Steve .... **CLC 64**
    See Erickson, Stephen Michael
    See also CANR 60, 68, 136; MTFW 2005;
    SUFW 2
Erickson, Walter
    See Fast, Howard (Melvin)
Ericson, Walter
    See Fast, Howard (Melvin)
Eriksson, Buntel
    See Bergman, (Ernst) Ingmar
Eriugena, John Scottus c.
    810-877 .... **CMLC 65**
    See also DLB 115
Ernaux, Annie 1940- .... **CLC 88, 184**
    See also CA 147; CANR 93; MTFW 2005;
    NCFS 3, 5
Erskine, John 1879-1951 .... **TCLC 84**
    See also CA 112; 159; DLB 9, 102; FANT
Eschenbach, Wolfram von
    See Wolfram von Eschenbach
    See also RGWL 3
Eseki, Bruno
    See Mphahlele, Ezekiel
Esenin, Sergei (Alexandrovich)
    1895-1925 .... **TCLC 4**
    See Yesenin, Sergey
    See also CA 104; RGWL 2, 3
Eshleman, Clayton 1935- .... **CLC 7**
    See also CA 33-36R, 212; CAAE 212;
    CAAS 6; CANR 93; CP 1, 2, 3, 4, 5, 6,
    7; DLB 5
Espriella, Don Manuel Alvarez
    See Southey, Robert
Espriu, Salvador 1913-1985 .... **CLC 9**
    See also CA 154; 115; DLB 134; EWL 3
Espronceda, Jose de 1808-1842 ..... **NCLC 39**
Esquivel, Laura 1951(?)- ... **CLC 141; HLCS**
    1
    See also AAYA 29; CA 143; CANR 68, 113;
    DA3; DNFS 2; LAIT 3; LMFS 2; MTCW
    2; MTFW 2005; NFS 5; WLIT 1
Esse, James
    See Stephens, James
Esterbrook, Tom
    See Hubbard, L(afayette) Ron(ald)
Estleman, Loren D. 1952- .... **CLC 48**
    See also AAYA 27; CA 85-88; CANR 27,
    74, 139, CMW 4; CPW; DA3; DAM
    NOV, POP; DLB 226; INT CANR-27;
    MTCW 1, 2; MTFW 2005; TCWW 1, 2
Etherege, Sir George 1636-1692 . **DC 23; LC**
    78
    See also BRW 2; DAM DRAM; DLB 80;
    PAB; RGEL 2
Euclid 306B.C.-283B.C. .... **CMLC 25**
Eugenides, Jeffrey 1960(?)- .... **CLC 81, 212**
    See also AAYA 51; CA 144; CANR 120;
    MTFW 2005
Euripides c. 484B.C.-406B.C. .... **CMLC 23,**
    51; DC 4; WLCS
    See also AW 1; CDWLB 1; DA; DA3;
    DAB; DAC; DAM DRAM, MST; DFS 1,
    4, 6; DLB 176; LAIT 1; LMFS 1; RGWL
    2, 3
Evan, Evin
    See Faust, Frederick (Schiller)
Evans, Caradoc 1878-1945 ... **SSC 43; TCLC**
    85
    See also DLB 162

Evans, Evan
    See Faust, Frederick (Schiller)
Evans, Marian
    See Eliot, George
Evans, Mary Ann
    See Eliot, George
    See also NFS 20
Evarts, Esther
    See Benson, Sally
Everett, Percival
    See Everett, Percival L.
    See also CSW
Everett, Percival L. 1956- .... **CLC 57**
    See Everett, Percival
    See also BW 2; CA 129; CANR 94, 134;
    CN 7; MTFW 2005
Everson, R(onald) G(ilmour)
    1903-1992 .... **CLC 27**
    See also CA 17-20R; CP 1, 2, 3, 4; DLB 88
Everson, William (Oliver)
    1912-1994 .... **CLC 1, 5, 14**
    See Antoninus, Brother
    See also BG 1:2; CA 9-12R; 145; CANR
    20; CP 2, 3, 4; DLB 5, 16, 212; MTCW 1
Evtushenko, Evgenii Aleksandrovich
    See Yevtushenko, Yevgeny (Alexandrovich)
    See also CWW 2; RGWL 2, 3
Ewart, Gavin (Buchanan)
    1916-1995 .... **CLC 13, 46**
    See also BRWS 7; CA 89-92; 150; CANR
    17, 46; CP 1, 2, 3, 4; DLB 40; MTCW 1
Ewers, Hanns Heinz 1871-1943 ..... **TCLC 12**
    See also CA 109; 149
Ewing, Frederick R.
    See Sturgeon, Theodore (Hamilton)
Exley, Frederick (Earl) 1929-1992 .... **CLC 6,**
    11
    See also AITN 2; BPFB 1; CA 81-84; 138;
    CANR 117; DLB 143; DLBY 1981
Eynhardt, Guillermo
    See Quiroga, Horacio (Sylvestre)
Ezekiel, Nissim (Moses) 1924-2004 .. **CLC 61**
    See also CA 61-64; 223; CP 1, 2, 3, 4, 5, 6,
    7; EWL 3
Ezekiel, Tish O'Dowd 1943- .... **CLC 34**
    See also CA 129
Fadeev, Aleksandr Aleksandrovich
    See Bulgya, Alexander Alexandrovich
    See also DLB 272
Fadeev, Alexandr Alexandrovich
    See Bulgya, Alexander Alexandrovich
    See also EWL 3
Fadeyev, A.
    See Bulgya, Alexander Alexandrovich
Fadeyev, Alexander .... **TCLC 53**
    See Bulgya, Alexander Alexandrovich
Fagen, Donald 1948- .... **CLC 26**
Fainzilberg, Ilya Arnoldovich 1897-1937
    See Ilf, Ilya
    See also CA 120; 165
Fair, Ronald L. 1932- .... **CLC 18**
    See also BW 1; CA 69-72; CANR 25; DLB
    33
Fairbairn, Roger
    See Carr, John Dickson
Fairbairns, Zoe (Ann) 1948- .... **CLC 32**
    See also CA 103; CANR 21, 85; CN 4, 5,
    6, 7
Fairfield, Flora
    See Alcott, Louisa May
Fairman, Paul W. 1916-1977
    See Queen, Ellery
    See also CA 114; SFW 4
Falco, Gian
    See Papini, Giovanni
Falconer, James
    See Kirkup, James

Field, Andrew 1938- .... **CLC 44**
See also CA 97-100; CANR 25

Field, Eugene 1850-1895 .... **NCLC 3**
See also DLB 23, 42, 140; DLBD 13; MAI-CYA 1, 2; RGAL 4; SATA 16

Field, Gans T.
See Wellman, Manly Wade

Field, Michael 1915-1971 .... **TCLC 43**
See also CA 29-32R

Fielding, Helen 1958- .... **CLC 146, 217**
See also AAYA 65; CA 172; CANR 127; DLB 231; MTFW 2005

Fielding, Henry 1707-1754 .... **LC 1, 46, 85; WLC**
See also BRW 3; BRWR 1; CDBLB 1660-1789; DA; DA3; DAB; DAC; DAM DRAM, MST, NOV; DLB 39, 84, 101; NFS 18; RGEL 2; TEA; WLIT 3

Fielding, Sarah 1710-1768 .... **LC 1, 44**
See also DLB 39; RGEL 2; TEA

Fields, W. C. 1880-1946 .... **TCLC 80**
See also DLB 44

Fierstein, Harvey (Forbes) 1954- ..... **CLC 33**
See also CA 123; 129; CAD; CD 5, 6; CPW; DA3; DAM DRAM, POP; DFS 6; DLB 266; GLL; MAL 5

Figes, Eva 1932- .... **CLC 31**
See also CA 53-56; CANR 4, 44, 83; CN 2, 3, 4, 5, 6, 7; DLB 14, 271; FW

Filippo, Eduardo de
See de Filippo, Eduardo

Finch, Anne 1661-1720 .... **LC 3; PC 21**
See also BRWS 9; DLB 95

Finch, Robert (Duer Claydon)
1900-1995 .... **CLC 18**
See also CA 57-60; CANR 9, 24, 49; CP 1, 2, 3, 4; DLB 88

Findley, Timothy (Irving Frederick)
1930-2002 .... **CLC 27, 102**
See also CA 25-28R; 206; CANR 12, 42, 69, 109; CCA 1; CN 4, 5, 6, 7; DAC; DAM MST; DLB 53; FANT; RHW

Fink, William
See Mencken, H(enry) L(ouis)

Firbank, Louis 1942-
See Reed, Lou
See also CA 117

Firbank, (Arthur Annesley) Ronald
1886-1926 .... **TCLC 1**
See also BRWS 2; CA 104; 177; DLB 36; EWL 3; RGEL 2

Firdawsi, Abu al-Qasim
See Ferdowsi, Abu'l Qasem
See also WLIT 6

Fish, Stanley
See Fish, Stanley Eugene

Fish, Stanley E.
See Fish, Stanley Eugene

Fish, Stanley Eugene 1938- .... **CLC 142**
See also CA 112; 132; CANR 90; DLB 67

Fisher, Dorothy (Frances) Canfield
1879-1958 .... **TCLC 87**
See also CA 114; 136; CANR 80; CLR 71; CWRI 5; DLB 9, 102, 284; MAICYA 1, 2; MAL 5; YABC 1

Fisher, M(ary) F(rances) K(ennedy)
1908-1992 .... **CLC 76, 87**
See also CA 77-80; 138; CANR 44; MTCW 2

Fisher, Roy 1930- .... **CLC 25**
See also CA 81-84; CAAS 10; CANR 16; CP 1, 2, 3, 4, 5, 6, 7; DLB 40

Fisher, Rudolph 1897-1934 . **BLC 2; HR 1:2; SSC 25; TCLC 11**
See also BW 1, 3; CA 107; 124; CANR 80; DAM MULT; DLB 51, 102

Fisher, Vardis (Alvero) 1895-1968 .... **CLC 7; TCLC 140**
See also CA 5-8R; 25-28R; CANR 68; DLB 9, 206; MAL 5; RGAL 4; TCWW 1, 2

Fiske, Tarleton
See Bloch, Robert (Albert)

Fitch, Clarke
See Sinclair, Upton (Beall)

Fitch, John IV
See Cormier, Robert (Edmund)

Fitzgerald, Captain Hugh
See Baum, L(yman) Frank

FitzGerald, Edward 1809-1883 ...... **NCLC 9, 153**
See also BRW 4; DLB 32; RGEL 2

Fitzgerald, F(rancis) Scott (Key)
1896-1940 ... **SSC 6, 31, 75; TCLC 1, 6, 14, 28, 55, 157; WLC**
See also AAYA 24; AITN 1; AMW; AMWC 2; AMWR 1; BPFB 1; CA 110; 123; CDALB 1917-1929; DA; DA3; DAB; DAC; DAM MST, NOV; DLB 4, 9, 86, 219, 273; DLBD 1, 15, 16; DLBY 1981, 1996; EWL 3; EXPN; EXPS; LAIT 3; MAL 5; MTCW 1, 2; MTFW 2005; NFS 2, 19, 20; RGAL 4; RGSF 2; SSFS 4, 15, 21; TUS

Fitzgerald, Penelope 1916-2000 . **CLC 19, 51, 61, 143**
See also BRWS 5; CA 85-88; 190; CAAS 10; CANR 56, 86, 131; CN 3, 4, 5, 6, 7; DLB 14, 194; EWL 3; MTCW 2; MTFW 2005

Fitzgerald, Robert (Stuart)
1910-1985 .... **CLC 39**
See also CA 1-4R; 114; CANR 1; CP 1, 2, 3, 4; DLBY 1980; MAL 5

FitzGerald, Robert D(avid)
1902-1987 .... **CLC 19**
See also CA 17-20R; CP 1, 2, 3, 4; DLB 260; RGEL 2

Fitzgerald, Zelda (Sayre)
1900-1948 .... **TCLC 52**
See also AMWS 9; CA 117; 126; DLBY 1984

Flanagan, Thomas (James Bonner)
1923-2002 .... **CLC 25, 52**
See also CA 108; 206; CANR 55; CN 3, 4, 5, 6, 7; DLBY 1980; INT CA-108; MTCW 1; RHW; TCLE 1:1

Flaubert, Gustave 1821-1880 .... **NCLC 2, 10, 19, 62, 66, 135; SSC 11, 60; WLC**
See also DA; DA3; DAB; DAC; DAM MST, NOV; DLB 119, 301; EW 7; EXPS; GFL 1789 to the Present; LAIT 2; LMFS 1; NFS 14; RGSF 2; RGWL 2, 3; SSFS 6; TWA

Flavius Josephus
See Josephus, Flavius

Flecker, Herman Elroy
See Flecker, (Herman) James Elroy

Flecker, (Herman) James Elroy
1884-1915 .... **TCLC 43**
See also CA 109; 150; DLB 10, 19; RGEL 2

Fleming, Ian (Lancaster) 1908-1964 . **CLC 3, 30**
See also AAYA 26; BPFB 1; CA 5-8R; CANR 59; CDBLB 1945-1960; CMW 4; CPW; DA3; DAM POP; DLB 87, 201; MSW; MTCW 1, 2; MTFW 2005; RGEL 2; SATA 9; TEA; YAW

Fleming, Thomas (James) 1927- ...... **CLC 37**
See also CA 5-8R; CANR 10, 102; INT CANR-10; SATA 8

Fletcher, John 1579-1625 .... **DC 6; LC 33**
See also BRW 2; CDBLB Before 1660; DLB 58; RGEL 2; TEA

Fletcher, John Gould 1886-1950 .... **TCLC 35**
See also CA 107; 167; DLB 4, 45; LMFS 2; MAL 5; RGAL 4

Fleur, Paul
See Pohl, Frederik

Flieg, Helmut
See Heym, Stefan

Flooglebuckle, Al
See Spiegelman, Art

Flora, Fletcher 1914-1969
See Queen, Ellery
See also CA 1-4R; CANR 3, 85

Flying Officer X
See Bates, H(erbert) E(rnest)

Fo, Dario 1926- .... **CLC 32, 109; DC 10**
See also CA 116; 128; CANR 68, 114, 134; CWW 2; DA3; DAM DRAM; DLBY 1997; EWL 3; MTCW 1, 2; MTFW 2005; WLIT 7

Fogarty, Jonathan Titulescu Esq.
See Farrell, James T(homas)

Follett, Ken(neth Martin) 1949- .... **CLC 18**
See also AAYA 6, 50; BEST 89:4; BPFB 1; CA 81-84; CANR 13, 33, 54, 102; CMW 4; CPW; DA3; DAM NOV, POP; DLB 87; DLBY 1981; INT CANR-33; MTCW 1

Fondane, Benjamin 1898-1944 ..... **TCLC 159**

Fontane, Theodor 1819-1898 . **NCLC 26, 163**
See also CDWLB 2; DLB 129; EW 6; RGWL 2, 3; TWA

Fonte, Moderata 1555-1592 .... **LC 118**

Fontenot, Chester .... **CLC 65**

Fonvizin, Denis Ivanovich
1744(?)-1792 .... **LC 81**
See also DLB 150; RGWL 2, 3

Foote, Horton 1916- .... **CLC 51, 91**
See also CA 73-76; CAD; CANR 34, 51, 110; CD 5, 6; CSW; DA3; DAM DRAM; DFS 20; DLB 26, 266; EWL 3; INT CANR-34; MTFW 2005

Foote, Mary Hallock 1847-1938 .. **TCLC 108**
See also DLB 186, 188, 202, 221; TCWW 2

Foote, Samuel 1721-1777 .... **LC 106**
See also DLB 89; RGEL 2

Foote, Shelby 1916-2005 .... **CLC 75**
See also AAYA 40; CA 5-8R; 240; CANR 3, 45, 74, 131; CN 1, 2, 3, 4, 5, 6, 7; CPW; CSW; DA3; DAM NOV, POP; DLB 2, 17; MAL 5; MTCW 2; MTFW 2005; RHW

Forbes, Cosmo
See Lewton, Val

Forbes, Esther 1891-1967 .... **CLC 12**
See also AAYA 17; BYA 2; CA 13-14; 25-28R; CAP 1; CLR 27; DLB 22; JRDA; MAICYA 1, 2; RHW; SATA 2, 100; YAW

Forche, Carolyn (Louise) 1950- .... **CLC 25, 83, 86; PC 10**
See also CA 109; 117; CANR 50, 74, 138; CP 4, 5, 6, 7; CWP; DA3; DAM POET; DLB 5, 193; INT CA-117; MAL 5; MTCW 2; MTFW 2005; PFS 18; RGAL 4

Ford, Elbur
See Hibbert, Eleanor Alice Burford

Ford, Ford Madox 1873-1939 ... **TCLC 1, 15, 39, 57, 172**
See Chaucer, Daniel
See also BRW 6; CA 104; 132; CANR 74; CDBLB 1914-1945; DA3; DAM NOV; DLB 34, 98, 162; EWL 3; MTCW 1, 2; RGEL 2; TEA

Ford, Henry 1863-1947 .... **TCLC 73**
See also CA 115; 148

Ford, Jack
See Ford, John

Ford, John 1586-1639 .... **DC 8; LC 68**
See also BRW 2; CDBLB Before 1660;
DA3; DAM DRAM; DFS 7; DLB 58;
IDTP; RGEL 2

Ford, John 1895-1973 .... **CLC 16**
See also CA 187; 45-48

Ford, Richard 1944- .... **CLC 46, 99, 205**
See also AMWS 5; CA 69-72; CANR 11,
47, 86, 128; CN 5, 6, 7; CSW; DLB 227;
EWL 3; MAL 5; MTCW 2; MTFW 2005;
RGAL 4; RGSF 2

Ford, Webster
See Masters, Edgar Lee

Foreman, Richard 1937- .... **CLC 50**
See also CA 65-68; CAD; CANR 32, 63,
143; CD 5, 6

Forester, C(ecil) S(cott) 1899-1966 . **CLC 35;
TCLC 152**
See also CA 73-76; 25-28R; CANR 83;
DLB 191; RGEL 2; RHW; SATA 13

Forez
See Mauriac, Francois (Charles)

Forman, James
See Forman, James D(ouglas)

Forman, James D(ouglas) 1932- .... **CLC 21**
See also AAYA 17; CA 9-12R; CANR 4,
19, 42; JRDA; MAICYA 1, 2; SATA 8,
70; YAW

Forman, Milos 1932- .... **CLC 164**
See also AAYA 63; CA 109

Fornes, Maria Irene 1930- .... **CLC 39, 61,
187; DC 10; HLCS 1**
See also CA 25-28R; CAD; CANR 28, 81;
CD 5, 6; CWD; DLB 7; HW 1, 2; INT
CANR-28; LLW; MAL 5; MTCW 1;
RGAL 4

Forrest, Leon (Richard)
1937-1997 .... **BLCS; CLC 4**
See also AFAW 2; BW 2; CA 89-92; 162;
CAAS 7; CANR 25, 52, 87; CN 4, 5, 6;
DLB 33

Forster, E(dward) M(organ)
1879-1970 ...... **CLC 1, 2, 3, 4, 9, 10, 13,
15, 22, 45, 77; SSC 27; TCLC 125;
WLC**
See also AAYA 2, 37; BRW 6; BRWR 2;
BYA 12; CA 13-14; 25-28R; CANR 45;
CAP 1; CDBLB 1914-1945; DA; DA3;
DAB; DAC; DAM MST, NOV; DLB 34,
98, 162, 178, 195; DLBD 10; EWL 3;
EXPN; LAIT 3; LMFS 1; MTCW 1, 2;
MTFW 2005; NCFS 1; NFS 3, 10, 11;
RGEL 2; RGSF 2; SATA 57; SUFW 1;
TEA; WLIT 4

Forster, John 1812-1876 .... **NCLC 11**
See also DLB 144, 184

Forster, Margaret 1938- .... **CLC 149**
See also CA 133; CANR 62, 115; CN 4, 5,
6, 7; DLB 155, 271

Forsyth, Frederick 1938- .... **CLC 2, 5, 36**
See also BEST 89:4; CA 85-88; CANR 38,
62, 115, 137; CMW 4; CN 3, 4, 5, 6, 7;
CPW; DAM NOV, POP; DLB 87; MTCW
1, 2; MTFW 2005

Forten, Charlotte L. 1837-1914 .... **BLC 2;
TCLC 16**
See Grimke, Charlotte L(ottie) Forten
See also DLB 50, 239

Fortinbras
See Grieg, (Johan) Nordahl (Brun)

Foscolo, Ugo 1778-1827 .... **NCLC 8, 97**
See also EW 5; WLIT 7

Fosse, Bob .... **CLC 20**
See Fosse, Robert Louis

Fosse, Robert Louis 1927-1987
See Fosse, Bob
See also CA 110; 123

Foster, Hannah Webster
1758-1840 .... **NCLC 99**
See also DLB 37, 200; RGAL 4

Foster, Stephen Collins
1826-1864 .... **NCLC 26**
See also RGAL 4

Foucault, Michel 1926-1984 . **CLC 31, 34, 69**
See also CA 105; 113; CANR 34; DLB 242;
EW 13; EWL 3; GFL 1789 to the Present;
GLL 1; LMFS 2; MTCW 1, 2; TWA

**Fouque, Friedrich (Heinrich Karl) de la
Motte** 1777-1843 .... **NCLC 2**
See also DLB 90; RGWL 2, 3; SUFW 1

Fourier, Charles 1772-1837 .... **NCLC 51**

Fournier, Henri-Alban 1886-1914
See Alain-Fournier
See also CA 104; 179

Fournier, Pierre 1916-1997 .... **CLC 11**
See Gascar, Pierre
See also CA 89-92; CANR 16, 40

Fowles, John (Robert) 1926- . **CLC 1, 2, 3, 4,
6, 9, 10, 15, 33, 87; SSC 33**
See also BPFB 1; BRWS 1; CA 5-8R;
CANR 25, 71, 103; CDBLB 1960 to
Present; CN 1, 2, 3, 4, 5, 6, 7; DA3; DAB;
DAC; DAM MST; DLB 14, 139, 207;
EWL 3; HGG; MTCW 1, 2; MTFW 2005;
NFS 21; RGEL 2; RHW; SATA 22; TEA;
WLIT 4

Fox, Paula 1923- .... **CLC 2, 8, 121**
See also AAYA 3, 37; BYA 3, 8; CA 73-76;
CANR 20, 36, 62, 105; CLR 1, 44, 96;
DLB 52; JRDA; MAICYA 1, 2; MTCW
1; NFS 12; SATA 17, 60, 120; WYA;
YAW

Fox, William Price (Jr.) 1926- .... **CLC 22**
See also CA 17-20R; CAAS 19; CANR 11,
142; CSW; DLB 2; DLBY 1981

Foxe, John 1517(?)-1587 .... **LC 14**
See also DLB 132

Frame, Janet .. **CLC 2, 3, 6, 22, 66, 96; SSC
29**
See Clutha, Janet Paterson Frame
See also CN 1, 2, 3, 4, 5, 6, 7; CP 2, 3, 4;
CWP; EWL 3; RGEL 2; RGSF 2; TWA

France, Anatole .... **TCLC 9**
See Thibault, Jacques Anatole Francois
See also DLB 123; EWL 3; GFL 1789 to
the Present; RGWL 2, 3; SUFW 1

Francis, Claude .... **CLC 50**
See also CA 192

Francis, Dick
See Francis, Richard Stanley
See also CN 2, 3, 4, 5, 6

Francis, Richard Stanley 1920- ... **CLC 2, 22,
42, 102**
See Francis, Dick
See also AAYA 5, 21; BEST 89:3; BPFB 1;
CA 5-8R; CANR 9, 42, 68, 100, 141; CD-
BLB 1960 to Present; CMW 4; CN 7;
DA3; DAM POP; DLB 87; INT CANR-9;
MSW; MTCW 1, 2; MTFW 2005

Francis, Robert (Churchill)
1901-1987 .... **CLC 15; PC 34**
See also AMWS 9; CA 1-4R; 123; CANR
1; CP 1, 2, 3, 4; EXPP; PFS 12; TCLE
1:1

Francis, Lord Jeffrey
See Jeffrey, Francis
See also DLB 107

Frank, Anne(lies Marie)
1929-1945 .... **TCLC 17; WLC**
See also AAYA 12; BYA 1; CA 113; 133;
CANR 68; CLR 101; DA; DA3; DAB;
DAC; DAM MST; LAIT 4; MAICYA 2;
MAICYAS 1; MTCW 1, 2; MTFW 2005;
NCFS 1; SATA 87; SATA-Brief 42; WYA;
YAW

Frank, Bruno 1887-1945 .... **TCLC 81**
See also CA 189; DLB 118; EWL 3

Frank, Elizabeth 1945- .... **CLC 39**
See also CA 121; 126; CANR 78; INT CA-
126

Frankl, Viktor E(mil) 1905-1997 ...... **CLC 93**
See also CA 65-68; 161

Franklin, Benjamin
See Hasek, Jaroslav (Matej Frantisek)

Franklin, Benjamin 1706-1790 .... **LC 25;
WLCS**
See also AMW; CDALB 1640-1865; DA;
DA3; DAB; DAC; DAM MST; DLB 24,
43, 73, 183; LAIT 1; RGAL 4; TUS

**Franklin, (Stella Maria Sarah) Miles
(Lampe)** 1879-1954 .... **TCLC 7**
See also CA 104; 164; DLB 230; FW;
MTCW 2; RGEL 2; TWA

Franzen, Jonathan 1959- .... **CLC 202**
See also AAYA 65; CA 129; CANR 105

Fraser, Antonia (Pakenham) 1932- . **CLC 32,
107**
See also AAYA 57; CA 85-88; CANR 44,
65, 119; CMW; DLB 276; MTCW 1, 2;
MTFW 2005; SATA-Brief 32

Fraser, George MacDonald 1925- ...... **CLC 7**
See also AAYA 48; CA 45-48, 180; CAAE
180; CANR 2, 48, 74; MTCW 2; RHW

Fraser, Sylvia 1935- .... **CLC 64**
See also CA 45-48; CANR 1, 16, 60; CCA
1

Frayn, Michael 1933- .... **CLC 3, 7, 31, 47,
176; DC 27**
See also BRWC 2; BRWS 7; CA 5-8R;
CANR 30, 69, 114, 133; CBD; CD 5, 6;
CN 1, 2, 3, 4, 5, 6, 7; DAM DRAM,
NOV; DFS 22; DLB 13, 14, 194, 245;
FANT; MTCW 1, 2; MTFW 2005; SFW
4

Fraze, Candida (Merrill) 1945- .... **CLC 50**
See also CA 126

Frazer, Andrew
See Marlowe, Stephen

Frazer, J(ames) G(eorge)
1854-1941 .... **TCLC 32**
See also BRWS 3; CA 118; NCFS 5

Frazer, Robert Caine
See Creasey, John

Frazer, Sir James George
See Frazer, J(ames) G(eorge)

Frazier, Charles 1950- .... **CLC 109**
See also AAYA 34; CA 161; CANR 126;
CSW; DLB 292; MTFW 2005

Frazier, Ian 1951- .... **CLC 46**
See also CA 130; CANR 54, 93

Frederic, Harold 1856-1898 .... **NCLC 10**
See also AMW; DLB 12, 23; DLBD 13;
MAL 5; NFS 22; RGAL 4

Frederick, John
See Faust, Frederick (Schiller)
See also TCWW 2

Frederick the Great 1712-1786 .... **LC 14**

Fredro, Aleksander 1793-1876 .... **NCLC 8**

Freeling, Nicolas 1927-2003 .... **CLC 38**
See also CA 49-52; 218; CAAS 12; CANR
1, 17, 50, 84; CMW 4; CN 1, 2, 3, 4, 5,
6; DLB 87

Freeman, Douglas Southall
1886-1953 .... **TCLC 11**
See also CA 109; 195; DLB 17; DLBD 17

Freeman, Judith 1946- .... **CLC 55**
See also CA 148; CANR 120; DLB 256

Freeman, Mary E(leanor) Wilkins
1852-1930 .... **SSC 1, 47; TCLC 9**
See also CA 106; 177; DLB 12, 78, 221;
EXPS; FW; HGG; MAWW; RGAL 4;
RGSF 2; SSFS 4, 8; SUFW 1; TUS

Freeman, R(ichard) Austin
1862-1943 .... **TCLC 21**
See also CA 113; CANR 84; CMW 4; DLB
70

Gent, Peter 1942- .... **CLC 29**
   See also AITN 1; CA 89-92; DLBY 1982
Gentile, Giovanni 1875-1944 .... **TCLC 96**
   See also CA 119
Gentlewoman in New England, A
   See Bradstreet, Anne
Gentlewoman in Those Parts, A
   See Bradstreet, Anne
Geoffrey of Monmouth c.
   1100-1155 .... **CMLC 44**
   See also DLB 146; TEA
George, Jean
   See George, Jean Craighead
George, Jean Craighead 1919- .... **CLC 35**
   See also AAYA 8; BYA 2, 4; CA 5-8R;
   CANR 25; CLR 1; 80; DLB 52; JRDA;
   MAICYA 1, 2; SATA 2, 68, 124; WYA;
   YAW
George, Stefan (Anton) 1868-1933 . **TCLC 2,
   14**
   See also CA 104; 193; EW 8; EWL 3
Georges, Georges Martin
   See Simenon, Georges (Jacques Christian)
Gerald of Wales c. 1146-c. 1223 ... **CMLC 60**
Gerhardi, William Alexander
   See Gerhardie, William Alexander
Gerhardie, William Alexander
   1895-1977 .... **CLC 5**
   See also CA 25-28R; 73-76; CANR 18; CN
   1, 2; DLB 36; RGEL 2
Gerson, Jean 1363-1429 .... **LC 77**
   See also DLB 208
Gersonides 1288-1344 .... **CMLC 49**
   See also DLB 115
Gerstler, Amy 1956- .... **CLC 70**
   See also CA 146; CANR 99
Gertler, T. .... **CLC 34**
   See also CA 116; 121
Gertsen, Aleksandr Ivanovich
   See Herzen, Aleksandr Ivanovich
Ghalib .... **NCLC 39, 78**
   See Ghalib, Asadullah Khan
Ghalib, Asadullah Khan 1797-1869
   See Ghalib
   See also DAM POET; RGWL 2, 3
Ghelderode, Michel de 1898-1962 ..... **CLC 6,
   11; DC 15**
   See also CA 85-88; CANR 40, 77; DAM
   DRAM; DLB 321; EW 11; EWL 3; TWA
Ghiselin, Brewster 1903-2001 .... **CLC 23**
   See also CA 13-16R; CAAS 10; CANR 13;
   CP 1, 2, 3, 4, 5, 6, 7
Ghose, Aurabinda 1872-1950 .... **TCLC 63**
   See Ghose, Aurobindo
   See also CA 163
Ghose, Aurobindo
   See Ghose, Aurabinda
   See also EWL 3
Ghose, Zulfikar 1935- .... **CLC 42, 200**
   See also CA 65-68; CANR 67; CN 1, 2, 3,
   4, 5, 6, 7; CP 1, 2, 3, 4, 5, 6, 7; EWL 3
Ghosh, Amitav 1956- .... **CLC 44, 153**
   See also CA 147; CANR 80; CN 6, 7;
   WWE 1
Giacosa, Giuseppe 1847-1906 .... **TCLC 7**
   See also CA 104
Gibb, Lee
   See Waterhouse, Keith (Spencer)
Gibbon, Edward 1737-1794 .... **LC 97**
   See also BRW 3; DLB 104; RGEL 2
Gibbon, Lewis Grassic .... **TCLC 4**
   See Mitchell, James Leslie
   See also RGEL 2
Gibbons, Kaye 1960- .... **CLC 50, 88, 145**
   See also AAYA 34; AMWS 10; CA 151;
   CANR 75, 127; CN 7; CSW; DA3; DAM
   POP; DLB 292; MTCW 2; MTFW 2005;
   NFS 3; RGAL 4; SATA 117

Gibran, Kahlil 1883-1931 . **PC 9; TCLC 1, 9**
   See also CA 104; 150; DA3; DAM POET,
   POP; EWL 3; MTCW 2; WLIT 6
Gibran, Khalil
   See Gibran, Kahlil
Gibson, Mel 1956- .... **CLC 215**
Gibson, William 1914- .... **CLC 23**
   See also CA 9-12R; CAD; CANR 9, 42, 75,
   125; CD 5, 6; DA; DAB; DAC; DAM
   DRAM, MST; DFS 2; DLB 7; LAIT 2;
   MAL 5; MTCW 2; MTFW 2005; SATA
   66; YAW
Gibson, William (Ford) 1948- ... **CLC 39, 63,
   186, 192; SSC 52**
   See also AAYA 12, 59; BPFB 2; CA 126;
   133; CANR 52, 90, 106; CN 6, 7; CPW;
   DA3; DAM POP; DLB 251; MTCW 2;
   MTFW 2005; SCFW 2; SFW 4
Gide, Andre (Paul Guillaume)
   1869-1951 ..... **SSC 13; TCLC 5, 12, 36;
   WLC**
   See also CA 104; 124; DA; DA3; DAB;
   DAC; DAM MST, NOV; DLB 65, 321;
   EW 8; EWL 3; GFL 1789 to the Present;
   MTCW 1, 2; MTFW 2005; NFS 21;
   RGSF 2; RGWL 2, 3; TWA
Gifford, Barry (Colby) 1946- .... **CLC 34**
   See also CA 65-68; CANR 9, 30, 40, 90
Gilbert, Frank
   See De Voto, Bernard (Augustine)
Gilbert, W(illiam) S(chwenck)
   1836-1911 .... **TCLC 3**
   See also CA 104; 173; DAM DRAM, POET;
   RGEL 2; SATA 36
Gilbreth, Frank B(unker), Jr.
   1911-2001 .... **CLC 17**
   See also CA 9-12R; SATA 2
Gilchrist, Ellen (Louise) 1935- .. **CLC 34, 48,
   143; SSC 14, 63**
   See also BPFB 2; CA 113; 116; CANR 41,
   61, 104; CN 4, 5, 6, 7; CPW; CSW; DAM
   POP; DLB 130; EWL 3; EXPS; MTCW
   1, 2; MTFW 2005; RGAL 4; RGSF 2;
   SSFS 9
Giles, Molly 1942- .... **CLC 39**
   See also CA 126; CANR 98
Gill, Eric .... **TCLC 85**
   See Gill, (Arthur) Eric (Rowton Peter
   Joseph)
Gill, (Arthur) Eric (Rowton Peter Joseph)
   1882-1940
   See Gill, Eric
   See also CA 120; DLB 98
Gill, Patrick
   See Creasey, John
Gillette, Douglas .... **CLC 70**
Gilliam, Terry (Vance) 1940- .... **CLC 21, 141**
   See Monty Python
   See also AAYA 19, 59; CA 108; 113; CANR
   35; INT CA-113
Gillian, Jerry
   See Gilliam, Terry (Vance)
Gilliatt, Penelope (Ann Douglass)
   1932-1993 .... **CLC 2, 10, 13, 53**
   See also AITN 2; CA 13-16R; 141; CANR
   49; CN 1, 2, 3, 4, 5; DLB 14
Gilligan, Carol 1936- .... **CLC 208**
   See also CA 142; CANR 121; FW
Gilman, Charlotte (Anna) Perkins (Stetson)
   1860-1935 ...... **SSC 13, 62; TCLC 9, 37,
   117**
   See also AMWS 11; BYA 11; CA 106; 150;
   DLB 221; EXPS; FL 1:5; FW; HGG;
   LAIT 2; MAWW; MTCW 2; MTFW
   2005; RGAL 4; RGSF 2; SFW 4; SSFS 1,
   18

Gilmour, David 1946- .... **CLC 35**
Gilpin, William 1724-1804 .... **NCLC 30**
Gilray, J. D.
   See Mencken, H(enry) L(ouis)
Gilroy, Frank D(aniel) 1925- .... **CLC 2**
   See also CA 81-84; CAD; CANR 32, 64,
   86; CD 5, 6; DFS 17; DLB 7
Gilstrap, John 1957(?)- .... **CLC 99**
   See also AAYA 67; CA 160; CANR 101
Ginsberg, Allen 1926-1997 .... **CLC 1, 2, 3, 4,
   6, 13, 36, 69, 109; PC 4, 47; TCLC
   120; WLC**
   See also AAYA 33; AITN 1; AMWC 1;
   AMWS 2; BG 1:2; CA 1-4R; 157; CANR
   2, 41, 63, 95; CDALB 1941-1968; CP 1,
   2, 3, 4, 5, 6; DA; DA3; DAB; DAC; DAM
   MST, POET; DLB 5, 16, 169, 237; EWL
   3; GLL 1; LMFS 2; MAL 5; MTCW 1, 2;
   MTFW 2005; PAB; PFS 5; RGAL 4;
   TUS; WP
Ginzburg, Eugenia .... **CLC 59**
   See Ginzburg, Evgeniia
Ginzburg, Evgeniia 1904-1977
   See Ginzburg, Eugenia
   See also DLB 302
Ginzburg, Natalia 1916-1991 .... **CLC 5, 11,
   54, 70; SSC 65; TCLC 156**
   See also CA 85-88; 135; CANR 33; DFS
   14; DLB 177; EW 13; EWL 3; MTCW 1,
   2; MTFW 2005; RGWL 2, 3
Giono, Jean 1895-1970 .... **CLC 4, 11; TCLC
   124**
   See also CA 45-48; 29-32R; CANR 2, 35;
   DLB 72, 321; EWL 3; GFL 1789 to the
   Present; MTCW 1; RGWL 2, 3
Giovanni, Nikki 1943- ...... **BLC 2; CLC 2, 4,
   19, 64, 117; PC 19; WLCS**
   See also AAYA 22; AITN 1; BW 2, 3; CA
   29-32R; CAAS 6; CANR 18, 41, 60, 91,
   130; CDALBS; CLR 6, 73; CP 2, 3, 4, 5,
   6, 7; CSW; CWP; CWRI 5; DA; DA3;
   DAB; DAC; DAM MST, MULT, POET;
   DLB 5, 41; EWL 3; EXPP; INT CANR-
   18; MAICYA 1, 2; MAL 5; MTCW 1, 2;
   MTFW 2005; PFS 17; RGAL 4; SATA
   24, 107; TUS; YAW
Giovene, Andrea 1904-1998 .... **CLC 7**
   See also CA 85-88
Gippius, Zinaida (Nikolaevna) 1869-1945
   See Hippius, Zinaida (Nikolaevna)
   See also CA 106; 212
Giraudoux, Jean(-Hippolyte)
   1882-1944 .... **TCLC 2, 7**
   See also CA 104; 196; DAM DRAM; DLB
   65, 321; EW 9; EWL 3; GFL 1789 to the
   Present; RGWL 2, 3; TWA
Gironella, Jose Maria (Pous)
   1917-2003 .... **CLC 11**
   See also CA 101; 212; EWL 3; RGWL 2, 3
Gissing, George (Robert)
   1857-1903 .... **SSC 37; TCLC 3, 24, 47**
   See also BRW 5; CA 105; 167; DLB 18,
   135, 184; RGEL 2; TEA
Gitlin, Todd 1943- .... **CLC 201**
   See also CA 29-32R; CANR 25, 50, 88
Giurlani, Aldo
   See Palazzeschi, Aldo
Gladkov, Fedor Vasil'evich
   See Gladkov, Fyodor (Vasilyevich)
   See also DLB 272
Gladkov, Fyodor (Vasilyevich)
   1883-1958 .... **TCLC 27**
   See Gladkov, Fedor Vasil'evich
   See also CA 170; EWL 3
Glancy, Diane 1941- .... **CLC 210; NNAL**
   See also CA 136, 225; CAAE 225; CAAS
   24; CANR 87; DLB 175

Glanville, Brian (Lester) 1931- .... **CLC 6**
See also CA 5-8R; CAAS 9; CANR 3, 70; CN 1, 2, 3, 4, 5, 6, 7; DLB 15, 139; SATA 42

Glasgow, Ellen (Anderson Gholson)
1873-1945 .... **SSC 34; TCLC 2, 7**
See also AMW; CA 104; 164; DLB 9, 12; MAL 5; MAWW; MTCW 2; MTFW 2005; RGAL 4; RHW; SSFS 9; TUS

Glaspell, Susan 1882(?)-1948 ..... **DC 10; SSC 41; TCLC 55**
See also AMWS 3; CA 110; 154; DFS 8, 18; DLB 7, 9, 78, 228; MAWW; RGAL 4; SSFS 3; TCWW 2; TUS; YABC 2

Glassco, John 1909-1981 .... **CLC 9**
See also CA 13-16R; 102; CANR 15; CN 1, 2; CP 1, 2, 3; DLB 68

Glasscock, Amnesia
See Steinbeck, John (Ernst)

Glasser, Ronald J. 1940(?)- .... **CLC 37**
See also CA 209

Glassman, Joyce
See Johnson, Joyce

Gleick, James (W.) 1954- .... **CLC 147**
See also CA 131; 137; CANR 97; INT CA-137

Glendinning, Victoria 1937- .... **CLC 50**
See also CA 120; 127; CANR 59, 89; DLB 155

Glissant, Edouard (Mathieu)
1928- .... **CLC 10, 68**
See also CA 153; CANR 111; CWW 2; DAM MULT; EWL 3; RGWL 3

Gloag, Julian 1930- .... **CLC 40**
See also AITN 1; CA 65-68; CANR 10, 70; CN 1, 2, 3, 4, 5, 6

Glowacki, Aleksander
See Prus, Boleslaw

Gluck, Louise (Elisabeth) 1943- .. **CLC 7, 22, 44, 81, 160; PC 16**
See also AMWS 5; CA 33-36R; CANR 40, 69, 108, 133; CP 1, 2, 3, 4, 5, 6, 7; CWP; DA3; DAM POET; DLB 5; MAL 5; MTCW 2; MTFW 2005; PFS 5, 15; RGAL 4; TCLE 1:1

Glyn, Elinor 1864-1943 .... **TCLC 72**
See also DLB 153; RHW

Gobineau, Joseph-Arthur
1816-1882 .... **NCLC 17**
See also DLB 123; GFL 1789 to the Present

Godard, Jean-Luc 1930- .... **CLC 20**
See also CA 93-96

Godden, (Margaret) Rumer
1907-1998 .... **CLC 53**
See also AAYA 6; BPFB 2; BYA 2, 5; CA 5-8R; 172; CANR 4, 27, 36, 55, 80; CLR 20; CN 1, 2, 3, 4, 5, 6; CWRI 5; DLB 161; MAICYA 1, 2; RHW; SAAS 12; SATA 3, 36; SATA-Obit 109; TEA

Godoy Alcayaga, Lucila 1899-1957 .. **HLC 2; PC 32; TCLC 2**
See Mistral, Gabriela
See also BW 2; CA 104; 131; CANR 81; DAM MULT; DNFS 1; HW 1, 2; MTCW 1, 2; MTFW 2005

Godwin, Gail 1937- ...... **CLC 5, 8, 22, 31, 69, 125**
See also BPFB 2; CA 29-32R; CANR 15, 43, 69, 132; CN 3, 4, 5, 6, 7; CPW; CSW; DA3; DAM POP; DLB 6, 234; INT CANR-15; MAL 5; MTCW 1, 2; MTFW 2005

Godwin, Gail Kathleen
See Godwin, Gail

Godwin, William 1756-1836 .. **NCLC 14, 130**
See also CDBLB 1789-1832; CMW 4; DLB 39, 104, 142, 158, 163, 262; GL 2; HGG; RGEL 2

Goebbels, Josef
See Goebbels, (Paul) Joseph

Goebbels, (Paul) Joseph
1897-1945 .... **TCLC 68**
See also CA 115; 148

Goebbels, Joseph Paul
See Goebbels, (Paul) Joseph

Goethe, Johann Wolfgang von
1749-1832 . **DC 20; NCLC 4, 22, 34, 90, 154; PC 5; SSC 38; WLC**
See also CDWLB 2; DA; DA3; DAB; DAC; DAM DRAM, MST, POET; DLB 94; EW 5; GL 2; LATS 1; LMFS 1:1; RGWL 2, 3; TWA

Gogarty, Oliver St. John
1878-1957 .... **TCLC 15**
See also CA 109; 150; DLB 15, 19; RGEL 2

Gogol, Nikolai (Vasilyevich)
1809-1852 .... **DC 1; NCLC 5, 15, 31, 162; SSC 4, 29, 52; WLC**
See also DA; DAB; DAC; DAM DRAM, MST; DFS 12; DLB 198; EW 6; EXPS; RGSF 2; RGWL 2, 3; SSFS 7; TWA

Goines, Donald 1937(?)-1974 ... **BLC 2; CLC 80**
See also AITN 1; BW 1, 3; CA 124; 114; CANR 82; CMW 4; DA3; DAM MULT, POP; DLB 33

Gold, Herbert 1924- ... **CLC 4, 7, 14, 42, 152**
See also CA 9-12R; CANR 17, 45, 125; CN 1, 2, 3, 4, 5, 6, 7; DLB 2; DLBY 1981; MAL 5

Goldbarth, Albert 1948- .... **CLC 5, 38**
See also AMWS 12; CA 53-56; CANR 6, 40; CP 3, 4, 5, 6, 7; DLB 120

Goldberg, Anatol 1910-1982 .... **CLC 34**
See also CA 131; 117

Goldemberg, Isaac 1945- .... **CLC 52**
See also CA 69-72; CAAS 12; CANR 11, 32; EWL 3; HW 1; WLIT 1

Golding, Arthur 1536-1606 .... **LC 101**
See also DLB 136

Golding, William (Gerald)
1911-1993 ..... **CLC 1, 2, 3, 8, 10, 17, 27, 58, 81; WLC**
See also AAYA 5, 44; BPFB 2; BRWR 1; BRWS 1; BYA 2; CA 5-8R; 141; CANR 13, 33, 54; CD 5; CDBLB 1945-1960; CLR 94; CN 1, 2, 3, 4; DA; DA3; DAB; DAC; DAM MST, NOV; DLB 15, 100, 255; EWL 3; EXPN; HGG; LAIT 4; MTCW 1, 2; MTFW 2005; NFS 2; RGEL 2; RHW; SFW 4; TEA; WLIT 4; YAW

Goldman, Emma 1869-1940 .... **TCLC 13**
See also CA 110; 150; DLB 221; FW; RGAL 4; TUS

Goldman, Francisco 1954- .... **CLC 76**
See also CA 162

Goldman, William (W.) 1931- ...... **CLC 1, 48**
See also BPFB 2; CA 9-12R; CANR 29, 69, 106; CN 1, 2, 3, 4, 5, 6, 7; DLB 44; FANT; IDFW 3, 4

Goldmann, Lucien 1913-1970 .... **CLC 24**
See also CA 25-28; CAP 2

Goldoni, Carlo 1707-1793 .... **LC 4**
See also DAM DRAM; EW 4; RGWL 2, 3; WLIT 7

Goldsberry, Steven 1949- .... **CLC 34**
See also CA 131

Goldsmith, Oliver 1730-1774 .... **DC 8; LC 2, 48, 122; WLC**
See also BRW 3; CDBLB 1660-1789; DA; DAB; DAC; DAM DRAM, MST, NOV, POET; DFS 1; DLB 39, 89, 104, 109, 142; IDTP; RGEL 2; SATA 26; TEA; WLIT 3

Goldsmith, Peter
See Priestley, J(ohn) B(oynton)

Gombrowicz, Witold 1904-1969 .... **CLC 4, 7, 11, 49**
See also CA 19-20; 25-28R; CANR 105; CAP 2; CDWLB 4; DAM DRAM; DLB 215; EW 12; EWL 3; RGWL 2, 3; TWA

Gomez de Avellaneda, Gertrudis
1814-1873 .... **NCLC 111**
See also LAW

Gomez de la Serna, Ramon
1888-1963 .... **CLC 9**
See also CA 153; 116; CANR 79; EWL 3; HW 1, 2

Goncharov, Ivan Alexandrovich
1812-1891 .... **NCLC 1, 63**
See also DLB 238; EW 6; RGWL 2, 3

Goncourt, Edmond (Louis Antoine Huot) de
1822-1896 .... **NCLC 7**
See also DLB 123; EW 7; GFL 1789 to the Present; RGWL 2, 3

Goncourt, Jules (Alfred Huot) de
1830-1870 .... **NCLC 7**
See also DLB 123; EW 7; GFL 1789 to the Present; RGWL 2, 3

Gongora (y Argote), Luis de
1561-1627 .... **LC 72**
See also RGWL 2, 3

Gontier, Fernande 19(?)- .... **CLC 50**

Gonzalez Martinez, Enrique
See Gonzalez Martinez, Enrique
See also DLB 290

Gonzalez Martinez, Enrique
1871-1952 .... **TCLC 72**
See Gonzalez Martinez, Enrique
See also CA 166; CANR 81; EWL 3; HW 1, 2

Goodison, Lorna 1947- .... **PC 36**
See also CA 142; CANR 88; CP 7; CWP; DLB 157; EWL 3

Goodman, Paul 1911-1972 ..... **CLC 1, 2, 4, 7**
See also CA 19-20; 37-40R; CAD; CANR 34; CAP 2; CN 1; DLB 130, 246; MAL 5; MTCW 1; RGAL 4

GoodWeather, Harley
See King, Thomas

Googe, Barnabe 1540-1594 .... **LC 94**
See also DLB 132; RGEL 2

Gordimer, Nadine 1923- ...... **CLC 3, 5, 7, 10, 18, 33, 51, 70, 123, 160, 161; SSC 17, 80; WLCS**
See also AAYA 39; AFW; BRWS 2; CA 5-8R; CANR 3, 28, 56, 88, 131; CN 1, 2, 3, 4, 5, 6, 7; DA; DA3; DAB; DAC; DAM MST, NOV; DLB 225; EWL 3; EXPS; INT CANR-28; LATS 1:2; MTCW 1, 2; MTFW 2005; NFS 4; RGEL 2; RGSF 2; SSFS 2, 14, 19; TWA; WLIT 2; YAW

Gordon, Adam Lindsay
1833-1870 .... **NCLC 21**
See also DLB 230

Gordon, Caroline 1895-1981 . **CLC 6, 13, 29, 83; SSC 15**
See also AMW; CA 11-12; 103; CANR 36; CAP 1; CN 1, 2; DLB 4, 9, 102; DLBD 17; DLBY 1981; EWL 3; MAL 5; MTCW 1, 2; MTFW 2005; RGAL 4; RGSF 2

Gordon, Charles William 1860-1937
See Connor, Ralph
See also CA 109

Gordon, Mary (Catherine) 1949- .... **CLC 13, 22, 128, 216; SSC 59**
See also AMWS 4; BPFB 2; CA 102; CANR 44, 92; CN 4, 5, 6, 7; DLB 6; DLBY 1981; FW; INT CA-102; MAL 5; MTCW 1

Gordon, N. J.
See Bosman, Herman Charles

Gordon, Sol 1923- .... **CLC 26**
See also CA 53-56; CANR 4; SATA 11

Guillen, Nicolas (Cristobal)
1902-1989 .... **BLC 2; CLC 48, 79; HLC 1; PC 23**
See also BW 2; CA 116; 125; 129; CANR 84; DAM MST, MULT, POET; DLB 283; EWL 3; HW 1; LAW; RGWL 2, 3; WP
Guillen y Alvarez, Jorge
See Guillen, Jorge
Guillevic, (Eugene) 1907-1997 .... **CLC 33**
See also CA 93-96; CWW 2
Guillois
See Desnos, Robert
Guillois, Valentin
See Desnos, Robert
Guimaraes Rosa, Joao 1908-1967 .... **HLCS 2**
See Rosa, Joao Guimaraes
See also CA 175; LAW; RGSF 2; RGWL 2, 3
Guiney, Louise Imogen
1861-1920 .... **TCLC 41**
See also CA 160; DLB 54; RGAL 4
Guinizelli, Guido c. 1230-1276 ...... **CMLC 49**
See Guinizzelli, Guido
Guinizzelli, Guido
See Guinizelli, Guido
See also WLIT 7
Guiraldes, Ricardo (Guillermo)
1886-1927 .... **TCLC 39**
See also CA 131; EWL 3; HW 1; LAW; MTCW 1
Gumilev, Nikolai (Stepanovich)
1886-1921 .... **TCLC 60**
See Gumilyov, Nikolay Stepanovich
See also CA 165; DLB 295
Gumilyov, Nikolay Stepanovich
See Gumilev, Nikolai (Stepanovich)
See also EWL 3
Gump, P. Q.
See Card, Orson Scott
Gunesekera, Romesh 1954- .... **CLC 91**
See also BRWS 10; CA 159; CANR 140; CN 6, 7; DLB 267
Gunn, Bill .... **CLC 5**
See Gunn, William Harrison
See also DLB 38
Gunn, Thom(son William)
1929-2004 . **CLC 3, 6, 18, 32, 81; PC 26**
See also BRWS 4; CA 17-20R; 227; CANR 9, 33, 116; CDBLB 1960 to Present; CP 1, 2, 3, 4, 5, 6, 7; DAM POET; DLB 27; INT CANR-33; MTCW 1; PFS 9; RGEL 2
Gunn, William Harrison 1934(?)-1989
See Gunn, Bill
See also AITN 1; BW 1, 3; CA 13-16R; 128; CANR 12, 25, 76
Gunn Allen, Paula
See Allen, Paula Gunn
Gunnars, Kristjana 1948- .... **CLC 69**
See also CA 113; CCA 1; CP 7; CWP; DLB 60
Gunter, Erich
See Eich, Gunter
Gurdjieff, G(eorgei) I(vanovich)
1877(?)-1949 .... **TCLC 71**
See also CA 157
Gurganus, Allan 1947- .... **CLC 70**
See also BEST 90:1; CA 135; CANR 114; CN 6, 7; CPW; CSW; DAM POP; GLL 1
Gurney, A. R.
See Gurney, A(lbert) R(amsdell), Jr.
See also DLB 266
Gurney, A(lbert) R(amsdell), Jr.
1930- .... **CLC 32, 50, 54**
See Gurney, A. R.
See also AMWS 5; CA 77-80; CAD; CANR 32, 64, 121; CD 5, 6; DAM DRAM; EWL 3

Gurney, Ivor (Bertie) 1890-1937 ... **TCLC 33**
See also BRW 6; CA 167; DLBY 2002; PAB; RGEL 2
Gurney, Peter
See Gurney, A(lbert) R(amsdell), Jr.
Guro, Elena (Genrikhovna)
1877-1913 .... **TCLC 56**
See also DLB 295
Gustafson, James M(oody) 1925- ... **CLC 100**
See also CA 25-28R; CANR 37
Gustafson, Ralph (Barker)
1909-1995 .... **CLC 36**
See also CA 21-24R; CANR 8, 45, 84; CP 1, 2, 3, 4; DLB 88; RGEL 2
Gut, Gom
See Simenon, Georges (Jacques Christian)
Guterson, David 1956- .... **CLC 91**
See also CA 132; CANR 73, 126; CN 7; DLB 292; MTCW 2; MTFW 2005; NFS 13
Guthrie, A(lfred) B(ertram), Jr.
1901-1991 .... **CLC 23**
See also CA 57-60; 134; CANR 24; CN 1, 2, 3; DLB 6, 212; MAL 5; SATA 62; SATA-Obit 67; TCWW 1, 2
Guthrie, Isobel
See Grieve, C(hristopher) M(urray)
Guthrie, Woodrow Wilson 1912-1967
See Guthrie, Woody
See also CA 113; 93-96
Guthrie, Woody .... **CLC 35**
See Guthrie, Woodrow Wilson
See also DLB 303; LAIT 3
Gutierrez Najera, Manuel
1859-1895 .... **HLCS 2; NCLC 133**
See also DLB 290; LAW
Guy, Rosa (Cuthbert) 1925- .... **CLC 26**
See also AAYA 4, 37; BW 2; CA 17-20R; CANR 14, 34, 83; CLR 13; DLB 33; DNFS 1; JRDA; MAICYA 1, 2; SATA 14, 62, 122; YAW
Gwendolyn
See Bennett, (Enoch) Arnold
H. D. .... **CLC 3, 8, 14, 31, 34, 73; PC 5**
See Doolittle, Hilda
See also FL 1:5
H. de V.
See Buchan, John
Haavikko, Paavo Juhani 1931- .. **CLC 18, 34**
See also CA 106; CWW 2; EWL 3
Habbema, Koos
See Heijermans, Herman
Habermas, Juergen 1929- .... **CLC 104**
See also CA 109; CANR 85; DLB 242
Habermas, Jurgen
See Habermas, Juergen
Hacker, Marilyn 1942- ...... **CLC 5, 9, 23, 72, 91; PC 47**
See also CA 77-80; CANR 68, 129; CP 3, 4, 5, 6, 7; CWP; DAM POET; DLB 120, 282; FW; GLL 2; MAL 5; PFS 19
Hadewijch of Antwerp fl. 1250- ... **CMLC 61**
See also RGWL 3
Hadrian 76-138 .... **CMLC 52**
Haeckel, Ernst Heinrich (Philipp August)
1834-1919 .... **TCLC 83**
See also CA 157
Hafiz c. 1326-1389(?) .... **CMLC 34**
See also RGWL 2, 3; WLIT 6
Hagedorn, Jessica T(arahata)
1949- .... **CLC 185**
See also CA 139; CANR 69; CWP; DLB 312; RGAL 4

Haggard, H(enry) Rider
1856-1925 .... **TCLC 11**
See also BRWS 3; BYA 4, 5; CA 108; 148; CANR 112; DLB 70, 156, 174, 178; FANT; LMFS 1; MTCW 2; RGEL 2; RHW; SATA 16; SCFW 1, 2; SFW 4; SUFW 1; WLIT 4
Hagiosy, L.
See Larbaud, Valery (Nicolas)
Hagiwara, Sakutaro 1886-1942 .... **PC 18; TCLC 60**
See Hagiwara Sakutaro
See also CA 154; RGWL 3
Hagiwara Sakutaro
See Hagiwara, Sakutaro
See also EWL 3
Haig, Fenil
See Ford, Ford Madox
Haig-Brown, Roderick (Langmere)
1908-1976 .... **CLC 21**
See also CA 5-8R; 69-72; CANR 4, 38, 83; CLR 31; CWRI 5; DLB 88; MAICYA 1, 2; SATA 12; TCWW 2
Haight, Rip
See Carpenter, John (Howard)
Hailey, Arthur 1920-2004 .... **CLC 5**
See also AITN 2; BEST 90:3; BPFB 2; CA 1-4R; 233; CANR 2, 36, 75; CCA 1; CN 1, 2, 3, 4, 5, 6, 7; CPW; DAM NOV, POP; DLB 88; DLBY 1982; MTCW 1, 2; MTFW 2005
Hailey, Elizabeth Forsythe 1938- ..... **CLC 40**
See also CA 93-96, 188; CAAE 188; CAAS 1; CANR 15, 48; INT CANR-15
Haines, John (Meade) 1924- .... **CLC 58**
See also AMWS 12; CA 17-20R; CANR 13, 34; CP 1, 2, 3, 4; CSW; DLB 5, 212; TCLE 1:1
Hakluyt, Richard 1552-1616 .... **LC 31**
See also DLB 136; RGEL 2
Haldeman, Joe (William) 1943- .... **CLC 61**
See Graham, Robert
See also AAYA 38; CA 53-56, 179; CAAE 179; CAAS 25; CANR 6, 70, 72, 130; DLB 8; INT CANR-6; SCFW 2; SFW 4
Hale, Janet Campbell 1947- .... **NNAL**
See also CA 49-52; CANR 45, 75; DAM MULT; DLB 175; MTCW 2; MTFW 2005
Hale, Sarah Josepha (Buell)
1788-1879 .... **NCLC 75**
See also DLB 1, 42, 73, 243
Halevy, Elie 1870-1937 .... **TCLC 104**
Haley, Alex(ander Murray Palmer)
1921-1992 .... **BLC 2; CLC 8, 12, 76; TCLC 147**
See also AAYA 26; BPFB 2; BW 2, 3; CA 77-80; 136; CANR 61; CDALBS; CPW; CSW; DA; DA3; DAB; DAC; DAM MST, MULT, POP; DLB 38; LAIT 5; MTCW 1, 2; NFS 9
Haliburton, Thomas Chandler
1796-1865 .... **NCLC 15, 149**
See also DLB 11, 99; RGEL 2; RGSF 2
Hall, Donald (Andrew, Jr.) 1928- ...... **CLC 1, 13, 37, 59, 151**
See also AAYA 63; CA 5-8R; CAAS 7; CANR 2, 44, 64, 106, 133; CP 1, 2, 3, 4, 5, 6, 7; DAM POET; DLB 5; MAL 5; MTCW 2; MTFW 2005; RGAL 4; SATA 23, 97
Hall, Frederic Sauser
See Sauser-Hall, Frederic
Hall, James
See Kuttner, Henry
Hall, James Norman 1887-1951 ..... **TCLC 23**
See also CA 123; 173; LAIT 1; RHW 1; SATA 21
Hall, Joseph 1574-1656 .... **LC 91**
See also DLB 121, 151; RGEL 2

Hoffman, Eva 1945- .... **CLC 182**
  See also CA 132; CANR 146
Hoffman, Stanley 1944- .... **CLC 5**
  See also CA 77-80
Hoffman, William 1925- .... **CLC 141**
  See also CA 21-24R; CANR 9, 103; CSW;
  DLB 234; TCLE 1:1
Hoffman, William M.
  See Hoffman, William M(oses)
  See also CAD; CD 5, 6
Hoffman, William M(oses) 1939- ..... **CLC 40**
  See Hoffman, William M.
  See also CA 57-60; CANR 11, 71
Hoffmann, E(rnst) T(heodor) A(madeus)
  1776-1822 .... **NCLC 2; SSC 13**
  See also CDWLB 2; DLB 90; EW 5; GL 2;
  RGSF 2; RGWL 2, 3; SATA 27; SUFW
  1; WCH
Hofmann, Gert 1931-1993 .... **CLC 54**
  See also CA 128; CANR 145; EWL 3
Hofmannsthal, Hugo von 1874-1929 ... **DC 4;**
  TCLC 11
  See also CA 106; 153; CDWLB 2; DAM
  DRAM; DFS 17; DLB 81, 118; EW 9;
  EWL 3; RGWL 2, 3
Hogan, Linda 1947- ..... **CLC 73; NNAL; PC**
  35
  See also AMWS 4; ANW; BYA 12; CA 120,
  226; CAAE 226; CANR 45, 73, 129;
  CWP; DAM MULT; DLB 175; SATA
  132; TCWW 2
Hogarth, Charles
  See Creasey, John
Hogarth, Emmett
  See Polonsky, Abraham (Lincoln)
Hogarth, William 1697-1764 .... **LC 112**
  See also AAYA 56
Hogg, James 1770-1835 .... **NCLC 4, 109**
  See also BRWS 10; DLB 93, 116, 159; GL
  2; HGG; RGEL 2; SUFW 1
Holbach, Paul-Henri Thiry
  1723-1789 .... **LC 14**
  See also DLB 313
Holberg, Ludvig 1684-1754 .... **LC 6**
  See also DLB 300; RGWL 2, 3
Holcroft, Thomas 1745-1809 .... **NCLC 85**
  See also DLB 39, 89, 158; RGEL 2
Holden, Ursula 1921- .... **CLC 18**
  See also CA 101; CAAS 8; CANR 22
Holderlin, (Johann Christian) Friedrich
  1770-1843 .... **NCLC 16; PC 4**
  See also CDWLB 2; DLB 90; EW 5; RGWL
  2, 3
Holdstock, Robert
  See Holdstock, Robert P.
Holdstock, Robert P. 1948- .... **CLC 39**
  See also CA 131; CANR 81; DLB 261;
  FANT; HGG; SFW 4; SUFW 2
Holinshed, Raphael fl. 1580- .... **LC 69**
  See also DLB 167; RGEL 2
Holland, Isabelle (Christian)
  1920-2002 .... **CLC 21**
  See also AAYA 11, 64; CA 21-24R; 205;
  CAAE 181; CANR 10, 25, 47; CLR 57;
  CWRI 5; JRDA; LAIT 4; MAICYA 1, 2;
  SATA 8, 70; SATA-Essay 103; SATA-Obit
  132; WYA
Holland, Marcus
  See Caldwell, (Janet Miriam) Taylor
  (Holland)
Hollander, John 1929- .... **CLC 2, 5, 8, 14**
  See also CA 1-4R; CANR 1, 52, 136; CP 1,
  2, 3, 4, 5, 6, 7; DLB 5; MAL 5; SATA 13
Hollander, Paul
  See Silverberg, Robert
Holleran, Andrew .... **CLC 38**
  See Garber, Eric
  See also CA 144; GLL 1

Holley, Marietta 1836(?)-1926 .... **TCLC 99**
  See also CA 118; DLB 11; FL 1:3
Hollinghurst, Alan 1954- .... **CLC 55, 91**
  See also BRWS 10; CA 114; CN 5, 6, 7;
  DLB 207; GLL 1
Hollis, Jim
  See Summers, Hollis (Spurgeon, Jr.)
Holly, Buddy 1936-1959 .... **TCLC 65**
  See also CA 213
Holmes, Gordon
  See Shiel, M(atthew) P(hipps)
Holmes, John
  See Souster, (Holmes) Raymond
Holmes, John Clellon 1926-1988 ...... **CLC 56**
  See also BG 1:2; CA 9-12R; 125; CANR 4;
  CN 1, 2, 3, 4; DLB 16, 237
Holmes, Oliver Wendell, Jr.
  1841-1935 .... **TCLC 77**
  See also CA 114; 186
Holmes, Oliver Wendell
  1809 1894 .... **NCLC 14, 81**
  See also AMWS 1; CDALB 1640-1865;
  DLB 1, 189, 235; EXPP; RGAL 4; SATA
  34
Holmes, Raymond
  See Souster, (Holmes) Raymond
Holt, Victoria
  See Hibbert, Eleanor Alice Burford
  See also BPFB 2
Holub, Miroslav 1923-1998 .... **CLC 4**
  See also CA 21-24R; 169; CANR 10; CD-
  WLB 4; CWW 2; DLB 232; EWL 3;
  RGWL 3
Holz, Detlev
  See Benjamin, Walter
Homer c. 8th cent. B.C.- .... **CMLC 1, 16, 61;**
  PC 23; WLCS
  See also AW 1; CDWLB 1; DA; DA3;
  DAB; DAC; DAM MST, POET; DLB
  176; EFS 1; LAIT 1; LMFS 1; RGWL 2,
  3; TWA; WP
Hongo, Garrett Kaoru 1951- .... **PC 23**
  See also CA 133; CAAS 22; CP 7; DLB
  120, 312; EWL 3; EXPP; RGAL 4
Honig, Edwin 1919- .... **CLC 33**
  See also CA 5-8R; CAAS 8; CANR 4, 45,
  144; CP 1, 2, 3, 4, 5, 6, 7; DLB 5
Hood, Hugh (John Blagdon) 1928- . **CLC 15,**
  28; SSC 42
  See also CA 49-52; CAAS 17; CANR 1,
  33, 87; CN 1, 2, 3, 4, 5, 6, 7; DLB 53;
  RGSF 2
Hood, Thomas 1799-1845 .... **NCLC 16**
  See also BRW 4; DLB 96; RGEL 2
Hooker, (Peter) Jeremy 1941- .... **CLC 43**
  See also CA 77-80; CANR 22; CP 2, 3, 4,
  5, 6, 7; DLB 40
Hooker, Richard 1554-1600 .... **LC 95**
  See also BRW 1; DLB 132; RGEL 2
hooks, bell
  See Watkins, Gloria Jean
Hope, A(lec) D(erwent) 1907-2000 .... **CLC 3,**
  51; PC 56
  See also BRWS 7; CA 21-24R; 188; CANR
  33, 74; CP 1, 2, 3, 4; DLB 289; EWL 3;
  MTCW 1, 2; MTFW 2005; PFS 8; RGEL
  2
Hope, Anthony 1863-1933 .... **TCLC 83**
  See also CA 157; DLB 153, 156; RGEL 2;
  RHW
Hope, Brian
  See Creasey, John
Hope, Christopher (David Tully)
  1944- .... **CLC 52**
  See also AFW; CA 106; CANR 47, 101;
  CN 4, 5, 6, 7; DLB 225; SATA 62

Hopkins, Gerard Manley
  1844-1889 .... **NCLC 17; PC 15; WLC**
  See also BRW 5; BRWR 2; CDBLB 1890-
  1914; DA; DA3; DAB; DAC; DAM MST,
  POET; DLB 35, 57; EXPP; PAB; RGEL
  2; TEA; WP
Hopkins, John (Richard) 1931-1998 .. **CLC 4**
  See also CA 85-88; 169; CBD; CD 5, 6
Hopkins, Pauline Elizabeth
  1859-1930 .... **BLC 2; TCLC 28**
  See also AFAW 2; BW 2, 3; CA 141; CANR
  82; DAM MULT; DLB 50
Hopkinson, Francis 1737-1791 .... **LC 25**
  See also DLB 31; RGAL 4
Hopley-Woolrich, Cornell George 1903-1968
  See Woolrich, Cornell
  See also CA 13-14; CANR 58; CAP 1;
  CMW 4; DLB 226; MTCW 2
Horace 65B.C.-8B.C. .... **CMLC 39; PC 46**
  See also AW 2; CDWLB 1; DLB 211;
  RGWL 2, 3
Horatio
  See Proust, (Valentin-Louis-George-Eugene)
  Marcel
Horgan, Paul (George Vincent
  O'Shaughnessy) 1903-1995 .. **CLC 9, 53**
  See also BPFB 2; CA 13-16R; 147; CANR
  9, 35; CN 1, 2, 3, 4, 5; DAM NOV; DLB
  102, 212; DLBY 1985; INT CANR-9;
  MTCW 1, 2; MTFW 2005; SATA 13;
  SATA-Obit 84; TCWW 1, 2
Horkheimer, Max 1895-1973 .... **TCLC 132**
  See also CA 216; 41-44R; DLB 296
Horn, Peter
  See Kuttner, Henry
Horne, Frank (Smith) 1899-1974 ...... **HR 1:2**
  See also BW 1; CA 125; 53-56; DLB 51;
  WP
Horne, Richard Henry Hengist
  1802(?)-1884 .... **NCLC 127**
  See also DLB 32; SATA 29
Hornem, Horace Esq.
  See Byron, George Gordon (Noel)
Horney, Karen (Clementine Theodore
  Danielsen) 1885-1952 .... **TCLC 71**
  See also CA 114; 165; DLB 246; FW
Hornung, E(rnest) W(illiam)
  1866-1921 .... **TCLC 59**
  See also CA 108; 160; CMW 4; DLB 70
Horovitz, Israel (Arthur) 1939- .... **CLC 56**
  See also CA 33-36R; CAD; CANR 46, 59;
  CD 5, 6; DAM DRAM; DLB 7; MAL 5
Horton, George Moses
  1797(?)-1883(?) .... **NCLC 87**
  See also DLB 50
Horvath, odon von 1901-1938
  See von Horvath, Odon
  See also EWL 3
Horvath, Oedoen von -1938
  See von Horvath, Odon
Horwitz, Julius 1920-1986 .... **CLC 14**
  See also CA 9-12R; 119; CANR 12
Hospital, Janette Turner 1942- .... **CLC 42,**
  145
  See also CA 108; CANR 48; CN 5, 6, 7;
  DLBY 2002; RGSF 2
Hostos, E. M. de
  See Hostos (y Bonilla), Eugenio Maria de
Hostos, Eugenio M. de
  See Hostos (y Bonilla), Eugenio Maria de
Hostos, Eugenio Maria
  See Hostos (y Bonilla), Eugenio Maria de
Hostos (y Bonilla), Eugenio Maria de
  1839-1903 .... **TCLC 24**
  See also CA 123; 131; HW 1
Houdini
  See Lovecraft, H(oward) P(hillips)
Houellebecq, Michel 1958- .... **CLC 179**
  See also CA 185; CANR 140; MTFW 2005

Cumulative Author Index

Hougan, Carolyn 1943- .... **CLC 34**
See also CA 139

Household, Geoffrey (Edward West)
1900-1988 .... **CLC 11**
See also CA 77-80; 126; CANR 58; CMW
4; CN 1, 2, 3, 4; DLB 87; SATA 14;
SATA-Obit 59

Housman, A(lfred) E(dward)
1859-1936 .... **PC 2, 43; TCLC 1, 10;**
WLCS
See also AAYA 66; BRW 6; CA 104; 125;
DA; DA3; DAB; DAC; DAM MST,
POET; DLB 19, 284; EWL 3; EXPP;
MTCW 1, 2; MTFW 2005; PAB; PFS 4,
7; RGEL 2; TEA; WP

Housman, Laurence 1865-1959 .... **TCLC 7**
See also CA 106; 155; DLB 10; FANT;
RGEL 2; SATA 25

Houston, Jeanne (Toyo) Wakatsuki
1934- .... **AAL**
See also AAYA 49; CA 103, 232; CAAE
232; CAAS 16; CANR 29, 123; LAIT 4;
SATA 78

Howard, Elizabeth Jane 1923- ..... **CLC 7, 29**
See also BRWS 11; CA 5-8R; CANR 8, 62,
146; CN 1, 2, 3, 4, 5, 6, 7

Howard, Maureen 1930- .... **CLC 5, 14, 46,**
151
See also CA 53-56; CANR 31, 75, 140; CN
4, 5, 6, 7; DLBY 1983; INT CANR-31;
MTCW 1, 2; MTFW 2005

Howard, Richard 1929- .... **CLC 7, 10, 47**
See also AITN 1; CA 85-88; CANR 25, 80;
CP 1, 2, 3, 4, 5, 6, 7; DLB 5; INT CANR-
25; MAL 5

Howard, Robert E(rvin)
1906-1936 .... **TCLC 8**
See also BPFB 2; BYA 5; CA 105; 157;
FANT; SUFW 1; TCWW 1, 2

Howard, Warren F.
See Pohl, Frederik

Howe, Fanny (Quincy) 1940- .... **CLC 47**
See also CA 117, 187; CAAE 187; CAAS
27; CANR 70, 116; CP 7; CWP; SATA-
Brief 52

Howe, Irving 1920-1993 .... **CLC 85**
See also AMWS 6; CA 9-12R; 141; CANR
21, 50; DLB 67; EWL 3; MAL 5; MTCW
1, 2; MTFW 2005

Howe, Julia Ward 1819-1910 .... **TCLC 21**
See also CA 117; 191; DLB 1, 189, 235;
FW

Howe, Susan 1937- .... **CLC 72, 152; PC 54**
See also AMWS 4; CA 160; CP 7; CWP;
DLB 120; FW; RGAL 4

Howe, Tina 1937- .... **CLC 48**
See also CA 109; CAD; CANR 125; CD 5,
6; CWD

Howell, James 1594(?)-1666 .... **LC 13**
See also DLB 151

Howells, W. D.
See Howells, William Dean

Howells, William D.
See Howells, William Dean

Howells, William Dean 1837-1920 ... **SSC 36;**
TCLC 7, 17, 41
See also AMW; CA 104; 134; CDALB
1865-1917; DLB 12, 64, 74, 79, 189;
LMFS 1; MAL 5; MTCW 2; RGAL 4;
TUS

Howes, Barbara 1914-1996 .... **CLC 15**
See also CA 9-12R; 151; CAAS 3; CANR
53; CP 1, 2, 3, 4; SATA 5; TCLE 1:1

Hrabal, Bohumil 1914-1997 ...... **CLC 13, 67;**
TCLC 155
See also CA 106; 156; CAAS 12; CANR
57; CWW 2; DLB 232; EWL 3; RGSF 2

Hrabanus Maurus 776(?)-856 .... **CMLC 78**
See also DLB 148

Hrotsvit of Gandersheim c. 935-c.
1000 .... **CMLC 29**
See also DLB 148

Hsi, Chu 1130-1200 .... **CMLC 42**

Hsun, Lu
See Lu Hsun

Hubbard, L(afayette) Ron(ald)
1911-1986 .... **CLC 43**
See also AAYA 64; CA 77-80; 118; CANR
52; CPW; DA3; DAM POP; FANT;
MTCW 2; MTFW 2005; SFW 4

Huch, Ricarda (Octavia)
1864-1947 .... **TCLC 13**
See Hugo, Richard
See also CA 111; 189; DLB 66; EWL 3

Huddle, David 1942- .... **CLC 49**
See also CA 57-60; CAAS 20; CANR 89;
DLB 130

Hudson, Jeffrey
See Crichton, (John) Michael

Hudson, W(illiam) H(enry)
1841-1922 .... **TCLC 29**
See also CA 115; 190; DLB 98, 153, 174;
RGEL 2; SATA 35

Hueffer, Ford Madox
See Ford, Ford Madox

Hughart, Barry 1934- .... **CLC 39**
See also CA 137; FANT; SFW 4; SUFW 2

Hughes, Colin
See Creasey, John

Hughes, David (John) 1930-2005 ..... **CLC 48**
See also CA 116; 129; 238; CN 4, 5, 6, 7;
DLB 14

Hughes, Edward James
See Hughes, Ted
See also DA3; DAM MST, POET

Hughes, (James Mercer) Langston
1902-1967 ..... **BLC 2; CLC 1, 5, 10, 15,**
35, 44, 108; DC 3; HR 1:2; PC 1, 53;
SSC 6; WLC
See also AAYA 12; AFAW 1, 2; AMWR 1;
AMWS 1; BW 1, 3; CA 1-4R; 25-28R;
CANR 1, 34, 82; CDALB 1929-1941;
CLR 17; DA; DA3; DAB; DAC; DAM
DRAM, MST, MULT, POET; DFS 6, 18;
DLB 4, 7, 48, 51, 86, 228, 315; EWL 3;
EXPP; EXPS; JRDA; LAIT 3; LMFS 2;
MAICYA 1, 2; MAL 5; MTCW 1, 2;
MTFW 2005; NFS 21; PAB; PFS 1, 3, 6,
10, 15; RGAL 4; RGSF 2; SATA 4, 33;
SSFS 4, 7; TUS; WCH; WP; YAW

Hughes, Richard (Arthur Warren)
1900-1976 .... **CLC 1, 11**
See also CA 5-8R; 65-68; CANR 4; CN 1,
2; DAM NOV; DLB 15, 161; EWL 3;
MTCW 1; RGEL 2; SATA 8; SATA-Obit
25

Hughes, Ted 1930 1998 . **CLC 2, 4, 9, 14, 37,**
119; PC 7
See Hughes, Edward James
See also BRWC 2; BRWR 2; BRWS 1; CA
1-4R; 171; CANR 1, 33, 66, 108; CLR 3;
CP 1, 2, 3, 4, 5, 6; DAB; DAC; DLB 40,
161; EWL 3; EXPP; MAICYA 1, 2;
MTCW 1, 2; MTFW 2005; PAB; PFS 4,
19; RGEL 2; SATA 49; SATA Brief 27;
SATA-Obit 107; TEA; YAW

Hugo, Richard
See Huch, Ricarda (Octavia)
See also MAL 5

Hugo, Richard F(ranklin)
1923-1982 .... **CLC 6, 18, 32; PC 68**
See also AMWS 6; CA 49-52; 108; CANR
3; CP 1, 2, 3; DAM POET; DLB 5, 206;
EWL 3; PFS 17; RGAL 4

Hugo, Victor (Marie) 1802-1885 .... **NCLC 3,**
10, 21, 161; PC 17; WLC
See also AAYA 28; DA; DA3; DAB; DAC;
DAM DRAM, MST, NOV, POET; DLB
119, 192, 217; EFS 2; EW 6; EXPN; GFL

1789 to the Present; LAIT 1, 2; NFS 5,
20; RGWL 2, 3; SATA 47; TWA

Huidobro, Vicente
See Huidobro Fernandez, Vicente Garcia
See also DLB 283; EWL 3; LAW

Huidobro Fernandez, Vicente Garcia
1893-1948 .... **TCLC 31**
See Huidobro, Vicente
See also CA 131; HW 1

Hulme, Keri 1947- .... **CLC 39, 130**
See also CA 125; CANR 69; CN 4, 5, 6, 7;
CP 7; CWP; EWL 3; FW; INT CA-125

Hulme, T(homas) E(rnest)
1883-1917 .... **TCLC 21**
See also BRWS 6; CA 117; 203; DLB 19

Humboldt, Wilhelm von
1767-1835 .... **NCLC 134**
See also DLB 90

Hume, David 1711-1776 .... **LC 7, 56**
See also BRWS 3; DLB 104, 252; LMFS 1;
TEA

Humphrey, William 1924-1997 .... **CLC 45**
See also AMWS 9; CA 77-80; 160; CANR
68; CN 1, 2, 3, 4, 5, 6; CSW; DLB 6, 212,
234, 278; TCWW 1, 2

Humphreys, Emyr Owen 1919- .... **CLC 47**
See also CA 5-8R; CANR 3, 24; CN 1, 2,
3, 4, 5, 6, 7; DLB 15

Humphreys, Josephine 1945- ..... **CLC 34, 57**
See also CA 121; 127; CANR 97; CSW;
DLB 292; INT CA-127

Huneker, James Gibbons
1860-1921 .... **TCLC 65**
See also CA 193; DLB 71; RGAL 4

Hungerford, Hesba Fay
See Brinsmead, H(esba) F(ay)

Hungerford, Pixie
See Brinsmead, H(esba) F(ay)

Hunt, E(verette) Howard, (Jr.)
1918- .... **CLC 3**
See also AITN 1; CA 45-48; CANR 2, 47,
103; CMW 4

Hunt, Francesca
See Holland, Isabelle (Christian)

Hunt, Howard
See Hunt, E(verette) Howard, (Jr.)

Hunt, Kyle
See Creasey, John

Hunt, (James Henry) Leigh
1784-1859 .... **NCLC 1, 70**
See also DAM POET; DLB 96, 110, 144;
RGEL 2; TEA

Hunt, Marsha 1946- .... **CLC 70**
See also BW 2, 3; CA 143; CANR 79

Hunt, Violet 1866(?)-1942 .... **TCLC 53**
See also CA 184; DLB 162, 197

Hunter, E. Waldo
See Sturgeon, Theodore (Hamilton)

Hunter, Evan 1926-2005 .... **CLC 11, 31**
See McBain, Ed
See also AAYA 39; BPFB 2; CA 5-8R; 241;
CANR 5, 38, 62, 97; CMW 4; CN 1, 2, 3,
4, 5, 6, 7; CPW; DAM POP; DLB 306;
DLBY 1982; INT CANR-5; MSW;
MTCW 1; SATA 25; SFW 4

Hunter, Kristin
See Lattany, Kristin (Elaine Eggleston)
Hunter
See also CN 1, 2, 3, 4, 5, 6

Hunter, Mary
See Austin, Mary (Hunter)

Hunter, Mollie 1922- .... **CLC 21**
See McIlwraith, Maureen Mollie Hunter
See also AAYA 13; BYA 6; CANR 37, 78;
CLR 25; DLB 161; JRDA; MAICYA 1,
2; SAAS 7; SATA 54, 106, 139; SATA-
Essay 139; WYA; YAW

Ives, Morgan
See Bradley, Marion Zimmer
See also GLL 1
Izumi Shikibu c. 973-c. 1034 .... **CMLC 33**
J. R. S.
See Gogarty, Oliver St. John
Jabran, Kahlil
See Gibran, Kahlil
Jabran, Khalil
See Gibran, Kahlil
Jackson, Daniel
See Wingrove, David (John)
Jackson, Helen Hunt 1830-1885 .... **NCLC 90**
See also DLB 42, 47, 186, 189; RGAL 4
Jackson, Jesse 1908-1983 .... **CLC 12**
See also BW 1; CA 25-28R; 109; CANR
27; CLR 28; CWRI 5; MAICYA 1, 2;
SATA 2, 29; SATA-Obit 48
Jackson, Laura (Riding) 1901-1991 .... **PC 44**
See Riding, Laura
See also CA 65-68; 135; CANR 28, 89;
DLB 48
Jackson, Sam
See Trumbo, Dalton
Jackson, Sara
See Wingrove, David (John)
Jackson, Shirley 1919-1965 . **CLC 11, 60, 87;**
SSC 9, 39; WLC
See also AAYA 9; AMWS 9; BPFB 2; CA
1-4R; 25-28R; CANR 4, 52; CDALB
1941-1968; DA; DA3; DAC; DAM MST;
DLB 6, 234; EXPS; HGG; LAIT 4; MAL
5; MTCW 2; MTFW 2005; RGAL 4;
RGSF 2; SATA 2; SSFS 1; SUFW 1, 2
Jacob, (Cyprien-)Max 1876-1944 .... **TCLC 6**
See also CA 104; 193; DLB 258; EWL 3;
GFL 1789 to the Present; GLL 2; RGWL
2, 3
Jacobs, Harriet A(nn)
1813(?)-1897 .... **NCLC 67, 162**
See also AFAW 1, 2; DLB 239; FL 1:3; FW;
LAIT 2; RGAL 4
Jacobs, Jim 1942- .... **CLC 12**
See also CA 97-100; INT CA-97-100
Jacobs, W(illiam) W(ymark)
1863-1943 .... **SSC 73; TCLC 22**
See also CA 121; 167; DLB 135; EXPS;
HGG; RGEL 2; RGSF 2; SSFS 2; SUFW
1
Jacobsen, Jens Peter 1847-1885 .... **NCLC 34**
Jacobsen, Josephine (Winder)
1908-2003 .... **CLC 48, 102; PC 62**
See also CA 33-36R; 218; CAAS 18; CANR
23, 48; CCA 1; CP 2, 3, 4, 5, 6, 7; DLB
244; PFS 23; TCLE 1:1
Jacobson, Dan 1929- .... **CLC 4, 14**
See also AFW; CA 1-4R; CANR 2, 25, 66;
CN 1, 2, 3, 4, 5, 6, 7; DLB 14, 207, 225,
319; EWL 3; MTCW 1; RGSF 2
Jacqueline
See Carpentier (y Valmont), Alejo
Jacques de Vitry c. 1160-1240 ...... **CMLC 63**
See also DLB 208
Jagger, Michael Philip
See Jagger, Mick
Jagger, Mick 1943- .... **CLC 17**
See also CA 239
Jahiz, al- c. 780-c. 869 .... **CMLC 25**
See also DLB 311
Jakes, John (William) 1932- .... **CLC 29**
See also AAYA 32; BEST 89:4; BPFB 2;
CA 57-60, 214; CAAE 214; CANR 10,
43, 66, 111, 142; CPW; CSW; DA3; DAM
NOV, POP; DLB 278; DLBY 1983;
FANT; INT CANR-10; MTCW 1, 2;
MTFW 2005; RHW; SATA 62; SFW 4;
TCWW 1, 2
James I 1394-1437 .... **LC 20**
See also RGEL 2

James, Andrew
See Kirkup, James
James, C(yril) L(ionel) R(obert)
1901-1989 .... **BLCS; CLC 33**
See also BW 2; CA 117; 125; 128; CANR
62; CN 1, 2, 3, 4; DLB 125; MTCW 1
James, Daniel (Lewis) 1911-1988
See Santiago, Danny
See also CA 174; 125
James, Dynely
See Mayne, William (James Carter)
James, Henry Sr. 1811-1882 .... **NCLC 53**
James, Henry 1843-1916 .... **SSC 8, 32, 47;**
TCLC 2, 11, 24, 40, 47, 64, 171; WLC
See also AMW; AMWC 1; AMWR 1; BPFB
2; BRW 6; CA 104; 132; CDALB 1865-
1917; DA; DA3; DAB; DAC; DAM MST,
NOV; DLB 12, 71, 74, 189; DLBD 13;
EWL 3; EXPS; GL 2; HGG; LAIT 2;
MAL 5; MTCW 1, 2; MTFW 2005; NFS
12, 16, 19; RGAL 4; RGEL 2; RGSF 2;
SSFS 9; SUFW 1; TUS
James, M. R.
See James, Montague (Rhodes)
See also DLB 156, 201
James, Montague (Rhodes)
1862-1936 .... **SSC 16; TCLC 6**
See James, M. R.
See also CA 104; 203; HGG; RGEL 2;
RGSF 2; SUFW 1
James, P. D. .... **CLC 18, 46, 122**
See White, Phyllis Dorothy James
See also BEST 90:2; BPFB 2; BRWS 4;
CDBLB 1960 to Present; CN 4, 5, 6; DLB
87, 276; DLBD 17; MSW
James, Philip
See Moorcock, Michael (John)
James, Samuel
See Stephens, James
James, Seumas
See Stephens, James
James, Stephen
See Stephens, James
James, William 1842-1910 .... **TCLC 15, 32**
See also AMW; CA 109; 193; DLB 270,
284; MAL 5; NCFS 5; RGAL 4
Jameson, Anna 1794-1860 .... **NCLC 43**
See also DLB 99, 166
Jameson, Fredric (R.) 1934- .... **CLC 142**
See also CA 196; DLB 67; LMFS 2
James VI of Scotland 1566-1625 .... **LC 109**
See also DLB 151, 172
Jami, Nur al-Din 'Abd al-Rahman
1414-1492 .... **LC 9**
Jammes, Francis 1868-1938 .... **TCLC 75**
See also CA 198; EWL 3; GFL 1789 to the
Present
Jandl, Ernst 1925-2000 .... **CLC 34**
See also CA 200; EWL 3
Janowitz, Tama 1957- .... **CLC 43, 145**
See also CA 106; CANR 52, 89, 129; CN
5, 6, 7; CPW; DAM POP; DLB 292;
MTFW 2005
Japrisot, Sebastien 1931- .... **CLC 90**
See Rossi, Jean-Baptiste
See also CMW 4; NFS 18
Jarrell, Randall 1914-1965 .... **CLC 1, 2, 6, 9,**
13, 49; PC 41
See also AMW; BYA 5; CA 5-8R; 25-28R;
CABS 2; CANR 6, 34; CDALB 1941-
1968; CLR 6; CWRI 5; DAM POET;
DLB 48, 52; EWL 3; EXPP; MAICYA 1,
2; MAL 5; MTCW 1, 2; PAB; PFS 2;
RGAL 4; SATA 7

Jarry, Alfred 1873-1907 .... **SSC 20; TCLC 2,**
14, 147
See also CA 104; 153; DA3; DAM DRAM;
DFS 8; DLB 192, 258; EW 9; EWL 3;
GFL 1789 to the Present; RGWL 2, 3;
TWA
Jarvis, E. K.
See Ellison, Harlan (Jay)
Jawien, Andrzej
See John Paul II, Pope
Jaynes, Roderick
See Coen, Ethan
Jeake, Samuel, Jr.
See Aiken, Conrad (Potter)
Jean Paul 1763-1825 .... **NCLC 7**
Jefferies, (John) Richard
1848-1887 .... **NCLC 47**
See also DLB 98, 141; RGEL 2; SATA 16;
SFW 4
Jeffers, (John) Robinson 1887-1962 .. **CLC 2,**
3, 11, 15, 54; PC 17; WLC
See also AMWS 2; CA 85-88; CANR 35;
CDALB 1917-1929; DA; DAC; DAM
MST, POET; DLB 45, 212; EWL 3; MAL
5; MTCW 1, 2; MTFW 2005; PAB; PFS
3, 4; RGAL 4
Jefferson, Janet
See Mencken, H(enry) L(ouis)
Jefferson, Thomas 1743-1826 . **NCLC 11, 103**
See also AAYA 54; ANW; CDALB 1640-
1865; DA3; DLB 31, 183; LAIT 1; RGAL
4
Jeffrey, Francis 1773-1850 .... **NCLC 33**
See Francis, Lord Jeffrey
Jelakowitch, Ivan
See Heijermans, Herman
Jelinek, Elfriede 1946- .... **CLC 169**
See also AAYA 68; CA 154; DLB 85; FW
Jellicoe, (Patricia) Ann 1927- .... **CLC 27**
See also CA 85-88; CBD; CD 5, 6; CWD;
CWRI 5; DLB 13, 233; FW
Jelloun, Tahar ben 1944- .... **CLC 180**
See Ben Jelloun, Tahar
See also CA 162; CANR 100
Jemyma
See Holley, Marietta
Jen, Gish .... **AAL; CLC 70, 198**
See Jen, Lillian
See also AMWC 2; CN 7; DLB 312
Jen, Lillian 1955-
See Jen, Gish
See also CA 135; CANR 89, 130
Jenkins, (John) Robin 1912- .... **CLC 52**
See also CA 1-4R; CANR 1, 135; CN 1, 2,
3, 4, 5, 6, 7; DLB 14, 271
Jennings, Elizabeth (Joan)
1926-2001 .... **CLC 5, 14, 131**
See also BRWS 5; CA 61-64; 200; CAAS
5; CANR 8, 39, 66, 127; CP 1, 2, 3, 4, 5,
6, 7; CWP; DLB 27; EWL 3; MTCW 1;
SATA 66
Jennings, Waylon 1937-2002 .... **CLC 21**
Jensen, Johannes V(ilhelm)
1873-1950 .... **TCLC 41**
See also CA 170; DLB 214; EWL 3; RGWL
3
Jensen, Laura (Linnea) 1948- .... **CLC 37**
See also CA 103
Jerome, Saint 345-420 .... **CMLC 30**
See also RGWL 3
Jerome, Jerome K(lapka)
1859-1927 .... **TCLC 23**
See also CA 119; 177; DLB 10, 34, 135;
RGEL 2
Jerrold, Douglas William
1803-1857 .... **NCLC 2**
See also DLB 158, 159; RGEL 2

Jordan, June (Meyer)
1936-2002 .. **BLCS; CLC 5, 11, 23, 114; PC 38**
See also AAYA 2, 66; AFAW 1, 2; BW 2, 3; CA 33-36R; 206; CANR 25, 70, 114; CLR 10; CP 3, 4, 5, 6, 7; CWP; DAM MULT, POET; DLB 38; GLL 2; LAIT 5; MAICYA 1, 2; MTCW 1; SATA 4, 136; YAW

Jordan, Neil (Patrick) 1950- .... **CLC 110**
See also CA 124; 130; CANR 54; CN 4, 5, 6, 7; GLL 2; INT CA-130

Jordan, Pat(rick M.) 1941- .... **CLC 37**
See also CA 33-36R; CANR 121

Jorgensen, Ivar
See Ellison, Harlan (Jay)

Jorgenson, Ivar
See Silverberg, Robert

Joseph, George Ghevarughese .... **CLC 70**

Josephson, Mary
See O'Doherty, Brian

Josephus, Flavius c. 37-100 .... **CMLC 13**
See also AW 2; DLB 176

Josiah Allen's Wife
See Holley, Marietta

Josipovici, Gabriel (David) 1940- ...... **CLC 6, 43, 153**
See also CA 37-40R, 224; CAAE 224; CAAS 8; CANR 47, 84; CN 3, 4, 5, 6, 7; DLB 14, 319

Joubert, Joseph 1754-1824 .... **NCLC 9**

Jouve, Pierre Jean 1887-1976 .... **CLC 47**
See also CA 65-68; DLB 258; EWL 3

Jovine, Francesco 1902-1950 .... **TCLC 79**
See also DLB 264; EWL 3

Joyce, James (Augustine Aloysius)
1882-1941 .... **DC 16; PC 22; SSC 3, 26, 44, 64; TCLC 3, 8, 16, 35, 52, 159; WLC**
See also AAYA 42; BRW 7; BRWC 1; BRWR 1; BYA 11, 13; CA 104; 126; CD-BLB 1914-1945; DA; DA3; DAB; DAC; DAM MST, NOV, POET; DLB 10, 19, 36, 162, 247; EWL 3; EXPN; EXPS; LAIT 3; LMFS 1, 2; MTCW 1, 2; MTFW 2005; NFS 7; RGSF 2; SSFS 1, 19; TEA; WLIT 4

Jozsef, Attila 1905-1937 .... **TCLC 22**
See also CA 116; 230; CDWLB 4; DLB 215; EWL 3

Juana Ines de la Cruz, Sor
1651(?)-1695 ...... **HLCS 1; LC 5; PC 24**
See also DLB 305; FW; LAW; RGWL 2, 3; WLIT 1

Juana Inez de La Cruz, Sor
See Juana Ines de la Cruz, Sor

Judd, Cyril
See Kornbluth, C(yril) M.; Pohl, Frederik

Juenger, Ernst 1895-1998 .... **CLC 125**
See Junger, Ernst
See also CA 101; 167; CANR 21, 47, 106; DLB 56

Julian of Norwich 1342(?)-1416(?) . **LC 6, 52**
See also DLB 146; LMFS 1

Julius Caesar 100B.C.-44B.C.
See Caesar, Julius
See also CDWLB 1; DLB 211

Junger, Ernst
See Juenger, Ernst
See also CDWLB 2; EWL 3; RGWL 2, 3

Junger, Sebastian 1962- .... **CLC 109**
See also AAYA 28; CA 165; CANR 130; MTFW 2005

Juniper, Alex
See Hospital, Janette Turner

Junius
See Luxemburg, Rosa

Junzaburo, Nishiwaki
See Nishiwaki, Junzaburo
See also EWL 3

Just, Ward (Swift) 1935- .... **CLC 4, 27**
See also CA 25-28R; CANR 32, 87; CN 6, 7; INT CANR-32

Justice, Donald (Rodney)
1925-2004 .... **CLC 6, 19, 102; PC 64**
See also AMWS 7; CA 5-8R; 230; CANR 26, 54, 74, 121, 122; CP 1, 2, 3, 4, 5, 6, 7; CSW; DAM POET; DLBY 1983; EWL 3; INT CANR-26; MAL 5; MTCW 2; PFS 14; TCLE 1:1

Juvenal c. 60-c. 130 .... **CMLC 8**
See also AW 2; CDWLB 1; DLB 211; RGWL 2, 3

Juvenis
See Bourne, Randolph S(illiman)

K., Alice
See Knapp, Caroline

Kabakov, Sasha .... **CLC 59**

Kabir 1398(?)-1448(?) .... **LC 109; PC 56**
See also RGWL 2, 3

Kacew, Romain 1914-1980
See Gary, Romain
See also CA 108; 102

Kadare, Ismail 1936- .... **CLC 52, 190**
See also CA 161; EWL 3; RGWL 3

Kadohata, Cynthia (Lynn)
1956(?)- .... **CLC 59, 122**
See also CA 140; CANR 124; SATA 155

Kafka, Franz 1883-1924 ... **SSC 5, 29, 35, 60; TCLC 2, 6, 13, 29, 47, 53, 112; WLC**
See also AAYA 31; BPFB 2; CA 105; 126; CDWLB 2; DA; DA3; DAB; DAC; DAM MST, NOV; DLB 81; EW 9; EWL 3; EXPS; LATS 1:1; LMFS 2; MTCW 1, 2; MTFW 2005; NFS 7; RGSF 2; RGWL 2, 3; SFW 4; SSFS 3, 7, 12; TWA

Kahanovitsch, Pinkhes
See Der Nister

Kahn, Roger 1927- .... **CLC 30**
See also CA 25-28R; CANR 44, 69; DLB 171; SATA 37

Kain, Saul
See Sassoon, Siegfried (Lorraine)

Kaiser, Georg 1878-1945 .... **TCLC 9**
See also CA 106; 190; CDWLB 2; DLB 124; EWL 3; LMFS 2; RGWL 2, 3

Kaledin, Sergei .... **CLC 59**

Kaletski, Alexander 1946- .... **CLC 39**
See also CA 118; 143

Kalidasa fl. c. 400-455 .... **CMLC 9; PC 22**
See also RGWL 2, 3

Kallman, Chester (Simon)
1921-1975 .... **CLC 2**
See also CA 45-48; 53-56; CANR 3; CP 1, 2

Kaminsky, Melvin 1926-
See Brooks, Mel
See also CA 65-68; CANR 16; DFS 21

Kaminsky, Stuart M(elvin) 1934- ..... **CLC 59**
See also CA 73-76; CANR 29, 53, 89; CMW 4

Kamo no Chomei 1153(?)-1216 .... **CMLC 66**
See also DLB 203

Kamo no Nagaakira
See Kamo no Chomei

Kandinsky, Wassily 1866-1944 .... **TCLC 92**
See also AAYA 64; CA 118; 155

Kane, Francis
See Robbins, Harold

Kane, Henry 1918-
See Queen, Ellery
See also CA 156; CMW 4

Kane, Paul
See Simon, Paul (Frederick)

Kanin, Garson 1912-1999 .... **CLC 22**
See also AITN 1; CA 5-8R; 177; CAD; CANR 7, 78; DLB 7; IDFW 3, 4

Kaniuk, Yoram 1930- .... **CLC 19**
See also CA 134; DLB 299

Kant, Immanuel 1724-1804 ..... **NCLC 27, 67**
See also DLB 94

Kantor, MacKinlay 1904-1977 .... **CLC 7**
See also CA 61-64; 73-76; CANR 60, 63; CN 1, 2; DLB 9, 102; MAL 5; MTCW 2; RHW; TCWW 1, 2

Kanze Motokiyo
See Zeami

Kaplan, David Michael 1946- .... **CLC 50**
See also CA 187

Kaplan, James 1951- .... **CLC 59**
See also CA 135; CANR 121

Karadzic, Vuk Stefanovic
1787-1864 .... **NCLC 115**
See also CDWLB 4; DLB 147

Karageorge, Michael
See Anderson, Poul (William)

Karamzin, Nikolai Mikhailovich
1766-1826 .... **NCLC 3**
See also DLB 150; RGSF 2

Karapanou, Margarita 1946- .... **CLC 13**
See also CA 101

Karinthy, Frigyes 1887-1938 .... **TCLC 47**
See also CA 170; DLB 215; EWL 3

Karl, Frederick R(obert)
1927-2004 .... **CLC 34**
See also CA 5-8R; 226; CANR 3, 44, 143

Karr, Mary 1955- .... **CLC 188**
See also AMWS 11; CA 151; CANR 100; MTFW 2005; NCFS 5

Kastel, Warren
See Silverberg, Robert

Kataev, Evgeny Petrovich 1903-1942
See Petrov, Evgeny
See also CA 120

Kataphusin
See Ruskin, John

Katz, Steve 1935- .... **CLC 47**
See also CA 25-28R; CAAS 14, 64; CANR 12; CN 4, 5, 6, 7; DLBY 1983

Kauffman, Janet 1945- .... **CLC 42**
See also CA 117; CANR 43, 84; DLB 218; DLBY 1986

Kaufman, Bob (Garnell) 1925-1986 . **CLC 49**
See also BG 1:3; BW 1; CA 41-44R; 118; CANR 22; CP 1; DLB 16, 41

Kaufman, George S. 1889-1961 ...... **CLC 38; DC 17**
See also CA 108; 93-96; DAM DRAM; DFS 1, 10; DLB 7; INT CA-108; MTCW 2; MTFW 2005; RGAL 4; TUS

Kaufman, Moises 1964- .... **DC 26**
See also CA 211; DFS 22; MTFW 2005

Kaufman, Sue .... **CLC 3, 8**
See Barondess, Sue K(aufman)

Kavafis, Konstantinos Petrou 1863-1933
See Cavafy, C(onstantine) P(eter)
See also CA 104

Kavan, Anna 1901-1968 .... **CLC 5, 13, 82**
See also BRWS 7; CA 5-8R; CANR 6, 57; DLB 255; MTCW 1; RGEL 2; SFW 4

Kavanagh, Dan
See Barnes, Julian (Patrick)

Kavanagh, Julie 1952- .... **CLC 119**
See also CA 163

Kavanagh, Patrick (Joseph)
1904-1967 .... **CLC 22; PC 33**
See also BRWS 7; CA 123; 25-28R; DLB 15, 20; EWL 3; MTCW 1; RGEL 2

Keynes, John Maynard
1883-1946 .... **TCLC 64**
See also CA 114; 162, 163; DLBD 10;
MTCW 2; MTFW 2005

Khanshendel, Chiron
See Rose, Wendy

Khayyam, Omar 1048-1131 ... **CMLC 11; PC 8**
See Omar Khayyam
See also DA3; DAM POET; WLIT 6

Kherdian, David 1931- .... **CLC 6, 9**
See also AAYA 42; CA 21-24R, 192; CAAE
192; CAAS 2; CANR 39, 78; CLR 24;
JRDA; LAIT 3; MAICYA 1, 2; SATA 16,
74; SATA-Essay 125

Khlebnikov, Velimir .... **TCLC 20**
See Khlebnikov, Viktor Vladimirovich
See also DLB 295; EW 10; EWL 3; RGWL
2, 3

Khlebnikov, Viktor Vladimirovich 1885-1922
See Khlebnikov, Velimir
See also CA 117; 217

Khodasevich, Vladislav (Felitsianovich)
1886-1939 .... **TCLC 15**
See also CA 115; DLB 317; EWL 3

Kielland, Alexander Lange
1849-1906 .... **TCLC 5**
See also CA 104

Kiely, Benedict 1919- ... **CLC 23, 43; SSC 58**
See also CA 1-4R; CANR 2, 84; CN 1, 2,
3, 4, 5, 6, 7; DLB 15, 319; TCLE 1:1

Kienzle, William X(avier)
1928-2001 .... **CLC 25**
See also CA 93-96; 203; CAAS 1; CANR
9, 31, 59, 111; CMW 4; DA3; DAM POP;
INT CANR-31; MSW; MTCW 1, 2;
MTFW 2005

Kierkegaard, Soren 1813-1855 ..... **NCLC 34, 78, 125**
See also DLB 300; EW 6; LMFS 2; RGWL
3; TWA

Kieslowski, Krzysztof 1941-1996 .... **CLC 120**
See also CA 147; 151

Killens, John Oliver 1916-1987 .... **CLC 10**
See also BW 2; CA 77-80; 123; CAAS 2;
CANR 26; CN 1, 2, 3, 4; DLB 33; EWL
3

Killigrew, Anne 1660-1685 .... **LC 4, 73**
See also DLB 131

Killigrew, Thomas 1612-1683 .... **LC 57**
See also DLB 58; RGEL 2

Kim
See Simenon, Georges (Jacques Christian)

Kincaid, Jamaica 1949- ...... **BLC 2; CLC 43, 68, 137; SSC 72**
See also AAYA 13, 56; AFAW 2; AMWS 7;
BRWS 7; BW 2, 3; CA 125; CANR 47,
59, 95, 133; CDALBS; CDWLB 3; CLR
63; CN 4, 5, 6, 7; DA3; DAM MULT,
NOV; DLB 157, 227; DNFS 1; EWL 3;
EXPS; FW; LATS 1:2; LMFS 2; MAL 5;
MTCW 2; MTFW 2005; NCFS 1; NFS 3;
SSFS 5, 7; TUS; WWE 1; YAW

King, Francis (Henry) 1923- .... **CLC 8, 53, 145**
See also CA 1-4R; CANR 1, 33, 86; CN 1,
2, 3, 4, 5, 6, 7; DAM NOV; DLB 15, 139;
MTCW 1

King, Kennedy
See Brown, George Douglas

King, Martin Luther, Jr. 1929-1968 . **BLC 2; CLC 83; WLCS**
See also BW 2, 3; CA 25-28; CANR 27,
44; CAP 2; DA; DA3; DAB; DAC; DAM
MST, MULT; LAIT 5; LATS 1:2; MTCW
1, 2; MTFW 2005; SATA 14

King, Stephen 1947- .... **CLC 12, 26, 37, 61, 113; SSC 17, 55**
See also AAYA 1, 17; AMWS 5; BEST
90:1; BPFB 2; CA 61-64; CANR 1, 30,
52, 76, 119, 134; CN 7; CPW; DA3; DAM
NOV, POP; DLB 143; DLBY 1980; HGG;
JRDA; LAIT 5; MTCW 1, 2; MTFW
2005; RGAL 4; SATA 9, 55, 161; SUFW
1, 2; WYAS 1; YAW

King, Stephen Edwin
See King, Stephen

King, Steve
See King, Stephen

King, Thomas 1943- .... **CLC 89, 171; NNAL**
See also CA 144; CANR 95; CCA 1; CN 6,
7; DAC; DAM MULT; DLB 175; SATA
96

Kingman, Lee .... **CLC 17**
See Natti, (Mary) Lee
See also CWRI 5; SAAS 3; SATA 1, 67

Kingsley, Charles 1819-1875 .... **NCLC 35**
See also CLR 77; DLB 21, 32, 163, 178,
190; FANT; MAICYA 2; MAICYAS 1;
RGEL 2; WCH; YABC 2

Kingsley, Henry 1830-1876 .... **NCLC 107**
See also DLB 21, 230; RGEL 2

Kingsley, Sidney 1906-1995 .... **CLC 44**
See also CA 85-88; 147; CAD; DFS 14, 19;
DLB 7; MAL 5; RGAL 4

Kingsolver, Barbara 1955- .... **CLC 55, 81, 130, 216**
See also AAYA 15; AMWS 7; CA 129; 134;
CANR 60, 96, 133; CDALBS; CN 7;
CPW; CSW; DA3; DAM POP; DLB 206;
INT CA-134; LAIT 5; MTCW 2; MTFW
2005; NFS 5, 10, 12; RGAL 4; TCLE 1:1

Kingston, Maxine (Ting Ting) Hong
1940- .... **AAL; CLC 12, 19, 58, 121; WLCS**
See also AAYA 8, 55; AMWS 5; BPFB 2;
CA 69-72; CANR 13, 38, 74, 87, 128;
CDALBS; CN 6, 7; DA3; DAM MULT,
NOV; DLB 173, 212, 312; DLBY 1980;
EWL 3; FL 1:6; FW; INT CANR-13;
LAIT 5; MAL 5; MAWW; MTCW 1, 2;
MTFW 2005; NFS 6; RGAL 4; SATA 53;
SSFS 3; TCWW 2

Kinnell, Galway 1927- ..... **CLC 1, 2, 3, 5, 13, 29, 129; PC 26**
See also AMWS 3; CA 9-12R; CANR 10,
34, 66, 116, 138; CP 1, 2, 3, 4, 5, 6, 7;
DLB 5; DLBY 1987; EWL 3; INT CANR-
34; MAL 5; MTCW 1, 2; MTFW 2005;
PAB; PFS 9; RGAL 4; TCLE 1:1; WP

Kinsella, Thomas 1928- .... **CLC 4, 19, 138; PC 69**
See also BRWS 5; CA 17-20R; CANR 15,
122; CP 1, 2, 3, 4, 5, 6, 7; DLB 27; EWL
3; MTCW 1, 2; MTFW 2005; RGEL 2;
TEA

Kinsella, W(illiam) P(atrick) 1935- . **CLC 27, 43, 166**
See also AAYA 7, 60; BPFB 2; CA 97-100,
222; CAAE 222; CAAS 7; CANR 21, 35,
66, 75, 129; CN 4, 5, 6, 7; CPW; DAC;
DAM NOV, POP; FANT; INT CANR-21;
LAIT 5; MTCW 1, 2; MTFW 2005; NFS
15; RGSF 2

Kinsey, Alfred C(harles)
1894-1956 .... **TCLC 91**
See also CA 115, 170, MTCW 2

Kipling, (Joseph) Rudyard 1865-1936 . **PC 3; SSC 5, 54; TCLC 8, 17, 167; WLC**
See also AAYA 32; BRW 6; BRWC 1, 2;
BYA 4; CA 105; 120; CANR 33; CDBLB
1890-1914; CLR 39, 65; CWRI 5; DA;
DA3; DAB; DAC; DAM MST, POET;
DLB 19, 34, 141, 156; EWL 3; EXPS;
FANT; LAIT 3; LMFS 1; MAICYA 1, 2;

MTCW 1, 2; MTFW 2005; NFS 21; PFS
22; RGEL 2; RGSF 2; SATA 100; SFW
4; SSFS 8, 21; SUFW 1; TEA; WCH;
WLIT 4; YABC 2

Kircher, Athanasius 1602-1680 .... **LC 121**
See also DLB 164

Kirk, Russell (Amos) 1918-1994 .. **TCLC 119**
See also AITN 1; CA 1-4R; 145; CAAS 9;
CANR 1, 20, 60; HGG; INT CANR-20;
MTCW 1, 2

Kirkham, Dinah
See Card, Orson Scott

Kirkland, Caroline M. 1801-1864 . **NCLC 85**
See also DLB 3, 73, 74, 250, 254; DLBD
13

Kirkup, James 1918- .... **CLC 1**
See also CA 1-4R; CAAS 4; CANR 2; CP
1, 2, 3, 4, 5, 6, 7; DLB 27; SATA 12

Kirkwood, James 1930(?)-1989 .... **CLC 9**
See also AITN 2; CA 1-4R; 128; CANR 6,
40; GLL 2

Kirsch, Sarah 1935- .... **CLC 176**
See also CA 178; CWW 2; DLB 75; EWL
3

Kirshner, Sidney
See Kingsley, Sidney

Kis, Danilo 1935-1989 .... **CLC 57**
See also CA 109; 118; 129; CANR 61; CD-
WLB 4; DLB 181; EWL 3; MTCW 1;
RGSF 2; RGWL 2, 3

Kissinger, Henry A(lfred) 1923- ..... **CLC 137**
See also CA 1-4R; CANR 2, 33, 66, 109;
MTCW 1

Kivi, Aleksis 1834-1872 .... **NCLC 30**

Kizer, Carolyn (Ashley) 1925- ... **CLC 15, 39, 80; PC 66**
See also CA 65-68; CAAS 5; CANR 24,
70, 134; CP 1, 2, 3, 4, 5, 6, 7; CWP; DAM
POET; DLB 5, 169; EWL 3; MAL 5;
MTCW 2; MTFW 2005; PFS 18; TCLE
1:1

Klabund 1890-1928 .... **TCLC 44**
See also CA 162; DLB 66

Klappert, Peter 1942- .... **CLC 57**
See also CA 33-36R; CSW; DLB 5

Klein, A(braham) M(oses)
1909-1972 .... **CLC 19**
See also CA 101; 37-40R; CP 1; DAB;
DAC; DAM MST; DLB 68; EWL 3;
RGEL 2

Klein, Joe
See Klein, Joseph

Klein, Joseph 1946- .... **CLC 154**
See also CA 85-88; CANR 55

Klein, Norma 1938-1989 .... **CLC 30**
See also AAYA 2, 35; BPFB 2; BYA 6, 7,
8; CA 41-44R; 128; CANR 15, 37; CLR
2, 19; INT CANR-15; JRDA; MAICYA
1, 2; SAAS 1; SATA 7, 57; WYA; YAW

Klein, T(heodore) E(ibon) D(onald)
1947- .... **CLC 34**
See also CA 119; CANR 44, 75; HGG

Kleist, Heinrich von 1777-1811 ...... **NCLC 2, 37; SSC 22**
See also CDWLB 2; DAM DRAM; DLB
90; EW 5; RGSF 2; RGWL 2, 3

Klima, Ivan 1931- .... **CLC 56, 172**
See also CA 25-28R; CANR 17, 50, 91;
CDWLB 4; CWW 2; DAM NOV; DLB
232; EWL 3; RGWL 3

Klimentev, Andrei Platonovich
See Klimentov, Andrei Platonovich

Klimentov, Andrei Platonovich
1899-1951 .... **SSC 42; TCLC 14**
See Platonov, Andrei Platonovich; Platonov,
Andrey Platonovich
See also CA 108; 232

Kubrick, Stanley 1928-1999 .... **CLC 16; TCLC 112**
See also AAYA 30; CA 81-84; 177; CANR 33; DLB 26

Kumin, Maxine (Winokur) 1925- ..... **CLC 5, 13, 28, 164; PC 15**
See also AITN 2; AMWS 4; ANW; CA 1-4R; CAAS 8; CANR 1, 21, 69, 115, 140; CP 2, 3, 4, 5, 6, 7; CWP; DA3; DAM POET; DLB 5; EWL 3; EXPP; MTCW 1, 2; MTFW 2005; PAB; PFS 18; SATA 12

Kundera, Milan 1929- . **CLC 4, 9, 19, 32, 68, 115, 135; SSC 24**
See also AAYA 2, 62; BPFB 2; CA 85-88; CANR 19, 52, 74, 144; CDWLB 4; CWW 2; DA3; DAM NOV; DLB 232; EW 13; EWL 3; MTCW 1, 2; MTFW 2005; NFS 18; RGSF 2; RGWL 3; SSFS 10

Kunene, Mazisi (Raymond) 1930- ... **CLC 85**
See also BW 1, 3; CA 125; CANR 81; CP 1, 7; DLB 117

Kung, Hans .... **CLC 130**
See Kung, Hans

Kung, Hans 1928-
See Kung, Hans
See also CA 53-56; CANR 66, 134; MTCW 1, 2; MTFW 2005

Kunikida Doppo 1869(?)-1908
See Doppo, Kunikida
See also DLB 180; EWL 3

Kunitz, Stanley (Jasspon) 1905- .. **CLC 6, 11, 14, 148; PC 19**
See also AMWS 3; CA 41-44R; CANR 26, 57, 98; CP 1, 2, 3, 4, 5, 6, 7; DA3; DLB 48; INT CANR-26; MAL 5; MTCW 1, 2; MTFW 2005; PFS 11; RGAL 4

Kunze, Reiner 1933- .... **CLC 10**
See also CA 93-96; CWW 2; DLB 75; EWL 3

Kuprin, Aleksander Ivanovich 1870-1938 .... **TCLC 5**
See Kuprin, Aleksandr Ivanovich; Kuprin, Alexandr Ivanovich
See also CA 104; 182

Kuprin, Aleksandr Ivanovich
See Kuprin, Aleksander Ivanovich
See also DLB 295

Kuprin, Alexandr Ivanovich
See Kuprin, Aleksander Ivanovich
See also EWL 3

Kureishi, Hanif 1954- .. **CLC 64, 135; DC 26**
See also BRWS 11; CA 139; CANR 113; CBD; CD 5, 6; CN 6, 7; DLB 194, 245; GLL 2; IDFW 4; WLIT 4; WWE 1

Kurosawa, Akira 1910-1998 ..... **CLC 16, 119**
See also AAYA 11, 64; CA 101; 170; CANR 46; DAM MULT

Kushner, Tony 1956- .... **CLC 81, 203; DC 10**
See also AAYA 61; AMWS 9; CA 144; CAD; CANR 74, 130; CD 5, 6; DA3; DAM DRAM; DFS 5; DLB 228; EWL 3; GLL 1; LAIT 5; MAL 5; MTCW 2; MTFW 2005; RGAL 4; SATA 160

Kuttner, Henry 1915-1958 .... **TCLC 10**
See also CA 107; 157; DLB 8; FANT; SCFW 1, 2; SFW 4

Kutty, Madhavi
See Das, Kamala

Kuzma, Greg 1944- .... **CLC 7**
See also CA 33-36R; CANR 70

Kuzmin, Mikhail (Alekseevich) 1872(?)-1936 .... **TCLC 40**
See also CA 170; DLB 295; EWL 3

Kyd, Thomas 1558-1594 .... **DC 3; LC 22**
See also BRW 1; DAM DRAM; DFS 21; DLB 62; IDTP; LMFS 1; RGEL 2; TEA; WLIT 3

Kyprianos, Iossif
See Samarakis, Antonis

L. S.
See Stephen, Sir Leslie

Laȝamon
See Layamon
See also DLB 146

Labe, Louise 1521-1566 .... **LC 120**

Labrunie, Gerard
See Nerval, Gerard de

La Bruyere, Jean de 1645-1696 .... **LC 17**
See also DLB 268; EW 3; GFL Beginnings to 1789

Lacan, Jacques (Marie Emile) 1901-1981 .... **CLC 75**
See also CA 121; 104; DLB 296; EWL 3; TWA

Laclos, Pierre-Ambroise Francois 1741-1803 .... **NCLC 4, 87**
See also DLB 313; EW 4; GFL Beginnings to 1789; RGWL 2, 3

Lacolere, Francois
See Aragon, Louis

La Colere, Francois
See Aragon, Louis

La Deshabilleuse
See Simenon, Georges (Jacques Christian)

Lady Gregory
See Gregory, Lady Isabella Augusta (Persse)

Lady of Quality, A
See Bagnold, Enid

La Fayette, Marie-(Madelaine Pioche de la Vergne) 1634-1693 .... **LC 2**
See Lafayette, Marie-Madeleine
See also GFL Beginnings to 1789; RGWL 2, 3

Lafayette, Marie-Madeleine
See La Fayette, Marie-(Madelaine Pioche de la Vergne)
See also DLB 268

Lafayette, Rene
See Hubbard, L(afayette) Ron(ald)

La Flesche, Francis 1857(?)-1932 ...... **NNAL**
See also CA 144; CANR 83; DLB 175

La Fontaine, Jean de 1621-1695 .... **LC 50**
See also DLB 268; EW 3; GFL Beginnings to 1789; MAICYA 1, 2; RGWL 2, 3; SATA 18

Laforgue, Jules 1860-1887 . **NCLC 5, 53; PC 14; SSC 20**
See also DLB 217; EW 7; GFL 1789 to the Present; RGWL 2, 3

Lagerkvist, Paer (Fabian) 1891-1974 ..... **CLC 7, 10, 13, 54; TCLC 144**
See Lagerkvist, Par
See also CA 85-88; 49-52; DA3; DAM DRAM, NOV; MTCW 1, 2; MTFW 2005; TWA

Lagerkvist, Par .... **SSC 12**
See Lagerkvist, Paer (Fabian)
See also DLB 259; EW 10; EWL 3; RGSF 2; RGWL 2, 3

Lagerloef, Selma (Ottiliana Lovisa) .... **TCLC 4, 36**
See Lagerlof, Selma (Ottiliana Lovisa)
See also CA 108; MTCW 2

Lagerlof, Selma (Ottiliana Lovisa) 1858-1940
See Lagerloef, Selma (Ottiliana Lovisa)
See also CA 188; CLR 7; DLB 259; RGWL 2, 3; SATA 15; SSFS 18

La Guma, (Justin) Alex(ander) 1925-1985 . **BLCS; CLC 19; TCLC 140**
See also AFW; BW 1, 3; CA 49-52; 118; CANR 25, 81; CDWLB 3; CN 1, 2, 3; CP 1; DAM NOV; DLB 117, 225; EWL 3; MTCW 1, 2; MTFW 2005; WLIT 2; WWE 1

Laidlaw, A. K.
See Grieve, C(hristopher) M(urray)

Lainez, Manuel Mujica
See Mujica Lainez, Manuel
See also HW 1

Laing, R(onald) D(avid) 1927-1989 . **CLC 95**
See also CA 107; 129; CANR 34; MTCW 1

Laishley, Alex
See Booth, Martin

Lamartine, Alphonse (Marie Louis Prat) de 1790-1869 .... **NCLC 11; PC 16**
See also DAM POET; DLB 217; GFL 1789 to the Present; RGWL 2, 3

Lamb, Charles 1775-1834 ..... **NCLC 10, 113; WLC**
See also BRW 4; CDBLB 1789-1832; DA; DAB; DAC; DAM MST; DLB 93, 107, 163; RGEL 2; SATA 17; TEA

Lamb, Lady Caroline 1785-1828 ... **NCLC 38**
See also DLB 116

Lamb, Mary Ann 1764-1847 .... **NCLC 125**
See also DLB 163; SATA 17

Lame Deer 1903(?)-1976 .... **NNAL**
See also CA 69-72

Lamming, George (William) 1927- ... **BLC 2; CLC 2, 4, 66, 144**
See also BW 2, 3; CA 85-88; CANR 26, 76; CDWLB 3; CN 1, 2, 3, 4, 5, 6, 7; CP 1; DAM MULT; DLB 125; EWL 3; MTCW 1, 2; MTFW 2005; NFS 15; RGEL 2

L'Amour, Louis (Dearborn) 1908-1988 .... **CLC 25, 55**
See also AAYA 16; AITN 2; BEST 89:2; BPFB 2; CA 1-4R; 125; CANR 3, 25, 40; CPW; DA3; DAM NOV, POP; DLB 206; DLBY 1980; MTCW 1, 2; MTFW 2005; RGAL 4; TCWW 1, 2

Lampedusa, Giuseppe (Tomasi) di .... **TCLC 13**
See Tomasi di Lampedusa, Giuseppe
See also CA 164; EW 11; MTCW 2; MTFW 2005; RGWL 2, 3

Lampman, Archibald 1861-1899 ... **NCLC 25**
See also DLB 92; RGEL 2; TWA

Lancaster, Bruce 1896-1963 .... **CLC 36**
See also CA 9-10; CANR 70; CAP 1; SATA 9

Lanchester, John 1962- .... **CLC 99**
See also CA 194; DLB 267

Landau, Mark Alexandrovich
See Aldanov, Mark (Alexandrovich)

Landau-Aldanov, Mark Alexandrovich
See Aldanov, Mark (Alexandrovich)

Landis, Jerry
See Simon, Paul (Frederick)

Landis, John 1950- .... **CLC 26**
See also CA 112; 122; CANR 128

Landolfi, Tommaso 1908-1979 .... **CLC 11, 49**
See also CA 127; 117; DLB 177; EWL 3

Landon, Letitia Elizabeth 1802-1838 .... **NCLC 15**
See also DLB 96

Landor, Walter Savage 1775-1864 .... **NCLC 14**
See also BRW 4; DLB 93, 107; RGEL 2

Landwirth, Heinz 1927-
See Lind, Jakov
See also CA 9-12R; CANR 7

Lane, Patrick 1939- .... **CLC 25**
See also CA 97-100; CANR 54; CP 3, 4, 5, 6, 7; DAM POET; DLB 53; INT CA-97-100

Lang, Andrew 1844-1912 .... **TCLC 16**
See also CA 114; 137; CANR 85; CLR 101; DLB 98, 141, 184; FANT; MAICYA 1, 2; RGEL 2; SATA 16; WCH

Lang, Fritz 1890-1976 .... **CLC 20, 103**
See also AAYA 65; CA 77-80; 69-72; CANR 30

Leblanc, Maurice (Marie Emile)
1864-1941 .... **TCLC 49**
See also CA 110; CMW 4

Lebowitz, Fran(ces Ann) 1951(?)- ... **CLC 11, 36**
See also CA 81-84; CANR 14, 60, 70; INT CANR-14; MTCW 1

Lebrecht, Peter
See Tieck, (Johann) Ludwig

le Carre, John .... **CLC 3, 5, 9, 15, 28**
See Cornwell, David (John Moore)
See also AAYA 42; BEST 89:4; BPFB 2; BRWS 2; CDBLB 1960 to Present; CMW 4; CN 1, 2, 3, 4, 5, 6, 7; CPW; DLB 87; EWL 3; MSW; MTCW 2; RGEL 2; TEA

Le Clezio, J(ean) M(arie) G(ustave)
1940- .... **CLC 31, 155**
See also CA 116; 128; CWW 2; DLB 83; EWL 3; GFL 1789 to the Present; RGSF 2

Leconte de Lisle, Charles-Marie-Rene
1818-1894 .... **NCLC 29**
See also DLB 217; EW 6; GFL 1789 to the Present

Le Coq, Monsieur
See Simenon, Georges (Jacques Christian)

Leduc, Violette 1907-1972 .... **CLC 22**
See also CA 13-14; 33-36R; CANR 69; CAP 1; EWL 3; GFL 1789 to the Present; GLL 1

Ledwidge, Francis 1887(?)-1917 .... **TCLC 23**
See also CA 123; 203; DLB 20

Lee, Andrea 1953- .... **BLC 2; CLC 36**
See also BW 1, 3; CA 125; CANR 82; DAM MULT

Lee, Andrew
See Auchincloss, Louis (Stanton)

Lee, Chang-rae 1965- .... **CLC 91**
See also CA 148; CANR 89; CN 7; DLB 312; LATS 1:2

Lee, Don L. .... **CLC 2**
See Madhubuti, Haki R.
See also CP 2, 3, 4

Lee, George W(ashington)
1894-1976 .... **BLC 2; CLC 52**
See also BW 1; CA 125; CANR 83; DAM MULT; DLB 51

Lee, (Nelle) Harper 1926- . **CLC 12, 60, 194; WLC**
See also AAYA 13; AMWS 8; BPFB 2; BYA 3; CA 13-16R; CANR 51, 128; CDALB 1941-1968; CSW; DA; DA3; DAB; DAC; DAM MST, NOV; DLB 6; EXPN; LAIT 3; MAL 5; MTCW 1, 2; MTFW 2005; NFS 2; SATA 11; WYA; YAW

Lee, Helen Elaine 1959(?) .... **CLC 86**
See also CA 148

Lee, John .... **CLC 70**

Lee, Julian
See Latham, Jean Lee

Lee, Larry
See Lee, Lawrence

Lee, Laurie 1914-1997 .... **CLC 90**
See also CA 77-80; 158; CANR 33, 73; CP 1, 2, 3, 4; CPW; DAB; DAM POP; DLB 27; MTCW 1; RGEL 2

Lee, Lawrence 1941-1990 .... **CLC 34**
See also CA 131; CANR 43

Lee, Li-Young 1957- .... **CLC 164; PC 24**
See also AMWS 15; CA 153; CANR 118; CP 7; DLB 165, 312; LMFS 2; PFS 11, 15, 17

Lee, Manfred B(ennington)
1905-1971 .... **CLC 11**
See Queen, Ellery
See also CA 1-4R; 29-32R; CANR 2; CMW 4; DLB 137

Lee, Nathaniel 1645(?)-1692 .... **LC 103**
See also DLB 80; RGEL 2

Lee, Shelton Jackson 1957(?)- .. **BLCS; CLC 105**
See Lee, Spike
See also BW 2, 3; CA 125; CANR 42; DAM MULT

Lee, Spike
See Lee, Shelton Jackson
See also AAYA 4, 29

Lee, Stan 1922- .... **CLC 17**
See also AAYA 5, 49; CA 108; 111; CANR 129; INT CA-111; MTFW 2005

Lee, Tanith 1947- .... **CLC 46**
See also AAYA 15; CA 37-40R; CANR 53, 102, 145; DLB 261; FANT; SATA 8, 88, 134; SFW 4; SUFW 1, 2; YAW

Lee, Vernon .... **SSC 33; TCLC 5**
See Paget, Violet
See also DLB 57, 153, 156, 174, 178; GLL 1; SUFW 1

Lee, William
See Burroughs, William S(eward)
See also GLL 1

Lee, Willy
See Burroughs, William S(eward)
See also GLL 1

Lee-Hamilton, Eugene (Jacob)
1845-1907 .... **TCLC 22**
See also CA 117; 234

Leet, Judith 1935- .... **CLC 11**
See also CA 187

Le Fanu, Joseph Sheridan
1814-1873 .... **NCLC 9, 58; SSC 14, 84**
See also CMW 4; DA3; DAM POP; DLB 21, 70, 159, 178; GL 3; HGG; RGEL 2; RGSF 2; SUFW 1

Leffland, Ella 1931- .... **CLC 19**
See also CA 29-32R; CANR 35, 78, 82; DLBY 1984; INT CANR-35; SATA 65

Leger, Alexis
See Leger, (Marie-Rene Auguste) Alexis Saint-Leger

Leger, (Marie-Rene Auguste) Alexis
Saint-Leger 1887-1975 .. **CLC 4, 11, 46; PC 23**
See Perse, Saint-John; Saint-John Perse
See also CA 13-16R; 61-64; CANR 43; DAM POET; MTCW 1

Leger, Saintleger
See Leger, (Marie-Rene Auguste) Alexis Saint-Leger

Le Guin, Ursula K(roeber) 1929- ..... **CLC 8, 13, 22, 45, 71, 136; SSC 12, 69**
See also AAYA 9, 27; AITN 1; BPFB 2; BYA 5, 8, 11, 14; CA 21-24R; CANR 9, 32, 52, 74, 132; CDALB 1968-1988; CLR 3, 28, 91; CN 2, 3, 4, 5, 6, 7; CPW; DA3; DAB; DAC; DAM MST, POP; DLB 8, 52, 256, 275; EXPS; FANT; FW; INT CANR-32; JRDA; LAIT 5; MAICYA 1, 2; MAL 5; MTCW 1, 2; MTFW 2005; NFS 6, 9; SATA 4, 52, 99, 149; SCFW 1, 2; SFW 4; SSFS 2; SUFW 1, 2; WYA; YAW

Lehmann, Rosamond (Nina)
1901-1990 .... **CLC 5**
See also CA 77-80; 131; CANR 8, 73; CN 1, 2, 3, 4; DLB 15; MTCW 2; RGEL 2; RHW

Leiber, Fritz (Reuter, Jr.)
1910-1992 .... **CLC 25**
See also AAYA 65; BPFB 2; CA 45-48; 139; CANR 2, 40, 86; CN 2, 3, 4, 5; DLB 8; FANT; HGG; MTCW 1, 2; MTFW 2005; SATA 45; SATA-Obit 73; SCFW 1, 2; SFW 4; SUFW 1, 2

Leibniz, Gottfried Wilhelm von
1646-1716 .... **LC 35**
See also DLB 168

Leimbach, Martha 1963-
See Leimbach, Marti
See also CA 130

Leimbach, Marti .... **CLC 65**
See Leimbach, Martha

Leino, Eino .... **TCLC 24**
See Lonnbohm, Armas Eino Leopold
See also EWL 3

Leiris, Michel (Julien) 1901-1990 ..... **CLC 61**
See also CA 119; 128; 132; EWL 3; GFL 1789 to the Present

Leithauser, Brad 1953- .... **CLC 27**
See also CA 107; CANR 27, 81; CP 7; DLB 120, 282

le Jars de Gournay, Marie
See de Gournay, Marie le Jars

Lelchuk, Alan 1938- .... **CLC 5**
See also CA 45-48; CAAS 20; CANR 1, 70; CN 3, 4, 5, 6, 7

Lem, Stanislaw 1921- ...... **CLC 8, 15, 40, 149**
See also CA 105; CAAS 1; CANR 32; CWW 2; MTCW 1; SFW 1, 2; SFW 4

Lemann, Nancy (Elise) 1956- .... **CLC 39**
See also CA 118; 136; CANR 121

Lemonnier, (Antoine Louis) Camille
1844-1913 .... **TCLC 22**
See also CA 121

Lenau, Nikolaus 1802-1850 .... **NCLC 16**

L'Engle, Madeleine (Camp Franklin)
1918- .... **CLC 12**
See also AAYA 28; AITN 2; BPFB 2; BYA 2, 4, 5, 7; CA 1-4R; CANR 3, 21, 39, 66, 107; CLR 1, 14, 57; CPW; CWRI 5; DA3; DAM POP; DLB 52; JRDA; MAICYA 1, 2; MTCW 1, 2; MTFW 2005; SAAS 15; SATA 1, 27, 75, 128; SFW 4; WYA; YAW

Lengyel, Jozsef 1896-1975 .... **CLC 7**
See also CA 85-88; 57-60; CANR 71; RGSF 2

Lenin 1870-1924
See Lenin, V. I.
See also CA 121; 168

Lenin, V. I. .... **TCLC 67**
See Lenin

Lennon, John (Ono) 1940-1980 .. **CLC 12, 35**
See also CA 102; SATA 114

Lennox, Charlotte Ramsay
1729(?)-1804 .... **NCLC 23, 134**
See also DLB 39; RGEL 2

Lentricchia, Frank, (Jr.) 1940- .... **CLC 34**
See also CA 25-28R; CANR 19, 106; DLB 246

Lenz, Gunter .... **CLC 65**

Lenz, Jakob Michael Reinhold
1751-1792 .... **LC 100**
See also DLB 94; RGWL 2, 3

Lenz, Siegfried 1926- .... **CLC 27; SSC 33**
See also CA 89-92; CANR 80; CWW 2; DLB 75; EWL 3; RGSF 2; RGWL 2, 3

Leon, David
See Jacob, (Cyprien-)Max

Leonard, Elmore (John, Jr.) 1925- . **CLC 28, 34, 71, 120**
See also AAYA 22, 59; AITN 1; BEST 89:1, 90:4; BPFB 2; CA 81-84; CANR 12, 28, 53, 76, 96, 133; CMW 4; CN 5, 6, 7; CPW; DA3; DAM POP; DLB 173, 226; INT CANR-28; MSW; MTCW 1, 2; MTFW 2005; RGAL 4; SATA 163; TCWW 1, 2

Leonard, Hugh .... **CLC 19**
See Byrne, John Keyes
See also CBD; CD 5, 6; DFS 13; DLB 13

Leonov, Leonid (Maximovich)
1899-1994 .... **CLC 92**
See Leonov, Leonid Maksimovich
See also CA 129; CANR 76; DAM NOV; EWL 3; MTCW 1, 2; MTFW 2005

Limonov, Edward 1944- .... **CLC 67**
   See Limonov, Eduard
   See also CA 137
Lin, Frank
   See Atherton, Gertrude (Franklin Horn)
Lin, Yutang 1895-1976 .... **TCLC 149**
   See also CA 45-48; 65-68; CANR 2; RGAL 4
Lincoln, Abraham 1809-1865 .... **NCLC 18**
   See also LAIT 2
Lind, Jakov .... **CLC 1, 2, 4, 27, 82**
   See Landwirth, Heinz
   See also CAAS 4; DLB 299; EWL 3
Lindbergh, Anne (Spencer) Morrow
   1906-2001 .... **CLC 82**
   See also BPFB 2; CA 17-20R; 193; CANR 16, 73; DAM NOV; MTCW 1, 2; MTFW 2005; SATA 33; SATA-Obit 125; TUS
Lindsay, David 1878(?)-1945 .... **TCLC 15**
   See also CA 113; 187; DLB 255; FANT; SFW 4; SUFW 1
Lindsay, (Nicholas) Vachel
   1879-1931 .... **PC 23; TCLC 17; WLC**
   See also AMWS 1; CA 114; 135; CANR 79; CDALB 1865-1917; DA; DA3; DAC; DAM MST, POET; DLB 54; EWL 3; EXPP; MAL 5; RGAL 4; SATA 40; WP
Linke-Poot
   See Doeblin, Alfred
Linney, Romulus 1930- .... **CLC 51**
   See also CA 1-4R; CAD; CANR 40, 44, 79; CD 5, 6; CSW; RGAL 4
Linton, Eliza Lynn 1822-1898 .... **NCLC 41**
   See also DLB 18
Li Po 701-763 .... **CMLC 2; PC 29**
   See also PFS 20; WP
Lipsius, Justus 1547-1606 .... **LC 16**
Lipsyte, Robert (Michael) 1938- ...... **CLC 21**
   See also AAYA 7, 45; CA 17-20R; CANR 8, 57; CLR 23, 76; DA; DAC; DAM MST, NOV; JRDA; LAIT 5; MAICYA 1, 2; SATA 5, 68, 113, 161; WYA; YAW
Lish, Gordon (Jay) 1934- ... **CLC 45; SSC 18**
   See also CA 113; 117; CANR 79; DLB 130; INT CA-117
Lispector, Clarice 1925(?)-1977 .... **CLC 43; HLCS 2; SSC 34**
   See also CA 139; 116; CANR 71; CDWLB 3; DLB 113, 307; DNFS 1; EWL 3; FW; HW 2; LAW; RGSF 2; RGWL 2, 3; WLIT 1
Littell, Robert 1935(?)- .... **CLC 42**
   See also CA 109; 112; CANR 64, 115; CMW 4
Little, Malcolm 1925-1965
   See Malcolm X
   See also BW 1, 3; CA 125; 111; CANR 82; DA; DA3; DAB; DAC; DAM MST, MULT; MTCW 1, 2; MTFW 2005
Littlewit, Humphrey Gent.
   See Lovecraft, H(oward) P(hillips)
Litwos
   See Sienkiewicz, Henryk (Adam Alexander Pius)
Liu, E. 1857-1909 .... **TCLC 15**
   See also CA 115; 190
Lively, Penelope 1933- .... **CLC 32, 50**
   See also BPFB 2; CA 41-44R; CANR 29, 67, 79, 131; CLR 7; CN 5, 6, 7; CWRI 5; DAM NOV; DLB 14, 161, 207; FANT; JRDA; MAICYA 1, 2; MTCW 1, 2; MTFW 2005; SATA 7, 60, 101, 164; TEA
Lively, Penelope Margaret
   See Lively, Penelope

Livesay, Dorothy (Kathleen)
   1909-1996 .... **CLC 4, 15, 79**
   See also AITN 2; CA 25-28R; CAAS 8; CANR 36, 67; CP 1, 2, 3, 4; DAC; DAM MST, POET; DLB 68; FW; MTCW 1; RGEL 2; TWA
Livy c. 59B.C.-c. 12 .... **CMLC 11**
   See also AW 2; CDWLB 1; DLB 211; RGWL 2, 3
Lizardi, Jose Joaquin Fernandez de
   1776-1827 .... **NCLC 30**
   See also LAW
Llewellyn, Richard
   See Llewellyn Lloyd, Richard Dafydd Vivian
   See also DLB 15
Llewellyn Lloyd, Richard Dafydd Vivian
   1906-1983 .... **CLC 7, 80**
   See Llewellyn, Richard
   See also CA 53-56; 111; CANR 7, 71; SATA 11; SATA-Obit 37
Llosa, (Jorge) Mario (Pedro) Vargas
   See Vargas Llosa, (Jorge) Mario (Pedro)
   See also RGWL 3
Llosa, Mario Vargas
   See Vargas Llosa, (Jorge) Mario (Pedro)
Lloyd, Manda
   See Mander, (Mary) Jane
Lloyd Webber, Andrew 1948-
   See Webber, Andrew Lloyd
   See also AAYA 1, 38; CA 116; 149; DAM DRAM; SATA 56
Llull, Ramon c. 1235-c. 1316 .... **CMLC 12**
Lobb, Ebenezer
   See Upward, Allen
Locke, Alain (Le Roy)
   1886-1954 .... **BLCS; HR 1:3; TCLC 43**
   See also AMWS 14; BW 1, 3; CA 106; 124; CANR 79; DLB 51; LMFS 2; MAL 5; RGAL 4
Locke, John 1632-1704 .... **LC 7, 35**
   See also DLB 31, 101, 213, 252; RGEL 2; WLIT 3
Locke-Elliott, Sumner
   See Elliott, Sumner Locke
Lockhart, John Gibson 1794-1854 .. **NCLC 6**
   See also DLB 110, 116, 144
Lockridge, Ross (Franklin), Jr.
   1914-1948 .... **TCLC 111**
   See also CA 108; 145; CANR 79; DLB 143; DLBY 1980; MAL 5; RGAL 4; RHW
Lockwood, Robert
   See Johnson, Robert
Lodge, David (John) 1935- .... **CLC 36, 141**
   See also BEST 90:1; BRWS 4; CA 17-20R; CANR 19, 53, 92, 139; CN 1, 2, 3, 4, 5, 6, 7; CPW; DAM POP; DLB 14, 194; EWL 3; INT CANR-19; MTCW 1, 2; MTFW 2005
Lodge, Thomas 1558-1625 .... **LC 41**
   See also DLB 172; RGEL 2
Loewinsohn, Ron(ald William)
   1937- .... **CLC 52**
   See also CA 25-28R; CANR 71; CP 1, 2, 3, 4
Logan, Jake
   See Smith, Martin Cruz
Logan, John (Burton) 1923-1987 .... **CLC 5**
   See also CA 77-80; 124; CANR 45; CP 1, 2, 3, 4; DLB 5
Lo Kuan-chung 1330(?)-1400(?) .... **LC 12**
Lombard, Nap
   See Johnson, Pamela Hansford
Lombard, Peter 1100(?)-1160(?) ... **CMLC 72**
London, Jack 1876-1916 .. **SSC 4, 49; TCLC 9, 15, 39; WLC**
   See London, John Griffith
   See also AAYA 13; AITN 2; AMW; BPFB 2; BYA 4, 13; CDALB 1865-1917; DLB

8, 12, 78, 212; EWL 3; EXPS; LAIT 3; MAL 5; NFS 8; RGAL 4; RGSF 2; SATA 18; SFW 4; SSFS 7; TCWW 1, 2; TUS; WYA; YAW
London, John Griffith 1876-1916
   See London, Jack
   See also CA 110; 119; CANR 73; DA; DA3; DAB; DAC; DAM MST, NOV; JRDA; MAICYA 1, 2; MTCW 1, 2; MTFW 2005; NFS 19
Long, Emmett
   See Leonard, Elmore (John, Jr.)
Longbaugh, Harry
   See Goldman, William (W.)
Longfellow, Henry Wadsworth
   1807-1882 .... **NCLC 2, 45, 101, 103; PC 30; WLCS**
   See also AMW; AMWR 2; CDALB 1640-1865; CLR 99; DA; DA3; DAB; DAC; DAM MST, POET; DLB 1, 59, 235; EXPP; PAB; PFS 2, 7, 17; RGAL 4; SATA 19; TUS; WP
Longinus c. 1st cent. - .... **CMLC 27**
   See also AW 2; DLB 176
Longley, Michael 1939- .... **CLC 29**
   See also BRWS 8; CA 102; CP 1, 2, 3, 4, 5, 6, 7; DLB 40
Longstreet, Augustus Baldwin
   1790-1870 .... **NCLC 159**
   See also DLB 3, 11, 74, 248; RGAL 4
Longus fl. c. 2nd cent. - .... **CMLC 7**
Longway, A. Hugh
   See Lang, Andrew
Lonnbohm, Armas Eino Leopold 1878-1926
   See Leino, Eino
   See also CA 123
Lonnrot, Elias 1802-1884 .... **NCLC 53**
   See also EFS 1
Lonsdale, Roger ed. .... **CLC 65**
Lopate, Phillip 1943- .... **CLC 29**
   See also CA 97-100; CANR 88; DLBY 1980; INT CA-97-100
Lopez, Barry (Holstun) 1945- .... **CLC 70**
   See also AAYA 9, 63; ANW; CA 65-68; CANR 7, 23, 47, 68, 92; DLB 256, 275; INT CANR-7, -23; MTCW 1; RGAL 4; SATA 67
Lopez de Mendoza, Inigo
   See Santillana, Inigo Lopez de Mendoza, Marques de
Lopez Portillo (y Pacheco), Jose
   1920-2004 .... **CLC 46**
   See also CA 129; 224; HW 1
Lopez y Fuentes, Gregorio
   1897(?)-1966 .... **CLC 32**
   See also CA 131; EWL 3; HW 1
Lorca, Federico Garcia
   See Garcia Lorca, Federico
   See also DFS 4; EW 11; PFS 20; RGWL 2, 3; WP
Lord, Audre
   See Lorde, Audre (Geraldine)
   See also EWL 3
Lord, Bette Bao 1938- .... **AAL; CLC 23**
   See also BEST 90:3; BPFB 2; CA 107; CANR 41, 79; INT CA-107; SATA 58
Lord Auch
   See Bataille, Georges
Lord Brooke
   See Greville, Fulke
Lord Byron
   See Byron, George Gordon (Noel)
Lorde, Audre (Geraldine)
   1934-1992 .... **BLC 2; CLC 18, 71; PC 12; TCLC 173**
   See Domini, Rey; Lord, Audre
   See also AFAW 1, 2; BW 1, 3; CA 25-28R; 142; CANR 16, 26, 46, 82; CP 2, 3, 4; DA3; DAM MULT, POET; DLB 41; FW; MAL 5; MTCW 1, 2; MTFW 2005; PFS 16; RGAL 4

Marley, Bob .... **CLC 17**
See Marley, Robert Nesta
Marley, Robert Nesta 1945-1981
See Marley, Bob
See also CA 107; 103
Marlowe, Christopher 1564-1593 . **DC 1; LC 22, 47, 117; PC 57; WLC**
See also BRW 1; BRWR 1; CDBLB Before 1660; DA; DA3; DAB; DAC; DAM DRAM, MST; DFS 1, 5, 13, 21; DLB 62; EXPP; LMFS 1; PFS 22; RGEL 2; TEA; WLIT 3
Marlowe, Stephen 1928- .... **CLC 70**
See Queen, Ellery
See also CA 13-16R; CANR 6, 55; CMW 4; SFW 4
Marmion, Shakerley 1603-1639 .... **LC 89**
See also DLB 58; RGEL 2
Marmontel, Jean-Francois 1723-1799 .. **LC 2**
See also DLB 314
Maron, Monika 1941- .... **CLC 165**
See also CA 201
Marquand, John P(hillips)
1893-1960 .... **CLC 2, 10**
See also AMW; BPFB 2; CA 85-88; CANR 73; CMW 4; DLB 9, 102; EWL 3; MAL 5; MTCW 2; RGAL 4
Marques, Rene 1919-1979 .. **CLC 96; HLC 2**
See also CA 97-100; 85-88; CANR 78; DAM MULT; DLB 305; EWL 3; HW 1, 2; LAW; RGSF 2
Marquez, Gabriel (Jose) Garcia
See Garcia Marquez, Gabriel (Jose)
Marquis, Don(ald Robert Perry)
1878-1937 .... **TCLC 7**
See also CA 104; 166; DLB 11, 25; MAL 5; RGAL 4
Marquis de Sade
See Sade, Donatien Alphonse Francois
Marric, J. J.
See Creasey, John
See also MSW
Marryat, Frederick 1792-1848 .... **NCLC 3**
See also DLB 21, 163; RGEL 2; WCH
Marsden, James
See Creasey, John
Marsh, Edward 1872-1953 .... **TCLC 99**
Marsh, (Edith) Ngaio 1895-1982 .. **CLC 7, 53**
See also CA 9-12R; CANR 6, 58; CMW 4; CN 1, 2, 3; CPW; DAM POP; DLB 77; MSW; MTCW 1, 2; RGEL 2; TEA
Marshall, Allen
See Westlake, Donald E(dwin)
Marshall, Garry 1934- .... **CLC 17**
See also AAYA 3; CA 111; SATA 60
Marshall, Paule 1929- .. **BLC 3; CLC 27, 72; SSC 3**
See also AFAW 1, 2; AMWS 11; BPFB 2; BW 2, 3; CA 77-80; CANR 25, 73, 129; CN 1, 2, 3, 4, 5, 6, 7; DA3; DAM MULT; DLB 33, 157, 227; EWL 3; LATS 1:2; MAL 5; MTCW 1, 2; MTFW 2005; RGAL 4; SSFS 15
Marshallik
See Zangwill, Israel
Marsten, Richard
See Hunter, Evan
Marston, John 1576-1634 .... **LC 33**
See also BRW 2; DAM DRAM; DLB 58, 172; RGEL 2
Martel, Yann 1963- .... **CLC 192**
See also AAYA 67; CA 146; CANR 114; MTFW 2005
Martens, Adolphe-Adhemar
See Ghelderode, Michel de
Martha, Henry
See Harris, Mark

Marti, Jose
See Marti (y Perez), Jose (Julian)
See also DLB 290
Marti (y Perez), Jose (Julian)
1853-1895 .... **HLC 2; NCLC 63**
See Marti, Jose
See also DAM MULT; HW 2; LAW; RGWL 2, 3; WLIT 1
Martial c. 40-c. 104 .... **CMLC 35; PC 10**
See also AW 2; CDWLB 1; DLB 211; RGWL 2, 3
Martin, Ken
See Hubbard, L(afayette) Ron(ald)
Martin, Richard
See Creasey, John
Martin, Steve 1945- .... **CLC 30, 217**
See also AAYA 53; CA 97-100; CANR 30, 100, 140; DFS 19; MTCW 1; MTFW 2005
Martin, Valerie 1948- .... **CLC 89**
See also BEST 90:2; CA 85-88; CANR 49, 89
Martin, Violet Florence 1862-1915 .. **SSC 56; TCLC 51**
Martin, Webber
See Silverberg, Robert
Martindale, Patrick Victor
See White, Patrick (Victor Martindale)
Martin du Gard, Roger
1881-1958 .... **TCLC 24**
See also CA 118; CANR 94; DLB 65; EWL 3; GFL 1789 to the Present; RGWL 2, 3
Martineau, Harriet 1802-1876 ...... **NCLC 26, 137**
See also DLB 21, 55, 159, 163, 166, 190; FW; RGEL 2; YABC 2
Martines, Julia
See O'Faolain, Julia
Martinez, Enrique Gonzalez
See Gonzalez Martinez, Enrique
Martinez, Jacinto Benavente y
See Benavente (y Martinez), Jacinto
Martinez de la Rosa, Francisco de Paula
1787-1862 .... **NCLC 102**
See also TWA
Martinez Ruiz, Jose 1873-1967
See Azorin; Ruiz, Jose Martinez
See also CA 93-96; HW 1
Martinez Sierra, Gregorio
1881-1947 .... **TCLC 6**
See also CA 115; EWL 3
Martinez Sierra, Maria (de la O'LeJarraga)
1874-1974 .... **TCLC 6**
See also CA 115; EWL 3
Martinsen, Martin
See Follett, Ken(neth Martin)
Martinson, Harry (Edmund)
1904-1978 .... **CLC 14**
See also CA 77-80; CANR 34, 130; DLB 259; EWL 3
Martyn, Edward 1859-1923 .... **TCLC 131**
See also CA 179; DLB 10; RGEL 2
Marut, Ret
See Traven, B.
Marut, Robert
See Traven, B.
Marvell, Andrew 1621-1678 .... **LC 4, 43; PC 10; WLC**
See also BRW 2; BRWR 2; CDBLB 1660-1789; DA; DAB; DAC; DAM MST, POET; DLB 131; EXPP; PFS 5; RGEL 2; TEA; WP
Marx, Karl (Heinrich)
1818-1883 .... **NCLC 17, 114**
See also DLB 129; LATS 1:1; TWA
Masaoka, Shiki -1902 .... **TCLC 18**
See Masaoka, Tsunenori
See also RGWL 3

Masaoka, Tsunenori 1867-1902
See Masaoka, Shiki
See also CA 117; 191; TWA
Masefield, John (Edward)
1878-1967 .... **CLC 11, 47**
See also CA 19-20; 25-28R; CANR 33; CAP 2; CDBLB 1890-1914; DAM POET; DLB 10, 19, 153, 160; EWL 3; EXPP; FANT; MTCW 1, 2; PFS 5; RGEL 2; SATA 19
Maso, Carole (?)- .... **CLC 44**
See also CA 170; CN 7; GLL 2; RGAL 4
Mason, Bobbie Ann 1940- ... **CLC 28, 43, 82, 154; SSC 4**
See also AAYA 5, 42; AMWS 8; BPFB 2; CA 53-56; CANR 11, 31, 58, 83, 125; CDALBS; CN 5, 6, 7; CSW; DA3; DLB 173; DLBY 1987; EWL 3; EXPS; INT CANR-31; MAL 5; MTCW 1, 2; MTFW 2005; NFS 4; RGAL 4; RGSF 2; SSFS 3, 8, 20; TCLE 1:2; YAW
Mason, Ernst
See Pohl, Frederik
Mason, Hunni B.
See Sternheim, (William Adolf) Carl
Mason, Lee W.
See Malzberg, Barry N(athaniel)
Mason, Nick 1945- .... **CLC 35**
Mason, Tally
See Derleth, August (William)
Mass, Anna .... **CLC 59**
Mass, William
See Gibson, William
Massinger, Philip 1583-1640 .... **LC 70**
See also BRWS 11; DLB 58; RGEL 2
Master Lao
See Lao Tzu
Masters, Edgar Lee 1868-1950 ...... **PC 1, 36; TCLC 2, 25; WLCS**
See also AMWS 1; CA 104; 133; CDALB 1865-1917; DA; DAC; DAM MST, POET; DLB 54; EWL 3; EXPP; MAL 5; MTCW 1, 2; MTFW 2005; RGAL 4; TUS; WP
Masters, Hilary 1928- .... **CLC 48**
See also CA 25-28R, 217; CAAE 217; CANR 13, 47, 97; CN 6, 7; DLB 244
Mastrosimone, William 1947- .... **CLC 36**
See also CA 186; CAD; CD 5, 6
Mathe, Albert
See Camus, Albert
Mather, Cotton 1663-1728 .... **LC 38**
See also AMWS 2; CDALB 1640-1865; DLB 24, 30, 140; RGAL 4; TUS
Mather, Increase 1639-1723 .... **LC 38**
See also DLB 24
Matheson, Richard (Burton) 1926- .. **CLC 37**
See also AAYA 31; CA 97-100; CANR 88, 99; DLB 8, 44; HGG; INT CA-97-100; SCFW 1, 2; SFW 4; SUFW 2
Mathews, Harry (Burchell) 1930- ..... **CLC 6, 52**
See also CA 21-24R; CAAS 6; CANR 18, 40, 98; CN 5, 6, 7
Mathews, John Joseph 1894-1979 .. **CLC 84; NNAL**
See also CA 19-20; 142; CANR 45; CAP 2; DAM MULT; DLB 175; TCWW 1, 2
Mathias, Roland (Glyn) 1915- .... **CLC 45**
See also CA 97-100; CANR 19, 41; CP 1, 2, 3, 4, 5, 6, 7; DLB 27
Matsuo Basho 1644(?)-1694 ...... **LC 62; PC 3**
See Basho, Matsuo
See also DAM POET; PFS 2, 7, 18
Mattheson, Rodney
See Creasey, John
Matthews, (James) Brander
1852-1929 .... **TCLC 95**
See also CA 181; DLB 71, 78; DLBD 13

McGinley, Patrick (Anthony) 1937- . **CLC 41**
See also CA 120; 127; CANR 56; INT CA-127

McGinley, Phyllis 1905-1978 .... **CLC 14**
See also CA 9-12R; 77-80; CANR 19; CP 1, 2; CWRI 5; DLB 11, 48; MAL 5; PFS 9, 13; SATA 2, 44; SATA-Obit 24

McGinniss, Joe 1942- .... **CLC 32**
See also AITN 2; BEST 89:2; CA 25-28R; CANR 26, 70; CPW; DLB 185; INT CANR-26

McGivern, Maureen Daly
See Daly, Maureen

McGrath, Patrick 1950- .... **CLC 55**
See also CA 136; CANR 65; CN 5, 6, 7; DLB 231; HGG; SUFW 2

McGrath, Thomas (Matthew)
1916-1990 .... **CLC 28, 59**
See also AMWS 10; CA 9-12R; 132; CANR 6, 33, 95; CP 1, 2, 3, 4; DAM POET; MAL 5; MTCW 1; SATA 41; SATA-Obit 66

McGuane, Thomas (Francis III)
1939- .... **CLC 3, 7, 18, 45, 127**
See also AITN 2; BPFB 2; CA 49-52; CANR 5, 24, 49, 94; CN 2, 3, 4, 5, 6, 7; DLB 2, 212; DLBY 1980; EWL 3; INT CANR-24; MAL 5; MTCW 1; MTFW 2005; TCWW 1, 2

McGuckian, Medbh 1950- .... **CLC 48, 174; PC 27**
See also BRWS 5; CA 143; CP 4, 5, 6, 7; CWP; DAM POET; DLB 40

McHale, Tom 1942(?)-1982 .... **CLC 3, 5**
See also AITN 1; CA 77-80; 106; CN 1, 2, 3

McHugh, Heather 1948- .... **PC 61**
See also CA 69-72; CANR 11, 28, 55, 92; CP 4, 5, 6, 7; CWP

McIlvanney, William 1936- .... **CLC 42**
See also CA 25-28R; CANR 61; CMW 4; DLB 14, 207

McIlwraith, Maureen Mollie Hunter
See Hunter, Mollie
See also SATA 2

McInerney, Jay 1955- .... **CLC 34, 112**
See also AAYA 18; BPFB 2; CA 116; 123; CANR 45, 68, 116; CN 5, 6, 7; CPW; DA3; DAM POP; DLB 292; INT CA-123; MAL 5; MTCW 2; MTFW 2005

McIntyre, Vonda N(eel) 1948- .... **CLC 18**
See also CA 81-84; CANR 17, 34, 69; MTCW 1; SFW 4; YAW

McKay, Claude .... **BLC 3; HR 1:3; PC 2; TCLC 7, 41; WLC**
See McKay, Festus Claudius
See also AFAW 1, 2; AMWS 10; DAB; DLB 4, 45, 51, 117; EWL 3; EXPP; GLL 2; LAIT 3; LMFS 2; MAL 5; PAB; PFS 4; RGAL 4; WP

McKay, Festus Claudius 1889-1948
See McKay, Claude
See also BW 1, 3; CA 104; 124; CANR 73; DA; DAC; DAM MST, MULT, NOV, POET; MTCW 1, 2; MTFW 2005; TUS

McKuen, Rod 1933- .... **CLC 1, 3**
See also AITN 1; CA 41-44R; CANR 40; CP 1

McLoughlin, R. B.
See Mencken, H(enry) L(ouis)

McLuhan, (Herbert) Marshall
1911-1980 .... **CLC 37, 83**
See also CA 9-12R; 102; CANR 12, 34, 61; DLB 88; INT CANR-12; MTCW 1, 2; MTFW 2005

McManus, Declan Patrick Aloysius
See Costello, Elvis

McMillan, Terry (L.) 1951- . **BLCS; CLC 50, 61, 112**
See also AAYA 21; AMWS 13; BPFB 2; BW 2, 3; CA 140; CANR 60, 104, 131; CN 7; CPW; DA3; DAM MULT, NOV, POP; MAL 5; MTCW 2; MTFW 2005; RGAL 4; YAW

McMurtry, Larry 1936- .... **CLC 2, 3, 7, 11, 27, 44, 127**
See also AAYA 15; AITN 2; AMWS 5; BEST 89:2; BPFB 2; CA 5-8R; CANR 19, 43, 64, 103; CDALB 1968-1988; CN 2, 3, 4, 5, 6, 7; CPW; CSW; DA3; DAM NOV, POP; DLB 2, 143, 256; DLBY 1980, 1987; EWL 3; MAL 5; MTCW 1, 2; MTFW 2005; RGAL 4; TCWW 1, 2

McNally, T. M. 1961- .... **CLC 82**

McNally, Terrence 1939- ... **CLC 4, 7, 41, 91; DC 27**
See also AAYA 62; AMWS 13; CA 45-48; CAD; CANR 2, 56, 116; CD 5, 6; DA3; DAM DRAM; DFS 16, 19; DLB 7, 249; EWL 3; GLL 1; MTCW 2; MTFW 2005

McNamer, Deirdre 1950- .... **CLC 70**

McNeal, Tom .... **CLC 119**

McNeile, Herman Cyril 1888-1937
See Sapper
See also CA 184; CMW 4; DLB 77

McNickle, (William) D'Arcy
1904-1977 .... **CLC 89; NNAL**
See also CA 9-12R; 85-88; CANR 5, 45; DAM MULT; DLB 175, 212; RGAL 4; SATA-Obit 22; TCWW 1, 2

McPhee, John (Angus) 1931- .... **CLC 36**
See also AAYA 61; AMWS 3; ANW; BEST 90:1; CA 65-68; CANR 20, 46, 64, 69, 121; CPW; DLB 185, 275; MTCW 1, 2; MTFW 2005; TUS

McPherson, James Alan 1943- . **BLCS; CLC 19, 77**
See also BW 1, 3; CA 25-28R; CAAS 17; CANR 24, 74, 140; CN 3, 4, 5, 6; CSW; DLB 38, 244; EWL 3; MTCW 1, 2; MTFW 2005; RGAL 4; RGSF 2

McPherson, William (Alexander)
1933- .... **CLC 34**
See also CA 69-72; CANR 28; INT CANR-28

McTaggart, J. McT. Ellis
See McTaggart, John McTaggart Ellis

McTaggart, John McTaggart Ellis
1866-1925 .... **TCLC 105**
See also CA 120; DLB 262

Mead, George Herbert 1863-1931 . **TCLC 89**
See also CA 212; DLB 270

Mead, Margaret 1901-1978 .... **CLC 37**
See also AITN 1; CA 1-4R; 81-84; CANR 4; DA3; FW; MTCW 1, 2; SATA-Obit 20

Meaker, Marijane (Agnes) 1927-
See Kerr, M. E.
See also CA 107; CANR 37, 63, 145; INT CA-107; JRDA; MAICYA 1, 2; MAICYAS 1; MTCW 1; SATA 20, 61, 99, 160; SATA-Essay 111; YAW

Medoff, Mark (Howard) 1940- .... **CLC 6, 23**
See also AITN 1; CA 53-56; CAD; CANR 5; CD 5, 6; DAM DRAM; DFS 4; DLB 7; INT CANR-5

Medvedev, P. N.
See Bakhtin, Mikhail Mikhailovich

Meged, Aharon
See Megged, Aharon

Meged, Aron
See Megged, Aharon

Megged, Aharon 1920- .... **CLC 9**
See also CA 49-52; CAAS 13; CANR 1, 140; EWL 3

Mehta, Deepa 1950- .... **CLC 208**

Mehta, Gita 1943- .... **CLC 179**
See also CA 225; CN 7; DNFS 2

Mehta, Ved (Parkash) 1934- .... **CLC 37**
See also CA 1-4R, 212; CAAE 212; CANR 2, 23, 69; MTCW 1; MTFW 2005

Melanchthon, Philipp 1497-1560 .... **LC 90**
See also DLB 179

Melanter
See Blackmore, R(ichard) D(oddridge)

Meleager c. 140B.C.-c. 70B.C. ...... **CMLC 53**

Melies, Georges 1861-1938 .... **TCLC 81**

Melikow, Loris
See Hofmannsthal, Hugo von

Melmoth, Sebastian
See Wilde, Oscar (Fingal O'Flahertie Wills)

Melo Neto, Joao Cabral de
See Cabral de Melo Neto, Joao
See also CWW 2; EWL 3

Meltzer, Milton 1915- .... **CLC 26**
See also AAYA 8, 45; BYA 2, 6; CA 13-16R; CANR 38, 92, 107; CLR 13; DLB 61; JRDA; MAICYA 1, 2; SAAS 1; SATA 1, 50, 80, 128; SATA-Essay 124; WYA; YAW

Melville, Herman 1819-1891 ..... **NCLC 3, 12, 29, 45, 49, 91, 93, 123, 157; SSC 1, 17, 46; WLC**
See also AAYA 25; AMW; AMWR 1; CDALB 1640-1865; DA; DA3; DAB; DAC; DAM MST, NOV; DLB 3, 74, 250, 254; EXPN; EXPS; GL 3; LAIT 1, 2; NFS 7, 9; RGAL 4; RGSF 2; SATA 59; SSFS 3; TUS

Members, Mark
See Powell, Anthony (Dymoke)

Membreno, Alejandro .... **CLC 59**

Menand, Louis 1952- .... **CLC 208**
See also CA 200

Menander c. 342B.C.-c. 293B.C. .... **CMLC 9, 51; DC 3**
See also AW 1; CDWLB 1; DAM DRAM; DLB 176; LMFS 1; RGWL 2, 3

Menchu, Rigoberta 1959- .. **CLC 160; HLCS 2**
See also CA 175; CANR 135; DNFS 1; WLIT 1

Mencken, H(enry) L(ouis)
1880-1956 .... **TCLC 13**
See also AMW; CA 105; 125; CDALB 1917-1929; DLB 11, 29, 63, 137, 222; EWL 3; MAL 5; MTCW 1, 2; MTFW 2005; NCFS 4; RGAL 4; TUS

Mendelsohn, Jane 1965- .... **CLC 99**
See also CA 154; CANR 94

Mendoza, Inigo Lopez de
See Santillana, Inigo Lopez de Mendoza, Marques de

Menton, Francisco de
See Chin, Frank (Chew, Jr.)

Mercer, David 1928-1980 .... **CLC 5**
See also CA 9-12R; 102; CANR 23; CBD; DAM DRAM; DLB 13, 310; MTCW 1; RGEL 2

Merchant, Paul
See Ellison, Harlan (Jay)

Meredith, George 1828-1909 .. **PC 60; TCLC 17, 43**
See also CA 117; 153; CANR 80; CDBLB 1832-1890; DAM POET; DLB 18, 35, 57, 159; RGEL 2; TEA

Meredith, William (Morris) 1919- .... **CLC 4, 13, 22, 55; PC 28**
See also CA 9-12R; CAAS 14; CANR 6, 40, 129; CP 1, 2, 3, 4, 5, 6, 7; DAM POET; DLB 5; MAL 5

Merezhkovsky, Dmitrii Sergeevich
See Merezhkovsky, Dmitry Sergeyevich
See also DLB 295

Merezhkovsky, Dmitry Sergeevich
See Merezhkovsky, Dmitry Sergeyevich
See also EWL 3

Merezhkovsky, Dmitry Sergeyevich
1865-1941 .... **TCLC 29**
See Merezhkovsky, Dmitrii Sergeevich;
Merezhkovsky, Dmitry Sergeyevich
See also CA 169

Merimee, Prosper 1803-1870 ... **NCLC 6, 65;
SSC 7, 77**
See also DLB 119, 192; EW 6; EXPS; GFL
1789 to the Present; RGSF 2; RGWL 2,
3; SSFS 8; SUFW

Merkin, Daphne 1954- .... **CLC 44**
See also CA 123

Merleau-Ponty, Maurice
1908-1961 .... **TCLC 156**
See also CA 114; 89-92; DLB 296; GFL
1789 to the Present

Merlin, Arthur
See Blish, James (Benjamin)

Mernissi, Fatima 1940- .... **CLC 171**
See also CA 152; FW

Merrill, James (Ingram) 1926-1995 .. **CLC 2,
3, 6, 8, 13, 18, 34, 91; PC 28; TCLC
173**
See also AMWS 3; CA 13-16R; 147; CANR
10, 49, 63, 108; CP 1, 2, 3, 4; DA3; DAM
POET; DLB 5, 165; DLBY 1985; EWL 3;
INT CANR-10; MAL 5; MTCW 1, 2;
MTFW 2005; PAB; PFS 23; RGAL 4

Merriman, Alex
See Silverberg, Robert

Merriman, Brian 1747-1805 .... **NCLC 70**

Merritt, E. B.
See Waddington, Miriam

Merton, Thomas (James)
1915-1968 . **CLC 1, 3, 11, 34, 83; PC 10**
See also AAYA 61; AMWS 8; CA 5-8R;
25-28R; CANR 22, 53, 111, 131; DA3;
DLB 48; DLBY 1981; MAL 5; MTCW 1,
2; MTFW 2005

Merwin, W(illiam) S(tanley) 1927- ... **CLC 1,
2, 3, 5, 8, 13, 18, 45, 88; PC 45**
See also AMWS 3; CA 13-16R; CANR 15,
51, 112, 140; CP 1, 2, 3, 4, 5, 6, 7; DA3;
DAM POET; DLB 5, 169; EWL 3; INT
CANR-15; MAL 5; MTCW 1, 2; MTFW
2005; PAB; PFS 5, 15; RGAL 4

Metastasio, Pietro 1698-1782 .... **LC 115**
See also RGWL 2, 3

Metcalf, John 1938- .... **CLC 37; SSC 43**
See also CA 113; CN 4, 5, 6, 7; DLB 60;
RGSF 2; TWA

Metcalf, Suzanne
See Baum, L(yman) Frank

Mew, Charlotte (Mary) 1870-1928 .. **TCLC 8**
See also CA 105; 189; DLB 19, 135; RGEL
2

Mewshaw, Michael 1943- .... **CLC 9**
See also CA 53-56; CANR 7, 47; DLBY
1980

Meyer, Conrad Ferdinand
1825-1898 .... **NCLC 81; SSC 30**
See also DLB 129; EW; RGWL 2, 3

Meyer, Gustav 1868-1932
See Meyrink, Gustav
See also CA 117; 190

Meyer, June
See Jordan, June (Meyer)

Meyer, Lynn
See Slavitt, David R(ytman)

Meyers, Jeffrey 1939- .... **CLC 39**
See also CA 73-76; 186; CAAE 186; CANR
54, 102; DLB 111

**Meynell, Alice (Christina Gertrude
Thompson)** 1847-1922 .... **TCLC 6**
See also CA 104; 177; DLB 19, 98; RGEL
2

Meyrink, Gustav .... **TCLC 21**
See Meyer, Gustav
See also DLB 81; EWL 3

Michaels, Leonard 1933-2003 ..... **CLC 6, 25;
SSC 16**
See also CA 61-64; 216; CANR 21, 62, 119;
CN 3, 45, 6, 7; DLB 130; MTCW 1;
TCLE 1:2

Michaux, Henri 1899-1984 .... **CLC 8, 19**
See also CA 85-88; 114; DLB 258; EWL 3;
GFL 1789 to the Present; RGWL 2, 3

Micheaux, Oscar (Devereaux)
1884-1951 .... **TCLC 76**
See also BW 3; CA 174; DLB 50; TCWW
2

Michelangelo 1475-1564 .... **LC 12**
See also AAYA 43

Michelet, Jules 1798-1874 .... **NCLC 31**
See also EW 5; GFL 1789 to the Present

Michels, Robert 1876-1936 .... **TCLC 88**
See also CA 212

Michener, James A(lbert)
1907(?)-1997 .. **CLC 1, 5, 11, 29, 60, 109**
See also AAYA 27; AITN 1; BEST 90:1;
BPFB 2; CA 5-8R; 161; CANR 21, 45,
68; CN 1, 2, 3, 4, 5, 6; CPW; DA3; DAM
NOV, POP; DLB 6; MAL 5; MTCW 1, 2;
MTFW 2005; RHW; TCWW 1, 2

Mickiewicz, Adam 1798-1855 . **NCLC 3, 101;
PC 38**
See also EW 5; RGWL 2, 3

Middleton, (John) Christopher
1926- .... **CLC 13**
See also CA 13-16R; CANR 29, 54, 117;
CP 1, 2, 3, 4, 5, 6, 7; DLB 40

Middleton, Richard (Barham)
1882-1911 .... **TCLC 56**
See also CA 187; DLB 156; HGG

Middleton, Stanley 1919- .... **CLC 7, 38**
See also CA 25-28R; CAAS 23; CANR 21,
46, 81; CN 1, 2, 3, 4, 5, 6, 7; DLB 14

Middleton, Thomas 1580-1627 ...... **DC 5; LC
33, 123**
See also BRW 2; DAM DRAM, MST; DFS
18, 22; DLB 58; RGEL 2

Migueis, Jose Rodrigues 1901-1980 . **CLC 10**
See also DLB 287

Mikszath, Kalman 1847-1910 .... **TCLC 31**
See also CA 170

Miles, Jack .... **CLC 100**
See also CA 200

Miles, John Russiano
See Miles, Jack

Miles, Josephine (Louise)
1911-1985 .... **CLC 1, 2, 14, 34, 39**
See also CA 1-4R; 116; CANR 2, 55; CP 1,
2, 3, 4; DAM POET; DLB 48; MAL 5;
TCLE 1:2

Militant
See Sandburg, Carl (August)

Mill, Harriet (Hardy) Taylor
1807-1858 .... **NCLC 102**
See also FW

Mill, John Stuart 1806-1873 .... **NCLC 11, 58**
See also CDBLB 1832-1890; DLB 55, 190,
262; FW 1; RGEL 2; TEA

Millar, Kenneth 1915-1983 .... **CLC 14**
See Macdonald, Ross
See also CA 9-12R; 110; CANR 16, 63,
107; CMW 4; CPW; DA3; DAM POP;
DLB 2, 226; DLBD 6; DLBY 1983;
MTCW 1, 2; MTFW 2005

Millay, E. Vincent
See Millay, Edna St. Vincent

Millay, Edna St. Vincent 1892-1950 ..... **PC 6,
61; TCLC 4, 49, 169; WLCS**
See Boyd, Nancy
See also AMW; CA 104; 130; CDALB
1917-1929; DA; DA3; DAB; DAC; DAM
MST, POET; DLB 45, 249; EWL 3;
EXPP; FL 1:6; MAL 5; MAWW; MTCW
1, 2; MTFW 2005; PAB; PFS 3, 17;
RGAL 4; TUS; WP

Miller, Arthur 1915-2005 ..... **CLC 1, 2, 6, 10,
15, 26, 47, 78, 179; DC 1; WLC**
See also AAYA 15; AITN 1; AMW; AMWC
1; CA 1-4R; 236; CABS 3; CAD; CANR
2, 30, 54, 76, 132; CD 5, 6; CDALB
1941-1968; DA; DA3; DAB; DAC; DAM
DRAM, MST; DFS 1, 3, 8; DLB 7, 266;
EWL 3; LAIT 1, 4; LATS 1:2; MAL 5;
MTCW 1, 2; MTFW 2005; RGAL 4;
TUS; WYAS 1

Miller, Henry (Valentine)
1891-1980 .... **CLC 1, 2, 4, 9, 14, 43, 84;
WLC**
See also AMW; BPFB 2; CA 9-12R, 97-
100; CANR 33, 64; CDALB 1929-1941;
CN 1, 2; DA; DA3; DAB; DAC; DAM
MST, NOV; DLB 4, 9; DLBY 1980; EWL
3; MAL 5; MTCW 1, 2; MTFW 2005;
RGAL 4; TUS

Miller, Hugh 1802-1856 .... **NCLC 143**
See also DLB 190

Miller, Jason 1939(?)-2001 .... **CLC 2**
See also AITN 1; CA 73-76; 197; CAD;
CANR 130; DFS 12; DLB 7

Miller, Sue 1943- .... **CLC 44**
See also AMWS 12; BEST 90:3; CA 139;
CANR 59, 91, 128; DA3; DAM POP;
DLB 143

Miller, Walter M(ichael, Jr.)
1923-1996 .... **CLC 4, 30**
See also BPFB 2; CA 85-88; CANR 108;
DLB 8; SCFW 1, 2; SFW 4

Millett, Kate 1934- .... **CLC 67**
See also AITN 1; CA 73-76; CANR 32, 53,
76, 110; DA3; DLB 246; FW; GLL 1;
MTCW 1, 2; MTFW 2005

Millhauser, Steven (Lewis) 1943- .... **CLC 21,
54, 109; SSC 57**
See also CA 110; 111; CANR 63, 114, 133;
CN 6, 7; DA3; DLB 2; FANT; INT CA-
111; MAL 5; MTCW 2; MTFW 2005

Millin, Sarah Gertrude 1889-1968 ... **CLC 49**
See also CA 102; 93-96; DLB 225; EWL 3

Milne, A(lan) A(lexander)
1882-1956 .... **TCLC 6, 88**
See also BRWS 5; CA 104; 133; CLR 1,
26; CMW 4; CWRI 5; DA3; DAB; DAC;
DAM MST; DLB 10, 77, 100, 160; FANT;
MAICYA 1, 2; MTCW 1, 2; MTFW 2005;
RGEL 2; SATA 100; WCH; YABC 1

Milner, Ron(ald) 1938-2004 ..... **BLC 3; CLC
56**
See also AITN 1; BW 1; CA 73-76; 230;
CAD; CANR 24, 81; CD 5, 6; DAM
MULT; DLB 38; MAL 5; MTCW 1

Milnes, Richard Monckton
1809-1885 .... **NCLC 61**
See also DLB 32, 184

Milosz, Czeslaw 1911-2004 .... **CLC 5, 11, 22,
31, 56, 82; PC 8; WLCS**
See also AAYA 62; CA 81-84; 230; CANR
23, 51, 91, 126; CDWLB 4; CWW 2;
DA3; DAM MST, POET; DLB 215; EW
13; EWL 3; MTCW 1, 2; MTFW 2005;
PFS 16; RGWL 2, 3

Milton, John 1608-1674 ..... **LC 9, 43, 92; PC
19, 29; WLC**
See also AAYA 65; BRW 2; BRWR 2; CD-
BLB 1660-1789; DA; DA3; DAB; DAC;
DAM MST, POET; DLB 131, 151, 281;
EFS 1; EXPP; LAIT 1; PAB; PFS 3, 17;
RGEL 2; TEA; WLIT 3; WP

Niven, Laurence Van Cott 1938-
See Niven, Larry
See also CA 21-24R, 207; CAAE 207; CAAS 12; CANR 14, 44, 66, 113; CPW; DAM POP; MTCW 1, 2; SATA 95; SFW 4

Nixon, Agnes Eckhardt 1927- .... **CLC 21**
See also CA 110

Nizan, Paul 1905-1940 .... **TCLC 40**
See also CA 161; DLB 72; EWL 3; GFL 1789 to the Present

Nkosi, Lewis 1936- .... **BLC 3; CLC 45**
See also BW 1, 3; CA 65-68; CANR 27, 81; CBD; CD 5, 6; DAM MULT; DLB 157, 225; WWE 1

Nodier, (Jean) Charles (Emmanuel)
1780-1844 .... **NCLC 19**
See also DLB 119; GFL 1789 to the Present

Noguchi, Yone 1875-1947 .... **TCLC 80**

Nolan, Christopher 1965- .... **CLC 58**
See also CA 111; CANR 88

Noon, Jeff 1957- .... **CLC 91**
See also CA 148; CANR 83; DLB 267; SFW 4

Norden, Charles
See Durrell, Lawrence (George)

Nordhoff, Charles Bernard
1887-1947 .... **TCLC 23**
See also CA 108; 211; DLB 9; LAIT 1; RHW 1; SATA 23

Norfolk, Lawrence 1963- .... **CLC 76**
See also CA 144; CANR 85; CN 6, 7; DLB 267

Norman, Marsha (Williams) 1947- . **CLC 28, 186; DC 8**
See also CA 105; CABS 3; CAD; CANR 41, 131; CD 5, 6; CSW; CWD; DAM DRAM; DFS 2; DLB 266; DLBY 1984; FW; MAL 5

Normyx
See Douglas, (George) Norman

Norris, (Benjamin) Frank(lin, Jr.)
1870-1902 .... **SSC 28; TCLC 24, 155**
See also AAYA 57; AMW; AMWC 2; BPFB 2; CA 110; 160; CDALB 1865-1917; DLB 12, 71, 186; LMFS 2; NFS 12; RGAL 4; TCWW 1, 2; TUS

Norris, Leslie 1921- .... **CLC 14**
See also CA 11-12; CANR 14, 117; CAP 1; CP 1, 2, 3, 4, 5, 6, 7; DLB 27, 256

North, Andrew
See Norton, Andre

North, Anthony
See Koontz, Dean R.

North, Captain George
See Stevenson, Robert Louis (Balfour)

North, Captain George
See Stevenson, Robert Louis (Balfour)

North, Milou
See Erdrich, (Karen) Louise

Northrup, B. A.
See Hubbard, L(afayette) Ron(ald)

North Staffs
See Hulme, T(homas) E(rnest)

Northup, Solomon 1808-1863 ...... **NCLC 105**

Norton, Alice Mary
See Norton, Andre
See also MAICYA 1; SATA 1, 43

Norton, Andre 1912-2005 .... **CLC 12**
See Norton, Alice Mary
See also AAYA 14; BPFB 2; BYA 4, 10, 12; CA 1-4R; 237; CANR 68; CLR 50; DLB 8, 52; JRDA; MAICYA 2; MTCW 1; SATA 91; SUFW 1, 2; YAW

Norton, Caroline 1808-1877 .... **NCLC 47**
See also DLB 21, 159, 199

Norway, Nevil Shute 1899-1960
See Shute, Nevil
See also CA 102; 93-96; CANR 85; MTCW 2

Norwid, Cyprian Kamil
1821-1883 .... **NCLC 17**
See also RGWL 3

Nosille, Nabrah
See Ellison, Harlan (Jay)

Nossack, Hans Erich 1901-1978 .... **CLC 6**
See also CA 93-96; 85-88; DLB 69; EWL 3

Nostradamus 1503-1566 .... **LC 27**

Nosu, Chuji
See Ozu, Yasujiro

Notenburg, Eleanora (Genrikhovna) von
See Guro, Elena (Genrikhovna)

Nova, Craig 1945- .... **CLC 7, 31**
See also CA 45-48; CANR 2, 53, 127

Novak, Joseph
See Kosinski, Jerzy (Nikodem)

Novalis 1772-1801 .... **NCLC 13**
See also CDWLB 2; DLB 90; EW 5; RGWL 2, 3

Novick, Peter 1934- .... **CLC 164**
See also CA 188

Novis, Emile
See Weil, Simone (Adolphine)

Nowlan, Alden (Albert) 1933-1983 ... **CLC 15**
See also CA 9-12R; CANR 5; CP 1, 2, 3; DAC; DAM MST; DLB 53; PFS 12

Noyes, Alfred 1880-1958 ...... **PC 27; TCLC 7**
See also CA 104; 188; DLB 20; EXPP; FANT; PFS 4; RGEL 2

Nugent, Richard Bruce
1906(?)-1987 .... **HR 1:3**
See also BW 1; CA 125; DLB 51; GLL 2

Nunn, Kem .... **CLC 34**
See also CA 159

Nussbaum, Martha Craven 1947- .. **CLC 203**
See also CA 134; CANR 102

Nwapa, Flora (Nwanzuruaha)
1931-1993 .... **BLCS; CLC 133**
See also BW 2; CA 143; CANR 83; CD-WLB 3; CWRI 5; DLB 125; EWL 3; WLIT 2

Nye, Robert 1939- .... **CLC 13, 42**
See also BRWS 10; CA 33-36R; CANR 29, 67, 107; CN 1, 2, 3, 4, 5, 6, 7; CP 1, 2, 3, 4, 5, 6, 7; CWRI 5; DAM NOV; DLB 14, 271; FANT; HGG; MTCW 1; RHW; SATA 6

Nyro, Laura 1947-1997 .... **CLC 17**
See also CA 194

Oates, Joyce Carol 1938- .. **CLC 1, 2, 3, 6, 9, 11, 15, 19, 33, 52, 108, 134; SSC 6, 70; WLC**
See also AAYA 15, 52; AITN 1; AMWS 2; BEST 89:2; BPFB 2; BYA 11; CA 5-8R; CANR 25, 45, 74, 113, 129; CDALB 1968-1988; CN 1, 2, 3, 4, 5, 6, 7; CP 7; CPW; CWP; DA; DA3; DAB; DAC; DAM MST, NOV, POP; DLB 2, 5, 130; DLBY 1981; EWL 3; EXPS; FL 1:6; FW; GL 3; HGG; INT CANR-25; LAIT 4; MAL 5; MAWW; MTCW 1, 2; MTFW 2005; NFS 8; RGAL 4; RGSF 2; SATA 159; SSFS 1, 8, 17; SUFW 2; TUS

O'Brian, E. G.
See Clarke, Arthur C(harles)

O'Brian, Patrick 1914-2000 .... **CLC 152**
See also AAYA 55; CA 144; 187; CANR 74; CPW; MTCW 2; MTFW 2005; RHW

O'Brien, Darcy 1939-1998 .... **CLC 11**
See also CA 21-24R; 167; CANR 8, 59

O'Brien, Edna 1932- ..... **CLC 3, 5, 8, 13, 36, 65, 116; SSC 10, 77**
See also BRWS 5; CA 1-4R; CANR 6, 41, 65, 102; CDBLB 1960 to Present; CN 1, 2, 3, 4, 5, 6, 7; DA3; DAM NOV; DLB 14, 231, 319; EWL 3; FW; MTCW 1, 2; MTFW 2005; RGSF 2; WLIT 4

O'Brien, Fitz-James 1828-1862 ..... **NCLC 21**
See also DLB 74; RGAL 4; SUFW

O'Brien, Flann .... **CLC 1, 4, 5, 7, 10, 47**
See O Nuallain, Brian
See also BRWS 2; DLB 231; EWL 3; RGEL 2

O'Brien, Richard 1942- .... **CLC 17**
See also CA 124

O'Brien, (William) Tim(othy) 1946- . **CLC 7, 19, 40, 103, 211; SSC 74**
See also AAYA 16; AMWS 5; CA 85-88; CANR 40, 58, 133; CDALBS; CN 5, 6, 7; CPW; DA3; DAM POP; DLB 152; DLBD 9; DLBY 1980; LATS 1:2; MAL 5; MTCW 2; MTFW 2005; RGAL 4; SSFS 5, 15; TCLE 1:2

Obstfelder, Sigbjoern 1866-1900 .... **TCLC 23**
See also CA 123

O'Casey, Sean 1880-1964 .... **CLC 1, 5, 9, 11, 15, 88; DC 12; WLCS**
See also BRW 7; CA 89-92; CANR 62; CBD; CDBLB 1914-1945; DA3; DAB; DAC; DAM DRAM, MST; DFS 19; DLB 10; EWL 3; MTCW 1, 2; MTFW 2005; RGEL 2; TEA; WLIT 4

O'Cathasaigh, Sean
See O'Casey, Sean

Occom, Samson 1723-1792 .... **LC 60; NNAL**
See also DLB 175

Ochs, Phil(ip David) 1940-1976 .... **CLC 17**
See also CA 185; 65-68

O'Connor, Edwin (Greene)
1918-1968 .... **CLC 14**
See also CA 93-96; 25-28R; MAL 5

O'Connor, (Mary) Flannery
1925-1964 .... **CLC 1, 2, 3, 6, 10, 13, 15, 21, 66, 104; SSC 1, 23, 61, 82; TCLC 132; WLC**
See also AAYA 7; AMW; AMWR 2; BPFB 3; BYA 16; CA 1-4R; CANR 3, 41; CDALB 1941-1968; DA; DA3; DAB; DAC; DAM MST, NOV; DLB 2, 152; DLBD 12; DLBY 1980; EWL 3; EXPS; LAIT 5; MAL 5; MAWW; MTCW 1, 2; MTFW 2005; NFS 3, 21; RGAL 4; RGSF 2; SSFS 2, 7, 10, 19; TUS

O'Connor, Frank .... **CLC 23; SSC 5**
See O'Donovan, Michael Francis
See also DLB 162; EWL 3; RGSF 2; SSFS 5

O'Dell, Scott 1898-1989 .... **CLC 30**
See also AAYA 3, 44; BPFB 3; BYA 1, 2, 3, 5; CA 61-64; 129; CANR 12, 30, 112; CLR 1, 16; DLB 52; JRDA; MAICYA 1, 2; SATA 12, 60, 134; WYA; YAW

Odets, Clifford 1906-1963 ..... **CLC 2, 28, 98; DC 6**
See also AMWS 2; CA 85-88; CAD; CANR 62; DAM DRAM; DFS 3, 17, 20; DLB 7, 26; EWL 3; MAL 5; MTCW 1, 2; MTFW 2005; RGAL 4; TUS

O'Doherty, Brian 1928- .... **CLC 76**
See also CA 105; CANR 108

O'Donnell, K. M.
See Malzberg, Barry N(athaniel)

O'Donnell, Lawrence
See Kuttner, Henry

O'Donovan, Michael Francis
1903-1966 .... **CLC 14**
See O'Connor, Frank
See also CA 93-96; CANR 84

Pinsky, Robert 1940- .... **CLC 9, 19, 38, 94, 121, 216; PC 27**
See also AMWS 6; CA 29-32R; CAAS 4; CANR 58, 97, 138; CP 3, 4, 5, 6, 7; DA3; DAM POET; DLBY 1982, 1998; MAL 5; MTCW 2; MTFW 2005; PFS 18; RGAL 4; TCLE 1:2

Pinta, Harold
See Pinter, Harold

Pinter, Harold 1930- .. **CLC 1, 3, 6, 9, 11, 15, 27, 58, 73, 199; DC 15; WLC**
See also BRWR 1; BRWS 1; CA 5-8R; CANR 33, 65, 112, 145; CBD; CD 5, 6; CDBLB 1960 to Present; CP 1; DA; DA3; DAB; DAC; DAM DRAM, MST; DFS 3, 5, 7, 14; DLB 13, 310; EWL 3; IDFW 3, 4; LMFS 2; MTCW 1, 2; MTFW 2005; RGEL 2; TEA

Piozzi, Hester Lynch (Thrale)
1741-1821 .... **NCLC 57**
See also DLB 104, 142

Pirandello, Luigi 1867-1936 .. **DC 5; SSC 22; TCLC 4, 29, 172; WLC**
See also CA 104; 153; CANR 103; DA; DA3; DAB; DAC; DAM DRAM, MST; DFS 4, 9; DLB 264; EW 8; EWL 3; MTCW 2; MTFW 2005; RGSF 2; RGWL 2, 3; WLIT 7

Pirsig, Robert M(aynard) 1928- ... **CLC 4, 6, 73**
See also CA 53-56; CANR 42, 74; CPW 1; DA3; DAM POP; MTCW 1, 2; MTFW 2005; SATA 39

Pisarev, Dmitrii Ivanovich
See Pisarev, Dmitry Ivanovich
See also DLB 277

Pisarev, Dmitry Ivanovich
1840-1868 .... **NCLC 25**
See Pisarev, Dmitrii Ivanovich

Pix, Mary (Griffith) 1666-1709 .... **LC 8**
See also DLB 80

Pixerecourt, (Rene Charles) Guilbert de
1773-1844 .... **NCLC 39**
See also DLB 192; GFL 1789 to the Present

Plaatje, Sol(omon) T(shekisho)
1878-1932 .... **BLCS; TCLC 73**
See also BW 2, 3; CA 141; CANR 79; DLB 125, 225

Plaidy, Jean
See Hibbert, Eleanor Alice Burford

Planche, James Robinson
1796-1880 .... **NCLC 42**
See also RGEL 2

Plant, Robert 1948- .... **CLC 12**

Plante, David (Robert) 1940- . **CLC 7, 23, 38**
See also CA 37-40R; CANR 12, 36, 58, 82; CN 2, 3, 4, 5, 6, 7; DAM NOV; DLBY 1983; INT CANR-12; MTCW 1

Plath, Sylvia 1932-1963 ..... **CLC 1, 2, 3, 5, 9, 11, 14, 17, 50, 51, 62, 111; PC 1, 37; WLC**
See also AAYA 13; AMWR 2; AMWS 1; BPFB 3; CA 19-20; CANR 34, 101; CAP 2; CDALB 1941-1968; DA; DA3; DAB; DAC; DAM MST, POET; DLB 5, 6, 152; EWL 3; EXPN; EXPP; FL 1:6; FW; LAIT 4; MAL 5; MAWW; MTCW 1, 2; MTFW 2005; NFS 1; PAB; PFS 1, 15; RGAL 4; SATA 96; TUS; WP; YAW

Plato c. 428B.C.-347B.C. .... **CMLC 8, 75; WLCS**
See also AW 1; CDWLB 1; DA; DA3; DAB; DAC; DAM MST; DLB 176; LAIT 1; LATS 1:1; RGWL 2, 3

Platonov, Andrei
See Klimentov, Andrei Platonovich

Platonov, Andrei Platonovich
See Klimentov, Andrei Platonovich
See also DLB 272

Platonov, Andrey Platonovich
See Klimentov, Andrei Platonovich
See also EWL 3

Platt, Kin 1911- .... **CLC 26**
See also AAYA 11; CA 17-20R; CANR 11; JRDA; SAAS 17; SATA 21, 86; WYA

Plautus c. 254B.C.-c. 184B.C. ...... **CMLC 24; DC 6**
See also AW 1; CDWLB 1; DLB 211; RGWL 2, 3

Plick et Plock
See Simenon, Georges (Jacques Christian)

Plieksans, Janis
See Rainis, Janis

Plimpton, George (Ames)
1927-2003 .... **CLC 36**
See also AITN 1; CA 21-24R; 224; CANR 32, 70, 103, 133; DLB 185, 241; MTCW 1, 2; MTFW 2005; SATA 10; SATA-Obit 150

Pliny the Elder c. 23-79 .... **CMLC 23**
See also DLB 211

Pliny the Younger c. 61-c. 112 ...... **CMLC 62**
See also AW 2; DLB 211

Plomer, William Charles Franklin
1903-1973 .... **CLC 4, 8**
See also AFW; BRWS 11; CA 21-22; CANR 34; CAP 2; CN 1; CP 1, 2; DLB 20, 162, 191, 225; EWL 3; MTCW 1; RGEL 2; RGSF 2; SATA 24

Plotinus 204-270 .... **CMLC 46**
See also CDWLB 1; DLB 176

Plowman, Piers
See Kavanagh, Patrick (Joseph)

Plum, J.
See Wodehouse, P(elham) G(renville)

Plumly, Stanley (Ross) 1939- .... **CLC 33**
See also CA 108; 110; CANR 97; CP 3, 4, 5, 6, 7; DLB 5, 193; INT CA-110

Plumpe, Friedrich Wilhelm
1888-1931 .... **TCLC 53**
See also CA 112

Plutarch c. 46-c. 120 .... **CMLC 60**
See also AW 2; CDWLB 1; DLB 176; RGWL 2, 3; TWA

Po Chu-i 772-846 .... **CMLC 24**

Podhoretz, Norman 1930- .... **CLC 189**
See also AMWS 8; CA 9-12R; CANR 7, 78, 135

Poe, Edgar Allan 1809-1849 ..... **NCLC 1, 16, 55, 78, 94, 97, 117; PC 1, 54; SSC 1, 22, 34, 35, 54, 88; WLC**
See also AAYA 14; AMW; AMWC 1; AMWR 2; BPFB 3; BYA 5, 11; CDALB 1640-1865; CMW 4; DA; DA3; DAB; DAC; DAM MST, POET; DLB 3, 59, 73, 74, 248, 254; EXPP; EXPS; GL 3; HGG; LAIT 2; LATS 1:1; LMFS 1; MSW; PAB; PFS 1, 3, 9; RGAL 4; RGSF 2; SATA 23; SCFW 1, 2; SFW 4; SSFS 2, 4, 7, 8, 16; SUFW; TUS; WP; WYA

Poet of Titchfield Street, The
See Pound, Ezra (Weston Loomis)

Pohl, Frederik 1919- .... **CLC 18; SSC 25**
See also AAYA 24; CA 61-64; 188; CAAE 188; CAAS 1; CANR 11, 37, 81, 140; CN 1, 2, 3, 4, 5, 6; DLB 8; INT CANR-11; MTCW 1, 2; MTFW 2005; SATA 24; SCFW 1, 2; SFW 4

Poirier, Louis 1910-
See Gracq, Julien
See also CA 122; 126; CANR 141

Poitier, Sidney 1927- .... **CLC 26**
See also AAYA 60; BW 1; CA 117; CANR 94

Pokagon, Simon 1830-1899 .... **NNAL**
See also DAM MULT

Polanski, Roman 1933- .... **CLC 16, 178**
See also CA 77-80

Poliakoff, Stephen 1952- .... **CLC 38**
See also CA 106; CANR 116; CBD; CD 5, 6; DLB 13

Police, The
See Copeland, Stewart (Armstrong); Summers, Andrew James

Polidori, John William 1795-1821 . **NCLC 51**
See also DLB 116; HGG

Poliziano, Angelo 1454-1494 .... **LC 120**
See also WLIT 7

Pollitt, Katha 1949- .... **CLC 28, 122**
See also CA 120; 122; CANR 66, 108; MTCW 1, 2; MTFW 2005

Pollock, (Mary) Sharon 1936- .... **CLC 50**
See also CA 141; CANR 132; CD 5; CWD; DAC; DAM DRAM, MST; DFS 3; DLB 60; FW

Pollock, Sharon 1936- .... **DC 20**
See also CD 6

Polo, Marco 1254-1324 .... **CMLC 15**
See also WLIT 7

Polonsky, Abraham (Lincoln)
1910-1999 .... **CLC 92**
See also CA 104; 187; DLB 26; INT CA-104

Polybius c. 200B.C.-c. 118B.C. ...... **CMLC 17**
See also AW 1; DLB 176; RGWL 2, 3

Pomerance, Bernard 1940- .... **CLC 13**
See also CA 101; CAD; CANR 49, 134; CD 5, 6; DAM DRAM; DFS 9; LAIT 2

Ponge, Francis 1899-1988 .... **CLC 6, 18**
See also CA 85-88; 126; CANR 40, 86; DAM POET; DLBY 2002; EWL 3; GFL 1789 to the Present; RGWL 2, 3

Poniatowska, Elena 1933- . **CLC 140; HLC 2**
See also CA 101; CANR 32, 66, 107; CD-WLB 3; CWW 2; DAM MULT; DLB 113; EWL 3; HW 1, 2; LAWS 1; WLIT 1

Pontoppidan, Henrik 1857-1943 .... **TCLC 29**
See also CA 170; DLB 300

Ponty, Maurice Merleau
See Merleau-Ponty, Maurice

Poole, Josephine .... **CLC 17**
See Helyar, Jane Penelope Josephine
See also SAAS 2; SATA 5

Popa, Vasko 1922-1991 . **CLC 19; TCLC 167**
See also CA 112; 148; CDWLB 4; DLB 181; EWL 3; RGWL 2, 3

Pope, Alexander 1688-1744 ...... **LC 3, 58, 60, 64; PC 26; WLC**
See also BRW 3; BRWC 1; BRWR 1; CD-BLB 1660-1789; DA; DA3; DAB; DAC; DAM MST, POET; DLB 95, 101, 213; EXPP; PAB; PFS 12; RGEL 2; WLIT 3; WP

Popov, Evgenii Anatol'evich
See Popov, Yevgeny
See also DLB 285

Popov, Yevgeny .... **CLC 59**
See Popov, Evgenii Anatol'evich

Poquelin, Jean-Baptiste
See Moliere

Porete, Marguerite (?)-1310 .... **CMLC 73**
See also DLB 208

Porphyry c. 233-c. 305 .... **CMLC 71**

Porter, Connie (Rose) 1959(?)- .... **CLC 70**
See also AAYA 65; BW 2, 3; CA 142; CANR 90, 109; SATA 81, 129

Porter, Gene(va Grace) Stratton .. **TCLC 21**
See Stratton-Porter, Gene(va Grace)
See also BPFB 3; CA 112; CWRI 5; RHW

Porter, Katherine Anne 1890-1980 ... **CLC 1, 3, 7, 10, 13, 15, 27, 101; SSC 4, 31, 43**
See also AAYA 42; AITN 2; AMW; BPFB 3; CA 1-4R; 101; CANR 1, 65; CDALBS; CN 1, 2; DA; DA3; DAB; DAC; DAM MST, NOV; DLB 4, 9, 102; DLBD 12; DLBY 1980; EWL 3; EXPS; LAIT 3;

MAL 5; MAWW; MTCW 1, 2; MTFW
2005; NFS 14; RGAL 4; RGSF 2; SATA
39; SATA-Obit 23; SSFS 1, 8, 11, 16;
TCWW 2; TUS

Porter, Peter (Neville Frederick)
  1929- .... **CLC 5, 13, 33**
  See also CA 85-88; CP 1, 2, 3, 4, 5, 6, 7;
  DLB 40, 289; WWE 1

Porter, William Sydney 1862-1910
  See Henry, O.
  See also CA 104; 131; CDALB 1865-1917;
  DA; DA3; DAB; DAC; DAM MST; DLB
  12, 78, 79; MAL 5; MTCW 1, 2; MTFW
  2005; TUS; YABC 2

Portillo (y Pacheco), Jose Lopez
  See Lopez Portillo (y Pacheco), Jose

Portillo Trambley, Estela 1927-1998 .. **HLC 2**
  See Trambley, Estela Portillo
  See also CANR 32; DAM MULT; DLB
  209; HW 1

Posey, Alexander (Lawrence)
  1873-1908 .... **NNAL**
  See also CA 144; CANR 80; DAM MULT;
  DLB 175

Posse, Abel .... **CLC 70**

Post, Melville Davisson
  1869-1930 .... **TCLC 39**
  See also CA 110; 202; CMW 4

Potok, Chaim 1929-2002 ... **CLC 2, 7, 14, 26,
  112**
  See also AAYA 15, 50; AITN 1, 2; BPFB 3;
  BYA 1; CA 17-20R; 208; CANR 19, 35,
  64, 98; CLR 92; CN 4, 5, 6; DA3; DAM
  NOV; DLB 28, 152; EXPN; INT CANR-
  19; LAIT 4; MTCW 1, 2; MTFW 2005;
  NFS 4; SATA 33, 106; SATA-Obit 134;
  TUS; YAW

Potok, Herbert Harold -2002
  See Potok, Chaim

Potok, Herman Harold
  See Potok, Chaim

Potter, Dennis (Christopher George)
  1935-1994 .... **CLC 58, 86, 123**
  See also BRWS 10; CA 107; 145; CANR
  33, 61; CBD; DLB 233; MTCW 1

Pound, Ezra (Weston Loomis)
  1885-1972 .. **CLC 1, 2, 3, 4, 5, 7, 10, 13,
  18, 34, 48, 50, 112; PC 4; WLC**
  See also AAYA 47; AMW; AMWR 1; CA
  5-8R; 37-40R; CANR 40; CDALB 1917-
  1929; CP 1; DA; DA3; DAB; DAC; DAM
  MST, POET; DLB 4, 45, 63; DLBD 15;
  EFS 2; EWL 3; EXPP; LMFS 2; MAL 5;
  MTCW 1, 2; MTFW 2005; PAB; PFS 2,
  8, 16; RGAL 4; TUS; WP

Povod, Reinaldo 1959-1994 .... **CLC 44**
  See also CA 136; 146; CANR 83

Powell, Adam Clayton, Jr.
  1908-1972 .... **BLC 3; CLC 89**
  See also BW 1, 3; CA 102; 33-36R; CANR
  86; DAM MULT

Powell, Anthony (Dymoke)
  1905-2000 .... **CLC 1, 3, 7, 9, 10, 31**
  See also BRW 7; CA 1-4R; 189; CANR 1,
  32, 62, 107; CDBLB 1945-1960; CN 1, 2,
  3, 4, 5, 6; DLB 15; EWL 3; MTCW 1, 2;
  MTFW 2005; RGEL 2; TEA

Powell, Dawn 1896(?)-1965 .... **CLC 66**
  See also CA 5-8R; CANR 121; DLBY 1997

Powell, Padgett 1952- .... **CLC 34**
  See also CA 126; CANR 63, 101; CSW;
  DLB 234; DLBY 01

Powell, (Oval) Talmage 1920-2000
  See Queen, Ellery
  See also CA 5-8R; CANR 2, 80

Power, Susan 1961- .... **CLC 91**
  See also BYA 14; CA 160; CANR 135; NFS
  11

Powers, J(ames) F(arl) 1917-1999 ..... **CLC 1,
  4, 8, 57; SSC 4**
  See also CA 1-4R; 181; CANR 2, 61; CN
  1, 2, 3, 4, 5, 6; DLB 130; MTCW 1;
  RGAL 4; RGSF 2

Powers, John J(ames) 1945-
  See Powers, John R.
  See also CA 69-72

Powers, John R. .... **CLC 66**
  See Powers, John J(ames)

Powers, Richard (S.) 1957- .... **CLC 93**
  See also AMWS 9; BPFB 3; CA 148;
  CANR 80; CN 6, 7; MTFW 2005; TCLE
  1:2

Pownall, David 1938- .... **CLC 10**
  See also CA 89-92; 180; CAAS 18; CANR
  49, 101; CBD; CD 5, 6; CN 4, 5, 6;
  DLB 14

Powys, John Cowper 1872-1963 ... **CLC 7, 9,
  15, 46, 125**
  See also CA 85-88; CANR 106; DLB 15,
  255; EWL 3; FANT; MTCW 1, 2; MTFW
  2005; RGEL 2; SUFW

Powys, T(heodore) F(rancis)
  1875-1953 .... **TCLC 9**
  See also BRWS 8; CA 106; 189; DLB 36,
  162; EWL 3; FANT; RGEL 2; SUFW

Pozzo, Modesta
  See Fonte, Moderata

Prado (Calvo), Pedro 1886-1952 ... **TCLC 75**
  See also CA 131; DLB 283; HW 1; LAW

Prager, Emily 1952- .... **CLC 56**
  See also CA 204

Pratchett, Terry 1948- .... **CLC 197**
  See also AAYA 19, 54; BPFB 3; CA 143;
  CANR 87, 126; CLR 64; CN 6, 7; CPW;
  CWRI 5; FANT; MTFW 2005; SATA 82,
  139; SFW 4; SUFW 2

Pratolini, Vasco 1913-1991 .... **TCLC 124**
  See also CA 211; DLB 177; EWL 3; RGWL
  2, 3

Pratt, E(dwin) J(ohn) 1883(?)-1964 . **CLC 19**
  See also CA 141; 93-96; CANR 77; DAC;
  DAM POET; DLB 92; EWL 3; RGEL 2;
  TWA

Premchand .... **TCLC 21**
  See Srivastava, Dhanpat Rai
  See also EWL 3

Prescott, William Hickling
  1796-1859 .... **NCLC 163**
  See also DLB 1, 30, 59, 235

Preseren, France 1800-1849 .... **NCLC 127**
  See also CDWLB 4; DLB 147

Preussler, Otfried 1923- .... **CLC 17**
  See also CA 77-80; SATA 24

Prevert, Jacques (Henri Marie)
  1900-1977 .... **CLC 15**
  See also CA 77-80; 69-72; CANR 29, 61;
  DLB 258; EWL 3; GFL 1789 to the
  Present; IDFW 3, 4; MTCW 1; RGWL 2,
  3; SATA-Obit 30

Prevost, (Antoine Francois)
  1697-1763 .... **LC 1**
  See also DLB 314; EW 4; GFL Beginnings
  to 1789; RGWL 2, 3

Price, (Edward) Reynolds 1933- ... **CLC 3, 6,
  13, 43, 50, 63, 212; SSC 22**
  See also AMWS 6; CA 1-4R; CANR 1, 37,
  57, 87, 128; CN 1, 2, 3, 4, 5, 6, 7; CSW;
  DAM NOV; DLB 2, 218, 278; EWL 3;
  INT CANR-37; MAL 5; MTFW 2005;
  NFS 18

Price, Richard 1949- .... **CLC 6, 12**
  See also CA 49-52; CANR 3; CN 7; DLBY
  1981

Prichard, Katharine Susannah
  1883-1969 .... **CLC 46**
  See also CA 11-12; CANR 33; CAP 1; DLB
  260; MTCW 1; RGEL 2; RGSF 2; SATA
  66

Priestley, J(ohn) B(oynton)
  1894-1984 .... **CLC 2, 5, 9, 34**
  See also BRW 7; CA 9-12R; 113; CANR
  33; CDBLB 1914-1945; CN 1, 2, 3; DA3;
  DAM DRAM, NOV; DLB 10, 34, 77,
  100, 139; DLBY 1984; EWL 3; MTCW
  1, 2; MTFW 2005; RGEL 2; SFW 4

Prince 1958- .... **CLC 35**
  See also CA 213

Prince, F(rank) T(empleton)
  1912-2003 .... **CLC 22**
  See also CA 101; 219; CANR 43, 79; CP 1,
  2, 3, 4, 5, 6, 7; DLB 20

Prince Kropotkin
  See Kropotkin, Peter (Aleksieevich)

Prior, Matthew 1664-1721 .... **LC 4**
  See also DLB 95; RGEL 2

Prishvin, Mikhail 1873-1954 .... **TCLC 75**
  See Prishvin, Mikhail Mikhailovich

Prishvin, Mikhail Mikhailovich
  See Prishvin, Mikhail
  See also DLB 272; EWL 3

Pritchard, William H(arrison)
  1932- .... **CLC 34**
  See also CA 65-68; CANR 23, 95; DLB
  111

Pritchett, V(ictor) S(awdon)
  1900-1997 ... **CLC 5, 13, 15, 41; SSC 14**
  See also BPFB 3; BRWS 3; CA 61-64; 157;
  CANR 31, 63; CN 1, 2, 3, 4, 5, 6; DA3;
  DAM NOV; DLB 15, 139; EWL 3;
  MTCW 1, 2; MTFW 2005; RGEL 2;
  RGSF 2; TEA

Private 19022
  See Manning, Frederic

Probst, Mark 1925- .... **CLC 59**
  See also CA 130

Procaccino, Michael
  See Cristofer, Michael

Proclus c. 412-485 .... **CMLC 81**

Prokosch, Frederic 1908-1989 ...... **CLC 4, 48**
  See also CA 73-76; 128; CANR 82; CN 1,
  2, 3, 4; CP 1, 2, 3, 4; DLB 48; MTCW 2

Propertius, Sextus c. 50B.C.-c.
  16B.C. .... **CMLC 32**
  See also AW 2; CDWLB 1; DLB 211;
  RGWL 2, 3

Prophet, The
  See Dreiser, Theodore (Herman Albert)

Prose, Francine 1947- .... **CLC 45**
  See also CA 109; 112; CANR 46, 95, 132;
  DLB 234; MTFW 2005; SATA 101, 149

Proudhon
  See Cunha, Euclides (Rodrigues Pimenta)
  da

Proulx, Annie
  See Proulx, E. Annie

Proulx, E. Annie 1935- .... **CLC 81, 158**
  See also AMWS 7; BPFB 3; CA 145;
  CANR 65, 110; CN 6, 7; CPW 1; DA3;
  DAM POP; MAL 5; MTCW 2; MTFW
  2005; SSFS 18

Proulx, Edna Annie
  See Proulx, E. Annie

**Proust, (Valentin-Louis-George-Eugene)
  Marcel** 1871-1922 ..... **SSC 75; TCLC 7,
  13, 33; WLC**
  See also AAYA 58; BPFB 3; CA 104; 120;
  CANR 110; DA; DA3; DAB; DAC; DAM
  MST, NOV; DLB 65; EW 8; EWL 3; GFL
  1789 to the Present; MTCW 1, 2; MTFW
  2005; RGWL 2, 3; TWA

Prowler, Harley
  See Masters, Edgar Lee

Prudentius, Aurelius Clemens 348-c. 405 .... **CMLC 78**
See also EW 1; RGWL 2, 3

Prus, Boleslaw 1845-1912 .... **TCLC 48**
See also RGWL 2, 3

Pryor, Richard (Franklin Lenox Thomas) 1940-2005 .... **CLC 26**
See also CA 122; 152

Przybyszewski, Stanislaw 1868-1927 .... **TCLC 36**
See also CA 160; DLB 66; EWL 3

Pteleon
See Grieve, C(hristopher) M(urray)
See also DAM POET

Puckett, Lute
See Masters, Edgar Lee

Puig, Manuel 1932-1990 .... **CLC 3, 5, 10, 28, 65, 133; HLC 2**
See also BPFB 3; CA 45-48; CANR 2, 32, 63; CDWLB 3; DA3; DAM MULT; DLB 113; DNFS 1; EWL 3; GLL 1; HW 1, 2; LAW; MTCW 1, 2; MTFW 2005; RGWL 2, 3; TWA; WLIT 1

Pulitzer, Joseph 1847-1911 .... **TCLC 76**
See also CA 114; DLB 23

Purchas, Samuel 1577(?)-1626 .... **LC 70**
See also DLB 151

Purdy, A(lfred) W(ellington) 1918-2000 .... **CLC 3, 6, 14, 50**
See also CA 81-84; 189; CAAS 17; CANR 42, 66; CP 1, 2, 3, 4, 5, 6, 7; DAC; DAM MST, POET; DLB 88; PFS 5; RGEL 2

Purdy, James (Amos) 1923- .... **CLC 2, 4, 10, 28, 52**
See also AMWS 7; CA 33-36R; CAAS 1; CANR 19, 51, 132; CN 1, 2, 3, 4, 5, 6, 7; DLB 2, 218; EWL 3; INT CANR-19; MAL 5; MTCW 1; RGAL 4

Pure, Simon
See Swinnerton, Frank Arthur

Pushkin, Aleksandr Sergeevich
See Pushkin, Alexander (Sergeyevich)
See also DLB 205

Pushkin, Alexander (Sergeyevich) 1799-1837 .... **NCLC 3, 27, 83; PC 10; SSC 27, 55; WLC**
See Pushkin, Aleksandr Sergeevich
See also DA; DA3; DAB; DAC; DAM DRAM, MST, POET; EW 5; EXPS; RGSF 2; RGWL 2, 3; SATA 61; SSFS 9; TWA

P'u Sung-ling 1640-1715 .... **LC 49; SSC 31**

Putnam, Arthur Lee
See Alger, Horatio, Jr.

Puttenham, George 1529(?)-1590 ...... **LC 116**
See also DLB 281

Puzo, Mario 1920-1999 .... **CLC 1, 2, 6, 36, 107**
See also BPFB 3; CA 65-68; 185; CANR 4, 42, 65, 99, 131; CN 1, 2, 3, 4, 5, 6; CPW; DA3; DAM NOV, POP; DLB 6; MTCW 1, 2; MTFW 2005; NFS 16; RGAL 4

Pygge, Edward
See Barnes, Julian (Patrick)

Pyle, Ernest Taylor 1900-1945
See Pyle, Ernie
See also CA 115; 160

Pyle, Ernie .... **TCLC 75**
See Pyle, Ernest Taylor
See also DLB 29; MTCW 2

Pyle, Howard 1853-1911 .... **TCLC 81**
See also AAYA 57; BYA 2, 4; CA 109; 137; CLR 22; DLB 42, 188; DLBD 13; LAIT 1; MAICYA 1, 2; SATA 16, 100; WCH; YAW

Pym, Barbara (Mary Crampton) 1913-1980 .... **CLC 13, 19, 37, 111**
See also BPFB 3; BRWS 2; CA 13-14; 97-100; CANR 13, 34; CAP 1; DLB 14, 207; DLBY 1987; EWL 3; MTCW 1, 2; MTFW 2005; RGEL 2; TEA

Pynchon, Thomas (Ruggles, Jr.) 1937- ...... **CLC 2, 3, 6, 9, 11, 18, 33, 62, 72, 123, 192, 213; SSC 14, 84; WLC**
See also AMWS 2; BEST 90:2; BPFB 3; CA 17-20R; CANR 22, 46, 73, 142; CN 1, 2, 3, 4, 5, 6, 7; CPW 1; DA; DA3; DAB; DAC; DAM MST, NOV, POP; DLB 2, 173; EWL 3; MAL 5; MTCW 1, 2; MTFW 2005; RGAL 4; SFW 4; TCLE 1:2; TUS

Pythagoras c. 582B.C.-c. 507B.C. . **CMLC 22**
See also DLB 176

Q
See Quiller-Couch, Sir Arthur (Thomas)

Qian, Chongzhu
See Ch'ien, Chung-shu

Qian, Sima 145B.C.-c. 89B.C. .... **CMLC 72**

Qian Zhongshu
See Ch'ien, Chung-shu
See also CWW 2

Qroll
See Dagerman, Stig (Halvard)

Quarles, Francis 1592-1644 .... **LC 117**
See also DLB 126; RGEL 2

Quarrington, Paul (Lewis) 1953- ..... **CLC 65**
See also CA 129; CANR 62, 95

Quasimodo, Salvatore 1901-1968 .... **CLC 10; PC 47**
See also CA 13-16; 25-28R; CAP 1; DLB 114; EW 12; EWL 3; MTCW 1; RGWL 2, 3

Quatermass, Martin
See Carpenter, John (Howard)

Quay, Stephen 1947- .... **CLC 95**
See also CA 189

Quay, Timothy 1947- .... **CLC 95**
See also CA 189

Queen, Ellery .... **CLC 3, 11**
See Dannay, Frederic; Davidson, Avram (James); Deming, Richard; Fairman, Paul W.; Flora, Fletcher; Hoch, Edward D(entinger); Kane, Henry; Lee, Manfred B(ennington); Marlowe, Stephen; Powell, (Oval) Talmage; Sheldon, Walter J(ames); Sturgeon, Theodore (Hamilton); Tracy, Don(ald Fiske); Vance, John Holbrook
See also BPFB 3; CMW 4; MSW; RGAL 4

Queen, Ellery, Jr.
See Dannay, Frederic; Lee, Manfred B(ennington)

Queneau, Raymond 1903-1976 ..... **CLC 2, 5, 10, 42**
See also CA 77-80; 69-72; CANR 32; DLB 72, 258; EW 12; EWL 3; GFL 1789 to the Present; MTCW 1, 2; RGWL 2, 3

Quevedo, Francisco de 1580-1645 .... **LC 23**

Quiller-Couch, Sir Arthur (Thomas) 1863-1944 .... **TCLC 53**
See also CA 118; 166; DLB 135, 153, 190; HGG; RGEL 2; SUFW 1

Quin, Ann (Marie) 1936-1973 .... **CLC 6**
See also CA 9-12R; 45-48; CN 1; DLB 14, 231

Quincey, Thomas de
See De Quincey, Thomas

Quindlen, Anna 1953- .... **CLC 191**
See also AAYA 35; CA 138; CANR 73, 126; DA3; DLB 292; MTCW 2; MTFW 2005

Quinn, Martin
See Smith, Martin Cruz

Quinn, Peter 1947- .... **CLC 91**
See also CA 197

Quinn, Simon
See Smith, Martin Cruz

Quintana, Leroy V. 1944- ...... **HLC 2; PC 36**
See also CA 131; CANR 65, 139; DAM MULT; DLB 82; HW 1, 2

Quintilian c. 40-c. 100 .... **CMLC 77**
See also AW 2; DLB 211; RGWL 2, 3

Quintillian 0035-0100 .... **CMLC 77**

Quiroga, Horacio (Sylvestre) 1878-1937 .... **HLC 2; TCLC 20**
See also CA 117; 131; DAM MULT; EWL 3; HW 1; LAW; MTCW 1; RGSF 2; WLIT 1

Quoirez, Francoise 1935-2004 .... **CLC 9**
See Sagan, Francoise
See also CA 49-52; 231; CANR 6, 39, 73; MTCW 1, 2; MTFW 2005; TWA

Raabe, Wilhelm (Karl) 1831-1910 . **TCLC 45**
See also CA 167; DLB 129

Rabe, David (William) 1940- .. **CLC 4, 8, 33, 200; DC 16**
See also CA 85-88; CABS 3; CAD; CANR 59, 129; CD 5, 6; DAM DRAM; DFS 3, 8, 13; DLB 7, 228; EWL 3; MAL 5

Rabelais, Francois 1494-1553 .... **LC 5, 60; WLC**
See also DA; DAB; DAC; DAM MST; EW 2; GFL Beginnings to 1789; LMFS 1; RGWL 2, 3; TWA

Rabinovitch, Sholem 1859-1916
See Aleichem, Sholom
See also CA 104

Rabinyan, Dorit 1972- .... **CLC 119**
See also CA 170

Rachilde
See Vallette, Marguerite Eymery; Vallette, Marguerite Eymery
See also EWL 3

Racine, Jean 1639-1699 .... **LC 28, 113**
See also DA3; DAB; DAM MST; DLB 268; EW 3; GFL Beginnings to 1789; LMFS 1; RGWL 2, 3; TWA

Radcliffe, Ann (Ward) 1764-1823 ... **NCLC 6, 55, 106**
See also DLB 39, 178; GL 3; HGG; LMFS 1; RGEL 2; SUFW; WLIT 3

Radclyffe-Hall, Marguerite
See Hall, (Marguerite) Radclyffe

Radiguet, Raymond 1903-1923 ...... **TCLC 29**
See also CA 162; DLB 65; EWL 3; GFL 1789 to the Present; RGWL 2, 3

Radnoti, Miklos 1909-1944 .... **TCLC 16**
See also CA 118; 212; CDWLB 4; DLB 215; EWL 3; RGWL 2, 3

Rado, James 1939- .... **CLC 17**
See also CA 105

Radvanyi, Netty 1900-1983
See Seghers, Anna
See also CA 85-88; 110; CANR 82

Rae, Ben
See Griffiths, Trevor

Raeburn, John (Hay) 1941- .... **CLC 34**
See also CA 57-60

Ragni, Gerome 1942-1991 .... **CLC 17**
See also CA 105; 134

Rahv, Philip .... **CLC 24**
See Greenberg, Ivan
See also DLB 137; MAL 5

Raimund, Ferdinand Jakob 1790-1836 .... **NCLC 69**
See also DLB 90

Raine, Craig (Anthony) 1944- .. **CLC 32, 103**
See also CA 108; CANR 29, 51, 103; CP 3, 4, 5, 6, 7; DLB 40; PFS 7

Raine, Kathleen (Jessie) 1908-2003 .. **CLC 7, 45**
See also CA 85-88; 218; CANR 46, 109; CP 1, 2, 3, 4, 5, 6, 7; DLB 20; EWL 3; MTCW 1; RGEL 2

Rainis, Janis 1865-1929 .... **TCLC 29**
See also CA 170; CDWLB 4; DLB 220; EWL 3

Rakosi, Carl .... **CLC 47**
See Rawley, Callman
See also CA 228; CAAS 5; CP 1, 2, 3, 4, 5, 6, 7; DLB 193

Robbins, Tom .... **CLC 9, 32, 64**
See Robbins, Thomas Eugene
See also AAYA 32; AMWS 10; BEST 90:3;
BPFB 3; CN 3, 4, 5, 6, 7; DLBY 1980
Robbins, Trina 1938- .... **CLC 21**
See also AAYA 61; CA 128
Roberts, Charles G(eorge) D(ouglas)
1860-1943 .... **TCLC 8**
See also CA 105; 188; CLR 33; CWRI 5;
DLB 92; RGEL 2; RGSF 2; SATA 88;
SATA-Brief 29
Roberts, Elizabeth Madox
1886-1941 .... **TCLC 68**
See also CA 111; 166; CLR 100; CWRI 5;
DLB 9, 54, 102; RGAL 4; RHW; SATA
33; SATA-Brief 27; TCWW 2; WCH
Roberts, Kate 1891-1985 .... **CLC 15**
See also CA 107; 116; DLB 319
Roberts, Keith (John Kingston)
1935-2000 .... **CLC 14**
See also BRWS 10; CA 25-28R; CANR 46;
DLB 261; SFW 4
Roberts, Kenneth (Lewis)
1885-1957 .... **TCLC 23**
See also CA 109; 199; DLB 9; MAL 5;
RGAL 4; RHW
Roberts, Michele (Brigitte) 1949- .... **CLC 48,
178**
See also CA 115; CANR 58, 120; CN 6, 7;
DLB 231; FW
Robertson, Ellis
See Ellison, Harlan (Jay); Silverberg, Robert
Robertson, Thomas William
1829-1871 .... **NCLC 35**
See Robertson, Tom
See also DAM DRAM
Robertson, Tom
See Robertson, Thomas William
See also RGEL 2
Robeson, Kenneth
See Dent, Lester
Robinson, Edwin Arlington
1869-1935 .... **PC 1, 35; TCLC 5, 101**
See also AMW; CA 104; 133; CDALB
1865-1917; DA; DAC; DAM MST;
POET; DLB 54; EWL 3; EXPP; MAL 5;
MTCW 1, 2; MTFW 2005; PAB; PFS 4;
RGAL 4; WP
Robinson, Henry Crabb
1775-1867 .... **NCLC 15**
See also DLB 107
Robinson, Jill 1936- .... **CLC 10**
See also CA 102; CANR 120; INT CA-102
Robinson, Kim Stanley 1952- .... **CLC 34**
See also AAYA 26; CA 126; CANR 113,
139; CN 6, 7; MTFW 2005; SATA 109;
SCFW 2; SFW 4
Robinson, Lloyd
See Silverberg, Robert
Robinson, Marilynne 1944- ...... **CLC 25, 180**
See also CA 116; CANR 80, 140; CN 4, 5,
6, 7; DLB 206; MTFW 2005
Robinson, Mary 1758-1800 .... **NCLC 142**
See also DLB 158; FW
Robinson, Smokey .... **CLC 21**
See Robinson, William, Jr.
Robinson, William, Jr. 1940-
See Robinson, Smokey
See also CA 116
Robison, Mary 1949- .... **CLC 42, 98**
See also CA 113; 116; CANR 87; CN 4, 5,
6, 7; DLB 130; INT CA-116; RGSF 2
Roches, Catherine des 1542-1587 ...... **LC 117**
Rochester
See Wilmot, John
See also RGEL 2

Rod, Edouard 1857-1910 .... **TCLC 52**
Roddenberry, Eugene Wesley 1921-1991
See Roddenberry, Gene
See also CA 110; 135; CANR 37; SATA 45;
SATA-Obit 69
Roddenberry, Gene .... **CLC 17**
See Roddenberry, Eugene Wesley
See also AAYA 5; SATA-Obit 69
Rodgers, Mary 1931- .... **CLC 12**
See also BYA 5; CA 49-52; CANR 8, 55,
90; CLR 20; CWRI 5; INT CANR-8;
JRDA; MAICYA 1, 2; SATA 8, 130
Rodgers, W(illiam) R(obert)
1909-1969 .... **CLC 7**
See also CA 85-88; DLB 20; RGEL 2
Rodman, Eric
See Silverberg, Robert
Rodman, Howard 1920(?)-1985 .... **CLC 65**
See also CA 118
Rodman, Maia
See Wojciechowska, Maia (Teresa)
Rodo, Jose Enrique 1871(?)-1917 .... **HLCS 2**
See also CA 178; EWL 3; HW 2; LAW
Rodolph, Utto
See Ouologuem, Yambo
Rodriguez, Claudio 1934-1999 .... **CLC 10**
See also CA 188; DLB 134
Rodriguez, Richard 1944- .... **CLC 155; HLC
2**
See also AMWS 14; CA 110; CANR 66,
116; DAM MULT; DLB 82, 256; HW 1,
2; LAIT 5; LLW; MTFW 2005; NCFS 3;
WLIT 1
Roelvaag, O(le) E(dvart) 1876-1931
See Rolvaag, O(le) E(dvart)
See also CA 117; 171
Roethke, Theodore (Huebner)
1908-1963 .... **CLC 1, 3, 8, 11, 19, 46,
101; PC 15**
See also AMW; CA 81-84; CABS 2;
CDALB 1941-1968; DA3; DAM POET;
DLB 5, 206; EWL 3; EXPP; MAL 5;
MTCW 1, 2; PAB; PFS 3; RGAL 4; WP
Rogers, Carl R(ansom)
1902-1987 .... **TCLC 125**
See also CA 1-4R; 121; CANR 1, 18;
MTCW 1
Rogers, Samuel 1763-1855 .... **NCLC 69**
See also DLB 93; RGEL 2
Rogers, Thomas Hunton 1927- .... **CLC 57**
See also CA 89-92; INT CA-89-92
Rogers, Will(iam Penn Adair)
1879-1935 .... **NNAL; TCLC 8, 71**
See also CA 105; 144; DA3; DAM MULT;
DLB 11; MTCW 2
Rogin, Gilbert 1929- .... **CLC 18**
See also CA 65-68; CANR 15
Rohan, Koda
See Koda Shigeyuki
Rohlfs, Anna Katharine Green
See Green, Anna Katharine
Rohmer, Eric .... **CLC 16**
See Scherer, Jean-Marie Maurice
Rohmer, Sax .... **TCLC 28**
See Ward, Arthur Henry Sarsfield
See also DLB 70; MSW; SUFW
Roiphe, Anne (Richardson) 1935- .. **CLC 3, 9**
See also CA 89-92; CANR 45, 73, 138;
DLBY 1980; INT CA-89-92
Rojas, Fernando de 1475-1541 ... **HLCS 1, 2;
LC 23**
See also DLB 286; RGWL 2, 3
Rojas, Gonzalo 1917- .... **HLCS 2**
See also CA 178; HW 2; LAWS 1
Roland (de la Platiere), Marie-Jeanne
1754-1793 .... **LC 98**
See also DLB 314

**Rolfe, Frederick (William Serafino Austin
Lewis Mary)** 1860-1913 .... **TCLC 12**
See Al Siddik
See also CA 107; 210; DLB 34, 156; RGEL
2
Rolland, Romain 1866-1944 .... **TCLC 23**
See also CA 118; 197; DLB 65, 284; EWL
3; GFL 1789 to the Present; RGWL 2, 3
Rolle, Richard c. 1300-c. 1349 .... **CMLC 21**
See also DLB 146; LMFS 1; RGEL 2
Rolvaag, O(le) E(dvart) .... **TCLC 17**
See Roelvaag, O(le) E(dvart)
See also DLB 9, 212; MAL 5; NFS 5;
RGAL 4
Romain Arnaud, Saint
See Aragon, Louis
Romains, Jules 1885-1972 .... **CLC 7**
See also CA 85-88; CANR 34; DLB 65,
321; EWL 3; GFL 1789 to the Present;
MTCW 1
Romero, Jose Ruben 1890-1952 .... **TCLC 14**
See also CA 114; 131; EWL 3; HW 1; LAW
Ronsard, Pierre de 1524-1585 . **LC 6, 54; PC
11**
See also EW 2; GFL Beginnings to 1789;
RGWL 2, 3; TWA
Rooke, Leon 1934- .... **CLC 25, 34**
See also CA 25-28R; CANR 23, 53; CCA
1; CPW; DAM POP
Roosevelt, Franklin Delano
1882-1945 .... **TCLC 93**
See also CA 116; 173; LAIT 3
Roosevelt, Theodore 1858-1919 ..... **TCLC 69**
See also CA 115; 170; DLB 47, 186, 275
Roper, William 1498-1578 .... **LC 10**
Roquelaure, A. N.
See Rice, Anne
Rosa, Joao Guimaraes 1908-1967 ... **CLC 23;
HLCS 1**
See Guimaraes Rosa, Joao
See also CA 89-92; DLB 113, 307; EWL 3;
WLIT 1
Rose, Wendy 1948- . **CLC 85; NNAL; PC 13**
See also CA 53-56; CANR 5, 51; CWP;
DAM MULT; DLB 175; PFS 13; RGAL
4; SATA 12
Rosen, R. D.
See Rosen, Richard (Dean)
Rosen, Richard (Dean) 1949- .... **CLC 39**
See also CA 77-80; CANR 62, 120; CMW
4; INT CANR-30
Rosenberg, Isaac 1890-1918 .... **TCLC 12**
See also BRW 6; CA 107; 188; DLB 20,
216; EWL 3; PAB; RGEL 2
Rosenblatt, Joe .... **CLC 15**
See Rosenblatt, Joseph
See also CP 3, 4, 5, 6, 7
Rosenblatt, Joseph 1933-
See Rosenblatt, Joe
See also CA 89-92; CP 1, 2; INT CA-89-92
Rosenfeld, Samuel
See Tzara, Tristan
Rosenstock, Sami
See Tzara, Tristan
Rosenstock, Samuel
See Tzara, Tristan
Rosenthal, M(acha) L(ouis)
1917-1996 .... **CLC 28**
See also CA 1-4R; 152; CAAS 6; CANR 4,
51; CP 1, 2, 3, 4; DLB 5; SATA 59
Ross, Barnaby
See Dannay, Frederic
Ross, Bernard L.
See Follett, Ken(neth Martin)
Ross, J. H.
See Lawrence, T(homas) E(dward)
Ross, John Hume
See Lawrence, T(homas) E(dward)

Ryder, Jonathan
   See Ludlum, Robert
Ryga, George 1932-1987 .... **CLC 14**
   See also CA 101; 124; CANR 43, 90; CCA
   1; DAC; DAM MST; DLB 60
S. H.
   See Hartmann, Sadakichi
S. S.
   See Sassoon, Siegfried (Lorraine)
Sa'adawi, al- Nawal
   See El Saadawi, Nawal
   See also AFW; EWL 3
Saadawi, Nawal El
   See El Saadawi, Nawal
   See also WLIT 2
Saba, Umberto 1883-1957 .... **TCLC 33**
   See also CA 144; CANR 79; DLB 114;
   EWL 3; RGWL 2, 3
Sabatini, Rafael 1875-1950 .... **TCLC 47**
   See also BPFB 3; CA 162; RHW
Sabato, Ernesto (R.) 1911- .... **CLC 10, 23;
   HLC 2**
   See also CA 97-100; CANR 32, 65; CD-
   WLB 3; CWW 2; DAM MULT; DLB 145;
   EWL 3; HW 1, 2; LAW; MTCW 1, 2;
   MTFW 2005
Sa-Carneiro, Mario de 1890-1916 . **TCLC 83**
   See also DLB 287; EWL 3
Sacastru, Martin
   See Bioy Casares, Adolfo
   See also CWW 2
Sacher-Masoch, Leopold von
   1836(?)-1895 .... **NCLC 31**
Sachs, Hans 1494-1576 .... **LC 95**
   See also CDWLB 2; DLB 179; RGWL 2, 3
Sachs, Marilyn 1927- .... **CLC 35**
   See also AAYA 2; BYA 6; CA 17-20R;
   CANR 13, 47; CLR 2; JRDA; MAICYA
   1, 2; SAAS 2; SATA 3, 68, 164; SATA-
   Essay 110; WYA; YAW
Sachs, Marilyn Stickle
   See Sachs, Marilyn
Sachs, Nelly 1891-1970 .... **CLC 14, 98**
   See also CA 17-18; 25-28R; CANR 87;
   CAP 2; EWL 3; MTCW 2; MTFW 2005;
   PFS 20; RGWL 2, 3
Sackler, Howard (Oliver)
   1929-1982 .... **CLC 14**
   See also CA 61-64; 108; CAD; CANR 30;
   DFS 15; DLB 7
Sacks, Oliver (Wolf) 1933- .... **CLC 67, 202**
   See also CA 53-56; CANR 28, 50, 76;
   CPW; DA3; INT CANR-28; MTCW 1, 2;
   MTFW 2005
Sackville, Thomas 1536-1608 .... **LC 98**
   See also DAM DRAM; DLB 62, 132;
   RGEL 2
Sadakichi
   See Hartmann, Sadakichi
Sa'dawi, Nawal al-
   See El Saadawi, Nawal
   See also CWW 2
Sade, Donatien Alphonse Francois
   1740-1814 .... **NCLC 3, 47**
   See also DLB 314; EW 4; GFL Beginnings
   to 1789; RGWL 2, 3
Sade, Marquis de
   See Sade, Donatien Alphonse Francois
Sadoff, Ira 1945- .... **CLC 9**
   See also CA 53-56; CANR 5, 21, 109; DLB
   120
Saetone
   See Camus, Albert
Safire, William 1929- .... **CLC 10**
   See also CA 17-20R; CANR 31, 54, 91

Sagan, Carl (Edward) 1934-1996 .... **CLC 30,
   112**
   See also AAYA 2, 62; CA 25-28R; 155;
   CANR 11, 36; CPW; DA3; MTCW 1,
   2; MTFW 2005; SATA 58; SATA-Obit 94
Sagan, Francoise .... **CLC 3, 6, 9, 17, 36**
   See Quoirez, Francoise
   See also CWW 2; DLB 83; EWL 3; GFL
   1789 to the Present; MTCW 2
Sahgal, Nayantara (Pandit) 1927- .... **CLC 41**
   See also CA 9-12R; CANR 11, 88; CN 1,
   2, 3, 4, 5, 6, 7
Said, Edward W. 1935-2003 .... **CLC 123**
   See also CA 21-24R; 220; CANR 45, 74,
   107, 131; DLB 67; MTCW 2; MTFW
   2005
Saint, H(arry) F. 1941- .... **CLC 50**
   See also CA 127
St. Aubin de Teran, Lisa 1953-
   See Teran, Lisa St. Aubin de
   See also CA 118; 126; CN 6, 7; INT CA-
   126
Saint Birgitta of Sweden c.
   1303-1373 .... **CMLC 24**
Sainte-Beuve, Charles Augustin
   1804-1869 .... **NCLC 5**
   See also DLB 217; EW 6; GFL 1789 to the
   Present
**Saint-Exupery, Antoine (Jean Baptiste
   Marie Roger) de** 1900-1944 .... **TCLC 2,
   56, 169; WLC**
   See also AAYA 63; BPFB 3; BYA 3; CA
   108; 132; CLR 10; DA3; DAM NOV;
   DLB 72; EW 12; EWL 3; GFL 1789 to
   the Present; LAIT 3; MAICYA 1, 2;
   MTCW 1, 2; MTFW 2005; RGWL 2, 3;
   SATA 20; TWA
St. John, David
   See Hunt, E(verette) Howard, (Jr.)
St. John, J. Hector
   See Crevecoeur, Michel Guillaume Jean de
Saint-John Perse
   See Leger, (Marie-Rene Auguste) Alexis
   Saint-Leger
   See also EW 10; EWL 3; GFL 1789 to the
   Present; RGWL 2
Saintsbury, George (Edward Bateman)
   1845-1933 .... **TCLC 31**
   See also CA 160; DLB 57, 149
Sait Faik .... **TCLC 23**
   See Abasiyanik, Sait Faik
Saki .... **SSC 12; TCLC 3**
   See Munro, H(ector) H(ugh)
   See also BRWS 6; BYA 11; LAIT 2; RGEL
   2; SSFS 1; SUFW
Sala, George Augustus 1828-1895 . **NCLC 46**
Saladin 1138-1193 .... **CMLC 38**
Salama, Hannu 1936- .... **CLC 18**
   See also EWL 3
Salamanca, J(ack) R(ichard) 1922- .. **CLC 4,
   15**
   See also CA 25-28R, 193; CAAE 193
Salas, Floyd Francis 1931- .... **HLC 2**
   See also CA 119; CAAS 27; CANR 44, 75,
   93; DAM MULT; DLB 82; HW 1, 2;
   MTCW 2; MTFW 2005
Sale, J. Kirkpatrick
   See Sale, Kirkpatrick
Sale, Kirkpatrick 1937- .... **CLC 68**
   See also CA 13-16R; CANR 10
Salinas, Luis Omar 1937- ... **CLC 90; HLC 2**
   See also AMWS 13; CA 131; CANR 81;
   DAM MULT; DLB 82; HW 1, 2
Salinas (y Serrano), Pedro
   1891(?)-1951 .... **TCLC 17**
   See also CA 117; DLB 134; EWL 3

Salinger, J(erome) D(avid) 1919- .. **CLC 1, 3,
   8, 12, 55, 56, 138; SSC 2, 28, 65; WLC**
   See also AAYA 2, 36; AMW; AMWC 1;
   BPFB 3; CA 5-8R; CANR 39, 129;
   CDALB 1941-1968; CLR 18; CN 1, 2, 3,
   4, 5, 6, 7; CPW 1; DA; DA3; DAB; DAC;
   DAM MST, NOV, POP; DLB 2, 102, 173;
   EWL 3; EXPN; LAIT 4; MAICYA 1, 2;
   MAL 5; MTCW 1, 2; MTFW 2005; NFS
   1; RGAL 4; RGSF; SATA 67; SSFS 17;
   TUS; WYA; YAW
Salisbury, John
   See Caute, (John) David
Sallust c. 86B.C.-35B.C. .... **CMLC 68**
   See also AW 2; CDWLB 1; DLB 211;
   RGWL 2, 3
Salter, James 1925- ... **CLC 7, 52, 59; SSC 58**
   See also AMWS 9; CA 73-76; CANR 107;
   DLB 130
Saltus, Edgar (Everton) 1855-1921 . **TCLC 8**
   See also CA 105; DLB 202; RGAL 4
Saltykov, Mikhail Evgrafovich
   1826-1889 .... **NCLC 16**
   See also DLB 238;
Saltykov-Shchedrin, N.
   See Saltykov, Mikhail Evgrafovich
Samarakis, Andonis
   See Samarakis, Antonis
   See also EWL 3
Samarakis, Antonis 1919-2003 .... **CLC 5**
   See Samarakis, Andonis
   See also CA 25-28R; 224; CAAS 16; CANR
   36
Sanchez, Florencio 1875-1910 .... **TCLC 37**
   See also CA 153; DLB 305; EWL 3; HW 1;
   LAW
Sanchez, Luis Rafael 1936- .... **CLC 23**
   See also CA 128; DLB 305; EWL 3; HW 1;
   WLIT 1
Sanchez, Sonia 1934- .... **BLC 3; CLC 5, 116,
   215; PC 9**
   See also BW 2, 3; CA 33-36R; CANR 24,
   49, 74, 115; CLR 18; CP 2, 3, 4, 5, 6, 7;
   CSW; CWP; DA3; DAM MULT; DLB 41;
   DLBD 8; EWL 3; MAICYA 1, 2; MAL 5;
   MTCW 1, 2; MTFW 2005; SATA 22, 136;
   WP
Sancho, Ignatius 1729-1780 .... **LC 84**
Sand, George 1804-1876 ..... **NCLC 2, 42, 57;
   WLC**
   See also DA; DA3; DAB; DAC; DAM
   MST, NOV; DLB 119, 192; EW 6; FL 1:3;
   FW; GFL 1789 to the Present; RGWL 2,
   3; TWA
Sandburg, Carl (August) 1878-1967 . **CLC 1,
   4, 10, 15, 35; PC 2, 41; WLC**
   See also AAYA 24; AMW; BYA 1, 3; CA
   5-8R; 25-28R; CANR 35; CDALB 1865-
   1917; CLR 67; DA; DA3; DAB; DAC;
   DAM MST, POET; DLB 17, 54, 284;
   EWL 3; EXPP; LAIT 2; MAICYA 1, 2;
   MAL 5; MTCW 1, 2; MTFW 2005; PAB;
   PFS 3, 6, 12; RGAL 4; SATA 8; TUS;
   WCH; WP; WYA
Sandburg, Charles
   See Sandburg, Carl (August)
Sandburg, Charles A.
   See Sandburg, Carl (August)
Sanders, (James) Ed(ward) 1939- .... **CLC 53**
   See Sanders, Edward
   See also BG 1:3; CA 13-16R; CAAS 21;
   CANR 13, 44, 78; CP 1, 2, 3, 4, 5, 6, 7;
   DAM POET; DLB 16, 244
Sanders, Edward
   See Sanders, (James) Ed(ward)
   See also DLB 244
Sanders, Lawrence 1920-1998 .... **CLC 41**
   See also BEST 89:4; BPFB 3; CA 81-84;
   165; CANR 33, 62; CMW 4; CPW; DA3;
   DAM POP; MTCW 1

Sanders, Noah
See Blount, Roy (Alton), Jr.
Sanders, Winston P.
See Anderson, Poul (William)
Sandoz, Mari(e Susette) 1900-1966 .. **CLC 28**
See also CA 1-4R; 25-28R; CANR 17, 64;
DLB 9, 212; LAIT 2; MTCW 1, 2; SATA
5; TCWW 1, 2
Sandys, George 1578-1644 .... **LC 80**
See also DLB 24, 121
Saner, Reg(inald Anthony) 1931- .... **CLC 9**
See also CA 65-68; CP 3, 4, 5, 6, 7
Sankara 788-820 .... **CMLC 32**
Sannazaro, Jacopo 1456(?)-1530 .... **LC 8**
See also RGWL 2, 3; WLIT 7
Sansom, William 1912-1976 . **CLC 2, 6; SSC 21**
See also CA 5-8R; 65-68; CANR 42; CN 1,
2; DAM NOV; DLB 139; EWL 3; MTCW
1; RGEL 2; RGSF 2
Santayana, George 1863-1952 .... **TCLC 40**
See also AMW; CA 115; 194; DLB 54, 71,
246, 270; DLBD 13; EWL 3; MAL 5;
RGAL 4; TUS
Santiago, Danny .... **CLC 33**
See James, Daniel (Lewis)
See also DLB 122
Santillana, Inigo Lopez de Mendoza, Marques de 1398-1458 .... **LC 111**
See also DLB 286
Santmyer, Helen Hooven
1895-1986 .... **CLC 33; TCLC 133**
See also CA 1-4R; 118; CANR 15, 33;
DLBY 1984; MTCW 1; RHW
Santoka, Taneda 1882-1940 .... **TCLC 72**
Santos, Bienvenido N(uqui)
1911-1996 ... **AAL; CLC 22; TCLC 156**
See also CA 101; 151; CANR 19, 46; CP 1;
DAM MULT; DLB 312; EWL; RGAL 4;
SSFS 19
Sapir, Edward 1884-1939 .... **TCLC 108**
See also CA 211; DLB 92
Sapper .... **TCLC 44**
See McNeile, Herman Cyril
Sapphire
See Sapphire, Brenda
Sapphire, Brenda 1950- .... **CLC 99**
Sappho fl. 6th cent. B.C.- ... **CMLC 3, 67; PC 5**
See also CDWLB 1; DA3; DAM POET;
DLB 176; FL 1:1; PFS 20; RGWL 2, 3;
WP
Saramago, Jose 1922- ..... **CLC 119; HLCS 1**
See also CA 153; CANR 96; CWW 2; DLB
287; EWL 3; LATS 1:2
Sarduy, Severo 1937-1993 .... **CLC 6, 97; HLCS 2; TCLC 167**
See also CA 89-92; 142; CANR 58, 81;
CWW 2; DLB 113; EWL 3; HW 1, 2;
LAW
Sargeson, Frank 1903-1982 .... **CLC 31**
See also CA 25-28R; 106; CANR 38, 79;
CN 1, 2, 3; EWL 3; GLL 2; RGEL 2;
RGSF 2; SSFS 20
Sarmiento, Domingo Faustino
1811-1888 .... **HLCS 2**
See also LAW; WLIT 1
Sarmiento, Felix Ruben Garcia
See Dario, Ruben
Saro-Wiwa, Ken(ule Beeson)
1941-1995 .... **CLC 114**
See also BW 2; CA 142; 150; CANR 60;
DLB 157
Saroyan, William 1908-1981 ... **CLC 1, 8, 10, 29, 34, 56; SSC 21; TCLC 137; WLC**
See also AAYA 66; CA 5-8R; 103; CAD;
CANR 30; CDALBS; CN 1, 2; DA; DA3;
DAB; DAC; DAM DRAM, MST, NOV;
DFS 17; DLB 7, 9, 86; DLBY 1981; EWL

3; LAIT 4; MAL 5; MTCW 1, 2; MTFW
2005; RGAL 4; RGSF 2; SATA 23; SATA-
Obit 24; SSFS 14; TUS
Sarraute, Nathalie 1900-1999 .... **CLC 1, 2, 4, 8, 10, 31, 80; TCLC 145**
See also BPFB 3; CA 9-12R; 187; CANR
23, 66, 134; CWW 2; DLB 83, 321; EW
12; EWL 3; GFL 1789 to the Present;
MTCW 1, 2; MTFW 2005; RGWL 2, 3
Sarton, (Eleanor) May 1912-1995 ..... **CLC 4, 14, 49, 91; PC 39; TCLC 120**
See also AMWS 8; CA 1-4R; 149; CANR
1, 34, 55, 116; CN 1, 2, 3, 4, 5, 6; CP 1,
2, 3, 4; DAM POET; DLB 48; DLBY
1981; EWL 3; FW; INT CANR-34; MAL
5; MTCW 1, 2; MTFW 2005; RGAL 4;
SATA 36; SATA-Obit 86; TUS
Sartre, Jean-Paul 1905-1980 . **CLC 1, 4, 7, 9, 13, 18, 24, 44, 50, 52; DC 3; SSC 32; WLC**
See also AAYA 62; CA 9-12R; 97-100;
CANR 21; DA; DA3; DAB; DAC; DAM
DRAM, MST, NOV; DFS 5; DLB 72,
296, 321; EW 12; EWL 3; GFL 1789 to
the Present; LMFS 2; MTCW 1, 2; MTFW
2005; NFS 21; RGSF 2; RGWL 2, 3;
SSFS 9; TWA
Sassoon, Siegfried (Lorraine)
1886-1967 .... **CLC 36, 130; PC 12**
See also BRW 6; CA 104; 25-28R; CANR
36; DAB; DAM MST, NOV, POET; DLB
20, 191; DLBD 18; EWL 3; MTCW 1, 2;
MTFW 2005; PAB; RGEL 2; TEA
Satterfield, Charles
See Pohl, Frederik
Satyremont
See Peret, Benjamin
Saul, John (W. III) 1942- .... **CLC 46**
See also AAYA 10, 62; BEST 90:4; CA 81-
84; CANR 16, 40, 81; CPW; DAM NOV,
POP; HGG; SATA 98
Saunders, Caleb
See Heinlein, Robert A(nson)
Saura (Atares), Carlos 1932-1998 .... **CLC 20**
See also CA 114; 131; CANR 79; HW 1
Sauser, Frederic Louis
See Sauser-Hall, Frederic
Sauser-Hall, Frederic 1887-1961 ...... **CLC 18**
See Cendrars, Blaise
See also CA 102; 93-96; CANR 36, 62;
MTCW 1
Saussure, Ferdinand de
1857-1913 .... **TCLC 49**
See also DLB 242
Savage, Catharine
See Brosman, Catharine Savage
Savage, Richard 1697(?)-1743 .... **LC 96**
See also DLB 95; RGEL 2
Savage, Thomas 1915-2003 .... **CLC 40**
See also CA 126; 132; 218; CAAS 15; CN
6, 7; INT CA-132; SATA-Obit 147;
TCWW 2
Savan, Glenn 1953-2003 .... **CLC 50**
See also CA 225
Sax, Robert
See Johnson, Robert
Saxo Grammaticus c. 1150-c.
1222 .... **CMLC 58**
Saxton, Robert
See Johnson, Robert
Sayers, Dorothy L(eigh) 1893-1957 . **SSC 71; TCLC 2, 15**
See also BPFB 3; BRWS 3; CA 104; 119;
CANR 60; CDBLB 1914-1945; CMW 4;
DAM POP; DLB 10, 36, 77, 100; MSW;
MTCW 1, 2; MTFW 2005; RGEL 2;
SSFS 12; TEA
Sayers, Valerie 1952- .... **CLC 50, 122**
See also CA 134; CANR 61; CSW

Sayles, John (Thomas) 1950- .... **CLC 7, 10, 14, 198**
See also CA 57-60; CANR 41, 84; DLB 44
Scammell, Michael 1935- .... **CLC 34**
See also CA 156
Scannell, Vernon 1922- .... **CLC 49**
See also CA 5-8R; CANR 8, 24, 57, 143;
CN 1, 2; CP 1, 2, 3, 4, 5, 6, 7; CWRI 5;
DLB 27; SATA 59
Scarlett, Susan
See Streatfeild, (Mary) Noel
Scarron 1847-1910
See Mikszath, Kalman
Scarron, Paul 1610-1660 .... **LC 116**
See also GFL Beginnings to 1789; RGWL
2, 3
Schaeffer, Susan Fromberg 1941- ..... **CLC 6, 11, 22**
See also CA 49-52; CANR 18, 65; CN 4, 5,
6, 7; DLB 28, 299; MTCW 1, 2; MTFW
2005; SATA 22
Schama, Simon (Michael) 1945- ..... **CLC 150**
See also BEST 89:4; CA 105; CANR 39,
91
Schary, Jill
See Robinson, Jill
Schell, Jonathan 1943- .... **CLC 35**
See also CA 73-76; CANR 12, 117
Schelling, Friedrich Wilhelm Joseph von
1775-1854 .... **NCLC 30**
See also DLB 90
Scherer, Jean-Marie Maurice 1920-
See Rohmer, Eric
See also CA 110
Schevill, James (Erwin) 1920- .... **CLC 7**
See also CA 5-8R; CAAS 12; CAD; CD 5,
6; CP 1, 2, 3, 4
Schiller, Friedrich von 1759-1805 ...... **DC 12; NCLC 39, 69**
See also CDWLB 2; DAM DRAM; DLB
94; EW 5; RGWL 2, 3; TWA
Schisgal, Murray (Joseph) 1926- .... **CLC 6**
See also CA 21-24R; CAD; CANR 48, 86;
CD 5, 6; MAL 5
Schlee, Ann 1934- .... **CLC 35**
See also CA 101; CANR 29, 88; SATA 44;
SATA-Brief 36
Schlegel, August Wilhelm von
1767-1845 .... **NCLC 15, 142**
See also DLB 94; RGWL 2, 3
Schlegel, Friedrich 1772-1829 .... **NCLC 45**
See also DLB 90; EW 5; RGWL 2, 3; TWA
Schlegel, Johann Elias (von)
1719(?)-1749 .... **LC 5**
Schleiermacher, Friedrich
1768-1834 .... **NCLC 107**
See also DLB 90
Schlesinger, Arthur M(eier), Jr.
1917- .... **CLC 84**
See also AITN 1; CA 1-4R; CANR 1, 28,
58, 105; DLB 17; INT CANR-28; MTCW
1, 2; SATA 61
Schlink, Bernhard 1944- .... **CLC 174**
See also CA 163; CANR 116
Schmidt, Arno (Otto) 1914-1979 ...... **CLC 56**
See also CA 128; 109; DLB 69; EWL 3
Schmitz, Aron Hector 1861-1928
See Svevo, Italo
See also CA 104; 122; MTCW 1
Schnackenberg, Gjertrud (Cecelia)
1953- .... **CLC 40; PC 45**
See also AMWS 15; CA 116; CANR 100;
CP 7; CWP; DLB 120, 282; PFS 13
Schneider, Leonard Alfred 1925-1966
See Bruce, Lenny
See also CA 89-92

Shepherd, Michael
See Ludlum, Robert
Sherburne, Zoa (Lillian Morin)
1912-1995 .... **CLC 30**
See also AAYA 13; CA 1-4R; 176; CANR
3, 37; MAICYA 1, 2; SAAS 18; SATA 3;
YAW
Sheridan, Frances 1724-1766 .... **LC 7**
See also DLB 39, 84
Sheridan, Richard Brinsley
1751-1816 .... **DC 1; NCLC 5, 91; WLC**
See also BRW 3; CDBLB 1660-1789; DA;
DAB; DAC; DAM DRAM, MST; DFS
15; DLB 89; WLIT 3
Sherman, Jonathan Marc 1968- .... **CLC 55**
See also CA 230
Sherman, Martin 1941(?)- .... **CLC 19**
See also CA 116; 123; CAD; CANR 86;
CD 5, 6; DFS 20; DLB 228; GLL 1; IDTP
Sherwin, Judith Johnson
See Johnson, Judith (Emlyn)
See also CANR 85; CP 2, 3, 4; CWP
Sherwood, Frances 1940- .... **CLC 81**
See also CA 146, 220; CAAE 220
Sherwood, Robert E(mmet)
1896-1955 .... **TCLC 3**
See also CA 104; 153; CANR 86; DAM
DRAM; DFS 11, 15, 17; DLB 7, 26, 249;
IDFW 3, 4; MAL 5; RGAL 4
Shestov, Lev 1866-1938 .... **TCLC 56**
Shevchenko, Taras 1814-1861 .... **NCLC 54**
Shiel, M(atthew) P(hipps)
1865-1947 .... **TCLC 8**
See Holmes, Gordon
See also CA 106; 160; DLB 153; HGG;
MTCW 2; MTFW 2005; SCFW 1, 2;
SFW 4; SUFW
Shields, Carol (Ann) 1935-2003 ...... **CLC 91,
113, 193**
See also AMWS 7; CA 81-84; 218; CANR
51, 74, 98, 133; CCA 1; CN 6, 7; CPW;
DA3; DAC; MTCW 2; MTFW 2005
Shields, David (Jonathan) 1956- ...... **CLC 97**
See also CA 124; CANR 48, 99, 112
Shiga, Naoya 1883-1971 .... **CLC 33; SSC 23;
TCLC 172**
See Shiga Naoya
See also CA 101; 33-36R; MJW; RGWL 3
Shiga Naoya
See Shiga, Naoya
See also DLB 180; EWL 3; RGWL 3
Shilts, Randy 1951-1994 .... **CLC 85**
See also AAYA 19; CA 115; 127; 144;
CANR 45; DA3; GLL 1; INT CA-127;
MTCW 2; MTFW 2005
Shimazaki, Haruki 1872-1943
See Shimazaki Toson
See also CA 105; 134; CANR 84; RGWL 3
Shimazaki Toson .... **TCLC 5**
See Shimazaki, Haruki
See also DLB 180; EWL 3
Shirley, James 1596-1666 .... **DC 25; LC 96**
See also DLB 58; RGEL 2
Sholokhov, Mikhail (Aleksandrovich)
1905-1984 .... **CLC 7, 15**
See also CA 101; 112; DLB 272; EWL 3;
MTCW 1, 2; MTFW 2005; RGWL 2, 3;
SATA-Obit 36
Shone, Patric
See Hanley, James
Showalter, Elaine 1941 .... **CLC 169**
See also CA 57-60; CANR 58, 106; DLB
67; FW; GLL 2
Shreve, Susan
See Shreve, Susan Richards
Shreve, Susan Richards 1939- .... **CLC 23**
See also CA 49-52; CAAS 5; CANR 5, 38,
69, 100; MAICYA 1, 2; SATA 46, 95, 152;
SATA-Brief 41

Shue, Larry 1946-1985 .... **CLC 52**
See also CA 145; 117; DAM DRAM; DFS
7
Shu-Jen, Chou 1881-1936
See Lu Hsun
See also CA 104
Shulman, Alix Kates 1932- .... **CLC 2, 10**
See also CA 29-32R; CANR 43; FW; SATA
7
Shuster, Joe 1914-1992 .... **CLC 21**
See also AAYA 50
Shute, Nevil .... **CLC 30**
See Norway, Nevil Shute
See also BPFB 3; DLB 255; NFS 9; RHW;
SFW 4
Shuttle, Penelope (Diane) 1947- .... **CLC 7**
See also CA 93-96; CANR 39, 84, 92, 108;
CP 3, 4, 5, 6, 7; CWP; DLB 14, 40
Shvarts, Elena 1948- .... **PC 50**
See also CA 147
Sidhwa, Bapsi
See Sidhwa, Bapsy (N.)
See also CN 6, 7
Sidhwa, Bapsy (N.) 1938- .... **CLC 168**
See Sidhwa, Bapsi
See also CA 108; CANR 25, 57; FW
Sidney, Mary 1561-1621 .... **LC 19, 39**
See Sidney Herbert, Mary
Sidney, Sir Philip 1554-1586 . **LC 19, 39; PC 32**
See also BRW 1; BRWR 2; CDBLB Before
1660; DA; DA3; DAB; DAC; DAM MST,
POET; DLB 167; EXPP; PAB; RGEL 2;
TEA; WP
Sidney Herbert, Mary
See Sidney, Mary
See also DLB 167
Siegel, Jerome 1914-1996 .... **CLC 21**
See Siegel, Jerry
See also CA 116; 169; 151
Siegel, Jerry
See Siegel, Jerome
See also AAYA 50
Sienkiewicz, Henryk (Adam Alexander Pius)
1846-1916 .... **TCLC 3**
See also CA 104; 134; CANR 84; EWL 3;
RGSF 2; RGWL 2, 3
Sierra, Gregorio Martinez
See Martinez Sierra, Gregorio
Sierra, Maria (de la O'LeJarraga) Martinez
See Martinez Sierra, Maria (de la
O'LeJarraga)
Sigal, Clancy 1926- .... **CLC 7**
See also CA 1-4R; CANR 85; CN 1, 2, 3,
4, 5, 6, 7
Siger of Brabant 1240(?)-1284(?) . **CMLC 69**
See also DLB 115
Sigourney, Lydia H.
See Sigourney, Lydia Howard (Huntley)
See also DLB 73, 183
Sigourney, Lydia Howard (Huntley)
1791-1865 .... **NCLC 21, 87**
See Sigourney, Lydia H.; Sigourney, Lydia
Huntley
See also DLB 1
Sigourney, Lydia Huntley
See Sigourney, Lydia Howard (Huntley)
See also DLB 42, 239, 243
Siguenza y Gongora, Carlos de
1645-1700 .... **HLCS 2; LC 8**
See also LAW
Sigurjonsson, Johann
See Sigurjonsson, Johann
Sigurjonsson, Johann 1880-1919 ... **TCLC 27**
See also CA 170; DLB 293; EWL 3
Sikelianos, Angelos 1884-1951 .... **PC 29; TCLC 39**
See also EWL 3; RGWL 2, 3

Silkin, Jon 1930-1997 .... **CLC 2, 6, 43**
See also CA 5-8R; CAAS 5; CANR 89; CP
1, 2, 3, 4, 5, 6; DLB 27
Silko, Leslie (Marmon) 1948- .... **CLC 23, 74,
114, 211; NNAL; SSC 37, 66; WLCS**
See also AAYA 14; AMWS 4; ANW; BYA
12; CA 115; 122; CANR 45, 65, 118; CN
4, 5, 6, 7; CP 4, 5, 6, 7; CPW 1; CWP;
DA; DA3; DAC; DAM MST, MULT,
POP; DLB 143, 175, 256, 275; EWL 3;
EXPP; EXPS; LAIT 4; MAL 5; MTCW
2; MTFW 2005; NFS 4; PFS 9, 16; RGAL
4; RGSF 2; SSFS 4, 8, 10, 11; TCWW 1,
2
Sillanpaa, Frans Eemil 1888-1964 ... **CLC 19**
See also CA 129; 93-96; EWL 3; MTCW 1
Sillitoe, Alan 1928- .. **CLC 1, 3, 6, 10, 19, 57,
148**
See also AITN 1; BRWS 5; CA 9-12R, 191;
CAAE 191; CAAS 2; CANR 8, 26, 55,
139; CDBLB 1960 to Present; CN 1, 2, 3,
4, 5, 6; CP 1, 2, 3, 4; DLB 14, 139; EWL
3; MTCW 1, 2; MTFW 2005; RGEL 2;
RGSF 2; SATA 61
Silone, Ignazio 1900-1978 .... **CLC 4**
See also CA 25-28; 81-84; CANR 34; CAP
2; DLB 264; EW 12; EWL 3; MTCW 1;
RGSF 2; RGWL 2, 3
Silone, Ignazione
See Silone, Ignazio
Silver, Joan Micklin 1935- .... **CLC 20**
See also CA 114; 121; INT CA-121
Silver, Nicholas
See Faust, Frederick (Schiller)
Silverberg, Robert 1935- .... **CLC 7, 140**
See also AAYA 24; BPFB 3; BYA 7, 9; CA
1-4R, 186; CAAE 186; CAAS 3; CANR
1, 20, 36, 85, 140; CLR 59; CN 6, 7;
CPW; DAM POP; DLB 8; INT CANR-
20; MAICYA 1, 2; MTCW 1, 2; MTFW
2005; SATA 13, 91; SATA-Essay 104;
SCFW 1, 2; SFW 4; SUFW 2
Silverstein, Alvin 1933- .... **CLC 17**
See also CA 49-52; CANR 2; CLR 25;
JRDA; MAICYA 1, 2; SATA 8, 69, 124
Silverstein, Shel(don Allan)
1932-1999 .... **PC 49**
See also AAYA 40; BW 3; CA 107; 179;
CANR 47, 74, 81; CLR 5, 96; CWRI 5;
JRDA; MAICYA 1, 2; MTCW 2; MTFW
2005; SATA 33, 92; SATA-Brief 27;
SATA-Obit 116
Silverstein, Virginia B(arbara Opshelor)
1937- .... **CLC 17**
See also CA 49-52; CANR 2; CLR 25;
JRDA; MAICYA 1, 2; SATA 8, 69, 124
Sim, Georges
See Simenon, Georges (Jacques Christian)
Simak, Clifford D(onald) 1904-1988 . **CLC 1,
55**
See also CA 1-4R; 125; CANR 1, 35; DLB
8; MTCW 1; SATA-Obit 56; SCFW 1, 2;
SFW 4
Simenon, Georges (Jacques Christian)
1903-1989 .... **CLC 1, 2, 3, 8, 18, 47**
See also BPFB 3; CA 85-88; 129; CANR
35; CMW 4; DA3; DAM POP; DLB 72;
DLBY 1989; EW 12; EWL 3; GFL 1789
to the Present; MSW; MTCW 1, 2; MTFW
2005; RGWL 2, 3
Simic, Charles 1938- .... **CLC 6, 9, 22, 49, 68,
130; PC 69**
See also AMWS 8; CA 29-32R; CAAS 4;
CANR 12, 33, 52, 61, 96, 140; CP 2, 3, 4,
5, 6, 7; DA3; DAM POET; DLB 105;
MAL 5; MTCW 2; MTFW 2005; PFS 7;
RGAL 4; WP
Simmel, Georg 1858-1918 .... **TCLC 64**
See also CA 157; DLB 296

Spacks, Barry (Bernard) 1931- .... **CLC 14**
   See also CA 154; CANR 33, 109; CP 3, 4,
   5, 6, 7; DLB 105

Spanidou, Irini 1946- .... **CLC 44**
   See also CA 185

Spark, Muriel (Sarah) 1918- ..... **CLC 2, 3, 5,
   8, 13, 18, 40, 94; SSC 10**
   See also BRWS 1; CA 5-8R; CANR 12, 36,
   76, 89, 131; CDBLB 1945-1960; CN 1, 2,
   3, 4, 5, 6, 7; CP 1, 2, 3, 4, 5, 6, 7; DA3;
   DAB; DAC; DAM MST, NOV; DLB 15,
   139; EWL 3; FW; INT CANR-12; LAIT
   4; MTCW 1, 2; MTFW 2005; NFS 22;
   RGEL 2; TEA; WLIT 4; YAW

Spaulding, Douglas
   See Bradbury, Ray (Douglas)

Spaulding, Leonard
   See Bradbury, Ray (Douglas)

Speght, Rachel 1597-c. 1630 .... **LC 97**
   See also DLB 126

Spence, J. A. D.
   See Eliot, T(homas) S(tearns)

Spencer, Anne 1882-1975 .... **HR 1:3**
   See also BW 2; CA 161; DLB 51, 54

Spencer, Elizabeth 1921- .... **CLC 22; SSC 57**
   See also CA 13-16R; CANR 32, 65, 87; CN
   1, 2, 3, 4, 5, 6, 7; CSW; DLB 6, 218;
   EWL 3; MTCW 1; RGAL 4; SATA 14

Spencer, Leonard G.
   See Silverberg, Robert

Spencer, Scott 1945- .... **CLC 30**
   See also CA 113; CANR 51; DLBY 1986

Spender, Stephen (Harold)
   1909-1995 .... **CLC 1, 2, 5, 10, 41, 91**
   See also BRWS 2; CA 9-12R; 149; CANR
   31, 54; CDBLB 1945-1960; CP 1, 2, 3, 4;
   DA3; DAM POET; DLB 20; EWL 3;
   MTCW 1, 2; MTFW 2005; PAB; PFS 23;
   RGEL 2; TEA

Spengler, Oswald (Arnold Gottfried)
   1880-1936 .... **TCLC 25**
   See also CA 118; 189

Spenser, Edmund 1552(?)-1599 ...... **LC 5, 39,
   117; PC 8, 42; WLC**
   See also AAYA 60; BRW 1; CDBLB Be-
   fore 1660; DA; DA3; DAB; DAC; DAM
   MST, POET; DLB 167; EFS 2; EXPP;
   PAB; RGEL 2; TEA; WLIT 3; WP

Spicer, Jack 1925-1965 .... **CLC 8, 18, 72**
   See also BG 1:3; CA 85-88; DAM POET;
   DLB 5, 16, 193; GLL 1; WP

Spiegelman, Art 1948- .... **CLC 76, 178**
   See also AAYA 10, 46; CA 125; CANR 41,
   55, 74, 124; DLB 299; MTCW 2; MTFW
   2005; SATA 109, 158; YAW

Spielberg, Peter 1929- .... **CLC 6**
   See also CA 5-8R; CANR 4, 48; DLBY
   1981

Spielberg, Steven 1947- .... **CLC 20, 188**
   See also AAYA 8, 24; CA 77-80; CANR
   32; SATA 32

Spillane, Frank Morrison 1918-
   See Spillane, Mickey
   See also CA 25-28R; CANR 28, 63, 125;
   DA3; MTCW 1, 2; MTFW 2005; SATA
   66

Spillane, Mickey .... **CLC 3, 13**
   See Spillane, Frank Morrison
   See also BPFB 3; CMW 4; DLB 226; MSW

Spinoza, Benedictus de 1632-1677 .. **LC 9, 58**

Spinrad, Norman (Richard) 1940- ... **CLC 46**
   See also BPFB 3; CA 37-40R, 233; CAAE
   233; CAAS 19; CANR 20, 91; DLB 8;
   INT CANR-20; SFW 4

Spitteler, Carl (Friedrich Georg)
   1845-1924 .... **TCLC 12**
   See also CA 109; DLB 129; EWL 3

Spivack, Kathleen (Romola Drucker)
   1938- .... **CLC 6**
   See also CA 49-52

Spofford, Harriet (Elizabeth) Prescott
   1835-1921 .... **SSC 87**
   See also CA 201; DLB 74, 221

Spoto, Donald 1941- .... **CLC 39**
   See also CA 65-68; CANR 11, 57, 93

Springsteen, Bruce (F.) 1949- .... **CLC 17**
   See also CA 111

Spurling, Hilary 1940- .... **CLC 34**
   See also CA 104; CANR 25, 52, 94

Spurling, Susan Hilary
   See Spurling, Hilary

Spyker, John Howland
   See Elman, Richard (Martin)

Squared, A.
   See Abbott, Edwin A.

Squires, (James) Radcliffe
   1917-1993 .... **CLC 51**
   See also CA 1-4R; 140; CANR 6, 21; CP 1,
   2, 3, 4

Srivastava, Dhanpat Rai 1880(?)-1936
   See Premchand
   See also CA 118; 197

Stacy, Donald
   See Pohl, Frederik

Stael
   See Stael-Holstein, Anne Louise Germaine
   Necker
   See also EW 5; RGWL 2, 3

Stael, Germaine de
   See Stael-Holstein, Anne Louise Germaine
   Necker
   See also DLB 119, 192; FL 1:3; FW; GFL
   1789 to the Present; TWA

Stael-Holstein, Anne Louise Germaine
   Necker 1766-1817 .... **NCLC 3, 91**
   See Stael; Stael, Germaine de

Stafford, Jean 1915-1979 .. **CLC 4, 7, 19, 68;
   SSC 26, 86**
   See also CA 1-4R; 85-88; CANR 3, 65; CN
   1, 2; DLB 2, 173; MAL 5; MTCW 1, 2;
   MTFW 2005; RGAL 4; RGSF 2; SATA-
   Obit 22; SSFS 21; TCWW 1, 2; TUS

Stafford, William (Edgar)
   1914-1993 .... **CLC 4, 7, 29**
   See also AMWS 11; CA 5-8R; 142; CAAS
   3; CANR 5, 22; CP 1, 2, 3, 4; DAM
   POET; DLB 5, 206; EXPP; INT CANR-
   22; MAL 5; PFS 2, 8, 16; RGAL 4; WP

Stagnelius, Eric Johan 1793-1823 . **NCLC 61**

Staines, Trevor
   See Brunner, John (Kilian Houston)

Stairs, Gordon
   See Austin, Mary (Hunter)

Stalin, Joseph 1879-1953 .... **TCLC 92**

Stampa, Gaspara c. 1524-1554 .. **LC 114; PC
   43**
   See also RGWL 2, 3; WLIT 7

Stampflinger, K. A.
   See Benjamin, Walter

Stancykowna
   See Szymborska, Wislawa

Standing Bear, Luther
   1868(?)-1939(?) .... **NNAL**
   See also CA 113; 144; DAM MULT

Stanislavsky, Konstantin (Sergeivich)
   1863(?)-1938 .... **TCLC 167**
   See also CA 118

Stannard, Martin 1947- .... **CLC 44**
   See also CA 142; DLB 155

Stanton, Elizabeth Cady
   1815-1902 .... **TCLC 73**
   See also CA 171; DLB 79; FL 1:3; FW

Stanton, Maura 1946- .... **CLC 9**
   See also CA 89-92; CANR 15, 123; DLB
   120

Stanton, Schuyler
   See Baum, L(yman) Frank

Stapledon, (William) Olaf
   1886-1950 .... **TCLC 22**
   See also CA 111; 162; DLB 15, 255; SCFW
   1, 2; SFW 4

Starbuck, George (Edwin)
   1931-1996 .... **CLC 53**
   See also CA 21-24R; 153; CANR 23; CP 1,
   2, 3, 4; DAM POET

Stark, Richard
   See Westlake, Donald E(dwin)

Staunton, Schuyler
   See Baum, L(yman) Frank

Stead, Christina (Ellen) 1902-1983 ... **CLC 2,
   5, 8, 32, 80**
   See also BRWS 4; CA 13-16R; 109; CANR
   33, 40; CN 1, 2, 3; DLB 260; EWL 3;
   FW; MTCW 1, 2; MTFW 2005; RGEL 2;
   RGSF 2; WWE 1

Stead, William Thomas
   1849-1912 .... **TCLC 48**
   See also CA 167

Stebnitsky, M.
   See Leskov, Nikolai (Semyonovich)

Steele, Richard 1672-1729 .... **LC 18**
   See also BRW 3; CDBLB 1660-1789; DLB
   84, 101; RGEL 2; WLIT 3

Steele, Timothy (Reid) 1948- .... **CLC 45**
   See also CA 93-96; CANR 16, 50, 92; CP
   7; DLB 120, 282

Steffens, (Joseph) Lincoln
   1866-(1936) .... **TCLC 20**
   See also CA 117; 198; DLB 303; MAL 5

Stegner, Wallace (Earle) 1909-1993 .. **CLC 9,
   49, 81; SSC 27**
   See also AITN 1; AMWS 4; ANW; BEST
   90:3; BPFB 3; CA 1-4R; 141; CAAS 9;
   CANR 1, 21, 46; CN 1, 2, 3, 4, 5; DAM
   NOV; DLB 9, 206, 275; DLBY 1993;
   EWL 3; MAL 5; MTCW 1, 2; MTFW
   2005; RGAL 4; TCWW 1, 2; TUS

Stein, Gertrude 1874-1946 .... **DC 19; PC 18;
   SSC 42; TCLC 1, 6, 28, 48; WLC**
   See also AAYA 64; AMW; AMWC 2; CA
   104; 132; CANR 108; CDALB 1917-
   1929; DA; DA3; DAB; DAC; DAM MST,
   NOV, POET; DLB 4, 54, 86, 228; DLBD
   15; EWL 3; EXPS; FL 1:6; GLL 1; MAL
   5; MAWW; MTCW 1, 2; MTFW 2005;
   NCFS 4; RGAL 4; RGSF 2; SSFS 5;
   TUS; WP

Steinbeck, John (Ernst) 1902-1968 ... **CLC 1,
   5, 9, 13, 21, 34, 45, 75, 124; SSC 11, 37,
   77; TCLC 135; WLC**
   See also AAYA 12; AMW; BPFB 3; BYA 2,
   3, 13; CA 1-4R; 25-28R; CANR 1, 35;
   CDALB 1929-1941; DA; DA3; DAB;
   DAC; DAM DRAM, MST, NOV; DLB 7,
   9, 212, 275, 309; DLBD 2; EWL 3;
   EXPS; LAIT 3; MAL 5; MTCW 1, 2;
   MTFW 2005; NFS 1, 5, 7, 17, 19; RGAL
   4; RGSF 2; RHW; SATA 9; SSFS 3, 6;
   TCWW 1, 2; TUS; WYA; YAW

Steinem, Gloria 1934- .... **CLC 63**
   See also CA 53-56; CANR 28, 51, 139;
   DLB 246; FW; MTCW 1, 2; MTFW 2005

Steiner, George 1929- .... **CLC 24**
   See also CA 73-76; CANR 31, 67, 108;
   DAM NOV; DLB 67, 299; EWL 3;
   MTCW 1, 2; MTFW 2005; SATA 62

Steiner, K. Leslie
   See Delany, Samuel R(ay), Jr.

Steiner, Rudolf 1861-1925 .... **TCLC 13**
   See also CA 107

Stendhal 1783-1842 .. **NCLC 23, 46; SSC 27;
   WLC**
   See also DA; DA3; DAB; DAC; DAM
   MST, NOV; DLB 119; EW 5; GFL 1789
   to the Present; RGWL 2, 3; TWA

Szirtes, George 1948- .... **CLC 46; PC 51**
See also CA 109; CANR 27, 61, 117; CP 4, 5, 6, 7

Szymborska, Wislawa 1923- ... **CLC 99, 190; PC 44**
See also CA 154; CANR 91, 133; CDWLB 4; CWP; CWW 2; DA3; DLB 232; DLBY 1996; EWL 3; MTCW 2; MTFW 2005; PFS 15; RGWL 3

T. O., Nik
See Annensky, Innokenty (Fyodorovich)

Tabori, George 1914- .... **CLC 19**
See also CA 49-52; CANR 4, 69; CBD; CD 5, 6; DLB 245

Tacitus c. 55-c. 117 .... **CMLC 56**
See also AW 2; CDWLB 1; DLB 211; RGWL 2, 3

Tagore, Rabindranath 1861-1941 .... **PC 8; SSC 48; TCLC 3, 53**
See also CA 104; 120; DA3; DAM DRAM, POET; EWL 3; MTCW 1, 2; MTFW 2005; PFS 18; RGEL 2; RGSF 2; RGWL 2, 3; TWA

Taine, Hippolyte Adolphe
1828-1893 .... **NCLC 15**
See also EW 7; GFL 1789 to the Present

Talayesva, Don C. 1890-(?) .... **NNAL**

Talese, Gay 1932- .... **CLC 37**
See also AITN 1; CA 1-4R; CANR 9, 58, 137; DLB 185; INT CANR-9; MTCW 1, 2; MTFW 2005

Tallent, Elizabeth (Ann) 1954- .... **CLC 45**
See also CA 117; CANR 72; DLB 130

Tallmountain, Mary 1918-1997 .... **NNAL**
See also CA 146; 161; DLB 193

Tally, Ted 1952- .... **CLC 42**
See also CA 120; 124; CAD; CANR 125; CD 5, 6; INT CA-124

Talvik, Heiti 1904-1947 .... **TCLC 87**
See also EWL 3

Tamayo y Baus, Manuel
1829-1898 .... **NCLC 1**

Tammsaare, A(nton) H(ansen)
1878-1940 .... **TCLC 27**
See also CA 164; CDWLB 4; DLB 220; EWL 3

Tam'si, Tchicaya U
See Tchicaya, Gerald Felix

Tan, Amy (Ruth) 1952- . **AAL; CLC 59, 120, 151**
See also AAYA 9, 48; AMWS 10; BEST 89:3; BPFB 3; CA 136; CANR 54, 105, 132; CDALBS; CN 6, 7; CPW 1; DA3; DAM MULT, NOV, POP; DLB 173, 312; EXPN; FL 1:6; FW; LAIT 3, 5; MAL 5; MTCW 2; MTFW 2005; NFS 1, 13, 16; RGAL 4; SATA 75; SSFS 9; YAW

Tandem, Felix
See Spitteler, Carl (Friedrich Georg)

Tanizaki, Jun'ichiro 1886-1965 ... **CLC 8, 14, 28; SSC 21**
See Tanizaki Jun'ichiro
See also CA 93-96; 25-28R; MJW; MTCW 2; MTFW 2005; RGSF 2; RGWL 2

Tanizaki Jun'ichiro
See Tanizaki, Jun'ichiro
See also DLB 180; EWL 3

Tannen, Deborah F(rances) 1945- .. **CLC 206**
See also CA 118; CANR 95

Tanner, William
See Amis, Kingsley (William)

Tao Lao
See Storni, Alfonsina

Tapahonso, Luci 1953- .... **NNAL; PC 65**
See also CA 145; CANR 72, 127; DLB 175

Tarantino, Quentin (Jerome)
1963- .... **CLC 125**
See also AAYA 58; CA 171; CANR 125

Tarassoff, Lev
See Troyat, Henri

Tarbell, Ida M(inerva) 1857-1944 . **TCLC 40**
See also CA 122; 181; DLB 47

Tarkington, (Newton) Booth
1869-1946 .... **TCLC 9**
See also BPFB 3; BYA 3; CA 110; 143; CWRI 5; DLB 9, 102; MAL 5; MTCW 2; RGAL 4; SATA 17

Tarkovskii, Andrei Arsen'evich
See Tarkovsky, Andrei (Arsenyevich)

Tarkovsky, Andrei (Arsenyevich)
1932-1986 .... **CLC 75**
See also CA 127

Tartt, Donna 1964(?)- .... **CLC 76**
See also AAYA 56; CA 142; CANR 135; MTFW 2005

Tasso, Torquato 1544-1595 .... **LC 5, 94**
See also EFS 2; EW 2; RGWL 2, 3; WLIT 7

Tate, (John Orley) Allen 1899-1979 .. **CLC 2, 4, 6, 9, 11, 14, 24; PC 50**
See also AMW; CA 5-8R; 85-88; CANR 32, 108; CN 1, 2; CP 1, 2; DLB 4, 45, 63; DLBD 17; EWL 3; MAL 5; MTCW 1, 2; MTFW 2005; RGAL 4; RHW

Tate, Ellalice
See Hibbert, Eleanor Alice Burford

Tate, James (Vincent) 1943- ..... **CLC 2, 6, 25**
See also CA 21-24R; CANR 29, 57, 114; CP 1, 2, 3, 4, 5, 6, 7; DLB 5, 169; EWL 3; PFS 10, 15; RGAL 4; WP

Tate, Nahum 1652(?)-1715 .... **LC 109**
See also DLB 80; RGEL 2

Tauler, Johannes c. 1300-1361 ...... **CMLC 37**
See also DLB 179; LMFS 1

Tavel, Ronald 1940- .... **CLC 6**
See also CA 21-24R; CAD; CANR 33; CD 5, 6

Taviani, Paolo 1931- .... **CLC 70**
See also CA 153

Taylor, Bayard 1825-1878 .... **NCLC 89**
See also DLB 3, 189, 250, 254; RGAL 4

Taylor, C(ecil) P(hilip) 1929-1981 .... **CLC 27**
See also CA 25-28R; 105; CANR 47; CBD

Taylor, Edward 1642(?)-1729 . **LC 11; PC 63**
See also AMW; DA; DAB; DAC; DAM MST, POET; DLB 24; EXPP; RGAL 4; TUS

Taylor, Eleanor Ross 1920- .... **CLC 5**
See also CA 81-84; CANR 70

Taylor, Elizabeth 1912-1975 ..... **CLC 2, 4, 29**
See also CA 13-16R; CANR 9, 70; CN 1, 2; DLB 139; MTCW 1; RGEL 2; SATA 13

Taylor, Frederick Winslow
1856-1915 .... **TCLC 76**
See also CA 188

Taylor, Henry (Splawn) 1942- .... **CLC 44**
See also CA 33-36R; CAAS 7; CANR 31; CP 7; DLB 5; PFS 10

Taylor, Kamala (Purnaiya) 1924-2004
See Markandaya, Kamala
See also CA 77-80; 227; MTFW 2005; NFS 13

Taylor, Mildred D(elois) 1943- .... **CLC 21**
See also AAYA 10, 47; BW 1; BYA 3, 8; CA 85-88; CANR 25, 115, 136; CLR 9, 59, 90; CSW; DLB 52; JRDA; LAIT 3; MAICYA 1, 2; MTFW 2005; SAAS 5; SATA 135; WYA; YAW

Taylor, Peter (Hillsman) 1917-1994 .. **CLC 1, 4, 18, 37, 44, 50, 71; SSC 10, 84**
See also AMWS 5; BPFB 3; CA 13-16R; 147; CANR 9, 50; CN 1, 2, 3, 4, 5; CSW; DLB 218, 278; DLBY 1981, 1994; EWL 3; EXPS; INT CANR-9; MAL 5; MTCW 1, 2; MTFW 2005; RGSF 2; SSFS 9; TUS

Taylor, Robert Lewis 1912-1998 .... **CLC 14**
See also CA 1-4R; 170; CANR 3, 64; CN 1, 2; SATA 10; TCWW 1, 2

Tchekhov, Anton
See Chekhov, Anton (Pavlovich)

Tchicaya, Gerald Felix 1931-1988 .. **CLC 101**
See Tchicaya U Tam'si
See also CA 129; 125; CANR 81

Tchicaya U Tam'si
See Tchicaya, Gerald Felix
See also EWL 3

Teasdale, Sara 1884-1933 .... **PC 31; TCLC 4**
See also CA 104; 163; DLB 45; GLL 1; PFS 14; RGAL 4; SATA 32; TUS

Tecumseh 1768-1813 .... **NNAL**
See also DAM MULT

Tegner, Esaias 1782-1846 .... **NCLC 2**

Teilhard de Chardin, (Marie Joseph) Pierre
1881-1955 .... **TCLC 9**
See also CA 105; 210; GFL 1789 to the Present

Temple, Ann
See Mortimer, Penelope (Ruth)

Tennant, Emma (Christina) 1937- .. **CLC 13, 52**
See also BRWS 9; CA 65-68; CAAS 9; CANR 10, 38, 59, 88; CN 3, 4, 5, 6, 7; DLB 14; EWL 3; SFW 4

Tenneshaw, S. M.
See Silverberg, Robert

Tenney, Tabitha Gilman
1762-1837 .... **NCLC 122**
See also DLB 37, 200

Tennyson, Alfred 1809-1892 ... **NCLC 30, 65, 115; PC 6; WLC**
See also AAYA 50; BRW 4; CDBLB 1832-1890; DA; DA3; DAB; DAC; DAM MST, POET; DLB 32; EXPP; PAB; PFS 1, 2, 4, 11, 15, 19; RGEL 2; TEA; WLIT 4; WP

Teran, Lisa St. Aubin de .... **CLC 36**
See St. Aubin de Teran, Lisa

Terence c. 184B.C.-c. 159B.C. ...... **CMLC 14; DC 7**
See also AW 1; CDWLB 1; DLB 211; RGWL 2, 3; TWA

Teresa de Jesus, St. 1515-1582 .... **LC 18**

Teresa of Avila, St.
See Teresa de Jesus, St.

Terkel, Louis 1912-
See Terkel, Studs
See also CA 57-60; CANR 18, 45, 67, 132; DA3; MTCW 1, 2; MTFW 2005

Terkel, Studs .... **CLC 38**
See Terkel, Louis
See also AAYA 32; AITN 1; MTCW 2; TUS

Terry, C. V.
See Slaughter, Frank G(ill)

Terry, Megan 1932- .... **CLC 19; DC 13**
See also CA 77-80; CABS 3; CAD; CANR 43; CD 5, 6; CWD; DFS 18; DLB 7, 249; GLL 2

Tertullian c. 155-c. 245 .... **CMLC 29**

Tertz, Abram
See Sinyavsky, Andrei (Donatevich)
See also RGSF 2

Tesich, Steve 1943(?)-1996 .... **CLC 40, 69**
See also CA 105; 152; CAD; DLBY 1983

Tesla, Nikola 1856-1943 .... **TCLC 88**

Teternikov, Fyodor Kuzmich 1863-1927
See Sologub, Fyodor
See also CA 104

Tevis, Walter 1928-1984 .... **CLC 42**
See also CA 113; SFW 4

Tey, Josephine .... **TCLC 14**
See Mackintosh, Elizabeth
See also DLB 77; MSW

Ustinov, Peter (Alexander)
  1921-2004 .... CLC 1
  See also AITN 1; CA 13-16R; 225; CANR
  25, 51; CBD; CD 5, 6; DLB 13; MTCW
  2

U Tam'si, Gerald Felix Tchicaya
  See Tchicaya, Gerald Felix

U Tam'si, Tchicaya
  See Tchicaya, Gerald Felix

Vachss, Andrew (Henry) 1942- .... CLC 106
  See also CA 118, 214; CAAE 214; CANR
  44, 95; CMW 4

Vachss, Andrew H.
  See Vachss, Andrew (Henry)

Vaculik, Ludvik 1926- .... CLC 7
  See also CA 53-56; CANR 72; CWW 2;
  DLB 232; EWL 3

Vaihinger, Hans 1852-1933 .... TCLC 71
  See also CA 116; 166

Valdez, Luis (Miguel) 1940- ..... CLC 84; DC
  10; HLC 2
  See also CA 101; CAD; CANR 32, 81; CD
  5, 6; DAM MULT; DFS 5; DLB 122;
  EWL 3; HW 1; LAIT 4; LLW

Valenzuela, Luisa 1938- .... CLC 31, 104;
  HLCS 2; SSC 14, 82
  See also CA 101; CANR 32, 65, 123; CD-
  WLB 3; CWW 2; DAM MULT; DLB 113;
  EWL 3; FW; HW 1, 2; LAW; RGSF 2;
  RGWL 3

Valera y Alcala-Galiano, Juan
  1824-1905 .... TCLC 10
  See also CA 106

Valerius Maximus fl. 20- .... CMLC 64
  See also DLB 211

Valery, (Ambroise) Paul (Toussaint Jules)
  1871-1945 .... PC 9; TCLC 4, 15
  See also CA 104; 122; DA3; DAM POET;
  DLB 258; EW 8; EWL 3; GFL 1789 to
  the Present; MTCW 1, 2; MTFW 2005;
  RGWL 2, 3; TWA

Valle-Inclan, Ramon (Maria) del
  1866-1936 .... HLC 2; TCLC 5
  See del Valle-Inclan, Ramon (Maria)
  See also CA 106; 153; CANR 80; DAM
  MULT; DLB 134; EW 8; EWL 3; HW 2;
  RGSF 2; RGWL 2, 3

Vallejo, Antonio Buero
  See Buero Vallejo, Antonio

Vallejo, Cesar (Abraham)
  1892-1938 .... HLC 2; TCLC 3, 56
  See also CA 105; 153; DAM MULT; DLB
  290; EWL 3; HW 1; LAW; RGWL 2, 3

Valles, Jules 1832-1885 .... NCLC 71
  See also DLB 123; GFL 1789 to the Present

Vallette, Marguerite Eymery
  1860-1953 .... TCLC 67
  See Rachilde
  See also CA 182; DLB 123, 192

Valle Y Pena, Ramon del
  See Valle-Inclan, Ramon (Maria) del

Van Ash, Cay 1918-1994 .... CLC 34
  See also CA 220

Vanbrugh, Sir John 1664-1726 .... LC 21
  See also BRW 2; DAM DRAM; DLB 80;
  IDTP; RGEL 2

Van Campen, Karl
  See Campbell, John W(ood, Jr.)

Vance, Gerald
  See Silverberg, Robert

Vance, Jack .... CLC 35
  See Vance, John Holbrook
  See also DLB 8; FANT; SCFW 1, 2; SFW
  4; SUFW 1, 2

Vance, John Holbrook 1916-
  See Queen, Ellery; Vance, Jack
  See also CA 29-32R; CANR 17, 65; CMW
  4; MTCW 1

Van Den Bogarde, Derek Jules Gaspard
  Ulric Niven 1921-1999 .... CLC 14
  See Bogarde, Dirk
  See also CA 77-80; 179

Vandenburgh, Jane .... CLC 59
  See also CA 168

Vanderhaeghe, Guy 1951- .... CLC 41
  See also BPFB 3; CA 113; CANR 72, 145;
  CN 7

van der Post, Laurens (Jan)
  1906-1996 .... CLC 5
  See also AFW; CA 5-8R; 155; CANR 35;
  CN 1, 2, 3, 4, 5, 6; DLB 204; RGEL 2

van de Wetering, Janwillem 1931- ... CLC 47
  See also CA 49-52; CANR 4, 62, 90; CMW
  4

Van Dine, S. S. .... TCLC 23
  See Wright, Willard Huntington
  See also DLB 306; MSW

Van Doren, Carl (Clinton)
  1885-1950 .... TCLC 18
  See also CA 111; 168

Van Doren, Mark 1894-1972 .... CLC 6, 10
  See also CA 1-4R; 37-40R; CANR 3; CN
  1; CP 1; DLB 45, 284; MAL 5; MTCW
  1, 2; RGAL 4

Van Druten, John (William)
  1901-1957 .... TCLC 2
  See also CA 104; 161; DLB 10; MAL 5;
  RGAL 4

Van Duyn, Mona (Jane) 1921-2004 .. CLC 3,
  7, 63, 116
  See also CA 9-12R; 234; CANR 7, 38, 60,
  116; CP 1, 2, 3, 4, 5, 6, 7; CWP; DAM
  POET; DLB 5; MAL 5; MTFW 2005;
  PFS 20

Van Dyne, Edith
  See Baum, L(yman) Frank

van Itallie, Jean-Claude 1936- .... CLC 3
  See also CA 45-48; CAAS 2; CAD; CANR
  1, 48; CD 5, 6; DLB 7

Van Loot, Cornelius Obenchain
  See Roberts, Kenneth (Lewis)

van Ostaijen, Paul 1896-1928 .... TCLC 33
  See also CA 163

Van Peebles, Melvin 1932- .... CLC 2, 20
  See also BW 2, 3; CA 85-88; CANR 27,
  67, 82; DAM MULT

van Schendel, Arthur(-Francois-Emile)
  1874-1946 .... TCLC 56
  See also EWL 3

Vansittart, Peter 1920- .... CLC 42
  See also CA 1-4R; CANR 3, 49, 90; CN 4,
  5, 6, 7; RHW

Van Vechten, Carl 1880-1964 ... CLC 33; HR
  1:3
  See also AMWS 2; CA 183; 89-92; DLB 4,
  9, 51; RGAL 4

van Vogt, A(lfred) E(lton) 1912-2000 . CLC 1
  See also BPFB 3; BYA 13, 14; CA 21-24R;
  190; CANR 28; DLB 8, 251; SATA 14;
  SATA-Obit 124; SCFW 1, 2; SFW 4

Vara, Madeleine
  See Jackson, Laura (Riding)

Varda, Agnes 1928- .... CLC 16
  See also CA 116; 122

Vargas Llosa, (Jorge) Mario (Pedro)
  1936- .... CLC 3, 6, 9, 10, 15, 31, 42, 85,
  181; HLC 2
  See Llosa, (Jorge) Mario (Pedro) Vargas
  See also BPFB 3; CA 73-76; CANR 18, 32,
  42, 67, 116, 140; CDWLB 3; CWW 2;
  DA; DA3; DAB; DAC; DAM MST,
  MULT, NOV; DLB 145; DNFS 2; EWL
  3; HW 1, 2; LAIT 5; LATS 1:2; LAW;
  LAWS 1; MTCW 1, 2; MTFW 2005;
  RGWL 2; SSFS 14; TWA; WLIT 1

Varnhagen von Ense, Rahel
  1771-1833 .... NCLC 130
  See also DLB 90

Vasari, Giorgio 1511-1574 .... LC 114

Vasiliu, George
  See Bacovia, George

Vasiliu, Gheorghe
  See Bacovia, George
  See also CA 123; 189

Vassa, Gustavus
  See Equiano, Olaudah

Vassilikos, Vassilis 1933- .... CLC 4, 8
  See also CA 81-84; CANR 75; EWL 3

Vaughan, Henry 1621-1695 .... LC 27
  See also BRW 2; DLB 131; PAB; RGEL 2

Vaughn, Stephanie .... CLC 62

Vazov, Ivan (Minchov) 1850-1921 . TCLC 25
  See also CA 121; 167; CDWLB 4; DLB
  147

Veblen, Thorstein B(unde)
  1857-1929 .... TCLC 31
  See also AMWS 1; CA 115; 165; DLB 246;
  MAL 5

Vega, Lope de 1562-1635 ... HLCS 2; LC 23,
  119
  See also EW 2; RGWL 2, 3

Vendler, Helen (Hennessy) 1933- ... CLC 138
  See also CA 41-44R; CANR 25, 72, 136;
  MTCW 1; MTFW 2005

Venison, Alfred
  See Pound, Ezra (Weston Loomis)

Ventsel, Elena Sergeevna 1907-2002
  See Grekova, I.
  See also CA 154

Verdi, Marie de
  See Mencken, H(enry) L(ouis)

Verdu, Matilde
  See Cela, Camilo Jose

Verga, Giovanni (Carmelo)
  1840-1922 .... SSC 21, 87; TCLC 3
  See also CA 104; 123; CANR 101; EW 7;
  EWL 3; RGSF 2; RGWL 2, 3; WLIT 7

Vergil 70B.C.-19B.C. ... CMLC 9, 40; PC 12;
  WLCS
  See Virgil
  See also AW 2; DA; DA3; DAB; DAC;
  DAM MST, POET; EFS 1; LMFS 1

Vergil, Polydore c. 1470-1555 .... LC 108
  See also DLB 132

Verhaeren, Emile (Adolphe Gustave)
  1855-1916 .... TCLC 12
  See also CA 109; EWL 3; GFL 1789 to the
  Present

Verlaine, Paul (Marie) 1844-1896 .. NCLC 2,
  51; PC 2, 32
  See also DAM POET; DLB 217; EW 7;
  GFL 1789 to the Present; LMFS 2; RGWL
  2, 3; TWA

Verne, Jules (Gabriel) 1828-1905 ... TCLC 6,
  52
  See also AAYA 16; BYA 4; CA 110; 131;
  CLR 88; DA3; DLB 123; GFL 1789 to
  the Present; JRDA; LAIT 2; LMFS 2;
  MAICYA 1, 2; MTFW 2005; RGWL 2, 3;
  SATA 21; SCFW 1, 2; SFW 4; TWA;
  WCH

Verus, Marcus Annius
  See Aurelius, Marcus

Very, Jones 1813-1880 .... NCLC 9
  See also DLB 1, 243; RGAL 4

Vesaas, Tarjei 1897-1970 .... CLC 48
  See also CA 190; 29-32R; DLB 297; EW
  11; EWL 3; RGWL 3

Vialis, Gaston
  See Simenon, Georges (Jacques Christian)

Vian, Boris 1920-1959(?) .... TCLC 9
  See also CA 106; 164; CANR 111; DLB
  72, 321; EWL 3; GFL 1789 to the Present;
  MTCW 2; RGWL 2, 3

Viaud, (Louis Marie) Julien 1850-1923
See Loti, Pierre
See also CA 107
Vicar, Henry
See Felsen, Henry Gregor
Vicente, Gil 1465-c. 1536 .... **LC 99**
See also DLB 318; IDTP; RGWL 2, 3
Vicker, Angus
See Felsen, Henry Gregor
Vidal, (Eugene Luther) Gore 1925- .. **CLC 2, 4, 6, 8, 10, 22, 33, 72, 142**
See Box, Edgar
See also AAYA 64; AITN 1; AMWS 4; BEST 90:2; BPFB 3; CA 5-8R; CAD; CANR 13, 45, 65, 100, 132; CD 5, 6; CDALBS; CN 1, 2, 3, 4, 5, 6, 7; CPW; DA3; DAM NOV, POP; DFS 2; DLB 6, 152; EWL 3; INT CANR-13; MAL 5; MTCW 1, 2; MTFW 2005; RGAL 4; RHW; TUS
Viereck, Peter (Robert Edwin) 1916 .... **CLC 4; PC 27**
See also CA 1-4R; CANR 1, 47; CP 1, 2, 3, 4, 5, 6, 7; DLB 5; MAL 5; PFS 9, 14
Vigny, Alfred (Victor) de 1797-1863 .... **NCLC 7, 102; PC 26**
See also DAM POET; DLB 119, 192, 217; EW 5; GFL 1789 to the Present; RGWL 2, 3
Vilakazi, Benedict Wallet 1906-1947 .... **TCLC 37**
See also CA 168
Villa, Jose Garcia
See Villa, Jose Garcia
See also CP 1, 2, 3, 4; DLB 312
Villa, Jose Garcia 1914-1997 .... **AAL; PC 22**
See Villa, Jose Garcia
See also CA 25-28R; CANR 12, 118; EWL 3; EXPP
Villard, Oswald Garrison 1872-1949 .... **TCLC 160**
See also CA 113; 162; DLB 25, 91
Villarreal, Jose Antonio 1924- .... **HLC 2**
See also CA 133; CANR 93; DAM MULT; DLB 82; HW 1; LAIT 4; RGAL 4
Villaurrutia, Xavier 1903-1950 ...... **TCLC 80**
See also CA 192; EWL 3; HW 1; LAW
Villaverde, Cirilo 1812-1894 .... **NCLC 121**
See also LAW
Villehardouin, Geoffroi de 1150(?)-1218(?) .... **CMLC 38**
Villiers, George 1628-1687 .... **LC 107**
See also DLB 80; RGEL 2
Villiers de l'Isle Adam, Jean Marie Mathias Philippe Auguste 1838-1889 ... **NCLC 3; SSC 14**
See also DLB 123, 192; GFL 1789 to the Present; RGSF 2
Villon, Francois 1431-1463(?) . **LC 62; PC 13**
See also DLB 208; EW 2; RGWL 2, 3; TWA
Vine, Barbara .... **CLC 50**
See Rendell, Ruth (Barbara)
See also BEST 90:4
Vinge, Joan (Carol) D(ennison) 1948- .... **CLC 30; SSC 24**
See also AAYA 32; BPFB 3; CA 93-96; CANR 72; SATA 36, 113; SFW 4; YAW
Viola, Herman J(oseph) 1938- .... **CLC 70**
See also CA 61-64; CANR 8, 23, 48, 91; SATA 126
Violis, G.
See Simenon, Georges (Jacques Christian)
Viramontes, Helena Maria 1954- .... **HLCS 2**
See also CA 159; DLB 122; HW 2; LLW
Virgil
See Vergil
See also CDWLB 1; DLB 211; LAIT 1; RGWL 2, 3; WP

Visconti, Luchino 1906-1976 .... **CLC 16**
See also CA 81-84; 65-68; CANR 39
Vitry, Jacques de
See Jacques de Vitry
Vittorini, Elio 1908-1966 .... **CLC 6, 9, 14**
See also CA 133; 25-28R; DLB 264; EW 12; EWL 3; RGWL 2, 3
Vivekananda, Swami 1863-1902 .... **TCLC 88**
Vizenor, Gerald Robert 1934- .... **CLC 103; NNAL**
See also CA 13-16R, 205; CAAE 205; CAAS 22; CANR 5, 21, 44, 67; DAM MULT; DLB 175, 227; MTCW 2; MTFW 2005, TCWW 2
Vizinczey, Stephen 1933- .... **CLC 40**
See also CA 128; CCA 1; INT CA-128
Vliet, R(ussell) G(ordon) 1929-1984 .... **CLC 22**
See also CA 37-40R; 112; CANR 18; CP 2, 3
Vogau, Boris Andreyevich 1894-1938
See Pilnyak, Boris
See also CA 123; 218
Vogel, Paula A(nne) 1951- ... **CLC 76; DC 19**
See also CA 108; CAD; CANR 119, 140; CD 5, 6; CWD; DFS 14; MTFW 2005; RGAL 4
Voigt, Cynthia 1942- .... **CLC 30**
See also AAYA 3, 30; BYA 1, 3, 6, 7, 8; CA 106; CANR 18, 37, 40, 94, 145; CLR 13, 48; INT CANR-18; JRDA; LAIT 5; MAICYA 1, 2; MAICYAS 1; MTFW 2005; SATA 48, 79, 116, 160; SATA-Brief 33; WYA; YAW
Voigt, Ellen Bryant 1943- .... **CLC 54**
See also CA 69-72; CANR 11, 29, 55, 115; CP 7; CSW; CWP; DLB 120; PFS 23
Voinovich, Vladimir (Nikolaevich) 1932- .... **CLC 10, 49, 147**
See also CA 81-84; CAAS 12; CANR 33, 67; CWW 2; DLB 302; MTCW 1
Vollmann, William T. 1959- .... **CLC 89**
See also CA 134; CANR 67, 116; CN 7; CPW; DA3; DAM NOV, POP; MTCW 2; MTFW 2005
Voloshinov, V. N.
See Bakhtin, Mikhail Mikhailovich
Voltaire 1694-1778 . **LC 14, 79, 110; SSC 12; WLC**
See also BYA 13; DA; DA3; DAB; DAC; DAM DRAM, MST; DLB 314; EW 4; GFL Beginnings to 1789; LATS 1:1; LMFS 1; NFS 7; RGWL 2, 3; TWA
von Aschendrof, Baron Ignatz
See Ford, Ford Madox
von Chamisso, Adelbert
See Chamisso, Adelbert von
von Daeniken, Erich 1935- .... **CLC 30**
See also AITN 1; CA 37-40R; CANR 17, 44
von Daniken, Erich
See von Daeniken, Erich
von Hartmann, Eduard 1842-1906 .... **TCLC 96**
von Hayek, Friedrich August
See Hayek, F(riedrich) A(ugust von)
von Heidenstam, (Carl Gustaf) Verner
See Heidenstam, (Carl Gustaf) Verner von
von Heyse, Paul (Johann Ludwig)
See Heyse, Paul (Johann Ludwig von)
von Hofmannsthal, Hugo
See Hofmannsthal, Hugo von
von Horvath, Odon
See von Horvath, Odon
von Horvath, Odon
See von Horvath, Odon

von Horvath, Odon 1901-1938 .... **TCLC 45**
See von Horvath, Oedoen
See also CA 118; 194; DLB 85, 124; RGWL 2, 3
von Horvath, Oedoen
See von Horvath, Odon
See also CA 184
von Kleist, Heinrich
See Kleist, Heinrich von
von Liliencron, (Friedrich Adolf Axel) Detlev
See Liliencron, (Friedrich Adolf Axel) Detlev von
Vonnegut, Kurt, Jr. 1922- . **CLC 1, 2, 3, 4, 5, 8, 12, 22, 40, 60, 111, 212; SSC 8; WLC**
See also AAYA 6, 44; AITN 1; AMWS 2; BEST 90:4; BPFB 3; BYA 3, 14; CA 1-4R; CANR 1, 25, 49, 75, 92; CDALB 1968-1988; CN 1, 2, 3, 4, 5, 6, 7; CPW 1; DA; DA3; DAB; DAC; DAM MST, NOV, POP; DLB 2, 8, 152; DLDD 3; DLBY 1980; EWL 3; EXPN; EXPS; LAIT 4; LMFS 2; MAL 5; MTCW 1, 2; MTFW 2005; NFS 3; RGAL 4; SCFW; SFW 4; SSFS 5; TUS; YAW
Von Rachen, Kurt
See Hubbard, L(afayette) Ron(ald)
von Rezzori (d'Arezzo), Gregor
See Rezzori (d'Arezzo), Gregor von
von Sternberg, Josef
See Sternberg, Josef von
Vorster, Gordon 1924- .... **CLC 34**
See also CA 133
Vosce, Trudie
See Ozick, Cynthia
Voznesensky, Andrei (Andreievich) 1933- .... **CLC 1, 15, 57**
See Voznesensky, Andrey
See also CA 89-92; CANR 37; CWW 2; DAM POET; MTCW 1
Voznesensky, Andrey
See Voznesensky, Andrei (Andreievich)
See also EWL 3
Wace, Robert c. 1100-c. 1175 .... **CMLC 55**
See also DLB 146
Waddington, Miriam 1917-2004 .... **CLC 28**
See also CA 21-24R; 225; CANR 12, 30; CCA 1; CP 1, 2, 3, 4, 5, 6, 7; DLB 68
Wagman, Fredrica 1937- .... **CLC 7**
See also CA 97-100; INT CA-97-100
Wagner, Linda W.
See Wagner-Martin, Linda (C.)
Wagner, Linda Welshimer
See Wagner-Martin, Linda (C.)
Wagner, Richard 1813-1883 ..... **NCLC 9, 119**
See also DLB 129; EW 6
Wagner-Martin, Linda (C.) 1936- .... **CLC 50**
See also CA 159; CANR 135
Wagoner, David (Russell) 1926- .... **CLC 3, 5, 15; PC 33**
See also AMWS 9; CA 1-4R; CAAS 3; CANR 2, 71; CN 1, 2, 3, 4, 5, 6, 7; CP 1, 2, 3, 4, 5, 6, 7; DLB 5, 256; SATA 14; TCWW 2
Wah, Fred(erick James) 1939- .... **CLC 44**
See also CA 107; 141; CP 1, 7; DLB 60
Wahloo, Per 1926-1975 .... **CLC 7**
See also BPFB 3; CA 61-64; CANR 73; CMW 4; MSW
Wahloo, Peter
See Wahloo, Per
Wain, John (Barrington) 1925-1994 . **CLC 2, 11, 15, 46**
See also CA 5-8R; 145; CAAS 4; CANR 23, 54; CDBLB 1960 to Present; CN 1, 2, 3, 4, 5; CP 1, 2, 3, 4; DLB 15, 27, 139, 155; EWL 3; MTCW 1, 2; MTFW 2005

Wajda, Andrzej 1926- .... **CLC 16**
    See also CA 102
Wakefield, Dan 1932- .... **CLC 7**
    See also CA 21-24R, 211; CAAE 211;
    CAAS 7; CN 4, 5, 6, 7
Wakefield, Herbert Russell
    1888-1965 .... **TCLC 120**
    See also CA 5-8R; CANR 77; HGG; SUFW
Wakoski, Diane 1937- ...... **CLC 2, 4, 7, 9, 11,**
    40; PC 15
    See also CA 13-16R, 216; CAAE 216;
    CAAS 1; CANR 9, 60, 106; CP 1, 2, 3, 4,
    5, 6, 7; CWP; DAM POET; DLB 5; INT
    CANR-9; MAL 5; MTCW 2; MTFW
    2005
Wakoski-Sherbell, Diane
    See Wakoski, Diane
Walcott, Derek (Alton) 1930- ... **BLC 3; CLC**
    2, 4, 9, 14, 25, 42, 67, 76, 160; DC 7;
    PC 46
    See also BW 2; CA 89-92; CANR 26, 47,
    75, 80, 130; CBD; CD 5, 6; CDWLB 3;
    CP 1, 2, 3, 4, 5, 6, 7; DA3; DAB; DAC;
    DAM MST, MULT, POET; DLB 117;
    DLBY 1981; DNFS 1; EFS 1; EWL 3;
    LMFS 2; MTCW 1, 2; MTFW 2005; PFS
    6; RGEL 2; TWA; WWE 1
Waldman, Anne (Lesley) 1945- .... **CLC 7**
    See also BG 1:3; CA 37-40R; CAAS 17;
    CANR 34, 69, 116; CP 1, 2, 3, 4, 5, 6, 7;
    CWP; DLB 16
Waldo, E. Hunter
    See Sturgeon, Theodore (Hamilton)
Waldo, Edward Hamilton
    See Sturgeon, Theodore (Hamilton)
Walker, Alice (Malsenior) 1944- .... **BLC 3;**
    CLC 5, 6, 9, 19, 27, 46, 58, 103, 167;
    PC 30; SSC 5; WLCS
    See also AAYA 3, 33; AFAW 1, 2; AMWS
    3; BEST 89:4; BPFB 3; BW 2, 3; CA 37-
    40R; CANR 9, 27, 49, 66, 82, 131;
    CDALB 1968-1988; CN 4, 5, 6, 7; CPW;
    CSW; DA; DA3; DAB; DAC; DAM MST,
    MULT, NOV, POET, POP; DLB 6, 33,
    143; EWL 3; EXPN; EXPS; FL 1:6; FW;
    INT CANR-27; LAIT 3; MAL 5; MAWW;
    MTCW 1, 2; MTFW 2005; NFS 5; RGAL
    4; RGSF 2; SATA 31; SSFS 2, 11; TUS;
    YAW
Walker, David Harry 1911-1992 ...... **CLC 14**
    See also CA 1-4R; 137; CANR 1; CN 1, 2;
    CWRI 5; SATA 8; SATA-Obit 71
Walker, Edward Joseph 1934-2004
    See Walker, Ted
    See also CA 21-24R; 226; CANR 12, 28,
    53
Walker, George F(rederick) 1947- .. **CLC 44,**
    61
    See also CA 103; CANR 21, 43, 59; CD 5,
    6; DAB; DAC; DAM MST; DLB 60
Walker, Joseph A. 1935-2003 .... **CLC 19**
    See also BW 1, 3; CA 89-92; CAD; CANR
    26, 143; CD 5, 6; DAM DRAM, MST;
    DFS 12; DLB 38
Walker, Margaret (Abigail)
    1915-1998 .... **BLC; CLC 1, 6; PC 20;**
    TCLC 129
    See also AFAW 1, 2; BW 2, 3; CA 73-76;
    172; CANR 26, 54, 76, 136; CN 1, 2, 3,
    4, 5, 6; CP 1, 2, 3, 4; CSW; DAM MULT;
    DLB 76, 152; EXPP; FW; MAL 5; MTCW
    1, 2; MTFW 2005; RGAL 4;
    RHW
Walker, Ted .... **CLC 13**
    See Walker, Edward Joseph
    See also CP 1, 2, 3, 4, 5, 6, 7; DLB 40
Wallace, David Foster 1962- ... **CLC 50, 114;**
    SSC 68
    See also AAYA 50; AMWS 10; CA 132;
    CANR 59, 133; CN 7; DA3; MTCW 2;
    MTFW 2005

Wallace, Dexter
    See Masters, Edgar Lee
Wallace, (Richard Horatio) Edgar
    1875-1932 .... **TCLC 57**
    See also CA 115; 218; CMW 4; DLB 70;
    MSW; RGEL 2
Wallace, Irving 1916-1990 .... **CLC 7, 13**
    See also AITN 1; BPFB 3; CA 1-4R; 132;
    CAAS 1; CANR 1, 27; CPW; DAM NOV,
    POP; INT CANR-27; MTCW 1, 2
Wallant, Edward Lewis 1926-1962 ... **CLC 5,**
    10
    See also CA 1-4R; CANR 22; DLB 2, 28,
    143, 299; EWL 3; MAL 5; MTCW 1, 2;
    RGAL 4
Wallas, Graham 1858-1932 .... **TCLC 91**
Waller, Edmund 1606-1687 .... **LC 86**
    See also BRW 2; DAM POET; DLB 126;
    PAB; RGEL 2
Walley, Byron
    See Card, Orson Scott
Walpole, Horace 1717-1797 .... **LC 2, 49**
    See also BRW 3; DLB 39, 104, 213; GL 3;
    HGG; LMFS 1; RGEL 2; SUFW 1; TEA
Walpole, Hugh (Seymour)
    1884-1941 .... **TCLC 5**
    See also CA 104; 165; DLB 34; HGG;
    MTCW 2; RGEL 2; RHW
Walrond, Eric (Derwent) 1898-1966 . **HR 1:3**
    See also BW 1; CA 125; DLB 51
Walser, Martin 1927- .... **CLC 27, 183**
    See also CA 57-60; CANR 8, 46, 145;
    CWW 2; DLB 75, 124; EWL 3
Walser, Robert 1878-1956 ..... **SSC 20; TCLC**
    18
    See also CA 118; 165; CANR 100; DLB
    66; EWL 3
Walsh, Gillian Paton
    See Paton Walsh, Gillian
Walsh, Jill Paton .... **CLC 35**
    See Paton Walsh, Gillian
    See also CLR 2, 65; WYA
Walter, Villiam Christian
    See Andersen, Hans Christian
Walters, Anna L(ee) 1946- .... **NNAL**
    See also CA 73-76
Walther von der Vogelweide c.
    1170-1228 .... **CMLC 56**
Walton, Izaak 1593-1683 .... **LC 72**
    See also BRW 2; CDBLB Before 1660;
    DLB 151, 213; RGEL 2
Wambaugh, Joseph (Aloysius), Jr.
    1937- .... **CLC 3, 18**
    See also AITN 1; BEST 89:3; BPFB 3; CA
    33-36R; CANR 42, 65, 115; CMW 4;
    CPW 1; DA3; DAM NOV, POP; DLB 6;
    DLBY 1983; MSW; MTCW 1, 2
Wang Wei 699(?)-761(?) .... **PC 18**
    See also TWA
Warburton, William 1698-1779 .... **LC 97**
    See also DLB 104
Ward, Arthur Henry Sarsfield 1883-1959
    See Rohmer, Sax
    See also CA 108; 173; CMW 4; HGG
Ward, Douglas Turner 1930- .... **CLC 19**
    See also BW 1; CA 81-84; CAD; CANR
    27; CD 5, 6; DLB 7, 38
Ward, E. D.
    See Lucas, E(dward) V(errall)
Ward, Mrs. Humphry 1851-1920
    See Ward, Mary Augusta
    See also RGEL 2
Ward, Mary Augusta 1851-1920 ... **TCLC 55**
    See Ward, Mrs. Humphry
    See also DLB 18
Ward, Nathaniel 1578(?)-1652 .... **LC 114**
    See also DLB 24
Ward, Peter
    See Faust, Frederick (Schiller)

Warhol, Andy 1928(?)-1987 .... **CLC 20**
    See also AAYA 12; BEST 89:4; CA 89-92;
    121; CANR 34
Warner, Francis (Robert le Plastrier)
    1937- .... **CLC 14**
    See also CA 53-56; CANR 11; CP 1, 2, 3, 4
Warner, Marina 1946- .... **CLC 59**
    See also CA 65-68; CANR 21, 55, 118; CN
    5, 6, 7; DLB 194; MTFW 2005
Warner, Rex (Ernest) 1905-1986 ...... **CLC 45**
    See also CA 89-92; 119; CN 1, 2, 3, 4; CP
    1, 2, 3, 4; DLB 15; RGEL 2; RHW
Warner, Susan (Bogert)
    1819-1885 .... **NCLC 31, 146**
    See also DLB 3, 42, 239, 250, 254
Warner, Sylvia (Constance) Ashton
    See Ashton-Warner, Sylvia (Constance)
Warner, Sylvia Townsend
    1893-1978 .. **CLC 7, 19; SSC 23; TCLC**
    131
    See also BRWS 7; CA 61-64; 77-80; CANR
    16, 60, 104; CN 1, 2; DLB 34, 139; EWL
    3; FANT; FW; MTCW 1, 2; RGEL 2;
    RGSF 2; RHW
Warren, Mercy Otis 1728-1814 ..... **NCLC 13**
    See also DLB 31, 200; RGAL 4; TUS
Warren, Robert Penn 1905-1989 .. **CLC 1, 4,**
    6, 8, 10, 13, 18, 39, 53, 59; PC 37; SSC
    4, 58; WLC
    See also AITN 1; AMW; AMWC 2; BPFB
    3; BYA 1; CA 13-16R; 129; CANR 10,
    47; CDALB 1968-1988; CN 1, 2, 3, 4;
    CP 1, 2, 3, 4; DA; DA3; DAB; DAC;
    DAM MST, NOV, POET; DLB 2, 48, 152,
    320; DLBY 1980, 1989; EWL 3; INT
    CANR-10; MAL 5; MTCW 1, 2; MTFW
    2005; NFS 13; RGAL 4; RGSF 2; RHW;
    SATA 46; SATA-Obit 63; SSFS 8; TUS
Warrigal, Jack
    See Furphy, Joseph
Warshofsky, Isaac
    See Singer, Isaac Bashevis
Warton, Joseph 1722-1800 .... **NCLC 118**
    See also DLB 104, 109; RGEL 2
Warton, Thomas 1728-1790 .... **LC 15, 82**
    See also DAM POET; DLB 104, 109;
    RGEL 2
Waruk, Kona
    See Harris, (Theodore) Wilson
Warung, Price .... **TCLC 45**
    See Astley, William
    See also DLB 230; RGEL 2
Warwick, Jarvis
    See Garner, Hugh
    See also CCA 1
Washington, Alex
    See Harris, Mark
Washington, Booker T(aliaferro)
    1856 1915 .... **BLC 3; TCLC 10**
    See also BW 1; CA 114; 125; DA3; DAM
    MULT; LAIT 2; RGAL 4; SATA 28
Washington, George 1732-1799 .... **LC 25**
    See also DLB 31
Wassermann, (Karl) Jakob
    1873-1934 .... **TCLC 6**
    See also CA 104; 163; DLB 66; EWL 3
Wasserstein, Wendy 1950-2006 . **CLC 32, 59,**
    90, 183; DC 4
    See also AMWS 15; CA 121; 129; CABS
    3, CAD; CANR 53, 75, 128; CD 5, 6;
    CWD; DA3; DAM DRAM; DFS 5, 17;
    DLB 228; EWL 3; FW; INT CA-129;
    MAL 5; MTCW 2; MTFW 2005; SATA
    94

Waterhouse, Keith (Spencer) 1929- . **CLC 47**
    See also CA 5-8R; CANR 38, 67, 109;
    CBD; CD 6; CN 1, 2, 3, 4, 5, 6, 7; DLB
    13, 15; MTCW 1, 2; MTFW 2005

INT CANR-29; MAL 5; MTCW 1, 2;
MTFW 2005; PAB; PFS 11, 12, 16;
RGAL 4; SATA 9, 108; WP

Wild, Peter 1940- .... **CLC 14**
See also CA 37-40R; CP 1, 2, 3, 4, 5, 6, 7;
DLB 5

Wilde, Oscar (Fingal O'Flahertie Wills)
1854(?)-1900 .... **DC 17; SSC 11, 77;
TCLC 1, 8, 23, 41; WLC**
See also AAYA 49; BRW 5; BRWC 1, 2;
BRWR 2; BYA 15; CA 104; 119; CANR
112; CDBLB 1890-1914; DA; DA3;
DAB; DAC; DAM DRAM, MST, NOV;
DFS 4, 8, 9, 21; DLB 10, 19, 34, 57, 141,
156, 190; EXPS; FANT; GL 3; LATS 1:1;
NFS 20; RGEL 2; RGSF 2; SATA 24;
SSFS 7; SUFW; TEA; WCH; WLIT 4

Wilder, Billy .... **CLC 20**
See Wilder, Samuel
See also AAYA 66; DLB 26

Wilder, Samuel 1906-2002
See Wilder, Billy
See also CA 89-92; 205

Wilder, Stephen
See Marlowe, Stephen

Wilder, Thornton (Niven)
1897-1975 .. **CLC 1, 5, 6, 10, 15, 35, 82;
DC 1, 24; WLC**
See also AAYA 29; AITN 2; AMW; CA 13-
16R; 61-64; CAD; CANR 40, 132;
CDALBS; CN 1, 2; DA; DA3; DAB;
DAC; DAM DRAM, MST, NOV; DFS 1,
4, 16; DLB 4, 7, 9, 228; DLBY 1997;
EWL 3; LAIT 3; MAL 5; MTCW 1, 2;
MTFW 2005; RGAL 4; RHW; WYAS 1

Wilding, Michael 1942- ...... **CLC 73; SSC 50**
See also CA 104; CANR 24, 49, 106; CN
4, 5, 6, 7; RGSF 2

Wiley, Richard 1944- .... **CLC 44**
See also CA 121; 129; CANR 71

Wilhelm, Kate .... **CLC 7**
See Wilhelm, Katie (Gertrude)
See also AAYA 20; BYA 16; CAAS 5; DLB
8; INT CANR-17; SCFW 2

Wilhelm, Katie (Gertrude) 1928-
See Wilhelm, Kate
See also CA 37-40R; CANR 17, 36, 60, 94;
MTCW 1; SFW 4

Wilkins, Mary
See Freeman, Mary E(leanor) Wilkins

Willard, Nancy 1936- .... **CLC 7, 37**
See also BYA 5; CA 89-92; CANR 10, 39,
68, 107; CLR 5; CP 2, 3, 4; CWP; CWRI
5; DLB 5, 52; FANT; MAICYA 1, 2;
MTCW 1; SATA 37, 71, 127; SATA-Brief
30; SUFW 2; TCLE 1:2

William of Malmesbury c. 1090B.C.-c.
1140B.C. .... **CMLC 57**

William of Ockham 1290-1349 ..... **CMLC 32**

Williams, Ben Ames 1889-1953 ..... **TCLC 89**
See also CA 183; DLB 102

Williams, C(harles) K(enneth)
1936- .... **CLC 33, 56, 148**
See also CA 37-40R; CAAS 26; CANR 57,
106; CP 1, 2, 3, 4, 5, 6, 7; DAM POET;
DLB 5; MAL 5

Williams, Charles
See Collier, James Lincoln

Williams, Charles (Walter Stansby)
1886-1945 .... **TCLC 1, 11**
See also BRWS 9; CA 104; 163; DLB 100,
153, 255; FANT; RGEL 2; SUFW 1

Williams, Ella Gwendolen Rees
See Rhys, Jean

Williams, (George) Emlyn
1905-1987 .... **CLC 15**
See also CA 104; 123; CANR 36; DAM
DRAM; DLB 10, 77; IDTP; MTCW 1

Williams, Hank 1923-1953 .... **TCLC 81**
See Williams, Hiram King

Williams, Helen Maria
1761-1827 .... **NCLC 135**
See also DLB 158

Williams, Hiram Hank
See Williams, Hank

Williams, Hiram King
See Williams, Hank
See also CA 188

Williams, Hugo (Mordaunt) 1942- ... **CLC 42**
See also CA 17-20R; CANR 45, 119; CP 1,
2, 3, 4, 5, 6, 7; DLB 40

Williams, J. Walker
See Wodehouse, P(elham) G(renville)

Williams, John A(lfred) 1925- . **BLC 3; CLC
5, 13**
See also AFAW 2; BW 2, 3; CA 53-56; 195;
CAAE 195; CAAS 3; CANR 6, 26, 51,
118; CN 1, 2, 3, 4, 5, 6, 7; CSW; DAM
MULT; DLB 2, 33; EWL 3; INT CANR-6;
MAL 5; RGAL 4; SFW 4

Williams, Jonathan (Chamberlain)
1929- .... **CLC 13**
See also CA 9-12R; CAAS 12; CANR 8,
108; CP 1, 2, 3, 4, 5, 6, 7; DLB 5

Williams, Joy 1944- .... **CLC 31**
See also CA 41-44R; CANR 22, 48, 97

Williams, Norman 1952- .... **CLC 39**
See also CA 118

Williams, Sherley Anne 1944-1999 ... **BLC 3;
CLC 89**
See also AFAW 2; BW 2, 3; CA 73-76; 185;
CANR 25, 82; DAM MULT, POET; DLB
41; INT CANR-25; SATA 78; SATA-Obit
116

Williams, Shirley
See Williams, Sherley Anne

Williams, Tennessee 1911-1983 . **CLC 1, 2, 5,
7, 8, 11, 15, 19, 30, 39, 45, 71, 111; DC
4; SSC 81; WLC**
See also AAYA 31; AITN 1, 2; AMW;
AMWC 1; CA 5-8R; 108; CABS 3; CAD;
CANR 31, 132; CDALB 1941-1968; CN
1, 2, 3; DA; DA3; DAB; DAC; DAM
DRAM, MST; DFS 17; DLB 7; DLBD 4;
DLBY 1983; EWL 3; GLL 1; LAIT 4;
LATS 1:2; MAL 5; MTCW 1, 2; MTFW
2005; RGAL 4; TUS

Williams, Thomas (Alonzo)
1926-1990 .... **CLC 14**
See also CA 1-4R; 132; CANR 2

Williams, William C.
See Williams, William Carlos

Williams, William Carlos
1883-1963 .... **CLC 1, 2, 5, 9, 13, 22, 42,
67; PC 7; SSC 31**
See also AAYA 46; AMW; AMWR 1; CA
89-92; CANR 34; CDALB 1917-1929;
DA; DA3; DAB; DAC; DAM MST,
POET; DLB 4, 16, 54, 86; EWL 3; EXPP;
MAL 5; MTCW 1, 2; MTFW 2005; NCFS
4; PAB; PFS 1, 6, 11; RGAL 4; RGSF 2;
TUS; WP

Williamson, David (Keith) 1942- ..... **CLC 56**
See also CA 103; CANR 41; CD 5, 6; DLB
289

Williamson, Ellen Douglas 1905-1984
See Douglas, Ellen
See also CA 17-20R; 114; CANR 39

Williamson, Jack .... **CLC 29**
See Williamson, John Stewart
See also CAAS 8; DLB 8; SCFW 1, 2

Williamson, John Stewart 1908-
See Williamson, Jack
See also CA 17-20R; CANR 23, 70; SFW 4

Willie, Frederick
See Lovecraft, H(oward) P(hillips)

Willingham, Calder (Baynard, Jr.)
1922-1995 .... **CLC 5, 51**
See also CA 5-8R; 147; CANR 3; CN 1, 2,
3, 4, 5; CSW; DLB 2, 44; IDFW 3, 4;
MTCW 1

Willis, Charles
See Clarke, Arthur C(harles)

Willy
See Colette, (Sidonie-Gabrielle)

Willy, Colette
See Colette, (Sidonie-Gabrielle)
See also GLL 1

Wilmot, John 1647-1680 .... **LC 75; PC 66**
See Rochester
See also BRW 2; DLB 131; PAB

Wilson, A(ndrew) N(orman) 1950- .. **CLC 33**
See also BRWS 6; CA 112; 122; CN 4, 5,
6, 7; DLB 14, 155, 194; MTCW 2

Wilson, Angus (Frank Johnstone)
1913-1991 . **CLC 2, 3, 5, 25, 34; SSC 21**
See also BRWS 1; CA 5-8R; 134; CANR
21, CN 1, 2, 3, 4; DLB 15, 139, 155;
EWL 3; MTCW 1, 2; MTFW 2005; RGEL
2; RGSF 2

Wilson, August 1945-2005 .. **BLC 3; CLC 39,
50, 63, 118; DC 2; WLCS**
See also AAYA 16; AFAW 2; AMWS 8; BW
2, 3; CA 115; 122; CAD; CANR 42, 54,
76, 128; CD 5, 6; DA; DA3; DAB; DAC;
DAM DRAM, MST, MULT; DFS 3, 7,
15, 17; DLB 228; EWL 3; LAIT 4; LATS
1:2; MAL 5; MTCW 1, 2; MTFW 2005;
RGAL 4

Wilson, Brian 1942- .... **CLC 12**

Wilson, Colin (Henry) 1931- .... **CLC 3, 14**
See also CA 1-4R; CAAS 5; CANR 1, 22,
33, 77; CMW 4; CN 1, 2, 3, 4, 5, 6; DLB
14, 194; HGG; MTCW 1; SFW 4

Wilson, Dirk
See Pohl, Frederik

Wilson, Edmund 1895-1972 .. **CLC 1, 2, 3, 8,
24**
See also AMW; CA 1-4R; 37-40R; CANR
1, 46, 110; CN 1; DLB 63; EWL 3; MAL
5; MTCW 1, 2; MTFW 2005; RGAL 4;
TUS

Wilson, Ethel Davis (Bryant)
1888(?)-1980 .... **CLC 13**
See also CA 102; CN 1, 2; DAC; DAM
POET; DLB 68; MTCW 1; RGEL 2

Wilson, Harriet
See Wilson, Harriet E. Adams
See also DLB 239

Wilson, Harriet E.
See Wilson, Harriet E. Adams
See also DLB 243

Wilson, Harriet E. Adams
1827(?)-1863(?) .... **BLC 3; NCLC 78**
See Wilson, Harriet; Wilson, Harriet E.
See also DAM MULT; DLB 50

Wilson, John 1785-1854 .... **NCLC 5**

Wilson, John (Anthony) Burgess 1917-1993
See Burgess, Anthony
See also CA 1-4R; 143; CANR 2, 46; DA3;
DAC; DAM NOV; MTCW 1, 2; MTFW
2005; NFS 15; TEA

Wilson, Lanford 1937- .. **CLC 7, 14, 36, 197;
DC 19**
See also CA 17-20R; CABS 3; CAD; CANR
45, 96; CD 5, 6; DAM DRAM; DFS 4, 9,
12, 16, 20; DLB 7; EWL 3; MAL 5; TUS

Wilson, Robert M. 1941- .... **CLC 7, 9**
See also CA 49-52; CAD; CANR 2, 41; CD
5, 6; MTCW 1

Wilson, Robert McLiam 1964- .... **CLC 59**
See also CA 132; DLB 267

Wilson, Sloan 1920-2003 .... **CLC 32**
See also CA 1-4R; 216; CANR 1, 44; CN
1, 2, 3, 4, 5, 6

Wilson, Snoo 1948- .... **CLC 33**
  See also CA 69-72; CBD; CD 5, 6
Wilson, William S(mith) 1932- .... **CLC 49**
  See also CA 81-84
Wilson, (Thomas) Woodrow
  1856-1924 .... **TCLC 79**
  See also CA 166; DLB 47
Wilson and Warnke eds. .... **CLC 65**
Winchilsea, Anne (Kingsmill) Finch
  1661-1720
  See Finch, Anne
  See also RGEL 2
Windham, Basil
  See Wodehouse, P(elham) G(renville)
Wingrove, David (John) 1954- .... **CLC 68**
  See also CA 133; SFW 4
Winnemucca, Sarah 1844-1891 .... **NCLC 79;**
  NNAL
  See also DAM MULT; DLB 175; RGAL 4
Winstanley, Gerrard 1609-1676 .... **LC 52**
Wintergreen, Jane
  See Duncan, Sara Jeannette
Winters, Arthur Yvor
  See Winters, Yvor
Winters, Janet Lewis .... **CLC 41**
  See Lewis, Janet
  See also DLBY 1987
Winters, Yvor 1900-1968 .... **CLC 4, 8, 32**
  See also AMWS 2; CA 11-12; 25-28R; CAP
  1; DLB 48; EWL 3; MAL 5; MTCW 1;
  RGAL 4
Winterson, Jeanette 1959- .... **CLC 64, 158**
  See also BRWS 4; CA 136; CANR 58, 116;
  CN 5, 6, 7; CPW; DA3; DAM POP; DLB
  207, 261; FANT; FW; GLL 1; MTCW 2;
  MTFW 2005; RHW
Winthrop, John 1588-1649 .... **LC 31, 107**
  See also DLB 24, 30
Wirth, Louis 1897-1952 .... **TCLC 92**
  See also CA 210
Wiseman, Frederick 1930- .... **CLC 20**
  See also CA 159
Wister, Owen 1860-1938 .... **TCLC 21**
  See also BPFB 3; CA 108; 162; DLB 9, 78,
  186; RGAL 4; SATA 62; TCWW 1, 2
Wither, George 1588-1667 .... **LC 96**
  See also DLB 121; RGEL 2
Witkacy
  See Witkiewicz, Stanislaw Ignacy
Witkiewicz, Stanislaw Ignacy
  1885-1939 .... **TCLC 8**
  See also CA 105; 162; CDWLB 4; DLB
  215; EW 10; EWL 3; RGWL 2, 3; SFW 4
Wittgenstein, Ludwig (Josef Johann)
  1889-1951 .... **TCLC 59**
  See also CA 113; 164; DLB 262; MTCW 2
Wittig, Monique 1935-2003 .... **CLC 22**
  See also CA 116; 135; 212; CANR 143;
  CWW 2; DLB 83; EWL 3; FW; GLL 1
Wittlin, Jozef 1896-1976 .... **CLC 25**
  See also CA 49-52; 65-68; CANR 3; EWL
  3
Wodehouse, P(elham) G(renville)
  1881-1975 . **CLC 1, 2, 5, 10, 22; SSC 2;**
  TCLC 108
  See also AAYA 65; AITN 2; BRWS 3; CA
  45-48; 57-60; CANR 3, 33; CDBLB
  1914-1945; CN 1, 2; CPW 1; DA3; DAB;
  DAC; DAM NOV; DLB 34, 162; EWL 3;
  MTCW 1, 2; MTFW 2005; RGEL 2;
  RGSF 2; SATA 22; SSFS 10
Woiwode, L.
  See Woiwode, Larry (Alfred)
Woiwode, Larry (Alfred) 1941- ... **CLC 6, 10**
  See also CA 73-76; CANR 16, 94; CN 3, 4,
  5, 6, 7; DLB 6; INT CANR-16

Wojciechowska, Maia (Teresa)
  1927-2002 .... **CLC 26**
  See also AAYA 8, 46; BYA 3; CA 9-12R,
  183; 209; CAAE 183; CANR 4, 41; CLR
  1; JRDA; MAICYA 1, 2; SAAS 1; SATA
  1, 28, 83; SATA-Essay 104; SATA-Obit
  134; YAW
Wojtyla, Karol (Jozef)
  See John Paul II, Pope
Wojtyla, Karol (Josef)
  See John Paul II, Pope
Wolf, Christa 1929- .... **CLC 14, 29, 58, 150**
  See also CA 85-88; CANR 45, 123; CD-
  WLB 2; CWW 2; DLB 75; EWL 3; FW;
  MTCW 1; RGWL 2, 3; SSFS 14
Wolf, Naomi 1962- .... **CLC 157**
  See also CA 141; CANR 110; FW; MTFW
  2005
Wolfe, Gene 1931- .... **CLC 25**
  See also AAYA 35; CA 57-60; CAAS 9;
  CANR 6, 32, 60; CPW; DAM POP; DLB
  8; FANT; MTCW 2; MTFW 2005; SATA
  118, 165; SCFW 2; SFW 4; SUFW 2
Wolfe, Gene Rodman
  See Wolfe, Gene
Wolfe, George C. 1954- .... **BLCS; CLC 49**
  See also CA 149; CAD; CD 5, 6
Wolfe, Thomas (Clayton)
  1900-1938 ...... **SSC 33; TCLC 4, 13, 29,**
  61; WLC
  See also AMW; BPFB 3; CA 104; 132;
  CANR 102; CDALB 1929-1941; DA;
  DA3; DAB; DAC; DAM MST, NOV;
  DLB 9, 102, 229; DLBD 2, 16; DLBY
  1985, 1997; EWL 3; MAL 5; MTCW 1,
  2; NFS 18; RGAL 4; SSFS 18; TUS
Wolfe, Thomas Kennerly, Jr.
  1931- .... **CLC 147**
  See Wolfe, Tom
  See also CA 13-16R; CANR 9, 33, 70, 104;
  DA3; DAM POP; DLB 185; EWL 3; INT
  CANR-9; MTCW 1, 2; MTFW 2005; TUS
Wolfe, Tom .... **CLC 1, 2, 9, 15, 35, 51**
  See Wolfe, Thomas Kennerly, Jr.
  See also AAYA 8, 67; AITN 2; AMWS 3;
  BEST 89:1; BPFB 3; CN 5, 6, 7; CPW;
  CSW; DLB 152; LAIT 5; RGAL 4
Wolff, Geoffrey (Ansell) 1937- .... **CLC 41**
  See also CA 29-32R; CANR 29, 43, 78
Wolff, Sonia
  See Levitin, Sonia (Wolff)
Wolff, Tobias (Jonathan Ansell)
  1945- .... **CLC 39, 64, 172; SSC 63**
  See also AAYA 16; AMWS 7; BEST 90:2;
  BYA 12; CA 114; 117; CAAS 22; CANR
  54, 76, 96; CN 5, 6, 7; CSW; DA3; DLB
  130; EWL 3; INT CA-117; MTCW 2;
  MTFW 2005; RGAL 4; RGSF 2; SSFS 4,
  11
Wolfram von Eschenbach c. 1170-c.
  1220 .... **CMLC 5**
  See Eschenbach, Wolfram von
  See also CDWLB 2; DLB 138; EW 1;
  RGWL 2
Wolitzer, Hilma 1930- .... **CLC 17**
  See also CA 65-68; CANR 18, 40; INT
  CANR-18; SATA 31; YAW
Wollstonecraft, Mary 1759-1797 .... **LC 5, 50,**
  90
  See also BRWS 3; CDBLB 1789-1832;
  DLB 39, 104, 158, 252; FL 1:1; FW;
  LAIT 1; RGEL 2; TEA; WLIT 3
Wonder, Stevie .... **CLC 12**
  See Morris, Steveland Judkins
Wong, Jade Snow 1922- .... **CLC 17**
  See also CA 109; CANR 91; SATA 112
Woodberry, George Edward
  1855-1930 .... **TCLC 73**
  See also CA 165; DLB 71, 103

Woodcott, Keith
  See Brunner, John (Kilian Houston)
Woodruff, Robert W.
  See Mencken, H(enry) L(ouis)
Woolf, (Adeline) Virginia 1882-1941 .. **SSC 7,**
  79; TCLC 1, 5, 20, 43, 56, 101, 123,
  128; WLC
  See also AAYA 44; BPFB 3; BRW 7;
  BRWC 2; BRWR 1; CA 104; 130; CANR
  64, 132; CDBLB 1914-1945; DA; DA3;
  DAB; DAC; DAM MST, NOV; DLB 36,
  100, 162; DLBD 10; EWL 3; EXPS; FL
  1:6; FW; LAIT 3; LATS 1:1; LMFS 2;
  MTCW 1, 2; MTFW 2005; NCFS 2; NFS
  8, 12; RGEL 2; RGSF 2; SSFS 4, 12;
  TEA; WLIT 4
Woollcott, Alexander (Humphreys)
  1887-1943 .... **TCLC 5**
  See also CA 105; 161; DLB 29
Woolrich, Cornell .... **CLC 77**
  See Hopley-Woolrich, Cornell George
  See also MSW
Woolson, Constance Fenimore
  1840-1894 .... **NCLC 82**
  See also DLB 12, 74, 189, 221; RGAL 4
Wordsworth, Dorothy 1771-1855 . **NCLC 25,**
  138
  See also DLB 107
Wordsworth, William 1770-1850 .. **NCLC 12,**
  38, 111; PC 4, 67; WLC
  See also BRW 4; BRWC 1; CDBLB 1789-
  1832; DA; DA3; DAB; DAC; DAM MST,
  POET; DLB 93, 107; EXPP; LATS 1:1;
  LMFS 1; PAB; PFS 2; RGEL 2; TEA;
  WLIT 3; WP
Wotton, Sir Henry 1568-1639 .... **LC 68**
  See also DLB 121; RGEL 2
Wouk, Herman 1915- .... **CLC 1, 9, 38**
  See also BPFB 2, 3; CA 5-8R; CANR 6,
  33, 67, 146; CDALBS; CN 1, 2, 3, 4, 5,
  6; CPW; DA3; DAM NOV, POP; DLBY
  1982; INT CANR-6; LAIT 4; MAL 5;
  MTCW 1, 2; MTFW 2005; NFS 7; TUS
Wright, Charles (Penzel, Jr.) 1935- .. **CLC 6,**
  13, 28, 119, 146
  See also AMWS 5; CA 29-32R; CAAS 7;
  CANR 23, 36, 62, 88, 135; CP 3, 4, 5, 6,
  7; DLB 165; DLBY 1982; EWL 3;
  MTCW 1, 2; MTFW 2005; PFS 10
Wright, Charles Stevenson 1932- ...... **BLC 3;**
  CLC 49
  See also BW 1; CA 9-12R; CANR 26; CN
  1, 2, 3, 4, 5, 6, 7; DAM MULT, POET;
  DLB 33
Wright, Frances 1795-1852 .... **NCLC 74**
  See also DLB 73
Wright, Frank Lloyd 1867-1959 .... **TCLC 95**
  See also AAYA 33; CA 174
Wright, Jack R.
  See Harris, Mark
Wright, James (Arlington)
  1927-1980 ... **CLC 3, 5, 10, 28; PC 36**
  See also AITN 2; AMWS 3; CA 49-52; 97-
  100; CANR 4, 34, 64; CDALBS; CP 1, 2;
  DAM POET; DLB 5, 169; EWL 3; EXPP;
  MAL 5; MTCW 1, 2; MTFW 2005; PFS
  7, 8; RGAL 4; TUS; WP
Wright, Judith (Arundell)
  1915-2000 .... **CLC 11, 53; PC 14**
  See also CA 13-16R; 188; CANR 31, 76,
  93; CP 1, 2, 3, 4, 5, 6, 7; CWP; DLB 260;
  EWL 3; MTCW 1, 2; MTFW 2005; PFS
  8; RGEL 2; SATA 14; SATA-Obit 121
Wright, L(aurali) R. 1939- .... **CLC 44**
  See also CA 138; CMW 4
Wright, Richard (Nathaniel)
  1908-1960 ... **BLC 3; CLC 1, 3, 4, 9, 14,**
  21, 48, 74; SSC 2; TCLC 136; WLC
  See also AAYA 5, 42; AFAW 1, 2; AMW;
  BPFB 3; BW 1; BYA 2; CA 108; CANR
  64; CDALB 1929-1941; DA; DA3; DAB;

DAC; DAM MST, MULT, NOV; DLB 76, 102; DLBD 2; EWL 3; EXPN; LAIT 3, 4; MAL 5; MTCW 1, 2; MTFW 2005; NCFS 1; NFS 1, 7; RGAL 4; RGSF 2; SSFS 3, 9, 15, 20; TUS; YAW

Wright, Richard B(ruce) 1937- .... **CLC 6**
See also CA 85-88; CANR 120; DLB 53

Wright, Rick 1945- .... **CLC 35**

Wright, Rowland
See Wells, Carolyn

Wright, Stephen 1946- .... **CLC 33**
See also CA 237

Wright, Willard Huntington 1888-1939
See Van Dine, S. S.
See also CA 115; 189; CMW 4; DLBD 16

Wright, William 1930- .... **CLC 44**
See also CA 53-56; CANR 7, 23

Wroth, Lady Mary 1587-1653(?) .... **LC 30; PC 38**
See also DLB 121

Wu Ch'eng-en 1500(?)-1582(?) .... **LC 7**

Wu Ching-tzu 1701-1754 .... **LC 2**

Wulfstan c. 10th cent. -1023 .... **CMLC 59**

Wurlitzer, Rudolph 1938(?)- ... **CLC 2, 4, 15**
See also CA 85-88; CN 4, 5, 6, 7; DLB 173

Wyatt, Sir Thomas c. 1503-1542 . **LC 70; PC 27**
See also BRW 1; DLB 132; EXPP; RGEL 2; TEA

Wycherley, William 1640-1716 .... **LC 8, 21, 102**
See also BRW 2; CDBLB 1660-1789; DAM DRAM; DLB 80; RGEL 2

Wyclif, John c. 1330-1384 .... **CMLC 70**
See also DLB 146

Wylie, Elinor (Morton Hoyt) 1885-1928 .... **PC 23; TCLC 8**
See also AMWS 1; CA 105; 162; DLB 9, 45; EXPP; MAL 5; RGAL 4

Wylie, Philip (Gordon) 1902-1971 ... **CLC 43**
See also CA 21-22; 33-36R; CAP 2; CN 1; DLB 9; SFW 4

Wyndham, John .... **CLC 19**
See Harris, John (Wyndham Parkes Lucas) Beynon
See also DLB 255; SCFW 1, 2

Wyss, Johann David Von 1743-1818 .... **NCLC 10**
See also CLR 92; JRDA; MAICYA 1, 2; SATA 29; SATA-Brief 27

Xenophon c. 430B.C.-c. 354B.C. ... **CMLC 17**
See also AW 1; DLB 176; RGWL 2, 3

Xingjian, Gao 1940-
See Gao Xingjian
See also CA 193; DFS 21; RGWL 3

Yakamochi 718-785 .... **CMLC 45; PC 48**

Yakumo Koizumi
See Hearn, (Patricio) Lafcadio (Tessima Carlos)

Yamada, Mitsuye (May) 1923- .... **PC 44**
See also CA 77-80

Yamamoto, Hisaye 1921- .... **AAL; SSC 34**
See also CA 214; DAM MULT; DLB 312; LAIT 4; SSFS 14

Yamauchi, Wakako 1924- .... **AAL**
See also CA 214; DLB 312

Yanez, Jose Donoso
See Donoso (Yanez), Jose

Yanovsky, Basile S.
See Yanovsky, V(assily) S(emenovich)

Yanovsky, V(assily) S(emenovich) 1906-1989 .... **CLC 2, 18**
See also CA 97-100; 129

Yates, Richard 1926-1992 .... **CLC 7, 8, 23**
See also AMWS 11; CA 5-8R; 139; CANR 10, 43; CN 1, 2, 3, 4, 5; DLB 2, 234; DLBY 1981, 1992; INT CANR-10

Yau, John 1950- .... **PC 61**
See also CA 154; CANR 89; CP 4, 5, 6, 7; DLB 234, 312

Yeats, W. B.
See Yeats, William Butler

Yeats, William Butler 1865-1939 . **PC 20, 51; TCLC 1, 11, 18, 31, 93, 116; WLC**
See also AAYA 48; BRW 6; BRWR 1; CA 104; 127; CANR 45; CDBLB 1890-1914; DA; DA3; DAB; DAC; DAM DRAM, MST, POET; DLB 10, 19, 98, 156; EWL 3; EXPP; MTCW 1, 2; MTFW 2005; NCFS 3; PAB; PFS 1, 2, 5, 7, 13, 15; RGEL 2; TEA; WLIT 4; WP

Yehoshua, A(braham) B. 1936- .. **CLC 13, 31**
See also CA 33-36R; CANR 43, 90, 145; CWW 2; EWL 3; RGSF 2; RGWL 3; WLIT 6

Yellow Bird
See Ridge, John Rollin

Yep, Laurence Michael 1948- .... **CLC 35**
See also AAYA 5, 31; BYA 7; CA 49-52; CANR 1, 46, 92; CLR 3, 17, 54; DLB 52, 312; FANT; JRDA; MAICYA 1, 2; MAICYAS 1; SATA 7, 69, 123; WYA; YAW

Yerby, Frank G(arvin) 1916-1991 ..... **BLC 3; CLC 1, 7, 22**
See also BPFB 3; BW 1, 3; CA 9-12R; 136; CANR 16, 52; CN 1, 2, 3, 4, 5; DAM MULT; DLB 76; INT CANR-16; MTCW 1; RGAL 4; RHW

Yesenin, Sergei Alexandrovich
See Esenin, Sergei (Alexandrovich)

Yesenin, Sergey
See Esenin, Sergei (Alexandrovich)
See also EWL 3

Yevtushenko, Yevgeny (Alexandrovich) 1933- ...... **CLC 1, 3, 13, 26, 51, 126; PC 40**
See Evtushenko, Evgenii Aleksandrovich
See also CA 81-84; CANR 33, 54; DAM POET; EWL 3; MTCW 1

Yezierska, Anzia 1885(?)-1970 .... **CLC 46**
See also CA 126; 89-92; DLB 28, 221; FW; MTCW 1; RGAL 4; SSFS 15

Yglesias, Helen 1915- .... **CLC 7, 22**
See also CA 37-40R; CAAS 20; CANR 15, 65, 95; CN 4, 5, 6, 7; INT CANR-15; MTCW 1

Yokomitsu, Riichi 1898-1947 .... **TCLC 47**
See also CA 170; EWL 3

Yonge, Charlotte (Mary) 1823-1901 .... **TCLC 48**
See also CA 109; 163; DLB 18, 163; RGEL 2; SATA 17; WCH

York, Jeremy
See Creasey, John

York, Simon
See Heinlein, Robert A(nson)

Yorke, Henry Vincent 1905-1974 ..... **CLC 13**
See Green, Henry
See also CA 85-88; 49-52

Yosano Akiko 1878-1942 .... **PC 11; TCLC 59**
See also CA 161; EWL 3; RGWL 3

Yoshimoto, Banana .... **CLC 84**
See Yoshimoto, Mahoko
See also AAYA 50; NFS 7

Yoshimoto, Mahoko 1964-
See Yoshimoto, Banana
See also CA 144; CANR 98; SSFS 16

Young, Al(bert James) 1939- ... **BLC 3; CLC 19**
See also BW 2, 3; CA 29-32R; CANR 26, 65, 109; CN 2, 3, 4, 5, 6, 7; CP 1, 2, 3, 4, 5, 6, 7; DAM MULT; DLB 33

Young, Andrew (John) 1885-1971 .... **CLC 5**
See also CA 5-8R; CANR 7, 29; CP 1; RGEL 2

Young, Collier
See Bloch, Robert (Albert)

Young, Edward 1683-1765 .... **LC 3, 40**
See also DLB 95; RGEL 2

Young, Marguerite (Vivian) 1909-1995 .... **CLC 82**
See also CA 13-16; 150; CAP 1; CN 1, 2, 3, 4, 5, 6

Young, Neil 1945- .... **CLC 17**
See also CA 110; CCA 1

Young Bear, Ray A. 1950- ... **CLC 94; NNAL**
See also CA 146; DAM MULT; DLB 175; MAL 5

Yourcenar, Marguerite 1903-1987 ... **CLC 19, 38, 50, 87**
See also BPFB 3; CA 69-72; CANR 23, 60, 93; DAM NOV; DLB 72; DLBY 1988; EW 12; EWL 3; GFL 1789 to the Present; GLL 1; MTCW 1, 2; MTFW 2005; RGWL 2, 3

Yuan, Chu 340(?)B.C.-278(?)B.C. . **CMLC 36**

Yurick, Sol 1925- .... **CLC 6**
See also CA 13-16R; CANR 25; CN 1, 2, 3, 4, 5, 6, 7; MAL 5

Zabolotsky, Nikolai Alekseevich 1903-1958 .... **TCLC 52**
See Zabolotsky, Nikolay Alekseevich
See also CA 116; 164

Zabolotsky, Nikolay Alekseevich
See Zabolotsky, Nikolai Alekseevich
See also EWL 3

Zagajewski, Adam 1945- .... **PC 27**
See also CA 186; DLB 232; EWL 3

Zalygin, Sergei -2000 .... **CLC 59**

Zalygin, Sergei (Pavlovich) 1913-2000 .... **CLC 59**
See also DLB 302

Zamiatin, Evgenii
See Zamyatin, Evgeny Ivanovich
See also RGSF 2; RGWL 2, 3

Zamiatin, Evgenii Ivanovich
See Zamyatin, Evgeny Ivanovich
See also DLB 272

Zamiatin, Yevgenii
See Zamyatin, Evgeny Ivanovich

Zamora, Bernice (B. Ortiz) 1938- .. **CLC 89; HLC 2**
See also CA 151; CANR 80; DAM MULT; DLB 82; HW 1, 2

Zamyatin, Evgeny Ivanovich 1884-1937 .... **TCLC 8, 37**
See Zamiatin, Evgenii; Zamiatin, Evgenii Ivanovich; Zamyatin, Yevgeny Ivanovich
See also CA 105; 166; SFW 4

Zamyatin, Yevgeny Ivanovich
See Zamyatin, Evgeny Ivanovich
See also EW 10; EWL 3

Zangwill, Israel 1864-1926 ... **SSC 44; TCLC 16**
See also CA 109; 167; CMW 4; DLB 10, 135, 197; RGEL 2

Zanzotto, Andrea 1921- .... **PC 65**
See also CA 208; CWW 2; DLB 128; EWL 3

Zappa, Francis Vincent, Jr. 1940-1993
See Zappa, Frank
See also CA 108; 143; CANR 57

Zappa, Frank .... **CLC 17**
See Zappa, Francis Vincent, Jr.

Zaturenska, Marya 1902-1982 ..... **CLC 6, 11**
See also CA 13-16R; 105; CANR 22; CP 1, 2, 3

Zayas y Sotomayor, Maria de 1590-c. 1661 .... **LC 102**
See also RGSF 2

Zeami 1363-1443 .... **DC 7; LC 86**
See also DLB 203; RGWL 2, 3

Zelazny, Roger (Joseph) 1937-1995 . **CLC 21**
See also AAYA 7, 68; BPFB 3; CA 21-24R;
148; CANR 26, 60; CN 6; DLB 8; FANT;
MTCW 1, 2; MTFW 2005; SATA 57;
SATA-Brief 39; SCFW 1, 2; SFW 4;
SUFW 1, 2
Zhang Ailing
See Chang, Eileen
See also CWW 2; RGSF 2
Zhdanov, Andrei Alexandrovich
1896-1948 .... **TCLC 18**
See also CA 117; 167
Zhukovsky, Vasilii Andreevich
See Zhukovsky, Vasily (Andreevich)
See also DLB 205
Zhukovsky, Vasily (Andreevich)
1783-1852 .... **NCLC 35**
See Zhukovsky, Vasilii Andreevich
Ziegenhagen, Eric .... **CLC 55**
Zimmer, Jill Schary
See Robinson, Jill
Zimmerman, Robert
See Dylan, Bob
Zindel, Paul 1936-2003 ...... **CLC 6, 26; DC 5**
See also AAYA 2, 37; BYA 2, 3, 8, 11, 14;
CA 73-76; 213; CAD; CANR 31, 65, 108;
CD 5, 6; CDALBS; CLR 3, 45, 85; DA;

DA3; DAB; DAC; DAM DRAM, MST,
NOV; DFS 12; DLB 7, 52; JRDA; LAIT
5; MAICYA 1, 2; MTCW 1, 2; MTFW
2005; NFS 14; SATA 16, 58, 102; SATA-
Obit 142; WYA; YAW
Zinn, Howard 1922- .... **CLC 199**
See also CA 1-4R; CANR 2, 33, 90
Zinov'Ev, A. A.
See Zinoviev, Alexander (Aleksandrovich)
Zinov'ev, Aleksandr (Aleksandrovich)
See Zinoviev, Alexander (Aleksandrovich)
See also DLB 302
Zinoviev, Alexander (Aleksandrovich)
1922- .... **CLC 19**
See Zinov'ev, Aleksandr (Aleksandrovich)
See also CA 116; 133; CAAS 10
Zizek, Slavoj 1949- .... **CLC 188**
See also CA 201; MTFW 2005
Zoilus
See Lovecraft, H(oward) P(hillips)
Zola, Emile (Edouard Charles Antoine)
1840-1902 ...... **TCLC 1, 6, 21, 41; WLC**
See also CA 104; 138; DA; DA3; DAB;
DAC; DAM MST, NOV; DLB 123; EW
7; GFL 1789 to the Present; IDTP; LMFS
1, 2; RGWL 2; TWA

Zoline, Pamela 1941- .... **CLC 62**
See also CA 161; SFW 4
Zoroaster 628(?)B.C.-551(?)B.C. ... **CMLC 40**
Zorrilla y Moral, Jose 1817-1893 .... **NCLC 6**
Zoshchenko, Mikhail (Mikhailovich)
1895-1958 .... **SSC 15; TCLC 15**
See also CA 115; 160; EWL 3; RGSF 2;
RGWL 3
Zuckmayer, Carl 1896-1977 .... **CLC 18**
See also CA 69-72; DLB 56, 124; EWL 3;
RGWL 2, 3
Zuk, Georges
See Skelton, Robin
See also CCA 1
Zukofsky, Louis 1904-1978 ... **CLC 1, 2, 4, 7, 11, 18; PC 11**
See also AMWS 3; CA 9-12R; 77-80;
CANR 39; CP 1, 2; DAM POET; DLB 5,
165; EWL 3; MAL 5; MTCW 1; RGAL 4
Zweig, Paul 1935-1984 .... **CLC 34, 42**
See also CA 85-88; 113
Zweig, Stefan 1881-1942 .... **TCLC 17**
See also CA 112; 170; DLB 81, 118; EWL 3
Zwingli, Huldreich 1484-1531 .... **LC 37**
See also DLB 179

Literary Criticism Series
Cumulative Topic Index

This index lists all topic entries in Gale's *Children's Literature Review* (CLR), *Classical and Medieval Literature Criticism* (CMLC), *Contemporary Literary Criticism* (CLC), *Drama Criticism* (DC), *Literature Criticism from 1400 to 1800* (LC), *Nineteenth-Century Literature Criticism* (NCLC), *Short Story Criticism* (SSC), and *Twentieth-Century Literary Criticism* (TCLC). The index also lists topic entries in the Gale Critical Companion Collection, which includes the following publications: *The Beat Generation* (BG), and *Harlem Renaissance* (HR).

Topic Index

Topic Index

SSC Cumulative Nationality Index

SSC-88 Title Index

Title Index

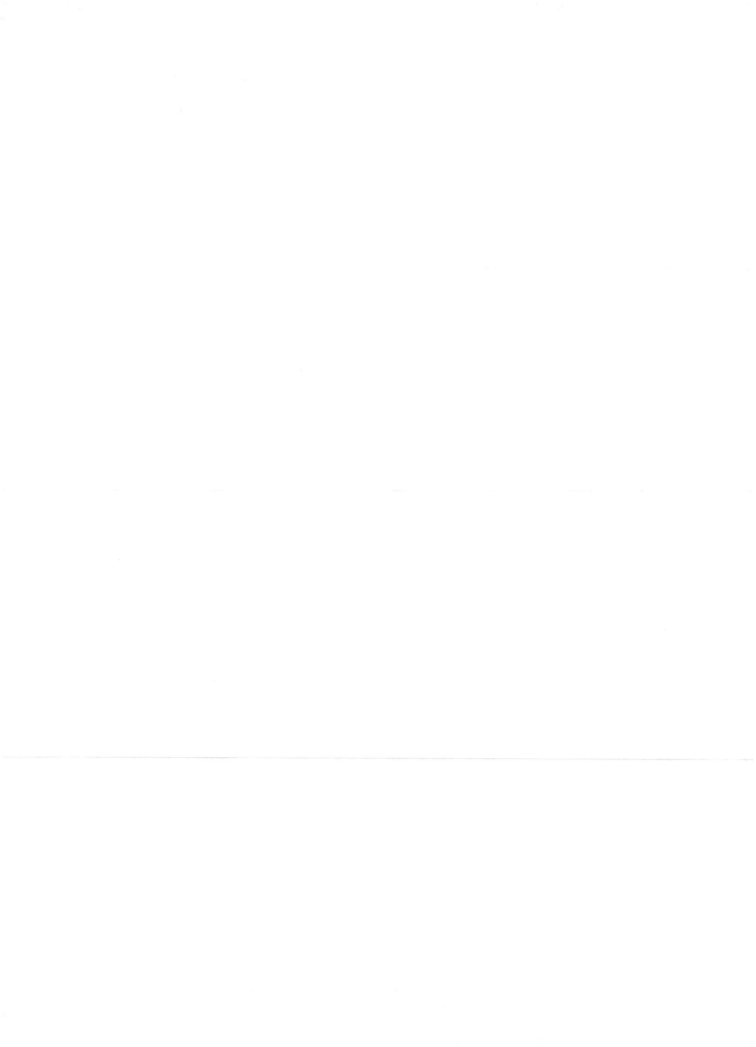

ISBN 0-7876-8885-1

90000